Acclaim for *The War, 1939–1945*

"A brilliant achievement." —*Times Literary Supplement*

"A fascinating book and a valuable record, providing a very illuminating picture of the war." **—B.H. Liddell Hart**

"For the person with insufficient space or money for a comprehensive collection of World War II books, here is a one-volume substitute." —*San Francisco Chronicle*

"Very welcome." **—Field Marshal Erich Von Manstein**

"I congratulate the editors on an excellent and entertaining anthology. They have produced a truly worldwide picture of a worldwide conflict and have shown many of its participants on every level, and have permitted them to tell their stories." **—Admiral Chester W. Nimitz**

"It is a poignant book, yet at the same time exciting and fascinating. It is also uniquely revealing. It sheds light on those countless facets of World War II which so often escape notice in conventional accounts." —*Chicago Sunday Tribune*

"Very interesting." **—Paul Reynaud**

"Eminently readable." **—Grand Admiral Karl Doenitz**

"The editors have used their scissors and paste with discrimination. At times, by juxtaposing the accounts written by adversaries in the same action, they throw a fresh and vivid light on the fortunes of war." —*Spectator*

"Unique and highly interesting. . . . No one can read this book without achieving a personal sense of the tragedy of war." **—General Mark Clark**

"An extremely valuable addition to any World War II collection. . . . [Full of] brutality, terror, death, courage, occasional humor and finally triumph." —*Kirkus*

THE WAR, 1939–1945

A Documentary History

Edited By

DESMOND FLOWER

and

JAMES REEVES

New Introduction by John S.D. Eisenhower

DA CAPO PRESS • NEW YORK

Library of Congress Cataloging in Publication Data

Taste of courage.

The war, 1939–1945: a documentary history / edited by Desmond Flower and James Reeves.—1st Da Capo Press ed. / new introduction by John S. Eisenhower.

   p.   cm.

Originally published: The taste of courage: the war, 1939–1945. New York: Harper, [1960]. Simultaneously published as: The war, 1939–1945. London: Cassell, [1960].

Includes index.

ISBN 0-306-80763-7 (alk. paper)

1. World War, 1939–1945. I. Flower, Desmond, 1908–   . II. Reeves, James. III. Title.

D743.F55   1997

940.53—dc20   96-44131

                                                     CIP

First Da Capo Press edition 1997

This Da Capo Press paperback edition of *The War, 1939–1945* (originally published in the U.S. as *The Taste of Courage*) is an unabridged republication of the edition published in London in 1960, here supplemented with a new introduction by John S.D. Eisenhower. It is reprinted by arrangement with HarperCollins Publishers, Inc.

Published by Da Capo Press, Inc.
A Member of the Perseus Books Group

Manufactured in the United States of America

Grateful acknowledgment is made to the following for permission to reprint selections included in this book:

Brandt & Brandt
  I Was There by Admiral William D. Leahy. Published by McGraw-Hill Book Co.
  Admiral Halsey's Story by William F. Halsey and Joseph Bryan. Published by McGraw-Hill Book Co.

Curtis Brown, Ltd.
  Still Digging by Mortimer Wheeler. Copyright © 1955 by Eric Robert Mortimer Wheeler. Published by E. P. Dutton & Co.
  The Green Beret by Hilary St. George Saunders. Reprinted by permission of the author's estate.

Coward-McCann, Inc.

At Whatever Cost (Dieppe at Dawn) by R. W. Thompson. Copyright © 1956 by R. W. Thompson.

The John Day Company

The Invisible Flag by Peter Bamm.

Dodd, Mead & Company

Going to the Wars by John Verney. Copyright © 1955 by John Verney.

Doubleday & Company, Inc.

The Goebbels Diaries edited by Louis P. Lochner. Copyright 1948 by Fireside Press, Inc.

Action in the East (Retreat in the East) by O. D. Gallagher. Copyright 1942 by Doubleday & Company, Inc.

I Saw the Fall of the Philippines by Carlos P. Romulo. Copyright 1942 by Carlos P. Romulo.

Crusade in Europe by Dwight D. Eisenhower. Copyright 1948 by Doubleday & Company, Inc.

The Diary of a Young Girl by Anne Frank. Copyright 1952 by Otto H. Frank.

The Turn of the Tide by Arthur Bryant. Copyright 1957 by Arthur Bryant.

E. P. Dutton & Co., Inc.

Memoirs of Marshal Mannerheim translated by Count Eric Lewenhaupt. Copyright 1954 by E. P. Dutton & Co., Inc.

A Sailor's Odyssey by Admiral of the Fleet Viscount Cunningham of Hyndhope. Copyright 1951 by E. P. Dutton & Co., Inc.

Panzer Leader by General Heinz Guderian. Translated by Constantine Fitz Gibbon.

Stalingrad by Heinz Schroter. Translated by Constantine FitzGibbon. Copyright 1958 by E. P. Dutton & Co., Inc.

Hitler and His Admirals by Anthony Martienssen. Copyright 1949 by Anthony Martienssen.

Defeat in the West by Milton Shulman. Copyright 1948 by Milton Shulman.

Harcourt, Brace and Company, Inc.

The Rommel Papers, edited by B. H. Liddell Hart. Copyright 1953 by B. H. Liddell Hart.

A Thousand Shall Fall by Hans Habe. Copyright 1941 by Harcourt, Brace and Company, Inc.

Flight to Arras by Antoine de Saint-Exupéry. Copyright 1942 by Harcourt, Brace and Company, Inc.

Harper & Brothers

Flight Above Cloud (Ten Summers) by John Pudney. Copyright 1944 by John Pudney.

Rommel by Desmond Young. Copyright 1950 by Desmond Young.

The Labyrinth (The Schellenberg Memoirs) edited by Louis Hagen. Copyright © 1956 by Harper & Brothers.

The Time for Decision by Sumner Welles. Copyright 1944 by Sumner Welles.

Soldier by General Matthew B. Ridgway. Copyright © 1956 by Matthew B. Ridgway and Harold H. Martin.

Calculated Risk by General Mark Clark. Copyright 1950 by Mark W. Clark.

Hill and Wang, Inc.

The Fall of France, Vol. II, Assignment to Catastrophe, by Major-General Sir Edward L. Spears. Copyright 1955 by Roland Thomas Outen and Randolph Henry Albert Lerse.

Henry Holt & Co., Inc.

Sunk by Mochitsura Hashimoto. Copyright 1954 by Henry Holt & Co., Inc.

The First and the Last by Adolf Galland. Copyright 1954 by Henry Holt & Co., Inc.

Houghton Mifflin Company

The Monastery by Fred Majdalany.

War as I Knew It by George S. Patton, Jr.

The Second World War, Vols. 1–6 by Winston Churchill.

The Second World War, Abridged Edition by Winston Churchill.

Cassino: Portrait of a Battle by Fred Majdalany.

The Small Back Room by Nigel Balchin.

Alfred A. Knopf, Inc.

The Retreat by P. H. Newby. Copyright 1953 by P. H. Newby.

The Cruel Sea by Nicholas Monsarrat. Copyright 1951 by Nicholas Monsarrat.

The Last Days of Sevastopol by Boris Voyetekhov. Copyright 1943 by Alfred A. Knopf, Inc.

The Year of Stalingrad by Alexander Werth. Copyright 1946 by Alexander Werth.

Fires on the Plain by Shohei Ooka. Copyright 1957 by Alfred A. Knopf, Inc.

J. B. Lippincott Company

Graf Spee (The Battle of the River Plate) by Dudley Pope. Copyright 1956 by Dudley Bernard Egerton Pope.

The Colditz Story by P. R. Reid. Copyright 1952 by P. R. Reid.

Little, Brown & Company

Escape to Adventure (Eastern Approaches) by Fitzroy Maclean. Copyright 1949, 1950 by Fitzroy Maclean.

Three Came Home by Agnes Newton Keith. Copyright 1946, 1947 by Agnes Newton Keith.

War Fish by George Grider and Lydel Sims. Copyright © 1958 by George Grider and Lydel Sims.

The Macmillan Company

Ill Met by Moonlight by W. Stanley Moss. *Bomber Offensive* by Sir Arthur Harris.

Macmillan & Co. Ltd. (London) and St. Mar-

TO THE
30,000,000
DEAD

INTRODUCTION
TO THE DA CAPO EDITION

WORLD War Two was the greatest cataclysm of the twentieth century. Few came through the period without experiencing major disruptions in their lives, and those of us who survived found our lives after the war forever changed. Some Americans were affected only after Pearl Harbor in December 1941, but for my family the war was a reality long before United States involvement. I will always remember the date when it began for us: September 3, 1939. I was seventeen years old at the time. My father, Lieutenant Colonel Dwight D. Eisenhower, was an Army officer stationed in Manila in the Philippine Islands. The atmosphere there was tense, exposed as we were to the might of the Japanese empire, only a few hundred miles away. My parents and I learned that British Prime Minister Neville Chamberlain was scheduled to make a radio address that evening, and since Adolf Hitler's Nazi legions had two days earlier poured across the borders of Poland despite the warnings of Britain and France, we harbored very little doubt as to what we would hear.

As we hunched over the small shortwave radio in the Manila Hotel, the crackling voice of Mr. Chamberlain came through from London: "Now Great Britain is at war with Germany," he said. "You can imagine what a bitter blow this is to me."

We were not surprised, but we were stunned nevertheless. We cared little for Mr. Chamberlain's personal disappointment, though we knew how sincerely he had worked to prevent this tragedy. Nor were we thinking of what this news would mean to our own immediate family. Our thoughts instead returned to the horrors of the First World War—the "war to end all wars"—and we hoped that the tragedy would not be repeated. Maybe, we said to each other, this one might be confined to a minor fracas on the perimeters of continental Europe and terminated once the European powers regained their senses.

Our hopes for a short, easy war were dashed. How much so is summarized by the book's dedication: "To the 30,000,000 Dead." Such a figure is too much for the human imagination to cope with. Josef Stalin, the wartime dictator of the Soviet Union, expressed it well. "In matters of human perception," he is reputed to have said, "one death constitutes a tragedy, but a million deaths represent only a statistic." Cynical as that statement was, old "Uncle Joe" had a point: our individual capacity for dealing with tragedy is limited and, when overburdened with stark reality, we quickly take refuge in denying and intellectualizing. So it has become with World War II. Selective memory has dulled the fears and the horror, and in our benign recollections we sometimes refer to it as the "last good war." When we develop such a rosy glow, it is time to be reminded otherwise. True, the objectives of the Allies were laudable; survival itself dictated that the Nazi regime in Germany and the Fascist one in Italy be eliminated. And it is natural to long wistfully for the spirit of national unity that prevailed, for days when people pulled together, almost without complaint, in a common cause. There *were* moments of joy and humor among those of fear and sorrow. But few people who participated actively in that war would like to repeat the experience. For some, whose exposure to danger and hardship exceeded human capacity to bear, the effects have been lasting.

The War, 1939–1945 bridges the gap between glowing nostalgia and the nightmare of reality. No one's individual story can provide that crucial link. Only in a collective experience can anything approaching a satisfactory perspective be achieved. The editors, therefore, have brought together a vast collection of accounts from persons varied in rank, station, and nationality. It is a book about the men, women, and children who were involved in the fighting and dying, about the terrors of the prisoners, and about the endless waiting. Its wide variety of viewpoints reminds the modern-day reader of the war's breadth—how many miles of ocean had to be traveled, how different were the friends and foes of soldiers, sailors, airmen, and marines in one theater as contrasted with another. An infantryman facing the Nazi war machine in France, Italy, or Germany can well be expected to view Operation Overlord as the center of the entire Allied effort. But how differently would a sailor on the *U.S.S. Enterprise* see things as he searches the seas for Japanese fleets and withstands the terror of kamikazes? The answer is, of course, that while roles differed, all were important.

This collection, however, does not confine itself to the Allied point of view, but contains articles by Germans, Italians, and Japanese as well. It is fortunate that the editors waited until 1960 to publish this volume, for it required some fifteen years (with Germany and Italy part of NATO for six of those years) for most people to recognize that the average Axis soldier was every bit as patriotic and brave as his Allied counterpart.

High-level strategy, from either Allied or Axis viewpoints, is not the subject of this book. Suffice it to say that the Allied governments and their military service chiefs directed the war with remarkable success. The United States and Britain, the two allies who bore the brunt of the Axis onslaught in the West from the fall of France in 1940 to D-Day in 1944, wielded a joint instrument of war, the power of which nearly staggers the imagination. Although they did not shed their own national interests, they hammered out a compromise strategy that eventually triumphed, first over Germany in May 1945 and then over Japan three months later. That task was easier said than done. It involved national psychologies, affected by different social mores and by the experiences of the two nations in the First World War. The Americans could never quite understand, for example, the impact on the British of losing nearly an entire generation of their young manhood in the fields of the Somme and Flanders. The goal of achieving peace was also impacted by the differing views concerning British and French colonialism after the end of the war. It is a monument to the leadership of President Franklin D. Roosevelt, Prime Minister Winston S. Churchill, and their military chiefs that the amalgamation was so successful.

As I perused this book, which is really a small library of World War II material, I was surprised to discover how much emotion some of the articles could still evoke in me. I had spent my high school years in the Philippines during the 1930s, and recollecting our fears of the Japanese, I was particularly struck when I read

"The Execution of an Intelligence Officer." [1] The article describes the last moments of a young British officer, probably a spy, before his ceremonial execution by Japanese authorities. Although the incident was only one among many in a cruel war, this Japanese account aroused emotions that had been ingrained in me by nearly four years of wartime indoctrination—our tendency to cast every member of the enemy's armed forces into a single, bestial mold. I can still remember a wartime photograph of a British officer, kneeling with his hands tied behind his back, about to be decapitated by a Japanese officer with a poised Samurai sword. The words bring the picture and the feelings back, fortunately only momentarily.

The lighter side of the war is also depicted. One incident that Americans like to recall is a scene at Bastogne, Belgium on December 22, 1944. The Ardennes Campaign, better known as the Battle of the Bulge, had been under way for six days, and the United States 101st Airborne Division had just been surrounded in that city by the spearheads of Panzer General Hasso Von Manteuffel's Fifth German Panzer Army. On that morning two Germans approached the American lines with a message addressed to General Anthony McAuliffe, demanding that he and his paratroopers surrender. The language was pompous:

> The fortune of war is changing. This time the U.S.A. forces in and near Bastogne have been encircled by strong German armored units. . . . There is only one possibility of saving the encircled U.S.A. troops from total annihilation: that is the honorable surrender of the encircled town. . . . If this proposal should be rejected, one German artillery corps and six heavy anti-aircraft battalions are ready to annihilate the U.S.A. troops in or near Bastogne. The order for firing will be given immediately after [a] two-hour period.

Just below that message is this inscription: "The reply to this message is generally known. It was: 'Nuts.'" [2]

I witnessed much during the last days of the European phase of the war, but my most vivid memory remains the sight of stacked-up corpses of starved Nazi victims in the horror camp of Buchenwald, near Weimar. I have long wondered how the Germans, among whom I have warm friends today, could have been parties to the Holocaust. Within the pages of *The War, 1939–1945* I found articles written from the German viewpoint. Generally they depict themselves as victims. Regarding the Dresden bombing of February 13, 1945, Else Wendel quotes Gerhardt Hauptmann, the German poet, thus:

> He who has forgotten how to weep, learns again at Dresden's ruin. . . . I am at the end of my life, and I envy my dead friends who have been saved this terrible sight. I weep, and I am not ashamed of my tears. . . . I am nearly eighty-three years old and I am standing before God beseeching him with my whole heart

---

[1] p. 736.
[2] p. 965.

to show us His love more clearly, to show mankind how to purify ourselves, to show us how to reach our salvation.[3]

But the other side of the German psyche is also represented, again in connection with Buchenwald. After a grisly description of the camp by Colonel Charles Codman,[4] a short squib reveals a remarkable side of the German attitude of the day:

> Bruce tells me that quite a nice young German hospital nurse came to see him in his Company H.Q. He showed her the pictures of the Buchenwald concentration camp. She looked horrified, then suddenly her face cleared. "But it's only the Jews," she said.[5]

These are only a few examples out of hundreds, illustrating that there is something for everyone in this monumental and memorable book. The overall effect of the collection is, as it should be, sobering. As Antoine de Saint-Exupéry is quoted in the introductory pages, "War is not a true adventure. . . . [T]here is no adventure in heads-or-tails, in betting that the toss will come out life or death. War is . . . a disease. It is like typhus."

JOHN S.D. EISENHOWER
Trappe, Maryland

A West Point graduate, retired Army brigadier general, former ambassador to Belgium, and military historian, John S.D. Eisenhower is the author of The Bitter Woods: The Battle of the Bulge (*available from Da Capo Press*), Intervention!: The United States & the Mexican Revolution, So Far From God: The U.S. War with Mexico, 1846–1848, *among others, and editor of the Major Battles and Campaigns series (also available from Da Capo Press).*

---

[3] pp. 576–577.
[4] General George S. Patton's aide.
[5] pp. 996–998.

INTRODUCTION

THIS is a documentary conspectus of the worst war in history, beginning at the German invasion of Poland on 1 September 1939 and ending with the last Japanese surrenders in September and October 1945. But it is not a history of the war: that has been written—by Sir Winston Churchill and by other historians, official and unofficial. This book could not have been written by one man, for it is an attempt to put together a chronicle of how it actually felt to be alive twenty years ago; to see, to hear, to smell, to feel the war at first hand. As service men and women, politicians and diplomats, workers in the resistance movements and victims of aggression, as men and women in civil occupations, and even as children, millions were aware of the war as a world-wide cataclysm hanging over the whole of life. Some, comparatively few but still numerous, wrote down their experience of that part of the war in which they were immediately involved; this book is a mosaic of such records. The contributors are world leaders, soldiers, sailors and airmen, journalists, firemen, hospital staff, factory workers, peasants—anyone who has written down in the spirit of an eye-witness or a participant his impressions of some aspect of war experience, of greater or lesser significance.

What must impress the reader of these pages is the vastness of the war: its totality, the extent to which it penetrated like an evil contagion into every corner of the inhabited world. As Marshal Pétain, the misguided master of Vichy, remarked at one stage—'Now for the first time the whole world is at war.' In these pages will be found the views and feelings of housewives in London, Berlin, Moscow and Tokyo: their problems, joys and sorrows are much the same. Here, too, we present the views of British and Germans facing one another at El Alamein, of Russians and Germans creeping forward through the frozen ruins of Stalingrad, of Americans and Japanese inching through a sodden Pacific jungle. All these, and many more, were men and women committed the world over to a problem from which none could escape once the politicians had decreed that the shooting should begin. This second World War produced heroism comparable with anything which had gone before, cowardice, inefficiency, brilliance, greatness, and a dedication to one object—on whichever side it might be—of more people that have ever before been involved in a single, terrifying catastrophe.

One of us responsible for this volume was concerned in 1937 with the production of a similar book describing the first World War: it was called *Vain Glory*. In our present task we find a difference. About the second World War there was little either vain or glorious. It was a bitter, sordid affair—for even the horrors of Passchendaele had an heroic dignity which cannot be equalled. It was not in vain, since it was begun to remove the evil men of Nuremberg, and in that at least it succeeded. But, to the surprise of those who found themselves involved in it, it developed into a display of hard-hitting brutality—sparing neither men, women, nor children—which only the mythical depredations of Genghis Khan may have challenged.

If there is ever a third world war, it will no doubt be a very clean job of

destruction started at a range of thousands of miles by technicians suitably protected below ground and pressing a knob. But when the first scientific flurry is
over, the destruction will be so great that it will be left to the surviving men,
women and children to stick it out and somehow try to get the mess through to
a conclusion.

In compiling this book we have paid our respects to military prowess—the
actions of the professional soldiers who have triumphed with all the skill to
which their lives have been devoted; but the victims of any war are the people:
people in uniform, people out of uniform, people fighting, and people fleeing.
There will be nowhere to flee next time, so this book offers a record of what
may be the last of its kind: for better or for worse.

D. F.
Headley, Hants

J. R.
Chalfont St. Giles, Bucks

NOTE

The contributions to this book are chosen from documentary sources. In one
or two cases, where no eye-witness account is available, a reliable historian has
been drawn upon for the record. Fiction has only been used when the Editors
are satisfied that the writer was present at and witnessed the events which he
has woven into his narrative. The war and its ramifications were so great and
so many that some aspects have not been mentioned in these pages. To those on
all sides whose work has not been recognized, we offer our apologies and hope
that they will find some satisfaction in the overall picture of the vast struggle.

D. F.
J. R.

CONTENTS

CONTENTS

MAPS

ACKNOWLEDGMENTS

WE wish to express our gratitude to the individuals, libraries, and other bodies listed below, all of whom have been of the greatest possible assistance in the preparation of this book. The authors and publishers of the extracts used are acknowledged in full between pages 1069 and 1076.

> The American Embassy Library
> The Guildhall Library
> The Imperial War Museum Library
> The Information Bureau, Chatham House
> The Book Information Bureau, National Book League
> The Walter Hines Page Memorial Library
> The War Office Library
> Mr. J. A. Williams

We would also like to thank the many publishers and literary agents who have lent us new books in typescript, proof, or bound copy form, a kindness which has allowed the inclusion of much recently-published material. We also wish to thank Mr. T. R. Nicholson for his great editorial help in the closing stages of the preparation of the book for the printer, Mrs. Herta Ryder, who throughout has kept under her control the vast amount of material which accumulated, and Mr. Antony Brett-James for his assistance in checking proofs.

D. F.   J. R.

IDENTIFICATION
OF EXTRACTS

IN order to discover the source of any extract, the reader should note the number of the page on which it begins and its heading and first words, and then refer to the section entitled *Key to the Sources of Extracts* (pages 1043 to 1068). There, following the page number and brief identification of the passage, will be found a key number. Reference to this key number in the following section, entitled *Sources* (pages 1069 to 1076), will reveal the title, author, publisher and publication date of the work drawn upon.

The italicized passages between extracts have been interpolated by the Editors to provide a consecutive narrative.

Signatures: A very few extracts are not signed. These are the small minority of completely impersonal passages written by historians, inserted, when of a sufficiently high standard, for lack of first-hand material. Of the signed extracts, a few are anonymous; for example, 'British gunner'. In these cases the Editors have been unable to ascertain the writer's identity, or else the writer has wished to remain anonymous. In some cases the signatures of servicemen do not include ranks. These are omitted either because the appropriate rank could not be ascertained, or because it was thought more effective to omit them. Where a rank is given, it changes appropriately in the cases of the most famous men, and in other cases remains the same throughout, the rank likely to sound most familiar or natural to the reader being given. These are broad principles, but individual circumstances may have had to dictate some exceptions, at the expense of rules of consistency.

.... THERE is a great danger in this war. But if we are among those that get back, we shall have nothing to tell. I have had adventures— pioneering mail lines; flying the Andes; being forced down among rebellious Arabs in the Sahara. But war is not a true adventure. It is a mere *ersatz*. Where ties are established, where problems are set, where creation is stimulated—there you have adventure. But there is no adventure in heads-or-tails, in betting that the toss will come out life or death. War is not an adventure. It is a disease. It is like typhus.

Antoine de Saint-Exupéry

If it be Life that awaits, I shall live forever unconquered:
If Death, I shall die at last strong in my pride and free.

Scottish National Memorial

I

THE COMING OF WAR

In the summer of 1939 Hitler's Germany, having annexed Austria and Czecho-slovakia with the acquiescence of the rest of the world, turned eastward towards Poland. On 31 March, Britain, ending the policy of appeasement, had joined France in a guarantee of Poland against aggression. On 23 August Hitler secured Soviet connivance to his designs on the Poles. The stage was set.

WE WANT WAR

THE bloodless solution of the Czech conflict in the autumn of 1938 and the spring of 1939 and the annexation of Slovakia rounded off the territory of Greater Germany in such a way that it then became possible to consider the Polish problem on the basis of more or less favourable strategic premises.

General Jodl to the Gauleiters, 1943

I wanted to make sure for myself, and on 11 August I went to Salzburg. It was in his residence at Fuschl that Ribbentrop informed me, while we were waiting to sit down at the table, of the decision to start the fireworks, just as he might have told me about the most unimportant and commonplace administrative matter. 'Well, Ribbentrop,' I asked him, while we were walking in the garden, 'what do you want? The Corridor or Danzig?' 'Not any more,' and he stared at me through those cold *Musée Grévin* eyes. 'We want war.'

Count Ciano, Italian Foreign Minister, 1939

POLAND

An Act of Aggression is Arranged: 26 August 1939

Mehlhorn's voice grew more excited as he told me that Heydrich had asked him to come to his office and, surprisingly, had confided to him one of Hitler's secret orders. Before 1 September, if possible, an absolutely irreproachable cause for war had got to be created, one that would stand in history as a complete justification and would brand Poland in the eyes of the world as the aggressor against Germany. It had therefore been planned to dress troops in Polish uniforms and attack the Gleiwitz radio transmitter. Hitler had assigned Heydrich and Admiral Canaris, Chief of Army Intelligence, to carry out this operation. However, Canaris was so repelled by the order that he had managed to withdraw and Heydrich alone was in charge of it. Heydrich had explained to Mehlhorn the details of the plan. The Polish uniforms were to be supplied at Keitel's command by the O.K.W.—the Supreme Command of the Armed Forces.

1

I asked Mehlhorn where they would get the Poles who were to wear these uniforms. 'That's just it,' Mehlhorn replied. 'That's the devilish thing about this plan: the "Poles" will be convicts from the concentration camps. They're going to be armed with proper Polish weapons, but most of them will just be mown down, of course. They've been promised that any who get away with it will have their freedom immediately. But who's going to believe such a promise?'

Mehlhorn paused. Then he said, 'Heydrich has put me in command of the attack.' He gripped my arm hard: 'What am I to do?' he asked. 'Heydrich has given me this assignment to get rid of me. I know it. He wants my death! What can I do?'

Now it was my turn to be silent. What advice could I possibly give? Finally I said, 'The whole thing is insane. One can't make world history by tactics of that kind. The thing couldn't possibly be kept secret, not for long, anyway. Somewhere, somehow, it'll all come out. You must keep clear of it though. Try to talk your way out. Make some excuse—say you're ill—or just simply refuse. Whatever happens through your refusing that sort of order, it'll be preferable to the consequence of your carrying it out.'

Walter Schellenberg, German Foreign Intelligence Service

Most Secret

Directive No. 1 for the Conduct of War: 31 August

1. Now that all the political possibilities of disposing by peaceful means of a situation on the Eastern Frontier which is intolerable for Germany are exhausted, I have determined on a solution by force.
2. The attack on Poland is to be carried out in accordance with the preparations made for 'Fall Weiss', with the alterations which result, where the Army is concerned, from the fact that it has, in the meantime, almost completed its dispositions.

    Allotment of tasks and the operational target remain unchanged.

    The date of attack—1 September, 1939.

    Time of attack—04.45 [inserted in red pencil].

    This time also applies to the operation at Gdynia, Bay of Danzig, and the Dirschau Bridge.
3. In the West it is important that the responsibility for the opening of hostilities should rest unequivocally with England and France. At first, purely local action should be taken against insignificant frontier violations.

Adolf Hitler

Proclamation to the Armed Forces: 1 September

The Polish Government, unwilling to establish good neighbourly relations as aimed at by me, wants to force the issue by way of arms.

The Germans in Poland are being persecuted with bloody terror and driven from their homes. Several acts of frontiér violation, which cannot be tolerated by a great power, show that Poland is no longer prepared to respect the Reich's frontiers. To put an end to these mad acts, I can see no other way but from now onwards to meet force with force.

The German Armed Forces will with firm determination take up the struggle for the honour and the vital rights of the German people.

I expect every soldier to be conscious of the high tradition of the eternal German soldierly qualities and to do his duty to the last.

Remember always and in any circumstances that you are the representatives of National Socialist Greater Germany.

Long live our people and the Reich.   Adolf Hitler

BRITAIN

A Letter to America: 3 September 1939

It was a brilliantly sunny morning.

At ten o'clock the wireless said, 'Stand by for an announcement of national importance.' It was about our ultimatum and the time-limit of eleven o'clock. At quarter-hour intervals they announced that the Prime Minister would 'make an announcement of national importance at 11.15'; in between they played things like the Berceuse from *Jocelyn* and at the zero hour they were disseminating a talk by Mrs. Somebody on 'How to Make the Most of Tinned Foods: Some Useful Recipes'. . . .

11.15 a.m.

I am speaking to you from the Cabinet Room at 10 Downing Street. This morning the British Ambassador in Berlin handed the German Government a final note stating that, unless we heard from them by eleven o'clock that they were prepared at once to withdraw their troops from Poland, a state of war would exist between us. I have to tell you now that no such undertaking has been received, and that consequently this country is at war with Germany.

You can imagine what a bitter blow it is to me that all my long struggle to win peace has failed. Yet I cannot believe that there is anything more or anything different that I could have done and that would have been more successful.

Up to the very last it would have been quite possible to have arranged a peaceful and honourable settlement between Germany and Poland, but Hitler would not have it. He had evidently made up his mind to attack Poland whatever happened, and although he now says he put forward reasonable proposals which were rejected by the Poles, that is not a true statement.

The proposals were never shown to the Poles, nor to us, and, though they were announced in a German broadcast on Thursday night, Hitler did not wait to hear comments on them, but ordered his troops to cross the Polish frontier. His action shows convincingly that there is no chance of expecting that this man will ever give up his practice of using force to gain his will. He can only be stopped by force.

We and France are to-day, in fulfilment of our obligation, going to the aid of Poland, who is so bravely resisting this wicked and unprovoked attack on her people. We have a clear conscience. We have done all that any country could do to establish peace. The situation in which no word given by Germany's ruler could be trusted, and no people or country could feel themselves safe, has become intolerable. And now that we have resolved to finish it, I know that you will all play your part with calmness and courage.

At such a moment as this the assurances of support that we have received from the Empire are a source of profound encouragement to us.

Now may God bless you all. May He defend the right. It is the evil things that we shall be fighting against—brute force, bad faith, injustice, oppression, and persecution—and against them I am certain that the right will prevail.

Neville Chamberlain

. . . . His voice was firm, with an undertone of great sadness, and at certain moments you could hear indignation deepening the timbre. Immediately afterwards came the general directions what to do in air-raids, etc. I locked up, gave Mrs. C. the key, and accepted a lift from our landlord to Westminster Cathedral where I was going to the twelve o'clock Mass.

And hardly had we set out when, doggone it, the sirens started warbling, and the whistles shrilling and the A.R.P. wardens patrolling the streets. We got past about a hundred doorways, and all the people indoors were coming out to see the war start, and standing around craning their necks at the sky as if that would help. Finally a warden pulled us over to the kerb and advised us to take cover, assuring us that it was a genuine warning with about ten minutes allowed for taking cover. Mr. P., whose *sang-froid* is immense, remained in his car, but I elected to duck for the nearest likely place, because I'd had time to think about trying to explain to you how I came to be near Victoria at all, and I felt slightly conscience-stricken. Anyway, I crossed the street to that block of L.C.C. flats which you'll remember on the left coming away from Victoria—council houses with archway entrances. The paved courtyard inside was filling with people of the flats, each with that small square cardboard box that everybody carries now —the effect of an enormous picnic with each one carrying his own sandwiches— and we were all sent down to the laundry, a nice cool long room lined with tubs and well sandbagged on the outside. There were about fifty of us, men and women. They were all, of course, very poor and 'common' people and they were all pretty well convinced that 'that man', with his well-known instinct for the dramatic, was about to put over a really convincing reply to the Ultimatum. And they were as cool as cucumbers—just as gallantly matter-of-fact as you'd expect them to be. One young girl was sniffling a bit, and her friends were jollying her out of it. The men busied themselves in shifting a pile of sandbags. There was no joking, no talk to speak of; the only expression on their faces was one of deep disapproval—the incredulous, 'shocked' disapproval of a man who is serene enough in his own mind to feel morally outraged without feeling flustered.

Beatrice L. Warde

Mobilization: Britain

The plan was this. In the event of the international situation deteriorating to such an extent that the Government felt it could n>t carry on without the backing of the 54th (County of London) H.A.A. Regiment, R.A. (and perhaps some other units of the Territorial Army as well), the summons would be passed down through channels of ever-diminishing grandeur until it reached the permanent staff at the drill hall, Putney; the permanent staff would then ring up the keymen, and the keymen would ring up the sub-keymen, whose duty it was to inform what I can only call the sub-submen. The use of the word 'inform' rather than 'ring up' is noteworthy here. For whereas all sub-keymen were on the phone, such was by no means the case with all sub-submen, so that to the sub-keyman fell the responsible and arduous duty of getting out his car and actually calling in person at the doors of those whose names were inscribed on his folder. It will be seen that the position of sub-keymen was one of great trust—though, looking back, it is hard to resist the conclusion that possession of a telephone *and* a car may have been more of a recommendation for the post than a good bearing, say, or steadiness on parade.

Despite, or in ignorance of, these arrangements, Hitler continued his aggressive preparations against Poland, and on 24 August 1939 the call came. I wish I could say that I answered it with flashing eyes and a gesture of defiance. But when the sergeant rang me up at my office and told me to report at the drill hall without delay, my first feeling, as I remember it, was that this really was going a bit too far. Was this, I wonder, the instinctive reaction of others in A.A. units of the T.A.? We had recently got back from a month's 'embodiment'—a fortnight on operational gun positions 'just in case' and a fortnight at practice camp—and twenty-eight days in khaki seemed, in those far-off days, about as much as could reasonably be demanded of any private citizen. To be rung up with this peremptory order at 2.30 in the afternoon, in the sanctity of one's own office, was getting very near downright impertinence.

'Oh, but look here, Sergeant, this is getting beyond a joke. I mean, I've got my work to do, you know.'

I don't claim that these were my actual words. It is possible that, on reflection, I may have substituted the shorter form, 'Yes, Sergeant.' But I know what I was thinking.

I remember laying down the receiver and looking slowly round the office. It seemed much the same. The sun still streamed through the window on the papers on my desk, the half-written letter, the note to ring up So-and-so at four, the memo about to-morrow's meeting. On the window-sill lay the brown-paper parcel containing the new pullover to which I had treated myself during the lunch hour. Across the street a man suspended in a cradle of ropes and planks was busily cleaning the windows of the building opposite. Everything was just as it had been two minutes ago; only now it had no significance. It was incredible that I should have been concerned, a few short moments ago, with the phrasing of a letter that seemed to belong to so remote a point in time, to have been written by so dim and irrecoverable a personality. This sense of being suddenly cut off from one's own past, and future, is the strongest recollection I have of this peculiar day.

On the way home to pick up my car and my gear the feeling of numbness evaporated and a certain excitement came over me. After all, I was a sub-keyman. My own moment of shock was over, and I was now to be the bringer of startling news to others—always a pleasurable occupation. 'Get cracking,

Gunner Bones,' I should say. 'It's war!' And Gunner Bones, remembering that his only pair of boots was at the cobbler's, would pale beneath his tan, while I stood calm and collected on his doorstep. These unworthy thoughts sustained me through most of the journey, save for a grim moment as my bus passed the ground of my club and I remembered that I was due to play tennis there that evening, with perhaps a swim to follow. Tennis! The Lord alone knew when my next game would be. . . .

My recollections of rounding up my sub-submen and driving to the drill hall are vague. But a few random pictures remain of the drill hall itself. I remember a scene of some confusion. I remember sitting on my kit-bag, with that sensation of slight sickness one used to get on the first day at school, wishing, quite simply and unheroically, that I was back home again, and I remember falling in in full marching order and then falling out again to get stripped to the waist for a medical inspection. I remember the M.O. asking whether I felt all right as I halted in front of him, and dismissing me with a kindly nod when I assured him that I felt fine, thank you. I also remember reflecting, as I struggled into my uniform again, that if my own doctor had got me stripped to the waist and then declined even to lay a stethoscope against my chest I should rapidly have taken my custom elsewhere. But this, of course, was war—or pretty near it.

Somebody was shouting my name. What now? Could it be that they had decided to get along without me? 'Bit of a muddle. Didn't mean to trouble a busy man like you, sir. Get off home as soon as you like.' However, it turned out to be not quite that. They told me the sergeant wanted me.

'Yes, Sergeant?'

'Ah, there you are. Is that stinking old red car outside yours?'

'The thirty-two-horse La Salle?'

'I don't care what it is. Is it yours?'

'Yes, Sergeant.'

'Then say so. You're to take the Battery Commander down to the gun site.'

'The Battery Commander? Crikey!'

'He's ready now.'

'Yes, Sergeant.'

There's glory for you. Just the Battery Commander and me—leading the van. They piled his kit in the dickey, somebody stuck an *Air Defence of Great Britain: Priority* label on the windscreen, and we were off.

This was, without question, my finest hour. Never again throughout the war did I feel so important—never again, to be truthful, did I feel important at all; but just at this moment I felt terrific.

1440433 Gunner Ellis, H. F.

Mobilization: New Zealand

We had a week before the men came in. The huts were barely finished, showers and ablution stands not completed; but the carpenters took their kits with them one evening and the drafts to form the 3rd Rifle Battalion, the Machine-gun Battalion, a Field-Ambulance, and an A.S.C. Company came in by special trains. Most were ending a long journey. All were in old civilian clothes and many were far from sober. As I watched some of my men trudge in

I remarked to Gordon Washbourn, 'This is going to be the best infantry in the world.'

On the first night we did nothing more than give them their army numbers, feed them, and get them to bed; in beds, for the one and only time in their service, made up by the officers and the N.C.Os. All slept very well. Next day, with the aid of a big chart showing the establishment of a rifle battalion, we organized and allotted jobs.

The rifle companies were made up by their Provinces, but Headquarters Company was not so easy. Officers kept rushing into the Orderly Room, consulting the chart, and dashing out to collect another driver or signaller or water-cart man or range-finder or some such, those already acquired being left seated in puzzled groups under the strictest injunctions not to stray. Gradually the parade ground emptied as the completed platoons were moved away, some already being asked to do so in step; and about midday there were only a few stragglers left who collected and sat themselves down together. Frank Davis and I checked our chart and discovered that we had omitted to provide for the anti-aircraft platoon, which had no officer. There should have been fourteen in that platoon. I went out and counted the survivors. There were fourteen, so establishment was completed, though as a matter of fact this was the only platoon up to strength. Several days later I found three innocents sunning themselves behind one of the huts and found that somehow they had been missed altogether and were apparently quite happy about it. They promptly became riflemen.

Three months later we embarked at Lyttleton in the first transport to leave New Zealand for the war. In the meantime the mob which had tramped in that afternoon had become a battalion, very young, very partially trained, but already possessing its own memories and beginning to be proud.

Brigadier Howard Kippenberger

The Reason for Fighting

From a broadcast prepared by George Bernard Shaw, but banned by the Minister of Information.

.... What am I, a superannuated non-combatant, encouraging young men to fight against? It is not German National Socialism: I was a National Socialist before Mr. Hitler was born. I hope we shall emulate and surpass his great achievements in that direction. I have no prejudice against him personally: much that he has written and spoken echoes what I myself have written and said. He has adopted even my diet. I am interested in his career as one of the great psychological curiosities of political history; and I fully appreciate his physical and moral courage, his diplomatic sagacity, and his triumphant rescue of his country from the yoke the Allies imposed on her after her defeat in 1918. I am quite aware of the fact that his mind is a twentieth-century mind, and that our governing class is mentally in the reign of Edward III, six centuries out of date. I can pay him a dozen compliments which I could not honestly pay to any of our present rulers.

My quarrel with him is a very plain one. I happen to be what he calls a Nordic. In stature, in colour, in length of head, I am the perfect blond beast whom Mr. Hitler classes as the salt of the earth, divinely destined to rule over all lesser breeds. Trace me back as far as you can; and you will not find a Jew in my ancestry. But I have a friend who happens to be a Jew. His name is Albert Einstein: and he is a far greater human prodigy than Mr. Hitler and myself rolled into one. And the nobility of his character has made his gift an unmixed benefit to his fellow-creatures. Well, Adolf Hitler would compel me, the Nordic Shaw, to insult Albert Einstein; to claim moral superiority to him and unlimited power over him, drive him out of his house, exile him, be punished for miscegenation if I allow a relative of mine to marry a relative of his, and finally to kill him as part of a general duty to exterminate his race. Adolf has actually done these things to Albert, bar the killing, as he carelessly exiled him first and thus made the killing impossible. Since then he has extended the list of reprobates from Semites to Celts and from Poles to Slavs: in short, to all who are not what he calls Nordics. If he conquers these islands he will certainly add the Irish to the list, as several authorities have maintained that the Irish are the lost tribes of Israel.

Now this is not the sort of thing that sane men can afford to argue with. It is on the face of it pernicious nonsense; and the moment any ruler starts imposing it as a political philosophy on his nation or any other nation by physical force, there is nothing for it but for the sane men to muster their own physical forces and go for him. We ought to have declared war on Germany the moment his police stole Einstein's violin. When the work of a police force consists not of suppressing robbery with violence but actually committing it, it becomes a recruiting ground for the most infernal blackguards, of whom every country has its natural-born contingent. Unless such agents are very strictly disciplined and controlled, their heads are turned by the authority they possess as a State police; and they resort to physical torture as the easiest way to gratify their tastes and execute their function at the same time. How is that discipline and control to be maintained? Not by an autocrat, because, as Napoleon said when he heard of the defeat of his navy at Trafalgar, an autocrat cannot be everywhere. And when his police get out of hand and give his prisons and concentration camps a bad name, he has to back them up because he cannot do without them, and thus becomes their slave instead of their master.

George Bernard Shaw

GERMANY

War broke quietly and as if under a cloud. There were no frenzied people in the streets such as we had read about in 1914. No flags, no processions. No cheering and marching troops and flowers. The streets of Berlin seemed empty and there were no troops to be seen. There was only a particularly dull sense of waiting, which gradually faded, and then, with the finish of the 'siege' of Poland, completely changed to a wild excitement.

Werner Harz, journalist

There was only one topic of conversation in the homes and cafés during those last days of August 1939, the Non-Aggression Treaty with Russia. It had come as a complete shock to all of us. Ever since the Reichstag fire in February

1933, Communism had been expelled from German political life. Members of the Communist Party had been bitterly pursued and put in prison. Russia was declared the arch-enemy. In February 1933 we had been told that Russia had prepared a revolution in Germany, and had it not been for Hitler we would all have been swallowed up in the Communist régime, and now, after six years of hate campaign, the Press suddenly declared unanimously that Russia had no wish to export her ideology to Germany. Nor did Germany wish to export National Socialism to Russia. The world, our Press said firmly, was wide enough for both ideologies to flourish side by side. . . . Our feelings now were a jumble of relief and astonishment at the quick change. Towards Hitler we had nothing but admiration and respect. A man who had the courage to step over the abyss between Germany and Russia to prevent war was a man worthy of the highest praise.

Mr. Wolter told us all to read the writings of Machiavelli. 'Get a copy of Machiavelli's book *Il Principe*,' he told me. 'Keep yourself up to date. Learn about politics, my dear comrade-assistant. The key is "no morals"; forget the Salvation Army; be ruthless and have no remorse. No price is too high for peace for your home-country.' He said all this in a stern voice with a half-twinkle in his eye. Then he became gentler and added: 'You know, in the long run this ruthlessness may be best. It's more merciful than a long "decent, human" war, don't you agree?

I agreed.

'In time you will get used to seeing the flag with the hammer and sickle flying in the Unter den Linden,' said Mr. Wolter ironically.

On 1 September, 1939, however, my personal views changed. The radio and newspapers announced the attack on Poland.

'You look like the Mater Dolorosa,' Mr. Wolter said to me that morning. 'You want your sons to live, don't you? Well, how can they live if Germany is to be cramped up—*ein Volk ohne Raum* [a people without living room]? Twenty years after the Treaty of Versailles and we are still separated from our own people by the Polish Corridor! Danzig is a German town. If the Poles won't give it back to us voluntarily, then, all right, we march in and take it. . . .

'It's all trash when they accuse Germany of being responsible for the first World War, and say we must be punished. They talk of freedom to us, but where is freedom when a big town like Danzig can't come back into its Fatherland? Do you seriously think we would have got the Rhineland back if we hadn't marched into it?; or Austria?; or Czechoslovakia?; and our Army?; and our rivers; we weren't even masters of our own rivers till Hitler came! Now we have got our Army and no more foreign restrictions in our country.' He looked at me with a certain pity. 'But, of course, you women don't understand politics. You have to be hard and strong to grasp such things. Women have the brains of babies over politics. My wife is just the same.'

Somehow I just had to answer back. 'But up till now Hitler has done everything peacefully. I *do* admire his foresight and diplomacy, as long as it means peace. But this is war!'

Mr. Wolter commented, 'No need to worry at all. You take my word for it, this war against Poland will be just a Blitzkrieg. It will be over in a flash.'

Else Wendel, housewife

I regarded England's and France's interference and declaration of war as nothing else but a formality. There was no doubt that as soon as they realized the utter hopelessness of Polish resistance and the vast superiority of German arms they would begin to see that we had always been in the right and it was quite senseless to meddle in our private business. But of course we had to let these warmongers know that this was the last time that Germany would stand for any sort of foreign interference. It was only as a result of their guarantee of something that wasn't their business that the war had ever started. If Poland had been alone she would certainly have given in quietly.

Otherwise, we had no quarrel with France or England. Our West Wall was perfectly secure, and we never thought that we would have to invade these countries or fight them actively.

Fritz Muehlebach, Storm Trooper

AMERICA

The only interest here, as everywhere, is the war, and I believe that we really can keep out of it. Fortunately there is no great sentiment in this country for getting into it, although I think almost everyone wants to see England and France win.

Harry L. Hopkins, Presidential adviser, to his brother Emory, October 1939

. . . . Americans in 1939 were fortified with the experience that the previous generation had conspicuously lacked, the experience of involvement in European war, and they wanted no more of it. The impulse to let 'Europe stew in its own juice' was a very powerful one, and an entirely understandable one, for there were too many Americans who considered that their country's only reward for coming to the aid of Britain and France in 1918 was to be given the name of 'Uncle Shylock'. (As Roosevelt remarked many times, 'We fortunately never had a chance to find out what our "reward" would have been if Germany had won that war.') Thus isolationist sentiment in 1939 was not limited to Americans of German birth or descent, or to those who loved German music and admired German science and industry, or to those who were pure pacifists: it was representative of the entire American people save for a diminutive minority of those who believed that a victory for Hitler would put the security of our own country and our own constitutional democracy in deadly peril.

Harry L. Hopkins

INVASION

The ordering of general mobilization came almost on top of Britain's and France's guarantee of Poland; reservists were called up, vehicles and troops mobilized and ammunition distributed. We loaded our tanks and trucks on to the train and travelled for three days to Paprad in Slovakia, where we waited about ten miles from the Polish border. Several of us went up to the frontier to reconnoitre, and after the third day we got orders to move up during the night. At dawn we crossed into Poland.

The whole thing was so like an occupation or a manœuvre that we could hardly believe this was really war; it all seemed too well-ordered and familiar. There was virtually no resistance, and for days on end we advanced towards the Polish Ukraine. There were rumours of sharpshooters and partisans, but I never saw or heard anything of them, except for the occasional sound of a shot in the distance. There was a certain amount of sporadic fighting when we got to the river barriers, but the Luftwaffe had already cleared the way for us. Their Stuka dive-bombers were deadly accurate, and as there was no opposition they had it all their own way. The roads and fields were swarming with unhappy peasants who had fled in panic from their villages when the bombing began, and we passed hundreds and hundreds of Polish troops walking dejectedly towards Slovakia. The Poles seemed to be completely apathetic, and there were so many prisoners that nobody bothered to guard them or even tell them where to go.

Lieutenant Baron Tassilo von Bogenhardt, 6th Motorized Regiment

On 5 September our corps had a surprise visit from Adolf Hitler. I met him near Plevno on the Tuchel-Schwetz road, got into his car and drove with him along the line of our previous advance. We passed the destroyed Polish artillery, went through Schwetz, and then, following closely behind our encircling troops, drove to Graudenz, where he stopped and gazed for some time at the blown bridges over the Vistula. At the sight of the smashed artillery regiment, Hitler had asked me, 'Our dive-bombers did that?' When I replied, 'No, our Panzers!' he was plainly astonished. Between Schwetz and Graudenz those elements of 3 Panzer Division not needed for the encirclement of the Poles were drawn up: these included the 6th Panzer Regiment and the 3rd Armoured Reconnaissance Battalion with my son Kurt. We drove back through parts of 23 and 2 (Motorized) Infantry Divisions. During the drive we discussed at first the course of events in my corps area. Hitler asked about casualties. I gave him the latest figures that I had received, some one hundred and fifty dead and seven hundred wounded for all the four divisions under my command during the Battle of the Corridor. He was amazed at the smallness of these figures and contrasted them with the casualties of his own old regiment, the List Regiment, during the first World War: on the first day of battle that one regiment alone had lost more than two thousand dead and wounded. I was able to show him that the smallness of our casualties in this battle against a tough and courageous enemy was primarily due to the effectiveness of our tanks. Tanks are a life-saving weapon. The men's belief in the superiority of their armoured equipment had been greatly strengthened by their successes in the Corridor. The enemy had suffered the total destruction of between two and three infantry divisions and one cavalry brigade. Thousands of prisoners and hundreds of guns had fallen into our hands.

General Heinz Guderian

Warsaw: The End

Upon the capitulation of the city on 29 September, we left the special trains for a few days and travelled to Warsaw by road. Our three-day stay in the capital made one of the deepest and most disturbing impressions on me of all my war experiences. I was shocked at what had become of the beautiful city I had known—ruined and burnt-out houses, starving and grieving people. The nights were already unpleasantly chilly and a pall of dust and smoke hung over the city, and everywhere there was the sweetish smell of burnt flesh. There was no running water anywhere. In one or two streets isolated resistance by Polish nationalist bands was being continued. Elsewhere everything was quiet. Warsaw was a dead city.

Walter Schellenberg

When signing the instrument of capitulation, the Polish general said: 'A wheel always turns.' He was to prove right in the end, though hardly—as far as the subsequent fate of his fatherland was concerned—in the sense his words had been meant to convey.

General Erich von Manstein

THE SOLDIER'S CATECHISM

If it moves, salute it.
If it doesn't move, pick it up.
If you can't pick it up, paint it.

2

PHONEY WAR AND WINTER WAR

For six months after the conquest of Poland, land and air warfare in Europe virtually came to a standstill, with the exception of Russia's campaign against Finland. An uneasy truce prevailed on the Western Front, where the French and the British Expeditionary Force, despatched to France a week after war broke out, faced the Germans, each side sitting behind its fixed fortifications.

PHONEY WAR

The Birth of a Catch-phrase

FOR some reason which still seems inexplicable public imagination in this country* had been captured by the phrase employed by Senator Borah when he referred to the European war as a 'phoney' war. It was true that after the devastation of Poland the Germans had refrained from undertaking any air offensive against the Western powers. Nor had the German armies as yet made any move to invade the Low Countries or to break through the Maginot Line. But even to the most casual observer familiar with the working of Hitler's mind it was obvious that Hitler was waiting for two developments. First, he hoped that Germany's overwhelming superiority in the air and in mechanized equipment, as evidenced in the invasion of Poland, would persuade Great Britain and France that a negotiated peace granting Germany, as a first step, hegemony over Europe would be preferable to the probability of annihilation and occupation. Second, should this hope fail, he knew that the winter months would give his propaganda and subversive agencies much valuable time in which to break down the morale of the French armies. In this manner he would improve his chances for a military pushover as soon as the approach of summer made weather conditions more propitious for an all-out offensive.

Why any considerable segment of public opinion in the United States should have regarded the war as a 'phoney' war in view of constantly accumulating evidence of Hitler's military strength, and in view of the ruin which Poland had already suffered, must always remain a mystery. Moreover, many people appeared to feel, like Senator Borah, that the failure of Great Britain and France to undertake the offensive was somehow reprehensible. This feeling was almost sadistic. It had in it something of the 'boos' howled out by the spectators at a prize-ring when the two contestants are not putting on as bloody an exhibition as they have paid to witness.

Sumner Welles, U.S. Under-Secretary of State

Britain: Comment

In a Blackpool pub:
    'Nothing doing yet.'
    'Looks like another bloody hundred years' war.'

* The United States (Ed.)

'Rummest bloody war *I* ever knew.'

'Fighting with bloody pamphlets.'

'Strikes me they've both got the wind up.'

'It's a war of nerves.'

'Nerves my arse. It's boring me bloody well stiff. No football neither.'

From Cardiff:

'It's hard to believe there's a war on at all.'

'I shan't be happy until I see a really satisfactory casualty list.'

'Why don't they start something?'

'A couple of real air raids is what we want.'

From Harrow:

'This is a funny war; wish they would do something.'

'It's another trick of Hitler's. He thinks we shall get so bored with doing nothing that we shall start bombing, and then he can say we began it.'

'It's just another way of waging a war of nerves.'

Black-out

A woman: 'There's no need for all this darkness.'

Another: 'It's the same as everything they do—daft. They started rationing coal, and now they can't get shot of it, and they're asking you to buy as much as you can. Same with fish, and butter, and bacon; I don't know what things are coming to.'

Pub manageress:

'Wasn't Tuesday an awful night? I couldn't see a thing because the rain got on my glasses, and what with the black-out I walked into the sandbags under the clock, just by there. I hurt my leg, and it isn't better yet. That's a week ago, and I haven't been out since. It makes you frightened to go out, doesn't it, in case you get hurt again?'

Other women who are frightened:

'I'm all alone, with no one beside me, and it's terrible if they black-out before anyone comes back.'

'This black-out is simply cruel. I daren't go to chip shop of a night, and t'boss does like chips for his supper.'

'This darkness gets on my nerves. I don't know what to do with myself of an evening, when my husband is out. I can't go out anywhere unless he comes to fetch me. I wouldn't dare to come home alone in the dark—why, I'd never find my way.'

'I'm afraid of being molested. One of our girls was, going home from work last night.'

'It's all right for you; you're married. But I can't go out any more at night. I'm disgusted with this black-out.'

An insurance manager in Blackpool, married, forty:

'Had a nice night last night. Tommy bloody Handley on the wireless again; read every book in the house. Too dark to walk to the library, bus every forty-five minutes, next one too late for the pictures. "Freedom is in peril"—they're telling me!'

South Croydon porter:

'I fell off the platform the other night. Clean over the edge I fell. Thought I had turned far enough left and I hadn't. Mind you, there was a fog at the time.'

A bus conductor in Macclesfield:

'The number of times I been fooled wi' coins since black-out. . . . Last week I paid up four and sixpence from me wages.'

Amateur Inventors

Backroom scientists of a research group under the War Ministry consider suggestions for new weapons.

'Come on,' I said. 'Keystone Komics. Let's get going.'

They came and sat at my table and Joe produced the Keystone Komics file. The Komics were bright ideas which had been sent in to Mair. Joe and Tilly and I used to run through the week's bag every Wednesday.

Some of them were sent in by departments who'd received them and wanted Mair's view or wanted to be rid of them. But the others were from all over the place. The thing which always puzzled me was how these people got to know the address.

Joe opened the file and took out the first one.

'Poisoned barbed wire,' he said. 'You scratch yourself on it and die in agony two hours later. Any bidders?'

'What's the poison?' I said. 'Curare?'

'Oh, he doesn't go into *that*,' said Joe. 'He says he isn't a scientist himself. He just has ideas.'

'If I had ideas like that I'd see a doctor,' I said. 'Out.'

Joe put the letter aside and picked up the next.

'"Specification of the Barnes Retractable Bayonet. The bayonet is carried in a housing in the forepiece of the rifle. When the bayonet is required, a button is depressed and the bayonet is forced forward into the 'Ready' position by a strong spring, and locks itself rigidly. After use it can be pressed back into the housed position where it is retained by a catch."'

I said, 'I like "after use". Nice phrase.'

Tilly said, 'It's not a bad idea, though. Saves carrying the bayonet separately or having it sticking out all the time.'

'"An experimental model, fitted to a sporting rifle, works perfectly",' Joe read. '"The device costs very little." He's sent a drawing of it.'

We looked at it. It was quite a workmanlike drawing.

'I think it's a darned good idea,' said Tilly. He was always a perfect customer for the Komics.

'Hardly that,' I said. 'If it works and doesn't jam or break or mind being buried in mud or anything like that, it might have been a good idea before the war. That's about the size of it.'

'Why?'

'Well, damn it, we can't start re-equipping the whole army with joke bayonets. Anyhow, if the poor devil but knew it, what's really wanted is a bayonet that will open a bully beef tin without cutting you. Send him a nice note though, Joe.'

'Sure,' said Joe, 'and a free entry form for next week's competition. *A bas* the Barnes Bayonet.' He pulled out a big blueprint. 'The next's a radio thing which Williams has sent across. Leave that to the Old Man?'

'Yes. He wants to see all the radio. What is it?'

'Search me,' said Joe. 'I'm not a radio man myself. I saw something about the Heaviside Layer and decided it was out of my class. Now *this* is much more my sort of thing: "Dear Sirs, I have always been interested in birds. . . ."' He stopped and laughed a lot. 'Can you beat it?'

'Funny joke,' I said. 'What's he invented?'

'"It occurs to me,"' read Joe,' "that migrating birds are one of the few agencies which can enter enemy occupied territory without arousing suspicion."'

'Oh God!' I said. 'Which does he want them to take? Little bombs round their necks or bacteria?'

Joe looked on down the page. 'You've got it,' he said, looking up. 'Or nearly. Plant diseases. Out, I take it?'

'Yes. Y'know it's amazing what *dirty* ideas people get. That using animals one is a hardy annual, and it always gets me. There was the chap who trained dogs and wanted to teach them to take explosive booby traps across to the enemy.'

Nigel Balchin

The Venlo Incident

In the late autumn of 1939, *Holland was still a neutral country. Captain Payne Best, a British intelligence officer stationed there, was trying to make contact with a mysterious German 'general' who was said to be at the head of an underground resistance movement in Germany aimed at displacing Hitler and coming to terms with the Allies. Captain Best had several abortive clandestine meetings just over the frontier in Holland with German officers who claimed to represent the 'general'. In fact these officers were loyal, and were party to a plan to kidnap Captain Best and his associates and carry them off to Germany. On* 9 *November, Captain Best, Major Stevens and Lieutenant Klop of the Dutch Army were again due to meet the German officers near Venlo, a Dutch frontier town. Owing to the prevailing quiet, the events which followed created a great uproar.*

All the way down from The Hague we had noticed that military precautions had been intensified and we had been held up at every road block and tank barrier. Even now, between Venlo and our café, we were stopped twice. The first time the sentry said something about having orders to allow no cars to pass, and although Klop showed him his authority, insisted that he must first go to the guard-room and speak to the N.C.O. in charge. Both Stevens and I, I believe, felt alike and hoped that he would come back with the news that we could go no farther; but in a few minutes he was with us: 'Everything is all right. The N.C.O. had a message for me which had been phoned through from the office. Carry on.'

The second sentry did not actually stop us, but only made signs that we should drive slowly. He was stationed at a bend in the road just before we entered the straight along which one had a view of the frontier. Somehow or other, it seemed to me that things looked different from what they had on the previous days. Then I noticed that the German barrier across the road which had always been closed was now lifted; there seemed to be nothing between us and the enemy. My feeling of impending danger was very strong. Yet the scene was peaceful enough. No one was in sight except a German customs officer in uniform lounging along the road towards us and a little girl who was playing at ball with a big black dog in the middle of the road before the café.

I must have rather checked my speed, for Klop called out, 'Go ahead, everything is quite all right.' I felt rather a fool to be so nervous. I let the car drift slowly along to the front of the café on my left and then reversed into the car park on the side of the building farthest from the frontier. Schaemmel was standing on the veranda at the corner and made a sign which I took to mean that our bird was inside. I stopped the engine and Stevens got out on the right. My car had left-hand drive. I had just wriggled clear of the wheel and was following him out when there was a sudden noise of shouting and shooting. I looked up, and through the windscreen saw a large open car drive up round the corner till our bumpers were touching. It seemed to be packed to overflowing with rough-looking men. Two were perched on top of the hood and were firing over our heads from sub-machine guns; others were standing up in the car and on the running-board, all shouting and waving pistols. Four men jumped off almost before their car had stopped and rushed towards us shouting: 'Hands up!'

I don't remember actually getting out of the car, but by the time the men reached us I was certainly standing next to Stevens, on his left. I heard him say, 'Our number is up, Best.' The last words we were to exchange for over five years. Then we were seized. Two men pointed their guns at our heads, the other two quickly handcuffed us.

I heard shots behind me on my right. I looked round and saw Klop. He must have crept out behind us under cover of the car door which had been left open. He was running diagonally away from us towards the road; running sideways in big bounds, firing at our captors as he ran. He looked graceful with both arms outstretched—almost like a ballet dancer. I saw the windscreen of the German car splinter into a star, and then the four men standing in front of us started shooting, and after a few more steps Klop just seemed to crumple and collapse into a dark heap of clothes on the grass.

'Now, march!' shouted our captors, and prodding us in the small of our backs with their guns, they hurried us, with cries of 'Hup! Hup! Hup!' along the road towards the frontier. As we passed the front of the café I saw my poor Jan held by the arms by two men who were frog-marching him along. It seemed to me that his chin was reddened as from a blow. Then we were across the border. The black and white barrier closed behind us. We were in Nazi Germany.

Captain S. Payne Best

WINTER WAR

Russia invaded Finland at the end of November in order to occupy territories considered strategically necessary for her security. Such a move could only be directed against Germany, yet so unpopular was Russia and so unprovoked her aggression that Allied sympathy for the Finns resulted in preparations to send them active help. Such help was also being given, less openly, by the Germans. This extraordinary state of affairs was concluded by the signing of peace between Russia and Finland in March 1940.

An Analysis of the Russian Failure

If the general impression of the performance of the Soviet Union in the Finnish War had not been so unfavourable, Germany would hardly have underestimated the war potential of the Russian giant to the extent she did.

On what was this view of the Red Army, produced by the Winter War, based?

The most striking factor was no doubt the disproportion between the enormous effort and the small result achieved. Even in the first week of the war, unexpectedly large forces were thrown against Finland. . . . About half of the regular Russian divisions in Europe and Western Siberia had been mobilized for the Finnish War. Including the specialist formations, the enemy's strength amounted to nearly a million men, of whom part possessed a certain experience of war from the Polish campaign.

It was a characteristic mistake of the Red High Command to start military operations without paying necessary attention to the basic factors in the war against Finland, the character of the theatre of war and the strength of the enemy. It is understandable that the latter was under-estimated because of our obvious material weakness. It is more remarkable that the Russian High Command did not realize that its army organization was too cumbersome in northern country and winter conditions. How could troops coming from plains, even if they were accustomed to severe winters, be expected to fight in a barren wilderness the like of which they had never seen? The failure to estimate our powers of resistance shows the lack of foresight with which their plan of war had been drawn up, and also the blind faith of the Russians in the unlimited possibilities of modern technique.

That every order must first be approved by the political leaders necessarily led to delay and confusion, not to speak of a lessening of initiative and fear of responsibility. The political commissars were undoubtedly a driving force to be reckoned with. This became apparent in the first phase of the war when they had to restore order in detachments whose discipline had suffered through unsuccessful attacks, and also when it was a question of forcing unwilling troops to attack. The fact that surrounded units refused to surrender in spite of cold and hunger was largely due to the political commissars. Soldiers were prevented from surrendering by threats of reprisals against their families and the assurance that they would be killed after torture if they fell into the hands of the enemy. There were innumerable cases where officers as well as men preferred suicide to surrender.

The Russian officers were generally brave men who were little concerned about casualties, but in the higher ranks there were signs of a kind of inertia. This displayed itself in the formalism and simplicity of the operative plan, which excluded manœuvring and was obstinately pursued to victory or defeat. The Russians based their art of war on weight of material, and were clumsy, ruthless and extravagant. There was a striking absence of creative imagination where the fluctuations of the situation demanded quick decisions. The commanders were often unable to follow up initial successes.

The Russian infantryman showed himself brave, tough and frugal, but lacking in initiative. Contrary to his Finnish adversary, he was a mass fighter who was incapable of independent action when out of contact with his officers or comrades. Especially in the beginning, the Russians for this reason went in principally for mass attack, which often resulted in the attackers being mown down to the last man by a few well-placed automatic weapons. In spite of this, one attacking wave after another would follow, with a similar result. It happened in the initial fighting in December that the Russians would advance in close formation, singing, and even hand in hand, against the Finnish minefields, apparently indifferent to the explosions and the accurate fire of the defenders. The fatalistic submission which characterized the infantry was astonishing. The Russian soldier was not very susceptible to outward impressions and in every situation quickly regained his composure. Even if political terror played its part, the real explanation is to be found in the Russian people's hard struggle against nature, which in the course of ages had created a capacity for suffering and deprivation, a passive courage, and a fatalism incomprehensible to Europeans, and which has had, and continues to have, an important part in political development.

In this connection, the Russians' phenomenal ability to dig themselves in deserves special mention. It seemed second nature with them, and they were masters of engineering. In spite of long military service, the Russian infantry showed a number of defects. Their musketry with automatic arms and rifles was very poor. Though many of the divisions against us came from wooded country, the troops were unable to manœuvre successfully and fight in forests. As they lacked compasses, even orientation presented difficulties, and the forests, the ally of the Finnish fighter, filled them with terror. Here the 'White Death' (*Bielaja Smert*), the Finnish commando in his winter garb, harried them. But the greatest weakness of the troops was their lack of familiarity with skis. Even though they started systematic training of their troops immediately after the outbreak of the war, this meant little, because the technique of ski-ing, especially as practised in war, cannot be mastered in a few weeks.

In the Tsarist army the artillery had, from a technical as well as from a tactical point of view, been regarded as an *élite* arm. Now its level had naturally sunk because of the lack of education of the Officer Corps. But the material had kept up well to modern development. This was illustrated by the astonishingly great mass of modern artillery of great rapidity of fire and range as well as by the apparently inexhaustible stocks of ammunition.

In spite of tactical deficiencies, it was the enormous mass of artillery which formed the base of the Russians' activity on the Isthmus, but their artillery, such as it was, was not capable of meeting the demands of a war of movement.

There can be no question but that their armour was a disappointment to them. Already, the country in Finland made the dense and deep advances favoured by Russian tactics impossible. Instead, they had to work with smaller numbers attached to the infantry, and at what price? The total of tanks captured or destroyed by us was one thousand six hundred, which amounted to half of those opposed to us. In other words, a quarter of the Red Army's modern armour, not to mention the loss of three to four thousand politically picked and technically trained specialists. It should be mentioned, however, that the co-operation of armour with infantry improved considerably in the latter phase of the war. Their twenty-eight- and forty-five-ton tanks, armed with two guns and four or five machine-guns, contributed decisively to their penetration of our lines.

In spite of their crushing superiority—they had about two thousand five hundred planes—Russian air power was not to prove a factor of decisive importance. Its activity against ground troops was, especially in the beginning of the war, hesitant, and it was not able to break the defensive spirit of the nation. Total air war was in our country met by a calm and intelligent population whom danger merely steeled and united more strongly. The destruction was nevertheless considerable, for about a hundred and fifty thousand explosive and incendiary bombs were dropped with a total weight of seven thousand five hundred tons. Seven hundred civilians were killed and twice that number injured.

The Russians failed completely in their strategic task of severing our channels with the outside world and in producing chaos in our communications. Shipping traffic had been concentrated in Turku, which was subjected to sixty air attacks without becoming paralyzed. It is difficult to understand why the Russians had not for this purpose based light naval forces in Baltic ports, but the explanation may be that they had from the beginning counted on a lightning victory. Our only railway connection with the outside world was the line Kemi-Tornio, which carried most of our exports as well as our imports of war material. This line remained intact until the end of the war.

That their effort in the air did not produce corresponding results is unquestionable, and what did it cost them? According to figures from General Headquarters, 684 planes were shot down, but a later examination of war reports show that the actual number was 725. If one includes the 'unconfirmed' cases, the figure rises to 975.

The Finnish Air Force at the outbreak of war possessed ninety-six machines, a large part of which were antiquated. The total number of our planes during the whole of the war numbered 287, of which 162 were fighters. Our losses amounted to sixty-one, corresponding to 21 per cent of the total.

In men, our losses were 24,923 killed, missing and died from wounds, and 43,557 wounded.

It is unlikely that the exact Russian losses will ever be revealed, but they can at least be estimated in the light of known facts as approximately two hundred thousand killed.

Two causes contributed to these heavy losses, and should be especially noted—i.e. the severe winter and the deficiencies in the medical service. The continuous cold caused the death of thousands of wounded while awaiting succour.

There is no doubt that the experiences of the Finnish campaign were made full use of by Marshal Timoshenko in his reorganization of the Red Army. In his own words, to our Military Attaché in Moscow, 'The Russians have learnt much in this hard war in which the Finns fought with heroism.'

Marshal Mannerheim

ALL QUIET . . .

The Siegfried Line

Even before the end of the Polish Campaign, III Corps was transferred to the west, and at the beginning of October we arrived in the sector north of Trier. My elder brother was serving as a platoon commander in a reserve division near Saarbrücken, and I was able to visit him. This gave me an opportunity of inspecting the famous West Wall, or Siegfried Line, at first hand.

I soon realized what a gamble the Polish campaign had been, and the grave risks which were run by our High Command. The second-class troops holding the Wall were badly equipped and inadequately trained, and the defences were far from being the impregnable fortifications pictured by our propaganda. Concrete protection of more than three feet was rare, and as a whole the positions were by no means proof against heavy-calibre shelling. Few of the strong points were sited to fire in enfilade and most of them could have been shot to pieces by direct fire, without the slightest risk to the attackers. The West Wall had been built in such a hurry that many of the positions were sited on forward slopes. The anti-tank obstacles were of trivial significance, and the more I looked at the defences the less I could understand the completely passive attitude of the French.

Apart from sending some local patrols into the outlying areas (very 'outlying') of Saarbrücken, the French had kept very quiet and left the West Wall alone. This negative attitude was bound to affect the fighting morale of their troops, and was calculated to do much more harm than our propaganda, effective though it was.

General von Mellenthin

Boxing Day

The B.E.F. has had two Christmases—one white, one green. On the Maginot Line, sharp frost created rime on the woods and grass so thick that it resembled a fall of snow. A dense mist has at times shrouded their positions so that you could not see much more than forty or fifty yards ahead. Christmas morning was quiet. The sound of folk-songs drifted over from the German lines. But the truce, if truce there was, was probably more accidental than purposeful. Little activity beyond patrols and intermittent gunfire, which lasts only a few minutes, as a rule, has marked the festive season.

The bulk of the B.E.F. has had a different Christmas. In our other positions on the Belgian frontier frost suddenly changed to a wet mist, and Christmas Day and to-day saw rain falling. French children romped round British Christmas trees, colonels presented toys, and thousands of French youngsters will not forget the first Christmas of this war, nor their parents either, nor we.

J. L. Hodson, British war correspondent

Montgomery in France

My own divisional area was south of Lille. My operational task was to work on defences which were being undertaken in order to prolong the Maginot Line behind the Belgian frontier. Until 10 May Belgium was a strictly neutral country. Apart from the defensive tasks, I concentrated on training the division for the active operations which I was certain must come. My soul revolted at what was happening. France and Britain stood still while Germany swallowed Poland; we stood still while the German armies moved over to the West, obviously to attack *us* later on; we waited patiently to be attacked; and during all this time we occasionally bombed Germany *with leaflets*. If this was war, I did not understand it.

I well remember the visit of Neville Chamberlain to my division; it was on 16 December 1939. He took me aside after lunch and said in a low tone so that no one could hear, 'I don't think the Germans have any intention of attacking us. Do you?'

I made it quite clear that in my view the attack would come at the time of their own choosing; it was now winter and we must get ready for trouble to begin when the cold weather was over.

3 Division certainly put that first winter to good use and trained hard. If the Belgians were attacked, we were to move forward and occupy a sector astride Louvain behind the River Dyle. I trained the division for this task over a similar distance moving westwards, i.e. backwards into France. We became expert at a long night move, and then occupying a defensive position in the dark, and by dawn being fully deployed and in all respects ready to receive attack. This is what I felt we might have to do; and it was.

. . . . During the winter G.H.Q. arranged for divisions to send infantry brigades in turn down to the active front in the Saar, holding positions in front of the Maginot Line in contact with the German positions in the Siegfried Line. I went down there in January 1940 to visit one of my brigades and spent a few days having a look round. That was my first experience in the war of the French Army in action; I was seriously alarmed, and on my return I went to see my Corps Commander, and told him of my fears about the French Army and what we might have to expect from that quarter in the future. Brooke had been down there himself and had formed the same opinion.

The popular cries in the Maginot Line were: *Ils ne passeront pas* and *On les aura*.

But the general attitude did not give me any confidence that either of these two things would happen. Brooke and I agreed not to talk about it to our subordinates; I believe he discussed the matter with Gort.

I got into serious trouble during that first winter of the war. It happened in this way. After a few months in France the incidence of venereal disease in 3 Division gave me cause for alarm. To stop it I enlisted the aid of the doctors and even the padres; but all efforts were unsuccessful and the figures increased. Finally I decided to write a confidential letter to all subordinate commanders in which I analysed the problem very frankly and gave my ideas about how to solve it. Unfortunately a copy of the letter got into the hands of the senior chaplains at G.H.Q., and the Commander-in-Chief (Gort) was told of my action. My views on how to tackle the problem were not considered right and proper and there was the father-and-mother of a row. They were all after my blood at G.H.Q. But my Corps Commander (Brooke) saved me by insisting on being allowed to handle the matter himself. This he did in no uncertain manner and I received from him a proper backhander. He said, amongst other things, that he didn't think much of my literary effort. Anyhow it achieved what I wanted, since the venereal disease ceased.

General Montgomery

Live and Let Live

'Live and let live' was still the policy in the Saar, and anybody who loosed off a rifle was thought to be thoroughly anti-social. Twenty years of peace-time training made one hesitate to take life; and there was a marked reluctance among the Jocks to raise one's rifle to one's shoulder and have a shot at an unprovocative German. Twice in April the Germans went through the motions of an attack, and the second time overran some French posts on our flank; this was considered to be extremely bad form, and not to be imitated.

Bernard Fergusson

Leaflet Raids

In the earliest stages of the war we were not allowed to bomb anything on land, and our only possible targets were therefore warships, which we could attack only by day. Our losses from enemy fighters and flak were prohibitive and we therefore desisted before we had done ourselves or the enemy much harm. Meanwhile the Whitleys and Wellingtons were put to the questionable employment of dropping pamphlets all over Europe, a game in which we never had the slightest faith. My personal view is that the only thing achieved was largely to supply the Continent's requirements of toilet paper for the five long years of war. You have only to think what any man of sense would do with an obviously enemy pamphlet when he picked it up, how he would regard it, and how he would react to the statements in it. Our reaction to enemy pamphleteering had always been to jeer and at the most to keep some of their leaflets as souvenirs. News to occupied territory was another matter.

Years before, the idiotic expansion of secret files at the Air Ministry once drove me to send a minute round pointing out that at the rate we were going we should be making newspapers secret next. But never did I think to see the day when not only were newspapers made secret, but moreover newspapers expressly produced for the sole purpose of being delivered as rapidly as possible and by any and every means to the enemy. Yet they still had to be handled under all the complicated secret document procedure on our bomber stations and, in spite of repeated applications, we could never get these instructions withdrawn. Many of these pamphlets were patently so idiotic and childish that it was perhaps just as well to keep them from the knowledge of the British public, even if we did risk and waste crews and aircraft in dropping them on the enemy.

Air Vice-Marshal Arthur Harris

First Air Raid: Paris 1940

At dawn the siren sounded. By the second wail we were up and dressing, so quickly does one's mind readjust to past experience. In the lobby the night *concierge* was stretching and rubbing his eyes. We went out into the street. Chimney pots and the trees of the Champs Elysées black against a grey sky. The crackle of anti-aircraft guns. People in doorways and on the pavement. Men in dressing-gowns and slippers, smoking cigarettes. Women in every stage of dress and undress, some of them exercising lap dogs. Bored little girls in curl papers.

Someone said: 'There they are', and pointed directly overhead. Eyes turned upward and voices hushed. In the silence the drone of engines plainly audible. Then, we saw them. Five dark birds flying close formation. Clusters of air bursts, pink in the morning sun, surrounded them. A prayer that at least one burst might find its target, but with slow, deliberate progress the marauders passed safely out of sight. A little later the all-clear sounded.

Colonel Charles Codman, U.S. Army

In February 1940, Mr. Sumner Welles, U.S. Under-Secretary of State, was sent by President Roosevelt on a fact-finding tour of the belligerent nations of Europe.

Mussolini: February 1940

My first impression was one of profound astonishment at Mussolini's appearance. In the countless times I had seen him in photographs and in motion pictures and in the many descriptions I had read of him I had always gained the impression of an active, quick-moving, exceedingly animated personality. The man I saw before me seemed fifteen years older than his actual age of fifty-six. He was ponderous and static rather than vital. He moved with an elephantine motion; every step appeared an effort. He was heavy for his height, and his face in repose fell in rolls of flesh. His close-cropped hair was snow-white. During our long and rapid interchange of views he kept his eyes shut a considerable part of the time. He opened them with his dynamic and often-described wide stare only when he desired particularly to underline some remark. At his side was a large cup of some hot brew which he sipped from time to time.

Mussolini impressed me as a man labouring under a tremendous strain. One could almost sense a leaden oppression.

Impressions of Germany: March 1940

When our interview was over Goering insisted upon showing me the vast and innumerable rooms of his palace. It would be difficult to find an uglier building or one more intrinsically vulgar in its ostentatious display. The walls of the reception rooms and of the halls were hung with hundreds of paintings. Many examples of the best Italian and old German masters were placed side by side with daubs by modern German painters. He had made a speciality of collecting Cranachs. Two of them I recognized as being from the collection in the Alte Pinakothek in Munich.

In the entrance hall, lined like the first reception room with glass vitrines, there were displayed gifts presented to the Marshal by foreign governments. In this collection were shown a large number of objects recently given to him by the Government of Japan. Goering told me that he had personally arranged the placing of every object in the house.

In March the twilight sets in early in North Germany. It was already getting dark as we come out through the entrance gate of Goering's preserve. I had ample time for meditation on the long drive back to Berlin.

Various things had become fully clear. The key to the question whether Hitlerism was going to dominate Europe, and possibly succeed in dominating the rest of the world, was to be found in Berlin and nowhere else. It was far more evident than I had previously realized that Mussolini's influence, if it had ever possessed even some slight weight, had vanished. It had all along been more than obvious that both the British and French Governments had kept on appeasing until, if they were to retain even a semblance of independence, they could appease no longer. But never before in the history of Europe had the Western powers fought a more wholly defensive war than that in which they were now engaged. The allegations of Hitler, Ribbentrop and Goering that the Western powers wanted the war might have had some deceptive effect in 1914. They were farcical in 1939.

There was only one power on earth which could give Hitler and his associates pause. That would be their conviction that, in a war of devastation forced upon Europe by Germany, the United States, in its own interest, would come to the support of the Western democracies. Equally clearly, however, there was at that moment not the remotest chance that our Government could tell the Nazi Government that this would prove to be the case. The great majority of the American people were altogether confident that they could keep out of the war. No executive in Washington with any sense of his responsibility to the American electorate, or with any regard for his constitutional limitations, could assume the authority for bluntly informing the Government of the Third Reich that the United States would support Great Britain and France should Germany persist in her policy of world conquest. And yet it was only that threat which would have the remotest chance of averting the greatest calamity that the modern world had known.

As we drove through the dreary Berlin suburbs, night was just settling down. Long queues were patiently standing in the streets, as they had been when I had earlier passed through, waiting to obtain provisions or to enter a motion-picture theatre. It struck me that the temper of the Berlin people had radically changed during the years since I had last been there. Even in the inflation days and in the days of desperate poverty of my last visits the crowds in the streets had seemed good-natured. One saw smiling faces. Through the miles of Berlin streets that I traversed on this final visit I never saw one smiling face.

Hitler: 1940

He said: 'I am fully aware that the Allied powers believe a distinction can be made between National Socialism and the German people. There was never a greater mistake. The German people to-day are united as one man and I have the support of every German. 'I can see no hope for the establishment of any lasting peace until the will of England and France to destroy Germany is itself destroyed. I feel that there is no way by which the will to destroy Germany can itself be destroyed except through a complete German victory. I believe that German might is such as to make the triumph of Germany inevitable, but, if not, we will all go down together.' And here he added the extraordinary phrase, 'Whether that be for better or for worse.'

He paused a moment and then said textually, rapidly, and in high and raucous pitch, 'I did not want this war. It has been forced upon me against my will. It is a waste of my time. My life should have been spent in constructing and not in destroying.'

Sumner Welles

> We're gonna hang out the washing on the Siegfried Line
> Have you any dirty washing, mother dear?
> We're gonna hang out the washing on the Siegfried Line
> 'Cos the washing day is here.
> Whether the weather may be wet or fine
> We'll just rub along without a care.
> We're gonna hang out the washing on the Siegfried Line
> If the Siegfried Line's still there.

British 'Phoney War' song hit

3

THE WAR AT SEA,
1939-1940

The war at sea began on the same day as the war itself with the sinking of the liner Athenia *by a U-boat. There was never any 'phoney' war for the men at sea. German submarines and aircraft immediately began to attack Allied and then neutral merchant vessels, though the main German effort was still to come, in 1941-43.*

At this early stage, combats involving heavy warships were the most prominent, largely because the Germans at once sent their pocket battleships to sea as commerce raiders. The Graf Spee *was the most successful of these.*

THE SINKING OF THE *ROYAL OAK:*
SCAPA FLOW, OCTOBER 1939

In September 1939 one of the 'canoes'* operating east of the Orkneys found herself off the Pentland Firth, the passage between Scotland and the Orkneys. A strong westerly current caught the boat and swept her through the turbulent narrows. Finding that his engines were not powerful enough to pull him free, the captain, making a virtue out of necessity, carefully surveyed the movement of ships and the defences in the area. On his return he made a detailed report to Doenitz, who at once saw the possibilities of a special operation. After much deliberation he ordered one of his best young officers, Lieutenant Gunther Prien, to report on board the depot-ship *Weichsel* at Kiel.

As Prien entered the Commodore's cabin he found Doenitz in conference with his own flotilla-commander and Lieutenant Wellner, the captain of the 'canoe'. Charts lay spread on the table before them and Prien's eye was immediately caught by the words 'Scapa Flow'. The Commodore addressed him.

'Do you think that a determined C.O. could take his boat into Scapa Flow and attack the ships there? Don't answer now, but let me have your reply by Tuesday. The decision rests entirely with you, and without prejudice to yourself.' It was then Sunday. Prien saluted and withdrew, his heart beating fast. He went straight to his quarters and settled down to a thorough study of the problem. He worked away hour after hour, calculating, figuring, checking and re-checking. On the appointed day he stood once again before the Commodore.

'Yes or no?' — 'Yes, sir.' A pause. 'Have you thought it all out? Have you thought of Emsmann and Henning who tried the same thing in the first World War and never came back?' 'Yes, sir.' 'Then get your boat ready.'

The crew could make no sense of the preparations for their next patrol. Why were they disembarking part of their food supplies and taking so little fuel

* U-boats (Ed.)

27

and fresh water with them? Apart from giving essential orders the captain was uncommunicative, and on the appointed day the U-boat slipped quietly through the Kiel Canal into the North Sea. The nights were dark, the seas running high. While on passage the crew watched their captain closely; although funnel-smoke was sighted several times he never attempted to attack. At last, early in the morning of 13 October, the Orkneys were in sight. Prien gave the order to dive and when the U-boat was resting easily on the sea-bed, he ordered all hands to muster forward. 'To-morrow we go into Scapa Flow', he began, and went on talking quietly, making sure that every man knew what he had to do. Then he ordered every available man off watch to turn in; they would need all their strength when the time came.

At four o'clock in the afternoon the boat came to life again and the cook served a specially good meal. Jokes were bandied about and Prien wrote in his log: 'The morale of the ship's company is superb.' At 7.15 all hands went to diving-stations, and the chief engineer began to lift the boat off the bottom; the ballast-pumps sang and the boat began to move as the motors stirred into life. Prien took a first cautious glimpse through the periscope. All clear. He gave the order to surface. The wind had dropped but the sky was covered with light clouds; although there was a new moon, the Northern Lights made the night almost as bright as day.

Log of the U-47

. . . . We are in Scapa Flow.

14.10.39. It is disgustingly light. The whole bay is lit up. To the south of Cava there is nothing. I go farther in. To port, I recognize the Hoxa Sound coastguard, to which in the next few minutes the boat must present itself as a target. In that event all would be lost; at present south of Cava no ships are to be seen, although visibility is extremely good. Hence decisions:

South of Cava there is no shipping; so before staking everything on success, all possible precautions must be taken. Therefore, turn to port is made. We proceed north by the coast. Two battleships are lying there at anchor, and further inshore, destroyers. Cruisers not visible, therefore attack on the big fellows.

Distance apart, three thousand metres. Estimated depth, seven and a half metres. Impact firing. One torpedo fired on northern ship, two on southern. After a good three and a half minutes, a torpedo detonates on the northern ship; of the other two nothing is to be seen.

About! Torpedo fired from stern; in the bow two tubes are loaded; three torpedoes from the bow. After three tense minutes comes the detonation on the nearer ship. There is a loud explosion, roar, and rumbling. Then come columns of water, followed by columns of fire, and splinters fly through the air. The harbour springs to life. Destroyers are lit up, signalling starts on every side, and on land, two hundred metres away from me, cars roar along the roads. A battleship had been sunk, a second damaged, and the other three torpedoes have gone to blazes. All the tubes are empty. I decide to withdraw, because: (1) With my periscopes I cannot conduct night attacks while submerged. . . . (2) On a bright night I cannot manœuvre unobserved in a calm sea. (3) I must assume that I was observed by the driver of a car which stopped opposite us, turned around, and drove off towards Scapa at top speed. (4) Nor can I go farther north, for there, well hidden from my sight, lie the destroyers which were previously dimly distinguishable.

At full speed both engines we withdraw. Everything is simple until we reach Skildaenoy Point. Then we have more trouble. It is now low tide. The current is against us. Engines at slow and dead slow; I attempt to get away. I must leave by the south through the narrows, because of the depth of the water. Things are again difficult. Course, 058°, slow—ten knots. I make no progress. At full speed I pass the southern blockship with nothing to spare. The helmsman does magnificently. Full speed ahead both, finally three-quarter speed and full ahead all out. Free of the blockships—ahead a mole! Hard over and again about, and at 02.15 we are once more outside. A pity that only one was destroyed. The torpedo misses I explain as due to faults of course, speed and drift. In tube 4, a misfire. The crew behaved splendidly throughout the operation.

Lieutenant Gunther Prien

THE BATTLE OF THE RIVER PLATE:
DECEMBER 1939

.... On the 11th and 12th the *Graf Spee* continued on a south-westerly course towards the Plate Estuary. By the 12th Langsdorff* reached what he estimated would be the shipping lane and he took the *Graf Spee* along it with the intention of patrolling to and fro across it during the night.

If, by the following day, 13 December, nothing had been sighted, he intended to turn right round and cross the South Atlantic again to an area off the West African coast near the Gulf of Lagos. There he would search along and either side of the peacetime shipping lanes.

So it came about that shortly before dawn on Wednesday, 13 December, 1939, the *Panzerschiff Admiral Graf Spee* was cruising at fifteen knots on a course of 155 degrees in a position 34° 27' south, 49° 55' west. She had destroyed nine British ships, totalling 50,089 tons, without the loss of a single life. The man who made that proud claim, *Kapitän zur See* Hans Langsdorff, was at that moment in his sea cabin on the bridge, his task as a commerce raider nearly finished and his life, at the age of forty-two, almost over.

The British Warships Close In

At noon Commodore Harwood made a signal to Captain Parry in the *Achilles* and Captain Bell in the *Exeter*, which gave, in a few words, his plan for battle. It was brief and it was clear.

Harwood's small force, which would be outgunned from the start, could only sink or cripple a pocket battleship by superior tactics. There would be no scope for the unexpected move which would take the enemy unawares that Nelson had employed at the Nile; but there was just as much scope for mistakes.

The Commodore planned to attack immediately by day or by night, and he

* Captain of the *Graf Spee* (Ed.)

would split his force into two divisions—the *Exeter*, with her heavier 8-inch guns forming one, and the *Ajax* and *Achilles*, with their less effective and shorter ranged 6-inch guns, forming the other. Both divisions would attack from slightly different directions, so that each could spot the other's fall of shot (flank marking) and also force the enemy to divide his attention. This splitting of his main force was unorthodox—it would have been more usual to keep the three ships concentrated—but it might keep the enemy guessing.

. . . . The rest of the hunting groups were in the following positions:

Force H (*Sussex* and *Shropshire*) sweeping off the West African coast, more than four thousand miles away.

Force I (*Eagle*, *Cornwall* and *Gloucester*) were at Durban, more than four thousand one hundred miles away, short of fuel after a wild goose chase into the Indian Ocean.

Force K (*Ark Royal* and *Renown*), the most powerful hunting group in the South Atlantic, were off Pernambuco, two thousand miles northwards.

Force X (*Hermes* and the French cruisers *Dupleix* and *Foch*) with the *Neptune*, *Hardy*, *Hostile* and *Hero*, were still farther north off St. Paul Rocks.

The *Cumberland* was at the Falkland Islands; and the *Dorsetshire* was on the eve of sailing from Simonstown to relieve the *Exeter*. The submarine *Severn* was halfway between St. Helena and Bahia, on her way to the Falklands, and the submarine *Clyde* was approaching Dakar.

That, then, was the scene in the South Atlantic on 12 December, 1939, the eve of the Battle of the River Plate.

13 December

The captain of the *Graf Spee* . . . thought at first that he had been sighted by only one cruiser and hence turned immediately to attack. Too late he realized the true situation, and a running fight ensued throughout the day.

The Crippling of the *Exeter*

From Captain Bell's report: . . . *After the eighth salvo B turret received a direct hit from an 11-inch shell and was put out of action. The splinters also killed or wounded all the bridge personnel with the exception of the Captain, Torpedo Control and Firing Officers, and wrecked the wheelhouse communications. . . .*

. . . . The *Graf Spee*, after firing four salvoes of base-fused shells, switched over to impact fuses 'in order to obtain the greatest possible damage to the lightly-armoured turrets and super-structure and through hits on its hull to reduce the ship's speed'.*

One of these shells landed on B turret just between the two guns, ripping off the front armour plate and killing eight men at the front of the gunhouse.

They had fired seven broadsides and the Number Ones of the two guns were just about to ram home the next rounds when the shell burst. All the lights went out, leaving the gunhouse in darkness, and dense, acrid fumes started to burn the nostrils and throats of the stunned survivors.

Sergeant Arthur Wilde, R.M., groped for the Number Ones who should

* Later in the action she reverted to base-fused shells.

have been either side of him, but they were not in their seats. Then he saw day-light coming in through the left rear door of the gunhouse, which had been blown open, and he made his way out on deck.

'As I was going aft,' Wilde reported later, 'Marine Attwood called for me to assist him with Marine W. A. Russell. I turned and saw Russell had lost a fore-arm and was badly hurt in the other arm.

'Attwood and I assisted Russell down to the port 4-inch gundeck, and as we reached it there was another violent explosion which seemed to be in the vicinity of B turret. I dropped to the deck, pulling Russell with me.

'After the splinters had stopped I cut off two lengths of signal halyard, which were hanging loose, and put a clove hitch for a tourniquet around both of Russell's arms above the elbows.

'I went to the Sick Bay and told someone that I had left Russell sitting against the funnel casing, port side. I proceeded down to the waist and turned forward, intending to go to B magazine and shell room, but was ordered back as the gangway was blocked by C.P.O. Evans, who was attending to a man who was seriously injured around the legs. . . .

'Some time later I collected Marines Camp, Attwood and Thomas, and we went back to B turret to see what could be done. I observed several small fires, some of which were put out by sand, the fire hydrants being dry.

'Marine Thomas drew my attention to a small fire near the left elevating standard, and I sent him for water and sand. Then, remembering I had seen water in the starboard waist, I went down for some. When I returned Lieutenant Toase, assisted by Marine Thomas, had extinguished the fire and we proceeded to take the cordite from both rammers and pass it overboard. . . .'

While this was being done, the badly wounded Russell, his clothing blood-stained and his arms still bound with signal halyard, walked round making cheering remarks and, in the words of Captain Bell, 'encouraging all by his fortitude'. (He stayed on deck until after the action, when he collapsed.)

But although the shell had hit B turret, the worst damage was done on the bridge just above: a withering shower of splinters, like spray from a big sea, had been flung up at more than the speed of sound and cut through the thin armour and window openings, ricocheted down from the metal roof and killed or wounded nearly every man standing on the bridge.

Within a fraction of a second the *Exeter* was changed from a perfectly handled fighting ship to an uncontrolled machine. The wheelhouse was wrecked; all communications to the engine room and Lower Steering Position were cut. Captain Bell had been wounded in the face. Among the dead were the Navigating Officer, plotting staff and the men standing either side of Captain Bell.

. . . . By now the forward part of the ship was slowly flooding. Water streamed out of a shattered fire main and from hoses pouring water on to the fo'c'sle fire; and the sea was spurting in through splinter holes caused by the hit on the anchor and the many near misses. The flow was increased by the forward thrust of the ship, which was now steaming at full speed.

From Captain Bell's report: . . . *Two more* 11-*inch hits were received, one on A turret, putting it out of action, and one which penetrated the Chief Petty Officer's flat, where it burst, causing very extensive damage.* . . .

Just before the Chief Petty Officer's flat was hit another shell, not mentioned in the above report, hit the Navigating Officer's cabin, passed through the Armament Office, killed five telegraphists and went on for sixty feet before bursting on the barrel of 'S-one' (Starboard one) 4-inch gun, killing or wounding several more men.

The foremost ready-use locker, containing 4-inch shells, immediately caught fire and the ammunition started bursting, sending up showers of debris and splinters. At that moment a man ran up to Midshipman Cameron, in command of the 4-inch guns, and warned him that the fore topmast was just about to fall down.

'I gave the order to clear the fore end of the gun deck,' Cameron reported later. 'As it did not appear to be coming down immediately I started the crews working again.'

The men in A turret had fired between forty and fifty rounds when, at this moment, an 11-inch shell hit the right gun. Once again the explosion tore at the armour plate on the front of the turret. Inside all the lights were put out and fumes streamed in.

Petty Officer Pierce tried to get through to the bridge by telephone, but it was wrecked. Ordering the telegraphists to stay at their posts, he climbed out of the gunhouse to go up to warn the bridge, but finding it had already been wrecked he went back to the gunhouse to tell the men to abandon it.

By this time an 11-inch shell had burst in the Chief Petty Officers' flat and started a bad fire above the 4-inch magazine. After checking that it was being dealt with, Midshipman Cameron returned with Ordinary Seaman Gwilliam to find the 4-inch ready-use locker still burning from the earlier hit.

'There were still several live shells in the bottom of the locker. Without any hesitation, Gwilliam removed his greatcoat and attempted to smother the flames with it,' Cameron reported later. 'At the same time somebody else threw a bucket of sand over it. The flames were extinguished and we proceeded to throw over the side what was left in the locker.

'Gwilliam reported to me that there were still several cans of petrol underneath the port catapult. These we threw overboard.

'As the fire on the messdecks was still raging, I got more hands on to the job of carrying buckets to it. At the same time Lieutenant Kemball and I kept the remainder occupied in breaking up blocks of holystone in an effort to make sand out of them. . . .

'At this time an effort, which subsequently proved to be successful, was being made to get the planes over the side, they having been badly holed and showering out quantities of petrol.'

The shell which burst in the C.P.O.'s flat did so much damage that the *Exeter* later had to discontinue the action. It penetrated the light plating of the ship's amidships, as if it were cardboard, cut through three bulkheads and then burst on the lower deck above the 4-inch magazine and the torpedo-gunner's store, blasting a hole measuring sixteen feet by fourteen feet.

The *Exeter*'s tall topmasts were still in danger. Flying splinters had cut through many of the wire shrouds supporting them, and when finally the triatic stay joining the heads of the two masts was severed they had started to whip so violently that all the main aerials parted and the ship's wireless link with the Commodore was cut. As soon as the sets had gone dead Chief Petty Officer Telegraphist Harold Newman began the dangerous and laborious job of rigging jury aerials.

The topmasts were so tall that they undoubtedly helped the *Graf Spee*'s gunners in finding the range; and had the weather not been exceptionally calm they almost certainly would have toppled down.

A Tribute

'You English are hard. You do not know when you are beaten. The *Exeter* was beaten, but would not know it!'

Captain Langsdorff

Commodore Harwood's tactics were successful; the Graf Spee *suffered considerably, and her captain became convinced that the cruisers would not have pressed home their attack so persistently if they were not expecting immediate support from heavier ships.*

Damaged, and a considerable distance from his home bases, Langsdorff decided to make for a neutral port where he could carry out temporary repairs before attempting to break through once more into the North Atlantic and so back to Germany. Unaware of the pro-Allied feeling in Uruguay, he shaped course for Montevideo.

Graf Spee reached Montevideo on the evening of the same day, 13 December, and began a prolonged diplomatic argument in an effort to remain in port beyond the legal seventy-two hours. Meanwhile skilful British propaganda created the impression of a large fleet in the vicinity of the La Plata estuary waiting to annihilate the *Graf Spee*. H.M. Ships *Ark Royal* and *Renown* were reported to be at Rio de Janeiro while in reality they were many thousands of miles away. The cruiser force had in fact been reinforced by only one more ship, another cruiser, H.M.S. *Cumberland*.

Langsdorff signalled his appreciation of the situation and his intentions to Berlin. On 16 December Raeder consulted Hitler:

Report of the Commander-in-Chief, Navy, to the Führer on 16 December 1939 :

The C.-in-C., Navy, reports that at least two weeks are needed to make the *Graf Spee* seaworthy, and that the Government of Uruguay has granted only seventy-two hours. The Foreign Office is requested to continue efforts to obtain an extension of the time allowed; this appears hopeless, however, as Britain and France are exerting great pressure, and Uruguay will conform to their wishes. Uruguay is unreliable as a neutral, and is not able to defend her neutrality.

The Commander's telegram of 16 December follows:

1. Strategic position off Montevideo: Besides the cruisers and destroyers, *Ark Royal* and *Renown*. Close blockade at night. Escape into open sea and breakthrough to home waters hopeless.

2. Propose putting out as far as neutral boundary. If it is possible to fight our way through to Buenos Aires, using remaining ammunition, this will be attempted.

3. If a break-through would result in certain destruction of *Graf Spee* without opportunity of damaging enemy, request decision on whether the ship should be scuttled in spite of insufficient depth in the estuary of the La Plata, or whether internment is to be preferred.

4. Decision requested by radiogram.

Commander, Graf Spee

The text of the instructions follows (sent as Radiogram 1347/16 to *Graf Spee*):

1. Attempt by all means to extend the time in neutral waters in order to guarantee freedom of action as long as possible.

2. With reference to No. 2: Approved.

3. With reference to No. 3: *No* internment in Uruguay. Attempt effective destruction if ship is scuttled.

Raeder

Note: The envoy in Montevideo reports in the afternoon that further attempts to extend the time limit were without result.

Confirmation was therefore sent by radiogram to the Commander of the *Graf Spee* that the instructions in Radiogram 1347 with reference to No. 2 and No. 3 remain in force.

The text of the radiogram is as follows:

As envoy reported impossibility of extending time limit, instructions according to Radiogram 1347/16 Nos. 2 and 3 remain in force.

Sent at 00.40 on 17 December.

On the following morning, watched by a vast crowd of sightseers, *Graf Spee* put to sea. The British ships cleared for action, but, before they could engage the enemy, their spotting aircraft reported that the *Graf Spee* had been scuttled and blown up by her own crew.

The End of the *Graf Spee*

. . . At 20.54, as the sun dipped below the coastline, a sudden flash of flame leapt from the ship, followed by a vast double explosion. The centre of the *Graf Spee* seemed to dissolve into swirling black smoke which twisted upwards in tortured spirals towards the darkening sky.

The pocket battleship's crew, scattered in the tugs, the barge and the *Tacoma*, stood to attention, giving the Nazi salute. . . .

But the first rumbling reverberation had not lost itself in receptive space before another curtain of flame leapt up aft, high above the masthead, to be followed by another explosion which seemed to erupt under the *Graf Spee*, lift her, and drop her back crumpled into the waiting sea. Wreckage showered out in neat parabolas, the main-mast collapsed like a stalk of corn before a scythe, and the great after-turret, which had successfully withstood the shells of the British cruisers, was flung upwards as the magazine beneath exploded.

Now the violent dying spasms were over and self-induced cremation was to follow. Eager, seeking flames swept along the whole length of the ship; and ashore, while excited radio commentators regained their breath, the German Naval Attaché sent a cable to Berlin. It said:

> Pocket battleship *Graf Spee* left Montevideo 18.20 [German time]; blown up by her crew 19.54. Crew at present embarked in *Tacoma*.*

Langsdorff: The End

Three days later, on 20 December, Captain Langsdorff committed suicide, leaving this letter addressed to the German Ambassador and meant for onward transmission to Germany and his Führer.

Your Excellency,

After a long struggle I reached the grave decision to scuttle the pocket battleship *Admiral Graf Spee*, in order to prevent her from falling into enemy hands. I am still convinced that under the circumstances this decision was the only one left, once I had taken my ship into the trap of Montevideo. For with the ammunition remaining, any attempt to fight my way back to open and deep water was bound to fail. And yet only in deep water could I have scuttled the ship, after having used the remaining ammunition, thus avoiding her falling to the enemy.

Sooner than expose my ship to the danger that after a brave fight she would fall partly or completely into enemy hands, I decided not to fight but to destroy the equipment and then scuttle the ship. It was clear to me that this decision might be consciously or unwittingly misconstrued by persons ignorant of my motives, as being attributable entirely or partly to personal considerations. Therefore I decided from the beginning to bear the consequences involved in this decision. For a Captain with a sense of honour, it goes without saying that his personal fate cannot be separated from that of his ship.

I postponed my intention as long as I still bore responsibility for decisions concerning the welfare of the crew under my command. After to-day's decision of the Argentine Government, I can do no more for my ship's company. Neither will I be able to take an active part in the present struggle of my country. I can now only prove by my death that the fighting services of the Third Reich are ready to die for the honour of the flag.

I alone bear the responsibility for scuttling the pocket battleship *Admiral Graf Spee*. I am happy to pay with my life for any possible reflection on the honour of the flag. I shall face my fate with firm faith in the cause and the future of the nation and of my Führer.

I am writing this letter to Your Excellency in the quiet of the evening, after calm deliberation, in order that you may be able to inform my superior officers, and to counter public rumours if this should become necessary.

Langsdorff

---

* They spent the rest of the war interned in Argentina (Ed.)

THE MAGNETIC MINE: DEGAUSSING

By the end of October 1939 *over fifty thousand tons of Allied and British ship-*
ping had been sunk by magnetic mines sown by aircraft, and in November Hitler
boasted of this new 'secret weapon' as being without counter. On 23 November a
magnetic mine was recovered intact off Shoeburyness, and effective counter-measures
were devised by the Admiralty.

Hitler's 'secret weapon' had yielded its design and powers and manner of
operation and the antidote lay in a belt of energized electrical cable which they
were planning to instal in the ship. As I understood it, the object was to neutralize the ship's magnetic field by a counter-current passing through the cable and
in this way render the magnetic needle in the German mine ineffective to
detonate its explosive charge. For operation of the belt, no special schooling
would be needed. The ship's engineer or electrical officers could attend to it.
The only adjustment the navigator would need to make was in respect of the
compass course that was being steered and, for that, a fairly simple instrument
would be fitted on the bridge. We were warned to 'keep the juice running' at all
times when in port or in shallow waters. An instance of over-confidence was
quoted: that of a ship only recently equipped. Upon arrival at her next port,
the master thought he might safely switch off the protective energy when moored
at his familiar wharf—with the result that the ship's stern was shattered by the
explosion of a magnetic mine that had been dropped from the air, probably on
the night before. It is not often that one has the key of extinction so readily at
hand. We would need to guard that switch.

During my term of relief duty in the ship I watched the shipyard workers
harness the insulated belt around the hull on the level of the main-deckline:
there seemed to be miles of it, for she was a sizeable vessel. When the fitting was
completed and the wiring tested by ammeter, she was said to be immunized and
it only remained for the formulae to be approved by the results of the ranging
off Helensburgh Pier before sailing. Certification was important before a programme could be prepared for the sequence of that test and I was required to
call at Naval Headquarters to obtain the document. I found the newly established
division in the throes of settling in to what must speedily have become a major
department of the Admiralty. Despite its newness and understandable congestion and apparent disorder, the experts so recently gazetted had found a slogan
or motto for their 'trade'. That they had enrolled a classical scholar in their
ranks was evident from a typewritten slip pinned up above the desk at which
certificates were issued. It was a paraphrase from Pope's translation of the
Odyssey—

> This potent girdle round thy bosom bind
> And sail: throw all thy terrors to the wind.

Sir David W. Bone

4

NORWAY

Early in the war both Britain and Germany were looking anxiously towards Norway, the neutral route from Sweden by which iron ore was transported in large quantities to the Reich. On 19 September 1939 the First Lord of the Admiralty, Winston Churchill, sent a memorandum to the First Sea Lord which began, 'I brought to the notice of the Cabinet this morning the importance of stopping the Norwegian transportation of Swedish iron ore from Narvik'. Less than two weeks later Admiral Raeder submitted a proposal in which he asked 'that the Fuehrer be informed as soon as possible of the opinions of the Naval War Staff on the possibility of extending the operational base to the north. It must be ascertained whether it is possible to gain bases in Norway under the combined pressure of Russia and Germany, with the aim of improving our strategic and operational position.'

Both sides watched one another warily. In early 1940 Hitler made active preparations for the occupation of Norway, while the British Cabinet debated whether they should or should not infringe Norwegian neutrality by mining her territorial waters. Although German plans were more deep-laid, it was in fact the British who moved first.

PRELUDE TO INVASION

Quisling

SUPPLEMENTARY to earlier information, I wish to report that Quisling is one of the best-known Norwegian general staff officers. He was Military Attaché in Finland, and from 1927 to 1930, before diplomatic relations between the Soviet Union and Great Britain were broken off, he represented British interests in Moscow. From 1931 to 1933 he was Norwegian War Minister, representing the Norwegian Peasant Party; he then resigned and formed a radical national and socialist party called the National Unity Party. This party had, and still has, anti-semitic views and it recommends closest co-operation with Germany. It has fifteen thousand registered members, and Quisling estimates the number of his direct followers at two to three hundred thousand; this comprises that 10 per cent of the population which is in favour of co-operation with Germany even at the present time, when the general attitude in Norway and Sweden is definitely anti-German. His party also did not participate in voting for the Storthing. . . .

Quisling knows the King very well from the time when he was in office and he believes that the King holds him in esteem, even though the latter is on the whole pro-British.

A plan for possible procedure has been suggested.

According to this plan a number of picked Norwegians will be given training in Germany for this particular task. They will be told exactly what to do, and will be assisted by seasoned National Socialists who are experienced in such matters. These trained men are then to be sent back to Norway as quickly as possible, where details will be discussed. Several focal points in Oslo will have to be occupied with lightning speed, and simultaneously the German Navy with contigents of the German Army will have to put in an appearance at a pre-arranged bay outside Oslo in answer to a special summons from the new Norwegian Government. Quisling has no doubt that such a coup, achieved instantaneously, would at once meet with the approval of those sections of the Army with which he now has connections. Of course, he has never discussed political action with them. As regards the King, he believes that he would accept such a *fait accompli*.

Quisling's estimate of the number of German troops needed for the operation coincides with the German estimates.

Alfred Rosenberg, Nazi Party foreign affairs expert, December 1939

The German plan for the invasion of Norway was christened Operation Weser.

13 March 1940
Führer does not give order yet for 'W'. He is still looking for an excuse.

14 March
English keep vigil in the North Sea with fifteen to sixteen submarines; doubtful whether reason to safeguard own operations or prevent operations by Germans. Führer has not yet decided what reason to give for Weser Exercise.

General Jodl, Chief of Hitler's personal staff, diary

General Orders for Operation Weser

The barrage-breaking vessels, *Sperrbrecher*, will penetrate inconspicuously, and with lights on, into Oslo Fjord disguised as merchant steamers.

Challenge from coastal signal stations and look-outs are to be answered by the deceptive use of the names of English steamers. I lay particular stress on the importance of not giving away the operation before zero hour.

Adolf Hitler, 4 April

8 April
His Majesty's Government in the United Kingdom and the French Government have . . . resolved to deny the continued use by the enemy of stretches of territorial waters which are clearly of particular value to him, and they have therefore decided to prevent unhindered passage of vessels carrying contraband of war through Norwegian territorial waters. They accordingly hereby give notice that . . . areas of Norwegian territorial waters have been rendered dangerous on account of mines. Vessels entering these areas will do so at their peril.

OPERATION WESER

The German Minister in Oslo called upon Herr Koht, the Norwegian Foreign Minister, at 4 a.m. on 9 April and presented him with a list of demands. Even by

Nazi standards the timing was bad, for at midnight four German warships had forced an entry into Oslo Fjord, shots had been exchanged and the invasion had begun. Denmark was occupied on the same day. The 'phoney war' was over.

Appeal to his People by the King: 13 April

.... In the situation to-day I cannot report to you the whereabouts in Norway of myself, the Crown Prince, and the Government. The German forces have in fact engaged in a violent attack on us, while we were staying in a little place which was unfortified and undefended. High explosive and incendiary bombs and machine-gun fire were used against the civilian population and ourselves in the most unscrupulous and brutal fashion. The attack could have had but one object—immediately to annihilate all of us who were assembled to resolve questions in the bests interests of Norway. . . . God Save Norway.

Haakon R.

The German Proclamation: 14 April

It is my task to protect Norway against attack by the Western Powers. The Norwegian Government have declined several offers of co-operation. The Norwegian people must now themselves determine the future of their fatherland. If my proclamation meets with the obedience which was very sensibly accorded by the Danish people when faced with similar circumstances, Norway will be spared the horrors of war.

If opposition is offered and the hand of friendship is rejected I shall be forced to employ the severest and most relentless means to crush such opposition.

General von Falkenhorst, C.-in-C., Norway

In response to an appeal from Norway, which previously had been almost belligerently neutral, the British and French Governments decided to send what troops they could to the northern part of the country, the south being considered as already beyond redemption.

The Cabinet heartily approved all possible measures for the rescue and defence of Narvik and Trondheim. The troops . . . lacked aircraft, anti-aircraft guns, anti-tank guns, tanks, transport and training. The whole of Northern Norway was covered with snow to depths which none of our soldiers had ever seen, felt, or imagined. There were neither snow-shoes nor skis—still less skiers. We must do our best. Thus began this ramshackle campaign.

Winston Churchill

The Norwegian Failure

The fact was that, whilst the Germans were disembarking a division each week in Norway, we still had not a man there.

On the 18th,* I wrote to Chamberlain, 'It is the pace of enemy reinforcements which should control the pace at which our own troops arrive . . . I am,

* April (Ed.)

therefore, asking you to try to make the necessary effort to place at our disposal
the tonnage which we need.'

On the other hand, the British Fleet gained a great success. During fights
which took place up to the 13th, the Navy of the Reich suffered heavy losses.
The Vichy Press has scoffed at me for having called the sailing of the German
Fleet into the North Sea a strategic error. It is true that the Reich forces established themselves in the port of Narvik on the 9th at 5.15 in the morning and
that they held on there until 28 May, the day when the Allied troops finally
succeeded in dislodging them. Nevertheless, the fact still remains that the British
Fleet, after having destroyed, during engagements between 10 and 13 April,
ten of the most modern and speedy destroyers of the Kriegsmarine—which
were escorting General Dietl's convoy—blockaded closely all the fjords around
Narvik. Not another German boat could, from that date to the end of May, the
date of our voluntary evacuation, enter the port. It was therefore . . . a matter of
prestige for Hitler to continue holding Narvik. This was why he clung so
desperately to it. On 20 April, Mussolini wrote to him: . . . 'If you have any
means whatever to help you to hold on to Narvik, you must use them. If the
evacuation of Narvik took place it would become the subject of noisy exploitation by Allied propaganda.'

The future expeditionary force was being organized at this time. If my
suggestions were not entirely followed, it was at least decided to form three
light divisions (with two infantry regiments) and the equivalent of a fourth
(Polish and Foreign Legion). Unfortunately each of these divisions was only to
be supplied with very insufficient equipment: an artillery group, two companies
with 22 mm. guns for attacking low-flying aircraft, but none which had a ceiling
above one thousand metres, a company of out-of-date tanks (except that of 1
Division), and finally as the sole 'recce' element for all the expeditionary corps,
a squadron of machine-gun carriers, which, however, were to be dispersed
within the different sectors. The Germans were less parsimonious. It seems probable that they sent a dozen infantry and two armoured divisions into Norway.

Were these slender resources at least compensated for by our rapidity in
preparing our troops? And, if we had been forestalled in seizing the ports, was
the pace of our movement going to allow us to reconquer them rapidly? Unfortunately the timetable laid down was not in the least inspired by the battle
for speed which I had never ceased to advocate. 1 Light Division (six battalions),
the Polish brigade (four battalions) and the two battalions of the Foreign Legion
were to embark between the 12th and the 23rd. The first echelon of 2 Light
Division would in its turn only embark on the 24th and the second echelon was
not to leave Brest. As regards 3 Light Division, its departure was dependent on
the British providing the necessary ships. In actual fact it was destined never to
leave Britanny. Finally, on the 19th, ten days after the first German landing, the
first French troops disembarked in Norway. The port chosen was Namsos, from
which the Wehrmacht were still some distance, and which was the terminus of
roads leading to Sweden. But, though our troops were able to disembark there
without interference, they were completely incapable of moving off or of offering any action whatsoever. Their artillery, tanks, anti-aircraft guns, their mules
and even their skis and snowshoes had remained in the auxiliary cruiser *Ville*

d'Alger, which had not been able to enter harbour because of her length—a detail which had been forgotten. It was only a week later that some anti-aircraft guns began to be unloaded. In the meantime, our forces had suffered violent bombing raids.

The British disembarkations had been carried out on the 13th in the area of Narvik, then at Namsos in the centre, and at Andalsnes, farther south.

The essential problem was to free Trondheim. It was only the road which went from this port which would permit the future support of the Swedish Army and the defence of central Scandinavia, the essential aim which our Supreme Command had allotted itself.

The operation should have been successful. About the 20th, after the major disembarkations had been accomplished, the Germans had in the area only five thousand or six thousand men. Now, the Allied forces comprised in the north (Namsos), eight thousand British and French whom, it was hoped, would finally recover their equipment—and four battalions of Norwegian troops; in the south (Andalsnes), five thousand British and Norwegian troops. The Germans, who had to face simultaneously enemy forces to the north and south and also to defend the sea, were thus at a decided numerical disadvantage. Therefore, at a meeting of the Supreme Council on the 22nd, Chamberlain revealed himself fairly optimistic despite the Germans' aerial superiority.

But three days later the situation had changed. German forces disembarking at Oslo had reinforced those at Trondheim. The Luftwaffe, which occupied the bases, became increasingly stronger and more aggressive. Norwegian troops remained inactive. They had carried out no destruction. Thus the Foreign Office informed M. Corbin on the 26th that the Trondheim expedition was doomed to failure, and that it was necessary to take steps for the withdrawal of troops in this area. Our Ambassador tried in vain to convince the Foreign Office of the contrary. The War Committee, which met on the same day, unanimously declared itself opposed to this withdrawal, which Gamelin considered deplorable. I wrote on the same day to Chamberlain in order to instruct him about our attitude and to advise him to speed up the dispatch of men and material. 'One must plan on a big scale,' I told him, 'or abandon the struggle. One must act quickly or lose the war.'

The Supreme Council met on the 27th in London. The results of our delay had become worse, I told the Council; 'The expedition into central Scandinavia was based on a technical error. It was impossible to carry it out without first securing both an important port and aerial bases. Even without one of these things, the operation would have been difficult. But, lacking in both, one has cause to wonder if the Allies had the slightest chance of success.'

On the other hand the occupation of Narvik was attainable and of the utmost importance since it was the exit door to the mineral iron. Chamberlain stated that the capture of Trondheim was no longer possible, and that he thought this point of view was shared by Gamelin, who, however, insisted upon the importance to the Allies of holding Namsos in order to advance from there on Narvik, occupying different points along the coast. The British Government thought we should continue to fight at Namsos, but it believed that it was scarcely possible to keep a foothold there for long. At Narvik, on the contrary, Chamberlain continued, steps had already been taken to seize the port as quickly as possible when weather conditions would allow, and then to push to the Swedish frontier. But would the Swedish Government, intimidated by German successes, allow us to advance to the iron ore mines? The result, moreover, he added, 'would not be as immediate as that resulting from action against the German reserves of oil'.

I myself asked in the first place that at least we should save our face by not evacuating central Scandinavia before having attacked Narvik and, subsequently, that we should defend vigorously the road from Namsos to this port. During the night, the only wharf available at Andalsnes was destroyed by an air raid. The War Office ordered evacuation. 'Lord Halifax,' M. Corbin wrote to me on the 28th, 'has assured me that it is only the prospect of not being able to supply the Allied contingents at Andalsnes and Namsos any longer which has brought about the present situation. . . . It is none the less true that the British military leaders have almost completely re-adapted their plan . . . the first step of which has thus been organizing the withdrawal of half of the expedition.'

With this inglorious page we must contrast the glorious capture of Narvik on 28 May by our troops and those of our Allies, although they had received the order of evacuation from London on the 26th. On the 30th the Allied forces pinned the enemy on the Swedish frontier. The examinations at the Nuremberg trial have proved that, at this time, Hitler considered the Allies to have won the battle of Narvik, and that the Dietl corps was lost. It was Dunkirk that saved Dietl and his troops.

The disaster of Flanders entailed unfortunately a confirmation of the order for withdrawal. This was done at the request of Churchill, by the Supreme Council, which met in Paris on the 31st. Until our voluntary evacuation, 'the permanent road to iron ore supplies', was, I repeat, well and truly cut. The 'madcap enterprise' was based, therefore, on a healthy inspiration. It could have been realized, but its execution was defective.

Paul Reynaud, Prime Minister of France

Independent Companies

In order to delay to the utmost the northward advance of the enemy towards Narvik, we were now sending special companies raised in what was afterwards called 'Commando' style, under an enterprising officer, Colonel Gubbins, to Mosjoen, a hundred miles farther up the coast. I was most anxious that a small part of the Namsos force should make their way in whatever vehicles were available along the road to Grong. Even a couple of hundred would have sufficed to fight small rearguard actions. From Grong they would have to find their way on foot to Mosjoen. I hoped by this means to gain the time for Gubbins to establish himself so that a stand could be made against the very small numbers which the enemy could as yet send there.

Winston Churchill

Mission to Norway

Shortly after the Germans made their first landing in Norway, we responded by a gallant failure at Narvik. In the middle of one night there was a telephone message for me to report to the War Office. It dawned on me the reason might be Norway, especially as I had never been there and knew nothing about it. Norway it was, and I was ordered to go there immediately to take command of the Central Norwegian Expeditionary Force. Unfortunately I was not to take my own division, the 61st, for the Force was to consist of a brigade and some odd troops sent from Northern Command, together with a French force composed of Chasseurs Alpins under General Audet. These troops were to proceed to Namsos.

Having got my orders, I collected my kit and flew up to Scotland the next day, 13 April. We were to fly across to Norway the same night but were delayed by a blizzard, and took off next morning in a Sunderland.

The Norwegian coastline was lovely to look at, with the majesty of its rough mountains covered in snow, but from a fighting angle the view had no attraction for me, as obviously in this type of country one would need very specialized troops.

We reached Namsos in the evening and started to disembark troops at once. It was soon evident that the officers had little experience in handling men, although they had a first-class commander in Brigadier G. P. Phillips.

In Norway, at that time of the year, there were only about three hours of darkness, and landing troops with the whole country under snow, and a vigilant and attentive enemy, was no easy matter.

The troops were only too anxious to do what they were told, and to be quick about it, and it says much for them that not only did they succeed in landing, but they completely obliterated all traces of their landing. The Germans who flew over next morning suspected nothing.

My orders were to take Trondheim whenever a naval attack took place. The date was unnamed but I moved my troops up to Verdael and Steinjaer (both near Trondheim), from where I would lose no time in synchronizing with the naval attack when it came.

The following night we had to land French troops—the Chasseurs Alpins under General Audet. Although far better trained than we were, and experienced at looking after themselves, they did not obliterate the traces of their landings. The next morning the Germans saw that troops had been put ashore, and the French made themselves still more noticeable by loosing off their machine-guns at them, which succeeded in making matters much worse. The Germans responded by more and more bombs, and in a matter of hours Namsos was reduced to ashes. The casualties were not heavy, as by that time my troops were all forward, and the French were bivouacked outside the town. I went up to the front with Peter Fleming soon after the bombing started, and by the time we returned there was little of Namsos left.

The French Chasseurs Alpins were a fine body of troops and would have been ideal for the job in hand, but ironically they lacked one or two essentials, which made them completely useless to us. I had wanted to move them forward, but General Audet regretted they had no means of transport, as their mules had not turned up. Then I suggested that his ski-troops might move forward, but it was found that they were lacking some essential strap for their skis, without which they were unable to move. Their other equipment was excellent; each man carried some sixty pounds and managed his load with the utmost ease. They would have been invaluable to us if only I could have used them.

The British troops had been issued with fur coats, special boots and socks to compete with the cold, but if they wore all these things they were scarcely able to move at all and looked like paralyzed bears.

As far as planes, guns and cars went, I had no trouble at all, for we had none, though we commandeered what cars we could. Landing facilities were conspicuous by their absence, and to make matters worse we were being supplied by ships larger than the harbour could take. How the sailors got them in and out of these harbours remains a mystery never to be understood by a mere landsman.

The Hun bombers destroyed our small landing-stage. They had the time of their lives with no opposition whatsoever. Some of the ships carried A.A. guns, and a few days before the evacuation I was sent some Bofors guns. The Bofors never actually shot down a Hun plane, but they managed to disconcert them and had a nuisance value, at the same time giving us a fillip at being able to shoot at them.

On one of our more hopeful days an aircraft carrier miraculously cleared the skies of German planes and stayed several hours, but as there were German submarines about it was not able to remain close to the land, and had to go out to sea again where some of the planes could not return to it.

My headquarters in Namsos was one of the few houses to escape destruction, but after the bombardment I moved out to a small farm on the south side of the River Namsen, where we were not bothered much by the enemy, and it was easier for me to get to the front-line troops.

Two or three days after we had occupied Steinjaer and Verdael, about forty or fifty miles south of Namsos, the German Navy gained its one and only victory of the war, for their destroyers came up Trondheim Fjord and shelled my troops out of these two places. We had rifles, a few Bren guns and some 2-inch smoke bombs, but none of them were either comforting or effective against a destroyer.

The troops at Verdael had a particularly bad time. The road ran through the town on the shore of the fjord in full view of the ships, and the troops had to take to the snow-covered hills, ploughing through unknown country in eighteen inches of snow, only to be attacked by German ski-troops. There is no doubt that not many of them would have survived had it not been for the handling of the situation by Brigadier Phillips.

We retired to positions north of Steinjaer and out of reach of the German naval guns, where we were able to hold on. Steinjaer was being heavily bombed and shelled, and it was not surprising that the population in these small towns lived in deadly terror of our arrival. Our intentions were excellent, but our ideas of ultimate deliverance invariably brought the whole concentrated weight of bombing on top of the heads of the population. At the time I felt irritated by their lack of interest in us, but afterwards I realized that, unused as they were to the horror of war, they were stunned by the invasion, and had not had time to come round.

Still I waited for news of our naval attack which was to be my signal to take Trondheim, but still it did not come. Hourly it became more and more obvious to me that with my lack of equipment I was quite incapable of advancing on Trondheim, and could see very little point in remaining in that part of Norway sitting out like rabbits in the snow. I wired the War Office to tell them my conclusions, only to get back the reply that for political reasons they would be glad if I would maintain my positions. I agreed, but said that it was about all I could do. They were so relieved that they actually wired me their thanks.

Now that my chances of taking Trondheim had gone, I sent Peter Fleming to the War Office to find out their future plans. He came back after a couple of days and told me that plans and ideas about Norway were somewhat confused, and adding, 'You can really do what you like, for they don't know what they want done.'

About this time a complete staff turned up, but I was not very pleased to see them. They took up a lot of unavailable space, there was not much for them to do, and Peter Fleming and Martin Lindsay had more than fulfilled my requirements. We had already been given one most useful addition—Major R. Delacombe—and I felt that soon we would be all staff and no war.

During these last few days I was offered more men. Lack of accommodation and the fact that my only line of communication was a single road and a small railway line functioning spasmodically forced me to refuse them. They were the type of troops that I should have been delighted to have under me, for they were Poles and the French Foreign Legion, but if I had accepted them it would have made evacuation still more difficult.

Several staff officers were sent over in the role of liaison officers, but I don't think they cared much about the job, for they seemed very intent on departing as soon as they could. One of them was particularly amusing: he was so anxious that his plane should not go off without him that he thought he would like to go and sit quite near it in a sloop which was in the fjord. A Hun promptly dropped a bomb on the sloop and sank it, but the gallant officer was not drowned and made a safe return to England, where his report must have been illuminating.

My farmhouse headquarters provided us with some amusement and excitement from the air. My new staff had not seen these air antics played by the Hun, and were startled one day when a German plane came down the road, flying very low and machine-gunning us. It is a most unnerving and unpleasant sensation to be peppered at from a plane bearing straight down on one, and takes a lot of getting used to.

Just as we had settled to an uneventful routine with my troops in their new positions, wires started to flash to and from the War Office. First to evacuate, then to hold on, then to evacuate, then suddenly it was suggested that I should retire on Mosjoen, about a hundred miles to the north of Namsos. I knew the road to be covered in deep snow and impassable for infantry, and I could see no point in the move and wired the War Office to that effect. Meanwhile I sent Peter Fleming and Martin Lindsay to reconnoitre the route in a car, and they took twelve hours to cover forty miles.

I believe the War Office considered me very unenterprising for opposing their suggestion, but I felt at that moment the move only looked feasible on a map.

More orders came to evacuate, and this time I started to set about it. General

Audet came to see me and begged me not to leave his troops until the last when the hour came to embark. He seemed much moved, and on my assuring him that not a single British soldier would be embarked until every Frenchman was on board ship, I had a narrow escape from being embraced and was told that I was *un vrai gentleman.*

Gradually we retired towards Namsos, where we were to embark. The evacuation was to take place on two consecutive nights. I intended sending the French troops off the first night, and they had all gone down at dusk to be ready to embark. We waited—no ships turned up. There was no word from the Navy, and I must admit to feeling anxious. Just before dawn I had to move the troops up into their positions again, leaving them, depressed and disappointed, to await another night.

I was getting more and more anxious as Mr. Neville Chamberlain had told the House of Commons that General Paget's force had been evacuated from Andalsnes, which left me the only unenvied pebble on the beach. Alone against the might of Germany.

In the course of that last endless day I got a message from the Navy to say that they would evacuate the whole of my force that night. I thought it was impossible, but learned a few hours later that the Navy do not know the word.

Apparently there was a dense sea mist quite unsuspected by us on shore, and this had prevented their coming in the night before, but Lord Mountbatten managed to feel his way into the harbour, and the other ships followed him in. It was a tremendous undertaking to embark that whole force in a night of three short hours, but the Navy did it and earned my undying gratitude.

As day was breaking the Germans spotted us leaving the fjord and bombed us heavily. We lost the *Afridi* and a French destroyer and I lost my chance of being sunk. Having known the *Afridi* so well I asked to go on board, but had been told she was not coming in that night. When I found that she had come in after all I asked again to go in her, only to be told that my kit had been put on the *York* and it would be best for me to go in her instead. I did, and missed a very great experience. Unfortunately the wounded from the French destroyer had been put on board the *Afridi* and nearly all of them were drowned.

On my sixtieth birthday, 5 May, we arrived back at Scapa Flow exactly eighteen days after we had set forth. Captain Portal, who commanded the *York*, thought it was a most fitting occasion for a bottle of champagne. He must have known that to me the taste is extra good after a surgical operation or a major disaster.

General Sir Adrian Carton de Wiart

The King and the Government have at this moment seen themselves compelled to remove their abode and their activities outside the frontiers of the country. . . . The hard necessity of war has compelled the Allied Governments to muster all their strength to fight upon other fronts, and they have full scope for all their men and material on those fronts.

Under these conditions it is impossible to maintain the struggle in this country against a preponderance like that of Germany.

. . . . The Higher Command of our defence has therefore advised the King and the Government for the present to give up the struggle within the country, and the King and Government have considered it their duty to follow that advice. They are, therefore, now leaving the country.

Haakon R.
Johan Nygaardsvold*
7 June

* Norwegian Prime Minister (Ed.)

5

THE BATTLE IN THE WEST: TO DUNKIRK

On the traditional battlefields of the West, the 'phoney war' came to an end on 10 May, when Germany invaded Holland, Belgium and Luxembourg, having prepared the way with Fifth-Columnists and soldiers infiltrated in plain clothes.

HITLER TURNS WEST

FOR the first time in history we have to fight on only one front, the other front is at present free. But no one can know how long that will remain so. I have doubted for a long time whether I should strike in the East and then in the West. Basically I did not organize the Armed Forces in order not to strike. The decision to strike was always in me. Earlier or later, I wanted to solve the problem. Under pressure it was decided that the East was to be attacked first. If the Polish war was won so quickly, it was due to the superiority of our Armed Forces. The most glorious appearance in history. Unexpectedly small expenditures of men and material. Now the Eastern front is held by only a few divisions. It is a situation which we viewed previously as unachievable. Now the situation is as follows: The opponent in the West lies behind his fortification. There is no possibility of coming to grips with him. The decisive question is: How long can we endure this situation?

England cannot live without her imports. We can feed ourselves. The permanent sowing of mines on the English coasts will bring England to her knees. However, this can occur only if we have occupied Belgium and Holland. It is a difficult decision for me. None has ever achieved what I have achieved. My life is of no importance in all this. I have led the German people to a great height, even if the world does hate us now. I risk the loss of this achievement. I have to choose between victory or destruction. I choose victory. . . . My decision is unchangeable. I shall attack France and England at the most favourable and earliest moment. Breach of the neutrality of Belgium and Holland is meaningless. No one will question that when we have won. We shall not bring about the breach of neutrality as idiotically as it was done in 1914. If we do not break the neutrality, then England and France will. Without attack the war cannot be ended victoriously.

Adolf Hitler to the German High Command
3 November 1939

France: The Storm Breaks

Back in the line, as the weather gradually improved, there was a sense of heightening tension and a speeding-up of the tempo of training; fire programmes of enormous size and marvellous intricacy poured out of Corps H.Q., to be worked out in record time as the battery teams became more expert; short courses were held for adjutants, staff officers and even budding C.R.As, while many officers and other ranks attended a practice camp down in the French area.

There was, even so, time for some relaxation, and there were many cheerful dinners in Lille or in unit messes and visits to old friends of 1916–17.

But thoughts inevitably turned to the end of this phase of 'phoney' war and the famous Plan D began to be made known. It was unfortunate that the French slang for what the Navy so aptly called a 'shambles' should have been *système D*, for nothing could have been more fool-proof or more carefully worked out than that famous march table. More and more the C.O. wondered how long this calm could last, but he was less worried now; batteries had knit into efficient units, the unfit had been weeded out and he had a firm confidence in the sturdy common sense of these north-countrymen. They were fit, they were trained and he felt they would play a worthy part if only he could give them a fair chance.

But April drew into May and it was almost with a feeling of relief that at last the C.O. woke one fine morning to the sound of bombs dropping on the nearby aerodrome.

He realized that at long last the 'phoney' war was over and the hunt was up.

British gunner officer

Parachutists and Fifth Column

In the planning for the surprise invasion of Holland, Belgium and Luxembourg, a major preoccupation was whether it would be possible to seize the bridges over the Maas and the Albert Canal intact. Only if that could be done would the army be able swiftly to reach the Peel position in Holland and thereafter quickly relieve the paratroops dropped in the vicinity of Rotterdam.

In November 1939 a conference on the subject was held in the Reich Chancellery with Hitler presiding. As a result the Abwehr was ordered to prepare a plan for the seizure, by means of a *ruse de guerre*—by troops, that is, dressed in Dutch and Belgian uniforms—of the most important bridges over the Maas, the two road and one railway bridge at Maastricht and the one road and one railway bridge at Gennep.

Early in the preparations a most annoying setback was experienced. The agent who had been detailed to procure pattern uniforms was captured by the Belgians with the uniforms in his possession. In connection with this mysterious theft of uniforms a Flemish newspaper published a caricature of Goering, wearing the uniform of a Brussels tram conductor and admiring himself in a mirror, with the caption, 'This *does* suit me well!'

It is quite astonishing that this episode aroused no suspicions either in Holland or Belgium, and that no additional precautionary instructions were as a result issued to the frontier guards. Had the Dutch realized, for instance, what the significance of this abuse of their uniforms was to have been, they would have been spared the surprise overthrow they suffered at Gennep and might have caused a delay in the German advance, which, while it would probably not have affected the fate of the Western campaign, might well have led to the cutting off of the airborne troops landed behind the Dutch lines.

The operations against the Maastricht bridges were carried out by . . . a volunteer unit of Sub-station Breslau (Special Duty Battalion 100). An advance guard, dressed in uniforms surrended by Dutchmen, drove in the early hours of 10 May 1940 via Raedern and Sittart to Maastricht. What happened next is not generally known. The only certainty appears to be that one of the road bridges leading to Maastricht was seized, but the detonating charge could not be removed. After a wild shooting affray, in which the commander of the bogus Dutchmen, Lieutenant Hocke, lost his life, all three bridges blew up. The Maastricht enterprise had ended in complete failure, and it was a depressing sight for the Abwehr chief when on his arrival a few hours later he found whole columns of tanks and lorries jammed on the roads leading to Maastricht and waiting impatiently until the Engineer Corps had thrown a field-service bridge across the river. For it was precisely to avoid this loss of time in the blitz attack that the Maastricht operation had been devised.

The success of the operation at Gennep, carried out by a unit of the Brandenburg Special Duty Battalion 800 under the command of Lieutenant Walther, however, more or less counterbalanced the failure at Maastricht; and as soon as he heard that the Gennep bridges had been secured intact, General von Reichenau, the Commander-in-Chief of 6 Army, forcing its way through the narrow gap between Roermond and Liège, was able immediately to divert some of the units stuck fast at Maastricht to the Gennep route.

This Gennep enterprise was most carefully planned and was executed in partial camouflage. A reconnaissance platoon, disguised as German prisoners under Dutch escort, seized the bridge well before zero hour, and, before the Dutch could recover from their surprise, a column of German tanks was rolling across this important Meuse crossing. The 'prisoners' were men of the Brandenburg Regiment, with hand-grenades and automatic pistols concealed under their greatcoats. And the 'escort' were agents from the Flemish nationalist Mussert movement, disguised as men of the Dutch frontier guards. The gaining of a purely military objective by Secret Service methods—in other words, the tactical co-ordination of the action of regular troops and agents—was successfully employed for the first time in this Gennep affair.

Paul Leverkuehn, German intelligence officer

HOLLAND

Rotterdam: Friday, 10 May

Something terrible happened last night. War began!!! Uncle Pieter was *right*. The city has been *bombed* all day. Am writing this in the Baron's air-raid shelter. There are not many air-raid shelters here but the Baron and Father and Mevrouw Klaes had this one built for us, and all our neighbours said it was a waste of money. This has been a terrible day and everything is upset and people are very sad and excited. This is what happened. Before daylight I woke up and for several minutes did not know what had happened. I could hear explosions and people were shouting under our windows. Mother came running in in her nightie and dressing gown and told me to get my coat on and come quickly. On the way downstairs she told me there was bombing going on but no one knew yet what it meant but she supposed it was war all right. The noise seemed very near. Father had Keetje in his arms and we hurried across the street to the Baron's and went down into his air-raid shelter. Betje and Brenda and Grietje, Mother said, were already gone to the Baron's. Father pointed toward the city and Mother nodded. There were great flames shooting up into the sky and beams of light from the searchlights and the sirens were going very loud. They are on the tops of buildings and have things on them to make them very loud. We could see bullets going up from our guns. The Baron's air-raid shelter was full of people, all our neighbours and some people I didn't know. They were all talking loudly and no one was dressed, just coats over their nightclothes. Keetje began to cry and Father whispered something to her and kissed her and she stopped. Finally she went to sleep in his arms. We waited about two hours. At first most people thought the noise was only practice. All the time people kept running outside and coming back with news. It was war all right and the radio was giving the alarm and calling all the time for all men in the reserves to report for duty at the nearest place. The radio said this over and over. It was very exciting. The bombing kept on all the time, boom-boom-boom, and everyone said they were falling on Waalhaven, the air-port, which is only about five miles away. The Baron went upstairs and began telephoning. The voices on the radio sounded strange and terribly excited. Father put Keetje into Mother's arms and went away. A few minutes later he came back dressed and carrying a gas mask and a knapsack. He kissed Mother and Keetje and me very hard and then hurried out. He shouted back something about taking care of his animals and Mother nodded and told him to be careful, *please*.

After the radio called for the men they all left the shelter and there was no one but the old men and the women and children. At 6.30 the radio said the bombing was over. We all went outside and were glad to get out.

Saturday, 11 May

This was another bad day. The war didn't stop but got worse everywhere. Mother says the Germans have taken all of North Holland and she tried to telephone Grandfather and Grandmother Huyn but the telephone connections are gone now for good to that part of Friesland. To-day was not like yesterday although the bombing and trouble are the same. It is now night and I am going to write what happened all day. We are in the air-shelter again. People are not talking as much as yesterday. Everyone is very tired from working. Yesterday no one knew what to do because the war had come so quickly but to-day we all worked, even the Baron and Uncle Pieter. The radio told citizens what to do to protect themselves. We have been piling sandbags around the houses and digging trenches away from cellars and laying in lots of food. Mother went to the bank this morning to get some money in case we had to leave but there was a long line and no one could take out more than two thousand guilders. There have been many air raids but we worked on outside during some of them. Soldiers are patrolling our little street, just going up and down which is patrolling. There are some soldiers on the housetops farther away. They are looking for parachutists and Dutch Nazis. A few people have tin or steel helmets like the soldiers but I wore a kettle over my head and so did many other people. We do this to keep from getting hit by shrapnel from the anti-aircraft guns and machine-guns. People look very funny going around wearing kettles and pots over their heads and Keetje's keeps falling off all the time. The trolley cars have stopped running, to save electricity, the Baron says, and there is no drinking water in any of the houses in our section because the Germans blew up some of the water pipes yesterday. The telephone is not working either and all letters and telegrams have stopped coming. This is because of the traitors and parachutists. The radio says that no one is to go on the streets after 8.30 to-night unless he has the proper papers and not to go anyway unless it's absolutely necessary. There were seven air raid alarms between nine this morning and supper. The radio says not to depend on sirens for warning because some of the traitors are giving false alarms. Uncle Pieter is furious about this and says he will shoot all traitors on sight and he has an army pistol to do it with too. He carries it inside his coat. There are not so many people here to-night because some of them were called out to fight fires and stand guard and help rescue and dig for people in fallen buildings. I wish I could do more.

This afternoon we saw our first parachutist. We were pasting strips of paper across the Baron's windows—the ones not broken—and across the windows of our own house so they won't break any more when the bombs come. About half of them were broken in all the houses around here yesterday. The parachutist came down at three o'clock. About fifty came down at once. This one was separated from the others. We saw the planes drop them but they seemed far away at first. Keetje was the first to see him because she was not doing much work. Mijnheer van Helst was near Keetje and when he saw the parachutist he called out to the women to go inside and then ran toward the man. The man came down behind the Baron's barn. We saw Mijnheer van Helst take out his pistol and aim and then he fired three times. He came back a moment later looking very sad and said the German was shot. The Baron and several others ran forward to see the German but Brenda kept me from going. Heintje Klaes went and came back and said the German was really dead and he was glad. Mijnheer van Helst didn't look glad and his hands were trembling. He is an old and very kind man and not used to shooting people the way regular soldiers do.

The parachutist, Heintje said, wore a one-piece green suit like overalls and his uniform was like a pair of ski pants. He had a flying eagle on his helmet which was of metal. The Baron brought back the helmet and he said someone could use this but no one wanted to put it on. Heintje got it later and is wearing it now. It is too big for him and he looks silly in it. Heintje is pretty silly-looking anyway and his eyes stick out like tulip bulbs most of the time. Mevrouw Klaes went out to see the dead parachutist and came back very excited. She swore she knew him and that he was named Friedrich Buehler and had grown up in Holland after the other war. This caused a great deal of talk and excitement and Uncle Pieter said, 'The damned ungrateful swine. We took their war babies and fed them and this is what we get back.' Some soldiers came and took the dead parachutist away.

Some of the German planes dropped pieces of paper to-day and Max Blok brought one of the papers into our air-shelter. It said many things in Dutch and was written by the Germans. It said the Germans came as friends and they were sorry to be doing what they were doing but they had to protect us from the English and the French. This made everyone laugh at first and made them angry too. The paper also said that we should stop fighting for it was foolish and crazy for us to go on fighting when our country was almost completely beaten. Why did we want to fight against our friends the Germans?, the paper asked. Our friends the Germans, Mijnheer van Helst said, spitting. He stuck the paper on the wall and ran his pencil through it.

The worst air-raid of all has just come. About half the houses on our street are gone. One bomb landed on the lawn by our air-shelter and one side of the shelter is caved in but the Baron and others are repairing it now. Mevrouw Hartog broke down and cried during the air-raid and got everyone very nervous when she yelled. I think she almost went crazy.

Heintje Klaes was killed! He went outside to see the light from the big flares and incendiary bombs and didn't come back. He slipped out. Heintje was not afraid of anything but the bombs got him. The whole house rocked when the bombs came close. We put our fingers in our ears but it didn't help much. The fire engines are working outside now and half the people in the air-shelter including Uncle Pieter have gone out. I went out for a while and they were taking dead people out of the bombed houses. Uncle Pieter sent me back to stay with Keetje. There is a funny smell in the air like burnt meat and a funny yellow light all over the country from the incendiary bombs. Three men were killed trying to get a bomb away that hadn't gone off yet. One of the men was our postmaster and I loved him very much. He gave me my first bicycle ride. It is awful to watch the people standing by their bombed houses. They don't do much. They just walk around and look at them and look sad and tired. I guess there isn't anything else they can do, but it seems awful.

Our house wasn't hit but the street in front of it between our house and the Baron's is just a great big hole and all the cobblestones are thrown up on our lawn and the Baron's until it doesn't look as if there ever was a street there. Mother is going to be surprised when she sees it. The street was just made over last year and was very smooth and nice.

At the end of our street the water is coming in where the canal locks were hit and I guess it will just keep running over the land until it is fixed. No one does anything about it because there are too many people to be helped and fires to fight. Twelve people on our street were killed and I knew every one of them but I knew Heintje best. Mevrouw Klaes has been crying ever since the bombing. Some people prayed all the time and some sang the national anthem and some just sat and stared. A woman who is very sick with a bad heart looked as if she might die. She was very pale when she came and still is. Jan Klaes is Mevrouw Klaes' other son and he is fighting somewhere like my father is. I said a prayer to myself for Father and I hope God heard it in spite of all the noise. I told Uncle Pieter I had prayed but he didn't say anything, just laid his hand on my shoulder. Uncle Pieter has gone off to the hospital to try to find Mother. It is getting late and he is worried, I think. I know he will find her. Keetje has gone to sleep again but she talks in her sleep and wakes up all the time asking if the war is over and things like that. Poor Keetje, she is so little and doesn't know what is happening. I think I do and it is worse than anything I ever heard about and worse than the worst fight in the cinema. The ambulances coming and going and so many dead people make it hard for me not to cry. I did cry some while the bombing was going on but so many other little children were that no one noticed me, I think. I just got into bed with Keetje and hid my face. I was really frightened this time.

Later

Uncle Pieter came back. He didn't find Mother because she is dead. I can't believe it but Uncle Pieter wouldn't lie. We aren't going to tell Keetje yet. The ambulances are still screaming. I can't sleep or write any more now or anything.

'Dirk van der Heide', aged twelve

The Conquerors

A few days after the start of the offensive Velten was ordered to go as the messing officer's interpreter on a trip into newly-occupied territory. Just as Quickloot and Grabber in Goethe's *Faust* follow in the footsteps of the war-lord to get their greedy claws on enemy possessions, so now did a corps of administrative units, foragers and 'procurement men' move in behind the German armies. The troop began to live from the land even before the country was fully occupied. The headquarters paymaster had a copious supply of the newly printed scrip on a par with the currency of the conquered country. So when Second-Lieutenant Schloyka, the messing officer, drew out sufficient to cover his purchases, Velten, too, converted a portion of his cash.

When their open tourer drew up at the Dutch-German frontier, somewhere near Venlo, they found the road barred by a turnpike just as in the most balmy days of peace. But German soldiers and customs officials watched over it; and on the other side the Dutch frontier guards were missing. The countryside lay at peace in the sunlight, the lush green of the meadows alternating with the silvery grey of the cornfields. The houses in the villages and hamlets through which they passed shone prosperously in the cleanliness of their neat red bricks and white window-frames. Except for an occasional road-block one could drive unimpeded along the smooth well-kept highways of this rich little country. Only columns of prisoners slowed them down from time to time—tired, listless men in Belgian and French uniforms. Dutch prisoners were less frequently encountered, having already been marshalled on municipal sports grounds behind hastily erected barbed-wire entanglements. In the first flush of victory they were being magnanimously treated. Before long they were to regain full liberty.

Schloyka, who had already been in Holland the day before, was telling Velten of the treats to come at a café in the town where he had to make purchases for the mess kitchen.

They were not disappointed. If one ignored the slight restlessness of a people usually so stolid, there was an entirely peace-time atmosphere about the little place. All the businesses and shops were open and German soldiers and Dutch civilians mingled indiscriminately. When they sat down on the sunny terrace of the café and Schloyka ordered *Bohnenkaffee*, the waiter grinned and inquired what other kind of coffee they imagined there was. During the first months of the war it was not easy to make the citizens of this prosperous colonial power understand that in a country where the slogan 'Guns instead of Butter' was a mark of heroism rather than an imposition, the word coffee could signify a brew of malt and dried turnips.

As they walked through the town after their sumptuous repast, Velten noticed how Dutch women watched the German soldiers buying half a dozen pairs of artificial silk stockings at a time, as well as shirts, neckties and underclothing. 'They're hoarding, you know, hoarding!' he heard them whisper to each other excitedly.

Shortly afterwards Velten found himself in the narrow office of the wholesale dealer on whom they had called to buy coffee and cocoa at eighty cents per kilo. The sacks and cartons were already being loaded into the car outside. The dealer was a well-fed man with a thick gold watch-chain across his comfortable paunch. When Velten, having calculated what he owed in marks at the official rate of exchange, laid a roll of German scrip on the table, the Dutchman gazed at the notes in astonishment and suspicion.

'Come along with you,' said Velten, 'that's good money. If we win the war, you'll be glad to have it. And,' he added hesitatingly, 'if we lose, we shall still have to pay up.' At that a broad smile spread over the man's round face. 'If you poor devils lose this war,' he said good-naturedly in his heavy Limburg dialect, 'I don't believe you'll be able to pay a single *pfennig*.' Then he pocketed the notes without counting them and gave Velten the change in clinking silver guilders and those dainty little ten-cent pieces called *dubbeltjes* which are also made of silver.

Velten lost no time in leaving.   Gerhard Kramer

BELGIUM

10 May

At 8.30 a.m. the German Ambassador came to the Ministry of Foreign Affairs. When he entered the Minister's room, he began to take a paper from his pocket. M. Spaak—that is the Belgian Minister—stopped him: 'I beg your pardon, Mr. Ambassador. I will speak first.' And in an indignant voice, he read the Belgian Government's protest: 'Mr. Ambassador, the German Army has just attacked our country. This is the second time in twenty-five years that Germany has committed a criminal aggression against a neutral and loyal Belgium. What has just happened is perhaps even more odious than the aggression of 1914. No ultimatum, no note, no protest of any kind has ever been placed before the Belgian Government. It is through the attack itself that Belgium has learned that Germany has violated the undertakings given by her on 13 October, 1937, and renewed spontaneously at the beginning of the war. . . .'

An Invasion is Organized

We began to have some idea of the scope and importance of the German parachutists' activities when the police came around, about the third day, to remove from the hotel all advertising signs for 'Pacha' Chicory, a step being taken all over Belgium at that moment. As the police officer explained, it had been discovered that the 'Pacha' signs bore on the back information for the use of German parachutists; this was later confirmed by repeated radio warnings.

Chicory is widely used on the Continent, as a coffee substitute, or as a mixture with it, and 'Pacha' was the most widely used brand of chicory in Belgium. In consequence, every little food shop in the country had signs advertising 'Pacha'. These signs had been printed in Belgium, but complicity on someone's part had permitted the Germans to put on the back of them indications useful to parachutists landing in the locality where that particular sign was to be used. Thanks to this arrangement, a German parachutist needed to carry on his person no incriminating maps and addresses; wherever he might land, he needed only to find the nearest 'Pacha' chicory sign, which might be in a grocery shop or along a public highway, and on its back he would find cryptic indications giving him the location of the nearest German agent and how to find him.

Lars Moen, research worker

The B.E.F. Advances Into Belgium: 12 May

Yesterday, so overjoyed were the Belgian people to see our troops that the B.B.C. car was partly filled with tulips and narcissi, our drivers were taken to lunch and loaded with cigarettes. A Lancashire lad said, 'Ee, I'm havin' a terrible time'—he'd been kissed by half-a-dozen girls.

The bombing, so far as my colleagues have been able to judge at the moment, appears to be directed for the most part at military objectives—aerodromes, railway stations, level crossings and so forth. But on this, indeed, it is extremely difficult to form an opinion. The pilot tries to bomb a level crossing—he misses the crossing and demolishes a couple of villas two hundred yards away. Or a pilot is attacked by a fighter and, in making his escape, lightens his machine by dropping his bombs indiscriminately. That action kills half-a-dozen civilians. It seems to their friends deliberate murder; to the pilot no more than the chance of war.

I'm told four British airmen interned in Belgium through a forced landing have now been able to go to England, that they were not on parole, but found the life lonely because few besides members of the British Embassy could visit them.

This is a day of great beauty, and if the occasion were not so grave, one could enjoy it thoroughly. Even so, it is difficult not to enjoy it. The sun is always the sun, and flowers are no less lovely because bombers zoom overhead. Indeed, war puts an edge on beauty—it is as though beauty said, 'Take a long look at me, enjoy me while you may. Who knows for how long it will be?' It may seem incongruous that spring's foliage should be used to camouflage motorcycles and that steel helmets should be adorned with green leaves, but so it is.

The procession on the roads has drawn villagers to their doors. They sit on chairs on the pavement watching the cavalcade go by: British guns (medium and light) draped in dust-sheets, Bren carriers, motor lorries—all the impedimenta of war; and on the other side of the road, speeding towards us, those fleeing from war as from the plague—thousands upon thousands of refugees. I don't know how many passed this way yesterday but the numbers to-day are colossal. Somebody said last night to me, 'It is Poland over again.' But, I thought, hardly that, for these can, at least, put British troops between themselves and the German horde. These seem to be the richer folk with cars—some are large cars, and they go by at a great pace; others are ramshackle affairs—one with two people clinging to the running-board. A host of them carry a mattress on top, partly to guard against machine-gun bullets, partly because this is the most convenient way of carrying it.

And yet even this pitiful sight—and you cannot see it unmoved—bears from time to time, and for a swift instant or two, an air of holiday, a touch of Derby Day. For a lorry will come along holding a large family—grandfather driving the old horse, mother and grandmother sitting aloft surrounded by young children, and all of them raising a hand or waving a greeting. A moment later that impression is blotted out by the sight of a sick woman lying back on her pillows open to the sky.

The route by which we go is marked by sticks on which is painted a black upright arrow rather resembling a plane in flight. Within two or three hours of our entry into Belgium, roads were marked as clearly and traffic guided as efficiently as to the Aldershot Tattoo.

We drive along in the direction of Brussels. Here we pass a motor-lorry on which our lads have chalked: *Berlin or Bust*. My French colleague asks what it means, and is tickled when he learns. We pull up alongside a refugee motor-car broken down—a back wheel is off. They have come from near Liège—the grandmother, whose face wears that numbed, stricken look which is worst of all, was a refugee in the last war also. That is what one finds so repeatedly— people are enduring again what they suffered twenty-odd years ago. They've had no sleep for two nights; they have no food.

Here are two cottages half-obliterated by a bomb. That bomb killed people yesterday. But the hole it made in the road is mended—it almost seems a long time ago since the bomb fell.

Occasional gunfire thuds heavily, like someone beating a carpet a long way off; from time to time a shrill air-raid siren blows; but the procession does not stop. Refugees, exhausted, lie asleep in the fields beside their bicycles.

I talk to an old man leaning over his garden gate, brown eyes deep-sunken. He says, 'It is the Boche, monsieur. He does not change. I saw it coming—like a cloud of dust in the road concealing you know not what. And then, from the dust emerges a shape—a shape we knew before—the Boche, monsieur. Yes, I have seen it before.' He stops. Presently his face lightens. 'It is spring,' he says slowly, 'and in spring there is hope. Your men bring us hope; and since it is spring, we give them our flowers—lilac, tulips, narcissus.' He looks at our stolid lads with their brick-red faces, sweaty, dusty, rolling by in their lorries, some of them asleep in the sun, and for a moment there is a light in his old eyes. . . .

J. L. Hodson

On 13 May, Winston Churchill made his first speech to the House of Commons as Prime Minister.

I would say to the House, as I said to those who have joined this Government, 'I have nothing to offer but blood, toil, tears and sweat.'

We have before us an ordeal of the most grevious kind. We have before us many, many long months of struggle and of suffering. You ask what is our policy? I will say: it is to wage war, by sea, land and air, with all our might and with all the strength that God can give us: to wage war against a monstrous tyranny never surpassed in the dark, lamentable catalogue of human crime. That is our policy. You ask, what is our aim? I can answer in one word: victory—victory at all costs, victory in spite of all terror, victory, however long and hard the road may be; for without victory, there is no survival. Let that be realized; no survival for the British Empire; no survival for all that the British Empire has stood for, no survival for the urge and impulse of the ages, that mankind will move forward towards its goal. But I take up my task with buoyancy and hope. I feel sure that our cause will not be suffered to fail among men. At this time I feel entitled to claim the aid of all, and I say, 'Come, then, let us go forward together with our united strength.'

Winston Churchill

The Formation of the Home Guard: 14 May

I want to speak to you to-night about the form of warfare which the Germans have been employing so extensively against Holland and Belgium, namely, the dropping of troops by parachute behind the main defensive lines.

The success of such an attack depends on speed. Consequently, the measures to defeat such an attack must be prompt and rapid. It is upon this basis that our plans have been laid. You will not expect me to tell you, or the enemy, what our plans are, but we are confident that they will be effective. However, in order to leave nothing to chance, and to supplement, from sources as yet untapped, the means of defence already arranged, we are going to ask you to help us in a manner which I know will be welcome to thousands of you. Since the war began the Government have received countless inquiries from all over the Kingdom from men of all ages who are for one reason or another not at present engaged in military service and who wish to do something for the defence of the country.

Now is your opportunity. We want large numbers of such men in Great Britain who are British subjects between the ages of seventeen and sixty-five to come forward now and offer their service in order to make assurance doubly sure. . . .

Anthony Eden, Secretary of State for War

BLITZKRIEG

On 13 May the Germans broke through the line of the Meuse, and two days later had shattered the French 9 Army of General Corap. In the next seven days the Panzers swept west and north-west, cutting off the French, British and Belgian armies to the north, which soon had their backs to the sea.

The Master Plan

. . . . Each of us generals outlined what his task was and how he intended to carry it out. I was the last to speak. My task was as follows: On the day ordered

I would cross the Luxembourg frontier, drive through southern Belgium towards Sedan, cross the Meuse and establish a bridgehead on the far side so that the infantry corps following behind could get across. I explained briefly that my corps would advance through Luxembourg and southern Belgium in three columns; I reckoned on reaching the Belgian frontier posts on the first day and I hoped to break through them on that same day; on the second day I would advance as far as Neufchâteau; on the third day I would reach Bouillon and cross the Semois; on the fourth day I would arrive at the Meuse; on the fifth day I would cross it. By the evening of the fifth day I hoped to have established a bridgehead on the far bank. Hitler asked, 'And then what are you going to do?' He was the first person who had thought to ask me this vital question. I replied, 'Unless I receive orders to the contrary, I intend on the next day to continue my advance westwards. The supreme leadership must decide whether my objective is to be Amiens or Paris. In my opinion the correct course is to drive past Amiens to the English Channel.' Hitler nodded and said nothing more. Only General Busch, who commanded 16 Army on my left, cried out, 'Well, I don't think you'll cross the river in the first place!' Hitler, the tension visible in his face, looked at me to see what I would reply. I said, 'There's no need for you to do so, in any case.' Hitler made no comment.

General Heinz Guderian, G.O.C. Panzer Corps

Crossing the Meuse

On 13 May I drove off to Dinant at about 04.00 hours with Captain Schraepler. The whole of the divisional artillery was already in position as ordered, with its forward observers stationed at the crossing points. In Dinant I found only a few men of the 7th Rifle Regiment. Shells were dropping in the town from French artillery west of the Meuse, and there were a number of knocked-out tanks in the streets leading down to the river. The noise of battle could be heard from the Meuse valley.

The situation when I arrived was none too pleasant. Our boats were being destroyed one after the other by the French flanking fire, and the crossing eventually came to a standstill. The enemy infantry were so well concealed that they were impossible to locate even after a long search through glasses. Again and again they directed their fire into the area in which I and my companions— the commanders of the Rifle Brigade and the Engineer Battalion—were lying. A smoke screen in the Meuse valley would have prevented these infantry doing much harm. But we had no smoke unit. So I now gave orders for a number of houses in the valley to be set alight in order to supply the smoke we lacked.

Minute by minute the enemy fire grew more unpleasant. From up river a damaged rubber boat came drifting down to us with a badly wounded man clinging to it, shouting and screaming for help—the poor fellow was near to drowning. But there was no help for him here, the enemy fire was too heavy.

With Captain Schraepler, I now drove south down the Meuse valley road in a Panzer IV to see how things were going with the 7th Rifle Regiment. On the way we came under fire several times from the western bank and Schraepler

was wounded in the arm from a number of shell splinters. Single French
infantrymen surrendered as we approached.

By the time we arrived the 7th Rifle Regiment had already succeeded in
getting a company across to the west bank, but the enemy fire had then become
so heavy that their crossing equipment had been shot to pieces and the crossing
had had to be halted. Large numbers of wounded were receiving treatment in a
house close beside the demolished bridge. As at the northern crossing point,
there was nothing to be seen of the enemy who were preventing the crossing.
As there was clearly no hope of getting any more men across at this point without powerful artillery and tank support to deal with the enemy nests, I drove
back to Division Headquarters, where I met the Army commander, Colonel-
General von Kluge and the Corps commander, General Hoth.

After talking over the situation with Major Heidkaemper and making the
necessary arrangements, I drove back along the Meuse to Leffé [a village on the
outskirts of Dinant] to get the crossing moving there.

At Leffé weir we took a quick look at the footbridge, which had been barred
by the enemy with a spiked steel plate. The firing in the Meuse valley had
ceased for the moment and we moved off to the right through some houses to
the crossing point proper. The crossing had now come to a complete standstill,
with the officers badly shaken by the casualties which their men had suffered.
On the opposite bank we could see several men of the company which was
already across, among them many wounded. Numerous damaged boats and
rubber dinghies lay on the opposite bank. The officers reported that nobody
dared show himself outside cover, as the enemy opened fire immediately on
anyone they spotted.

Several of our tanks and heavy weapons were in position on the embankment east of the houses, but had seemingly already fired off almost all their
ammunition. However, the tanks I had ordered to the crossing point soon
arrived, to be followed shortly afterwards by two field howitzers from the Battalion Grasemann.

All points on the western bank likely to hold enemy riflemen were now
brought under fire, and soon the aimed fire of all weapons was pouring into
rocks and buildings. Lieutenant Hanke knocked out a pill-box on the bridge ramp
with several rounds. The tanks, with turrets traversed left, drove slowly north at
fifty yards' spacing along the Meuse valley, closely watching the opposite slopes.

Under cover of this fire the crossing slowly got going again, and a cable
ferry using several large pontoons was started. Rubber boats paddled backwards
and forwards and brought back the wounded from the west bank. One man who
fell out of his boat on the way grabbed hold of the ferry rope and was dragged
underwater through the Meuse. He was rescued by Private Heidenreich, who
dived in and brought him to the bank.

I now took over personal command of the 2nd Battalion of the 7th Rifle
Regiment and for some time directed operations myself.

With Lieutenant Most I crossed the Meuse in one of the first boats and at
once joined the company which had been across since early morning. From the
company command post we could see Companies Enkefort and Lichter were
making rapid progress.

I then moved up north along a deep gully to the Company Enkefort. As we arrived an alarm came in: 'Enemy tanks in front.' The company had no anti-tank weapons, and I therefore gave orders for small arms fire to be opened on the tanks as quickly as possible, whereupon we saw them pull back into a hollow about a thousand yards north-west of Leffé. Large numbers of French stragglers came through the bushes and slowly laid down their arms.

On arrival at Brigade Headquarters on the west bank I found the situation looking decidedly unhealthy. The commander of the 7th Motor-cycle Battalion had been wounded, his adjutant killed, and a powerful French counter-attack had severely mauled our men in Grange. There was a danger that enemy tanks might penetrate into the Meuse valley itself.

Leaving my signals truck on the west bank, I crossed the river again and gave orders for first the Panzer Company, and then the Panzer Regiment, to be ferried across during the night. However, ferrying tanks across the 120-yards-wide river by night was a slow job, and by morning there were still only fifteen tanks on the west bank, an alarmingly small number.

At daybreak [14 May] we heard that Colonel von Bismarck had pressed through his attack to close on Onhaye [three miles west of Dinant], where he was now engaged with a powerful enemy. Shortly afterwards a wireless message came in saying that his regiment was encircled, and I therefore decided to go to his assistance immediately with every available tank.

At about 09.00 hours the 25th Panzer Regiment, under the command of Colonel Rothenburg, moved off along the Meuse valley with the thirty tanks which had so far arrived on the west bank and penetrated as far as a hollow five hundred yards north-east of Onhaye without meeting any resistance. It transpired that von Bismarck had actually radioed 'arrived' instead of 'encircled'* and that he was now on the point of sending an assault company round the northern side of Onhaye to secure its western exit. This move, as had been shown by an exercise we had carried out earlier in Godesberg, was of the greatest importance for the next stages of the operation. Accordingly, five tanks were placed under von Bismarck's command for this purpose—not to make a tank attack in the usual sense, but to provide mobile covering fire for the infantry attack on the defile west of Onhaye. It was my intention to place the Panzer Regiment itself in a wood a thousand yards north of Onhaye and then to bring all other units up to that point, from where they could be employed to the north, north-west or west, according to how the situation developed.

I gave orders to Rothenburg to move round both sides of the wood into this assembly area, and placed myself in a Panzer III which was to follow close behind him.

Rothenburg now drove off through a hollow to the left with the five tanks which were to accompany the infantry, thus giving these tanks a lead of a hundred to a hundred and fifty yards. There was no sound of enemy fire. Some twenty to thirty tanks followed up behind. When the commander of the five tanks reached the rifle company on the southern edge of Onhaye wood, Colonel Rothenburg moved off with his leading tanks along the edge of the wood going west: we had just reached the south-west corner of the wood and were about to

* Translator's note: *eingetroffen* instead of *eingeschlossen*.

cross a low plantation, from which we could see the five tanks escorting the infantry below us to our left front, when suddenly we came under heavy artillery and anti-tank gunfire from the west. Shells landed all round us and my tank received two hits, one after the other, the first on the upper edge of the turret and the second in the periscope.

The driver promptly opened the throttle wide and drove straight into the nearest bushes. He had only gone a few yards, however, when the tank slid down a steep slope on the western edge of the wood and finally stopped, canted over on its side, in such a position that the enemy whose guns were in position about five hundred yards away on the edge of the next wood could not fail to see it. I had been wounded in the right cheek by a small splinter from the shell which had landed in the periscope. It was not serious though it bled a great deal.

I tried to swing the turret round so as to bring our 37 mm. gun to bear on the enemy in the opposite wood, but with the heavy slant of the tank it was immovable.

The French battery now opened rapid fire on our wood and at any moment we could expect their fire to be aimed at our tank, which was in full view. I therefore decided to abandon it as fast as I could, taking the crew with me. At that moment the subaltern in command of the tanks escorting the infantry reported himself seriously wounded, with the words, 'Herr General, my left arm has been shot off.' We clambered up through the sandy pit, shells crashing and splintering all round. Close in front of us trundled Rothenburg's tank with flames pouring out of the rear. The adjutant of the Panzer Regiment had also left his tank. I thought at first that the command tank had been set alight by a hit in the petrol tank and was extremely worried for Colonel Rothenburg's safety. However, it turned out to be only the smoke candles that had caught light, the smoke from which now served us very well. In the meantime Lieutenant Most had driven my armoured signals vehicle into the wood, where it had been hit in the engine and now stood immobilized. The crew was unhurt.

I now gave orders for the tanks to drive through the wood in a general easterly direction, a move which the armoured cars, which stood at my disposal, were of course unable to follow. Slowly Rothenburg's command tank forced its way through the trees, many of them tall and well grown. It was only the involuntary smoke-screen laid by this tank that prevented the enemy from shooting up any more of our vehicles. If only the tanks had sprayed the wood which the enemy was believed to be holding with machine-gun and 37 mm. gunfire during their advance, the French would probably have immediately abandoned their guns, which were standing in exposed positions at the edge of the wood, and our losses would almost certainly have been smaller. An attack launched in the evening by the 25th Panzer Regiment was successful, and we were able to occupy our assembly area.

General Erwin Rommel, G.O.C. 7 Panzer Division

Break-through: 15 May

The way to the west was now open. The moon was up and for the time being we could expect no real darkness. I had already given orders, in the plan for the break-through, for the leading tanks to scatter the road and verges with machine and anti-tank gunfire at intervals during the drive to Avesnes, which I hoped would prevent the enemy from laying mines. The rest of the Panzer Regiment was to follow close behind the leading tanks and be ready at any time to fire salvoes to either flank. The mass of the division had instructions to follow up the Panzer Regiment lorry-borne.

The tanks now rolled in a long column through the line of fortifications and on towards the first houses, which had been set alight by our fire. In the moonlight we could see the men of 7th Motor-cycle Battalion moving forward on foot beside us. Occasionally an enemy machine-gun or anti-tank gun fired, but none of their shots came anywhere near us. Our artillery was dropping heavy harassing fire on villages and the road far ahead of the regiment. Gradually the speed increased. Before long we were five hundred—a thousand—two thousand—three thousand yards into the fortified zone. Engines roared, tank tracks clanked and clattered. Whether or not the enemy was firing was impossible to tell in the ear-splitting noise. We crossed the railway line a mile or so south-west of Solre le Château, and then swung north to the main road which was soon reached. Then off along the road and past the first houses.

The people in the houses were rudely awoken by the din of our tanks, the clatter and roar of tracks and engines. Troops lay bivouacked beside the road, military vehicles stood parked in farmyards and in some places on the road itself. Civilians and French troops, their faces distorted with terror, lay huddled in the ditches, alongside hedges and in every hollow beside the road. We passed refugee columns, the carts abandoned by their owners, who had fled in panic into the fields. On we went, at a steady speed, towards our objective. Every so often a quick glance at the map by a shaded light and a short wireless message to Divisional H.Q. to report the position and thus the success of the 25th Panzer Regiment. Every so often to look out of the hatch to assure myself that there was still no resistance and that contact was being maintained to the rear. The flat countryside lay spread out around us under the cold light of the moon. We were through the Maginot Line!* It was hardly conceivable. Twenty-two years before we had stood for four and a half long years before this self-same enemy and had won victory after victory and yet finally lost the war. And now we had broken through the renowned Maginot Line and were driving deep into enemy territory. It was not just a beautiful dream. It was reality.

Suddenly there was a flash from a mound about three hundred yards away to the right of the road. There could be no doubt what it was, an enemy gun well concealed in a concrete pill-box, firing on the 25th Panzer Regiment from the flank. More flashes came from other points. Shell bursts could not be seen. Quickly informing Rothenburg of the danger—he was standing close beside me—I gave orders through him for the regiment to increase speed and burst through this second fortified line with broadsides to right and left.

Fire was opened quickly, the tank crews having been instructed in the method of fire before the attack. Much of our ammunition was tracer and the regiment drove on through the new defence line spraying an immense rain of

* In fact, this was the recently-built northward extension of the Maginot Line proper, which lay farther to the south (Ed.)

fire into the country on either side. Soon we were through the danger area, without serious casualties. But it was not now easy to get the fire stopped and we drove through the villages of Sars Poteries and Beugnies with guns blazing. Enemy confusion was complete. Military vehicles, tanks, artillery and refugee carts packed high with belongings blocked part of the road and had to be pushed unceremoniously to the side. All around were French troops lying flat on the ground, and farms everywhere were jammed tight with guns, tanks and other military vehicles. Progress towards Avesnes now became slow. At last we succeeded in getting the firing stopped. We drove through Semousies. Always the same picture, troops and civilians in wild flight down both sides of the road.

Rommel

Amiens

1 Panzer Division's attack went well, and by about noon we had taken the city and forced a bridgehead to a depth of some four miles. I had a quick look over the ground we had seized and also the city with its beautiful cathedral, before hurrying back to Albert where I expected to find 2 Panzer Division. I met the columns of my advancing troops and had to drive through crowds of fleeing refugees. I also ran into a number of enemy vehicles which, thick with dust, had joined the German columns and hoped in this fashion to reach Paris and avoid being taken prisoner. I thus quickly captured some fifteen Englishmen.

In Albert I found General Veiel. 2 Panzer Division had captured an English artillery battery, drawn up on the barrack square and equipped only with training ammunition, since nobody had reckoned on our appearance that day. Prisoners of all nationalities filled the market-place and the adjoining streets. 2 Panzer Division were almost out of fuel and were therefore proposing to stop where they were, but they were soon disillusioned. I ordered them to advance at once to Abbeville and by 19.00 hours they had reached this objective, passing through Doullens-Beaumetz-Saint Riquier.

The divisional commander was mistaken in thinking that his troops were out of fuel. After regulating the fuel stocks in the hands of the troops it proved possible to continue the advance. One must always distrust the report of troop commanders, 'We have no fuel.' Generally they have. But if they become tired they lack fuel. That is a common experience of war with the forward troops. During the campaign in France there was no lack of fuel—good staff work can avoid this calamity. Later in the war we often had a real scarcity of fuel because of the destruction of our industry. But in 1940 it was only a question of transport and easy to solve.

General Heinz Guderian

A Postcard

I received a postcard at my address, found on the body of an officer of Corap's army, who had just committed suicide in Le Mans station. He wrote, 'I am killing myself, Mr. President, to let you know that all my men were brave, but one cannot send men to fight tanks with rifles.'

Paul Reynaud

Sauve Qui Peut

For twenty-one hours Captain Billerot was cut off from the colonel's head-quarters. Then he decided to send out three men in search of the Ferme Saint-Denis. Adjudant Lesfauries, Sergeant Keruran, and I volunteered. We all had our bellyful of that wood. Sergeant-Major Gerber joined us at the last moment.

After four hours we found the Ferme and our colonel, but we had lost Gerber on our way. The colonel told us he had taken up position with his three battalions without knowing the whereabouts of the regiment we were supposed to relieve. This regiment, the 48th Infantry, had vanished, he said. A battalion of anti-tank guns that happened to be nearby had rushed to his assistance and for the moment was holding back the Germans. Captain Duvivier had gone off to find the divisional commander—his exact whereabouts were not known. Infuriated that the two companies had not yet arrived, Colonel de Buissy asked me if I could show him the exact location of the woods in which Captains Billerot and Berley were entrenched. I could not, because the colonel owned only a Michelin automobile map: the only military map in the regiment had been taken by Captain Duvivier.

The colonel asked me whether I would undertake to find my way back to the wood and guide both companies to the Ferme. I set out. Considering that the Germans seemed to be asleep and that the *Mouchard** had gone home, I decided to avoid the woods and follow the main road straight through Châtillon. This road offered an amazing spectacle. Everywhere I saw guns, knapsacks, tins of food, cartridge-cases in the ditch. Equipment worth hundreds of thousands of francs was strewn along the road: no one thought of picking it up. All these things had become too heavy for the infantrymen.

A short distance beyond Châtillon I met a soldier sitting on his knapsack and devouring a tin of meat.

'What regiment?' I asked him.

'48th Infantry.'

'Where's your regiment?'

'Don't know.'

He quietly went on eating.

'Where are you going now?'

He looked sullenly ahead. He was a square-built, dark-haired fellow. His dark eyes had so dull a look that I thought: he wouldn't notice if a bullet hit him.

'Don't know,' he said at last. 'I'm looking for my regiment.'

I asked him whether they had been ordered to retreat.

'How do I know?' said the soldier. He rubbed his knee, adding, 'All of a sudden someone began to yell, "*Sauve qui peut!*"—and then we ran for it.'

'Were the Germans there?'

He reflected a while.

'No, we didn't see any.'

He rose, looking at me with distrust.

'Let's go!'

* German reconnaissance plane.

He took his field flask and made ready to follow me.

'What about your gun?' I asked.

He cast a glance at his gun lying in the ditch—a farewell glance.

'Much too heavy,' he said. 'And rusty. Can't get it open. There's plenty of guns all over the place.'

He thrust his hands into his trouser pockets and limped along by my side. But there was nothing unusual in his limp. All of us limped.

We came to a house where two shell-stricken negroes sat smoking. They belonged to the 24th Colonials. They joined us. They, too, were 'looking for' their regiment. One of them was a corporal and understood French. He asked me whether it would soon be 'over'. He too, thought Germany hadn't done anything to him. I tried to explain that France was in danger. He didn't seem to understand.

'Hitler no come Senegal', he kept repeating. He smiled, showing his teeth, and spoke at quick intervals to his comrade. 'Hitler no come Senegal. I no come Germany. I and Hitler no enemy.'

A stray German shell exploded a few yards ahead of us. We threw ourselves on the ground. The Senegal negro—the one who did not speak French—shouted, 'Sauve qui peut!' It sounded like 'shof ki po'. He probably did not understand the meaning of his cry. He had heard it at a moment of great peril, and from that time on he repeated it whenever he thought himself in danger.

The Frenchman lay in the ditch beside me, the two negroes about five steps from us. The sound of bursting shrapnel grew clearer and clearer, closer and closer. I lay on an abandoned knapsack. At every explosion the Senegalese yelled, 'Shof ki po! Shof ki po!'

Soon it began to sound like an Oriental prayer.

The Germans shortened their range. Now the shrapnel burst on the field to the right of us. Suddenly I heard an inhuman cry. It was one of the negroes. The other, the black corporal, threw himself sobbing and lamenting over his comrade. I crawled as close to them as I could. The negro's whole back had been torn open by a shrapnel splinter.

He was the first dying man I saw at the front. His eyes were wide open, his mouth was foaming. His tongue, a thick black tongue, moved between his lips. And, like a last wish or the name of someone he loved, he mumbled the words, 'Shof ki po! Shof ki po!'

Run for your lives! This was the slogan of the French Army.

Run for your lives. *Shof ki po.*

Hans Habe

The Battle of Sainte-Menehould

When I went out of the church with Kohn Gabriel I heard the first German tanks entering the town.

The panic had started while we were inside. Soldiers ran up and down in the square looking for cover. There were practically no officers left; at least none appeared in the square. Even to-day I believe that some of the men lost their minds at this moment. I still can see Sergeant Rupin dashing madly about the square on his bicycle, round and round, like a participant in a six-day cycle race. Again and again he flitted by my nose, and I couldn't stop him. Adjudant Lesfauries stumbled by me asking, with an infinitely stupid look, whether there was anything new. He did not wait for my answer. Some lay flat on the pavement, pressing their guns to their shoulders. This gesture—only natural on the battle-field—here seemed grotesque. Men with rifles, with knapsacks on their backs, lay on the pavement of the main square like toy soldiers on the carpet of a nursery. The first planes appeared. We could no longer distinguish between the sound of the planes and the tanks. A bomb fell in the middle of the square. Stones hurtled through the air. You could hardly tell whether it was day or night. Each bomb that fell spread light and then darkness.

I lay in front of the church. Suddenly I heard a voice, 'Take cover, in the houses! Stop the tanks!'

No one knew who had cried out. We obeyed mechanically. I slipped under a gate at the corner of the square and the Rue Margraine. At the same moment the German tanks turned into the narrow street. They didn't seem to be moving down the street—the whole street seemed to be moving—moving with the armoured cars. They filled the street. They took it with them. The red maws of the tanks drilled their flaming tongues into the walls of the houses. It looked as though nothing could remain in their wake. It was as though each tank peeled a piece off the crust of the earth. But for this very reason we were not frightened. The whole thing seemed unreal. It was more like a bad film of the future, with warriors from Mars and synthetic men popping out of bottles. Everything moved as on a screen. We felt that it couldn't go on much longer.

Suddenly, in the midst of the deafening noise of the circling bombers and the slowly advancing tanks, I heard a familiar sound—the rattle of a machine-gun not far from me. The sound was almost friendly, almost musical. I looked up. From the second or third floor of the adjoining house a machine-gun was firing—firing at the approaching tanks. And the same thing happened that always happens when a man turns up in a faint-hearted crowd. Suddenly firing started from all sides. It was a childish effort. Our experience had taught us that even the anti-tank guns were powerless against the heavy German units. Only the seventy-fives obtained some success. And now we were firing our machine-guns and old carbines. But what did that matter? There was a sudden patter from all the houses. I quickly ran to the other side of the street. Bullets whistled past me on both sides. Our soldiers had made up their minds to lay a barrage across the street.

I ran up the steps. It was a little old house with wooden stairs. Half-way to the first floor a door was open—the door to the W.C. Nothing on earth is funnier than a W.C. when the whole world is collapsing.

I did not know the machine-gunners. But at the window of the adjoining room stood a man whom I immediately recognized, even from behind. It gave me a feeling of indescribable joy. I say 'indescribable', because a normal human being in his daily routine rises to the joys of his existence from a settled level of mediocrity. One must fall to the depths to understand what it means to find a friend. At the window stood Saint-Brice.

For some unknown reason the tank, followed by innumerable others—the

street was so narrow that they could move only in single file—halted. At the
same time the roar of the aeroplane engines redoubled in intensity. The tank
stood at the northern end of the Rue Camille Margraine. The machine-guns
stopped rattling. Half-hidden in our room, we looked down into the street.
Fallen soldiers lay on the asphalt. Blood ran down the gutter. It is so easy to
write these words, forgetting what they mean: blood running down the gutter.
In writing, everything seems two-dimensional in effect, without background.
Blood in the gutter: nothing behind it. No suffering, no pain, no meaning. Red
water in the drain. Gurgling red water. You move as in a film, watching yourself.
And that is what makes it all bearable.

A few steps from our house a wounded soldier was screaming. From time to
time the upper part of his body rose. Each time he fell down again he stopped
crying. Again and again we believed that he was dead. But at regular intervals
he sat up. At regular intervals the dead man screamed.

Behind the tank German motor-cycles appeared. As the street was too narrow they formed on the pavement. Each cycle had a sidecar with two men in it.
Each of them was armed with an automatic rifle. But they had not yet started
to move. My brain throbbed with the tension. Something seemed to be flying
through my temples. Behind street corners and windows a group of desperate
men was waiting. How many were they? Were we not alone? Alone with a few
dead and the half-dead whose cries rent the air. We did not know. Any sound
would have been more bearable than this silence in which you couldn't tell where
your comrades were. Even the machine-gunners in the next room did not
stir.

At last the motor-cyclists started. They emerged at the right and left of the
armoured car. One of the two men on each motor-cycle held his automatic
rifle upward, the other horizontally down the street. They fired without interruption. In less than a fraction of a minute they were in front of our house. At
least fifteen of them arrived at the same time. I was half-crouching under a
window. Saint-Brice bent forward. I saw that he was taking aim. I made ready
to shoot. Saint-Brice pulled the trigger. I followed him immediately. The miracle
occurred—my Remington went off! I reloaded in feverish haste. Despite the
infernal noise that was suddenly unleashed—motor-cycles, armoured cars,
aeroplanes, bombs, machine-gun fire, rifles—I distinctly heard orders shouted
in German. Somebody cried, *'Rein ins Haus!'* ('Into the house!') Simultaneously the pane splintered. They were firing at our window.

I crawled into the adjoining room for ammunition. A bullet whistled by me.
Curious, I thought unconsciously, this shot cannot come from the street. Then
I heard somebody saying beside me, *'Oh, les salauds!'*

I crawled to the three men at the machine-gun. And then I saw what, for the
first time, struck me with horror. In a window of one of the few undamaged
houses on the opposite side of the street—the same house under the gate of which
I had been hidden a short time before—a machine-gun had been set in place.
Behind the machine-gun a German steel helmet emerged and quickly disappeared. But the man could not disappear quickly enough; I saw his face. His
eyes stared at me. It was probably only my imagination, but it seemed to me that
I had never before seen more evil eyes. And though I had never feared all the

terrifying things invented by man, I was afraid of this man. Cannon, shells, and bombs are not terrifying. Only man is terrifying.

Suddenly I realized that Saint-Brice had seized me by the arm. . . .

'We've got to get out of here!' Saint-Brice whispered into my ear. I followed him. He pushed me forward and covered our retreat with his unloaded revolver. He must have explored the premises in advance; he took me through a narrow corridor, through a half-demolished room, down a wooden staircase, and finally through a store-room. And then we were outside.

We must have left the house by the back door. We stood in a little vegetable garden, bordered by an old stone wall. Suddenly we found ourselves in the midst of a summer morning. I stood still, breathing deeply. The din of the battle was muffled.

'Come on,' said Saint-Brice.

We ran across a field. What did we care whether planes spotted us? We breathed. We were alive.

And we knew what it meant to be alive.

But there was no time to pause. To reach the bridge we had to go back through the town. Meanwhile the Germans had moved in everywhere. But our regiments were resisting desperately. I saw soldiers firing from behind corpses, resting their guns on the bodies of their dead comrades. The town stank of corpses, smoke, and sugar. I had a glimpse of Colonel de Buissy trying with a few men to erect a tank barricade. The whole scene had a toylike effect, comic and tragic at once: on one side a few riflemen, the lieutenant with the revolver, the meagre fabric of barbed wire, the forlorn machine-gun; the other side, tanks, armoured cars that reached nearly to the second storey, motor-cycles, machine-guns on wheels.

A single machine-gun was holding the south bridge. A young Frenchman of the 11th Regiment whom I knew and a negro of the same regiment were firing the gun. Suddenly the negro clutched his chest and collapsed. From the bridge I saw Mayer-Mayerescu of Bucharest throw himself on the dead man. He lay on the negro's body and guided the machine-gun belt.

Soldiers of the engineering corps ran across the bridge with me. Quicker than I could think, with the town still full of our men, they carried out their orders. I had scarcely passed when the bridge blew up. It was the only avenue of retreat.

France had men. One of them was Pierre Saint-Brice.

We had separated when we saw the colonel. We agreed that I should wait on the other side of the bridge. Unseen to one another, we had crossed it at about the same time. Then suddenly we found ourselves side by side. I told him about little Mayer's exploit. He thought for a while. Then he said, 'Come on! Quick!'

We ran along the river bank. At one place the river was particularly narrow. Saint-Brice sat down on the grass and began silently to pull off his boots.

'What are you doing?' I asked.

'I'm going to get little Mayer!'

I said nothing. I sat beside him and tried to unbuckle my puttees.

'What are you doing?' Saint-Brice asked with annoyance.

'I'm going with you.'

'What for?'

'So that you won't be alone.'

He looked at me, smiling behind his glasses.

'All right,' he said. 'Let's take a bath.'

We both cursed as we pulled off our shoes. It was a real operation to take them off our swollen, bleeding feet.

'I am not tired any more,' said the lieutenant.

'Neither am I. I've forgotten all about it.'

He jumped into the water first.

When I left my watch—a gift from my father, to which I was particularly attached—in my shoes the time was two o'clock in the afternoon. When I came back with the soldiers whom I had found in the place indicated by Saint-Brice it was three o'clock. Little Mayer was sitting on the grass. But in the meantime Saint-Brice had returned to the burning town. He had 'delivered' Mayer only a short while before, and had immediately gone for another bath. Between two and seven in the evening he made three trips to the town, which had meanwhile been completely occupied by the enemy. Each time he saved seven or eight soldiers from certain death.

Hans Habe

Colonel de Buissy

Colonel de Buissy, at the head of his regiment, had defended Sainte-Menehould with heroism. De Buissy was nearly sixty years old. He had been wounded seven times in the Great War. He had spent eighteen years in Africa, commanding the 4th Foreign Legion, the most famous of all the famous regiments of the Foreign Legion. He had distinguished himself in the great Moroccan battles. At the outbreak of the present war the colonel, who had been pensioned shortly before, left his home in Lille and offered his services to France. In consideration of his particular abilities and merits, he was immediately appointed commander of the 1st Foreign Volunteer Regiment, which was later renamed the 21st. He was an officer of the Legion of Honour and bearer of almost every high distinction that a French officer can achieve.

Colonel de Buissy was ordered to appear at Passavant at nine o'clock on the night before Saint-Brice and myself reached that village. The general commanding our brigade waited for the colonel in the notary's house. It proved impossible, however, to interrupt the battle of Sainte-Menehould according to a prearranged schedule. If the retreat of the innumerable regiments streaming southward was to be even partly covered we had to hold the enemy in and around Sainte-Menehould. Colonel de Buissy reached Passavant at five in the morning, on foot, totally exhausted, having escaped death by a miracle. Lieutenant Costa, a brave Corsican who commanded our motor-cyclists—motor-cyclists without motor-cycles, mind you—had fallen on the battlefield only a few steps from the colonel.

The following conversation took place between the General and the Colonel:

The General: 'Why are you so late, Colonel de Buissy?'

The Colonel: 'We held Sainte-Menehould as long as we could.'

The General: 'You could have retreated long ago. I have been waiting here for twenty-one hours.'

The Colonel: 'I am sorry. We tried to resist. Unfortunately, *mon général,* our arms were more than deficient, as you well know.'

The General: 'How many men were killed?'

The Colonel: 'At least five hundred. With normal equipment we should have had four hundred less casualties.'

The General: 'Five hundred Jews the less.'

The Colonel: 'The Jews fought like the rest. Moreover, there were at least as many Christians as Jews.'

The General: 'You don't look well, Colonel.'

The Colonel: 'I am somewhat tired.'

The General: 'Excellent! Madame de Buissy will be very glad to have you back.'

The Colonel: 'Do you mean that I am relieved of my command?'

The General: 'I mean that within one hour you will be taken to the peaceful south in an ambulance.'

The Colonel: 'Thank you! But I am neither sick nor injured. I have been with this regiment from the first minute of its existence, and I intend to remain at the head of my men to my last breath. My regiment has fought heroically. I deserve ——'

The General: 'How old are you, Colonel de Buissy?'

The Colonel: 'Fifty-eight.'

The General: 'You deserve a rest, my dear de Buissy. Your nerves are frayed. You'll be taken to the rear in one hour. At the same time Lieutenant-Colonel Landry will arrive here.'

The Colonel: 'You mean that my successor has already been appointed?'

The General: 'Yes! And I hope you enjoy your well-deserved rest.'

The Colonel: 'Is that an order?'

The General: 'Yes.'

The Colonel: 'I accept under protest.'

The General: 'I am convinced that Madame de Buissy will not protest against having you back with her.'

One hour later our colonel was loaded on an ambulance sent by the High Command and taken to the divisional headquarters at Commercy. The colonel on his stretcher was brought to a hall where two generals—the commanders of the brigade and the division—were engaged in a conversation. The hall was large, and the two generals apparently thought that the colonel would not hear their whispering. Besides, Colonel de Buissy pretended to be asleep.

This is what he heard:

The Brigade Commander: 'Colonel Landry has taken over his post.'

The Divisional Commander: 'This de Buissy has given me enough trouble.'

The Brigade Commander: 'He wanted to resist at any cost.'

The Divisional Commander: 'These *Légionnaires* are intriguing politicians, all of them.'

The Brigade Commander: 'What shall I write in my report?'

The Divisional Commander: 'I don't know.'

The Brigade Commander: 'He told me he would protest against his dismissal on the ground of sickness.'

The Divisional Commander: 'I'm telling you, the man has caused us nothing but trouble. He has completely adapted himself to the rabble he commanded. Can't you find something? Something incriminating in his record?'

The Brigade Commander: 'No. I went through all his belongings. But there was nothing, except ——'

The Divisional Commander: 'Except ——?'

The Brigade Commander: 'Except an empty bottle.'

The Divisional Commander: 'Was there liquor in it?'

The Brigade Commander: 'Perhaps.'

The Divisional Commander: 'Excellent! Report that his alcoholic excesses necessitated his sudden dismissal.'

Colonel de Buissy had overheard this whole conversation. He opened his eyes. The Brigade Commander approached the stretcher. He assured de Buissy that he was happy to have been able to put through his well-deserved retirement. He asked whether Madame de Buissy had succeeded in reaching Perpignan. He whispered that he intended to propose the colonel for a high distinction on account of his regiment's magnificent bravery. The colonel did not answer. When the general had finished, de Buissy inquired, 'Has a bottle been found among my belongings: a bottle of iodine? It's a habit I acquired in Africa. I always carry a bottle of iodine.'

The general said with embarrassment that the colonel would have no further need for iodine.

The same day Colonel Paul de Buissy was sent south. We were given a new commander. Subsequent events demonstrated that the new chief was a man of his word, and that his superiors had no reason to regret his appointment. He offered the Germans no resistance.

Hans Habe

The Germans Enter Antwerp: 18 May

On Thursday afternoon, the police came around to notify us that for a period of forty-eight hours, no one might go out into the streets for any reason whatsoever. It was even forbidden to look out of a window. Newspapers had ceased publication, there was little news on the radio, and we had almost no idea of what was happening. It should be remembered that Antwerp was so near the border of Holland that some of the Antwerp tramway lines actually went to the Dutch frontier, so it was clear to us that, now that Holland had fallen, we should not have long to wait for the arrival of the Germans in Antwerp. Rumours had been rife for several days that Antwerp would not be defended, but would be handed over to the Germans in order to spare the civilian population, if it became clear that the Allies must fall back.

When the police told us that no one might go out for forty-eight hours, I had an intuitive feeling that this meant that Antwerp was being handed over—that twenty-four hours were for the retreat of the Allied armies, and twenty-four hours for the Germans to take over. The prohibition even to look out of windows sounded much more like a condition dictated by the Germans than anything emanating from the Allied command, which had shown no such nervousness when advancing to the front through Antwerp.

Friday, the first day indoors, passed without incident. Forbidden though it was, we peered out of the windows from time to time, but the streets were practically deserted. No movements of troops were visible, but occasionally a motor-cycle courier or an army truck sped through the town. Such movement as there was was always away from the front, never towards it. The most disquieting sign was the departure of groups of firemen and police officers, still in uniform, some with bicycles and all with parcels and valises.

On the second night of our confinement the bombardment became terrific, and to it was added a new note: for hours we heard the sound of big guns firing, not far from Antwerp; the battle had reached our doorstep. If, as I believed, the Allied armies were going to pass through Antwerp that night, they would have to go through the tunnel under the river, which would take them past our door.

Presently I heard the whine of falling shells, followed by shattering explosions, very near, which shook the basement. With the monotonous regularity of metronome beats, one shell followed another, and the blasts became more violent as the shells fell closer and closer to the nearby tunnel. First I heard the sound of the distant gun, then the whine of the shell overhead, and finally, the crash as it burst; each time the explosion seemed nearer, which may well have been the effect of my own imagination. As I lay there in the darkness, I knew that the others were awake as well, but no one spoke. There was little that could be said to comfort one another, and none of us, I suppose, wanted to say anything that would further depress the others. For that matter, I cannot remember that we ever spoke of that night in the months that followed; it was not something that we wanted to remember. For the first time since the beginning of the invasion, I felt deep, panic-stricken fear. The cellar seemed like a rat-trap. My imagination pictured what it would feel like if a shell came crashing and tearing through the floors above, to burst over our heads and bury us beneath the masonry which was our only bulwark against the battle going on above us. Worst of all was the feeling of total helplessness; I did not want to die, there— and if I went somewhere else, that might be the very place a shell was fated to fall.

Still the shells continued to fall near us, until finally the earth seemed split as a mighty explosion, which made the shell bursts insignificant and puny, rocked the hotel. The artillery fire ceased, and the rest was a dead silence.

Finally, unutterably weary from the hours of strain, I fell into an uneasy sleep.

Towards morning, as a little daylight began to filter down into the forward part of the cellar, which lay beneath the pavement, I was awakened by the sound of steel-shod boots running along the street. Belgian or French boots did not make that angry, metallic noise; I was not so sure about British Army footwear, but intuition told me that it was the Germans who were there. Bursts of automatic rifle and machine-gun fire became more frequent, and from time to time a heavier explosion suggested that hand grenades were being thrown.

The three women were now also awake, and we discussed in a low voice what the significance of these noises might be. Perhaps what we were hearing was the sound of Allied patrols left behind to delay the German advance—or had the Germans already arrived?

Shortly after eight o'clock I decided to end the uncertainty, and despite the protests of the others, I went upstairs to try to see what was happening. I passed through the kitchen and into the restaurant, half expecting to find it already filled with German soldiers. I could see nothing from there, for at the beginning of the forty-eight-hour quarantine period we had hastily boarded up the street windows and the front door. I went up to my room on the third floor, and cautiously advanced towards the window. There, below, just in front of the cathedral, was what I had dreaded to see—a German soldier. The moment was a bitter one, but its grimness was relieved by a ludicrous touch. The German soldier mounting guard over the great cathedral was short, squat and bow-legged, and his mushroom-like helmet suggested a man who had been flattened out by heavy pressure from above. As I peered down at his ludicrous figure, an automobile drove up and a flag officer in blue uniform with gold braid stepped smartly out. The sentry saluted, and the officer entered the door leading to the stairway which mounted to the top of the cathedral tower.

I had seen all I wanted. I returned to the cellar, and announced to the others, 'The Germans are here!'

Lars Moen

DESIGN FOR PANIC

I was given a special assignment. Working with experts of the Propaganda Ministry, I devised radio broadcasts and propaganda for other media designed to create the greatest possible confusion among our enemies, especially the French. Dr. Adolf Raskin, then Director of Radio Saarbrücken, and a close friend of mine, was the man chiefly responsible for the great successes we achieved. Working with three transmitters specially equipped with a very powerful signal, he sent a continual stream of news reports in French, purporting to be of official French origin but which were in fact his own imaginative inventions. These false news items were the chief cause of the fatal panic and confusion among the French civil population. Streams of refugees blocked all the highways of France and made troop movements behind the French lines almost impossible. Meanwhile, in spite of the difficulties created by the military situation, our agents in France continued to collect information, which was transmitted to us by a special network of frontier-crossing couriers and by telephone, a cable having been laid across the Maginot Line to Saaralben.

Another device which did great damage was a small and apparently innocuous pamphlet which was distributed in great numbers by our agents and also dropped from aircraft. Printed in French and described as being the prophecies of Nostradamus—many of whose prophecies were actually included—the pamphlet predicted terrifying destruction from 'flying fire-machines', stressing all the time that south-eastern France would be preserved from this horror. While preparing these brochures, I had never imagined that they would have such a tremendous effect. All the efforts of the civilian and military authorities to divert the great streams of refugees from attempting to reach south-eastern France proved useless.

Walter Schellenberg

Panic

It was six in the morning, and Dutertre and I, coming out of our billet, found ourselves in the midst of chaos. All the stables, all the sheds, all the barns and garages had vomited into the narrow streets a most extraordinary collection of contrivances. There were new motor cars, and there were ancient farm carts that for half a century had stood untouched under layers of dust. There were hay wains and lorries, carry-alls and tumbrils. Had we seen a mail-coach in this maze it would not have astonished us. Every box on wheels had been dug up and was now laden with the treasures of the home. From door to vehicle, wrapped in bedsheets sagging with hernias, the treasures were being piled in.

Together, these treasures had made up that greater treasure—a home. By itself each was valueless; yet they were the objects of a private religion, a family's worship. Each filling its place, they had been made indispensable by habit and beautiful by memory, had been lent price by the sort of fatherland which, together, they constituted. But those who owned them thought each precious in itself and for itself. These treasures had been wrenched from their fireside, their table, their wall; and now that they were heaped up in disorder, they showed themselves to be the worn and torn stock of a junk-shop that they were. Fling sacred relics into a heap, and they can turn your stomach.

'What's going on here? Are you mad?'

The café-owner's wife shrugged her shoulders.

'We're evacuating.'

'But why, in God's name!'

'Nobody knows. Mayor's orders.'

She was too busy to talk, and vanished up her staircase. Dutertre and I stood in the doorway and looked on. Every motor car, every lorry, every cart and charabanc was piled high with children, mattresses, kitchen utensils.

Of all these objects the most pitiful were the old motor cars. A horse standing upright in the shafts of a farm-cart gives off a sensation of solidity. A horse does not call for spare parts. A farm-cart can be put into shape with three nails. But all these vestiges of the mechanical age! This assemblage of pistons, valves, magnetos, and gear-wheels! How long would it run before it broke down?

'Please, captain. Could you give me a hand?'

'Of course. What is it?'

'I want to get my car out of the garage.'

I looked at the woman in amazement.

'Are you sure you know how to drive?'

'Oh, it will be all right. The road is so jammed, it won't be hard.'

There was herself, and her sister-in-law, and their children—seven children in all.

That road easy to drive? A road over which you made two or ten miles a day, stopping dead every two hundred yards? Braking, stopping, shifting gears, changing from low into second and back again every fifty yards in the confusion of an inextricable jam. Easy driving? The woman would break down before she had gone half a mile! And fuel! And oil! And water, which she was sure to forget!

'Better watch your water. Your radiator is leaking like a sieve.'

'Well, it's not a new car.'

'You'll be on the road a week, you know. How are you going to make it?'

'I don't know.'

She won't have gone three miles before running into half a dozen cars, stripping her gears and blowing out her tyres. Then she and her sister-in-law and the seven children will start to cry. And she and her sister-in-law and the seven children, faced by problems out of their ken, will give up. They will abandon the car, sit down by the side of the road, and wait for the coming of a shepherd.

'Why don't you stay home?'

'God knows, we'd rather stay.'

'Then why do you leave?'

'They said we had to.'

'Who said so?'

'The mayor.'

Always the mayor.

'Of course we'd rather stay home.'

It is a fact that these people are not panicky; they are people doing a blind chore. Dutertre and I tried to shake some of them out of it.

'Look here, why don't you unload and put that stuff back into your house. At least you'll have your pump-water to drink.'

'Of course that would be the best thing.'

'But you are free to do it. Why don't you?'

Dutertre and I are winning. A cluster of villagers has collected round us. They listen to us. They nod their heads approvingly.

'He's right, he is, the captain.'

Others come to our support. A roadmender, converted, is hotter about it than I am.

'Always said so. Get out on that road and there's nothing but asphalt to eat.'

They argue. They agree. They will stay. Some go off to preach to others. And they come back discouraged.

'Won't do. Have to go.'

'Why?'

'Baker's already left. Who will bake our bread?'

The village has already broken down. At one point or another it has burst; and through that hole its contents are running out. Hopeless.

Farther on, in the open country, the enemy fighters would be flying low and spitting forth their bursts of machine-gun fire upon this lamentable flock. But it was astonishing how on the whole the enemy refrained from total annihilation.

Here and there stood a car in flames, but very few. And there were few dead. Death was a sort of luxury, something like a bit of advice. It was the nip in the hock by which the shepherd dog hurried the flock along.

Antoine de Saint-Exupéry

It took us thirty-two hours to get from Nantes to Paris against the stream of refugees. I was driving the car. Beside me was Bordier, a brothel-keeper from Nantes. He had provided the car in exchange for the security my official pass afforded him. He did not much like teaming up with me, but he was a meticulous business man: he wanted to put his affairs in order, that is to say recover his silver from a safe in Paris and collect the last receipts from his fourteen slot-machines. We knew that the Germans were approaching Paris. He looked on my naval officer's badge of rank as a passport. No doubt he thought of the invading army as a horde which stole silver, rifled money from slot-machines, raped women, but respected uniforms.

It was one of the finest springtimes we had known in years, a springtime of battle. As far as Le Mans the roads were clear. Apart from the fact that the nation was wearing uniforms, had surrendered to the hopelessness of merely pretending and waiting, and apart from a few obstacles on the roads, over-turned carts laced with barbed wire, little rows of walls forming a defile through which one had to pass at walking pace under the eye of a bored Territorial, there were no signs of war or of the immediate likelihood of battle. Only the slowing down of life, caused by the creation of an enormous administrative machine and the sheep-like necessity of listening to the radio ten times a day, bore witness to an exceptional period, not of revolt or struggle, but of resignation, egoism and fear.

. . . . We felt surprised and to a certain extent cheated at seeing no signs of defeat: overflowing hospitals, trains of wounded crowding the stations, units being relieved and convoys of reinforcements going up to the line, as I had seen at Bourges in 1914.

It was only after Le Mans, and still more after Chartres that the signs of disaster became increasingly apparent—and these were all on the roads. In the sky, nothing. No activity or excitement in the fields; the corn was ripening. It was only in the towns and villages that the refugees crowded round the hotels, the cafés and the petrol pumps. Their fear was contagious: at the sight of them people who had never thought of leaving were suddenly seized with the urge to go. . . .

We covered twenty kilometres in eight hours. As night fell, our car was stuck behind a truck which was transporting a hundred and twenty men from a technical college to Pau. From eight o'clock to midnight they sang and told dirty stories. At Saint-Rémy the traffic jam was so dense that we decided, after standing still for two hours, that at the first forward move we would park in a side street. I went to sleep with my head on the steering wheel, weariness and the presence of the maidservant inducing an erotic dream.

At five o'clock in the morning, awakened by the chill in the air, we took the road again. It was less crowded: the stream flowed more rapidly. Bordier was snoring. Lambertine was sleeping in a heap, her mouth open. The sun made me so sleepy that I could not keep awake. I came to in a field of oats; the stalks slithering along the panels of the car made a noise like water. The ears of corn and the poppies cut off by the front bumper were thrown up against the windows, drowning them in a mist of grain and pollen. We decided to stop at the first village and sleep for two hours. Night was falling when we reached Nantes. At Pierrot's, the café opposite the brothel, there was so much noise that we could not hear ourselves speak. The hubbub was like a station. While awaiting disaster, the soldiers and sailors of the rear areas ate, drank and had a good time. I tried to find a room for Lambertine, who had become a problem. Bordier suggested making her 'hustle'. When I protested, he said, 'It would be good business. Refugees go to women like horses to a stable, and there aren't enough to go round. However, if you insist, she need only do the cleaning.'

Emmanuel d'Astier, naval officer

RETREAT TO DUNKIRK

The 15th dawned bright and sunny, and brought orders. The Battalion was to dig positions in the Seine Canal six miles north of Brussels, near Vilvorde. Next day there came a change of position and more orders, this time ominous. They were to hold a bridgehead for 3 Division to use in their withdrawal from Louvain. Less than a week had turned an eager advance into a withdrawal; and the withdrawal was to turn into one of the fastest and most disastrous of history.

17 May gave the Battalion its first view of the enemy. 3 Division had passed through, already bewildered at the turn of events; the pontoon bridge was blown, and the Battalion was preparing to hold the line of the Canal. A Belgian civilian appeared on the far side of it, inspected the wreckage of a steel bridge which had been blown some time before, and clambered cautiously across it. Close on his heels came the first Germans. A few shots sent them out of sight, and the Battalion turned its attention first to a Belgian who was claiming transport on the grounds that he was a trusted British agent, and secondly to a couple of messages which had just come in. The first ordered that a certain burial ground should be reconnoitred: it was already in enemy hands, so this message was ignored. The second ordered withdrawal that night.

. . . . They halted at Petegem, ten miles south-west of Ghent, on the Lys Canal. Petegem had panicked, and not a soul was left in the village. Cigarette ends had burned themselves away on tables, glasses and been left half-drained, there was a game of draughts half-finished. Despite their weariness, the Jocks went round releasing tame rabbits and canaries—and picking up what stores they could. Petegem was a gloomy experience.

That evening—it was 19 May—the Battalion at last took up a position again, and remained in this general area for four days. The Germans arrived and deployed, and shelling developed. On the 23rd it became really heavy, as heavy as anything experienced in later years. But now the Battalion was being constantly moved to meet various threats. There was a good deal of confusion, as when they were told to leave some half-completed trenches, to move forward and to conform with some troops on the flank—who proved to be Germans.

The night of the 23rd came near to being the end of the Battalion. The enemy was round the left rear, where he announced his presence with machine-guns and emphasized it with bombers. The only wireless set to Brigade H.Q. was out of order, and messages by other means were taking an hour to bring an answer. There was little touch between Battalion H.Q. and the forward companies; but when the order finally came to disengage it was got through somehow. A long trudge of thirty miles began, with men falling asleep almost as they walked. Hitherto the direction of the withdrawal had been a little to the north of west; now it turned south-west and followed the line of the Lys to Courtrai; here some magnificent hot soup was issued, but many found that it made them sleepier than ever. At last the somnambulant Battalion stumbled into Halluin, a small town on the French frontier, and dropped off to sleep in a carpet factory. A group of officers, before doing so, tuned in to the B.B.C., and heard that the Germans were already in Boulogne.

Bernard Fergusson

War Diary

Nothing but a miracle can save the B.E.F. now, and the end cannot be very far off. We carried out our withdrawal successfully last night back to the old frontier defences and by this morning we were established in the defences we spent the winter preparing. But where the danger lies is on our right rear. The German armoured divisions have penetrated to the coast; Abbeville, Boulogne and Calais have been rendered useless. We are, therefore, cut off from our sea communications, beginning to be short of ammunition. Supplies still all right for three days, but after that, scarcity.

Armentières has been very heavily bombed and we are well out of it; half the town is demolished, including the madhouse, and its inmates are now wandering about the country.

These lunatics let loose . . . were the last straw. With catastrophe on all sides, bombarded by rumours of every description, flooded by refugees and a demoralized French Army, bombed from a low altitude, and now on top of it all lunatics in brown corduroy suits standing at the side of the road grinning at one with an inane smile, a flow of saliva running from the corner of their mouths, and dripping noses! Had it not been that by then one's senses were numbed with the magnitude of the catastrophe that surrounded one, the situation would have been unbearable.

General Alan Brooke, diary 23–25 May

Not long after I received another message. Would I report to the Battery Command Post.

One of the B.C.P. Staff went round handing each of us a new map-sheet. I took mine without paying very much attention. We were already up in the corner of our last sheet, so I had expected we'd soon get a new issue.

Suddenly, glancing down at it, I noticed that a great proportion of the new sheet was occupied by the sea. Another look showed me a strip of coast. And the principal name on this strip was Dunkirk. It was the first time the word had struck us with any particular significance.

Y Battery pulled out at half-past four in the afternoon. We hadn't proceeded far when we were struck by what seemed, at first sight, an extraordinary phenomenon. The entire countryside was a-flutter with white. From every house in the villages, from church steeples, farms, cottages, from everywhere where people lived there flapped a white flag, and if not a real flag, a white table-cloth, sheet, towel, or handkerchief. They were, of course, the tokens of surrender which the inhabitants were in a great hurry to have on display by the time the Germans arrived. Most of the private houses were heavily shuttered. Here and there little knots of silent people stood by the wayside. But we all had the feeling that the vast majority were peeping at us from behind the shutters with mixed emotions. Relief that the tide of war was departing from their neighbourhood, mingled with apprehensions of what troubles the entry of the Germans would bring in its train.

Approaching the bridge over the canal we once more found ourselves in a main stream of military traffic, some French but mostly British. The road narrowed here, and to add to the confusion a truck full of *poilus*, who seemed to be in a panic to get away, insisted on trying to pass all the other vehicles on the road. They were blocking up the whole procession, and causing dangerous delays as aeroplanes could be heard overhead. Shouts of, 'Pull-in . . . pull-in . . . wait your turn . . . what's your hurry?' came from the angry British troops, mingled with oaths and curses. But the *poilus* took no heed. They insisted on forcing a passage through. At last they endeavoured to pass my truck. I didn't waste any words. I leaped out, drew my revolver, and told the driver that if he did not get back in line instantly I'd shoot him. He pulled in.

A few moments later, thirty yards from the bridge, the threatened air attack developed. Three bombers swooped low over the bridge and dropped their bombs. They missed the bridge but hit the banks. As the bombers swooped, everyone leaped from the vehicles and scattered over the fields on each side of the road. I crouched in a ditch. A few yards away a French soldier and a little boy had taken refuge. A bomb exploded and a fragment of it sliced head-and-shoulders off both. When the bombs finished, the machine-gunning started, the Germans, from only a short distance up, emptying belt after belt of bullets upon the troops in the fields. That over, we resumed our journey and passed through the village of Houthem.

The face of the countryside had now undergone a complete change. Miles and miles of low-lying marshy fields stretched far as the eye could see, all cut up by a network of canals and highways at right-angles to each other. Each field was below canal level, so each had its own diminutive dyke running round it. There were few trees to be seen anywhere, save the pollard oaks bordering the dead-straight roads.

Into this pancake of a land it seemed as if the whole of the B.E.F. was pouring. Every road scoring the landscape was one thick mass of transport and troops, great long lines of them stretching back far to the eastern horizon, and all the lines converging towards the one focus—Dunkirk. Ambulances, lorries, trucks, Bren-gun carriers, artillery columns—everything except tanks—all crawling along those roads in well-defined lines over the flat, featureless country in the late afternoon sunshine, provided an impressive and memorable picture of two modern armies in retreat. Under their greyish camouflage paint they resembled from a distance slow-moving rivers of muddy-coloured lava from some far-off eruption.

It was now that I saw, for the first time, regiments in the doleful process of wrecking their equipment. New wireless sets, costing perhaps £20 apiece, were placed in rows in the fields, twenty in a row, sometimes, while a soldier with a pick-axe proceeded up and down knocking them to pieces. Trucks were being dealt with just as drastically. Radiators and engines were smashed with sledge-hammers; tyres slashed and sawn after they had been deflated. Vehicles that were near the canals were finally pushed in. Some of the canals were choked with the wrecks, all piled on top of each other. There was more wreck than water.

Also, from this point you encountered another novel sight in this war-on-wheels . . . infantry marching on foot. Having destroyed their transport they had to walk the last ten miles to Dunkirk. This was the infantry due for immediate evacuation. Not the rearguard. They were allowed to use their transport up to a later point.

Now progress along the roads, filled with pedestrians, and dusk falling, became terribly slow. The troops marched in single file along each side of the road, weary, red-eyed and dust-begrimed. But cheerful, and still able to shoot off a bit of characteristic repartee when the occasion arose.

By now we weren't altogether unaware of what was happening on the beaches. Our progress along the road had been at a snail's pace. We went forward three or four yards, then made a forced halt sometimes lasting a quarter of an hour. It was during these halts that we picked up a very good idea of the horrors going on at Dunkirk from scraps of conversation with the infantry. These gave rise to scraps of uneasy conversation among ourselves.

'Have you heard that they're gunning 'em as well as bombing 'em? . . .'

'Some have been on the beach three days before they got a boat. . . .'

'Got safely on the destroyer and it was bombed. Most of 'em blown to bits. . . .'

'Hundreds of dead and dying on the beaches. No chance for them at all. . . .'

'I've just been told that they gun the fellows as they are swimming to the lifeboats. . . .'

'What'll it be like when we get there? . . .'

'Shall we get there? . . .'

'What d'you think our chance is? . . .'

'Evens. . . .'

'I put it just under. . . .'

It will be realized from these bits of talk among us that Y Battery was having its eyes opened.

It was at one of these halts that I asked our saddler, who had been a gunner in the Mons Retreat, how it compared with the present one. His view was that Dunkirk was the worse.

'At Mons we always had the possibility of going forward again, sooner or later. Here we know we shan't. That's what makes it bad.'

British gunner officer

The Beaches

Eventually we arrived at the spot on this side of the last canal separating us from the sea, where we had to abandon the vehicles. They were smashed up in the darkness and pushed into the canal. The men formed up by the roadside and the roll was called for the last time. A weird scene, the Troop sergeant-majors calling out the names of the gunners in loud whispers, and ticking them off on their lists by torch-light as the answers came back out of the darkness, from nowhere it seemed.

'All present and correct, sir.'

And once more the fifty of us started off, this time on foot, formed-up in threes, the Major and I walking at the head of the column. To our great joy we discovered that the bridge spanning the canal had not been smashed. Once over it, and another obstacle between us and the Unknown had been passed. We continued towards Malo-les-Bains, crossing the railway, and marching through the ruined street of Rosendaal, whose skeleton walls stood around us like the ruins of some bygone civilization. The only sound was the crunching of the broken glass under our feet, as if we were marching over hard ice-crystals on a winter's day. Mysterious shadows flitted about the streets, in and out of broken doorways, and disappearing silently round corners. They were stray inhabitants who had been cut-off by the swift march of events and were living in cellars. And a few looters. And, probably, a few spies. The German gun-fire was now incessant, the flash of the explosions continually lighting up the scene for a second or two on every side of us.

Now we were no longer alone. We began to meet little batches of our infantry marching in the same direction. Often as we approached we would be hailed out of the darkness:

'Is that A Company, King's Own Scottish Borderers? . . .' Or the name of some other unit would be shouted. These were bits of the rearguard coming back, and marching still in good formation down to the beaches.

We were now in the region of the dunes, which rose like humps of a deeper darkness. And these in their turn were dotted with the still blacker shapes of abandoned vehicles, half-sunk in the sand, fantastic twisted shapes of burned-out skeletons, and crazy-looking wreckage that had been heaped up in extraordinary piles by the explosions of bombs. All these black shapes were silhouetted against the angry red glare in the sky, which reflected down on us the agony of burning Dunkirk.

Slowly we picked our way between the wreckage, sinking ankle-deep in the loose sand, until we reached the gaunt skeletons of what had once been the houses on the promenade. The whole front was one long continuous line of blazing buildings, a high wall of fire, roaring and darting in tongues of flame, with the smoke pouring upwards and disappearing in the blackness of the sky above the roof-tops. Out seawards the darkness was as thick and smooth as black velvet, except for now and again when the shape of a sunken destroyer or paddle-steamer made a slight thickening on its impenetrable surface. Facing us, the great black wall of the Mole stretched from the beach far out into sea, the end of it almost invisible to us. The Mole had an astounding, terrifying background of giant flames leaping a hundred feet into the air from blazing oil tanks. At the shore end of the Mole stood an obelisk, and the high explosive shells burst around it with monotonous regularity.

Along the promenade, in parties of fifty, the remnants of practically all the last regiments were wearily trudging along. There was no singing, and very little talk. Everyone was far too exhausted to waste breath. Occasionally out of the darkness came a sudden shout:

'A Company, Green Howards. . . .'

'C Company, East Yorks. . . .'

These shouts came either from stragglers trying to find lost units, or guides on the look-out for the parties they were to lead on to the Mole for evacuation.

The tide was out. Over the wide stretch of sand could be dimly discerned little oblong masses of soldiers, moving in platoons and orderly groups down towards the edge of the sea. Now and again you would hear a shout:

'Alf, where are you? . . .'

'Let's hear from you, Bill. . . .'

'Over this way, George. . . .'

It was none too easy to keep contact with one's friends in the darkness, and amid so many little masses of moving men, all looking very much alike. If you stopped for a few seconds to look behind, the chances were you attached yourself to some entirely different unit.

From the margin of the sea, at fairly wide intervals, three long thin black lines protruded into the water, conveying the effect of low wooden breakwaters. These were lines of men, standing in pairs behind one another far out into the water, waiting in queues till boats arrived to transport them, a score or so at a time, to the steamers and warships that were filling up with the last survivors. The queues stood there, fixed and almost as regular as if ruled. No bunching, no pushing. Nothing like the mix-up to be seen at the turnstiles when a crowd is going into a football match. Much more orderly, even, than a waiting theatre queue.

About this time, afraid that some of our men might be tailing off, I began shouting, '2004th Field Regiment . . . 2004th Field Regiment. . . .'

A group of dead and dying soldiers on the path in front of us quickened our desire to quit the promenade. Stepping over the bodies we marched down the slope on to the dark beach. Dunkirk front was now a lurid study in red and black; flames, smoke, and the night itself all mingling together to compose a frightful panorama of death and destruction. Red and black, all the time, except for an occasional flash of white low in the sky miles away to the left and right where big shells from coastal defence guns at Calais and Nieuport were being hurled into the town.

Down on the beach you immediately felt yourself surrounded by a deadly evil atmosphere. A horrible stench of blood and mutilated flesh pervaded the place. There was no escape from it. Not a breath of air was blowing to dissipate the appalling odour that arose from the dead bodies that had been lying on the sand, in some cases for several days. We might have been walking through a slaughter-house on a hot day. The darkness, which hid some of the sights of horror from our eyes, seemed to thicken this dreadful stench. It created the impression that death was hovering around, very near at hand.

We set our faces in the direction of the sea, quickening our pace to pass through the belt of this nauseating miasma as soon as possible.

'Water . . . Water. . . .' groaned a voice from the ground just in front of us.

It was a wounded infantryman. He had been hit so badly that there was no hope for him. Our water-bottles had long been empty, but by carefully draining them all into one we managed to collect a mouthful or two. A sergeant knelt down beside the dying man and held the bottle to his lips. Then we proceeded on our way, leaving the bottle with the last few drains in it near the poor fellow's hand so that he could moisten his lips from time to time.

On either side, scattered over the sand in all sorts of positions, were the dark shapes of dead and dying men, sometimes alone, sometimes in twos and threes. Every now and then we had to pull ourselves up sharply in the darkness to avoid falling over a wooden cross erected by comrades on the spot where some soldier had been buried. No assistance that availed anything could be given to these dying men. The living themselves had nothing to offer them. They just pressed forward to the sea, hoping that the same fate would not be theirs. And still it remained a gamble all the time whether that sea, close though it was, would be reached in safety. Splinters from bursting shells were continually whizzing through the air, and occasionally a man in one of the plodding groups would fall with a groan.

British gunner officer

Small Craft at Dunkirk

Between 26 May and 4 June, 222 naval ships and 665 other vessels succeeded in bringing back to England 224,585 British and 112,546 French and Belgian troops.

Half an hour after they had left Ramsgate the yacht *Sundowner* began her crossing. *Sundowner* belonged to Commander C. H. Lightoller, D.S.C., R.N.R. (Retd.), who, as senior surviving officer of the *Titanic*, had been the principal witness at the inquiry into that disaster. She was a biggish craft, approximately sixty feet with a speed of ten knots, and with the assistance of his son and a Sea Scout, Commander Lightoller had taken her out of Cubitt's Yacht Basin at Chiswick on 31 May and had dropped down the river to Southend as part of a big convoy of forty boats which had mustered at Westminster. At dawn on 1 June he left Southend with five others and, reaching Ramsgate, was instructed in the casual manner of those days to 'proceed to Dunkirk for further orders'. His charts, he says, were somewhat antiquated, and he was fortunate enough to be able to obtain a new set. At ten o'clock he left by the route laid down. His account of the voyage is clear and detailed:

Half-way across we avoided a floating mine by a narrow margin, but having no firearms of any description—not even a tin hat—we had to leave its destruction to someone better equipped. A few minutes later we had our first introduction to enemy aircraft, three fighters flying high. Before they could be offensive, a British destroyer—*Worcester*, I think—overhauled us and drove them off. At 2.25 p.m. we sighted and closed the twenty-five-foot motor-cruiser *Westerly*; broken down and badly on fire. As the crew of two (plus three naval ratings she had picked up in Dunkirk) wished to abandon ship—and quickly—I went alongside and took them aboard, giving them the additional pleasure of again facing the hell they had only just left.

We made the fairway buoy to the Roads shortly after the sinking of a French transport with severe loss of life. Steaming slowly through the wreckage we entered the Roads. For some time now we had been subject to sporadic bombing and machine-gun fire, but as the *Sundowner* is exceptionally and extremely quick on the helm, by waiting till the last moment and putting the helm hard over—my son at the wheel—we easily avoided every attack, though sometimes near lifted out of the water.

It had been my intention to go right on to the beaches, where my second son, Second-Lieutenant R. T. Lightoller, had been evacuated some forty-eight hours previously; but those of the *Westerly* informed me that the troops were all away, so I headed up for Dunkirk piers. By now dive-bombers seemed to be eternally dropping out of the cloud of enemy aircraft overhead. Within half a mile of the pierheads a two-funnelled grey-painted transport had overhauled and was just passing us to port when two salvoes were dropped in quick succession right along her port side. For a few moments she was hid in smoke and I certainly thought they had got her. Then she reappeared, still gaily heading for the piers and entered just ahead of us.

The difficulty of taking troops on board from the quay high above us was obvious, so I went alongside a destroyer (*Worcester* again, I think) where they were already embarking. I got hold of her captain and told him I could take about a hundred (though the most I had ever had on board was twenty-one). He, after consultation with the military C.O., told me to carry on and get the troops aboard. I may say here that before leaving Cubitt's Yacht Basin, we had worked all night stripping her down of everything moveable, masts included, that would tend to lighten her and make for more room.

My son, as previously arranged, was to pack the men in and use every available inch of space—which I'll say he carried out to some purpose. On deck I detailed a naval rating to tally the troops aboard. At fifty I called below, 'How are you getting on?,' getting the cheery reply, 'Oh, plenty of room yet.' At seventy-five my son admitted they were getting pretty tight—all equipment and arms being left on deck.

I now started to pack them on deck, having passed word below for every man to lie down and keep down; the same applied on deck. By the time we had fifty on deck I could feel her getting distinctly tender, so took no more. Actually we had exactly a hundred and thirty on board, including three *Sundowners* and five *Westerlys*.

During the whole embarkation we had quite a lot of attention from enemy planes, but derived an amazing degree of comfort from the fact that the *Worcester*'s A.A. guns kept up an everlasting bark overhead.

Casting off and backing out we entered the Roads again; there it was continuous and unmitigated hell. The troops were just splendid and of their own initiative detailed look-outs ahead, astern, and abeam for inquisitive planes, as my attention was pretty wholly occupied watching the steering and passing orders to Roger at the wheel. Any time an aircraft seemed inclined to try its hand on us, one of the look-outs would just call quietly, 'Look out for this bloke, skipper', at the same time pointing. One bomber that had been particularly offensive, itself came under the notice of one of our fighters and suddenly plunged vertically into the sea just about fifty yards astern of us. It was the only time any man ever raised his voice above a conversational tone, but as that big black bomber hit the water they raised an echoing cheer.

My youngest son, Pilot Officer H. B. Lightoller (lost at the outbreak of war in the first raid on Wilhelmshaven), flew a Blenheim and had at different times given me a whole lot of useful information about attack, defence and evasive tactics (at which he was apparently particularly good) and I attribute, in a great measure, our success in getting across without a single casualty to his unwitting help.

On one occasion an enemy machine came up astern at about a hundred feet with the obvious intention of raking our decks. He was coming down in a gliding dive and I knew that he must elevate some ten to fifteen degrees before his guns would bear. Telling my son 'Stand by,' I waited till, as near as I could judge, he was just on the point of pulling up, and then 'Hard a-port.' (She turns a hundred and eighty degrees in exactly her own length.) This threw his aim completely off. He banked and tried again. Then 'Hard a-starboard,' with the same result. After a third attempt he gave it up in disgust. Had I had a machine-gun of any sort, he was a sitter—in fact, there were at least three that I am confident we could have accounted for during the trip.

Not the least of our difficulties was contending with the wash of fast craft, such as destroyers and transports. In every instance I had to stop completely, take the way off the ship and head the heavy wash. The M.C. being where it was, to have taken one of these seas on either the quarter or beam would have at once put paid to our otherwise successful cruise. The effect of the consequent plunging on the troops below, in a stinking atmosphere with all ports and skylights closed, can well be imagined. They were literally packed like the proverbial sardines, even one in the bath and another on the W.C., so that all the poor devils could do was sit and be sick. Added were the remnants of bully beef and biscuits. So that after discharging our cargo in Ramsgate at 10 p.m., there lay before the three of us a nice clearing-up job.

Arriving off the harbour I was at first told to 'lie off'. But when I informed them that I had a hundred and thirty on board, permission was at once given to 'come in' (I don't think the authorities believed for a minute that I had a hundred and thirty), and I put her alongside a trawler lying at the quay. Whilst entering, the men started to get to their feet and she promptly went over to a terrific angle. I got them down again in time and told those below to remain below and lying down till I gave the word. The impression ashore was that the fifty-odd lying on deck plus the mass of equipment was my full load.

After I had got rid of those on deck I gave the order, 'Come up from below,' and the look on the official face was amusing to behold as troops vomited up through the forward companionway, the after companionway, and the doors either side of the wheelhouse. As a stoker P.O., helping them over the bulwarks, said, 'God's truth, mate! Where did you put them?' He might well ask. . . .

Dieppe: Sunk

It was a silent ship. The decks were so crowded it was impossible to form queues for the meal that was being served below. The crowd was quiet enough for Knight, wedged against the rail of the promenade deck, to hear morse from the radio cabin. In theory the promenade deck was reserved for officers, but in reality all ranks were massed there—men, N.C.O.s, officers, and even a number of nursing sisters, though so far as Knight could see he was the only R.A.F. man on board. They were not going to England, the rumour went round; they were ordered to St. Nazaire; the Allies were to hold the line of the Seine, and a new medical base area was being established in the Loire valley. A white hospital ship followed them out of the harbour. That, presumably, was making for England. Knight searched the sky but there was not an aircraft in sight.

Nevertheless the anti-aircraft gun in the stern suddenly went into action, and neat puffs of brown were seen high in the clear atmosphere. All on board felt the kick of the gun beneath their feet. The ship's siren gave a number of short, sharp blasts, a bell rang on the bridge, and the vessel changed course so rapidly the following hospital ship appeared to swing out from the land.

'All personnel below decks!' said the loudspeaker. 'All personnel below decks!'

A middle-aged nursing sister with red hair peeping from beneath her steel helmet took his arm. 'Come on, sonny. Grandma doesn't like this.'

'Why pick on me?'

Already there was room to walk about on the deck, and the sister had merely paused to tie the strings on Knight's lifebelt when all the driving energy of the boat seeped into sound, a column of sound that was based on the bed of the sea itself. Knight tried to force the sister to the deck, but bewildered by the suddenness of the onset she fought against him and both, leaning against the rail for support, were drenched by the explosion of brine. The boat rocked on the edge of a crater. In the wildness of the moment it seemed possible for the vessel to fall to the bottom of the sea. The bomber had already pulled out of its dive. Water smacked against the hull like a hand.

'They're bombing, not gunning,' said Knight. He had swallowed so much sea water that he felt hungry and sick in the same moment. 'Take it from me, we're better off here than down below.'

'I thought you were trying to rape me, sonny,' said the sister. She lay on her belly and pressed her cheek to the deck. Drenched figures were lying all over the decks, some swearing, some laughing, but for the most part they were silent, waiting for the next attack. The ack-ack gun at the stern kicked away and the red hair, the flushed cheek and the smell of lilies of the valley were suddenly so close to Knight that he could have kissed her nose without moving. But she left him. First she lost her colour, then she looked indignant, then she rose above him, floating.

'We've been hit,' he thought.

He had been turned over. If it had not been for the intense cold, he would have been perfectly comfortable, lying there on his back, gazing up at the sea. Because it was an emergency of some sort he suspected that it would be foolish to turn his head. By moving his eyes, though, he could take in a great deal. There was a wave arrested at the very moment of breaking into a line of foam. Oil fumes, at the instant of combustion, froze in black and red, at right angles to the horizon. A coil of yellow rope hung in the sunshine like a flower. All the left side of his field of vision was taken up by a mountain of varnished gold that bore a delicate encrustation of elaborately worked metal; the hull of the ship, in fact, with its rust and barnacles streaming.

'Why not?' he asked himself, when the sea slipped like a carpet beneath his feet; and he set off running so lightly across the water he could feel the sharp ridges of the waves through the soles of his shoes. It was a matter of pride that he could make a quick decision and act upon it. He would go to Helen.

But in this stratagem he failed. Perhaps, unwittingly, he had spoken his intentions aloud; perhaps they had read his secret from his eyes or outstretched hands. But the whole brilliant and detailed picture suddenly started into motion; the green sea yawned with all its salty breath, an underwater explosion produced a magnificent growth of liquid on the surface, flame ran like a frightened animal over the nursing sister's mop of hair, and a sudden thunder was quickly choked into silence. He was detached from the world of matter. He had lost contact. There was neither hard nor soft, and there was no sound of any kind. He opened his eyes and looked up at the golden surface of the sea. Bubbles sped from his mouth and he thought that if he could but follow they would take him to Helen. He struck out and the morning air cut him like frost.

Physically he felt splendid. Until the bombing he had been stiff from the previous day's exertions. Now, the very violence he put into his swimming restored his circulation; although the waves rolled down upon him from all sides he inhabited a new, more vigorous body which could not be defeated. After an explosion the air sang with metal. A hundred fish jumped, or so it seemed. Fragments of timber, biscuit boxes, lifebelts, a towel, a pipe, bobbed within reaching distance. He was uninjured and quite safe—of this he was never for a moment in doubt. His only anxiety was his inability to travel to Helen as quickly as he would have liked. He thought he would go out of his mind with impatience.

When he was picked up twenty minutes later, clinging to one of the emergency rafts he had fortuitously come across, his first words were, 'I've got to get home quickly, you know.' Then he said, 'Oh, keep me out of that sea,' and fainted.

He awoke to find himself swaddled like a baby, and swinging in mid-air with no obvious means of support. He could neither move his arms nor flex his legs; but he could look out over the wreckage-strewn sea to the distant white cliffs of France.

A man in a white smock tried to stuff a cigarette into his mouth, but he spat it out. 'Let me out of this thing, will you? I itch like hell. I want to scratch myself, d'you understand? I want to scratch myself.'

'Would you give me your number, rank, name and regiment?' said a voice.

A helmeted corporal with a fountain-pen bent over him. They were unbuckling the straps that held him but they could not work fast enough for Knight.

'I'm all right. There's nothing the matter with me. I'm fine. For God's sake get me out of this thing. I'm itching, I tell you.'

'Oh, and I want your religion as well,' said the corporal.   P. H. Newby

THE GERMANS: POST-MORTEM

On this day (the 24th) the Supreme Command intervened in the operations in progress, with results which were to have a most disastrous influence on the whole future course of the war. *Hitler ordered the left wing to stop on the Aa.* It was forbidden to cross that stream. We were not informed of the reasons for this. The order contained the words, 'Dunkirk is to be left to the Luftwaffe. Should the capture of Calais prove difficult, this port too is to be left to the Luftwaffe.' (I quote here from memory.) We were utterly speechless. But since we were not informed of the reasons for this order, it was difficult to argue against it. The Panzer divisions were therefore instructed, 'Hold the line of the canal. Make use of the period of rest for general recuperation.'

Fierce enemy activity met little opposition from our air force.

Early on 25 May I went to visit the *Leibstandarte** and to make sure that they were obeying the order to halt. When I arrived there I found the *Leibstandarte* engaged in crossing the Aa. On the far bank was Mont Watten, a height of only some 235 feet, but that was enough in this flat marshland to dominate the whole surrounding countryside. On top of the hillock, among the ruins of an old castle, I found the divisional commander, Sepp Dietrich. When I asked why he was disobeying orders, he replied that the enemy on Mont Watten could 'look right down the throat' of anybody on the far bank of the canal. Sepp Dietrich had therefore decided on 24 May to take it on his own initiative. The *Leibstandarte* and the Infantry Regiment G.D. on its left were now continuing their advance in the direction of Wormhoudt and Bergues. In view of the success that they were having I approved the decision taken by the commander on the spot and made up my mind to order 2 Panzer Division to move up in their support.

On this day we completed the capture of Boulogne. 10 Panzer Division was fighting outside the Calais citadel. When a demand that he surrender was addressed to the English commandant, Brigadier Nicohlson sent the laconic reply, 'The answer is no, as it is the British Army's duty to fight as well as it is the German's.' So we had to take it by assault. . . .

On 26 May 10 Panzer Division captured Calais. At noon I was at the divisional headquarters and according to the orders I had received I asked Schaal whether he wanted to leave Calais to the Luftwaffe. He replied that he did not, since he did not believe that our bombs would be effective against the thick walls and earthworks of the old fortifications. Furthermore, if the Luftwaffe were to attack them it would mean that he would have to withdraw his troops from their advanced positions on the edge of the citadel, which would then have to be captured all over again. I was bound to agree with this. At 16.45

* *Leibstandarte* Adolf Hitler: the S.S. Division which was formerly Hitler's bodyguard (Ed.)

hours the English surrendered. We took twenty thousand prisoners, including three to four thousand British, the remainder being French, Belgian and Dutch, of whom the majority had not wanted to go on fighting and whom the English had therefore locked up in cellars.

In Calais, for the first time since 17 May, I met General von Kleist, who expressed his appreciation for the achievements of my troops.

On this day we attempted once again to attack towards Dunkirk and to close the ring about that sea fortress. But renewed orders to halt arrived. We were stopped within sight of Dunkirk! We watched the Luftwaffe attack. We also saw the armada of great and little ships by means of which the British were evacuating their forces.

General von Wietersheim appeared at my headquarters during the course of the day to discuss with me arrangements for the relief of XIX Army Corps by his XIV Army Corps. The advanced division of this corps, 20 (Motorized) Infantry Division, was placed under my command. I put it in on the right of the *Leibstandarte* Adolf Hitler. Before this discussion was over, a small incident occurred. The commander of the *Leibstandarte*, Sepp Dietrich, while driving from the front came under machine-gun fire from a party of Englishmen who were still holding out in a solitary house behind our lines. They set his car on fire and compelled him and his companions to take shelter in the ditch. Dietrich and his adjutant crawled into a large drain pipe, where the ditch ran under a cross road, and in order to protect himself from the burning petrol of his car covered his face and hands with damp mud. A wireless truck following his command car signalled for help and we were able to send part of the 3rd Panzer Regiment of 2 Panzer Division, whose sector this was, to get him out of his unpleasant predicament. He soon appeared at my headquarters covered from head to foot in mud and had to accept some very ribald comments on our part.

It was not until the afternoon of 26 May that Hitler gave permission for the advance on Dunkirk to be resumed. By then it was too late to achieve a great victory.

The corps was sent into the attack during the night of the 26–27th. 20 (Motorized) Infantry Division, with the *Leibstandarte* Adolf Hitler and the Infantry Regiment G.D. under command and reinforced by heavy artillery, was given Wormhoudt as its objective. 1 Panzer Division on its left was ordered to push forward, with point of main effort its right wing, in accordance with the progress that that attack should make.

The Infantry Regiment G.D. received useful support from 4 Panzer Brigade of 10 Panzer Division and secured its objective, the high ground Crochte-Pitgam. The Armoured Reconnaissance Battalion of 1 Panzer Division took Brouckerque.

Heavy enemy movement of transport ships from Dunkirk was observed.

On 28 May we reached Wormhoudt and Bourgbourgville. On the 29th Gravelines fell to 1 Panzer Division. But the capture of Dunkirk was after all completed without us. On 29 May XIX Army Corps was relieved by XIV Army Corps.

The operation would have been completed very much more quickly if Supreme Headquarters had not kept ordering XIX Army Corps to stop and thus hindered its rapid and successful advance. What the future course of the war would have been if we had succeeded at that time in taking the British Expeditionary Force prisoner at Dunkirk, it is now impossible to guess. In any event a military victory on that scale would have offered a great chance to capable diplomats. Unfortunately the opportunity was wasted owing to Hitler's nervousness. The reason he subsequently gave for holding back my corps—that the ground in Flanders with its many ditches and canals was not suited to tanks —was a poor one.

General Heinz Guderian

To me Dunkirk was one of the great turning-points of the war. If I had had my way the English would not have got off so lightly at Dunkirk. But my hands were tied by direct orders from Hitler himself. While the English were clambering into the ships off the beaches, I was kept uselessly outside the port unable to move. I recommended to the Supreme Command that my five Panzer divisions be immediately sent into the town and thereby completely destroy the retreating English. But I received definite orders from the Führer that under no circumstances was I to attack, and I was expressly forbidden to send any of my troops closer than ten kilometres from Dunkirk. The only weapons I was permitted to use against the English were my medium guns. At this distance I sat outside the town, watching the English escape, while my tanks and infantry were prohibited from moving.

This incredible blunder was due to Hitler's personal idea of generalship. The Führer daily received statements of tank losses incurred during the campaign, and by a simple process of arithmetic he deduced that there was not sufficient armour available at this time to attack the English. He did not realize that many of the tanks reported out of action one day could, with a little extra effort on the part of the repair squads, be able to fight in a very short time. The second reason for Hitler's decision was the fact that on the map available to him at Berlin the ground surrounding the port appeared to be flooded and unsuitable for tank warfare. With a shortage of armour and the difficult country, Hitler decided that the cost of an attack would be too high, when the French armies to the south had not yet been destroyed. He therefore ordered that my forces be reserved so that they could be strong enough to take part in the southern drive against the French, designed to capture Paris and destroy all French resistance.

Field-Marshal von Rundstedt, G.O.C.-in-C., Army Group

6

THE BATTLE IN THE WEST: TO VICHY

After the evacuation of over four-fifths of the B.E.F. at Dunkirk, France was given no respite. The final assault began on 5 June, when the German armies in Flanders launched their attack south-eastwards towards Paris. On the 10th, Mussolini, anxious to be in at the kill, declared war on the Allies. By the 16th the collapse of the French armies was complete.

ITALY DECLARES WAR

On 26 May, having gone to see him on a matter of routine business, I met Marshal Balbo* in the waiting-room. He had come to Rome to discuss the unhappy state of affairs in Libya, both from the military point of view and from that of the civilian population, which was suffering from a lack of food.

Mussolini sent us a message to come in together; I had hardly crossed the threshold of the vast room which he occupied when I realized that he had something of the greatest importance to say to us. He was standing behind his writing-table, his hands on his hips, looking intensely serious, almost solemn. He did not speak at once but silently transfixed us with his penetrating stare. What was he going to say? Suddenly I found that I had difficulty in breathing. Finally he decided to speak, and then with an air of inspiration he announced, 'I wish to tell you that yesterday I sent a messenger to Hitler with my written declaration that I do not intend to stand idly by with my hands in my pockets, and that after 5 June I am ready to declare war on England.'

We were dumbfounded and seemed to have lost the power of speech.

Mussolini opened his eyes very widely to show his surprise at the coldness with which we had received his news.

When I was able to speak I said:

'Your Excellency, you know perfectly well that we are absolutely unprepared—you have received complete reports every week. We have about twenty divisions with seventy per cent of the necessary equipment and training; and about another twenty divisions with fifty per cent. We have no tanks. The Air Force, as you know from General Pricolo's reports, is grounded. This is to say nothing of stores—we have not even sufficient shirts for the Army. In such a state of affairs how is it possible to declare war? Our colonies lack everything. Our merchant shipping is on the high seas.'

Feeling absolutely desperate, I added, 'It is suicide.'

Mussolini did not answer for a few minutes and then said quite calmly:

'You were right about the situation in Ethiopia in 1935. It is evident that

* Translator's note: Governor and Commander-in-Chief in Libya.

to-day you are too excited to judge the situation correctly. I assure you the war will be over in September, and that I need a few thousand dead so as to be able to attend the peace conference as a belligerent.'

General Pietro Badoglio, Chief of Staff

The Ambassador Goes Home

The fighting spirit of His British Majesty's Fleet is alive and still has the aggressive ruthlessness of the captains and pirates of the 17th century. Ambassador Bastianini, who is back from London, says that the morale of the British is very high and that they have no doubts about victory, even though it may come only after a long time.

Count Ciano

COLLAPSE

The Anglo-French War Council: 11 June

We arrived at Briare late in the afternoon, having made a considerable detour. Aerodromes seldom give an impression of being overpopulated, but this one seemed particularly flat and deserted. Winston, in black, leaning on his stick, strolled about beaming as if he had left all his preoccupations in the plane and had reached the one spot in the world he most wished to visit at that particular moment. He conveyed the impression that the long journey had been well worth while since at last it was vouchsafed to him to walk about the aerodrome of Briare.

I, on the other hand, thought it quite a beastly place and hoped I should never see it again. The fact that my wishes have been fulfilled does not make me feel more kindly towards it.

Three or four cars drove up at intervals, and the Prime Minister left in the first with a French colonel who, from his expression, might have been welcoming poor relations at a funeral reception.

We drove a few kilometres to a hideous house, the sort of building the *nouveau riche* French *bourgeoisie* delight in, a villa expanded by successful business in groceries or indifferent champagne into a large monstrosity of red lobster-coloured brick, and stone the hue of unripe Camembert.

This was Weygand's abode, where the Prime Minister was to sleep.

The place, to which I took an instant dislike, had, I was glad to hear, a ridiculous name; it was called *Le Château du Muguet*—Lily of the Valley Castle.

As soon as we walked into the building I felt that the impression conveyed by the colonel on the aerodrome was but a projection of the attitude of our hosts. It was like walking into a house thinking one is expected, to find one had been invited for the following week. Our presence was not really desired.

It was a subtle feeling, and I may have been wrong, for every form of politeness was shown, even to the extent of giving us tea, but I do not think so. The strain caused by a situation which had greatly deteriorated since I had last seen our hosts had relaxed the bonds of friendship, even in the cause of the staunchest of our French *vis-à-vis*.

Within a few minutes we all trooped into the large dining-room where the conference was to be held. Pétain, de Gaulle, de Margerie and Colonel de Villelume, followed Reynaud. I sat near the window between Pug Ismay and de Gaulle. It was now seven o'clock.

The Frenchmen sat with set white faces, their eyes on the table. They looked for all the world like prisoners hauled up from some deep dungeon to hear an inevitable verdict.

For relief I turned to de Gaulle, whose bearing alone among his compatriots matched the calm, healthy phlegm of the British. A strange-looking man, enormously tall; sitting at the table he dominated everyone else by his height, as he had done when walking into the room. No chin, a long drooping elephantine nose over a closely-cut moustache, a shadow over a small mouth whose thick lips tended to protrude as if in a pout before speaking, a high receding forehead and pointed head surmounted by sparse black hair lying flat and neatly parted. His heavily-hooded eyes were very shrewd. When about to speak he oscillated his head slightly, like a pendulum, while searching for words. I at once remembered and understood the nickname of 'Le Connétable' which Pétain said had been given him at St. Cyr. It was easy to imagine that head on a ruff, that secret face at Catherine de Medici's Council Chamber.

I studied him with great interest, little thinking that for a while we should both be bent with such complete concentration on the same task, nor that later we would be driven so far apart.

That afternoon he had a look of confidence and self-possession which was very appealing. He had, I thought, brought it from Abbeville where he had fought a successful tank action (the only one). Fresh air had given his sallow skin a healthy colour. His cheeks were almost pink. That freshness of complexion I never saw on his face again, nor, I think, did I often see him smile as he did when he turned towards me then. It was a frank confident smile that belied his usual expression and made me feel I should greatly like this man. I perceived that afternoon what was perhaps the real de Gaulle, or maybe that part of him which might have predominated had he remained a soldier, straight, direct, even rather brutal.

. . . . There was a rather awkward pause, then, after a few words of formal welcome, Reynaud turned towards Churchill with that stiff-necked movement of his, and again raising his eyebrows asked him, with a gesture of the hands and the slight facial twitch familiar to him, to address the conference.

The Prime Minister then spoke; the words came slowly, carefully selected but hammered together sharply into a vivid mosaic. He said, in substance, that he had come to France to consider with Monsieur Reynaud and his advisers, the realities of a situation which must be faced without flinching. The matter for discussion was how best to carry on with the struggle which nothing could prevent the British from pursuing. His own impression was that as soon as the Germans had stabilized themselves on a front in France, they would turn on England. He hoped they would do so for two reasons. It would give France relief and enable the British to take a fuller and more equal share in the struggle, but above all, it would give our R.A.F. the opportunity of smashing the German air power. He had complete confidence that they would do so. Every effort was being made in Great Britain to turn out arms and re-equip the armies. At this very moment the British were sending troops to France, and a British infantry division was deployed about Le Mans.

A Canadian division and seventy-two guns were landing that night, so that there were now four British divisions in France. Another division would arrive about 20 June. The dispatch of yet a further division would depend on the guns the French could provide. Then there were the troops from Narvik. If the French Army could hold out till the spring of 1941, the British would have from twenty to twenty-five divisions to place at the disposal of the French Command, to employ anywhere. They might, for example, be used to form continental bridgeheads. He realized, he said, that the numbers he had given were small in the face of the present emergency, but if the French could hold out, the British participation would grow rapidly. The whole problem was how to tide over the present period until the potential strength of the Allies materialized.

He stopped. Reynaud thanked him, but I felt his suppressed irritation and that of the other Frenchmen at the inadequacy of these driblets to halt a con-flagration whose flames were fast spreading from the Channel to the Atlantic. Reynaud added no word to his formal acknowledgement of Churchill's words and asked Weygand to report on the military situation. No one expected good news, but what we were told by the Commander-in-Chief was so bad that the sweat poured off my face as I listened. There was inescapable reality in the tale he unfolded while the light of the June evening faded under gathering clouds in the sky outside. The story had not carried the same conviction when reading reports or listened to at second hand. He appeared more intent on convincing his listeners that all was lost than on considering with them means of continuing the struggle. There was not a single battalion in reserve. The totality of the French forces were engaged. The fighting from Abbeville to Reims had been going on for more than six days without intermission. 'The troops fight all day, then fall back to new positions during the night. The men have neither food nor rest. They collapse into sleep when halted and·have to be shaken in the morning to open fire.'

. . . . The French command had hoped to hold the Somme-Aisne line, Wey-gand was saying, but, although, thanks to the R.A.F., heavy losses had been inflicted on the enemy's armour as well as on his air force, the overwhelming superiority of the Germans in aircraft, tanks and manpower had compelled a withdrawal. The result was that the French armies were falling back to their last line of defence. This ran along the lower Seine and the Paris defence positions, followed the Oise and the Marne to join the north-west extremity of the Marne line, thence on to the Maginot forts. This line had been attacked at most points and broken on the lower Seine, and quite recently on the Marne. Up to this point Weygand's voice had been calm, expostulatory; it now rose a note or two as he said, 'The German mechanized columns get through our lines, curl round and blow up the bridges behind our troops who, when they reach them, find themselves cut off. In other cases, as the enemy aircraft can spot French troop movements unhindered, they blow up the bridges they are making for from the air,' and he told the story I had already heard of the German plane which, flying low, had blown up the French explosive charges on the Oise bridges, cutting off the troops from the positions they were withdrawing to. 'It is,' he said, 'a race between the exhaustion of the French and the shortness of breath of the enemy divisions. . . . There is nothing to prevent the enemy reaching Paris. We are fighting on our last line and it has been breached.' His tone now as dramatic as his words, he rapped out, 'I am helpless, I cannot intervene for I have no reserves; there are no reserves. *C'est la dislocation'*—the break-up.

I looked round and read consternation on all the English faces. My own mouth was so dry, I could not swallow. I wrote quickly to make up for lost time as I found I had stopped to listen, for the picture evoked was slow to take shape in my mind.

I looked at Reynaud. Eyebrows raised, he was gazing at the middle of the table. Churchill, his face flushed, hunched over the table, was watching Weygand intently. His expression was not benevolent. But Weygand was now launched on his favourite theme, the folly of having embarked on the war at all. 'I wish to place on record that I consider that those responsible embarked upon the war very lightly and without any conception of the power of German armaments. As it is, we have lost something like two-fifths of our initial strength.'

Weygand had finished. He was drained dry like a squeezed lemon. Not an idea, not a suggestion was to be wrung out of him. This must have been Churchill's conclusion, for he put him no questions, did not even look at him again, and merely asked that General Georges should be summoned. . . . I looked at de Gaulle. I had already noted that he had been ceaselessly smoking cigarettes, lighting one from another, his lips pursed and rounded in the characteristic movement I had already observed. Not a muscle of his face had moved. Nothing had been said that had caused his expression to change. The Prime Minister had looked at him several times. He was searching for something he had failed to find in the other French faces. The fact that he returned several times to a study of de Gaulle made me think he had detected in him the thing he was looking for.

When Georges came in he looked ghastly, but later his expression became more normal. The close similarity of his account to that already given by Weygand was very striking. They both told the same story in almost similar words. There were only differences of detail.

He told us that the Allies had lost a minimum of thirty-five divisions out of 105, as well as all the mechanized cavalry and a substantial proportion of the armoured divisions.

Georges intended to speak up for the troops, and did so. He was proud of the way many of them were fighting and was determined that where heroism had been shown it should be recognized. There was no Englishman at that table who did not understand and appreciate his intention, and his sober words carried infinitely more weight and conviction than had Weygand's discourse, which had been larded with far too many exclamations about *'troupes sans défaillances'* —an army that had fought magnificently without any exception. Such statements had exactly the contrary effect on British ears to that intended.

In his usual matter-of-fact decided way Georges said, 'The fact is that some divisions have ceased to exist, they are only numbers. The Army is not in a position to oppose a powerful thrust.'

Reynaud chimed in as he had done at every meeting with: 'If this battle is lost, it will be through lack of aviation,' uttered in a resigned voice, as he might have said, 'Well, the poor chap is dead but it was his own fault.' This sentence, true as are most clichés, but as unenlightening, emphasized that we were getting nowhere. Not a single positive suggestion had been made, nor had the hint of a plan emerged.

The Prime Minister may have sensed this, and felt that it was time he intervened again. His mouth had been working, an indication that he was pouring an idea into the mould of words. His voice when he spoke was warm and deep, an admirable medium for giving utterance to his generous ideas. He wished, he said, to express his admiration for the heroic resistance of the French armies, and Great Britain's grief at not being able to take a more effective part in the struggle. The inescapable fact was that the B.E.F. had come out of Flanders almost literally naked. It could only resume the struggle after it had been re-armed. Had it not been for events in the north, some thirteen or fourteen British divisions would now be fighting by the side of the French. This was the gist of his words, but they conveyed far more; the longing of the British people to help their friends in distress, their determination to do so the moment they could, and his evocation of the disaster in the north, whilst conveying no hint of reproach, nevertheless did recall facts that explained Britain's momentary helplessness.

Then, returning to his constant purpose of instilling the will to fight into the French, of demonstrating that, come what might, the struggle must continue, he evoked the past. We had been near disaster before in the last war, and had survived. Now, as then, we were losing sight of the war as a whole in the contemplation of our own immediate losses. We must not be hypnotized by our defeats, discouraged by our temporary weakness, or blind to the enemy's difficulties. The German armies must now also be in a state of extreme exhaustion and feeling the strain of their immensely long lines of communication.

The pressure might diminish in forty-eight hours. Might it not be possible, while holding the main line, to mount a counter-attack with the help of the British forces that would then be in position in the region of Rouen?

If the front held for another three or four weeks, there would be a substantial British force available to attack the enemy's flank. He was convinced the enemy was feeling his losses acutely; there was a complete absence of exultation in Germany. Every hour, every day gained tended to retrieve our fortunes. Whereupon Weygand broke in to say discouragingly but truthfully that it was a question of hours, not of days and weeks.

I ceased taking notes and watched him [Churchill], hypnotized. He found wonderful flashing words with which to express his fiery eloquence. They came in torrents, French and English phrases tumbling over each other like waves racing for the shore when driven by a storm. Something of the impression he then made comes back to me as I read his account of what occurred that afternoon. He wanted the French to fight in Paris, describing how a great city, if stubbornly defended, absorbed immense armies. And the pageant of history, the lurid glow of burning cities, some as beautiful as Paris, collapsing on garrisons

who refused to accept defeat, arose before our eyes. The French perceptibly
froze at this.*

Incongruously perhaps, but with a slight sense of personal scorn, a half-
forgotten story took shape in my memory concerning three hundred Spartans
who on another summer day long ago sat 'combing their long hair for death in
the passes of Thermopylae'. If such men existed in France, they were not in
that room. Leonidas was there, but he was not French. But Churchill, if he had
noticed the perceptible movement which had led all the French to sit back in
their chairs with the tension of a motorist pressing hard on the brakes, save de
Gaulle, and de Margerie who was utterly detached in his work, he did not heed
it, or if he did, it merely spurred him on, for he went straight on, now counter-
attacking on the subject of the Royal Air Force. Weygand had asked that every
British fighting plane should be sent to France as this was the decisive battle
that would settle the fate of both nations. This, Churchill declared with great
force, was not so, there was a wider horizon, a vaster field to be considered.

To-day we had the battle of France, to-morrow we would have that of Britain,
and it was on this field that the fate of the war would be decided. If we won that
battle, all we had now lost would be retrieved. He looked very fierce, and it was
quite evident that nothing would make him surrender the last air defence of
Britain. And he said so. Although we were doing all we could in the air, the
French could not expect us to destroy irretrievably our only hope in the present
battle, the air arm. I remembered he had told me in London he would not give
way on this absolutely vital issue, and he was keeping faith with himself.

The fighter force would . . . break up the attack on their island and cripple
the might of Germany when it came, and it would surely come. But whatever
happened we would fight on and on and on, *toujours*, all the time, everywhere,
partout, pas de grâce, no mercy. *Puis la victoire!*

Reynaud, who had listened politely, easing his head in his collar now and
then, said he fully accepted that the British fighter force should be kept in
being, but he must assert that it was equally important to maintain the last line
of defence in France. It was evident that British fighters operating from England must be less effective than those based in France. After all, where was the
danger? If the worst befell, they could always regain their home bases. The
French High Command was persuaded that a large-scale air attack on the advancing Germans might reverse the situation. The air force was the only weapon
left to the Allies. Great Britain could therefore turn the scales of the present
battle in favour of the Allies if she so wished. He stopped, looked at Georges,
and made a movement of the chin in his direction. He knew that the General
had more influence on Churchill than any other Frenchman and had observed,
quick as he was, how carefully the Prime Minister had listened to him. He
wanted his support and got it. Very solemnly Georges said he fully agreed with
Reynaud.

It was quite plain from Churchill's expression that he had no intention of
giving way. He diverted the discussion by saying that an attack on the United
Kingdom would in all probability bring the United States into the war, since

* On this day General Weygand decided to declare Paris an open town and issued orders in
consequence.

the whole British population would resist the attack with the utmost fierceness. The losses the German Air Force would sustain might well be the turning-point of the war. . . .

It was of capital importance, he rapped out, to keep in existence the instrument on which depended the intervention of the United States in the conflict. It would be folly to ruin the only weapon capable of achieving this result. Moreover, it was far from certain that the contrary decision would reverse the position in France.

Reynaud dryly intervened to say that nothing was less desirable than the break-up of the British Air Force except that of the Western Front, and once more repeated that history would no doubt say that the battle of France had been lost because of weaknesses in the air.

As an approaching squall is heralded by choppy waters, so the rising tone of the French Premier's voice warned of impending trouble. Churchill perceived this, and in sentences warm and soothing, emphasizing by a deeper tone the first syllable of key words, moulded phrases rounded and smooth that fell like drops of oil flicked on a rising sea.

The acerbity had gone from Reynaud's voice when he answered, but his theme was unchanged, for he repeated almost word for word Georges' plea that more and still more British fighters should be based in France. The Prime Minister, having got the discussion back into his own hands, was a trifle blunt as he repeated the arguments for not doing so. But easing up a little, he said that the whole position would be reviewed on his return to England. 'We are always thankful, but always famished,' said Reynaud in a quite friendly way. . . .

Now Weygand was speaking again: 'We are at the last quarter of an hour.' If he says that again, I thought, I shall do something foolish, and, by the look of my notes, I broke my pencil.

Thereupon fancy came to my rescue as it often does, and I saw Big Ben with a French general's cap on, marking time at the double, chiming the last quarter of an hour incessantly, at ever-accelerating speed, whilst the dial of the clock became Weygand's face.

My mind wandered from the discussion, but I do not think I missed much; Weygand was saying that there was conceivably still a hope of winning through, and that was why any possible help was indispensable.

The heads of Governments and the generals had met to examine what would be the consequence of the eventual dislocation of the armies. The enemy already held bridgeheads across the Seine, and his armour was manœuvring to encircle Paris from both sides. If the present line was broken, there was no hope that it could be re-established, as there was nothing behind it. 'Once this defensive battle has been lost,' he said, 'there is nothing to prevent the total invasion of France owing to the strength and power of penetration of the German Panzer divisions.' Not only Paris but every large town in France would be occupied. Doubtless the remainder of the French forces would fight on until not a man remained, but this would be unco-ordinated warfare, and he himself, as Commander-in-Chief, would find himself completely powerless. He found it difficult to imagine how, if the worst happened, France could carry on with the war.

Well, now we had it. There was no mistaking the Commander-in-Chief's meaning.

I looked at Reynaud. He had bristled visibly. When he spoke, his voice was carefully controlled and modulated, but he was plainly very angry.

The Commander-in-Chief had given, he said in effect, the most competent view available on the military situation, but, and here he rapped out his words, the question of whether or not the war was to continue was the responsibility of the Government and of the Government alone.

The two men glared at each other. Reynaud's eyebrows were lifted so high that every wrinkle beneath them was ironed out. But if in consequence his face was blank, his eyes darted fury. Weygand opened and closed his mouth. His parchment skin, tightly stretched on his Mongolian face, looked as if it would crack under the strain of his moving jaw. But he said nothing for a few moments whilst all watched him. Then he recovered some control and with the playful *bonhomie* of the dog who persists in having a last snap at the postman's trousers, repeated that he would be only too glad to serve under anyone who could escape from the consequences of the present situation. His clear intention was to indicate that he maintained his previous statement.

The Prime Minister had been watching the two speakers very attentively. I guessed he had learnt much from the glimpse he had been given of the off-stage relations of the principal actors in the tragedy. What he did was to ring the curtain down and ask the cast if an entirely fresh approach could not be attempted in the next act.

What were the possibilities, he enquired, of establishing one or more bridge-heads on the Atlantic? If these were established British divisions could be put in at ever-increasing pace. He felt certain also that the United States would soon be taking her share. This meant Brittany. I wondered whether the true attitude of each would now emerge.

Reynaud answered that the problem was being studied. General Altmayer (the younger) was on the spot taking stock of the situation. Certain measures in view of this eventuality had been taken on his instructions some time back. I felt, perhaps because his interest in the plan had not been apparent for some time, that Reynaud had lost faith in the idea. In any case, he spoke without conviction and seemed anxious to hand over the discussion to Weygand. Nothing loth, the General proceeded finally to demolish the project. He said the problem presented two difficulties, the first strategic, the other concerning supplies.

It was difficult to fight to the last on a given position and at the same time to withdraw troops to another. Also, seventy per cent of the armies' needs were supplied from the Paris region. Brittany certainly offered the advantage of open communications with Great Britain, but it had neither fortifications nor resources. Everything should be done to hold it, but he did not think it could be long defended. The German Air Force could make things very difficult for all those in this restricted territory. Meanwhile, the Germans would systematically destroy every town, village and factory in occupied France.

Reynaud said he could not but concur with General Weygand's conclusions. The military difficulties of such a step were immense; nevertheless he fully appreciated the great political importance it might have, which meant exactly nothing.

The Prime Minister did not pursue the subject, and to my chagrin turned to his favourite hobbyhorse, guerrilla warfare.

The Prime Minister said he put forward his proposals with diffidence in the presence of the heads of the French Army, but if only some effective means of holding up the German tanks could be devised, the tactics he suggested might lead to some secure bridgeheads being held for a few months until Britain's great strength developed, which it was doing at tremendous pace, and until American help came in full measure.

Weygand showed ill-concealed scorn at the Prime Minister's suggestion, and Pétain anger. Evidently determined the proposal should be at once squashed, 'It would mean the destruction of the country,' Pétain growled. He was far more moved than he had been by anything so far. Real wrath rumbled behind his words. Reynaud evidently also believed the suggestion an impossible one, and his comment showed that at some points his thought did not diverge as widely from that of the Marshal as might have been expected. He also dwelt on the suffering it would impose on the country, towns would be destroyed. . . . All this is leading nowhere, I thought. It was becoming painfully clear to me that the battle of France was lost and that no one believed in miracles. The only reality consisted in planning the next stage of the war in Africa. But no one spoke of it. I became very depressed. Hope lay in planning campaigns for the future, in establishing a new base from which attacks could be launched. But the talk was only of make-believe operations in a prostrate country with armies that had ceased to exist. This much had been made clear. If matters were left where they were, faith and confidence would be allowed to vanish from the room, absorbed by the spirit of defeat as wavelets are by sand. Darkness rather than light was being shed from the chandeliers. A miasma, a despond had fallen on the conference like a fog. No one appeared able to see his way. Then Churchill reacted explosively. As a slap in the face is considered a remedy for hysteria, or for a swoon, so he interjected violently that if the destruction of towns was an unpleasant perspective, that of falling a helpless prey to the enemy was a worse one. Britain was not only willing to suffer as France was suffering, she would gladly draw upon herself the full weight of Nazi ferocity. Meanwhile the main thing was to be able to hold out. A bridgehead on the Atlantic or some other form of resistance might achieve this. There was nothing Great Britain would not do for France except give up the struggle. She would fight on, of that he was certain, until Hitlerism was destroyed. She would never give in, never. She would fight on for years, she would fight in the air, she would fight with her navy and impose on Europe the most severe blockade. England controlled the seas. Her Empire and that of France were intact, the Belgian and Dutch colonies depended on them. This war might well soon become a war of continents. Although the collapse of France evoked the most distressing picture, yet he felt certain that, in spite of it, Germany could at last be brought to her knees. 'It is possible that the Nazis may dominate Europe, but it will be a Europe in revolt, and in the end it is certain that a regime whose victories are in the main due to its machines will collapse. Machines will one day beat machines.'

The fog had gone, blown away by the great gusts of Churchill's eloquence. All could see one thing clearly; the path England was following. It lay straight ahead, steep, jagged and dangerous, but leading upward to where, high up, shone a light. I felt this so strongly that I lifted my eyes, as in dedication, and, grateful as a thirsty man is for a glass of water, I heard Victor Hugo's tremendous line sing in my ears: '*L'espoir changea de camp, le combat changea d'âme.*' Others than myself must, I think, have seen, as Churchill spoke, a dim vista of utter ruin, dust-clouds over collapsing cities, but in the far distance the sun of victory rising on a silent world of dead towns and rubble.

Major-General Sir Edward Spears

Weygand

. . . . Went to see Weygand at 8.30 a.m. Found him looking very wizened and tired with a stiff neck from a car smash on previous evening. He said he would speak very frankly. That the French Army had ceased to be able to offer organized resistance and was disintegrating into disconnected groups. That Paris had been given up and that he had no reserves whatever left. He then stated that at the Inter-Allied Council it had been decided to hold a position covering Brittany in front of Rennes. . . . He then suggested that I should go with him to Georges' headquarters to draw up an agreement for this manœuvre.

I therefore started off in the car with him for Georges' headquarters, and, as we were trundling along, he turned to me, and said, 'This is a terrible predicament that I am in.' I was just preparing to answer that I could well understand how heavy the responsibility must be to be entrusted with the task of saving France in her distress. To my astonishment he continued with: 'Yes, I had finished my military career which had been a most successful one.' I remained dumb and unable to make any adequate remark; it seemed impossible that the man destined to minister to France in her death agonies should be thinking of his military career.

General Alan Brooke, diary, 14 June

France From Six Miles Up

Burning is a great word when you look down from thirty-three thousand feet; for over the villages and the forests there is nothing to be seen but a pall of motionless smoke, a sort of ghastly whitish jelly. Below it the fires are at work like a secret digestion. At thirty-three thousand feet time slows down, for there is no movement here. There are no crackling flames, no crashing beams, no spirals of black smoke. There is only that greyish milk curdled in the amber air. Will that forest recover? Will that village recover? Seen from this height, France is being undermined by the secret gnawing of bacteria.

About this, too, there is much to be said. 'We shall not hesitate to sacrifice our villages.' I have heard these words spoken. And it was necessary to speak them. When a war is on, a village ceases to be a cluster of traditions. The enemy who hold it have turned it into a nest of rats. Things no longer mean the same. Here are trees three hundred years old that shade the home of your family. But they obstruct the field of fire of a twenty-two-year-old lieutenant. Wherefore he sends up a squad of fifteen men to annihilate the work of time. In ten minutes he destroys three hundred years of patience and sunlight, three hundred years of the religion of the home and of betrothals in the shadows round the grounds. You say to him, 'My trees!' but he does not hear you. He is right. He is fighting a war.

But how many villages have we seen burnt down only that war may be made to look like war? Burnt down exactly as trees are cut down, crews flung into the holocaust, infantry sent against tanks, merely to make war look like war. Small wonder that an unutterable disquiet hangs over the land. For nothing does any good.

One fact the enemy grasped and exploited—that men fill small space in the earth's immensity. A continuous wall of men along our front would require a hundred million soldiers. Necessarily, there were always gaps between the French units. In theory, these gaps are cancelled by the mobility of the units. Not, however, in the theory of the armoured division, for which an almost un-motorized army is as good as unmanœuvrable. The gaps are real gaps. Whence this simple tactical rule: 'An armoured division should move against the enemy like water. It should bear lightly against the enemy's wall of defence and advance only at the point where it meets with no resistance.' The tanks operate by this rule, bear against the wall, and never fail to break through. They move as they please for want of French tanks to set against them; and though the damage they do is superficial—capture of unit staffs, cutting of telephone cables, burning of villages—the consequences of their raids are irreparable. In every region through which they make their lightning sweep, a French army, even though it seem to be virtually intact, has ceased to be an army. It has been transformed into clotted segments. It has, so to say, coagulated. The armoured divisions play the part of a chemical agent precipitating a colloidal solution. Where once an organism existed they leave a mere sum of organs whose unity has been destroyed. Be-tween the clots—however combative the clots may have remained—the enemy moves at will.

Antoine de Saint-Exupéry

THE LAST OF THE B.E.F.

On 12 June, 51 Highland Division, which was the last major unit of the B.E.F. in France, and which had not been involved in Flanders, was cornered at Saint.-Valéry. Five days later the last British forces in France were evacuated.

Retreat

The weather was hot and still, gloriously blue and sunny, with fleecy white clouds high in the heavens. The country was pleasant and pastoral, some of it cultivated and dotted with copses, some of it hardwood forest. The streams ran placidly to the sea, the beasts still grazed. There is in France a cemetery of the earlier war, where French and Scottish soldiers lie buried side by side, and where the French, mindful of the oldest alliance in all Europe, have put the inscription:

'Ici parmi les lilas de la France fleurira pour toujours le chardon de l'Ecosse.' The
same will always be true of those dolorous sixty miles from Abbeville to Saint-
Valéry.

The two battalions had shaken down. There had been little fighting in the
Saar, but they had been shot over; in the old phrase, they had smelt powder.
They were now to face disaster unprepared, underarmed, and, except for their
comrades of the Highland Division, alone.

On 5 June, 1940, when the German attack came in, the 1st Battalion held a
front of two miles and a half, between the pretty little villages of Lambercourt
and Toeuffles. On their left were the 1st Gordons, who had lost heavily in the
attack of the previous day. Beyond the Gordons were the 7th Argylls, who were
even more widely dispersed than the rest of the Division. It was against the
Argylls that the Germans moved, at dawn on the 5th; and on such a wide front
it was easy for them to pass through, often unobserved and unimpeded.

What little could be done to meet this development was done at once. The
Argylls stood their ground; the Gordons fell back a little to avoid being outflanked. Their movement exposed in turn the flank of the 1st Battalion, and the
enemy approached to within a few hundred yards of it, opening up with machine-
guns and inflicting casualties. The 4th Battalion, under Rory Macpherson, which
was some miles back, was moved across to the village of Valines, to act as long-
stop to the 7th Argylls and to the 8th Argylls (a unit still farther to the left, of
whose situation at this moment little was known).

The 7th Argylls still held fast, and were at length surrounded in the village
of Franleu, to which their colonel, a stout-hearted officer called 'Copper'
Buchanan, had called in his scattered companies. The 4th Black Watch was
bidden to counter-attack, with a troop of French tanks in support. An hour or
two passed, but the tanks failed to arrive; and an effort to probe forward with
two rifle companies was blocked before it had progressed very far. Without
tanks no such attack had any hope of succeeding, and Rory Macpherson and his
officers helplessly watched the enemy's assault on Franleu. At dusk, Buchanan
and the few survivors left to him did their best to break out of Franleu by a
desperate effort; but his battalion lost twenty-three officers and five hundred
other ranks that day.

The front had now begun to crumble. It was wide, it was unsupported, it
had been defied and infiltrated. The defence of the Argylls could cover one
point in twenty; it could never stem the German advance, which now lapped
around the 4th Black Watch in the village of Valines.

Rory Macpherson expected to be asked to hold his position around Valines
. . . and was making all preparations to do so, although far from sanguine as to
the eventual fate of his battalion. But soon after dark he received urgent orders
to withdraw to the river Bresle. . . . But the Battalion had hardly settled there
before they were ordered to retire across the river to a new position. They were
to move at 9 p.m., but at 7 p.m. the enemy was already nearer to the solitary
bridge at Incheville than the Battalion itself. By 7.30 p.m., a number of Germans
had actually reached it. They were driven off by the Battalion's own anti-tank
guns, which were under command of the Brigade, but which happened by chance
at this moment to be on the critical spot. Most of the Battalion succeeded in

crossing at the correct time and place; two companies were cut off, crossed three miles upstream at Gamaches, and managed to rejoin the main body sometime on the following day.

For the next thirty-six hours the Battalion hung on by its toe-nails, overlooking the Bresle. Its position was again impossibly wide; the wooded and difficult country made it easy for the enemy to infiltrate, and difficult for Macpherson to communicate with his company commanders.

At dawn on 6 June, Major Lorne Campbell of Airds, of the 8th Argylls (whose name will recur often in this book), came marching in with the remnants of his company. They had been cut off two days before on the extreme left of the line near the sea at Ault; but they had made their way back, marching among the German columns as if they had been Germans themselves. The administrative difficulties hereabouts were acute, and all that Stuart-Fotheringham could offer Campbell as he passed through was a glass of neat gin. The 4th Battalion stayed all day on the Bresle, while the enemy poured through the gaps like clear soup through a sieve. That night, the 8th, orders were again received to withdraw at short notice, and they marched several miles to find some buses at Villebosc. By this time the whole brigade consisted of the Battalion; of three hundred men who were the sole survivors of two Argyll battalions, under Lorne Campbell; and of a battalion of the Scots Fusiliers, under Lord Rowallan, which had hitherto been pioneers, but had now been stepped up into the line. The enemy tried to interfere with this withdrawal, but was stemmed by an attack, in the course of which the commander of the carrier platoon was killed.

At the Battalion's next rendezvous—in the Forest of Arques, south-east of Dieppe—a scratch force, called Ark Force, was hastily thrown together. It was given the task of hastening to Le Havre and preparing its defence, while the rest of the Highland Division withdrew more slowly to that port to prepare for embarkation. Ark Force sought to move by the coast road, but found it too congested with refugees and fugitives. It therefore moved by sideroads; and the heroes of this journey were the Quartermaster, Glasier, and the Transport Officer, Walker, whose brother was a Regular officer in the 1st Battalion a few miles away. But the 4th Battalion's task in Le Havre was sadly different to the original intention. News came through that the withdrawal of the main body of the Division had been blocked, and that an effort would be made to take it off at Saint-Valéry.

Surrender

An ominous silence prevailed. The enemy could be seen, but there was little shooting. At twenty minutes past four, Colonel Honeyman left for Brigade H.Q., leaving Bill Bradford the Adjutant in command. Almost at once tanks appeared, and the enemy opened fire with mortars and machine-guns. Some dismounted French cavalry arrived, under a veteran major with a gallant heart; and in this penultimate position of the original Black Watch, Frenchmen and Scotsmen lay side by side and fought. When the tanks appeared, Noel Jardine-Paterson, the Signal Officer, went off to try to collect the anti-tank platoon in readiness for the attack which was obviously brewing. Casualties mounted; the old French major had his arm blown off, but insisted on being carried round his position to encourage his men. We do not know his name.

Still the anti-tank platoon had not arrived, and it was not established until long after that Alastair Telfer-Smollett, its commander, was killed, and his men either killed or captured, in trying to get forward. In the absence of orders, Bill Bradford decided to withdraw a little farther. He piled his wounded into the office truck, and sent it off with Lance-Corporal Farquharson driving it. Farquharson drove across the fields to the road, and actually reached the hospital and delivered the wounded. Then he tried to get back, but on the way was ambushed and badly wounded: he made his report to Bradford as a prisoner, and died soon afterwards.

Many more wounded had to be left when Bradford succeeded in withdrawing the remnants of his two companies, which now amounted to less than a hundred men. They journeyed across country in the dark, and at 7.45 a.m. in the morning of 12 June took up a position on the high ground above the cemetery, just outside Saint-Valéry. Bradford improvised platoons under such senior N.C.O.s as were available, armed them with abandoned weapons which were lying around in profusion, and formed additional sub-units from men who had become detached from their proper companies or battalions.

By 9 a.m. his strength had almost doubled, and four officers had arrived in addition to those already with him. The position was being heavily mortared from every direction, and a tank attack was coming into view, when Major Thomas Rennie of the Regiment, who was serving on General Fortune's staff, arrived. It had fallen to him to bring the saddest news of all. The Division had capitulated. . . .

There was nothing left to fight with, and nothing left to fight for. The Navy was powerless to take off what little remained of the Division; and early in the morning, acting on orders from home, General Fortune had been forced to surrender to the German general whose troops had surrounded him, whose name was Erwin Rommel.

When buglers blew the 'Cease Fire' at Saint-Valéry, few men could believe what they heard. They were physically and mentally exhausted; for the last fortnight they had never managed to win more than an hour or two of sleep in the twenty-four. They heard the bugles, paused, and then went on with whatever they were doing: digging in on the lip of the valley where most of them were, dragging ammunition boxes from the useless lorries, or shooting at German tanks with mere Bren guns. As verbal orders reached them, they collected slowly, and under the direction of the officers destroyed everything of value which still remained to them. Then they formed up in silent and disciplined bodies.

Major Nogy Dundas addressed all those who were near him. He explained how they would soon be separated from their officers, and exhorted them not to forget who they were in the captivity that lay before them. Then they moved off; and the Brigadier—himself to die in prison—stood to attention with a long Highland crook in his left hand. As each body of troops went past, the senior N.C.O. or private gave 'Eyes Left', and leaderless individuals saluted him.

Bernard Fergusson

The Victor

During the next few hours no less than twelve generals were brought in as prisoners, among them four divisional commanders. A particular joy for us was the inclusion among them of General Fortune, commander of 51 British* Division, and his staff. I now agreed divisional boundaries with my neighbour, General Cruewell, commander of 2 Motorized Division. Meanwhile, the captured generals and staff officers had been assembled in a house south of the market place. A German Luftwaffe lieutenant, who had just been liberated from captivity, was made responsible for the guard. He was visibly delighted by the change of role.

Particularly surprising to us was the *sang-froid* with which the British officers accepted their fate. The General, and even more, his staff officers, stalked round laughing in the street in front of the house. The only thing that seemed to disturb them was the frequent photographing and filming they had to endure by our Propaganda Company and some other photographers.

The captured generals were now invited to an open-air lunch at a German field kitchen, but they refused with thanks, saying that they still had supplies of their own. So we ate alone. There were still arrangements to be made for transporting away the prisoners, especially the numerous officers, for salvaging the equipment, securing the coast and evacuating Saint-Valéry. At about 20.00 hours we returned to Divisional H.Q. at Château Auberville.

It was impossible at that stage to estimate the total of prisoners and booty. Twelve thousand men, of whom eight thousand were British, were transported off by 7 Panzer Division's vehicles alone. The total number of prisoners captured at Saint-Valéry is said to have numbered forty-six thousand men.

General Erwin Rommel

Evacuation

Over three thousand men perished when the liner Lancastria *was bombed at St. Nazaire on 17 June.*

I then moved into St. Nazaire where I found 'Turtle' Hamilton in charge of the naval side of the embarkation. He was most obliging and helpful in our search for the armed trawler, H.M.T. *Cambridgeshire*. She had also gone to assist in the *Lancastria* rescues, and it was some time before she could be found. When she did arrive, it was after saving nine hundred men from swimming in fuel oil, and conveying them to another transport. During their time on the trawler they had most of them stripped off their oil-soaked clothing. The whole trawler was covered in that foul-smelling black treacly substance, heaps of clothes on the decks oozed out oil, whilst in the tiny cabin below the carpet was soaked with it, the walls covered with impressions of every part of the human anatomy printed in brown on the white walls; bandages, cotton-wool, iodoform, blood and the all-permeating smell of fuel oil. Ronnie Stanyforth came to me and said, 'The one reason why I like to serve you as A.D.C. is owing to the comfort and luxury that we travel in!'

* Highland (Ed.)

. . . . After embarking we lay at anchor in the harbour until 4 a.m., during which time there were several more air-raids. We were sleeping on deck and 'Rusty' Eastwood had his roll of bedding alongside of mine. The A.A. Lewis guns on the bridge were firing furiously. Suddenly I heard a thump followed by a grunt of discomfort from Eastwood. I asked him if he had been hit, he replied, 'Yes, by a Lewis gun drum thrown from the bridge, which landed on my stomach!'

We spent the whole of this day on the trawler, mostly lying on the deck in the sunshine and thanking God that we were safely out of France for the second time. Luckily it was a lovely calm day, and, in spite of the stink of fuel-oil, conditions were quite pleasant. Suddenly in the middle of this peaceful scene we were disturbed by piercing yells emanating from the lower parts of the trawler. The screams drew nearer and finally the individual responsible for them emerged on the deck. It was one of the stokers, a young boy who had been so seriously affected by the men of the *Lancastria* drowning in fuel-oil that he had temporarily become unhinged. He started tearing round the deck shouting, 'Can't you see they are all drowning? Why are you not doing anything? Oh God, we must do something for them.' We caught him and held him down, and then hunted for some bromide to give him, but there was none. We therefore got several aspirins and ground them down in some milk and poured it down his throat. He gradually quietened down and slept for a couple of hours, when the whole procedure had to be repeated.

General Alan Brooke, diary, 17–18 June

THE END

France Betrayed

We lay silent for a few minutes; then Saint-Brice asked, 'What are you sighing about?'

'Did I sigh?'

'You did.'

He too sighed. Then he said, 'No, it's not a pretty sight.'

'What do you think?' I asked. 'How long are we going to keep running like this?'

'I've no idea! Maybe till the Germans occupy all France.'

'And what about the Maginot Line? And the Daladier Line that's supposed to be waiting somewhere? And the resistance that's being organized on the Loire? Why shouldn't this war have its Marne, too? Don't you believe in it?'

I felt in the darkness that he had turned towards me with his head in his hands.

'No,' he said, 'I don't believe in it.'

I did not want to ask questions, but he went on talking, as he seldom did.

'I have stopped believing,' he said. 'We had not prepared for this war. No, I don't speak of armaments. We could have caught up in nine months. But no Frenchman knew what he was fighting for. The Germans, over there, wrapped their foulest plans in ideological tissue-paper. And we? We did the opposite. We were really fighting for freedom and humanity, and we were ashamed of those two words. We acted as though nothing but territory were at stake. Did we hate the Germans? Our young people didn't even know what the Germans meant. Even to-day the blockheads think they'll survive a Hitler victory. Yes, they *will* survive! But as slaves. The purpose of this whole war is to bring slavery back to the world. And the world will regard us as voluntary slaves!'

His voice sounded hoarse. I stretched out on the narrow school bench. Between us lay a desk with an inkpot and drawer.

'We Frenchmen forgot the meaning of freedom long ago,' he went on. 'Real freedom. We were in the midst of a civil war when the Germans overran us.'

'In times of war,' I objected, 'Frenchmen always dropped their internal quarrels.'

'That was true in the past,' said Saint-Brice. 'Patriotism is stronger than politics. It always was in our country. But philosophy is stronger than patriotism. The Germans armed themselves with a philosophy for this war. Their philosophy is a skeleton key that lets them into a country without resistance. But God help a country once the Germans have occupied it!'

Never before had he spoken like this. Despite our intimacy, we both had preserved the distance between superior and subordinate, between Frenchman and foreigner. This time Saint-Brice seemed to be speaking to himself.

'Recently,' he continued, 'a captain told me that he loved France more than he loved Hitler, but that he loved Hitler more than Léon Blum. What more do you want?'

He was interrupted by a fit of coughing.

'Yes,' he said at last, 'I know the old story of our deficiency in arms. But do you think that was the decisive factor? Didn't we win the Great War despite our inferior armament? They say that the greatest part of our aircraft was destroyed on the ground. Do you know what that means? There were officers who prevented our pilots, at the point of a gun, from taking off. Can you conceive of such a thing?'

'No, I can't.'

'I am beginning to understand; we were not sold out, but we were betrayed. And that's the worst part of it. A couple of corrupted generals can always be dealt with by a firing-squad. But we had no corrupt generals. You can't prove anything against them. There is no *bordereau* as in the Dreyfus Case. They betrayed us without having exchanged a single word with the Germans. They did not want to fight against Germany. They liked Germany. Bought by the Germans? If only they had been bought! But they weren't even bought! Once I was told that the people of some Balkan state were always ready to sell their country, but never to deliver it. We did worse than that. We delivered our country without even getting paid for it.'

'Aren't you painting too black a picture?'

I said this without conviction. But he was tormenting me, just as he was tormenting himself. We had loved this country and this people more than anything in the world: each of us in his own way.

'No,' he said, 'it can't be painted too black.'

We tried to sleep. But the day and the conversation had been too much for us. And the thunder of the guns was drawing nearer.

'Artillery preparation,' said Saint-Brice. 'They still expect resistance.'

I took up the thread of his thought.

'On this lousy, clogged road resistance is unthinkable.'

'Right', said the officer. 'That's what they want to show us. It's the same men who sabotaged our armament. Always the same. They started the Dreyfus Case—and lost it. After that they were dethroned in France. Now they're taking revenge for the Dreyfus Case. Now they expect to stage a triumphal come-back on German bayonets. People won't understand that. Not for a long time. Because, by accident, war was declared between Germany and France. Because our generals were not as straightforward as General Franco. He, at least, openly invited the foreigners into his country. . . . In the streets of Sainte-Menehould, couldn't you feel that this is not a war between two states, but a civil war? You did feel it, didn't you? And doesn't that explain everything? On the one side, free France. Like free Spain. And against it, a gang of bandits leaning on foreign support! Only here the plot was much more diabolic, the whole thing was much more subtly conceived, much more treacherously carried out. In Spain civil war was openly proclaimed. The motives were clearly stated. No false slogans, no false banners! You could take one side or the other. Here they all sail under a false banner. They make it look as though Frenchmen are fighting Germans. Never, never, I'm telling you, would France have lost the war against Germany. We would have beaten them even with our medieval guns. But this was a war of Frenchmen against Frenchmen. And no one told us. . . .'

Hans Habe

Waiting for the Germans: Paris, 12 June

I went first to the Invalides. The only officer I found there said: 'We are expecting them at any moment.' Beneath our feet, the Metro had fallen silent, the buses and taxis were no doubt with the Post Office and the other vehicles on the roads to the south. All traffic had ceased; the police had been withdrawn. I tried to get news from the houses of five or six friends: but the friends and their *concierges* had gone. I left Bordier near the Opera to attend to his business. He would have considerable difficulty in tracing his machines. Then I went home.

The house was empty. On the staircase, I heard a sound of sobbing. Seated on a step, a maidservant was weeping: 'I've been left behind, I've been left behind.' I sat down beside her, patted her on the back and promised to take her away.

. . . . When I got up to leave the house, nothing bound me any longer to the world which had come to an end. And yet, like the little mulatto girl, who had died in my arms ten years before and wanted to take three photographs with her, I looked round for some talisman to take with me. Even though I had conquered hope and desire for possessions, books remained my weakness. I put six in my pockets.

Bordier was waiting for me at a café in the Rue Richer; it seemed to be the only one open for a kilometre around. Two metal merchants were sitting with him. A news-boy gave us the last copy of a half-sized paper; it looked like the newspaper of a besieged city. Two women at the bar were questioning the cashier.

'Where are they?'

'At Saint-Denis.'

'It's all over then?'

'Perhaps it's a trap.'

The panic-stricken had left Paris. Those who remained were on holiday, if somewhat bewildered. From the Boulevards to the Porte de Châtillon, I do not believe we passed a single car. The choice had been made. But for a few pedestrians in the deserted streets all was still.

Emmanuel d'Astier

Paris fell on the 14th.

Britain's Offer of Union with France: 16 June

As the Ambassador and I argued with Reynaud, more acrimoniously than ever, on the subject of the Fleet, the telephone rang. Reynaud took up the receiver. The next moment his eyebrows went up so far they became indistinguishable from his neatly brushed hair; one eyebrow to either side of the parting. 'One moment,' he said, 'I must take it down,' and grasping a sheet of foolscap on the slippery table, he began to write, using a short gold pencil with an enormous lead. He repeated each word as he wrote it, and listening, I became transfixed with amazement. I was so absorbed I did not even look at the Ambassador to see if he shared my feelings. Reynaud was taking down in French from de Gaulle's dictation in London, the text of the Declaration of Union proposed by the British Government. On he wrote in a frightful scrawl, getting more excited as the message unfolded. The paper skidded on the smooth surface of the table. I held it. As each sheet was covered I handed him a fresh one. His pencil gave out. I handed him mine.

Finally he stopped and said into the elephone, 'Does he agree to this? Did Churchill give you this personally?' There was a moment's pause and now he was speaking in English. It was evident that de Gaulle had handed the receiver to Churchill, who was assuring him that the document was a decision of the Cabinet. If there were alterations, they would be merely verbal.

Reynaud put the receiver down. He was transfigured with joy and my old friendship for him surged out in a wave of appreciation at his response, for he was happy with a great happiness in the belief that France would now remain in the war. This was his thought as it was ours, and in those first moments this was all that mattered. The sense of the generosity of the offer was overwhelming, the sincerity of the gesture completely convincing.

I was as moved as when I used to hear at some Battalion Headquarters in Flanders of a great feat of bravery and self-sacrifice. Of a man who, exhausted, wet and tired, struggled back through the mud under heavy fire to rescue a friend. For that was it. Britain, having escaped so far, now turned back to help her stricken comrade, offering to share with her everything she possessed. The one-sided sacrifice of France seemed balanced in a moment by this gesture of absolute solidarity.

The text of the proposed joint declaration was as follows:

> At this most fateful moment in the history of the modern world the Governments of the United Kingdom and the French Republic make this declaration of indissoluble union and unyielding resolution in their common defence of justice and freedom against subjection to a system which reduces mankind to a life of robots and slaves.
>
> The two Governments declare that France and Great Britain shall no longer be two nations, but one Franco-British Union.
>
> The constitution of the Union will provide for joint organs of defence, foreign, financial, and economic policies.
>
> Every citizen of France will enjoy immediately citizenship of Great Britain; every British subject will become a citizen of France.
>
> Both countries will share responsibility for the repair of the devastation of war, wherever it occurs in their territories, and the resources of both shall be equally, and as one, applied to that purpose.
>
> During the war there shall be a single War Cabinet, and all the forces of Britain and France, whether on land, sea, or in the air, will be placed under its direction. It will govern from wherever it best can. The two Parliaments will be formally associated. The nations of the British Empire are already forming new armies. France will keep her available forces in the field, on the sea, and in the air. The Union appeals to the United States to fortify the economic resources of the Allies, and to bring her powerful material aid to the common cause.
>
> The Union will concentrate its whole energy against the power of the enemy, no matter where the battle may be.
>
> And thus we shall conquer.
>
> Major-General Sir Edward Spears

The offer was rejected, and on the 17th the French Government asked the Germans for armistice terms.

General de Gaulle Appeals to the French: 18 June

The leaders who, for many years past, have been at the head of the French armed forces, have set up a Government.

Alleging the defeat of our armies, this Government has entered into negotiations with the enemy with a view to bringing about a cessation of hostilities. It is quite true that we were, and still are, overwhelmed by enemy mechanized forces, both on the ground and in the air. It was the tanks, the planes, and the tactics of the Germans, far more than the fact that we were outnumbered, that forced our armies to retreat. It was the German tanks, planes, and tactics that provided the element of surprise which brought our leaders to their present plight.

But has the last word been said? Must we abandon all hope? Is our defeat final and irremediable? To those questions I answer—No!

Speaking in full knowledge of the facts, I ask you to believe me when I say that the cause of France is not lost. The very factors that brought about our defeat may one day lead us to victory.

For, remember this, France does not stand alone. She is not isolated. Behind her is a vast Empire, and she can make common cause with the British Empire, which commands the seas and is continuing the struggle. Like England, she can draw unreservedly on the immense industrial resources of the United States.

This war is not limited to our unfortunate country. The outcome of the struggle has not been decided by the Battle of France. This is a world war. Mistakes have been made, there have been delays and untold suffering, but the fact remains that there still exists in the world everything we need to crush our enemies some day. To-day we are crushed by the sheer weight of mechanized force hurled against us, but we can still look to a future in which even greater mechanized force will bring us victory. The destiny of the world is at stake.

I, General de Gaulle, now in London, call on all French officers and men who are at present on British soil, or may be in the future, with or without their arms; I call on all engineers and skilled workmen from the armaments factories who are at present on British soil, or may be in the future, to get in touch with me.

Whatever happens, the flame of French resistance must not and shall not die.

De Gaulle

A Letter from General de Gaulle to General Weygand: 20 June

Mon Général,

I have received your order to return to France. I therefore enquired at once about the means of doing so, for my one determination is, of course, to serve as a combatant.

I therefore expect to come and report to you within twenty-four hours if, between now and then, a capitulation has not been signed.

If it should have been, I would join any French resistance which might be organized no matter where. In London, in particular, there are some military elements—and doubtless there will come others—who are resolved to fight, whatever may happen in the Mother Country.

I feel it my duty to tell you quite simply that I wish, for the sake of France and for yours, *mon Général*, that you may be willing and able to escape disaster, reach overseas France and continue the war. There is at present no possible armistice with honour.

I add that my personal relations with the British Government—in particular with Mr. Churchill—could enable me to be useful to you yourself or to any other eminent Frenchman willing to place himself at the head of a continued French resistance.

I beg you to accept, *mon Général*, my most respectful and devoted regards.

De Gaulle

Note.—This letter, sent on to General Weygand by General Lelong, Military Attaché in London, was returned from Vichy to General de Gaulle in

September 1940 with a typed slip which ran as follows: 'If retired Colonel de Gaulle wishes to enter into communication with General Weygand, he should do so through the proper channels.'

The Armistice: 22 June

When in 1918 Germany had asked for an armistice, the question arose for Marshal Foch of the place where the conditions approved by the Allied Governments should be notified to the German plenipotentiaries. Marshal Foch excluded from his choice any town and even any inhabited spot. He wanted to place the conference out of reach of indiscretions, and at the same time to spare an unfortunate adversary from a humiliation, and to avoid any manifestation of hostility towards an enemy who had made himself hated by summary executions and needless destruction. In the centre of the forest of Rethondes, the clearing in which did not then exist, there was a railway siding where the trains of the two delegations could be brought close to each other. This was the spot chosen; it was known only to M. Clemenceau and Marshal Pétain. The secret was well kept. In this way the Germans were spared all contacts or spectacles humiliating to the vanquished. This meeting in 1918 will preserve in history the character of simplicity and dignity inseparable from true greatness.

If talion law led the German Chancellor to choose the same place, the 1940 meeting was organized in a diametrically opposite spirit. In the vast clearing, nothing less than a demonstration had been provided for German vindictiveness. Every sharpening of humiliation had been devised for the one whom the fortune of war had brought low—a crowd, music, cinema, and all the paraphernalia of the taking of a film.

Nothing was spared to the representative of France, not even words to which he had no opportunity to reply. For it was in front of Hitler and in his name that General Keitel read this monument of lying and vainglory, the record of which should be preserved:

> On the strength of the assurances given to the German Reich by President Wilson, and confirmed by the Allied Powers, the German Army laid down its arms in November 1918. So ended a war which the German people and its Government had not wanted, and in the course of which it had not been given to its adversaries, in spite of a crushing superiority, to achieve a decisive victory over the German Army, Navy, or Air Force.
>
> From the moment of the arrival of the German delegation sent to take part in the *pourparlers* for the conclusion of an armistice, there began the violations of the promise solemnly given. It was on 11 November 1918, in this same coach, that there thus began the Calvary of the German people. Every element of dishonour, moral humiliation, and material human sufferings that can be imposed on a people had its origin here. In this way violation of the pledged word and perjury crashed down upon a nation which, after a heroic resistance maintained through four years, had succumbed only through the one weakness of believing in the promises given by democratic statesmen.

On 3 September, 1939—that is to say, twenty-five years after the outbreak of the World War—England and France once more, without any reason, declared war on Germany. The decision at arms has now come.

France is beaten. The French Government has asked the Government of the Reich to make known to it the German conditions for the conclusion of an armistice.

To receive these conditions, the French delegation has been invited to come to the historic forest of Compiègne, and this spot has been chosen to efface once and for all, by an act of justice and reparation, a memory which, for France, was not an honourable page in her history, but which was considered by the German people as the deepest dishonour of all time.

France, after a heroic resistance that showed itself in an uninterrupted succession of sanguinary battles, is beaten and has collapsed. In these circumstances, Germany does not wish to give to the armistice conditions or to the *pourparlers* relating to them such a character as to humiliate so brave an adversary.

The conditions formulated by Germany aim first at preventing the resumption of hostilities, secondly at offering full security to Germany in the war against England imposed on her by this latter, and thirdly at creating the conditions necessary for the establishment of a new peace which would consist essentially in repairing the injustices done to Germany by force. . . .

Maxime Weygand

The War is Over

We really did feel that the war was over now. It looked as if we should not even have to land in England. With our U-boats blocking the sea routes, it seemed as if the British hadn't a dog's chance of getting help from the Empire or America. This meant that eventually they would simply have to throw up the sponge; all we had to do was to send in the Luftwaffe to help them make up their minds.

Lieutenant Baron Tassilo von Bogenhardt

The Truth about the Armoured Forces of the Wehrmacht

Free rein has been given to speculations about the armoured forces which faced each other in the battle.

A similar controversy has arisen about the armoured forces of the enemy. Let us examine the question.

Estimates which our specialist services gave to our Supreme Command on this subject ranged, roughly speaking, from one extreme to another. Gamelin emphasizes the divergence in this sphere between the General Staff of the northeast command and the Intelligence Service. The latter according to Gamelin . . . put the number of Panzers thrown into the fight against us at four thousand. According to the calculations of Georges' General Staff, the Wehrmacht had employed on 10 May between seven thousand and seven thousand five hundred tanks on all its fronts. . . . 'These,' says Major Lyet, . . . 'were divided into from twelve to fourteen armoured divisions, and some fifteen independent regiments or battalions.' But he adds, 'It has often been assumed that the German Army had actually engaged in the western campaign a total of seven thousand to seven thousand five hundred tanks.' Between these two extreme estimates lies that of our own Command of Armoured Forces which, according to Colonel Ferré . . . 'puts the number at about four thousand five hundred or five thousand tanks'.

In the confusion of defeat, imagination has still further magnified these figures. We shall see a figure of ten thousand Panzers constantly quoted by the most authoritative circles without it ever being contested. And Pétain, in his speech to the nation on 25 June 1940, was to appear a realist when he only attributed eleven Panzer divisions to the Wehrmacht.

We now know the truth. General Guderian has told it to us. There could be no better qualified authority. On the eve of the war, Guderian, in actual fact, was Inspector-General of Armoured Forces to the German Army. It was he who, during the campaign, was to be entrusted with the decisive movement, namely, the forcing of the Meuse at Sedan. Guderian states that the forces thrown in against us comprised ten Panzer divisions and six motorized. The Panzer divisions had a total number in each ranging from two hundred and fifteen to three hundred and twenty-four tanks, and not four hundred to five hundred as was estimated in 1940 by our experts. The number of Panzers came, therefore, to 3,003 at the most. To this figure must be added 848 heavy armoured cars. Thus there was a grand total of 3,851 vehicles, of which a certain number took no part in the battle. Colonel Ferré writes: . . . 'Guderian gives a definitive figure of two thousand eight hundred tanks and seven hundred armoured cars. Major Lyet estimates . . . for his part that the total was three thousand. A figure,' he adds, 'slightly higher than that of the Franco-British forces.'

'Thus,' writes Gamelin, 'is exploded the myth of a crushing German superiority in tanks.'

Is it not now a convenient time to recall once again that, materially speaking, it was not the number of vehicles but their organization, as I had emphasized so often to the Chamber, which was the decisive factor? A collection of tanks was not, I was never tired of explaining, an armoured division. The German Army had an *armoured corps*. We had not.

Did we not see our leaders, opposed to the massive use of armoured forces, deny that these contained a danger in an assault against a continuous front? When, on the morrow of the Polish campaign, General Billotte and Colonel de Gaulle each in his turn recommended, because we were lacking armoured divisions, the integration of infantry escort tanks as armoured divisions, our Supreme Command would not listen to their proposal. It is true that this proposal would have been of no avail unless we could have been certain that the enemy would give us the necessary respite to establish the divisions, whose creation was proposed. In actual fact there could have been no question of 'improvising' armoured divisions.

On this subject we also have the opinion of General Bruneau, who, as we have seen, led 1 Armoured Division into battle, the only division which, as we have also seen, was capable of standing up to the Panzer divisions. He gave his opinion to the Committee of Inquiry in his deposition, cited above of 6 July 1948. To one member who asked him if it were 'technically possible' to form divisions out of battalions of escort tanks, General Bruneau replied, 'No; a large armoured unit cannot be improvised.'

Paul Reynaud

Vichy

It has often been charged and it is altogether likely that Pétain and others were so ready to make peace partly because they feared that the country would lapse into Communism if the unequal struggle continued, and partly because they thought that defeat would perhaps be bought not too dearly if France could be saved from herself and remade along more godly lines. Granted the hopelessness of the military situation, their thoughts turned quickly to the opportunity for a national revolution. There was more than a bit of sheer fatalism in their acceptance of defeat.

Bullitt* spoke to most of these leaders within a week of the signing of the armistice. His report of 1 July is one of the most remarkable and revealing documents in the entire annals of this great war. Nothing but direct quotation will give anything like the flavour of his comments:

'The impression which emerges from these conversations is the extraordinary one, that the French leaders desire to cut loose from all that France has represented during the past two generations, that their physical and moral defeat has been so absolute that they have accepted completely for France the fate of becoming a province of Nazi Germany. Moreover, in order that they may have as many companions in misery as possible they hope that England will be rapidly and completely defeated by Germany and that the Italians will suffer the same fate. Their hope is that France may become Germany's favourite province—a new 'Gau' which will develop into a new Gaul. . . .'

Marshal Pétain told the ambassador in so many words that Germany would attempt to reduce France to the status of a province by securing complete control and by enforcing military impotence. He was extremely bitter about the politicians and insisted that the government of France must be radically altered.

'In his opinion one of the chief causes for the collapse of the French Army was that the reserve officers who had been educated by school teachers who were Socialists and not patriots had deserted their men and shown no fighting spirit whatsoever. . . .'

Darlan sounded the same note. He too was convinced that Hitler would unite all Europe in a customs union and make France his leading vassal state: 'France could do nothing but accept such a position for the moment.' The fault had all been with the political regime: 'The entire system of parliamentary government in France had been rotten and the high commander of the army [i.e. Gamelin] had proved to be equally rotten.' Chautemps, one of the leaders of the Radical Socialist Party, chimed in and remarked quite frankly to Bullitt, 'Pétain, Weygand and Laval intend to abolish the present French Constitution and to introduce a semi-dictatorial state in which Parliament would play a small

---

* United States Ambassador to France (Ed.)

role.' Pétain would be the Hindenburg of the new regime, and Laval the Hitler. 'Pétain, Weygand and Laval,' concluded the ambassador, 'all believe that if a dictatorship of this kind should be introduced in France before the peace, France would obtain much better terms than could be obtained under a parliamentary regime.'[*]

The concluding remark of Bullitt's report raises a consideration that is absolutely fundamental to an understanding of all that happened in the sequel. It must be remembered that Pétain and his followers looked upon the defeat of France as merely the prelude to the collapse of the entire resistance to Hitler and the Nazis. We know that the Führer at the time shared this view. The armistice terms as we know them betray a hastily drawn document—a document full of provisional arrangements and half-settlements that was intended only to tide over the situation until a definitive peace treaty could be drawn. We need not analyse it in detail to demonstrate the point. What is important here is the thought on the part of the French defeatists that if they at once recognized their failure and dropped out of the struggle, the whole sad business would be over so much the sooner and they might, by accepting Hitler, curry favour with him and figure in the new Nazi Europe as Germany's preferred province. Pétain and his friends saw in France's misfortune a golden opportunity to effect the national revolution and calculated that if France could be remade in the Nazi image, the conqueror would be more lenient in the terms he would finally impose. Recalling the fact that Britain was given only three weeks or a month before her day of doom, it is clear that haste was indicated. Actually the new France emerged less than three weeks after the signature of the armistice.

William L. Langer

THE TRAGEDY OF THE FRENCH FLEET

Winston Churchill Speaks to the House of Commons: 4 July

I said last week that we must now look with particular attention to our own salvation. I have never in my experience seen discussed in a Cabinet so grim and sombre a question as what we were to do about the French Fleet. It shows how strong were the reasons for the course which we thought it our duty to take, that every Member of the Cabinet had the same conviction about what should be done and there was not the slightest hesitation or divergence among them, and that the three Service Ministers, as well as men like the Minister of Information[†] and the Secretary of State for the Colonies, particularly noted for their long friendship with France, when they were consulted were equally convinced that no other decision than that which we took was possible. We took that decision, and it was a decision to which, with aching hearts but with clear vision, we unitedly came. Accordingly early yesterday morning, 3 July, after all preparations had been made, we took the greater part of the French Fleet under our control, or else called upon them, with adequate force, to comply with our requirements. Two battleships, two light cruisers, some submarines, including a very large one, the *Surcouf*, eight destroyers and approximately two hundred smaller but extremely useful minesweeping and anti-submarine craft which lay,

---

[*] Tel.(1 July, 1940) from Bullitt, at La Bourboule.   [†] Mr. Duff Cooper.

for the most part at Portsmouth and Plymouth, though there were some at Sheerness, were boarded by superior forces, after brief notice had been given wherever possible to their captains.

This operation was successfully carried out without resistance or bloodshed except in one instance. A scuffle arose through a misunderstanding in the submarine *Surcouf*, in which one British leading seaman was killed and two British officers and one rating wounded and one French officer killed and one wounded. For the rest, the French sailors, in the main, cheerfully accepted the end of a period of uncertainty.

Now I turn to the Mediterranean. At Alexandria, where a strong British battle fleet is lying, there are besides a French battleship, four French cruisers, three of them modern 8-inch gun vessels, and a number of smaller ships. These have been informed that they cannot be permitted to leave harbour and thus fall within the power of the German conquerors of France. Negotiations and discussions, with the details of which I need not trouble the House, have necessarily been taking place, and measures have now been taken to ensure that those ships, which are commanded by a very gallant Admiral, shall be sunk or otherwise made to comply with our wishes. . . .

But the most serious part of the story remains. Two of the finest vessels of the French Fleet, the *Dunkerque* and the *Strasbourg*, modern battle-cruisers much superior to *Scharnhorst* and *Gneisenau*—and built for the purpose of being superior to them—lay with two battleships, several light cruisers and a number of destroyers and submarines and other vessels at Oran and at its adjacent military port of Mers-el-Kebir on the northern African shore of Morocco. Yesterday morning, a carefully chosen British officer, Captain Holland, late Naval Attaché in Paris, was sent on in a destroyer and waited upon the French Admiral Gensoul. After being refused an interview, he presented the following document, which I will read to the House. The first two paragraphs of the document deal with the general question of the armistice, which I have already explained in my own words. The fourth paragraph begins as follows: This is the operative paragraph:

It is impossible for us, your comrades up to now, to allow your fine ships to fall into the power of the German or Italian enemy. We are determined to fight on to the end, and if we win, as we think we shall, we shall never forget that France was our ally, that our interests are the same as hers and that our common enemy is Germany. Should we conquer, we solemnly declare that we shall restore the greatness and territory of France. For this purpose, we must make sure that the best ships of the French Navy are not used against us by the common foe. In these circumstances, His Majesty's Government have instructed me—[that is, the British Admiral]—to demand that the French Fleet now at Mers-el-Kebir and Oran shall act in accordance with one of the following alternatives:

(*a*) Sail with us and continue to fight for victory against the Germans and Italians.

(*b*) Sail with reduced crews under our control to a British port. The reduced crews will be repatriated at the earliest moment.

If either of these courses is adopted by you, we will restore your ships to France at the conclusion of the war or pay full compensation, if they are damaged meanwhile.

(*c*) Alternatively, if you feel bound to stipulate that your ships should not be used against the Germans or Italians unless these break the Armistice, then sail them with us with reduced crews, to some French port in the West Indies, Martinique, for instance, where they can be demilitarized to our satisfaction or be perhaps entrusted to the United States and remain safe until the end of the war, the crews being repatriated.

If you refuse these fair offers, I must, with profound regret, require you to sink your ships within six hours.

Finally, failing the above, I have the orders of His Majesty's Government to use whatever force may be necessary to prevent your ships from falling into German or Italian hands.

We had hoped that one or other of the alternatives which we presented would have been accepted, without the necessity of using the terrible force of a British battle squadron. Such a squadron arrived before Oran two hours after Captain Holland and his destroyer. This battle squadron was commanded by Vice-Admiral Somerville, an officer who distinguished himself lately in the bringing-off of over a hundred thousand Frenchmen during the evacuation from Dunkirk. Admiral Somerville was further provided, besides his battleships, with a cruiser force and strong flotillas. All day the parleys continued, and we hoped until the afternoon that our terms would be accepted without bloodshed. However, no doubt in obedience to the orders dictated by the Germans from Wiesbaden, where the Franco-German Armistice Commission is in session, Admiral Gensoul refused to comply and announced his intention of fighting. Admiral Somerville was, therefore, ordered to complete his mission before darkness fell, and at 5:53 p.m. he opened fire upon this powerful French Fleet, which was also protected by its shore batteries. At 6 p.m. he reported that he was heavily engaged. The action lasted for some ten minutes and was followed by heavy attacks from our naval aircraft, carried in the *Ark Royal*. At 7.20 p.m. Admiral Somerville forwarded a further report, which stated that a battle-cruiser of the *Strasbourg* class was damaged and ashore; that a battleship of the *Bretagne* class had been sunk, that another of the same class had been heavily damaged, and that two French destroyers and a seaplane carrier, *Commandant Teste*, were also sunk or burned.

While this melancholy action was being fought either the battle-cruiser *Strasbourg* or the *Dunkerque*, one or the other, managed to slip out of harbour in a gallant effort to reach Toulon or a North African port and place herself under German control, in accordance with the Armistice terms of the Bordeaux Government—though all this her crew and captain may not have realized. She was pursued by aircraft of the Fleet Air Arm and hit by at least one torpedo. She may have been joined by other French vessels from Algiers, which were well placed to do so and to reach Toulon before we would overtake them. She will, at any rate, be out of action for many months to come.

I need hardly say that the French ships were fought, albeit in this unnatural cause, with the characteristic courage of the French Navy, and every allowance must be made for Admiral Gensoul and his officers who felt themselves obliged to obey the orders they received from their Government and could not look behind that Government to see the German dictation. I fear the loss of life among the French and in the harbour must have been very heavy, as we were compelled to use a severe measure of force and several immense explosions were heard. None of the British ships taking part in the action was in any way affected in gun-power or mobility by the heavy fire directed upon them. I have not yet received any reports of our casualties, but Admiral Somerville's fleet is, in all military respects, intact and ready for further action. . . .

A large proportion of the French Fleet has, therefore, passed into our hands or has been put out of action or otherwise withheld from Germany by yesterday's events. The House will not expect me to say anything about other French ships which are at large except that it is our inflexible resolve to do everything that is possible in order to prevent them falling into the German grip. I leave the judgment of our action, with confidence, to Parliament. I leave it to the nation, and I leave it to the United States. I leave it to the world and history.

Winston Churchill

7

THE BATTLE OF BRITAIN

The Germans were now confronted with the problem of invading Britain in the face of British naval supremacy and air cover in the Channel. The Luftwaffe was the weapon upon which the Germans relied to cow the British so that they would throw in their hand, or soften them so that a cross-Channel invasion would become easy. The Battle of Britain was therefore an air battle, with enormous consequences depending upon it. It fell into three stages, beginning on 10 July. The first and second involved the Luftwaffe's attempt to destroy British fighter strength, first by attacks on ports and coastal shipping and then by concentrated assaults on airfields. Following the failure of this plan, the Luftwaffe finally turned on the cities.

Meanwhile, in the face of his country's official state of neutrality and almost every American's dislike of involvement with any of the belligerents, President Roosevelt began his long battle to convince his people that the defence of Britain was a part of the defence of the United States and everything it stood for, and also began to do whatever could legally be done to help.

'WE SHALL NEVER SURRENDER'

TURNING once again, and this time more generally, to the question of invasion, I would observe that there has never been a period in all these long centuries of which we boast when an absolute guarantee against invasion, still less against serious raids, could have been given to our people. In the days of Napoleon the same wind which would have carried his transports across the Channel might have driven away the blockading fleet. There was always the chance, and it is that chance which has excited and befooled the imaginations of many Continental tyrants. Many are the tales that are told. We are assured that novel methods will be adopted, and when we see the originality of malice, the ingenuity of aggression, which our enemy displays, we may certainly prepare ourselves for every kind of novel stratagem and every kind of brutal and treacherous manœuvre. I think that no idea is so outlandish that it should not be considered and viewed with a searching, but at the same time, I hope, with a steady eye. We must never forget the solid assurances of sea-power and those which belong to air-power if it can be locally exercised.

I have, myself, full confidence that if all do their duty, if nothing is neglected, and if the best arrangements are made, as they are being made, we shall prove ourselves once again able to defend our island home, to ride out the storm of war, and to outlive the menace of tyranny, if necessary for years, if necessary alone. At any rate, that is what we are going to try to do. That is the resolve of His Majesty's Government—every man of them. That is the will of Parliament and the nation. The British Empire and the French Republic, linked together in their cause and in their need, will defend to the death their native soil, aiding each other like good comrades to the utmost of their strength. Even though large tracts of Europe and many old and famous states have fallen or may fall into the grip of the Gestapo and all the odious apparatus of Nazi rule, we shall not flag or fail. We shall go on to the end, we shall fight in France, we shall fight on the seas and oceans, we shall fight with growing confidence and growing strength in the air, we shall defend our island, whatever the cost may be, we shall fight ôn the beaches, we shall fight on the landing grounds, we shall fight in the fields and in the streets, we shall fight in the hills; we shall never surrender, and even if, which I do not for a moment believe, this island or a large part of it were subjugated and starving, then our Empire beyond the seas, armed and guarded by the British Fleet, would carry on the struggle, until, in God's good time, the new world, with all its power and might, steps forth to the rescue and the liberation of the old.

Winston Churchill, 4 June 1940

AMERICA'S REPLY

When the second World War started the defences of the United States consisted primarily of a scrap of paper called the Neutrality Law, which the Congress had passed and which President Roosevelt had signed 'with reluctance'. That piece of legislation, passed originally in 1936, was carefully designed to prevent us from getting into war in 1917. It was purely retroactive, as though its framers believed that it would restore life to the brave men who had died at Château Thierry and in the Argonne. It was born of the belief that we could legislate ourselves out of the war, as we had once legislated ourselves out of the saloons (and into the speakeasies).

Harry L. Hopkins

In our American unity, we will pursue two obvious and simultaneous courses; we will extend to the opponents of force the material resources of this nation; and, at the same time, we will harness and speed up the use of those resources in order that we ourselves in the Americas may have equipment and training equal to the task of any emergency and every defence.

President Roosevelt, 10 June

The President had scraped the bottom of the barrel in American arsenals for half a million rifles, eighty thousand machine-guns, a hundred and thirty million rounds of ammunition, nine hundred 75 mm. guns and a million shells, as well as some bombs, T.N.T., and smokeless powder, all to be shipped to Britain. This was done by means of more legal manipulation in a 'damn the torpedoes' spirit. It was done at a moment when many men close to the White House were shouting almost hysterically that this represented suicide for Roosevelt and quite possibly for the nation—that Britain was finished and that all this material would merely fall into the hands of Hitler, who would turn it against us in our own relatively defenceless state. But it was done, and it was of inestimable value to Britain in her hour of greatest need.

Harry L. Hopkins

BEFORE THE BATTLE

. . . . I see only one sure way through now, to wit, that Hitler should attack this country, and in so doing break his air weapon. If this happens he will be left to face the winter with Europe writhing under his heel, and probably with the United States against him after the Presidential Election is over.

Winston Churchill to General Smuts, 9 June

Armed Forces Supreme Headquarters was located near our airfield, and I took advantage of this fact to visit one or two old friends now serving on Hitler's staff, including Colonel-General Keitel, who had once been my commanding officer, and Captain von Below, who had served under me in the old days and was now Hitler's air adjutant. Both these officers were convinced that England was prepared to sue for peace, and that the war was as good as finished.

Nevertheless, despite this wave of optimism in high places, the Air Force was ordered to make good its relatively light casualties in crews and machines and to prepare for the next battles which must be fought over the Channel and in the English skies. Within a few days the German Air Force was ready.

Werner Kreipe, General of the Luftwaffe

'Their Finest Hour'

What General Weygand called the Battle of France is over. I expect that the Battle of Britain is about to begin. Upon this battle depends the survival of Christian civilization. Upon it depends our own British life, and the long continuity of our institutions and our Empire. The whole fury and might of the enemy must very soon be turned on us. Hitler knows that he will have to break us in this island or lose the war. If we can stand up to him, all Europe may be free and the life of the world may move forward into broad, sunlit uplands. But if we fail, then the whole world, including the United States, including all that we have known and cared for, will sink into the abyss of a new dark age made more sinister, and perhaps more protracted, by the lights of perverted science. Let us therefore brace ourselves to our duties, and so bear ourselves that, if the British Empire and its Commonwealth last for a thousand years, men will say, 'This was their finest hour'.

Winston Churchill, 18 June

Hitler Addresses the Reichstag: 19 July

In this hour I feel it to be my duty before my own conscience to appeal once more to reason and common sense in Great Britain as much as elsewhere. I consider myself in a position to make this appeal, since I am not a vanquished foe begging favours, but the victor, speaking in the name of reason. I can see no reason why this war need go on. I am grieved to think of the sacrifices it must claim. . . . Possibly Mr. Churchill will brush aside this statement of mine by saying it is merely born of fear and doubt of final victory. In that case I shall have relieved my conscience in regard to the things to come.

Adolf Hitler

. . . During the evening I waited impatiently for the speech of Lord Halifax which was to be delivered at 9.0 p.m. At ten I received a telephone message to the effect that the British Government had rejected any negotiation with Germany, and had taken up the challenge. The Anglo-German war is about to begin, and if the Germans do not master England this autumn they will have lost the war.

Paul Baudouin, French Foreign Minister, 22 July

The air war will start now, and will determine our ultimate relative strength. If the results of the air war are not satisfactory, [invasion] preparations will be stopped. But if we gain the impression that the English are being crushed and that the air war is, after a certain time, taking effect, then we shall attack. An attempt must be made to prepare the operation for 15 September 1940.

Adolf Hitler, 31 July

Directive No. 17: 1 August

In order to establish the preliminary conditions required for the final conquest of Britain . . . I intend to continue the air and naval war against metropolitan Britain more intensively than heretofore. . . . The German Air Force will use all available means to destroy the British Air Force as soon as possible. Attacks will be directed primarily against the flying units, ground organization, and supply installations of the Royal Air Force, and, further, against the air armaments industry, including factories producing anti-aircraft equipment.

Adolf Hitler

The Antagonists: 10 August

. . . . The Luftwaffe had marked numerical superiority. While the Royal Air Force could put six to seven hundred fighters into the air, the serviceable aircraft of *Luftflotten* 2 and 3 consisted of 929 fighters,* 875 long-range bombers, and 316 dive-bombers: *Luftflotte* 5 disposed of thirty-four twin-engined fighters and 123 long-range bombers.

THE BATTLE

The Luftwaffe

. . . Over the Thames Estuary we got involved in a heavy scrap with Spitfires, which were screening a convoy. Together with the Staff Flight, I selected one formation as our prey, and we made a surprise attack from a favourably higher altitude. I glued myself to the tail of the plane flying outside on the left flank and when, during a right-handed turn, I managed to get in a long burst, the Spitfire went down almost vertically. I followed it until the cockpit cover came flying towards me and the pilot baled out, then followed him down until he crashed into the water. His parachute had failed to open.

* 277 of these were twin-engined fighters or fighter-bombers.

The modern Vickers Supermarine Spitfires were slower than our planes by about ten to fifteen m.p.h., but could perform steeper and tighter turns. The older Hawker Hurricane, which was at that time still frequently used by the British, compared badly with our Messerschmitt 109 as regards speed and rate of climb. Our armament and ammunition were also undoubtedly better. Another advantage was that our engines had injection pumps instead of the carburettors used by the British, and therefore did not conk out through lack of acceleration in critical moments during combat. The British fighters usually tried to shake off pursuit by a half-roll or half-roll on top of a loop, while we simply went straight for them, with wide-open throttle and eyes bulging out of their sockets.

During this first action we lost two aircraft. That was bad, although at the same time we had three confirmed kills. We were no longer in doubt that the R.A.F. would prove a most formidable opponent.

Colonel Adolf Galland, Luftwaffe

The Royal Air Force

. . . . I climbed into the cockpit of my plane and felt an empty sensation of suspense in the pit of my stomach. For one second time seemed to stand still and I stared blankly in front of me. I knew that that morning I was to kill for the first time. That I might be killed or in any way injured did not occur to me. Later, when we were losing pilots regularly, I did consider it in an abstract way when on the ground; but once in the air, never. I knew it could not happen to me. I suppose every pilot knows that, knows it cannot happen to him; even when he is taking off for the last time, when he will not return, he knows that he cannot be killed. I wondered idly what he was like, this man I would kill. Was he young, was he fat, would he die with the Führer's name on his lips, or would he die alone, in that last moment conscious of himself as a man? I would never know. Then I was being strapped in, my mind automatically checking the controls, and we were off. We ran into them at eighteen thousand feet, twenty yellow-nosed Messerschmitt 109s, about five hundred feet above us. Our Squadron strength was eight, and as they came down on us we went into line astern and turned head on to them. Brian Carbury, who was leading the section, dropped the nose of his machine, and I could almost feel the leading Nazi pilot push forward on his stick to bring his guns to bear. At the same moment Brian hauled hard back on his own control stick and led us over them in a steep climbing turn to the left. In two vital seconds they lost their advantage. I saw Brian let go a burst of fire at the leading plane, saw the pilot put his machine into a half roll, and knew that he was mine. Automatically, I kicked the rudder to the left to get him at right angles, turned the gun-button to 'Fire', and let go in a four-second burst with full deflection. He came right through my sights and I saw the tracer from all eight guns thud home. For a second he seemed to hang motionless; then a jet of red flame shot upwards and he spun out of sight.

For the next few minutes I was too busy looking after myself to think of anything, but when, after a short while, they turned and made off over the Channel, and we were ordered to our base, my mind began to work again.

It had happened.

My first emotion was one of satisfaction, satisfaction at a job adequately done, at the final logical conclusion of months of specialized training. And then I had a feeling of the essential rightness of all. He was dead and I was alive; it could so easily have been the other way round; and that would somehow have been right too. I realized in that moment just how lucky a fighter pilot is. He has none of the personalized emotions of the soldier, handed a rifle and bayonet and told to charge. He does not even have to share the dangerous emotions of the bomber pilot who night after night must experience that childhood longing for smashing things. The fighter pilot's emotions are those of the duellist—cool, precise, impersonal. He is privileged to kill well. For if one must either kill or be killed, as now one must, it should, I feel, be done with dignity. Death should be given the setting it deserves; it should never be a pettiness; and for the fighter pilot it never can be.

Richard Hillary

Throughout it all the radio is never silent—shouts, oaths, exhortations and terse commands. You single out an opponent. Jockey for position. All clear behind! The bullets from your eight guns go pumping into his belly. He begins to smoke. But the wicked tracer sparkles and flashes over the top of your own cockpit and you break into a tight turn. Now you have two enemies. The 109 on your tail and your remorseless, ever-present opponent 'G', the force of gravity. Over your shoulder you can still see the ugly, questing snout of the 109. You tighten the turn. The Spit protests and shudders, and when the blood drains from your eyes you 'grey-out'. But you keep turning, for life itself is the stake. And now your blood feels like molten lead and runs from head to legs. You black out! And you ease the turn to recover in a grey, unreal world of spinning horizons. Cautiously you climb into the sun. You have lost too much height and your opponent has gone—disappeared. You are completely alone in your own bit of sky, bounded by the blue vault above and the coloured drapery of earth below.

'Johnnie' Johnson

We made a dash for our machines and within two minutes were off the ground. Twice we circled the aerodrome to allow all twelve planes to get in formation. We were flying in four sections of three: Red Section leading, Blue and Green to right and left, and the three remaining planes forming a guard section above and behind us.

I was flying No. 2 in the Blue Section.

Over the radio came the voice of the controller, 'Hullo, Red Leader', followed by instructions on course and height.

As always, for the first few minutes we flew on the reciprocal of the course given until we reached fifteen thousand feet. We then turned about and flew on 110° in an all-out climb, thus coming out of the sun and gaining height all the way.

During the climb Uncle George was in constant touch with the ground. We were to intercept about twenty enemy fighters at twenty-five thousand feet. I glanced across at Stapme and saw his mouth moving. That meant he was singing again. He would sometimes do this with his radio set on 'Send', with the result that, mingled with our instructions from the ground, we would hear a raucous rendering of *Night and Day*. And then quite clearly over the radio I heard the Germans excitedly calling to each other. This was a not infrequent occurrence and it made one feel that they were right behind, although often they were some distance away. I switched my set to 'Send' and called out *'Halts Maul!'* and as many other choice pieces of German invective as I could remember. To my delight I heard one of them answer, 'You feelthy Englishmen, we will teach you how to speak to a German.' I am aware that this sounds a tall story, but several others in the Squadron were listening out and heard the whole thing.

I looked down. It was a completely cloudless sky and way below lay the English countryside, stretching lazily into the distance, a quite extraordinary picture of green and purple in the setting sun.

I took a glance at my altimeter. We were at twenty-eight thousand feet. At that moment Sheep yelled 'Tally-ho' and dropped down in front of Uncle George in a slow dive in the direction of the approaching planes. Uncle George saw them at once.

'O.K. Line astern.'

I drew in behind Stapme and took a look at them. They were about two thousand feet below us, which was a pleasant change, but they must have spotted us at the same moment, for they were forming a protective circle, one behind the other, which is a defence formation hard to break.

'Echelon starboard,' came Uncle George's voice.

We spread out fanwise to the right.

'Going down!'

One after the other we peeled off in a power dive. I picked out one machine and switched my gun-button to 'Fire'. At three hundred yards I had him in my sights. At two hundred I opened up in a long four-second burst and saw the tracer going into his nose. Then I was pulling out, so hard that I could feel my eyes dropping through my neck. Coming round in a slow climbing turn, I saw that we had broken them up. The sky was now a mass of individual dog-fights. Several of them had already been knocked down. One I hoped was mine, but on pulling up I had not been able to see the result. To my left I saw Peter Pease make a head-on attack on a Messerschmitt. They were headed straight for each other and it looked as though the fire of both was striking home. Then at the last moment the Messerschmitt pulled up, taking Peter's fire full in the belly. It rolled on to its back, yellow flames pouring from the cockpit, and vanished.

Richard Hillary

Attack on an Advanced Fighter Aerodrome: August

After about a week of Hornchurch, I woke late one morning to the noise of machines running up on the aerodrome. It irritated me: I had a headache.

Having been on every flight the previous day, the morning was mine to do with as I pleased. I got up slowly, gazed dispassionately at my tongue in the mirror, and wandered over to the Mess for breakfast. It must have been getting on for twelve o'clock when I came out on to the aerodrome to find the usual

August heat haze forming a dull pall over everything. I started to walk across the aerodrome to the Dispersal Point on the far side. There were only two machines on the ground so I concluded that the Squadron was already up. Then I heard a shout, and our ground crew drew up in a lorry beside me. Sergeant Ross leaned out:

'Want a lift, sir? We're going round.'

'No, thanks, Sergeant. I'm going to cut across.'

This was forbidden for obvious reasons, but I felt like that.

'O.K., sir. See you round there.'

The lorry trundled off down the road in a cloud of dust. I walked on across the landing ground. At that moment I heard the emotionless voice of the controller.

'Large enemy bombing formation approaching Hornchurch. All personnel not engaged in active duty take cover immediately.'

I looked up. They were still not visible. At the Dispersal Point I saw Bubble and Pip Cardell make a dash for the shelter. Three Spitfires just landed, turned about and came past me with a roar to take off down-wind. Our lorry was still trundling along the road, maybe half-way round, and seemed suddenly an awfully long way from the Dispersal Point.

I looked up again, and this time I saw them—about a dozen slugs, shining in the bright sun and coming straight on. At the rising scream of the first bomb I instinctively shrugged up my shoulders and ducked my head. Out of the corner of my eye I saw the three Spitfires. One moment they were about twenty feet up in close formation; the next catapulted apart as though on elastic. The leader went over on his back and ploughed along the runway with a rending crash of tearing fabric; Number Two put a wing in and spun round on his air-screw, while the plane on the left was blasted wingless into the next field. I remember thinking stupidly, 'That's the shortest flight he's ever taken,' and then my feet were nearly knocked from under me, my mouth was full of dirt, and Bubble, gesticulating like a madman from the shelter entrance, was yelling, 'Run, you bloody fool, run!' I ran. Suddenly awakened to the lunacy of my behaviour, I covered the distance to that shelter as if impelled by a rocket and shot through the entrance while once again the ground rose up and hit me, and my head smashed hard against one of the pillars. I subsided on a heap of rubble and massaged it.

'Who's here?' I asked, peering through the gloom.

'Cardell and I and three of our ground crew,' said Bubble, 'and, by the Grace of God, you!'

I could see by his mouth that he was still talking, but a sudden concentration of the scream and crump of falling bombs made it impossible to hear him.

The air was thick with dust and the shelter shook and heaved at each explosion, yet somehow held firm. For about three minutes the bedlam continued, and then suddenly ceased. In the utter silence which followed nobody moved. None of us wished to be the first to look on the devastation which we felt must be outside. Then Bubble spoke. 'Praise God!' he said, 'I'm not a civilian. Of all the bloody frightening things I've ever done, sitting in that shelter was the worst. Me for the air from now on!'

It broke the tension and we scrambled out of the entrance. The runways were certainly in something of a mess. Gaping holes and great gobbets of earth were everywhere. Right in front of us a bomb had landed by my Spitfire, covering it with a shower of grit and rubble.

I turned to the aircraftsman standing beside me. 'Will you get hold of Sergeant Ross and tell him to have a crew give her an inspection.'

He jerked his head towards one corner of the aerodrome: 'I think I'd better collect the crew myself, sir. Sergeant Ross won't be doing any more inspections.'

I followed his glance and saw the lorry, the roof about twenty yards away, lying grotesquely on its side. I climbed into the cockpit, and, feeling faintly sick, tested out the switches. Bubble poked his head over the side.

'Let's go over to the Mess and see what's up: all our machines will be landing down at the reserve landing field, anyway.'

I climbed out and walked over to find that the three Spitfire pilots were quite unharmed but for a few superficial scratches, in spite of being machine-gunned by the bombers. 'Operations' was undamaged: no hangar had been touched and the Officers' Mess had two windows broken.

The Station Commander ordered every available man and woman on to the job of repairing the aerodrome surface and by four o'clock there was not a hole to be seen. Several unexploded bombs were marked off, and two lines of yellow flags were laid down to mark the runways. At five o'clock our Squadron, taking off for a 'flap' from the reserve field, landed without incident on its home base. Thus, apart from four men killed in the lorry and a network of holes on the landing surface, there was nothing to show for ten minutes' really accurate bombing from twelve thousand feet, in which several dozen sticks of bombs had been dropped. It was a striking proof of the inefficacy of their attempts to wipe out our advance fighter aerodromes.

Richard Hillary

'Sailor' Malan on Air Strategy

Sailor would never talk freely as did the others. I found him (leaning silently against the pub mantelpiece, a pint of beer in his hand which did him the whole evening) rather difficult to know, and exceedingly uncommunicative. As he had already established a reputation as a killer, and his silent stolidity was so much at variance with the extroversion of the others, I was at some pains to draw him out, and on one occasion devoted a whole evening to doing so.

'Tell me, Sailor, as a matter of technical interest, how exactly do you go about shooting down a bomber?'

After some rumination: 'I try not to now.'

'Whatever do you mean?'

'Well, I think it's a bad thing.'

'Now come, Sailor, I really want to know. Don't trifle with me.'

'I mean it. I think it's a thoroughly bad thing. You see, if you shoot them down they don't get back and no one in Germany is a whit the wiser. So I figure the right thing to do is to let them get back. With a dead rear gunner; a dead navigator, and the pilot coughing his lungs up as he lands . . . I think if you do that it has a better effect on their morale . . . that's what we want to aim at now. Of course, if you just mean to shoot them down, well, what I generally do is . . . knock out port and starboard engines. But, honestly, Doc, the other way is best.'

Hospital Surgeon

The Few

The gratitude of every home in our island, in our Empire, and indeed throughout the world, except in the abodes of the guilty, goes out to the British airmen who, undaunted by odds, unwearied in their constant challenge and mortal danger, are turning the tide of the world war by their prowess and their devotion. Never in the field of human conflict was so much owed by so many to so few.

Winston Churchill, 20 August

THE BLITZ

Hitler had failed to destroy the R.A.F. in the air or on the ground. On 7 September the Blitz began. London was attacked more heavily and persistently than any other city in Britain. The Luftwaffe opened its hostilities in daylight, but by 14 November they had sustained such heavy losses that they switched to night operations and so continued until mid-1941, from which time London and the cities of Britain were generally left in peace until the beginning of the VI raids in the summer of 1944.

The First Days

The barracks of the Middlesex Regiment are built on one of the highest pieces of ground to the north of London: the whole city lies spread out at your feet. I arrived there as a recruit in the middle of August 1940, when the sense of urgency had become almost unbearable. The Middlesex was a machine-gun regiment equipped with the .303 Vickers medium gun. They were specialists and proud of it, and the instructors were extraordinarily able. As a result, a large number of us were bulldozed into mastery of this complicated weapon in an incredibly short time. Perhaps the presence of a flying column in the barracks, ready to move at thirty minutes' notice in the event of invasion, brought home to us the perilous situation in which we and everyone else in Britain found ourselves at that time.

The weather was lovely, and we sweated day after day in our shirtsleeves as we went through the drill of: 'On this spot, in that direction MOUNT GUN!' I remember one day when we were doing a platoon drill, with two D.P. guns and two which did not exist at all. Numbers One and Four were there, but were considered too old to be used in action; Numbers Two and Three were left to the imagination. One of their gunners sat on the ground with legs crossed and hands raised in what he hoped was the required position, to be lashed by a falsetto scream from Sergeant Jacques: 'Number One on Number Two gun, how many times have I told you to get those forefingers correctly under the safety-catch!'

Suddenly we were gaping upwards. The brilliant sky was criss-crossed from horizon to horizon by innumerable vapour-trails. The sight was a completely novel one. We watched, fascinated, and all work stopped. The little silver stars sparkling at the heads of the vapour trails turned east. This display looked so insubstantial and harmless; even beautiful. Then, with a dull roar which made the ground across London shake as one stood upon it, the first sticks of bombs hit the docks. Leisurely, enormous mushrooms of black and brown smoke shot with crimson climbed into the sunlit sky. There they hung and slowly expanded, for there was no wind, and the great fires below fed more smoke into them as the hours passed.

On Friday and Saturday morning the sky grew darker and darker as the oily smoke rose and spread in heavy, immobile columns, shutting out the sun.

At the barracks, drill quickly became monotonous. We had work to do, and we weren't the target. But we couldn't keep our eyes off those sickening, solid columns climbing up like the convolutions of a lazy snake into a torpid sky.

I suppose our masters felt that, although the Battle of Britain had begun, the worst might already be over—I don't know; but they decided to put us recruits in the hat and draw out three for week-end leave. My name came out of the hat first, and I sent a wire to my parents in Sevenoaks to say that I was coming home. My pass was from midday on Saturday, and I got down to the centre of London by Underground. Bombers were coming over at monotonously regular intervals. I walked down to Charing Cross. There was a lot of noise still, and a lot of smoke. As I entered the station the loudspeakers were ordering everyone out because planes were overhead and they were frightened of casualties if the place were hit. I strolled out to the top of that long flight of stone steps down into Villiers Street and sat on the balustrade watching.

Up in the lonely sky there was still one bomber, gleaming silver, and then he dropped a stick just across the Thames from us. Back in the station the loudspeaker announced that the main line was gone and that there wouldn't be any more trains out for hours. Hundreds of people stood around like a flock of sheep which is frightened and can't make up its mind which way to turn. You could see the dead mask of indecision on their faces as they looked about, hoping someone would tell them what to do. I walked out of the station and decided to hitch-hike home. I was lucky; somewhere on the south bank of the river I met a man on a motor-cycle who was going through Blackheath, and he took me on his pillion.

Now we were nearer to the docks. The columns of smoke merged and became a monstrous curtain which blocked the sky; only the billows within it and the sudden shafts of flame which shot up hundreds of feet made one realize that it was a living thing and not just the backdrop of some nightmare opera. There were fire-hoses along the side of the road, climbing over one another like a helping of macaroni, with those sad little fountains spraying out from the leaks, as they always seem to do from all fire-hoses. Every two or three minutes we would pull into the gutter as a fire-bell broke out stridently behind us and an engine in unfamiliar livery tore past at full tilt: chocolate or green or blue, with gold lettering—City of Birmingham Fire Brigade, or Sheffield, or Bournemouth. The feeling was something you had never experienced before—the excitement and dash of fire-engines arriving to help from so far away, and the oily, evil smell of fire and destruction, with its lazy, insolent rhythm.

It looked terrible and hopeless, but there was a kind of *Götterdämmerung* grandeur about it.

I got home in one piece, and my parents welcomed me with a splendid dinner. But that night the *Luftwaffe*, already working round the clock, came again and dropped a stick of bombs straight down our quiet Sevenoaks road. They hit the town centre just by the historic Vine cricket ground with the first bomb. The last but one landed opposite our gate, and the last by the street corner. Apart from the destruction of the town hall, no damage was done, and I wonder why that particular pilot chose that particular target; I suppose he must have seen the main London–Dover railway line and his bomb-aimer let go too soon.

Sunday in Sevenoaks was the same as Sunday throughout Kent, Surrey, Sussex and Essex. The hot summer air throbbed with the steady beat of the engines of bombers which one could not see in the dazzling blue. Then the R.A.F. would arrive; the monotonous drone would be broken by the sudden snarl of a fighter turning at speed, and the vapour trails would start to form in huge circles. I lay on my back in the rose garden and watched the trails forming; as they broadened and dispersed a fresh set would be superimposed upon them. Then, no bigger than a pin's head, a white parachute would open and come down, growing slowly larger; I counted eight in the air at one time.

I had to be back in barracks on the Sunday night, and set off after supper. The twenty-three-mile journey took well over two hours, and no one could tell us what station we would be taken to. When we finally got there, it turned out to be Holborn. I stepped out into the darkness of the street, or what would have been darkness but for the fires; but as I did so a stick whistled down on the other side of the road and I ducked back inside. After a while I knew I had to begin to move. Hanging about in the station shelter wasn't doing me any good, so I started out on foot up Holborn. When I reached Gamages I was turned back: everything was cascaded down into the road as though two landslides had started simultaneously from opposite sides. There was utter silence, except for the crunch and crackle of my own feet treading a carpet of broken glass.

I was told to make a detour, and eventually got to Marble Arch, where I found a taxi. The driver said he would take me to the barracks, but we hadn't been going up the Edgware Road for long when the next wave came in and the stuff began dropping round us all the way to Mill Hill. As I paid him, the driver said, 'If I'd 'a known it was going to be like this, Guv, I'd never 'a taken the fare.' I felt desperately sorry for him as he drove away into the darkness; my bed and a few hours' sleep were only two minutes' walk away, while he had a long drive back to London alone. In those early days the indifference to death and danger which became so characteristic of the civilian was as yet hardly perceptible. I, a recruit of three weeks' standing, already thought of him as a 'civilian'. I hope he made it.

D. F.

Firemen

I signed on at Chelsea as a member of the London Auxiliary Fire Service. The assembled recruits, aided by casual residents of Wellington Square, were already in their shirt-sleeves, revelling in the lovely weather, the healthy occupation, the novelty of digging up municipal territory to fill sandbags, and the opportunity to meet strangers without introduction. Among them I found an attitude of almost incredible optimism. That it should take a war to produce this holiday-camp mood was a reflection of the dullness of people's lives and the prison of class distinction in English society. After months of brooding and preaching on the horrors of war I was astonished to find how little the prospect seemed to dismay people. There were bearded artists who talked of keeping their hands in by joining the Camouflage Corps. There were university graduates 'marking time' till their chance came to join one of the Services. There were middle-aged ladies whose lonely lives had been brightened by the announcement: 'Your Country Needs You.' I felt happy for them. They had little to lose and great energy to give. There were society girls who could hold open the neck of a sandbag with exquisite grace, declaring that this job was more fun than Ascot. One of them—I think she was a minor actress—was so pleased with the perspiring youth who was filling her sandbag that she stagily promised to get him a commission in her uncle's regiment. Then there were old soldiers who had been in 'the last lot'. They would have joined the ranks to-morrow if they had been ten years younger. Their talk was full of words like 'Blighty' and 'Jerry'; and gave me a strange feeling of recognition. I, too, had been through it before, in a score of war books from Raymond to Remarque. Some of the old soldiers were labourers, some cab drivers, some shopkeepers. I noted at once that the 'working class', if franker about their motives for joining National Service, were less public-spirited. Nor were they carried away by the community spirit the hour fostered. Many of them were there because they were out of a job, because they were lonely, or because business was bad. A few confessed that the A.F.S. was an easy alternative to the Army. 'They won't get me in the Kate Karney,' an unemployed truck driver declared. 'My old man was four years a private in the last lot, and he brought me up a pacifist. All the same I don't mind doing my bit.' He, too, seemed happy. Like everybody else, the war had provided him with a short-term object in life. We were in Civil Defence: we were firemen.

London fireman

An American Watches

All the fires were quickly brought under control. That's a common phrase in the morning communiqués. I've seen how it's done; spent a night with the London fire brigade. For three hours after the night attack got going, I shivered in a sandbag crow's-nest atop a tall building near the Thames. It was one of the many fire-observation posts. There was an old gun barrel mounted above a round table marked off like a compass. A stick of incendiaries bounced off roof-tops about three miles away. The observer took a sight on a point where the first one fell, swung his gun-sight along the line of bombs, and took another reading at the end of the line of fire. Then he picked up his telephone and shouted above the half gale that was blowing up there, 'Stick of incendiaries— between 190 and 220—about three miles away.' Five minutes later a German bomber came boring down the river. We could see his exhaust trail like a pale ribbon stretched straight across the sky. Half a mile downstream there were two eruptions and then a third, close together. The first two looked as though some giant had thrown a huge basket of flaming golden oranges high in the air. The third was just a balloon of fire enclosed in black smoke above the house-tops. The observer didn't bother with his gun sight and indicator for that one. Just reached for his night glasses, took one quick look, picked up his telephone, and said, 'Two high explosives and one oil bomb,' and named the street where they had fallen.

There was a small fire going off to our left. Suddenly sparks showered up from it as though someone had punched the middle of a huge camp-fire with a tree trunk. Again the gun sight swung around, the bearing was read, and the report went down the telephone lines: 'There is something in high explosives on that fire at 59.'

There was peace and quiet inside for twenty minutes. Then a shower of incendiaries came down far in the distance. They didn't fall in a line. It looked like flashes from an electric train on a wet night, only the engineer was drunk and driving his train in circles through the streets. One sight at the middle of the flashes and our observer reported laconically, 'Breadbasket at 90—covers a couple of miles.' Half an hour later a string of fire bombs fell right beside the Thames. Their white glare was reflected in the black, lazy water near the banks and faded out in midstream where the moon cut a golden swathe broken only by the arches of famous bridges.

We could see little men shovelling those fire bombs into the river. One burned for a few minutes like a beacon right in the middle of a bridge. Finally those white flames all went out. No one bothers about the white light, it's only when it turns yellow that a real fire has started.

I must have seen well over a hundred fire bombs come down and only three small fires were started. The incendiaries aren't so bad if there is someone there to deal with them, but those oil bombs present more difficulties.

As I watched those white fires flame up and die down, watched the yellow blazes grow dull and disappear, I thought, what a puny effort is this to burn a great city.

Edward Murrow

Incident

The volume of noise shut out all thought, there was no lull, no second in which to breathe and follow carefully the note of an oncoming bomber. It was an orchestra of madmen playing in a cupboard. I thought, 'God! what a stupid waste if I were to die now.' I wished with all my heart that I was down a shelter.

'We'd be better off underground to-night, sir, and no mistake.' It was my taxi-driver speaking.

'Nonsense,' I said. 'We couldn't be drinking this down there,' and I took a long pull at my beer.

I was pushing the glass across the counter for a refill when we heard it coming. The girl in the corner was still laughing and for the first time I heard her soldier speak. 'Shut up!' he said, and the laugh was cut off like the sound track in a movie. Then everyone was diving for the floor. The barmaid (she was of considerable bulk) sank from view with a desperate slowness behind the counter and I flung myself tight up against the other side, my taxi-driver beside me. He still had his glass in his hand and the beer shot across the floor, making a dark stain and setting the sawdust afloat. The soldier too had made for the bar counter and wedged the girl on his inside. One of her shoes had nearly come off. It was an inch from my nose: she had a ladder in her stocking.

My hands were tight-pressed over my ears but the detonation deafened me. The floor rose up and smashed against my face, the swing-door tore off its hinges and crashed over a table, glass splinters flew across the room, and behind the bar every bottle in the place seemed to be breaking. The lights went out, but there was no darkness. An orange glow from across the street shone through the wall and threw everything into a strong relief.

I scrambled unsteadily to my feet and was leaning over the bar to see what had happened to the unfortunate barmaid when a voice said, 'Anyone hurt?' and there was an A.F.S. man shining a torch. At that everyone began to move, but slowly and reluctantly as though coming out of a dream. The girl stood white and shaken in a corner, her arm about her companion, but she was un-hurt and had stopped talking. Only the barmaid failed to get up.

'I think there is someone hurt behind the bar,' I said. The fireman nodded and went out, to return almost immediately with two stretcher-bearers who made a cursory inspection and discovered that she had escaped with no more than a severe cut on the head. They got her on to the stretcher and disappeared.

Together with the man in the A.F.S., the taxi-driver and I found our way out into the street. He turned to us almost apologetically. 'If you have nothing very urgent on hand,' he said, 'I wonder if you'd help here for a bit. You see, it was the house next to you that was hit and there's someone buried in there.'

I turned and looked on a heap of bricks and mortar, wooden beams and doors, and one framed picture, unbroken. It was the first time that I had seen a building newly blasted. Often had I left the flat in the morning and walked up Piccadilly, aware vaguely of the ominously tidy gap between two houses, but further my mind had not gone.

We dug, or rather pushed, pulled, heaved, and strained, I somewhat in-effectually because of my hands*; I don't know for how long, but I suppose for a short enough while. And yet it seemed endless. From time to time I was aware of figures round me: an A.R.P. warden, his face expressionless under a steel helmet; once a soldier swearing savagely in a quiet monotone; and the taxi-driver, his face pouring sweat.

And so we came to the woman. It was her feet that we saw first, and whereas before we had worked doggedly, now we worked with a sort of frenzy, like

* The writer was recovering after being badly injured in action (Ed.)

prospectors at the first glint of gold. She was not quite buried, and through the gap between two beams we could see that she was still alive. We got the child out first. It was passed back carefully and with an odd sort of reverence by the warden, but it was dead. She must have been holding it to her in the bed when the bomb came.

Finally we made a gap wide enough for the bed to be drawn out. The woman who lay there looked middle-aged. She lay on her back and her eyes were closed. Her face, through the dirt and streaked blood, was the face of a thousand working women; her body under the cotton nightdress was heavy. The night-dress was drawn up to her knees and one leg was twisted under her. There was no dignity about that figure.

Around me I heard voices. 'Where's the ambulance?' 'For Christ's sake don't move her!' 'Let her have some air!'

I was at the head of the bed, and looking down into that tired, blood-streaked, work-worn face I had a sense of complete unreality. I took the brandy flask from my hip pocket and held it to her lips. Most of it ran down her chin, but a little flowed between those clenched teeth. She opened her eyes and reached out her arms instinctively for the child. Then she started to weep. Quite soundlessly, and with no sobbing, the tears were running down her cheeks when she lifted her eyes to mine.

'Thank you, sir,' she said, and took my hand in hers. And then, looking at me again, she said after a pause, 'I see they got you too.'

Richard Hillary

Ford began to run. He ran in what he thought was the direction of the noises, along Marlow Square, past the sub-post, deciding (probably wrongly) not to go in and report first, but to go straight for the incident. It did not cross his mind that there would be any difficulty in finding it. Nor did there seem to be. He ran into Gage Street, crossed Royal Walk and the top of James Street, which he glanced down. It touched his consciousness that the outline of its houses—a quarter seen in the blackness—looked unfamiliar. But he thought nothing of that. Now he saw a masked torch, switched on at the far end of Gage Street. In a moment he found Ivy Rawlings standing over a very small crater, just where the street joined the pavement. They used their torches and saw that a couple of cellars were broken in, but the houses seemed undamaged.

'It was quite a small one, then,' Ford said.

A white hat came up—Mr. Strong on his bicycle.

'Come with me to Royal Walk.'

'Is there another incident there?' Ford asked as they walked.

Strong said, 'Considerable damage reported in Royal Walk, but no crater found yet.'

Just then a car came up. Strong said, 'Stay and stop the traffic.' They were just back at the top of James Street. Ford stood about for a bit.

There was no traffic. He began to sense that they were on the fringe of something. He looked down James Street. He could see nothing at all. Surely even to-night one should be able to see the outline of the rows of houses? The darkness down James Street was, he now realized, something yet again. Thick, like rough woollen curtains. You looked into, or on to, total blankness. He felt that something simply wasn't there. (Nor was it.)

He began to walk down James Street. Immediately he was in another world. People were moving about and coming up. He saw that the houses opposite him were very considerably shattered. He looked farther down the street and saw that there were no houses. He became conscious of the smell. The unmistakable, indescribable, incident smell flooded into his nostrils. It is more than a smell really; it is an acute irritation of the nasal passages from the powdered rubble of dissolved houses; it is a raw, brutal smell. He realized that the particular darkness which hung over James Street was due, not to the moonless night, but to the fact that the whole of this area was still covered by an unsettled dust cloud. Here's the incident all right, he thought.

Before he had got opposite to the part of James Street that did not appear to be there, he met Miss Sterling. She pointed at the shattered-looking but still standing houses and said, 'There's a good many people in there.' Mrs. Morley came up, smooth and undisturbed. She said, 'The mobile unit [a sort of medical advance guard consisting of doctor, nurse, and stretcher-bearers] has just gone in there,' pointing to No. 50.

Ford went into this house. The ground- and first-floor rooms were more or less all right—nothing more than blown-out window frames and shattered plaster. But up from the first floor the stairs were ankle deep in rubble. He went up, passing the second-floor rooms. The two top-floor rooms and the top landing were deeply encumbered with debris, rubble, slates and roof timbers. He looked up; there was no roof overhead. There were dark clouds, picked out with momentary sparkles of shell bursts, reflected gun flashes and an uneasy searchlight waving its futility.

In the first room two men of a stretcher party, a nurse and another man were bending over a figure lying on a heap of the plaster rubble. Ford saw that it was an injured man. His breathing was violent and laboured. They seemed to be trying to get something down his throat through some sort of tube. One of the stretcher-bearers saw Ford. Pointing to the back room he said, 'There are two more in there.' Ford looked in, cautiously using his torch, supplementing its metal hood with his hand. This room was wrecked. One side of it was heaped halfway up to the ceiling with debris. Several roof timbers lay across it. Ford began to clamber his way into it. He saw something dark lying at his feet. He put the beam of his torch on it and saw that it was a girl. She lay partly in, partly out of, the heaped-up debris of plaster and brick, her body perhaps a third buried, like a high bas-relief. She lay in a pleasant attitude, one hand curved behind her head, her legs a little pulled up, to form, with her body, a gentle S shape. He had seen that attitude once before, in the little Museum of Prehistory in the Dordogne; a skeleton of a prehistoric girl of the Mousterian Age, from one of the *abri* (they had their *abri* too). Celia had said, 'I never knew that a skeleton could be attractive and elegant; that one's bones may be chic after twenty thousand years.' Here in the top floor back of James Street was the same charming position.

Ford hadn't much doubt that she was dead. She looked so small for one thing; and there was a severe head wound. But he wondered what could have caused fatal injuries. The roof timbers were fairly light and had had only a few feet to fall. With a feeling of intimacy, he took up her unresisting hand and felt for a pulse. To his surprise he felt, or thought he felt, a very feeble beat. He went back to the front room and said, 'Is there a doctor here?' One of the stretcher party said: 'He's a doctor, but he's busy.' He pointed at an oldish man bending over the other casualty. Ford said, 'I think the girl in here is alive. Will you come and see?' The doctor gave no sign of having heard. But after a time he came. He ran a hypodermic into the grey, debris-encrusted flesh of her arm. 'Just in case,' he said. He felt for the pulse, but said, 'Very improbable. Where's the injury?' Ford said, 'Her head, I think.' 'The *head*?' said the doctor, as if astonished. Then he ran his fingers over her skull, under her blood and rubble-matted hair. But he said nothing. Ford said, 'Shall I take her downstairs?' The doctor said, 'No.' So they left her, lying easily on the debris, looking through the roof at the sky.

John Strachey ('Ford')

The bomb was recorded by a telephonist in the Control Centre at 18.35. The message said that there was fire and casualties trapped in Holy Redeemer Church in Upper Cheyne Row. Requests followed in rapid succession for ambulances, blankets to cover the dead, fire services and reports came in that there were many casualties.

The bomb had struck the church at an angle through a window in a most extraordinary way and had penetrated the floor and burst among the shelterers, mostly women and small children. Here George Thorpe, whom we knew as 'Bert,' lost his life with those women and children whom he had visited to reassure them—as he always did, although he was not shelter warden. He knew that they were apt to become nervous and needed moral support in the heavy raids and he used to drop in there to boost up their courage and cheer them up. He had just despatched Jo on duty and gone there when the bomb fell. The bomb exploded right amongst the shelterers. A woman who was in the shelter told me about it when I visited her afterwards in St. Luke's Hospital. She was badly injured and said that the scene resembled a massacre—in fact, she compared it to an engraving she had seen of the massacre of the Cawnpore women and children in the Indian Mutiny, with bodies, limbs, blood and flesh mingled with little hats, coats and shoes and all the small necessities which people took to the shelters with them. She said that people were literally blown to pieces and the mess was appalling. She herself was behind a pillar or buttress which protected her somewhat—and there was a pile of bodies between her and the explosion, for it was still daylight—no one had gone to their bunks.

Jo and Len Lansdell were quickly at the scene, followed by the whole A.R.P. services. They could not get into the crypt at first because the body of a very heavy woman barred the only entrance. The explosion had set fire to the great heaps of coke stored there for heating the church and the smoke from it made it difficult to see. Jo and Len Lansdell immediately set to work with stirrup pumps to try and extinguish it before the whole place became a crematorium. The body of Bert lay there face downwards. Jo, who had spoken to him only a few minutes before the bomb fell, turned him over. She said afterwards that she wished so much that she hadn't, so that she could have remembered him as he had been when he had sent her on duty. His equipment, which was taken back to his Post, was described to me as being bright red with blood—as was everything which had been in that crypt.

The work of the A.R.P. services that night was magnificent—by nine o'clock in the evening the casualties were all extricated and were lain in the grounds of the church with the Home Guard in charge, and wonderful work was done by Dr. Castillo and Fr. Fali of Tarapore. In our F.A.P. we had numbers of casualties again, including some rare and interesting fractures which Dr. Graham Kerr commented on for the instruction of us V.A.Ds. To watch her at work, deft, neat, cheerful and competent, was a lesson in itself.

After a heavy raid with many casualties such as this one there was a task for which we were sometimes detailed from our F.A.P. and to which both our Commandants disliked having to send us. This was to help piece the bodies together in preparation for burial. The bodies—or rather the pieces—were in the mortuaries. It was a grim task and Betty Compton felt that we were too young and inexperienced for such a terrible undertaking—but someone had to do it and we were sent in pairs when it became absolutely necessary. Betty asked me if I would go as I had studied Anatomy at the Slade. The first time I went my partner was a girl I did not know very well called Sheila. It *was* pretty grim, although Mr. Leacock made it all as business-like and rapid as possible. We had somehow to form a body for burial so that the relatives (without seeing it) could imagine that their loved one was more or less intact for that purpose. But it was a very difficult task—there were so many pieces missing and, as one of the mortuary attendants said, 'Proper jigsaw puzzle, ain't it, Miss?' The stench was the worst thing about it—that, and having to realize that these frightful pieces of flesh had once been living, breathing people. We went out to smoke a cigarette when we simply could not go on—and some busybody saw Sheila smoking and reported her for smoking when in uniform and on duty. Betty Compton, who invariably supported her V.A.Ds, was most indignant about this, as indeed she was about us having to perform such a task at all. I thought myself that butchers should have done it.

After the first violent revulsion I set my mind on it as a detached, systematic task. It became a grim and ghastly satisfaction when a body was fairly constructed —but if one was too lavish in making one body almost whole, then another one would have sad gaps. There were always odd members which did not seem to fit and there were too many legs. Unless we kept a very firm grip on ourselves nausea was inevitable. The only way for me to stand it was to imagine that I was back in the anatomy class again—but there the legs and arms on which we studied muscles had been carefully preserved in spirit and were difficult to associate with the human body at all. I think that this task dispelled for me the idea that human life is valuable—it could be blown to pieces by blast just as dust was blown by wind. The wardens had to gather up pieces after a bad raid—they had no choice, and someone had to assemble them into shrouds for Christian burial, but it seemed monstrous that these human beings had been reduced to this revolting indignity by so-called Christians, and that we were doing the same in Germany and other countries. The feeling uppermost in my mind after every big raid was *anger*, anger at the lengths to which humans could go to inflict injury to one another.

. . . . About twenty past eleven we decided to settle down and read for a time. Neither of us felt like going to bed—it was far too noisy and exciting. A warden raced by shouting, and suddenly we heard a shout of *'lights, lights'* from the street. Richard wondered if the recent near explosion had caused the black-out curtains to shift in the studio and he said: 'I'll run up and have a look.'

He had scarcely gone when the lights all went out. There was a strange quiet—a dead hush, and prickles of terror went up my spine as a rustling, crackling, endless sound as of ripping, tearing paper began. I did not know what it was, and I screamed to Richard, *'Come down, come down!'* Before I could hear whether or not he was coming down the stairs, things began to drop—great masses fell—great crashes sounded all round me. I had flung myself down by the bed, hiding Vicki under my stomach, trying thus to save her and the coming baby from harm. I buried my face in the eiderdown of the bed as the rain of debris went on falling for what seemed ages . . . ages. . . . The bed was covered and so was I—I could scarcely breathe—things fell all round my head—some of it almost choked me as the stuff, whatever it was, reached my neck and my mouth.

At last there was a comparative silence and with great difficulty I raised my head and shook it free of heavy choking dusty stuff. An arm had fallen round my neck—a warm living arm—and for one moment I thought that Richard had entered in the darkness and was holding me, but when very, very cautiously I raised my hand to it, I found that it was a woman's bare arm with two rings on the third finger and it stopped short in a sticky mess. I shook myself free of it. Vicki, who had behaved absolutely perfectly, keeping so still that she could have been dead, became excited now as she smelt blood. I screamed again, *'Richard, Richard,'* and to my astonishment he answered quite near me. 'Where are you?' I cried—more things had begun falling. 'At the bottom of the stairs,' he said. 'Keep there. Keep still—there are more things falling,' I cried and buried my head again as more debris fell all round me. At last it appeared to have stopped. I raised my head again—I could see the sky and the searchlights and I knew that the whole of the three upper stories of the house had gone. 'We've been hit,' I said. *'One in a million!'*—and the only feeling I was conscious of was furious anger.

It was pitch dark—too dangerous to move without some idea of what the position was. I had had my torch in my hand but the blast had thrown it from me—'Light a match,' I said. He lit several matches, standing, as I saw by their light, in the entrance of the room. There were no ceilings, nothing above me as I crouched there. The front of the room had blown out—but the wall nearest to the one where I was crouching, the ferro-concrete one, was still there, as was the one to the hall. By the light of the matches I saw something more terrifying than the arm which was now partially covered with debris—the light lathes from the ceilings had all fallen down across me, so that their weight had not hurt me at all—but balanced on them were huge blocks and lumps of masonry. If I moved they might all crash down. 'Don't come any nearer,' I shouted to Richard. He said, 'Keep still—I'm going to try and get out—the front door is twisted and jammed.'

I had seen where my best exit passage lay when Richard had lit the matches for me, and while he was trying to shift the broken door I began wriggling very, very carefully and cautiously along the floor. It was not easy—for I was not as slim as normally, and I had Vicki. It was so perilous that I thought of loosing her and letting her find her own way out. Had she not behaved so wonderfully I would have been obliged to leave her—for the thought uppermost of anything else in my mind was to save my baby. The baby, hitherto a nebulous dream of the future, now became urgently real and my only thought was of it. I shouted again and again—for if only the Heavy Rescue would come—as they had always promised me they would if I were buried—I would not have to face this perilous crawl; but no sound came from the streets.

I have never been brave at doing dangerous things—I can only do them if I do them very quickly. As children we used to go fishing with my father in Devonshire, and had to cross some of the deep streams bridged only by a tree trunk—not even a flat one. My father always walked straight over without looking to left or right. This, he told me, was the only way. Sometimes I would not cross and he would simply leave me behind until I did.

There were constant terrific explosions and things fell each time there was a fresh thud. If I did not get out soon some of those huge blocks were bound to fall on me. I shouted again, 'Help, Help,' and so did Richard. The sounds echoed in the darkness and then far away I heard a woman's voice calling, 'They're coming . . . they'll come . . .' and it died away and we didn't know if it was to us they would come, because from the thuds and whooshes and violent explosions all round they must have been pretty busy.

'I've got the door open enough to squeeze through,' Richard called. 'Don't light any more matches; I can smell gas,' I warned him. I could not see him— nor he me. 'I'm going to try and crawl through this space to the door,' I said, and I began doing it immediately. I remembered what Tapper told me, '*Test it first, tap it gently,*' and his warning: 'Don't go scrabbling at anything in case it all comes down on you.' Very slowly and cautiously I squeezed my way along the tiny tunnel under the hanging lathes on which were balanced the concrete blocks which I had only caught sight of for a split second in the light of the matches. It seemed a life-time. There were two awful moments when my shoulders brushed something and there was a fall of stuff again—and then I was at the door and Richard had caught me and pulled me carefully up. We stood there for a minute clinging together. 'Anne's dead—her arm is in there,' I said. 'I'm afraid they're all dead—the whole storeys have gone,' he said. 'D'you think you can walk?'

We now had to squeeze through the jammed door, which he had managed to shift a little. I begged him not to put his weight on it again in case there was another collapse of what was left standing. It was almost impossible to get out because of the piled-up glass in the entrance to the flats under the archway. I had to climb, and even so I could feel the glass cutting my legs. At the back there was a solid mass of debris—and above it nothing remained of the Marsh-mans' flat—just this great pile of rubble. I rushed at it crying frantically, 'Kathleen, Kathleen! Cecil! Cecil!' but there wasn't a sound.

Frances Faviell, V.A.D.

The Germans dropped a number of huge parachute mines on London, and few who were close to one when it exploded survived to tell the tale.

On the night of 8 December 1940, I left the B.B.C. shortly after 10.45 and accompanied by a colleague . . . went to the cycle-shed in Chapel Mews. The customary nightly air-raid was in progress, and as we left the cycle-shed we could hear the distant sound of aircraft and A.A. gunfire. We were just entering Hallam Street from the mews when I heard the shrieking whistling noise like a large bomb falling. This noise continued for about three seconds, and then abruptly ceased as if in mid-air. There was no thud, explosion or vibration. I particularly remember this, as I'd heard this happen once before, and was curious as to what caused it and why it stopped. Then came the sound of something clattering down the roof of a building in the direction of Broadcasting House. I looked up, thinking that it might be incendiaries, but this was not so. . . . Whilst we were conversing I noticed a large, dark, shiny object approach the lamp-post and then recede. I concluded that it was a taxi parking. It made no noise. The night was clear, with a few small clouds. There was moonlight from a westerly direction, but Portland Place was mainly shadow.

A few seconds later I saw what seemed to be a very large tarpaulin of a drab or khaki colour fall on the same spot; the highest part of it was about ten or twelve feet above the road when I first saw it, and it seemed to be about twenty-five feet across. It fell at about the speed of a pocket handkerchief when dropped, and made no noise. . . . There were no other warnings of any imminent danger. I went towards the tarpaulin and had reached a spot . . . twenty-five to thirty feet from 'the thing', when Vaughan came running towards me at high speed. He shouted something which I did not hear. At that moment there was a very loud swishing noise, as if a plane were diving with engine cut off—or like a gigantic fuse burning. It lasted about three or four seconds; it did not come from the lamp-post end of 'the thing' but it may have come from the other end.

. . . . I had a momentary glimpse of a large ball of blinding, wild, white light and two concentric rings of colour, the inner one lavender and the outer one violet, as I ducked my head. The ball seemed to be ten to twenty feet high, and was near the lamp-post. Several things happened simultaneously. My head was jerked back due to a heavy blow on the dome and rim of the back of my steel helmet, but I do not remember this, for, as my head went back, I received a severe blow on my forehead and the bridge of my nose. The blast bent up the front rim of my helmet and knocked it off my head. The explosion made an indescribable noise—something like a colossal growl—and was accompanied by a veritable tornado of air blast. I felt an excruciating pain in my ears, and all sounds were replaced by a very loud singing noise, which I was told later was when I lost my hearing and had my eardrums perforated. I felt that consciousness was slipping from me, and that moment I heard a clear loud voice shouting, 'Don't let yourself go, face up to it—hold on.' It rallied me, and summoning all my willpower and energy I succeeded in forcing myself down into a crouching position with my knees on the ground and my feet against the kerb behind me and my hands covering my face.

I remember having to move them over my ears because of the pain in them, doubtless due to the blast. This seemed to ease the pain. Then I received another hit on the forehead and felt weaker. The blast seemed to come in successive waves, accompanied by vibrations from the ground. I felt as if it were trying to spin me and clear me away from the kerb. Then I received a very heavy blow just in front of the right temple which knocked me down flat on my side, in the gutter. Later, in our first-aid post, they removed what they described as a piece of bomb from that wound. Whilst in the gutter I clung on to the kerb with both hands and with my feet against it. I was again hit in the right chest, and later found that my double-breasted overcoat, my coat, leather comb-case and papers had been cut through, and the watch in the top right-hand pocket of my waistcoat had the back dented in and its works broken.

Just as I felt that I could not hold out much longer I realized that the blast pressure was decreasing and a shower of dust, dirt and rubble swept past me. Pieces penetrated my face, some skin was blown off, and something pierced my left thumbnail and my knuckles were cut, causing me involuntarily to let go my hold on the kerb. Instantly, although the blast was dying down, I felt myself being slowly blown across the pavement towards the wall of the building. I tried to hold on but there was nothing to hold on to. Twice I tried to rise but seemed to be held down. Eventually I staggered to my feet. I looked around and it seemed like a scene from Dante's *Inferno*. The front of the building was lit by a reddish-yellow light; the saloon car was on fire to the left of me, and the flames from it were stretching out towards the building, and not upwards; pieces of brick, masonry and glass seemed to appear on the pavement, making, to me, no sound; a few dark huddled bodies were round about, and right in front of me were two soldiers; one, some feet from a breach in the wall of the building where a fire seemed to be raging, was propped up against the wall with his arms dangling by him, like a rag doll.

The other was nearer, about twelve feet from the burning car; he was sitting up with his knees drawn up and supporting himself by his arms—his trousers had been blown off him. I could see that his legs were bare and that he was wearing short grey underpants. He was alive and conscious.

I told him to hang on to an upright at the entrance and to shout like hell for assistance should he see or hear anyone approaching. I went back to look at the other soldier. He was still in the same posture and I fear that he was dead. I ooked around. There was a long, dark body lying prone, face downwards close to the kerb in front of the building—it may have been Vaughan. There appeared to be one or two dark, huddled bodies by the wall of the building. I had not the strength to lift any of them. I wondered where the water was coming from which I felt dripping down my face, and soon discovered that it was blood from my head wounds.

B.B.C. employee

German Naval Staff War Diary: 14 September

From a series of reports, sent by the Military Attaché in Washington, on the morale of the population and the situation in London, it emerges that the will to fight of the London population is considerably affected by lack of sleep. This physical weakness is regarded as the worst danger to morale. As regards damage, he reports that twenty-four large docks were totally burnt out and four gaso-meters were destroyed. The stations of Sherrycross [*sic*] and Waterloo, and several Underground stations are damaged. Of ten good airfields round London, seven are almost completely unusable.

Secret Weapon

Mr. Mallet, who in 1940 was living in Chelsea—'carting X-ray equipment for the hospitals' is his own description of his job—was a fire-watcher. He has said how people at his post were always discussing strange and weird bombs. One new weapon of which he heard tell contained a huge coil spring, like the spring inside a gramophone, '. . . and if you got in the way of this thing, they said that it'd either cut your legs off, or your head off, or cut you in half. You just laugh at things like that at the time, you think they're talking out of the back of their necks, you don't take any more notice of it. But those things flash through your mind later on.' One windy night, during a raid, he was down by the Chelsea Old Church. 'They was dropping different things all over London again. Presently I heard something come down and go with a dull thud. It may have gone in the river, I don't know. Then I heard this noise.' It was a strange, scraping, metallic sound, which seemed to be coming closer in the semi-darkness. 'Well, immediately I heard this noise it reminded me of what they were saying about this coil spring. I didn't stop to look, I just took to my heels and started to go. I went up Church Street as far and as fast as I could. All I could see was the houses on either side of me, and I didn't even bother to look whether any doors were open or not.' Because, as he started up Old Church Street, he had realized that this thing, this noise was following him, rattling and scraping along the street just about as fast as he could run. It was, indeed, gaining on him. 'I just belted hell for leather up the road. I thought, this darned thing, whatever it is, can't turn round a corner surely. So when I got to Paultons Street I turned the corner, and as I did this thing went by me. It stopped up the road about a hundred yards farther on.' He saw it, in the half-light, a dome-shaped object in the centre of the road. For some minutes he waited at the corner of the street, ready to dodge back should it show any sign of life. After a little while curiosity won, and he made his way cautiously towards it. 'And when I got up to it, what I found was this bloody dustbin lid that had chased me up the road.' . . . 'You can laugh at it now, but by Christ you never did then.'

Constantine Fitz Gibbon

The Barrage

It was difficult for civilians to understand why there should be no more than spasmodic gunfire when hordes of enemy aircraft streamed over London most of the night. The intricate and enormous problems of night shooting were unknown to them, and impossible to explain. Londoners wanted to hear the guns hit back; they wanted to feel that, even if aircraft were not being brought down, at least the pilots were being made uncomfortable.

It was abundantly apparent that every effort must be made to defend the Londoner more effectively, and to uphold his morale in so doing.

Anti-aircraft guns take a little time to become effective after they have moved into new positions. Telephone lines have to be laid, gun positions levelled, the warning system co-ordinated, and so on. It was, however, very disappointing that, although the increase in the number of guns by the second night of the battle was very considerable, there did not appear to be much more anti-aircraft fire. And, after about three bad nights' bombing in London, in which it was obvious to me, sleeping in my bed, that our system was no good, I became both angry and frightened at the same time, and lay awake the rest of the night thinking how to deal with this business.

During the nights of 8 and 9 September my staff had been round the gun-sites and Gun Operations Rooms to try to find some more effective answer to the Hun. But, though they laid on variations of all sorts in an attempt to achieve greater accuracy, everyone was most dissatisfied with the results. So, on 10 September, we held a conference at Command Headquarters and determined that, whatever had gone before, we would meet the enemy that night with a barrage the like of which had never been seen or heard before.

The commanders of every gun position in London with their Battery, Brigade, and Divisional commanders met me in the Signals Drill-hall in the Brompton Road, and I told them personally what I wanted them to do. Every gun was to fire every possible round. Fire was not to be withheld on any account. Guns were to go to the approximate bearing and elevation and fire. Searchlights were not to expose. R.A.F. fighters were not going to operate over London, and every unseen target must be engaged without waiting to identify the aircraft as hostile.

The result was as astonishing to me as it appears to have been to the citizens of London—and, apparently, to the enemy as well. For, although few of the bursts can have been anywhere near the target, the heights of aircraft steadily increased as the night went on, and many of them turned away before entering the inner artillery zone. What, in effect, we were doing was to use our predictors, with all the information we could feed into them from any source, to engage the enemy by predicted fire from all the guns that could bear on any particular target. It was in no sense a barrage, though I think by that name it will always be known.

Anyway, it bucked people up tremendously. The midnight news said some nice things about us, and when I put through a phone call to my wife the telephone operator said, 'By God, this is the stuff. All the girls here are hugging each other.' Next day everyone said they had slept better, and for the first time A.A. Command hit the headlines. Apart from comforting the civilians, it stimulated the gunners, who had been feeling pretty frustrated during the long nights when they had been compelled to hear aircraft flying overhead and dropping their bombs without being engaged.

But not everyone was pleased. There were some angry voices raised, for instance, in the southern and eastern suburbs, upon which the retreating Luftwaffe jettisoned their bombs. Worse still, the council of another suburb wrote to say that lavatory pans were being cracked in the council houses by the vibration of the guns, and would we mind very much moving the barrage somewhere else.

We didn't move the barrage, and until people got used to it and could see no dead birds on the ground as a result of it, it served its purpose. As a matter of fact, almost six years to a day after the opening of the barrage, and while I was writing this chapter, I came upon a belated testimonial. In a silversmith's attic near my office I saw hanging upon the wall a pair of earplugs. There was a notice under them:

ANTIQUES OF THE FUTURE

Issued by the Ministry of Home Security to Londoners (and never used) so that we should not hear our guns, which were Music.

General Sir Frederick Pile, O.C. Anti-Aircraft Command

Unexploded Bomb

At 9 a.m. Archer received a message from the Assistant Military Liaison Officer of the Regional Commissioner's staff ordering him to take his section to Swansea where unexploded bombs were hampering efforts to control a fire at the Llandarcy oil refinery, at that time held to be the largest establishment of the kind in the kingdom. Fifteen miles from the refinery, not only the smoke of the conflagration but the huge leaping flames were clearly visible in the morning light, and as they got nearer its appearance suggested that any operations in the immediate area would be for the time impossible.

However, at ten o'clock when they arrived they were met by the officer of the local bomb disposal section who were already at work there. He guided Lieutenant Archer to an entry into the storage area of the refinery where there were a great many gasometer-like tanks arranged in rows. Some were alight and others, though still intact, fiercely hot.

In one section of this storage area there were four unexploded bombs. One had penetrated to a position directly beneath an un-ignited tank, another was some one hundred and fifty yards away between two tanks, also un-ignited, and the remaining pair were at a safer distance from the stored oil. Since the first object was to prevent further fires from breaking out, Archer decided to deal with the bomb under the tank first.

It was a bad site to work on. Fifty yards away in one direction and eighty in another a tank was on fire. The heat caused by their burning was very great; as the flames on their tops worked their way down they melted the steel walls so that the tanks flared like gigantic Roman candles. Smoke and flames whirled up hundreds of feet into the air, simultaneously darkening the daylight and lighting the place with their own unsteady glare.

The heat at the entry hole where the bomb had torn its way diagonally into the concrete plinth at the base of the tank was such that Archer and his men were only able to work for short periods at a time. They dug in relays, working as energetically as they could to reach the bomb before it exploded or the tank above caught fire.

At midday the bomb one hundred and fifty yards away detonated. They all threw themselves flat, none of them was struck, and no further fires were started. At two, just as they were starting to uncover the bomb case, one of the two further bombs went off. This second explosion lent even greater urgency to their efforts, and shortly afterwards they completed the uncovering.

The bomb proved to be of the 250 kg. S.C. type, and its case had split, presumably as a result of its passage through the concrete plinth. The main explosive filling was clearly visible through the break. There was only one fuse-pocket and the fuse-boss had been ripped away, disclosing a fuzz of wires and other electrical components.

Archer decided that if he was to prevent a major explosion he would have to remove the base-plate at the rear end of the bomb and then scoop out the main filling, which was the powder variety. By means of a hammer and chisel the heavy base-plate was slowly turned on its threads and eventually removed. He could then see that the fuse-pocket was more or less loose inside the bomb. The spot-weld by which the closed end of the tube had been fastened to the inside of the bomb-case had been completely sheared, and the weld at the open, or fuse-box end partly so. By manual force he tore the tube with its dangling wires free and removed it from the bomb. The tank was now for practical purposes safe, his men could empty the filling into sandbags and cart it and the case away. It was 2.50 p.m.; the operation had taken just over four and a half hours, during which time all concerned had been aware that it was unlikely they would see the job completed. Moreover, in addition to the heat and the perpetual extra hazard of one of the adjacent tanks exploding, they had been constantly choked and confused by smoke.

Having secured the fuse-pocket, Lieutenant Archer left his section to complete the removal of the bomb and retired to examine it. He gripped the exposed wires with pliers and pulled until the fuse came away, disclosing the clockwork delayed-action apparatus at the rear. He unscrewed the gaine* and put the electric and clockwork components in his pocket. He then again looked into the tube. There was something else there besides the picric booster-pellets he had expected to find. He shook the tube gently and another mechanism with another gaine attached slid into view.

He had hardly unscrewed this second gaine when there was a crack and a flash from the mechanism. A small cap inside had detonated. At least he knew it would not crack again—so into his pocket it went. After destroying the booster-pellets at the bottom of the tube he next went to find the local Swansea bomb disposal officer, who told him that the immediate danger to the refinery having been overcome, he could return to his station at Cardiff.

. . . . Answers to the questions set disclosed a great range of capacities and often produced an illuminating side-light on the character of the student or his local instructor. The question—*What do you consider the ideal qualification of character for a member of a Bomb Disposal Unit?*—evoked several very different responses:

'The first and foremost qualification is caution. If a B.D.S. man is a hundred per cent careful he is a hundred per cent safe—if he is ninety-nine per cent careful he is a danger to the Squad.'

'A member of the B.D.S. should be strong, unmarried, and a fast runner.'

'A member of the squad should not be indispensable to the factory. He should be of excellent character and prepared for the after-life.'

Major A. B. Hartley

* A type of detonator (Ed.)

MEN . . .

I was in it from the first. Like the volunteers of 1914, I 'leapt to arms unbidden'—only there were no arms to leap to. There was nothing but an armband of white cotton crudely lettered 'L.D.V.' This we were instructed to dye with tea or coffee. The drilling of the L.D.V. with pikes and muskets instantly became a national joke. Actually it was propaganda to frighten the enemy, for in our company, somewhere in the Home Counties, we had not even these aids to morale. We assembled at the local drill-hall and shot off a few precious rounds of miniature ammunition; for the rest, we drilled and marched about the streets to inspire confidence. Eventually a few actual rifles were distributed—I never received one of my own, or at least not a whole one, because, although I could hit a target, I could not master the niceties of arms drill: presenting, sloping, shouldering, as taught by retired sergeants of the first World War, seemed to me useless and archaic.

Twice a week I went on patrol with two companions. It might be at dusk, at midnight, or towards dawn. We enforced the black-out on careless householders, checked cars to see that they had been properly 'immobilized', and kept our ears open for spies and fifth columnists. For relief we occasionally retailed the latest pleasantries of 'Lord Haw-Haw', the Irishman William Joyce, whose insinuating propaganda over the German radio was one of the ingredients of that pre-invasion atmosphere. The old soldiers returned in spirit to the Somme and Ypres; the younger ones had to be content with speculating on the immediate future. The dawn patrol was in some ways the worst. The weather, that summer, seemed to be always indescribably calm and beautiful. First the rising sun would reveal the sensuous contours of the silver barrage balloons that hung over a near-by aircraft factory. One of them, which was larger than the rest and always sagged as if from weariness, had been lovingly christened Göring. Then I could make out the details of the little suburban houses with their gardens full of lupins and delphiniums.

July passed with mounting anxiety but still no invasion. We got battledress, boots, forage-caps. We paraded on Sunday mornings at the grammar school and were sent for what was called a 'walk', while the officers discussed what to do with us when we came back. The whole thing was so haphazard and impromptu that it soon became obvious that, in the mind of the central authority which presumably was responsible for some sort of overall plan, either our area was regarded as safe from invasion, or, as was more likely, of no military importance since by the time the enemy reached us we should have lost the war. I realize of course that in coastal areas things were very different; indeed, my father-in-law, who lived near the south coast and was twice my age, was even then undergoing a far more rigorous training.

We were instructed in the use of new weapons. In particular, I remember one which consisted of a length of sawn-off iron piping mounted on a sketchily constructed tripod. This was set up behind a hedge, and imaginary bottle-bombs were lobbed out of the tube as a deterrent to approaching tanks. Mercifully we were never given any ammunition, or the casualties among the gun-crews would have been terrific. At first we evolved a very smart drill for operating the thing with a crew of three; after that, we unlearned it all in order to employ only two.

.... The climax of that autumn was the all-night stand-to: whether this was a large-scale exercise or a genuine false alarm we were never sure. I was lent a rifle and half-a-dozen rounds, and despatched on my bicycle to guard a telephone-box a quarter of a mile from my house. I stood there all night and well on into the next day. The weather was fine and warm, and the night was filled with a profound and unbroken calm. It will, I suppose, always seem odd that I should have spent a whole night of my life guarding a telephone-box with a rifle of whose precise mode of operation I had not a perfectly clear idea. At the time it seemed natural enough, yet even in those days I could see the humour of the situation when, at eight o'clock in the morning, another member of the company cycled past me on his way to work and asked if nobody had told me the order to dismiss had been given hours ago.

But I should not judge my company by myself: if I was not quite the most inefficient and craven member of it, I must have been pretty nearly so. We had some keen and competent men, and by mid-October, when the invasion was called off, I should think we might have put up a very fair show; by the following June, when the Germans crossed into Russia, we were almost well organized. We had a greatcoat and a service gas-mask apiece; there may even have been a few who harboured a secret regret that our mettle had never been put to the test.

                                                                J. R.

. . . AND GUNS

The vital task was to put into the hands of the troops every gun that could be found and to build up as quickly as possible a crust of artillery defence around the most threatened coasts.

The search for weapons produced the most remarkable results. The equipment that came to light in the greatest numbers was the 6-pounder Hotchkiss gun that had been fitted into the tanks of the 1914–1918 war. Some of these had already been sent to France to thicken up the anti-tank defence there, and had of course been lost, but several hundreds still remained. Some were put on pedestal mountings in the concrete pillboxes which formed the so-called 'Stop Lines' across England; others were mounted on the back-axles of old motor-cars and so made mobile. Unfortunately the ammunition supply for them was hardly adequate, being about seventy rounds in all per gun. Moreover, it was always doubtful if they would have penetrated the armour of the German tanks which were likely to be opposed to them.

The Navy produced about a hundred 4-inch and 12-pounder guns. It was said that they had been concealed under a mountain of coal at one of the Royal Dockyards since they had been taken out of warships scrapped under one of the Disarmament Agreements. Of these some also were mounted on fixed bases, mostly on the coast, and some on commercial steam lorries. There were also a number of 'freaks'. There were two German 105 mm. guns which a medium regiment had captured complete with first-line ammunition in France and had managed to bring home. The saluting gun from Edinburgh Castle, the successor of Mons Meg, moved down and went into action near Berwick. The Navy offered the pack guns that were used in the Inter-Port obstacle race at Olympia, but as the only ammunition available for them was blank, they were reluctantly refused. One unit was said to have detached a German 5·9-inch of the 1914 war from its place on some war memorial, to have cleaned it up and to be asking for ammunition for it. At Dunbar two 6-inch guns were deployed which were reported to be two of the 'Long Toms' used by the Naval Brigade in the Boer War. As for the old wooden-wheeled 13-pounders, once the equipment of the R.H.A., any unit that received one or more of these considered itself greatly favoured.

Even with all these makeshifts not all Gunners could be fully equipped at first, and in several places R.A. units were used as infantry, notably a group of medium regiments, popularly known as 'John Barry's Private Army',* in Lincolnshire and Leicestershire.

Then came a great windfall. The United States of America offered to us (this was before Lease-Lend) several hundred 75 mm. guns that had been in store in America since the 1914 war. They were joyfully accepted and shipped over in haste. They proved to be of three types: genuine French 75 mm. of 1897 vintage, British 18-pounders Mk I, which had been converted to take 75 mm. ammunition, and a few of more recent date, made to an American design. With them came a device by which the carriages of earlier design could quickly be converted from wooden to pneumatic wheels.

Lieutenant-Colonel C. J. Burlison

Coastal Artillery

. . . . Mr. Winston Churchill was anxious to be able to announce as soon as possible after the Germans began to shoot across the Channel that we had done the same thing. He therefore took great interest in the installations of the first of these naval 14-inch guns; and it was in consequence named 'Winnie' after him. (Its mate inevitably became 'Pooh'.) When 'Winnie' was to open fire for the first time, it was ordered that the Battery Commander should report direct to the Prime Minister, through G.H.Q. Home Forces, when and how many rounds it had fired. The following is the essence of the interchange of signals that followed:

R.M. Siege Battery to Prime Minister:
   '"Winnie" fired three rounds to-day. Two direct hits obtained.'

P.M. to R.M.S.B.:
   'Direct hits on what?'

R.M.S.B. to P.M.:
   'Direct hits on France.'

* Brigadier J. R. Barry, C.B.E., D.S.O., was then C.C.R.A. I Corps.

PRESIDENT ROOSEVELT TO CONGRESS: 3 SEPTEMBER

. . . . This Government has acquired the right to lease naval and air bases in Newfoundland, and in the islands of Bermuda, the Bahamas, Jamaica, St. Lucia, Trinidad, and Antigua, and in British Guiana. . . .

The right to bases in Newfoundland and Bermuda are gifts—generously given and gladly received. The other bases mentioned have been acquired in exchange for fifty of our over-age destroyers.

President Roosevelt

BERLIN 1940

Naturally we were all intoxicated by our victories. And if my personal life had not been sad, I too should have joined in the celebrations and victory parties. No doubt we now and then (at least the women amongst us) thought of our defeated enemies and were sorry for them, but the strongest feeling of all was our pride in Germany, showing the world that the Treaty of Versailles, with its bitter humiliations, had been broken. I was proud to be German. I was also proud of Hitler. Indeed, all those who formerly had had doubts about Hitler were now carried away in respect and admiration. He had put Germany back as a great nation in the world.

Feverishly we waited for the invasion of England. Some of us were astonished that it did not at once follow the defeat of the British Army at Dunkirk. But this time I did not become sceptical. I had learnt my lesson that I really could not judge political or military situations at all. We must leave these things to Hitler and trust his judgment. The Press, too, assured us daily that the day was not far distant when we would land in England.

Else Wendel, housewife

THE STAND-TO

Autumn met me to-day as I walked over Castle Hill.
The wind that had set our corn by the ears was blowing still:
Autumn, who takes the leaves and the long days, crisped the air
With a tang of action, a taste of death; and the wind blew fair.

From the east for men and barges massed on the other side—
Men maddened by numbers or stolid by nature, they have their pride
As we in work and children, but now a contracting will
Crumples their meek petitions and holds them poised to kill.

Last night a Stand-to was ordered. Thirty men of us here
Came out to guard the star-lit village—my men who wear
Unwitting the seasons' beauty, the received truth of the spade—
Roadmen, farm labourers, masons, turned to another trade.

A dog barked over the fields, the candle stars put a sheen
On the rifles ready, the sandbags fronded with evergreen:
The dawn wind blew, the stars winked out on the posts where we lay,
The order came, Stand Down and thirty went away.

Since a cold wind from Europe blows back the words in my teeth,
Since autumn shortens the days and the odds against our death,
And the harvest moon is waxing and high tides threaten harm,
Since last night may be the last night all thirty men go home.

I write this verse to record the men who have watched with me—
Spot who is good at darts, Squibby at repartee,
Mark and Cyril, the dead shots, Ralph with a ploughman's gait,
Gibson, Harris and Long, old hands for the barricade.

Whiller the lorry-driver, Francis and Rattlesnake,
Fred and Charl and Stan, these nights I have lain awake
And thought of my thirty men and the autumn wind that blows
The apples down too early and shatters the autumn rose.

Destiny, History, Duty, Fortitude, Honour—all
The words of the politicians seem too big or too small
For the ragtag fighters of lane and shadow, the love that has grown
Familiar as working-clothes, faithful as bone to bone.

Blow, autumn wind, upon orchard and rose! Blow leaves along
Our lanes, but sing through me for the lives that are worth a song!
Narrowing days have darkened the vistas that hurt my eyes,
But pinned to the heart of darkness a tattered fire-flag flies.

C. Day Lewis

OPERATION SEA LION

On 1 and 2 September, 'the invasion of England' was filmed for the German newsreels in the harbour of Antwerp, with the bathing beach at St. Anne serving to represent the shores of Albion. St. Anne is directly across from Antwerp, on the opposite side of the Scheldt River which forms the vast harbour, and is a favourite spot for excursionists during the summer.

Here, for two days, invasion barges drew in to the shore and men leapt into the shallow water as light tanks and motor-cycles sped from the concrete decks to the sandy beach, firing as they went. One of the men in charge explained to me the reason:

'You see,' he said, 'when we invade England it will be at night, or very early in the morning, and there won't be enough light to photograph it. Since this will be the decisive event of the war, it must be covered for the newsreel—so we're staging it here, exactly as it will be done later on the English coast.'

Lars Moen

Case History

Planning for a landing in England began on 15 November 1939, when Raeder issued an order to his staff to investigate and prepare the operation. This was an order to the Naval Staff only, and neither Hitler nor the other two Services were informed. The plans were apparently prepared not so much because Raeder considered the invasion of England essential, but because he did not want to be confronted with a sudden directive from Hitler ordering the invasion at short notice.

. . . When it became obvious that, weak as she was, England had no intention of capitulating, the Supreme Command decided to investigate the possibilities of direct attack.

The three branches of the Armed Forces set to work and produced rough plans. The operation was not yet considered necessary, however, and on 11 July Raeder informed Hitler: 'That for a speedy termination of the war with Britain the impact of the war must be forcibly brought home to the British public itself.' He suggested that heavy air attacks should be made on the principal towns, and in particular pointed out the importance of London: 'The great mass of people who cannot be evacuated, difficulties of food supply, and the fact that forty per cent of the imports come through the Port of London.' On the subject of invasion, Raeder stated, 'I consider that an invasion should be used only as a last resort to force Britain to sue for peace. I am convinced that Britain can be made to ask for peace simply by cutting off her import trade by means of submarine warfare, air attacks on convoys, and heavy air attacks on her main centres, Liverpool, for instance. I cannot for my part, therefore, advocate an invasion of Britain as I did in the case of Norway. The prerequisites are complete air superiority and the creation of a mine-free area for transports and disembarkation.'

Hitler appeared to agree, but in the next few days he changed his mind, and, on 16 July, issued the directive for the invasion of England—operation 'Sea Lion'.

Top Secret   16 July 1940
Directive No. 16
Preparations for the Invasion of England

As England, in spite of the hopelessness of her military position, has so far shown herself unwilling to come to any compromise, I have decided to begin to prepare for, and if necessary to carry out, an invasion of England.

This operation is dictated by the necessity of eliminating Great Britain as a base from which the war against Germany can be fought, and if necessary, the island will be occupied.

I therefore issue the following orders:

1. The landing operation must be a surprise crossing on a broad front extending approximately from Ramsgate to a point west of the Isle of Wight. Elements of the Air Force will do the work of the artillery and elements of the Navy the work of engineers. I ask each of the fighting services to consider the advantage from their respective point of view of preliminary operations such as the occupation of the Isle of Wight or the Duchy of Cornwall prior to the full-scale invasion, and to inform me of the result of their deliberations. I shall be responsible for the final decision.

The preparations for the large scale invasion must be completed by the middle of August. . . .

On 19 July, Raeder, through his staff, sent to the Supreme Command a long memorandum explaining the difficulties from the naval point of view:

The task allotted to the Navy in operation 'Sea Lion' is out of all proportion to the Navy's strength and bears no relation to the tasks that are set the Army and the Air Force. . . .

The principal difficulties confronting the Navy are as follows:

The transport of Army troops must take place from a coast whose harbour installations and adjacent inland waterways have been extensively damaged through the fighting in the campaign against France, or are of limited capacity. . . .

The gaining of air supremacy is vital to the possibility of assembling the requisite Naval Forces and shipping in the relatively restricted area of embarkation. . . .

So far the enemy has not needed to use his fleet fully, as a matter of life and death, but the landing operations on the English coast will find him resolved to throw in fully and decisively all his naval forces. It cannot be assumed that the Luftwaffe alone will succeed in keeping the enemy naval forces clear of our shipping, as its operations are very dependent on weather conditions. . . .

These reflections cause the Naval Staff to see exceptional difficulties that cannot be assessed individually until a detailed examination of the transport problem has been made.

Meanwhile German Intelligence was trying to estimate the strength of England's defences. On 17 July an extract from the War Diary of the Naval Staff stated:

> The whole foreign Press, in particular the English Press, comments that a major German attack is expected. Thousands of barges and vessels are said to be standing by on the Channel and Atlantic coast. The attack is expected in the Dover area, though the defences here are strongest.
> Strong air attacks lasting several days will precede the landing.

Two days later a further report was received:

> English defence measures: coastal defence by the Army. Defence is based on mobility and concentration of all available fire-power. No fixed defence line with built-in defences. The task of the fleet and the R.A.F. would be to render impossible the landing of armoured units or surprise landing by troops. The R.A.F. is so organized that strong units can be quickly concentrated at any danger spot, and also to attack the new German bases in Northern France and Holland and to search for indications of German activity, such as the assembly of ships and barges.

These reports, though lacking in definite information, impressed upon the Naval Staff the difficulties of invasion, and on 21 July Raeder reported yet again to Hitler. Only rough notes of this conference are available, but additional information shows that in Hitler's opinion the war was already won, but that England had not yet recognized the situation. From being averse to the landing the German Supreme Command (i.e. Keitel and Jodl) had entirely changed its views, and, to the alarm of the Naval Staff, now considered the landing quite a simple operation. Hitler himself was not, however, convinced:

Notes of Conference on 21 July 1940

The Führer raised the following points:
. . . The invasion of Britain is an exceptionally daring undertaking, because even if the way is short, this is not just a river crossing, but the crossing of a sea which is dominated by the enemy. This is not a case of a single crossing operation as in Norway; operational surprise cannot be expected; a defensively prepared and utterly determined enemy faces us and dominates the sea area which we must use. For the Army operation forty divisions will be required; the most difficult part will be the continued reinforcement of material and stores. We cannot count on supplies of any kind being available to us in England. The prerequisites are complete mastery of the air, the operational use of powerful artillery in the Dover Straits, and protection by minefields. The time of year is an important factor, since the weather in the North Sea and in the Channel during the second half of September is very bad and the fogs begin by the middle of October. The main operation would therefore have to be completed by 15 September; after this date co-operation between the Luftwaffe and the heavy weapons becomes too unreliable. But

as air co-operation is decisive, it must be regarded as the principal factor in fixing the date.

The following must be established:

1. How long does the Navy require for its technical preparations?
2. How soon can the guns be in place?
3. To what extent can the Navy safeguard the crossing?

If it is not certain that preparations can be completed by the beginning of September, other plans must be considered.

On the following day it was reported to Hitler that the preparations could not in any event be completed by the middle of August, and that the actual date of invasion could only be determined when air supremacy in the Channel had been achieved.

The Army then sent their theoretical demands to the Naval Staff:

> The General Staff of the Army has given its intentions for carrying out the operation, as follows: about a hundred thousand men with appropriate equipment, including heavy gear, must be transported in the first wave from the area Dunkirk-Cherbourg to the area between Ramsgate and Lyme Bay. Further waves must follow in quickest succession, so that the formation of a local bridgehead may be followed in the shortest time by a war of movement on the island. This demands the most rapid turn round of transports after disembarkation of the first echelon.

The amount of shipping required to carry out the Army demands was estimated as: 1,722 barges, 471 tugs, 1,161 motor boats, 155 transports.

The assembly of this armada would impose a severe strain on German economy and, on 25 July, Raeder again reported to Hitler:

Conference with the Führer on 25 July 1940

Placement of batteries at the Straits of Dover: (Report by Captain Voss.)

The guns are to be ready by 15 August. The 38 cm. battery will not be ready until the middle of September. Concrete covers will be built later as a protection against air attack.

The C.-in-C., Navy, emphasizes the necessity for making use of the batteries as soon as they are ready in order to protect minesweepers and to close the Straits of Dover. (The 28 cm. Kurfürst battery will be ready about 1 August.) As British air reconnaissance is obviously closely watching the placing of the guns, firing them will not disclose German plans to any greater degree.

The Führer agrees.

Operation 'Sea Lion':

The C.-in-C., Navy, describes forcefully once again the effects of these preparations on the German economy; cessation of inland shipping and a great part of maritime shipping, strain on shipyards, etc. The C.-in-C., Navy, requests that an order be issued that these preparations be given preference over anything else.

The Führer and the Chief of Staff, Armed Forces High Command, agree.

There follows a report on the state of preparations on 25 July 1940. The C.-in-C., Navy, again stresses the necessity of establishing air superiority soon in order to carry out preparations. At the present time, the following can be said:

Every effort is being made to complete preparations by the end of August. Provided that there are no special difficulties and that air superiority is established soon, it will be possible to do the following:

1. Provide and convert barges.
2. Make available the necessary personnel.
3. Prepare ports for embarkation.
4. Reconnoitre the enemy coast.
5. Clear the invasion area of mines.
6. Lay protecting minefields.
7. Set up the organization.

It is still very uncertain whether a sufficient number of ships can be obtained along the Belgian–French coast and how long it will take to convert them. The C.-in-C., Navy, will try to give a clear picture by the middle of next week.

The Führèr orders a conference for the middle of next week.

Preparations for 'Sea Lion' now began in earnest, but the essential air superiority over the Channel was elusive.

Top Secret   14 September 1940

At the conference with the Commanders-in-Chief of the Armed Forces on 14 September the Führer has decided:

1. *'Sea Lion'*:
   (a) The start of the operation is again postponed. A new order follows on 17 September. All preparations are to be continued.
   (b) As soon as preparations are complete, the Luftwaffe is to carry out attacks against the British long-range batteries.
   (c) The measures planned for the evacuation of the coastal area are not to be set in motion to the full extent. Counter-espionage and deception measures are, however, to be increased.

2. *Air attacks against London:*
   The air attacks against London are to be continued and the target area is to be expanded against military and other vital installations (e.g., railway stations).

   Terror attacks against purely residential areas are reserved for use as an ultimate means of pressure, and are therefore not to be employed at present.

Heavy air attacks by both sides continued for the next two days, and on 17 September an entry in the War Diary stated:

The enemy air force is still by no means defeated; on the contrary, it shows increasing activity. The weather situation as a whole does not permit us to expect a period of calm. . . . *The Führer therefore decides to postpone 'Sea Lion' indefinitely.*

On 19 September, a Supreme Command directive was issued confirming the postponement. The Naval Staff summed up the situation:

1. The preparations for a landing on the Channel coast are extensively known to the enemy, who is taking more counter-measures. Symptoms are, for example, operational use of his aircraft for attacks and reconnaissance over the German operational harbours; frequent appearance of destroyers off the South Coast of England, in the Straits of Dover, and on the Franco-Belgian coast; stationing of his patrol vessels off the North Coast of France; Churchill's last speech, etc.

2. The main units of the Home Fleet are being held in readiness to repel the landing, though the majority of the units are still in Western bases.

3. Already a large number of destroyers (thirty) has been located by air reconnaissance in the southern and south-eastern harbours.

4. All available information indicates that the enemy's naval forces are solely occupied with this theatre of operations.

Although there was still a possibility of invading in October, shipping was dispersed to prevent further losses. By 21 September the state of the invasion armada was:

Shipping previously available			Lost or damaged
Transports .	.	. 168	21 (i.e., 12·5%)
Barges	.	. 1,697	214 (i.e., 12·6%)
Tugs .	.	. 360	5 (i.e., 1.4%)

Troops and ships were kept at readiness until 12 October, when the operation was postponed until the spring of 1941.

12 October 1940

Top Secret

The Führer has decided that from now until the spring, preparations for 'Sea Lion' shall be continued solely for the purpose of maintaining political and military pressure on England.

Should the invasion be reconsidered in the spring or early summer of 1941, orders for a renewal of operational readiness will be issued later. In the meantime military conditions for a later invasion are to be improved. . . .

But, by the spring of 1941, Hitler and his staff were deeply involved in the preparations for invading Russia, and Operation 'Sea Lion' was shelved. It was finally cancelled in January 1942.

Anticipation

To:
SS Colonel Professor Dr. Six,
Berlin.

By virtue of *Reichsmarschall* Göring's authority I appoint you Representative of the Chief of the Security Police and S.D. in Great Britain. Your task is to combat, with the requisite means, all anti-German organizations, institutions, opposition, and opposition groups which can be seized in England, to prevent the removal of all available material, and to centralize and safeguard it for future exploitation. I designate the capital, London, as the location of your headquarters as Representative of the Chief of the Security Police and S.D.; and I authorize you to set up small action groups in other parts of Great Britain as the situation dictates and the necessity arises.

Reinhard Heydrich, Chief, German Security Service (S.D.)

. . . . All the organs of the political and military leadership worked on the preparation of Operation 'Sea Lion' at top speed and with typical Prussian thoroughness. For example, at the end of June 1940, I was ordered to prepare a small handbook for the invading troops and the political and administrative units that would accompany them, describing briefly the most important political, administrative and economic institutions of Great Britain and the leading public figures. It was also to contain instructions on the necessary measures to be taken in occupying the premises of the Foreign Office, the War Office, the Home Office and the various departments of the Secret Service, and Special Branch. This task occupied a great deal of my time, involving the collection and assembly of material from various sources by a selected staff of my own people. When it was finished an edition of twenty thousand copies was printed, and stored in a room next to my office. They were burned in 1943 in a fire started in one of the air raids.

Walter Schellenberg

LEASE-LEND

President Roosevelt's hand was strengthened by his victory in the Presidential Election of November 1940, and, in spite of opposition which was still strong, the 'Lease-Lend' scheme was prepared.

I think we are doing Great Britain a great disservice in urging her to go and fight until she is exhausted. . . . Peace has got to come sometime, and I don't think there is any sane, intelligent military or naval officer . . . who thinks that England can land troops on German soil and drive the Germans back to Berlin before that time arrives. And even if our own warmongers get us into the war, as it looks now they will, I doubt that the joint efforts of Great Britain and the United States could succeed in that project.

Senator Burton K. Wheeler, Christmas 1940

President Roosevelt to the Press: 17 December

Now, what I am trying to do is to eliminate the dollar sign. That is something brand new in the thoughts of practically everybody in this room, I think—get rid of the silly, foolish old dollar sign.

Well, let me give you an illustration: Suppose my neighbour's home catches fire, and I have a length of garden hose four or five hundred feet away. If he can take my garden hose and connect it up with his hydrant, I may help him to put out his fire. Now, what do I do? I don't say to him before that operation, 'Neighbour, my garden hose cost me $15; you have to pay me $15 for it.'—I want my garden hose back after the fire is over. All right. If it goes through the fire all right, intact, without any damage to it, he gives it back to me and thanks me very much for the use of it. But suppose it gets smashed up—holes in it—during the fire; we don't have to have too much formality about it, but I say to him, 'I was glad to lend you that hose; I see I can't use it any more, it's all smashed up.' He says, 'How many feet of it were there?' I tell him, 'There were a hundred and fifty feet of it.' He says, 'All right, I will replace it.' Now, if I get a nice garden hose back, I am in pretty good shape.

In other words, if you lend certain munitions and get the munitions back at the end of the war, if they are intact—haven't been hurt—you are all right; if they have been damaged or have deteriorated or have been lost completely, it seems to me you come out pretty well if you have them replaced by the fellow to whom you have lent them.

President Roosevelt to the American People: 29 December

The Nazi masters of Germany have made it clear that they intend not only to dominate all life and thought in their own country, but also enslave the whole of Europe, and then to use the resources of Europe to dominate the rest of the world.

. . . . Does anyone seriously believe that we need to fear attack anywhere in the Americas while a free Britain remains our most powerful naval neighbour in the Atlantic? Does anyone seriously believe, on the other hand, that we could rest easy if the Axis powers were our neighbours there?

If Great Britain goes down, the Axis powers will control the continents of Europe, Asia, Africa, Australasia, and the high seas—and they will be in a position to bring enormous military and naval resources against this hemisphere. It is no exaggeration to say that all of us, in all the Americas, would be living at the point of a gun—a gun loaded with explosive bullets, economic as well as military.

. . . . The British people and their allies to-day are conducting an active war against this unholy alliance. Our own future security is greatly dependent on the outcome of that fight. Our ability to 'keep out of war' is going to be affected by that outcome.

Thinking in terms of to-day and to-morrow, I make the direct statement to the American people that there is far less chance of the United States getting into war, if we do all we can now to support the nations defending themselves against attack by the Axis than if we acquiesce in their defeat, submit tamely to an Axis victory, and wait our turn to be the object of attack in another war later on.

. . . . The people of Europe who are defending themselves do not ask us to do their fighting. They ask us for the implements of war, the planes, the tanks, the guns, the freighters which will enable them to fight for their liberty and for our security. Emphatically we must get these weapons to them in sufficient volume and quickly enough, so that we and our children will be saved the agony and suffering of war which others have had to endure.

Let not the defeatists tell us that it is too late. It will never be earlier. To-morrow will be later than to-day.

Certain facts are self-evident.

In a military sense Great Britain and the British Empire are to-day the spear-head of resistance to world conquest. They are putting up a fight which will live forever in the story of human gallantry.

. . . . Democracy's fight against world conquest is being greatly aided, and must be more greatly aided, by the rearmament of the United States and by sending every ounce and every ton of munitions and supplies that we can possibly spare to help the defenders who are in the front lines. It is no more un-neutral for us to do that than it is for Sweden, Russia and other nations near Germany to send steel and ore and oil and other war materials into Germany every day of the week.

. . . . We must be the great arsenal of democracy. For us this is an emergency as serious as war itself. We must apply ourselves to our task with the same resolution, the same sense of urgency, the same spirit of patriotism and sacrifice as we would show were we at war.

President Roosevelt to Congress: 6 January 1941

I also ask this Congress for authority and for funds sufficient to manufacture additional munitions and war supplies of many kinds, to be turned over to those nations which are now in actual war with aggressor nations.

Our most useful and immediate role is to act as an arsenal for them as well as for ourselves. They do not need man-power, but they do need billions of dollars' worth of the weapons of defence.

The time is near when they will not be able to pay for them all in ready cash. We cannot, and we will not, tell them that they must surrender, merely because of present inability to pay for the weapons which we know they must have.

I do not recommend that we make them a loan of dollars with which to pay for these weapons—a loan to be repaid in dollars.

I recommend that we make it possible for those nations to continue to obtain war materials in the United States, fitting their orders into our own programme. Nearly all their material would, if the time ever came, be useful for our own defence.

. . . . For what we send abroad we shall be repaid within a reasonable time following the close of hostilities, in similar materials, or, at our option, in other goods of many kinds, which they can produce and which we need.

Let us say to the democracies, 'We Americans are vitally concerned in your defence of freedom. We are putting forth our energies, our resources and our organizing powers to give you the strength to regain and maintain a free world. We shall send you, in ever-increasing numbers, ships, planes, tanks, guns. This is our purpose and our pledge.'

. . . . In the future days, which we seek to make secure, we look forward to a world founded upon four essential human freedoms.

The first is freedom of speech and expression—everywhere in the world.

The second is freedom of every person to worship God in his own way—everywhere in the world.

The third is freedom from want—which, translated into world terms, means economic understandings which will secure to every nation a healthy peacetime life for its inhabitants—everywhere in the world.

The fourth is freedom from fear—which, translated into world terms, means a world-wide reduction of armaments to such a point and in such a thorough fashion that no nation will be in a position to commit an act of physical aggression against any neighbour—anywhere in the world.

. . . . This nation has placed its destiny in the hands and heads and hearts of its millions of free men and women; and its faith in freedom under the guidance of God. Freedom means the supremacy of human rights everywhere. Our support goes to those who struggle to gain those rights or keep them. Our strength is our unity of purpose.

To that high concept there can be no end save victory.

On 10 January 1941 the Lease-Lend Bill was put before the United States Congress; on 11 March it was approved and signed by the President.

A NEW YEAR MESSAGE

It is the will of the democratic war inciters and their Jewish-capitalistic wire-pullers that the war must be continued. . . . We are ready! . . . The year 1941 will bring completion of the greatest victory in our history.

Adolf Hitler to his troops, New Year's Eve 1940

8

THE END OF
THE ITALIAN EMPIRE

In the late summer of 1940, *Mussolini stood ready in his African domains to emulate his erstwhile pupil's sweeping victories in Europe. In North Africa over two hundred thousand men began to gather themselves for a descent on Egypt and the Suez Canal, faced only by a thin screen of British troops. In Italy's East African possessions an even stronger army, composed of her best units splendidly equipped, invaded British Somaliland on* 3 *August, expelling the greatly outnumbered British forces without much difficulty. The position of the Allies in Africa took a further turn for the worse towards the end of September, when General de Gaulle's efforts to rally France's colonial possessions suffered a hard knock at Dakar, on the west coast.*

FOG OVER DAKAR

THE expedition left Liverpool on 31 August. I myself, with part of the French units and a small staff, was on board the *Westerland*, which flew the French flag beside the Dutch, and whose commander (Captain Plagaay), officers and crew were to prove, like those of the *Pennland*, models of friendly devotion. Spears accompanied me, delegated by Churchill as liaison officer, diplomat and informant. In England I left our forces in course of formation under the orders of Muselier, an embryo administration under the direction of Antoine, and, in the person of Dewavrin, an element of liaison and direct information. In addition, General Catroux was expected shortly from Indo-China; and in a letter which was to be handed to him as soon as he arrived I explained to him my projects as a whole and what I had in mind for him. I reckoned that, in spite of my absence, and provided it did not last long, the reserves of wisdom accumulated by my companions would prevent internal quarrels and intrigues from outside from shaking the still very fragile edifice too profoundly! None the less, on the deck of the *Westerland*, after leaving the port in the middle of an air-raid warning with my small troop and my tiny ships, I felt crushed, as it were, by the dimensions of duty. Out in the open, in black night, on the swell of the ocean, a poor foreign ship, with no guns, with all lights extinguished, was carrying the fortunes of France.

Our first destination was Freetown. . . . During the voyage, radiograms received from London had given us a piece of news about the Vichy forces which might well lead to everything being reconsidered. On 11 September three large modern cruisers, the *Georges Leygues*, *Gloire* and *Montcalm*, and three light cruisers, the *Audacieux*, *Fantasque* and *Malin*, having started from Toulon, had passed the Straits of Gibraltar without being stopped by the British Fleet. But hardly had we anchored at Freetown when a new and grave piece of information completed our perplexity. The squadron, reinforced at Dakar by the cruiser *Primauguet*, had just weighed anchor and was heading southwards at full speed. A British destroyer, detached to watch it, was keeping in touch with it at a distance.

I could have no doubt that this powerful naval force was bound for Equatorial Africa, where the port of Libreville was open to it, and where it would find it easy to retake Pointre-Noire and Duala. If such a thunder-clap did not suffice to reverse the situation in the Congo and Cameroons, these magnificent ships could easily cover the transport and landing of forces of repression from Dakar, Konakry or Abidjan. . . . It was clear that Vichy was starting a large-scale operation to re-establish itself in the territories which had rallied to Free France, and that the despatch of seven cruisers towards the Equator was conceivable only with the full consent, if not at the orders, of the Germans. Admiral Cunningham fell in with my view that the Vichy squadron must be stopped at once.

In fact, the British cruisers which made contact with Admiral Bourragué, the commander of the untimely squadron, had no difficulty in making it change course when its leader learned, to his complete surprise, of the presence of a Franco-British fleet in the region. But the Vichy ships, defying all pursuit, made straight for Dakar.

In this way Free French Africa escaped a very great danger. . . . But after congratulating ourselves on having made our adversaries' plan come to nothing, we had to admit that our own was gravely compromised. In fact, the Dakar authorities were henceforward on their guard and had received a most valuable reinforcement of ships. We learned almost at once, through our intelligence agents, that to serve the shore batteries naval gunners had been substituted for the men of the colonial artillery, who were considered less reliable. In short, our chances of occupying Dakar appeared, from now on, very small.

In London Mr. Churchill and the Admiralty reckoned that, in these circumstances, it was better to do nothing. They had telegraphed this to us as early as 16 September, proposing that the fleet should simply escort our vessels as far as Duala and then move on elsewhere. I must say that to give up in this way seemed to me the worst possible solution. In fact, if we left everything at Dakar as it was, all Vichy would have to do, to resume its attempt on Equatorial Africa, would be to wait for the British ships to return northwards, as they soon would. With the sea open to them, Bourragué's cruisers would swoop once more towards the Equator. In this way the combatants under the Cross of Lorraine, including General de Gaulle, would sooner or later be mewed up in these distant territories and, even if they did not succumb to it, absorbed by a sterile struggle carried on against other Frenchmen in the bush and forest. No prospect for them, in these conditions, of fighting Germans or Italians. I had no doubt that those were the intentions of the enemy, of which the Vichy puppets inevitably made themselves the instruments, conscious or not. It seemed to me that, at the stage things had now reached, we ought in spite of everything to try to enter Dakar.

Admiral Cunningham reacted in the same way. We telegraphed to London, arguing, most pressingly, that we should be allowed to attempt the operation. Mr. Churchill, as he told me later, was surprised and enchanted by this insistence. He willingly consented and the action was decided on.

. . . . At dawn on the 23rd,* in the midst of a very thick fog, we were before Dakar.

The fog was bound to compromise our enterprise seriously. In particular, the moral effect which, according to Churchill, the sight of our fleet was to produce upon the garrison and population would not come into play at all, since not a thing was to be seen. But postponement was obviously impossible. The plan as prepared was therefore put into execution. At six o'clock I addressed the Navy, the troops and the inhabitants by radio, announcing our presence and our friendly intentions. Immediately afterwards two small *Lucioles*, French touring aircraft, unarmed, took off from the deck of *Ark Royal*: they were to land at the aerodrome of Ouakam and there set down three officers—Gaillet, Scamaroni and Soufflet—with a fraternization mission. In fact, I quickly learned that the *Lucioles* had landed without difficulty, and that the signal 'Success' was displayed on the airfield.

Suddenly ack-ack fire was heard at various points. Some of the guns of the *Richelieu* and of the fortress were firing at the Free French and British machines which were beginning to fly over the town, dropping friendly leaflets. And yet, sinister though this cannonade might be, it seemed to me to have something hesitant about it. I therefore gave the order to the two pinnaces with the spokesmen on board to enter the port, while the Free French sloops, together with the *Westerland* and *Pennland*, approached in the mist as far as the entrance to the roads.

There was at first no reaction. Commander d'Argenlieu, Major Gotscho, Captains Bécourt-Foch and Perrin and Sub-Lieutenant Porgés ordered their boats to be moored, landed on the quay, and asked for the port commander. When he presented himself, d'Argenlieu told him that he was the bearer of a letter from General de Gaulle for the Governor-General, which letter he was instructed to deliver to him personally. But the port commander, with unconcealed embarrassment, informed the spokesmen that he had orders to have them arrested. At the same time he showed his intention of calling the guard. Seeing which, my envoys returned to the pinnaces. As these drew away, some machine-guns opened fire on them. D'Argenlieu and Perrin were brought on board the *Westerland*, seriously wounded.

Thereupon, the Dakar batteries began aiming at the British and French ships an intermittent fire which for several hours remained without reply. The *Richelieu*, having been moved within the harbour by tugs so that its guns might be put to better use, began firing in its turn. Towards eleven the cruiser *Cumberland*, having been badly hit, Admiral Cunningham addressed this message by radio to the fortress: 'I am not firing on you. Why are you firing on me?' The reply was, 'Retire to twenty miles' distance.' Upon which, the British in their turn sent some broadsides. Meanwhile time was passing without a sign, on one side or the other, of real fighting ardour. No Vichy aeroplane had taken off up to midday.

* September (Ed.)

From these indications as a whole I did not draw the impression that the place was determined on a desperate resistance. Perhaps the Navy, garrison and Governor were waiting for something to happen which could serve them as pretext for conciliation? Towards noon, Admiral Cunningham sent me a signal to let me know that this was his feeling too. Certainly, there could be no thought of getting the squadron into the harbour. But would it not be possible to land the Free French somewhere near the fortress, which they would then attempt to approach by land? This alternative had been considered in advance. The small port of Rufisque, outside the range of the works, seemed suitable for the operation, provided always that this did not meet with determined resistance. In fact, while our sloops could reach Rufisque, our transports could not, because of their draught. The troops would therefore have to be disembarked by lighter, which would deprive them of their heavy weapons and make complete peace essential. However, having received from Cunningham the assurance that he was covering us from the sea, I set all in motion towards Rufisque.

Towards 3 p.m., still in the fog, we arrived at the spot. The *Commandant Duboc*, with a section of marines on board, entered the port and sent some sailors ashore in a boat to prepare the berthing. On shore a crowd of natives was already running up to welcome the patrol, when the Vichy troops in position in the neighbourhood opened fire on our sloop, killing and wounding several men. A few moments earlier, two Glenn-Martin bombers had flown over our little force at a low altitude, as if to show it that they held it at their mercy—which was indeed the case. Lastly, Admiral Cunningham signalled that the cruisers *Georges Leygues* and *Montcalm* had left Dakar roads and were in the mist at a mile's distance from us, and that the British ships, occupied elsewhere, could not protect us from them. Decidedly, the affair was a failure! Not only was the landing not possible, but, what was more, a few shots fired by the Vichy cruisers would be enough to send the whole Free French expedition to the bottom. I decided to make for the open again, which was done without further incident.

We passed the night on tenterhooks. Next morning the British Fleet, having received from Mr. Churchill a telegram inviting it to push on actively with the affair, addressed an ultimatum to the Dakar authorities. They replied that they would not surrender the place. From then on, the day was spent by the British in exchanging a rather lively cannonade with the shore batteries and ships in the roads, firing blind in the mist, which was thicker than ever. By the end of the afternoon it seemed evident that no decisive result could be obtained.

As evening fell, the *Barham* came up quite close to the *Westerland*, and Admiral Cunningham asked me to come and see him, to discuss the situation. On board the British battleship the atmosphere was gloomy and strained. They were sorry, certainly, not to have succeeded. But the dominant feeling was that of surprise. The British, being practical people, could not understand how and why the authorities, naval forces and troops at Dakar expended such energy upon fighting against their compatriots and against their allies at a time when France lay beneath the invader's boot. As for me, I had from that moment given up being astonished at it. What had just happened showed me, once for all, that the Vichy rulers would never fail to misuse, against the interests of France, the courage and discipline of those who were in subjection to them.

Admiral Cunningham summed up the situation. 'Given,' he declared, 'the attitude of the place and of the squadron supporting it, I do not think bombardment can result in a solution.' General Irwin, who commanded the landing units, added that he was ready to send his troops ashore to assault the fortifications, but that it must be clearly understood that this would mean a great risk for each boat and each soldier. Both of them asked me what would become of the Free France 'movement' if an end were put to the expedition.

'Up to now,' I said, 'we have not made an all-out attack on Dakar. The attempt to enter the harbour peaceably has failed. Bombardment will decide nothing. Lastly, a landing against opposition and an assault on the fortifications would lead to a pitched battle which, for my part, I desire to avoid and of which, as you yourselves indicate, the issue would be very doubtful. We must, therefore, for the moment, give up the idea of taking Dakar. I propose to Admiral Cunningham that he should announce that he is stopping the bombardment at the request of General de Gaulle. But the blockade must be maintained in order not to allow the ships now at Dakar their liberty of action. Next, we shall have to prepare a fresh attempt by marching against the place by land, after disembarking at undefended or lightly defended points, for instance at Saint-Louis. In any case, and whatever happens, Free France will continue.'

The British admiral and general fell in with my view as regards the immediate future. In the falling night I left the *Barham* on board a launch which danced on the waves, while the officers and crew, drawn up along the hand-rails, sadly gave me a ceremonial send-off.

But during the night two facts were to make Admiral Cunningham go back on what we had agreed. First, a fresh telegram from Mr. Churchill expressly called upon him to pursue the enterprise. In it the Prime Minister showed astonishment and irritation at the idea of the affair coming to nothing—the more so because, already, political circles in London and, above all, in Washington, were beginning to grow agitated, impressed by the Vichy and Berlin radios. At the same time the fog was lifting, and this at once seemed to give the bombardment another chance. The fighting therefore began again at dawn—this time without my having been consulted—with an exchange of gunfire between the fortress and the British. But towards evening the battleship *Resolution*, torpedoed by a submarine and in danger of sinking, had to be taken in tow. Several other British ships had been badly hit. Four aircraft from the *Ark Royal* had been shot down. On the other side, the *Richelieu* and various other ships had taken some hard punishment. The destroyer *Audacieux*, the submarines *Persée* and *Ajax* had been sunk; a British destroyer had managed to pick up the latter's crew. But the stalwarts of the fortress still went on firing. Admiral Cunningham decided to cut the losses. I could not but agree. We headed for Freetown.

The days which followed were cruel for me. I went through what a man must feel when an earthquake shakes his house brutally and he receives on his head the rain of tiles falling from the roof.

In London a tempest of anger, in Washington a hurricane of sarcasms were let loose against me. For the American Press and many English newspapers it was immediately a matter of course that the failure of the attempt was due to de

Gaulle. 'It was he,' the echoes repeated, 'who thought of this absurd adventure, misled the British by imaginative reports on the situation at Dakar, and insisted, out of Don Quixotism, that the place be attacked when the reinforcements sent by Darlan made any success impossible. . . . Besides, the cruisers from Toulon had come only as the result of the incessant indiscretions of the Free French, which had put Vichy on the alert. . . . Once for all, it was clear that no reliance could be placed on people incapable of keeping a secret.' Soon Mr. Churchill, too, was roughly handled for having, so it was said, so easily let himself be carried away. Spears, with a long face, kept bringing me telegraphed reports from his correspondents suggesting it as probable that de Gaulle in despair, abandoned by his partisans, dropped by the British into the bargain, would renounce all activity, while the British Government would take up afresh with Catroux or Muselier, on a much more modest scale, the recruitment of French auxiliaries.

As for the Vichy propaganda, it triumphed without restraint. The Dakar communiqués gave the impression that the thing had been a great naval victory. Innumerable messages of congratulation, addressed to Governor-General Boisson and to the heroic fighters of Dakar, were published and commented upon by newspapers of both zones and by the so-called 'French' radios. And I, in my narrow cabin, in a harbour crushed by the heat, was completing my education in what the reactions of fear could be, both among adversaries taking revenge for having felt it and among allies suddenly alarmed by a set-back.

General de Gaulle

COLLAPSE IN EAST AFRICA

In East and North Africa troops were assembling under the command of General Wavell who were to win the first land victories achieved by the Allies in the second World War. In January 1941 a mixed force of British and Commonwealth units took the offensive from the Sudan, driving in the Italian forces which had occupied Kassala and Gallabat, just over the frontier from Eritrea and Abyssinia.

Compared with the subsequent campaigns in the Western Desert, Italy, North-West Europe and Burma, the campaign in Eritrea in the early part of 1941 was probably very small beer. But to those who took part in it from January to March 1941 it seemed a big and important show. Important it certainly was as a means of preventing any interference by the Italians with our communications through the Red Sea and Suez Canal and with our bases in Egypt. From a prestige point of view also it was important. After all, it was the only completely successful campaign in the second World War until 1943, when the North African campaign was finished.

Those who advanced into Eritrea in January 1941 and expected to meet the same sort of opposition as they met in Wavell's Sidi Barrani campaign in December 1940 got a rude shock. The Italian army in Eritrea and Abyssinia were much stouter fighters than Graziani's troops in Libya. Their black troops, too, fought well right up to the moment they decided to come in and surrender.

Lieutenant-Colonel J. L. Gardner-Brown

Gallabat

. . . . Patrolling in the tall elephant grass was a nervy procedure, and small patrols might well come unexpectedly face to face with an Italian party. Then the men in front would shoot it out while their companions behind tried to outflank the opposite side. Already the vultures were feasting in Gallabat, or what remained of it, after the fighting and bombardments. Care was essential when approaching the fort, because the sudden rising of a flock of these sinister birds could reveal our presence to a watchful foe. False alarms were many, and often caused by the baboons which abounded in the district.

The tinder-like elephant grass was also a problem to the Gunners. Several fires started in the gun-pits when fragments of burning cordite set the grass alight. Buckets of water had constantly to be kept at hand, and smoking was strictly forbidden. Because of the visits of hostile aircraft day after day, these gun-pits were elaborate with their camouflage nets draped on poles. The Gunners went to the length of cutting sods with the grass attached and of 'planting' these on top of the camouflage nets to simulate the normal jungle grass growing on every side. As these covers had to be taken down every time the guns were fired, and then replaced immediately afterwards, the trouble involved was great, but amply repaid. Never once were the Gunners spotted by Italian pilots.

The local superiority enjoyed by the enemy in the air was a salutary training in care and concealment to our men. Track discipline was rigorously enforced. Trucks of all kinds were parked under trees and liberally draped with foliage. The troops lived in huts constructed of boughs and named *tukls*. These had to be dug in, for protection against the 'egg-basket' type of Italian bomb, a series of anti-personnel grenades that were virtually shovelled out of the enemy bombers. Along the banks of the local *khors* the trees were particularly heavy and green. At this season the streams were mostly dry, with an occasional pool, and away from their proximity the bush was scorched by heat and drought, the leaves burnt off, and the landscape consequently more open than a few months earlier when the vegetation had been dense and tall.

The mirage whose outline faded and then vanished as you drew near, the heat shimmer from which tree-ringed lakes and the likeness of still water might be stared at, were a frequent memorable feature of many a drive over the desert. Wells became important and recognizable by the swarms of flies as well as by the camels, cows, goats and donkeys that watered there in daylight. To pick out the one camel track to be followed among many such tracks was often perplexing, and a glance at the sun or a compass would be necessary to avoid taking the wrong route. Patches of long *tubbas* grass grew on the sand now that the rains were falling, and camel-thorn bushes studded the ground. Where these bushes flourished, particularly round Gedaref, men found it difficult to walk any distance without getting caught up in thorns like fish-hooks. The scratches festered into septic sores, and in certain units there was hardly a man without bandages on one or both arms and knees.

Antony Brett-James

Keren

Fighting back doggedly, the Italians retired on Keren, the formidable position covering Asmara, capital of Eritrea. Here they concentrated their strength for a decisive stand.

The town of Keren, which lies over four thousand feet above sea-level, is protected on all sides, except on the east, by a formidable barrier of gaunt and rugged mountains. From the direction of Agordat, the only gap is the narrow, winding Dongolaas Gorge that takes both road and railway through to Keren. High on the left of the Gorge are Mounts Samanna and Amba and also the towering Mount Sanchil, which appears to dominate the entire range. On the other side of the Gorge are the high, jagged formations of Falestoh and Zeban, before and below which lies the fortified feature of Dologorodoc. In front of the fort, in the direction of Agordat, lies the long, wide bed of the 'Happy Valley', from which the surrounding features shoot heavenwards some two thousand feet. Rising sharply in the east corner of the valley stands the Aqua Col.

The strategic value of this mass of natural defences had long since been fully appreciated by the Italian High Command, and it was here that General Luigi Frusci, Governor of Eritrea and Commander-in-Chief of the Italian Northern Army, decided to concentrate the bulk of his forces in one final effort to hold Eritrea.

The Key

The Italian stronghold of Fort Dologorodoc, the key position covering Keren and the main approach road to Asmara, capital of Eritrea, provided one of the bloodiest of battlegrounds, and its capture was largely responsible for the sudden and total collapse of Italy's mighty colonial empire, comprising Abyssinia, Somaliland and Eritrea.

The Battleground

Since the Gallabat showdown, we had concentrated largely on marching and assaulting the precipitous heights round Sabderat, which lies between Kassala and Keren. As intended, the latter form of activity obviously fitted us well for the Keren operations. Lord, how we sweated and toiled to master those monstrous heights, and yet the dry humour common to the sturdy Yorkshireman continued to flow freely. Between their puffs and grunts, one caught such apt and expressive remarks as: 'Think we're bloody mountain goats' and 'We'll be sprouting horns soon.'

One felt that to scale those almost unclimbable heights, fully armed and equipped for battle, was a feat in itself, requiring supreme physical effort. It was not surprising therefore that one of the major problems with which we were faced at Keren was that of arriving high up on the enemy strongpoints in a fit state to fight.

The soil between the hard, jagged boulders crumbled underfoot, and many of the smaller rocks were so easily dislodged that they proved to be an extremely risky aid to climbing. One had also to contend with the thick, thorny scrub and the hard sharp-pointed grass that, together with the boulder-studded slopes, made up the general pattern of the Eritrean countryside around Keren.

The enemy, on the other hand, held every advantage. He could sit tight in comparative comfort and await the approaching mass of struggling humanity. As a general rule, the greater proportion of his forces were established behind and just below the crest of whatever height they occupied. It was only when our artillery barrage lifted, and they thought that an assault on their position was imminent, that their defences were fully manned and their full strength exposed. Time and time again our troops got to within a stone's throw of the enemy strongpoints, only to be literally blasted back by automatic fire and showers of the comparatively small, red, tinny grenades with which the Italians were well supplied.

.... On the night of 15–16 March the battle was joined. We moved off quietly with the object of making a wide detour to the right and crossing into the immediate battle zone at a point known as White Ridge.

We had already been told of the magnificent display of courage by the 3rd/5th Mahrattas, who had advanced to the attack at last light. After fierce hand-to-hand fighting, and at least four spirited attacks, they had finally succeeded in driving the enemy from the summit of 'Pimple'. In doing so, they had expended their entire reserves. We were later to learn that the task of taking 'Pimple', the next and final objective before the Fort, had been taken over by the 3rd/12th Frontier Force.

Throughout our advance the noise was deafening. We scrambled forward and upwards at a good if erratic pace among the scrub and between the juts of jagged rock. The roar of our guns, now seemingly well behind us, was relieved only by the blinding flashes and the crashing of our shells immediately in front. So close to us were many of these shells that I gained the impression that we were not regulating the pace of our advance to timed artillery concentrations, but that we were following closely in the wake of a creeping barrage.

We passed through the 3rd/12th Frontier Force on 'Pimple' soon after they had beaten off an exceptionally fierce counter-attack. It was first light, and we passed on at staggering pace past many of that gallant regiment, who appeared to be half-standing and half-lying against the large sloping rocks as if in moment-ary repose. To all appearances these men, with their rifles in the immediate-action position, were keeping vigilant watch towards Dologorodoc: it was only on hurrying past that one realized that they would see no further action.

Supported by the guns of the 144th and the 28th Field Regiments, we passed on along the knife-edged ridge between 'Pimple' and Fort Dologorodoc. The going was tough and the fighting hard but spasmodic. Small, independent pockets of resistance were soon overcome at the point of the bayonet. The last hundred yards or so up to the Fort were difficult to negotiate, owing to the crumbling and powdery nature of the ground—a state our artillery had un-doubtedly helped to produce. At about 6.30 a.m. the success signal, in the form of Verey lights, indicated that we were at last in possession of Fort Dologorodoc.

The Fort consisted of a concrete trench running most of the way round and just below the rock-faced summit of the hill. As the concreted half of the newly-won dug-outs now faced away from the enemy, we were set the immediate task of building sand-bag walls on the reverse side of Dologorodoc, from which direction the enemy would surely counter-attack.

The fighting which followed our capture of Fort Dologorodoc was close and bitter in the extreme. Between counter-attacks the enemy pumped shells and mortar bombs into the Fort by day and by night.

That the enemy considered Fort Dologorodoc to be the key position in his defence system was indicated by the ferocity and determination of his attempts to oust us from it. These heavy and costly attacks with such crack troops as the Savoy Grenadiers and the Alpini and Bersaglieri Regiments eventually sapped his strength and cracked his morale.

In the early hours of 25 March, attacks were successfully pressed home by the West Yorks and the 3rd/12th Frontier Force on three small features which lay just forward and to the left of the Fort between Falestoh and Zeban.

On the night of 26–27 March, 29 Brigade passed through the newly-won 9 Brigade positions and assaulted Falestoh and Zeban. By dawn we had occupied both features.

At first light on 27 March a white flag was to be seen flying from the impregnable Mount Sanchil, and a little later others appeared on 'Brigs Peak' and Mounts Amba and Samanna.

British infantry officer

So Keren fell after fifty-three days of siege. It is estimated that the Italians employed in battle a total of thirty-nine battalions and thirty-six batteries, and that during the period of operations they disposed in all of something over thirty thousand infantry, supported by 144 guns. Many of these were fresh troops, and although the British forces never succeeded in driving their opponents from the main peaks on either side of the Dongolaas Gorge, and suffered over four thousand casualties in their attempts to do so, it is true to say that the enemy brought defeat on himself and finally wore himself out in his eight fierce but fruitless attempts to retake Dologorodoc Fort. It was here that his best and freshest units were driven back with crippling losses. In General Frusci's own situation reports, which were captured, he reveals that three thousand dead were left in Keren, including General Lorenzini and five senior officers. Practically all had been staked in holding this natural fortress, with the result that, at the end, there were but three battalions and a few batteries uncommitted between Keren and Asmara. The fall of Keren was the beginning of the end of Italian influence and power in East Africa. The road lay open to the capital city of Eritrea. On 1 March our troops marched into Asmara. Massawa, the enemy's principal port on the Red Sea coast, surrendered with ten thousand prisoners on 8 April.

Lieutenant-Colonel J. E. B. Barton

Meanwhile East and South African forces under General Cunningham had executed a rapid and brilliant advance northward, overrunning Italian Somaliland, and, in conjunction with troops landed from Aden, had by mid-March cleared British Somaliland of the enemy. By April the Italians were being driven from

Abyssinia. On the 6th of the month General Cunningham's soldiers entered Addis Ababa. The remnants of the Italian armies in East Africa, under the Duke of Aosta, were hemmed in at Amba Alagi by General Mayne.

Indians at Amba Alagi

I had puffed and panted my way to the top of a sheer peak which afforded the best available observation of the enemy's position at Toselli. The Garhwali tactical headquarters were there, and so was an important O.P. from the 28th Field Regiment. As I arrived exhausted at my destination, a party of British gunners caught me up and were hailed with obvious enthusiasm by some Garhwali signallers, who were brewing tea in a dugout. I stopped for a breather before scaling the last fifty feet to the look-out, and saw out of the tail of my eye much hand-shaking and then the Englishmen squatting down beside the Indians and accepting the tea and cigarettes that they offered.

Having finished my own business in half an hour or so, I began stumbling down the hill again, only to be stopped by the same Garhwali signallers and led into the dugout. There I, too, was given tea, biscuits, and a cigarette. I took them thankfully, but with mild protest, knowing that every half-pint of water and morsel of everything else had to be carried by hand from a water point over a mile away and nearly a thousand feet lower down, and I asked the Garhwalis whether it was their habit to entertain every Tom, Dick and Harry who came their way. Their answer was a flat denial. Not a bit of it. It was business enough to keep their own tummies full, and normal hospitality had to go hang. But in my case it was different. I was, after all, the Divisional Commander and a very old man too! Then what about the British soldiers, I asked. 'Oh, that's quite different,' they replied, 'they belong to the 28th. They belong to us.'

General Mayne

At about 7.30 a.m. on 6 May, when plans for an all-out assault on the enemy's main defences were almost complete, envoys from the Duke of Aosta arrived at General Mayne's headquarters. They first asked for an armistice, in order that they might hand over to us their many casualties. It was also requested that they should be given access to fresh water supplies. When a truce was refused, General Mayne was asked to receive one of the Duke of Aosta's senior officers, with the object of discussing surrender terms. To this he agreed.

The reason for this sudden desire to capitulate was soon evident. On the night before the Duke sent his envoys to General Mayne, a burst from our artillery had hit an Italian fuel dump high up on Amba Alagi. The contents of the dump had cascaded downhill and contaminated the enemy's only source of drinking water.

British infantry officer

Surrender with Honour

'Surrender with Honour' was an idea that had never occurred to me and nothing of the kind was included in the terms of surrender which I sent by hand of Colonel Russell to the Duke of Aosta. The suggestion originated with the

Duke himself, and as soon as it was communicated to me I felt that I could make capital out of it—that it was I who would benefit much more than the Italians. This is why I thought of it that way.

Amongst my terms of surrender, which Colonel Russell was to elaborate verbally, was a demand that the battlefield should be handed over 'clean'; all mines, booby traps and such like were to be clearly defined and their location shown to those troops of mine who were to take over the area; there was to be no sabotage or destruction of any kind of guns, equipment and stores; none were to be hidden and all were to be handed over intact to my representatives. All that was very easy to say and equally easy for the Italians to accept. But would they play up honestly? Obviously not, I thought. It would be nothing else than normal, underhand, war-time practice for them to spend the intervening hours between now and the march-out hiding or sabotaging the breech-blocks of valuable guns and anything else that might be of use to us; and it would be only natural for an enemy conveniently to forget to show us some of the places where mines and booby-traps had been laid, and many of our men would be blown up for the price of their 'forgetfulness'.

But if I put the Duke of Aosta 'on his honour' it might, I thought, put things on an entirely different footing. He was, as I knew, an honourable man and, as a popular Prince, his word ought to be unbreakable law to every single soldier in his army. So, for the price of allowing the Italian troops to march out in military formation—handing over their arms a couple of miles away from the battlefield instead of on the battlefield itself—I should, as I hoped, get a clean and complete hand-over of valuable equipment and stores. And, more important still to my way of thinking, I should save the lives of men who might otherwise stroll over ground that looked harmless, but, in fact, concealed death-dealing contraptions of many kinds.

As events proved, I was quite right. The Duke of Aosta was delighted with my concession and, as he told me, gave a rigid and unmistakable edict that the hand-over was to be complete and clean, making it quite clear that any breach of his orders would mean that he had broken his own word. So the Italians did play up. We got everything intact and no one, save Abyssinian patriots who broke all bounds in their search for loot and deserved their fate, suffered so much as a scratch from a hidden mine, although there were plenty of them about.

General Mayne

A Message to the Emperor: 9 May

It is with deep and universal pleasure that the British nation and Empire have learned of Your Imperial Majesty's welcome home to your capital at Addis Ababa. Your Majesty was the first of the lawful sovereigns to be driven from his throne and country by the Fascist-Nazi criminals, and you are now the first to return in triumph.

Winston Churchill to the Emperor Haile Selassie of Abyssinia

THE WESTERN DESERT

During the long months needed to conquer Italian East Africa, the deserts of the north had been the scene of spectacular attack and counter-attack. After three months of skirmishing, the main Italian army advanced into Egypt on 13 September 1940, but so successfully were they harried by the inferior British forces slowly retiring before them that they halted at Sidi Barrani only four days and sixty-odd miles later.

Introduction to the Desert

The desert has been described, acidly but with no little justice, as 'miles and miles and bloody miles of absolutely damn all'. There was a seeming eternity of barren, inhospitable nothingness. And this lack of physical features and recognizable landmarks by which to find your way made navigation a problem to all, and was particularly baffling to the newcomer to the desert. You learned to move by map, compass and speedometer. You were never really certain that you were actually at the point from which you thought you were starting, and you had to take your map reference on trust: there was no guarantee. It was hard to tell how far away the horizon was. Your sense of direction became befuddled, you were haunted by the constant risk of losing your way. After a time you developed a sense of direction in daylight; but at night, though to proceed in a general direction was tolerably simple, it was no light matter to pin-point a unit or a rendezvous. You might search for a group of tanks reported to be leaguered at a certain map reference, and you might spend hours driving round the sand, when all the time the tanks were only a mile distant. Unless it was extremely urgent that they be found, it was wiser to camp down for the night and wait until daybreak. Usually the tanks were then visible towards the horizon.

You had to step out of your truck or jeep, lorry or staff car whenever you needed to take a new compass bearing. You kept a watchful eye on the speedometer. And you found your way back by observation of tiny details: a pile of stones or jerry cans that someone had dropped, or a strip of red flag on a hillside, or a tin of bully-beef lying in the sand. All vehicles looked alike, and to search for your unit was sometimes like looking at a sea of transport as though in a nightmare. You gazed upon acres of flat desert studded with scores of trucks, and these were poor landmarks—they might move at any time.

All vehicles could be seen moving from afar because of the trail of dust that billowed up behind or to one side. When two trucks did meet, each driver tried desperately to steer to windward and so avoid the dust of the other vehicle. You might wear sand goggles, but your face was coated with sand that caked itself into a beige mask, clinging to the sweat of your countenance, collecting in the corners of your eyes. Hands and arms, necks and knees became coated with this same sand, which penetrated under your shirt, and caught in your throat, and made your eyes smart. Your hair became matted and bistre. Along your limbs the trickling sweat would cleave little rivulets through the sandy coating.

All day long thousands of vehicles shod with balloon tyres or with tracks were moving about, each with its plume of sand that poured up over the mudguards, penetrated into the carburettor, came through chinks in the truck's body, or round the edge of a staff car's windows. The tanks cut deep ruts in the sand. Half the surface of the desert might appear to be in the air at one time, and drivers would keep their windscreen-wipers going in order to clear the dust and so see a few yards ahead. For in a sandstorm, with its blown and gritty sand that lashed the human body and was blasted everywhere that particles of sand can go, there was an opaque yellowish fog ahead, into which you could peer for but a yard or two. It was as though some shuddering beige curtain had been drawn across the face of the desert; the light of day became unreal in its strange hues; you stumbled over tent ropes and into slit trenches; minefields became a still greater source of danger; while maps were invisible beneath the layer of dust. . . .

Although you were permanently coated with sand when driving or when the wind blew up, baths were impossible and you grew accustomed to being dirty, to washing seldom. Water was short in the desert, scarcer by far than petrol. On a gallon a day for all purposes it became an art to wash, shave, clean your teeth, wash your feet, all in a mug of water, with the resultant glutinous fluid being strained and poured into the radiator of your truck. Some men planned to wash a third of their bodies each day, for the sand became matted in the hairy parts of the body, and they felt the imperative need for washing it away, even though a fresh lot of sand was picked up at once.

Antony Brett-James

The Art of War

It was after we had left the coastal road that Templeton stopped the truck and said, 'Now, if you two are going to learn to drive in the desert, you might as well start now. You'll find it's not so easy as you may think. Stannard, you take first crack.'

He allowed each of us a turn and, being novices at what we later recognized as something of an art, our efforts were exhausting. It was not so much that we lacked practice in driving, but that with unfailing regularity each of us had managed to pick just those soft patches of sand into which the truck sank axle-deep each time. Then followed the business of digging out the wheels, placing the sand channels and driving forward or backward to the limit of the channels, so that, repeating the process time after time until firm ground was reached again, we could drive on until we struck the next patch of soft sand. It was after yet another of these incidents that Egerton, his normal cheerfulness somewhat subdued, was heard to remark, "If the whole —— desert's like this, it's going to be a bloody long war.'

This was almost despair from Egerton, for nothing in our so far brief association had ever seemed to worry him unduly. But we were all feeling tired and irritable by now and were thankful when Templeton decided on a meal halt.

We now made our first attempt at the recognized Desert Army method of a 'brew-up' of tea. We cut in half one of the thin sheet-metal four-gallon petrol tins used at that time, punched it with holes and filled it with sand and gravel. We then poured on a generous splash of petrol and set it alight. The tea was brewed in the other half of the tin. When the water was boiling, tea, sugar and milk were all added and the whole potion was vigorously stirred. The resulting brew was strong and sweet, like no other tea that we had tasted before.

Cyril Joly

THE ITALIANS ADVANCE

At last, on 13 September, the Italians advanced into Egypt. It was with a fanfare of triumphant threats that they launched the new campaign.

For three days before the advance actually began the indications had been so clear that we had already started to take the preliminary action before withdrawal. The track down the escarpment at Halfaya Pass had been torn up and mined, as had the coastal track from Sollum to the east. Mines had been sown, too, at various vital places in the desert and the available water supplies had been salted.

The Italians' advance was entirely down 'Hellfire' Pass and along the coastal road.

The move down the pass was bombed by the R.A.F., shelled by our artillery and hampered by exploding mines, until such confusion reigned that the Italian troops were forced to dismount from their lorries and scrambled down on foot. The subsequent advance along the coast was preceded, as usual, by motor-cyclists to reconnoitre, supported by groups of tanks to execute the main thrusts and assaults, backed by guns to clear each new objective and disperse opposition, and finally reinforced by the infantry, whose task it was to occupy the ground captured and to repel any counter-attacks.

For four days, from the 13th to the 16th of September, the slow, fumbling, hesitant advance continued until it had reached Sidi Barrani, sixty-five miles from the Italian starting positions. Each small ridge was contested. The Italian columns were bombed by day by the R.A.F. and by night were shelled by the guns, who found it easy to locate and hit the Italian night leaguers, since their positions were given away by searchlights which continually swept the surrounding desert.

At Sidi Barrani the advance halted and, to our surprise and indignation, the Italians started to dig in and prepare defended positions—surprise because till then the Italians had not had to overcome any prepared positions nor had they suffered excessive losses; indignation because a strong counter-thrust had been prepared farther east and the remainder of 7 Armoured Division was lying in wait.

From the beginning of the war in June the Italians had suffered some three thousand five hundred killed and wounded and had lost seven hundred prisoners; many guns, tanks and lorries also had been destroyed. Our losses had been a hundred and fifty men killed, wounded and missing and not more than fifty tanks and lorries destroyed or captured. Despite the disparity in numbers and the distance from the base, we had, for three months, not only contained a vastly superior enemy, but had also made ourselves such masters of the open desert that, even with five divisions, the Italians now felt obliged to bring their ponderous advance to a grinding halt, to secure the sixty-five miles of communications against the mere threat of action which might have cut them off from their base.

Cyril Joly

THE DESERT GALLOP

The Italians remained inactive for nearly three months, a breathing-space which allowed the British forces in Egypt to be built up for a counter-offensive. On 8 December 1940 General O'Connor's assault was launched.

All through the night of Sunday, 8 December, the R.A.F. bombed Sidi Barrani and aerodromes to the west, the Navy bombarded Maktila and the guns of 7 Armoured Division shelled the camps of Nibeiwa and Rabia. Under cover of this noise the final moves to complete the concentration were made. Guided by specially posted marker lights organized by the Support Group, the Matilda tanks and 11 Indian Infantry Brigade moved until they were in position to the west and north-west of Nibeiwa, facing the less heavily defended portion of the perimeter and a gap through which, the previous evening, twenty-three Italian M.11 light tanks had been seen to move—a reassuring sign that it had not been mined.

Punctually at 07.00 hours the next morning the guns began to register their targets. At 07.15 the bombardment by about two hundred guns started, and the Matildas and the infantry moved in to attack Nibeiwa.

Meanwhile we in 4 Armoured Brigade had begun our advance to the coastal road some thirty-five miles away. As the sky lightened in the east and the guns started their bombardment, I could not help feeling awed and exhilarated. To my right, as we moved, the desert was bare and deserted, but it was from here that in due course the enemy might attack or the desert might become filled with enemy surprised by our move. However empty and tranquil it looked then, there was the lurking threat of sudden action, and action on a scale that I had not experienced before.

However preoccupied I was with the stark, ominous desert to my right, I could not resist occasionally glancing at the scene on my left. As far as the eye could see, stretching across the horizon to my left front and flank and rear, there were vehicles moving: the tanks of the leading and the other flanking regiment to my front and left, and behind me the other two squadrons of my own regiment. Each tank was followed by a plume of sand, lit and high-lighted by the slanting rays of the early sun, as it pitched and rolled and tossed over the uneven, stony surface of the desert. Within the three-sided box formed by the tanks were the supply vehicles, the fitters' lorries, the doctors' trucks, the ambulances. In the centre of the whole array I could see the few vehicles of the Brigade Headquarters. In front of them, and behind the centre of the leading regiment, was the small group of tanks from which I knew the Brigadier was controlling the whole move and ready to give instant orders the moment the enemy was met. The contrast between the scene on my left and that on my right continued to enthral me as we advanced towards the coast.

As the light spread over the sky to the east I felt, rather than heard, the dull concussion of the guns as they fired on Nibeiwa. I could imagine the consternation of the unsuspecting Italians and the confusion which would follow. In my mind's eye I followed the Matildas in their attack.

Cyril Joly

The fall of Sidi Barrani, Sollum, Fort Capuzzo, Bardia, Tobruk and Ben-
ghazi were the landmarks in the breathless onset of General O'Connor's mobile
forces. At the end of two months, five hundred miles of territory had been won and
an enemy army destroyed.

We were all desperately tired, until sometime during the siege of Tobruk, when I, for one, got my second wind. Starting with the sandstorm during the attack on Sidi Barrani, the weather had been persistently bad. High winds had either lashed the desert sand into storms of unusual intensity or had brought torrential downpours of rain, which had swamped the pits we dug for shelter or penetrated the hastily rigged bivouacs and seeped through every crack and crevice in tank or lorry. After the intense heat of the summer I found that I took time to get used to the cold and wet. Nor, to begin with, was I accustomed to the endless lack of sleep and the inadequate food. Eighteen hours of intense watchfulness and alert wakefulness, followed by six hours of so-called rest disturbed by a tour of guard duty and the ceaseless turmoil and noise of the leaguer, for forty days at a stretch—that had been our lot. When, at last, at the end of each day I crept into my blankets to get what sleep I could, I found that my earlier life of ease and luxury made it difficult for me to sleep soundly in these conditions. Either the blankets were wet from the day's heavy rain, or, muffled beneath a ground-sheet as protection against more night rain, the air was too close for comfort; or the ground was hard and pebbly; or it was just too cold for the blankets to afford enough warmth for sound repose. Whatever the reasons, I found that each night it was an effort to sleep.

Cyril Joly

Tobruk: 22 January 1941

The morning after the battle ended, smoke from smouldering dumps and ships still drifted over the town and harbour of Tobruk, though the front had already jumped a hundred miles westward to the heights above Derna. Before continuing their advance the Australian and British troops who had stormed Tobruk could rest, swim and look around. Only a few were supposed to have access to the town, but several hundred spirited themselves inside.

Driving in that morning, we turned up Via Mussolini, already renamed 'Pitt Street', and past 'Albergo Tobruch', which now bore the sign 'Young and Jackson's'. Down the road swaggered a party of Diggers, Italian national and regimental pennants flying from their bayonets, gay Fascist badges, cockades and ribbons stuck in their hats or pinned to their jackets. Their pockets bulged with miscellaneous souvenirs—monogrammed ashtrays, and cutlery from 'Albergo Tobruch', knick-knacks from officers' houses, revolvers, Fascist badges, sashes, swords, whistles and knives from Italian ordnance stores. They reminded me of an incident that occurred earlier in the campaign. A Digger who was escorting some prisoners had acquired an Italian captain's insignia and badges of rank. I asked him how he got them and he said: 'I swapped 'em—for a coupla fags; for 'arf a bloody packet, I coulda been a blasted general.'

Further down the road I saw some Australians with a pile of Italian paper money and it soon became fashionable to light a cigarette with a fifty or a hundred lire or to post an autographed note back to Australia. Useless in Tobruk, these same notes were real money in Benghazi, as the troops ruefully discovered a few weeks later. Through the streets troops were driving anything that moved; little Fiats, big Lancias, captured motor-cycles and Diesel trucks. Some of these and a number of British trucks were drawn up in front of the Italian Navy and Army stores, where there was all the food the troops wanted—and they lost no time in supplementing their rations.

. . . . Tobruk was stocked with enough tinned food for a garrison of twenty-five thousand for two months—a windfall for our troops who had been existing on little but bully-beef, biscuits, butter, jam and tea. The Italian tinned fruit and vegetables were as good as Australia's best. In one store in Tobruk there were supplies of tinned cherries, strawberries, pears, apricots, beans, peas and carrots, and these were soon being issued along with regular British rations. Most welcome of all were square two-gallon tins of pulped tomatoes and great boxes of spaghetti; but packets of powdered garlic had few takers. Even the cool-store was well stocked with meat, and in one dump there were several hundred tons of flour which went straight to our field bakeries.

Chester Wilmot, war correspondent

Victory

On 7 February 1941 *the remains of the Italian army in Cyrenaica were trapped near Beda Fomm, beyond Benghazi, and there they surrendered.*

The battlefield was an amazing sight. It was strewn with broken and abandoned equipment, tattered uniforms, piles of empty shell and cartridge cases. It was littered with paper, rifles and bedding. Here and there small groups of men tended the wounded who had been gathered together. Others were collecting and burying the dead. Others still, less eager to surrender than the majority, stood or lay waiting to be captured. Some equipment was still burning furiously, more was smouldering. There were many oil and petrol fires emitting clouds of black smoke.

There were few incidents. Soon the generals and the high-ranking officers had been discovered and taken away. The remaining officers were piled unceremoniously into Italian lorries and driven off. The thousands of men were formed into long columns guarded at head and tail by only one or two of our impassive, imperturbable and perpetually cheerful soldiers, who shouldered the unaccustomed new duties with the same confident assurance with which they had met and mastered all the other trials of the campaign.

It was the work of some days to clear the battlefield of all that was worth salvaging and to muster and despatch on their long march to the prison camps in Egypt the thousands of prisoners. At Benghazi, which had fallen into Australian hands on the same day as the surrender to us farther south, and at Beda Fomm, the Italians had lost some twenty thousand men killed and captured, as well as fifteen hundred lorries, 112 tanks and 216 guns.

Cyril Joly

During February, 7 *Armoured Division pushed ahead as far as El Agheila, on the borders of Tripolitania, but by now General O'Connor's little army had reached the end of its endurance. The 'gallop' was over.*

9

GERMANY STRIKES SOUTH

Even while the Italian Empire crumbled before Wavell's forces, storm-clouds were gathering to the north. Hitler was preparing to overrun the Balkans, in order to cover his preparations for an assault on Russia, to establish himself on the Mediterranean and thus threaten the Middle East, and incidentally to afford succour to the battered Italians, who had been faring as badly in their war with Greece as elsewhere. The victorious British forces in Africa were hurriedly depleted so as to allow aid to be sent to Greece. However ill-fated this was, Germany's intervention in Greece led to a delay which was to prove fatal to Hitler's designs on Russia.

THE GREEK ADVENTURE

THE more we examined the problem, the more unsound the venture appeared. There were so many uncertain quantities. What would Turkey do? Would Jugoslavia resist an Axis move through her country? Would Germany attack Turkey before Greece? The answer to any of these questions would have a decided influence upon our plans. One thing was quite certain, and that was if Germany decided to attack Greece it would be in full strength, and by all practicable routes.

In February, 1941, a very high-powered party arrived in Cairo. There were Eden (then Secretary of State for War), Dill (Chief of the Imperial General Staff), and their advisers. Discussions took place behind closed doors and we on the lower levels were all agog to know what was happening, and what decisions were being made. As far as I can remember the Planners were not asked to produce a paper giving their views as to the feasibility of the project. We certainly held some very decided ones.

The D.M.I., Brigadier Shearer, did produce a paper drawing attention to the great dangers of this campaign in view of the German resources and methods. I remember this paper coming back from the C.-in-C., General Wavell. There was a short note written in his own hand across the top—it said:

'"War is an option of difficulties."—Wolfe. A.P.W.'

Major-General Sir Francis de Guingand

Winston Churchill to General Smuts: 28 February

We have taken a grave and hazardous decision to sustain the Greeks and try to make a Balkan Front.

Landing in Greece: March

Because of a bad bloomer on someone's part, we were issued with tropical kit of 'Bombay bloomers' (those frightful turned-up shorts), 'Bombay bowlers' (pith helmets) and shirts. As practical kit for crossing the Med. and fighting in a Greek spring, the clothing was just fantastic, and the 'bowler' an unmitigated bloody nuisance. I threw mine into a snowdrift on Mount Olympus. Despite instructions to hand in battle-dress, all Kiwis wore it, packing the tropical gear, except the helmet. Only place for the confounded thing was on the head—hence the extraordinary spectacle of British and New Zealand troops disembarking at Piraeus in battle-dress and pith helmets. That must have shaken the German Embassy, as they watched us pass.

Another point worth mentioning is the secrecy of our move to Greece. Officially, the verdict is that the destination was not known to the bulk of the troops. My impression is rather different. Anyone who was interested knew perfectly well, including the enemy! There were Gyppo and other money changers at most dock gates, and in Amiriya, peddling drachmae notes: 'Very good money—veree cheap! You need, Kiwi—in Athens!'

Brigadier George Clifton

We landed at the Piraeus and for a few days camped in the pines on Mount Hymettos, on the outskirts of Athens. Our camp was inspected by some smart-looking Evzones, the German Consul, and a number of half-starved citizens. The 18th Battalion, the first to land, had already gone forward. It was impossible to do any serious training, and we waited impatiently. At last orders arrived for us to entrain and also for me to leave six out of my forty officers and forty-six of my 813 other ranks. This meant more painful selections and I had to withstand some most urgent protests. But I was determined to have good people in the reinforcements and made no concessions, promising them all plenty of fighting in the good time to come. After a church parade I told the battalion what I could remember about Greece and what it stood for, and we marched through Athens past the crowded balcony of the German Embassy and entrained for the front, now being built up north of Mount Olympus.

Brigadier Kippenberger

Retreat—Break-up

The British forces, consisting of the New Zealand Division, 6 Australian Division and 1 Armoured Brigade, were to help seven weak Greek divisions to hold the Aliakhmon line, which ran across northern Greece from the Jugoslav frontier on the west to the Aegean on the east. In Bulgaria the Germans had massed fifteen divisions and ten times the Allies' strength in aircraft for their assault, which could fall on both Greece and Jugoslavia.

Two days after the Germans attacked on 6 April the Jugoslav armies crumbled, leaving the western flank of the Aliakhmon line completely exposed, and five days later the withdrawal from this position began. As the Germans poured down into Greece the Greek forces disintegrated, rendering the British plan of making a stand at Thermopylae impracticable. Evacuation was then the only course left open to the British troops.

Germany declared war on Greece,* and to our surprise we still made no move forward. Across the bay one evening we heard the faint rolling thunder of

* 6 April (Ed.).

distant bombing and saw the dull glow of fires in Salonika. It could not be long now.

Next day there was rain. About four in the afternoon I was ordered to report to Brigade Headquarters. On the way down I saw the 6th Field Regiment hauling and winding and manhandling its guns out of their muddy pits on to the equally muddy road. Obviously we were going forward. The Brigadier, to my extreme surprise, said that we were giving up the Aliakhmon position, 6 Brigade going back behind 5 Brigade somewhere, 4 Brigade to move through the Olympus pass and up to Servia to cover the left of the army. There had been disaster in Jugoslavia and the position might become serious.

Brigadier Kippenberger

We had been preparing a defensive position in support of the Rangers, the motor battalion of 1 Armoured Brigade, to meet the expected German attack from Bulgaria to our north-east. As usual our gunpits were to be wasted. For on the evening of 8 April came a message that the Germans had smashed their way across southern Jugoslavia and were pushing south through the Florina Gap behind us, threatening to cut us off. Our orders were to move at once forty miles west into the mountains and join the rest of 1 Armoured Brigade on a line south of Florina. The position of the Germans was unknown and there were rumours that they had already cut our route at the road junction of Veve. If so, our prospects would not be cheerful.

It was a long, cold, wet drive. As we passed through the villages in the dark, Greek soldiers and civilians came out to cheer us, thinking that we were on our way north to attack the enemy. Little did they know that the retreat had already begun. Their enthusiasm brought back memories of the 'triumphant' march into Belgium in May 1940, and we hoped that this time there would be a less dismal ending. We reached Veve about 1 a.m. As we wound down into the village we could see a long line of tiny pinpricks of light moving slowly along the road from Florina. Luckily for us we soon discovered that it was not the enemy, but a column of mules and bullock-carts of the Greek and Jugoslav armies, mixed up with civilian refugees. A few minutes later we were hailed out of the darkness by a cheery Aussie voice and we knew that the Australians had arrived from the south and we were not cut off.

. . . . We moved back thirty-five miles, across the Aliakhmon river, leaving a small brigade rearguard to follow us later. There had been much talk of the Aliakhmon as the main line of defence in Greece. When we crossed the river in bright moonlight and saw not a sign of troops, not even a slit trench dug, we realized that our retreat was very far from going according to plan. We were on the extreme left of the Imperial forces in Greece. The only Greek troops we saw were by now thoroughly disorganized, for with horsed transport they hadn't a chance of getting away. Next day we spent lying up just north of Grevena. The scrub-covered valleys offered little concealment and the first morning flight of Messerschmitts spotted us.

That evening we got orders for a further fifteen-mile retreat to a position behind the river Venetikos. A message from our C.O., Lieutenant-Colonel

Aikenhead, prepared us for the worst: 'You will hold your positions at all costs till the flanks are turned, when you will extricate your troops as best you can and, unless other orders are received, move to rejoin the British troops in Greece, in a south-easterly direction. I am confident that the Regiment will continue to give a fine account of itself. . . . Good luck.' Much later we were to hear that G.H.Q. had given the Brigade up for lost and never expected us to emerge from the mountains.

After dark we started on a nightmare drive. Grevena was full of burning dumps and lorries and houses, bewildered Greek troops and confused columns of mules and bullock carts. The road on to the Venetikos was narrow and twisting, sometimes with steep ravines or precipices on both sides. We were a mixed cavalcade. Vehicles were jammed nose to tail for miles, double- and even treble-banked wherever the road was wide enough. Buses and private cars, Greeks on horseback and foot, were all jumbled in between our guns. Halts were interminable and we crawled forward a few hundred yards at a time. Weary drivers fell asleep in their cabs and had to be roused by cursing officers and N.C.Os. Our route was strewn with all the litter of a retreat: discarded clothing, ammunition and harness, dead mules and horses, sodden papers and office files, and dozens of abandoned vehicles—ramshackle requisitioned lorries from every province of Greece, British three-tonners side by side with Italian tractors and mobile workshops captured by the Greek Army in Albania and now waiting for their original owners; some bogged down in the ditches, some tipped at crazy angles into bomb craters, others burnt out or shattered by machine-gun bullets. All the time dawn was getting nearer and we could look forward to being caught by the first air sortie like rats in a trap, unable to disperse off the narrow road. But at first light the miracle occurred and the column began to move. As we twisted down into the Venetikos valley, a single Messerschmitt flew along the bottom of the gorge below us. But we were safely in action across the river and well camouflaged before the first air attacks began. It had taken us twelve hours to cover fifteen miles.

We never fired a round on the Venetikos, for the enemy found more to interest him in our flanks and was slow to follow down our road. But the Luftwaffe showed no lack of interest in us, treating us every few hours to a display of machine-gunning and dive-bombing which brought home to us as never before what monopoly of the air meant. Our guns were well off the road and were not attacked, but our B Echelons had a grim day. On the 16th we woke to grey skies and clouds low down over the hills. The rain saved us, and for thirty-six hours we didn't see a single enemy plane. But our road became a morass of pot-holes, mud and slime. About 3 p.m. we were on the move southwards again, wondering whether we would get through. The track was a new one, unmarked on our maps, and it was not certain whether it had ever been completed. There were also rumours that the Germans had cut it a few miles ahead. Working parties travelling in front of each unit performed wonders. They felled pine-trees to fill the axle-deep ruts, put down wire-netting, filled in craters and pushed crocks and abandoned lorries off the road. The rain poured steadily down. But we met no Germans and our skid chains got us through. Next day the pace quickened, and at midday on the 17th we emerged from the misty, wooded mountains and reached the plains, sunshine and a metalled road. We had regained contact with the main Imperial forces—and simultaneously with the Luftwaffe.

Major C. I. W. Seton-Watson

When to 'blow' and who orders the engineer firer to press his exploder handle are two problems which have given many soldiers and staff officers headaches in many wars. Coming back down Greece, whenever New Zealanders tailed the withdrawal, a squadron of the Divisional Cavalry were last men out. They had a Demolition Officer, who stood by each successive firing party, tallied his squadron past like sheep through a drafting race, and when either the last vehicle or the first enemy appeared said, 'O.K. Let her go!' And she went. Simple but most effective. My engineers blew up ninety-five bits and pieces of Greece and we only slipped once.

Brigadier Clifton

My idea was the obvious one: to travel south during the day, cross the road down which the German army would be pouring by night, and then head east for the coast. First we must get some food and perhaps help from the villagers, and so two of the party set off for a village near by. We were out of sight of the road and all the countryside was bright and silent. Before they had gone out of earshot we heard, startlingly, the thudding of guns far to the south. I jumped up. 'That's our rearguard at Elassona; they are certain to have orders to stay till night,' I said. And at once we all started southwards as fast as we could walk.

For an hour we plodded on. Small groups of peasants were tramping towards high hills to the west and we passed a few shepherds with little flocks. We said 'Elassona?' to one, and he pointed the way we were going. The thudding and rumble of guns continued, almost seemed a little nearer, and we began to have hope. I called a halt and said that we would observe the regulation ten minutes' halt before every clock hour, and otherwise would walk on all day; that we had a chance, just a chance. We were very weary and hungry, the ground was rough and tumbled; but we trudged on hour after hour, crossing little streams, scrambling through scrub, literally over hill and dale. Soon after midday we came in sight of the road again, packed solid with German transport, head to tail, tanks and guns, lorry-loads of infantry, all halted, with the men strolling about. We turned out of sight, crossed a difficult ravine very slowly, and started to climb up a steep valley leading to the crest of a distinct line of low hills. The guns were undoubtedly nearer, though muffled by the hills, and I thought I could distinguish the nearer crumps of shell-bursts. The valley was steep and we were desperately tired, but we were hopeful now and somehow kept going.

From there on we alternated formations, moving as a clump when the ground concealed us from the Germans and we could be seen by our own gunners, extending to forty paces when the Germans could see us, and moving in bounds from one piece of cover to the next. It was a slow business; we were all tired out and starving, the day was hot, and at each halt half the party would fall asleep and have to be kicked awake for the next bound. The ground was covered with spring flowers and the birds were singing. Evidently we puzzled the gunners of both sides, for sometimes we would make our move in peace, the next time be fired on, and once both parties joined in to fire on us.

Brigadier Kippenberger

Then came three busy days under command of the New Zealand Division at Molos, on the east coast near Thermopylae. On the third day the enemy pressure was becoming formidable and the shelling and dive-bombing were the most intense of the whole campaign. But the New Zealanders held them and the final withdrawal went magnificently according to plan. At 11 p.m. on the 24th we fired off our last rounds with buffers and recuperators drained, left our wrecked guns in their pits and started south for the last time. Next day when we drove through Athens the Greeks lined the streets in thousands, many of them in tears, yet cheering and throwing flowers and shouting, 'You will be back; we'll be waiting for you.' Few retreating armies can have had such a send-off.

Major C. I. W. Seton-Watson

Evacuation: 21–29 April

Anzac Corps allotted 6 Australian Division the honour of following Leonidas and his Spartans in holding the famous Pass of Thermopylae where the main bitumen road zigzagged up nearly three thousand feet of mountain wall. The New Zealanders were spread out for probably ten miles along the coastal sector among the pines, olive groves, and occasional villages fringed by small bays and lovely blue sea. Across a narrow inlet were more hills, and the road winding round from Volos down which some of us had withdrawn. Easy enough to cross by boat, as many of our stragglers did—and as the Boche could do too, if he was so minded. So part of the plot involved coast watchers and even sea patrols in borrowed power-craft. For nearly forty-eight hours everyone worked hell for leather on defences, which the first orders from Force H.Q. decreed would be held for at least one month. Then sometime on 21 April, the unfortunate Greeks finally gave up the unequal struggle and surrendered,* but insisted on two days' grace for the British forces to leave their beautiful country! Easy enough to plan but not so easy to execute. My diary speaks for everyone—'22 Apr.— Called to Div. Conference about 11.00 hrs. regarding plot for withdrawal and embarkation. Move by night by brigades. Lie up by day. Embark by night. All nicely worked out by Anzac Corps. Only disturbing factors are enemy and Force H.Q. who will change scheme for certain. Found Kiwis providing rearguard, and as demolitions were the vital factor asked for command and got it— to my astonishment. Wrote my first complete Engineer Order to take Companies out; saw them all and said good-bye. Then started on my first fighting job.'

Brigadier Clifton

The Peloponnese

. . . . As the light went, the Sunderland crept round the far headland at nought feet to make a perfect landing, perfectly timed. Then a motley collection from Generals to batmen spilled out of various vehicles on to the jetty and prepared to depart. Limited to one suitcase each, great men, accustomed to settle the

* Actually 24 April (Ed.)

lives and destinies of thousands by quick snappy decisions, rummaged over masses of kit, trying to decide what should be jettisoned. Having already taken similar action back at Thermopylae, we stood round sardonic-like and vulturish, waiting for the pickings. A pathetic sight. They took so long and fussed so much that finally the skipper of the Sunderland climbed on to a bollard and roared out: 'Gentlemen! If you don't make up your bloody minds and get aboard the tender, I'm leaving in ten minutes time, otherwise we'll be shot down in daylight to-morrow morning. For God's sake, make it snappy.' Nobody arrested him and they made it very snappy. Within five minutes sixty of them were aboard and away. Not many minutes later we had transferred our gear into a sleek Humber Pullman and gladly jettisoned an historic, battered Utility, veteran of two campaigns. The transfer included four tins of an excellent brand of smoking mixture and two boxes of good cigars which the late, unknown owner, had left behind, doubtless with regret.

Brigadier Clifton

By 2 May a total of 43,000 Imperial troops had been evacuated, many of them going to Crete, where on 5 May Major-General Freyberg, the most famous of all New Zealand soldiers, took up his appointment as Commander-in-Chief. Eleven thousand men together with the whole of the army's matériel *remained on Greek soil.*

CRETE

For about a fortnight there was an uneasy lull.

It was the end of April 1941, in Germany.

A bright spring day dawned over the moorland, and across the broad tracts of the artillery range the young grass sparkled in the morning dew. It felt like the first Sunday after the creation of the world: everything was new and clean and good. A group of young soldiers had fallen in, the early sunlight glinting on their fresh faces. They were wearing the rimless helmets and copious, apparently ill-fitting jumping suits of German parachutists, and their variegated apparel— a mixture of green, grey, brown, and black patches—gave them the appearance of harlequins.

In my capacity of commander of the 1st Battalion of the 3rd Parachute Regiment, it was my duty, on that beautiful spring morning, to decorate each of the twelve young men in the group with a parachutist's badge, for they had just completed their jumping course.

. . . . The small black cases, in which the gilt bronze badges depicting a plunging eagle in an oval garland of oak and laurel leaves lay upon dark blue velvet, were handed to me one by one by my adjutant (who happened to have been a student of theology in civilian life). When I had affixed the last badge, it was up to me to say a few words to the men. I spoke of the obligations which the wearing of this decoration entailed. 'Our formation is young. We have not yet any traditions. We must create tradition by our actions in the future. It depends upon us whether or not the sign of the plunging eagle—the badge which unites us—will go down in history as a symbol of military honour and valour.'

Baron von der Heydte, O.C. 1st Battalion, 3rd Parachute Regiment

Winston Churchill to General Wavell: 28 April

It seems clear from our information that a heavy airborne attack by German troops and bombers will soon be made on Crete. Let me know what forces you have in the island and what your plans are. It ought to be a fine opportunity for killing the parachute troops. The island must be stubbornly defended.

General Freyberg to General Wavell: 1 May

Forces at my disposal are totally inadequate to meet attack envisaged. Unless fighter aircraft are greatly increased and naval forces made available to deal with sea-borne attack I cannot hope to hold out with land forces alone, which as result of campaign in Greece are now devoid of any artillery, have insufficient tools for digging, very little transport, and inadequate war reserves of equipment and ammunition. Force here can and will fight, but without full support from Navy and Air Force cannot hope to repel invasion. If for other reasons these cannot be made available at once, urge that question of holding Crete should be reconsidered.

Plans for Invasion

One look at the hermetically-sealed and shuttered room in the Hotel Grande Bretagne,* where the commanders of all the paratroop regiments and battalions were gathered to receive their orders, was sufficient to dispel the secret of our target: a large map of Crete was prominently displayed upon the wall.

In a quiet but clear and slightly vibrant voice, General Student explained the plan of attack. It was his own, personal plan. He had devised it, had struggled against heavy opposition for its acceptance, and had worked out all the details. One could perceive that this plan had become a part of him, a part of his life. He believed in it and lived for it and in it.

.... When the General had finished, the corps intelligence officer rose to speak. He sketched a broad picture of the enemy's situation. On the island were the remnants of two or three Greek divisions, much weakened by the battles on the mainland, and a British force of divisional strength consisting mainly of Dominion troops under command of the well-known General Freyberg. A portion of the population would be sympathetic towards a German attack. There was also on the island a secret resistance group which would be prepared to fight alongside the Germans and would make itself known to us by the code-words 'Major Bock'.

Next, the quartermaster dealt with the question of supplies, the medical officer with that of hospital arrangements, the commander of the air-transport fleet with matters relating to the air sortie, an admiral with nautical plans, and finally, when it came to the turn of unit commanders to ask questions, there were still some whose egos would not permit them to lose the opportunity of posing questions either which they could well have answered themselves or to which no one could provide any answers at all.

* In Athens (Ed.)

It was already afternoon when the conference came to an end. Before we dispersed, our regimental commander called his three battalion commanders together and ordered us to visit his headquarters in the early evening to receive his operational instructions. Only a short time was left to us in which to snatch a hasty luncheon before returning to our troops. And I was in Athens, no more than a few hundred yards from the foot of the Acropolis. . . . But there was no time for that sort of enjoyment. I felt like a child at the open door of a room full of toys and not being allowed to enter.

Baron von der Heydte

General Freyberg to General Wavell: 16 May

Have completed plan for defence of Crete and have just returned from final tour of defences. I feel greatly encouraged by my visit. Everywhere all ranks are fit and morale is high. All defences have been extended, and positions wired as much as possible. We have forty-five field guns placed, with adequate ammunition dumped. Two infantry tanks are at each aerodrome. Carriers and transport still being unloaded and delivered. 2nd Leicesters have arrived, and will make Heraklion stronger. I do not wish to be over-confident, but I feel that at least we will give excellent account of ourselves. With help of Royal Navy I trust Crete will be held.

20 May

As it grew dark we were transported in lorries to the airfield, where we were greeted by the ear-splitting roar of a hundred and twenty air-transports as they tested their engines in preparation for the take-off. Through clouds of dust we could see red glowing sparks flaring from the exhausts of the machines, and only by this light was it possible to discern the silhouettes of our men. Flashing the pale green beams of their torches in order to indicate their whereabouts, the hundred and twenty officers and N.C.O.s of my battalion tried their best to make themselves heard above the thundering of the engines. The picture reminded me of glow-worms in August.

During the hours which precede a sortie everything seems to become bewitched. Arms containers being hoisted into the racks spill open, aircraft are not where they should be, and the most important machine is liable, for some reason or another, to pack up. But the most extraordinary thing is that despite these numerous hitches the take-off invariably seems to proceed satisfactorily.

Later:

I was roused by my adjutant and started awake, still drowsy, to hear a roar of engines growing louder and louder, as if coming from a great distance. It took me a moment or two to remember where I was and what lay before me.

'We are nearing Crete, sir.'

I got up and moved towards the open door, beside which the dispatcher whose duty it was to see that all final preparations for the jump were ready was seated. Our plane was poised steady in the air, almost as though motionless. Looking out, beyond the silver-grey wing with its black cross marking, I could

see our target—still small, like a cliff rising out of the glittering sea to meet us—
the island of Crete.

Slowly, infinitely slowly, like the last drops wrung from a drying well, the
minutes passed. Again and again I glanced stealthily at my wristwatch. There is
nothing so awful, so exhausting, as this waiting for the moment of a jump. In
vain I tried to compel myself to be calm and patient. A strange unrest had also
gripped most of those who were flying with me.

.... Scarcely able to bear it any longer, I stepped once again to the open door.
We were just flying over the beaches. The thin strip of surf which looked from
above like a glinting white ribbon, separated the blue waters from the yellow-
green of the shore. The mountains reared up before us, and the planes approaching them looked like giant birds trying to reach their eyries in the rocks.

We were still flying inland as if to run against a dark mountainside. It seemed
almost as though we could touch the steep slopes upon which trees and solitary
buildings appeared like toys. Then our left wing dipped and we swung away
from the mountain and the plane started to circle; but soon we straightened out
again, and at that moment there came the pilot's order, 'Prepare to jump!'

Everyone rose and started to fasten his hook to the static line which ran down
the centre of the body of the plane. And while we stood there, securing our
hooks, we noticed that we were losing height, and the pressure of air became
hard, almost painful, to the ear.

Next came the order, 'Ready to jump!'

In two strides I was at the door, my men pressing close behind me, and
grasped the supports on either side of it. The slipstream clutched at my cheeks,
and I felt as though they were fluttering like small flags in the wind.

Suddenly, a lot of little white clouds appeared from nowhere and stood
poised in the air about us. They looked harmless enough, like puffs of cotton-
wool, for the roar of the plane's engines had drowned the sound of the ack-ack
shells' detonation.

Below me was the village of Alikianou. I could see people in the streets
staring up at us, others running away and disappearing into doorways. The
shadows of our planes swept like ghostly hands over the sun-drenched white
houses, while behind the village there gleamed a large mirror—the reservoir—
with single coloured parachutes, like autumn leaves, drifting down towards it.

Our plane slowed down. The moment had come.

'Go!'

I pushed with hands and feet, throwing my arms forward as if trying to
clutch the black cross on the wing. And then the slipstream caught me, and I
was swirling through space with the air roaring in my ears. A sudden jerk upon
the webbing, a pressure on the chest which knocked the breath out of my lungs,
and then—I looked upwards and saw, spread above me, the wide-open, motley
hood of my parachute. In relation to this giant umbrella I felt small and insignificant.

Baron von der Heydte

The morning of 20 May was calm and cloudless, as was every day during the
battle. Before the sunlight had reached the valleys the German reconnaissance

plane appeared. Shortly afterwards a fighter arrived and started to roar up and down the main street of Galatos firing bursts at anything it could see. This struck me as a bit unusual so I hurriedly finished shaving and looked with some caution out of my first-floor window. Other fighters were swooping over the Canea road and there was a great deal of noise from aeroplane engines. Nothing appeared imminent, however, so I finished dressing and went down for breakfast under the trees outside. The plane was still tearing up and down the street and maybe the cooks were bustled, for the porridge was mere oatmeal and water. I was grumbling about this when someone gave an exclamation that might have been an oath or a prayer or both. Almost over our heads were four gliders, the first we had ever seen, in their silence inexpressibly menacing and frightening. Northwards was a growing thunder. I shouted, 'Stand to your arms!', and ran upstairs for my rifle and binoculars. I noticed my diary lying open on the table. Four years later it was returned to me, having meanwhile been concealed by some Cretan girl.

When I reached the courtyard again the thunder had become deafening, the troop-carriers were passing low overhead in every direction one looked, not more than four hundred feet up, in scores. As I ran down the Prison road to my battle headquarters the parachutists were dropping out over the valley, hundreds of them, and floating quietly down.

Brigadier Kippenberger

More like a tramp than a soldier at war I walked along the road towards the white wall before me. And now, as the last of the aircraft turned north towards base, the sound of engines grew fainter and fainter, more and more distant. Somewhere on the high ground ahead of me, to the left of the road, where the village of Galatos was situated, a machine-gun started stuttering. Another answered, followed by rifle-shots. Part of the 2nd Battalion must have contacted the enemy. I registered this fact appreciatively, yet practically without concern, for I was not responsible for what happened over there. Then suddenly, from the mountains behind me, there came a screech of engines—not the ponderous roar of a transport plane, but a sound more like a siren—followed by a fierce crackle of machine-gun fire. Automatically I hurled myself into the ditch—a deep, concrete ditch bordering a large field of corn—and at that moment a German fighter with all guns blazing swept over within a few feet of where I lay. A stream of bullets threw up fountains of dust on the road, and ricochets sang away into the distance. Then, as suddenly as it had appeared, the apparition passed. The fighter pulled up high and disappeared over the olive groves in the direction of what I took to be Canea. So the first shots to be aimed at me during this attack had been fired by one of my own countrymen! No one could have thought of laying out identification signals so soon after landing, and the fighter-pilot, whose task it was to support our attack, had obviously never imagined that this lackadaisical figure wandering in such unmilitary fashion down the centre of the road could possibly have been the commanding officer of a German battalion. . . .

Baron von der Heydte

General Freyberg to General Wavell: 10 p.m., 20 May

To-day has been a hard one. We have been hard pressed. So far, I believe, we hold aerodromes at Retimo, Heraklion, and Maleme, and the two harbours. Margin by which we hold them is a bare one, and it would be wrong of me to paint optimistic picture. Fighting has been heavy and we have killed large numbers of Germans. Communications are most difficult. Scale of air attacks upon Canea has been severe. Everybody here realizes vital issue and we will fight it out.

The Battle

The third day dawned—Thursday, 22 May 1941. In the early morning I went once again with Willi Riese to visit the positions. Nothing had changed during the past twenty-four hours. The ammunition and food situation had not improved. What little ammunition we had received during the previous day had already been used up, and food was virtually unobtainable. According to plan, each company had started to explore the backward areas for supplies. In the abandoned British and Greek positions one would find a tin here, a packet of cigarettes there, and in some deserted farmhouse there might be bread and cheese; but there was nothing like enough to go round. The soldiers were hungry, and in the awful monotony of waiting their morale sank. They tried to make themselves more comfortable by utilizing the paraphernalia which they had found in the abandoned enemy positions. One of the men in 3 Company discovered a most welcome piece of loot in a deserted British dug-out: a gramophone and several records. A sound of dance music was consequently to be heard all day long in the region of 'Little Castle Hill', where 3 Company was in position, and the men took an especial delight in playing English numbers whenever the enemy artillery opened up. A barrage would usually last for about the same length of time as it took to play a record; but once, when the firing continued rather longer, one of the men shouted over the parapet, 'Wait a moment while I change the record!'

Baron von der Heydte

During the day the valley would ring to the volleys of rifle and machine-gun fire sent hurtling across it by both sides, but after darkness set in shooting ceased; for, by a tacit and mute understanding, no firing took place at night; it would have inconvenienced both sides equally. For this was the time when whatever had to be done was done, when the casualties were evacuated, the dead were buried, the rations and ammunition distributed, and the men were able to walk and stretch their legs.

Before dawn we would all be back in our trenches, the hum of aeroplanes would fill the sky, and so would start another day.

After breakfast there was nothing to do except go to sleep, or try to, all except one who acted as sentry. But it was not usually long before someone would cock an ear and exclaim, 'Listen! Here they come!' Whereupon we would scramble to our feet and gaze out towards the sea near the promontory a mile

or two up the coast. Then the faintly audible drone that we knew so well came
floating towards us from over the sea, followed by the dark shapes of troop
transports flying in low over the water. Punctually at nine o'clock every morning
the armada arrived.

At the end of each day, when I visited the posts and talked with the soldiers,
it was always the same question they asked me: how was the battle going, and
what was the news? Their high spirits had been replaced by a grim determination; for they were now playing that hardest of all games—namely, sitting tight,
under orders to defend their positions to the last man, and with no prospect of
relief.

And so the cycle of days continued. Relief was out of the question: there was
no one to relieve us. Not a man had taken off his boots during this past week, or
had been able to have a proper wash; but fortunately the nights had been cool,
thus preventing bodies from attaining that unhygienic state they would have
done in a hotter climate.

British infantry officer

About four o'clock a dozen Stukas dive-bombed Galatos. We had no anti-
aircraft defences and they must have enjoyed it. My headquarters had one or
two very near misses. At this stage I was standing on a table looking through a
window that gave a view over the line from the village to the sea, and every few
minutes I had to stand aside to avoid being seen by one of the planes continuously cruising over the tree-tops shooting at everything in sight. Fountaine,
O'Callaghan and Carson were with me, waiting the order to counter-attack.
Carson's batman kept us all going with cups of tea.

Immediately after the bombing the main infantry attack started against the
18th, and the crackle of musketry swelled to a roar, heavily punctuated by mortar
bursts. Inglis rang and asked what all the noise was about and I could only say
that things were getting warm. I estimated the mortar bursts at six a minute on
one company sector alone. 'Overs' from the German machine-guns were crackling all round our building in the most alarming manner. The telephone system
had been almost destroyed by the bombing; the line to Brigade now went out and,
though the linesmen worked gallantly, was never restored.

I went a few hundred yards forward to get a view of Wheat Hill, and for a
few minutes watched, fascinated, the rain of mortar bursts. In a hollow, nearly
covered by undergrowth, I came on a party of women and children huddled
together like little birds. They looked at me silently, with black, terrified eyes.

Brigadier Kippenberger

Suddenly—almost frighteningly, like a rifle-shot—there sounded from the
bushes all around us a loud, joyous tremolo. The birds were greeting the dawn.
From every side there came an answer, and the air was filled with the echo of
their song. Lucky creatures, I thought, they did not know about the murder in
their midst. Their polyphonic concert was almost painful with its cruel sweet-
ness, for the contrast between the carefree singing and all the inhuman and
terrible things which we had experienced, and which still lay before us, was
almost too much to bear. And then the bird-song stopped almost as suddenly as

it had started, and the dawn of the new day broke in eerie silence. Only the recollection of the choral greeting still hung in the air, just as alien as, but no less real than, the stench of decomposing bodies.

And now it was day—Monday, 26 May 1941. Since early morning the sounds of heavy fighting on the heights of Galatos had indicated that our alpine troops had renewed their assault on the positions of the New Zealanders.

Baron von der Heydte

General Freyberg to General Wavell: 26 May

I regret to have to report that in my opinion the limit of endurance has been reached by the troops under my command here at Suda Bay. No matter what decision is taken by the Commanders-in-Chief from a military point of view, our position here is hopeless. A small, ill-equipped and immobile force such as ours cannot stand up against the concentrated bombing that we have been faced with during the last seven days. I feel I should tell you that from an administrative point of view the difficulties of extricating this force in full are insuperable. Provided a decision is reached at once, a certain proportion of the force might be embarked.

The End

It was one of the strangest quirks of fortune of the war that on the very day that the British decided that they must evacuate Crete, General Student, his men exhausted and with little ammunition, saw his dive-bombers taken from him for use in another theatre. His assault on Canea on 27 May was his last despairing throw, but it was enough.

The Victors

The garden suburb of Chaleppas on the coast was reported by our scouts to have escaped the bombardment, so my adjutant sensibly suggested that we should transfer our headquarters there.

'The battle for Canea is over, sir,' he said. 'The fight for comfortable billets has now begun.'

I agreed to his proposal, and selected as my headquarters a small villa of the coast near the building which, until now, had housed the British Consulate. The villa, like most of the other houses in the district, had been evacuated. It had a pleasant terrace and a well in the garden from which we were able to draw delicious cold water. Since we had nothing better to do for the moment I suggested to my staff that we should take advantage of the lull to have a bathe. We undressed and started splashing each other like fifteen-year-olds, and it was while we were thus disporting ourselves that a British soldier suddenly appeared at the garden gate. The villa had apparently been used as a British headquarters, and I suppose the soldier, in his ignorance, had arrived with a message for the staff. I do not know who was the more astonished, he or ourselves, but in any event he realized his mistake more quickly than we and hastily beat a retreat.

He was the last British soldier I saw in the battle for Canea.

General Student visited us almost immediately after the fall of Canea. Had fourteen days really elapsed since I had last seen him issuing orders in Athens? He had visibly altered. He seemed much graver, more reserved, and older. There was no evidence in his features that he was joyful over the victory—his victory—and proud at the success of his daring scheme. The cost of victory had evidently proved too much for him. Some of the battalions had lost all their officers, and in several companies there were only a few men left alive.

.... The battle for Crete was to prove the overture to the great tragedy which reached its climax at El Alamein and Stalingrad. For the first time there had stood against us a brave and relentless opponent on a battleground which favoured him. On this occasion things had gone well with us, but it seemed almost a miracle that our great and hazardous enterprise had succeeded. How it did, I cannot say to this day. Success had suddenly come to us at a moment when, as so often happens in war, we had ceased to believe in the possibility of success.

My interview with General Student was brief and to the point. In answer to his questions I concisely reported our experiences in the attack and told him of our losses. When I had finished he grasped me firmly by the hand and held it for a long time.

'I thank you,' was all he said; but the grasp of his hand and those three short words were quite sufficient for me.

Once the action was over, one of our primary tasks was to collect and bury our dead. I ordered that a common cemetery should be made on the road from Alikianou to Canea, near the spot where my first company had been held up, for the dead of both my own battalion and the British and Greek troops who had opposed us. At the entrance to the cemetery we erected a large cross. On one side of its pedestal was the following inscription:

In these olive groves and on the heights of Perivolia these men of the 1st Battalion of the 3rd Parachute Regiment fought, and won and died.

On tablets to the left and right of this inscription the names of our dead were engraved, while the reverse side of the pedestal carried an inscription as follows:

In valiant combat against the Battalion one hundred and fifty-six members of the following British regiments died for their King and Country.

Beneath were inscribed the names of the units to which the British troops who had fought against us had belonged.

Once the bodies of the dead had been retrieved and the cemetery been completed, I invited the British officers who had fought in our sector and been taken prisoner to attend the consecration of the memorial.

The survivors of my battalion paraded at the cemetery. I spoke first to them in German, then added a few words in English. The senior British officer replied. And at that moment we did not consider ourselves enemies, but friends who had been defeated by the same harsh fate.

.... During that very same evening the sentry at my headquarters reported that a young Greek lady had arrived and wished to speak to me. Automatically I thought of Ariadne; but this young woman did not bear a sword. She had brought a large bunch of white flowers which she asked me to lay on the graves of the German, British and Greek soldiers who had been buried in the cemetery.

Baron von der Heydte

Evacuation Again

The companies made their selections and Jim Burrows started to organize his rear-party and to take over water and food from those who were to go. Fountaine's company came back, very hot and tired. When they were collected, Fountaine told them how many were to stay and asked for volunteers. There was a gasp and then Grooby, the C.S.M., stepped forward. He was followed at once by Fraser, the C.Q.M.S., and by Kirk and Vincent, the two sergeants, and then the remaining forty men. The N.C.Os insisted on staying, and after much argument lots had to be drawn for the men.

The afternoon wore miserably on, but at last there was nothing for it but to say good-bye and go. I spoke as reassuringly as I could to the rear-party, shook hands with Jim, and went off very sadly.

We had a tramp of some miles to the beach, the last part lined with men who had lost their units and were hoping for a place with us. Some begged and implored, most simply watched stonily, so that we felt bitterly ashamed. There was a cordon round the beach with orders to shoot any man who tried to break in. I had to count my men through. We were the last unit to pass, and on the principle that there is always room for one more, I bullied the cordon officer into letting me take Frank Davis, with some of Divisional Headquarters as well. I had Brian Basset with me, and just before embarking found that John Russell was in an A.D.S. on the beach and insisted on taking him also.

We embarked on the Australian destroyer *Napier* and were at once led to great piles of bread and butter, jugs of cold water, and urns of coffee. We ate and drank incredible quantities. An Australian colonel and his adjutant got aboard, but just before sailing discovered that their battalion had not embarked and went hurriedly ashore again. We sailed after midnight and made for Alexandria at full speed.

Brigadier Kippenberger

It has been said that the losses suffered by the German airborne troops in their Cretan landings were so severe that Hitler was discouraged from ever again undertaking a similar venture. If that was the case, all those who fought on the island— including nearly six thousand New Zealand casualties—had struggled not only manfully but with success—however clouded their glory may have seemed at the time.

THE MIDDLE EAST

While the Germans overran Greece and Crete and (as will be told) turned the tide in the Western Desert, they were also planning to gain control of Syria, Iraq and Persia through puppet governments. Here was a deadly threat to Suez and Britain's communications with India, and to her Middle Eastern oil supplies.

During March Rashid Ali's pro-German party seized power in Iraq. German and Italian aircraft were actually being landed on Iraqi airfields when British forces, advancing from the Persian Gulf and across the desert from Palestine, forestalled them and forced Rashid Ali to flee on 30 May.

Syria

Syria was strongly held for Vichy France, and thus was a potential base for German bombers and airborne troops now established in the Balkans. To avert such a disastrous situation, British and Free French forces entered Syria on 8 June 1941. The Vichy French, better equipped, more numerous and supported by German aircraft, resisted with determination and skill, and the fighting, complicated by the uncomfortable feeling that each side should have been the ally, not the enemy, of the other, was bitter and costly. One of the Allied columns, under Major-General William Slim, invaded Syria from the east.

.... About the middle of June, my division was suddenly transferred from the Iraq to the Syrian Command, and I was told to advance as speedily as possible up the Euphrates into Syria. My objective, a hundred miles inside the French frontier, was the town of Deir-ez-Zor, the capital of Eastern Syria, where desert routes from all directions converged on the only bridge spanning the river for the five hundred miles between Habbaniyeh and the Turkish Frontier. Once there, I should outflank the French line across Syria and might menace Aleppo, far in their rear. At the moment the British and Australian forces were fighting slowly northward against strong opposition in a two-pronged drive on Damascus and on Palmyra. My division would make a third prong a hundred miles to the east.

Major-General William Slim

For the attack on Deir-ez-Zor, General Slim divided his force into two parts, one to make a frontal assault while the other, a flying column, set off into the desert to make a long flanking march which would take the defenders in the rear.

Towards us flowed the winding Euphrates, broad, placid and now beginning to reflect the sun. East and west on either side stretched, mile after mile, the desert, flat and featureless, a muddy brown. To the north, a low *café-au-lait* ridge ran obliquely away from us to the north-west. We saw only its rounded end, coming down in a steep but even slope to within a few hundred yards of the river bank. Through the gap between ridge and river the white thread of the road ran on past the airfield into Deir-ez-Zor. The ridge screened a large part of the town and all but a corner of the aerodrome from our view. Judging by the size and height of the flat-topped houses we could see, the town promised to be bigger and more imposing than I had expected. If we got our small force involved in fighting through those streets, it would be soaked up like water in a sponge—not a very comforting thought.

It was now full daylight. Weld and I walked slowly up and down, waiting. I looked surreptitiously at my watch, *six-thirty*—surely the column *must* be there! Soon it would break silence and call up! The hands of my watch crawled on. *Seven.* French could not have failed to locate the column by now. Still no signal came. *Seven-thirty . . . eight.* If the column was ever going to reach the Aleppo road it must have done so already and, wherever it was, the enemy must have seen it! I told the Signal Officer to call it up. No answer; obviously something had gone wrong—very wrong.

We resumed our measured pacing, stopping every now and then to gaze through field-glasses at the enemy positions. No visible movement there and a silence broken only once by the French guns firing again at their first love, the wrecked trucks on the road. As we walked, to conceal our mounting anxiety we spoke of old days in India, of our friends, of casual things, yet our minds were elsewhere. What had gone wrong? Where *was* that blasted column? If only I had an aeroplane, just one aeroplane, to send out to look for it! A couple of armoured cars? No, they would take too long. I glanced sideways at Weld; I hoped I appeared as unperturbed as he did.

Nine . . . conversation languished; we walked in silence. *Nine-thirty!* As at a signal, we stopped and faced one another. I was quite sure my plan had failed. We had pushed Weld and his brigade into a far worse position than they had been at the end of their first attempt. Then he could reunite his force; now the flank column could not possibly get back—it would have no petrol left. Should I order a frontal attack with what we had in hand or call the whole thing off and concentrate on an attempt to rescue the column?—how, I had no idea. It is always a nasty moment when one faces a disaster knowing it has been caused by one's own obstinacy in persisting in a plan against advice. I was having such a moment now.

Weld's common-sense came to my rescue. 'We haven't heard any firing north of the town,' he pointed out. 'If the French had spotted the column there would have been din enough. Better hang on a bit. All the chaps down there have their orders—we can start an attack in a matter of minutes if we want to.'

'All right,' I agreed, grateful to him for this excuse to put off decision. 'We'll wait another half-hour.'

We resumed our silent promenade.

No gun fired, no aeroplane flew, no bomb crumped—all was quiet. Quiet except that it required an increasing effort of will to continue this steady march up and down, up and down. . . .

Footsteps behind us. We turned and there, charging towards us, waving a signal form in his hand, was the Brigade Signals Officer.

'The column's come through,' he gasped. 'They're on the Aleppo road a couple of miles north of Deir-ez-Zor and advancing. Leading troops nearing town. No opposition so far!'

Ten years and a ton of weight dropped off my shoulders. I turned to Weld to say 'Let battle begin' or words to that effect, but he and the Signals Officer were already sliding down the mound to the signal truck.

A quarter of an hour later, our guns started with a grand and simultaneous crash. I dare say there have been bigger and better bombardments, before and since, but no general ever listened to one with more relief than I did on that mound. The upper part of the ridge vanished in rolling clouds of fawn dust. The racket grew as rifles and automatics joined in and the French guns thumped away at ours.

The bombardment of the ridge was at its height when uneven lines of Gurkhas began to move forward across the flat ground at its foot. Luckily for them the billowing curtain of dust half way up the slope blinded the French earthworks. The distant lines of little figures pushed on up the steep incline at a real hillman's pace and disappeared into the smoke and dust. Our guns had by now lifted and were firing over the ridge; I could see some of their shells bursting beyond the aerodrome.

The cloud on the ridge thinned rapidly and drifted away. The Gurkhas were half way up, some of them shooting from the hip. Suddenly, on the top of the ridge, silhouetted against the smoke and sky, appeared an agitated figure or two, arms waving, bodies bent. Then more, then a crowd of them, scrambling wildly over the crest and vanishing down the other side. The French native troops were abandoning their entrenchments. A few moments later the Gurkhas reached the top of the ridge and plunged out of sight after them.

The noise of gun and rifle fire died away except for the chattering of light automatics from the aerodrome. I turned my glasses in that direction and could see our men advancing each side of the road, some already at the corner of the airfield. As the din wavered towards silence, I heard for the first time a strange confused murmur from the town itself, punctuated by bursts of machine-gun fire, rifle shots and the crump of shells—the column! A vehicle, leaving a trail of dust behind it, fled madly down the road from the aerodrome into the town; others followed it and rifle fire started again. Coloured Verey lights—success signals—leapt up from the ridge and from the aerodrome. The enemy was on the run. The double attack had been too much for his nerves. We were into Deir-ez-Zor!

General Slim

The Enemies

In the earlier stages of the engagement, before heat and tiredness had worn the edge off enthusiasm, I crawled forward to an outpost to see what I could of our enemy. At dawn, when we had reached the mountain-top, we had seen a few unidentifiable figures silhouetted against the rising sun. Since then the enemy had been invisible, shooting at us through loopholes in the fort or from the neighbouring hillsides. I lay down beside a trooper. More for the fun of the thing than because he had a target, he was firing a Hotchkiss sporadically at a low built-in stone parapet about fifty yards away. Suddenly, behind the parapet, two black French soldiers (Senegalese, I believe) popped their heads up. Their two faces, under steel helmets, grinned at us, and I can still see the whiteness of their teeth and eyeballs. God knows what they thought they were doing. Probably they had never been in a battle before and, like myself, they were childishly curious to have a look at their enemy.

Or were they attempting to do something more? If men are ever to cease destroying one another, if the everlasting tit-for-tat process is ever to be halted, it will perhaps only come by an individual, a simple black man, for example, standing up suddenly in the face of bullets and crying out:

'See, here I am. I don't want to kill you. Why kill me? Let us stop the battle and be friends.'

The trooper beside me was so astonished by the apparition of the two black men that he never thought of firing his Hotchkiss.

'Shoot!' I hissed at him.

He pressed the trigger and nothing happened. A cartridge had jammed. There was a simple drill for curing the stoppage, but now, in his excitement, the trooper bungled it. I pushed him out of the way, grabbed the gun and ejected the cartridge.

Over the sights, I saw my burst hit the top of the parapet. The two grinning faces vanished like puppets. A little dust lingered in the air where they had been. Thus, with the wantonness of a boy destroying some harmless bird for 'sport', I contributed my share towards the never-ending story of man's inhumanity to man. But at the time I thought I had behaved rather splendidly and the trooper was impressed too.

John Verney

By 11 July this unhappy campaign was over. Syria was lost to Vichy France, and to Germany.

Persia

Thousands of German agents flourished in Persia, harboured by a government which refused to expel them. General Slim was appointed to command the British force which on 25 August 1941 entered Persia to enforce Allied demands. By this time the situation had become doubly dangerous, for on 22 June Germany had invaded Russia, and a pro-Axis Persia on her southern flank could not be tolerated.

.... I was fully occupied going over with Aizlewood, the Brigadier of the Armoured Brigade, the plans he had already prepared for the first phase of our invasion—the forcing of the formidable Pai Tak Pass, which within thirty miles of our crossing the frontier would bar our way. With time so short it was fortunate that I could heartily approve his plans, and I decided to act on them without serious alteration.

Accordingly, before dawn on 25 August, led by the Hussars in their always gallant but decrepit and slightly ridiculous old Mark VII tanks, whose only armament was a single Vickers machine-gun apiece and whose armour almost anything could pierce, we crossed the frontier. By that time I was becoming accustomed to invasions; this was the fifth frontier I had crossed in the past year. All the same, there was a thrill about it. But very little happened. A few harmless shots from vanishing frontier guards greeted us as we encircled the village of Qasr-i-Shirin, about ten miles inside Persia, but we met no real opposition. As it grew lighter, Aizlewood and I pushed on with the advance guard, and by midmorning we were almost at the entrance to the Pai Tak Pass. Here we stopped and, covered by a screen of light tanks, stood on the roof of my station wagon to study this historic gate through which, over the centuries, so many armies had passed or tried to pass.

Viewed from below it was a most formidable and threatening obstacle. The interminable flat plains of the Tigris and Euphrates which stretched behind us for hundreds of miles here came to an abrupt end at the great boundary wall of a mighty escarpment stretching from north to south across our path. The road to Kermanshah which we must follow rose sharply into the mouth of the Pass and, climbing in curves and loops, vanished among cliffs and gorges to emerge, three thousand feet higher, on to the plateau of Gilan. It looked as if a handful of men could hold it against an army many times the size of mine.

At the moment there was no sign of even the proverbial handful in the Pass or on the crest of the escarpment. Both appeared completely deserted. Yet our intelligence was quite firm that there was a Persian force, reliably reported to have been reinforced to a strength of five thousand, well dug in on and around the Pass. It was so still and deserted that we began to wonder if there really were any enemy at all. Curiously but cautiously we drove on a few hundred yards and again searched the hills and cliffs. Not a sign of movement; not the sound of a shot. Proceeding in this way, growing bolder with continued impunity, we reached the point where the road entered a sinister and narrowing gorge, the jaws of the Pass itself. The road, quite empty, ran uphill from us to disappear with surprising suddenness round a sharp corner a couple of hundred yards farther on. At this corner stood a white-washed *chai khana*, a tea shop, the Persian equivalent of a tavern, with a few small trees growing at the roadside in front of it; all utterly peaceful, drowsing deserted in the sunlight.

The irresistible urge to look round the corner that comes on every winding road fell upon us. Why not? It looked safe enough! Standing boldly upright, our heads and shoulders through the open roof, we drove slowly to the corner, cautiously poked our bonnet round it and peered up the Pass. I had just spotted above the road what I took to be the oil pumping station marked on our map when a bang, well behind us and off to one side, made me jump.

'What's that?' I asked Aizlewood.

His reply was emphasized by a much louder and nearer *crump* and a cloud of dust, smoke and stones level with us but some way off the road. Almost simultaneously with it came the *crack* of a gun ahead.

'By God, they're shooting at us!' exclaimed the Brigadier in an aggrieved voice.

Our driver had already realized this unpleasant fact, and we jerked in reverse round the corner as a couple more shells from the anti-tank gun smacked into the road at the spot we had just left. The driver needed no orders to turn the car behind the *chai khana*, and we left the Pai Tak Pass a good deal more briskly than we had entered it.

There was an interesting postscript to this incident. Some days later the anti-tank battery fell into our hands and we were told that just as it was ordered to the Pai Tak Pass it had been issued with brand-new guns. The first shot its crew had ever fired from one of these was the opening round at us and, as a Persian gunner wistfully remarked, a little more practice would have made them shoot better!

We could now, at any rate, be sure there were enemy on the Pass and that they meant to hold it against us. The idea of a frontal attack up the rugged and in places almost vertical escarpment was not attractive, but the Brigadier when studying his map before my arrival had spotted a route by which any position at the Pai Tak itself could be by-passed. This was a track which crossed the escarpment some twenty miles further south and went via the village of Gilan to Shahabad on the main Kermanshah road, about thirty miles south-east of the main pass. It was a long—about ninety miles—and rough track but it was said to be passable by wheels. Although we could hardly expect it not to be blocked by the enemy, all reports agreed that their strength there was small and, even if we were delayed, the threat to the Persian rear would, we could hope, at least divide their force. I therefore decided to send the Armoured Brigade by this track and, as soon as the enemy began to feel the threat against their rear, to attack on each side of the Pai Tak Pass with the rest of my force.

On the 26th, the R.A.F. located enemy defences in the Pass and along the escarpment, and later in the afternoon bombed them. Throughout the day the infantry carried out their reconnaissances and preparations for the attack while the Armoured Brigade began its arduous and hazardous march, the first stages of which were to be completed before daylight. About Gilan the column was delayed for a time by road blocks and some infantry and machine-gun fire. An overheard radio conversation when this skirmish was at its height, while it did not diminish our fear that the column might be seriously held up, did at least give us a smile:

First Signaller: 'This is getting a bit too hot! I'm going under my truck. Over.'

Second Signaller: 'I *am* under my truck! Out!'

Before dawn on the 27th, two Gurkha battalions, one each side of the Pai Tak Pass, began in real mountain warfare style to scramble up the escarpment. Hardly had they got going when I was most relieved to receive a signal from the flank column that it had taken Shahabad. The news of this had proved too much for the Persians, already shaken by the bombing, and they had pulled out hurriedly across country north of the road while it was still dark.

General Slim

No other opposition was offered to the British troops, and within three days the Persian Government had agreed to expel German influence from Persia.

10

OPERATION BARBAROSSA

Having secured his lines of communication by means of his conquests in the Balkans, Hitler launched his offensive against Soviet Russia on 22 June 1941. One hundred and twenty divisions were massed on the eastern frontier for this task.

The Northern Army Group, commanded by von Loeb, was to deploy twenty-nine divisions in the direction of Leningrad; von Bock's Central Army Group consisted of fifty divisions and was to drive for Smolensk; the Southern Army Group, under von Rundstedt, contained forty-one divisions with the lower Dnieper as its objective. There were twenty-six divisions in reserve, and a considerable quantity of Finnish and Roumanian troops available for use on the northern and southern fronts respectively.

THE GRAND DESIGN

THE German armed forces must be prepared to crush Soviet Russia in a quick campaign before the end of the war against England (case 'Barbarossa').

For this purpose the army will have to employ all available units with the reservation that the occupied territories will have to be safeguarded against surprise attacks.

For the Eastern campaign the air force will have to free such strong forces for the support of the army that a quick completion of the ground operations may be expected and that damage of the eastern German territories will be avoided as much as possible. This concentration of the main effort in the East is limited by the following reservation: that the entire battle against enemy air attacks and that the attacks on England and especially the supply for them must not be permitted to break down.

Concentration of the main effort of the navy remains unequivocally against England also during an Eastern campaign.

If occasion arises I will order the concentration of troops for action against Soviet Russia eight weeks before the intended beginning of operations.

Preparations requiring some time to start are—if this has not yet been done—to begin presently and are to be completed by 15 May 1941.

Great caution has to be exercised that the intention of the attack will not be recognized. . . .

Adolf Hitler, 18 December 1940

When 'Barbarossa' commences, the world will hold its breath and make no comment.

Adolf Hitler, 3 February 1941

This war with Russia is a nonsensical idea, to which I can see no happy ending. But if, for political reasons, the war is unavoidable, then we must face the fact that it can't be won in a single summer campaign. Just look at the distances involved. We cannot possibly defeat the enemy and occupy the whole of western Russia, from the Baltic to the Black Sea, within a few short months. We should prepare for a long war and go for our objectives step by step.

Field-Marshal von Rundstedt, May 1941

Canaris was terribly worried about the approaching campaign. He criticized in the strongest terms the Wehrmacht leaders who, despite their expert knowledge, were irresponsible and foolish enough to support the views of a man like Hitler in his assumption that we should be able to conclude the Russian campaign within three months. He would not be a party to this, and could not understand how the Generals, von Brauchitsch, Halder, Keitel and Jodl, could be so complacent, so unrealistic, and so optimistic. But any attempt at opposition was useless; he had already made himself unpopular by his repeated warnings. Only a few days earlier Keitel had said to him, 'My dear Canaris, you may have some understanding of the Abwehr, but you belong to the navy, you really should not try to give us lessons in strategic and political planning.' When Canaris repeated such remarks he would usually rein in his horse, look at me with wide eyes and say quite seriously, 'Wouldn't you find all this quite comic —if it weren't so desperately serious?'

Walter Schellenberg

From the report of the Ambassador in Moscow: 'All observations show that Stalin and Molotov, who alone are responsible for Russian foreign policy, are doing everything to avoid a conflict with Germany. The entire behaviour of the Government, as well as the attitude of the Press, which reports all events concerning Germany in a factual, indisputable manner, supports this view. The loyal fulfilment of the economic treaty with Germany proves the same thing.'

German Foreign Office docket, 7 June 1941

From every source at my disposal, including some most trustworthy, it looks as if a vast German onslaught on Russia was imminent. Not only are the main German armies deployed from Finland to Roumania, but the final arrivals of air and armoured forces are being completed.

Winston Churchill to Franklin D. Roosevelt, 15 June 1941

On the evening of Friday, 20 June, I drove down to Chequers alone. I knew that the German onslaught upon Russia was a matter of days, or it might be hours. I had arranged to deliver a broadcast on Saturday night dealing with this event. It would of course have to be in guarded terms. Moreover, at this time the Soviet Government, at once haughty and purblind, regarded every warning we gave as a mere attempt of beaten men to drag others into ruin. As a result of my reflexions in the car I put off my broadcast till Sunday night, when I thought that all would be clear.

Winston Churchill

Tension rose steadily on the German side. By the evening of the 21st we assumed that the Russians must have realized what was happening, yet across the River Bug on the front of 4 Army and Second Panzer Group, that is to say between Brest-Litovsk and Lomza, all was quiet. The Russian outposts were behaving quite normally. At a little after midnight, when the entire artillery of the assault divisions and of the second wave too was already zeroed in on its targets, the international Berlin–Moscow train passed without incident through Brest-Litovsk. It was a weird moment.

General Gunther Blumentritt, Chief of Staff, 4 Army

Ribbentrop to Count Schulenburg, German Ambassador in Moscow

Berlin, 21 June 1941

1. Upon receipt of this telegram all of the cipher material still there is to be destroyed. The radio set is to be put out of commission.

2. Please inform Herr Molotov at once that you have an urgent communication to make to him and would therefore like to call upon him immediately. Then please make the following declaration to him:

'.... The Government of the Reich declares that the Soviet Government, contrary to the obligations it assumed,
(1) has not only continued, but even intensified, its attempts to undermine Germany and Europe;
(2) has adopted a more and more anti-German foreign policy;
(3) has concentrated all its forces in readiness at the German border.

Thereby the Soviet Government has broken its treaties with Germany and is about to attack Germany from the rear, in its struggle for life. The Führer has therefore ordered the German armed forces to oppose this threat with all the means at their disposal.'

Please do not enter into any discussion of this communication.

Ribbentrop

At six o'clock in the morning of 22 June 1941, the German Ambassador, Count von Schulenburg, handed Molotov a Note of the German Government declaring war on the Soviet Union.

Both Count von Schulenburg and Molotov were pale with emotion. The Commissar for Foreign Affairs took the Note wordlessly, spat on it and then tore it up. He rang for his secretary Poskrebichev.

'Show this gentleman out through the back door.'

Ivan Krylov, Soviet staff officer

BARBAROSSA IS LAUNCHED

At dawn the next day, 22 June 1941, the Wehrmacht began the offensive on all sectors of the front, from the Black Sea to the northern regions of Finland. In General Halder's diary is the following entry:

'I have just described the plan for the Russian Campaign to the Führer; the Russian armies will be destroyed in six weeks.'

Reactions

The Russians were clearly taken entirely by surprise on our front. Almost at once our signals intercept service listened in to a Russian message: 'We are being fired on. What shall we do?' They heard the reply from the senior headquarters to whom this request for orders was addressed: 'You must be insane. And why is your signal not in code?'

General Blumentritt

I saw Poskrebichev at nine o'clock. He had come to Colonel Smaguine to ask for a list of the personnel of our military attaché in Berlin.

'Molotov is so calm you'd almost think he didn't realize what was at stake,' he said. 'Stalin isn't in Moscow at the moment, but he'll be returning to-morrow. The Politburo is meeting in special session to discuss the conduct of operations. To-day those members who are already in Moscow will hold a meeting.'

'To discuss the war?'

'No, to discuss the situation at home. Beria is presenting a rather alarming report. He's afraid the reservists will honour the old Russian custom of raiding the vodka before going to the front. The townspeople are calm enough, but when the peasants come to Moscow they are bound to be a bit turbulent.'

'Well, what's Beria proposing to do? Machine-gun them?'

'Not at all. I'm beginning to think that Lavrenti Pavlovitch is a highly intelligent man. He proposes to supply each reservist arriving in Moscow with two litres of alcohol and then confine them to barracks for two or three days and have them guarded by N.K.V.D. troops. After that they'll go to the front like lambs.'

I went to see Muraviev. I found him very calm.

'Everything's going well, Vania. They're fighting.'

'Who is?'

'Our men. I've just had a talk with Brest-Litovsk. There's been no trouble except with 2 Infantry division, and they're all *Khokli*,* as you know. They made an attempt to murder their commanders and political commissars and surrender to the Germans. There is some cause for apprehension. You know the peasants get awkward when war starts; in particular the *Khokli* and the men from Northern Caucasia. They expect the Germans to proclaim the independence of their republics.'

Ivan Krylov

The mood of Britain towards Russia had for a long time been far from friendly, but the Prime Minister, with characteristic statesmanship, promptly associated his country with Russia's struggle against Nazism, and assured Russia of the utmost material assistance.

At four o'clock this morning Hitler attacked and invaded Russia. All his usual formalities of perfidy were observed with scrupulous technique. A non-aggression treaty had been solemnly signed and was in force between the two

---

* Contemptuous expression used by Russians to describe Ukrainians.

countries. No complaint had been made by Germany of its non-fulfilment. Under its cloak of false confidence, the German armies drew up in immense strength along a line which stretches from the White Sea to the Black Sea; and their air fleets and armoured divisions slowly and methodically took their stations. Then, suddenly, without declaration of war, without even an ultimatum, German bombs rained down from the air upon the Russian cities, the German troops violated the frontiers; and an hour later the German Ambassador, who till the night before was lavishing his assurances of friendship, almost of alliance, upon the Russians, called upon the Russian Foreign Minister to tell him that a state of war existed between Germany and Russia. . . .

All this was no surprise to me. In fact, I gave clear and precise warnings to Stalin of what was coming. I gave him warning as I have given warning to others before. I can only hope that this warning did not fall unheeded. All we know at present is that the Russian people are defending their native soil and that their leaders have called upon them to resist to the utmost.

Any man or State who fights on against Nazidom will have our aid. Any man or State who marches with Hitler is our foe. This applies not only to organized States but to all representatives of that vile race of quislings who make themselves the tools and agents of the Nazi régime against their fellow-countrymen and the lands of their birth. They—these quislings—like the Nazi leaders themselves, if not disposed of by their fellow-countrymen, which would save trouble, will be delivered by us on the morrow of victory to the justice of the Allied tribunals. That is our policy and that is our declaration. It follows, therefore, that we shall give whatever help we can to Russia and the Russian people. We shall appeal to all our friends and allies in every part of the world to take the same course and pursue it, as we shall, faithfully and steadfastly to the end. . . .

Winston Churchill, 22 June 1941

The entire Soviet people is rising in defence of the Fatherland at the side of the Red Army. It is a question of life and death for the Soviet State, for the people of the U.S.S.R.—a question whether the peoples of the Soviet Union shall be free or reduced to slavery.

Great Lenin, who founded our State, used to say that the basic qualities of the Soviet men should be valour and daring: they should be fearless in battle and resolved to fight against the enemies of our country. The Red Army and Navy and all the citizens of the Soviet Union must defend every inch of the Soviet soil, fight to the last drop of their blood, defend their towns and villages, and show their daring and ingenuity—qualities that are characteristic of our people.

In the event of the retreat of the Red Army all railway rolling stock must be brought away. We must not leave a single engine to the enemy, nor a single railway coach. We must not leave a single pound of grain or a single gallon of petrol to the enemy. The collective farmers must take away all their cattle and place their corn in the care of State organizations to be transported to the rear zone. All valuable materials which cannot be taken away must be resolutely destroyed.

In the areas occupied by the enemy, foot and horse guerrilla detachments must be created, as well as groups of saboteurs entrusted with fighting against the units of the enemy army, with the launching of guerrilla warfare everywhere, with blowing up bridges and roads, with wrecking telephone and telegraph communications, and with setting forests, depots and trains on fire. It is necessary to create in invaded areas conditions unbearable for the enemy and all his accomplices. . . .

In this war of liberation we shall not be alone. In this great war we shall have faithful allies in the person of the peoples of Europe and America. Our war for the freedom of our Fatherland is merged into the struggle of the peoples of Europe and America for their independent freedom. It is the united front of the peoples who stand for freedom against the threat of enslavement by Hitler's Fascist armies.

In this connection the historic utterance of the British Prime Minister, Mr. Churchill, about aid to the Soviet Union, and the declaration of the Government of the United States signifying readiness to give assistance to our country are fully comprehensible and symptomatic.

Comrades! Our forces are numberless. The over-weening enemy will soon learn this to his cost. Side by side with the Red Army many thousand workers, collective farmers, and intellectuals are rising to fight the enemy aggressor. The masses of our people will rise up in their millions.

Stalin

ADVANCE

At first, like Napoleon's invasion more than a century before, everything went almost too well. All three German Army Groups advanced rapidly, and the pattern was the same, the Russians were prepared always to sacrifice their two inexhaustible assets—men and space—to gain time. For example, at the end of July when the Germans took Smolensk after four weeks' fighting, they took a hundred and eighty thousand prisoners, but they could not quite shut the trap, and the hard core of the Soviet forces drew away, just out of reach. And although it was summer, there was rain—a mere shadow of the horror to come, but one with its own problems.

The infantry had a hard time keeping up. Marches of twenty-five miles in the course of a day were by no means exceptional, and that over the most atrocious roads. A vivid picture which remains of these weeks is the great clouds of yellow dust kicked up by the Russian columns attempting to retreat and by our infantry hastening in pursuit. The heat was tremendous, though interspersed with sudden showers which quickly turned the roads to mud before the sun reappeared and as quickly baked them into crumbling clay once again.

By 2 July the first battle was for all intents and purposes won. The haul was astounding. A hundred and fifty thousand prisoners taken, some twelve hundred tanks and six hundred guns captured or destroyed. First impressions revealed that the Russian was as tough a fighter as ever. His tanks, however, were not particularly formidable and his air force, so far as we could see, non-existent.

The conduct of the Russian troops, even in this first battle, was in striking contrast to the behaviour of the Poles and of the Western allies in defeat. Even when encircled, the Russians stood their ground and fought. The vast extent of the country, with its forests and swamps, helped them in this. There were not enough German troops available completely to seal off a huge encirclement such as that of Bialystok-Slonim. Our motorized forces fought on or near to the roads: in the great trackless spaces between them the Russians were left largely unmolested. This was why the Russians were able not infrequently to break out of our encirclements, whole columns moving by night through the forests that stretched away eastwards. They always attempted to break out to the east, so that the eastern side of each encirclement had to be held by our strongest troops, usually Panzer troops. Nevertheless, our encirclements were seldom entirely successful.

General Blumentritt

By late afternoon we had pressed the retreating Russians right to the edge of the marshlands, across which the only passage was the bridge of logs. They fled across it, but our heavy machine-guns raked the bridge and picked them off at will. As we saw them being mown down, unable to jump either to right or left to escape the cross-fire, we thought uneasily of our own fate when we reached the other end of the crossing, which was likely to be under equally murderous fire from the Reds. But there was no alternative. We had to take our chance on the log bridge.

At dusk our assault troops and pioneers set off across the logs and the rest of the battalion followed them after a short interval. If we could only make the crossing safely during the darkness, we would be in an excellent position the following morning to press home our advantage against the fleeing Red Army. The bridge was only six yards wide. On the more solid ground, the poles lay directly on the earth: in the swampier places, they were supported by wooden piles. Our marching column stretched like eerie shadows into the fast-falling night. The logs slowly sank under our weight and marsh gases gurgled on either side of us. Random and apparently aimless bursts of tracer bullets arced play-fully and fantastically over our heads. Farther and farther we marched. Monoton-ously we heard the tramp of our own marching feet. Nobody spoke a word. Our ears strained to catch any sound coming across the treacherous marshes.

Then to the right of the causeway I heard a voice calling pitifully. It became more and more distinct as we got nearer. The ghostly cries were in a foreign tongue—the pleading cries for help of a Russian soldier, only a few yards from the bridge. He was being sucked into the swamp, deeper and deeper. Silently, the German troops marched by.

'Surely we can help him,' I found myself whispering to Neuhoff.

'How?' asked Neuhoff. 'I don't like leaving any poor devil to a fate like that. But anybody who leaves these logs will get sucked in himself. These marshes are bottomless.'

Again and again came the agonized cries. I dropped out of the column and let the marching troops pass me. With the help of a soldier, I removed a loose pole from the bridge. We heaved the heavy log as hard as we could into the direction of the sinking man. The cries ceased and for a few moments we could hear the man splashing and struggling to reach the pole. We could see nothing through the darkness, and there was something uncanny in hearing a human being fighting for his life with every bit of strength he had le°. He again shouted. There was a gurgling sound and I felt every hair on my body crawl. Then all was quiet. Dead quiet.

Heinrich Haape, German medical officer

German Difficulties

It was appallingly difficult country for tank movement—great virgin forests, widespread swamps, terrible roads, and bridges not strong enough to bear the weight of tanks. The resistance also became stiffer, and the Russians began to cover their front with minefields; it was easier for them to block the way because there were so few roads.

The great motor highway leading from the frontier to Moscow was unfinished—the one road a Westerner would call a 'road'. We were not prepared for what we found because our maps in no way corresponded to reality. On those maps all supposed main roads were marked in red, and there seemed to be many, but they often proved to be merely sandy tracks. The German intelligence service was fairly accurate about conditions in Russian-occupied Poland, but badly at fault about those beyond the original Russian frontier.

Such country was bad enough for the tanks, but worse still for the transport accompanying them—carrying their fuel, their supplies, and all the auxiliary troops they needed. Nearly all this transport consisted of wheeled vehicles, which could not move off the roads, nor move on it if the sand turned into mud. An hour or two of rain reduced the Panzer forces to stagnation. It was an extraordinary sight, with groups of them strung out over a hundred miles stretch, all stuck—until the sun came out and the ground dried.

General Blumentritt

Information concerning Russia was comparatively scanty. We had in our possession the captured archives of Holland, Belgium, Greece, Jugoslavia and even of the French General Staff, but none of these countries was any better informed about the Russians than we were. The information concerning the troops we would first meet on the border was fairly correct, but we had no statistical data as to the future potentialities of this vast state. Of course, during our first six months' advance we found out a lot more.

Colonel-General Franz Halder, Chief of the General Staff

I realized soon after the attack was begun that everything that had been written about Russia was nonsense. The maps we were given were all wrong. The roads that were marked nice and red and thick on a map turned out to be tracks, and what were tracks on the map became first-class roads. Even railways which were to be used by us simply didn't exist. Or a map would indicate that there was nothing in the area, and suddenly we would be confronted with an American-type town, with factory buildings and all the rest of it.

Field-Marshal von Rundstedt, G.O.C.-in-C., Army Group South

Bolski was not particularly amused.

'What do distances matter to us?' he demanded.

'A hell of a lot,' Kageneck growled. 'As much as they meant to Napoleon.'

'Nonsense!' said Bolski scornfully. 'This is the twentieth century and we have Adolf Hitler for a leader—not Napoleon.'

'So what?' asked Jakobi.

'We have the greatest army and the greatest military leader of all time. Distance means nothing to-day.' He was encouraged to greater heights of oratory: 'Let us not forget: we are not a spear thrown haphazardly into space, which may or may not find the target. We are the sword of the new Germany, wielded by the best hands, and when called upon are always ready to cut and thrust until our enemies are completely destroyed.'

Heinrich Haape

No More Castles

We did not waste time looking for accommodation. In France castles and mansions had been ours for the asking. The small wooden huts of the East held little appeal, particularly in view of the ubiquity of certain 'domestic pets'. Consequently our tactical headquarters lived almost the whole time in tents and the two command wagons which, together with a few wartime *Volkswagen* and the vehicles of the wireless section and telephone exchange, carried our other ranks when we changed location. I myself slept in a sleeping-bag in the small tent I shared with my A.D.C., and do not remember having used a proper bed more than three times throughout this Panzer drive. The one man with any objection to living under canvas was our senior military assistant, who preferred to sleep in his car. Unfortunately he had to leave his long legs sticking out through the door, with the result that he could never get his wet boots off after a rainy night.

General Erich von Manstein, G.O.C. LVI Panzer Corps

The First Reserves

We were forty in our wagon. All day long we hung in the openings, the sliding doors right back, and tried to see as much as we could of the landscape flitting by. Positions went by rank: first a row sitting on the floor, with their legs dangling out; then a row on a narrow board, leaning themselves on the diagonally placed barrier; behind these standing room—the gallery—leaning on the shoulders of those in front. It worked jolly well like that, only one or other of the front seats turning round swearing when one of the gallery trod on his fingers. On the other hand, one could hardly speak of harmony at night. When a chap stirred in his sleep, his cheesy toes would dig into another man's nose, and when that one jerked his head away he would ram another fellow in the belly, so he in turn would wake up and start taking it out of yet another.

Washing, too, was a business. When the train halted, every man looked to the chance of cleaning up, but you could never go far from the train; nobody could tell you whether it was there for minutes or hours. Nor were there any privies; at every halt the chaps squatted along the line with their trousers down and tried to reduce the necessary business to the minimum of time. If the whistle blew, there would be faces scarlet with a final effort and trousers pulled up on the run. You also had to see you weren't counted a deserter; none of the swine up above would ever admit that it was a job of that sort made you miss the bus.

We touched Breslau and entered Poland. Children and womenfolk surrounded the train, begging for bread. It was a foreign lingo now, but their gestures were understandable enough. We gave them food and still had enough for ourselves.

Once the train halted bang in the heart of a little town; men and women alike flocked down in curiosity, and the children came right up to us, but as the train had not halted for some hours that meant we had to take full advantage of the halt, so in no time the whole train was flanked by a row of naked backsides and the Poles scurried their children out of range.

We crossed the Soviet frontier at Przemysl, and saw the first extensive damage. The formerly Russian part of the place had been badly hit. This was where the attack had begun. We were silent as we passed this destruction. An impression of the great misery which this war was going to inflict was forced on us. Hopeless piles of ruin, fireplaces sticking out of the rubble, grim reminders indeed; houses cut in two, revealing all the intimacies of each floor; iron girders snapped like matches, beams shattered, collapsed walls, utter confusion, where once had been normal life; the labour of centuries in a few short hours turned to illusion.

On we went, past ruins, crashed trees and shell craters. Here and there were the first corpses of tanks, death-dealing steel beasts shattered by steel. The farther we went, the more frequent this wreckage was; over there one obviously just bogged in the marsh, here one off which a mine had ripped the giant tracks, now another decapitated, minus its conning tower. Of how many destroyed lives could these dead monsters have told?

We began to reflect rather gloomily. Our thoughts turned to home. A sunset like this brought heartache; I could have howled. Then one of the chaps began singing to himself. It was a gloomy tune, but others joined in, humming at first. Soon we had all picked it up and that tune soared strongly against the monotonous roll and beat of the train's wheels on the rails. Lost in dreams, one felt one's eyes trying to penetrate the sombre shadows of the endless ghost-ridden expanses of this foreign land. What did lie ahead?

Benno Zieser

Russian Prisoners

We suddenly saw a broad, earth-brown crocodile slowly shuffling down the road towards us. From it came a subdued hum, like that from a beehive. Prisoners of war. Russians, six deep. We couldn't see the end of the column. As they drew near the terrible stench which met us made us quite sick; it was like the biting stench of the lion house and the filthy odour of the monkey house at the same time.

But these were not animals, they were men. We made haste out of the way of the foul cloud which surrounded them, then what we saw transfixed us where we stood and we forgot our nausea. Were these really human beings, these grey-brown figures, these shadows lurching towards us, stumbling and staggering, moving shapes at their last gasp, creatures which only some last flicker of the will to live enabled to obey the order to march? All the misery in the world seemed to be concentrated here. There was also that gruesome barrage of shouts and wails, groans, lamentations and curses which combined with the cutting orders of the guards into a hideous accompaniment.

We saw one man shuffle aside from the ranks, then a rifle butt crash between his shoulder-blades and drive him gasping back into place. Another with a head wound lost in bloodstained bandages ran a few paces out with gestures almost ludicrous in their persuasiveness to beg one of the nearby local inhabitants for a scrap of bread. Then a leather thong fetched him a savage lash round his shoulders and yanked him, too, back into place. Another, a lanky fellow, a regular giant, stepped aside to pump ship, and when he too was forced back he could not stop nature and it all drenched the man in front, but he never even turned his head.

Stray dogs were legion, among them were the most unbelievable mongrels; the only thing they were all alike in was that they were thin. The Sheikh said one could have learned to play the harp on their ribs. That was no hindrance to the prisoners. They were hungry, so why not eat roast dog? They were always trying to catch the scary beasts. They would also beg us with gestures and *bow-wows* and *bang-bangs* to kill a dog for them. There it was, shoot it! And we almost always did; it was a bit of sport anyway, and at the same time it delighted those human skeletons. Besides, those wild dogs were a regular pest.

When we brought one down, there followed a performance that could make a man puke. Yelling like mad, the Russkies would fall on the animal and tear it in pieces with their bare hands, even before it was quite dead. The pluck they would stuff their pockets with, like tobacco, whenever they got hold of any of that—it made a sort of iron ration. Then they would light a fire, skewer shreds of the dog's meat on sticks and roast it. There were always fights over the bigger bits. The burnt flesh stank frightfully; there was almost no fat in it.

But they did not have roast dog every day. Behind the huts there was a big midden, a regular mountain of stinking waste, and if we did not look out they would poke about in it and eat such things as decaying onions, the mere sight of which was enough to turn you up. If one of us came near they would scatter like dung-flies. I once found one roasting dried pig's dung.

Benno Zieser

A German Prisoner

The day we arrived we were invited by Krassovsky to come to his head-quarters. He was anxious to examine a German prisoner personally. One of our patrols had crossed the Dnieper for the express purpose of bringing in prisoners. Krassovsky had only one officer on his staff who spoke German fairly well, Commandant Fechner, and he was anxious that I should be present at the examination.

The prisoner was a Company Sergeant-Major, and with his horn-rimmed glasses, his fine hands and his slim figure, he seemed to be a man of some education and intelligence. On the way back he had tried to escape from our patrols by jumping from the boat into the Dnieper, but a blow from a rifle butt had prevented his escape. His head was bandaged, and blood trickled from his lips from time to time as he talked. He had lost his front teeth, which made it difficult for him to talk and difficult for us to understand him. He spoke with a strong Berlin accent.

'Your name, rank and unit?'

'Heinrich Fechner, Company Sergeant-Major of 147 Infantry Division.'

'Fechner.' General Krassovsky smiled. 'No relation of yours, I suppose, comrade Fechner?'

I noticed that the man was listening intently. He seemed to understand Russian.

'Who is in command of your regiment?'

'General von Falz.'

'What sort of a general?'

'Brigadier-General.'

'What army does your unit belong to? What other units are there at Kriukov? Who commands them? What equipment have they?'

'I don't know.'

'You mean you don't want to say.'

'No. I really don't know.'

'Do you speak Russian?'

'No.'

'Do you understand Russian?'

'No.'

'Good. Very well, tell him, comrade Fechner, that we shall send him to Kharkov escorted by Cossacks.'

The man turned pale and didn't wait for Krassovsky's words to be translated.

'Shoot me straight away,' he said in Russian.

'Oh, so that loosens your tongue, eh? You do speak Russian, after all. And almost without an accent. Where were you born?'

'Lodz.'

'So you're not German at all? You're Polish.'

'I was born in 1908. Lodz was in Russian hands then.'

'So much the worse for you. You're Russian, and you're fighting against us. You'll be hanged.'

'Hang me then, but don't hand me over to the Cossacks.'

'Lieutenant Petrov, call Cossack Lieutenant Kromov.'

'Excellency, I'll talk. I'll answer your questions.'

The prisoner swayed.

'Give the man a glass of water.'

Within a short space of time we had all the information we wanted. The German attack was to begin at dawn the next day.

Ivan Krylov

Deserters

Sometimes the steppes would be white with the leaflets which our airmen dropped to the Soviet forces. These informed the Russians they should give up their senseless resistance and come over to us. The bottom part of the leaflets was detachable and counted as 'Pass for officers or men up to fifty in number.' There was the promise, in German and Russian, of 'good treatment and an early return to your homeland after the war is over'.

Most deserters showed us these passes when they came over. There were others who were only mastered at the cost of fierce fighting but who when beaten would suddenly pull out one of these passes, in a crumpled state, as if they thought they would prove trump cards and ensure them against any more worries.

However, those passes did not bring any of them any advantage whatsoever. They were only a propaganda trick; 'Birdlime,' said the Sheikh, 'to catch stupid peasants.' It bore the fine name of Psychological Warfare. Actually, all prisoners, without distinction, were marched to the nearest assembly camp, and there nobody cared two hoots whether they really were deserters or had fought us like furies to the last; though, it is true, there were a number of deserters kept at base for menial tasks. As a matter of fact, they had a far better time than any of us.

Benno Zieser

A Captured German Colonel's Diary: September 1941

Russia has double the population of Germany and is able to put twice the number of troops in the field.

There is no need for us to be in a hurry for Moscow. The fact that the Russians are throwing in more and more troops against us makes no difference to us. We will take Moscow when we want to.

The young people of both sexes are a great danger. They belong to the Bolshevist organization. Whenever these ragamuffins are discovered they must be detained and inquiries made at the burgomeister's office as to whether they are local residents. If they are not residents, they are to be arrested immediately, but they must not be shot before they have been interrogated by the Gestapo. Adults who are not local residents or who arouse suspicion must also be detained. The question of shooting them can be decided by each officer individually.

The Russians are very tenacious in defence and particularly skilful in constructing field fortifications.

In the Gaisin district the Russians discovered that our situation was serious, and for that reason they began to bomb us daily.

Only a reserve field battalion saved us from encirclement by counter-attacking.

Young soldiers must remember that even during a protracted war a soldier remains a soldier. Care must be taken that they do not get out of hand, otherwise we shall go downhill without noticing it with ever-increasing speed, as happened in the last war.

We cannot deny the Bolsheviks' courage and contempt for death. We have not been confronted by such an opponent hitherto.

As yet our troops have not been exterminating all prisoners and wounded. But the longer the war goes on, the more ruthlessly must we wage it. We will set aside all who were Bolsheviks, either officially or by virtue of their conduct. We will kill ten Bolsheviks for every German. Without attempting to prophesy—prophecy in wartime is always dangerous—and without using any fine language, I am bound to say the following: We are going to cross the Dnieper. We have no time to lose and must make short work of the Russians before the bad weather sets in. Obviously, we shall be exposed to attack by their cavalry.

The heavy fighting near Moscow has now been going on for three weeks. Apparently we are allowing the Russians to counter-attack and even to advance in some sectors. The situation at Leningrad looks very promising. But we must not forget that the Russians, unlike the French, are able to throw in more and more masses of men.

Conclusions:

1. Our communication lines have been considerably lengthened. Every bullet has to be brought by railway, then by motor transport and finally across country. Do not abandon ammunition under the influence of panic and do not waste it. Keep calm.

2. We have experienced a shortage of petrol and will continue to do so, as well as a shortage of supplies, provisions, etc. Actually the bread ration has already decreased to three hundred grammes. We are not receiving sugar or butter. Therefore food that has been seized must be dealt out economically.

3. We have only two lorries of necessary articles for the whole regiment. Everybody must send home for razor-blades and boot polish.

4. We shall soon enter the malarial region. Malaria is a very unpleasant disease, although not necessarily fatal. It is carried by mosquitoes. When we get twenty-one miles beyond the Dnieper there will no longer be any danger of malaria.

5. In future no leave will be granted except in special cases.

I leave it to those experts with sufficient leisure to clarify the future course of events.

Colonel Kress

A Prophecy

Shortly before sunset we heard the soft melody of a lute coming from the bower adjoining the house. Lammerding and I found an old Lithuanian seated near the house playing to a few soldiers. His long, snow-white beard made him look like an ancient bard. We asked him into the house to play for us. He sat by the fireplace, his hands quivering over his instrument. Officers and men stood about or leaned against the walls and doorway listening in silence.

As if out of distant depths that we could not at first comprehend came weird chords, first searching and appealing, then gradually developing into a coherent theme of exquisite melody, sad, almost melancholic, yet with no touch of morbidness. To me these plaintive melodies were the expression of the soul of a frontier nation, which had suffered subjection and bondage for many centuries. And then, gradually, the mood changed; turbulent and provocative tones grew into a throbbing and angry rhythm. The old man's face, which had been serene, as if no longer interested in worldly matters, was transformed. His eyes flashed with an inner fire and he started to sing in a foreign tongue. His voice was feeble with age, but true to every note. It seemed that he was conveying the thanks of a nation that had regained its freedom.

Those who followed the German Army and took over administration of Lithuania made a sad blunder when they failed to recognize this cry for freedom and did not call upon the help of these people in the fight against the Reds. There was a reservoir of goodwill waiting to be tapped. Instead it was dammed up by short-sighted oppression.

Some of the soldiers who had been listening to the old man took the opportunity to have a look at the inside of the farmhouse. The massive stone oven in the centre of the living-room amused them; it was about twenty feet square, had an open fireplace and a number of apertures in which stood primitive-looking pots. The thick walls of the oven divided the house into semi-enclosed rooms.

'Hey, Uncle!' called one of the soldiers. 'You must have a big family. Why do you want an oven as big as this?'

The old man smiled. He knew enough German to understand what they were getting at. 'Will you be in Russia this winter?' he asked in his thin voice.

'Perhaps.'

'Then you will find out! And perhaps you won't laugh.'

Heinrich Haape

The German forces pressed on. In spite of all the space which they could play with, the Russians were cutting it fine by the late summer—Leningrad was besieged and Moscow, the holy city, was almost within sight of the most forward German elements. But there was a late summer of quite exceptional wetness, and on 12 September the first snow fell.

The Fall of Kiev

On 26 September the Battle of Kiev was brought to a successful conclusion. The Russians surrendered. 665,000 men were taken prisoner. The Commander-in-Chief South-west Front and his chief of staff fell in the last phase of the battle while attempting to break out. The Commander of the Fifth Army was among the prisoners captured. I had an interesting conversation with this officer, to whom I put a number of questions. 'When did you learn that my tanks had penetrated behind you?' 'About the 8th of September.' 'Why did you not evacuate Kiev at once?' 'We had received orders from the Army Group to evacuate the area and withdraw eastwards and had already begun to do so, when we received contrary orders to turn about and defend Kiev in all circumstances.' The carrying out of this second order resulted in the destruction of the Kiev Army Group. The enemy was never to make the same mistake again. Unfortunately, though, we were to suffer the direst calamities as a result of just such interference from higher levels.

The Battle of Kiev was undoubtedly a great tactical victory. But whether great strategic advantages were to be garnered from this tactical success remained questionable. It all depended on this: would the German Army, before the onset of winter and, indeed, before the autumnal mud set in, still be capable of achieving decisive results? It is true that the planned assault on Leningrad had already had to be abandoned in favour of a tight investment. But the O.K.H.* believed that the enemy was no longer capable of creating a firm defensive front or of offering serious resistance in the area of Army Group South. The O.K.H. wanted this Army Group to capture the Donetz Basin and reach the River Don before winter.

But the main blow was to be dealt by the reinforced Army Group Centre, with objective Moscow. Was there still sufficient time for this to succeed?

General Heinz Guderian, G.O.C. Panzer Group 2

The steel ring that would tighten on Moscow was to be the greatest pincer movement of all time. We on the left flank were to be the claw of the pincers that would surround Moscow from the north-west, while the right flank of the Army Group was advancing on Kaluga and Tula and would squeeze the capital city from the south-east.

But the rain continued—rain such as this part of Russia had never in living memory experienced at this time of the year. So the Russian peasants told us. We marched on, but it got colder and colder and we were soaked through and depressed. The roads became quagmires and we thought bitterly of the winter clothing that had been promised us.

Heinrich Haape

On 2 October the Führer announced that the drive to Moscow would be 'the last decisive battle of this year', and on the 6th the assault began. Three days later Molotov proclaimed a state of siege in the city, and on the following day the Government, with the exception of Stalin himself, packed its bags and moved eastwards to Kiubyzhev. Heavy industrial plant was transferred en masse *to Siberia. The German advance continued along the whole front, and before long the forward troops were within easy reach of Moscow.*

The Evacuation of Moscow

In the early days of the war our people had to be told what the Nazis were, and with other writers I was asked to describe with hatred the horrible thing that was hanging over our land. On the second day of the war I began to write for the Vakhtangov Theatre the play *Welcome Arms*. Its theme concerned a second European front.

The play was written in two months, and then during the period of heavy air raids, when we slept in the theatre, we rehearsed. One night I went home. A bomb hit and destroyed the theatre and until the next afternoon I was thought to have perished. But actually I was already rewriting my burned manuscript from memory. We began to rehearse again elsewhere, but the day before the première was billed, the company was given short notice to evacuate to Omsk in Siberia, for the position in Moscow was becoming critical.

Boris Voyetekhov

* The Army High Command.

Among the mountains and pine forests there is spread out the beautiful capital of the Urals, Sverdlovsk. It has many fine buildings, but I want to tell you of the two most remarkable buildings of the whole area. Winter had already come when Sverdlovsk received Comrade Stalin's order to erect the two buildings for the plant evacuated from the south. The trains packed with machinery and people were on the way. In its new home the war factory had to start production, and it had to do so in not more than a fortnight. Fourteen days—not an hour more! It was then that the people of the Urals came to this empty spot with shovels, bars and pickaxes: students, typists, accountants, shop assistants, housewives, artists, teachers. The earth was like stone, frozen hard by our fierce Siberian frost. Axes and pickaxes could not break the stony soil. In the light of arc-lamps people hacked at the earth all night. They blew up the stones and the frozen earth, and they laid the foundations. Comrade Sivach, the grey-bearded decorator from the Sverdlovsk theatre, and his team were leading.

People's hands and feet were swollen with frostbite, but they did not leave work. Over the charts and blueprints, laid out on packing-cases, the blizzard was raging. Hundreds of trucks kept rolling up with building materials.

Rapidly the steel structures rose from the ground. . . . On the twelfth day, into the new buildings with their glass roofs, the machinery, covered with hoar-frost, began to arrive. Braziers were kept alight to unfreeze the machines. . . . And two days later, the war factory began production.

V. Ilyenkov

On to Moscow

Two days after we had left Butovo, late in the afternoon, the first snow fell in heavy flakes on the silently-marching columns. Every man's thoughts turned in the same direction as he watched the flakes drop on the slushy roads. The first manifestations of winter! How cold and how long would the winter be? The black soil immediately dissolved the white flakes as if sucking them in, but as the late afternoon frost set in and snow fell more thickly, the countryside took on itself a white mantle. We watched it uneasily.

But by the evening we had reached the upper Dnieper and were lying exactly seventy-five miles from Vyasma and one hundred and seventy miles west of Moscow. Facing us across the river, which was narrow at this point, lay a strong line of Russian bunkers. Next morning we launched our assault across the river and by 6.30 a.m. the Russian defensive system was in our hands and the enemy was in full retreat. We thrust towards our next objective—the town of Sychevka.

The weather deteriorated. It became colder and snowed the whole day. But the snow did not remain for long. It was churned into the black earth, into which our vehicles sank deeper and deeper. The troops hauled and pushed the wheels of the transport; the gallant little *panje* horses sweated and strained; at times we had to take a brief ten-minute rest from sheer exhaustion; then back to the transport, our legs in black mud up to the knees. Anything to keep the wheels moving. To make up for lost time, and in a desperate race against the weather

that we knew would worsen, we marched the night through and reached the area
north of Sychevka on 11 October.

Heinrich Haape

And now, when Moscow itself was almost in sight, the mood both of commanders and troops changed. With amazement and disappointment we discovered in late October and early November that the beaten Russians seemed
quite unaware that as a military force they had almost ceased to exist. . . .
Skilfully camouflaged strongpoints, wire entanglements and thick minefields
now filled the forests which covered the western approach to Moscow.

One began to hear sarcastic references to the military leaders far away in
Germany. The troops felt that it was high time our political leaders came and
had a look at the front. Our soldiers were over-tired now, our units under
strength. This was particularly so among the infantry, where many companies
were reduced to a mere sixty or seventy men. The horses, too, had suffered
grievously and the artillery had difficulty in moving its guns. The number of
serviceable tanks in the Panzer divisions was far below establishment. Since
Hitler had believed that the campaign was over, he had ordered that industry at
home cut down on its production of munitions. Only a trickle of replacements
reached the fighting units. Winter was about to begin, but there was no sign of
any winter clothing to be seen anywhere.

By mid-November the mud period was over and frost heralded the approach
of winter. Both the roads and the open country were now passable for vehicles
of all kinds. Tractors extricated the heavy artillery from the mud far behind the
front and one gun after another was towed forward. It happened, however, that
in the process of dragging these guns out of the ground into which many had
become frozen fast, a number of them were literally torn to pieces.

General Blumentritt

Winter

Then the weather suddenly broke and almost overnight the full fury of the
Russian winter was upon us. The thermometer suddenly dropped to thirty degrees of frost. This was accompanied by heavy falls of snow. Within a few days
the countryside presented the traditional picture of a Russian winter. With
steadily decreasing momentum and increasing difficulty the two Panzer groups
continued to battle their way towards Moscow.

General Blumentritt

On 13 November we awoke and shivered. An icy blast from the north-east
knifed across the snowy countryside. The sky was cloudless and dark blue, but
the sun seemed to have lost its strength and instead of becoming warmer towards noon as on previous days, the thermometer kept falling and by sundown
had reached minus twelve degrees Centigrade.

The soldiers, who up to now had not regarded the light frosts too seriously,
began to take notice. One man who had been walking outside for only a short
distance without his woollen *Kopfschutzer* or 'head-saver' came into the sick
bay. Both ears were white and frozen stiff.

It was our first case of frost-bite.

We gently massaged the man's ears, taking care not to break the skin, and they thawed out. We powdered them and covered them with cotton-wool and made a suitable head-dressing. Perhaps we had managed to save the whole of the ears; we should have to wait and see.

This minor case of frost-bite was a serious warning. The icy winds from Siberia—the breath of death—were blowing across the steppes; winds from where all life froze, from the Arctic ice-cap itself. Things would be serious if we could not house ourselves in prepared positions and buildings, and I stopped to think of the armies marching on Moscow across open country at this very moment. All that those men had received so far were their woollen *Kopfschutzers*; the winter clothing had still not arrived. What was happening to the men's feet, for the ordinary army boot retained very little warmth?

Then, too, the thermometer showed only twelve degrees below zero. Temperatures would drop to minus twenty-four degrees—minus thirty-six degrees—minus forty-eight degrees—perhaps even lower. It was beyond comprehension —a temperature four times colder than a deep freezer. To attempt any movement without warm clothing in those conditions would be sheer suicide. Surely the older generals had been right when, after the battle of Vyasma and Bryansk, they had counselled: 'Dig in for the winter.' Some of them were men with experience of Russia during the 1914–1918 War. At the most they had said, continue the war through the winter only with a few thoroughly-equipped and well-provisioned divisions. Make the big push in the spring.

If only the battle for Moscow had started fourteen days earlier, the city would now have been in our hands. Or even if the rains had held off for fourteen days. If—if—if. If Hitler had started 'Barbarossa' six weeks earlier as originally planned; if he had left Mussolini on his own in the Balkans and had attacked Russia in May; if we had continued our sweeping advance instead of stopping at the Schutsche Lake; if Hitler had sent us winter clothing. Yes, if, if, if—but now it was too late.

Those Arctic blasts that had taken us by surprise in our protected positions had scythed through our attacking troops. In a couple of days there were one hundred thousand casualties from frost-bite alone; one hundred thousand first-class, experienced soldiers fell out because the cold had surprised them.

A couple of days later our winter clothing arrived. There was just enough for each company to be issued with four heavy fur-lined greatcoats and four pairs of felt-lined boots. Four sets of winter clothing for each company! Sixteen greatcoats and sixteen pairs of winter boots to be shared among a battalion of eight hundred men! And the meagre issue coincided with a sudden drop in the temperature to minus twenty-two degrees.

Reports reached us that the issue of winter clothing to the troops actually advancing on Moscow had been on no more generous scale. More and more reports were being sent to Corps and Army Headquarters recommending that the attack on Moscow by a summer-clad army be abandoned and that winter positions be prepared. Some of these reports were forwarded by Central Army Group to the Führer's Headquarters, but no reply or acknowledgment ever came. The order persisted: 'Attack!' And our soldiers attacked.

Heinrich Haape

Moscow Tram-stop

There was a deathly silence all round. In front of us lay the tramway shelter and the telegraph poles silently pointed the way to the great city beyond the curtain of snow.

'Let's walk across and have a look at that tramway station,' Kageneck said. 'Then we can tell Neuhoff that we were only a tram ride from Moscow.'

We walked silently down the road to the stone shed. There was not a movement around us as we stopped and stared at the wooden seats on which thousands of Muscovites had sat and waited for the tram to clang down the road from Moscow.

There was an old wooden bin attached to one wall. I felt inside and dragged out a handful of old tram tickets. We picked out the cyrillic letters, which by now we knew spelled *Moskva*.

Slowly we trudged back to the car. Kagenck broke the silence and spoke for both of us: 'It must fall, yet . . . I wonder. . . .'

Fischer turned the car round and we headed back along the white road.

The snow was falling a little more heavily now.

Heinrich Haape

Every soldier outside Moscow knew that this was a battle for life or death. If the Russians succeeded in defeating us here, there could be no hope. In 1812 Napoleon had at least returned with the shattered remnants of his Grand Army. In 1941 the choice for the Germans was only to hold fast or to be annihilated. Russian propaganda took the form of postcards, dropped from the air. These bore crude pictures of the snow-covered Russian plains dotted with the corpses of German soldiers. Such propaganda made no impression on our troops.

General Blumentritt

On Leave from Russia

'At first it was fine,' went on Rudolf. 'We swept on, adding towns and villages by the score. Then the troops began to get stale. Do you know how we behaved to the civilians? Shall I tell you?' he asked. We didn't reply before he began his story.

'We behaved like devils out of hell,' he said. 'We have left those villagers to starve to death behind us, thousands and thousands of them. How can you win a war in this way? Do you think they won't revenge themselves somehow? Of course they will.'

'You mean you leave nothing behind? No homes, no food, no animals?'

'Those are the orders,' said Rudolf. 'Just to leave enough for the occupying troops.'

'It's utter madness,' said Heiner. 'Whoever gave such orders are out of their minds. Surely not the generals?'

'No,' said Rudolf. 'The Russian front is really in the hands of the S.S., the generals have little say. It is Hitler's revenge for being told he couldn't win a war against Russia. He is trying to prove all the army officers wrong.'

We sat in an awful silence for a moment. Then Rudolf went on to tell us more details of the partisans behind their lines.

'We shoot the prisoners on the slightest excuse,' he said. 'Just stick them up against the wall and shoot the lot. We order the whole village out to look while we do it, too.'

'Yes,' said Dr. Schmitt. 'And I have heard too that Hitler ordered that every officer or political commissar made prisoner on the Eastern Front was to be shot immediately after questioning.'

Rudolf jumped up. 'No,' he declared, 'you are wrong there. The officers are not shot after questioning. I, at least, have seen that that's not true.'

'Calm down,' said Dr. Schmitt. 'I only said "ordered", I didn't say it was being carried out. Hitler signed a secret document to have it done, but the high Army officers are refusing to carry the order out. That is one reason why Hitler is getting so wild and allowing the S.S. and the Gestapo terrible powers in the villages after you have passed on.'

'My God,' said Rudolf. 'If it is really true, then everything is lost. Not only the Russian war, but the whole war.'

Heiner made a sign to Dr. Schmitt not to say anything more on that subject, but Rudolf would go on talking.

'You can't imagine what happens behind the lines. We had orders to try and clear partisans out of a wood. We combed that wood for two days in the most bitter weather. But no partisans. I was just about to withdraw my troops, when suddenly whistles began to blow, and the wood was full of Russians in a second. They were in such a terrible condition, however, that we beat them off. They had been lying in holes in the ground covered only with straw and brushwood and had had no food or drink, indeed they must scarcely have dared to take breath. They were so cold their limbs would not move properly when the order came to attack us.'

'The courage of desperation,' said Dr. Schmitt. 'Men in those conditions will do anything.'

'They do do anything,' said Rudolf. 'As terrible things as we do to them. When we passed through another village where the partisans had caught some of our troops we found men stripped naked except for their steel helmets which still stuck on their heads. A long line of them were tied together and water had been poured over them until they had frozen into a solid block of ice. You see, it's a vicious circle. We hate them, they hate us, and on and on it goes, everyone getting more and more inhuman.'

Rudolf's last words echoed round the room. No one spoke. I put out a hand and touched Dr. Schmitt lightly; he was sitting quite close to me. He looked up and saw that I wanted him to try to help Rudolf.

'Yes,' he said slowly, as if coming out of a coma. 'It *is* a vicious circle.'

'Another of our mistakes was in the Ukraine,' said Rudolf, now a little calmer. 'I was one of those who marched in to be received, not as a conqueror but as a friend. The civilians were all ready to look on us as saviours. They had had years of oppression from the Soviet. They thought we had come to free them. Does it sound absurd? Perhaps it does. What did we do? Turn them into slaves under Hitler. Worse, we deported their women for labour in Germany, and did not bother if they were married or single, had children or not. To add insult to injury we forced every woman and girl to undergo medical inspection. Ninety-nine per cent of the unmarried girls were virgins, but we took no notice of that, just ordered one and all to line up for medical inspection as though they were prostitutes. After inspection a clean medical report was made in their labour books, then they were loaded into wagons and transported to work for the Fatherland.'

In the deep silence that followed I was very near to tears. To try and overcome them I hastily refilled the glasses and offered one to Rudolf to cheer him up.

'Come on, Rudolf, try and cheer up, we are together for only a short time. Come on,' I pleaded.

Dr. Schmitt and his wife also took glasses, and Hermann and Heiner. We lifted them, and perhaps stupidly, but anyway with the best of intentions, we began to hum an old German drinking song. 'Drink, dear brother, drink, and let worry look after itself.' (*Trink, Brüderlein, trink, lasse die Sorgen zu Haus!*)

Rudolf took the glass and stared at me and said, 'You can take my word for it, Else, if the Russians should ever knock at this door and only pay back one half of what we have done to them, you wouldn't ever smile or sing again!'

Else Wendel, housewife

Rejoining One's Unit

The cart track led past the charred remains of a cottage, now no more than foundations of walls with charred and shivered beams sticking oddly out of the cinders. In many places the mass was still smouldering, thin smoke coiled slowly up into the air. A few paces farther, I saw some military graves. The earth was freshly turned, the crosses new. *Tenth Company*, I read. My heart shrank. My own company. *Rifleman Georg Haunstein*. Didn't know him. Must be a new chap. *Corporal Dieter Hufnagel*. Must be one of the heavy machine-gunners. *N.C.O. Karl Mansch*. A stranger. Then a lot more I did not know. But stop, this one—was that not the fellow who had collected those prisoners' rings? And there was Habacher, too, one of the real front-line veterans. So Habacher too had now been knocked out. When Habacher had to shoot that commissar he said afterwards he was sure the commissar would have his revenge. *Hartman, Kulbeck, Strangel*. Strangel was in my platoon, a lad bubbling over with good spirits and humour.

Racked with anxiety, I now ran through all the names on the remaining crosses, and found another and yet another whom I knew. Then my breath caught in my throat. I bent low to see it clearly. The letters swam in front of me. It could not be! *Corporal Willi Scholz*.

Our Willi! I stared at the rough lettering in sheer dismay, and my thoughts began a mad whirl. How cold and supercilious that lettering did look, the second *l* was partly smudged, somebody had corrected it, started first to put *h*—for *Wilhelm*, I suppose. They thought Willi could not possibly be his baptismal name, till someone must have said: 'Yes, that was his name all right, *Willi*.' How I hated that cursed cross! I felt I could have flung the thing into the smoking ruins of the house to feed the flames.

The tin hat set on the cross was a bit crooked, just a little bit, precisely the way he had always worn it; it had always been a bit on the large side for him. I took it down. My hands shook. In the leather band inside was scratched *W. Scholz*, in Willi's own hand. But it was not at all easy to read, the leather was smeared with dark brown stains. Blood. Dried blood. And at the side the tin hat had a hole, with the usual sharp, in-bent edges, and they too were dark brown, like the patches on the leather.

Benno Zieser

RETREAT FROM MOSCOW

In mid-November the Russians, jealous for their holy city, counter-attacked both north and south—at Kalinin and Tula. They counter-attacked also in the south, and retook Rostov-on-Don before the month was out. On 1 December they successfully mounted a major operation at Tula, and the threat to Moscow was removed for ever. Twelve days later von Bock, the Army Commander, was relieved because of his failure and was succeeded by List. By mid-December the Germans were in retreat along the entire front, and on the 19th the Führer decided that drastic measures were required—he relieved von Brauchitsch and took supreme command of the armies himself.

A bombshell burst on 8 December—Japan was at war with America! It seemed like an act of senseless bravado. Did we not already have enough enemies? Was not the position on the Russian front serious enough—an army without winter clothing facing an enemy with allies? Must we be at war with a hostile world?

Then came reports that fresh Siberian troops, equipped with superb w nter clothing, were attacking our lines on both sides of Kalinin. Stalin must have had a secret agreement with Japan for some time past, otherwise how dared he withdraw these divisions from the East?

Over the Volga the Siberian troops came, and threw themselves against our 127 and 162 Divisions. The Volga was no longer a barrier—it was completely frozen over; an army could have marched across it. Desperately I prayed that the Russians would not break through and set the whole front aflame. It was a selfish prayer; at any moment I feared the instruction would be issued: 'All leave cancelled.' I wanted to be away before the order was given.

. . . . The retreat from Moscow had begun.

It was a retreat that involved the entire Germany Army from before the capital. Three armies were falling back from the rich prize and were being hammered as they went by Marshal Zhukov and his hordes of warmly-clad reinforcements.

For our ill-equipped troops, retreat in many instances spelt death. Death with the thermometer standing at fifty degrees below zero. Fiercely, the wind from the far steppes of Asia continued to blow, driving the loose snow and ice before it. The highways could no longer be recognized except as lanes of hard-packed snow. During the blizzards it was cold, bitterly cold, but when the clouds cleared and the sun hung low in the sky it was colder still. It was as if the sky itself had frozen into a crystal of cold lead. Death came with icy pinions and stood at our elbow. But our troops fought him just as, again and again, they formed up and fought the Russians. They retreated across the snow desert with their faces to the enemy.

Every day we fought bitterly, threw back the Russians with bloody losses to themselves and every evening disentangled ourselves from the grip of the enemy so that we could warm our frozen bodies in the shelter of some deserted hamlet.

In this unearthly cold, in which the breath froze and icicles hung from nostrils and eyelashes all day long, where thinking became an effort, the German soldiers fought—no longer for an ideal or an ideology, no longer for the Fatherland. They fought blindly without asking questions, without wanting to know what lay ahead of them. Habit and discipline kept them going; that and the flicker of an instinct to stay alive. And when the soldier's mind had become numb, when his strength, his discipline and his will had been used up, he sank into the snow. If he was noticed, he was kicked and slapped into a vague awareness that his business in the world was not finished and he staggered to his feet and groped on. But if he lay where he had collapsed until it was too late, as if forgotten he was left lying at the side of the road and the wind blew over him and everything was levelled indistinguishably.

We fought our way southwards towards Staritsa, and on 22 December found ourselves back in Vassilevskoye. We had arrived there at the end of our sweeping march through Poland and Russia with practically a full battalion of eight hundred men. The fighting strength of the battalion was now 189 men, including officers and N.C.O.s. It had shrunk pitifully, but was still battleworthy.

Heinrich Haape

Only for a few hours each day was there limited visibility at the front. Until nine o'clock in the morning the wintry landscape was shrouded in a thick fog. Gradually a red ball, the sun, became visible in the eastern sky and by about eleven it was possible to see a little. At three o'clock in the afternoon dusk set in, and an hour later it was almost completely dark again.

Supplies were usually short. Only a few railways ran into the area behind the front. These were frequently cut by the partisans. The water froze inside the boilers of the engines, which were not built to withstand the Russian climate. Each engine could draw only half the normal number of wagons. Many of them became stuck for days on end in the snow and ice. Our urgent requests for artillery shells could scarcely be met. Yet in order to encourage the soldiers on the Eastern Front trainloads of red wine were shipped to us from France and Germany. The anger of a unit which received a trainload of wine instead of the shells it urgently needed can be readily imagined. Even as wine such a cargo was frequently useless. At forty degrees Centigrade below zero, not an unusual temperature, it had often frozen in transit, burst its bottles, and all that remained were chunks of red ice.

Defensive positions which offered shelter to their occupants were almost non-existent. This resulted in a tactical development whereby both sides fought bitterly for possession of the scattered villages where there was at least some cover to be found against the cruel cold. A further result was that both sides shelled these villages and set fire to the wood and thatch houses in order to deprive the enemy of the relief which they provided. There could be no question of digging in; the ground was frozen to the consistency of iron.

General Blumentritt

The Christmas Present

Little Becker and I walked on together on silence; there was nothing to say. The wind blew up and drove the snow and flakes of ice past us in almost horizontal lines. Fortunately the wind was at our backs. Kageneck and Lammerding came out of a house and rejoined us when, about an hour later, we came to a small hamlet. *Oberst* Becker and von Kalkreuth followed them, got into their jeep, covered themselves with blankets and drove off.

Stolze joined us and asked Kageneck, 'What's happening?'

'A hell of a lot. It's a bastard,' replied Kageneck bitterly. 'The enemy has broken through at Vassilevskoye and nobody knows his head from his arse at the moment. The Russians might be anywhere—at our backs, on our flanks, or even in front of us. We'll have to send out flank patrols.'

'Through those snowdrifts?' asked Stolze.

'It will have to be done,' Kageneck replied.

'And what about the rest of the front?' Stolze asked. 'Surely it can't be as bad as this everywhere?'

'We're retreating from Moscow along the whole of the Central Army Group front,' said Kageneck. 'Three German armies, all with their backs turned on Moscow.'

Lammerding took up the tale: 'The situation has deteriorated to an alarming extent.'

'And the foulest part of it all,' Kageneck burst out, 'is that nearly all our generals have been relieved of their posts.'

'Brauchitsch?' asked Stolze.

'Yes.'

'Guderian?'

'Yes.'

'Von Bock?'

'Yes.'

'Kluge?'

'Field-Marshal von Kluge is practically the only one of the old brigade left. He's taken the Central Army Group from von Bock. Strauss has been relieved of command of 9 Army; Rundstedt's gone; so has Hoth; even Auleb has had 6 Division taken away from him.'

'Then who the hell is our commander now that all the generals have been sent into the desert?' demanded Stolze. He grabbed Kageneck by the arm and for a moment we all stopped while the blizzard swept round us.

'We have a Christmas present, gentlemen,' said Kageneck. 'A new commander.'

'Who is it?' Stolze demanded urgently.

Kageneck pulled his *Kopfschutzer* firmly round his ears and looked hard at Stolze: '*Gefreiter* Adolf Hitler has assumed complete command of the entire German Wehrmacht.'

Heinrich Haape

Winter Clothing—a Solution

Now we had an opportunity to equip our men with more winter clothing. Kageneck ordered that the seventy-three dead Russians be carried to the village and stripped of their felt-lined boots and warm clothing.

But the bodies were frozen stiff. And those invaluable boots were frozen to the Russians' legs.

'Saw their legs off,' ordered Kageneck.

The men hacked off the dead men's legs below the knee and put legs, with boots still attached, into the ovens. Within ten or fifteen minutes the legs were sufficiently thawed for the soldiers to strip off the vital boots.

Stolze had captured his own little personal booty. In hand-to-hand combat he had killed a Russian commissar and he came up to me, his face beaming beneath a wonderful fox-fur cap that he had taken from the dead commissar. I was lavish in my admiration of the prize. Stolze turned to his orderly: 'If ever anything happens to me, see to it that the doctor gets this cap. Understand?'

'*Jawohl, Herr Oberleutnant*,' said the orderly with a grin. . . .

. . . . Stolze's body lay in a barn at the eastern end of the village—among the 10th Company men he had loved so well, men, who, after his death, had shown how close had been the bond between them. They had not dug a grave in the snow for him. They did not trust the Staritsa Line and wanted to inter his body in a proper German war cemetery behind the lines. They laid out his body on a long narrow sledge, rested his head on a pillow and folded his hands across his chest. This improvised bier was placed in the open barn in such a way that if we had to evacuate our positions in a hurry they could take him along at a moment's notice, either by hitching a horse to the sledge or pulling it themselves. They had gone to all this trouble in spite of dead weariness, hunger and long hours of danger and strain. Stolze could have had no finer tribute.

Black rafters stuck out from the thick snow on the roof of the barn like badly decayed teeth. Inside it was still light enough to pick out details. Gently I pulled back the ground-sheet that covered Stolze's body and powdery grains of snow rolled to the ground. Like sculptured marble, Stolze lay on the sledge. His eyes were closed and there was a suspicion of a smile on his mouth. If winter lasted for ever, I thought, Stolze's body would lie embalmed like this until the end of time.

Stolze's orderly was waiting for me outside. He saluted and said: '*Herr Oberleutnant* Stolze ordered me to give *Herrn Assistenzarzt* this fox-fur cap.'

Heinrich Haape

Scorched Earth

The retreating army marched against a back-drop of flame. Special 'scorched-earth commandos' were organized to carry out Hitler's adaptation of Stalin's earlier policy. But our men carried it out more thoroughly than ever the Russians had done. The night shone red as buildings, whole villages, broken-down vehicles, everything of any conceivable value to the enemy, went up in flames. Nothing had to be left to the Red Army—and nothing was left. We marched with the flames licking our footsteps, marched day and night, with only short halts, for we well knew that we were the rearguard of the army that had fallen back from Kalinin; there were no troops between us and the pursuing Russians.

On the evening of 29 December we had crossed the Volga at Terpilovo; we marched the whole of that night, right through the next day and the next night, with the Russians on our heels. But if our spur was the enemy, the whip that flayed us as we marched was the unholy cold. Like mummies we padded along, only our eyes visible, but the cold relentlessly crept into our bodies, our blood, our brains. Even the sun seemed to radiate a steely cold and at night the blood-red skies above the burning villages merely hinted a mockery of warmth.

For long periods at a stretch each man was conscious only of the man who walked in front of him as the shrunken grey column marched ceaselessly towards Staritsa.

And silently with our column went the sledge carrying Stolze's body. The 10th Company men had captured a horse from the Reds for the sole purpose of pulling the sledge. But on the afternoon of 30 December a flight of six Heinkel 111s flew over us from the south, turned and came at us in a shallow dive. We threw ourselves off the road, into snowdrifts or into the ditch. Some men stood up and shouted, 'We're Germans!'; others swore as they dived for cover. But the Heinkels came in and dropped their bombs. In our winter clothing and in our rearguard position, the airmen's mistake was understandable. The bombs exploded, throwing up showers of snow and frozen earth, but nobody was hit. But a near-miss had killed the horse and shattered the sledge carrying Stolze's body. The half-smile was still on the big fellow's face when the 10th Company men went to retrieve the corpse, which was as stiff as a gun-barrel and unharmed. With shovels, Stolze's men set to work to enlarge a bomb crater which would act as a grave for their dead leader, for there was no other sledge they could commandeer.

Then the Heinkels regrouped and came in for another attack. The six men in the burial party threw themselves into the grave on top of Stolze. Another cluster of bomb-craters appeared in the snow and the Heinkels set course southwards. From fragments of the smashed sledge the men fashioned a cross for Stolze's grave and the gallant warrior was left to his rest beside the road of retreat from Moscow.

Heinrich Haape

11

EIGHTH ARMY VERSUS AFRIKA KORPS

In February 1941 *the war in North Africa and Egypt was about to enter into a new and critical phase. Hitler decided to send German troops to North Africa to stiffen his hard-pressed Italian allies. These soldiers and their commander were to write a page in history, together with their opponents, the British desert forces later christened the Eighth Army.*

AN OBSCURE GENERAL ARRIVES

'DETACHMENTS of a German expeditionary force under an obscure general, Rommel, have landed in North Africa.'

The announcement was perfunctory but rather interesting. It had been issued in an Intelligence summary by the British High Command early in March 1941.

Lieutenant Heinz Werner Schmidt, Afrika Korps

In view of the highly critical situation with our Italian allies, two German divisions—one light and one Panzer—were to be sent to Libya to their help. I was to take command of this German Afrika Korps and was to move off as soon as possible to Libya to reconnoitre the ground.

The middle of February would see the arrival of the first German troops in Africa; the movement of 5 Light Division would be complete by mid-April and of 15 Panzer Division at the end of May.

The Italian motorized forces in North Africa were to be placed under my command, while I myself was to be subordinate to Marshal Graziani.

In the afternoon I reported to the Führer, who gave me a detailed account of the situation in Africa and informed me that I had been recommended to him as the man who would most quickly adapt himself to the altogether different conditions of the African theatre. The Führer's chief adjutant, Colonel Schmundt, was to accompany me for the first stage of my tour of reconnaissance. I was advised to start by assembling the German troops in the area round Tripoli so that they could go into action as one body. In the evening the Führer showed me a number of British and American illustrated papers describing General Wavell's advance through Cyrenaica. Of particular interest was the masterly co-ordination these showed between armoured land forces, air force and navy.

General Erwin Rommel

It was not then known that Rommel had given his Afrika Korps special desert training in Germany. On a sandy peninsula in the Baltic, he had found terrain which approximated to that in Libya and there had worked out tactical and maintenance problems. The troops had lived and worked in over-heated barracks and artificial sandstorms, and on strictly rationed water and limited food. After this 'hot-house' training they were ready for desert action when they stepped off the ships at Tripoli.

The New Broom

Before von dem Borne, the Chief of Staff, had an opportunity of checking the number of officers present, Rommel entered unexpectedly. The officers snapped to attention. Von dem Borne announced resonantly, 'Staff Officers and Panzer Regiment officers ready for the conference!' I was surprised at what seemed rather an informal way of 'reporting'. (Normally in the German Army the General would be advised briefly how many officers, and from which units, were present, how many were absent, and so on.) But without further ceremony Rommel launched himself into his address:

'Gentlemen,' he said, 'I am pleased to know that after strenuous days the gentlemen of the 5th Panzer Regiment are now in Tripoli almost up to full strength. With the arrival of your Panzers the situation in North Africa will be stabilized. The enemy's thrust towards Tripolitania has been brought to a standstill. Our reconnaissance units [a battalion of armoured cars] under Lieutenant-Colonel von Wegmar have reached the Italians' advanced positions on the Gulf of Sirte at El Agheila, and have morally and materially strengthened the front. It is our task to restore the confidence of the Italian people in their arms, and to bolster up the fighting spirit of our allies.'

Rommel paused between sentences, clenching his fists with elbows bent and thrust slightly forward. That powerful chest, those energetic facial gestures, and his abrupt, precise, military manner of expressing himself clearly indicated a resolute will. The officers, all standing, listened intently to his review of the situation.

Rommel raised his voice. He shook his fist lightly.

'We *must* save Tripolitania from the attack of the British Army. We *will* hold them.'

Lieutenant Heinz Werner Schmidt

Lili Marlene

Vor der Kaserne, vor dem grossen Tor
Steht eine Laterne, und steht sie noch davor.
Wenn sich die späten Nebel drehn,
Bei der Laterne woll'n wir stehn
Wie einst Lili Marlene
Wie einst Lili Marlen'.

The Desert

The war in Africa is quite different from the war in Europe. It is absolutely individual. Here there are not masses of men and material. Nobody and nothing can be concealed. Whether in battle between opposing land forces or between those of the air or between both it is the same sort of fight, face to face; each side thrusts and counter-thrusts. If the struggle were not so brutal, so entirely without rules, one would be inclined to think of the romantic idea of a knight's tourney.

Lieutenant Schorm, Afrika Korps, diary, 16 April 1941

Two main considerations governed warfare in the Libyan-Egyptian desert: supply, and the balance of 'mobile striking power'—a term which may be used to cover the combined power of tanks, anti-tank guns and field artillery working together as a common force. The chief geographical factor influencing tactics in this desert is that, except at El Alamein near Alexandria and at El Agheila on the border of Tripolitania, there are no defensive positions that cannot be out-flanked. At both these places secure flanks are provided by narrow bottlenecks—between the Mediterranean and the Qattara Depression in one case, and the Great Sand Sea in the other. Everywhere else there is an open desert flank, the cause of constant anxiety to the commander who has not superiority in mobile striking power. Even the most gallant infantry cannot hold fixed positions in this desert when once enemy armoured forces have outflanked them. Then, if they are not to be cut off, they must withdraw and keep on withdrawing until wear and tear or supply difficulties reduce the enemy's superiority in armoured and mobile forces to such an extent that he loses control of the open desert flank. Their only alternative is to establish themselves behind a fortified perimeter covering a water-point and harbour like that at Tobruk.

THE FIRST BLOW: 30 MARCH 1941

We went for the little fort in the desert, and the British positions round it, from three directions. The engagement was sharp but lasted only a couple of hours. We took the British commander, Major-General Gambier-Parry, in his tent. The haul of prisoners numbered almost three thousand. We had a further spectacular success. A mobile force of motor-cyclists caught up with the British column moving eastward across the desert below the Jebel Akhdar nearby, and to their astonishment held up the two heroes of the British advance to Ben-ghazi: Lieutenant-General Sir Richard O'Connor, who had just been knighted for his successes against the Italians, and Lieutenant-General Sir Philip Neame, V.C. So we had three generals in the bag.

Mechili landing-ground was littered with destroyed planes. British machines swooped down to attack it afresh at short intervals. At the height of one assault, 'my' Fieseler Storch dropped in out of the sky. Out stepped Rommel, smiling buoyantly, fresh from a personal reconnaissance of the desert scene.

The command trucks of the captured British generals stood on a slight rise. They were large, angular vehicles on caterpillar tracks, equipped inside with wireless and facilities for 'paper' work. We christened them 'Mammoths' then, but I did not realize that these useful trucks would be used by Rommel and his staff and commanders right through the long struggle that was now beginning in the desert.

Rommel inspected the vehicles with absorbed interest after a brief interview with the captured British generals. He watched them emptied of their British gear. Among the stuff turned out he spotted a pair of large sun-and-sand goggles. He took a fancy to them. He grinned, and said, 'Booty—permissible, I take it, even for a General.' He adjusted the goggles over the gold-braided rim of his cap peak.

Those goggles for ever after were to be the distinguishing insignia of the 'Desert Fox'.

Lieutenant Heinz Werner Schmidt

Rommel Writes to His Wife

3 April 1941

Dearest Lu,

We've been attacking since the 31st with dazzling success. There'll be consternation amongst our masters in Tripoli and Rome, perhaps in Berlin too. I took the risk against all orders and instructions because the opportunity seemed favourable. No doubt it will all be pronounced good later and they'll all say they'd have done exactly the same in my place. We've already reached our first objective, which we weren't supposed to get to until the end of May. The British are falling over each other to get away. Our casualties small. Booty can't yet be estimated. You will understand that I can't sleep for happiness.

Rommel

TOBRUK

Weakened and faced by a new and determined foe, the British withdrew eastwards with celerity and not without some disorder. They left behind them a citadel destined to prove a thorn in the flank of their enemies.

Seven weeks after the capture of Cyrenaica 9 Division was fleeing helter-skelter for Tobruk with Rommel in close pursuit.

Vehicles shouldered each other crazily on the crammed roadway. To keep fleeing was the only thought. Some of the battered transport broke down and was abandoned. Some of the division were overtaken and made prisoner. In Nazi prison camps Australians came to talk of the 'Breakfast Battalion'. Its commander, perhaps under the delusion that he was still engaged in leisurely manœuvring with his militia company somewhere back in Australia, ordered the battalion to 'stop for breakfast'. His officers demurred, pointing out that Nazi scout cars were only a few miles away. The colonel repeated serenely that 'the battalion would stop for breakfast'. Those of the companies who could manage it disobeyed and kept on fleeing. The colonel and about a hundred of his men stopped for breakfast. For the next four years they partook of that meal in Nazi prison camps: a long time to stop for breakfast.

The tide had turned against the impudent force that occupied Cyrenaica. Rommel recaptured Benghazi. Six days after, 9 Division and the remnants of a British armoured division reached Tobruk. The Benghazi Derby was over. In Tobruk they turned to stand before Rommel and all that he had to hurl against them.

That was the day before Good Friday. But the troops came to call it Black Friday.

Eric Lambert

Churchill on Tobruk

I have never known Churchill at a loss on any question of pure strategy; naturally enough, the service representatives would often have to press him to reject or alter a solution he proposed when the right decision on grounds of pure strategy was unacceptable for lack of resources or for reasons of time and space—which were perhaps not Winston's strongest suit. On grounds of pure strategy Winston was therefore arguing passionately—I never knew him over-rule—for the retention of Tobruk. When Winston asked for my opinion, I supported his desire to hold on, not because it was his idea but because it seemed to me to offer absolutely the only hope of stopping the rot. I pointed out that though there would indeed be difficulties for the Navy and Air Force in supplying and supporting Tobruk, these difficulties on our side, even though our forces were inadequate, would be as nothing to the fears and uncertainties of the enemy when he came to advance far beyond a by-passed Tobruk, with our forces there threatening his communications while they were at extreme stretch across hundreds of miles of desert. The alternative for Rommel would be to devote so large a part of his force to the investment and capture of Tobruk that with what was left he would find it impossible to advance farther into Egypt. To leave a force in Tobruk, on that first occasion, to threaten Rommel's tenuous communications seemed the one chance left of giving pause to an otherwise victorious enemy who at that time looked like stopping nowhere short of Alexandria or Cairo.

Winston greeted this support for his own ideas with unfeigned delight. And at once he found the right phrase for Tobruk: 'A sally port,' he said, pronouncing this with his slight lisp between the 's' and the 'a'. He rolled the phrase round his mouth and repeated it. 'Yes, a sally port, a sally port; that is what we want, that is the thing to do with them. The farther he advances the more you threaten, the more he has to fear. That is the answer, a sally port. . . .'

Air Vice-Marshal Arthur Harris

The Siege Begins

There'll be no Dunkirk here. If we should have to get out, we shall fight our way out. There is to be no surrender and no retreat.

General Morshead, G.O.C. Tobruk garrison

The final count showed more than forty thousand men inside the perimeter. On 12 April there were some five thousand Axis prisoners, and 35,307 British,

Australians and Indians, but many of these were not front-line troops. There were far more Ordnance, Army Service Corps and medical personnel than the garrison needed; five British engineer companies, which had been working on roads and installations throughout Cyrenaica; hundreds of Air Force ground staff, and a number of stragglers. Fortunately the fighting units had reached Tobruk in good order, and they were now joined by two urgently-needed regiments of Royal Horse Artillery, which were rushed up from Egypt.

Before the end of April some twelve thousand troops and airmen and more than seven thousand prisoners of war were withdrawn from Tobruk by sea and the final streamlined garrison—stripped down to essential personnel—from early May to late August averaged little more than twenty-three thousand and fell as low as 22,026 in July. Of these nearly fifteen thousand were Australians and about five hundred were Indians. The rest came from Great Britain.

Chester Wilmot

All our energies and ingenuity were required to guard effectively the twenty-five miles of the perimeter, at any point of which the Germans might have attacked. The defence lines were in the form of a semi-circle, whose radius was about ten miles, with Tobruk as the centre. Within this area we, in the tanks, had to be prepared to move at a moment's notice to any part of the perimeter which was threatened.

Cyril Joly

The First Attacks: Amateur Gunners

On this morning our Transport Officer was in command of the guns and, when the first enemy vehicles appeared, Battalion H.Q. said he could engage them. The guns had no sights but we got direction by squinting down the barrel, and range by trial and error. As it happened, a British artillery colonel was there and he gave us expert advice. Our gun drill wasn't very good and our fire orders would have shocked the R.H.A., but we got the shells away. When the vehicles were about five hundred yards out, the T.O. called, 'All ready boys, let 'er go.' The first shell fell short. 'Cock 'em up a bit, boys,' said the colonel. We did, and the second shot fell dead between the two leading vehicles. We kept on firing and they disappeared in a cloud of dust—and stayed out of range for the rest of the day.

Sergeant E. D. Rule

Repulse

There was terrible confusion at the only gap as tanks and infantry pushed their way through it. The crossing was badly churned up and the tanks raised clouds of dust as they went. In addition, there was the smoke of two tanks blazing just outside the wire.

Into this cloud of dust and smoke we fired anti-tank weapons, Brens, rifles, and mortars, and the gunners sent hundreds of shells. We shot up a lot of infantry as they tried to get past, and many, who took refuge in the anti-tank ditch, were later captured. It was all I could do to stop the troops following them outside the wire. The Germans were a rabble, but the crews of three tanks did keep their heads. They stopped at the anti-tank ditch and hitched on behind them the big guns, whose crews had been killed. They dragged these about a thousand yards, but by then we had directed our artillery on to them. They unhitched the guns and went for their lives. That was the last we saw of the tanks, but it took us several hours to clean up small parties of infantry who hadn't been able to get away.

Major J. W. Balfe

Disillusionment

The information distributed before the action told us that the enemy was about to withdraw, his artillery was weak and his morale had become very low. We had been led to believe that the enemy would retire immediately on the approach of German tanks. Before the beginning of the third attack* the regiment had not the slightest idea of the well-designed and executed defences of the enemy, nor of a single battery position, nor of the terrific number of anti-tank guns. Also it was not known that he had heavy tanks. The regiment went into battle with firm confidence and iron determination to break through the enemy and take Tobruk. Only the vastly superior enemy, the frightful loss and the lack of any supporting weapons, caused the regiment to fail in its task.

Afrika Korps officer

25 April 1941

Things are very warm in front of Tobruk. I shan't be sorry to see more troops arrive, for we're still very thin on the long fortress front. I've seldom had such worries—militarily speaking—as in the last few days. However, things will probably look different soon.

.... Greece will probably soon be disposed of and then it will be possible to give us more help. Paulus is due to arrive in a few days. The battle for Egypt and the Canal is now on in earnest and our tough opponent is fighting back with all he's got.

Rommel

Stukas

It was an ordinary Libyan day, furnace-hot, with a glare that was like a knife across the eyes. Striking the stone-littered surface of the desert the light quivered vaporously. The sky was the colour of smoke. It was motionless. The sun was seen through it like a coin in a dim pool.

But there was life in that sky.

Six Platoon sat in their pits. They were not the men who, attired correctly and uniformly, had marched around the roads of Palestine or stalked the streets of Jerusalem and Tel Aviv in quest of adventures. Their shorts were bleached to a dirty yellow and their boots were worn to whiteness by the sand. Gone was the slouch hat; in its place they wore the round steel helmet, painted yellow. Those who had discarded their shirts showed skins as brown as the wood in the

* The one on 14 April.

butts of their rifles. They eyes were keener, their faces leaner, their lips drawn finer.

For the umpteenth time, Dooley Franks wiped an oily rag over the Bren gun and covered it carefully with an empty sandbag, and for the thousandth time Tommy Collins, his 'Number Two', checked the magazines. Sergeant Lucas glanced approvingly along his Italian Breda machine-gun. Corporal Percy Gribble fingered a boil on his neck. Andy Caine amused himself with a chameleon he kept on the end of a piece of string. Dick Brett shovelled some fallen sand out of a pit. The whole platoon busied itself in a casual sort of fashion. Then, with one accord, they stopped and looked upwards.

There was a faint pulsing in the sky.

'Here the bastards come!' said Dooley.

The pulsing became a trembling, the trembling became a hum.

Then suddenly the noise of the dive-bombers burst out of the blue like a snarl.

'Here they are!' cried Dick, and pointed to the east.

They came out of the sun, black and evil-looking. Stukas. Their curiously-shaped wings were like those of hawks, poised to drop on their prey. There were two flights of them. One flight peeled off, dwindling in the direction of the invisible town.

The world became all noise. Around them the Bofors guns coughed out a torrent of explosions and the sky flowered with little white pom-poms of smoke. Farther back the heavy anti-aircraft brayed hideously upwards.

One by one the black shapes came earthwards, as if they hurtled down a gigantic slide. The shrieks of their downward passage pierced the sound of exploding bombs. The earth around the Australians vomited upwards in great black clouds.

The air became a fog of yellow dust and black smoke and through the frightful din came faintly the cries of men. Tortured ears rejected the concussions and grew dulled, hearing the bombing as muffled convulsions of the earth.

Then, as suddenly as it began, the raid ceased. The anti-aircraft fire dwindled to isolated bangs. The noise of the Stukas grew fainter and fainter in the distance. Human voices carried through the drifting smoke. One of the voices called, high-pitched and urgent:

'Stretcher-bearer!'

Forms came running through the haze.

'You all right, Dick?' Andy called.

'I'm all right,' said a dazed Dick. But echoes of the bombing still thundered in his ears.

'They got a couple from Three Section.'

Gradually the smoke was clearing.

Six Platoon came out of their pits to discover who were their two latest casualties. Dick clambered across the parapet and made towards the wadi where men were already gathered. Leaping across a trench, he noticed a figure huddled against its side. For a moment he thought it to be a corpse; but it was unmarked and a faint regular trembling ran through it.

'Who's that?' he called.

The figure raised its head slowly. Percy Gribble's chalk-white face stared up at him dimly. The lips moved but said nothing. Dick turned and hurried away. He felt as though in seeing what he had he was guilty of something shameful.

The two dead men had been placed on stretchers. Neither of them was well-known to Dick. One was a small grey man approaching middle age who had joined the battalion only a few days before it left Palestine. His remains formed an unnatural heap beneath a blanket through which the blood oozed. The other lay uncovered, his eyes looking up sightlessly to the sky. None of Six Platoon had known him very well either. He had been a big, fair, smiling young fellow, always pleasant, but shy. All they knew about him was that he had been a motor mechanic and had a young wife to whom he wrote every day. He was not marked, but his clothes hung from him in a thousand small tatters where the blast had ripped across his body.

Watched by the men of Six Platoon, the stretcher-bearers bore the dead men slowly down the wadi. Andy Cain gazed expressionlessly after them.

'That's that,' he said.

Eric Lambert

Rommel Breaks Through

When the fog lifted we saw about thirty tanks lined up near R2—half a mile to the west of us. The tanks dispersed, four or five going to each of the posts near by. Infantry followed in parties of about sixty. As they got within range we opened up and they went to ground, but four tanks came on. Their machine-guns kept our heads down and their cannon blasted away our sandbag parapets. The sand got into our M.Gs and we spent as much time cleaning them as we did firing them, but we sniped at the infantry whenever we got a chance. Our anti-tank rifle put one light tank out of action, but it couldn't check the heavier ones, which came right up to the post. We threw hand grenades at them but these bounced off, and the best we could do was to keep the infantry from getting closer than a hundred yards.

After about an hour of this fighting the tanks withdrew, but about ten o'clock more came back. They drove through the wire and one even cruised up and down over our communication trench dropping stick bombs into it. We held their infantry off most of the morning, but eventually under cover of this attack they got into one end of the post, where the Bren crew had all been wounded. Then the Germans worked along the trench while the rest of us were still firing from the other pits. By this time more than half our chaps—we'd only had fifteen—had been killed or wounded, and the Germans got command of the post before we survivors realized what had happened. Just then our artillery began shelling it heavily and the German tanks must have been driven off. So there we were, Germans and Aussies stuck in the post together with shells falling outside. A Jerry sergeant said, 'I don't know who'll be the prisoners—you or us. We'd better wait awhile until the shelling stops.' When the shelling stopped more Germans came in and the sergeant said, 'You're the prisoners.' And we were.

Corporal R. McLeish

Rommel at the Front

Rommel in these days was always present in person when any attack went in against a point on the Tobruk perimeter—not with the staff of the attacking formation, but with the front-line troops. Often, to the annoyance of the tactical staff, he would give orders in person on the spot, changing plans to meet the situation. His subordinate commanders found this a real thorn in the flesh, and resented it bitterly.

We left the Mammoth at Advanced H.Q. and drove off in the usual little battle party—the two open cars and the armoured car, Aldinger, Berndt, and I with the General.

A report had come in that the Australians in the sector facing the Italians had been feverishly active during the night. Rommel wanted a precise picture of the situation now, and so went to see in person. As we approached the sector, we thought it completely calm and were ready to conclude that the reports of enemy activity overnight had been, as so often before, exaggerated by our allies. Even the enemy artillery in Tobruk seemed quiet.

But the puzzle was soon solved: we found not a single Italian in the whole sector, barring a few isolated artillery batteries in the rear, entirely unprotected by infantry. We peered cautiously over a rise and were met by the sight of hundreds of discarded sun-helmets gaily decorated with multi-coloured cocks' feathers—Bersaglieri helmets. Otherwise, not a thing. It dawned on us that the Australians must have 'collected' the entire battalion of our allies during the night.

Rommel hurriedly ordered up a scratch assortment of troops from Acroma to act as a stop-gap in the denuded sector. Then he issued a sharp order . . . to the effect that he would, in future, expect the immediate execution of officers who showed cowardice in the face of the enemy.

Lieutenant Heinz Werner Schmidt

The Australians: An Appreciation

The Australians, who are the men our troops have had opposite them so far, are extraordinarily tough fighters. The German is more active in the attack, but the enemy stakes his life in the defence and fights to the last with extreme cunning. Our men, usually easy-going and unsuspecting, fall easily into his traps, especially as a result of their experiences in the closing stages of the European campaign.

The Australian is unquestionably superior to the German soldier: 1. In the use of individual weapons, especially as snipers. 2. In the use of ground camouflage. 3. In his gift of observation, and the drawing of correct conclusions from his observation. 4. In using every means of taking us by surprise.

Enemy snipers achieve astounding results. They shoot at anything they recognize. Several N.C.Os of the battalion have been shot through the head with the first bullet while making observations in the front line. Protruding sights in gun directors have been shot off, observation slits and loopholes have been fired on, and hit, as soon as they were seen to be in use (i.e. when the light background became dark). For this reason loopholes must be kept plugged with a wooden plug to be taken out when used so that they always show dark.

Major Bellerstedt, O.C. 2nd Battalion, 115th Motorized Infantry Regiment

Our opponents are Englishmen and Australians. Not trained attacking troops, but men with nerves and toughness, tireless, taking punishment with obstinacy, wonderful in defence. Ah well, the Greeks also spent ten years before Troy.

Lieutenant Schorm, diary, 6 May

Courtesies of War

We didn't know what sort of reception we'd get, as almost any truck which came near the perimeter in daylight used to get shelled. But I stood on the bonnet, holding up a big Red Cross flag and hoping for the best. They didn't fire a shot. When we were four hundred yards south of R7 we stopped the truck and I went forward with a stretcher-bearer named Keith Pope, and our padre, Father Gard, followed along behind us. I still had a flag, and when we were about two hundred and fifty yards from the post, a German stood up with another flag like mine.

He shouted what sounded like: '*Halten Minen.*' We could tell we were on the edge of a minefield because we could see the bodies of thirteen of our chaps lying there. A couple of Jerries came out with an electrical mine-detector and guided a lieutenant and a doctor out to us. I told the officer we wanted to pick up our dead and wounded. He replied in English, 'Very well, but only one truck and only two men at a time. You must not come closer than this. We will send your wounded out.'

They brought four wounded and let the truck come up to take them away. Then they carried out the bodies of fifteen dead and helped us with those in the minefield. I told the doctor we were four short and he replied that three of our wounded had been taken away in ambulances early that morning; another taken prisoner. When the last of our dead had been brought to us, the lieutenant told me we were not to move until they were all back in the post and had taken in their flag. He went back; his men went below. He lowered his flag and I lowered mine. I saluted him, and he saluted back, but he gave me the salute of the Reichswehr, not of the Nazis. Our armistice was over.

Sergeant W. Tuit

Inside Tobruk: After Five Months

It is August of that same year. Tobruk, and its miles of trench, are quiet for the moment in the glowing dusk. The floor of the wadi is level and spacious; this is a well-known spot. It is several miles behind the Red Line, and they call it Happy Valley. Some say it should be Bomb-happy Valley, for it escapes the attention of neither dive-bombers nor Nazi guns. Perhaps, originally, it was Bomb-happy Valley. Who knows for certain? So many tales have been told around it already, for, like all places where men live, die and work together, it has its legends.

Down the wadi comes a file of men. They march slowly, out of step, and mostly in silence. The dull clink of their weapons is clear in the evening air. At first their faces look all the same, burnt deep, with several days of beard, their eyes red-rimmed with the whites gleaming, cheeks hollowed, lips straight and grave. Their shirts and shorts are stiff like canvas with mingled dust and sweat, and streaked again with the sweat of that day. Their legs are bare and burnt almost black; their boots are worn pure white. Some who still have them wear their tunics, for the air will soon be deathly cold; and their headgear is, as before, motley: a steel helmet, a crumpled slouch hat and an Italian pith helmet. Their packs, haversacks and ammunition pouches have become as white as their boots, and their weapons gleam dully in the spots where they have worn, for they have had five months of use.

They are a strange spectacle. They were once ordinary men, but now they do not belong among ordinary men; in the city they would seem like a vision. Their sameness is not only that of their dark brown faces, their silence, their fatigue, for they have shared together, for many months, the most abysmal, the most terrible of human emotions; each has in turn, and in his own way, been a hero, a panting coward, an entity with a mind crying its anguish at death. And while each has shown to his fellows most of his deepest self, each hugs to himself, grimly and pitiably, what is left. No one of them will ever be quite the same again.

As he reaches a turn in the wadi, Henry Gilbertson stops, turns round and says, 'B Company—halt!'

They gather in close, for it has become very dark.

Eric Lambert

Bugs—Anti-British

All day we lay in a dug-out just big enough for three Diggers and me stretched out. Four feet above us was a roof of corrugated iron resting on sleepers and over that sandbags, earth and bits of camel-bush, which made the top of the dug-out just one more piece of desert to German snipers scanning the level plain from five hundred yards away. The late afternoon sun beat down on the sandbags. We were clammy with sweat. The wind died away and dust stopped drifting in through the small air vent and the narrow low doorway that led to the crawl trench outside. The air was heavy with dust, cigarette smoke and the general fug we'd been breathing in and out for the past thirteen hours. We waited for darkness when we could stretch our legs and fill our lungs with fresh, cool air, and the troops could crack at the Hun who had been lying all day in his dug-out, too.

. . . . I woke about seven in the evening and started to scratch. I seemed to be itching all over—the itchiness of being dirty. You get that way after the flies and fleas have been at you all day. You don't know whether you've been bitten or not, and you just scratch as a matter of routine. In the far corner Mick was doing a bit of hunting. He had his shirt off. Seriously, deliberately he ran his thumb nail under the seam and a slow smile of success spread across his face. 'Got you, you little —— That makes four less, anyway!'

Chester Wilmot

Bugs—Anti-German

Nothing new. The heat's frightful, night time as well as day time. Liquidated four bugs. My bed is now standing in tins filled with water and I hope the nights will be a little more restful from now on. Some of the others are having a bad time with fleas. They've left me alone so far.

Rommel

The Lost Men

We have immense fun over 'the lost men'. Wherever you go in the desert, you come across little pockets of men camped by their vehicles: they are invariably unshaven, cheerful, and brewing up tea in a petrol tin. Similarly they can *always* tell you which way to go ('Y Track, sir? Straight on till you get to the Rifleman's Grave; can't miss it, sir'; or: 'Barrel Track, mate? W'y you just come from it.') Nine times out of ten they give you the directions wrong. They appear to belong to nobody, and seem perfectly contented to camp out in the blue. Arthur has now decided that they are all deserters from Wavell's first campaign. He is planning for both of us to go 'missing' one day. Then we will ensconce ourselves in a jolly little camp, and spend our days waving people in the direction of the Diamond Track, or the Gebel Something-or-other.

C.O., 1st Battalion, Black Watch

The Navy Runs In Supplies

Then above the roar of engines, wind and sea, from the rear gun-platform an officer shouts through a megaphone, 'Stand by. Action stations.' We wait again. Then: 'Stand by, Enemy aircraft.'

Suddenly we're snatching at the nearest rail or bulkhead as the destroyer heels over in a wild zigzag and seems to leap forward. On the slippery deck the cargo slides crashing into the scuppers and spray drenches everything.

Above the turmoil that voice again: 'Stand by. Blitz barrage.' Behind us a great white swath of wash is even more tell-tale than before, but they'll have seen us now and the only way to trick them is to zigzag. I look across at *Havock*—a great stream of black smoke is pouring from her funnels. Then we hear the bomber's drone and *Havock*'s guns stab the darkness with red flashes. She rolls over in a ninety-degree turn and a hundred yards or so ahead of her a great white water-spout tells us that the Stuka has missed its mark.

Out of the darkness ahead we see two pin-points of light, the harbour lights of Tobruk, shielded from the air but visible to us. We slacken speed. There is no wash now, and a welcome cloud cloaks the moon and other bombers cannot see us.

But they are over Tobruk and are going for the harbour. We can hear the muffled crack of the ack-ack guns and see the flashes of bursting shells high in the sky; only the 'heavies' are firing, so apparently the bombers are well up.

We slip in between the lights, past the black ghosts of wrecks, under the lee of the white sepulchre of a town. The ack-ack is still speeding the raider home, but another is coming in—lower. The Bofors are firing too, so it must be well under ten thousand feet. But we have no time to think of the fireworks display above us. As *Decoy* stops moving two barges and two launches come alongside. Troops clamber over the side, pitching their kitbags ahead of them. Unloading parties swarm aboard and slide ammunition down wooden chutes into one barge, while the rest of the cargo is dumped anyhow into the other. As soon as the troops are off, the crew start bringing wounded aboard in stretchers.

They are getting a warm farewell. One stick of bombs screams down on the south shore of the harbour; the next is closer—in the water five hundred yards away. The old hands continue working, unworried, but some of the new ones, like us, pause momentarily, shrinking down behind the destroyer's after-screen. From the man with the megaphone comes a sharp rebuke—'What are you stopping for? Those bloody bombs are nothing to do with you.'

Chester Wilmot

Winston Churchill to General Morshead

To General Morshead from Prime Minister England. The whole Empire is watching your steadfast and spirited defence of this important outpost of Egypt with gratitude and admiration.

While Tobruk held on, Rommel's main force drove on to the east. Wavell's counter-attack in June on the Egyptian frontier was a failure. There the 88 mm. A.A. gun established its formidable reputation in an anti-tank role. General Auchinleck assumed command of the British forces, and the Eighth Army as such was born.

In constructing our positions at Halfaya and on Hill 208 great skill was shown in building in batteries of 88 mm. guns for anti-tank work, so that with the barrels horizontal there was practically nothing to be seen above ground. I had great hopes of the effectiveness of this arrangement.

Rommel

On the second day, 16 June, thrust and counter-thrust around Capuzzo ended in stalemate. The enemy still held Halfaya, and twenty miles south-west in a series of running skirmishes his 5th Tank Regiment, with superior numbers and fire-power, forced 7 Armoured Brigade back across the frontier. Rommel mustered every tank he could to press home his advantage. One column, with seventy-five tanks of the 5th Regiment, carried its outflanking movement twenty miles into Egypt south of Halfaya. Simultaneously another column fought its way through nearer the coast towards Halfaya. Threatened by these two moves, the Anglo-Indian forces, which had held Capuzzo for nearly two days, had to withdraw, leaving on the battlefield a large number of disabled, but recoverable, British tanks.

It had been a disastrous three days. Captured German documents (secret German military reports and not propaganda) allege that 143 British tanks were destroyed. This was a slight exaggeration, for the actual British losses were 123. However G.H.Q. admitted later that 'two-thirds of the British armour was out of action' after the battle, and it did not claim that the Germans had lost more than fifty tanks. The battle had been decided by two factors—a new German anti-tank weapon and Rommel's bold handling of his armour. The weapon was the 88 mm. A.A. gun, used for the first time (on the frontier at least) in an anti-tank role. Rommel had only twelve of these, but, if German official documents are to be believed, they knocked out seventy-nine British tanks—one for every twenty rounds they fired.

At the two German frontier positions that held, eight of these guns destroyed thirty-six British tanks. The tanks, firing a 2-pounder with an effective range of eight hundred yards at most, were no match for the 88 mm. with its 20-pound shell that could knock out an 'I' tank at a range of a mile. In these positions the 88 mm. guns were dug in flush with the ground and so well camouflaged that the British tank crews did not even know what had hit them.

MALTA

Throughout the war in North Africa, the island of Malta was a constant thorn in the side of the Axis. The outcome of the desert battle depended largely on the rate of reinforcement achieved by both sides, and air and submarine attacks from Malta on the convoys supplying Rommel were a serious hindrance to him. The Italians had been attacking Malta to little effect since June 1940, but in January 1941 the Luftwaffe joined in, trying to destroy Malta's offensive capacity and starve it out by attacks on the island itself and on the Allied convoys supplying it. The crisis of the battle came in the spring of 1942, when Malta's strength was almost neutralized and its power to resist greatly weakened.

The Luftwaffe Attacks

The drone of the bombers was getting louder now as they approached Gozo Island, just north of Malta. Squadrons of Me.109s could be seen spreading out to the left and to the right, slightly above. Much higher up in the clear, bright blue, a coop top flashed in the sun revealing the presence of a top cover of enemy fighters. From this higher group two squadrons took more definite shape and, breaking away from the others, advanced towards the island at a very fast clip. Over St. Paul's Bay, near the north tip of Malta, they spread out wide into pairs, and in that position roared over the island at some ten thousand feet.

. . . . More guns barked near St. Paul's Bay. The flak burst in among the leading bombers, and some of the bursts were white. More ack-ack batteries cracked and in a few seconds all the guns of that part of the island were slamming away. Up in the sky the white bursts were being outnumbered by brown-black ones, their closeness intensifying the speed of the enemy planes that were now like groaning spiders crawling through peppered blue.

Then the gaggle began to split.

One wave turned east and flew out over the sea. The second swung west and crossed the pilots' line of vision, while the third kept on for the centre of the island. Now the three prongs resembled a giant leaf-rake in the sky.

. . . . From one of the leading bombers in the centre group a jet of white smoke spouted from the starboard engine, followed by black. The maimed Junkers turned to its left and ploughed into another. There was a simultaneous flash that snuffed out like an altar candle. The pressure of the explosion chewed and pushed at the waves of black flak ahead of it, encircling and rolling up wave upon wave until suddenly the whole of it burst into a gigantic ball of flame, and the enemy bombers shattered into a million pieces and were no more than the flak. Two Spitfires dived through the murk, zoomed up again and were lost to sight. Me.s weaved back and forth, some in the flak, but most of them above it.

. . . . The east wave came in from the sea and hit Sliema, Valetta and the harbour first. The 88s held their incredibly vertical dives till they were about four thousand feet from the earth, then, synchronized by gyroscope with the bomb release, were pulling up in a back-breaking climb, twisting and weaving crazily towards the sea again. Meanwhile, others dived and bombs plummeted into the ground, and the dust and sand spouted like geysers. In a few minutes that part of the island, nearly eight miles away, was going up and down, while the rumbling crept along and through the earth like an approaching earthquake, the tremor reaching the feet of the watching pilots. The centre wave was starting its dive. The west group was turning and diving. Then all hell broke loose. . . . A thousand flashes of orange, red and purple were pipping the ground and the dust rose and spread to blot out the far side of the island. Overhead, the west wave was screaming in, the whine of the brakes so close now, unhindered, unopposed. Aircraft, near enough to see the big black crosses edged in white, were milling in, mad, anxious, in ones and twos, trying not to be the first, nor yet the last.

. . . . And the first bombs were leaving the bellics of the crazy diving planes of the west wave; strings of small bombs dribbling end over end, big bombs, black and shooting down in their tantalizing arc. [Wallace] had seen many bombs drop before, heard a good many more, but never did he realize that they dropped with such ferocity, such complete certainty and yet with no apparent control, falling like loose shale from an unpropped mine just before it finally caves in. There were big bombs, singly and in pairs, small ones in strings, all black, screaming and whistling in that hideous flat curve across the hill town of Rabat, over M'dima, the ancient capital of Malta, the vicious arc ending at the foot of the hill which was Takali aerodrome, the whistling straining, like high winds over iced wires in winter, all ending in rumbling explosions.

Charles MacLean

The Ordeal of *Penelope*

Thursday, 26 March 1942

Ju. 87s were employed for the first time on the Grand Harbour area. H.M.S. *Penelope*, lying at Hamilton Wharf, her bows south, was damaged forward and aft by near misses, causing the flooding of all compartments below the two foremost mess decks and a number of compartments aft, and also putting A and B turrets out of action. The forward near miss lifted all the decks forward, resulting in the straining of most of the watertight doors.

The after near miss caused severe blast-damage to the after superstructure, waist screens and watertight doors.

. . . . The keel plate had been bent upwards for a distance of thirty feet in a large dent six to eight feet deep. At the centre of this dent, the keel plate and lower plate were cracked across for a distance of twelve feet.

It was decided that *Penelope* must sail as soon as possible.

A scheme of first-aid repairs was devised. This subsequently proved thoroughly efficient and capable of rapid execution.

It was estimated that the repairs would take four weeks if too many raids did not take place.

Saturday, 4 April

This was a black day. From 11.15 a.m. to 7.40 p.m. heavy and sustained attacks were made on *Penelope*.

In the first raid a near miss damaged the dock caisson, and the dock started to leak. The dock pump was put out of action and only got going again at 11 p.m.

Another near miss struck the dockyard wall on the port side of *Penelope*, abreast of the quarter deck. This bomb hurled great piles of masonry and debris on to the quarter deck, the 4-inch gun deck and boat deck. Other bombs blew large stones from adjacent buildings on to the upper deck. So after 'dinner' it was a matter of all hands to remove the rock garden from the ship.

It was during the last attack on this day that a bomb hit *Penelope*'s port after brow and exploded just beneath it. Many hundreds of small holes were made in the port side aft in all compartments. The port outer shaft was punctured with three large and several smaller holes.

Some damage was done to the propellers. Fires broke out in the Captain's store and in some of the port after cabins.

This extra damage entailed a lot more repair work. I sent an appeal to the Army for welders. A prompt response was made and five sappers, qualified welders, joined the ship at 9.30 a.m. on Easter Sunday.

They worked with great skill and endurance.

Easter Sunday, 5 April

Another black day. Three heavy attacks on *Penelope* were made at 7.55 a.m., 11.25 a.m. and 5.05 p.m. *Penelope* made a signal to the Vice-Admiral, Malta: 'We take a poor view of Hitler's Easter eggs.' The Vice-Admiral replied: 'I agree. They are not even like the curate's.' The raids in each case were made by large formations attacking in waves. Each raid lasted about an hour. A huge bomb hit the dock abreast of the starboard side of the bridge. Large blocks of masonry and debris were thrown up as high as the bridge, which looked like the Mappin Terrace. The direct route between the ammunition lighter and the ship was blocked. To add to the difficulties a lighter with five hundred rounds was hit by a bomb and another lighter had to be quickly loaded. The dock was flooding rapidly, the water rose to twenty-one feet and there was a danger of the ship coming off the blocks. When the last raider had passed, the dockyard electricians gave us the blessed news that the pumps would soon be working. At 7.24 p.m. I reported to the Vice-Admiral: 'Pump is working again and water has been lowered by eighteen inches—Atta pump.'

Wednesday, 8 April

At 3.45 a.m. the hands commenced ammunitioning and working dock machinery.

At 8.15 a two-hour mass attack on *Penelope* began, and a bomb hit the starboard brow, making hundreds of holes in the starboard side forward. Only the most serious could be patched in the time and all the remainder had to be plugged with wooden pegs (the ship looked rather like a porcupine when she sailed).

There was a total of seven separate and heavy raids that day. The A.A. ammunition situation was acute throughout the day. The guns were firing 4-inch shells faster than they could be fused and embarked.

At the end of daylight raiding there was no 4-inch and very little close-range ammunition on board for the sea passage.

It had been intended to put a lighter with five hundred tons fuel alongside, but there were so many delays that at 4 p.m. I decided to wait no longer but to get the ship out of the dock and alongside Canteen Wharf to oil. This move was a tricky business as the tugs had been sunk—but Mr. Murphy, the pilot, handled the ship with skill.

The enemy redoubled his efforts and the fifth and sixth raids were intense. I am convinced that it was in the main the resolute firing of the ship's guns which defeated the enemy's aim and saved the ship. During the sixth raid the Gunnery Officer was killed. I myself received a flesh wound in an undignified place, and had to go to the dockyard dressing station.

This left Lieutenant Hamilton temporarily in command and in control of the guns.

I have in previous reports remarked on the outstanding ability of Lieutenant Hamilton.

In the course of this last raid he was at his best—fought off the raid magnificently and then dealt brilliantly with the ammunition situation.

The ship had no 4-inch ammunition left and we were due to sail in two hours.

Captain A. D. Nicholl, H.M.S. *Penelope*

After successfully dodging further air attacks, Penelope *reached Gibraltar on* 10 *April.*

AFRICA: THE PENDULUM SWINGS BACK

Meanwhile, throughout the summer and autumn of 1941, both armies in North Africa built up their forces. It appeared that the British would be ready to strike first, and in fact the Eighth Army under General Cunningham attacked on 18 November, with initial success. For the first four days the two Corps—XXX and XIII—fought brilliantly, but trouble followed at Sidi Rezegh.

'It has come in a way we did not expect,' wrote a German officer on Afrika Korps H.Q., 'and there's hell let loose. On the evening of the 18th, while I was still continuing my afternoon sleep, there came a telephone call summoning me to pack my kit immediately. Position: the enemy is attacking with very strong forces in the southern sector.' Actually, by this time the leading column was near El Gobi—fifty miles west of the frontier.

Sidi Rezegh: The Battle Begins

I woke the next morning to the certain knowledge that there would be fierce and desperate battles all day. Without my own bedding, with a crew who were not yet used to my ways and fads, almost smothered by the fug under the tarpaulin which had been necessary to keep off the rain which beat down all night, I could not have been less ready for instant and exhausting action. My beard was at the most uncomfortable stage of its growth, my clothes were damp and foul-smelling, my face and hands cold and numb. I left the operator to complete the net and walked over to Kinnaird's tank. I was such a picture of misery and despondence that Kinnaird, despite his many anxieties, grinned and said, 'Cheer up, Tony. You're still alive. It could be worse. But you've come just at the right moment. Here are the others, and these are the orders. 7 Armoured and the Support Group are already being attacked from the north-west. We have got to get to them. But as far as is known both 15 and 21 Panzer are between us and them. So we shall have a bloody battle before we can even give them any help. Right—we move off in five minutes.'

Within a few minutes of starting the reports began to come in, all telling the same story of tanks and anti-tank guns on the escarpments to the east and south-west of Sidi Rezegh, preventing us from moving to join the desperate battle on the airfield.

All morning the battles swayed forwards and backwards round the airfield and the high ground to the north. While 7 Armoured and the Support Group beat off the first attacks, we and 22 Armoured fought to get through to them.

I lost all count of time, and only the growing aches of my empty stomach and the parched dryness of my mouth indicated the passage of the hours. I lost, too, all count of the casualties in my squadron and the losses which each tank claimed to have inflicted on the enemy. The early battles were fought in the mist of the damp of the sodden ground evaporating in the sun. Later a dark pall of smoke and dust overhung the whole battlefield, hiding friend and foe alike. In the turmoil and confusion it was miraculous that more mistakes were not made in shooting against friends. Gradually we pushed the Germans farther and farther back, with the loss of many tanks on both sides. My own tank was penetrated by a shot which spent itself in the effort of piercing the armour and only fell to the floor at my driver's feet, doing no damage. There was a momentary relief of the tension when, referring to the many rumours of the desperate methods the Germans were reputed to be resorting to in their search for metals, he remarked, 'Not bad for bloody church railings, I calls it.'

Cyril Joly

Confusion

By now it was pretty dark and we joined up with the Brigadier (Davy) and some of our tanks and most of our N.H. guns and huddled together in a 'night leaguer'. As we collected, I looked back and could see our foes doing likewise about one and a half miles to two miles behind us, silhouetted against the remaining light. We made our usual type of huddle, with trucks inside and our guns, etc. on the perimeter . . . I had no overcoat—nothing but what I stood in; same for Dick except, poor devil, he was in shorts and a jersey. It was horribly cold by then. We were three windy cats all the time and kept walking out to listen. We could hear distant sounds of a lot of tanks moving, but otherwise quiet—a good many Verey lights going up from the foe. About 9.30 we heard the unmistakable noise of tanks, so we all took post on our guns, etc. One could see two hundred to three hundred yards in the moonlight. First came a single tank about one hundred and fifty yards on our north: when it had just passed us it fired a Verey light towards us but I don't think it saw us for its own dust. A few minutes later about twelve tanks followed the first and again fired a light. This waiting was awful, and we all breathed a sigh as they passed. This lot turned south after passing us. Then a number more approached, obviously on a line to meet us. Not a nice moment. Before they arrived a truck stopped about sixty yards away and a man approached us with a tommy-gun. A party of four led by John Cookson went to meet and challenge him. He was a German and we hauled him in. His truck drove away towards the oncoming tanks and I think warned them. Anyhow, a few minutes later they appeared alongside us and I heard our Brigadier shout, 'If they fire a light, shoot.' They fired a light which fell into our middle. Then each party let fly with everything which would bear on our foe. My and Dick's guns were on the far corner from them and we could not shoot.

We all started our engines and got going. Our truck would not start. We tried for about twenty seconds but 'no go'. The Sergeant-Major shouted, 'Let's get on another'—so we hopped out and jumped on a passing Bofors gun and tractor and rode out of the hotch-potch, everyone going off in every kind of direction. We went like hell for about two miles. I was clinging to the back of the tractor expecting to be jolted off under the gunwheels. Actually I scrambled on to the top. After about two miles we came on a stopped truck which was Ted Key's. One of our guns drew alongside. So Ted, the Sergeant-Major and I got on to it and, in company with our Bofors friends, continued south. The afternoon's push of the German tanks and column had been south of us and towards the east, i.e. behind us. As we went we could see their lights on each side of us and had to keep a sharp look out in case we bumped into one of their night leaguers.

Captain W. Williamson

Brewed Up

'Driver, halt,' I ordered. 'Gunner, 2-pounder—traverse left—on—tank—German Mark III—eight five zero yards. Fire.' I watched Basset carefully turn the range-drum to the right range, saw him turn to his telescope and aim, noticed out of the corner of my eye that King was ready with the next round, and then the tank jolted slightly with the shock of the gun firing. Through the smoke and dust and the spurt of flame I watched intently through my binoculars the trace of the shot in flight. It curved upwards slightly and almost slowly, and then seemed to plunge swiftly towards the target. There was the unmistakable dull glow of a strike of steel on steel. 'Hit, Basset! Good shot! Fire again,' I called. Another shot and another hit, and I called, 'Good shot; but the bastard won't brew.'

As I spoke I saw the flame and smoke from the German's gun, which showed that he was at last answering. In the next instant all was chaos. There was a clang of steel on the turret front and a blast of flame and smoke from the same place, which seemed to spread into the turret, where it was followed by another dull explosion. The shock-wave which followed swept past me, still standing in the cupola, singed my hands and face and left me breathless and dazed. I looked down into the turret. It was a shambles. The shot had penetrated the front of the turret just in front of King, the loader. It had twisted the machine-gun out of its mounting. It, or a jagged piece of the torn turret, had then hit the round that King had been holding ready—had set it on fire. The explosion had wrecked the wireless, torn King's head and shoulders from the rest of his body and started a fire among the machine-gun boxes stowed on the floor. Smoke and the acrid fumes of cordite filled the turret. On the floor, licking menacingly near the main ammunition stowage bin, there were innumerable small tongues of flame. If these caught on, the charge in the rounds would explode, taking the turret and all in it with it.

I felt too dazed to move. My limbs seemed to be anchored, and I wondered vaguely how long I had been standing there and what I ought to do next. It was a miracle that the explosion had left me unharmed, though shaken. I wondered what had happened to Basset and bent into the cupola to find out. Shielded behind the gun and the recoil guard-shield, Basset, too, had escaped the main force of the explosion. The face that turned to look at me was blackened and scorched and the eyes, peering at me from the black background, seemed to be unnaturally large and startlingly terrified. For once Basset's good humour had deserted him, and the voice which I heard was shaking with emotion.

'Let's get out of 'ere, sir. Not much we can do for King, poor bastard!— 'e's 'ad it and some. An' if we 'ang around we'll catch a packet too. For Gawd's sake let's —— off quick.'

At last I awoke from my daze. 'O.K., Basset. Tell Newman to bale out, and be bloody quick about it.'

As Basset bent to shout at the driver the tank was struck again, but this time on the front of the hull. When the smoke and dust cleared, Basset bent again to shout at Newman. A moment later he turned a face now sickened with horror and disgust and blurted out:

''E's ad it too, sir. It's took 'alf 'is chest away. For ——'s sake let's get out of 'ere.' In a frenzy of panic he tried to climb out of the narrow cupola past me, causing me to slip and delaying us both. Through my mind there flashed the thought that the German would still continue to fire until he knew that the tank was knocked out, and as yet no flames would be visible from the outside. Inside the turret there was now an inferno of fire.

Without knowing how I covered the intervening distance, I found myself lying in a small hollow some twenty yards from my stricken tank, watching the first thin tongues of flame and black smoke emerging from the turret top.

Cyril Joly

First Round to Rommel

The wide plain south of Sidi Rezegh was now a sea of dust, haze and smoke. Visibility was poor and many British tanks and guns were able to break away to the south and east without being caught. But a great part of the enemy force still remained inside. Twilight came, but the battle was still not over. Hundreds of burning vehicles, tanks and guns lit up the field of that *Totensonntag*. It was long after midnight before we could get any sort of picture of the day's events, organize our force, count our losses and gains and form an appreciation of the general situation upon which the next day's operations would depend. The most important results of the battle were the elimination of the direct threat to the Tobruk front, the destruction of a large part of the enemy armour and the damage to enemy morale caused by the complete ruin of his plans.

Rommel

At about 10.30 hours on the 24th Rommel put himself at the head of 21 Panzer Division, and drove off at a furious pace. Late that afternoon he reached the Wire,* with the whole Afrika Korps stretched out behind him over forty miles of desert, and 7 Armoured Division and 1 S.A. Division stampeding in all directions. Rommel's bold move had thrown 30 Corps into complete disorder, and according to British accounts General Cunningham wanted to retire at once into Egypt. . . . But very fortunately for the British, General Auchinleck had arrived at Eighth Army Headquarters; he disagreed with Cunningham, and ordered the continuation of the offensive. This was certainly one of the great decisions of the war; Auchinleck's fighting spirit and shrewd strategic insight had saved the 'Crusader' battle and much else besides.

General von Mellenthin

General Auchinleck was convinced that his attack should be pushed home in spite of the initial reverse of Sidi Rezegh and Rommel's counter-stroke. He replaced General Cunningham with General Ritchie, and the offensive continued. For a few days each side struggled for the advantage in confused fighting, then the British once more went forward. On the night of 25/26 November the New Zealanders captured Sidi Rezegh. Tobruk was on the point of relief.

The Wandering General

The Mammoth, now carrying all the most senior officers of the Panzer Group, drove on to the wire fence. Unfortunately, no way through could be found, and it was impossible to make one. Finally, Rommel grew impatient. 'I'll

* The Frontier (Ed.)

take over myself,' he said, and dismissed the A.D.C., who had been directing the vehicle up till then. But this time even Rommel's legendary sense of direction did not help. To make matters worse, they were in an area completely dominated by the enemy. Indian dispatch riders buzzed to and fro past the Mammoth, British tanks moved up forward and American-built lorries ground their way through the desert. None of them had any suspicion that the highest officers of the German-Italian Panzer Group were sitting in a captured command vehicle, often only two or three yards away. The ten officers and five men spent a restless night.

During the days that followed, Rommel continued to drive from one unit to another, usually through the British lines, in order to deal with the continually recurring crises. On one occasion he went into a New Zealand hospital, which was still occupied by the enemy. By this time no one really knew who was captor and who captive—except Rommel, who was in no doubt. He inquired if anything was needed, promised the British medical supplies and drove on unhindered. He also crossed an air strip occupied by the British, and was several times chased by British vehicles, but always escaped.

The Relief of Tobruk: 27 November 1941

One more determined concerted heave would do it. The honour of making the junction went to the 19th N.Z. Battalion and a squadron of the 44th R.T.R., commanded by an Irish giant of the Royal Tanks, Major 'Stump' Gibbon. Led by seventeen Valentines rumbling along through the night, the 19th Battalion made excellent progress. Unseen tanks, moving at night, are demoralizing enough, because of the noise; but when backed up by determined bayonets, the attack becomes terrifying. German resistance collapsed like a house of cards; and the junction with the men of Essex and, most appropriately, more Valentines of Royal Tanks, finally took place on Ed Duda at one o'clock in the small hours of 27 November. The news, awaited so anxiously throughout the free nations, flashed round the world. Nowhere was it so welcome as in the Anzac countries. The Australians had held Tobruk, tenaciously and with typical offensive spirit for many months of hard fighting and harder living; one battalion still remained to share in the 'fight out'. And the New Zealanders had finally forged the link on Ed Duda. Significantly, both thrusts were supported by determined Valentine crews of the Royal Tanks and good gunners.

If the 19th Battalion got the limelight, 6 N.Z. Brigade made an equally solid contribution by clearing their area in stubborn night fighting. The New Zealanders now occupied a big bulge stuck on the end of the Tobruk corridor. The corridor provided access to the base supplies and facilities; limited access only, because through movement was restricted to night and hampered by minefields. So into Tobruk went New Zealand wounded and Army Service Corps units; and also 13 Corps Headquarters (General Godwin-Austen is credited with announcing his entry by the signal: 'Tobruk and I both relieved').

Brigadier Clifton

The Afrika Korps withdrew, the British followed. Rommel first stood for five days at Gazala, and then pulled back again. Benghazi was occupied by the Royal

Dragoons on Christmas Eve; the garrisons left far behind at Bardia and Halfaya were overcome a few days later. On 7 January 1942 Rommel withdrew to his old lair at El Agheila on the Bay of Sirte. Two weeks later, on 21 January, he started to advance again against the over-extended Eighth Army. He pushed on for a month, regaining most of his lost ground as far as Gazala, where an equilibrium was established until May.

THE SECRET OF THE AFRIKA KORPS

The terrific armoured battles in the Western Desert cannot be understood without some reference to the weapons and equipment on both sides. Contrary to the generally accepted view, the German tanks did not have any advantage in quality over their opponents, and in numbers we were always inferior.

To what, then, are we to ascribe the brilliant successes of the Afrika Korps? To my mind, our victories depended on three factors—the superior quality of our anti-tank guns, our systematic practice of the principle of *Co-operation of Arms*, and—last but not least—our tactical methods. While the British restricted their 3·7 in. anti-aircraft gun (a very powerful weapon) to an anti-aircraft role, we employed our 88 mm. gun to shoot at tanks as well as aeroplanes. In November 1941 we only had thirty-five 88s, but moving in close touch with our Panzers these guns did terrific execution among the British tanks. Moreover, our high-velocity 50 mm. anti-tank gun was far superior to the British 2-pounder, and batteries of these guns always accompanied our tanks in action. Our field artillery, also, was trained to co-operate with the Panzers. In short, a German Panzer division was a highly flexible formation of all arms, which always relied on artillery in attack or defence. In contrast, the British regarded the anti-tank gun as a defensive weapon, and they failed to make adequate use of their powerful field artillery, which should have been taught to eliminate our anti-tank guns.

General von Mellenthin

THE SECOND RETREAT

On 27 May 1942 Rommel attacked. The British line extended from Gazala (held by 1 South African Division) in the north, to Bir Hacheim, held by the Free French in the south. Rommel raced below Bir Hacheim and swung up into the centre of the Eighth Army. The latter's defensive positions behind the outflanked Gazala Line, notable the Knightsbridge Box, suffered heavy attacks, which were at this stage repulsed. Rommel next pierced the Gazala Line from its rear, and built up a bridge-head in an area known as 'The Cauldron'.

Gazala: The Knightsbridge Box

The Knightsbridge Box was selected by the O.C. 2nd R.H.A. as a 'pivot of manœuvre'. The term conveyed little to any of us, involving as it did a technique which was as foreign to our mobile methods as is an anchorage to a fleet in action. The orders were to select and prepare a defensive position to be contained by the 2nd R.H.A., C Battery Northumberland Hussars (Anti-Tank), two troops of the 43rd L.A.A. Regiment, the 3rd Coldstream Guards and one company of the 2nd Scots Guards.

The area given for choice of position was one of fifty square miles, and here had to be formed a long-stop somewhere behind the Gazala Line, which was a string of similar positions between the sea and Bir Hacheim. The area chosen was a small plateau. It could only be overlooked from a distance and could not be looked into. A shallow depression in the middle gave bare cover for the troops of I Battery commanded by Major Blacker and L Battery commanded by Major Livingstone-Learmonth. After three days' reconnaissance this small saucer was discovered about six miles east of the centre of the Gazala Line. It was pear-shaped, about half a mile long and a quarter of a mile wide, but it possessed the outstanding advantage that the gun positions and the 'observation' were in one and the same area and could be defended simultaneously by the troops available. Standing alone on this very ordinary looking bit of sand one wondered at the circumstances which made it necessary to enclose it in such a way as to prohibit its occupants all possibility of manœuvre. It seemed like anchoring battle-ships in mid-ocean. Such thoughts were forgotten as the battle developed with increasing intensity around it—sometimes nearer, sometimes farther, closing in as the days went by—until at the end it became a fortress of the first importance, at least in one's own eyes, when the chances of escape had diminished and all guns were firing 'charge one'.

On 26 May rumour on a high level was offering odds against a German attack. The following morning, with admirable daring and efficiency, Rommel turned our southern flank, south of Bir Hacheim, with tanks in force. After a long march, he overran our outpost screen and surprised an armoured brigade at breakfast. It was a bad start for us. There followed some exciting days. First, the attempts of the enemy to attack and overrun our position. Heavy enemy shelling was accompanied by infantry attacks which were repeatedly repelled by our fire. Our observation was good, especially to the south, where the attacks were made, and a life-time of 'practice' shooting could be fulfilled in an hour. The attacks were soon followed by enemy tanks, who approached up the steep escarpment to the north. These were accounted for by the Northumberland Hussars, who used their new guns to great effect.

Brigadier L. Bolton

The First Check

After a peaceful breakfast on 27 May, a great deal of gun fire developed to the south and the noise of battle approached rapidly. I very soon got orders to proceed to 'The Bobble', a feature just west of the Box on which the 2nd R.H.A. O.P. was situated and which it was deemed important to hold. I went with my party of four 6-pounder guns, which we knew very little about and had never fired. On my way I put up an old fox which cheered me considerably: later he was to return past my truck as the battle got too close to be healthy.

My first view of the enemy was when about sixty-five tanks appeared in a cloud of smoke and dust over a crest about sixteen hundred yards distant. My guns opened fire—one of them later claimed a hit—but it soon became obvious that we had no chance of stemming the avalanche, and, after a lot of waving of blue flags—the guns carried no wireless—I was ordered to make my way back to the Box. This manœuvre was accomplished without loss, although one gun had been put out of action by a solid shot earlier on. As we skirted round the north side of the Box, under the Escarpment, we fired a lot of rounds at about twelve hundred yards into this mass of German tanks and vehicles, which continued north and sat on a ridge about two miles from the Box. The advance tanks and guns were followed by an enormous quantity of 'soft' vehicles, which for the rest of the day made an excellent target for the R.H.A. batteries. Inside the Box it was hardly a picnic; shells from guns and tanks landed at very regular intervals, but, strange to say, our losses were nil; our strenuous efforts to get underground more than paid a dividend.

About 6 p.m. a German tank attack developed on our front, the tanks climbing the Escarpment, halting on meeting the minefield, getting turret-down and raking the whole area with machine-gun fire, very unpleasant for those being shot at, but remarkably ineffective. We had two guns put out of action temporarily, and two portees burnt, but when the attack was eventually beaten off, the fires in the Box indicated that the other units had suffered more than we had.

Major R. I. G. Taylor

As our position proved for the present impregnable to the enemy, Rommel decided to ignore it. Thousands of German vehicles parked within easy range of our guns, but as a rule we had neither the time nor the ammunition to engage them. Rommel came himself to see, and his lone tank, stationary at about three thousand six hundred yards' range, made good shooting for one of the L Battery O.Ps. The tank was visited frequently by German staff cars and Storch aircraft, and the O.P. officer 'split' a twenty-five yard bracket on it several times, but this only made it move a few hundred yards each time.

Brigadier L. Bolton

British armoured forces counter-attacked, but in spite of their new tanks suffered severely at the hands of a more skilful commander.

Grants in Action

Now a shiver went through me. From out of the dip emerged rank after rank of the new tanks—a good sixty in all. They came at us with every muzzle blazing.

I got my right gun into action. It stopped one tank. Several others were burning. But the bulk of them came on relentlessly. What was wrong with my left gun, I wondered? It was silent, its muzzle still drooping to the ground. I leaped from my trench despite the stuff whistling all round and raced to the gun.

Two of the crew were sprawled on the ground. The breech of the gun was shattered. The loader lay beside a wheel, bleeding from a machine-gun bullet in the chest. 'Water, water,' he gasped.

A fresh salvo burst beside the gun. Tanks were obviously attacking it at almost point-blank range. To stop there meant death.

I dropped prone, and tried to cradle the head of the wounded man in my arms.

He shook his head at me.

'I'll carry you to my trench—there's water there,' I shouted in his ear. He shook his head again. To my consternation, he heaved himself to his feet and half stumbled, half ran towards my slit-trench.

Now the tanks were right on top of the front lines in the sector to my right. I scrambled back towards my trench. Muller was not there. I dragged the wounded gun-number halfway into the hole with me. My Italian water-bottle, half-full of coffee, lay there, and I thrust it into the man's shaking hand. He drank greedily, and then sagged back, dead. His legs dangled in the hole; his torso lay twisted on the rim of it.

Shell-bursts were now erupting all round. Was I alone out here now? As I wondered this, there came a reply from behind, where Sergeant Weber was firing my third gun. He pumped out shell after shell. But there was little help in his valour.

Twelve tanks swung at us to neutralize this menace. Their guns blazed insistently at us, and they came straight on.

I dropped my glasses and rolled to the bottom of my trench, where Muller had spread a blanket. I dragged it over myself in ineffectual protection. The toes of the dead man's boots dangled six inches from my eyes.

The earth trembled. My throat was like sandpaper. This, then, was the end. I had escaped at Sidi Rezegh. But now this was it. My fiancée would be told: 'With deep regret we have to inform you that. . . .' She would read that I had died a hero's death for the Fatherland. And what would it mean? That I was just a bloody mess in the sand at an unidentified spot near an unimportant point in the desert called Acroma.

A tank crunched by at the edge of my trench. I heard an English voice calling. Was it a man in the tank, or an infantryman following up with bayonet fixed?

A blanket is not much good against a bayonet. But perhaps they would not see me. Perhaps I should just lie here and go mad. Perhaps I should be killed by a shell. Perhaps another tank would crush me.

The minutes crawled by. I now heard German voices. Apparently the British were rounding up prisoners in my own sector. And here was I in the trench.

Firing had ceased. After perhaps a quarter of an hour I heard the tanks rolling off towards the south. Silence descended on the battlefield. But I still lay there like a sleeping man.

When I lifted my head the sky had dimmed from its brassy afternoon glare. Evening was coming. I saw no sign of life all round. Then I was startled by a figure that burst like a jack-in-the-box from a slit-trench some way back. It was my man Muller.

He had an anguished expression on his face. 'Are you well, *Herr Ober-leutnant*?' he called to me. And he added oddly, 'I am not.'

'Get down here,' I ordered Muller. 'We shall wait until it is dark before we move.'

'*Herr Oberleutnant*,' said Muller, 'that venison was just ready when the Tommies came.'

As soon as darkness had fallen on the battlefield Muller led me back to the wadi, where the gazelle had been roasted. A haunch, still warm, lay on a sheet of iron there. Muller's flask still held coffee. We tore off hunks of the tasty but exceedingly tough meat and swallowed it.

I can still remember the feeling of the juice running down from the corners of my mouth. It was good to be alive. That sense of futility and the inevitability of death that had overwhelmed me in the slit-trench had gone. The will to live is strong in us.

Lieutenant Heinz Werner Schmidt

Rommel takes Stock

I will not deny that I was seriously worried that evening. Our heavy tank losses were no good beginning to the battle (far more than a third of the German tanks had been lost in this one day). 90 Light Division under General Kleemann had become separated from the Afrika Korps and was now in a very dangerous position. British motorized groups were streaming through the open gap and hunting down the transport columns which had lost touch with the main body. And on these columns the life of my army depended.

However, in spite of the precarious situation and the difficult problems with which it faced us, I looked forward that evening full of hope to what the battle might bring. For Ritchie had thrown his armour into the battle piecemeal and had thus given us the chance of engaging them on each separate occasion with just about enough of our own tanks. This dispersal of the British armoured brigades was incomprehensible. In my view the sacrifice of 7 Armoured Division south of Bir el Harmat served no strategical or tactical purpose whatsoever, for it was all the same to the British whether my armour was engaged there or on the Trigh Capuzzo, where the rest of the British armour later entered the battle. The principal aim of the British should have been to have brought all the armour they had into action at one and the same time. . . . The full motorization of their units would have enabled them to cross the battlefield at great speed to wherever danger threatened. Mobile warfare in the desert has often and rightly been compared with a battle at sea—where it is equally wrong to attack piecemeal and leave half the fleet in port during the battle.

Rommel

The tank battles around us had not gone our way. In spite of our new tanks with the bigger armament and thicker armour, the 88 mm. dual-purpose gun was proving deadly. Time and again our tanks were led on to them by the withdrawal of the enemy, who then engaged them over open sights at two or three thousand yards' range and took heavy toll.

Brigadier L. Bolton

Bir Hacheim

Having destroyed a British brigade which lay across their communications to the west, the Germans next attacked Bir Hacheim in strength. After a defence which commanded Rommel's unqualified admiration, the Free French had to withdraw.

On the night 1–2 June, 90 Light Division and the Trieste moved against Bir Hacheim. They crossed the minefields without heavy casualties, thus shutting off the fortress from the east.

After our summons to surrender had been rejected, the attack opened at about midday. The Trieste from the north-east and 90 Light from the south-east advanced against the fortifications, field positions and minefields of the French defenders. With our preliminary barrage there began a battle of extra-ordinary severity, which was to last for ten whole days. I frequently took over command of the assault forces myself and seldom in Africa was I given such a hard-fought struggle. The French fought in a skilfully planned system of field positions and small defence works—slit trenches, small pill-boxes, machine-gun and anti-tank gun nests—all surrounded by dense minefields. This form of defence system is extraordinarily impervious to artillery fire or air attack, since a direct hit can destroy at the most one slit trench at a time. An immense ex-penditure of ammunition is necessary to do any real damage to an enemy holding a position of this kind.

It was a particularly difficult task to clear lanes through the minefields in face of the French fire. Superhuman feats were performed by the sappers, who suffered heavy casualties. Working under the cover of smoke-screens and artil-lery fire, they were frequently forced to sap their way direct through to the mines. Our victory was in a great measure due to their efforts.

Under non-stop attacks by our Luftwaffe (from 2 June up to the capture of the last French positions on the 11th, the Luftwaffe flew thirteen hundred sorties against Bir Hacheim) the French positions were attacked in the north by mixed assault groups drawn from various formations and in the south by 90 Light Division. Attack after attack came to a halt in the excellent British defence system.

During the first days of our attack on Bir Hacheim the mass of the British forces kept astonishingly quiet. Their only move was on 2 June against the Ariete, who resisted stubbornly. After a counter-attack by 21 Panzer Division, the situation quietened down again. British raiding parties from the area south of Bir Hacheim were continually harrying our supply traffic, to our great dis-comfort. Mines were laid on the desert tracks and attacks made against our supply columns. The British Motorized Group 'August' particularly distinguished itself in this work. We were forced to use armoured cars and self-propelled guns for convoy protection.

Rommel

The battle still hung in the balance, both armies having suffered reverses. The British forces were still largely intact, and on the night of 4 June XXX Corps was to attack to drive a wedge into the Cauldron.

Away in the desert south of Knightsbridge, where the forces concentrated for the attack, an Indian Army officer observed that 'the moon was late and the night was chill. A great quiet hung over the desert. A few tanks took station ahead followed by Bren-carriers. Behind them the lorry-borne infantry formed up. The men wore their greatcoats; while they waited they sat around their trucks. . . . The old moon climbed the sky and the night passed. At ten minutes to three the night exploded with the shock of heavy guns. The earth rocked. . . .'

The Battle for the Cauldron

All vehicles were lightened and precious possessions thrown away. A spare pair of boots, a cherished battery for a wireless, spare kit—they all went, and every drop of water that could be procured was carried in their place. All that night of 4–5 June the men stood to, and at about 2 a.m. they fired a long programme of concentrations on areas where the enemy were thought to be.

Then off in the moonlight, westwards—just such a silent move as when the Regiment trekked at speed, a little over a year previously, to the help of Tobruk. As dawn broke, and shortly after passing Bir 180, the Brigade Group topped the western lip of the Cauldron and were received with heavy and accurate fire. At once the guns dropped into action and each group shook out, guns in the centre, anti-tank and machine-guns on the flanks, vehicles and remaining infantry in rear.

After a short, fierce gun duel the enemy shelling ceased, and as the sun rose our tanks poured through the guns and joined battle with the German tanks over to the west. By about 10.00 hrs. the battle had become more or less stabilized, and from a commanding position on the escarpment in the H.L.I. area Captains Barber and Chadburn of the 426th Battery, on O.P. duty in their Honey tanks, could see down into the Cauldron proper, which was seething with German troops of all arms. It was an O.P. officer's dream. Fortunately they had plenty of ammunition and tremendous execution was done until the H.L.I. were counterattacked by tanks and forced to withdraw. Captain Barber's Honey had a track blown off and had to be towed out by Captain Chadburn's.

About midday the tanks broke off to refuel, bringing with them the tattered remains of the H.L.I. Regiment, who had found themselves caught in daylight between the opposing tank forces. Each tank had its load of badly wounded men, a grim and weary lot. Their colonel, blood pouring down his face, passed through three times collecting what was left of his men.

The enemy shelling went on all day, though as long as our tanks and O.Ps held the high ground to the west the Germans were unable to overlook our gun positions. But since the ground was paved with stone slabs digging was impossible, and each shell took a heavy toll.

Towards evening a reinforcement battalion started to arrive and take up position in the Cauldron in the rear of the Support Group, and as dusk fell the Armoured Brigadier came up and told the leaders of the Support Group that he was withdrawing the tanks and that the Group were to 'stand and fight where they were to the last man and the last round'. He promised to be back with his armour at first light on the 6th, but the tanks ran into trouble in their leaguer area and could not return. This completely altered the situation on the morrow, for it meant that we lost possession of the high ground to the west.

British gunner

The attack had gone astray, and the Germans counter-attacked with devastating success.

Few knew what was now our main object, for the original plan of attack had been thwarted and turned against us. The troops who had set out that morning in darkness were now being smashed and decimated and split and driven in flight, overrun and captured, pursued and harried, shelled and dive-bombed, encircled and crushed by armoured forces.

Antony Brett-James

As darkness approached, the fighting intensified, the shelling increased and brew-ups flared up all round. At last light a Jat battalion drove out to take up a position on the ridge six hundred yards in front. It was caught as it was deploying; all the officers were killed and what was left melted away. The night was very dark and every man on the guns 'stood to' in view of the infantry attack that had seemed to be boiling up when darkness fell.

As the tanks rumbled off to their rallying point, quiet descended on the Cauldron and it was possible to take stock of the situation. All ammunition was brought up and spread round the guns. The wounded were loaded up in fifteen-hundredweights and sent off eastwards. The men had a substantial, though cold, meal. Most of the guns were still in action, but many had been hit, and gun detachments were made up to at least three men per gun. . . .

On the left the Baluchis, commanded by a most capable and phlegmatic colonel, had dug in and prepared to meet any onslaught. In rear as night fell Gurkhas could be seen digging in hard, and on the right rear another infantry battalion seemed to be arriving. There was also a company of those most excellent and experienced machine-gunners the Northumberland Fusiliers, who in the days of peace had challenged the Abbasia gunners at every sport. One of their officers, just arrived back from Cairo, brought a very opportune parcel of food and drink. Arriving at dusk in the midst of heavy shelling, he threw it out and drove off to his company.

The night passed quietly enough with spasmodic shelling, and at dawn everyone brewed up and had a good breakfast. The day had every promise of being exciting and the Gunners were thrilled at the certain prospect of a tank shoot. They wanted badly to get their own back for the shelling they had had to put up with, for the incessant dive-bombing and for all the good chaps dead. . . .

Meanwhile the Germans had been massing their tanks and lorried infantry in the gap a few thousand yards westwards. As the dawn spread quickly over the desert the shelling started once more and our guns answered back. Our O.Ps attempted to get forward on to the high ground again but in the absence of our own armour found it already occupied by German tanks, with of course *their* O.Ps. More and more German tanks appeared in the west and spread round the position in a double ring, shooting up the F.O.Os in their Honeys, but remaining just out of range of our 25-pounder solid shot. They gave the impression of hounds holding a stag at bay, but not daring to go in.

Suddenly at 8.30 a.m. the enemy fire was concentrated on Birkin's battery, then into the Baluchis. The German tanks moved in, making for E Troop of 425th, and a brisk and deadly exchange took place. Then, as the dust and smoke cleared away, the enemy withdrew, leaving ten tanks behind, knocked out a few hundred yards from the guns of 425th Battery. The Gunners were delighted and settled down to await the next attack. It was not long in coming. The enemy moved farther west, to attack the units on 425th's left flank. A few minutes of intense small arms and machine-gun fire—and then dead silence. The position had been overrun. A handful of men were seen staggering off under heavy escort. This left 425th Battery with an exposed flank, and a hasty rearrangement had to be made. But a little later Stukas flew over the position and the ring of purple smoke sent up by the enemy to show his forward positions to the planes made it clear that the box was now completely surrounded.

Never for a moment did the shelling stop. Casualties became heavier and heavier. Vehicles were burning everywhere. The enemy with their guns just out of sight could direct their fire with great accuracy on the mass of men and vehicles and guns in the Cauldron below. Captain Bennett, hit through the leg, arrived at the Command Post to report his troop position untenable. Three of his gun detachments had been knocked out, but the guns themselves were intact. B.S.M. Hardy and a driver were immediately despatched in a quad to pull the guns in four hundred yards, a feat which they accomplished most gallantly in spite of heavy machine-gun fire.

Ammunition was now running short, particularly A.P., and orders were given for all fire to be held until the attack came in to close quarters. The position was exceedingly unhealthy and on the left flank had every prospect of soon becoming untenable. It was suggested to Colonel de Graz, commander of the Support Group, that the whole force should move back to the Knightsbridge Ridge, some three and a half miles to the east, and so have its flanks assured on the minefield before it was completely surrounded. But in view of the orders given him, he would not contemplate it.

More and more enemy tanks kept spreading round the area and presently a large column many miles long (actually the German 90 Light Division) appeared from the south behind the position, thus sealing the fate of this luckless brigade.

About 10 a.m. there was a very welcome lull—but it was short-lived. Down came the shells again, and a number of the Command Post staff were hit.

The Germans could now observe our every move. At about this time Colonel de Graz and Colonel Seely held a small conference at the Regimental Command Post, roughly in the centre of the box, and though there were only some ten people present the enemy at once started shelling.

The next attack came in very quickly and soon German tanks had overrun the infantry battalion in the rear and were nosing about amongst the burning vehicles round the Bir. Captain Trippier and his Northumberland Hussars were quite magnificent. Under heavy fire they man-handled their anti-tank guns across to try to safeguard our rear, but they were all knocked out. He then drove back with his truck full of badly wounded men to report that he had not a man left. As he spoke a shell exploding beside him wounded him severely. Events moved quickly now and amazing things happened as the fighting raged at close quarters. A sergeant of the Recce Regiment with what was left of his section leaped on a German tank, trying to ram hand grenades through the turret. They were killed to a man. The machine-gun fire was intense. Cartridge boxes went up in a sheet of flame. Four lorry loads of Germans in British three-tonners drove straight past the guns untouched. A staff car and two generals drove up to the Command Post, and as the gunners jumped at it, accelerated and got away. The doctor and his orderly worked unceasingly in a murderous fire round the Command Post, which was a shambles of dead and wounded. As the gun detachments were killed signallers, drivers and Northumberland 'Geordies' crawled over to take their places.

Colonel Seely, who had been constantly on the move around his Regiment in his Honey tank, encouraging the men by his splendid example, arrived at 426th Battery Command Post during the early afternoon and suddenly observed three German infantry lorries appearing over the escarpment about a thousand yards north of F Troop. The German infantry jumped out, but before they could get into action with their light automatics they were met by the concentrated fire of F Troop, the 6-pounder anti-tank guns of the Northumberland Hussars and the small arms of the Recce Regiment. In a few moments the lorries were in flames and the scattered German survivors rounded up.

About 3 p.m. the Germans were attacking the right of the position. Of the anti-tank guns one only now remained, but there was no one to man it until a young lance-bombardier, with one arm blown off at the elbow, crawled out in a vain attempt to reach it. Colonel de Graz walked over from his blazing and useless vehicle, but was killed immediately as he tried to fire the anti-tank gun. Communication still remained. For sixteen hours the Signal Sergeant had sat in his vehicle keeping on the air to Brigade. The second-in-command spoke to the Brigadier and told him that if he would get some ammunition through with some tanks, we could hold out until dark. The Brigadier wished him luck, but at that moment the vehicle was hit and up it went.

As evening approached, everywhere the German tanks were moving in. The Indian Infantry Brigade was completely overrun—there was nothing left. Nearly every vehicle was burning and heavy smoke obliterated the sky. Still the South Notts Hussars held out and kept the tanks at bay. Guns were facing every direction—wherever a tank could be seen working up through the smoke. Solid shot tore up the ground all round. As a last desperate measure it was decided to move the guns of Captain Pringle's E Troop to the rear, despite the enemy's immediate reaction to any sign of movement.

The quads drove up and the men—all that were left of them—leapt to hook in the guns. But before they had gone two hundred yards all four of the quads went up in flames. Major Birkin, hurrying to see what could be done, had his armoured car hit by an A.P. shot and his invaluable B.S.M. Hardy killed beside him. By the time he had regained his remaining A Troop, of which only two guns were still in action, the enemy tanks were on top of the position and the gallant fight of the 425th Battery was over.

Down in the hollow, Alan Chadburn's guns were still intact, but on all sides the German tanks were closing in, machine-guns blazing. Colonel Seely and Bish Peal, his adjutant, who had continued to ply indomitably about the battlefield, had their tank hit and set on fire. Both died later in enemy hands. The end was very near now. 426th Battery Command Post fell to the advancing tanks; and though in a last defiant gesture Chadburn's F Troop scored two direct hits at eight hundred yards they could do no more. The groups of British prisoners appearing over the escarpment put further firing out of the question, and the survivors of 426th Battery turned sadly to their final task—the battering of their gun sights. For a few moments more the air sang with machine-gun bullets; then all was quiet, and that deep silence that descends on a battlefield when the contest is over spread over the Cauldron.

British gunner

12 June was the day on which the vast battle of Gazala was finally lost. The British armour met disaster and the Knightsbridge Box was evacuated.

By nightfall the British armour was only a shadow of its former strength, and the desert was strewn with the wrecks of Grants, Crusaders and Stuarts which, since the Eighth Army had been driven off the field, were irrecoverable, even when the damage was slight. The German tanks had broken through the main line of defence covering the road between Gazala and Tobruk and several miles of the escarpment between Knightsbridge and El Adem were in their hands.

The Victors Sum Up

The C.-in-C., coming from the sector of 15 Panzer Division (Via Balbia), says that although part of the rearguard of 1 S.A. Division has been captured, the bulk of the Gazala formations have got away; therefore 21 Panzer Division was ordered at noon to pursue the enemy by swinging east of Tobruk.

. . . . Messages from 90 Light say that although local penetrations have been made in the east and west sectors of the El Adem Box, enemy resistance is on the whole unbroken. The three German reconnaissance units report that in the area south and south-east of El Adem they have thrown back enemy reconnaissance forces. Italian XX (Motorized) Corps is assembling around Knightsbridge, Italian X and XXI Corps are moving east through the Gazala position.

Enemy situation. The enemy has succeeded in evading our pincer movement and is escaping from the Gazala position. These forces (1 S.A. Division and 50 British Division) and the armoured brigades—no longer fit for battle—of 1 and 7 Armoured Divisions are assembling on the Libyan-Egyptian frontier; air reconnaissance confirms continuous movements from Tobruk eastwards; wireless intercept has confirmed that 1 S.A. Division and 50 Division together with the two armoured divisions are on the frontier [this was not entirely correct, but the reports are given as I made them at the time]. Therefore in the Tobruk zone we can reckon on 2 S.A. Division only, with 11 and 29 Indian Brigades in the outer approaches of the fortress.

C.-in-C.: 'It is my intention to take Tobruk by a *coup de main*. For this purpose the outlying area of Tobruk, south and east of the Fortress, must be gained without delay, and the British Eighth Army pressed away farther to the east.'

General von Mellenthin

A plan was proposed for a wholesale British withdrawal eastwards, but General Auchinleck opposed this.

Tobruk must be held and the enemy must not be allowed to invest it. This means that Eighth Army must hold the line Acroma–El Adem and southward and resist any enemy attempt to pass it. Having reduced your front by evacuating Gazala and reorganized your forces, this should be feasible and I order you to do it.

Auchinleck to Ritchie

The Prime Minister was urging a firm stand, the Eighth Army Commander was optimistic, but General Auchinleck then began to have doubts.

The conditions required for good maintenance were absent, and it is reasonable to conclude that the defences had indeed fallen into considerable neglect, that their detailed layout was largely unknown, and that they were very much in a state of being nobody's business.

A British Brigadier

Although I have made it clear to you that Tobruk must not be invested I realize that its garrison may be isolated for short periods until our counter-offensive can be launched. With this possibility in mind you are free to organize the garrison as you think best and to retain whatever administrative services and stocks of all sorts you consider necessary either for the service of the garrison or to assist the counter-offensive.

Auchinleck to Ritchie

Had I seen this order I should not have been content with it.

Winston Churchill

The Fall of Tobruk: 20–21 June

At 05.00 [20 June] I stood with Rommel on the escarpment to the north-east of El Adem; Battle Headquarters had been set up there and when daylight came we had excellent observation as far as the Tobruk perimeter. Promptly at 05.20 the Stukas flew over. Kesselring had been as good as his word and sent hundreds of bombers in dense formations; they dived on to the perimeter in one of the most spectacular attacks I have ever seen. A great cloud of dust and smoke rose from the sector under attack, and while our bombs crashed on to the defences, the entire German and Italian Army artillery joined in with a tremendous and well co-ordinated fire. The combined weight of the artillery and bombing was terrific, and as we soon realized, had a crushing effect on the morale of the Mahratta battalion in that sector. The Stukas kept it up all day, flying back to the airfields at Gazala and El Adem, replenishing with bombs, and then returning to the fray. On this occasion the Air Force bombing was directed through the Operations Section of Army Headquarters, with very fruitful results.

After a time the assault engineers released orange smoke as a signal that the range should be lengthened, and at 06.35 the report came back that the wire had been cut in front of Strong Point 69. Group Menny, and the infantry of the

Afrika Korps, now attacked the forward line of bunkers and made rapid progress against feeble resistance. At 07.03 Group Menny reported that a whole company of Indians had been taken prisoner, and by 07.45 a wide breach had been made and about ten strong points had been taken. Bridges were laid across the anti-tank ditch and the way was prepared for the tanks to enter the perimeter.

The weak resistance of the defenders was due primarily to the bombardment, and paradoxically to the excellent concrete shelters built by the Italians. Under the crushing weight of bombs and shells the Indians were driven below ground, where they were relatively secure, but could not bring any fire to bear on our attacking troops, who followed closely behind the barrage. Another important factor was the weakness of the defenders' artillery fire. There seems to have been a complete lack of co-ordination of the various batteries; a few South African guns were firing during the break-through, but apparently the 25th Field Regiment R.A., which was in immediate support of 11 Indian Brigade, did not fire until 07.45. The guns of this regiment had been sited in an anti-tank role, and it appears that they were relying on the medium artillery to bombard the perimeter gap, and the German troops assembling beyond it. But the mediums remained silent, and it was not until 08.45 that the Afrika Korps reported that the enemy's fire was 'increasing', particularly that of the 'heavy calibres'. I well remember our surprise, when watching the battle that morning, at the small volume of fire put down by the Tobruk artillery. Meanwhile Rommel had gone forward to take direct command of the break-through.

General von Mellenthin

General Ritchie to General Klopper, G.O.C. Tobruk Garrison

Army Commander: Every day and hour of resistance materially assists our cause. I cannot tell tactical situation and must therefore leave you to act on your own judgment regarding capitulation.

Report if you can extent to which destruction P.O.L. effected.

G.O.C. Situation shambles. Terrible casualties would result. Am doing the worst. Petrol destroyed.

Army Comd.: Whole of Eighth Army has watched with admiration your gallant fight. You are an example to us all and I know South Africa will be proud of you. God bless you and may fortune favour your efforts wherever you be. . . .

Surrender

After his message that he was 'doing the worst', which went in clear about 06.30, General Klopper sent out *parlementaires* under the white flag to the enemy forces lying east and west of his position with an offer to surrender. A huge white flag was hauled up over 6 Brigade Headquarters by some native drivers and 'a sort of cry or moan,' wrote one observer, 'went up from the South African Police. It gave an extraordinary impression of anguish and misery.'

Rommel Enters Tobruk

At 05.00 hours on 21 June, I drove into the town of Tobruk. Practically every building of the dismal place was either flat or little more than a heap of rubble, mostly the result of our siege in 1941. Next I drove off along the Via Balbia to the west. The staff of 32 British Army Tank Brigade offered to surrender, which brought us thirty serviceable British tanks. Vehicles stood in flames on either side of the Via Balbia. Wherever one looked there was chaos and destruction.

At about 09.40 hours, on the Via Balbia about four miles west of the town, I met General Klopper, G.O.C. 2 South African Infantry Division and Garrison Commandant of Tobruk. He announced the capitulation of the fortress of Tobruk. He had been unable to stave off the defeat any longer, although he had done all he could to maintain control over his troops.

I told the General, who was accompanied by his Chief of Staff, to follow me in his car along the Via Balbia to Tobruk. The road was lined with about ten thousand prisoners of war.

On arrival at the Hotel Tobruk, I talked for a while with General Klopper. It seemed that he had no longer been in possession of the necessary communications to organize a break-out. It had all gone too quickly. I instructed the South African general to make himself and his officers responsible for order among the prisoners, and to organize their maintenance from the captured stores.

Rommel

Twenty-five thousand men and enormous quantities of supplies fell into Rommel's hands. Before the day ended, Hitler had promoted him Field-Marshal. We all celebrated—with captured tinned fruit, Irish potatoes, cigarettes and canned beer.

For a day or so we rejoiced in the blessings of the British Naafi. It was a pleasure to snuffle round the field-kitchens, where pork sausages and potatoes, so long a rarity, were being fried. There was British beer to drink, and tinned South African pineapples for desert.

We spurned our own rations, especially '*Alte Mann*',* with distaste and contempt. Instead we gloried in Australian bully beef, of which the Australians were as sick as we were of '*Alte Mann*'. It was some time, however, before we could find ourselves agreeing with the sentiments expressed in captured enemy letters, which were far from extolling the deliciousness of bully. When conditions permitted, we used to send home parcels of Australian bully. It was regarded in Germany as a luxury.

Lieutenant Heinz Werner Schmidt

The fall of Tobruk made an enormous impression in Berlin and throughout Germany. Public spirits rose at once to a peak not experienced since the conclusion of the Battle of France in 1940. Rommel was the man of the day to whom nothing seemed impossible. Perhaps we can win the war after all, everybody said, and gave themselves up to jubilation over a victory which they really felt was a victory.

Arvid Fredborg, Swedish journalist

---

* *Alte Mann*—Italian sausage, labelled A.M.

Post-Mortem

As things turned out, I don't think the scratch garrison of Tobruk had a hope of survival. The garrison was not strong enough, and insufficient time was available to sort things out and get the defence organized properly. Air support, through no fault of the gallant Desert Air Force, was quite inadequate, and the enemy were in a position to form up and lay on their attack without interference. There were some hard things said about the South Africans after the capitulation, but I could never myself blame that division; they never had a chance. Under Montgomery at Alamein and before, the South Africans conducted themselves magnificently.

Much petrol, transport and supplies fell into Rommel's hands, and it was this that no doubt persuaded the German Commander, and eventually Hitler, that the capture of the Nile Valley was now a practical proposition.

Major-General Sir Francis de Guingand

Urgent conferences were held at Rommel's headquarters to consider further action.

A grave decision had to be made now. In the original plan agreed upon between Hitler and Mussolini at the end of April, it was laid down that after Rommel had taken Tobruk, the *Panzerarmee* would stand on the defensive on the Egyptian Frontier, and that all available aircraft and shipping would then be diverted to the attack on Malta. With the fall of the island our communications would be secure, and an advance to the Nile could follow. On 21 June Field-Marshal Kesselring flew to Africa, and I was present at his conference with Rommel in our Command Vehicle. Rommel insisted that he must follow up his victory without waiting for an attack on Malta, but Kesselring pointed out that an advance into Egypt could not succeed without full support from the Luftwaffe. If this were given, the Luftwaffe would not be available for operations against Malta, and should the island recover, Rommel's communications would be in serious jeopardy. Kesselring maintained that the only sound course was to stick to the original plan, and postpone an invasion of Egypt until Malta had fallen.

Rommel disagreed emphatically and the discussions became exceedingly lively. He admitted that the *Panzerarmee* had suffered heavily in the Gazala battles, but maintained that Eighth Army was in far worse plight and we now had a unique opportunity for a thrust to the Suez Canal. A delay of even a few weeks would give the enemy time to move up new forces and prevent any further advance. The two commanders failed to reach agreement, and before leaving, Kesselring made no secret of his intention to withdraw his air units to Sicily.

Rommel had made up his mind irrevocably. The vanguard of the Afrika Korps was already on its way to the frontier, and on the evening of the 21st Rommel sent off a personal liaison officer to put his views before Hitler. He also signalled to Rome, and assured the Duce that 'the state and morale of the troops, the present supply position owing to captured dumps, and the present weakness of the enemy, permit our pursuing him into the depths of the Egyptian area'.

Rommel carried the day with Hitler, in spite of the reasoned and powerful objections of the Italian General Staff, the German Naval Staff, Field-Marshal Kesselring, and also General von Rintelen, the German military attaché in Rome. Hitler signalled to Mussolini that 'it is only once in a lifetime that the Goddess of Victory smiles', and the fateful decision was made to postpone the Malta attack until September, and throw everything behind Rommel's invasion of Egypt.

General von Mellenthin

The Last Invasion

On the evening of 23 June the advance guard of the Afrika Korps crossed the Egyptian frontier. Rommel's aim was to outflank the formidable minefields and 'boxes' which the British had built up in the frontier area, but in fact Ritchie had already decided to fall back to Matruh. During the next twenty-four hours our advance guard made a sensational advance of over a hundred miles and reached the coast road between Matruh and Sidi Barrani. The morale of the troops was high and the victories of the past month went far to balance the strain and exhaustion of incessant fighting at the height of a desert summer. Tank strength, however, was ominously low, for there had been many breakdowns in the march from Tobruk, and the Afrika Korps entered Egypt with only forty-four Panzers.

Our advance on 24/25 June met with little interference from British ground forces, but was exposed to heavy and determined attacks by the Desert Air Force; the pace of the advance was outstripping our available fighter cover and we had to pay a heavy toll in casualties; indeed from the moment we entered Egypt the writing was on the wall as far as air support was concerned. Rommel never again enjoyed the advantage of air superiority, and the enemy's air forces grew with terrifying strength.

General von Mellenthin

On 25 June General Auchinleck decided that the precarious position of his forces was such that he must assume personal responsibility for the battle, and he himself relieved General Ritchie. He made up his mind to halt the enemy in the area between Matruh and Alamein. The area which was to prove critical was due south of Matruh: Minqa Qaim, occupied by seven New Zealand battalions newly arrived from Syria.

Minqa Qaim

The general situation was extremely vague, and I could see no merits in the position we stood in, though I knew of no better and could not see one. We moved on to the ground on the late afternoon of the 26th and dug in that night and until nine o'clock next morning. On top of the escarpment the solid rock was within eighteen inches of the surface, and it was not possible to do very much.

Soon after midday we could see that the enemy had worked round the right flank of the Division. There was a steady thudding of gunfire, much dust and the smoke of many explosions and burning vehicles, and occasionally the distant mutter of automatics, but we could form little idea of what was happening. Everything remained quiet with 5 Brigade but we could see that 4 Brigade was heavily engaged and that the enemy was steadily moving east of us. North of 5 Brigade the great enemy mass remained out of range. We moved headquarters to a safer area with the 22nd Battalion.

Early in the afternoon Division informed us that General Freyberg had been wounded. Inglis had taken command and Jim Burrows had taken over 4 Brigade.

. . . . I was called to Division for a conference about eight o'clock that evening. We stood in a group at the back of the command truck. Inglis said that all attacks had been repulsed so far, but the enemy was fairly round behind us and we obviously were in a grave position. The going to the south was reported bad, the only sure going was due east, which meant that we must make a break through.

Brigadier Kippenberger

The entire 2 New Zealand Division lined up in their vehicles and prepared to make a mad dash for safety.

. . . . The trucks were packed to the limit and the hundreds of men whom they could carry were crammed on to the fighting vehicles. Men were hanging on wherever there was standing room, squeezed inside the gun quads, on the guns themselves, on carriers and anti-tank portées, everywhere imaginable. The loading was completed in a quiet and orderly manner and I walked round to check up. I found about twenty men still unaccommodated and they followed me round while I found places for them one by one.

Brigadier Kippenberger

Break-Out

At last, well after midnight, we started to move forward, the column led by the C.R.A. 4 Brigade had not completed its attack, but we were forced to begin the break-out so that we should have a long enough period of darkness in which to get well clear of the enemy. We passed slowly through 4 Brigade's old area. There was little small-arms fire ahead of us, and later we learned that 4 Brigade had done tremendous execution with the bayonet.

We had gone only a short distance past the original forward posts when the scouting carriers moving just ahead of the column halted. A moment later the darkness in front exploded into fire. Tank shells and machine-gun bullets poured into the column, and a number of our vehicles burst into flames, illuminating the whole area. We remained halted in reality for only a few seconds, uncertain what to do. Then the C.R.A. roared out from his jeep, 'Follow me.' Several of us in the leading vehicles did so, and we drove hard right, i.e. south, skirting the enemy tanks. The whole column followed. The going was poor, but any thought of cautious driving was abandoned. We had gone about five hundred yards when more enemy tanks immediately in front of us opened fire. We halted again, and our predicament was obviously much more serious this time. Many of the leading vehicles went up in flames, a single shell in some cases going through two or three trucks in line.

My recollections are a little vague at this point; but I remember that, with no alternative, we started up and drove straight into the enemy's fire. I can well imagine the feelings of those tank crews when they saw an irresistible tide of vehicles and guns bearing down upon them. Trucks were still exploding in flames, but nothing could have halted that onrush, the product more of instinct than of command. The air was so heavy with dust and smoke that one could do nothing but follow the vehicle in front into the thick blanket ahead. A number of unfortunate men were thrown off motor-cycles or tossed out of trucks. Their death was certain, for vehicles behind had no chance of avoiding them.

Lieutenant-Colonel G. P. Hanna

Escape

My car was jammed on all sides and could not move. I told Ross and Joe to get out and for a moment we lay flat on the ground. Many others had done the same. A few seconds later I saw the truck ahead of us turning to the left, and beyond it quite clearly saw John Gray standing with his head through the roof of his car and pointing in the same direction. 'We'll give it a go, Ross,' I said. 'Very good, sir,' he replied, as polite as ever. We scrambled back and followed the trucks ahead, all bolting like wild elephants. For a few moments we ran on amid a pandemonium, overtaking and being overtaken by other frantic vehicles, dodging slit trenches, passing or crashing into running men, amid an uproar of shouts and screams. I recognized the men as Germans, pulled out my revolver and was eagerly looking out for a target when suddenly there was silence and we were out running smoothly on level desert. We were through.

Brigadier Kippenberger

The wild flare-up which ensued involved my own battle headquarters, which lay to the south. . . . Soon my headquarters were surrounded by burning vehicles, making them the target for continuous enemy fire at close range. I had enough of this after a while and ordered the troops, with the staff, to move back south-eastward. The confusion reigning on that night can scarcely be imagined. It was impossible to see one's hand before one's eyes. The R.A.F. bombed their own troops, German units were firing on each other, the tracer was flying in all directions.

Rommel

One more grave blow was to fall upon the Eighth Army before the battle came to an end: X Corps, already deprived of 2 New Zealand Division, which had fought its way to Alamein and was busy sorting itself out, took a beating on the Fuka escarpment and struggled back minus eight thousand prisoners. As General Auchinleck watched his battered army stream into the Alamein positions, there was little hope to be found in anyone's mind.

The Middle East situation is about as unhealthy as it can be, and I do not very well see how it can end.

General Sir Alan Brooke, C.I.G.S., diary, 28 June

Panic

General Gott was in his Armoured Command Vehicle (A.C.V.), the first I had seen. He came out at once and walked a few yards clear of it. 'Inglis has gone to Cairo,' he said, and handed me a letter. It was a short note from General Corbett, then General Auchinleck's M.G.G.S. I remember very clearly the opening sentence: 'The Chief has decided to save Eighth Army.' The note then went on to say that the South Africans would retire through Alexandria and the rest of us down the desert road through Cairo.

I asked what was meant by the first sentence. 'It means what it says—he means to save the Field Army,' the General said. He went on to explain: a general retirement and evacuation of Egypt was in contemplation and Inglis had gone to Cairo to arrange for the evacuation of 2 N.Z.E.F. rear installations and hospitals; he supposed we would go back to New Zealand. I protested that we were perfectly fit to fight and that it was criminal to give up Egypt to twenty-five thousand German troops and a hundred tanks (disregarding the Italians)—the latest Intelligence estimate—and to lose as helpless prisoners perhaps two hundred thousand Base troops. Strafer replied sadly that N.Z. Division was battle-worthy but very few other people were and he feared the worst.

Inglis returned on the afternoon of the 30th, nothing else of importance having occurred in his absence, and I returned to 5 Brigade. He drew a vivid picture of the confusion he had seen on the Cairo road and of the prodigious 'flap' in Cairo itself. This was the time of the famous Ash Wednesday when Middle East and B.T.E. (it was customary to say 'Middle East', meaning Middle East Headquarters, and B.T.E., meaning 'Headquarters, British Troops in Egypt') were said to have burned many of their records and the Navy left Alexandria in haste. Paddy Costello, later one of our best divisional intelligence officers, was always very upset that the elaborate draft he had prepared for a handbook on the Italian Army was destroyed at this time. We heard all sorts of peculiar and perhaps libellous stories, such as the one that all the reserve store of binoculars had been thrown into Alexandria Harbour, but despite General Gott's warning I do not remember that we were particularly depressed. We thought it too bad to be true.

Brigadier Kippenberger

It is nonsense to talk of the Alamein 'Line'. When the Riflemen heard the suave voice of the B.B.C. announcer reporting that the Eighth Army had reached the Alamein 'Line', they looked round at the empty desert, indistinguishable from the miles of sand to east and west, and commented as only Riflemen can.

Rommel is Stopped

On the morning of 30 June Rommel formed his plan for piercing the Alamein Line. Strictly speaking there was no such thing as an 'Alamein Line', although the gap between the Qattara Depression and the sea was filled by a number of boxes. He decided that the Afrika Korps should make a feint in the direction of the Qattara Depression, but should move on the night of 30 June/1 July to a position about ten miles south-west of El Alamein station. We believed that the British X Corps, with 50 Division and 10 Indian Brigade, was holding the Alamein Box and a position to the south-west of it at Deir el Abyad. We thought that XIII Corps with 1 Armoured Division, 2 N.Z. Division, and 5 Indian Division was holding the southern sector of the line, between the Qaret el Abd Box and the Qattara Depression. Rommel decided to repeat the tactics which had served him so well at Matruh; under cover of the darkness the Afrika Korps was to penetrate between the boxes at Alamein and Deir el Abyad and get in the rear of XIII Corps. 90 Light Division was to swing south of the Alamein Box and cut the coast road to the east of it—exactly the same orders as at Mersa Matruh. If we could once get our troops in rear of the British, Rommel was convinced that their defence would collapse.

In view of our experiences at Matruh I think that this plan offered a real hope of victory. The German forces were too weak for any heavy fighting, but they were still capable of manœuvre. It is quite possible that if Rommel had got his divisions across the British rear, they would have been stampeded once more into a headlong flight.

Unfortunately Rommel's theory was never put to the test. . . . The Afrika Korps was late—its night move from El Quseir to the concentration area near Tell el Aqqaqir was delayed by broken ground—and when it advanced on the morning of 1 July the corps found that there was no box at Deir el Abyad, but that the enemy was holding a box three miles farther east at Deir el Shein. It might have been possible for the Afrika Korps to by-pass the Deir el Shein Box and continue its move into the rear of XIII Corps, but in that case another enemy position—actually held by 1 S.A. Brigade north of Ruweisat Ridge— would have had to be eliminated. General Nehring decided to attack Deir el Shein, and when Rommel came up later that morning he approved of this decision.

On the afternoon of 1 July the Afrika Korps broke into the Deir el Shein Box, and after very severe fighting destroyed 18 Indian Brigade. But we lost eighteen tanks out of fifty-five, and the fighting edge of the Afrika Korps was finally blunted. 90 Light advanced during the afternoon, and attempted to by-pass the El Alamein Box; it ran into a crescent of fire from 1, 2 and 3 S.A. Brigades and their supporting artillery, and was thrown into confusion not far removed from panic. Rommel himself went to 90 Light to try and urge the division forward, but the volume of fire was so heavy that even he was pinned down.

On 3 July Rommel abandoned the hope of getting in rear of XIII Corps, and sought to use the Afrika Korps, 90 Light, and Littorio for a concentrated thrust round the Alamein Box. We suffered a sharp reverse that morning when the New Zealanders came out of their box at Qaret el Abd, attacked Ariete Division, and captured all their artillery. Nevertheless, Rommel ordered the main attack to go in on the afternoon of 3 July, and under cover of a heavy bombardment the Afrika Korps made a determined attempt to advance. Some ground was gained on Ruweisat Ridge, but with only twenty-six tanks it was impossible to break through. When darkness fell Rommel ordered the Panzer divisions to dig in where they stood; everyone realized that the offensive which opened on 26 May, and which had achieved such spectacular victories, had at last come to an end.

That night Rommel signalled to Kesselring that he had been forced to

suspend his attack 'for the time being'. This check was all the more disappoint-
ing because our air reconnaissance reported that the British fleet had left
Alexandria, and that there was much traffic *en route* from Egypt to Palestine.
We had just failed.

General von Mellenthin

*The Afrika Korps slowly but inevitably weakened for lack of reinforcements and
supplies. Heavy fighting continued to rage around the Ruweisat Ridge, and what
decision there was went to the British. By late July the inability of the Axis forces
to make progress was worrying their commander, who by now was even more tired
than his men.*

18 July 1942

Dearest Lu,
    Yesterday was a particularly hard and critical day. We pulled through again.
But it can't go on like it for long, otherwise the front will crack. Militarily, this
is the most difficult period I've ever been through. There's help in sight, of
course, but whether we will live to see it is a question. You know what an in-
curable optimist I am. But there are situations where everything is dark.
However, this period, too, will pass.

Rommel

Dear Frau Rommel,   26 August 1942
    You'll no doubt be surprised at hearing from me from Africa. . . . The reason
for my letter is to inform you about the state of the Marshal's health. Your
husband has now been nineteen months in Africa, which is longer than any
other officer over forty has stood it so far, and, according to the doctors, an
astonishing physical feat. After the rigours of the advance, he has had to carry
the immense responsibility of the Alamein front, anxiety for which has for many
nights allowed him no rest. Moreover, the bad season has come again.
    All this has, in the nature of things, not failed to leave its mark, and thus, in
addition to all the symptoms of a heavy cold and the digestive disturbances
typical of Africa, he has recently shown signs of exhaustion which have caused
great anxiety to all of us who were aware of it. True, there is no immediate
danger, but unless he can get a thorough rest some time, he might easily suffer
an overstrain which could leave organic damage in its train.
    The doctor who is treating him, Professor Dr. Horster of Würzburg Uni-
versity—one of the best-known stomach specialists in Germany—is constantly
available to him for medical advice and to watch over his health. The Führer
has been informed, and it has been agreed that he will receive a long period of
sick leave in Europe once the future of this theatre has been decided. Until that
time, we will do everything we can to make his life easier and to persuade him
to look after himself. We prepare and keep handy everything he needs for his
health. I have installed a small kitchen and obtained a good cook. Fresh fruit
and vegetables arrive by air daily. We fish, shoot pigeons, obtain chickens and
eggs, etc., in order to keep his strength up.

Lieutenant Alfred Ingemar Berndt

12

PEARL HARBOR

When in 1940 most of the world expected Britain's collapse to follow that of the other Western colonial powers, Japan's imperial designs on south-east Asia, long cherished by the Army, the dominant force in Japanese society, suddenly seemed closer to realization. The European colonies were cut off and would be easy prey. Japan's former neutrality with regard to Europe turned to warmth towards Germany and Italy, with whom she came to an understanding. Vichy France was induced to give up bases in northern Indo-China.

A PACT IS SIGNED: BERLIN, 27 SEPTEMBER 1940

JAPAN recognizes and respects the leadership of Germany and Italy in the establishment of a new order in Europe.

Germany and Italy recognize and respect the leadership of Japan in the establishment of a new order in Greater East Asia.

Germany, Italy and Japan agree . . . to assist one another with all political, economic, and military means when one of the three contracting powers is attacked by a power at present not involved in the European War or in the Chinese-Japanese conflict. . . .

Germany, Italy and Japan affirm that the aforesaid terms do not in any way affect the political status which exists at present between each of the contracting parties and Soviet Russia.

President Roosevelt to Ambassador Grew in Tokyo: 21 January 1941

I believe that the fundamental proposition is that we must recognize that the hostilities in Europe, in Africa, and in Asia are all parts of a single world conflict. We must, consequently, recognize that our interests are menaced both in Europe and in the Far East. . . . Our strategy of self-defence must be a global strategy.

Ambassador Grew to Washington: 27 January 1941

A member of the embassy was told by my Peruvian colleague that from many quarters, including a Japanese one, he had heard that a surprise mass attack on Pearl Harbor was planned by the Japanese military forces, in case of 'trouble' between Japan and the United States; that the attack would involve the use of all the Japanese military forces. My colleague said that he was prompted to pass this on because it had come to him from many sources, although the plan seemed fantastic.

275

Admiral Stark, Chief of Naval Operations, Washington, to Admiral Kimmel,
C.-in-C. Pacific Fleet, Pearl Harbor: 13 January 1941

In my humble opinion we may wake up any day . . . and find ourselves in
another undeclared war. . . . I have told the gang here for months past that in
my opinion we were heading straight for this war, that we could not assume
anything else and personally I do not see how we can avoid [it] . . . many months
longer. And of course it may be a matter of weeks or days. . . . I have been
moving Heaven and Earth trying to meet such a situation, and am terribly
impatient at the slowness with which things move here.

The Axis Confer: Ribbentrop and Matsuoka, Japanese Foreign Minister,
Berlin, 29 March 1941

Next, the R.A.M.* turned again to the Singapore question. In view of the
fears expressed by the Japanese of possible attacks by submarines based on the
Philippines, and of the intervention of the British Mediterranean and Home
Fleets, he had again discussed the situation with General-Admiral Raeder. The
latter had stated that the British Navy, during this year, would have its hands so
full in the English home waters and in the Mediterranean, that it would not be
able to send even a single ship to the Far East. General-Admiral Raeder had
described the U.S. submarines as so bad that Japan need not bother about them
at all.

Matsuoka replied immediately that the Japanese Navy had a low estimate
of the threat from the British Navy; it also held the view, that in case of a clash
with the American Navy, it would be able to smash the latter without trouble.

The R.A.M. replied that America could not do anything against Japan in
the case of the capture of Singapore. Perhaps, for this reason alone, Roosevelt
would think twice before deciding on active measures against Japan; for, while
on the one hand he could not achieve anything against Japan, on the other hand
there was the probability of losing the Philippines to Japan. For the American
President, of course, this would mean a considerable loss of prestige; and because of the inadequate rearmament he would have nothing to offset such a loss.

In this connection Matsuoka pointed out that he was doing everything to
reassure the English about Singapore. He acted as if Japan had no intention at
all regarding this key position of England in the East. Therefore it might be
possible that the attitude towards the British would appear to be friendly in
words and in acts. However, Germany should not be deceived by that. He
assumed this attitude not only in order to reassure the British, but also in order
to fool the pro-British and pro-American elements until, one day, he would
suddenly open the attack on Singapore.

[Ribbentrop concluded by expressing his view that] Germany had already
won the war. With the end of this year, the world would realize this. Even England would have to concede it, if she had not collapsed before then, and America
would also have to resign herself to this fact.

* *Reichaussenminister* (= Foreign Minister; i.e. Ribbentrop) (Ed.)

Britain's fighting survival and the growing hostility of the United States towards Japanese expansion in China and Indo-China cooled the militarists' ardour for a while. Japan began negotiations with America in the spring of 1941, to try to secure the latter's acquiescence to her conquests by peaceful means. However, the United States Government was by now thoroughly aroused by Japan's advances, and economic sanctions were laid on her. Throughout the summer and autumn the talks dragged on, neither side being willing to give ground. The Japanese soon realized that they could not get what they wanted short of war. The military party, with General Tojo as Prime Minister, won complete control.

Manila: State of Readiness, 3 November

The idea of an imminent war seemed far removed from the minds of most. Work hours, training schedules, and operating procedure were still based on the good old days of peace conditions in the tropics. There was a comprehensive project on paper for the construction of additional airfields, but unfortunately little money had been provided prior to my arrival.

General Brereton, C.-in-C. U.S. Far Eastern Air Forces

Admiral Nomura, Japanese Ambassador in Washington, contacts Foreign Minister Togo in Tokyo: 15 November 1941

.... He emphasized the firmness of the American determination, the certainty that if Japan plunged into the 'southward venture' she would have to fight the United States as well as Britain, and the fact that in spite of American involvements in the Atlantic the United States could still throw its 'main strength' into a Pacific war. He gave his estimate that in Russia 'the apex of German victories had been passed'. And he ventured to suggest, though he knew he would be 'harshly criticized for it', that his government use 'patience for one or two months in order to get a clear view of the world situation'.

Foreign Minister Togo to Japanese Ambassador, Washington: 16 November 1941

In your opinion we ought to wait and see what turn the war takes and remain patient. However, I am awfully sorry to say that the situation renders this out of the question. I set the deadline for the solution of these negotiations . . . and there will be no change. . . . Press them for a solution on the basis of our proposals.

Admiral Stark, Chief of Naval Operations, to Admiral Hart, Manila, and Admiral Kimmel, Pearl Harbor: 24 November

Top secret

Chances of favourable outcome of negotiations with Japan very doubtful. This situation coupled with statements of Japanese Government and movements of their naval and military forces indicate in our opinion that a surprise aggressive movement in any direction including attack on Philippines or Guam is a possibility. Chief of Staff (Marshall) has seen this dispatch, concurs and requests action, addressees to inform senior Army officers their areas. Utmost necessary secrecy in order not to complicate an already tense situation or precipitate Japanese action. Guam will be informed separately.

State Department to General Douglas MacArthur, C.-in-C. Far East: 27 November

Negotiations with Japan appear to be terminated to all practical purposes with only barest possibilities that Japanese Government might come back and offer to continue. Japanese future action unpredictable but hostile action possible at any moment. If hostilities cannot, repeat cannot, be avoided the United States desires that Japan commit the first overt act.

Not only the Washington negotiations were used to screen Japanese intentions.

As November ran out, various other carefully planned devices of 'deception' were put into effect—unfortunately with all too much success. The Japanese knew that they could not conceal their movement against Malaya, and doubtless were at pains not to do so; for by focusing all attention on the Gulf of Siam, this movement was in itself admirable 'deceptive' cover for the operations elsewhere. Towards the end of November a programme of false radio traffic was begun, to mislead our radio trackers into placing the various ships and squadrons where they were not. It was announced that one of Japan's crack liners, the *Tatsuta Maru*, would sail for the Americas on 2 December to pick up Japanese nationals. This seemed to imply that the war must still be at least some weeks away. She actually did sail on schedule, carrying among others a score of Americans who were taking this last chance to get home—in happy ignorance of the fact that she was under orders to run out to the International Date Line and then return.

The Die is Cast

28 November. Domei informed the Japanese people to-day that America had submitted to Japan a note which was tantamount to 'a sort of ultimatum', and which, by reiterating America's well-known principles, had brought the negotiations back to where they started eight months ago. 'There is little hope of bridging the gap between the views of Japan and those of the United States,' it declared. 'There is little room for prolonging the negotiations, and just as little room for optimism.' There was also the theme of the rest of the Press, and the mere fact that the Government had lifted the veil of secrecy surrounding the negotiations and had notified the people that they were face to face with 'a sort of ultimatum' was in itself ominous.

The *Asahi* said: 'The American memorandum is America's last word. The die is cast. A showdown has come, and the next few days will reveal which way the dice have fallen.'

1 December. Foreign Minister Togo to-day rejected the American proposals as 'fantastic, unrealistic and regrettable'. In a formal statement issued by the Foreign Office, he said:

'The United States does not understand the real situation in East Asia. It is trying forcibly to apply to East Asiatic countries fantastic principles and rules not adapted to the actual situation in the world, and is thereby tending to obstruct the construction of the New Order. This is extremely regrettable.'

Chief of Naval General Staff to C.-in-C. Combined Fleet, Admiral Yamamoto: 1 December

Japan, under the necessity of self-preservation, has reached a decision to declare war on the United States of America, British Empire and the Netherlands. The C.-in-C. Combined Fleet shall at the start of the war direct an attack on the enemy fleet in the Hawaiian area and reduce it to impotency, using the 1st Air Fleet as the nucleus of the attack force.

Chief of Naval General Staff to Admiral Yamamoto: 2 December

The hostile action against the United States of America, the British Empire, and the Netherlands shall be commenced on 8 December.* Bear in mind that, should it appear certain that Japanese-American negotiations will reach an amicable settlement prior to the commencement of hostile action, all forces of the Combined Fleet are to be ordered to reassemble and return to their bases.

Admiral Yamamoto to Pearl Harbor Task Force

Execute attack. 8 December designated as X day.

Japan Waits

7 December [6 December, U.S. time]. It was a bright, warm, and pleasant December Sunday. But under the circumstances, ominously quiet. The Press seemed to have exhausted itself and for lack of any new developments was devoid of any interest. Even the diatribes against America and Great Britain had ceased. The only news that caught my eye was a small item that Thai troops were at last marching towards the south, and I made a note of it for my next story. All Japan seemed to be waiting for something.

Otto D. Tolischus, American journalist

DAY OF INFAMY

Sunday morning, 7 December 1941, I went to my office, as I had done almost every Sunday since I entered the State Department in 1933. The faces of my visitors were grim. From all our reports it appeared that zero hour was a matter of hours, perhaps minutes.

During the morning I received a series of decoded intercepts consisting of fourteen parts of a long telegram from Foreign Minister Togo to Nomura and Kurusu. This was the answer to our proposals of 26 November. There was also a short message instructing the Ambassadors to present this to our Government, if possible to me, at one o'clock that afternoon. Here then was the zero hour.

* 7 December in the United States, east of the International Date Line (Ed.).

The Japanese note was little more than an insult. It said that our proposal 'ignores Japan's sacrifices in the four years of the China affair, menaces the Empire's existence itself, and disparages its honour and prestige'. It accused us of conspiring with Great Britain and other countries 'to obstruct Japan's efforts towards the establishment of peace through the creation of a new order in East Asia'. It concluded by saying that, in view of the attitude of the American Government, the Japanese Government considered it impossible to reach an agreement through further negotiations.

The note did not declare war. Neither did it break off diplomatic relations. Japan struck without such preliminaries.

Towards noon Ambassador Nomura telephoned my office to ask for an appointment with me at one o'clock for himself and Kurusu. I granted his request.

A few minutes after one, Nomura telephoned again to ask that the appointment be postponed until 1.45 p.m. I agreed.

The Japanese envoys arrived at the Department at 2.05, and went to the diplomatic waiting room. At almost that moment the President telephoned me from the White House. His voice was steady but clipped.

He said, 'There's a report that the Japanese have attacked Pearl Harbor.'

'Has the report been confirmed?' I asked.

He said, 'No.'

While each of us indicated his belief that the report was probably true, I suggested that he have it confirmed, having in mind my appointment with the Japanese Ambassadors.

As I thought it over, I decided that, since the President's report had not been confirmed and there was one chance out of a hundred that it was not true, I would receive the envoys.

Nomura and Kurusu came into my office at 2.20. I received them coldly and did not ask them to sit down.

Nomura diffidently said he had been instructed by his Government to deliver a document to me at one o'clock, but that difficulty in decoding the message had delayed him. He then handed me his Government's note.

I asked him why he had specified one o'clock in his request for an interview.

He replied that he did not know, but that was his instruction.

I made a pretence of glancing through the note. I knew its contents already but naturally could give no indication of this fact.

After reading two or three pages, I asked Nomura whether he had presented the document under instructions from his Government.

He replied that he had.

When I finished skimming the pages, I turned to Nomura and put my eye on him.

'I must say,' I said, 'that in all my conversations with you during the last nine months I have never uttered one word of untruth. This is borne out absolutely by the record. In all my fifty years of public service I have never seen a document that was more crowded with infamous falsehoods and distortions—infamous falsehoods and distortions on a scale so huge that I never imagined until to-day that any Government on this planet was capable of uttering them.'

Nomura seemed about to say something. His face was impassive, but I felt he was under great emotional strain. I stopped him with a motion of my hand. I nodded towards the door. The Ambassadors turned without a word and walked out, their heads down.

Nomura's last meeting with me was in keeping with the ineptitude that had marked his handling of the discussions from the beginning. His Government's intention, in instructing him to ask for the meeting at one o'clock, had been to give us their note a few minutes in advance of the attack on Pearl Harbor. Nomura's Embassy had bungled this by its delay in decoding. Nevertheless, knowing the importance of a deadline set for a specific hour, Nomura should have come to see me precisely at one o'clock, even though he had in his hand only the first few lines of his note, leaving instructions with the Embassy to bring him the remainder as it became ready.

It was therefore without warning that the Japanese struck at Pearl Harbor, more than an hour before Nomura and Kurusu delivered their note.

Cordell Hull, U.S. Secretary of State

Radar, a British invention, was being slowly developed by the Americans. They had a set at Pearl Harbor, exercise upon which was regarded as largely academic.

Thirty miles away at the Opana Station, Private Lockard had started to close down the radar set. Private Elliott protested. Although the 'problem' was over, their relief had not come. Elliott wanted instruction in the operation of this fascinating gadget; why not keep it going and give him a chance to work it? Lockard consented, and Elliott sat down at the oscilloscope. Almost immediately there sprang up out of the dancing line of light a 'blip' so big as to suggest that the machine must be out of order. Lockard displaced Elliott, tested the controls, found nothing wrong. There was the 'blip' still shimmering before them, telling them that there was something out there bigger than they had ever picked up before and far beyond the greatest range at which they had ever previously got an indication. Bearing three degrees east of north, it was 137 miles away; and though the radar of that time afforded no means of telling just what it was, it looked like a lot of aircraft, perhaps as many as fifty or more.

Elliott was pretty excited about it. This was the best thing their new radar had done yet, and he wanted to send in a report. Lockard told him, in effect, not to be silly; the exercise was over and it was no more of their business. But Elliott insisted. Entertaining a grossly exaggerated idea of the real capabilities of the Information Center, he thought that this might be a bunch of Navy planes about which the Army knew nothing, and that if the report went in it might give Army a chance for a nice bit of practice in the technique of interception. Lockard finally told him to go ahead if he wanted to. The 'blip' had been obediently recording the approach of the planes; they had come down to 132 miles and were still advancing at a fair speed. The direct telephone lines to the plotting board had been shut down by that time, but Elliott called the Center over the service line used for routine business. The operator said there was nobody there. But Elliott continued to insist, and the note of excitement in his voice bestirred the operator to say that he would find the officer and get him to call back. Violating orders, the operator left the switchboard to hunt up the lieutenant. Tyler called back. Lockard, answering the telephone, reported the news. It was all more or less incomprehensible to Tyler. Whatever these guys at Opana were seeing in their oscilloscope, Tyler had no means of knowing what it was. It might be anything. It might be a flight of Navy planes off a carrier. It might be . . . another flight of B-17s from the mainland. Probably was. Tyler told Opana to forget it, hung up, and stepped out into the fresh morning air. It was then about 7.20 a.m., just as the Navy was beginning to be really aroused over the submarine contact. Tyler found the morning pleasant, but with a good deal of low-hanging cloud, especially over the mountains.

Though snubbed from headquarters, Lockard and Elliott still thought they had made quite an interception, and continued to plot the advancing planes until, at about twenty miles out, the latter entered the 'dead space' of the machine and the 'blip' broke up among the echoes from the neighbouring heights. The two privates then secured the set and made a copy of their record to show their commanding officer. About 7.45 their relief appeared. Lockard and Elliott climbed into the car, made their way down the wood road to the highway, and set off for their barracks some nine miles away. As they tooled cheerfully along, they saw one of the trucks of their own Aircraft Warning company tearing up the road towards them. It appeared to have the accelerator on the floorboards; it was filled with their comrades from the company, and the men were apparently provided with full battle equipment. Lockard and Elliott honked politely. The truck thundered past without response. Lockard and Elliott thought it rather strange.

The first plane, a dive bomber, streaked in low over Pearl Harbor at 7.55 a.m., coming in from the south with its consorts close behind it. Two reconnaissance float planes had been catapulted from the Japanese cruisers before them, but if they reached Oahu they were not observed. The first wave of the main body, 189 aircraft in all, had been flown off the carrier decks at 6.00 a.m., Hawaiian time. As they sighted the north point of Oahu, at ten minutes before eight, they split up. In accordance with sound air warfare doctrine, the first objective was the American defensive aviation. One dive bomber unit, swerving only a little to the right, went in from the north over the ranked and helpless Army fighters on Wheeler Field. Another, swinging wide around the west coast of the island, came up from the south against the Army bombers on Hickam Field and the Navy PBYs on Ford Island. Immediately behind these were forty torpedo bombers, launching their deadly missiles from a low altitude at the 'sitting ducks' in Battleship Row. Fifty horizontal bombers were on the heels of the torpedo planes, in case the first should fail against nets or baffles; and after them all there came forty-five fighters, to put down any opposition which might get into the air or, failing that, to polish off the remains at Wheeler and Hickam, at Ford Island, Kaneohe and the Marine base at Ewa.

The whole of this massive force was flung within the space of a few minutes at virtually every prominent naval and air installation on Oahu. The Japanese pilots knew that an hour behind them a second wave of 171 aircraft—fifty-four horizontal bombers, eighty-one dive bombers, and thirty-six fighters—was on its way in support. But most of the damage was done within the first quarter of an hour. The Ford Island air station and the twenty-nine PBY patrol planes parked there was a shambles within a few minutes, the planes blazing and exploding. This one attack finished Ford Island, and the Japanese did not return. The Marine field at Ewa, to the westward, was worked over more methodically with dive bombing and strafing; and at the end of a rather leisurely fifteen minutes all the forty-nine planes there—fighters, scout bombers and utility types—had either been totally destroyed or put out of action. At Kaneohe, the Navy patrol base on the east coast, there were two principal attacks, one at 7.55 and the second about twenty-five minutes later. Of the thirty-three PBYs there, most of them moored out in the bay, twenty-seven had been destroyed by the end of the attack and the remainder put out of commission. Save for the seven PBYs which were out on local patrol or manœuvres when the attack began, the Navy and Marine Corps did not get a single plane into the air from Oahu during the action.

At just about eight o'clock twenty-five Japanese dive bombers roared low—not more than fifty or seventy-five feet from the ground—over the long lines of parked fighter planes on the Army's main fighter base at Wheeler Field, in the centre of the island. The bursting bombs, the rattle of the enemy machineguns, and the red ball insignia on the wings were the first intimation of war that anyone had at Wheeler. In a few moments the parked aircraft, many with their fuel tanks filled, were blazing; great clouds of oily smoke were rolling up on the still air to obscure everything and hamper the frantic efforts to pull the planes apart and get them armed. They managed to put six operable fighters into the air by 8.30 and a couple more just before the Japanese returned, in lesser strength, around nine, while another half-dozen or so got up in the final minutes of the action. But that was the extent of Wheeler's contribution to the defence. Forty-two planes were totally destroyed at Wheeler; and out of the 126 modern or fairly modern fighters on the field at the start, only forty-three were listed as in commission afterwards.

Hickam Field, like Ford Island, was a shambles within the first five minutes, and repeated attacks thereafter did a pretty thorough job. But since most of the planes there were the obsolete B-18 bombers, it did not matter so much. Of Short's twelve B-17s, as luck would have it, four were still serviceable after the attack and only four were destroyed. The Japanese had given a low priority to Bellows Field, across the island next to Kaneohe, and it was not until 8.30 that a single enemy plane made one ineffective pass at the parked aircraft of the fighter squadron which was there for gunnery practice. But although they were thus warned, the planes were without fuel or ammunition and it took time to ready them. It was not until about nine that they were taxi-ing for a take-off; and just as that moment seven Japanese appeared. Two American fighters got into the air, but were shot down as they did so. One pilot was saved, but that ended Bellows' contribution.

Meanwhile, two American air elements had flown, utterly unsuspecting, into the middle of the action. At dawn Admiral Halsey, returning from Wake Island with the *Enterprise* task force, was some two hundred miles west of Pearl. He flew off a squadron of scout bombers to perform the usual patrol ahead of the ships, but with orders to continue on in and land at Ewa. One pilot, on the extreme left wing of the patrol, was heard suddenly speaking over the voice radio circuit: 'Don't shoot, this is an American plane!' and was never heard from again. Another, seeing the sky over Pearl filled with anti-aircraft bursts, wondered what crazy nonsense the Army was up to, holding anti-aircraft drills on a Sunday. When the truth dawned on him, he could not clear his machine-gun; the plane, however, managed to land. In all, seven planes of this squadron were shot down; eight of the fourteen men in them were killed and others wounded. The eleven B-17s from the mainland, though completely unarmed, had better fortune. One, trying to get into Bellows, was hit, set on fire, and destroyed just as she landed, but most of the crew were saved. Six managed to land amid the wreckage at Hickam; one landed at Wheeler, one on a golf course, and two got into the Haleiwa air-strip.

The Japanese missed only one of all our air elements—the fighter squadron at Haleiwa, about which the enemy apparently knew nothing. They were like-wise unready, but the commander, Major George S. Welsh, got into the air with one wing man about 8.15 and three more pilots got up later. Major Welsh claimed four Japanese; and the others, together with the fighters which took off from Wheeler and the *Enterprise* scout bombers, got a number more. But the net result was that in the first fifteen minutes of the action the Japanese had successfully destroyed or paralyzed virtually the entire air strength of Oahu. In the same space of time they had gone far towards the accomplishment of their main objective, the destruction of the United States Pacific Fleet.

Seven of Kimmel's eight battleships were moored along the south-easterly face of Ford Island, at big concrete bollards or mooring posts set just off the shore line. *California* was at the southern end of the row, then the tanker *Neosho*, full of aviation fuel, then *Maryland* and *Oklahoma* side by side with *Oklahoma* outboard, then *Tennessee* and *West Virginia* with the latter outboard, then *Arizona* with the repair ship *Vestal* outboard of her, then *Nevada* alone. *Pennsylvania*, the eighth battleship, was in the big dry dock at the Navy Yard across the channel, together with a couple of destroyers ahead of her in the same dock. Several cruisers were in relative security in the Navy Yard slips; but the modern light cruiser *Helena* was moored at '10-10 Dock', the long quay parallel-ing the channel on the eastern side, with the old converted minelayer *Oglala* outboard of her. Around on the north-westerly side of Ford Island there was another row of four ships lying at bollards. In order from the north end these were the light cruiser *Detroit*, the light cruiser *Raleigh*, the old battleship *Utah* converted into a target ship, and the seaplane tender *Tangier*. Most of the des-troyers were anchored in nests in the broad basin of East Loch, north of Ford Island, and the submarines were in slips at their base.

Over this great fleet the forty Japanese torpedo bombers broke like a storm just before eight o'clock. They came from every direction, each pilot carefully briefed on the particular angle from which to launch his torpedo in order to get the best run and cause the maximum confusion in the defence. Taking the gunners by complete surprise, they were almost impossible to hit; in a few moments the harbour was crisscrossed by the white wakes of their missiles, and tremendous explosions were leaping up against the steel sides of the battleships. The horizontal and dive bombers were immediately behind them; and the bombs were landing even as the torpedoes went home. Every one of the five outboard battleships took one or more torpedo hits in the first few minutes, and the two inboard ships, *Maryland* and *Tennessee*, were hit by bombs. Other torpedo planes and bombers were at the same time attacking the ships moored along the north-west face of the island. The old target ship *Utah*, lying in a berth often used by the aircraft-carriers, took two torpedoes, turned over, and sank at 8.13, the first total casualty. The light cruiser *Raleigh*, lying just ahead of her, received one torpedo and later a bomb hit, and only heroic measures kept her from turning turtle.

In Battleship Row, the repair ship *Vestal*, lying alongside of *Arizona*, had afforded the latter slight protection. Two torpedoes streaked past the smaller vessel to reach the battleship,* while a heavy armour-piercing bomb found its way to *Arizona*'s forward magazine, and she blew up with a terrific detonation. The whole forward half of the ship was a total wreck, through which tremendous oil fires now poured up their flames and great billows of smoke. Just south of her *West Virginia* had taken four or five torpedo and bomb hits. Enormous rents had been torn in her plating; there was a fierce fire amidships, and she was settling now to the bottom, fortunately on an even keel. *Tennessee*, lying inboard, was not too badly damaged; but she was pinned against the bollards by the sinking *West Virginia* and was imperilled by the oil fires raging in the *Arizona* and across the water between them. South of this pair, the old *Oklahoma*, lying outboard of *Maryland*, had received four torpedo hits in the first minutes; she was soon listing extravagantly, and at 8.32 she rolled completely over and lay, like an immense whale, with her bottom and propellers showing to the now densely smoke-filled sky.

Meanwhile, a single torpedo plane, streaking in from the west, had loosed its 'fish' against 10-10 Dock; passing under *Oglala*, the torpedo exploded against the bottom of *Helena*, lying inboard of the old minelayer. The light cruiser was severely damaged, but *Oglala* had her whole side stove in. Tugs dragged her away from *Helena* in time, but presently she went over, sinking on her beam ends. Across from 10-10 Dock the battleship *California*, alone at the southern end of the row, had taken two torpedoes and bomb hits; there were fires in her; the fact that her compartments had been open hindered damage control, and she was slowly settling at her moorings.

All this had been accomplished in the first half-hour of the attack, and most of it in the first ten or fifteen minutes. The torpedo planes, their missiles expended, faded away. There were still horizontal and dive bombers ranging unhindered over the scene.

Walter Millis

President Roosevelt to Congress: 8 December

Yesterday, 7 December 1941—a date which will live in infamy—the United States of America was suddenly and deliberately attacked by naval and air forces of the Empire of Japan.

---

* This is uncertain. Later investigation was to throw doubt on the question of whether *Arizona* was torpedoed, but it was so reported at the time.

Imperial Rescript: the 8th day of the 12th month of the 16th year of Showa

We, by the grace of heaven, Emperor of Japan, seated on the Throne of a line unbroken for ages eternal, enjoin upon ye, Our loyal and brave subjects:

We hereby declare war on the United States of America and the British Empire. The men and officers of Our Army and Navy shall do their utmost in prosecuting the war, Our public servants of various departments shall perform faithfully and diligently their appointed tasks, and all other subjects of Ours shall pursue their respective duties; the entire nation with a united will shall mobilize their total strength so that nothing will miscarry in the attainment of our war aims.

Fascists Jubilant

A night telephone call from Ribbentrop. He is over-joyed about the Japanese attack on America. He is so happy about it that I am happy with him, though I am not too sure about the final advantages of what has happened. One thing is now certain; that America will enter the conflict, and that the conflict will be so long that she will be able to release all her potential forces. This morning I told this to the King, who had been pleased about the event. He ended by admitting that, in the long run, I may be right. Mussolini was happy, too. For a long time he has favoured a definite clarification of relations between America and the Axis.

Count Ciano

I Shall Never Look Back

All of Japan went to war singing this song. Roughly translated, *Umi Yukaba* goes:

> Across the sea,
> Corpses in the water;
> Across the mountain,
> Corpses heaped upon the field;
> I shall die only for the Emperor,
> I shall never look back.

Tokyo

A train passes under the viaduct, and the first travellers appear at the gates of the station. Hearing the jingling of his bell, they flock round the newsvendor, hand over their pennies and seize the paper. It is a very small sheet, almost like a pamphlet. The amazing news item figures there alone, in a few vertical lines in thick Japanese characters. 'From to-day at dawn the Imperial Army and Navy are at war with the forces of the United States and Great Britain in the waters of the Western Pacific.'

I watch the reactions of the people who read it. They walk on for two or three steps, then they stop suddenly in order to read it again, bend their heads and start back. Then they raise their faces that have once again become expressionless, transformed into the mask of apparent indifference. Nobody says a word to the newsvendor, none of the readers exchange a remark with each other. . . . I know them well enough to understand their reactions; under their assumed impassivity they can barely control their stupefaction and consternation. They wanted this war and yet they did not want it. They talked about it all the time, out of bravado and in imitation of their leaders, but they never really believed in it. . . . Tokyo is afraid, the Japanese are panic-stricken by their own daring.

Robert Guillain

13

DEFEAT IN THE FAR EAST

MALAYA

On the same day that Pearl Harbor was attacked, Japanese forces landed in Thailand and upon the north-east coast of Malaya. Thailand ceased resistance and allowed the passage of Japanese troops twenty-four hours later. On 8 December 1941 began the Japanese attack upon Hong Kong, which held out for seventeen days. In seventy days, the Japanese were to advance the length of the Malaya peninsula.

PEARL HARBOR was the opening note in what became one of the great clashes of peoples and principles. Singapore was the full-struck chord.

George Weller, war correspondent

A Correspondent Cables to America: 7 December

Strong indications Japanese are moving up ships and troops to launch an imminent attack with landing parties against Thailand with immediate objectives of capturing Bangkok. Reconnaissance by American-made Catalinas and Hudson bombers discovered units of Japanese Navy, including cruisers and merchant ships believed containing troops, are now steaming down the Gulf of Siam along the Indo-China coast in the direction of Thailand. . . .

War Comes to Singapore

The war began with a bang.

Maria and I lived on the top of the highest building in Singapore, the Cathay Building, which also housed the offices of the Malayan Broadcasting Corporation and the Far Eastern headquarters of the Ministries of Information and Economic Warfare. We had gone to bed early. Suddenly, shortly after four in the morning, the first siren began to wail. Rising and falling, rising and falling, it cut across the stillness of the tropic night like some frightful oath uttered in a polite drawing-room. One after the other the sirens from different parts of the city chimed in until they formed one shrill cacophony. If it was eerie for the white people, what chill fear that sound must have struck into the breasts of hundreds of thousands of poor natives in their ramshackle houses of brick and timber! I leapt out of bed and pulled back the curtain. With complete certainty I knew that it was war. A ring of searchlights from their positions round the islands were focused straight up into the air, moving backwards and forwards, trying to spot the planes that had caused the alarm. The black-out was not at all good and all the street lights were burning. Suddenly there were bright flashes and loud explosions in the direction of the docks and the centre of the town. The anti-aircraft guns were firing. From where we watched there were no planes visible, although we could hear the drone of bombers, that low vibration

288

that one *feels* as much as hears. Then some bombs fell down in the same quarter where the guns had been firing, not many, but they made a deeper rumbling sound quite disinct from the loud report of the guns. Then silence. The drone gradually died away. The searchlights continued their search for the raiders. The lights in the streets still shone brightly. One or two cars with dimmed lights sped through the streets. The voices of air-raid wardens, bustling about their duties, drifted up from below. One by one the searchlights were switched off. A long time later the all-clear sounded.

Ian Morrison, war correspondent

From the very beginning of the Malayan campaign, the pattern was set: Japanese troops, trained and equipped for jungle fighting, infiltrated, outflanked and attacked from the rear their road-bound, ill-prepared opponents, cutting them off or forcing them to withdraw hurriedly to avoid that fate.

The First Retreat

We were all so busy that we often failed to remember—though we knew we were working against time—that time would soon be up; but the signs had become pretty obvious. R.A.F. Buffaloes at Alor Star had for days been trying to chase away a Japanese plane that came over regularly to photograph our poor old Jitra Line: Thais on the border were becoming stricter in their train searches; we had news that Sikh agitators had crossed the frontier with orders to contact Sikh troops in Malaya. Even so it came as something of a shock—perhaps a shock of relief—when news came through in the early morning of 8 December that a Japanese convoy was off Kota Bahru, on the west coast, and was being engaged by our planes and artillery. We gave a cheer for 'our artillery', knowing that it consisted solely of four guns of our detached 21st Mountain Battery. Plan Matador was still on (we were to advance into Thailand and get as far as Singgora at least) and we moved out to the railway station long before dawn. But by ten o'clock that morning—in the meantime we had sat passively watching Alor Star aerodrome being bombed—the plan was altered and we were ordered into defensive positions on the road. That night and most of the next day we spent in one of our well-known and well-prepared gun positions, about six miles from the frontier. 1st/14th Punjab Regiment, under Lieutenant-Colonel Fitzpatrick, were the advance guard and the four guns of 4th Mountain Battery were to support them as they fell back, gracefully and gradually we hoped, on to the Jitra Line. An ambush party, consisting mainly of Bren carriers from 1st/8th Punjab, rattled past us into Thailand during the night. It returned in the morning, reporting only partial success. Someone had committed the original military sin of firing before he got the order.

By tea-time on 9 December we had managed to make our gun position fairly comfortable, and the gunners, who were convinced that the Japanese were a most *mamouli* enemy, were quite impatient for their arrival. At five o'clock I had sudden and unexpected orders to take my Sikh section and its two guns to a position from which I could fire on a road demolition that had been made just inside Thailand. Once again we went through the motions of going out of action and proceeding up the road; but this was the last time we ever travelled it in a

northward direction. By 5.30 we were in position near the 27th milestone. So
much for the completeness of our preparations—not only had we never surveyed
this position—we had never even seen it. We surveyed it just before dark. We
were under cover of a small Chinese village, which stank with rare violence—
even for a Chinese village—and contained more mosquitoes to the cubic inch of
heated air than I met with in any other place in Malaya.

Soon after midnight came the sound of light machine-gun fire from the
front and Lieutenant R. M. Hare of the O.P. told us to open up on the demolition. He called me to the phone to say that the first shell fired into Thailand had
landed smack in the middle of the road. Jemadar Jogindar Singh, when I told
him, smiled politely and asked in a slightly injured tone whether I had had any
doubts about it.

For two hours or so we fired at regular intervals on the demolition. The
mosquitoes clustered upon us gratefully; a *naik* off duty snored under the muzzle
of No. 1 gun; it was all very peaceful. We finished our firing task and the quiet
was disturbed only by nightjars and cicadas and very infrequent small-arms fire.
Suddenly a burst of light machine-gun fire came from the left and behind us; it
was followed by another and another. Orders came through; we were to pull out
and return to the old position; we had better hurry, the Japs were nearly round
us. It was a pattern we got to know far too well in the next couple of months.
Three nights later the Japanese were through the Jitra Line and we were south
of Alor Star and had seen the last of the road. The sorry trek to Singapore
was on and three months of preparation had been proved futile in three days.

Rawle Knox

Disaster at Sea

On 10 December two of the finest battleships in the British Navy, H.M.S.
Prince of Wales *and H.M.S.* Repulse, *sailed from Singapore accompanied by four
destroyers to seek and destroy enemy landing barges coming down the east coast.
Admiral Phillips wore his pennant on the* Prince of Wales.

The landings carried out on the east coast of the Malay peninsula at dawn
on 7 December were mostly successful except at Kota Bharu. On this day our
reconnaissance planes had reported two British battleships at anchor in Singapore. At 3.15 p.m. the next day two battleships were sighted by I.165 at a point
three hundred miles north of Singapore. She recognized them as the *Prince of
Wales* and *Repulse*. The ships were proceeding northwards at high speed; their
target was the supply line of our landings. Although they were clearly visible,
they were out of torpedo range, but Commander Harada, I.165's captain, sent
off a cipher message giving course and bearings. It duly reached the Malayan
operational H.Q., and all submarines in the area surfaced and immediately took
up the pursuit at speed.* The entire Malayan naval force, consisting of the

* H.M.S. *Prince of Wales* and *Repulse* were sighted by a Japanese submarine at 2 p.m., 9
December 1941, in position 7° N. latitude, 105° E. longitude, steering north. (This position was
very inaccurate.)

At 3.15 a.m., 10 December, the Japanese received a report from a second submarine which
indicated that the British squadron was steering south. Bad weather precluded any form of air
search on 9 December.

battleships *Kongo* and *Haruna,* together with the cruiser squadron and destroyer squadron under the command of Vice-Admiral Nobutake Kondo, was not really a match for the opponents, but our ships forged ahead with all speed in the hope of forcing a night action, in which was their best chance of achieving good results. However, contact with the enemy was lost in the dark night. At 3.40 a.m. on 10 December, I.156 attacked the ships on a southerly course in a position slightly to the westward of the original sighting, but missed in the darkness. At dawn the air units, keyed up with the news from Pearl Harbor, joined in their search for the enemy.

Mochitsura Hashimoto

Reporter on *Repulse*

Wednesday, 10 December

06.30—We are putting on cover-alls, anti-flash helmets and battle helmets. Off to the beam the sky is streaked with gold. All the gun crews are at the action stations. Gallagher and I went down for breakfast of coffee, cold ham, bread and marmalade.

07.20—Back on the flag deck. We are pushing in towards shore very fast. The *Prince of Wales* is ahead; we follow; the destroyers are about a mile or a mile and a half on each side of us. We still have four of them. We can see the shore line and an island far ahead of us.

10.45—One twin-engined Jap is reported shadowing us. It is the same type that bombed Singapore the first night of the war. It is a type 96 Mitsubishi of the Naval Air Service.

The clouds have gone now, and the sky is a robin's-egg blue and the sun is bright yellow. Our ships plough through pea-green water, white where the hulls cleave it.

11.07—The communications loudspeaker announces: 'Enemy aircraft approaching—action stations!'

I see them: one—two—three—four—five—six—seven—eight—nine. There are nine, flying line astern, one behind the other.

I would judge them about twelve thousand feet, coming straight over the *Repulse*.

11.14—And here they come.

11.15—The guns of the *Prince of Wales* just let go. At the same instant I see the flame belching from the guns of the *Wales,* ours break into a chattering, ear-splitting roar. The nine Japanese aircraft were stretched out across the bright blue, cloudless sky like star sapphires of a necklace.

I gape open-mouthed at those aircraft coming directly over us, flying so that they will pass from bow to stern over the *Repulse.* The sky is filled with black puffs from our ack-ack. They seem a discordant profanation of that beautiful sky. But the formation of Japanese planes, coming over one behind the other, is undisturbed.

Now they are directly overhead. For the first time I see the bombs coming down, materializing suddenly out of nothingness and streaming towards us like ever-enlarging tear-drops. There's a magnetic, hypnotic, limb-freezing fascination in that sight.

It never occurs to me to try and duck or run. Open-mouthed and rooted, I watch the bombs getting larger and larger. Suddenly, ten yards from me, out in the water, a huge geyser springs out of the sea, and over the side, showering water over me and my camera.

I instinctively hunch over, sort of a semi-crouch, and at the same instant there is a dull thud. The whole ship shudders. Pieces of paint fall from the deck over the flag deck.

11.17—'Fire on the boat deck. Fire below!' That just came over the loudspeakers. There are fountains of water all around the ship. Some are near misses. Most of the bombs are hitting the water ten to thirty yards off the port side. Beautiful fountains of thick white at the base and then tapering up into fine spray.

That first bomb was a direct hit. Someone on the flag deck says, 'Fire in marines' mess and hangar.'

That bomb struck the catapult deck, penetrated, exploded underneath. The bomb hit twenty yards astern of my position on the flat deck. A number of men [fifty] were killed.

11.45–. . . The torpedo-carrying bombers are coming in. We are putting up a beautiful barrage, a wall of fire. But the bombers come on, in a long glide, from all angles, not simultaneously but alternately. Some come head-on, some astern and from all positions on both sides of the ship. They level out.

About three hundred yards distant from the ship and a hundred yards above the water they drop their torpedoes.

The torpedoes seem small, dropping flat into the water, sending up splashes, then streaking towards us. Those bombers are so close you can almost see the colour of the pilot's eyes. The bombers are machine-gunning our decks as they come in.

11.51½—Captain Tennant is sending a message to the *Wales*: 'Have you sustained any damage?'

The answer comes back: 'We are out of control. Steering gear is gone.'

The decks of the *Repulse* are littered with empty shell-cases. Upon the faces of the sailors there's a mixture of incredulity and a sort of sensuous pleasure, but I don't detect fear. There's an ecstatic happiness, but strangely, I don't see anything approaching hate for the attackers. For the British this is a contest. The facial expression is interpreted by an officer. He turns to me and says, 'Plucky blokes, those Japs. That was as beautiful an attack as ever I expect to see.'

Cecil Brown, war correspondent

The End

A new wave of planes appeared at 12.20 p.m. The end was near, though we did not know it. *Prince of Wales* lay about ten cables astern of our port side. She was helpless. Not only was her steering-gear destroyed, but also her screws by that first torpedo. Unlike the German *Bismarck* caught by the Navy in the Atlantic, which lost only her steering-gear and was able to keep moving in a circle, *Prince of Wales* was a hulk.

All the aircraft made for her. I do not know how many there were in this last attack, but it was afterwards estimated that there were between fifty and eighty Japanese torpedo-bombers in operation during the entire action. *Prince of Wales* fought desperately to beat off the determined killers who attacked her like a pack of dogs on a wounded buck. *Repulse* and the destroyers formed a rough circle around her, to add our fire-power. All ships fired with the intention of protecting *Prince of Wales*, and in doing so each neglected her own defences.

It was difficult to make out her outline through the smoke and flame from all her guns except the 14-inchers. I saw one plane drop a torpedo. It fell nose-heavy into the sea and churned up a thin wake as it drove straight at the immobile *Prince of Wales*. It exploded against her bows. A couple of seconds later another hit her—and another.

I gazed at her turning slowly over on her port side, her stern going under, and dots of men jumping into the sea, and was thrown against the bulkhead by a tremendous shock as *Repulse* was hit by a torpedo on her port side.

O. D. Gallagher, war correspondent

The torpedo strikes the ship about twenty yards astern of my position. It feels as though the ship has crashed into dock. I am thrown four feet across the deck but I keep my feet. Almost immediately, it seems, the ship lists.

The command roars out of the loudspeaker, 'Blow up your life belts!'

I take down mine from the shelf. It is a blue-serge affair with a rubber bladder inside. I tie one of the cords around my waist and start to bring another cord up around the neck. Just as I start to tie it the command comes, 'All possible men to starboard.'

Captain Tennant's voice is coming over the ship's loudspeaker, a cool voice: 'All hands on deck. Prepare to abandon ship.' There is a pause for just an instant, then: 'God be with you.'

There is no alarm, no confusion, no panic. We on the flag deck move towards a companionway leading to the quarter deck. Abrahams, the Admiralty photographer, Gallagher and I are together. The coolness of everyone is incredible. There is no pushing, but no pausing either. One youngster seems in a great hurry. He tries to edge his way into the line at the top of the companionway to get down faster to the quarter deck.

A young sub-lieutenant taps him on the shoulder and says quietly, 'Now, now, we are all going the same way, too.'

The youngster immediately gets hold of himself.

The *Repulse* is going down.

The torpedo-smashed *Prince of Wales*, still a half to three-quarters of a mile ahead, is low in the water, half shrouded in smoke, a destroyer by her side.

Japanese bombers are still winging around like vultures, still attacking the *Wales*. A few of those shot down are bright splotches of burning orange on the blue South China Sea.

Men are tossing overboard rafts, lifebelts, benches, pieces of wood, anything that will float. Standing at the edge of the ship, I see one man (Midshipman Peter Gillis, an eighteen-year-old Australian from Sydney) dive from the air defence control tower at the top of the main mast. He dives a hundred and seventy feet and starts to swim away.

Men are jumping into the sea from the four or five defence control towers that segment the main mast like a series of ledges. One man misses his distance, dives, hits the side of the *Repulse*, breaks every bone in his body and crumples into the sea like a sack of wet cement. Another misses his direction and dives from one of the towers straight down the smokestack.

Men are running all along the deck of the ship to get further astern. The ship is lower in the water at the stern and their jump therefore will be shorter. Twelve Royal Marines run back too far, jump into the water and are sucked into the propeller.

The screws of the *Repulse* are still turning. There are five or six hundred heads bobbing in the water. The men are being swept astern because the *Repulse* is still making way and there's a strong tide here, too.

**Captain Tennant on the bridge turns to the navigating officer: 'It looks a bit different from this angle, doesn't it, pilot?'

The navigating officer nods, but says nothing. The group of officers on the bridge look at each other, and at the skipper.

'Well, gentlemen,' Captain Tennant says quietly, 'you had better get out of it now.'

'Aren't you coming with us, sir?' two or three eagerly demand simultaneously.

The Captain smiles, shakes his head negatively, then says impatiently, 'Off you go now. There's not much time.' They are all hanging on to something, one leg braced to keep an even keel as the ship heels over more and more.

'But, Captain,' the lieutenant commander says, 'you must come with us. You've done all you could for this ship. More than most men could.'

Captain Tennant does not budge. The men are getting restive. Almost by pre-arrangement they all move towards their skipper. They push him forcibly through the narrow doorway and on to the deck. The *Repulse* is almost on her beam-ends. Captain Tennant will go no farther. The officers and men of the bridge seize Captain Tennant and push him over the side. Then they jump into the sea.**

The jump is about twenty feet. The water is warm; it is not water, but thick oil. My first action is to look at my stop watch. It is smashed at 12.35, one hour and twenty minutes after the first Japanese bomb came through twelve thousand feet to crash into the catapult deck of the *Repulse*.

It doesn't occur to me to swim away from the ship until I see others striking out. Then I realize how difficult it is. The oil soaks into my clothes, weighting them and I think under-water demons are tugging at me, trying to drag me down. The airless lifebelt, absorbing oil too, tightens and tautens the preserver cords around my neck. I say to myself, 'I'm going to choke to death, I'm going to choke to death.'

The oil burns in my eyes as though someone is jabbing hot pokers into the eyes. That oil in the eyes is the worst thing. I've swallowed a bit of oil already, and it's beginning to sicken me.

** Cecil Brown wrote the passage between double asterisks from the accounts of eye-witness survivors.

Fifty feet from the ship, hardly swimming at all now, I see the bow of the *Repulse* swing straight into the air like a church steeple. Its red under-plates stand out as stark and as gruesome as the blood on the faces of the men around me. Then the tug and draw of the suction of thirty-two thousand tons of steel sliding to the bottom hits me. Something powerful, almost irresistible, snaps at my feet. It feels as though someone were trying to pull my legs out by the hip sockets. But I am more fortunate than some others. They are closer to the ship. They are sucked back.

When the *Repulse* goes down it sends over a huge wave, a wave of oil. I happen to have my mouth open and I take aboard considerable oil. That makes me terribly sick at the stomach.

After being picked up by one of the escorting destroyers:

Down there in the wardroom I am told the sequence of attacks on the *Prince of Wales*.

The attack was similar to our own. High-level bombers and torpedo-carrying bombers. With four torpedoes in the *Wales*, Admiral Phillips said, 'Tell the *Express* (which was then alongside the *Wales*) to signal to Singapore for tugs to tow us home.'

It was obvious the Admiral hadn't yet made up his mind that the ship was going to sink.

I ask a lieutenant-commander from the *Wales* about Admiral Phillips and Captain Leach.

They were last seen standing on the bridge of the *Prince of Wales*.

'The Admiral and the Captain stood there together,' the officer says. 'They would not go. As we started away, Captain Leach waved, and called out, "Good-bye. Thank you. Good luck. God bless you".'

Then the water rose up to meet them, meeting and then covering them.

Cecil Brown

I still remember the chill sense of calamity which was caused by the loss of these two ships. It was worse than calamity. It was calamity that had the premonitions of further calamity. No details were available that evening although most people had visions of Japanese suicide squads flying their loaded planes straight into the ships. For the first time we had an inkling of what the true balance of factors was in this Pacific war. We saw before us, still vaguely perhaps, that long dark tunnel through which we should have to pass before we emerged in the sunlight on the far side. Blown clean away at one fell swoop was one of the main pillars on which our sense of security rested.

Ian Morrison

On the same day that the Prince of Wales *and* Repulse *went down, the Japanese took Kota Bahru airfield, the most advanced striking base which the Allies possessed. Within a week they were within a very few miles of Penang, and the loss of the island was the first of many shocks to come in the land battle.*

Penang Bombed: 12 December

At least six hundred people were killed in this raid, and an equal number wounded. The correspondents in Singapore were allowed to say that the casualties numbered seventy. Penang was the first city to demonstrate the depths of Chinese courage and Malay stoicism. The Asiatics had refused to take cover, and were machine-gunned in the streets. The hospitals were filled with terribly wounded people; they were still bringing them in two days afterwards. Here sat a wrinkled old man, his body curled like a sea shell around his grandchild, the only living member of his son's family of eight. On Saturday they found an old woman, wounded and with both her legs broken. When they brought her to the hospital grounds and laid her on the bare floor—there were not nearly enough cots—she piped up, 'I'm not going to die yet. I'm going to live to see the Japs beaten.'

George Weller

Disposing of the Dead

It was horrible. We had to work with gas masks and stick bayonets into the bodies and pitch them into a truck. We didn't bury them but just poured some kerosene over them and charred the bodies a bit.

A volunteer

Doubt: 13 December

Raffles Hotel still has dancing every night, but there are not as many dancers. A good deal of the apathy about war has gone. In any event, it is true that the certainty that war would not come to Singapore has disappeared.

Cecil Brown

Realization: 18 December

The Japanese troops are now fourteen miles from Penang. This news came as a terrific shock to everyone in Singapore, and, as I understand it, throughout Malaya. People can hardly believe the Japs now have Alor Star and Sungei Patani. It was the first news they had that the Japanese had penetrated more than seventy-five miles from the Thai border. Up to now the people of Malaya thought that the Japs were being held almost at the frontier; instead they are well within Malaya and are about to take Penang.

. . . . The usual official communique came out this evening. It said, 'We have successfully disengaged the enemy and are south of the River Krain.'

I stared at that phrase—'successfully disengaged the enemy'. It made no sense to me and I mulled over it for minutes. Then it suddenly occurred to me that someone had coined a beautiful phrase of defeatist optimism. I rolled it around on my tongue—*successfully disengaged the enemy.*

It also meant to me that the British were south of Penang, since the River Krain is south of that island. . . .

. . . . Refugees are streaming into Singapore, and since the British refuse to admit the Penang débâcle, the people fear the worst. You can almost see morale collapsing like a punctured tyre.

Cecil Brown

The Invaders

The Japanese not only outfought us in Malaya—they out-thought us too. In everything they showed that they had devoted considerable care and study to the special requirements of a campaign taking place in the tropical jungle of the Malayan peninsula.

Thus they wore the lightest of uniforms, a singlet, cotton shorts, rubber-soled shoes. There was no uniformity about either the colour or the form of their dress. Both dress and equipment were as light as they could be, and all our commanders agreed that their cross-country capacity was remarkable. There was no uniformity about the headgear. Various types were worn, steel helmets, cotton khaki caps, slouch hats taken from prisoners or our own dead. Often they wore Malay sarongs. Two prisoners captured near Batu Pahat were disguised as Chinese coolies. This adoption of native dress troubled our troops, since the country through which the war was being fought was fairly thickly populated and our men were never able to distinguish between friend and foe. On my first trip to the front I heard innumerable 'fifth-column' stories. The British Tommy began to think that the entire native population was fighting against him. He could never be quite certain that the young Malay lolling on the far side of the road or the Tamil coolie just disappearing into a rubber plantation was not a Japanese in disguise.

The Asiatic appearance of the enemy was also an enormous advantage to him. It enabled him to masquerade as a native of the country. The British troops would not have been able to distinguish between Chinese, Japanese and Malays if they had been wearing their respective national dresses, let alone when they were all wearing sarongs.

In the matter of food also the Japanese were at an advantage. Being rice-eaters, they were able to live off the country, eating the same food as the Malays and the Chinese used to eat. The British troops were dependent upon elaborate catering arrangements. The Japanese soldier would set off through the jungle carrying a bottle of water and a large ball of rice, with some preserved seaweed and a few pickles to make the rice palatable. Those were his rations for three or four days.

Nearly all the Japanese infantry were armed with tommy-guns or other light automatic weapons. They were ideal for this close-range jungle fighting. Our men were armed chiefly with rifles and the percentage of automatic weapons was small. There were several bayonet engagements, a form of warfare for which the enemy seemed to have a marked distaste. Many of our officers continued to swear by the rifle right up to the end of the campaign, and there are sound arguments on both sides in the rifle-versus-tommy-gun controversy. But it always seemed to me that the rifle's chief use is as an accurate long-range weapon, and in Malaya there was rarely an extended field of fire. The advanced Japanese units would carry perhaps six or eight drums of ammunition with them and further supplies would be brought up in boxes on the carriers of push-bikes.

After the tommy-gun the next most popular weapon of the enemy was a light 2-inch mortar. Again, it was a weapon ideally suited to jungle warfare. It was very mobile and was easily transported and operated by two men. It was very accurate. The shell burst with a very loud report. There was also a 4-inch mortar which was seen mounted on armoured carriers. Except for the 2-inch mortar, Japanese artillery, until the siege of Singapore, played a comparatively small part in the fighting.

Hand-grenades were another weapon, extremely practicable in close fighting, of which the enemy made extensive use. Cases were reported in which Japanese climbed up trees and then tried to lob them down on to our vehicles.

Their local knowledge was excellent. They had good maps with them, and their guides were mostly former Japanese residents of Malaya whose job it had been to gain a detailed knowledge of the terrain.

They were fond of arboreal tactics and snipers would often climb up trees to shoot at our outposts. One of our casualties was shot in the foot while standing in a trench three feet deep. A British officer who went after a Japanese sniper reported to be concealed in a tree told me that he felt as if he was walking up to game at home.

One of the most conspicuous features of the campaign was the great use which the Japanese made of bicycles. They may have brought some with them from Japan, but most were simply commandeered from natives in the villages, possibly being paid for in the notes which the Japanese Army brought with them. (These notes were the same size, colour, and design as the British notes but said, 'The Japanese Government promises to pay the bearer on demand' the sum of ten dollars, fifty cents, or whatever the denomination was. These notes must have been printed long in advance of the outbreak of war, still further evidence of the care and thoroughness with which the Japanese planned their campaign in the Pacific. In the Philippines, in the Netherlands East Indies, in Burma, the Japanese Army brought their own specially printed notes with them.) Bicycles still further increased the mobility of the Japanese and enabled their forward troops to progress at great speed.

They made full use of the numerous rivers and 'crocodile-infested' streams up-country, sometimes using collapsible rubber boats, sometimes native craft commandeered or bought from the local inhabitants, sometimes native rafts made of bamboo poles lashed together with rattan. The Chinese sampans, capable of carrying forty men and their equipment, proved ideal for entering the mangrove swamps owing to their shallow draught. The first landings at Kota Bahru were made from specially constructed iron barges, brought overland from Singora. At a later date these barges were taken overland to the Straits of Johore and used in landings on the island.

It will be seen that the highest degree of mobility was the keynote of the enemy's equipment. The British forces were nothing like so mobile. One only had to see the British soldier on his way to the front, seemingly borne down with heavy boots, tin helmet, gas-mask, heavy pack, canvas webbing, rifle and bayonet, to sense that he lacked a certain freedom of movement. He had also been trained to be very dependent on his vehicular transport and this complicated, if it did not impede, movement. One used to see British troops seemingly immobilized by their own transport.

In their tactics the Japanese practised an extreme devolution of command. Small groups of men, even single individuals, would be told to make their way as best they could to a point on the map a number of miles ahead. It would be up to them to get there. They would set off through the jungle, quietly picking their way, sometimes lying concealed for hours. Arrived at the given point behind our lines they would re-form. Contact with their forces in the rear would be maintained by portable wireless apparatus. If they came up against one of our outposts they would attack it from the front, but, if the opposition were severe, would make no attempt to press home the frontal attack. Instead, they would creep round and attack it either from the flank or from the rear. Similarly, if our troops advanced, the enemy would simply melt into the jungle on each side and again attack from the flank. Such were the tactics employed by the Japanese not only against sections but against whole brigades and divisions. The landings on the west coast which later caused us so much trouble, when sometimes one or two thousand men would slip ashore under cover of darkness, were simply attempts to outflank our positions on a much larger scale.

These tactics were made possible by several things—by the Japanese superiority in numbers; by the fact that the terrain in Malaya favoured the attacker at every turn and hindered the defender; by the remarkable cross-country capacity of the Japanese infantryman who was the spearhead of the attack; by the enemy's superior local knowledge.

Ian Morrison

The Defenders: An Officer Speaks

It's like this. Before the war we would be working from a map to conduct our manœuvres. Our colonel or the brigadier would say, 'Now this is thick jungle here and this is mangrove swamp. We can rule this out. In this sector all we have to concern ourselves with is the main road.'

Thus we based our strategy on that type of operation. We kept to the roads everywhere. Why, I went through a mangrove swamp the other day and nowhere did I go down in the mud over my ankles. Anyhow, you can walk on the roots in almost any swamp and in that way avoid sinking down.

Japanese Propaganda

Not only did the Japanese drop bombs on Malaya; they also dropped leaflets by the thousand, in every language spoken in the peninsula, English, Malay, Chinese, Hindustani, Urdu, Gurmukhi. The leaflets were usually remarkable as much for the fatuity of their contents as for the incorrectness of the idiom in which they were couched. From a Japanese aircraft, flying so high that it was invisible to the naked eye, they would flutter down out of the sky on Singapore or on the towns up-country. I remember one in English purporting to be a newspaper extra and carrying a spurious Lisbon date-line, which declared that the United States had opened separate peace negotiations with Japan. Another, addressed to the officers and men of the British Army, asked, 'Why do you submit to the intolerable torture of malarial mosquitoes merely to pamper the British aristocrat? Do not dedicate your lives merely to fatten the British high-hat.' One addressed to the Indian troops would show a British officer sheltering in the rear while the Indians fought the enemy. One in Malay would contain a crude drawing of a fat white man with a whisky-glass in his hand treading a Malay underfoot, or a map of the Malayan peninsula with the Rising Sun flags all round it and the Union Jack flying only in the middle of the peninsula. One addressed to the Australians showed a blonde floozy tossing restlessly on her bed and crying out, 'Oh, Johnny, come back to me. I am so lonely without you.' One dropped on Singapore on Christmas Day had a drawing of what looked like several cavemen brandishing torches, with the legend underneath in Chinese and Malay—'Burn all the white devils in the sacred white flame of victory.' Bedrock in crudity was reached with a leaflet containing a reprint of a letter taken from the body of a dead Australian, written by his wife in Australia and giving him all the news about home and children. Pamphlets of this nature simply made the few white men who saw them feel that they were pitted against a brutal and barbaric foe. A pamphlet of another type, however, had a certain effect on the Asiatic population. One which fell on Singapore simply advised the native population to evacuate the city on a certain date. Fearing a terrific blitz on the date mentioned, a certain number of natives did evacuate, causing, if they were labourers or men engaged on essential services, still further complications in the problem of native labour. The day in question passed quite uneventfully, nor was the scale of Japanese air attacks noticeably intensified during the days following. Occasionally the natives received advance information whether there was going to be a raid that day or not, and the British staff at aerodromes would always prepare for a raid if they noticed any unusual movement on the part of the native inhabitants.

Ian Morrison

Japanese supremacy in the air was as obvious as their other advantages.

.... For the most part the night marches were our sorest trial. They were for us the reality of the Japanese superiority in the air. While the planes wheeled overhead we could not move without risk. We moved by night. We fought by day. In our impotence we watched the Japanese airmen searching for their target, coming closer to make doubly sure, then diving to the attack. There was a rattle of small-arms fire and somewhere behind the pump-pump of a Bofors, but always, it seemed, the planes soared away unharmed. Then one morning a squadron of British bombers skimmed low over the rubber trees and every man sprang up to cheer. False hopes! Within the week they had vanished from the fighting areas, and were not seen there any more.

Lieutenant C. A. R. Smallwood

Unless additional aircraft are supplied to the British forces in Malaya, Singapore stands in grave danger from the land advance. The wishful thinking and almost country-wide conviction among the military that the Japanese would back down as well as the underestimation of the Japanese strength plus the suddenness of the Japanese attack are responsible for the present situation.

There is throughout Singapore great criticism of the amazing unwillingness of the high command to inform the people what is going on. This method of treating Asiatics as well as Europeans as children who are unable to stand bad news is inevitably causing internal repercussions.

Cecil Brown

On 12 January 1942 Kuala Lumpur, second city of the peninsula, fell, but as the British and Commonwealth forces were inexorably driven southwards down the length of the Malay Peninsula their resistance became more effective in some places. The advancing Japanese did not always have things their own way.

Penang radio used to announce that 'Kuala Lumpur will be bombed to-morrow at eleven in the morning and five in the afternoon'. It usually was.

The Fall of Kuala Lumpur

On the outskirts of the city there were two or three high columns of black smoke—they had been a feature of Kuala Lumpur for several days past—as some remaining stocks of rubber were destroyed. We visited one such fire. The latex was burning fiercely, giving out such heat that one could not go within fifty yards, sending an enormous mushroom of inky smoke straight up into the air. The manager of this estate, an Australian who had been in Malaya for many years, had everything packed up in his car and was just about to leave for the south. The stocks of rice from the godown were being distributed to the Indian and Chinese labourers. Two Indian clerks were keeping a tally. It was quite orderly. Each labourer would have enough rice to keep him for at least two months. In the processing plant next door to the godown all the machinery had been smashed up.

. . . . The scene that met one's eyes in the city was fantastic. Civil authority had broken down. The European officials and residents had all evacuated. The white police officers had gone and most of the Indian and Malay constables had returned to their homes in the surrounding villages. There was looting in progress such as I have never seen before. Most of the big foreign department stores had already been whittled clean since the white personnel had gone. There was now a general sack of all shops and premises going on.

. . . . Radios, rolls of cloth, tins of preserved foods, furniture, telephones, carpets, golf-clubs, there was every conceivable object being fiercely fought for and taken away. One man had even brought an ox-cart into town and was loading it up in the main street outside Whiteaways. The most striking sight I saw was a young Tamil coolie, naked except for a green loincloth, who had had tremendous luck. He had found a long cylindrical tin, three inches in diameter and a foot long, well wrapped up. What could it contain? Obviously a tin like this could only contain some rare and luxurious Western delicacy. He sat on the kerbstone turning the tin round in his hands. He wished that he could read that Western language so that he might know what the tin contained. Should he open it now or should he wait until he got home? Curiosity got the better of him and he decided to open the tin. Carefully he peeled off the paper and took off the lid. Three white Slazenger tennis-balls rolled slowly out, bounced on the pavement and then trickled into the gutter, where they soon lost their speckless whiteness.

.... The only thing that was not being looted was booze. Several days previously the army had collected as much of the liquor in Kuala Lumpur as it could find. Tens of thousands of bottles and cases were amassed. When the time came for a move south, Local Defence Volunteers laid into the cases of gin and whisky and other intoxicants with sledge-hammers and destroyed them. It was a wise precaution.

.... Meanwhile the milling crowd of looters in the streets seemed to be becoming larger. Men were coming in from miles around to see what they could bag. Others were coming in for second and third trips. Only in some areas did the Chinese shopkeepers, with that toughness of fibre which is the secret of their country's greatness, arm themselves with long wooden staves and band together to protect their property from the ravages of would-be despoilers. Such were the last hours of the largest city on the Malayan mainland.

Ian Morrison

Fighting Back

It's difficult to find much optimism in these steady withdrawals. But it *is* noteworthy that British resistance shows signs of stiffening. This is due to the British forces becoming more concentrated, and to their increasing ability to fight the kind of jungle guerrilla warfare that the Japanese have found successful.

This does not mean that the Japanese drive to Singapore is being stopped. And the speed of the Japanese advance has decreased in the past few weeks. To many people here, it still seems rapid because the Japanese are about two hundred miles nearer to Singapore than they were when they crossed the Thai border into Malaya a month ago.

Cecil Brown

Australians in Ambush

He* resolved, in this opening engagement, to try and lead the Japanese into a trap. He chose a bridge on the main road a few miles north of Gemas. The bridge was prepared for demolition and a small group of men, upon whom would devolve the task of blowing it up, concealed themselves in the jungle near the bridge. One company took up positions in the jungle on each side of the road, and behind them were strung out the rest of the battalion. The scheme was to let the Japanese through and then fall upon them from each side of the road. The men took up their positions and were given four days' rations. Only two days' rations would have sufficed, for the Japanese appeared very much earlier than we thought.

They cannot have expected anything at all. They came marching along the road about four in the afternoon of 15 January in small groups, many of them wheeling bicycles. Several companies came over the bridge and walked down the road blissfully unaware that keen eyes were watching them from out of the jungle on each side. The officer in charge of blowing up the bridge decided at last that he had let enough Japanese over. He waited until there were as many actually on the bridge as he thought there were likely to be at any one moment and then released the fuse. There was a tremendous explosion. The Japanese on

---

* Major-General Gordon Bennett, commanding the Australians in Malaya (Ed.)

the bridge were blown sky-high. Bridge, bodies and bicycles went soaring up. The explosion was the signal for the battalion to fall upon the Japanese, which they did with loud yells. Rifles barked, tommy-guns sputtered, many of the Australians dashed in with their bayonets. Nearly all the Japanese who were on the hither side of the bridge were killed. Later it was estimated that between eight hundred and a thousand of the enemy were killed, while the Australians suffered less than a hundred killed and wounded. The Australians then fell back south of Segamat.

It was a triumphant beginning. It set all the Australians cock-a-hoop. It had a tonic effect on all the British forces. But more was still to come.

Foiled in their attempt to come straight down the main road, the Japanese did what they always did and tried to come round the side. They switched their main push from Gemas to the coast. Bennett astutely foresaw what the probable Japanese strategy would be and took appropriate measures.

Our line along the south bank of the Muar river was originally held by 45 Indian Brigade. It was a recently-formed unit, the men were raw and untrained, and they had only been in the country a few days. When the Japanese attacked in the Muar river sector two days later, the Indians failed to hold them. The fighting was severe and several of the senior white officers of the brigade were killed. There was great confusion. When the 45th finally extricated themselves from the mess, they were sent back to Singapore and played little further part in the fighting. In an effort to stabilize the situation in the Muar sector, Bennett had to divert, first the 19th Battalion, and then the 29th, in the direction of the coast. The Australian anti-tank gunners went with them and took up a position nine miles south of Muar on the coast road. Bennett suspected that the Japanese might try to use their tanks down this coast road. He read the enemy's intentions correctly.

The 19th Battalion established contact with the enemy south of Muar late on the afternoon of 17 January. Japanese units had filtered through the jungle. At dawn they launched an attack with tanks down the main road. They appear to have used only ten tanks, all of the medium type. Tank-traps had been constructed and two anti-tank guns, well concealed with thick foliage, were trained down the road, the first some distance ahead of the other. A point was chosen where the road ran through a cutting with banks on each side so that any tanks would have difficulty in turning there and would not be able to escape into the rubber plantations on each side. The tanks came rumbling down the road at dawn, each flying the pennant of the Rising Sun. The first gun allowed six tanks to pass down the road so that they could be dealt with by the gun in the rear, and it was actually the rear gun that was the first to go into action. The Australian gunners, tense with expectancy, waited until the leading tank was only fifty yards away. Then, with loud shouts of 'Whacko!' they let the Japanese have everything they'd got. The rear gun had a perfect field of fire. Five tanks were picked off, one after the other. They tried to turn round but could not do so in the cutting. Several caught fire and the ammunition inside them began to explode. The sixth tank was screened by the others and the gun could not sight it effectively, so one of the Australians picked up two hand-grenades, ran along the top of the cutting and threw them under the sixth tank, putting it out of action. Most of the Japanese crews were killed inside the tanks. A few scrambled out but were promptly picked off by rifle-fire. Meanwhile the forward gun, farther up the road, had let loose against the four remaining tanks, which were also close behind each other. They too were picked off, one after the other. In this second engagement a remarkable incident is reported to have occurred. I give it for what it is worth, although I was never able to obtain proper confirmation. A foreign officer in uniform was reported by two of the Australian gunners to have clambered out of one of the rearmost tanks, seized a bicycle that was affixed to the rear of the tank, and pedalled madly off up the road. If it was indeed a foreign officer, he could only have been one of the German military experts who had been advising the Japanese.

Ian Morrison

By 30 January the Malay Peninsula was lost. Less than two hundred survivors of the Argyll and Sutherland Highlanders marched across the Causeway on to Singapore Island with their pipers playing. They were the last; behind them the Causeway was blown, and on the following day the British Commander-in-Chief broadcast to the island:

'The battle of Malaya has come to an end and the battle of Singapore is started. For more than two months our troops have fought the enemy on the mainland. The enemy has had the advantage of great air superiority and considerable freedom of movement by sea.

'Our task has been both to impose losses on the enemy and to gain time to enable forces of the Allies to be concentrated for this struggle in the Far East.

'To-day we stand beleaguered in our island fortress until help can come, as assuredly it will come. This we are determined to do. In carrying out this task we want the active help of every man and woman in the fortress.

'There is work for all to do. Any enemy who sets foot in the fortress must be dealt with immediately. The enemy within our gates must be ruthlessly weeded out. There must be no more loose talk and rumour-mongering. Our duty is clear. With firm resolve and fixed determination we shall win through.'

It's a bit late in the day for Percival to call on 'every man and woman' of the seven hundred thousand natives. Their will to fight is gone.

Cecil Brown

Air attacks on the island grew in intensity. The outnumbered and dwindling defenders took heavy toll of the bombers, but they could not stop them. Below them, the city lay almost defenceless.

Fighters over Singapore

'We sailed right through the formation from one side to the other, shooting at everything in sight. Then when I came out the other side I saw two fighters coming at me—little chubby fellows with great big radial engines in front and painted bright green all over. I thought "All right, you——s!" and I started climbing for all I was worth. They couldn't keep up with me at all. I got well above them and then turned and dived on the nearest one. I got real close before I let him have it, and honest, you never saw anything like it. His machine just seemed to explode, with pieces flying off and smoke pouring out. He whipped up sort of, right in front of me, and then spun over sideways. The last I saw of him he was just a ball of fire going down. I gave the other one a burst, too, and I think I damaged him, but I was out of ammunition then so I dived away and headed for home. . . .'

. . . . There was a Chinese businessman in Singapore who had a standing offer of a bottle of champagne for every Jap plane destroyed, so that evening Red and Denny, accompanied by some of the others, drove into town to collect the two bottles they had earned by their victories.

Arthur G. Donahue

The Opposition is Very Strong

The British interception of the Japanese pilots talking to each other over their radio telephones is very good.

One Japanese pilot over Singapore called his base and shouted frantically, 'The opposition is very strong—the opposition is very strong!'

'What is very strong,' his base called, 'the air opposition or the anti-aircraft?'

'My observer is dying,' the pilot shouted.

Then there was a pause.

'He is dead. May I return now? The opposition is very strong', the pilot kept insisting, 'My observer is dead—may I return now—may I return now?'

'Continue with your mission,' he was told.

'I must return now—the opposition is too strong.'

'Yes, return now,' he finally was told.

There was another Japanese bomber in a flight of twenty-seven over Singapore. The aircraft fire was considerable and the British intercepted one pilot talking to his wing commander: 'I think I should release my bombs now,' he said.

'No, not yet,' the commander told him.

The firing continued very heavily and he called his squadron leader again nervously: 'I think I should release my bombs now.'

He was told to await orders, but he kept pestering and finally was told: 'All right, you can release your bombs and return to your base. But remember,' the squadron leader said, 'you have another mission this afternoon.'

Cecil Brown

Air-Raid Precautions

They are not building any air-raid shelters underground in Singapore and the safest shelters appear to be the concrete sewers, a foot wide and three feet deep, which line all the streets. People are being urged to use them. An A.R.P. warden said, 'Personally, if I were caught in the open I would just put my pride in my pocket and dive into a sewer. It is recommended, however, that those jumping in the sewers use respirators because of the stink.'

On Orchard Road, one of the main shopping districts, there is one deep trench which has been improved by the British, who have put wooden boards across the top and covered it over with sandbags.

The idea is a good one but when it rains the water in the trench reaches the wooden top. A person thus has the choice of jumping into the water and keeping his nose pressed against the boards to keep from drowning or sitting outside and dodging the bomb splinters.

Cecil Brown

On 8–9 February the Japanese secured footholds on the island itself.

The Japs have crossed the Straits of Johore and landed on Singapore Island. It happened late Saturday night and it was not officially announced until this morning—thirty-six hours afterwards. I can just imagine what a shock it must have been to the people to find out that the enemy had been on the island for thirty-six hours.

The other day General Percival said, 'We intend to hold Singapore. Everyone must realize that it's a common fight for military and civilians alike.'

And the *Sydney Telegraph* editorial comments bitterly to-day: 'So, when Singapore is in deadly danger, the civilian is expected to fight! With what? What has trained him? A month ago the brass hats in Singapore would have turned away in horror at the thought of inviting civilians to fight.'

Cecil Brown

Last Stand

On the night of 8 February we heard a tremendous bombardment going on over in the west of the island, and later learned that the Japs had got ashore there and were making progress eastwards. This was about ten miles to our left rear; no enemy activity appeared on our sector, but we intensified our harassing fire.

Next day we were ordered to withdraw to a perimeter round Singapore city, to conform to the Australians on our left, who were being hard pressed. Some of our guns were able to pull their trails round and support the troops on our left, but the close country made observation almost impossible. No attack or landing took place on our front; we had worked unceasingly on our gun positions and we felt desperately disappointed at having to leave them.

In the Singapore perimeter we held the central sector in the north and west of the suburbs. The gun area was necessarily very congested and batteries had to fit in where they could, in between buildings, on car parks and playing-fields, etc., all huddled together. Divisional H.Q. was between them and the forward posts. Here we fought the last bitter battle for Singapore. The Japs pressed us mainly from the west up the Bukit Timar road and from the north towards the reservoirs and Thompson Village.

We had F.O.Os with the infantry and were continuously firing tasks, but observation was very difficult, our wireless did not work and our lines were cut repeatedly. We constantly put down divisional artillery concentrations on both Bukit Timar villages and the main roads through them; later we knew from the numerous Jap graves in these places how effective our fire had been; but it was always at night that the Japs managed to infiltrate through our positions in the jungle country and in the morning the situation had invariably deteriorated. Enemy aircraft were over continuously; they had given up high-level attack now and were dive-bombing instead. Many were shot down by the L.A.A. gunners, but more came. Medium and heavy artillery now joined in and especially bombarded our congested gun area. They even had an observation balloon up some miles to the northward, which we presumed was directing the fire; but it was of course an impossible target—in any case our ammunition was dwindling fast. One's mind felt deadened and one could not believe this was really the end. Vain rumours spread of vast British reinforcements of aircraft and of landings behind the Japs. The sticky heat and frequent torrential rainstorms increased one's physical exhaustion. Already atrocity stories were beginning to come in.

Lieutenant-Colonel S. E. Skey

Thomson Road was now a veritable deathtrap, for transport from the north, west and east was converging on this main Singapore artery, and movement on the choked highway was slow and tedious. Enemy artillery was shelling many targets, snipers were harassing the drivers, and every now and then the enemy planes unloosed their loads of horror. The screams of the wounded and dying, the roar of burning trucks and cars, the deafening explosions of shells and bombs and the sickening whine and thud of small-arms bullets was something to instil fear into the stoutest heart.

On a little side road, nearly in the centre of the carnage, was a Tommy private, with a Vickers, mounted for ack-ack, pouring fire from a red-hot barrel at every plane that passed. Right in the centre of the road he stayed and carried on, no camouflage and no fear, and his answer to all and sundry was, 'The bloody ——s will never think of looking for me in the open, and I want to see a bloody plane brought down.'

Surrender

An invitation to our Command to surrender was dropped on 11 February by an aeroplane. The leaflets were signed by Yamashita and began: 'I advise immediate surrender of the British forces at Singapore, from the standpoint of *bushido*, to the Japanese Army and Navy forces, which have already dominated Malaya, annihilated the British Fleet in the Far East, and acquired complete control of the China Sea and the Pacific and Indian Oceans, as well as south-western Asia.'

Ian Morrison

This demand was ignored, and the fighting continued. Three days later it was obvious that further resistance was hopeless, and General Percival sent a white flag to the Japanese.

The unceasing blitz continued throughout the night and next morning, 15 February. Company areas received a heavy battering, but few shells fell in the immediate vicinity of the palace itself, which was undamaged. The shelling was very accurate and obviously targets were selected deliberately, notably 8 Divisional H.Q. in Tanglin Barracks and the Cathay Building in the city. A map taken from a captured Japanese officer showed in detail the dispositions of the defending troops on the island and, interestingly enough, a plan of their own attack from the north-west. The only error in positions shown was that of Brigade H.Q. which had, however, only moved some hours previously. Espionage was then very thorough, and though the enemy had not yet broken through the perimeter his artillery and aerial successes could not be checked, and he was content to shell and bomb the city into submission. It became known during the afternoon that a cessation of hostilities would be asked for at 3.30 p.m. This was inevitable, as conditions in the city were worsening, and, adding to the general confusion, there was a breakdown of all essential services. The appalling number of native casualties was estimated at thirty-five thousand.

Consequently, while the defending army never for one moment expected to see the raising of the white flag, this sacrifice of innocent human beings could not go on. Shells became fewer, the noise of battle gradually subsided, and at six o'clock all was quiet, except the drone of watchful planes overhead and a few stray enemy shells. Orders to cease fire at 8.30 p.m. came from headquarters, and the Malayan campaign of seventy weary days' duration came to an end.

A strange quiet settled over the Battalion positions. The men could not but feel thankful for the relief from the bombs and shells and the continuous strain of the past five weeks, but to the many who had never entertained the idea of capitulation it came as a staggering and sorrowful blow. It was difficult to realize that they were beaten and were prisoners of war. They were prepared to fight on in the streets, but they had no choice. They felt, at least, the consolation of a job done to the utmost of their ability, and had to be satisfied with that.

The personal message of the G.O.C. A.I.F., Malaya, Major-General Gordon Bennett, was accepted with appreciation. It was as follows: 'The G.O.C. A.I.F., Malaya, wishes to thank all ranks for their fine fighting and excellent co-operation in the war in Malaya. You have maintained the highest traditions of the A.I.F. and have done your tasks nobly. You can at least march out with pride in your achievement.'

Finally, Lieutenant-General Percival's last message came to hand: 'It has been necessary to give up the struggle but I want the true reason explained to all ranks. The forward troops continue to hold their ground, but the essentials of war have run short. In a few days we shall have neither food nor petrol. Many types of ammunition are short and the water supply, on which the vast population and many of the fighting forces are dependent, threatens to fail. . . . This has been brought about by being driven off our dumps by hostile air and artillery action. Without these sinews of war we cannot fight on. I thank all ranks for their efforts throughout the campaign.'

The Opening Battle

Prime Minister Curtin issued a statement to-day describing the fall of Singapore as the opening battle of Australia.

'I tell this nation that, as things stand to-day, brains and brawn are better than even bets or beer.'

Cecil Brown

JAVA—THE PHILIPPINES

While the British were being pitchforked out of Malaya, the Japanese swept through the Netherlands East Indies. Having first secured southern Sumatra, they turned on Java, where British, Dutch and some American units concentrated after the fall of Singapore. The last remaining Allied naval force in these waters was destroyed in the Java Sea at the end of February, and on 8 March the outmatched land forces in Java surrendered to the Japanese.

Meanwhile, the Americans were heavily set upon in the Philippines. The Japanese landed on Luzon twenty-four hours after Malaya had been invaded, while their major attack—setting between eighty and a hundred thousand men ashore—came on 22 December 1941. It was preceded by violent attacks from the air, during which Manila and the nearby naval base at Cavite were savagely bombed. American resistance was fierce.

JAVA: LANDING PLANES

A few minutes later twelve P-40 Es, the Kittyhawks, came in. This is a huge field at Daly Waters—in many respects a perfect field. There are no barriers and visibility is excellent on all sides. We stood beside our bombers, watching the Kittyhawks circle to follow their leader down. The leader made a perfect landing, the next one bounced but got down. The next one seemed to be coming down too low, short of the aerodrome, and heading for a field. He came down in the field and hit a ditch. The next one did the same—down on the field and half turned over. The following Kittyhawk did the same. Lieutenant Rose was shouting and screaming, 'What the hell's the matter with them? They've got all the field in the world here to land on and they are coming down in the grass and weeds.'

The others came in all right, until the final one of the twelve. He made five attempts to get down but when four or five feet off the ground he decided he couldn't make it, put on the gas, and zoomed up and away again for another circle. Five times he did that.

'You can just imagine,' Lieutenant Rose said, 'what that poor kid in there is going through.'

A sergeant mechanic with us said, 'The only way we'll get him down is shoot him down.'

I remarked to some of the airmen standing by that if a pilot couldn't make a simple landing in a strange and good field, how could he fight in combat, when the enemy is on his tail.

'These boys are going to be slaughtered out here,' one pilot said.

He finally came down on the aerodrome, and unlike the three others, did not crack up. These pilots were youngsters just out of flying school, with insufficient experience. There's no help for that, I suppose. Men, even untrained, are needed desperately if Java is to be saved.

Cecil Brown

THE PHILIPPINES

Bombs on Manila: 8 December

We hadn't long to wait after Pearl Harbor.

The next day I stood on the balcony of the *Herald* building and saw the first enemy planes cut down through the skies like great aerial bolos.

Fifty-four Japanese sky monsters, flashing silver in the bright noonday, were flying in two magnificently formed Vs.

Above the scream of the sirens the church bells solemnly announced the noon hour.

Unprotected and unprepared, Manila lay under the enemy planes—a city of ancient nunneries and chromium-fronted night clubs, or skyscrapers towering over *nipa* shacks, of antiquity and modernity, of East and West.

I heard the *Herald* staff clattering out of the building into Muralla Calle, where citizens in the customary spotless white were being herded by the police under the moss-covered old Spanish wall. Women clustered under the acacia-trees in the park. I found myself grinning—a few of them had opened their umbrellas for additional protection!

Half-a-dozen bearded Fathers came out of the College of San Juan de Letran next door, looked up and saw the planes, and, gathering up their white robes, rushed back into the building.

Colonel Carlos P. Romulo

The Defenders

We hopped a truck, threw our guns and ammunition aboard, and raced to the Cavite docks just as the Japs unloaded their first stick of bombs over Nichols Field across the bay below Manila. I had watched the merciless bombing of Chinese cities, but they were nothing like this. These Japs were using a new technique. They flew out of the clouds, with the sun at their tails, in two formations of twenty-seven planes each. They hummed along like a swarm of bees, high and flying straight.

Approaching the target, the squadron leader flipped sideways, then dived. The others followed quickly. After the longest minute I ever lived through, the leader let go of the first stick of bombs. They looked like silvery eggs glistening in the sun as they were detached in a bunch from beneath the plane, then scattered out over a wide area. Then came a strange rattle of machine-guns from the plane. They hadn't done this over Chapei. There in China they had just unloaded their bombs, climbed back again, and come in for another run. But this time they were firing machine-guns from the planes—strafing.

On they came, until fifty-four planes had unloaded their bombs and strafed the ground. Then they climbed back up to an open sky to rendezvous high. Off they flew, over Manila.

When the bombs hit Nichols Field, great showers of earth and debris shot skyward. As a boy I remember throwing handfuls of dust into the sky. This was the way it looked now, except that the clouds of dust we saw contained sticks and bricks and human bodies and pieces of machinery. No sooner had the dust clouds descended than great puffs of smoke followed; then flames leaped above the tree-tops. We couldn't see the Army flying-field, because it was too far away, but the bursting bombs, smoke and flames were plainly visible as we raced along in the truck to the docks. The earth quaked, and a roar of hot air puffed into our faces. Then came the crackling of flames and the deep rumble of falling debris.

. . . . I glanced skyward. The Japs were coming back towards us, still flying high. The anti-aircraft fire had stopped. Our planes were skimming the tree-tops now. Suddenly they shot upward, one ahead of the other in a single file.

'Here it comes, boys!'

'Yeah. This is it!'

Our planes kept climbing, straight for the bellies of those big twin-engined jobs. They still hadn't spotted our planes. They thought they had complete mastery of the skies, and they roared along like migrating ducks chased by a handful of sparrows.

Our fighters were now within range of the bombers and climbing fast. The leading plane now had the leading Jap bomber in his gun sight. There was a burst of fire and tracer bullets from the nose of the American fighter as he flew straight for the bomber. For a second it looked as if they would crash in mid-air. A tiny trickle of blue smoke trailed from the leading bomber. He wavered a little, then slanted earthwards, his wings whining like a crying baby.

'Got him!' someone cried, and we shouted and danced like little boys, clapping our hands and hugging each other.

The leader of our fighters zoomed up and over the Jap bombers, flipped back, and dived down towards them again. At the same time our second fighter came within range of the second squadron of twenty-seven Jap bombers. He opened up with guns in his wings and nose, giving the Japs everything he had. Another bomber trailed bluish smoke, then seemed to stop in mid-air and spin earthwards. Just then there was a terrific explosion as the first Jap bomber hit the earth and burst into flames. This was followed by another crash and a burst of flames as the second bomber buried itself in the ground.

By this time all eight of our fighters had made a run at the Japs, flying between their formations, over them and circling back behind them, attacking the planes in the rear of the formation.

'Now you're cookin' with gas!' the gun captain yelled, as if the American fliers could hear him.

The Japs didn't fly over Nichols Field as they had before. This time they headed straight for the sea and the cloud bank which had moved farther out over the water.

The Americans followed them all the way. A third bomber crashed in flames shortly after the second. A fourth and fifth went down soon after the others, with the American fighters still climbing beneath them and diving back in a wide circle to gun the bombers trailing the formation. Unescorted by fighter planes, the bombers were easy targets. It was like shooting bottles lined up on a fence. They would crack, then fall to explode as they bounded on the earth.

The sixth plane was shot out of the formation before the Japs split up to fly in three directions from about twenty miles south-east of Manila. The sixth big bomber didn't spin and crash like the others but descended in a wide circle, turning back across the bay towards us. He seemed to be heading straight for Cavite on a wide circle across the tree-tops and the bay.

'He's coming at us!' I cried.

'Yeah. Get ready,' the gun captain ordered.

Every man lifted his rifle or tommy-gun to his shoulder and waited. The ·50-calibre machine-gun on the truck was lowered so that its muzzle was trained on the big bomber as he came nearer, flying more than a thousand yards away from us and coming in fast on a wide circle. He was wobbling, almost out of control. Our fighters must have hit the controls, and the pilot seemed to be trying to pull her out. Her engines would idle, then they would cough and roar again as the pilot gunned her, trying to keep from crashing. Now the Jap had cleared the trees lining the shore, and he was approaching Cavite with the wind whistling through his wings and his motor groaning. The Jap was less than five hundred yards away now, low over the water and within easy range of us.

'When he comes in, let him have it!' the gunner ordered.

'Here he comes!'

The bomber's engines roared over the water, and the big plane seemed to settle on an even keel, its wings ceased wobbling, and he began to climb slowly.

'O.K., boys!' the gunner yelled. 'Fire!'

The tracers hit right in the nose and ploughed back through the fuselage and tail as the plane passed through the driving bullets. It was now less than four hundred yards away, flying straight over the water, so close that I could see the faces of the men at the controls as they grinned in defiance at us.

The plane lunged upwards, stalled, then flipped its tail up as the nose went straight down. There was a geyser of water, a hiss of steam as the hot motors caught fire and the detonators set the bomb load off. There was a hell of an explosion. A second later, and bits of wreckage splashed on the dock at our feet, and the plane disappeared from the surface, leaving a burning pool of oil and fuel where she went down.

William Martin Camp, U.S.M.C.

Cavite Abandoned

Finally came the order to advance. Truck motors roared and carbon monoxide fumes lay heavy beneath the smoke-clouds. The trucks started with a jerk as the wheels began to roll. There was no more talking. Everyone looked back and saw the dying embers and the ghostly shadows and the rising smoke. It was like a graveyard, deathly quiet, deserted and silent except for the last consuming flames which crackled like the inferno of Hell.

Thus began the retirement from Cavite at 1.30 a.m. on the morning of 11 December. A very small force under a fighting Marine officer of the fleet was remaining behind: they would man a few A.A. batteries to prevent the Japs from knowing we were evacuating the yard. They were to leave in small boats after we were well under way.

'That's stupid,' someone said. 'We ain't foolin' the Japs. Why, they know every move we've made so far. Ten to one they know we're leavin' right now. We'll be lucky if we ain't bombed along the road.'

The road to Manila was once a broad four-laned highway of concrete pan macadam, hard and smooth, but the dust from fallen buildings and great clouds of dirt had descended upon it in a thin layer which was stirred up as we rolled along in the heavy convoy. The road was crowded with refugees loaded in automobiles, *carabao*-drawn carts, *carranatas*, push-carts with heavy wooden wheels, wagons and all kinds of vehicles from the primitive farm carts to modern limousines. Those who lived in Manila were swarming to get out of the city, and country people were streaming into it, hoping to find safety there from the bombs.

In the light of the fires I could see on every face that drawn, terrified look, the same expression I recalled on the faces of the Chinese who had streamed into the International Settlement of Shanghai when the Japs bombed their homes and destroyed their towns. In every vehicle were the same things—blankets, chairs, boxes. Bundles of clothing and cooking utensils were tied up in sheets and blankets. Some of the wealthier families had mattresses piled upon the tops of their cars, with favourite chairs or tables or bicycles lashed to the rear. In the carts and wagons of the poor were chairs, tables, copper kettles, oil stoves, blankets and bundles of clothing. The poor were taking everything they owned, but the rich were leaving all but a few treasures behind.

William Martin Camp

Manila, Open City: 27 December

In order to spare the metropolitan area from possible ravages of attack either by air or ground, Manila is hereby declared an open city with the characteristics of a military objective. In order that no excuse may be given for a possible mistake, the American High Commissioner, the Commonwealth Government, and all combatant military installations will be withdrawn from its environs as rapidly as possible.

General MacArthur

In the New Year General MacArthur's forces were pinned down in the fortress island of Corregidor off Manila and in the Bataan peninsula. There they held out for several months.

Retreat to Corregidor: 1 January 1942

We drove through a city dark except for its burning areas. The port area was still in flames. Not a civilian showed himself against that back-drop of fire. The flames were hot on my face as I stumbled wearily up the gang-plank of the old steamer *Hyde*.

Even the boat was dark. An officer called our names in the dark. I answered mine and, slumping to the deck, and with my musette bag for a pillow, was instantly asleep.

I woke once in mid-channel. Captain John Christiansen, lying beside me, asked what was the matter. I told him I was cold. When I awoke again I discovered the sun was up and that the blanket he had given me was his only one.

The *Hyde* was against the dock of Corregidor. I looked at that hunk of rock surrounded by water. My first thought was, 'What a hole!' My second was, 'We'll be trapped here!'

To the east was Cavite, still in flames. To the west was the jungle peninsula of Bataan, where our boys were making their last fight.

Still numb from sleep on the deck of the old steamer, I hooked my musette strap over my shoulder. With weariness riding my shoulders I stumbled down the gang-plank on to the gritty soil of Corregidor.

At that very moment just twelve miles behind me Japanese soldiers were goose-stepping into Manila.

. . . . At 6.30 in the morning that New Year's Day I walked into the Malinta Tunnel on Corregidor.

The smell of the place hit me like a blow in the face. There was the stench of sweat and dirty clothes, the coppery smell of blood and disinfectant, coming from the lateral where the hospital was situated, and over all, the heavy stink of creosote hanging like a blanket in the air that moved sluggishly when it moved at all.

It had been taken for granted that in the event of war all the inhabitants of Corregidor would take shelter in the tunnel and its cluster of branching laterals sunk into the solid stone of the 'Rock'.

As many as five thousand people gathered there during raids. Those who could not get in were unprotected. I think the population of Corregidor at this time was about nine thousand—a number that would shrink rapidly in the death-dealing months to come.

I stood there gaping, bewildered and alarmed by the bedlam going on about me. This was the final refuge of a fortress we had all assumed had been prepared and impregnable for years.

Now that disaster was upon us, soldiers were rushing about belatedly installing beds and desks and sewage drains and electric lights.

The tunnel was wide enough to permit two ambulances to drive side by side down its length. Its stone arch was damp. Everywhere was the graveyard smell of wet rock—where it wasn't overwhelmed by sharper and even less pleasant odours.

Soldiers were sleeping along the sides of the tunnel, on camp-beds and ammunition-cases or curled up on the cement floor. Their boots were in one another's faces. Ambulances rolled within a few inches of their heads. The bombs that fell night and day shook the furthermost stone laterals of the tunnel.

Nobody paid any attention to me. I wandered in and out of the laterals carrying my luggage. These cave-like places were the offices for Ordnance, Quartermaster, Anti-aircraft, Harbour Defence, Finance, Signal Corps, and U.S.A.F.F.E. headquarters. The hospital was the largest and the best-organized lateral in the tunnel. From it jutted perhaps a dozen smaller laterals. These were for the women, the President and High Commissioner, the doctors and officer patients, the operating ward, the medical ward, the dental ward and other wards, the laboratory, X-ray department, and the hospital mess. In this mess, President Quezon, his family, and Cabinet, Commissioner Sayre, and his staff took their meals.

Colonel Romulo

Retreat to Bataan

I looked at the road ahead, and all I could see was a line of Filipino children standing by the road, holding their little brown fingers up in a V-sign. Their faces were wreathed in smiles.

I looked down. A little fellow was running along beside me.

'Hi, Marine!' he said, smiling up at me.

'Hello there, sonny.'

'How are you to-day, Marine?'

'Fine. How're you?'

'I'm fine. Say, Marine, you are not leavin' us here all alone, are you? You're not running away, are you?'

I squeezed his hand. He was about ten years old. His smile was only a half-smile, half eager, half afraid.

'No, sonny. Not running away. Just retiring to prepared positions. That's all.'

. . . . That's the way it was. *'To the rear! To the rear!'*

From Lingayen to the tar-covered Olongapo Road, then to Abucay, farther down Bataan. Infantry, artillery, cavalry, and machine-gun units tried to hold them back, but they just kept coming, all the way, head on, at point-blank range. There was nothing to stop them. They came in by the hundreds, the thousands. Their blood ran down the hills, seeped into the earth until it was sticky, then ran over the surface like water, down the valleys into the streams, and down the streams into the sea. Bodies cascaded down the hills like waterfalls, rolling and tumbling and lying still. Others followed, and the command was always:

'To the rear . . . to the rear. . . .'

The Filipino Scouts held them off for the first eleven days and eleven nights after the Lingayen invasion. It was continuous attacking, retreating to new positions, stopping long enough to slaughter a few hundred more, then being driven back by the sheer force of overwhelming numbers. There weren't enough guns to stop them.

'They're mad! They're crazy. Why, if one of our officers sent men to their deaths like that, he would be court-martialled and shot by firing-squads,' said the colonel from Spokane.

'It's mass suicide, that's what it is, sir. Mass suicide.'

'Just keep firing, men. Keep firing. We'll go to the rear after this wave. . . . Keep firing. . . .'

This was the retirement to Bataan. Wainwright's forces from the north just made it in time. So did the forces coming back up over the bridge at San Fernando Pampanga. The last convoy crossed the bridge. Then came the South Corps. The last man across the bridge stopped just long enough to dynamite it.

William Martin Camp

Persuasion

The first night I found myself looking forward to sleeping in the open air. I curled up in my borrowed blanket on the bank of the creek and prepared to enjoy the beauty of the stars and the symphony of running water and cicadas.

'Here's where I get my first night's sleep since Pearl Harbor,' I said drowsily to Colonel Lauro Hernandez, a former classmate of mine, who stretched out near by.

I thought some meaning was hidden in his silence. I knew there was when a few minutes later all round us in the darkness a thousand enemy guns seemed to open fire. I nearly jumped out of my blanket.

'Take it easy,' said Lauro; 'it's just the fire-cracker gag.'

I settled back on the ground. I hadn't recognized the Japanese firecracker trick, although we heard plenty about it. It was one of the many stunts the enemy were using in their attempt to break down the morale of the boys in the lines. Their planes circled overhead all night long scattering bombs hit and miss over Bataan. Their pistol-shots rang all night in the forest. They had a device for hurling long strings of firecrackers over the trees and on to our front lines. They hoped the boy in the fox-hole, hearing them, would think he was surrounded and shoot back, thereby making himself a target for the enemy.

I listened, my body tense. The cicadas had stopped humming. Then I heard a drawn-out human sigh. It was like the last intake of a man that is dying. Only it sounded inhuman and monstrous, because it came from everywhere and nowhere; as if the trees were in anguish. Then silence—then groans from the forests, and later, a scream.

The sounds were nerve-wracking. But I was on a river bank surrounded by men I knew, who were listening with me. I was not alone, weak with hunger and sleeplessness, in a fox-hole in the dead of night. Lauro spoke to me again in a whisper. He explained that these sounds were being broadcast from Japanese sound trucks on the very front of their lines.

Out of the night came a woman's voice, sweet and persuasive. In sentimental words it announced the dedication of a programme to 'the brave and gallant defenders of Bataan'. Songs followed, quavering through the forest. They were selected to arouse nostalgia to breaking-point in a boy facing death and longing for home. *Home, Sweet Home, Old Folks at Home*—this was the kind of song the Japanese broadcast in the dead of night, alternating heartbreak with horror.

Colonel Romulo

The Tokyo radio gave us the business. They called upon us for immediate surrender.

'Dear friends . . . Lay down your arms . . . It is useless to resist . . . You are completely encircled . . . You will get no assistance . . . What dishonour is there in following the example of the defenders of Hong Kong, Singapore and the Netherlands East Indies, in the acceptance of an honourable defeat?'

That's what the Japanese radio broadcast. Not long afterwards, the Japanese bombers flew over. They dropped no bombs that day. Instead, they dropped shiny tin cans which floated down from the skies and popped as they hit the earth. Inside were notes addressed to the commanding general of the forces of Americans and Filipinos.

'Your Excellency. Your duty has been performed. Accept our sincere advice and save the lives of those officers and men under your command. Surrender. Make an honourable surrender. There is no dishonour in an honourable defeat.'

William Martin Camp

Death in a Fox-hole

I lay there for about half an hour when Oakley grabbed his stomach and began groaning.

'Try what I did,' I told him. 'It'll make you feel better.'

He crawled to the end of the hole and squatted there, grunting and groaning with pain. There are two kinds of dysentery in the Orient, one a mild form, which we called the 'Yangtse rapids', and another which is more serious and requires a doctor's treatment.

'I've had the "rapids" for a week,' Oakley groaned. 'Now this. . . .'

He rolled over, writhing in pain.

'We gotta get him out of here,' Witherspoon said to me. 'He's got to go to hospital. He'll die if we don't get him out of here.'

It was about ten o'clock in the morning, and the sun was high. We had been there since about ten o'clock the night before. Somewhere ahead of us were the Jap snipers. I was trying to decide which was worse, having him killed by the snipers or die of the awful cramps which were causing him to roll his eyes and froth at the mouth.

At last I decided it was worth a try. I stood up and started to climb out of the hole, so Witherspoon could help him up to me, and we could both drag him back. If we could cross that narrow strip of open space which lay between our fox-hole and the trees behind we would be safe. From there on we could carry him back in a stretcher made of our shirts and a couple of saplings.

I had no sooner raised my head about the earth than a sudden burst of machine-gun fire splashed in the dust around me. I dropped back down, and Witherspoon shook his head.

'No use,' he said. 'We can't make it.'

Oakley was clawing the earth now, and his finger-tips were bleeding. If I hadn't known what it was, I might have thought it was sunstroke or epilepsy. He was chewing his tongue, and the saliva which ran down his chin was pink with blood. His eyeballs were turned back in his head with only a little bit of the pupils showing.

'God! We've got to do something!' Witherspoon cried, his face ashen with fright. 'We can't let him die like this!'

I dropped down and crawled over to where he lay. I took his head in my hands and tried to prise his jaws apart to release his tongue.

'Gimme something. Quick!' I said.

Witherspoon looked around, but there was nothing we could use to put in his mouth to prevent him eating his tongue.

'Here!' Witherspoon said, handing me a bayonet. 'Try this.'

'No! He'll kill himself with that. What if he falls on it or rolls over! It'll kill him.'

But there was nothing else to do, so I pulled his jaws apart and Witherspoon placed the tip of the bayonet between his teeth. I released his jaws gently until his teeth touched the cold steel, and they began grinding against it. He was twitching convulsively, and with each breath his cries were becoming weaker and weaker until they were no more than a whisper. I held his head in my lap, while Witherspoon stroked his stomach, pressing down hard with downward strokes. Whatever it was inside him, it had to come out.

We did this for about an hour. The pain seemed to go away, and he stopped gritting his teeth against the tip of the bayonet.

'He's coming along all right now,' I said. 'He'll be over it in a minute.'

'God! What is this?' Witherspoon exclaimed, looking at the back of his trousers. 'It's blood!'

I put his head down and crawled towards his feet. His trousers were soaked with blood, and it was running down, seeping into the ground. I ripped off his trousers to his knees. They were soaked with it. There was an odour like rotted flesh, the same odour which hovered over Bataan day and night from the thousands of dead which lay in the sun.

'Haemorrhages,' I said. 'He's bleeding from behind.'

'He'll bleed to death.'

We rolled him over on his stomach and parted his legs. I placed my hand over him to try to stop the blood, but it came through my fingers. I tried stopping him up with the slimy dirt, but it was useless. The blood forced the mud poultice away.

He died a few minutes later without opening his eyes again. Since we couldn't move out of the hole we dug the sides in until his body was covered with the fresh earth.

William Martin Camp

This Is It!

That night the flares of the Sakdalista and the Ganaps* lit up Bataan like a birthday cake. The Japs couldn't have given us a more positive warning. Those flares, lighting up prospective targets and bombing routes, were as infallible as a barometer at sea. At Cavite, in Manila, and in northern Bataan they forecast the next day's offensives without fail. Burning now in the hills behind Mariveles naval base, near the hospital up the zig-zag at Cabcaben, along the beaches near our embattlements, and in the trees near field headquarters locations, they were ample warning of what was to come at dawn. Time to prepare, time to double the watch, time to check equipment and rush arms and ammunition to fill up the gaps.

'This is it, guys! This is it!' everyone was saying.

'Yeah, it's it, all right.'

It was strange to note the varied effect those lights had upon some of the men around me. To some it meant a relief from the constant strain of expectancy; to others it only increased their anxiety and filled them with awe and fear, for you never knew where one would pop up next. It might be right behind you, in the trees above you, or at some distant, difficult pinnacle. It never failed to produce psychological fear and foreboding. I had a weird premonition which I could not shake as I watched them burn fiercely at every vital installation, including those which had been known only to a few. A chill on my neck and at the roots of my hair came over me, and the more I thought of it, the more con-

---

* Filipino Fifth Column (Ed.)

vinced I became that this was really 'it'. Just what 'it' meant I didn't or couldn't imagine.

William Martin Camp

Bombardment

All that day it continued with increased fury, from the air, from Jap shore batteries across the bay, and from ships anchored off-shore beyond the range of our artillery. Several Jap destroyers had slipped up in the night, blacked out and in the dark of the moon, and had measured the distance to us so that their ship batteries could open up at daylight. They were softening us up for an invasion, and there was nothing we could do about it except to hope they would be withdrawn as the fourteenth day passed and the fifteen-day limit of the Jap general's threat had expired.

That night, 6 April, we heard of the general's order to his Filipino and American forces to renew the attack, all along the line in every sector.

'The reserves have arrived,' said the Marine who relieved me at midnight. 'What about us?' I asked eagerly.

The Marine shrugged and shook his head. 'We hold on,' he said.

There wasn't much to hold on to by this time. The Jap destroyers had kept up a steady fire, lobbing their shells all around our positions, on the rocks of the beach in front of us and in the hills behind us.

As darkness came on, they ceased firing and began playing beams of their searchlights against the shore, sweeping up and down, surveying the situation. Just before midnight they had fired a few star shells which descended over our heads, lighting Bataan with a weird, artificial, white glow. Twice our anti-aircraft batteries exploded the star shells, and we were safe in the darkness once more. But the Jap destroyers had found us and were probably moving in closer under cover of darkness for a renewed assault at dawn.

William Martin Camp

On 9 April 1942 Bataan surrendered. On 6 May General Wainwright finally lowered his flag on Corregidor, and the fighting in the Philippines was left to the Resistance. As soon as the position had become hopeless, General MacArthur had been evacuated to Australia to take command of the Allied forces gathering there.

MacArthur Leaves Corregidor: 11 March

Corregidor rises abruptly from the water's edge where Bulkely's P.T. stood by. All boarded promptly except the General, who stopped and turned slowly to look back. What a transformation had taken place in that normally beautiful spot. Its vivid green foliage was gone with its trees, its shrubs, its flowers, all bruised and torn by the hail of relentless and devastating bombardment. That warped and twisted face of scorched rock seemed to reflect the writhings of a tortured body. It had become a black mass of destruction. Up on Topside the heavy guns still rent the air with their red blasts and deep roars. They were commanded by Paul Bunker, MacArthur's classmate at West Point, a famous all-American back in the team MacArthur had managed. He and many others of those thousands were old, old friends, bound by ties of deepest comradeship.

What thoughts must have crowded his mind as he looked his farewell. And then I saw him slowly raise his cap in salute, there in the twilight, as he glanced up through the smoky haze with its smell of death and stench of destruction thick in the night air. And it seemed to me that I could see a sudden convulsive twitch in the muscles of his jaw, a sudden whitening in the bronze of his face. I said to the man next to me, 'What's his chance of getting through?' 'About one in five,' was the reply. And then the General's quiet voice as he stepped aboard the boat: 'You may cast off, Buck, when you are ready.' And then they moved off into the night.

American eye-witness

The Fall

Down below we can hear the great thunder. The bombs have loosened the ceiling in some of the tunnels, and they have caved in at some places, cutting off any possible escape. We have heard that some of our boys are trapped in the tunnels farther along, but there is no confirmation of it. Everyone has turned to and is preparing his own little shelter, just in case we have to duck behind a rock in the tunnels and stop them as they come through the entrances.

Three times during the afternoon the Japs tried to make a landing, but we have repulsed them. They haven't learned yet how to take advantage of air support in attacking a stronghold and gaining a foothold. We didn't know it until to-day. But we have learned how effective is their bombing and strafing, and we know that if they tried it once they would be swarming all over the Rock.

Funny how long it takes a Jap to catch on. But they do catch on, and there's no denying the fact. It is sundown now, and the transports have all moved in a little closer. They are gunwale to gunwale now, or so we hear from the topside.

Word has been passed that we've made our last radio contact with the States. It happened about four o'clock this afternoon. No one knows what the last message was, but soon after it was sent a well-placed bomb blew the works all to hell, and the operators with it.

Time is short. Witherspoon and Weaver and I are lying on our backs. There is a little light coming in from a hole in the ceiling where a bomb crashed through. The last rays of the red sun are shining over Mariveles: although we can't see the lonely mountain silhouetted against the sunset, we know that's the way it was yesterday, the day before, and the day before. And that's the way it will be to-morrow and the next day and the next day. Hereafter, it will remind all who view it of the blood that was spilled here.

Everyone is in high spirits. That old Marine Corps spirit. Even as they brought around the last of the mule-meat everyone ate it and there was plenty of grumbling. As long as there's plenty of belly-aching, men will not lose heart.

The Army officer who plays the violin is still alive. We heard him a few minutes ago. He sang the 'Shepherd' song we all love.

William Martin Camp

Intrinsically it is but a barren, war-worn rock, hallowed, as so many other places, by death and disaster. Yet it symbolizes within itself that priceless, deathless thing, the honour of a nation. Until we lift our flag from its dust, we stand unredeemed before mankind. Until we claim again the ghastly remnants of its last gaunt garrison, we can but stand humble supplicants before Almighty God.

General MacArthur

BURMA

Once the Japanese had control of Thailand, it was obvious that they must soon attack Burma and open for themselves a way into India.

The people of the country were quite unprepared for invasion, and, as the British suffered defeat after defeat and the Japanese swept forward, they were stunned at the collapse of a Power they had always thought, if they thought about it at all, invincible and part of nature. The vast majority had no feeling that the war was their business; they wished only to avoid it. A small minority, mostly soldiers and officials, were actively loyal; about the same number, nationalist politicians, the relics of the old rebels of 1924, students, and some political *pongyis* (Buddhist priests) were actively hostile. These elements were rendered more formidable by the leadership of Japanese-trained Burmans, imported with the invading army, and by the flocking to their standards of numbers of dacoits and bad characters attracted by the prospect of loot.

Lieutenant-General William Slim

On 16 January 1942 the Japanese advance began, through Tenasserim and into Lower Burma. The British 17 Division was forced to retreat with heavy losses.

The army commander, however, as I was afraid he would, insisted on a continuance of his forward defence policy and, to start with, a strong defence of the very unsuitable Moulmein position. I perfectly well realized that great pressure must have been put upon him by the Governor of Burma to hold this politically important town, and that its loss would have a bad effect upon civilian morale. But that really was a very short-sighted view compared to the much more devastating effect of decisive military defeat.

Now the result of this appreciation of mine, and its rejection by the army commander, formed a major difference of opinion between us which widened and deepened as the days went by, and as it became more and more clear to me that the tactics imposed on me might lead to the loss of my whole division, on which the defence of Rangoon at that time almost solely depended. I quite understood the army commander's objections to my plan. He was being pressed strongly by General Wavell to fight as far forward as possible 'to gain time'; and he was also constantly pressed politically by the Governor that I should hold on to 'bits of Burma'. Dreadful bottlenecks like Moulmein, from which withdrawal had to be made over a wide stretch of water by river steamer, had to be held as long as possible because otherwise it might be bad for the morale of the civil population. Kawkareik, with a river obstacle and ferry behind it, was just as bad.

. . . . The Japanese intentions were now fairly clear. As expected, their main forces were advancing directly on to Moulmein from the east via Kawkareik. In addition they had diverted a regiment, equivalent to a British brigade, as a northern flanking force in the direction of Paan on the Salween river. From the south they had followed up their Tavoy success by a minor advance along the coast and another advance by a small force through the Three Pagodas Pass. They were closing on Moulmein from all directions, therefore, and the force advancing on Paan was directly threatening our line of withdrawal. These continued to be the stock Japanese tactics throughout the fighting in 1942, 1943 and the first part of 1944. Such tactics were extremely difficult to counter from our point of view, and we did not do so with any real effect until our air supply had been built up in 1944 to such proportions that the troops outflanked could stand fast and fight on in the knowledge that their food and ammunition would arrive by air.

.... On Sunday, 25 January, the army commander arrived up from Rangoon and we had a good look round and a long talk on the situation. It was quite obvious that the morale of the troops was poor. In the first place they felt keenly their lack of training in jungle war, their lack of artillery and air support, and their inability to move where they wanted owing to our acute lack of transport. The Indian troops had absolutely no confidence in the Burmese and the Burmese had no confidence in themselves as regular soldiers. They suffered the same depression as did our troops earlier at Dunkirk, Crete and Singapore, in seeing hostile aircraft continually in the air and very few of our own. The sick rate was also very high. I spent nearly all my time in morale-raising. On the 26th I spent the whole day going round brigades and units. Up at Moulmein things seemed fairly quiet; but two days later, on Friday the 30th, the Japanese attack developed after a good deal of preliminary reconnaissance and probing.

By this time my signallers had managed to run me up an excellent telephone line, by means of which I was in constant verbal communication with Roger Ekin, who had been appointed to command the Moulmein defences. Eventually, after some severe fighting, the defences were breached and the brigade fought its way down to the quays and embarked on the waiting steamers. The Indian mountain battery did magnificently to get all their guns away, but the final withdrawal was a nightmare with the steamers shelled and machine-gunned all the way across the Gulf of Martaban, and we were extremely lucky not to have more casualties than we did. The Japanese pressed their assault without regard for losses and suffered fairly heavily. Actually this extremely difficult operation was very creditable to the commanders and troops concerned; had there been the slightest panic or confusion the operation would have resulted in complete disaster.

.... By the capture of Moulmein the Japanese had advanced a big step towards the complete occupation of Burma, and had gained yet another airfield within striking distance of Rangoon.

Major-General Smyth, G.O.C. 17 Division

The Division fought a last, bitter delaying action on the Sittang river, but was pushed back towards Rangoon. The capital was now doomed. Thus, in the last week of February, ended the first phase of the Japanese invasion.

Rangoon: The First Invasion

Pilots of the meagre Allied air force, who constantly and effectively assailed the advancing Japanese, were unwelcome guests at the Mingalodon Golf Club.

We were present at the fall of the *Burra Sahib*'s last bastion in Rangoon, this club. While our member was engaged in 'avoiding as much of the unpleasantness of war as possible' (which apparently entailed living exactly as he had done before the Japanese came to Burma), the club was invaded by a group of some twenty boisterous young roughnecks who shouted with laughter, drank up all the club's refreshing iced beer, and smoked as many of the club's cigarettes as they could afford to buy. They slept on beds and benches all over the cool, big lounge where the *Burra Sahib* and his ladies used to drink their *chota-pegs* on Saturday afternoons after golf and on Sundays before eating throat-blistering curry which sent them to sleep.

They showed no respect whatsoever for the strait-laced conventions ruling the club. They stripped off their shirts and lay on the sacred lawn in front of the club-house sunning themselves. They actually had long talks with the Burmese waiters, learning about Burma and the customs of its people. An unheard-of thing, this fraternizing with the 'boys' whose job it was to wait on their *Burra Sahib*.

Then the club hit back. The managing member, Sidney Bush, a dear old man somewhat flustered by the war, was told not to serve the club's iced beer to the young roughnecks; nor the club's cigarettes. 'After all, the members' needs must be considered first. If we sell our stocks to all these young fellows there'll be nothing left for the members.'

O. D. Gallagher

The Last Days

With few exceptions the normal civilian population had gone, including the fire-brigade and all municipal employees. The empty streets were patrolled by troops carrying tommy-guns and rifles. The only other inhabitants were criminals, criminal lunatics, lunatics and lepers.

They had been released from the gaols and institutions on the order of an officer of the Indian Civil Service. He had misread an order sent to him regarding their disposal. The convicts numbered some five thousand. At night they made Rangoon a city of the damned. They prowled the deserted streets in search of loot. When they were seen looting they were shot by the soldiers. Numerous fires burned. Some were houses (many in neglected slum areas) set alight by their owners before they, too, evacuated. Other fires were laid by the looters, gone amuck, unbalanced by their sudden, unexpected freedom. Yet others were laid by fifth-columnists.

The senior civil servant who had given the criminals, lunatics and lepers their freedom committed suicide. Another did the same soon afterwards.

Lepers and lunatics wandered aimlessly about in search of food, some sharing pickings of the refuse-heaps with the many mongrel dogs. An occasional Buddhist monk walked the street going about his business, protected from assault by the long saffron robes of his faith.

Down at the docks all was chaos. Burmese looters were rummaging about and had found some medical supplies in cases. On examining these they judged them to be of no use except for the bottles. They tossed them away on the concrete wharves and watched them explode.

An A.V.G. ground-crew man, who went to the docks to see what there was that might be useful for the unit, saw them at it. 'They were having a great time,' he said. 'They were tickled pink by the explosions.'

O. D. Gallagher

Rangoon fell to the Japanese on 9 March. The British forces in the city escaped only through the lack of imagination of a Japanese commander, who removed a road-block at the critical moment. The battered defenders, reinforced by Chinese troops but now cut off from the outside world, retreated north, concentrated and turned to face their enemies once more. General William Slim was appointed to lead the troops in the field, under General Alexander as Army Commander.

General Slim Arrives

A day at Mandalay while we waited for an aircraft gave us an opportunity to look round. We saw a number of units and details that had been withdrawn for various reasons from the fighting to reform or to be used as reinforcements. Gunners who had lost their guns—the most pathetic people in the world—staffs of broken-up formations and evacuated camps, a hotchpotch of bits and pieces, odd groups and individuals. The British looked worried, the Indians puzzled, and the Burmese sulky. I had a suspicion that, unless someone very quickly took hold pretty tightly, a rot might set in behind the front.

. . . . There was, however, one bright gleam on the otherwise murky scene— the Chinese. At Christmas 1941, Generalissimo Chiang Kai-Shek had generously offered the Chinese 5 and 6 Armies to co-operate in the defence of Burma. General Wavell had accepted at once 93 Division of 6 Army, the most readily available, and moved it into the Shan States; 49 Division of the same Army was to be brought through Lashio to the Salween at Takaw. The third division, the 55th, which was scattered and not as ready as the others, was to concentrate at Wanting, there to equip and train. At the end of January, when arrangements for their maintenance had been hurriedly made, the Generalissimo, at Hutton's request, agreed that 5 Army should take over the Toungoo area. This Army consisted of 22, 96 and 200 Divisions, and was considered the best equipped and trained force in China. During February the Chinese troops, much hampered by lack of transport, moved forward into Burma.

. . . . A Chinese 'Army' corresponded to a European Corps and consisted usually of two or three divisions. The division itself was not only much smaller than its British or American equivalent, having a strength of from seven to nine thousand, but only two-thirds of the men were armed; the other third replaced the absent animal or motor transport and acted as carriers. As a result the rifle power of a Chinese division at full strength rarely exceeded three thousand, with a couple of hundred light machine-guns, thirty or forty medium machine-guns, and a few 3-inch mortars. There were no artillery units except a very occasional anti-tank gun of small calibre, no medical services, meagre signals, a staff car or two, half a dozen trucks, and a couple of hundred shaggy, ill-kept ponies. Nevertheless the Chinese soldier was tough, brave and experienced—after all, he had already been fighting on his own without help for years. He was the veteran among the Allies, and could claim up to this time that he had held back the Japanese more successfully than any of the others. Indeed, he registered his arrival in the forward areas by several minor but marked successes against enemy detachments.

General Slim

The Chinese Arrive in Burma

A junior Chinese officer and four men walked into the Pyinmana Club the second night they were there. There was no one about as most of the population had fled since a light Japanese bombing a week or two before. Naturally enough, the Chinese helped themselves to a drink. Whisky, brandy, gin, and all the rest were on the shelves, but the abstemious Chinese took two bottles of ginger-ale and four of soda-water. The Indian butler left in charge of the club walked in, saw the party in progress, and ran for help.

He returned with a senior Chinese officer who immediately made the revellers pay for their ginger-ale and soda. The careful Indian butler examined the till and declared that it lacked one rupee. In the search the senior officer found a silver rupee in the pocket of one of the soldiers. He gave this to the butler and drew his Mauser pistol. . . .

'Oh, please don't shoot him,' begged the Indian, on his knees. 'Perhaps it is not my rupee.'

And the senior officer returned his pistol to its holster; instead he drew his sword. Before you could say 'antidisestablishmentarianism' he had lopped a piece off the top of the soldier's ear. Everyone spoke of the Chinese troops in Burma up to this date as the best-behaved troops they had seen.

O. D. Gallagher

In Burma as elsewhere, Japanese air superiority was almost complete.

Now great wedges of silver bombers droned across the sky and one after another the cities of Burma spurted with flame and vanished in roaring holocausts. Prome, Meiktila, Mandalay, Thazi, Pyinmana, Maymyo, Lashio, Taung-gyi, largely wooden towns, all of them crumbled and burned. The Japanese used pattern bombing, coming over in faultless formation, giving themselves a leisurely dummy run or two, and then letting all their bombs go in one shattering crump. They were very accurate. We always said they had in each formation only one leader capable of aiming and all took the time from him. It was certainly effective, but I personally preferred it to the methods of the Italians and the French when they also had no air opposition. They had cruised round, dropping a few sticks at a time, and keeping one in suspense. With the Japanese it was all over quickly; you had either had it, or were alive till next time. Whatever the method, it was effective enough with the civil population. The police, hospital staffs, air-raid precaution units, public services, railways, collapsed. Labour vanished into the jungle; towns were evacuated. Only a few devoted British, Anglo-Burmans and Burmese carried nobly on.

.... One raid occurred as divisional commanders and others were assembled at Corps Headquarters for a conference. Some of us were just finishing breakfast when the alarm went. In a group we walked towards the slit trenches, I still carrying a cup of tea. Looking up, we could see the usual tight wedge of twenty or thirty bombers coming straight over. The mess servants and others saw them too and began to run for shelter. I had been insistent on stopping people running at these times as it had led to panic, so continuing our move at a slow and dignified pace, I called out to them to stop running and walk. I remember shouting in Hindustani, 'There's plenty of time. Don't hurry!'—a remark that almost qualified for the Famous Last Words series. At that instant we heard the unmistakable scream of bombs actually falling. With one accord two or three generals and half a dozen other senior officers, abandoning dignity, plunged for the nearest trench. Scott, being no mean athlete, arrived first, took a leap and landed with shattering impact on a couple of Indian sweepers already crouching out of sight. I followed, a cup of tea and all; the rest piled in on top, and the whole salvo of bombs went off in one devastating bang.

Poor Scott, crushed under our combined weight, feeling warm liquid dripping over him, was convinced that I had been blown into the trench and was now bleeding to death all over him. His struggles to come to my assistance were heroic, but almost fatal to the wretched bottom layer of sweepers. We hauled ourselves and them out, and, slightly shamefacedly, returned to our conference.

General Slim

On 24 March the rot set in once again. The Chinese forces in eastern Burma were attacked and driven out of Toungoo by the Japanese. Now the long retreat began for the last time; the British up the Irrawaddy and Chindwin and the Chinese between the Sittang and Salween. Time after time fierce battles were fought as the Japanese tried to cut off the withdrawing armies, who attacked desperately to hold them back and secure the line of escape.

The April Retreat: Battle for the Oilfields

North of the Pin Chaung at the old Corps Headquarters location, the enemy had reappeared in greater strength and re-established their block. This time in addition to Price and his Frontier Force Gurkhas, there were available some West Yorkshires and a few tanks coming up from the south. A concerted attack again cleared the road, inflicting heavy casualties, the Japanese leaving many bodies in our uniforms. Transport then moved over the ford again, but numbers of vehicles had been lost by air attack during the enforced halt. More enemy appeared south of the cleared block, about a thousand of them being shelled by our artillery with effect, but again they established a block, this time near the ford. The situation was not encouraging and I was greatly relieved to hear that the 113th Regiment of the Chinese 38 Division was just arriving at Kyauk-padaung. I dashed off in my jeep to meet their commander and give him his orders.

Apart from the Guerrilla Battalion that had so reluctantly come to us at Taungdwingyi, this was the first time I had had Chinese troops under me. I found the Regimental Commander in the upstairs room of one of the few houses still standing in Kyaukpadaung village. He was a slight but tough-looking little Chinaman, with a real poker face, a pair of field-glasses and a huge Mauser pistol. We were introduced by the British liaison officer with the regiment, who spoke perfect Chinese. We shook hands, and got down to business with a map. As I described the situation the Chinese colonel struck me as intelligent and quick to grasp what I wanted. This was to bring his regiment, in lorries which I had ready, down to the Pin Chaung at once, and then send back the transport to fetch the next regiment as quickly as possible. I explained that it was my intention to attack with those two regiments, or, if possible, with the whole division, across the Pin Chaung early on the 18th in co-operation with a break-out by 1 Burma Division. Having explained all this fully I asked him, through the interpreter, if he understood. He replied that he did.

'Then let's get moving,' I said cheerfully. The translation of this remark brought a flow of Chinese. He could not, he said, budge from Kyaukpadaung until he had the orders of General Sun, his Divisional Commander.

'But,' I explained, 'General Sun has been placed under my orders. If he were here I should tell him to do what I have told you to do, and he would do it. Isn't that right?'

'Yes,' agreed my Regimental Commander readily.

'All right, then let's get going.'

'But I cannot move until I get the orders of General Sun.'

And so it went on for an hour and a half, at the end of which I could cheerfully have shot the colonel with his own pistol. At last, just when I was feeling desperate, he suddenly smiled and said, 'All right, I will do it!'

Why he changed his mind I do not know. I suspect some of the Chinese of various ranks who had flowed in and out of the room through our interview must have brought a message from Sun, telling him to do whatever I wanted. Once he got moving, I had no complaints about my Chinaman. Indeed, within the next few days I got to like him very much.

. . . . Meanwhile the Burma Division had begun in real earnest the Battle of the Oilfields. And a brutal battle it was.

At 6.30 in the morning the Burma Division attacked. Progress was made, under cover of artillery, but the guns were running short of shells. Then some Burman troops faltered. In spite of this, a by-pass road was cleared, and a good deal of transport got down almost to the Pin Chaung itself, only to be held up by Japanese on the south bank. The British and Indian troops of the Division fought doggedly over low ridge after ridge, the Japanese defending each one to the last man. A detachment of the Inniskillings struggled through to the Pin Chaung and enthusiastically greeted the troops it found there, believing them to be Chinese. They were Japanese, who lured the Irishmen into an ambush. The tanks made a last attack on the road block, but it was defended by several anti-tank guns and the tanks, bogged in the soft sand, became sitting targets. The attack, like that of the Chinese from the other side, petered to a standstill.

More Japanese were coming in from the east and were reported on the river.

The situation was grave. At half-past four in the afternoon, Scott reported on the radio that his men were exhausted from want of water and continuous marching and fighting. He could hold that night, he thought, but if he waited until morning his men, still without water, would be so weakened they would have little or no offensive power to renew the attack. He asked permission to destroy his guns and transport and fight his way out that night. Scott was the last man to paint an unduly dark picture. I knew his men were almost at the end of their strength and in a desperate position. I could not help wishing that he had not been so close a friend. I thought of his wife and of his boys. There were lots of other wives, too, in England, India and Burma whose hearts would be under that black cloud a couple of miles away. Stupid to remember that now! Better get it out of my head.

I thought for a moment, sitting there with the headphones on, in the van with the operator crouching beside me, his eyes anxiously on my face. Then I told Scott he must hang on. I had ordered a Chinese attack again with all available tanks and artillery for the next morning. If Burma Division attacked then we ought to break through, and save our precious guns and transport. I was afraid too that if our men came out in driblets as they would in the dark, mixed up with Japanese, the Chinese and indeed our own soldiers would fail to recognize them and their losses would be heavy. Scott took it as I knew he would. He said, 'All right, we'll hang on and we'll do our best in the morning, but, for God's sake, Bill, make those Chinese attack.'

I stepped out of the van feeling about as depressed as a man could. There, standing in a little half-circle waiting for me, were a couple of my own staff, an officer or two from the Tank Brigade, Sun, and the Chinese liaison officers. They stood there silent and looked at me. All commanders know that look. They see it in the eyes of their staffs and their men when things are really bad, when even the most confident staff officer and the toughest soldier want holding up, and they turn where they *should* turn for support—to their commander. And sometimes he does not know what to say. He feels very much alone.

'Well, gentlemen,' I said, putting on what I hoped was a confident, cheerful expression, 'It might be worse!'

One of the group, in a sepulchral voice, replied with a single word: 'How?'

I could cheerfully have murdered him, but instead I had to keep my temper. 'Oh,' I said, grinning, 'it might be raining!'

Two hours later, it was—hard. As I crept under a truck for shelter I thought of that fellow and wished I *had* murdered him.

Throughout the night, as we sat inside a circle of leaguered tanks just above the Pin Chaung, we could hear and see the crump and flash of Japanese shells and mortar bombs flailing Scott's wretched men. His guns did not reply. They were down to about twenty rounds per gun now and he was keeping those for the morning. Time and again the Japanese put in infantry attacks, attempting to infiltrate under cover of darkness and shelling. These attacks, one after the other, were beaten off, but certain of the Burma troops panicked, abandoned their positions, throwing extra strain on the British and Indians.

The day began for me before dawn with a severe blow. The Chinese attack across the Pin Chaung to take Twingon, a village about a mile south of the ford, which I had hoped would start soon after daylight, could not be got ready in time. After a good deal of talk it was promised for 12.30 as the earliest possible hour. I was then faced with the problem of either telling Scott to hold his attack, which was due to go in at seven o'clock, or to let it go as arranged. I decided to let it go, rather than keep his men and transport sitting cramped and waterless under artillery, mortar and air attack.

At seven o'clock the Burma Division resumed the attack, but a reinforced Japanese defence held it after it had made some progress. Meanwhile on the north bank, while still urging the Chinese to hurry their preparations, we had managed to scrape up a small British force which attacked and during the morning actually got a squadron of tanks and some of the West Yorkshire Regiment across the Chaung. This small success might have been expanded had not one of those infuriating mishaps so common in battle occurred. An officer some distance in rear received a report that strong enemy forces were advancing to cut off the transport assembled about Gwegyo. Without realizing the situation forward, or still less, that the threatening forces advancing on him were not Japanese but Chinese, he ordered back the tanks and accompanying infantry to deal with this new, but imaginary, danger.

Burma Division was once more halted in a tight perimeter and was being heavily shelled. The heat was intense, there was still no water, the troops were exhausted and they had suffered heavy casualties, their wounded, of course, being still with them. At this stage, the Burma battalions, in spite of the efforts of their officers, really disintegrated. 1 Burma Brigade reported that the bulk of their troops were no longer reliable; even 13 Brigade said that some of theirs were shaky. It was hardly to be wondered at; their ordeal had been terribly severe.

The Chinese attack, promised for 12.30, had now been postponed to 14.00 hours. Just before that time it was again put back to 16.00 hours. We managed, however, to get it off at 15.00 instead.

Unhappily before that time communication with Scott had ceased and his last desperate effort to break out could not be co-ordinated with the Chinese attack. His squadron of tanks had found and cleared a rough track, leading east, down to the Pin Chaung, over which it was hoped vehicles could move. Scott himself formed up the column, guns in front, wounded in ambulances and trucks next, followed by such vehicles as had survived the bombardment. With a spearhead of tanks and infantry, the column lurched down the narrow, uneven path, through the low hillocks. But the trail turned to sand; the leading ambulances were bogged and the column stopped. As many wounded as possible were piled on the tanks, and Scott gave the order to abandon vehicles and fight a way out on foot, across the Pin Chaung. This his men did, some in formed bodies, some in small groups, and on the other side they met the Chinese. At the sight of the water in the Chaung the mules which had come out with them went mad and the men flung themselves face downwards into it. The haggard, red-eyed British, Indian and Burmese soldiers who staggered up the bank were a terrible sight, but every man I saw was still carrying his rifle. The two brigades of the Division had reached Yenangyaung at a strength of not more than one; there they had lost in killed and wounded twenty per cent of that small number, with a considerable portion of their guns, mortars and vehicles. None of these losses, in either men or equipment, could be replaced. After its ordeal, the Division would be of no fighting value until it had rested, and, as best it could, re-organized. We collected it that night about Gwegyo.

When the Chinese did attack they went in splendidly. They were thrilled at the tank and artillery support they were getting and showed real dash. They took Twingon, rescuing some two hundred of our prisoners and wounded. Next day, 19 April, 38 Division attacked again and with tanks penetrated into Yenang-yaung itself, repulsing a Japanese counter-attack. The fighting was severe and the Chinese acquitted themselves well, inflicting heavy losses, vouched for by our own officers. Sun now expected a really heavy Japanese attack at dawn on the 21st. I discussed this with him and agreed that he should come out of the town, back to the Pin Chaung. His Division had done well and I did not want it frittered away in a house-to-house dogfight for the shell of Yenangyaung. In spite of the stories I had heard from American sources of Chinese unwillingness to fight, I had remembered how enthusiastic officers, who had served with our own Chinese Hong Kong regiment, had been about their men, and I had expected the Chinese soldier to be tough and brave. I was, I confess, surprised at how he responded to the stimulus of proper tank and artillery support, and at the aggressive spirit he had shown. I had never expected, either, to get a Chinese general of the calibre of Sun.

As I talked this over with Davies, my chief of staff and my mainstay in these difficult times, we thought we saw a chance of striking back at 33 Japanese Division. True, our 1 Burma Division, never really a division in either establish-ment or equipment, was at the moment incapable of action, but it was definitely recovering in the peace of Mount Popa, where we had sent it. In a week or two we might hope to have it back in the field at a strength of, say, a brigade. If we could get 17 Division, still in Taungdwingyi, we might, with the Chinese 38 Division and anything else we could scrape up, try a counter-stroke. We were always building up our house of cards, Davies and I, and seeing it fall down—but we went on. So we renewed our attempts to persuade Burma Army to let us take 17 Division from Taungdwingyi. Meanwhile 38 Division and, as usual, 7 Armoured Brigade covered 1 Burma Division as it lay gasping but not dying.

A number of our badly wounded had of necessity been left in the ambulances when the Burma Division had finally broken out. A young gunner officer volunteered to go back to discover their fate. Under cover of darkness, he did so. The ambulances were still standing on the track but every man in them had had his throat cut or been bayoneted to death.

General Slim

Mandalay Falls

Mandalay was full of dumps, stores and camps of every kind—almost all of them deserted. A few officers and men of the administrative services and depart-ments remained, but there had been a general and not very creditable exodus. We were to find more and more that demoralization behind the line was spread-ing. From now on, while the fighting troops, knowing that their object—to get out intact to India—was at last clear, actually improved in morale and fighting power, the amorphous mass of non-fighting units on the line of communication deteriorated rapidly. In its withdrawal the Corps was from now on preceded by an undisciplined mob of fugitives intent only on escape. No longer in organized units, without any supply arrangements, having deserted their officers, they banded together in gangs, looting, robbing and not infrequently murdering the unfortunate villagers on their route. They were almost entirely Indians and very few belonged to combatant units of the Army. Most of them were soldiers only in name, but their cowardice and their conduct brought disrepute on the real Indian soldiers who followed. It was not to be wondered that as we retreated we found villages burnt and abandoned and such inhabitants as were not in hiding frightened and unfriendly.

It was impossible to guard all the stores lying unattended in Mandalay. On one dump we did, however, put a small guard—that of special octane petrol for our tanks. We were growing greatly anxious about their fuel supply and the find was a godsend, but, when the tanks arrived next day to refill they found nothing but twisted and blackened drums. A senior staff officer, alleged to be from Burma Army, had appeared, and ordered it to be destroyed, and so, with the help of the guard, it was. In the growing confusion mistakes of this kind were almost inevitable, but none the less damaging.

Numbers of 5 Army Chinese were collected in Mandalay and attempts were being made to get them away to the north by train. At the same time I was anxious to rescue some of the more important items such as rifles, Bren guns, ammunition, medical stores and boots, without which we could not continue to fight. With this object two or three small trains were being loaded under the direction of a few stout-hearted British and Anglo-Burmese railway officials who set a magnificent example of devotion to duty. My Chinese of 38 Division came one afternoon and told me that a certain Chinese general had discovered these trains and was coming that night with his troops to seize them and to escape north. I was in a quandary. I had not enough troops to guard them against the numbers who would appear, nor did I want a fight with our allies. I sent warning to our railway friends and asked them to steam the engines ten miles up the line. In due course the Chinese arrived, piled themselves in, on, and all over the wagons. The General ordered the trains to start. He was then told there were no engines, as on my orders they had been taken away. There was nothing for my Chinese friend to do but to call off his men and think of some other way of stealing a train. Eventually he succeeded in doing so and got away, but it was not one of my trains. I met him frequently afterwards in India. We never mentioned trains, but I noticed that he regarded me with an increased respect.

The Corps, with the exception of 63 Brigade that still held the approaches to the Ava Bridge on the south bank, was now all safely over the Irrawaddy. There had been an anxious moment with the tanks. I found a line of them halted on the south side of the bridge with officers in consultation. A Stuart tank weighs some thirteen tons and a notice warned us that the roadway running across the bridge on brackets each side of the railway had a maximum capacity of six tons. I asked who had built the bridge and was shown a tablet with the name of a well-known British engineering firm. My experience has been that any permanent bridge built by British engineers will almost certainly have a safety factor of one hundred per cent, and I ordered the tanks to cross, one by one. I confess I watched nervously to see if the roadway sagged under the first as it made a gingerly passage, but all was well. Good old British engineers! At last even the Chinese C.-in-C. agreed that all his men were over, and so 63 Brigade was withdrawn across the bridge. With a resounding thump it was blown at 23.59 hours on 30 April, and its centre spans fell neatly into the river—a sad sight, and a signal that we had lost Burma.

General Slim

The physical condition, morale, and spirit of the British Army was at a low ebb. Three months of bitter campaigning and worse hardship had enfeebled the whole Imperial Army and exacted a heavy toll in fighting fitness. Moreover, the average soldier in the Imperial Army no longer wanted to fight in Burma. The Indians were anxious to get back to their native land, and the British wanted to clear out of that forsaken country. This was obvious from their oft-repeated greetings of 'See you in India', but it was more apparent from hundreds of bitter comments that increased in violence as the days wore on. Though the high British authorities had delayed the Chinese from originally coming into Burma, a typical comment heard on the retreat past Mandalay was: 'If the Chinese want the goddam country, give it to them.'

But it is doubtful if the Chinese, at least their Army, at that particular time, wanted anything to do with Burma. They were just as fed up with Burma as their British comrades-in-arms. In addition, they were handicapped by being less familiar with Burma than the British.

Jack Belden, American journalist

The End of the Road: India, mid-May

The men of Burma Corps, when they reached Imphal, were physically and mentally very near the end of their strength. They had endured casualties, hardships, hunger, sickness and, above all, the heartbreaking frustration of retreat to a degree that few armies have suffered and yet held together as armies. They were, even at the last, as I had proved, ready if called upon to turn and fight again, but they had been buoyed up by the thought that once over the border into India, not only would other troops interpose between them and the enemy to give them relief from the strain they had supported so long, but that welcome and rest would await them.

. . . . As the wasted units marched wearily into Imphal, through the sheets of monsoon rain, they were directed into areas of jungle on the steep hillsides and told to bivouac there. It seemed to them that no preparations at all had been made for their reception. They had arrived with nothing but the soaked, worn and filthy clothing they stood up in; they had no blankets, no waterproof sheets, no tentage. Nor did they find any awaiting them. On those dripping, gloomy hillsides there was no shelter but the trees, little if any clothing or blankets, no adequate water or medical arrangements. As Taffy Davies, indefatigable in labouring to ease the sufferings of our troops, wryly said, 'The slogan in India seems to be, "Isn't that Burma Army annihilated yet?".'

General Slim

While the British walked the long nine hundred miles back to India, the Chinese under their tough, hard-bitten leader General 'Vinegar Joe' Stilwell, found their own way out. In mid-April those Chinese troops not already involved in their first defeat had been completely shattered by a new Japanese attack. Henceforth their military value was slight.

Stilwell

He already had something of a reputation for shortness of temper and for distrust of most of the rest of the world. I must admit he surprised me a little, when, at our first meeting, he said, 'Well, general, I must tell you that my motto in all dealings is "buyer beware",' but he never, as far as I was concerned, lived up to that old horse-trader's motto. He was over sixty, but he was tough, mentally and physically; he could be as obstinate as a whole team of mules; he could be, and frequently was, downright rude to people whom, often for no good reason, he did not like. But when he said he would do a thing he did it. True, you had to get him to *say* that he would, quite clearly and definitely—and that was not always easy—but once he had, you knew he would keep to his word. He had a habit, which I found very disarming, of arguing most tenaciously against some proposal and then suddenly looking at you over the top of his glasses with the shadow of a grin, and saying, 'Now tell me what you want me to do and I'll do it!' He was two people; one when he had an audience, and a quite different person when talking to you alone. I think it amused him to keep up in public the 'Vinegar Joe, Tough Guy' attitude, especially in front of his staff. Americans, whether they liked him or not—and he had more enemies among Americans than among British—were all scared of him. He had courage to an extent few people have, and determination, which, as he usually concentrated it along narrow lines, had a dynamic force. He was not a great soldier in the highest sense, but he was a real leader in the field; no one else I know could have made his Chinese do what they did. He was, undoubtedly, the most colourful character in south-east Asia—and I liked him.

General Slim

The Disintegration of Dynamite Chen

At the time of the Japanese attack Dynamite Chen had his division strung out in great depth, on an extremely narrow front, along the Lashio road leading from Mawchi through Bawlake. His units in general were echeloned on the road. In brief, Chen had committed two grave errors: he had echeloned in depth to an unbelievable extent so that not one of his units formed an adequate defence force; and he had formed such a narrow front that the Japanese could envelop any one of his units at will. American staff officers on the spot warned him of his dangerous position and tried to get him to change his dispositions, but Chen was so slow in moving that the corrections came too late. General Stilwell personally ordered Chen to get busy. If he had obeyed promptly and fought with determination, his division might conceivably have held on.

In the middle of April the Japanese struck these dispositions with the speed and force of a thunderbolt. Moving slightly off the road, the Japanese enveloped Chen's battalions on both flanks. When the Chinese division commander sought to attack these enveloping columns by bringing up his rear units, he found his rear echelons in turn enveloped by the enemy. The Japanese thrust quick striking forces between Chen's companies and battalions; between the battalions and the regiments; and finally interposed themselves between his regiments and the division command.

Just what happened after that is not exactly clear. Chinese units were cut off from one another. Innumerable Japanese infiltrated between them. With a mass of road blocks woven around them, the Chinese troops were thrown into indescribable confusion. The soldiers, who had been confined so strictly to a narrow valley by their commander, now fled to the hills. Liaison between different units was lost and finally the division disintegrated.

Suddenly one morning the whole of 55 Division disappeared. It disappeared as completely as if a hole had opened in the earth and swallowed all the soldiers.

What had happened to the division, how all the soldiers could so completely vanish from the face of the earth, was a complete mystery to everyone. General Stilwell, talking to me shortly afterwards, said, 'There's not a trace of them. It's the damnedest thing I ever heard of.'

For two days not a single soldier of the 55th was heard from or seen. When finally a few stragglers staggered into 6 Army headquarters, they could not tell what had happened. The only thing certain was that a great yawning gap had been opened in the lines.

Through this hole the Japanese now poured a motor column with the speed of an express train. During the first days of the battle the enemy had moved at a rate of ten miles a day; this rate soon increased to twenty-five miles a day, and finally to forty and fifty miles on a tortuous road in very rugged terrain northwest of the Salween valley, which should have been simple to defend.

Jack Belden

The Road North

There was no known highway leading to the north. Numerous reconnaissance parties sent out in all directions had finally discovered a cart track following close along the railway and through a dry bamboo forest. This track had been explored for fifty miles in a jeep by Major Frank Merrill, who reported that it might be passable for trucks and sedans, but beyond that fifty miles was unknown territory. On the morning of 2 May, amid circumstances of uncertainty, with the Japanese seeking to cut us off, Stilwell put his Chinese divisions and his American staff officers on that road, on that rutted cart track in that burning, arid, desolate country, and we struck northward, following the railway, moving without information of the enemy and driving towards an undetermined goal.

. . . . A growing mass of Chinese soldiery ahead of us crowded between the thickets and blocked passage; artillery bogged down in hollows and stuck in dried-up sandy washes; soldiers grunted and strained to pull them out; huge trucks loaded with forty and fifty soldiers, clinging to the framework of the sides, to mudguards and radiator bonnets, caught in the thickets and branches of dead trees overhanging the cart track; traffic halted, went forward, came to a standstill again.

We went so slowly that at nine o'clock we had not gone five miles. We had got down many times to help stuck guns extricate themselves and to unsnarl trucks tangled up with the thickets. We began to be disturbed by our slow pace and we despaired of ever getting by the Chinese column. Finally Merrill spied an opening in the thickets and rushed through it across the fields, thereby getting ahead of the Chinese. I followed swiftly and on coming to the upper end of the opening halted my jeep across the face of the leading Chinese truck so that Stilwell could come up and get by.

. . . . Again Colonel Williams ran after Stilwell, saying, 'The men can't stand this sun, general. They're not in condition yet. We've got to march only early in the morning and late in the afternoon.'

'We also have to average at the very least fourteen miles a day, and so far we've done less than five and it's almost eleven o'clock,' said the general.

In about half an hour, however, by a small sandy, gravel beach, the general called a noonday halt. As officers and young enlisted men came up one by one and flopped on the sand with their arms stretched out at full length in an attitude of extreme fatigue, the general . . . looked at me and remarked: 'When I was their age, if I couldn't do this before breakfast, I would have been ashamed.'

He began to divest himself of his pants and his shirt, and, with his campaign hat still on his head to protect him from the noonday sun, went into the stream, sat down, and bathed. Others soon roused themselves, lay in the stream, and tried to suck water back into their pores. The girls, now quieter than before, but still more lively than the men, dug small holes in the sand, placed leaves in the bottom of them, and when the water seeped through the sand as through a filter they scooped it up and drank. There seemed to be a trick in this, for when Jones and I tried it, our water always remained muddy and full of sand, never clearing like that of the girls.

Jack Belden

General Stilwell and his men reached India at about the same time as General Slim.

As well as the retreating armies, many thousands of refugees were struggling away through the jungle. Twenty thousand reached India between May and July. Thousands more trickled in throughout the summer and autumn. By the end of November all those still alive had come in.

Survival of the fittest was the order of the day. At the few hastily-erected camps along the road only those with energy enough to fight their way near the cookhouse were fed. The nights, even in May, were bitterly cold, and about sixty miles of the road were over four thousand feet above sea-level. When the rains started the plight of these people, with no more clothing than the flimsy rags they clutched about them, defies description. Every day dozens gave up the struggle and died where they fell by the roadside.

None who witnessed them can ever forget the innumerable scenes of individual tragedy. There were two children not more than eight years old, with abdomens grossly distended and the limbs of skeletons, trying to awaken a mother who had passed beyond human aid; there was a little girl of four or five having to be forcibly separated from her dead father, and an old woman who dropped exhausted by the roadside while her husband, reduced to a mere automaton with only the will to live, staggered on.

Some carried small bundles, and it was pathetic to see how they clung to the last to things that represented home—a brass flower-vase, a pair of ornate candle-sticks, and in one case an ancient gramophone.

British Nursing Sister

Starvation

Each morning about dawn people started wandering into camp, some of them having spent the night a few hundred yards away, unaware of the camp close by. Others would wander up from the refugee camp and demand a second issue of food. We were so short of food and there were so many people that it was only possible to feed them once. Our war cry was 'Keep them hungry, keep them moving'. We did not want people to get that comfortable feeling under their belts because it made them relax and deprived them of the necessary urge to get out of the jungle as quickly as possible. The new arrivals in camp had to wait until the food was cooked, which was seldom before half past-eight. In the meantime, we would take a walk round the camp and tell people to get a move on.

. . . . For the first three days we fed the refugees on Tagung Hka stew. We had no rice to spare, or any other food that we had brought from India, but our stew contained plenty of nutriment. Many Hindus who, under normal conditions, would have found beef loathsome to their taste, now, poor things, in their extremity hungrily ate this nourishing stew. We had refugees of every caste, and for very religiously-minded people who were really hungry and were still not prepared to eat meat, we kept a stew made principally of plantain.

. . . . It was also necessary to make the refugees fight both physically and mentally for their life. When no drugs were available this was done by shouting and insulting them until they got angry. If this did not work they were slapped all over and their legs and arms rubbed. When their faces showed signs of flushing they were shown a cup of glucose D and water. This they were allowed to sniff but not drink for a little while. Then they were given a few drops at a time. All this time things were said to the refugees which were calculated to arouse their emotions. After they had drunk two ounces of glucose and water they were given nothing more until they started to react. It usually took twenty minutes before they would start to gurk and belch. When this happened we knew they would live and not die. They were then allowed another two ounces of glucose and water. Half an hour later they would be put in a position where they could see everyone eating and drinking tea. They were given nothing until all the others had finished. Then they were given a small cup of tea with lots of milk, sugar and salt in it. The refugees were now ready to be carried for about four miles, where they would again be given a small amount of glucose water. On reaching a camp for the night they were given only tea, milk, salt and glucose or sugar. By this time their kidneys had started to work and the refugees wanted to urinate. If this did not happen they were given very strong tea, which generally did the trick. In the morning the refugees were made to watch the coolies eat, but were kept hungry and longing for food. They were then given half a biscuit softened in a hot cup of Marmite or tea. The refugees would then be carried to a permanent camp where they would be kept for a week. For the first few days they were given mainly tea, milk, sugar, salt, Marmite and biscuit. Then they were introduced to germinated gram and onions, garlic and rice. In a week or so these people were fit enough to be carried over the next pass, and after a day's rest went on to India.

The main thing to remember about refugees is that their morale must be kept up. Their desire to fight for their life must be continually stimulated. They must never be allowed to stop seeing the flag still flying or to feel they have no further responsibility towards themselves or their families.

A. R. Tainsh, supply and transport officer

POSTSCRIPT

I claim we got a hell of a beating. We got run out of Burma, and it is humiliating as hell. I think we should find out what caused it and go back and retake it.

General Stilwell, May 1942

14

RUSSIA, 1942:
THE LAST TRIUMPHS
OF GERMANY

THE WINTER RETREAT

Throughout the winter of 1941–42 the Russian forces, better equipped for and more accustomed to the frightful conditions, continued to hammer at the Germans, who fell back along almost the whole of their vast front.

The Barn

THE next ten days were concentrated hell as the Russians hammered ceaselessly at Gridino in an effort to break our defensive line and clear the way to Rzhev and Smolensk. The whole of the Central Army Group's front was called upon to repel the Red steam-roller offensive, but the Gridino corner of the defensive bulge round Rzhev was the nearest point to Moscow of the whole front and took a tremendous pounding. Major Klostermann's outlook was bounded by the shrinking, disintegrating village. And my field of vision extended only from the dressing station to the big Kolchoze barn, forty yards behind the house. That Kolchoze barn became our main concern.

On 8 January, the Russians captured it again and every man able to hold a weapon—stretcher-bearers, wounded men, Heinrich and myself—ran out into the bitter cold to engage them in fierce hand-to-hand fighting. The small infantry gun was used at point-blank range against the massive barn. We were inevitably being overwhelmed by weight of numbers when Klostermann staged a counter-attack with some of his men and the Reds were thrown out. A renewed Russian attack during the night petered out in the face of concentrated fire from small-arms and our heavy 21 cm. mortars. Towards morning, the Reds retaliated from a safe distance by plastering us with artillery shell-fire.

The Russian artillery fire stopped at about 5 a.m. and we heard a screaming mob coming towards us from the east again. Their high-pitched '*Oorair! Oorair!*' came across the snow to us. On they came towards the barn, yelling and screaming at the top of their voices. A flare picked them out—a close-packed body of charging men. From our holes in the snow and our wooden barricades behind the dressing station we fired our automatics and rifles into the advancing mass. They went down by the dozen, but the men behind trod the bodies into the snow. They took the Kolchoze barn again, but this time we fired grenades into the barn, where the Russians were still kicking up an infernal din. Some of the Reds charged out of the barn right into the muzzles of our guns. Confused hand-to-hand fighting developed, but suddenly the mass of Russians in the barn took to their heels and fled into the darkness.

Cautiously some of our men entered the barn. There were dead and wounded Russians littering the floor, victims of the grenades. But in a corner were two Russians singing raucously, quote oblivious of what was going on around them. Then it dawned on us—the Russians were blind drunk! From the less seriously wounded we gathered that the commissars, becoming desperate at the Red Army's inability to break through our lines in night attacks, had issued their troops with generous rations of alcohol, and when all the men were thoroughly drunk, had launched the attack.

And then something even more grotesque came to our notice. Two old women were cowering against the wall—in their muffled state we had taken them for men. They and about fifty more old men and women, civilians from the Russian-held villages, had been forced to run in front of the Red troops when they charged our positions. All but the two old women of this human shield had been shot down by us and trampled underfoot by the troops behind. But they had served the diabolical Russian purpose—fifty useless civilians had perished instead of fifty soldiers. We went outside and, lying in the snow, was the evidence; defenceless, unarmed civilians bore testimony in death. Three were wounded but still alive. They were carried into the dressing station along with our own thirty wounded. Eight of our men were dead.

Our village was shrinking round us as house after house was burnt down or destroyed by artillery fire. Never-ending alarms kept us on edge day and night. Next day, 10 January, we were bombed by the Luftwaffe and nine of our men were killed. We cursed our own airmen for their stupidity and their accuracy. Then a patrol of twelve men was surprised by the Russians and practically annihilated; two badly wounded men staggered back. Two more Russian attacks were hurled back; in one of them, one of our own mortars was misdirected in the confusion and eight of our soldiers were severely wounded as a result. The Reds brought their terrifying 'Stalin-organ' into the fight and plastered the village with mortar shells. While the 'Stalin-organ' was playing its devilish tune, every man in the battalion lay flat wherever he was and prayed that none of the shells from that battery of destruction was inscribed with his name. Fortunately after Gridino had been plastered thoroughly the 'organ' was moved to another sector to repeat its tune.

Heinrich Haape

The Major

A second blow fell almost immediately. The commander of the division's anti-tank battalion shot himself. He had been a friend of mine. He was a much-decorated soldier of the first World War; during the second he had gained further military distinction in France, Greece and Russia. In ten years of war I met very few men who were genuinely quite without fear. He was one of them. He loved danger. He was dauntless. He was also an excellent strategist and tireless in striving for the welfare of his men. Through some odd coincidence it had come to light that he had allowed some friends in Bucharest to lend him

Roumanian money and had repaid the amounts in Germany in German money. This was a currency offence. From the legal point of view the soldier was considered to be German territory wherever he might be. An offence of this kind seemed rather ridiculous in circumstances as they were then. Presumably it could have been settled without fuss by some disciplinary action which the divisional commander could have devised as principal judicial administrator. But there was another matter as well. For months a lieutenant on my friend's staff had been taking notes of the major's remarks about the régime. These the lieutenant had sent to one of the Party's offices in Germany and they came back to the division by way of circuitous official channels for 'opinion and report'. . . . The major faced degradation and removal to a punitive unit as a private, second class. He was a man of forty-five who had led a blameless life. He shot himself. Military honours for his funeral were refused and the regulations even forbade the chaplain to speak at the graveside. However, owing to the general's magnanimity, permission for a dignified burial was given.

Peter Bamm, German medical officer

Spring: German Winter Clothing arrives

The difference between new and old hands at this game of making war in the snow was further accentuated on 25 March, when there was a three-hour thaw at midday. Then it became cold again and by evening a blizzard was raging across the wide snowfields. For the newcomers the brief thaw was of little consequence, but on us it made a great impression—it was the first sign of the approach of a new spring.

And the next day our winter clothing arrived! Huge quantities of fur coats, woollens, fur-lined boots, thick overcoats—all of it collected from the civilians in Germany after a moving appeal to the nation by Goebbels in December. He had told the people at home that we were equipped with warm clothing—we had plenty of it—but it was impossible to have too much in a Russian winter. So the good folk in Germany had sacrificed their fur coats, warm boots, jerseys, overcoats, anything that looked vaguely as if it would keep out the Russian cold, little knowing that we should all have frozen to death had we not been able to shoot the enemy down and pillage their dead bodies to warm our own. The patriotic pile of clothing looked rather ridiculous as it lay in the command-post stable the day after the first thaw of spring.

Heinrich Haape

In September 1941 Leningrad, the second city of Russia, had been invested by the Germans. From then until the spring of 1943, Leningrad was more or less closely blockaded. A lifeline could be kept open across the frozen waters of Lake Ladoga during the winter, but with the thaw, this road across the ice disappeared.

Flight into Leningrad: Spring 1942

All my life I shall preserve the memory of that evening towards the end of April 1942, when our plane, escorted by fighters, flew very low over Lake Ladoga and beneath us, on the ice, which was cracked and fissured, with surging tides of water in between, stretched the road, the only road, which throughout the winter had linked Leningrad with the rest of the country. The people of Leningrad called it The Road of Life. It had already been torn to shreds— virtually obliterated—and in places was a mere flood of water. The plane flew straight towards the misty, crimson, diffuse globe of the sun, which caught the tops of the pines and firs along the entire length of the lakeshore behind us in the tender glow of spring.

A. Fadeyev

Fighting in the Suburbs

When the Germans approached Kolpino the workers of the Izhorsky plant took a vow not to yield either the factory or the town; the Germans would have to force a passage over their dead bones. In the result the front came right up to Kolpino itself. The town and the factory were subjected to systematic assault from the air and to an artillery bombardment which went on without pause day and night. Several generations of Izhorsky people, from infants at the breast to the most ancient men and women, were represented among those killed by bomb or shell fragments. But Kolpino remained in the hands of the Izhorsky workers, and the factory, in spite of everything, went on producing.

Much of Kolpino is ruins. When I was with Lieutenant-Colonel Shubin at the artillery observation post, the enemy's field guns were methodically, remorselessly and senselessly pounding the little wooden houses and huts. Our forward line was a few kilometres in front of us, almost on the edge of the town; the firing there was particularly heavy. But the peacetime ways of the town had not altogether ceased. Women did their washing at the pond. Two girls at the crossroads chatted and laughed. An old woman in a black dress walked slowly along the road, carrying in her arms a grandchild a few months old. The infant slept.

Snipers

Lieutenant Gorbatenko . . . told us about a singular duel in which he engaged for a whole day with an enemy sniper. Having taken up his position at night, towards dawn Lieutenant Gorbatenko detected a faint stir behind a bush on the edge of the enemy trench ahead. With this position as his proximate target Gorbatenko fired. A few seconds later a soldier's spade was thrust up above the enemy trench and waved from side to side. His opponent was signalling a miss. Gorbatenko kept quiet and waited a long time in the hope that his opponent would show himself. But nothing at all stirred in the enemy trench. Gorbatenko, whose position was well camouflaged, moved cautiously to obtain a closer view, but he had scarcely shifted his head when a shot rang out from the enemy trench and a bullet whistled past his ear, singeing his hair. Gorbatenko dived back into his trench, hung out his own spade and waved it from side to side, in his turn showing that he hadn't been hit.

In this way, changing their positions and spying on each other's faintest movement, they stuck to their duel for a good many hours, each of them signalling with his spade on every occasion that the other's shot had missed.

In the end Gorbatenko killed his man: he caught him out. After one of the enemy sniper's shots he made no attempt to signal with the spade, but kept still, feigning death. A little later his opponent decided to make certain and began to peer over the trench. Still Gorbatenko gave no sign of life. As he had reckoned in advance, the other abandoned all caution in a short time and hung boldly over the trench, so Gorbatenko dispatched him without difficulty.

Leningrad Landscape

The sight of somebody—man, woman or child—dragging a child's sledge on which lay a dead body wrapped up in a blanket or a bit of canvas became a daily commonplace of the winter Leningrad landscape. The spectacle of somebody dying of hunger in a snow-covered street was by no means rare. Pedestrians passed by, removed their caps and muttered a word or two in sympathy, or sometimes did not even stop, since there was no help they could offer.

The Widow

In one of the bays of the shop a group of women were standing at enormous milling machines, milling mines, scattering sparks in all directions. There were stacks of mines, still hot from the moulds, on the floor near them. I stopped next to one of the women. Her face was visible only in profile. A dark kerchief was drawn low over her brow and I could not guess her age. Her hands protected by huge gauntlets, she picked up a mine from the heap and then, using the whole weight of her body, held it against the rapidly revolving wheel of the machine. A sheaf of sparks flew round her. This was the preliminary process of rough milling before the mines reached the lathes for turning. Without paying any attention to me she picked up mine after mine and pressed them with all the force of her body against the wheel. It was plain that to do this involved a very considerable physical strain, for the woman's whole body quivered with the effort.

This was a man's work, and heavy work at that. I wanted to see the woman's face and I remained where I was until she turned towards me. She seemed to me a woman of about forty. Her face had a strange beauty. Delicate and stern of feature, it was the face of a saint.

'Is it hard work?' I asked.

'Yes, at first it was very hard,' she said, picking up a mine and holding it against the revolving wheel, making the sparks fly once more.

'Where is your husband?' I asked after a brief interval, during which she put the mine down and picked up another.

'He died last winter.'

Blockade Jelly

When I entered the room my cousin, who had a friend with her, a woman as emaciated as herself, was having her dinner. Because of the increased rations for the First of May, their dinner, judged by Leningrad standards, might have been called luxurious. It included even beer and vodka prepared from dried orange rind. Among the dishes was the famous Leningrad-blockade jelly—a jelly made from carpenter's glue. Here was the reverse process: you cooked the glue, removed all the bone scum—or, rather, the scum of what had once been bone—and added gelatine to the rest. Then you let it cool.

This jelly was absolutely tasteless and its nutritive value was dubious, but it was a stay and comfort for many people in Leningrad.

The White Nights

Over Leningrad descended the white nights. You could stand for hours on the Troitsky Bridge when on a white night the moon rose over the Summer Garden, and below, along the Neva, motionless and beautiful in the lilac mist, rose the great colonnades of the Bourse, the Winter Palace, the Admiralty.

And day and night the windows of Leningrad's dwellings were flung wide open. The sounds of wireless music or of gramophone records descended into the street. Wandering along a quiet shady street you would hear, from somewhere inside a wide-flung window, a girl carefully attacking her piano exercises and from time to time the severe voice of the piano teacher. And it was comforting, walking at night along the Neva, to see between the wings of the Kazan Cathedral the huge silver fish of a barrage balloon faintly stirring on its rigging and capable at a moment's notice of rising to the sky.

But there were few air-raid alarms during those summer months. The Leningrad airmen protected their own city and air battles took place some way from its approaches. Sometimes a single plane broke through the defences on the outskirts and dropped its bombs. The artillery bombardment of the city was by now of a stealthy, thieving character only. Suddenly on a clear sunny day or during a beautiful white night the distant sound of a big gun would be heard and a shell would scream overhead and burst somewhere near the Griboyedov canal or Uritsky Square. A second, a third—now here, now there—and the thief would make off.

A. Fadayev

With the departure of all Germany's hopes of a quick end to the war in the East, the official German attitude to the Russian people suffered a radical change for the worse.

Russian Volunteers

During their leave most of our men had been deeply shocked; the discontent all over Germany had left them perplexed and worried. A number had been detailed to accompany trains to Germany as medical orderlies. These trains carried Russians—both men and women—who had been enrolled . . . on a purely voluntary basis for service in the war industries. The men had been greatly disturbed by the complete lack of consideration with which these civilians had been treated on the journey. We still felt that we were on friendly terms with the Russians. The men, ignorant of the fact that these workers were heading straight for slavery, put down what they had witnessed to shortcomings in organization.

There was no longer any rhyme or reason in these things. The party was ceremoniously proclaiming the liberation of the Russian people from Soviet enslavement and going through the farce of setting up a Ukrainian puppet government in Kiev which was allowed to do little more than draft its own constitution. Hundreds of thousands of Russians were already fighting in the German Army and were displaying the same bravery that they had shown when they had been in the Red Army only a short while before. They were fighting for the deliverance of their country from the system of the Soviets. Simultaneously, hundreds of thousands of prisoners-of-war who would have been just as willing to take up the struggle against communism were left to starve in prison camps in the Ukraine. This too our people had learned from accounts given to them by escort troops whom they had come across occasionally on leave trains.

Peter Bamm

The Slavs are to work for us. In so far as we do not need them, they may die. They should not receive the benefits of the German public health system. We do not care about their fertility. They may practice abortion and use contraceptives; the more the better. We do not want them educated; it is enough if they can count up to one hundred. Such stooges will be the more useful to us. Religion we leave to them as a diversion. As to food, they will not get any more than is absolutely necessary. We are the masters; we come first.

Martin Bormann, Chief of the Nazi Party

The winter campaign in Russia is nearing its close. The outstanding bravery and self-sacrificing effort of our troops on the Eastern Front have achieved a great defensive success. The enemy suffered very severe losses in men and material. . . . As soon as weather and terrain conditions are favourable the superior German command and German forces must take the initiative once again to force the enemy to do our bidding.

Adolf Hitler, 5 April 1942

THE LAST TRIUMPHS

The main German offensive on the Eastern Front for 1942 was directed towards the south-east, in order to overrun the Caucasian oilfields. The first objective was to neutralize the Crimea, so securing the right flank of the main thrust. Then one army crossed the Don and thrust far down between the Black Sea and the Caspian, while another advanced east upon Stalingrad to control the Volga and protect the left flank of the main penetration.

The capture of Stalingrad will close the isthmus between the Don and the Volga, as well as the river itself: fast mobile units will also advance down the Volga to block the river at Astrakhan. . . .

Adolf Hitler, 2 July 1942

'The Russians are Finished'

Halder: 'The Russians have assembled a million troops in the Saratov area and a further half-million east of the Caucasus. The Soviet High Command will go over to the offensive, when the German forces reach the Volga. Stalin will launch an attack in this area, exactly similar to the one he launched against Denikin during the Russian revolution.'

He added: 'The Russians are producing fifteen hundred tanks per month, against a German figure of six hundred. I am warning you that a crisis is coming, and for sure.'

Hitler: 'Spare me this idiotic nonsense. The Russians are finished. In four weeks' time they will collapse.'

The Road to the Crimea

When one sees one of the roads along which reinforcements go forward to the front, the time-worn phrase 'an army worming its way along' describes the scene perfectly. Every man, every horse, every vehicle had its being twice over. Once in the control office of any command and once out here in the mud. At headquarters everything is neat and tidy; out here chaos is complete. Units become separated by many miles. No one can do anything to stop a new unit slipping from the left or right into a small gap between the marching columns. The 'road' is little more than a track—over which the light Russian peasant carts just manage to travel—hurriedly reinforced with gravel and a few broken stones. Stones are at a premium in the steppe. In a matter of hours an army's reinforcements grind a peasant track like that out of existence. This one had the added inconvenience of a ditch on either side which made it practically impossible to avoid an obstruction by cutting out into the fields.

This is the sort of thing that would happen: The back wheel of some horse-drawn vehicle in the mile-long column slips into a deep shell crater concealed by a puddle of water. The wheel breaks. The shaft rises in the air. The horses, wrenched upwards, shy and kick over the traces. One of the leads parts. The vehicle behind tries to overtake on the left but is unable to drive quite clear of the deep ruts. The right-hand back wheel of the second vehicle catches in the left-hand back wheel of the first. The horses rear and start kicking in all directions. There is no going forwards or backwards. An ammunition lorry returning empty from the front tries to pass the hopeless tangle on the narrow strip of roadway that remains. Shouts—'We must get through!' It slowly subsides into the ditch and sticks fast. It is a private van converted to army use and is quite incapable of getting out on its own.

Now there is an impassable obstruction on the roads, on the army's supply route! Everyone becomes infected with uncontrollable fury. Everyone shouts at everyone else. Sweating, swearing, mud-spattered men start laying into sweating, shivering, mud-caked horses that are already frothing at the mouth. All at once the fury passes. Someone lights a cheroot. Someone takes the initiative. The horses are unhitched. The lorry is dragged out backwards from the ditch by horses harnessed to a swingletree attached to a rope. The vehicle with a broken wheel is emptied of its load. There is general laughter if a pale blue eiderdown or a few live geese come to light in the process. The men step into the pool of water which runs over the tops of their boots. They seize hold of the muddy wheel, and shouting 'Heave! Heave!', manhandle the empty vehicle to the side. The horses are re-harnessed to the second wagon and it sets off once more. The lorry passes them, backfiring as it goes, on its way to the ammunition depot in the rear.

This scene is repeated a hundred times a day with monotonous regularity. But by each evening there has been a progression of twelve, six, occasionally only three miles. At one point a few fascines of intertwined gorse have been laid across the ditch. The whole crawling mass has meandered twenty yards on to the open field to by-pass a dud bomb which lies unexploded in the middle of the road. To left and right the fields are strewn with a weird assortment of stoves, milking stools, bedsteads, wireless-sets, munition boxes, lamps. It is like the aftermath of a flood. Every few hundred yards is a broken-down vehicle; or a dead horse with swollen belly; or a corpse. Crows rise with a heavy flapping of wings. Tattered grey clouds chase without pause high above the living and the dead.

Peter Bamm

Sevastopol

The colossal battle for Sevastopol lasted a full month.

On the morning of 7 June, as dawn turned the eastern sky to gold and swept the shadows from the valleys, our artillery opened up in its full fury by way of a prelude to the infantry assault. Simultaneously the squadrons of the Luftwaffe hurtled down on to their allotted targets. The scene before us was indescribable, since it was unique in modern warfare for the leader of an army to command a view of his entire battlefield. To the north-west the eye could range from the woodlands that hid the fierce battles of LIV Corps' left wing from view right over to the heights south of the Belbek valley, for which we were to fight so bitterly. Looking due west, one could see the heights of Gaytany, and behind them, in the far distance, the shimmer of Severnaya Bay where it joined the Black Sea. Even the spurs of the Khersones peninsula, on which we were to find vestiges of Hellenic culture, were visible in clear weather. To the south-west there towered the menacing heights of Zapun and the rugged cliffs of the coastal range. At night, within the wide circumference of the fortress, one saw the flashes of enemy gunfire, and by day the clouds of rock and dust cast up by the bursts of our heavy shells and the bombs dropped by German aircraft. It was indeed a fantastic setting for such a gigantic spectacle!

.... The second phase of the offensive, lasting up to 17 June, was marked on both fronts by a bitter struggle for every foot of ground, every pill-box and every trench. Time and again the Russians tried to win back what they had lost by launching violent counter-attacks. In their big strong-points, and in the smaller pill-boxes too, they often fought till the last man and the last round. While the main burden of these battles was borne by the infantry and engineers, the advanced observation posts of our artillery still deserve special mention, since it was chiefly they who had to direct the fire which made it possible to take individual strong-points and pill-boxes. They, together with the assault guns, were the infantry's best helpmates.

On 13 June the valiant 16th Infantry Regiment of 22 Division, led by Colonel von Choltitz, succeeded in taking Fort Stalin, before which its attack had come to a standstill the previous winter. The spirit of our infantry was typified by one wounded man of this regiment who, pointing to his smashed arm and bandaged head, was heard to cry: 'I can take this lot now we've got the Stalin!'

. . . . 22 Division gained control along its whole front of the cliffs overlooking Severnaya Bay. There was extremely hard fighting for the railway tunnel on the boundary between 22 and 50 Divisions, out of which the enemy launched a strong counter-attack with a brigade that had recently arrived by cruiser. The tunnel was finally captured by shelling its entrance. Not only hundreds of troops came out but an even greater number of civilians, including women and children. Particular difficulty was experienced in winkling the enemy out of his last hideouts on the northern shore of the bay, where deep galleries for storing supplies and ammunition had been driven into the sheer wall of rock. These had been equipped for defence by the addition of steel doors. Since the occupants, under pressure from their commissars, showed no sign of surrendering, we had to try to blow the doors open. As our engineers approached the first of them, there was an explosion inside the casemate and a large slab of cliff came tumbling down, burying not only the enemy within but also our own squad of engineers. The commissar in command had blown the casemate and its occupants sky-high. In the end a second lieutenant from an assault battery, who had brought up his gun along the coastal road regardless of enemy shelling from the southern shore, managed to force the other casemates to open up after he had fired on their embrasures at point-blank range. Crowds of completely worn-out soldiers and civilians emerged, their commissars having committed suicide.

General von Manstein, G.O.C. 11 Army

Inside Sevastopol: An Underground Factory

At last, through a long dark tunnel, I reached typical Sevastopol, underground. The noise was incredible. The Admiralty was a monastery compared with this. The vast cellar was subdivided by heavy metal screens where hundreds of lathes hummed and rattled, turning out grenades. A tractor motor was roaring. It was generating electricity, but was puffing and smoking like a bad old samovar. When the motor stopped, the lights went out; immediately every worker lit a cigarette, and the cave glowed with hundreds of faint lights. It has been agreed among them that only when work was held up by a failure of current should there be smoking. On the same table a cook and a compositor worked side by side, the one peeling potatoes, the other setting up the front page of a newspaper. The potatoes lay among the type.

The machines worked twenty-four hours daily, their noise not stopping a moment. With the tobacco smoke mingled the smells of the kitchen, gas, and stale air.

The whole front was relying on this factory for its grenades.

Boris Voyetekhov

The Docks

Into the shoving, swirling crowd the infantrymen from the ship moved with vigour, pushing away from the gangways old men and women who were waiting to be evacuated, till they had formed a line and had answered their roll call. They were going straight to the front.

The crew, who rarely slept, so constant was the crowd of people and the mass of cases in their quarters, unloaded the cargo themselves, working the noisy derricks quickly but efficiently. Soon the quay was crowded with new aeroplane engines, boxes of shells, bombs, freshly-painted machine-guns, mobile artillery, flasks of oil and acids, spare parts for tank caterpillars, sacks of flour, salt, canned meat, and much more besides.

The pile grew between the ship and the waiting evacuees and wounded. I remember two voices among all this confusion, one a woman's crying, 'Where is my aspidistra?', the other that of a tall, gaunt Red Army man who was quietly passing through the crowd with a child's toy rifle in his hand, phlegmatically shouting, 'Whose rifle? Whose rifle?' As I listened, the voices were drowned by the clamour of people coming aboard the destroyer.

The crew had just finished unloading the munitions from deep holds and now began to take on the thousands of pieces of evacuees' luggage. No restriction had been put on what could be transported. Even plants were allowed. Only in this way could the stubborn reluctance of the people of Sevastopol to leave their beloved city be broken down. That is why now, on abandoning their homes, these people were taking with them every object which reminded them of their childhood, youth, or old age, of their joys and woes, anything that in unknown cities or villages could bring back to these southern people memories of their life beside the sea. The Navy understood this, and with solicitude sailors carried up the gangway ancient models of sailing ships, knick-knacks, family portraits framed in lifebelts, old seascapes, deck chairs, ornamental tables and screens which for decades had stood unmoved in front parlours.

Amid these tears, the hurtling of shells, the skirmishes with the fire and the business of loading, the commissar of the destroyer was approached by a small, pale-faced man who took out a notebook and in his toneless voice asked, 'How many meetings did you hold during the trip? Did you read any articles aloud?' The commissar looked coldly at this intruder and said abruptly, 'We had a meeting to discuss the liquidation of fools like you. It was a very successful meeting, too. Aren't you ashamed to ask such questions when there isn't a man you can see here who has slept for the last ten days or eaten except at night on the journey back? Get away.'

The little man fidgeted where he stood for a moment and then went away. I saw neither shame nor regret in his dim fish-like eyes.

Divers

The commissar was insatiable. He knew that before Sevastopol the Germans had massed fourteen divisions with a huge force of aircraft and that these were now being hurled at the city in their third offensive. Wiping sweat from his brow and drinking yet more water, he carefully thumbed sunk ships' papers and bills of lading, asking persistently, 'Where are those six aeroplane engines? Why haven't I had those cases of dry bread? Where are the bandages, the cotton-wool, and drugs? What are you doing there on the bottom? Playing chess with the dead?'

'Just that,' replied the chief diver, 'and you had better come and take a hand down below; then you will be satisfied that it is impossible to get up those motors. They are covered with piles of dead horses and cavalrymen in the hold. Drugs'—he hesitated—'I can't go there.'

'Why not?'

'I have been a diver for thirty years. During that time I have seen things that drove people who were working next to me mad, or else they would come up grey-haired, but to go into that cabin where, if I open the door, dead bodies of children rush towards me—no, I can't and I won't.'

'Well,' said the commissar, 'that means you are letting living children die for the lack of food and bandages.'

The discussions ended as always with the divers going straight back to their cutters and down below.

The Battle of the Loudspeakers

The loudspeakers fell silent. Each side made use of this form of propaganda, and when night fell a regular radio duel began. Actually it was more of a scramble than a duel—a scrambling fight among announcers, drivers and gunners. Heavily-armoured radio vans would dash wildly from valley to valley trying to avoid the gunfire that would be directed at them as they gave their positions away by their sound. The announcers would compete not only in volume but in the presentation of their material. Each talked the enemy's language—we, German and Roumanian; they, Russian. The announcers came to know each other well during the siege and loudly reproached each other for professional faults, for bad grammar, poor jokes, traces of drunkenness in their voices, and other technical shortcomings. These exchanges of personalities were highly popular in the trenches, and every time the quips and the cracks of our announcer were heard, roars of laughter would be audible from the German trenches.

The Last Assault

At this moment something remarkable happened in the enemy trenches, the like of which had never happened before on the Sevastopol front. It was solemn religious chanting that reached our ears from the enemy lines, a great chorus that surged across the bitter, stony ground. The gramophone was stopped and every-body listened. It was the Roumanians, praying for victory, despairingly, as they faced the sun on the Crimean hills.

Boris Voyetekhov

After our experience of Soviet methods to date we were bound to assume that the enemy would make a last stand behind Sevastopol's perimeter defences and finally in the city itself. An order from Stalin had been repeatedly wirelessed to the defenders to hold out to the last man and the last round, and we knew that every member of the civil population capable of bearing arms had been mustered.

And so 1 July began with a massed bombardment of the perimeter fortifications and the enemy's strong-points in the interior of the city. Before long our reconnaissance aircraft reported that no further serious resistance need be anticipated. The shelling was stopped and the divisions moved in. It seemed probable that the enemy had pulled the bulk of his forces out to the west the previous night.

But the struggle was still not over. Although the Soviet Coast Army had given up the city, it had only done so in order to offer further resistance from behind the defences which sealed off the Khersones peninsula—either in pursuance of Stalin's backs-to-the-wall order or else in the hope of still getting part of the army evacuated by Red Fleet vessels at night from the deep inlets west of Sevastopol. As it turned out, only very few of the top commanders and commissars were fetched away by motor-torpedo boat, one of them being the army commander, General Petrov. When his successor tried to escape in the same way he was intercepted by our Italian E-boat.

Thus the final battles on the Khersones peninsula lasted up till 4 July. While 72 Division captured the armour-plated fort of 'Maxim Gorki II', which was defended by several thousand men, the other divisions gradually pushed the enemy back towards the extreme tip of the peninsula. The Russians made repeated attempts to break through to the east by night, presumably in the hope of joining up with the partisans in the Yaila Mountains. Whole masses of them rushed at our lines, their arms linked to prevent anyone from hanging back. At their head, urging them on, there were often women and girls of the Communist Youth, themselves bearing arms. Inevitably the losses which sallies of this kind entailed were extraordinarily high.

In the end the remnants of the Coast Army sought refuge in big caverns on the shore of the Khersones peninsula, where they waited in vain to be evacuated. When they surrendered on 4 July, thirty thousand men emerged from this small tip of land alone.

In all, the number of prisoners taken in the fortress was over ninety thousand, and the enemy's losses in killed amounted to many times our own. The amount of booty captured was so vast that it could not immediately be calculated. A naturally strong fortress, reinforced and consolidated in every conceivable way and defended by a whole army, had fallen. The army was annihilated and the entire Crimea now in German hands. At just the right time from the operational point of view, 11 Army had become free for use in the big German offensive on the southern wing of the Eastern Front.

General von Manstein

The Fallen City

We had been surprised to find no civilian casualties until Sergeant Kienzle discovered them in the vaults of the cathedral. I made my way there with a few medical orderlies. Old women, young women, children and old men lay next to each other on piles of straw. Their wounds have been well cared for surgically, but the dressings consisted of the barest emergency bandages. Probably the Russians had had no proper bandaging material left.

In one corner a priest belonging to the Russian Orthodox Church was kneeling on the straw. In his raised hand he bore a crucifix. The feeble light of the candle hardly reached to the ceiling of the vault but it sparkled on the jewels with which the crucifix was adorned. He was murmuring a prayer. Before him an old woman was dying, one of the bony, arthritic hands clawing the air. Her fellow sufferers repeated the prayers in unison. A deep rattling sound came from the old woman's throat and then she died. The priest got up; the old woman's hand remained poised in mid-air.

When I got back to our quarters which were situated at the edge of the town above the Khersones peninsula, Rombach was already waiting for me. I wanted to tell him what I had just seen but I didn't get a chance. He only said, 'Come with me.'

We drove a mile southwards out of the town. Among the vineyards on the southern slopes of Sevastopol—not far from the spot where Iphigenia had looked over the waters of the Propontis towards Hellas—the Russians had abandoned their wounded.

They lay scattered in their thousands between the vines. For days they had had nothing to eat and for forty-eight hours nothing to drink. For the most part they had received no surgical attention. Hour after hour the sun blazed down on them. Over the hills there passed a wind of sighs. The misery of these men who had been crushed by war did not cry out to heaven; it merely stirred gently like a light breeze across the hills. Down in the valley one could see several wire enclosures into which thirty thousand uninjured prisoners had been crowded together to await their fate. Now and then a shot rang out.

. . . . The miserable little trickle of warm and dirty water was nothing like enough to prevent the danger of hundreds of men dying from thirst. The wounded began to gain fresh hope but we couldn't provide sufficient *voda* or water as quickly as all that.

Every hour or so I went among them to pick out those in most urgent need of surgical attention. As I went through the tents they turned towards me with raised hands and the words: '*Voda, Gospodin! Voda!*' swirled in my wake like the rushing of a ship's backwater.

Sometimes in my dreams I still hear that cry: '*Voda, Gospodin! Voda!*'

Then they began to die.

We tried and tried to think of a way out. In the meantime down in the Severnaya Bay, about two and a half miles away, a few of the larger wells had been restored to working order and we decided to bring all the walking wounded there. This would reduce the number of those whom we still had to supply to about twelve hundred.

Only a small proportion of the total number of wounded had as yet been accommodated in the tents. The majority still lay out in the open. We had selected a number of lightly injured Russians to assist us as supervisors, and in order to distinguish them they wore a gauze bandage around their left arm. We sent these men through the vineyards to tell everybody who could walk to collect together and to march down to the wells. The prisoners, totally apathetic, didn't stir. Thereupon the supervisors tore the vine-props from the ground and started jumping about among the men cudgelling and beating them. That at last brought all those who still had them on to their legs. We stood by and watched. To have interfered with the brutality of this procedure would have been pure sentimentality, for it saved a host of seriously injured men from death by thirst.

With dragging gait, supporting themselves on sticks or leaning against each other, surrounded by myriads of flies, they shuffled towards the wells. A long, heart-rending procession, they trailed through Iphigenia's landscape under the dazzling Crimean sun.

They would quench their thirst. They would gain a little strength. But it would only help them to keep on along the dreary route into the realm of the barbarians. And of that realm we were the frontier.

Fortitude without justice is the tool of the wicked. Saint Ambrose said so fifteen hundred years ago.

Peter Bamm

The main thrust of the Germans under von Kleist to the south-east continued with extraordinary momentum into the heart of the Caucasian oilfields, which the Russians had destroyed. One railway, winding down the shores of the Caspian Sea, enabled the Russians to send reinforcements southwards which could meet head on and combat the German advance, which, so incredibly far from its firm base, was losing momentum.

Into the Caucasus

Late each evening we would radio the approximate positions of our subordinate units to the Army Headquarters. This Headquarters in turn would radio the information back to Supreme Headquarters during the night. Halder and his colleagues—the 'Boesemüller squad', as they were nicknamed after the famous book about the first World War—reported to Hitler at about 11.00 hours on the next morning, and issued orders immediately after this conference. These orders could not arrive at the front line until late afternoon, by which time the situation was completely altered, the divisions having moved perhaps fifty or a hundred miles in the meantime!

Our advance drove further and further south. The seriousness of our manœuvres could be judged by the Russian reaction. While Tukhachevski, the Russian Commander-in-Chief, had a narrow escape from 29 Mechanized, the Russians scraped together what tanks they could muster. They were defeated in a fierce tank battle near Chertkovo by my 23 Panzer on 12 July, and on 14 July a large Russian force was trapped near the important railway centre of Millerovo.

For somebody who has never lived in such an atmosphere, watching the disintegration of an enemy army from its rear, it is hard to imagine the details: surrendering units, individual and massed refugees, broken-down vehicles, retreating enemy columns, streams of prisoners with and without guards, attacks of enemy aircraft. It is an indescribable turmoil.

. . . . As Rostov-on-Don fell to the German forces the southern part of the Russian front appeared to disintegrate. The Russians, pouring back from the

Rostov area, were constantly pressing in upon my units, while from the east the Caucasian Cavalry Corps, bolstered with strong tank formations, tried to relieve the situation for the defeated and retreating troops.

The mission of protecting von Kleist's eastern flank meant advancing southward with complete disregard for our flanks and lines of communication. While my 3 Panzer Division, in the lead, cut the railway leading from Stalingrad to the Black Sea in the neighbourhood of Proletarskaya, winning a bridgehead over the Manych in a dramatic and bitter night battle against N.K.W.P. troops and forces from Krasnodar Officers' School, 23 Panzer Division dealt a decisive defeat to the Caucasian Cavalry Corps, knocking out sixty-eight tanks, mostly heavy types, in one hour, and capturing the chief-of-staff of the formation.

Our eastern flank was meanwhile being covered in a very nominal fashion by a mobile regiment of grenadiers (armoured infantry), and the lines of communication, although often cut for a period by the Russians who were streaming eastward, were maintained by the establishment of a convoy system, with independent tank companies protecting and escorting supplies over stretches. In fact, XL Panzer Corps fought in three directions at once in an eccentric battle, the main effort being made southwards.

. . . . The heat of the Kuban steppe was stifling. We were glad to approach the Caucasus mountains and breathe cooler air. By this time my corps had spent over a month behind the Soviet lines. Rumours of disagreements at Supreme Headquarters on account of the eccentricity of the manœuvres—southward toward the Caucasus and north-eastward against Stalingrad—did not worry us at this time, but difficulties with fuel supply were already being felt.

. . . . There was bitter street fighting in Piatigorsk, with N.K.W.P. troops, *women* signal formations and the Krasnodar Officers' School participating on the Russian side.

The tank regiment of 3 Panzer could participate in this murderous struggle only with advance parties. The regimental commander, Baron von Liebenstein, Guderian's former Chief of Staff, was immobilized through lack of fuel on the outskirts of Pushkin's town when, like a highwayman, he 'took over' a couple of Russian columns, thus providing us with fuel and well-manufactured American Lease-Lend trucks.

At this time (9 August) the troops of XL Panzer Corps were covering about three hundred miles in depth. This situation was not due to tactical measures. A similar situation had arisen during 1941 south of Moscow. Leadership had ceased to mean taking measures appropriate to the tactical situation, but merely restricting them to whatever fuel the supply would permit.

When we remonstrated we were informed by those in the highest quarters that 'We could not expect you to rush forward like this, could we?' As a matter of fact, Hitler had been warned by his experts that the available fuel supply of six thousand cubic metres would suffice either for the Stalingrad *or* the Caucasus operation. But quite illogically he expected his subordinates to go on 'with fanatical energy,' if without fuel, in both directions!

. . . . The guide book issued by our general staff stated that the many rivers streaming down from the mountains and crossing our path would be dry in summer time. The opposite was the case, since the snowy summits melting under the August sun sent down plenty of water. Bridging equipment soon became scarce, especially under the successful bombing attacks by the Russian Air Force. We asked for more aerial protection than could be given by the few fighters which were available. The answer was always: 'In a fortnight or so Stalingrad will be taken. Then you can get plenty of aerial cover.'

General Baron Leo Geyr von Schweppenburg, G.O.C. XL Panzer Corps

Farthest South

It was now the middle of August. Our operations were being slowed down by two factors, the lack of fuel and the growing strength of the Russian Air Force, the fastest and first reserves to appear in strength. The Air Force did much to delay us and thus saved the situation for the Russians.

A few days earlier we had still hoped to rush the passes over the Caucasus and thus reach the Turkish border. We wanted to do this by combining mountaineer battalions with Panzers, although this was an unusual group of task forces. In a single night my Chief of Staff had worked out special orders for this sort of co-operation with the help of the staff of a Bavarian mountaineer battalion. Unfortunately the idea had to be dropped.

. . . . XL German Panzer Corps had covered during its great raid, mostly in rear of the Southern Russian front, almost a thousand miles between the end of June and 8 August. It reached the Grozny oilfields but was unable to capture them.

Hitler's preliminary objective, the Baku oilfields, also remained unconquered and intact.

. . . . The most decisive factor during these weeks, from our point of view, was the growing stream of American Lease-Lend supply to the Russians, which our air reconnaissance saw and our intelligence reported upon. Only this could sustain the tottering giant in his hour of weakness.

General von Schweppenburg

As the Germans reached the fullest extent of their conquests, Russia's demands on her allies to open a 'Second Front' in the West, to relieve pressure on her, became insistent.

Second Front Now!

The talk I had to-day with Oumansky was typical of the present nervousness and also of the desire on the part of official Russians to do some propaganda among Allied correspondents.

Oumansky said, 'I am afraid resentment against the Allies, against England in particular, is going to rise very rapidly, as things go on deteriorating at our front. And, mind you, the Germans have already started the old stunt they practised so successfully in France. Their leaflets keep saying: "Russians, where are your Allies?" or else: "The Hungarians and Roumanians are better Allies to us than the British are to you." And in these leaflets are contained peace offers to the Russians—in terms you can imagine.

'It has no effect on our troops yet; most of them believe that the Germans are doing it just *because* they are scared of the Second Front, and that they are in a hurry to make peace with us, so as to be able to turn against England. But it may have a very bad effect after a while; it will not create defeatism, but certainly strong anti-British sentiment. For remember, this country has a traditional distrust of England, dating back to the time of Palmerston and Disraeli. . . .'

Feeling against the Allies continues to be quite bad. In a tramcar to-day there was an old woman—fairly well educated, judging by her way of speech—who was saying, 'Never trust the English. You young people know nothing about it, but I am old enough to remember how Lord Beaconsfield, otherwise D'Isra-eli' (she pronounced the four-syllable name viciously) 'let us down over Turkey in 1878.'

Alexander Werth, war correspondent

The Russian Soldier

What we soldiers are interested in above all else are three things: a wash, food and sleep. Nothing else matters much. We don't sing songs—only sometimes, usually under compulsion. Perhaps they do in the rear; but we frontliners aren't interested in songs. It isn't what you people in Moscow imagine. We aren't interested in women either—not much. Oh yes, there *are* girls at the front—girls serving in canteens, and typists, and all that. But they won't look at anything below the rank of lieutenant-colonel—not they!

Sometimes we get staff officers arriving at our local headquarters, and when they are offered to sleep on the floor, among the lice, they say, 'Oh no, really; I'll be quite comfortable sitting up in this chair, really quite comfortable!' It makes us snigger every time we see them sitting there pretending to sleep, and scared stiff of the lice getting into their spick-and-span uniform! Oh, I know, these people also do their job; I suppose it's just the old antagonism between the front and the rear. It's always existed; you can't help it. Take, for instance, our general. Some of us went to see him about an important matter. A young and pretty blonde came out: 'No,' she said, 'you can't go straight in; the General is still resting.' (You never say of a superior he's sleeping; you must always say 'resting'.) 'You will have to wait till I announce you.' 'And who are you, miss?' we said. 'I'm the typist,' she said. The General was, of course, sleeping comfortably in a real bed.

The Germans fight very ferociously, and I suppose this winter they'll be much better equipped than last winter. They've learned their lesson. Recently, it's true, I watched through a periscope in the front line the fellows on the hill opposite. I could see them putting up their collars, and stamping their feet, and generally looking distinctly cold; but then they were Hungarians, as many of them are at Voronezh; and I don't suppose the Germans will bother much about *their* winter equipment.

Our one aim now is to get to Germany, to give them what's coming to them. Last year we still used to give cigarettes to some miserable shivering Fritzes— but not now.

Russian private soldier

15

RESISTANCE

The Europe which the Third Reich brought under its heel between 1939 and 1941 did not submit tamely to German rule. At first, following their total defeat and occupation by a police state, the nations were stunned and quiescent. Then, from about 1942–43, resistance began to grow, ranging from sporadic acts by individuals to full-scale sabotage and overt military action by widespread underground organizations, sometimes acting independently and sometimes with the material aid, advice or direction of the Allies. The greater part of the populations remained inactive, or at best lent passive and fluctuating support to the resistance—more could not be expected of human nature and frailty. A good many organizations existed to promote their own highly questionable post-war objectives and to fight each other, and a few people were active traitors. But the actions of the minority who were not afraid to suffer and who were prepared to die for their cause were of very great value to the war effort of the free world. They distracted and tied down the Axis armed forces, hampered their communications and damaged their morale, carried out espionage for the Allies, committed sabotage, and did a good deal to preserve the morale of their own people. Faced with their own and their compatriots' human weaknesses and the efficiency of the German secret police, their failures and sacrifices were many, but the sum of their contribution to the winning of the war was incalculable.

· · · — The Symbol of Resistance

THE V sign is the symbol of the unconquerable will of the occupied territories, and a portent of the fate awaiting the Nazi tyranny. So long as the peoples of Europe continue to refuse all collaboration with the invader, it is sure that his cause will perish, and that Europe will be liberated.

Winston Churchill, 20 July 1941

The Invader

Our shops and farms wide open lie;
Still the invader feels a lack:
Disquiet whets his gluttony
For what he may not carry back.

He prowls about in search of wealth
But has no skill to recognize
Our things of worth: we need no stealth
To mask them from his pauper eyes.

He calls for worship and amaze;
We give him yes-men in a row,
Reverberating that self-praise
He wearied of a while ago.

He casts around for some new whim,
Something preposterously more:
'Love me,' he bids. We offer him
The slack embraces of a whore.

And when he spitefully makes shift
To share with us his pauperdom,
By forcing on us as a gift
The shoddy wares he brought from home,

And watches that we sell and buy
Amongst us his degrading trash,
He gets no gain at all. Though sly
With what he knows, the guns and cash.

What he knows not he may not touch:
Those very spoils for which he came
Are still elusive to his clutch—
They swerve and scorch him like a flame.

Invader—outcast of all lands,
He lives condemned to gorge and crave,
To foul his feast with his own hands:
At once the oppressor and the slave.

                                   Norman Cameron

NORWAY

An Agent is Dropped

It was the night of 19–20 April 1943; the time was one forty-five. For the third time I was sitting at the edge of the hole in the after-part of the Halifax. This was the last night of the full moon, the last night before the summer months, in which agents could not be dropped into Norway. It was the last chance I really had of carrying out the task I had undertaken.

The aircraft had a Polish crew. I sat staring hard at the dispatcher, trying to guess his thoughts from the movements of his features. Again we circled round, again the plane was flung from side to side by a too-strong wind; again I sat for seconds and minutes on the edge of the open hole, undergoing the worst mental torture. The plane began to climb again!

There must be some limits to what a man can endure. This time it was not at a dispatcher's request that I took off my rubber helmet for a talk with the captain on the intercom. He gave three reasons for not letting me jump: (1) there was a good thirty-mile wind force, i.e. fifteen miles too much; (2) he could not find any stretch of open moss which should be there according to the map, only mountains and forests everywhere; (3) he dared not go too low because of the violent gusts of wind, and he could not reduce speed to less than 160 miles, against the normal 115–120 miles, because if he did he would lose steering way in the violent air currents.

I will not report the discussion that went on for a quarter of an hour, but will only state that in the hearing of witnesses—the rest of the crew by intercom—I took the whole responsibility on myself.

I was sitting on the edge of the hole again; the time was 2.7 a.m. This time the dispatcher had inherited my nervousness, and for me there was only one thing to do: to take the chance of things going right, and jump. The Halifax went lower—the contours of water, mountain and forest grew sharper—there was a terrible lot of snow—the plane swung—went straight for a few seconds—swung again—speed was reduced slightly, and the propellers set at high pitch—we went steadily lower—I was heaved to and fro—I stared at the dispatcher—green light, and 'action stations' from the dispatcher, who had now raised his arm—I flung both my legs into the hole—fractions of seconds—red light . . . 'Go!' I started and—was out. . . .

The wind howled in my face. I was slung round—struck my head against something, the rear wheel of the Halifax—I saw stars—many stars—a terrific jerk—more stars—a sharp pain in my back, my head—everywhere—the night was dark—I became unconscious.

The next thing I knew was that I was being jerked and flung about pretty violently; it was a little while before I really paid any attention to what was happening—and there—a few yards away, against the fearful wind, I saw the rear turret of the Halifax and the rest of the plane silhouetted against the sky. I was hanging from the plane!

If it was fear or pain which made me faint again, I cannot say, most probably both. I recovered consciousness, feeling that I was still hanging, that I was being flung up and down, to and fro at a furious pace—and I fainted again.

Before I finally recovered consciousness a miracle must have happened: I was on my way to the ground far below. I looked up instinctively: yes, the para-chute was open, but only partly. It looked to me as if some of the many silk cords which went up to the parachute had got entangled in the material and divided the whole 'umbrella' into several sections.

I looked down—far below in the darkness lay water, mountain tops and forest. I could only feel that I was falling a good deal faster than I had ever done before. But there was nothing I could do about it one way or the other. Yet there was something seriously wrong with my right foot or leg. It was hanging all wrong in relation to the left, almost at a right angle. I tried to lift my leg as I hung—but the only reaction was a stab of pain.

It was blowing hard: I was approaching a ridge just below me—dense wood —no, I was caught again by a violent gust, passed the top of the ridge and went at full speed down into the valley on the other side. I held my breath—now for it! A bunch of big fir-tops came rushing at me—the noise of branches breaking

—something like a big besom hit me in the face—everything became still and strange—I had fainted again.

How long I was unconscious I do not know, but gradually and surely I came to myself again. A strange noise in my ears, a strange silence, and for a few seconds, minutes perhaps, I felt that I was dreaming—felt that I had come into quite a new world. At first I dared not move, but at last I tried. A burning pain in my back brought me back to reality, and I looked up, sideways and down.

I had landed in the top of a tree: I was hanging with my back against the trunk, and above me, a dark mass against the lighter sky, hung my pack. The fir-top itself was broken off and lay across a tree next to it and beyond, while the remains of the parachute were entangled in another. What a fantastic piece of luck! So fantastic that it could hardly be true.

It did not take me long to get hold of my commando knife and cut away the parachute straps: at the same time I twisted myself round to face the trunk, and slid down through the fir-boughs as carefully as possible. I now understood what was the matter with my right leg; the knee had been dislocated and the whole lower part of my leg, with the foot, had been twisted ninety degrees out to one side. I could only hope that nothing was broken; but that a knee out of joint could be so horribly painful I should never have believed.

I just collapsed at the foot of the fir-tree like a pile of wet rags and lay there with closed eyes. I stretched out my hand, caught hold of a piece of reindeer moss, and inhaled its scent. Never, never, would anyone make me do another parachute jump; indeed, I never wanted to see a plane again!

This was Norway: Norwegian fir and pine, Norwegian bilberry and reindeer moss. Despite the burning pain in my back and knee I could not help enjoying their familiar scent, taking long draughts of the night air.

Oluf Reed Olsen

Sabotage

The factory worked in shifts all round the clock. The Kjeller aircraft factories had been bombed a little while before by sixty American Flying Fortresses. The result was that everything had been moved down to Korsvoll. This was very unpopular with the people at Sagene, for the bombing of the factory would mean a catastrophe for all the dwelling-houses round about. It was typical of the Germans to protect their war industry by putting it in the midst of a dense civilian population. Naturally the Germans took all possible precautions: they posted guards at the most incredible places. After having studied the area and the Germans' security measures we came to a solution which really was quite simple.

The Germans had naturally posted sentries at all the entrances to the area, and they had placed searchlights and machine-guns in the yard. When the alarm went the searchlights were switched on, and we should be rather badly placed. We knew that there were seven guards at one end of the building alone, and that three Germans and one Norwegian watchman patrolled the sheds regularly, ready to set bells ringing and so on.

Nevertheless, when we decided to make an attempt, it was not because our own plan was so clever as that the Germans' defence system was very absurd despite all those security measures. There was one very weak point in the system, a hole in the wall of the fortress which gave us our great chance; part of the buildings were still at the disposal of Oslo Tramways. We reckoned that we could, with a bit of luck, reach without being seen a door which led to Oslo Tramways' office. We could wait for the watchman in the office, overpower him when he came, and use his keys to lock ourselves into the actual tram shed. Thence we could go down into a cellar which ran from the Norwegian part right over to the German. The Germans had tried to show foresight and had set up three thick wire fences right up to the roof to keep saboteurs away. Ridiculous things! With the cutters we had it would be like cutting soft butter. We would lay our charges down in the basement and try to blow up the whole roof, which was identical with the floor of the factory building. We learnt that the floor was three feet thick and of reinforced concrete.

Roy and I had at first thought of taking on the job alone, but when we realized how exacting it was we decided not to take any chances. We asked whether the boys of the Oslo gang would not join us. It was decided that 24, Rolf, Egil, Hermann, Roy and I should participate. We also took with us one of Hermann's men to guard the car and act as driver if necessary. His name was Erik, and he took part in many tough jobs later along with Hermann.

We pondered a good deal over the sort of charge we should use, and how large it should be. What we wanted was lifting, not cutting power, so the right thing would certainly have been to use amonal, i.e. explosive in powdered form. It burns comparatively slowly and has great lifting power. But we had no amonal, so we had to use plastic. I had got hold of some dynamite and we laid a charge consisting of two hundred and seventy pounds of plastic and seventy pounds of dynamite. We divided this among five suitcases with seventy pounds in each. We laid the charges in such a way that we could place all the suitcases on top of one another and couple together the fuses which stuck out of each suitcase. We calculated that we must do the job in twelve minutes and must therefore have everything ready beforehand in the smallest detail. The job must be done on Saturday night, the only night when there were not people working there. We did not want to risk blowing up good Norwegians along with the aircraft.

We met on Saturday in Fru Oeynebraaten's flat. She guessed with good reason that something was going to happen again. We had had some of the American plastic in the house, and it had the peculiar strong smell which some kinds of explosive have. She tried to conceal her nervousness, but that is not easy for a woman when she has, figuratively speaking, to wade in 250 lb. of explosive. It may be said that it was very imprudent of us to have it in the house at all, and that it would have been a bad business if we had blown up the whole of Frichsgate, but there was no other way of dealing with it at the moment, and Frichsgate, I am glad to say, came out of it almost intact. We had also a place up in Sagene which we called the office. We used to make our charges there, and there we had our main dump. So we were a menace to everyone at that time.

Fru Oeynebraaten took it as a man, or rather as a woman. Women in such cases were as a rule much less frightened than men. She made coffee for us and served home-made cakes, so we had something to stiffen ourselves up with.

We made the following plan for the evening: Roy and I were to drive the car containing the explosive up to the cross-street where we were to go into action. Here we were to meet the other boys at the tram terminus. At 1.45 a.m. everything would be ready. Two men would creep up to the door and hold up the guard when he came to open it. These were to be Roy and 24. When the door was opened, two other men would go into the factory with Roy and 24. They would start cutting the wire in the cellar at once. The two of us who remained were to act as cover till the signal was given. Then we would drive the car up, and each man would take a suitcase and bring it down to Rolf, who would tie the fuses together and light them.

To begin with everything went more or less according to plan. It was no light matter to drive through the town with the car full of arms and explosives, but we got through all right. Then we had to begin handing out Sten guns to the boys. Now the time had come, and we set to work.

Hermann and I took our places, likewise Rolf and Egil, Roy and 24 crept off, and we saw them gliding along the wall towards the door. We could hear the German guards talking as they walked to and fro behind the fence.

We waited and waited, but nothing happened. No one who has not been through it can imagine what a strange feeling one has when one is waiting for something to happen. Anything can happen on a job like that. And yet it is just when nothing happens that the strain is worst. The time grew long; people passed suspecting nothing; a young fellow stopped and asked if I had any spirits to sell.

Suddenly Roy and 24 returned. The job had miscarried. The watchman had not opened the door when they knocked. Presumably he had heard nothing. We agreed to meet on Monday at Fru Oeynebraaten's and lay our plans afresh.

We talked it over on Monday and came to the conclusion that the only thing to do was to break in, so that we should be independent of the guard. The door was fitted with a Yale lock and was comparatively easy to open. To open an ordinary Yale lock we used a celluloid plate of the thickness of a razor blade. This was pressed into the door-frame and the lock pushed back. (A certain degree of technical skill is required for this.)

Another week of tension passed, and then we tried again. Everything seemed to favour a successful operation. Even the moon was considerate and kept away.

Rolf was absent too; for one reason or another he had not turned up. This was not quite so good, but there were plenty of us and we decided to do the job without him. All went well. We got the door open, slipped in and waited for the watchman with the vital keys. Just before he was due to come, Egil suddenly burst into roars of laughter. It was not exactly the place for loud laughter, and we were all sure that Egil had gone mad. Such things had happened before in similar situations. 'The fuse, the fuse!' Egil stammered. 'Oh, hell!' we said, and what else could we say? It was Rolf who had the fuse which was to connect all the suitcases. So we cleared out again, and pretty quick too.

We could not help laughing when we were out in the street. But we were terribly anxious about Rolf and felt sure that he had been shot or at any rate arrested. But it turned out that he had gone to sleep in the flat where he was hiding; and his alarm had not sounded. A man must have very strong nerves to be able to sleep so undisturbed just before a job like ours.

Rolf was much upset about the whole business, but we consoled him with the thought that we should try again on Saturday. Certainly there would be a full moon then, but we were so tired and sick of the whole job that we wanted to be through with it.

On Saturday everyone was there in time. The moon was almost full, but slightly obscured by clouds.

Roy and 24 crept along in the shadow of the houses. In a little while we saw a light from the door, which showed that it was open. Then came the signal. Hermann and I took a look round and set off. We reached the door and went in. And now we six were standing in a small room, all armed to the teeth. Roy and 24 were nearest to the door which the watchman would pass. It was dead silent in the little room; not a word passed between us, but we all had our own thoughts. Some of us were thinking of our families, some of girls, and all of us of the Germans, who perhaps had already detected us and were surrounding the whole building. Then we heard the guards coming. We knew that the Germans would part from the Norwegian outside our door, and that he would come in to us in a moment. The steps came nearer. I moved a little in the direction of the door, where 24 and Roy stood ready for action. Then we heard the Germans go on, while the Norwegian watchman came towards us. A key was put into the lock, the door was opened, there was a gulp, and the man was dragged into the room. He looked bewildered as he stood there, one man against us six. We explained to him the cause of our visit, and promised him his life if he obeyed our instructions. This he did in every detail. He had all the keys of the cellar, so it looked promising. It was his first day as watchman, he said. He usually worked on a bus, but he had a bad heart, and he had now been appointed watchman. This was supposed to be the softest job of all!

Rolf and Egil set to work immediately to cut the wire fences down in the cellar. 24 attended to the women cleaners who were washing the buses without suspicion of trouble or danger: he courted them as vigorously as he could to remove the risk of any disturbance from that quarter. Hermann and I acted as cover, and Roy looked after the watchman. I went out into the little room which we had first entered, and set the door slightly ajar in order to listen. I heard the German guards going up and down talking, while Rolf and Egil were working their way forward underneath them. I wished that Gregers had been there; it was just the sort of job he would have liked.

Hermann came and said all the fences would have been removed in a moment. I went out into the street, where Erik was keeping the engine running, and we drove the valuable load in. Each man took a suitcase and carried it down into the cellar; Rolf tied the fuses together, while I went up to warn the old porter who lived over the office. I thundered and kicked at the door, but no one answered. It was an awkward situation. I did not want him to be killed, but on account of the Germans there were limits to the amount of noise one could make. Hermann came up with the watchman and said that the explosion would take place in two minutes. We tried to break the door down with our combined strength, but had to give it up. The watchman thought the porter was not at home, and we consoled ourselves with that thought. 24 told the cleaners that the building would go up in two minutes, and they cleared out in a hurry. One of them, however, would not go till she had fetched her tobacco which she had in the cloak-room. They can be cold-blooded, these women.

We took the watchman out into the street, and asked if he wished to be sent to Sweden. But he said no, on account of his family. We advised him to give an exact report of what had happened; he could go straight down to the first telephóne box and ring up. Now the women cleaners and the watchmen were running down the street, and at last the Germans too began to realize that something was happening. They shouted and beckoned, but I had already stepped on the gas and was about to turn the first corner. We rushed past Rolf and 24, who were both bicycling. I drove like fury, and we were a good way off when the explosion came. We had used a four-minute fuse, to the best of my recollection, so we had come quickly.

We stopped down in Vogtsgate, where we dropped Erik, Hermann and Egil, and then swept on, Roy and I, out to Egil's home on Nordstrand. Vesla gave us a splendid meal, and we spent the rest of the night in the highest good-humour. We were equally delighted that Korsvoll had at last been dealt with.

The job had meant a great deal of work. It is not so easy to explain now in a few words all the difficulties we met with beforehand, and it is always easier to preserve the good recollections than the bad ones. But in any case we felt that we had worked very hard.

Max Manus

When it was discovered that the Germans were producing heavy water in Norway for the purpose of atomic research, repeated attacks were made on their installations near Hardanger Fjord, and production was seriously hampered. Early in 1944 they attempted to ferry their entire stock of heavy water to Germany.

Armed with Sten guns, pistols and hand-grenades, we crept past Mel station and down towards the ferry. The bitterly cold night set everything creaking and crackling; the ice on the road snapped sharply as we went over it. When we came out on the bridge by the ferry station, there was as much noise as if a whole company was on the march.

Rolf and the other Rjukan men were told to cover me while I went on board to reconnoitre. All was quiet there. Was it possible that the Germans had omitted to place a guard at the weakest point in the whole route of the transport?

Hearing voices in the crew's quarters, forward, I stole to the companion and listened. There must be a party going on down there, and a game of poker. The other two followed me on to the deck of the ferry. We went down to the third-class accommodation and found a hatchway leading to the bilges. But before we had got the hatch open we heard steps, and took cover behind the nearest table or chair. The ferry watchman was standing in the doorway. He must have left the game of poker on hearing that there were other people on board. The situation was awkward, but not dangerous. We hurriedly explained to the watchman that we had to hide and were looking for a suitable place. The watchman immediately showed us the hatchway in the deck, and told us that they had several times had illicit things with them on their trips.

The Rjukan man now proved invaluable. He talked and talked with the watchman, while Rolf and I flung our sacks down under the deck and began to work.

It was an anxious job, and it took time. The charge and the wire had to be connected; then the detonators had to be connected to the wire and the ignition mechanism. Everything had to be put together and properly laid. It was cramped and uncomfortable down there under the deck, and about a foot of water was standing in the bilge.

The charge was placed in the water and concealed. It consisted of nineteen pounds of high explosive laid in the form of a sausage. We laid it forward, so that the rudder and propeller would rise above the surface when water began to come in. There was also a possibility that the railway trucks would roll off the deck and go to the bottom first.

When the charge exploded, it would blow about eleven square feet out of the ship's side. As the Tinnsjö is narrow, the ferry must sink in less than five minutes, or else it would be possible to beach her. I had spent many hours sitting and calculating how large the hole must be for the ferry to sink quickly enough.

To be on the safe side we used two alarm clocks. The operation must not fail, for everything was at stake. The hammer of the clock would short-circuit the current when it began to strike. The alarm clocks were set up on a rib of the vessel, and a wire led from them down to the charge. We counted on the train being ten minutes late. The clock was set to strike at a quarter to eleven, when the ferry would be over the deepest part of the lake.

Making the last connections was a dangerous job; for an alarm clock is an uncertain instrument, and contact between the hammer and the alarm was avoided by not more than a third of an inch. Thus there was one-third of an inch between us and disaster.

In the meantime the Rjukan man had had a long and well-thought-out talk with the watchman, and had explained to him that we must go back to Rjukan to fetch some things. We should be on board in the morning in good time before the ferry started.

When I left the watchman I was not clear in my mind as to what I ought to do. He had shown himself to be a good and useful Norwegian. It was very probable that he was just the person whom the Germans would interrogate after the ferry was sunk, and I should have liked to warn him and get him out of the danger zone. I was tempted, too, to take him with us and try to bring him into safety. I remembered the fate of the two Norwegian guards at Vemork, who had been sent to a German concentration camp after the attack there. I did not want to hand over a Norwegian to the Germans. But if the watchman disappeared, there was danger of the Germans' suspicions being aroused next morning.

I contented myself with shaking hands with the watchman and thanking him—which obviously puzzled him.

The car was waiting for us as arranged, and it turned out that we had been away for nearly two hours. Rolf was to take to the hills and keep Einar company while I was away. We said good-bye to him, and the journey to Sweden began.

At Jondalen the car had to turn and go home; for the driver was afraid of getting back to Rjukan too late. We reached Kongsberg railway station and took tickets for the first part of our journey. We booked from Kongsberg to Hokksund, then from Hokksund to Drammen; and at Drammen we took tickets for Oslo.

Halfway between Hokksund and Drammen I looked at my watch; it was a quarter to eleven. If everything had gone according to plan the ferry should just be sinking; the heavy water would be done for and the Germans' last chance of having it for their atomic experiments would have gone. It had cost us immense toil. We had been maintaining ourselves in the wilds of the Hardanger Vidda for nearly a year and a half. Snow and cold had been our constant companions, and we had carried danger with us wherever we went. Our best friends in Rauland and Vinje had not known what important work they were doing when they helped us. The certainty that a mistake on our part would bring death and destruction on many districts had been a heavy burden to us; for the Germans would have shown no mercy if they had found out who our helpers were.

What would happen now at Rjukan? How many Norwegian lives would be lost through this piece of devilry? The explosion on board the ferry must cost lives, and the reprisals at Rjukan certainly no fewer. Larsen and I did not talk much on the journey. I was thinking of the past.

The English had sacrificed thirty-four men with the gliders. Those men had known they would not be able to get away after they had done their work. The bombing had cost twenty-two lives. How many would it be this time? I was glad to know that one of those who were most in the danger zone at Rjukan would probably escape. The engineer Nielsen, who had been concerned with the transport, was, according to our plan, to be taken to hospital and operated on for appendicitis the next morning, before the ferry went down. The doctors would not ask if he were ill or not.

To be on the safe side, Rolf had given me a contact on Heröya, whence the heavy water was to be shipped to Germany. If anything had gone wrong I could take up the work again there. But I found that London too had been prepared for a hitch. Without my knowing it they had sent another sabotage party to Heröya to attack the transport there if we should fail. Submarines were lying in wait in the Skagerak. In Oslo we stayed with Trond as usual.

It was in the papers on Monday evening:

RAILWAY FERRY *HYDRO* SUNK IN THE TINNSJÖ

This was the headline on every front page. The ferry had sunk in a few minutes and was lying in deep water.

Fourteen Norwegians and four Germans had gone down with her.

Knut Haukelid

DENMARK

Gernant has reported to me about conditions in Denmark. From his report, prepared at the request of Best, I gather a situation has arisen which can only be called critical, because of the rather lax and feeble way in which the Danes were handled by the Reich's Plenipotentiary, Dr. Best. The Danes put a wrong interpretation on the generous treatment accorded them. Especially in Copenhagen events occurred that are more than shocking. German soldiers could hardly appear on the streets; German girls had swastikas branded on their bodies; acts of sabotage against Wehrmacht barracks and communication in-stallations increased day by day; and the government was neither willing nor able to do anything about it. Best was ordered to the Führer's G.H.Q. and given a vigorous dressing-down. He thereupon had to transfer his powers to the military command. The Danes at first tried to oppose martial law by a few stupid tricks, but when German tanks appeared they quickly became subdued. Since then everything has been going its normal way.

Dr. Goebbels, 8 September 1943

FRANCE

The Beginning

There was really no one. And one could not gauge the price one might have to pay. The enthusiasts were prepared to take a chance on anyone, yet everyone was reluctant or afraid with the excuse of being realistic.

The beginners had lost their nerve at the first disaster early in December 1940, when Edouard, my second-in-command, had been arrested in Marseilles and placed in solitary confinement in Fort Saint-Nicolas. Though we had gone so far as to sabotage a locomotive on its way to Italy, it was musical comedy stuff: sunshine, women bathing, petrol from the growing black market, traffic in gold and jewels. . . . Terrified crowds of emasculated, cowardly Jews, re-pentant Left wingers, petrified deputies and dubious capitalists, whose protecting régime had collapsed, were prepared to deny it now in the hope that some ar-rangement was possible with the new bunch. They groused in secret but avoided trouble, or prepared for flight to more clement lands when their affairs had gone too far awry.

In that Midi, where people, saturated with the sun and the landscape, perpetuated the mirage of happier days, it was difficult, wherever one turned one's eyes, to discover a trace of decent feeling or find men who, unless they themselves or their possessions were in danger, were prepared to take a stand because what was being done was a disgrace, for the whole scene was pervaded with a stench of swindling, in a sort of comic opera set, representing the end of the world. To my eyes it appeared the first sign of the Apocalypse.

. . . . After three months I had found five disinterested people, who were pre-pared to act without counting the cost and take a deliberate chance rather than resign themselves to the ignominy of a profitable conformity—five people sincerely concerned with Utopia, fired with rational despair or irrational hope: a Professor of Philosophy, a journalist who squinted, a manufacturer of bedding, an Amazon with a history degree and a Métro employee. . . . Add to them Bertrande and Jean—the family, that part of the family who, in their youth, refused to admit certain realities and rebelled against the dishonesty of certain social forms and conventions—who could travel without a ticket and stand for fifteen hours at a stretch.

At three o'clock in the morning, Jean woke up with a start because I was whistling to stop him snoring.

'What did you think when you met me in Vichy in November 1940?'

'That you were mad . . . I didn't know what you were up to when you spoke of the "last column".'

'It was for *Libération*, the newspaper. The "last column"—one could not call it the sixth, seventh or eighth.'

Emmanuel d'Astier, Resistance leader

A Recruit

I went to see my friends the Saint-Denises and met there a Dr. Meeus from Nantes, who offered his services and became Rivière in our organization. Madame de Hautecloque said to me:

'I'd like to introduce to you to the son of a woman I know very well. He is very eager to work for you. His name is Paul Mauger.'

Together, we went to see Madame Mauger. She lived in a little house in the new part of town. Paul was quite young, hardly eighteen. I was particularly struck by his eyes. They were a blue I had never seen before, a blue with a tinge of violet beneath great black lashes. His hair was cut short.

'Sit down, Paul,' I told him. 'What gave you the idea of working for me?' He was shy and stammered a little.

'I felt I ought to do something, monsieur,' he managed to get out.

'What Paul hasn't told you,' added Nicole de Hautecloque, 'is that he has already tried to get through Spain to join up with General de Gaulle.'

'Oh, yes?' I said. 'Tell me about it.'

Paul turned bewildered eyes towards his mother. She looked at him encouragingly.

'There were two of us,' he went on at length, 'a friend and myself. We had asked our parents' permission. . . .'

His mother smiled further encouragement.

'They told us we could. So we went off together and got over the frontier all right. We were arrested in the station at Madrid.'

'And then?'

'They put us in prison, at the Puerta del Sol, in the cellars. There were two or three hundred of us there. My friend died. I was brought back by train to Cerbère, with a civil guard on either side of me. French gendarmes were waiting for me, and I was put in prison again after having had my hair clipped short. An officer told me that if I joined the *Armée de l'Armistice* they would let me out, otherwise I would have to stay in prison for the rest of my life. So I joined up. The first day that they let me out of barracks I deserted, crossed the Line,* and got home. I am stuck now because I don't know how to get to England to join the general.'

I looked at the youth, almost a child, he seemed, who had given proof of real heroism, but could still keep such surprising simplicity. I read great anxiety in his eyes and in those of his mother. It was just as if his mother were introducing her boy to the manager of a business and was waiting to know whether her son would be taken on.

---

* Dividing Vichy France from Occupied France (Ed.)

'I am in no position to get you to England, Paul,' I told him. 'But would you like to work for me?'

'Yes, please,' he replied eagerly.

'You realize that I shall have to give you dangerous things to do.'

'That doesn't matter.'

'You realize, too, that you will be travelling all the time, often very uncomfortably?'

'That doesn't matter.'

'If they ever discover the papers you are carrying, you will be shot.'

'That doesn't matter.'

'Of course they will torture you first to make you talk. In no case must you ever say anything.'

The tears came to his eyes. I had already seen much the same look of reproach in Lhermite's eyes.

'I know all that,' was his answer.

'I shall be very exacting, very severe.'

'Yes,' he said.

'Right you are then, Paul. I'll take you on.'

I can still see the smile on Paul's lips as I agreed to let him work for me. He took to heart what I told him that day.

'From to-day on I shall give you another name. Among us you will be known as Pierre.'

He was as pleased as if I had given him a medal.

I rose. His mother shook hands with me warmly.

'I am very grateful to you,' she said. 'When can he begin?'

'This evening,' I replied. 'We shall leave together for Brest.'

Colonel Rémy

Crossing the Line

After he had left me near the Pont Mirabeau on that sunny afternoon of 30 May 1942, Maurice Rossi (Maurice we called him), had quickly put his more urgent affairs in order. On 1 June, he heard that the day before the Gestapo had turned up at the Traktir, the restaurant Prunier in the Avenue Victor Hugo, in order to arrest him. No one at the Traktir, save the manager, Monsieur Barnagaud, knew his address at the Place Saint-André-des-Arts; he thought, therefore, that he could leave his wife and small boy there without exposing them to any great risk, whilst he crossed over to the Unoccupied Zone. They could join him later when he had found them a safe place.

On 2 June he took the train at the Gare de Lyon, meaning to cross the Line secretly at Montchanin, but the station there was closely watched by the Germans, and they were getting into the carriages of the trains to examine the travellers' papers. Maurice had not had time to get himself fixed up with a false identity card; and it was probable that his real name had been telegraphed to all frontier stations. He thought it more prudent, therefore, to get out on the wrong side of the compartment and jump into a train that was just leaving in the opposite direction for Creusot. There was a woman in the compartment. Maurice took his place opposite her and proceeded quietly but painstakingly to tear his identity card into small pieces which he scattered through the open window.

At Montceau-les-Mines a German appeared and demanded his papers.

'I haven't got them,' replied Maurice. 'They were asked for at Montchanin and your people kept them. Didn't they, Madame?'

The unknown woman took her cue. 'Why, yes,' she replied.

But the *Feldgendarm* was by no means convinced.

'You must stay here until your papers arrive from Montchanin; we'll have them sent up. Open that bag.'

The only luggage that Maurice had taken with him was a leather satchel. This the German searched methodically. He found nothing but underwear, an ordinary razor, toilet articles, a few unimportant papers, a bottle of Alsatian sloe gin and twenty packets of cigarettes.

'How about letting me have some cigarettes?' asked the German.

Maurice, usually so quiet and smiling, foolishly lost his temper.

'If you want cigarettes,' he told the German, 'all you've got to do is to ask your Führer for them!'

So direct a snub was hardly calculated to please the German. He made Maurice leave the train and shut him up in the lamp room of the station under the guard of an armed sentry. In the corner was a young man who had also been arrested for having no papers.

Maurice considered him in silence for a while.

'Were you trying to get across the Line?' he asked him finally.

'Yes.'

'Shall we work this together?'

'I'm willing.'

'All right, then; but let me deal with the sentry.'

Maurice tapped on the door; the sentry opened it.

'I want to go to the lavatory.'

'*Was?*' enquired the sentry, who understood nothing.

'Lavatory, W.C., *cabinets*,' explained Maurice.

'Oh, *ja, gut.*'

The lavatory was next door. As he came back to the lamp room Maurice said to the sentry:

'You're a good chap. Like a drink?'

'*Was?*'

'Drink,' insisted Maurice, explaining at the same time in dumb-show. The sentry accepted immediately and followed him in. Maurice took the sloe gin from his satchel, uncorked it and gave the German a full glass; he swallowed it at one gulp.

'*Gut, gut,*' he gasped.

As a consequence the sentry saw no valid reason why Maurice should not be allowed to go to the lavatory several times, since each time he returned he was overwhelming with his thanks for the favour and did not fail to offer another glass of sloe gin which was always accepted with alacrity. In this way the German drank three-quarters of the bottle. Having tossed off a final glassful he slipped slowly to the ground, a vacant smile on his face, and, his back to the partition, fell asleep at once.

Maurice, in the course of his different peregrinations, had had ample opportunity to spy out the lie of the land. It was dark outside now. The moment for action had come.

'I'm not too happy about that bloke,' he said to his companion with a nod in the direction of the sentry. 'Suppose he opens an eye, just as we are slipping out, and starts shouting at the top of his lungs. We'd be in a worse mess than when we started.'

'What shall we do?' enquired the other.

'I see nothing for it but to kill him. Anyhow, it'll make one German less in the world.'

'What with? His rifle?'

'My word, no. Think what the noise would be like. Haven't you got anything in your bag?'

'Only tools.'

'Let's have a look.'

The other opened his bag. He must have been a mechanic; there was nothing but files, screw-drivers, spanners. Maurice pouted. The young man offered him a hammer, but Maurice shook his head.

'No good. We might miss, and then he'd only make a row,' he explained.

'That's all I have,' said the young man.

'I've got something better. A razor. We'll cut his throat.'

'We did it together,' Maurice told me afterwards. 'The mechanic chap held his head and I used the razor. When we'd finished the job, we slipped out. The German never opened his eyes.'

Fifty yards from the frontier line Maurice told his companion:

'You don't know my name, and I've not asked yours. You go your way, and I'll go mine. Good-bye.'

They separated, and Maurice crossed over the Line during the night without difficulty.

Colonel Rémy

Resistance Leaders in London

. . . . It is here in London that I feel lonely.

Everyone with whom I have talked seems to be making war at a distance, a distance in life and space. Eggs and bacon, hot baths and the morning taxi are transformed into a thought, a report, which will bear fruit to-morrow in Athens or Bordeaux, via the high seas, factories, ships and how much else, perhaps!

I have had a harassing day. The men I see have nothing to say to me as yet: perhaps they think that's what newspapers are for. But they have a great deal to ask me.

The Security people made me recount my whole life for two hours on end: they seem to know it better than I do myself and are trying to discover whether I am an impostor. Their tireless courtesy, therefore, changes to anxiety when I confess that I do not know my mother-in-law's maiden name, nor what I was doing in 1927.

After the Security people, the Intelligence people endeavoured to sum me up, in order to classify me: desire for money, patriotism, ambition, political objectives. . . . I am left with the impression that if they examined me with the X-rays of their universe, they would class me as an adventurer. But above all they're conscientious: I am a tool, either good or mediocre. Why leave it to others: de Gaulle, the *Deuxième Bureau* or Utopia. . . . It is with grains of sand that mountains are made.

At midday, I saw my first Frenchman: Colonel Bourse,* fair-haired—what remained of it—his eyes pale and red-rimmed, something rather porcine in the texture of his skin and hair, a high voice: immediate antipathy.

'What have you come to do here?'

I did not reply, I thought I had simply come to ask that we should be taken seriously. . . . Also, perhaps, that I had come to seek hope and confirmation of a plan which was both desperate and unreasonable. But since, in spite of his growing power, Bourse is still only an agent, he sent me to Symbole.†

'You'll dine with him to-night at nine o'clock.'

I went there at nine.

It was at the Connaught Hotel, the most exquisitely old-fashioned of hotels in London. A porter, as padded as the carpets and the life, led me to an empty drawing-room where a table was laid for two.

I stood waiting. Symbole came in.

He's even taller than one expects.

His movements are slow and heavy like his nose. His small head and waxen face are carried on a body of indeterminate structure. His most habitual gesture is to raise his forearms while keeping his elbows to his side. At these moments, his inert, very white, rather feminine hands, their palms turned downwards and attached to his arms by too-slender wrists, seem to be raising a whole world of abstract burdens.

He asked me no questions. We dined.

He does not love his fellow men: he loves their history, above all the history of France, in which he is acting a chapter that he seems to be writing concurrently in his head, like an impassioned Michelet.

As for me, traveller and seeker that I am, I said things which were either much too precise or much too confused, in which were mingled concrete details and Utopian sentiments. He gathered up only odds and ends here and there and put them in his history.

As with the others this morning, I had so great an impression of insurmountable incredulity—that incredulity in which I have been living in France for the last eighteen months as if in a cloud of cotton-wool—that I pleaded both his cause and our own. But why should he be incredulous? Suspicious, yes, because he despises men too much and too many things in the universe. Incredulous, no, because I am a French ant bringing him a fragment of straw, a piece of material for his history about which revolves a world of supernumerary friends and enemies, as Henri, Charles, Isabeau and Calixte revolve about Jeanne in a phrase-book.

I came out with my head in a whirl.

* Colonel Passy.   † General de Gaulle.

I had been in a theatre of history, I wanted to go out into life, my life.

Down below, the night porter reduced everything to scale again: insomnia of the cloakroom attendant, the mixture of keys to heart and mind, food, sleep, childhood and old age, women and their scent atoning for war and its uniforms. I went to the telephone: a familiar voice replied . . . remote, sunk in time. But it re-awakened a past life, stifled by the clamour of brotherhood and the passions of one race among races.

Emmanuel d'Astier

Supplies for the Maquis

Although she was vastly useful, the countess could only get comparatively small things, personal things, or presents for my friends and helpers. For the bulk needs of our headquarters or the Maquis we fell back on Paincheau.

The first thing I desired to end was the tobacco situation. And Paincheau ended it for us. He sent some men and trucks to Besançon and, working with a gang he ran in the town, they went to the place where French tobacco for the use of the German military garrison was stored. Breaking into the warehouse, these men coolly loaded their trucks with hundreds of cases of cigarettes. Germans passing in the street never imagined that anything illegal was going on. One night's work in the grand manner had provided enough cigarettes for all our Maquis for months. Paincheau had killed the '*bureau de tabac*' menace.

Next we asked him for boots, and these he supplied in the same grand manner. The Frisé also captured a truck-load of boots. All the Maquisards, including the officers, now appeared in brand-new lemon or banana-coloured boots. This became such a menace to security that we had to issue an order that all boots were to be dirtied or stained dark before worn. It was said that when a customer entered a shoe-shop in Besançon to ask for a pair of boots, the salesman said:

'But why not join the '*Equipes Boulaya*,' monsieur? There you get boots without disbursement and without coupons.'

The next thing was petrol. Paincheau already had fairly large stocks of this which he had requisitioned. But he decided that these must be increased. With his Besançon gang he devised the following plan. The main German petrol supply in Besançon was kept in tanks which were in a guarded building. One night Paincheau's men drew up in a large tanker truck beside one wall of the building which was not guarded. One of the men was a mason. Scientifically and silently he cut a hole in the brick wall. His comrades ran a pipe through the hole and into a tank in the interior. All night they pumped petrol out of the German store into their truck. As the first light of dawn came over the hills surrounding the city they stopped pumping and the mason re-built the wall. The tanker returned to Rougemont to empty its precious load. The following night the operation was repeated successfully. But now the level of the petrol in the tanks had sunk so drastically that the Germans discovered the loss. Since there were always guards on the door of the building, the Gestapo arrested all German soldiers who had been on this guard in the past seven days. Paincheau decided that we would get no more petrol. So that night four of his men volunteered to go back into the store building, to put two hundred pounds of sugar into the remaining stocks. They entered the building by the same route. The same mason closed the hole after them. The operation was an entire success.

Once Boulaya was short of money. All our Maquisards were paid like soldiers regularly by the week on a fixed scale according to the number of their dependants. Their pay was small, but it was important that it should not be interrupted. Paincheau could get anything from a bottle of absinthe to a funeral cortège with a black-and-silver hearse, lilies, and black Belgian horses. He met us in a wood between Devecey and Bonnay and unstrapped from the back of his 'pétrolette' an enormous sack.

'What have you there?' Boulaya asked.

'Eight million francs,' he replied calmly.

It was Gestapo money deposited in banks in Besançon. Paincheau explained that four men had succeeded in getting this money by several visits to banks with an accomplice, a woman who worked for the Gestapo. But the story was so complicated that I could not follow it. Perhaps it was because he spoke so softly. At any rate, the men who did the coup had only, we understood, kept two million of the German money for themselves, and the rest they presented to the Resistance. They were real patriots. Boulaya and I were greatly touched by the patriotism of the experts. We laughed a lot.

Jacques Paincheau was a magician. With his help we were able to organize the food situation. Where lesser beings thought in kilos, he thought in terms of truck-loads, barge-loads, warehouses. He could produce sugar, rice, gruyère, yes, even tyres for vehicles and chocolate by the ton. And all taken from the enemy. Although, like a skilful prestidigitator, he produced all those valuable things without apparent effort, his coups were all the result of faultless planning and execution. He worked everything out to the minutest detail, and he was prepared to lead his men into anything that he planned. He and I became close friends. We were not able to meet very frequently because we were both too busy. But each time that I met him I found that his mind was packed with ideas for work, and each time they were new ideas.

George Millar, British agent

The Patriot

In November 1941, Espadon had given me in Paris a blade of metal, about the size of two postage stamps.

'Send it off to London,' he requested, 'it's the sample they asked for by wireless.'

I turned the little blade over in my hand. The metal of which it was made seemed extraordinarily light and very hard. It was of a bluish-grey colour. It was not aluminium.

'I reported to London,' Espadon informed me, 'that the S.N.C.A.S.O. factory [*Société Nationale de Constructions Aeronautiques du Sud-Ouest*] at Bordeaux was making this metal in great secrecy on behalf of the Luftwaffe.'

'Yes,' I told him, 'I read your report. You said there that the Germans were taking extraordinary precautions against any leakage of the material through the workpeople; that they were obliged to take off their clothes and put on special overalls which had the hems unsewn; that they were very carefully searched when they left the factory, and that they were obliged to wash their hands and brush their nails in case they took away even the tiniest particle or filing in that way.'

'That's right.'

'How did you manage to get hold of this bit, then?'

'Do you remember,' he recounted, 'that on 11 November, five minutes of silence was observed everywhere, together with a general stoppage or slowing down of work, according to the request General de Gaulle made over the radio? In the S.N.C.A.S.O. factory all the workpeople downed tools, except one who went on working as if there was nothing unusual on. When the five minutes were up, all his neighbours turned on him, and knocked him down. The Germans intervened, and the man, who had fainted, was carried home. The next day I had the piece of metal.'

'So it was he . . .' I concluded his story for him.

'Yes, he was one of our men. I had asked him for the sample. He had heard the General's order and had said to himself that the attention of the Germans would be entirely occupied with those who stopped working. He was wearing clogs, underneath which were fixed strips of rubber cut from old motor tyres. Many of them do that. On the morning of 11 November, he managed to cut off a piece of metal the right size. When the others downed tools, he went on working and let this piece fall to the ground without the Germans noticing. By pushing his foot against the bench he managed to slip the piece of metal between two bits of rubber on one of his clogs.'

'What a marvellous man!' I exclaimed.

'There's better than that,' Espadon went on. 'I went to see him and told him that it was absolutely essential that the Germans should not know that we had a piece of the metal. He went on with his work at the factory and never told a soul. None of his companions would speak to him now after that business on 11 November; they treated him as a pariah and avoided him like the plague. They looked on him as a traitor.'

Colonel Rémy

The Mountain of Miserey

One day after lunch Philippe asked if he might take some of the others out and do a job on the Vesoul railway. We had just heard a train pass below us in the valley, and this was such an unusual sound that it roused us to action. Boulaya refused permission, but I persuaded him to let Philippe take out the Pointu and two new lads, Communists whom Maurice and Philippe together had rescued from imprisonment in the German hospital in Besançon, where they had been convalescing from German-inflicted wounds. The four of them departed happily on foot, carrying an arsenal of miscellaneous weapons and the heavy tools we used for unscrewing the railway lines. They promised to work as far afield as Miserey. Things appeared to go badly. That afternoon we heard the sound of firing, and the story came back to us that while they were derailing a train near Miserey a German truck full of soldiers passed on the road and opened fire. The Maquisards replied and then withdrew.

One by one that evening the young men dribbled back into the camp, bringing with them all their weapons and the tools. The story of the Germans was true, but Philippe had turned their arrival to our profit, for while the little battle was going on he had walked into Miserey station, found another train there and obliged the railwaymen to start it at full speed. This, crashing into the derailed train in the cutting, broke up the battle and allowed the other three Maquisards to withdraw in good order. On the way home Philippe and the Pointu seized a third train near Devecey, made all the occupants descend, and hurled this train on to the wreckage near Miserey. This was a wonderful day's work. I cycled out to see it, and I knew that if the enemy still had a crane he would need it for this, and it would be a long job. The cutting was deep, and the wreckage was well wedged in.

But our Philippe was irresistible. Boulaya gave him a holiday in Besançon to celebrate this important victory. He spruced himself up and left on a new bicycle. (We had just taken eight new ones from the police in Besançon, and Boulaya and I each bought one on the black market, so we were now astoundingly well off for bicycles.) Bronzed and bleached by the sun now, Philippe looked more cherubic than ever.

Unable to avoid the scene of his crime, he cycled past the still smoking remains where the Gestapo were examining tracks and questioning civilians and railwaymen. He saw another locomotive in Miserey station. Unarmed as he was, he cursed and swore at the railwaymen until they sent their engine rushing down the track. It hit the wreckage while the Gestapo were still there, and jumping, said onlookers, thirty feet into the air it landed upside down on the other side of the heap of twisted metal. Its wheels continued to revolve for some time. Already crowds were gathering for this fantastic sight. Cycling excursions were setting out from all the villages. Many of them were to have their money's worth. Philippe, tranquilly continuing on his way to Besançon, found another train and again, with only his gruff and determined voice to help him, succeeded in getting it launched at full speed on the right rails. In front of a large audience this train added itself to the heap in the cutting.

Sightseers were still visiting the place six weeks later. And it was known locally as 'the mountain of Miserey'. This closed the Vesoul line until (and, alas, after) the Allied armies arrived.

George Millar

HOLLAND

As everybody knows, the Dutch are the most insolent and obstreperous people in the entire West.

Dr. Goebbels, 10 September 1943

Jews in Hiding

Saturday, 20 June 1942

My father was thirty-six when he married my mother, who was then twenty-five. My sister Margot was born in 1926 in Frankfort-on-Main. I followed on 12 June 1929, and, as we are Jewish, we emigrated to Holland in 1933, where my father was appointed Managing Director of Travies N.V. This firm is in close relationship with the firm of 'Kolen & Co.' in the same building, of which my father is a partner.

The rest of our family, however, felt the full impact of Hitler's anti-Jewish laws, so life was filled with anxiety. In 1938 after the pogroms, my two uncles (my mother's brothers) escaped to the U.S.A. My old grandmother came to us; she was then seventy-three. After May, 1940, good times rapidly fled: first the war, then the capitulation, followed by the arrival of the Germans. That is when the sufferings of us Jews really began. Anti-Jewish decrees followed each other in quick succession. Jews must wear a yellow star, Jews must hand in their bicycles, Jews are banned from trams and are forbidden to drive. Jews are only allowed to do their shopping between three and five o'clock and then only in shops which bear the placard 'Jewish shop'. Jews must be indoors by eight o'clock and cannot even sit in their own gardens after that hour. Jews are forbidden to visit theatres, cinemas, and other places of entertainment. Jews may not take part in public sports. Swimming baths, tennis courts, hockey fields, and other sports grounds are all prohibited to them. Jews may not visit Christians. Jews must go to Jewish schools, and many more restrictions of a similar kind.

Thursday, 19 November 1942

Apart from that, all goes well. Dussel has told us a lot about the outside world, which we have missed for so long now. He had very sad news. Countless friends and acquaintances have gone to a terrible fate. Evening after evening the green and grey army lorries trundle past. The Germans ring at every front door to enquire if there are any Jews living in the house. If there are, then the whole family has to go at once. If they don't find any, they go on to the next house. No one has a chance of evading them unless one goes into hiding. Often they go round with lists, and only ring when they know they can get a good haul. Sometimes they let them off for cash—so much per head. It seems like the slave hunts of olden times. But it's certainly no joke; it's much too tragic for that. In the evenings, when it's dark, I often see rows of good, innocent people accompanied by crying children, walking on and on, in charge of a couple of these chaps, bullied and knocked about until they almost drop. No one is spared—old people, babies, expectant mothers, the sick—each and all join in the march of death.

How fortunate we are here, so well cared for and undisturbed. We wouldn't have to worry about all this misery were it not that we are so anxious about all those dear to us whom we can no longer help.

I feel wicked sleeping in a warm bed, while my dearest friends have been knocked down or have fallen into a gutter somewhere out in the cold night. I get frightened when I think of close friends who have now been delivered into the hands of the cruellest brutes that walk the earth. And all because they are Jews!

Wednesday, 13 January 1943

Everything has upset me again this morning, so I wasn't able to finish a single thing properly.

It is terrible outside. Day and night more of those poor miserable people are being dragged off, with nothing but a rucksack and a little money. On the way they are deprived even of these possessions. Families are torn apart, the men, women and children all being separated. Children coming home from school find that their parents have disappeared. Women return from shopping to find their homes shut up and their families gone.

Wednesday, 29 March 1944

People have to queue for vegetables and all kinds of other things; doctors are unable to visit the sick, because if they turn their backs on their cars for a moment they are stolen; burglaries and thefts abound, so much so that you wonder what has taken hold of the Dutch for them suddenly to have become such thieves. Little children of eight and eleven years break the windows of people's homes and steal whatever they can lay their hands on. No one dares to leave his house unoccupied for five minutes, because if you go, your things go too. Every day there are announcements in the newspapers offering rewards for the return of lost property, typewriters, Persian rugs, electric clocks, cloth, etc. Electric clocks in the streets are dismantled, public telephones are pulled to pieces—down to the last thread. Morale amongst the population can't be good, the weekly rations are not enough to last for two days except the coffee substitute. The invasion is a long time coming, and the men have to go to Germany. The children are ill or under-nourished, everyone is wearing old clothes and old shoes. A new sole costs 7.50 florins in the black market; moreover, hardly any of the shoemakers will accept shoe repairs, or if they do, you have to wait four months, during which time the shoes often disappear.

There's one good thing in the midst of it all, which is that as the food gets worse and the measures against the people more severe, so sabotage against the authorities steadily increases. The people in the food offices, the police, officials, they all either work with their fellow-citizens and help them or they tell tales on them and have them sent to prison. Fortunately, only a small percentage of Dutch people are on the wrong side.

Tuesday, 11 April 1944

We have been pointedly reminded that we are in hiding, that we are Jews in chains, chained to one spot, without any rights, but with a thousand duties. We Jews mustn't show our feelings, must be brave and strong, must accept all inconveniences and not grumble, must do what is within our power and trust in God. Some time this terrible war will be over. Surely the time will come when we are people again, and not just Jews.

Who has inflicted this upon us? Who has made us Jews different to all other people? Who has allowed us to suffer so terribly up till now? It is God that has made us as we are, but it will be God, too, who will raise us up again. If we bear all this suffering and if there are still Jews left, when it is over, then Jews, instead of being doomed, will be held up as an example. Who knows, it might even be our religion, from which the world and all peoples learn good, and for that reason and that reason only, do we have to suffer now. We can never become just Netherlanders, or just English, or representatives of any country for that matter, we will always remain Jews, but we want to, too.

Be brave! Let us remain aware of our task and not grumble, a solution will come; God has never deserted our people. Right through the ages there have been Jews, through all the ages they have had to suffer, but it has made them strong too; the weak fall, but the strong will remain and never go under!

Anne Frank, died Belsen concentration camp, 1945

CRETE

The Fighters

I tried hard not to judge Papadakis from his appearance alone. His swept-back grey hair and iron-grey clipped moustache were typical of any senior Greek Army officer; but his hard black eyes glittered with peasant cunning and his general expression could best be described by the American term of 'sour-puss'. His voice oscillated between arrogance and plaintiveness; at a moment's notice he would switch it from the didactic tone he used when exploiting his rank, of which he was exaggeratedly proud, to the wheedling notes of a pauper begging for alms.

But I did my best to overlook these unattractive qualities, remembering that he was the first man in the island to have established contact with the Allies and to have put himself at the disposal of our clandestine service. He alone had maintained Stockbridge and the wireless station ever since we started operations in Crete, and he had thereby reduced his own standard of living, which on his small pension would in any case not have been high, to a bare subsistence level —at Vouvoure there was nothing to eat but seed potatoes.

But his gestures of selfless patriotism, his quixotic plans for the freedom of Crete, were largely prompted by a personal ambition so vainglorious that he scarcely bothered to conceal it. He had set himself up as the head of a 'Supreme Liberation Committee', unrecognized by anyone except its four members, all of whom had been elected by himself. This would have been an admirable venture had it lived up to its rather grandiloquent name—for in Crete bombast and bluster were not necessarily divorced from courage and efficiency—but from the first conversations I had with Papadakis it became increasingly clear that, like himself, his fellow members were less interested in organizing immediate resistance than in securing post-war political positions.

Even this ulterior activity could have been put to good purpose had the committee been prepared to co-operate with the other local leaders whose names I had been given in Cairo; but Papadakis was reluctant to enlist their assistance in case, I suppose, he should have to surrender to them a vestige of his self-arrogated authority or, worse still, in case they should recognize that authority for what it was: a purely notional attribute. So during the first week I spent in Vouvoure, while I vainly enquired after the potential strength of his organization, its dispositions and eventual requirements, Papadakis not very craftily avoided the issue by claiming that nothing could be done until he received official recognition from G.H.Q. Middle East. Since I was not prepared to commit myself on this point, nothing practical was done.

Xan Fielding

June had ended, and in July—it must have been about two months since the fall of the island—three boys from a neighbouring village (Kastelos in Apokoronas), called Levtheri Daskalakis and George and Andrea Vernadakis, went down to the flat country near Aspouliano where the plane which had made the forced landing still lay. A German guard post had been set up to watch over it. But the boys went at midday when the men of the guard were inside eating, and, creeping up to the plane unobserved, they set fire to one of the petrol tanks. It went up in a flash, the whole plane catching in a moment and blazing like a firework. The Germans rushed out, but they did not see who had set fire to it, and (as we learnt later), fearing punishment by their superiors—for their only duty had been the guarding of this plane—they told the owners of the vegetable plots round about (if the military authorities should question them) to say that they had seen nobody: that the plane, in fact, had caught fire by itself. The gardeners said they would back them up in their report. Unfortunately, a 'bad Greek'* called Evangelos Stagakis of Dramia went to the local German command-post at Episkopi and asked to be taken to the Kommandant. When the interpreter learnt that he wanted to reveal the truth about the burning of the plane, he turned him out. But Stagakis started threatening the interpreter, and went on until he managed to appear before the Kommandant, to whom he betrayed the whole business. The men at the guard post were arrested at once and (we learnt) put in the lock-up where the Germans beat them up. To the devil with them. But what happened to the neighbourhood? A large German force immediately surrounded the villages of Dramia, Kastelos and Kourna and rounded up the male inhabitants. But the boys, forewarned, had left their villages. The Germans announced that unless the people who had burnt the aeroplane were given up, the villagers would all be shot. But how could the villagers have found them, even if they had wished to give them up? In the end, after all the denials of the villagers (who constantly repeated: 'We don't know anything. How could we find them?'), it was decided that the blame rested only with the boys' fellow-villagers, the Kastelians; so the Germans began to threaten the Kastelians and especially the relations of the three boys. But they were determined to die rather than hand their children over to be killed. The matter was very serious. If they did as the Germans demanded, the killing of their children would weigh heavy on their hearts for the rest of their lives. They would never be able to still their consciences. So they decided to warn them not to come near the village, but to flee far away and take care never to be caught by the Germans, even if everybody else were killed. And then they waited, resigned to the firing squad. Meanwhile the boys (who had gone into hiding near our village), learning that all their own people would be killed for shielding them, began to be tormented in their minds as to what they ought to do. Finally they decided to give themselves up. They lingered in the neighbourhood to observe the actions of the Germans, in order that, the moment they saw the Germans about to execute their relations, they might surrender and take the road to Golgotha. But here, too, bad Greeks were in evidence. The then Mayor of their village, Stavros Romanias, learning that the boys were in hiding nearby, sent a man to verify the fact, and, when he had made quite certain, took a large number of Germans who

* i.e. A traitor.

set out in ones and twos for Asi Gonia. Fortunately we saw them before they
reached the village, and had time to lead the English farther off and then to
escape ourselves. Unfortunately some villagers were mad enough not to escape,
so the Germans arrested about a dozen of them and led them away to Archontiki.
They gave them a certain time limit in which to betray the boys; otherwise
they were to be shot.

The luckless boys, learning all this, and seeing that the Germans were in no
joking mood, took the path of death with heavy hearts. Only Andrea, the youngest, was unwilling to give himself up, so he hid at the place called Koumara,*
where some Psychoundakis cousins of mine, who pastured their flocks there-
abouts, looked after him. As bad luck would have it, some fellow-villagers,
relations of the people who were being held in Archontiki, losing patience and
not knowing what the Germans were going to do with their kinsmen, set off one
day to Andrea's hiding-place to persuade or compel him to give himself up. But
the moment he saw them he took to his heels. They set off after him in pursuit,
and he ran tirelessly for many hours. Some of the ones in front fired shots at
him to make him stop, but it was all in vain. At last, when he had shaken them
off, he fell into the hands of some others, who caught him, half-dead with
exhaustion. They took him to Argyroupolis and handed him over to the Germans.
He showed no signs of fear but laughed at them as though it were all a game of
hide and seek.

The Germans took him to Canea along with the other two, where they were
tried. Andrea, being under age, was only sentenced to six months' hard labour
but the other two, who were nearing twenty if they had not actually reached it,
were condemned to death. So, after a few days, in a street in Archontiki and
under the eyes of all the inhabitants, these two martyrs to freedom and death-
deriders stood before the firing squad—naked, hungry, barefoot and in chains.
Their bonds were removed and their executioners, with rifles levelled at their
bare breasts, were waiting for the word 'Fire!' The leader of the German party
read out the sentence and asked if they had any last words to say. Daskalakis
asked for a glass of water which they gave him, and the question was repeated
to Vernadakis, who said, 'A glass of wine and permission to sing a *mantinada*.'†
Saying which, naked, barefoot and utterly exhausted as he was from thirst and
hunger (for, during their confinement in Ayia jail they had been given neither
food nor water), he mustered all the strength of his soul—and what greater
strength is there?—and took to his heels. Straight away the firing squad began
shooting after him as he ran. But neither the rifle bullets nor the bursts from the
sub-machine-guns could touch him. He ran like lightning from lane to lane until
he was out of the village. Then, as it was difficult to run farther without being
seen, he climbed up into an olive tree and stayed there until night fell. When it
was quite dark he climbed gently down and, slipping through the sentries, fled
far away. Later he escaped to the Middle East where he volunteered for the
Air Force.

* The arbutus-berries.
† A Cretan fifteen-syllable rhyming couplet, usually with a sting in it. Sung in solo to one of
half a dozen ritual tunes, the last half of each line being repeated, after the words 'Ela! Ela!
Ela!', by the rest of the company. They are sung and improvised by all Cretans, especially in the
mountains.

While they were chasing Vernadakis through the village, Daskalakis remained motionless in his place although he too had a chance of taking to his heels and escaping. 'Run for it!' several onlookers shouted, but he refused, saying the Germans would avenge themselves on his kinsmen. It would be better for him to die, he said. In a few moments the Germans were back again, and they opened fire on Daskalakis with fury. He fell at once, quite transformed and unrecognizable from the bursts of the German machine-guns.

George Psychoundakis

The Kidnapping of General Kreipe

I find it impossible to go to sleep because of the benzedrine which I took last night, so I shall try to put on paper all that I can remember of the events of the past twelve hours.

It was eight o'clock when we reached the T-junction. We had met a few pedestrians on the way, none of whom seemed perturbed at seeing our German uniforms, and we had exchanged greetings with them with appropriately Teutonic gruffness. When we reached the road we went straight to our respective posts and took cover. It was now just a question of lying low until we saw the warning torch-flash from Mitso, the buzzer-man. We were distressed to notice that the incline in the road was much steeper than we had been led to believe, for this meant that if the chauffeur used the foot-brake instead of the hand-brake when we stopped him there would be a chance of the car's running over the edge of the embankment as soon as he had been disposed of. However, it was too late at this stage to make any changes in our plan, so we just waited and hoped for the best.

There were five false alarms during the first hour of our watch. Two *Volkswagen*, two lorries, and one motor-cycle combination trundled past at various times, and in each of them, seated primly upright like tailors' dummies, the steel-helmeted figures of German soldiers were silhouetted against the night sky. It was a strange feeling to be crouching so close to them—almost within arm's reach of them—while they drove past with no idea that nine pairs of eyes were so fixedly watching them. It felt rather like going on patrol in action, when you find yourself very close to the enemy trenches, and can hear the sentries talking or quietly whistling, and can see them lighting cigarettes in their cupped hands.

It was already one hour past the General's routine time for making his return journey when we began to wonder if he could possibly have gone home in one of the vehicles which had already passed by. It was cold, and the canvas of our German garb did not serve to keep out the wind.

I remember Paddy asking me the time. I looked at my watch and saw that the hands were pointing close to half-past nine. And at that moment Mitso's torch blinked.

'Here we go.'

We scrambled out of the ditch on to the road. Paddy switched on his red lamp and I held up a traffic signal, and together we stood in the centre of the junction.

In a moment—far sooner than we had expected—the powerful headlamps of the General's car swept round the bend and we found ourselves floodlit. The chauffeur, on approaching the corner, slowed down.

Paddy shouted, '*Halt!*'

The car stopped. We walked forward rather slowly, and as we passed the beams of the headlamps we drew our ready-cocked pistols from behind our backs and let fall the life-preservers from our wrists.

As we came level with the doors of the car Paddy asked, '*Ist dies des Generals Wagen?*'

There came a muffled '*Ja, ja*' from inside.

Then everything happened very quickly. There was a rush from all sides. We tore open our respective doors, and our torches illuminated the interior of the car—the bewildered face of the General, the chauffeur's terrified eyes, the rear seats empty. With his right hand the chauffeur was reaching for his automatic, so I hit him across the head with my cosh. He fell forward, and George, who had come up behind me, heaved him out of the driving-seat and dumped him on the road. I jumped in behind the steering wheel, and at the same moment saw Paddy and Manoli dragging the General out of the opposite door. The old man was struggling with fury, lashing out with his arms and legs. He obviously thought that he was going to be killed, and started shouting every curse under the sun at the top of his voice.

The engine of the car was still ticking over, the hand-brake was on, everything was perfect. To one side, in a pool of torchlight in the centre of the road, Paddy and Manoli were trying to quieten the General, who was still cursing and struggling. On the other side George and Andoni were trying to pull the chauffeur to his feet, but the man's head was pouring with blood, and I think he must have been unconscious, because every time they lifted him up he simply collapsed to the ground again.

This was the critical moment, for if any other traffic had come along the road we should have been caught sadly unawares. But now Paddy, Manoli, Nikko and Stratis were carrying the General towards the car and bundling him into the back seat. After him clambered George, Manoli and Stratis—one of the three holding a knife to the General's throat to stop him shouting, the other two with their Marlin guns poking out of either window. It must have been quite a squash.

Paddy jumped into the front seat beside me.

The General kept imploring, 'Where is my hat? Where is my hat?'

The hat, of course, was on Paddy's head.

We were now ready to move. Suddenly everyone started kissing and congratulating everybody else; and Micky, having first embraced Paddy and me, started screaming at the General with all the pent-up hatred he held for the Germans. We had to push him away and tell him to shut up. Andoni, Grigori, Nikko and Wallace Beery were standing at the roadside, propping up the chauffeur between them, and now they waved us good-bye and turned away and started off on their long trek to the rendezvous on Mount Ida.

We started.

The car was a beauty, a brand-new Opel, and we were delighted to see that the petrol-gauge showed the tanks to be full.

We had been travelling for less than a minute when we saw a succession of lights coming along the road towards us; and a moment later we found ourselves driving past a motor convoy, and thanked our stars that it had not come this way a couple of minutes sooner. Most of the lorries were troop transports, all filled with soldiery, and this sight had the immediate effect of quietening George, Manoli and Stratis, who had hitherto been shouting at one another and taking no notice of our attempts to keep them quiet.

When the convoy had passed Paddy told the General that the two of us were British officers and that we would treat him as an honourable prisoner of war. He seemed mightily relieved to hear this and immediately started to ask a series of questions, often not even waiting for a reply. But for some reason his chief concern still appeared to be the whereabouts of his hat—first it was the hat, then his medal. Paddy told him that he would soon be given it back, and to this the General said, '*Danke, danke.*'

It was not long before we saw a red lamp flashing in the road before us, and we realized that we were approaching the first of the traffic-control posts through which we should have to pass. We were, of course, prepared for this eventuality, and our plan had contained alternative actions which we had hoped would suit any situation, because we knew that our route led us through the centre of Heraklion, and that in the course of our journey we should probably have to pass through about twenty control posts.

Until now everything had happened so quickly that we had felt no emotion other than elation at the primary success of our venture; but as we drew nearer and nearer to the swinging red lamp we experienced our first tense moment.

A German sentry was standing in the middle of the road. As we approached him, slowing down the while, he moved to one side, presumably thinking that we were going to stop. However, as soon as we drew level with him—still going very slowly, so as to give him an opportunity of seeing the General's pennants on the wings of the car—I began to accelerate again, and on we went. For several seconds after we had passed the sentry we were all apprehension, fully expecting to hear a rifle-shot in our wake; but a moment later we had rounded a bend in the road and knew that the danger was temporarily past. Our chief concern now was whether or not the guard at the post behind us would telephone ahead to the next one, and it was with our fingers crossed that we approached the red lamp of the second control post a few minutes later. But we need not have had any fears, for the sentry behaved in exactly the same manner as the first had done, and we drove on feeling rather pleased with ourselves.

Presently we found ourselves approaching the Villa Ariadne. The sentries, having recognized the car from a distance, were already opening the heavily-barbed gates in anticipation of our driving inside. I hooted the horn and did not slow down. We drove swiftly past them, and it was with considerable delight that we watched them treating us to hurried salutes.

We were now approaching Heraklion, and coming towards us we saw a large number of lorries. We remembered that Micky had told us that there was to be a garrison cinema-show in the town that evening, so we presumed that these lorries were transporting the audience back to various billets. We did not pass a single vehicle which was travelling in the same direction as ourselves.

Soon we had to slow down to about twenty-five k.p.h., because the road was chock-full of German soldiers. They were quick to respond to the hooting of our horn, however, and when they saw whose car it was they dispersed to the sides of the road and acknowledged us in passing. It was truly unfortunate that we should have arrived in the town at this moment; but once again luck was with us, and, apart from a near-miss on a cyclist, who swerved out of our way only just in time, we drove down the main street without let or hindrance. By the time we reached the market square in the centre of the town we had already left the cinema crowd behind us, and we found the large, open space, which by daylight is usually so crowded, now almost completely deserted. At this point we had to take a sharp turning to the left, for our route led us westward through the old West Gate to the Retimo road.

The West Gate is a relic of the old days when Heraklion was completely surrounded by a massive wall, and even to-day it remains a formidable structure. The gate itself, at the best of times not very wide, has been further narrowed by concrete anti-tank blocks; and a German guard is on duty there for twenty-four hours a day.

I remember saying 'Woops' as I saw the sentry signalling us to stop. I had proposed to slow down, as on the previous occasions, and then to accelerate upon drawing level with the sentry; but this time this was impossible, for the man did not move an inch, and in the light of the headlamps we saw several more Germans standing behind him. I was obliged to take the car forward at a snail's pace. We had previously decided that in the event of our being asked any questions our reply would be simply, '*Generals Wagen*', coupled with our hopes for the best. If any further conversation were called for Paddy was to do the talking.

George, Manoli and Stratis held their weapons at the ready and kept as low as they could in the back seat. The General was on the floor beneath them. Paddy and I cocked our pistols and held them on our laps.

The sentry approached Paddy's side of the car.

Before he had come too near Paddy called out that this was the General's car—which, after all, was true enough—and without awaiting the sentry's next word I accelerated and we drove on, calling out '*Gute Nacht!*' as we went. Everyone saluted.

We drove fast along the next stretch of road.

The General, coming to the surface, said he felt sorry for all the sentries at the control posts, because they would surely get into terrible trouble on the morrow.

W. Stanley Moss

JUGOSLAVIA

Tito Changes Headquarters

A few days after Vivian reached partisan headquarters an incident had occurred which aroused his suspicion. One morning a single German aircraft made its appearance over the valley, and, instead of dropping bombs or machine-gunning, as these aerial visitors usually did, had spent half an hour or more flying slowly up and down at a height of about two thousand feet. Each time it passed directly over the little house on the rising ground outside the village where he and the others were living. Standing outside in the orchard, in the warm spring sunshine, looking up at it, they discussed what it could be doing and came to the conclusion that it was making a photographic reconnaissance.

Now the Germans would not do this without a reason, and Vivian's guess was that the visit of the little aeroplane would be the forerunner of a heavy air attack that would put anything else we had experienced into the shade. Accordingly he sought out Tito in his cave and told him what he thought was going to happen, adding that in the circumstances he proposed to move a little farther out. That afternoon he and the others transferred themselves with wireless sets and escort to a little house in the hills a mile or two away from the village.

Two days passed; and nothing happened. Then a third day. Vivian began to wonder if he had not perhaps been rather over-cautious. That night he dined with Tito, and after a good meal walked home to bed through the orchards.

Next morning he was awakened, just as it was getting light, by the familiar shout of '*Avioni!*' from the partisans on guard outside. The shout was repeated, so he went out to see what was happening.

A number of small aircraft, considerably more than usual, were bombing the village, circling round and then, when they had dropped their bombs, pulling away to make room for others that were coming in from every direction. Then just as those who were watching were reflecting what short work a couple of Spitfires would make of the intruders, a deeper note fell on the ears of the watchers, and out of the sun came six great JU 52s, flying in formation down the valley. The Germans were doing things in style.

They waited for the whistle and crash of the bombs. The planes reached the village and circled it. Then, as they watched, something fell from the leading plane, and, falling, billowed out into a great canopy with a man dangling from it. Then more and more, from one plane after another. The air seemed full of them. More planes followed, and gliders, bringing guns and reinforcements to the parachutists, who by now were shooting their way into the village. A glider seemed to be landing almost on top of the little house which the Mission had left three days before.

For a few moments Vivian and the others stood and looked. Then, taking the wireless sets and anything else they could carry, they moved off along the hill-side to establish contact with the partisan corps headquarters situated farther up the valley.

Meanwhile, in Drvar itself, the partisans had driven back the Germans from the village. But they were firmly established on the slopes outside it. A glider which had come down on the flat ground immediately below Tito's cave had crashed and the crew had been killed. But now some other Germans had succeeded in gaining a position from which they commanded the mouth of the cave, and this was now under heavy fire. Tito's position was precarious, for to use the ordinary way down would have meant almost certain death. But, with the help of a rope he hoisted himself up a cleft in the rock to the high ground above his cave. From there he was able to join the main body of partisans.

Now came the news that, on top of the airborne attack, strong forces of the enemy were converging on Drvar from all sides. The partisans had already suffered heavy losses. They could not hope to hold Drvar in the face of such overwhelming odds. The order was given to withdraw into the hills.

After a ten hours' march Vivian and the others reached the little group of huts deep in the forest which we had left some months before, to find Tito and his staff already there. Soon the wireless was working and a message on its way to Bari saying what had happened and asking urgently for air support.

Meanwhile, the enemy had taken Drvar. They had inflicted severe casualties on the partisans, but at heavy cost to themselves, and they had failed to capture Tito or the Allied Missions. For this failure, they revenged themselves on the defenceless civilian population, known to be loyal to the partisans. When the village was recaptured some months later it was found that most of the inhabitants had been massacred. One of our officers who went back with the partisans tried to find some of the peasants who had lived near us. At last he found one who had somehow survived. He said that during the fighting the Germans had forced the civilians to carry ammunition for them at the point of the rifle, making them go on even after they had been wounded and could barely crawl: old men, women and even children. After the fighting was over and they no longer had any use for them, they had shot them. And the child Ginger? Ginger had been shot, too.

Having missed Tito at Drvar, the enemy began to close in on him in the woods. Soon they reached the edge of the forest. Firing could be heard coming nearer. Tito decided to break out.

The break-out took place at night. Fierce fighting was in progress. Flashes could be seen on the ridge above them. The sound of firing came ever closer. From time to time a Verey star shot up into the sky.

Then Vivian saw something that amazed him. There, on a siding in the woods, was drawn up the Partisan Express, with steam up and smoke and sparks belching from the funnel. Solemnly, Tito, his entourage and the dog Tigger entrained; the whistle blew; and, with much puffing and creaking, they started off down the five miles of track through the woods, with the enemy's bullets whining through the trees all round them.

During the days that followed, Tito and his staff, with the Allied Missions and a force of a few hundred partisans, were almost constantly on the move: dodging through the woods, lying up in the daytime, moving at night. Again and again they had narrow escapes from the enemy. German patrols, aircraft and light tanks seemed to be everywhere. Food and ammunition were getting desperately short, but once they managed to stop long enough to receive a supply dropped from British planes based in Italy. At the same time other British aircraft were giving much-needed air support, wherever they could. During the week that followed the attack on Drvar our planes flew over a thousand sorties in support of the partisans, thereby doing much to relieve the pressure on them.

All this time Vivian kept in close touch with Tito. He was, he told me afterwards, impressed throughout by the way in which Tito dominated the situation, remaining calm and collected under the severest strain, personally directing the operations of the small body of troops which accompanied him as well as those of the other partisan formations in the neighbourhood, quietly giving orders to the partisans round him. This from Vivian, an experienced soldier and a severe judge in such matters, was high praise.

Then one day, as they were resting after a long march, Tito sent for him. Vivian found the Marshal looking tired and depressed. He had, he said, reluctantly reached the conclusion that it was impossible for him to direct the operations of his forces throughout Jugoslavia while being chased through the woods and kept constantly on the move. The complexity of this task now made it essential for him to have a relatively firm base for his headquarters. Already he had lost touch with nearly all the formations under his command. He must ask Vivian to arrange for the evacuation of himself and his staff by air to Italy until such time as the situation permitted his return to Jugoslavia.

At first Vivian was surprised. Tito was connected in his mind with the hills and forests and it was hard to imagine him leaving them. But he soon realized that the decision which he had taken was the right one.

A signal was dispatched to Bari and the answer came back almost immediately. The R.A.F. would do everything in their power to pick them up from a nearby stretch of flat ground, now held by the partisans. That afternoon they set out for the landing-strip.

They reached it after dark. It was raining and there was low cloud. Not much hope, it seemed, of getting out. Then the moon came through the clouds and they cheered up a little. Anxiously they waited. At last came the sound they were waiting for: the faint hum of an aircraft engine in the distance. Bonfires were lighted and soon the Dakota was circling the field, ready to land. It touched down; they climbed in. Tito, his dog Tigger, half a dozen of his staff, Vivian and the Russian Mission. Almost immediately they were airborne.

As Vivian got into the plane, he saw that it was manned by Russians. It was a Dakota, supplied under Lease-Lend, which the Russians were operating from Bari under British operational control. The Soviet officer concerned had shown considerable astuteness in securing this particular assignment for his plane. Afterwards the Russians were to make great capital out of the claim that it was they who had rescued Tito in this emergency.

An hour or two later they reached Bari.

The next thing to be decided was where Tito and his headquarters staff were to establish themselves. I went and called on him at the suburban villa on the outskirts of Bari in which he had been temporarily installed and found him in favour of moving over to the island of Vis until such time as the military situation made it feasible to return to the interior. This, indeed, seemed the obvious solution. Vis was Jugoslav territory; at the same time, thanks to its now substantial garrison and ever-present British naval and air support, it offered a degree of security and stability which was not to be found on the mainland of Jugoslavia.

The task of conveying the Marshal to his new abode was entrusted to the Royal Navy and H.M.S. *Blackmore*, a Hunt Class destroyer, under the command of Lieutenant Carson, R.N., was allotted to us for the purpose, with another destroyer for the rest of the party.

Carson and the officers and crew of the *Blackmore* immediately entered into the spirit of the thing as only the Navy can. In order to avoid any risk of enemy interference, the crossing was made at night. At about six in the evening Tito, followed by Tigger, was piped on board in fine style, and at once taken below and plied with gin. His original Marshal's uniform had fallen into the hands of the Germans during the attack on Drvar and been taken away to grace a museum somewhere in Germany, but a substitute had been found, and he once more looked and, I think, felt the part.

By the time we weighed anchor any initial shyness had completely worn off and I could see that we were in for a convivial evening. We sat down to dinner in the wardroom to find ourselves confronted with a menu magnificently illuminated by one of the crew and written in Serb as well as English. I noticed at once that the wine list was a formidable one: sherry followed the gin, then red wine, then white, then port, then liqueurs. The Marshal drank some of everything, only hesitating momentarily when a large bottle was produced mysteriously draped in a napkin. For an instant he wavered.

'*Cheri-beri*?' he enquired cryptically.

'No, champagne,' said the Captain proudly.

'Ah, champagne!' said Tito and drained a tumbler of it.

It was not till later that we discovered that by *cheri-beri* he meant cherry brandy, though when, in due course, that stimulating beverage made its appearance, any distrust which he might have felt for it earlier in the evening had evidently vanished.

By this stage of dinner the Marshal, to my surprise, was speaking quite fluent English and rounded off the proceedings by giving a spirited recital of *The Owl and the Pussy-Cat*.

> The Owl and the Pussy-Cat went to sea
> In a beautiful pea-green boat.
> They dined on mince and slices of quince,
> Which they ate with a runcible spoon;
> And hand in hand, on the edge of the sand,
> They danced by the light of the moon. . . .

After that, we went up on deck.

By now the sky was starting to get lighter, and, outlined against it, we could already see the jagged outline of the Dalmatian mountains. Tito sat in an armchair on deck, contemplatively smoking a cigar. Soon we could make out the dark shape of Vis, rising from the sea, and twenty minutes later Carson, on the bridge, was bringing us skilfully alongside in the little harbour of Komisa.

Fitzroy Maclean

WARSAW

. . . Brief landing in Warsaw. But I take no notice of the city; I would only get angry anyway.

Dr. Goebbels

The Rising: August–October 1944

General Bor . . . commanded an underground force of three hundred thousand men, the Polish Home Army, whose anti-German efforts, including much of the actual liberating of Lvov and Vilna, had been lauded by Russian propaganda which at the same time continually demanded greater efforts. He had been instructed unequivocally by his government in London, having himself asked for directives when the Red Army penetrated Eastern Poland, that Russian commanders were to be accepted as hosts, that they should be helped to the utmost, and that Polish units were to be at their disposal. The Polish Home Army had then fought the Germans all over Poland in support of the 1944 spring–summer offensive of the Red Army; and when the Russians reached the River Bug, five days' march from Warsaw, General Bor summoned to his Warsaw headquarters the leaders of all the Polish political groups including the Communists (who had appealed ceaselessly for a general rising) and put it for decision, whether they should liberate the capital themselves or wait for the Red Army. Decision was unanimous for a rising.

No elaborate preliminaries were entailed. Plans had long since been worked out for a general rising all over Poland, and it was only necessary to excerpt the Warsaw section of the plans, in which all knew what they had to do without special orders. On 31 July, conveyed by messenger-girls from General Bor's H.Q. to all units in Warsaw, went the secret order: '5 p.m. to-morrow afternoon—X.' X was the code-letter for the project, 5 p.m. the hour chosen because workers would be leaving the factories and the city would be busy with casually unsuspicious movement.

1 August

Soldiers of the Capital!

To-day I have issued the order so long awaited by all of you, the order for an open fight against the German invader. After nearly five years of unceasing underground struggle, to-day you are taking up arms openly to restore the freedom of our country and to punish the German criminals for the terror and bestialities they have committed within our frontiers.

Bor, Home Army C.-in-C.

X-evening in fact completely surprised the unexpecting Germans. With machine-guns, machine-pistols, and hand-grenades three-quarters of Warsaw were quickly seized. German strongpoints in big buildings, occupied mainly by S.S. who had heavily prepared them for defence against the Russians, were approached and breached more slowly with explosives carried through the sewers.

At the time of this auspicious opening the Russian armies under Marshal Rokossovsky had pressed their rapid advance to within ten miles of Warsaw, east of the Vistula. General Bor had food and ammunition for a week; it seemed certain that that would be enough and that the Russians would in good time enter a city whose own people had hastened and facilitated its liberation.

The Fight for Mokotow

Mokotow was a residential district in the south of Warsaw. It was nearly lost by the insurgents during the first night's fighting, as described in the anonymous eye-witness account that follows. Owing to the stubborn resistance of Colonel Daniel, it was enabled to hold out for fifty-seven days.

It looked as if things were not going too well for us, either. To find out more about the situation Daniel, accompanied by Kubus, went out to establish personal contact with the commanders of Battalions B and O, who had been given the hardest assignments. Before leaving he told me to see to Woronicz's School, which was still in German hands.

It was after 8 p.m. Connected by telephone cable to all the centres of fighting in Mokotow, I sat and listened to reports coming in from the local commanders. Most of them confirmed my uneasiness and my fears. Nothing certain was known about the most distant units, but from scraps of information it emerged that Battalion K in Sluzewiec had been lost, and that Brigand's hand-picked company had been bled white in its assault on Mokotow Fort. The nearest troops, Burza's and Reda's companies, reported that they were still fighting desperately but only for their own survival now.

It was getting dark, and with the coming of dusk the fighting was losing in intensity. Our storm troops, for the last few hours interlocked in mortal combat with the Germans, had been kept pinned down in the open by accurate fire, and only now, using the last of their ammunition, were they fighting back, disengaging and pulling out to more advantageous positions.

The darkness allowed us to carry the wounded to safer places, and, helped by nurses, they were making their way in groups to the Elzbietanek Hospital.

More people were out in the streets; many were putting up barricades. Detachments of sappers were advancing boldly into the street openings and digging anti-tank trenches. There were numerous volunteers and the work was progressing swiftly.

Only now the picture of the burning capital assumed some sharpness of definition. Towering, billowing smoke topped the city like an immense parachute, lit from below by long tongues of flame. The roar issuing from that volcano of fire and smoke told us that the battle was not yet over, and this cheered us somewhat, though all the attempts of our radio-telegraphists to establish contact were unsuccessful.

Meanwhile the telephones in the Mokotow's H.Q. were ringing incessantly. The whole time the local commanders had something to report, and each one wanted to talk to Daniel personally, so that I couldn't put the receiver down for more than a second. Daniel was still out and I was beginning to worry, as the situation was difficult and important decisions had to be taken. I breathed at last when he returned from his tour of inspection, in complete darkness, shortly after ten. Though tired and evidently depressed, he at once went over all the reports received in his absence: we began summing up the results of the fighting so far and tried to appraise the situation. What we arrived at was not very encouraging. The results achieved were infinitesimal and the losses very serious.

The forces at our disposal had been considerably weakened without seriously incapacitating the Germans. But as long as the rest of the capital fought on we could not resign ourselves to the role of mere spectators.

Daniel came to a decision: we were to attack again, as we could not afford to give the Germans a breather. The attack would raise the morale of our own troops, too. Daniel answered all telephone enquiries with a curt and decided: 'One more effort.'

Before midnight I ran over to Garbaty's detachment near Woronicz's School. The platoons assembled there were silently moving up to base positions. The S.S. troops in the school opened up blindly from time to time with all their machine-guns hidden in concrete shelters. The fire did us no damage, but, at a distance of fifty paces, it caused an uneasiness which was increased by the darkness prevailing all around. We did not answer the fire and our lads kept very quiet. There were twenty minutes to go before the attack. Garbaty asked me to send up a few more pistols and more hand-grenades. I promised to do so, then checked the preparations and returned to H.Q.

The commanders at various points were reporting their readiness for renewed attack. I managed to send up the supplies to Garbaty, and, in a slightly better mood, waited for the attack to begin.

There was a loud explosion which rumbled on for some seconds, followed by the staccato of furious automatic fire. I was surprised and very pleased at the violence of our attack. Obviously the initiative was with our men and for the moment they had the upper hand. Storm units were reaching the entrance-halls and staircases of many buildings where the Germans were holding out. Those dull explosions meant that the doors and gates were being blown up by mining patrols and that the way was open for others to rush in through the breached defences. Lighter explosions of hand-grenades tossed in through the windows followed, and then another wave of dull and heavy rumbling. They had got through the barrier of automatic fire and were storming the inner pockets of resistance.

But our forces were expendable. The enemy fire showed no signs of abating, and our troops had to withdraw again without achieving tangible success; only the fighting round Woronicz's School lasted some time longer. The reports started coming in. Nowhere had we managed to overpower the Germans in their fortified positions; and again a wave of wounded men streamed towards the hospital. The fighting ceased. The darkness was no longer rent by tracer bullets, and only occasional German flares lit up the sky above the battle-ground below.

About 2 a.m. we had a complete picture of the situation. This time it was really bad. Out of twelve quite well-armed companies there were only four left in a condition to carry on the fight. Battalion K could be written off altogether, as, after some initial success at Sluzewiec, it had been forced to withdraw into the adjacent woods*; the company commanded by Zdzich had disintegrated, and only one platoon commanded by Bozydar made its way back to our lines. Zych's company suffered a similar fate. Other companies had shrunk enormously. The spirit of the men was flagging, the reversals were having a sad effect on morale.

---

* Some time later Battalion K returned to Mokotow.

The situation was not made easier by the remnants of defeated units from the neighbouring sectors who came streaming into our lines. They did not want to join us, but were all making for the woods. All round anxious voices were asking what was going to happen in the morning if the Germans attacked in full strength. Between 2 and 3 a.m. hardly anybody in Mokotow believed in the possibility of resisting a German attack, as so much ammunition had been used up and so many men killed, and as, with every person left lying in no-man's-land, a valuable rifle or pistol had been lost.

In the east, the sky over Praga* was beginning to be tinged with silver. The glow of fires over Warsaw was dying down and the sounds of battle were more subdued. In our part the silence was broken only by the Germans, who emptied their magazines in the air frequently and for no apparent purpose; while the freedom with which they spent their ammunition preyed on our minds and led to unpleasant guesses as to their stocks of it.

In their phone calls to H.Q. the unit commanders were betraying an increasing nervousness. More and more verbal phone reports suggested pulling out of Mokotow: the idea of withdrawing into the nearby woods was spreading even among the staff. Everybody was waiting for the commander's decision.

At 3 a.m. Daniel decided that we would remain as we were. Warsaw was still fighting on, and, anyway, we were not going to abandon the civilian population, whom the Germans would undoubtedly decimate after our withdrawal. It was up to us to stay on and share the fate of the rest of Warsaw and of the civilians. We threw ourselves into preparations for the battle, which was to begin again with daylight. The dawn of 2 August found us, with our ranks closed, holding a diminished perimeter between Goszczynskiego and Odynca Streets. The soldiers looked at each other and saw that not all had been killed the day before. Concentrated in a small area, our forces not only seemed larger but allowed a better tactical use to be made of them. The morale was much better than during the night.

It was raining and the low clouds overhead presaged a murky day. The advanced outposts found it very difficult to overcome their sleeplessness and fatigue. It was quiet except for concentrated bursts of German fire lasting about a minute each and, no doubt, preparing the way for some attack, though we had no means of knowing when and where it would develop.

At 8 a.m. enemy activity was reported from a few sectors. A fresh attack was signalled from Woronicz's School, where the Germans had received reinforcements in two armoured troop-carriers.

The fire from the detachment of our Battalions B and O stopped the swarm of S.S. men pouring forth from the school. But only for a time. More and more Germans joined the attack. Their fire was definitely superior to ours and the struggle became more vicious. The Germans were attacking due north, and their advance continued in spite of our efforts. They got through fences, jumped over walls and sprinted across streets, and one by one put our centres of resistance out of action. We saw that we were up against very good troops: the German success became more and more pronounced every minute. In places our units were beginning to retreat in disorder, as the battle reached its climax. Shortly

* A suburb of Warsaw on the right bank of the Vistula.

before noon the German attack had penetrated to within a short distance of our reserve detachments, and the tension among us had risen appreciably.

Only Daniel kept cool and followed the developments, waiting for the right moment to counter-attack. The companies from Burza's battalion had been ready for some time, and their commanders, Szwarc and Krzem, were only waiting for a sign from Daniel.

The Germans were level with Malczewskiego Street and small groups of them were infiltrating into the Elzbietanek Hospital. Not more than sixty yards separated us from the Germans. The line of steel helmets pressed forward with increasing audacity: they treated our weakening resistance with ever-diminishing respect. There were at least two full companies in the attack, and they were well aware of their strength.

The tension among our reserve detachments was rising to a climax. The time was ripe for a counter-attack. At a given sign the mass of men moved forward. The impetus and fury of this initial rush swept back the German line, while a second group cut them off from their starting base at the school. The back of the German attack was broken. Now it was their turn to pull out in disorder, and, leaving many wounded and dead behind, they retreated south, by-passing their stronghold in the school.

At 3 p.m. Woronicz's School had been completely cleared of the enemy, and our companies were fighting a long way farther south. This was our first major success, and it resulted in the capture of large quantities of arms and ammunition stored in the school.

But the moral success was even greater. The Mokotow garrison had come through its first crisis with flying colours, and, as a result of this valuable trial of strength, it held out through many more crises during the next eight weeks of the Rising, which for Mokotow came to an end on 27 September 1944.

Anon.

Kurt Heller's Diary*

1 August. Street fighting began this afternoon in Warsaw.

2 August. We're surrounded.

3 August. Ulrich has been killed. Still no help from outside. Hollweg has been seriously wounded.

5 August. Rudolf killed, as well as several others. We've reached the limit of endurance.

6 August. Got a little sleep this morning. Dinner was coffee with sugar. Death everywhere, but I want to live. Three men have committed suicide.

7 August. Our own artillery fired at us this afternoon, but no one was killed. An attempt to break out failed—one man killed, four badly hurt. We buried fourteen of our men to-day at 8 a.m. in the yard. The air smells bad.

8 August. Our positions are three hundred metres away, but the bandits' resistance is still strong.

9 August. Food very short.

* Kurt Heller, a German from Stettin, was taken prisoner in the Warsaw Telephone Exchange.

11 August. The police have taken what food we had, including our cigarettes. We're in no condition to resist longer.

12 August. Hungry. Some soup, six cigarettes. The police have seized everything, even what was left of the jam. When will this end?

13 August. Heavy tank fire against the Poles so that our Tower is being hit, but no casualties. A tank has brought in food supplies for five days. I can hardly stand. When will they get us out of here?

16 August. Hunger. The men are afraid at night. When I saw the first star I thought of my wife and the boy, lying in the earth in Stettin. Can't stop thinking of them; am in the same position myself.

17 August. The Poles are trying to smoke us out with petrol bottles. More men have lost their nerve and committed suicide. The dead smell horrible, lying in the streets.

18 August. Cut off entirely from the outer world.

19 August. No hope. The Poles are surrounding us.

Kurt Heller

The Betrayal

But suddenly during the first day of the rising the Russian front went dead. The sky that had been full of Russian aeroplanes was vacant. The streams of exhortation from Russian radio ceased all at once. For thirteen days this silence in the east continued. On the thirteenth day it was broken. The friendly, familiar voice of Russian radio sounded once again—but the words that General Bor heard were not quite so familiar. He heard himself described as a 'war criminal' and he heard the Rising stigmatized as 'irresponsible'. Then immediately with fatal clarity he saw that the struggle must fail, and knew equally that he 'could not now stop it'. The one hope, he thought, was that the importance of Warsaw might yet oblige the Red Army to intervene. But meanwhile the initially surprised Germans, who at first had reacted only defensively outside the city, had brought up two Panzer divisions, an S.S. division, and a quantity of bombers. They did not actually recapture much of what they had lost; but they did not have to. Their bombing, incessant and unhindered, brought havoc to the half-million civilian population, now foodless, and increasingly buried in collapsing cellars from which many could not be rescued. British aeroplanes from Italy dropped supplies, but so many were lost on their homeward journey that they had to desist. An American promise of a hundred Fortresses was doomed by the refusal of Russia to allow her airfields for refuelling; and when finally Stalin, after several telegrams from London reminding him that such contravention of the Anglo-Russian Treaty might have 'political consequences', professed to alter his decision, it was too late. Warsaw was in the last throes.

The Sewers

It was 26 September. For the last fortnight I and my radio group had been in Mokotow, where the situation was critical, not to say hopeless, just as it had been in the Old Town a month earlier. We were on a narrow strip of territory like an island, with the Germans all round.

I was given the decision of Colonel Karol, commanding the fighting in Mokotow, to retreat to the City Centre, as less than a month before we had retreated from the Old Town. As I radioed the message about the withdrawal— the last one from Mokotow—I felt an unspeakable sorrow. One more stage was coming to an end, and we had thought that each successive stage would bring us closer to freedom. What had been my pride—my transmitters—which had been carrying on conversations uninterruptedly with London and the High Command ever since my transfer to Mokotow on 11 September, now had to close down. Never again would they speak on the ether. A radio man's sending key is his faculty of speech, and I felt as if I had lost mine.

It was 11 p.m. when I set out with my group on the last stage of our retreat, the town drains. Through them we were to reach the City Centre. We forced ourselves into the ranks of this strange procession: all round us were gloomy faces, unwashed for many weeks, blood-stained rags hiding wounds, clothes in ribbons. The long file of people moved in silence. After the noise and uproar above, the silence was unbearable.

We waded into the stinking filth, moving terribly slowly. A few steps and then a long halt. A few more steps and again a halt. I began to lose count of the time; I was losing any power of judging the distance covered. I thought we should have come out long ago, while really it was only a few steps forward and then stop.

At one point I shook myself into consciousness. With some difficulty I began counting the number of stops. I added up the short distances between them, and came to the conclusion that we had covered a few hundred yards at best. I looked at my watch. It was nine, nine in the morning. So we'd been going all night and had only gone a few hundred yards. I felt myself sinking into a quiet dementia.

I was up to the waist in the stinking stuff. I was hot. There was a long row of people in front of me and another behind. All of us in a similar mood.

We moved forward again. At one point I came up against an obstacle blocking my passage. I felt that someone stood in front of me, though the column ahead was moving. I touched the motionless figure, trying to force it forward. But the man I was touching would never move again.

After that we came on more and more dead bodies. Sometimes on several at once. Each time it filled one with disgust, and worse, with very dark conjectures, for the dead men had also been soldiers and also full of youth and hope. I knew I mustn't think of it, not think of anything, or things might go ill for me. After all, it was only because I wanted to live again and hope again that I was pushing through the damned darkness.

My group was holding out well. But the sewer seemed endless. Suddenly from those in front came cries: 'Gas!' True, it was only tear gas. The Germans had discovered that we were passing and had gassed sections of the sewers. I didn't like to think what was happening at the front of the column, but we in our group were not spared the catastrophe either. Ewa, my cipher clerk, was seized with a fit of madness. I divided my men in two groups. One, under Smialy, I sent on after Karol's column; the other, consisting of Lieutenant Oko, the radio-telegraphist, Geniek and myself, stayed behind to help Ewa. Another girl, Stefa, Ewa's friend, decided to stay with us.

We carried her in turns, stumbling over corpses, knapsacks and arms. It was horrible. Ewa's demented howling mingled with other unearthly screams. She was not the only one.

I felt my strength ebbing away. At one point I lost my footing and fell heavily. My companions, Oko and Geniek, helped to put me on my feet again.

We set Ewa down and covered her with overcoats; we had to rest. She sat, propped against the side wall of the sewer, no longer screaming, and with glassy eyes. A procession of ghastly phantoms kept filing past us, some of them howling as Ewa did only a short time ago. Those screams, multiplied by echoes, were about as much as one could stand.

Then a new party approached. I wanted to warn them that we were resting, but before I could do so one of them had fallen, and the others, no longer aware of what they were doing, went over him, trampling him down into the bottom of the sewer—automatically, quite unconscious of the fact that he was still alive. In the same way they would have walked over us.

When they had passed we got up. Ewa no longer gave any sign of life, nor did the man who had been trampled on. We walked on.

We passed a barricade put across the sewer by the Germans. After some time we caught up with the group which had passed us. Then we came to another barricade. This one was well built and was a real obstacle. There was no way through here. I turned back with my group, and some of the others followed. When we came to the first barricade, the one we had just passed, we met a party of people who told us feverishly that the sewer beyond the barricade in the direction of Mokotow was flooded. So we should never get to the top!

A despairing argument took place between the two groups, the one that had brought the news of the flooding and the one that had come up against the impenetrable barricade. By then people had lost their senses; they were shouting in their fury and anguish.

Some remnant of judgment indicated a return to Mokotow. It was not very likely to succeed, but it was the only way of keeping alive—no matter for how long; the only thing that mattered was not to die in the sewer.

The gas was affecting our eyes more and more the whole time. I felt just as if I had sand under my eyelids; my head, too, was rolling to one side in a queer way. The mass of people all round were still arguing how to save themselves. From time to time a hideous bubbling was heard, as one more person whose strength had gone slipped into the foul liquid. But even more unbearable would be the voice of some woman pulling him out: 'Look, he's alive, he's smiling! My darling, you'll soon be on top again!' Oh God, not to see it, not to hear it!

I realized during my increasingly rarer spells of clarity that I was beginning to lose consciousness. I held on to one thought: to get back to the surface. I did not want someone else to hear the splash and the bubbling which my ears would not hear.

I shouted then, at the top of my voice:

'Make way, I'll lead you out!'

But the angry yells which met me on all sides were the worst thing yet.

'Who said that? Fifth columnist! Shoot him!'

This shouting, like a sharp lash, spurred me to an extra effort. I escaped. I had enough sense left to realize that at such a moment what they threatened could well happen. Edging sideways close to the wall, my group and I crossed the barricade unnoticed by the rest.

We were over on the other side. We were going back, come what might.

At once we were deep in it. After a few steps we could no longer feel the bottom, but with the help of planks, knapsacks and abandoned bundles, we managed to keep our heads above the surface. After a short time we again felt the ground under our feet. The cold water and the absence of the blasted gas helped to clear our heads, and, holding each other's hands, we crawled slowly forward. Forward, that was what mattered. I knew that by following that sewer we were bound to come out in Dworkowa Street. We had to make it.

At 4 p.m., seventeen hours after we first went down into the sewers, we were pulled out of them by S.S. men in Dworkowa Street.

Anon.

The Last Day of September

By radio telegram General Bor informed Marshal Rokossovsky that he would have to end resistance if within seventy-two hours he received no support or promise of support. He received neither. He received no reply at all; and when seventy-two hours had passed he sent two of his officers to General von den Bach, who had many times requested a meeting, and who now suggested, pleasantly if long-windedly, that there was 'nothing left to fight for' and that Warsaw might as well capitulate rather than be completely destroyed. On this report from his officers General Bor overnight drew up his 'conditions' for capitulation. The battle for Warsaw, planned for a week, had lasted sixty-three days; and perhaps the most remarkable testimony to the Polish defence, to General Bor, and to the blows that the Germans had received, was the alacrity with which General von den Bach accepted the 'conditions', in all their unpalatable clemency, that General Bor had laid down.*

Poland Lives

This is the stark truth. We were treated worse than Hitler's satellites, worse than Italy, Roumania, Finland. May God, Who is just, pass judgment on the terrible injustice suffered by the Polish nation, and may He punish accordingly all those who are guilty.

Your heroes are the soldiers whose only weapons against tanks, planes and guns were their revolvers and bottles filled with petrol. Your heroes are the women who tended the wounded and carried messages under fire, who cooked in bombed and ruined cellars to feed children and adults, and who soothed and comforted the dying. Your heroes are the children who went on quietly playing among the smouldering ruins. These are the people of Warsaw.

* Among the chief conditions agreed and signed were:
   (a) All Polish Home Army to have P.O.W. status as under Geneva Convention—a white-red armband sufficing as uniform.
   (b) This equally for women as for men.
   (c) All Communists to have the same combatant rights.
   (d) No civilian to be charged in respect of any earlier anti-German activity.

Immortal is the nation that can muster such universal heroism. For those who have died have conquered, and those who live on will fight on, will conquer and again bear witness that Poland lives when the Poles live.

This was one of the last messages broadcast from Warsaw.

PARTISANS IN RUSSIA

Organizing a Unit

Knocking a partisan unit into shape is a complicated business. Eugene is being assisted at the Combine by his former fellow students at the Institute. For years they attended lectures together, passed examinations and went on practical work, dreamed, argued, quarrelled, made it up, danced at socials, and courted young women. They know each other so well that one would think men could not know each other better; but even then it was hellishly difficult to pick our future partisans so that each retained his individual qualities and yet merged with the rest to form a single, indivisible whole.

In the hills we shall need primarily good fighters, men skilled in the use of all the different arms: snipers, machine-gunners, signallers, miners, sappers, mortar-gunners and artillerymen. Every one of these will be needed. Hence, the first question I put to every candidate is: 'What weapon can you handle?'

The unit must not be too large. I think it would be unwise to have more than fifty or sixty men. At the same time our operations will be extremely varied. Therefore, the men must be proficient in various departments. Those who can handle only one weapon must learn to handle others, and German weapons at that, because our chief source of supplies in the hills will come from the enemy.

.... In the hills we shall live like Robinson Crusoes. We shall get no orders for supplies or repairs up there, no shops will be open for us, no postman will bring us the latest newspapers. But we don't want, like Robinson Crusoe, to clothe ourselves in animals' skins and live in shacks. Hardships of that kind would certainly affect our operations. Hence, we need builders, surgeons, cooks, tailors, cobblers, hunters, truck-drivers, mechanics and radio operators. Each of our partisans must know several civilian trades. This raises new difficulties in selecting our men.

One thing is now clear, and that is that our unit will consist mainly of intellectuals. This has its good and bad sides.

Its good side is that culture is needed everywhere. Its bad side is that up to now we have all led urban lives, whereas the life of a partisan will demand the habits and knowledge of one accustomed to country life. Of what use will the partisan be if he is unable to harness oxen, cook a meal over a campfire and patch a pair of trousers? Far more useful for him to be able to mend a pair of boots than solve a problem in mathematics.

We have any numbers of builders and mechanics. Genya, I'm sure, will make quite a good truck-driver. My wife, of course, will be the surgeon. She did that sort of work even during the Civil War. Pavel Pavlovich Nadryag, an oil engineer, turns out to be a first-rate farrier and harness-maker. Nikolai Demyanovich Prichina is an ardent amateur radio operator. Yakov Ilyich Bibikov, the director of our margarine plant, seems to be quite a fair cobbler, and even Mikhail Denissovich, the director of the oil-extracting plant, is a skilful ox-driver.

P. K. Ignatov

Ambush

Genya and Pavlik were on outpost duty.

This was at night. The long hours passed very slowly.

At last the sun rose from behind the mountains, a dazzling bright orb. The mist dispersed. The birds twittered in the woods.

Suddenly a strange note was heard amidst the twittering. It was barely audible. It was difficult to determine what it was. Perhaps the distant patter of horses' hoofs?

Genya strained his ears. No, it was the rumble of an engine, far, far away. It was impossible to say as yet whether it came from the sky over the hills or from the road to Novo-Dmitriyevskaya Stanitsa.

The rumble grew into a distinct, steady drone.

'Pavlik!' whispered Genya. 'Run to Eugene and tell him that tanks are approaching the Afips.'

Gripping their grenades tightly in their hands, the men waited motionless in the roadside bushes.

The clang of tank treads and the rattle of heavy machines were now distinctly heard.

Suddenly a machine-gun burst split the air. A gun barked. Evidently the Germans feared the presence of partisans and to make sure were sweeping the bushes.

As usual the first to dash past was a tank. Behind it, wrapped in a cloud of yellow dust, came a heavy truck loaded with tommy-gunners. Standing close-packed against each other, they fired senselessly and aimlessly at the bushes.

Then came other trucks loaded with ammunition, with convoys of tommy-gunners and with provisions. These proceeded calmly and confidently, as if they were at home.

How infinitely long the seconds seemed! Surely the tank must have passed the spot where the mines were placed the night before!

Unexpectedly, although they had been waiting for it every second, an explosion caused the earth to tremble. At last! The leading tank was blown up.

Fire-bottles were flying, grenades bursting, and the machine-gun rattled without interruption.

Heavy trucks dashed down the road, crushing the wounded under their wheels in a desperate effort to find a way out of this fiery circle. But there was no way out. Bursting grenades, columns of fire, and the well-aimed bullets from partisan carbines and tommy-guns met them at every turn. Suddenly a new sound was heard amidst the din of battle.

A fascist tank, riding in the rear of the column, dashed into the bushes, to the rear of the partisans. Gaining speed every moment, it crushed the young trees under its treads with the greatest ease. In another instant it would have broken through the alder grove and have crushed this handful of men. But Genya rushed out to meet the tank, into the open, at full height.

A fascist spotted him and fired a short machine-gun burst at him, but the bullets flew wide. The tank pushed its way through the wood, Genya dashed forward to meet it. A long machine-gun burst came from the tank.

Unhurriedly, as if at his exercises, Genya swung his arm, hurled an anti-tank grenade and swiftly dodged behind a tree.

The tank halted and abruptly stopped firing.

Genya emerged from behind the tree and waited.

Several seconds later the tank came to life again. The muzzles of its machine-guns turned in Genya's direction.

Pavlik sprang towards his chum like a cat and, pulling him down by the arm, fell flat with him to the ground. A stream of bullets flew over their heads.

A short, sharp whistle was heard in the wood, repeated in quick succession. It was Eugene's signal to retreat. A second fascist column had arrived and the Germans were trying to surround the partisans. But the covering party went into action. Grenades were heard bursting in the woods while our riflemen held up the German tommy-gunners. In the same instant the main attacking group leapt out of the fiery ring.

Again the partisans proceeded in single file along the wild boar tracks, forded rivers, climbed the mountains, descended into deep gorges and again crossed the winding, capricious mountain rivers and at last arrived at the camp.

P. K. Ignatov

TERROR WITHOUT END

A leaflet duplicated and distributed in Germany by a group of Munich students in 1942. The leader, Hans Scholl, and five associates, including Professor Kurt Huber, were executed for these activities early in 1943.

One cannot argue intelligently with National Socialism because it is by nature unintelligent. To speak of a National Socialist philosophy is a mistake, for if such a thing existed one would have to try to prove it or disprove it by intellectual arguments. But the reality is totally different: even when it was first germinating this movement depended on deceiving the public; even then it was rotten through and through and could only maintain itself by continual lies. Hitler himself writes in an earlier edition of 'his' book (the worst-written book I have ever read, imposed as a bible on the 'nation of poets and thinkers'): 'You cannot believe how much you have to deceive a nation in order to govern it.' If this cancer of the German people was not all too obvious at the beginning, it was because there were enough healthy energies at work to restrain it. But as it grew and grew and at last, by a final piece of knavery, came to power, the cancer burst and made foul the whole political body. Then the majority of those who had opposed it went into hiding, German intellectuals took refuge in cellars, where they gradually suffocated, mere nocturnal shadows, cut off from light and the sun. Now we are facing the end. What matters now is to find the way to each other again, to enlighten each other, to keep the thought constantly in mind and give oneself no peace till everyone is convinced of the inescapable necessity of fighting against this system. If such a wave of revolt goes through the land, if revolt is 'in the air', if large numbers join us, then, by a last mighty effort, this system can be shaken off. An end with terror is better than terror without end.

It is not given to us to reach a final conclusion about the meaning of our history. But if out of this catastrophe good is to come, then only thus: by purification through suffering, by searching for the light while immersed in black darkness, by gathering one's powers and helping to shake off the yoke that oppresses the world.

We shall not deal in this leaflet with the Jewish question, nor write their justification—no, we only want to state this fact as a brief example: Since the conquest of Poland three hundred thousand Jews have been murdered in the most bestial fashion in this country. This is the most frightful crime ever committed against human dignity, a crime without parallel in all history. Jews, too, are men—whatever may be one's views on the Jewish question—and it was men on whom these crimes have been committed. Perhaps someone will say that the Jews deserved their fate—such a statement would be a piece of monstrous arrogance, but suppose someone made it—what would he say to the fact that all the youths and girls of the Polish nobility have been destroyed (though, pray God, some have escaped)? How, you ask, was this done? All males of noble family between the ages of fifteen and twenty were carried away to forced labour in concentration camps in Germany; all girls between the same ages were sent to the S.S. brothels in Norway.

Why do we tell you all this when you know it already? Or, if not this, other crimes equally terrible, committed by these horrifying sub-humans? Because it touches a question which deeply concerns us all and *must* make us all think. Why does the German people show such apathy towards all these frightful and inhuman crimes? Hardly anyone seems to trouble about them. They are accepted as facts and put aside, and the German people falls again into its dull obtuse sleep, giving these Fascist criminals the courage and the opportunity to continue their havoc—and they take it. Can this be a sign that the Germans have been blunted in their deepest human feelings, that no chord in them vibrates when they hear of such deeds, that they have sunk into a deadly sleep from which there can never, never, be an awakening? It seems so, and it certainly will be so unless the Germans awake at last from their stupor, unless they seize every opportunity to protest against this criminal gang, unless they suffer with the hundreds of thousands of victims. But it is not enough merely to sympathize. Much more is required. We must feel our share of the guilt. For it is the apathy of the Germans that enables these sinister men to act as they do; the Germans put up with this 'government', which bears such an immeasurable load of guilt; yes, they are themselves to blame for allowing such a government to exist. Everyone wishes to acquit himself of this guilt and, having succeeded in doing so, sleeps calmly again with a clear conscience. But he cannot acquit himself; we are all *guilty, guilty, guilty!*

Yet it is not too late to exterminate this most perverse and monstrous of governments, and thus to avoid adding still further to our guilt. In the last few years our eyes have been opened wide, we know with whom we have to deal, and it is now high time to eradicate this brown horde. Up to the outbreak of war the greater part of the German people were blinded, the National Socialists had not yet shown themselves in their true colours, but now we see them for what they are, and it is our most urgent, our sole duty, the most sacred duty of every German, to extirpate these wild beasts.

16

THE BATTLE OF THE LIFELINES

Her occupation of the Atlantic coast of Europe from the Pyrenees to North Cape gave Germany the submarine, warship and long-range aircraft bases she needed to launch her major onslaught on the shipping which supplied Britain and later Russia with food and war materials. The coming of this attack in its full intensity was heralded in a speech by Hitler on 30 January 1941, in which he declared that, with the coming of spring, Britain would be starved into surrender. The most important and long-drawn-out battle of the war was about to be joined; a battle whose fortunes fluctuated as one side or the other adopted improved techniques, weapons, tactics and strategy, or augmented the numbers of its ships and aircraft. As the tide of war slowly turned, the Germans found themselves fighting to delay or stave off the great counter-attacks which were coming—the landings in North Africa, southern Europe and Normandy. By the autumn of 1943 the crisis was past: the U-boats had summoned up their greatest strength; in 1942 had almost succeeded in crippling the Allied war effort; had failed and been defeated. They had sunk over fourteen million tons of shipping by the end of the war, and had lost 781 of their numbers at sea and in their harbours.

U-BOAT ATTACK

'OBJECT ahead!' The Commander spotted it first. All our eyes light up with excitement. 'What a stroke of luck! She's right ahead and four miles off.'

By now it is exactly ten o'clock. It'll take nine hours to manœuvre into the correct firing position, but at 5 a.m. it'll be steadily getting light, and before dawn the torpedoes must be out of their tubes. . . .

We can only make a guess at the position of the ship, for we dare not let her catch sight of us. But we can increase speed. Down goes the engineer to the engine-room—before long we're going all out, the white spray splashing over our conning-tower. Up on the bridge the watch are drenched to the skin, for nobody thinks of putting on oilskins at such times. All our blowers and compressors are screeching for all they're worth—we keep on blowing our diving tanks every five minutes, for we have to keep as high above the waterline as we can, since the higher we are the faster we go. True, the increase in our speed is only fractional, but it is an increase. We're all keyed up for the chase and the odd thing is that nobody has time to feel afraid, though we all know there'll probably be at least two guns mounted on the stern of the ship we're after, to say nothing of machine-guns and automatic weapons, for every ship that doesn't travel in convoy carries a whole armoury. One hit from any of those guns would cripple us when we came to dive, and that would mean the end. A hit on the diesel tank would be enough to finish us too, for it'd be sure to leave a long oil-slick in our wake which would make us a sitting bird target for any U-boat chaser that came along.

It is 4 a.m. at last, and now instead of getting darker the opposite is happening—we can distinguish the sky from the water-line. At five sharp we must fire; it'll be our last chance.

Fifteen minutes to go, and everyone is at their post—two men are operating the range-finder—one in the conning-tower, one in the control-room. The torpedoman and petty-officer torpedoman are at the for'ard torpedo tubes and there is another torpedoman aft. All this time the Commander is leaning against the rail at one corner of the bridge, his binoculars glued to his eyes and his long fair hair and beard hiding his face. He is like a being possessed, caught in the grip of our frenzied manhunt.

'Tubes one to five—ready!' the torpedo-officer's shouting—the tubes are wet and their outer doors open. Meanwhile the engineer is reckoning the quantity of water we'll need to have in our tanks to correct the boat's trim after the torpedoes have been discharged. All five of them are ready in case we need them.

'Tubes one to four—ready for surface fire', comes through the speaking-tube from the fo'c's'le, and from aft: 'Tube number five—ready for surface fire. Bridge control!' Torpedoes can be fired from several positions, from the fore and after compartments, the control-room, the conning-tower and the bridge. The order passes to the control-room and the switches are made. Dim white lamps in the conning-tower show the petty-officer at the range-finder that the order has been correctly carried out, and he reports to the torpedo-officer, who in his turn reports to the Commander.

We're still moving parallel with the enemy and slightly before his beam. The attack-sight is 'on', with the target in the centre of the crosswires.

'Target Red 90, speed sixteen and a half knots, range seven thousand metres, torpedo speed thirty knots, running depth seven metres.' Our torpedoes are set to run at a depth of seven metres below the surface, to pass about two metres beneath the target. A magnetic pistol fires the charge, which blows in the keel plates and causes the ship to break up.

During the first World War they had to aim with the whole boat, since after leaving the tubes the torpedoes continued on the same course as that of the U-boat, under the control of their gyroscopic automatic steering-gear. Attacks were difficult under these conditions, particularly when destroyers and other convoy escorts had to be avoided. But in the second World War our new torpedoes could take up a course automatically up to ninety degrees away from the direction in which they were fired—the latest models even up to a hundred and eighty degrees. The chances of success were in this way considerably increased, since the boat was no longer committed to a fixed course during an attack.

The torpedo-officer at the attack-table reports 'Lined-up', and the switch is made by which the attack-table is connected with the gyro-compass and the attack-sight. The mechanism churns round and two red lamps indicate that the process of calculating the information which has been fed into it is not yet completed. The lights go out after a few moments, and the petty-officer at the attack-table reports the resulting settings to the torpedo-officer. From this point onwards our own alterations of course are of little importance, being allowed for automatically. The target must simply be held in the cross-wires of the attack-sight in order that the apparatus can do its job. The torpedo-officer gives the order 'Follow' to the attack-table. A lamp glows, and the attack-table is now controlling the binoculars on the bridge. Meanwhile the constantly changing firing-settings are being transmitted automatically to the torpedoes and set on their angling mechanism. With this system we can fire at any moment and on any course, provided that the ninety-degree limiting angle is not exceeded. The torpedoes will run to a pattern that spreads over roughly a ship's length by the time they reach the range of the target. We turn to our attacking course.

We can now see the enemy clearly—a British tanker of eighteen thousand tons.

We are doing twelve knots and the range is now five thousand metres. The torpedo petty-officer at the attack-table reports the settings to the torpedo-officer whenever they alter, and the Commander is listening in.

Commander to torpedo-officer: 'Fire at four thousand five hundred metres. Aim at her foremast.' And then: 'Rate of turn, red 3.'

This is the speed at which the boat swings when the rudder is put hard-a-port. Our new torpedoes, combined with careful judgment of the moment to turn, which is helped by the attack-table, allow us to turn away before firing, which not only saves time but enables us to fire at shorter ranges.

Torpedo-officer to torpedo petty-officer: 'Red 3. Stand by for surface fire.'

Commander to helmsman: 'Hard-a-port.'

Torpedo petty-officer to bow tubes: 'Stand by for surface fire.'

The acknowledgement comes back: 'Tubes one, three and four ready.''

Commander to torpedo-officer: 'Fire when ready.'

Torpedo-officer: 'Ready.'

Torpedo petty-officer: 'On—on—on.' By this he indicates that the change settings are being accurately transmitted to the torpedoes as the boat swings.

The torpedo-officer at the attack-sight is holding the ship's foremast in the crosswires. . . . 'Fire!' and he presses the firing-push. 'Fire!' repeats the torpedo petty-officer, and the torpedo-gunner's mate at the fore tubes hears the order through the loudspeaker system; he has a hand on two of the firing levers and a leg across the third, in case of a failure of the remote-controlled firing-gear. The boat shivers three times in succession and three short heavy hissing sounds are heard—the noise of the compressed air by which the torpedoes are discharged. Firing is 'staggered' at $1\frac{1}{2}$-second intervals to prevent mutual interference between the discharges. At the order 'Fire', the Chief floods to a prescribed amount in order to compensate for the weight of the three torpedoes—for the boat must be ready for an instantaneous crash-dive if necessary. The Commander looks at his wristwatch—fifteen seconds running time yet.

Boom! 'Hurrah! hit!' The Commander at the periscope is the only man who can see anything. He switches his microphone in to the general loudspeaker system: 'Hit aft; stern seems to be buckled!' The magnetic pistol has worked well, it appears.

Her wireless is still working, however. An S.O.S. goes out on the six hundred-metre wavelength. *German submarine*—with our position.

'Very good,' remarks the chief quartermaster, 'it's friendly of the English to give us an exact position. No more need to worry to-day.'

She's no longer moving through the water and is giving off steam. Rudder and steering apparatus seem to be damaged. We attack again. It's easy now, for we are just over a thousand metres away. They've spotted our periscope, though, and with all their machine-guns and quick-firers let fly at us, endangering the periscope glass. We attack from the other quarter and dive under the ship at ten fathoms. The hydrophone-operator reports:

'She's right overhead!'

In a submarine attack the Commander controls the ship, gives the target information and fires the torpedoes himself. The torpedo-officer only sees that the proper settings are put on the attack-table. This time we are going to fire the stern tube, which we don't often get the chance to use.

'Range four hundred metres . . . fire!'

The roar's terrific. We've fired from much closer this time; underwater the noise is frightful. The tanker has broken in two.

Everyone has a look through the periscope. The fine ship before us is sinking into the sea. Emotion overcomes us. The daemonic madness of destruction that becomes law the moment a war breaks out has us in its grip. Under its spell as we are, what else can we do? Lifeboats and rafts are meanwhile being lowered, those aboard saving themselves as best they may. We can't help without running into grave danger, and in any case we've no room aboard—U-boats are built to allow space for the ship's company and no more. The enemy is well equipped with life-saving gear and these men on the tanker will certainly soon be picked up by a warship.

Heinz Schaeffer, U-boat officer

THE VICTIMS

Merchantman

At 11.30 p.m. that night the moon had just set. I was on the lower bridge talking to a half-English, half-Portuguese business man, Mr. D'Aguila, and his two sisters. We were having a nightcap before they turned in. I remarked that if we were attacked, and I thought it highly likely we would be, they were to make straight for the boat which was just below the bridge on the starboard side.

A few minutes later the D'Aguilas had just left me and were on their way down the ladder; I was about to go to the upper bridge to see the master and officer-of-the-watch. A violent tremor went through *Avoceta*. She staggered like a stumbling horse and shuddered to a lurching stop as a violent explosion came from the direction of the engine-room aft. My ears were buzzing from the crash of the exploding torpedo—I had no doubt but that that was what it was. My left arm was numb from being flung against the side of the bridge ladder. The vicious scream of escaping steam smothered some of the unearthly gargling sounds coming from the drowning and the tearing squeals of those trapped in the scalding agony of the engine-room. All these sounds darted into my ears during the two or three seconds before I picked myself up and stumbled across with Signalman Erskine to fire the distress rockets as an indication that we had been hit. As they whizzed up I glanced aft and saw the stern was already under water and the dreadful noises were ceasing from that part of the ship. The escape of steam was easing now as *Avoceta* sat back on her haunches and the bows rose to an ever more crazy angle into the air. No boats could be lowered. There was complete pandemonium; the thunderous bangs and crashes of furniture and cargo being hurled about below decks all mingled with the ghastly shrieks of the sleeping people waking to their deaths. As the bows went higher so did the shrieks. I clung to a stanchion feeling sick and helpless as I had to look on while the children were swept out into the darkness below by the torrent of water which roared through the smoking-room.

Instinctively I must have blown up my lifebelt and I thrust my false teeth into my jacket pocket—thinking, I suppose, of other commodores who had been sunk and not been compensated for the loss of their teeth.

By then I was standing on what was normally the vertical front of the bridge . . . then, scrabbling up the deck towards the forecastle, I caught on to a ring bolt at the edge of the hole, but the water overtook me and I found myself forced below the surface by the foremast and rigging. Everything became hazy. I suppose I was drowning. I felt curiously as if I was pleasantly drunk and enveloped in cotton wool. This was displaced by a sharp pain in my chest caused by the pressure of water from being forced so deep. The only way to stop this agony was, it seemed to me, to expel the remaining air in my lungs, swallow water and become unconscious and drown as soon as possible. I was about to do this when the pain suddenly eased. I looked up and saw the stars twinkling overhead. My lifebelt and an escaping bubble of air from the *Avoceta* had pushed me to the surface. During all this time I never saw a parade of my past life which is supposed to be traditional on these occasions. The whole affair from the time the torpedo struck until I found myself floating on the surface must have been less than four minutes.

The D'Aguilas, who had been with me on the lower bridge, I heard later from Miss D'Aguila, the only member of the family to survive, had reached the bottom of the ladder when they heard the explosion. They linked arms and tried to reach the boat I had pointed out. 'But before we got there,' she said, 'a wall of water forced us apart and I never saw my brother and sister again.'

Miraculously finding myself on the surface and alive I looked round and saw a raft about the size of a small sofa with a cluster of people on it. Dazed, sick and dopey, my eyes misting and with waves splashing over me I swam towards it. It can only have been around fifty yards away but it seemed ages before I got close.

Every so often I called out to the men on the raft; a faint noise reached me in reply.

As I came alongside I cried, 'Any room for another?'

I could see by the man's face that he was saying something. But only a faint unintelligible sound came through. I realized I must be deaf. Then I was hauled half on to the raft where I lay sodden, gasping and conscious now of feeling bitterly cold and quivering with a sort of ague. Dimly I saw the others on the raft and we huddled together trying to raise some kind of warmth between us. The temperature of the water, I learned afterwards, was forty-two degrees.

In the sky there was a glare from the starshell fired by the escorts trying to seek out the U-boats and find survivors. I was aware of the crump of depth charges coming from some way off. But generally everything was very hazy.

In the immediate vicinity of the raft there was complete silence; it may have seemed more so because of my deafness, but it was an awe-inspiring contrast to the cries of distress and the fearful sounds of the foundering ship a short while ago.

The master of *Avoceta* and six other men were on the raft with me. Several, their throats clogged with fuel oil, were choking and coughing. Gradually their strength ebbed, they became insensible and slipped off unnoticed in the darkness. The rest of us clung on for nearly three hours. All that time the spray and water sloshed over us as the raft rocked on the deep swell.

Sprinkled about in the darkness around us we could see little red lights bobbing up and down. These were the lamps attached to lifebelts and operated by a battery in a watertight container. Suddenly someone noticed that they were beginning to disappear; a ship must be picking up survivors, we thought.

It seemed a long time but when we were beginning to think we had been mistaken the shape of a corvette appeared close by. At last she drew alongside and we were hauled on board by sailors holding on to scrambling nets draped over the side.

Admiral Sir K. Creighton, Convoy Commodore

Escort

Next morning we were still sweeping in line abreast. It was a lovely clear morning, with bright sun, but bitterly cold. After 'Sunday Morning Rounds' I spent an hour practising radar control of the guns, and painting the arcs of fire of each gun on the gyro-repeater compass on the upper bridge. If we were to tackle E-boats we must shift our main interest in life from asdics to guns. At midday I sent for the Engineer Officer and the First Lieutenant to protest about the state of the stokers' messdeck at 'rounds' that morning. I also sent a message to the asdic officer of my own ship and to Commander Heath to say that I was not satisfied with the asdic, and would they please do something about it. As all these officers had gathered in the wardroom before lunch I unwittingly saved their lives when I brought them forward. Then the anti-submarine officer telephoned from the asdic compartment to say that he would like to shut down the set for half an hour and I agreed. I then turned to the First Lieutenant and the Engineer Officer to discuss the messdeck problem.

The sky suddenly turned to flame and the ship gave a violent shudder. Then the flame had gone, and as far as I could see everything was strangely the same. Looking ahead, I could see something floating and turning over in the water like a giant metallic whale. As I looked it rolled over farther still and I could make out our own pennant numbers painted on it. I was dumb-founded. It seemed beyond reason. I ran to the after-side of the bridge and looked over.

The ship ended just aft of the engine-room—everything abaft that had gone. What I had seen ahead of us *had really been the ship's own stern*. There were small fires all over the upper deck. The First Lieutenant was down there organizing the fire parties. He saw me and called, 'Will you abandon ship, sir?'

'Not bloody likely, Number One. Get those fires out, and then all the life-saving equipment over the side and secured by boat-ropes. We'll not get out till we have to.'

I went back to the compass platform.

'Signalman.'

'Sir?'

'Make to *Scimitar*—"I think I've been torpedoed." Then get down to the main deck. Yeoman, you go too—but first take all your books down to the wireless cabinet. Collect all the charts you can lay your hands on, and push them in there as well, and lock the door.'

The officer of the watch was still standing by the compass. I wondered how much longer he was going to stand there.

'Must have been hit in the magazine—the stern's been blown clean off,' I told him.

He leant forward to the wheelhouse voicepipe and called down: 'Stop both.'

'Both wizzers have been blown to glory.' I could not help laughing. 'Better get down to the main deck and give Number One a hand.'

When he had gone I was all alone on the bridge. It was strangely quiet. I took off my sea boots and tried to blow up my inflatable lifejacket. It would not fill with air. I put my hand behind my back and found that both the rubber tube and my jacket had been cut, I supposed by some flying fragment. I had often complained that lifejackets were left lying about the wheelhouse, so perhaps there would be one there now. I went down to see. But no, my recent words had taken effect. I seized a 'sorbo' cushion, and tucked it into the jacket of my battle dress. It gave me a feminine silhouette, but it could be a help if the worst was to happen. I went on to the wheelhouse deck. The ship was upright and apparently floating well. The carley-floats were by then all over the side, and secured by boat-ropes. The First Lieutenant had all the small fires out. We might save her yet.

I could hear a high windy sort of noise that I could not place. The deck began to take on an angle—suddenly—so suddenly. She was almost on her side. I was slithering, grasping all sorts of unlikely things. My world had turned through ninety degrees. I just caught sight of Harries, the navigator, going over the high side of the main deck. He had a polished wooden box in either hand, the chronometer and the sextant. I wished that I had someone to laugh with over that one. I jumped for the galley funnel which was now parallel with the water and about two feet clear, and flat-footed it to the end. I could see water pouring into the main funnel. It made a gurgling sound, like an enormous bath drain. The sea around me was covered with bobbing heads. I paused at the end of my small funnel to look at the faces. They were laughing as if this were part of some gigantic fun fair. The men called to me.

'Come on, sir. The water's lovely.'

'I'm waiting for the *Skylark*,' I shouted back. But the galley funnel dipped, and I was swimming too—madly. The man beside me turned to look over his shoulder. 'She's going!'

I turned to look. He was right. Her bow was pointed at the sky. 'Swim like hell—suction,' I shouted back. We swam like hell. I turned once more, but now there were very, very few bobbing heads behind me. I swam on. The destroyer of my old group was passing through us. I could see her men at action stations. They were attacking. They were attacking the wreck of the *Warwick*! I screamed at them in my frenzy. Wherever else the U-boat might have been it could not have been there. The depth-charges sailed up into the air. Funny how they wobbled from side to side, I'd never noticed that before. When, I wondered, would they explode? It was like being punched in the chest, not as bad as I had expected. I swam on. Things were a bit hazy. I was not as interested in going places as I had been. I could only see waves and more waves, and I wished that they would stop coming. I did not really care any more. Then I felt hands grasp my shoulders and a voice say, 'Christ, it's the skipper. Give me a hand to get the bastard in,' and I was dragged into a carley-float which was more than crowded to capacity.

Commander D. A. Rayner

Rescue

From the higher vantage-point of the bridge, Ericson had watched everything; he had seen the ship hit, the shower of sparks where the bomb fell, and then, a moment afterwards, the huge explosion that blew her to pieces. In the shocked silence that followed, his voice giving a routine helm-order was cool and normal: no one could have guessed the sadness and the anger that filled him, to see a whole crew of men like himself wiped out at one stroke. There was nothing to be done: the aircraft was gone, with this frightful credit, and if there were any men left alive—which was hardly conceivable—*Sorrel*, the stern escort, would do her best for them. It was so quick, it was so brutal. . . . He might have thought more about it, he might have mourned a little longer, if a second stroke had not followed swiftly; but even as he raised his binoculars to look at the convoy again, the ship they were stationed on, a hundred yards away, rocked to a sudden explosion and then, on the instant, heeled over at a desperate angle.

This time, a torpedo. . . . Ericson heard it: and even as he jumped to the voice-pipe to increase their speed and start zig-zagging, he thought: if that one came from outside the convoy, it must have missed us by a few feet. Inside the asdic-hut Lockhart heard it, and started hunting on the danger-side, without further orders: that was a routine, and even at this moment of surprise and crisis, the routine still ruled them all. Morell, on the fo'c'sle, heard it, and closed up his gun's crew again and loaded with star-shell: down in the wheel-house Tallow heard it, and gripped the wheel tighter and called out to his quartermasters: 'Watch that telegraph, now!' and waited for the swift orders that might follow. Right aft, by the depth-charges, Ferraby heard it, and shivered: he glanced downwards at the black water rushing past them, and then at the stricken ship which he could see quite clearly, and he longed for some action in which he could lose himself and his fear. Deep down in the engine-room, Chief E. R. A.

Watts heard it best of all: it came like a hammer-blow, hitting the ship's side a great splitting crack, and when, a few seconds afterwards, the telegraph rang for an increase of speed, his hand was on the steam-valve already. He knew what had happened, he knew what might happen next. But it was better not to think of what was going on outside: down here, encased below the water-line, they must wait, and hope, and keep their nerve.

Ericson took *Compass Rose* in a wide half-circle to starboard, away from the convoy, hunting for the U-boat down what he presumed had been the track of the torpedo; but they found nothing that looked like a contact, and presently he circled back again, towards the ship that had been hit. She had fallen out of line, like one winged bird in a flight of duck, letting the rest of the convoy go by: she was sinking fast, and already her screws were out of water and she was poised for the long plunge. The cries of men in fear came from her, and a thick smell of oil: at one moment, when they had her outlined against the moon, they could see a mass of men packed high in the towering stern, waving and shouting as they felt the ship under them begin to slide down to her grave. Ericson, trying for a cool decision in this moment of pity, was faced with a dilemma: if he stopped to pick up survivors he would become a sitting target himself, and he would also lose all chance of hunting for the U-boat: if he went on with the hunt, he would, with *Sorrel* busy elsewhere, be leaving these men to their death. He decided on a compromise, a not too dangerous compromise: they would drop a boat, and leave it to collect what survivors it could while *Compass Rose* took another cast away to starboard. But it must be done quickly.

Ferraby, summoned to the quarter-deck voice-pipe, put every effort he knew into controlling his voice.

'Ferraby, sir.'

'We're going to drop a boat, sub. Who's your leading hand?'

'Leading-Seaman Tonbridge, sir.'

'Tell him to pick a small crew—not more than four—and row over towards the ship. Tell him to keep well clear until she goes down. They may be able to get some boats away themselves, but if not, he'll have to do the best he can. We'll come back for him when we've had another look for the submarine.'

'Right, sir.'

'Quick as you can, sub. I don't want to stop too long.' Ferraby threw himself into the job with an energy which was a drug for all other feeling: the boat was lowered so swiftly that when *Compass Rose* drew away from it and left it to its critical errand the torpedoed ship was still afloat. But she was only just afloat, balanced between sea and sky before her last dive; and as Tonbridge took the tiller and glanced in her direction to get his bearings, there was a rending sound which carried clearly over the water, and she started to go down. Tonbridge watched, in awe and fear: he had never seen anything like this, and never had a job of this sort before, and it was an effort to meet it properly. It had been bad enough to be lowered into the darkness from *Compass Rose*, and to watch her fade away and be left alone in a small boat under the stars, with the convoy also fading and a vast unfriendly sea all round them; but now, with the torpedoed ship disappearing before their eyes, and the men shouting and crying as they splashed about in the water, and the smell of oil coming across to them thick and choking, it was more like a nightmare than anything else. Tonbridge was twenty-three years of age, a product of the London slums conditioned by seven years' naval training; faced by this ordeal, the fact that he did not run away from it, the fact that he remained effective, was beyond all normal credit.

They did what th~y could: rowing about in the darkness, guided by the shouting, appalled by the choking cries of men who drowned before they could be reached, they tried their utmost to rescue and to succour. They collected fourteen men: one was dead, one was dying, eight were wounded, and the rest were shocked and prostrated to a pitiful degree. It was very nearly fifteen men: Tonbridge actually had hold of the fifteenth, who was gasping in the last stages of terror and exhaustion, but the film of oil on his naked body made him impossible to grasp, and he slipped away and sank before a rope could be got round him. When there were no more shadows on the water, and no more cries to follow, they rested on their oars, and waited; alone on the enormous black waste of the Atlantic, alone with the settling wreckage and the reek of oil; and so, presently, *Compass Rose* found them.

Ferraby, standing in the waist of the ship as the boat was hooked on, wondered what he would see when the survivors came over the side: he was not prepared for the pity and horror of their appearance. First came the ones who could climb aboard themselves—half a dozen shivering, black-faced men, dressed in the filthy oil-soaked clothes which they had snatched up when the ship was struck: one of them with his scalp streaming with blood, another nursing an arm flayed from wrist to shoulder by scalding steam. They looked about them in wonder, dazed by the swiftness of disaster, by their rescue, by the solid deck beneath their feet. Then, while they were led to the warmth of the mess-deck, a sling was rigged for the seriously wounded, and they were lifted over the side on stretchers: some silent, some moaning, some coughing up the fuel oil which was burning and poisoning their intestines: laid side by side in the waist, they made a carpet of pain and distress so naked in suffering that it seemed cruel to watch them. And then, with the boat still bumping alongside in the eerie darkness, came Tonbridge's voice: 'Go easy—there's a dead man down here.' Ferraby had never seen a dead man before, and he had to force himself to look at this pitiful relic of the sea—stone-cold, stiffening already, its grey head jerking as it was bundled over the side: an old sailor, unseamanlike and disgusting in death. He wanted to run away, he wanted to be sick: he watched with shocked amazement the two ratings who were carrying the corpse: how can you bear what you are doing, he thought, how can you touch—it . . . ? Behind him he heard Lockhart's voice saying: 'Bring the whole lot into the fo'c'sle—I can't see anything here,' and then he turned away and busied himself with the hoisting of the boat, not looking behind him as the procession of wrecked and brutalized men was borne off. When the boat was inboard, and secure, he turned back again, glad to have escaped some part of the horror. There was nothing left now but the acrid smell of oil, and the patches of blood and water on the deck: nothing, he saw with a gasp of fear and revulsion, but the dead man lying lashed against the rail, a yard from him, rolling as the ship rolled, waiting for daylight ar.d burial. He turned and ran towards the stern, pursued by terror.

In the big seamen's mess-deck, under the shaded lamps, Lockhart was doing things he had never imagined possible. Now and again he recalled, with a spark of pleasure, his previous doubts: there was plenty of blood here to faint at, but that wasn't the way things were working out. . . . He had stitched up a gash in a man's head, from the nose to the line of the hair—as he took the catgut from its envelope he had thought: I wish they'd include some directions with this stuff. He had set a broken leg, using part of a bench as a splint. He bound up other cuts and gashes, he did what he could for the man with the burnt arm, who was now insensible with pain: he watched, doing nothing with a curious hurt detachment, as a man who had drenched his intestines and perhaps his lungs with fuel oil slowly died. Some of *Compass Rose*'s crew made a ring round him, looking at him, helping him when he asked for help: the two stewards brought tea for the cold and shocked survivors, other men offered dry clothing, and Tallow, after an hour or two, came down and gave him the largest tot of rum he had ever seen. It was not too large. . . . Once, from outside, there was the sound of an explosion, and he looked up: by chance, across the smoky fo'c'sle, the bandaged rows of wounded, the other men still shivering, the twisted corpse, the whole squalid confusion of the night, he met the eye of Leading-Seaman Phillips. Involuntarily, both of them smiled, to mark a thought which could only be smiled at: if a torpedo hit them now, there would be little chance for any of them, and all this bandaging would be wasted.

Then he bent down again, and went on probing a wound for the splinter of steel which must still be there, if the scream of pain which the movement produced was anything to go by. This was a moment to think only of the essentials, and they were all here with him, and in his care.

It was nearly daylight before he finished; and he went up to the bridge to report what he had done at a slow dragging walk, completely played out. He met Ericson at the top of the ladder: they had both been working throughout the night, and the two exhausted men looked at each other in silence, unable to put any expression into their stiff drawn faces, yet somehow acknowledging each other's competence. There was blood on Lockhart's hands, and on the sleeves of his dufflecoat: in the cold light it had a curious metallic sheen, and Ericson looked at it for some time before he realized what it was.

'You must have been busy, Number One,' he said quietly. 'What's the score down there?'

'Two dead, sir,' answered Lockhart. His voice was very hoarse, and he cleared his throat. 'One more to go, I think—he's been swimming and walking about with a badly-burned arm, and the shock is too much. Eleven others. They ought to be all right.'

'Fourteen. . . . The crew was thirty-six altogether.'

Lockhart shrugged. There was no answer to that one, and if there had been he could not have found it, in his present mood: the past few hours, spent watching and touching pain, seemed to have deadened all normal feeling. He looked round at the ships on their beam, just emerging as the light grew.

'How about things up here?' he asked.

'We lost another ship, over the other side of the convoy. That made three.'

'More than one submarine?'

'I shouldn't think so. She probably crossed over.'

'Good night's work.' Lockhart still could not express more than a formal regret. 'Do you want to turn in, sir? I can finish this watch.'

'No—you get some sleep. I'll wait for Ferraby and Baker.'

'Tonbridge did well.'

'Yes. . . . So did you, Number One.'

Lockhart shook his head. 'It was pretty rough, most of it. I must get a little book on wounds. It's going to come in handy, if this sort of things goes on.'

'There's no reason why it shouldn't,' said Ericson. 'No reason at all, that I can see. Three ships in three hours: probably a hundred men all told. Easy.'

'Yes,' said Lockhart, nodding. 'A very promising start. After the war, we must ask them how they do it.'

Nicholas Monsarrat

How is it with the Happy Dead?

The ship lay there on the bottom of the sea, as big as the whole world; quiet as a cathedral; gently breathing from the slanting ripple of light filtering down from above, through the grey North Sea water. She lay on her side, well down by the stern, the bow riding clear of the mud, a mile long in the water.

In the first mad rush of escaping steam, explosion and weaving lane of bubbles gouting from her sides, mixed with the cries of men, weak like babies at a baby show, everything buoyant had come away, to shoot to the surface, where later the gulls whirled, crazy screeching. Other objects followed the slow sinking of the ship.

The gear which broke surface was mixed and poor pickings for the birds, mops and brooms; the bosun's chair, odd cork jackets, an unused Carley float, oars, air-tight tins of duty-free tobacco, a cap, two cans; bottles and the ship model the Leading Seaman was making for his little boy.

Sinking to be lost forever in the soft mud was another array of gear; buckets, empty shell cases, tin hats, thrown away in the last scramble for the boat, the skipper's binoculars, a pair of boots that 'Bunts' was always on the point of mending, depth charges, broken from their lashings; smoke floats; rowlocks and pieces of torn rail and bridge-house. All these came down first, the ship herself followed, stern first, jerking uncertainly, as tank after tank burst or caved in, or as bulkheads carried away. Fiercely belching a wavering column of bubbles and debris, her buoyancy leaving her, the ship fought against gravity to the end, before finally accepting fate and settling quietly on the bottom.

Occasionally, as she settled still further, or as lashings parted or rotted away, various objects detached themselves and floated up to the surface. On the very first evening the body of a stoker found its way through the gash in her starboard side and drifted away, upwards and to the east with the young flood tide. On the third day the engineman and the coxswain, sworn enemies while alive, owing to a disagreement over a tot of rum, broke surface within three minutes of each other. Floating obscenely, stern uppermost, their drift overcame the light wind and they set out on a long voyage together until, the lashings of their clothes mercifully bursting, they both sank once more; soon to be two heaps of bones, white like pebbles, clean picked by the sea.

It was not long before the ex-trawler—she was one of the Footballers—lost her freshness and began to take on the colour of her new surroundings. Crabs and then small shoals of fish began to make her their home. The crabs, lumbering and sliding on the metal plates, like miniature tanks, found much food. The fish, suspended in tiny clouds, fed in the shadow of the cocked up bow; then, at a flick, darted off to reappear somewhere else. Eels came also, twining in and out of the rusting frames, and small green jellied growths appeared; to grow and spread and trail in the current.

The white ensign still floated at the stern. It was badly burnt, pierced by splinters, torn and discoloured, but the east-going current stirred it gently, so that it flapped against the staff. A depth charge, ready lashed in the Y thrower, looked as if it would overbalance, as it sprouted from the deck. The mizzen mast and its boom had altogether disappeared.

The galley door hung open. Inside, ashes from the fire, trapped in the roof, formed a thick scum up against the cork-flecked paint. The cook, suspended by his rubber lifebelt, floated up there, face downwards. He had gone back from the boat to get a joint of beef and some tinned apples, then, coming out, he slipped on the potatoes, broken from their bin and rolling on the deck—a ludicrous mishap, like a comic film. The last explosion from the boiler lifted the red-hot galley stove on top of him and there he lay—jammed; watching his skin blister and break and wishing the ship would soon go down so as to put the fire out. However, it was not until she listed on the bottom that the stove rolled off him and his body was released to rise majestically to the jobble of scum, like a stage fairy suspended on a wire.

He had never planned on going out like this. He was Hostilities Only, and in peace-time he and his wife ran a little boarding-house at a coast resort. He was disappointed when he realized that he was going to die lying beneath his own galley stove. However, when the sea did froth in over the coaming, the pain of the salt was so great that he fainted and never regained consciousness.

Above the engine-room casing the davits hung empty; the falls trailing, the first of the many ropy growths that would later spread and weave in the current, clinging to the hull as the ship settled lower and lower and fell away into little piles of rust and scrap.

The remains of the smoke-stack hung at a giddy angle, the stays parted and nothing supporting it. The whistle, somehow adrift from its fastenings, stood upright on its steam pipe, the lanyard now only the remains of a seized eye-slice. Most of the bridge and the skipper's cabin had disappeared. The first bomb had done that, shearing the steel like butter with a knife. Now there were only the queerly shaped jags of stanchions, twisted frames and the black charred or white splintered edges of the deck planking.

The starboard bridge wing remained and the gunner hung suspended in his harness, feet clear of the sloping deck, both ankles broken from the upward heaving explosion. His hair, escaping from the cap and the navy-blue chin-strap, floated out in the water like a fern. The barrels of the twin Lewis pointed up, rainbow-coloured with grease. Small fish fed on the ropy clots which trailed from his finger-tips.

In the well deck, the false hatch had carried away when the engine-room bulkhead blew in; little pieces of cork lining, straw, and charred wood floated up, eddying as they met the cross-current at the hatchway.

Below all was chaos.

Caught in the airlock on the starboard side, five unlashed sea-chests chafed their corners. A kapok mattress slimy with scum and trailing a blanket as a winding sheet remained pressed hard up against the pipe cot of an upper berth. His head jammed in a locker, a seaman knelt as if in prayer, his wide trousers gently weaving with the current. One foot was bare, the other covered in a soiled rubber gym shoe. He had gone back to look for the bottle of rum he had saved up, and when the boiler exploded it broke his neck.

Farther forward, the dart-board in the wardroom showed a double twenty and a nine, the steel points already corroding and the feathers spiked with the wet. In the corner a pile of broken glasses glinted in the grey-green light, not yet entirely silted over. On the settee, under a cushion, lay the body of a ship's cat. She had gone there when the alarm gong had sounded and a chance splinter, ricochetting off the companion way, entered her head—an unlucky chance.

On deck, the mainmast had gone by the board, the steel shrouds and rigging screws trailing, an unbelievable tangle of wire, over the port bow.

Forward, over the 'whale-back', the 'bandstand', shorn of its rails and iron ladder, remained intact. The gun, half-torn from its mounting, leaning at a giddy angle. Only one of the gun's crew remained. The second bomb, bursting just forward of the bow, had torn the remainder into queer and unanatomical shapes as they struggled to get elevation on a weapon not designed to beat off the attacks of aircraft.

The remaining gunner was the layer. The blast had removed most of his clothing and some of his flesh, the rest was stained a bluey-purple. The lifted gun mounting trapped the lower part of his body, pressing him down against the gun platform.

When they went for the boats they had thought he was along with the rest, but he awoke in time to feel her go down. Through a red curtain of mist he felt himself lifted up, like a swing at a fair, while the stern settled, then he watched the seethe of the advancing water. 'I'll never see the Argyle Bar again,' he thought. 'No more Saturday nights, no more wallop either.'

He was lying on his stomach, with no feeling at all below his thighs. His arms, stretched straight out to left and right, were pinned that way by the shoulder pad of the gun which lay across his back. He could, however, move his head from side to side, scraping his chin over the criss-cross pattern of the steel gun platform. He could move each arm from the elbow too, but because he was unable to raise his neck easily he could not see clearly outside the ship—everything was concentrated into a little circle close to his eyes. On the left hand third finger was the ring she had given him, and between the first finger and the thumb was the L-shaped white scar from a broken bottle gained in a scrap when he and Pincher Martin had beaten up the Thistle Bar and got thirty days No. 11 apiece. This scar hardly showed now, through the black grease which the handling of the gun had polished to a dull black-lead finish.

He turned his head painfully to look at his right hand.

The first joint of the little finger was missing—that was Bear Island, when he was deckie on the *Floral Queen*, trawling. The thumb-nail was blackened at the base from the crack he had caught it at target practice. Practice that wasn't at all like the rush and tumble of the real action, which had been over almost before it had started. A whining roar, the alarm gong, two bombs—one a direct, the other a near miss and that was all.

Tattooed on the back of his hand, blue and red against the scorched hair, was a swallow design with 'Mother' written on the scroll. On his forearm, three inches above the wrist, was a heart and arrow design and on the scroll was 'G' and 'M'—George and Maggie. He wouldn't see her again—or the kids either. He felt very sleepy—he would sleep and he would see no one ever again. Yet he wasn't afraid, why worry? Trawling all your life and then the war—always so near to death—seeing your mates lost overboard or smashed—always so near to death. Afraid? Why worry about a thing you've known of for so long. Still, perhaps it was a pity. No more beer, no more nights out with the boys—nothing ever any more. He felt so sleepy that it wasn't very difficult when the water did reach him.

The ship kicked hard under him, fighting. Then the bows shot up and he felt giddy with lying head down and the rush of her as she settled. The boiling waves rushed at him, brown with scum. He wondered how cold the water would be, how deep beneath him, how long ——

It reached him, snapping at his face, jumping, exultant. As he went down, the water darkening, he gave one frothy gulp and saw the spreading purple cloud go spiralling up to the surface above him.

Eric Joysmith

BATTLE OFF THE BEACHES

The U-boats scored some of their greatest successes in the six months after the United States entered the war, descending on the American seaboard and slaughtering shipping which was for some time unprotected by convoys or by adequate escorts.

December 1941

Should enemy submarines operate off this coast, this command has no forces available to take adequate action against them, either offensive or defensive.

Admiral Andrews, commanding U.S. Eastern Seaboard Defences

We have issued a special communiqué to the effect that German submarines have succeeded in sinking 125,000 tons of enemy shipping off the American Atlantic coast. This is an exceedingly good piece of news for the German people. It bears testimony to the tremendous activity of our submarines and their widely extended radius of action, as well as to the fact that German heroism conquers even the widest oceans. At last a special bulletin! We certainly needed it, and it acts like rain on parched land. Everybody regards the communiqué as a very effective answer to the warmonger Roosevelt, whom the whole German people curse. Many people are in a quandary whether to hate him or Churchill more.

Dr. Goebbels, 25 January 1942

On 6 February the cumbersome title North Atlantic Naval Coastal Frontier was officially established as the Eastern Sea Frontier, and the command itself was lengthened southward to Jacksonville, Florida, where it hooked into the newly made Gulf Sea Frontier. Andrews was now known as C.E.S.F.—Commander, Eastern Sea Frontier.

But change of name and additional areas to defend brought no appreciable new permanent forces to use against Doenitz, although Britain was sending over twenty-four anti-sub trawlers. A full two months after war had begun, Nazi U-boats could roam and strike at will.

Andrews' letter of 7 February to C.N.O. was indicative: 'The Eastern Sea Frontier has no long-range planes available for offshore work. Newport (Rhode Island) has one single-engined plane capable of carrying one bomb; the Fourth Naval District (Philadelphia headquarters) has no planes capable of attacking a sub. New York has a single squadron available for inshore patrol.'

March: The Score Mounts

It was no longer two or two and a half ships a day for the Nazis. U-boats were driving their average up to three every twenty-four hours. The Eastern Sea Frontier had the dubious international Allied distinction of being 'the most dangerous sea area in the world'.

The Climax

All the German boats operating in the Atlantic, Caribbean and Gulf of Mexico had impressive records for June. Forty-eight ships were lost in the Caribbean and its approaches; twenty-one ships in the Gulf; thirteen in the Eastern Sea Frontier; fourteen in the Bermuda area; and another fourteen along North Atlantic convoy routes.

Sinkings were heavy in all areas, but Doenitz seemed most pleased with his boats in the western seas. At a press conference late in the month, he said with obvious pride, 'Our submarines are operating close inshore along the coast of the United States, so that bathers and sometimes entire coastal cities are witnesses of that drama of war whose visual climaxes are constituted by the red glorioles of blazing tankers.'

There was fire on the beaches. The German submarine admiral was at the height of his career.

AID FOR RUSSIA: THE ARCTIC CONVOYS

P.Q. 16: Summer 1942

Whit Monday, 25 May

I don't know when exactly the little bastard joined us, but he's been circling round and round the convoy all day. He is keeping well outside the range of the guns on the destroyers, and sometimes he disappears, but before long he, or his relay, turns up again. He's a Focke-Wulf, and the crew, who are irritated by his presence, refer to him as 'George'. At five this morning the first alarm went, and I dressed in under three minutes, but nothing happened. Then, at dinner-time, the alarm bell rang again, and the destroyer fired several rounds at our German 'escort', but he was out of range, and for the rest of the afternoon he gave us no more trouble, except by being *there*. The crew looked longingly at the catapult Hurricane on the *Empire Lawrence*, but apparently it was decided not to waste the Hurricane on chasing George, especially as there was much cloud, and he would probably have escaped had the Hurricane been sent after him. At half-past six the alarm went again—and this time it was the real stuff.

They appeared in the distance, on the starboard side, low above the water: three—four—five, then three more, then four or five after that, farther to the right. We were all on deck—the R.A.F. boys, with their tin hats, and the deck-hands, the cabin boys—and we counted and watched. Eleven, twelve, thirteen. .... Something was already happening ahead of us. The gunners had rushed up to the gun-turrets. The two cruisers which had suddenly joined us earlier in the day, and the destroyers on the edge of the convoy were firing like mad. It was a beautiful bright day, the sea calm and blue like the Mediterranean, and the sky was now dotted with specks of smoke from the flak shells. They went in a half-circle round the front of the convoy, then, after a few seconds of suspense, they came right out of the sun. They swooped over us, two or three in succession, and from their yellow bellies the yellow eggs dropped, slowly, obscenely. They were after the cruisers, in the middle of the convoy. The tracer-bullets from our Oer-likons were rushing at the yellow belly of the Junkers as he swooped over us. A loud squeal, growing louder and louder, and then the explosion, as a stick of bombs landed between us and the destroyer, on the port side. Three pillars of water went high up in the air, and the ship shook. As he dived, almost to the water-level, our tracer-bullets followed him, but he got out of their way, and on the bridge Captain Dykes, wearing a wide navy-blue beret, was waving and shout-ing frantically: 'Don't fire so low! You're hitting the next ship!' Then after a few minutes they came again, out of the sun—three of them. This time they seemed to make a dead set at the cruisers. On the upper deck, on the fo'c'sle, the Flight Lieutenant was looking on, his long hair waving in the wind. He had his life-jacket on, with a drawing of naked 'Loulou'. The R.A.F. boys and I, and ginger-haired Harry with the blackheads, stood amidships, watching the battle. Suddenly something happened. The cruiser, which had put out a very impressive barrage, had got one. He began to reel and swoop down, on our port side, then he staggered over us. It was like a football match. Harry and the R.A.F. boys were shouting: 'He's on fire! He's on fire! That's it! He's down!' Harry jumped about with joy, frantically. He *was* down. Something brown and large and soft detached itself from the plane, and the plane itself slid into the water without much of a splash. The barrage was still going full blast, but a destroyer sailed up to the brown parachute or whatever it was, and proceeded to pick them up. Meantime the catapult Hurricane on the *Empire Lawrence* had leaped swiftly into the air, in pursuit of the dive-bombers. Swiftly it went in a wide circle round the convoy, ready to pounce on one of them; but here something unfortunate happened; one of the American cargoes, no doubt mistaking the

Hurricane for a German plane, fired what gun or machine-gun it had at him, and the next thing we saw was the pilot baling out by parachute, with nothing to show for his exploit, and with the Hurricane nothing to show for its £5,000.

Wednesday, 27 May

I am not likely ever to forget this day, and yet its exact sequence is hard to restore to one's mind, and what I remember, above all, is moments. I had had a good sleep; we had not been disturbed by anything all night, and one of the moments I remember is sitting on deck after breakfast, reading *Our Mutual Friend*, and feeling wonderfully contented. Life on the *Empire Baffin* seemed to have returned to normal. Pushkov was again giving his Russian lesson to the R.A.F. boys in the smoke-room, and, after yesterday's feeble attempts, the Luftwaffe was clearly not as terrifying as people were apt to imagine. But then, at half-past ten the alarm bell went. From the gun-turret somebody shouted: 'Here they come!' Again people rushed on deck—counting: three—three more, that's six—ten—twelve—fifteen. Now they came from all directions. Gun flashes and clouds of smoke came from the destroyers; then the barrage of the flak ship and the convoy ships went up; like a vulture pouncing on its prey, a dive-bomber swept down on to the submarine, right down to the water-level, but she crash-dived and the three pillars of water went high up in the air. For forty long minutes they attacked, usually in twos and threes, usually coming straight out of the sun, some diving low, others dropping their bombs from two hundred feet. From their yellow shark-like bellies, one could see the obscene yellow eggs dropping, and after a moment of suspense, one saw with relief the pillars of water leaping up. They were concentrating in that first attack on the forward part of the convoy, and we were, apparently, reserved for later. And then we saw the first casualty. The pale-blue and pale-green destroyer was smoking furiously, and signalling, signalling, signalling. What were those flashes saying? Was it the destroyer that had picked up those Huns on Monday? Somebody on board said, 'They are all right. They are not going to abandon her.' That didn't seem so bad. She was still smoking, but they seemed to have got the fire under control. Soon they put it out. The planes disappeared; the attack was over. That wasn't so bad, people said; and then we realized that it *was* bad. Not very far away from us was a Russian ship—I had realized for the first time that we had two or three Russian ships in the convoy—and her foredeck was enveloped in clouds of smoke, and flames were bursting out of the hold. 'They're going to abandon her,' somebody said. Were they? Yes, they were lowering their life-boats. But no. She was still keeping up steam, still keeping up with the other boats, but the clouds of smoke rising from her were growing larger and larger, her whole fo'c'sle was in a cloud of black smoke—but still she went on, and through the cloud of smoke one saw dim shapes of people running and doing something. I saw Alfred Adolphus rushing past me; he was streaming with sweat, and there was a look of panic in his yellowish eyes. 'Hullo, Alfred Adolphus!' I said. 'I think I'll go mad! I think I'll go mad!' he cried.

So the destroyer had been hit, and the Russian ship had been hit, and were fighting with the flames. And somebody said two more ships had been hit.

They came again in less than an hour. This was a short, sharp attack. They concentrated on the other end of the convoy. They dropped their bombs and disappeared. As we sailed on I saw a ship that had stayed behind, with a corvette by her side, blazing furiously. We were already a mile or two from her. And somebody said that another ship had received a direct hit, and had blown up.

Then there was a lull. Dinner was served punctually at noon; Cook wasn't a minute late. Everybody was there, as usual, the lanky first mate, and the young second mate, and the long skinny engineer's mate, with the fuzzy hair and the Hapsburg jaw, and our Flight Lieutenant and the R.A.F. boys. Everybody gulped tea, but appetites were at a low level and few words were exchanged. In their frames, the King and Queen were very calm. Like most of them I drank a lot of tea, but the food seemed to stick to my palate. Pushkov, with a wan smile, said the lesson could, he hoped, be resumed to-morrow. I went out on deck. The Russian ship was still enveloped in smoke though perhaps a little less than before. They had not abandoned ship. I saw Alfred Adolphus sauntering along the deck, now wearing his bright-blue suit with the red stripes and a new light-grey felt hat. 'I'm through with it,' he said defiantly. 'I have refused to go down to the engine-room.' 'Why did you dress up like this?' 'I want to save my clothes if we are torpedoed,' he said. He was much calmer than in the morning. 'It wouldn't matter,' he suddenly cried, 'but it's the *cargo*, the *cargo*!' With this remark, he slunk away. So that's what it is, I said to myself—T.N.T.? I had already heard somebody refer to it, but had taken no notice. The burning ship in the distance had now disappeared. Then the alarm bell went again. I forget what exactly happened at the beginning of that third attack, but this time they concentrated on our end of the convoy. The obscene yellow bellies were over us, and they dropped their eggs all round us. The bearded bank clerk with the Oxford accent was on one of the Oerlikons, and the man with the beret and the Soviet badge on another, and Steward was working a machine-gun, and the Flight Lieutenant, his hair waving in the wind, was, I think, on an Oerlikon, and aft, the little R.A.F. sergeant was on one of the two Lewis guns. And then something happened which I shall never forget. I was standing amidships with the R.A.F. boys and Pushkov and several others, and we realized that something had happened to our sister ship, the *Empire Lawrence*, now without her Hurricane on board. She was no longer steering a straight course. Her bows were pointing towards us—was she moving at all? She was showing a slight list. . . . And we realized that she was being abandoned. Already two of her lifeboats were bobbing on the water, and beside her was a little corvette, taking more men off. As we watched her, we heard all our guns fire like mad. Then one of the yellow-bellies swept over us with roaring engines, almost touching our topmast, and . . . they made a dead set at the helpless, dying ship. And suddenly from the yellow belly the five bombs detached themselves and went right into her. I don't think there was even a moment of suspense; there was an explosion that did not sound very loud, and a flash which, in the sun, was not very bright, and like a vomiting volcano a huge pillar of smoke and wreckage shot two hundred feet into the air—and then, slowly, terribly slowly, it went down to the sea. The *Empire Lawrence* was gone.

Alexander Werth

When daylight came on the fourth day there was, for the first time, no escorting aircraft. It made the men in the ships feel lonely not to see the familiar shape
of the Catalina flying-boat that had been with them on the previous day. It was
as though that last link with home had been cut, and they were alone on the
dark and dreary Arctic Ocean. The cold was hardening now, closing on them
with steely fingers, feeling for the blood in their veins; it took the wind for an
ally and came shrieking down from the North Pole, from the regions of eternal
ice. Snow came with it too, and the ships became pale ghosts, moving on under
the iron dome of the sky into a world of death and darkness, moving on towards
the rim of the ice.

Daylight came late, a weak shadow of its southern self, and stayed only an
hour or two. The sun, barely peeping above the grey horizon, rolled for a brief
while upon the lip of the ocean and then sank to rest. It had no power to warm
the men on watch, and they could observe it with undazzled eyes, observe it
appear and disappear, like a new penny thrust up through the slot of a money-
box, only to be withdrawn again.

At night the Aurora Borealis flickered across the sky, its streamers twisting
like cold flames, changing colour, growing and fading, casting an eerie glow
over the vessels of the convoy and holding all who watched them spellbound by
their wonder. It was as though a great luminous hand had been thrust up over
the northern horizon, its fingers groping across the heavens; at any moment it
seemed those fingers might fall upon the convoy and force it down into the
bottomless depths of the sea.

Then came the moon, hanging like a child's plaything amid the drifting
stars, and washing the ships with silver.

Vernon, for the first time in his life, was wearing long woollen underpants;
the gunners called them John L. Sullivans. He was glad to wear them, glad to
wear a thick vest, a flannel shirt, two pullovers, battle-blouse, lambswool
jerkin, army greatcoat, and dufflecoat; glad to wear two woollen Balaclava helmets
under the hood of his coat, two pairs of trousers, and thick sea-boot stockings
and leather sea-boots. Even so, dressed like a walking clothes-store, even so,
the wind came through; even so, the cold crept up from the feet, up and up as
the dead hours of the night watches dragged slowly past.

And still it grew colder.

On the fifth day the enemy found them. A Dornier 24 flying-boat came up
over the southern horizon and, keeping just beyond gunfire range, proceeded to
circle the convoy. Round and round, hour after hour, it flew; and the gunners,
standing at action stations, watched it with angry eyes and cursed their impotence.

'If only we had a carrier!' moaned Padgett. 'Even a Woolworth would do.
If only we had a carrier!'

But there was no aircraft carrier with the convoy, not even one of those converted merchant ships known irreverently as 'Woolworths'. There was nothing
—nothing but the outranged guns—and they were powerless to touch the
German plane, flying so leisurely in wide circles and signalling to its submarine
allies, signalling all the time.

When night fell they lost the Dornier, and in the night they altered course,
trying to throw their pursuers off the scent. But when day came the Dornier

found them again, and an hour later it was joined by six friends. Heinkel torpedo bombers. Then the alarm was really on; then the ships really awoke; then the air suddenly became full of glowing tracer and bursting steel, and the crackle, bark, and boom of the guns flung noise towards the sky as though to burst open that great steel door and drive on to the freedom of eternity.

Vernon sat on one side of the Bofors gun, watching through his sight a Heinkel coming in low across the line of ships. Andrews was in the other seat, and Miller was on the platform, loading. Vernon could see the Heinkel crawling along the wire of his gun-sight, and he waited for Sergeant Willis to give the order to fire. It was a sitter: it was not doing more than a hundred knots. Surely it was in range? Why did not Willis give the order? What was he waiting for? Was he waiting to see the colour of the pilot's eyes? Now, now, now!

'Fire!' yelled Willis in Vernon's ear.

Vernon pressed his foot on the firing pedal, and the gun began to rock on its pedestal, flinging out shells at the rate of two a second. It was a harsh, staccato song that the gun sang, but it was sweet music to the men on the platform.

Vernon could see the tracers curving away towards the Heinkel, and he could see that they were missing; Andrews was giving too much aim-off; you did not want so much with a plane coming in at that angle.

'Left, you idiot! Left!' he yelled; but he knew that he was wasting his breath, for the voice of the gun beat his voice aside and no one heard him. But Andrews was bringing the gun over, bringing it on to the correct line; the tracers were creeping nearer to their target.

Now, thought Vernon, now we've got the bastard.

And then the gun jammed, and Willis was swearing at Miller. 'You bloody, misbegotten fool! Don't you know how to load yet?'

Miller was struggling to free the shells in the auto-loader, but Willis thrust him aside.

'Gimme the unloading mask,' he yelled. 'You there, Payne! Don't stand gaping; gimme that mask. Hell! You'd think there was all day!'

But the action was over. Two Heinkels were in the sea, and the others were away, heading for base. And one ship lay crippled on the water, with a black column of smoke joining it to the grey ceiling of cloud.

James Pattinson

U-BOAT ATTACKED

It was a fine spring day without a cloud in the sky, and we could clearly see the Rock, that British fortress commanding the Mediterranean. So here were the pillars of Hercules, the Jebel Tarik, fresh from playing one more fateful role in history. Under its protection the invasion fleet had mustered and the African landings been carried out—since when the African campaign was drawing to its end and they were preparing to invade Italy.

Finally, the culmination of our monotonous waiting, we sighted great plumes of smoke and innumerable mastheads. But almost immediately planes appeared and we were obliged to dive. Had they spotted us? If so, warships would be on our trail within an hour. It was a fine day, but not too good for us, for the sea was glassily calm, perfect for their asdic. A report came from the hydrophone operator:

'Propellers at high speed. Probably destroyers. Trying to pick us up on their asdics.'

'Dive to seventy-five fathoms. Silent speed.'

We were all ready, with our felt shoes on and all but the most essential lighting shut off to save current, as we had no idea how long the hunt would last. The enemy were in triangular formation, with us in the middle, and I must say they worked superbly. We had never known the first charges to fall with such uncomfortable accuracy as these did, invariably six at a time. All the glass panels on our controls were shattered and the deck was strewn with splinters. Valve after valve loosened, and before long the water came trickling through. The attack went on unremittingly for three hours without a break, the charges falling thicker and thicker around us, cruising as we were now at a depth of a hundred fathoms. With the need to save current we were working the hydro-plane and steering-gear by hand, and meanwhile the hydrophone was picking up more destroyers, though only the men within earshot knew it. What was the point of upsetting the others?

Faces are pale, and every forehead's sweating. We all know what the other man's thinking. There are six destroyers now, three of them heading for Gibral-tar, but fresh ones always coming up in relay. Like this they'll never run out of depth-charges—our position's truly desperate, the fine weather dead against us. Why doesn't a storm blow up, as it always did when we were on our way here?

By the time we have had sixteen hours of it we have long given up counting the depth-charges. During this time no one's had any sleep, and we've all dark rings under our eyes. Plenty of bulbs have broken, but we don't change them—with the emergency lighting we can only guess the position of the various in-stallations. The darkness makes it all the more frightening.

There've been tricky moments before, but this time it's just hell. At times we have to dive to 125 fathoms. The steel bulkhead supports are buckling and may give at any moment. But perhaps just because of this we're calm.

'Well, it's not everyone who gets such an expensive coffin,' a dry voice re-marks. 'Four million marks it cost.'

Yes, when it happens it'll be quick enough.

If only we could defend ourselves, see something to shoot at—the sense of being trapped into inactivity is unbearable. The current is down to danger level, the compressed air cylinders almost empty and the air itself tastes leaden. Our oxygen is scarce, our carbon monoxide content continually increasing, so that we're breathing with difficulty like so many marathon runners in the last mile; at this rate we can last out twenty hours longer and then we'll just have to surface. We know what will happen then, we've read the dispatches: as soon as the U-boat surfaces all the warships open fire, and the bombardment goes on even though the crew have begun to jump overboard—they must be made to lose their nerve and forget to sink their boat. It was one of the enemy's dearest wishes to capture a U-boat, as that would have made it so much easier to devise means of countering the German underwater threat.

'Stand by for depth-charge attack!' They are falling right alongside now. A roar and a crash in the control-room enough to crack our eardrums—fragments of iron fly around—valves smash to bits. In spite of oneself one can't help stretching a hand out towards one's escape-gear. The petty officer in the control-room has his hand on the flood valve to let in compressed air for surfacing, but he's still awaiting the Commander's orders, and all the time they are still thundering at us. The helmsman shouts that the compass has been blown out of its frame—with its ten thousand revolutions a minute the gyro-wheel goes spinning round the boat, but luckily none of us is hit.

In a council of war with the officers, the Commander admitted the situation was pretty hopeless; it might even be that we should have to surface and sink the boat. On the other hand the moon would not rise until two in the morning and it would be dark till then—if we surfaced in the dark, there was still just a hundred-to-one chance we might break out of the trap that way. Meanwhile everything was ready to blow up the boat. Time fuses were laid against the torpedo warheads and in other vulnerable places all over the ship, so that if one didn't explode there was every chance that another would. In no circumstances must we fall into enemy hands and as a result be responsible for the deaths of many fellow U-boat men. Next we distributed escape-gear and life-boats—a one-man collapsible rubber dinghy per head. The Commander and bridge-watch put on red glasses to accustom their eyes to the dark so that they should be able to see the moment that we surfaced—I couldn't help thinking this super-fluous, for inside the boat it was as good as pitch dark anyway. Next the asdic decoys were thrown out, and we began to fill balloons with metal strips attached which were to be released when we surfaced to float low over the water and fox the enemy radar.

As we prepared to surface at fifty fathoms we caught the sound of asdics even more distinctly. Damn it, they'd still got us! As we shot up to twenty-five fathoms we could hear loud explosions. The hydrophone operator announced:

'Destroyers at close quarters. Six different propellers turning.'

Swearing, the Commander gave the order to surface. By now we couldn't make full speed as the batteries weren't up to it. We brought up ammunition for the A.A. guns, large magazines with fifty rounds in each. Five torpedo-tubes could fire simultaneously, and so could four machine-guns. The belts of these latter did not give out as they do on machine-guns ashore, but, stretching right down the conning-tower into the control-room, were constantly replenished so as to fire between them six thousand four hundred rounds a minute. We could turn them on like hoses. Up to two thousand metres we could menace a destroyer and outside two thousand metres the destroyer couldn't spot us. Yet we knew that if it did come to an engagement we would certainly get the worst of it. We just hoped that we would not have to open fire and might get away unnoticed.

We drove to the surface as depth-charges were still dropping around us. The asdic decoys were obviously fulfilling their purpose. All of a sudden the conning-tower hatch burst open and we almost shot out of it. The pressure was terrific. The Commander looked out to port and I to starboard. Thank heaven it was a dark night and the sky was overcast. We made out three destroyers, one five hundred metres away at most, still dropping depth-charges. We started up both diesel engines and rang down full speed at once—no time to let them warm up. The generators were going too, as we had to recharge our batteries, besides the two compressors recharging the compressed-air cylinders. The fans began to drive fresh air through the boat. The fresh air tore into our lungs; we could hardly stand up and were practically fainting. Guns and machine-guns were loaded and trained on the nearest destroyer, but we all hoped it wouldn't sight us for both our sakes. We had a new type of torpedo that could zig-zag or make circular tracks, but we weren't starting anything. Had we done so we couldn't have got away unmolested, since we lacked a good supply of two essentials: current and compressed air. The range started to increase and the ten gas-filled balloons we had released went up and drifted with the wind. The enemy radar would be amazed to pick up so many U-boats all at once. He presumably suspected the presence of still more where the asdic decoys were in action. . . .

At last we lost sight of the destroyers. The enemy radar was confused by all the echoes, and even if the destroyers did pick us out in the dark they could not go all out after us for fear of ramming other British ships.

After an hour we had taken in fresh air enough to cruise underwater for sixteen hours, and in two hours we were all fit for duty again, though terribly exhausted. We dived to fifty fathoms and left Gibraltar as far away and as fast as we could. I thought of the proverb, 'When an ass steps on thin ice he generally falls through.' Our ice had certainly been thin enough.

Heinz Schaeffer

COASTAL COMMAND

Ballad of Jack Overdue
1941

Come back, come back, Jolly Jack Straw,
    There's ice in the killer sea.
Weather at base closes down for the night:
    And the ash-blonde Waaf is waiting tea.

How many long Atlantic hours
    Has he hunted there alone:
Has he trimly weaved on the silent air
    The dullest patrol that's ever flown?

How can they know he found at last
    That he made a hunter's strike:
And swooped on a sly swift shark as it dived:
    Saw gouting oil mount carpet-like?

Jolly Jack Straw is beating it back,
    But his wireless set is blown.
He cannot report his long-sought luck,
    Or the ice-dark blinding the eye and bone.

Come back, come back, Jolly Jack Straw,
    For the ash-blonde Waaf drinks tea;
And the tea leaves tell her fortune as well.
    Come back, come back from the killer sea.

John Pudney

17

COMBINED OPERATIONS

The idea of forming small, permanent, specialized units of highly trained and highly skilled troops working on independent missions while supported by naval and air units was a British one, born naturally of her peculiar strategic situation and needs in the days of defeat in 1940. It originated in the mind of Lieutenant-Colonel Dudley Clarke, R.A., early in June. The prototypes for the force had been the hurriedly raised Independent Companies used to delay the Germans in Norway. The plan fitted in well with Winston Churchill's desire to hit back at the Germans, even in defeat, and was accepted.

The Commandos are Born

WE are greatly concerned—and it is certainly wise to be so—with the dangers of the German landing in England in spite of our possessing the command of the seas and having very strong defence by fighters in the air. Every creek, every beach, every harbour has become to us a source of anxiety. Besides this the parachutists may sweep over and take Liverpool or Ireland, and so forth. All this mood is very good if it engenders energy. But if it is so easy for the Germans to invade us, in spite of sea-power, some may feel inclined to ask the question, why should it be thought impossible for us to do anything of the same kind to them? The completely defensive habit of mind which has ruined the French must not be allowed to ruin all our initiative. It is of the highest consequence to keep the largest numbers of German forces all along the coasts of the countries they have conquered, and we should immediately set to work to organize raiding forces on these coasts where the populations are friendly.

Winston Churchill, 4 June 1940

We have got to get out of our minds the idea that the Channel ports and all the country between them are enemy territory. What arrangements are being made for good agents in Denmark, Holland, Belgium and along the French coast? Enterprises must be prepared, with specially-trained troops of the hunter class, who can develop a reign of terror down these coasts, first of all on the 'butcher and bolt' policy; but later on, or perhaps as soon as we are organized, we could surprise Calais or Boulogne, kill and capture the Hun garrison, and hold the place until all the preparations to reduce it by siege or heavy storm have been made, and then away. The passive resistance war, in which we have acquitted ourselves so well, must come to an end.

Winston Churchill, 6 June 1940

Utmost care was taken in selecting the men required for these irregular operations. There were failures, as in all walks of life, but most of those chosen were well-chosen.

Their view of their work was well summed up by one of their number, who died young with a D.S.O., M.C. and bar:

Of course, it is absolutely terrific; it is the greatest job in the Army that one could possibly get, and it is a job that, if properly carried out, can be of enormous value . . . no red tape, no paper work . . . just pure operations, the success of which depends principally on oneself and the men one has oneself picked to do the job with you . . . it's revolutionary.

Geoffrey Appleyard

The Technique of Staying Alive

Keep the sun behind you; you can control your own shadow and merge it with the others. . . . Fruit trees harbour many birds which set up a noise if disturbed. Steady shuffling through grass does not worry them but the slightest tinkle of metal causes a flurry. . . . Cattle not milked recently will lick your face and moo. The only solution is to lie on your back and milk the damn things. . . . We killed several Germans because they always went to the same latrine and we noticed it. . . . The sniper has to work long, long hours to kill one German. . . . Dirty your hands and face with burnt cork, graphite, soot, or lamp black, but do *not* use earth. . . . An antidote for sneezing is to press the upper lip against the base of the nose. . . . Do not wear gum boots; they go 'plop plop'.

Within three weeks of their formation, the Commandos' first raid was mounted. It was not a success; nor was the second, on Guernsey another three weeks later. In a sense, both served their purpose: the Commandos were learning fast.

The crews of the speedboats were R.N.V.R. volunteers of a most cheerful and happy-go-lucky disposition. The first thing we found as we left the destroyer was that they had forgotten to adjust their compasses which were many degrees wrong, so we had to take a chance and guess at our landing place. By great good luck we happened to strike the right one and make our landing approximately on time.

The time ashore was uneventful. The barracks we visited proved to be unoccupied so we were unable to make prisoners. We collected a certain amount of information from residents at Guernsey, most of whom were too frightened to talk properly, not being able to believe it was British soldiers and thinking it was some trick of the Gestapo to get information from them. The trouble started when we returned to the beach and tried to get off to the speedboats. A heavy swell had got up and the speedboats could not come nearer than about fifty yards, so we all had to swim for it, as the one small dinghy in use soon capsized and was smashed on the rocks. Three men, who had stated in their interviews that they could swim, proved to be non-swimmers and had to be left behind. This was one of our early lessons, and swimming instruction was pushed on pretty hard when we got back.

At this critical moment the Germans also came to life and started machine-gunning, fortunately not very accurately. We all had an exhausting swim through the surf, but bar the three non-swimmers all eventually got to the speedboats.

One of these then broke down, and aboard the other the crew were not very good at making up their minds what to do. Even the engine-room attendant emerged from the engine-room to take part in a discussion with the captain and give his advice. We finally got underway, making about two knots, with one boat towing the other.

By this time we were nearly an hour late for the rendezvous with the destroyer, and as we emerged from Telegraph Bay we could just see her disappearing at high speed. We managed to attract her attention with a torch and the captain very gallantly returned to pick us up, thereby leaving himself open to probable air attack the whole way back to England, as the dawn was just about breaking.

We got on board the destroyer and by a miracle avoided all air attacks and returned to Dartmouth, having achieved very little, but learnt a good deal.

Major Durnford-Slater

Churchill is not Satisfied: 25 August 1940

I hear that the whole position of the Commandos is being questioned. They have been told 'no more recruiting' and that their future is in the melting pot. . . . For every reason therefore we must develop the storm troop or Commando idea. I have asked for five thousand parachutists, and we must also have at least ten thousand of these small 'band of brothers' who will be capable of lightning war.

Winston Churchill

The Lofoten Raid

Some months of inaction followed the initial failures. Then on 4 March 1941 a combined operation was launched against the Lofoten Islands off the coast of Norway by Commandos and naval forces.

Tuesday 5.15 (scribbled in boat):

It is just light enough to write. We are packed sardine-wise and half asleep, being embarked in more than enough time. It is calm and clear twilight. In spite of the latitude, season of the year and early morning hour, I don't need gloves, though in an open boat at sea!

. . . . We are beginning to move in earnest. I can see nothing except a saxe-blue sky, a gull, and occasionally the mastheads of the man-of-war leading us.

Some spray coming in which *is* cold!

. . . . Whole silhouette of man-of-war. She is slowing down and we are passing her. I have seldom seen anything so dramatic and beautiful—every spar and rope clean-cut against the blue, every man standing rigid and motionless at his gun or instrument.

On land, Svolvaer:

Bang-banging everywhere. Presumably demolition, plus (?) men-o'-war sinking German trawlers.

A perfectly lovely morning. Beautiful little mountain peaks, pink in sunlight, round a rather picturesque little town.

8 a.m. (for address, see reverse side of page):

Guarding half-wrecked office.

Sapper has put one charge of explosive on safe and made a hole in it. But safe still resists and he has gone for more H.E. We don't want sappers so much as burglars!

No Germans this side of water. Must be dead or captured t'other side, because crowd is parading with Norwegian flag, cheering, etc.

10 a.m.:

Safe open. Little of interest. £5 worth of notes and coppers—to be returned to firm. Fine blaze in adjoining factory and yard.

We have captured one German soldier, a nasty-looking little twerp in a green uniform; he is smiling sheepishly and seems rather pleased to be captured. Officer has taken camera from him and is photographing fire.

Large crowd of Norsk children collecting. Much fraternization.

It *has* been very tame. Little danger now unless from air, or torpedo on return.

12 noon:

Back on S.S. *Domino* with many recruits for Norsk Army and Navy in England, one or two hundred prisoners, mainly sailors, but one flying officer and some soldiers. All objectives achieved. One casualty on our side—an officer has wounded himself with his own revolver. So it has been a mere tea-party for us, and all the heroics look a little silly.

4 p.m.:

All, or nearly all, is over. Norway is invisible to the left (PORT!). The last of the Lofotens sliding past on the right (STARBOARD!), looking like gigantic fairy icebergs in the evening sun.

. . . I must tell you that all my *arrière-pensées* about blowing up Norwegian cod liver oil factories prove unjustified. It appears that:

(i) The cod liver oil is not required for babies, but for making nitrogenous explosives, and so bombs.

(ii) The unemployment problem I feared is cancelled by the number of young men we are taking away from Svolvaer as volunteers for Norwegian Army, Navy and Merchant Services. Also, I was assured that the labour in the factory was more or less German-enforced, and that the men will be glad to go back to their own fishing. This is especially so in view of (iii), and (iii) is rather funny.

(iii) One of my jobs was to search the office for papers. I found very few of the slightest possible use. I found one or two referring to last week and then nothing between that and 1936. I naturally concluded that someone had got wind of our coming and hidden or removed the last five years' papers—though I couldn't quite make out why. I am now told that the factory closed down for lack of business in 1936: that the Nazi government ordered its re-opening for munition purposes: that last winter was spent in re-conditioning and repairing: that it re-opened yesterday. So we can say to Hitler, 'Open a factory in the Lofotens on Monday, and we'll blow it up for you on Tuesday.'

I was very glad of the little Norwegian I was able to learn (on top of my muddled and half-forgotten Swedish) during the voyage out. It enabled me to discover exactly what was going on, when I otherwise could not have known. It enabled me to help a lot of people, particularly a poor woman with a baby whom we had to get out of bed, and out of her home, in case the fire from the factory explosion spread. She was wife to the caretaker in the wooden office-warehouse I was responsible for, and she seemed sure we wanted to take her and her baby outside in order to bayonet them in the snow. She was the only Svolvaerian I saw who showed the slightest fear of us. I had to roar: '*For din egen Sikkerhet!*' at her about four times, and her husband and friends had to repeat it (in a rather better accent) before she began to look less terrified and prepare to come away. We helped her husband carry out most of their furniture, clothes, etc., in case of accidents, and make a dump of them at a safe distance from the burning factory. Incidentally, the fire didn't spread to their warehouse-office-home, so they'll be spending the afternoon carrying them all back again.

My bad Norwegian also enabled me to discover that some piles of timber which *were* beginning to burn were not for German consumption, and so to start our men and the crowd of Norwegian spectators on successful salvage. It meant I could help a little (a very little!) in the recruiting: most of this was going on in the main town t'other side of the harbour which I was itching to cross all the morning. It finally enabled me, as our boats pushed off at midday, to shout: '*Til vi komme tilbakke!*—Till we come back!'—to the crowd on the quay.

Evan John

Vaagso: 27 December 1941

This raid on Norway, directed against military installations, shipping and other targets, was much more seriously contested, but was equally successful.

As night fell, on Boxing Day, the ships sailed again for Vaagso, Admiral Tovey covering our approach with the major units of the Atlantic Fleet, including his flagship, *King George V*. The submarine *Tuna* had preceded us and was lying off the entrance to Vaagsfjord to act as a navigational beacon on our way in. H.M.S. *Kenya* led our particular convoy, flying the flag of Admiral Burrough. She was followed by the destroyer H.M.S. *Chiddingfold*; then came the *Charles* and *Leopold* carrying the troops with the destroyers *Onslow*, *Offa* and *Oribi* following close behind.

We were called at 4 a.m. I had often read in descriptions of naval battles that the sailors wore clean underclothes so as to minimize the risk of infection from wounds, so I put on a clean vest and pair of pants and told all the others to do the same. I took great trouble to check up on every item of my equipment. On this operation I carried a Colt ·45 pistol with three spare magazines. All these magazines were discharged by the end of the day, but I never again went into action carrying a pistol only, as these weapons do not give confidence when opposed to a man with a rifle. We had a good breakfast at 5 a.m. and carried with us a small compact haversack ration. In my case, and in nearly all other cases, this ration was untouched when we returned to the ship at 3 p.m. The excitement was too great to allow time off for eating.

Off Vaagsfjord at 7 a.m. we picked up the *Tuna* as planned. The surge of excitement which was running through our ship had erased all thought of sea-sickness. We entered the fjord, a spectacular passage between great, snow-covered hills. We were to land at first light, ten minutes to nine. The *Prince Charles* and *Prince Leopold* pulled into a small bay. The troops filed into the landing craft and these were lowered to the cold waters of the fjord. Then *Kenya*, two hundred yards behind us, opened the bombardment of Maaloy Island where the Germans manned a coast defence battery. We started the run-in in our landing craft.

About a hundred yards from our landing place, I fired ten red Verey light signals. This told the ships to stop firing and the aircraft to come in with their smoke bombs. As I leaped from the leading landing craft three Hampden bombers passed over me at zero feet with a roar. As they did so they loosed their bombs, which seemed to flash and then mushroom like miniature atom explosions. Some of the phosphorus came back in a great flaming sheet. Next thing I knew both my sleeves were on fire. Fortunately I wore leather gloves and beat the flames out before they could eat through my four layers of clothing to the skin. The beaching had been made, dry, against snow-covered rocks which rose thirty or forty feet in an almost sheer wall. For the moment, we were unopposed and hidden from the enemy by smoke.

Unfortunately, however, one of the Hampdens was hit by anti-aircraft fire as she came in. Out of control, she dropped a bomb on an incoming landing craft. Bursting, the phosphorus inflicted terrible burns amongst the men. The craft, too, burst into flames. Grenades, explosives, and small arms ammunition were detonated in a mad mixture of battle noises. We pushed the emptied craft out to sea where it could do us no harm, and Sam Corry, our big, efficiently calm Irish doctor, taking charge of the casualties, sent them back to the *Prince Charles*. The rest of us turned to the battle.

Major Durnford-Slater

The Capture of Maaloy Island

The Germans on the island had been caught unprepared. They were follow-ing their usual routine: the gunners were being roused by a loud-voiced N.C.O.; the officer commanding (Butziger, by name) was shaving; his batman, whose turn it was that morning to man the telephone connecting headquarters with the look-out post, was cleaning his officer's boots on the table beside the instrument. So busily engaged was he upon this task that he allowed the telephone bell to ring, and did not trouble to pick up the receiver. The German gunners thus received no warning. Outside the barracks on the island of Maaloy there was a naval signalling station established on the highest point. The signaller on duty received a message flashed by lamp telling of the advent of our forces. He ran down to the small bay on the north side of the island, leapt into a boat and rowed as fast as he could to the headquarters of the German Naval Commandant on the main island of Vaagso. Here he delivered the warning, but when asked whether he had warned the army gunners on Maaloy, he replied, 'Oh no, sir, it is a military battery, and this is a naval signal.' The Germans are a most methodical people.

Hilary St. George Saunders

Street Battle

Vaagso is built on one narrow street, three-quarters of a mile long, which runs parallel to, and about fifty yards from, the fjord. Behind the street, which was lined with unpainted wooden buildings, nearly sheer rocks rose to several hundred feet. I heard Johnny Giles yell, 'Come on', and saw him disappear with his 3 Troop into the smoke.

That was the last I saw of Johnny. Fifteen minutes later he was dead, killed in an assault on the back of a house. He and his men had shot three Germans who had been firing on them from the house, then rushed it. They went through the rooms and as Johnny entered the last room a fourth German jumped in front of him and shot him.

At about the time Johnny met his death I went into a large oil factory near our landing beach. I was looking for Johann Gotteberg, who had been named to us as the chairman of the local quislings and was the owner of this factory. Meanwhile Bill Bradley prepared the factory for demolition. I saw a middle-aged man who seemed to be attending the machinery with extraordinary concentration, considering the circumstances.

'Who is that man?' I asked my Norwegian guide, a native of Vaagso.

'That is Gotteberg, the owner.'

I had him arrested. A few minutes later he had a first-class view of his factory being blown up.

Algy Forrester went off like a rocket with his 4 Troop down the street of the town, leaving a trail of dead Germans behind him. The troop had just lost Arthur Komrower, who had suffered severe leg and back injuries when he was pinned between a landing craft and a rock. The third officer of 4 Troop was Bill Lloyd, who, with Algy, had developed the technique of landing on rough and rocky shores. Bill hardly got going before he was shot, clean through the neck. That was the end of him for this operation.

Algy waded in, shouting and cheering his men, throwing grenades into each house as they came to it and firing from the hip with his tommy gun. He looked wild and dangerous. I shouldn't have liked to have been a German in his path. He had absolutely no fear. He led an assault against the German headquarters, in the Ulvesund Hotel, and was about to toss a grenade in when one of the enemy, firing through the front door, shot him. As he fell he landed on his own grenade, which exploded a second later. This rough landing at Vaagso was the first time we had put into operational practice the system he and Bill Lloyd had developed. For Algy it was also the last.

Other casualties in Algy's troop were heavy. Captain Martin Linge, my Norwegian friend, had also been attached to No. 4. When the attack was briefly held up after Algy's death, he kept things moving, but only for a few minutes. He was killed in exactly the same way as Forrester, shot as he tried to force open a door. I had spoken to Martin just as he left the beach.

'This is good, Colonel,' he had said, laughing. 'We'll have a party at the Mayfair to celebrate when we get back.'

He was a very gallant and fearless ally and would have made an ideal Commando soldier.

The Germans had a tank in a garage near the Ulvesund Hotel, about a hundred and fifty yards up the street, a fact of which we were aware through our Intelligence. The tank was an old one, but if it were brought out on to the street it could wreak havoc amongst us with its gun. After Martin Linge's death, Sergeant Cork and Johnnie Dowling of 1 Troop managed to reach the tank, still in the garage, and blow it up. Unfortunately Cork used too heavy a charge and didn't get away quickly enough. He was caught in the explosion and died of wounds. Johnnie was untouched. Corporal 'Knocker' White was left in command of Forrester's troop. He performed the job so gallantly that he was to earn a Distinguished Conduct Medal for it.

From our out-of-doors, snow-covered headquarters near the landing place, I could see everything that took place on Maaloy. 5 and 6 Troops, only fifty yards from the beach when the naval barrage lifted, were up the slopes of the island like a flash. I saw them advancing through the smoke in perfect extended order. Jack Churchill, who had played them in with his bagpipes, was leading them with considerable dash. On landing, Peter Young saw a German running back to man his gun position. 'I was able to shoot him,' Peter told me later. Ten minutes after this, Young reached the company office on Maaloy. One of the German company clerks made the literally fatal mistake of trying to wrest Peter's rifle from him. Small pockets of resistance were quickly cleaned up and many prisoners were taken, including two Norwegian women of easy virtue who had been consoling the German soldiers.

The fighting in the town was still very hot and heavy, however, and I had Charlie Head, my Signals Officer for this raid, send a message to the headquarters ship asking for the floating reserve, and another to Jack Churchill on Maaloy asking if he, too, could help. Jack promptly sent 6 Troop under Peter Young: and Charles Haydon ordered the floating reserve to the far end of Vaagso. We were now attacking on two fronts.

Back in the main street, where our attack had been stalled, Peter Young with 6 Troop got things moving again. I left the Adjutant to control our headquarters and joined him. It was very noisy: there were the different sounds from the various calibres of small arms; artillery exchanges between *Kenya* and a coast defence battery somewhere down the fjord; anti-aircraft fire from the ships against the attacking Messerschmitts; the demolitions; and the crackling roar of flames. I heard one signaller complaining how difficult it was to receive messages.

'This is bloody awful! A man can hardly hear himself think!'

Our opposition was much stiffer than I had expected. It was not until later that I learned that about fifty men from an exceptionally good German unit were spending Christmas leave at Vaagso.

As I tried to catch up with Peter Young I saw him and George Herbert throwing grenades through windows and doors. They appeared to be enjoying themselves. I finally joined them in a timber yard which had only one entrance off the main street. Part of our plan had been to dump many sacks of grenades near the landing place. Our Administrative Officer had organized a gang of loyal Norwegian civilians who followed close behind the leading troops, carrying these sacks, and offering the troops replenishments of grenades as often as they were needed.

Suddenly, in a strange interval when artillery and demolitions seemed to pause for their wind, there was an eerie, unexpected stillness. Half of 6 Troop were clustered in the timber yard. A single rifle shot rang out and a man fell dead beside me. I thought the shot had come from a house, about twenty yards away, on the other side of the small yard. We all started firing furiously at the windows of the house. I emptied my revolver, feeling strangely helpless, for there was only one exit to the yard and unless we did something quickly it seemed certain the sniper would pick us all off, one by one. Another shot came from the house and another man fell dead. I think this was the first time in warfare that I truly felt fear. I didn't like it.

We crouched behind a pile of timber. The sniper fired whenever one of us moved. Soon he picked off a third of our number. He was shooting right down at us from a first floor window.

There was a shed just behind our cover and George Herbert disappeared into it. 'Captain Young,' he called, 'I've found a tin of petrol!'

'Put some in a bucket, Sergeant,' Peter called back. 'When you've done that we'll all stand up and give you covering fire while you toss it into the house.'

Herbert obeyed, and the others followed the petrol up by lobbing grenades through the windows. There was a great burst of flame. Very soon the wooden house was burned to the ground, a funeral pyre for the sniper. I wasn't sorry to leave that timber yard.

It was just about then that Lieutenant Denis O'Flaherty was wounded. He had been leading assault after assault on enemy-held houses and was leading an attack on the steamship wharf when a sniper, concealed in a warehouse, hit him in the eye. The bullet came out through his throat. O'Flaherty, a brave soldier, had been wounded twice before. This most serious wound was to cost him eight major operations and two years in hospital. He lost his eye but never his spirit. Later, still fighting for Britain, he was decorated by the Americans for gallantry in Korea.

After the affair of the timber yard, when the attack got moving down the main street again, a door on the fjord side of the street suddenly opened and a German lobbed out a grenade. It rolled between my feet and stopped. I was standing on a corner and instinctively took a tremendous dive for shelter round the edge of the building. I landed on my face, just in time to hear the grenade go off. I escaped with a couple of small bits of the grenade in my palm, but my orderly was badly wounded.

About thirty seconds later, the same door opened and the German who had tossed the grenade came out with his hands up and expressing his earnest desire to surrender. I was prepared to accept this, but one of my men thought otherwise. He advanced on the German. 'Nein! Nein!' the German yelled, a small man, yellow and scared.

Our man was so angry that he shot the German dead, through the stomach. This, of course, is one of the tricky problems in warfare. Can a man throw a death-dealing grenade one second and surrender the next? I hardly think he can expect much mercy.

Then I saw Bob Clement organizing an attack on another building farther down the street. With Lance-Sergeant Culling, he led the way. As they approached the front door a German threw a percussion grenade at Culling's face, killing him instantly. Clement kept a brisk fire going into the building and called for Sergeant Ramsey and the mortar detachment, posting men all around to prevent any German from escaping. Ramsey got a direct hit on the roof with his third round and then pumped several dozen mortar bombs through the hole. The place was soon blazing. On my way back, when the flames had died down, I counted twelve German corpses inside.

This incident was to end the most severe phase of the fighting.

Major Durnford-Slater

The Attempt on Rommel

Commando operations in the Mediterranean were under the direction of Colonel R. E. Laycock. There were many expeditions, of which the best-known was the attempt to catch Rommel at what was thought to be his headquarters behind the lines in North Africa.

The attack had been planned for midnight, 17/18 November 1941, so as to coincide with the opening of General Auchinleck's offensive against Rommel. Six hours before, the Commando soldiers 'fell in with almost parade-ground precision' for the final stage of the operation. They moved off, leaving behind them one man who had run a nail from the sole of his boot into his foot, to guard the spare rations. 'It was pouring with rain, and we were most of the way walking ankle deep in mud. It was not long before we were wet to the skin.' So bad were the conditions that they were soon compelled to move in single file 'to avoid knocking one another over as we slipped and staggered through the mud' and the streaming darkness. About 22.30 hours they reached the bottom of the escarpment, rested a short while, and then began to climb its two hundred and fifty feet of muddy turf and rock. Half-way up, their passage 'roused a watchdog and a stream of light issued from the door of a hut . . . a hundred yards on our flank. As we crouched motionless, hardly breathing, we heard a man shouting at the dog. Finally the door closed.'

At the top of the escarpment they found a muddy track which the guides had told them would lead them straight to the back of Rommel's headquarters. Here Cook departed with his detachment to find a pylon from which the telephone wires ran, and which he was to blow up. This task he successfully accomplished, but was captured on his way back to join Laycock, and spent the rest of the war a prisoner in Italy.

. . . . The men formed up for the assault, moving to the places assigned to them in the plan drawn up by Keyes. Then Keyes, with Campbell and Sergeant Terry, pushed through a hedge into the garden of the house and went round the corner 'on to a gravel sweep before a flight of steps, at the top of which were glass-topped doors'. Tommy-gun in hand, Keyes ran up the steps and Campbell pushed open the door.

'Just inside we were confronted by a German, an officer I think, in steel helmet and overcoat.

'Geoffrey at once closed with him, covering him with his tommy-gun. The man seized the muzzle of Geoffrey's gun and tried to wrest it from him. Before I or Terry could get round behind him he retreated, still holding on to Geoffrey, to a position with his back to the wall and his either side protected by the first and second pair of doors at the entrance. Geoffrey could not draw his knife and neither I nor Terry could get round Geoffrey as the doors were in the way, so I shot the man with my ·38 revolver which I knew would make less noise than Geoffrey's Tommy-gun. Geoffrey then gave the order to use tommy-guns and grenades, since we had to presume that my revolver shot had been heard. We found ourselves, when we had time to look round, in a large hall with a stone floor and stone stairway leading to the upper stories, and with a number of doors opening out of the hall. The hall was very dimly lit. We heard a man in heavy boots clattering down the stairs, though we could not see him or he us as he was hidden by a right-angle turn in the stairway. As he came to the turn and his feet came in sight, Sergeant Terry fired a burst with his tommy-gun. The man turned and fled away upstairs.

'Meanwhile Geoffrey had opened one door and we looked in and saw it (the room) was empty. Geoffrey pointed to a light shining from the crack under the next door and then flung it open. It opened towards him and inside were about ten Germans in steel helmets, some sitting and some standing. Geoffrey fired two or three rounds with his Colt ·45 automatic, and I said, "Wait, I'll throw a grenade in." He slammed the door shut and held it while I got a pin out of a grenade. I said "Right", and Geoffrey opened the door and I threw in the grenade which I saw roll to the middle of the room. Before Geoffrey (who said "Well done" as he saw the grenade go in) could shut the door, the Germans fired. A bullet struck Geoffrey just over his heart and he fell unconscious at the feet of myself and Terry. I shut the door and immediately afterwards the grenade burst with a shattering explosion. This was followed by complete silence and we could see that the light in the room had gone out. I decided Geoffrey had to be moved in case there was further fighting in the building, so between us Sergeant Terry and I carried him outside and laid him on the grass verge by the side of the steps leading up to the front door. He must have died as we were carrying him outside, for when I felt his heart it had ceased to beat.'

Campbell returned to the hall of the building, and then went round to its back, but while he was approaching it one of the Commando soldiers posted at the back entrance mistook him for a German and shot him through the leg, thus making it impossible for him to return to the beach. The men offered to carry Campbell back across the twenty-five miles, but he refused. They left him lying there, withdrawing under the command of Sergeant Terry. Campbell was presently found and taken by the Germans to hospital. Geoffrey Keyes they also took away and buried with military honours in the cemetery close by, the chaplain of the garrison church at Potsdam performing the ceremony. He was posthumously awarded the Victoria Cross.

General Rommel was not at the house attacked, and it is now known that he had never used it. Our Intelligence was faulty. The house was the headquarters of the German and Italian supply services. Nor, as was thought at the time, was Rommel in Rome attending a birthday celebration; he was close to the front line, then about to be attacked by General Auchinleck.

The raiders, with Sergeant Terry in charge, made their way, not without difficulty, back to Laycock who was awaiting them in the wadi; and then, still hoping, though in vain, that Cook and his men would arrive, sat down to wait the return of the *Torbay*. She arrived off the coast after dark on the 20th and flashed a message in Morse, which Laycock was able to read, saying that the sea was too rough and that she would return on the following night. She then moved off after successfully floating ashore a rubber dinghy containing food and water. This was thankfully received. The party prepared to spend the remainder of the night and the next day ashore, and to pray for better weather.

. . . . The Germans were by now maintaining a sustained fire, and about two o'clock in the afternoon it became evident that it would be impossible to hold the beach against such superior forces. When the enemy were no more than two hundred yards from the caves, Laycock ordered the detachment to split up into small parties, dash across the open and seek the cover of the hills inland. There they could either try to get in touch with H.M.S. *Talisman*, which they knew would be lying off an alternative beach that night, or they could hide in the wadis which abounded and await our forces. Lieutenant Pryor, who was grievously wounded, was left behind with a medical orderly to surrender. He eventually did so and was taken off to captivity on the back of a mule watched 'by a lovely great red-backed shrike sitting on a juniper bush'.

After the party had scattered, Laycock found himself with Sergeant Terry. They crossed half a mile of open country, being continually sniped, but neither of them was hit. Once in the shelter of the Jebel, which offered the excellent cover of thick scrub, they set out together to join the Eighth Army. After the first few days they made friends with various members of the local Senussi tribes, who helped them and hid them each night in the wadis which the enemy were known to have searched during the day. 'Neither of us,' records Laycock, 'could speak Arabic, and our conversation was mostly carried on by means of broken Italian and by making signs to each other. For instance, a Senussi holding up his five fingers, pointing at us and then drawing his forefinger across his throat, meant that five of our original raiding party had been murdered by the Arabs and handed over to the Germans. Our greatest problem,' he continues, 'was the lack of food, and though never desperate we were forced to subsist for periods, which never exceeded two and half consecutive days, on berries only, and we became appreciably weak from want of nourishment. At other times we fed well on goat and Arab bread, but developed a marked craving for sugar. Water never presented a serious proposition as it rained practically continuously.'

One evening they were making a thin stew out of some goat and bones— mostly bones—which they had flavoured with wild garlic picked by Laycock. As they were about to eat it a friendly Arab arrived, gave one loud sniff, and overturned the pot. He subsequently explained to the enraged and hungry pair that the garlic would have destroyed their sight. They ate all that goat, returning to dig up the lungs and entrails which they had buried.

Eventually the colonel and the sergeant joined the British forces at Cyrene, forty-one days after they had originally set out. 'On joining them we fell upon the marmalade offered to us and polished off a pot each.' They were the only members of the party to reach Cyrene.

St. Nazaire

On 27–28 March 1942, a combined Commando, Navy and R.A.F. raid was made on the port of St. Nazaire in order to render unserviceable the only dry dock on the Atlantic seaboard capable of holding the German battleship Tirpitz. *The following account was broadcast anonymously in June 1945.*

I was taken prisoner in the raid on St. Nazaire in March 1942. I was commanding a small party in the landing craft immediately astern of the destroyer *Campbeltown*. None of us expected to be taken prisoner. We thought we would all get away with it, blow up the docks, and return safely to England without a casualty. The raid was a success all right, but it didn't turn out quite like that; on the whole we were pretty lucky. Right up to the last moment it looked as if the raid was going to catch the Germans off their guard.

The sea journey took two days and a night and a half. We sailed from Falmouth. We didn't make straight for the French coast. We set a course way out into the Atlantic, so that if we were spotted the Germans might think we were only a submarine sweep. It was very calm, that was one blessing. No German aircraft came over, and I don't think we were sighted, so at evening on the second day we were feeling pretty optimistic.

We turned in towards the mouth of the river Loire from the south, and took up our assault formation. The destroyer *Campbeltown* was leading. She was an old destroyer converted for this job and she was followed by two flotillas of motor launches. She was stiff with explosive, five tons of it. It was her job to charge the gates of the St. Nazaire dry dock, about six miles up the river, and then she was to blow herself sky-high, and the dock gates were to go up with her. I was in the leading M.L. of the starboard flotilla. I saw our colonel and the naval commander go up and down the line of little ships in the M.G.B. They hailed us and wished us luck before taking their stations. The escorting destroyers left us, night fell, and soon we saw a light winking at us out of the darkness. The submarine *Sturgeon* had been waiting off the river mouth to give the direction. It was her light we saw. Commander Ryder, V.C., had led the whole convoy and the navigation of Lieutenant Green, his navigating officer, had been so accurate that we met the submarine exactly at the time scheduled. Everything was going very well. She signalled good-bye, good luck and then vanished.

Now we made straight for the entrance to the river Loire. Suddenly two white fringes, like very low clouds, emerged out of the dark ahead, to port and starboard. We went in between them. They were the surf on the French coast, the two banks of the Loire, and I realized now that we had reached the river.

Gradually the river narrowed. We could hear the thud of the R.A.F. bombing and could see the flash of the ack-ack batteries replying on shore. At first, they didn't pay any attention to us and we began to think we were going to get away with it. We were pretty lucky with the tide. The operation had been put forward a night to make the most of the good weather and the tide would have been better for us the night after. I could see the *Campbeltown* outlined just ahead of me, and as far as I could tell she was going along O.K. Her commander told me afterwards that he felt her jar and in fact she touched the bottom twice

going up the river. She just cleared, by a few inches, and went in very steadily
with the two flotillas of little ships aft to port and starboard. They were un-
armoured and we had come the whole way from England in them, that was a
good four hundred miles. The searchlights caught us first. They swung across
the black river from both banks and picked us up one by one. Then the coastal
batteries opened up—at first uncertainly. After a few minutes everything opened
up, and they let us have it. We knew we were for it then. Two searchlights were
like the ones at Plymouth Harbour. We had rehearsed the operation there a
week before and we never thought it would be quite like that. The *Campbeltown*
looked as if she was flood-lit for a naval review. I could see her clearly, just ahead.
The troops were lying down at their action stations. Commander Beattie—he
received the V.C. for his ship's crew and for his own conduct in this action—
Commander Beattie was on the bridge. I could see the shells all over the place,
bouncing off every part of the old destroyer. I don't know how she wasn't sunk
or crippled: everything in the harbour was focused on her.

Pretty quickly the searchlights began to pick up the little ships. They swept
over my own M.L., and then settled on it. For the last few minutes before we
landed, almost the whole convoy was floodlit. The coastal batteries began to
bracket us. Shells were rustling overhead and plopping into the water. Many
shells and machine-gun bullets went straight through the ships, from side to
side, killing men assembled below deck. We could see the docks now, our objective, and we could see the outline of jetties and warehouses which we had
memorized day after day from maps and air photographs. All of us knew the
place by heart. The *Campbeltown* changed course for the last time, and I saw her
turn towards the dry dock.

This was the big moment. She put on speed. She was flying the White
Ensign as she went in! She opened up with everything she had and charged the
boom and the huge dock gates at eighteen knots, head on, with a German
battery blazing at point-blank range across her decks. The troops were lying
down, firing back with their Brens; the deck was stripped and they hadn't much
cover. There was a mass of flame and smoke and gunfire. She went slap into the
dock gates, we saw it happen, and lay there dead centre. The gates were thirty-
five feet thick and the *Campbeltown* went in with such power that she didn't
stick till her bridge was level with them. The *Tirpitz* would think twice now
about coming out into the Atlantic to attack our convoys. The battle of the
Atlantic wasn't going too well for the Allies then, and we had been told that our
attack on St. Nazaire was not just a raid but an important part of Allied strategy.
The destroyer had done her job. She crashed the dock at 1.33 a.m., that was
three minutes after the time laid down in our orders. At 1.45 the troops were off.
At 1.50 the scuttling charges were set off. At two o'clock she was abandoned and
seen to be sinking. The five tons of explosive was concreted in and due to go off
some hours later. The troops poured over the sides and knocked out the coastal
battery alongside the dock. Another party blew up the pumping station and the
station operating the dock gate. There were many wounded on board the doomed
Campbeltown, and we got them all ashore.

The M.L.s carrying other troops to minor objectives came in behind. The
M.T.B. torpedoed the lock gates at the entrance to the U-boat basin and com-

pletely scuppered them. Our troops smashed up many installations and killed a good many Germans, but the shore batteries gave us a bad time. We saw ships manœuvring right under their noses to get into position to knock them out. Our petrol tanks were very vulnerable and many blew up. Just as my M.L. was coming alongside I felt the whole ship shudder. The tanks were hit, she was ablaze and adrift and her steering had gone. No, I didn't know it at the time. The naval commander said 'Jump', so I jumped, swam a bit, and was pulled ashore. Some men were blown into the water and got ashore and reached their objectives. Others I never saw again. Many of our men were last seen in blazing wrecks or swimming away from drifts of burning oil. Some reached shore, but others were too badly wounded.

Our colonel, Colonel Newman, managed to get ashore with what was left of his headquarters. The little area of the dock we had to knock out was under heavy fire. The Germans were pretty hysterical at first. Except in the strong battery positions, many ran away, thinking it was the invasion. Many of our men were in action for the first time. It may seem strange to you, but we had been training so long—and often with live ammunition—that honestly, it was hard to believe, in spite of what was happening, that we were on enemy coast. So curious things occurred. One man was clearing a house, for example. A German knocked heads with him as he opened the door; first he apologized, then he remembered himself and shot the German.

Most of us knew that the main task of the operation had been achieved, because we could see the destroyer jammed in the dry dock. And we were pretty clear by now that we weren't going to get back to England. When we collected on the Old Mole for our withdrawal and looked back along the river, the water seemed to be on fire. Ships were sinking in flames and streams of fire were pouring from every side. Troops were on rafts, far out in the river, and we heard some of them singing. There was nothing left, nothing to take us home. I don't know how we ever expected that there could be. The coastal batteries were still blazing away, and managed, among other things, to sink one of their own flak ships; and some German destroyers had got out of the dock into the river.

On shore the Germans had been strongly reinforced. They began to close in on us. The colonel organized a small perimeter to hold off the Germans. In this perimeter he issued orders to fight our way through the town into open country. He led the first party himself, crossing the bridge from the docks to the town under heavy fire, and fighting up the streets. He carried out this operation entirely on his own initiative and this helped to bewilder the Germans —they had brought in several armoured vehicles and they still thought it was an invasion. Another party got through a series of German posts using German phrases we had learnt on training. Some of the ships which came in last did not land. The troops in these ships were disappointed because they had not landed. One of them got several hours clear on the way home. A German destroyer caught up with it and came alongside it in the early morning. The Germans asked if the British commander of the M.L. wanted to surrender. They asked him in perfect English, through the megaphone. As soon as the troops heard it they opened up, although their ship hadn't a chance, using their Brens against the destroyer with her guns. The destroyer replied, but they refused to surrender. The ship was sunk in the end and many of them were killed.

Most of us on shore were caught in the morning hiding in cellars and boiler rooms, waiting for a chance to get away next night. About 10.30 in the morning we heard the hell of an explosion. The Germans panicked, windows all over the town were smashed, and a huge pillar of flame shot up from the dry dock. The explosive in the *Campbeltown* had gone off, and the huge dock gates and the two merchant ships inside had gone for six. So that was that. It was no good for a year after at least. Some Germans were nosing about aboard the destroyer the moment she went up and went up with her. We were told that some of our lads had taken them aboard, but we never knew which of them had done this. I suppose we shall never know their names.

I suppose we shall never know what happened to many of the men who had been training with us for so long. They'd been expecting something of this kind and hoping for it for many months. We were a very small force, not more than two hundred and eighty soldiers and three hundred and fifty navy personnel, though the Germans said there were several thousands. Those of us who have survived were very lucky. We have come home now and we would like to pay some tribute to the ones who have not survived. I don't know if we can do better than the French people did, a few days after the raid, and perhaps the families of the men who were killed would like to know what happened.

Many of the French had fought with us on the night and gone on fighting afterwards. Somehow they got to hear of the time when our dead were going to be buried. A huge crowd collected at the hospital to make a procession and the Germans cancelled the funeral service. They tried to keep the new time secret, but the French found out again, and there were many hundreds of them at the cemetery. It was a military funeral, with full honours. The French broke right through the German cordon of guards and heaped flowers on the graves of the men who had been killed. They gave money and food which they really couldn't afford to those of us who were there, and we shall never forget the risk they took. It was thanks to their help that five of our men managed to get to the Spanish frontier and so home by way of Gibraltar. The rest of us were taken into Germany, and while there we found out that the raid had succeeded. Admiral Mountbatten had told us that the loss of all the ships did not matter so long as the dock was smashed, and smashed it was.

Commando officer

DIEPPE: 19 AUGUST 1942

The raid on Dieppe was the largest single combined operation of its kind undertaken, in which the Commandos took a subsidiary but important part in support of the Canadians, who formed the great bulk of the attacking force.

Early in April 1942 the question of a raid in force on Dieppe was raised and referred to Combined Operations Headquarters. Its main object was to enable the planning staff of the Allies to learn how best to plan for that Second Front in Western Europe without which final victory could not be achieved. There was also a political motive. At that time the situation on the Eastern Front was far from good, and the Russians were clamouring for sufficient action in the West to contain in France at least forty first-line German divisions. In such circumstances, therefore, a raid on a scale much larger than any yet attempted was desirable and, the planners thought, not impracticable.

Canadians at Dieppe

Even before we put to sea some had an ominous feeling about what was ahead of them on the other side of the Channel. Nobody said anything but many were wondering how the security had been in the time since 7 July. Did the Germans know the Canadians were going to France and were they waiting? This was the question being asked in many minds.

They were puzzled, too, why the raid had been decided upon so suddenly. They would have liked more time to adjust themselves.

I shared most of their mental discomfort. For the first hour or so I ran over the plan and studied my maps and photographs and was surprised I had forgotten so much of the detail. I found misgivings growing in my mind. This seemed somewhat haphazard, compared with the serene way in which the cancelled raid was mounted.

The final Dieppe plan was altered only slightly from the one prepared for July. British Commandos were assigned to tasks on the flanks previously allotted to paratroopers.

.... It was one of the finest evenings of the summer. The sea was smooth, the sky was clear and there was the slightest of breezes. The ships cleared and the Royals went to dinner before making their final preparations. In the wardroom, the officers sat around the tables and dined in Navy style, as the last sunshine poured through the open portholes. We had a good meal and everyone ate hungrily, for on the way to the boats all we had had was haversack fare—a few bully-beef sandwiches.

The Royals officers were in good spirits at dinner. Looking around the table you would never have thought that they were facing the biggest test of their lives. They joked and bantered across the tables and renewed old friendships with the naval officers whom they had known in 'practice Dieppe' training days.

.... We were about ten miles from the French coast and until now there hadn't been a hitch in the plan. The minefield was behind us. The boats filled with infantrymen were lowered as the *Emma* stopped and anchored. Nobody spoke. Silence was the strict order but as our boat, which was the largest of the landing craft and was jammed with about eighty soldiers, pushed off from the *Emma*, a veteran sailor leaned over and in a stage whisper said, 'Cheerio, lads, all the best; give the bastards a walloping.' Then we were drifting off into the darkness and our coxswain peered through the night to link up with the rest of our assault flotilla.

.... Eyes were accustomed to the darkness now and we could discern practically all our little craft; the sea was glossy with starlight.

The boats plunged along, curling up white foam at their bows and leaving a phosphorescent wake that stood out like diamonds on black velvet.

We were about seven or eight miles from Dieppe when the first alarm shook us. To our left there was a streak of tracer bullets—light blue and white dots in the night—and the angry clatter of automatic guns. This wasn't according to plan and everyone in that boat of ours tightened up like a drum. We kept our heads down behind the steel bulwark of our little craft, but it was so crowded there that even to crouch was crowding someone beside you. I sat on a cartful of 3-inch mortar bombs. More tracer bullets swept across ahead of us and some pinged off our steel sides. A big sailor by my side rigged his Lewis gun through a slit at the stern of our boat and answered with a few short bursts. A blob in the night that was an enemy ship—an armed trawler or more likely an E-boat—was less than two hundred yards away. It was firing at half a dozen craft including ours, which was in the lead at that time. From other directions came more German tracer. There might have been four ships intercepting us.

There wasn't much we could do. There isn't any armament on these assault craft to engage in a naval action against E-boats or trawlers. Our support craft didn't seem to be about at that particular time. It looked as if we were going to be cut up piecemeal by this interception; our flotilla already had been broken up from the close pattern of two columns we had held before the attack.

I blew up my lifebelt a little more. A few more blasts of tracer whistled past and then there was a great flash and a bang of gun-fire behind us. In the flash we could see one of our destroyers speeding up wide-open to our assistance. It fired a dozen rounds at the enemy ships and they turned and disappeared towards the French coast. They probably went right into Dieppe harbour and spread the word that British landing craft were heading in.

.... Our coxswain tried to take us in to one section of the beach and it proved the wrong spot. Before he grounded he swung the craft out again and we fumbled through the smoke to the small strip of sand which was the Puits beach. The smoke was spotty and the last thirty yards was in the clear. Geysers from artillery shells or mortar bombs shot up in our path. Miraculously we weren't hit by any of them. The din of the German ack-ack guns and machine-guns on the cliff was so deafening you could not hear the man next to you shout.

The men in our boat crouched low, their faces tense and grim. They were awed by this unexpected blast of German fire, and it was their initiation to frightful battle noises. They gripped their weapons more tightly and waited for the ramp of our craft to go down.

We bumped on the beach and down went the ramp and out poured the first infantrymen. They plunged into about two feet of water and machine-gun bullets laced into them. Bodies piled up on the ramp. Some staggered to the beach and fell. Bullets were splattering into the boat itself, wounding and killing our men.

I was near the stern and to one side. Looking out the open bow over the bodies on the ramp, I saw the slope leading a short way up to a stone wall littered with Royals casualties. There must have been sixty or seventy of them, lying sprawled on the green grass and the brown earth. They had been cut down before they had a chance to fire a shot.

A dozen Canadians were running along the edge of the cliff towards the stone wall. They carried their weapons and some were firing as they ran. But some had no helmets, some were already wounded, their uniforms torn and bloody. One by one they were cut down and rolled down the slope to the sea.

I don't know how long we were nosed down on that beach. It may have been five minutes. It may have been twenty. On no other front have I witnessed such a carnage. It was brutal and terrible and shocked you almost to insensibility to see the piles of dead and feel the hopelessness of the attack at this point.

There was one young lad crouching six feet away from me. He had made several vain attempts to rush down the ramp to the beach but each time a hail of fire had driven him back. He had been wounded in the arm but was determined to try again. He lunged forward and a streak of red-white tracer slashed through his stomach.

I'll never forget his anguished cry as he collapsed on the blood-soaked deck: 'Christ, we gotta beat them; we gotta beat them!' He was dead in a few minutes.

.... For the rest of that morning one lost all sense of time and developments in the frantic events of the battle. Although the Puits landing had obviously failed and the headland to the east of Dieppe would still be held by the Germans, I felt that the main attack by three infantry battalions and the tanks had possibly fared better on the beach in front of the town.

Landing craft were moving along the coast in relays and the destroyers were going in perilously close to hit the headlands with shell-fire. I clambered from one landing craft to another to try to learn what was going on. Several times we were bombed too closely by long, black German planes that sailed right through our flak and our fighter cover.

Smoke was laid by destroyers and our planes along the sea and on the beach. Finally the landing craft in which I was at the time, with some naval ratings, touched down on the sloping pebble main beach which ran about sixty yards at that point to a high sea wall and the Esplanade, with the town beyond.

Smoke was everywhere and under its cover several of our ratings ran on to the beach and picked up two casualties by the barbed wire on the beach, lugging them back to the boat. I floundered through the loose shale to the sea-wall. There was heavy machine-gun fire down the beach towards the Casino. A group of men crouched twenty yards away under the shelter of the sea-wall.

The tobacco factory was blazing fiercely. For a moment there was no firing. It was one of those brief lulls you get in any battle. I thought our infantry were thick in the town but the Esplanade looked far too bare and empty.

There was no beach organization as there should have been. Some dead lay by the wall and on the shale. The attack here had not gone as planned either. A string of mortar bombs whanged on the Esplanade. The naval ratings waved and I lunged back to the boat as the beach battle opened up again. In choking smoke we pulled back to the boat pool.

.... Then the German air force struck with its most furious attack of the day. All morning long, British and Canadian fighters kept a constant patrol over the ships and the beaches, whole squadrons twisting and curling in the blue, cloud-flecked sky. Hundreds of other planes swept far over northern France, intercepting enemy fighters and bombers long before they reached Dieppe. Reconnaissance planes kept a constant lookout on the roads from Amiens and Abbeville and Rouen where reinforcements could be expected. There were air combats going on practically all morning long. It was the greatest air show since the Battle of Britain in the fall of 1940, and the R.A.F. and R.C.A.F. had overwhelming superiority. The High Command had hoped the German air force would be lured into the sky and most of the enemy strength in western Europe came up.

. . . Bullets screeched in every direction. The whole sky and sea had gone mad with the confusion of that sudden air attack, and a dozen times I clung to the bottom of the boat expecting that this moment was the last as we were cannoned or another stick of bombs churned the sea.

Several landing craft near us blew up, hit by bombs and cannon shells. There was nothing left. They just disintegrated. These craft had been trying to make the main beach again, as we had been, to take off troops on the withdrawal.

Ross Munro, Canadian War Correspondent

On the Ships

At about that time, within a minute or two of a quarter-past one o'clock, a JU88, hard pressed by fighters of the R.A.F., jettisoned a heavy bomb in a vain attempt to escape destruction, and sank the destroyer *Berkeley* with this single chance blow. The bomb struck slightly forward of amidships, destroying the bridge and wrecking the wardroom. The boiler-room and engine-room were at once flooded, and *Berkeley* broke her back.

Wing Commander S. H. Skinner, R.A.F., Observer of Combined Operations Headquarters, had been standing on the bridge at the side of Lieutenant I. J. S. Yorke, R.N., in command of *Berkeley*. Both were killed. A third man, Lieutenant-Colonel L. B. Hillsinger, of the U.S. Army Air Corps, was blown off the bridge to the forward deck, where he sat staring in anger and consternation at the place where his right foot had been. The foot, with the shoe still on it, could be seen floating a few yards from the sinking destroyer.

The vessel was at that moment alive with furious activity, with sailors running to aid the wounded and to the rescue of others who were trapped below. Two sailors came at once to the aid of the American colonel, and his behaviour impressed itself deeply upon them, even in their urgency. The colonel continued to sit up, staring alternately at his right stump and at his missing foot wearing the shoe. Suddenly with a gesture of intense irritation he tore the shoe from his good left foot and flung it after the other into the water.

'Take the goddam pair!'

The colonel turned then to the sailors.

'New shoes,' he said. 'Bought them this week. First time on. What d'you know!' He seemed unaware of pain.

One of the steam gunboats had at once come to the rescue, and was swiftly alongside the sinking destroyer, while *Albrighton* stood by. There was little time to lose, and the last of the wounded were transhipped within ten minutes.

By that time surgical dressings were getting scarce, but the naval medical personnel helped by R.C.A.M.C. did their best to make the wounded comfortable. Lieutenant-Colonel Hillsinger declined all but the treatment necessary to save his life. He refused injections. He refused a bunk, and insisted on lying out on the deck of the gunboat looking up at the sky.

'I'm meant to be observing this air battle,' he said.

Commandos at Dieppe

One question worried all of us in those last silent twenty minutes after the long, cramped voyage in the starlight. Would the Germans be ready for us? Thinking of it made my stomach flutter. I remembered that old R.A.F. saying, 'I had kittens', and suddenly knew what it meant. But I hung, in my rising funk,. on to the thought that 'the other bastards' were twice as scared as me.

The sergeant, still peering ahead from the back centre seat, began a whispered running commentary:

'About five hundred yards now. . . . See the cliffs? . . . There's the crack we want. . . . Look at the Jerry tracer-bullets. Don't think they're firing at us, though.... A hundred yards now.... Fifty.... God, there's a bloke on the cliff!'

Our question was answered. Throwing back my head, I could just make out a figure, silhouetted for an instant in the half-light.

Anderson, beside me, gave a little jerk, screwed up his face, and said: 'Blast! I've got cramp. Hell, damn and blast! I've got cramp.'

'All right,' I whispered. 'Take it easy. Nothing you can do. It'll pass.'

That was the worst moment, as we all said afterwards. The assault craft grounded, nosed a little to port, grounded again, and stayed put.

With great self-control, Anderson sat quite still while the ramp dropped and the forward men shuffled out on to the beach. By the time our turn came, his cramp had passed.

Just ahead of us the Frenchman, who had been bobbing up and down with excitement, stepped ashore muttering, '*C'est drôle.*' He had not been back since Dunkirk.

We had grounded on the shingle at full tide, a few yards from the foot of the cold-looking, unscalable, hundred-foot, overhanging chalk-white cliffs. As we blundered, bending, across the shingle to the cliff foot, a German machine-gun began to stutter from up above.

The Oerlikon guns from our support craft answered. Red-hot tracer bullets flashed past each other between cliff-top and sea, looking vicious and surprisingly slow, like the lighted matches boys flick across a room.

But for the moment we were under cover, brought in at the exact spot at exactly the appointed time—4.50 a.m.—by the sound seamanship of the Navy.

At the same moment the other half of 4 Commando, led by Lord Lovat himself, had made their landing a little farther west. They were beginning their movement across the low ground, and past the cottages and farms of Le Haut, to take the battery in the rear, while our forces, covered by mortar fire, made the frontal attack.

We found in the first few minutes that the crack in the cliffs to the left, nearest Dieppe, was so crammed full of barbed wire that we would not have time to risk it. The second crack, a little to the right, ended in an almost vertical beach staircase for holiday bathers and fishermen, about twenty feet wide between walls of chalk. Above that was a long gully, just as narrow as its bottom, running back to the woods and fields.

Had the Germans prepared their defences properly, we would not have had a chance. One platoon with a machine-gun could have held it against a fair-sized army. But the Commando leaders knew there was just a chance that the Germans would not believe anyone could be fool enough to try such a suicidal approach.

I waited at the foot of the cliff with the signallers, just round the corner from the crack. A pioneer section from A Troop (Commandos have troops, not .companies) were at the top of the stairs, thrusting their long, pipe-like bangalore torpedoes under the two banks of barbed wire. They lit the fuse and dodged back under cover.

In a few seconds we heard the bang, muffled by the cliffs, but still loud enough to make your head ring.

'And now,' I thought, 'the Germans will be really roused, and that gully will be impossible.'

But no. The Commando spearhead, scrambling through the chalk rubble, the smashed concrete and the flattened wire, and followed by the mortar platoon, were creeping cautiously up the gully.

At that moment the howitzers fired—a dull, hollow sound like an explosion in a quarry. The noise depressed me for a moment. It hadn't been the perfect surprise, after all. They might wreck our main force.

The light had grown just enough for their observers to spot craft a fair way out to sea. I watched the splashes and felt a little cheered. They were just spouts of water, not the smoke and steam of hits. Perhaps we'd be in time yet.

For a few minutes, as I sat by the signallers' portable wireless set, waiting for the spearhead troop to report back, I could see the soaring fireworks across the Dieppe approaches.

The naval bombardment of Dieppe, timed for twenty minutes after our landing, had begun. The shore batteries and all the light German guns were replying. The sky was scored with the slow tracks of incendiary shells, and the Dieppe basin was beginning to rumble and thud like the explosive growling of a volcano crater.

A formation of four-cannon Hurricanes dived out of the sky on to the cliffs above us, spitting fire at the machine-gun posts, and at the two German flak-guns to left and right of our position. The gun-flashes of the Hurricanes, coming in head on, made them look as if they were being pulled through the air by blades of flame instead of propellers.

Boston bombers, higher up, hurried across the coast on their way to strafe the German guns nearer Dieppe. Commando troopers beside me waved and shouted, 'Give them hell!' They were excited and pleased by their first sight of air support.

.... An explosion in front of us, louder and longer than anything we had heard that morning, made us crouch suddenly. It seemed to be the father and mother of all explosions, far louder than the biggest bomb I had heard in the London blitz.

We waited by the mortar battery wondering what had happened, and ducking when the shells from a German mortar, somewhere beyond the woods, came a little too near.

Presently Major Mills Roberts, Irish Guardsman, the leader of our part of the Commando force, came back through the trees, grinning with pleasure.

'We've got their ammunition dump,' he said. 'Mortar-shell bang on top of it. Bloody fools!—they'd got their ammunition all in one lot. Must have been drunk with power.'

'Doc. You'd better get your stretcher-bearers up the road quickly. There's a badly wounded man not far off.'

A few minutes later I was running down the cliff gully again with another message to pass to England.

It read, 'Battery demolished 06.50.'

A. B. Austin, war correspondent

German War Diary, H.Q. C.-in-C. West: 19 August

17.40 hours: No armed Englishman remains on the Continent.

The Cost

Of the 4,963 all ranks of the Canadian Army embarked, 2,211 returned to England; 589 of these were wounded but survived, while in twenty-eight cases wounds proved mortal. No less than 1,944 Canadian officers and men, however, became prisoners of war, at least 558 of them wounded. At Dieppe, from a force of fewer than five thousand men engaged for only nine hours, the Canadian Army lost more prisoners than in the whole eleven months of the later campaign in North-West Europe, or the twenty months during which Canadians fought in Italy. Sadder still was the loss in killed. As now computed, the total of fatal casualties was fifty-six officers and 851 other ranks; these include seven officers and sixty-four other ranks who died in captivity. Canadian casualties of all categories aggregated 3,369. Of the seven major Canadian units engaged, only one (Les Fusiliers Mont-Royal) brought its commanding officer back to England. Little was left of 4 Brigade, not much more of the 6th. Months of hard work were required before 2 Division became again the fine formation that had assaulted the beaches.

Dieppe served also to confirm the Germans in the belief that a basic consideration in the Allies' minds at the very outset of an invasion would be the capture of a major port, and thus encouraged them to devote their best efforts to developing heavy defences about such places. Thus the Germans were, as a result of the raid, centring their defence upon the ports when simultaneously the Allies, also in part as a result of the raid, were increasingly turning their attention to the possibility of invading over open beaches without immediately gaining a major port. The great conception of the prefabricated harbour owes something to the lessons learned at Dieppe concerning the difficulty of capturing a German-held port.

Hitler's Commando Order: 18 October 1942

For some time our enemies have been using, in their warfare, methods which are outside the International Geneva Conventions. Especially brutal and treacherous is the behaviour of the so-called Commandos, who, as is established, are partially recruited even from freed criminals in enemy countries. From captured orders it is divulged that they are directed not only to shackle prisoners, but also to kill defenceless prisoners on the spot at the moment in which they believe that the latter, as prisoners, represent a burden in the further pursuit of their purposes, or could otherwise be a hindrance. Finally, orders have been found in which the killing of prisoners has been demanded in principle.

I therefore order:

From now on all enemies on so-called Commando missions in Europe or Africa, challenged by German troops, even if they are to all appearances soldiers in uniform or demolition troops, whether armed or unarmed, in battle or in flight, are to be slaughtered to the last man. It does not make any difference whether they are landed from ships and aircraft for their actions, or whether they are dropped by parachute. Even if these individuals, when found, should apparently be prepared to give themselves up, no pardon is to be granted them on principle. In each individual case full information is to be sent to the O.K.W. for publication in the Report of the Military Forces.

If individual members of such Commandos, such as agents, saboteurs, etc., fall into the hands of the military forces by some other means, through the police in occupied territories, for instance, they are to be handed over immediately to the S.D. Any imprisonment under military guard, in P.W. stockades, for instance, etc., is strictly prohibited, even if this is only intended for a short time.

I will hold responsible under Military Law, for failing to carry out this order, all commanders and officers who either have neglected their duty of instructing the troops about this order, or acted against this order when it was to be executed.

This order is intended for commanders only and must not, under any circumstances, fall into enemy hands.

Adolf Hitler

THE OTHER SIDE OF THE HILL

The Commando idea suited Britain's war, in which manpower needed to be conserved and a long and vulnerable enemy-held coastline close by invited attack. The American Army faced totally different strategic problems in which raids by means of combined operations had comparatively little place, though the Rangers and other units became justly famous. Of the Axis powers, Germany was the only one to produce a comparable fighting force. This was led by Otto Skorzeny, whose most brilliant feat was the rescue of Mussolini after his arrest and imprisonment by the Italians in 1943.

Adolf Hitler to Captain Otto Skorzeny: 26 July 1943

I have a very important commission for you. Mussolini, my friend and our loyal comrade in arms, was betrayed yesterday by his king and arrested by his own countrymen. I cannot and will not leave Italy's greatest son in the lurch. To me the Duce is the incarnation of the ancient grandeur of Rome. Italy under the new government will desert us! I will keep faith with my old ally and dear friend; he must be rescued promptly or he will be handed over to the Allies.

Skorzeny lays his Plans

My own handful of Intelligence people now brought me the news—amounting to practical certainty—that Benito Mussolini was held in a mountain hotel in the Campo Imperatore (Gran Sasso *massif*) and was guarded by a Carabiniere unit.

.... A ground operation seemed hopeless from the start. An attack up the steep, rocky slopes would have cost us very heavy losses, apart from giving good notice to the enemy and leaving them time to conceal their prisoner. To forestall that eventuality the whole *massif* would have to be surrounded by good mountain troops. A division at least would be required. So a ground operation was ruled out.

The factor of surprise could be our only trump as it was to be feared that the prisoner's guards had orders to kill him if there was any danger of rescue. This supposition later also proved well founded. Such an order could only be frustrated by a lightning intervention.

There remained only two alternatives—parachute landings or gliders.

We pondered long over both and then decided in favour of the second. At such altitudes, and in the thin air, a parachute drop would involve too rapid a rate of descent for anyone equipped with the normal parachute only. We also feared that in this rocky region the parachutists would get scattered too widely, so that an immediate attack by a compact detachment would not be possible.

So a glider landing remained the only solution.

.... After this decision had been given, Radl and I worked out the details of our plan. We had to make careful calculations of the distances, make up our minds as to what arms and equipment the men should carry and, above all, prepare a large-scale plan showing the exact landing-place for each of the twelve gliders. Each glider could take ten men, i.e. a group, in addition to the pilot. Each group must know exactly what it had to do. I decided that I would go myself in the third glider so that the immediate assault by my own and the fourth group could be covered by the two groups already landed.

At the conclusion of these labours we spent a little time discussing our chances. We did not bluff ourselves that they were other than very slim. No one could really say whether Mussolini was still on the mountain and would not be spirited away elsewhere before we arrived. There was the further question whether we could overpower the guards quickly enough to prevent anyone killing him first, and we had not forgotten the warning given by the staff officers.

We must, in any event, allow for casualties in the landings. Even without any casualties we should only be 108 men and they could not all be available at the same moment. They would have to tackle a hundred and fifty Italians, who knew the ground perfectly, and could use the hotel as a fortress. In weapons the two opponents could be regarded as approximately equal, as our parachutists' tommy-guns gave us an advantage, compensating to some extent for the enemy's superiority in numbers, particularly if we had not suffered too badly at the outset.

12 September 1943

I glanced at my watch. One o'clock! I gave the signal to start. The engines began to roar and we were soon gliding along the tarmac and then rising into the air. We were off.

We slowly gained altitude in wide circles and the procession of gliders set course towards the north-east. The weather seemed almost ideal for our purpose. Vast banks of white cloud hung lazily at about three thousand metres. If they did not disperse we should reach our target practically unobserved and drop out of the sky before anyone realized we were there.

The interior of the glider was most unpleasantly hot and stuffy. I suddenly noticed that the corporal sitting behind me was being sick and that the general in front had turned as green as his uniform. Flying obviously did not suit him; he certainly was not enjoying himself. The pilot reported our position as best he could and I carefully followed his indications on my map, noting when we passed over Tivoli. From the inside of the glider we could see little of the country. The cellophane side-windows were too thick and the gaps in the fabric (of which there were many) too narrow to give us any view. The German glider, type DFS 230, comprised a few steel members covered with canvas. We were somewhat backward in this field, I reflected, thinking enviously of an elegant aluminium frame.

We thrust through a thick bank of clouds to reach the altitude of three thousand five hundred metres which had been specified. For a short time we were in a dense grey world, seeing nothing of our surroundings, and then we emerged into bright sunshine, leaving the clouds below us. At that moment the pilot of our towing machine, a Hentschel, came through on the telephone to the commander of my glider: 'Flights One and Two no longer ahead of us! Who's to take over the lead now?'

This was bad news. What had happened to them? At that time I did not know that I also had only seven machines instead of nine behind me. Two had fallen foul of a couple of bomb craters at the very start. I had a message put through: 'We'll take over the lead ourselves!'

I got out my knife and slashed right and left in the fabric to make a hole big enough to give us something of a view. I changed my mind about our old-fashioned glider. At least it was made of something we could cut!

My peephole was enough to let us get our bearings when the cloud permitted. We had to be very smart in picking up bridges, roads, river bends and other geographical features on our maps. Even so, we had to correct our course from time to time. Our excursion should not fail through going astray. I did not dwell on the thought that we should be without covering fire when we landed.

It was just short of zero-hour when I recognized the valley of Aquila below us and also the leading vehicles of our own formation hastening along it. It would clearly be at the right place at the right time, though it must certainly have had its troubles, too. We must not fail it!

'Helmets on!' I shouted as the hotel, our destination, came in sight and then: 'Slip the tow-ropes!' My words were followed by a sudden silence, broken only by the sound of the wind rushing past. The pilot turned in a wide circle, searching the ground—as I was doing—for the flat meadow appointed as our landing-ground. But a further, and ghastly, surprise was in store for us. It was triangular all right, but so far from being flat it was a steep, a very steep hillside! It could even have been a ski-jump.

. . . . I called out, 'Crash landing! As near to the hotel as you can get!' The pilot, not hesitating for a second, tilted the starboard wing and down we came with a rush. I wondered for a moment whether the glider could take the strain in the thin air, but there was little time for speculation. With the wind shrieking in our ears we approached our target. I saw Lieutenant Meyer release the para-chute brake, and then followed a crash and the noise of shattering wood. I closed my eyes and stopped thinking. One last mighty heave, and we came to rest.

The bolt of the exit hatch had been wrenched away, the first man was out like a shot and I let myself fall sideways out of the glider, clutching my weapons. We were within fifteen metres of the hotel! We were surrounded by jagged rocks of all sizes, which may have nearly smashed us up but had also acted as a brake so that we had taxied barely twenty metres. The parachute brake now folded up immediately behind the glider.

The first Italian sentry was standing on the edge of a slight rise at one corner of the hotel. He seemed lost in amazement. I had no time to bother about our Italian passenger, though I had noticed him falling out of the glider at my side, but rushed straight into the hotel. I was glad that I had given the order that no one must fire a shot before I did. It was essential that the surprise should be complete. I could hear my men panting behind me. I knew that they were the pick of the bunch and would stick to me like glue and ask no explanations.

We reached the hotel. All the surprised and shocked sentry required was a shout of 'mani in alto' (hands up). Passing through an open door, we spotted an Italian soldier engaged in using a wireless set. A hasty kick sent his chair flying from under him and a few hearty blows from my machine-pistol wrecked his apparatus. On finding that the room had no exit into the interior of the hotel we hastily retraced our steps and went outside again.

We raced along the façade of the building and round the corner, to find our-selves faced with a terrace two and a half to three metres high. Corporal Himmel offered me his back and I was up and over in a trice. The others followed in a bunch.

My eyes swept the façade and lit on a well-known face at one of the windows of the first storey. It was the Duce! Now I knew that our effort had not been in vain! I yelled at him, 'Away from the window!' and we rushed into the entrance hall, colliding with a lot of Italian soldiers pouring out. Two machine-guns were set up on the floor of the terrace. We jumped over them and put them out of action. The Carabinieri continued to stream out and it took a few far from gentle blows from my weapon to force a way through them. My men yelled out, 'Mani in alto.' So far no one had fired a shot.

I was now well inside the hall. I could not look round or bother about what was happening behind me. On the right was a staircase. I leaped up it three steps at a time, turned left along a corridor and flung open a door on the right. It was a happy choice. Mussolini and two Italian officers were standing in the middle of the room. I thrust them aside and made them stand with their backs to the door. In a moment my *Untersturmführer* Schwerdt appeared. He took in the situation in a glance and jostled the mightily surprised Italian officers out of the room and into the corridor. The door closed behind us.

We had succeeded in the first part of our venture. The Duce was safely in our hands. Not more than three or four minutes had passed since we arrived!

At that moment the heads of Holzer and Benz, two of my subordinates, appeared at the window. They had not been able to force their way through the crowd in the hall and so had been compelled to join me via the lightning-conductor. There was no question of my men leaving me in the lurch. I sent them to guard the corridor.

I went to the window and saw Radl and his S.S. men running towards the hotel. Behind them crawled *Obersturmführer* Menzel, the company commander of our Friedenthal special unit and in charge of glider No. 4 behind me. His glider had grounded about a hundred metres from the hotel and he had broken his ankle on landing. The third group in glider No. 5 also arrived while I was watching.

I shouted out, 'Everything's all right! Mount guard everywhere!'

I stayed a little while longer to watch gliders 6 and 7 crash-land with Lieutenant Berlepsch and his parachute company. Then before my very eyes followed a tragedy. Glider 8 must have been caught in a gust; it wobbled and then fell like a stone, landed on a rocky slope and was smashed to smithereens.

Sounds of firing could now be heard in the distance and I put my head into the corridor and shouted for the officer-in-command at the hotel. A colonel appeared from nearby and I summoned him to surrender forthwith, assuring him that any further resistance was useless. He asked me for time to consider the matter. I gave him one minute, during which Radl turned up. He had had to fight his way through and I assumed that the Italians were still holding the entrance, as no one had joined us.

The Italian colonel returned, carrying a goblet of red wine which he proffered to me with a slight bow and the words: 'To the victor!'

A white bedspread, hung from the window, performed the functions of a white flag.

After giving a few orders to my men outside the hotel I was able to devote attention to Mussolini, who was standing in a corner with *Untersturmführer* Schwerdt in front of him. I introduced myself: 'Duce, the Führer has sent me! You are free!'

Mussolini embraced me: 'I knew my friend Adolf Hitler would not leave me in the lurch,' he said.

Otto Skorzeny

The Uses of the Duce

A few hours later the Duce was in Vienna. Just before calling me the Führer had had a telephone conversation with him. He told me that the Duce was deeply shaken by developments. He informed the Führer that he was tired and sick and would first of all like to have a long sleep. On Monday he wanted to visit his family in Munich. We shall soon see whether he is still capable of large-scale political activity. The Führer thinks so. At any rate he will meet Mussolini at G.H.Q. on Tuesday.

However much I may be touched on the human side by the Duce's liberation, I am nevertheless sceptical about its political advantages. With the Duce out of the way, we had a chance to wipe the slate clean in Italy. Without any restraint, and basing our action on the grandiose treachery of the Badoglio régime, we could force a solution of all our problems regarding Italy.

To me it had seemed that, besides South Tyrol, our boundary ought to include Venetia. That will hardly be possible if the Duce re-enters politics. It will be very difficult for us even to put in our claim for South Tyrol. Under the leadership of the Duce, assuming he becomes active again, Italy will attempt to start a national rump government, towards which we shall have obligations in many respects. Both the English and ourselves could hack the Badoglio régime to pieces. A régime under the leadership of the Duce would presumably fall heir to all the rights and duties incident to the Three-Power Pact. A rather distressing prospect!

Dr. Goebbels

18

EL ALAMEIN

A STONY, waterless desert where bleak outcrops of dry rock alternated with stretches of sand sparsely clotted with camel-scrub beneath the pitiless African sun—such was the Alamein front in July of 1942. Lying between the rocky hillock of Tel el Eisa on the Mediterranean coast and the six-hundred-foot pyramid of Qaret el Hemeimat near the edge of the Qattara depression, it was the one position in the whole of the Western Desert which could not be out-flanked.

General Bayerlein, Afrika Korps

Early in August 1942, *the retreat to the Alamein Line and the state of the Eighth Army made Winston Churchill determine that changes of command must be made, despite the resolution which General Auchinleck had displayed in resisting the hard blows of Rommel. The new commander of the theatre was to be General Alexander and the new commander of the Eighth Army General Montgomery.*

1. Your prime and main duty will be to take or destroy at the earliest opportunity the German-Italian Army commanded by Field-Marshal Rommel, together with all its supplies and establishments in Egypt and Libya.

2. You will discharge or cause to be discharged such other duties as pertain to your Command, without prejudice to the task described in paragraph 1, which must be considered paramount to His Majesty's interests.

Winston Churchill to General Alexander

The New Broom

I believe it was in the second week in August that we were visited by the Prime Minister, the C.I.G.S. (now Lord Alanbrooke) and others. I think they only spent one day in the Desert, but it was a very full one. They saw and spoke with the senior commanders and saw a number of troops. They no doubt obtained a pretty accurate 'feel' of the state of the Eighth Army. Auchinleck had a long discussion with them, and went over the maps and future plans in his map lorry. Churchill was naturally eager for another offensive and wanted it soon. He was off to Moscow, and so this was important. The Commander-in-Chief would not promise anything very quickly—and how right he was. I thought perhaps he was a bit abrupt in the way he refused to be drawn over this matter. I remember noticing that the Prime Minister did not like this attitude, but he was an admirer of the 'Auk' and had been lavish in his praise for the way he had pulled the November offensive out of the fire.

Either the next day or the day after Auchinleck was summoned to Cairo. He appeared, I thought, a little worried before he left, but returned full of hope and heart. We went for our usual stroll that evening, and he discussed with the greatest enthusiasm our plans. Considerable reinforcements and new equipment were promised, and it now looked as if before many weeks were over we would be in a position to assume the offensive.

The next day one of the Prime Minister's staff came up during the afternoon with a letter. I guessed what it might contain. The Commander-in-Chief was very quiet at dinner, and afterwards asked me to come for a walk. He put his arm in mine and said, 'Freddie, I'm to go.'

. . . . It was a hot and sultry morning, and as I drove towards Alexandria I experienced considerable excitement. I was, of course, delighted that Montgomery had been selected, but I did not expect I should remain long in office. It was only natural that he (Montgomery) would bring out his own Chief of Staff. I was looking forward to the meeting, for I knew at the very least it would be exhilarating.

I arrived at the crossroads, and had only been there five minutes when his car turned up, and after a characteristic greeting with a wave of the hand, he asked me to jump in beside him, and off we started for the Ruweisat Ridge.

Montgomery was full of spirit and looking very fit. He said, 'Well, Freddie, you chaps seem to have been making a bit of a mess of things. Now what's the form?' I rather nervously tendered my paper, but he thrust it back, saying, 'I don't like reading papers, tell me about it.' I spent some time running through the various points, and then answered numerous questions. He then said, 'I was only told I was coming out here in London forty-eight hours ago, but I have been doing a lot of thinking since. Yesterday I spent at G.H.Q., Cairo, and worked out with Harding* how I want this Army organized. You'll never win a campaign as it is at the moment.'

He then went through his proposals for the future. It was extraordinary how he had spotted most of the weaknesses even before his arrival. And he gave out his ideas to a gathering of all the Headquarters Staff officers that very evening as the sun was setting below the Ruweisat Ridge. On arrival at the Headquarters —I saw at once that he didn't like the look of it—he said, 'I want to speak to all the staff.' I asked 'When sir?' 'Why, this evening of course,' was the reply. I had to get busy, as they had to be summoned from far and wide, but we just got them there in time.

Major-General Sir Francis de Guingand

It was clear to me that the situation was quite unreal and, in fact, dangerous. I decided at once to take action. I had been ordered not to take over command of the Eighth Army till 15 August; it was still only the 13th. I knew it was useless to consult G.H.Q. and that I must take full responsibility myself. I told General Ramsden he was to return at once to his corps; he seemed surprised as he had been placed in acting command of the Army, but he went. I then had lunch, with the flies and in the hot sun. During lunch I did some savage thinking. After lunch I wrote a telegram to G.H.Q. saying that I had assumed command of Eighth Army as from 2 p.m. that day, 13 August; this was disobedience,

---

* Now Lieutenant-General Sir John Harding, who was then a D.C.G.S. at Cairo, dealing with organization, training and equipment.

but there was no come-back. I then cancelled all previous orders about withdrawal.

I issued orders that in the event of enemy attack there would be *no* withdrawal; we would fight on the ground we now held and if we couldn't stay
there alive we would stay there dead.

General Montgomery

The new Army Commander made himself felt at once. I saw him first when
he called, unannounced, a few days after his arrival. He talked sharply and
curtly, without any soft words, asked some searching questions, met the battalion commanders, and left me feeling very much stimulated. For a long time
we had heard little from Army except querulous grumbles that the men should
not go about without their shirts on, that staff officers must always wear the
appropriate arm-bands, or things of that sort. Now we were told that we were
going to fight, there was no question of retirement to any reserve positions or
anywhere else, and to get ahead with our preparations. To make the intention
clear our troop-carrying transport was sent a long way back so that we could not
run away if we wanted to!

Brigadier Kippenberger

Rommel's final thrust was still awaited.

Alam Halfa

My orders from Alexander were quite simple; they were to destroy Rommel
and his army. I understood Rommel was expected to attack *us* shortly. If he
came soon it would be tricky, if he came in a week, all right, but give us two
weeks and Rommel could do what he liked; he would be seen off and then it
would be our turn. But I had no intention of launching *our* attack until we were
ready; when that time came we would hit Rommel for six right out of Africa.

.... It was soon pretty clear to me, after talking with de Guingand, that all
indications pointed to an early attack by Rommel; he would make a last attempt
to get to Cairo and Alexandria, and secure the Delta. It was evident that, if so,
he would probably make his main effort on the south or inland flank, and would
then carry out a right hook in order to get in behind the Eighth Army.

He could not leave the Army intact and pass on towards the flesh-pots of
Egypt; he must first destroy the Eighth Army, after which the flesh-pots were
all his for the asking.

General Montgomery

The Army Commander carried out a very detailed examination of the whole
front to decide how he would fight the defensive battle. The new policy meant
that a great deal of ammunition and supplies had to be moved to the forward
area, so that the troops there could fight in their present positions for a long
period. He appreciated at once that the Alam Halfa ridge was of vital importance,
but was virtually undefended. The ridge was in rear of the Alamein Line and

commanded a large area of desert, and was undoubtedly a key to the whole defensive system. Any 'right hook' by Rommel must capture this feature to be successful. No troops were available within the Army, and so he asked that 44 Division, which had recently arrived in Egypt, should be sent up. The story of the move of this division will give an idea of the change of tempo.

Before Montgomery's arrival G.H.Q. had said that 44 Division would not be available until the end of August at the earliest. Montgomery told me one evening at 5 or 6 p.m. to phone to Cairo and say he required the Division *at once*. I got on to the staff at G.H.Q. and was told that this was quite impossible, but that they would try and get elements of the Division moving in a few days' time. I reported this to the Army Commander. He seized the phone and had a few minutes' talk to Alexander. Later that night I was rung up and told that the division would start moving that night, and it arrived up complete, I believe, in a couple of days. This insistence probably helped considerably in repelling Rommel's attack at the end of the month.

Major-General Sir Francis de Guingand

I had pondered deeply over what I had heard about armoured battles in the desert and it seemed to me that what Rommel liked was to get our armour to attack him; he then disposed of his own armour behind a screen of anti-tank guns, knocked out our tanks, and finally had the field to himself. I was determined that would not happen if Rommel decided to attack us before we were ready to launch a full-scale offensive against him. I would not allow our tanks to rush out at him; we would stand firm in the Alamein position, hold the Ruweisat and Alam Halfa Ridges securely, and let him beat up against them. We would fight a static battle and my forces would not move; his tanks would come up against our tanks dug-in in hull-down positions at the western edge of the Alam Halfa Ridge.

During the day I met on the southern flank the general commanding 7 Armoured Division, the famous Desert Rats. We discussed the expected attack by Rommel and he said there was only one question to be decided: who would loose the armour against Rommel? He thought he himself should give the word for that to happen. I replied that no one would loose the armour; it would not be loosed and we would let Rommel bump into it for a change. This was a new idea to him and he argued about it a good deal.

When I got back to my headquarters that night the outline of my immediate plans for strengthening the Alamein position was clear in my mind. I was determined to make the position so strong that we would begin our preparations for our own great offensive and not become preoccupied by any attack that Rommel might decide to make. All information seemed to suggest that he would attack towards the end of the month in the full moon period; I wanted to begin my preparations for the battle of Alamein before then, and to continue those preparations whatever Rommel might do.

Therefore we must be strong, with our forces so 'balanced' that I need never react to his thrusts or moves: strong enough to see him off without disrupting the major preparations. That was my object.

General Montgomery

Rommel attacked the Alam Halfa position during the night of 30 August; by 5 September he had been met, held and repulsed. The final thrust upon Egypt had failed. The Eighth Army was now set to its preparations for attack.

Plan and Preparation

I was watching the training carefully and it was becoming apparent to me that the Eighth Army was very untrained. The need for training had never been stressed. Most commanders had come to the fore by skill in fighting and because no better were available; many were above their ceiling, and few were good trainers. By the end of September there were serious doubts in my mind whether the troops would be able to do what was being demanded; the plan was simple but it was too ambitious. If I was not careful, divisions and units would be given tasks which might end in failure because of the inadequate standard of training. The Eighth Army had suffered some eighty thousand casualties since it was formed, and little time had been spent in training the replacements.

The moment I saw what might happen I took a quick decision. On 6 October, just over two weeks before the battle was to begin, I changed the plan. My initial plan had been based on destroying Rommel's armour; the remainder of his army, the un-armoured portion, could then be dealt with at leisure. This was in accordance with the accepted military thinking of the day. I decided to reverse the process and thus alter the whole conception of how the battle was to be fought. My modified plan now was to hold off, or contain, the enemy armour while we carried out a methodical destruction of the infantry divisions holding the defensive system. These unarmoured divisions would be destroyed by means of a 'crumbling' process, the enemy being attacked from the flank and rear and cut off from their supplies. These operations would be carefully organized from a series of firm bases and would be within the capabilities of my troops.

General Montgomery

Large scale rehearsals for the coming battle were carried out, and the lessons learnt gone into very carefully by the commanders. And by the end of the third week in October we began to realize that all these vast preparations were successfully reaching their conclusion. From the staff point of view there was a healthy slackening in the tempo of work, denoting that the stage was set.

Montgomery had been indefatigable, and had satisfied himself that all was in readiness. He very rightly had decided that in order to get the best out of his troops it was necessary for them to know the whole plan so that they would realize how their particular contribution fitted in with the general scheme.

On 19 and 20 October he addressed all officers down to lieutenant-colonel level in XXX, XIII and X Corps. It was a real *tour de force*. These talks were some of the best he has ever given. Clear and full of confidence. I warrant there were no doubters after he had finished. He touched on the enemy situation, stressed his weaknesses, but was certain a long 'dog-fight' or 'killing match' would take place for several days—'it might be ten'. He then gave details of our great strength, our tanks, our guns and the enormous supplies of ammunition available. He drummed in the need never to lose the initiative, and how every-one—*everyone*—must be imbued with the burning desire to 'kill Germans'. 'Even the padres—one per weekday and two on Sundays!' This produced a roar. He explained how the battle was to be fought, and finished by saying that he was entirely and utterly confident of the result.

The men were let into the secret on 21 and 22 October, from which date no leave was granted. And, as a result of everything, a tremendous state of en-thusiasm was produced. I have never felt anything like it. Those soldiers just knew they were going to succeed.

Major-General Sir Francis de Guingand

In the open desert the possibilities of concealment were negligible, and it was impossible to disguise from the enemy the fact that the Eighth Army was preparing a major thrust. But nevertheless the army's camouflage experts were called upon for a deception plan on a vast scale—first to disguise from the enemy the full extent of the build-up of troops, weapons and stores, and second to convince him that the expected thrust was to come in the south instead of the north.

From the enemy's point of view on that morning of 22 October 1942, 'Martello' must have looked precisely as he had become accustomed to seeing it for the past few weeks—a fairly dense concentration of thin-skinned vehicles with nothing specially menacing about it. Down in the south, he could see that the new pipe-line was finished. He could put his own interpretation on the recent dumping of thousands of tons of petrol, ammunition and food, and on the appreciable massing of artillery at Munassib. In the Staging Areas, astride the system of tracks leading southwards, he could still see the whole array of our armour and take what comfort he could from the fact that so long as it stood there he still had some days of grace. The blow could hardly fall for another two days, or even three. In the north? Some new and possibly disquieting tracks leading up to the front? Yes—but in the absence of any appreciable increase of dumping or any massing of guns, might not these new tracks be a clumsy attempt to deceive? On the whole, the visible emphasis leaned towards the south.

And in reality? All the 'armour' in the Staging Areas, the 'guns', the 'dumps', and the 'pipe-line' in the south were stick and string, tin and canvas. Four hundred 25-pounders were in their barrage positions in 'Cannibal 2', ready to cast away their disguise and deluge the enemy with fire. The petrol, ammuni-tion, food and stores were all in their appointed places to feed the offensive. Safely tucked away under their sunshields, the tanks stood ready on their jumping-off points. The full strength of the Eighth Army was on its marks—in the north—not in two days' time, but *now*. All was in readiness for Alamein.

Southron and I stayed with the substitution scheme until it was complete. We had been given, in strict secrecy, the day and the hour of zero. There was nothing more for us to do, and so on the afternoon of 23 October we set out with Ashman in the Chevrolet for Cairo and the office, to catch up on the paper war. It was, I seem to remember, a lovely day. Towards sunset we decided to camp for the night beside the trail. We were far from any main track and apart from distant flights of aircraft no signs of war were to be seen or heard. It was a golden evening, serene and still.

We were too tired to be elated because the job was done, or apprehensive lest it had been done to no purpose. We lolled, while Ashman made tea and a meal. A few fleecy clouds rode overhead. All round us the reddish, stone-flecked sand was dotted with tufts of scrubby vegetation encrusted with the empty shells of dead snails.

The sun went down. We smoked and talked, our faces turned to the westward, towards the front line and beyond the long, low, distant horizon. I thought of what must be going through the minds of so many thousands up there beyond the skyline. I could see them checking things over, brewing up, singing their favourite mournful song, writing their letter home. It took me back twenty-six years to another night and another place where I too had waited in a trench and wondered what it would be like when the whistles blew and the moment came to climb out and take my chance.

Night fell and the stars came out. It was deeply quiet. We watched. Then on the very stroke of zero the sky to the north-west suddenly became alive with a faint continuous flickering. The four hundred guns in 'Cannibal 2' had opened the barrage.

Colonel Geoffrey Barkas

Attack

There was complete quiet all the afternoon. I strolled about and came on a party from the Scottish battalion holding the line being briefed for a patrol that night. They were completely unaware that anything particular was going to happen. Hardly anyone else was visible.

Immediately after dusk there was activity everywhere. The infantry got out of their cramped slits and made their final preparations. The cookers came up with the last meals for many of them. The tracks from the rear, Sun, Moon, Star, Bottle and Hat were lit with their distinctive signs and the transport moved up in orderly sequence. Exactly to the minute, the hundred first-line vehicles and anti-tank guns of the Brigade arrived and were parked close to headquarters. Equally punctually the heavy tanks of the Wiltshire Yeomanry rumbled up and Peter Sykes, their commander, reported in. John Currie called to make sure that everything was in order. It was evident that 9 Armoured Brigade meant business. The battalion commanders came in, all cheerful and confident, chatted a little while and went away with more than our casual good wishes. We all continually looked at our watches.

Brigadier Kippenberger

As the time drew near we got into our cars and drove to a good viewpoint to see the opening of the battle. We passed the never-ending stream of tanks and transport. All moving with clockwork precision. This was X Corps moving up to its starting line. The moon provided sufficient light to drive by, but the night protected them from the prying eyes of enemy aircraft. We had some of our own aircraft up over the enemy's forward positions making distracting noises. Otherwise all seemed fairly quiet and normal. An occasional Verey light and burst of machine-gun fire, a gun firing here and there, as would happen any night. We looked at our watches, 21.30 hours—ten minutes to go. I could hardly wait. The minutes ticked by, and then the whole sky was lit up, and a roar rent the air. Over a thousand of our guns had opened up. It was a great and heartening sight. I tried to picture what the enemy must be thinking; did he know what was coming? He must do now. How ready was he? Up and down the desert, from north to south, the twinkling of the guns could be seen in an unceasing sequence. Within the enemy's lines we could see an occasional deep red glow light up the western sky. Each time this happened the XXX Corps C.C.R.A.*—Dennis— let out a grunt of satisfaction. Another Axis gun position had gone up. We checked each change in the artillery plan; the pause whilst the guns switched to new targets. It was gun drill at its best. Now the infantry had started forward. We could see the periodic bursts of Bofors guns which, with their tracer shell, demarcated the direction of advance. Behind us great searchlight beams were directed towards the sky. These beacons were used to help the forward troops resect their positions, and so find out when they had reached their objectives, for few landmarks existed in this part of the desert.

Major-General Sir Francis de Guingand

At this critical moment, Rommel was in hospital in Germany: General Stumme had been left in command of the Axis forces.

Back in H.Q.—which was sited on the coast only a few miles behind the front—General Stumme heard this tornado of fire, but because of the meagre stocks of ammunition in Africa, did not authorize the artillery to open fire on the British assembly positions. This was a mistake, in my view, for it would have at least reduced the weight of the British attack. When the artillery did finally open fire it was unable to have anything like the effect it might have had earlier, for the British had by that time been able to instal themselves in the defence posts they had captured during the night. When dawn broke on 24 October, headquarters had still only received a few reports, and there was considerable obscurity about the situation. Accordingly, General Stumme decided to drive up to the front himself.

The acting Army Chief of Staff, Colonel Westphal, pressed him to take an escort vehicle and signals truck as I had always done. But he refused to take any escort apart from Colonel Buechting; he intended to go no farther than the headquarters of 90 Light Division and considered it unnecessary to take any other vehicles.

Concentric artillery fire began again in the early hours of the 24th, this time on the southern sector, where the British soon attacked with infantry and about a hundred and sixty tanks. After overrunning our outposts they were brought to a halt in front of the main defence line.

Rommel

* Commander Corps Royal Artillery.

We did not expect any news until after the first objective had been reached at 11 p.m. I got restless and went out on to the low ridge behind which we were sheltering. There was nothing to be seen, not even the hundreds of bursting shells, through the thick dust and smoke. The moonlight was dulled. There would plainly be trouble in keeping direction and touch. Far away on our right I could hear clearly the skirling of the Highland pipes, warlike, stirring music. It was not easy to return to the A.C.V. and sit down again. The minutes passed slowly. Whenever anyone opened the door the maddening incessant clamour of the guns became deafening. A whole field regiment was firing directly over us from a few hundred yards back. The waiting group of officers and orderlies stood on the lee side to get some shelter from the uproar and concussion.

Two signallers with a set had accompanied the sappers who were to make the left gap. We had no set to spare for the other gap. At about the expected time they called to say that the sappers had started clearing the gap and were under small-arms fire. They knew nothing about the infantry except that there was fighting going on ahead.

Brigadier Kippenberger

Crisis: 25 October

I have always thought that this was when the real crisis in the battle occurred.

General Montgomery

The Army Commander went to bed in his caravan that night at his usual time—between 9.30 and 10.0 p.m. As things appeared rather uncertain, I decided to stay up and keep a close touch with the Corps. Towards 2 a.m. on the 25th it was obvious that the situation in the southern corridor about the Miteiriya Ridge was not satisfactory. Various reports were coming in. Congestion was considerable in the cleared lane through the minefields, with a lot of damage being done by enemy shelling and mortar fire. Freyberg was personally directing operations from his tank in this critical zone. Altogether I gained the impression from these reports and those from liaison officers just back, that a feeling in some quarters was creeping in which favoured suspending the forward move, and pulling back under cover of the ridge. I decided, therefore, that this was an occasion when the Army Commander must intervene, and so I called a conference for 3.30 a.m. at our Tactical Headquarters, asking Leese (XXX Corps) and Lumsden (X Corps) to attend. In my long association with Montgomery I think I could count the times I have awakened him at night on my two hands. I went along to his caravan and woke him up. He appeared to be sleeping peacefully in spite of a lot of attention from the enemy air force outside. He agreed to the action I had taken, and told me to bring the two Corps Commanders along to his map lorry when they arrived. To my mind, this conference should be classed as the 'First Stepping Stone'.

Under the best circumstances, 3.30 a.m. is not a good time to hold a conference. The conditions surrounding this one called for the best qualities the Army Commander could produce. I led the generals along the little path to the lorry. Inside, Montgomery was seated on a stool carefully examining a map fixed to the wall. He greeted us all most cheerfully, motioned us to sit down, and then asked each Corps Commander to tell his story. He listened very quietly, only occasionally interrupting with a question. There was a certain 'atmosphere' present, and careful handling was required. Lumsden was obviously not very happy about the role his armour had been given. As the situation was being described, I looked out of the lorry door and saw the placid Mediterranean at our feet twinkling in the moonlight. In contrast to this peaceful scene was the constant fire of A.A. guns, the droning of aircraft overhead, and every now and again the vicious whistle and crump of a bomb nearby. A little later Montgomery spoke to the commander of 10 Armoured Division on the telephone. He heard his version of the situation, and then clearly and quickly made it very plain that there would be no alteration to his orders. The armour could and must get through. He also ordered the headquarters of this division to be moved farther forward.

Before this call had been put through there had been some discussion in the map lorry, in which the Army Commander, speaking very quietly, gave his views. I remember the reaction his words had on me. They were a tonic, and we felt not only that these orders would stand, but that there was no possible question that the plan could fail. The firm decision to make no change in the plan at that moment was a brave one, for it meant accepting considerable risks and casualties. Unless it had been made I am firmly convinced that the attack might well have fizzled out, and the full measure of success we achieved might never have been possible. The meeting broke up with no one in any doubt as to what was in the Commander's mind.

By 08.00 hours that morning the leading armoured brigade of 10 Armoured Division was reported to be two thousand yards west of the minefield area, and in touch with 1 Armoured Division to the north. In addition, we heard that the New Zealand Division and 8 Armoured Brigade were clear of the main minefields, and were advancing south-westwards in accordance with the plan. This was all very encouraging, and justified the Army Commander's confidence.

During the 25th, 15 Panzer Division carried out several counter-attacks against us, but they were all repulsed with heavy loss to the enemy. From now onwards fierce fighting took place around a feature we named 'Kidney Hill'. It was a small kidney-shaped contour on the map, and we had a great deal of difficulty in locating it exactly. Everyone gave it a different map reference. Eventually I believe it was established that the ring contour denoted a depression and not a hill! I was so exercised about this at one period that I sent out a special survey party to establish its position once and for all.

Major-General Sir Francis de Guingand

In the XIII Corps sector to the south, 7 Armoured Division got through the first minefield on the opening night, but was stopped in front of the second. As losses were rising, Montgomery discontinued the attack in the south, for he wanted to preserve 7 Armoured Division for further action elsewhere. Meanwhile the Germans were becoming very worried.

Rommel Returns

On the afternoon of the 24th, I was rung up on the Semmering by Field-Marshal Keitel, who told me that the British had been attacking at Alamein with powerful artillery and bomber support since the previous evening. General Stumme was missing. He asked whether I would be well enough to return to Africa and take over command again. I said I would. Keitel then said that he would keep me informed of developments, and would let me know in due course whether I was to return to my command. I spent the next few hours in a state of acute anxiety, until the evening, when I received a telephone call from Hitler himself. He said that Stumme was still missing—either captured or killed—and asked whether I could start for Africa immediately. I was to telephone him again before I actually took off, because he did not want me to interrupt my treatment unless the British attack assumed dangerous proportions. I ordered my aircraft for seven o'clock next morning and drove immediately to Wiener Neustadt. Finally, shortly after midnight, a call came through from the Führer. In view of developments at Alamein he found himself obliged to ask me to fly back to Africa and resume my command. I took off next morning. I knew there were no more laurels to be earned in Africa, for I had been told in the reports I had received from my officers that supplies had fallen far short of my minimum demands. But just how bad the supply situation really was I had yet to learn.

Rommel

He [Rommel] was at Panzer Gruppe Headquarters again a couple of hours after sunset that same night.

I think he knew then that El Alamein was lost: he had found out how short of petrol the Afrika Korps was. He told Bayerlein that we could not win, but he made desperate attempts to retrieve the situation. He was up almost all night planning a counter-attack against Kidney Ridge (Miteiriya) in the north.

Lieutenant Heinz Werner Schmidt

General von Thoma and Colonel Westphal reported to me that evening on the course of the battle to date, mentioning particularly that General Stumme had forbidden the bombardment of the enemy assembly positions on the first night of the attack, on account of the ammunition shortage. As a result the enemy had been able to take possession of part of our minefield and to overcome the occupying troops with comparatively small losses to himself. The petrol situation made any major movement impossible and permitted only local counter-attacks by the armour deployed behind the particular sector which was in danger. Units of 15 Panzer Division had counter-attacked several times on 24 and 25 October, but had suffered frightful losses in the terrible British artillery fire and non-stop R.A.F. bombing attacks. By the evening of the 25th, only thirty-one of their 119 tanks remained serviceable.

There were now only very small stocks of petrol left in North Africa, and a crisis was threatening. I had already—on my way through Rome—demanded the immediate employment of all available Italian submarines and warships for the transport of petrol and ammunition. Our own air force was still unable to prevent the British bombing attacks, or to shoot down any major number of British aircraft. The R.A.F.'s new fighter-bombers were particularly in evidence, as is shown by the fact that every one of the captured tanks belonging to the *Kampfstaffel* had been shot up by this new type of aircraft.

Our aim for the next few days was to throw the enemy out of our main defence line at all costs and to reoccupy our old positions, in order to avoid having a westward bulge in our front.

Rommel

The Australians Strike

By about mid-day* Montgomery realized that the 'crumbling' operations by the New Zealand Division would prove very expensive and made a decision to switch the axis to an operation by 9 Australian Division—northwards. The object was to destroy the Germans in the salient, and it might also reduce the strength facing the main drive. This movement proved so successful that I have always considered it 'Stepping Stone to Victory No. 2'.

1 Armoured Division were ordered to fight their way westwards with the object of threatening the enemy's supply routes in the Rahman track area. They would also threaten the rear of the enemy holding the coastal salient. This attack made no appreciable progress until the night of the 26th/27th, when a brigade of the division established themselves about Kidney Hill.

The Australian attack went very well, ground being gained and very heavy casualties being inflicted on the enemy. In this area the enemy's defences were very strong, and their garrison preponderantly German. I think this area saw the most determined and savage fighting of the campaign. No quarter was given, and the Australians fought some of the finest German troops in well-prepared positions to a standstill, and by their action did a great deal to win the battle of El Alamein. This division fought continuously for nine days under their fine commander, Morshead; and at the end of this period they were ready for a well-earned rest.

Major-General Sir Francis de Guingand

Attacks were now launched on Hill 28 by elements of 15 Panzer Division, the Littorio and a Bersaglieri battalion, supported by the concentrated fire of all the local artillery and A.A. Unfortunately, the attack gained ground very slowly. The British resisted desperately. Rivers of blood were poured out over miserable strips of land which, in normal times, not even the poorest Arab would have bothered his head about. Tremendous British artillery fire pounded the area of the attack. In the evening part of the Bersaglieri battalion succeeded in occupying the eastern and western edges of the hill. The hill itself remained in British hands, and later became the base for many enemy operations.

I myself observed the attack that day from the north. Load after load of bombs cascaded down among my troops. British strength round Hill 28 was increasing steadily. I gave orders to the artillery to break up the British move-

* 26 October (Ed.)

ment north-east of Hill 28 by concentrated fire, but we had too little ammunition to do it successfully. During the day I brought up 90 Light Divsion and the *Kampfstaffel*, in order to press home the attack on Hill 28. The British were continually feeding fresh forces into their attack from Hill 28 and it was clear that they wanted to win through to the area between El Daba and Sidi Abd el Rahman. Late in the afternoon German and Italian dive-bomber formations made a self-immolating attempt to break up the British lorry columns moving towards the north-west. Some sixty British fighters pounced on these slow machines and forced the Italians to jettison their bombs over their own lines, while the German pilots pressed home their attack with very heavy losses. Never before in Africa had we seen such a density of anti-aircraft fire. Hundreds of British tracer shells criss-crossed the sky and the air became an absolute inferno of fire.

British attacks supported by tanks tried again and again to break out to the west through our line south of Hill 28. Finally, in the afternoon, a thrust by a hundred and sixty tanks succeeded in wiping out an already severely mauled battalion of 164 Infantry Division and penetrated into our line towards the south-west. Violent fighting followed in which the remaining German and Italian tanks managed to force the enemy back. Tank casualties so far, counting in that day's, were sixty-one in 15 Panzer Division and fifty-six in the Littorio, all totally destroyed.

Following on their non-stop night attacks, the R.A.F. sent over formations of eighteen to twenty bombers at hourly intervals throughout the day, which not only caused considerable casualties, but also began to produce serious signs of fatigue and a sense of inferiority among our troops.

Rommel

The Decisive Phase

Montgomery has always been most careful to husband his forces, in fact ensures that he has fresh troops available for the decisive moment. This re-grouping now produced the nucleus of reserves for the decisive phase of the battle. I would, therefore, call it the 'Third Stepping Stone to Victory'.

2 New Zealand Division was pulled out of the line into reserve. Their place was taken by a side-stepping northwards of 1 South African and 4 Indian Divisions. The New Zealanders were made first priority for all tank replacements, and they spent a day or so resting and bathing. We could see this cheerful body of men spread out along the beach from Headquarters, the horrors of the Miteiriya Ridge forgotten, preparing themselves for the ordeal ahead.

27 October was a good day on the sea, in the air, and on land. News came in that two tankers and a merchantman had been sunk near the entrance to Tobruk harbour. The loss of these much needed supplies to the enemy, including vital petrol, no doubt had a great influence on the battle. The R.A.F. attacked with great gallantry, and their losses were very heavy. The Desert Air Force shot down at least eighteen enemy fighters during the day. On land the regrouping went smoothly ahead, and at 2 p.m. the Army Commander held a conference at his Tactical Headquarters. At this meeting the regrouping plan was given out,

and also plans for the continuance of the Australian attack. XIII Corps were ordered to make final arrangements for moving 7 Armoured Division and other troops to the northern sector. During the night of the 26th/27th 21 Panzer Division moved northwards, and so these forces could be spared. In the morning we had located, by wireless direction finding, the headquarters of this German armoured division opposite Kidney Hill.

For most of the day, the two German Panzer divisions launched attacks against our Kidney Hill positions. This suited us well, and 1 Armoured Division excelled themselves. They claimed fifty enemy tanks knocked out, as well as others damaged. In addition, the R.A.F. was doing good work bombing these attacks as they formed up. Good claims of transport destroyed were made. It was an exciting day, and during the afternoon I stood by our command vehicle listening to the loudspeaker which was tuned to the wireless 'net' which served the forward tanks. We heard a running commentary on the fight. One could hear the fire orders being given to the tank crews and the results of their shooting. This sort of thing:

'Look out, Bob, a couple sneaking up your right flank—you should see them any moment now.'

You would hear the fire order given by the tank commander as the enemy came into view. Then:

'Well done—good shooting—another brew-up.'

We ticked off the numbers claimed and felt very pleased. Looking westwards there were visible signs of success. Pillars of black smoke towering into the sky showed the truth of the reports we were hearing on the radio. Then, every three-quarters of an hour, the fleet of medium bombers would fly overhead, and drop their load with a terrific crump on the enemy concentrations. A great cloud of dust would rise up, interposed with black smoke which came from vehicles hit.

After this Montgomery decided that 1 Armoured Division needed a rest, and withdrew it into reserve. This particular sector would, for the moment, remain a defensive one.

Major-General Sir Francis de Guingand

28 October

Dearest Lu,

Who knows whether I'll have a chance to sit down and write in peace in the next few days or ever again. To-day there's still a chance.

The battle is raging. Perhaps we will still manage to be able to stick it out, in spite of all that's against us—but it may go wrong, and that would have very grave consequences for the whole course of the war. For North Africa would then fall to the British in a few days, almost without a fight. We will do all we can to pull it off. But the enemy's superiority is terrific and our resources very small.

Whether I would survive a defeat lies in God's hands. The lot of the vanquished is heavy. I'm happy in my own conscience that I've done all I can for victory and have not spared myself.

I realized so well in the few short weeks I was at home what you two mean to me. My last thought is of you.

Rommel

A real hard and very bloody fight has gone on now for eight days. It has been a terrific party and a complete slogging match, made all the more difficult in that the whole area is just one enormous minefield. . . . I have managed to keep the initiative throughout, and so far Rommel has had to dance entirely to my tune; his counter-attack and thrusts have been handled without difficulty up to date. I think he is now ripe for a real hard blow which may topple him off his perch. It is going in to-night and I am putting everything I can into it. . . . If we succeed it will be the end of Rommel's army.

General Montgomery to General Sir Alan Brooke, 1 November

Victory

At 1 a.m. on 2 November the divisions drawn out of the line by Montgomery were launched at the Germans around Kidney Ridge. In spite of furious resistance and counter-attacks, they burst through.

2 November

Dearest Lu,

Very heavy fighting again, not going well for us. The enemy, with his superior strength, is slowly levering us out of our position. That will mean the end. You can imagine how I feel. Air raid after air raid after air raid!

Rommel

At about midday* I returned to my command post, only just escaping by some frantic driving a carpet of bombs laid by eighteen British aircraft. At 13.30 hours an order arrived from the Führer. It read in roughly the following words:

To Field-Marshal Rommel:

In the situation in which you find yourself there can be no other thought but to stand fast and throw every gun and every man into the battle. The utmost efforts are being made to help you. Your enemy, despite his superiority, must also be at the end of his strength. It would not be the first time in history that a strong will has triumphed over the bigger battalions. As to your troops, you can show them no other road than that to victory or death.

Adolf Hitler

This order demanded the impossible. Even the most devoted soldier can be killed by a bomb. In spite of our unvarnished situation reports, it was apparently still not realized at the Führer's H.Q. how matters really stood in Africa. Arms, petrol and aircraft could have helped us, but not orders. We were completely stunned, and for the first time during the African campaign I did not know what to do. A kind of apathy took hold of us as we issued orders for all existing posi-

* 3 November (Ed.)

tions to be held on instructions from the highest authority. I forced myself to this action, as I had always demanded unconditional obedience from others and, consequently, wished to apply the same principle to myself. Had I known what was to come I should have acted differently, because from that time on we had continually to circumvent orders from the Führer or Duce in order to save the army from destruction. But this first instance of interference by higher authority in the tactical conduct of the African war came as a considerable shock.*

Rommel

4 November: Break-through—Retreat

At 2 a.m. I directed two hard punches at the 'hinges' of the final break-out area where the enemy was trying to stop us widening the gap which we had blown. That finished the battle.

The armoured car regiments went through as dawn was breaking and soon the armoured divisions got clean away into the open desert; they were now in country clear of minefields, where they could manœuvre and operate against the enemy rear areas and retreating columns.

The armoured cars raced away to the west, being directed far afield on the enemy line of retreat.

General Montgomery

Enormous dust-clouds could be seen south and south-east of headquarters, where the desperate struggle of the small and inefficient Italian tanks of XX Corps was being played out against the hundred or so British heavy tanks which had come round their open right flank. I was later told by Major von Luck, whose battalion I had sent to close the gap between the Italians and the Afrika Korps, that the Italians, who at that time represented our strongest motorized force, fought with exemplary courage. Von Luck gave what assistance he could with his guns, but was unable to avert the fate of the Italian armoured corps. Tank after tank split asunder or burned out, while all the time a tremendous British barrage lay over the Italian infantry and artillery positions. The last signal came from the Ariete at about 15.30 hours:

'Enemy tanks penetrated south of Ariete. Ariete now encircled. Location five kilometres north-west Bir el Abd. Ariete's tanks in action.'

By evening XX Italian Corps had been completely destroyed after a very gallant action. In the Ariete we lost our oldest Italian comrades, from whom we had probably always demanded more than they, with their poor armament, had been capable of performing.

A view over the battlefield from Corps H.Q. showed that strong British tank formations had also broken through the Afrika Korps and were pressing on to the west.

Thus the picture in the early afternoon was as follows: on the right of the Afrika Korps, powerful enemy armoured forces had destroyed the XX Italian Motorized Corps, and thus burst a twelve-mile hole in our front, through which

* *Note by Manfred Rommel:* The existence of such passages as this caused my father to decide, in 1944, to burn that part of the manuscript dealing with El Alamein. His death on 14 October of that year prevented him carrying out his design.

strong bodies of tanks were moving to the west. As a result of this, our forces in the north were threatened with encirclement by enemy formations twenty times their superior in tanks. 90 Light Division had defended their line magnificently against all British attacks, but the Afrika Korps' line had been penetrated after a very gallant resistance by their troops. There were no reserves, as every available man and gun had had to be put into the line.

Rommel

General Ritter von Thoma of the Afrika Korps threw his own headquarters unit into the breach in a forlorn attempt to stop the break-through.

'Go to the El Daba command post. I shall stay here and personally take charge of the defence of Tel el Mampsra.'

I could see that Thoma was utterly disheartened and foresaw no good. His A.D.C., Lieutenant Hartdegen, remained with the general: he had a wireless transmitter. The general put on his greatcoat and picked up a small canvas bag. I wondered whether the general intended to die. Then I left Tel el Mampsra and drove to the rear.

It was eight o'clock before the British attacked, after approximately one hour's artillery preparation. Their main effort was directed against Tel el Mampsra. By committing all its forces the Afrika Corps was able to hold attacks by two hundred British tanks.

At eleven o'clock Lieutenant Hartdegen appeared at my command post and said:

'General von Thoma has sent me back, with the radio transmitter. He doesn't need it any more. All our tanks, anti-tank guns and ack-ack have been destroyed on Tel el Mampsra. I don't know what has happened to the general.'

I immediately climbed into a small armoured reconnaissance car and drove off eastwards. Suddenly a hail of armour-piercing shot was whistling all about me. In the noontime haze I could see countless black monsters far away in front. They were Montgomery's tanks, the 10th Hussars. I jumped out of the armoured car and beneath the burning midday sun ran as fast as I could towards Tel el Mampsra. It was a place of death, of burning tanks and smashed flak guns, without a living soul. But then, about two hundred yards away from the sand-hole in which I was lying, I saw a man standing erect beside a burning tank, apparently impervious to the intense fire which criss-crossed about him. It was General von Thoma. The British Shermans which were closing up on Tel el Mampsra had halted in a wide half-circle. What should I do? The general would probably regard it as cowardice on my part were I not to go forward and join him. But to run through the curtain of fire which lay between General von Thoma and myself would have been to court certain death. I thought for a moment or two. Then the British tanks began to move forward once again. There was now no fire being put down on Tel el Mampsra. Thoma stood there, rigid and motionless as a pillar of salt, with his canvas bag still in his hand. A Bren carrier was driving straight towards him, with two Shermans just behind. The British soldiers signalled to Thoma. At the same time one hundred and fifty fighting vehicles poured across Tel el Mampsra like a flood.

.... The Afrika Korps signals officer brought Rommel a decoded message, from the 10th Hussars to Montgomery, which our people had intercepted. It read:

'We have just captured a general named Ritter von Thoma.'

The Field-Marshal took me aside, and said:

'Bayerlein, what we tried with all our might to prevent has now happened. Our front is smashed and the enemy is pouring through into our rear area. There can no longer be any question of obeying Hitler's order. We're withdrawing to the Fuka position so as to save what still can be saved.

.... 'Bayerlein,' Rommel went on, 'I'm putting you in command of the Afrika Korps. There's no one else to whom I can entrust it. And if it should happen later on that the Führer court-martials us for our disobedience, we'll both have to answer squarely for our decision to-day. Do your duty as best you can. All your orders to the troops carry my authority. You may say this to the senior commanders, in the event of your having any trouble with them.'

'I shall do my best, sir,' I replied. Then Rommel got into his armoured command vehicle, to visit the other units of his beaten army and to give the orders for the retreat.

General Bayerlein

This decision could at least be the means of saving the motorized part of the Panzer Army from destruction, although the army had already lost so much as a result of the twenty-four-hour postponement of its retreat—including practically the whole of its infantry and large numbers of tanks, vehicles and guns—that it was no longer in a position to offer effective opposition to the British advance at any point. Orders for the retreat went out at 15.30 hours, and the movement began immediately.

There was now no chance of getting order into our columns, for nothing short of a quick retreat could save us from the British air attacks which reached a climax that day. Anything that did not immediately reach the road and race off westwards was lost, for the enemy followed us up over a wide front and over-ran everything that came in his path.

Next morning—far too late—signals arrived from the Führer and the Commando Supremo authorizing the withdrawal of the army to the Fuka position.

Rommel

... The General* was certain. He said he had told the Army Commander that the battle was over and had sent a cable to the same effect to the New Zealand Government. In the late afternoon there was a divisional conference. The General said the gap was made to all intents and purposes and next morning we would go south through it and head westwards and north to Fuka on the desert road to cut off the Germans in the north. The six Italian divisions in the south, without troop-carrying transport, were doomed in any case. We were to load up with eight days' water, rations, petrol for five hundred miles, the gun-

* Montgomery (Ed.)

ners with three hundred and sixty rounds per 25-pounder and two hundred rounds per medium gun. This was great news.

Brigadier Kippenberger

The Field

Below them stretched nothing but death and destruction to the very horizon. Shattered trucks, burnt and contorted tanks, blackened and tangled heaps of wreckage not to be recognized; they scattered the landscape as thickly as stars in the sky. Like dead stalks in the sand, rifles were thrust upright—a denuded forest. And each one meant a man who had been maimed or killed. Inside each wrecked tank a putrid, blackening paste on the walls was what an armour-piercing shell had left of the men who had manned it. Over the miles of wire hung at intervals the bodies of men, like a ghastly and infinite tableau. In dug-outs, pits and trenches the dead lay tangled and piled. Here and there from a heap of dead a hand reached forth as if in supplication, or a pair of eyes stared up accusingly—and would stare so until they rotted into the skull. Here was a body with the limbs torn from it or without a head; and somewhere else a head lay on its own. Ripped-apart bellies with the viscera swelling outwards like some great sea-anemone; a throat impaled by the long shard of a shell. These were details of the scene repeated again and again in every corner of the desert landscape: a great rubbish-heap of metal and human flesh. So the victors sat, gazing across the gigantic desolation.

Graves: El Alamein

Live and let live.
No matter how it ended,
These lose and, under the sky,
Lie befriended.

For foes forgive,
No matter how they hated,
By life so sold and by
Death mated.

John Pudney

It may almost be said, 'Before Alamein we never had a victory. After Alamein we never had a defeat.'

Winston Churchill

19

STALINGRAD

In Russia in the autumn of 1942, the decisive battle was about to be fought. On the northern flank of their advancing troops in the Caucusus, the German onslaught on Stalingrad slowed. It was not until 15 September that Army Group B reached the outskirts of the city, and there its spearhead—6 Army commanded by General Paulus—remained.

STALINGRAD lies beside the Volga and the German enemy had reached the city's centre. The Russian troops holding the ruins received orders which left no room for misunderstanding:

'You can no longer retreat across the Volga. There is only one road, the road that leads forward. Stalingrad will be saved by you, or be wiped out with you.'

THE BATTLE OF ATTRITION

Our losses . . . were very heavy, especially during the first stages of the Stalingrad battle; they were then much heavier than the German losses; later, after we had dug in at Stalingrad, the German casualties began to pile up far beyond ours—not to mention the encirclement phase when the German losses became truly fantastic.

But during the first stage our losses were, of course, very heavy indeed. And yet, the people who survived acquired a tremendous experience in the technique of house-to-house fighting. Two or three men of such experience could be worth a whole platoon. They knew every drain pipe, every manhole, every shell-hole and crater in and around their particular building, they knew every brick that could serve as shelter. Among piles of rubble, which no tank could penetrate, a man would sit there, inside his manhole or crater, or hole in the floor, and, looking through his simple periscope, he would turn on his tommy-gun the moment he saw any German within firing distance. Seldom anything short of a direct hit could knock him out; he was very hard to pick out of his hole and bombing, as I said before, only tended to create new shelters.

In the nightmare of this positional warfare the nucleus of experienced men survived, in the main; it was the new people who perished most easily. . . . Snipers also played a great part in inflicting heavy losses on the Germans and in harassing them. And then there was the continuous activity—the technique of small counter-attacks—practised by the defenders of Stalingrad; they seldom gave the Germans a moment's peace. In October, and especially in November, it became hard to determine who was actually attacking—we or the Germans. The whole of Stalingrad became a seething cauldron of small attacks. In these small battles we had the initiative; in the big attacks, right through September and October, the Germans had the initiative; and the middle of October was the most terrifying period of all. From the end of October, though the Germans were showing signs of great weariness, we had a new and very serious cause of worry—the iceflows in the Volga and the river's reluctance to freeze.

General Talensky

.... On 14 October the Germans struck out; that day will go down as the bloodiest and most ferocious in the whole Battle of Stalingrad. Along a narrow front of four to five kilometres, the Germans threw in five brand-new or newly-reinforced infantry divisions, and two tank divisions, supported by masses of artillery and planes. It began in the morning with a terrible artillery and mortar barrage; and during the day there were over two thousand Luftwaffe sorties. That morning you could not hear the separate shots or explosions: the whole merged into one continuous deafening roar. At five yards you could no longer distinguish anything, so thick were the dust and the smoke. It was astonishing: in a dugout the vibration was such that a tumbler on a table would fly into a thousand bits. That day sixty-one men in my headquarters were killed. After four or five hours of this stunning barrage, the Germans started to attack with tanks and infantry, and they advanced one and a half kilometres, and finally broke through at the Tractor Plant. Our officers and soldiers did not retreat a step here, and if the Germans still advanced it was over the dead bodies of our men. But the losses the Germans had suffered during that day were so heavy that they could not maintain the power of their blow.

.... From then on till the end the two armies were left gripping each other in a deadly clutch; the front became virtually stabilized. Despite this virtual stabilization, we were ordered by the High Command in November to activize our front. It was essential that the Stalingrad group of divisions keep the Germans busy with constant attacks and divert their attention from the flanks. The rest of the story is known.

General Chuikov, G.O.C. 62 Army

The Germans

All our attempts to get the better of the Balka* held by the enemy had so far been in vain. We tried Stuka attacks and artillery shoots. We had assault troops attacking it; they achieved nothing, but suffered heavy losses. The Russians had dug themselves in too well. We thought that about four hundred men was a more or less correct estimate of the enemy's strength. In normal circumstances a force of that size should have surrendered after a fortnight. After all, the Russians were completely cut off from the outside world. Nor was there any chance of supply by air, as at that time we had undoubted air superiority. Now and then at night small single-seater open aircraft tried their luck and dropped an insignificant quantity of supplies to the encircled Russians. One must not forget that Russians are not like normal soldiers where supplies are concerned. On many occasions we found out how little they needed.

* Dry river bed (Ed.)

This Balka was a thorn in our side, but we could not count on reducing it by starving the garrison. Something had to be done.

Having exhausted all the wiles and arts which our training as staff officers had taught us, we thought it would be a good thing to allow the real fighting man a chance. Therefore we called in our lieutenants. Three of them were instructed to go into the matter and think up something useful. After three days they reported back and submitted their plan. They suggested subdividing the Balka into several sectors and putting tanks and anti-tank guns opposite the holes of the Russians on the slopes below. Then our assault troops were to work themselves down to these holes and smoke them out.

Everything went according to plan—the Russians didn't even wait to be fetched personally from their holes but followed the invitation of a few hand-grenades and other explosives. We were very surprised when we counted our prisoners and found that instead of four hundred men we had captured about *a thousand*. For nearly four weeks these thousand men had subsisted on grass and leaves and on a minimum of water which they dug up by sinking a deep hole into the ground. What is more, they not only had lived on so little, but put up a stiff fight to the very end.

Colonel H. R. Dingler, 3 Motorized Division

XIV Panzer Corps was losing up to five hundred men a day and on one occasion, after adding up the totals, General von Wietersheim informed his Commander-in-Chief:

'Sir, I can work out the exact day on which I shall lose my last man, if the situation is allowed to continue like this.' He received the reply:

'Are you commanding 6th Army, Wietersheim, or am I?'

Stalingrad-Holds Out

Stalingrad is still holding out, and the impression is gaining ground that it may well hold. The Germans, it seems, are no longer even trying to capture it at one swoop, but simply to slice it up like a sausage—and that will take some doing. A lot of people in Moscow think that if Stalingrad holds for another six weeks, the Germans may have to pull out of the Caucasus.

Alexander Werth

On 9 November, Adolf Hitler made his annual speech in the Bürgerbräu Beer Cellar before the Nazi 'old guard':

'I wanted to get to the Volga and to do so at a particular point where stands a certain town. By chance it bears the name of Stalin himself. I wanted to take the place, and do you know, we've pulled it off, we've got it really, except for a few enemy positions still holding out. Now people say: "Why don't they finish the job more quickly?" Well, the reason is that I don't want another Verdun. I prefer to do the job with quite small assault groups. Time is of no consequence at all.'

Many of the soldiers at Stalingrad listened to these words. They cannot even have shaken their heads over them, since they must have seemed so incomprehensible. One soldier, however, seated in a dug-out on the northern perimeter, buried his head in his hands and murmured:

'My God, quite small assault groups . . . if he had only at least reached full corporal!'

ENCIRCLEMENT

On 20 November things began to happen around Stalingrad. 16 Panzer Division, our neighbour on the right, received orders to leave their present positions at once and move to the western bank of the Don by way of Kalatsch. Something very serious must have happened.

On 21 November we heard from our supply troops who were stationed on the east bank of the Don and south of Kalatsch, that Russian tanks were approaching the town from the south. Other supply units stationed in the area west of the Don informed us by wireless that Russians were approaching Kalatsch from the north. It was clear that the *encirclement* of Stalingrad would soon be a reality. We realized how difficult it would be to break that ring with the forces at our disposal—their weakness was only too apparent.

If the Russians decided to advance with powerful forces in the area west of the Don their line of encirclement would be a very hard nut to crack.

Colonel Dingler

22 November, 18.00 hours

Army encircled. Despite heroic resistance whole of Tsaritsa Valley, railway from Sovietski to Kalatsch, the Don bridge at Kalatsch, high ground on west bank as far as Golubinskaia, Olskinskii and Krainii inclusive now in Russian hands.

Further enemy forces are advancing from the south-east through Businovska northwards and also in great strength from the west.

Situation at Surovikino and Chir unknown.

. . . . The Don now frozen and can be crossed. Fuel supplies almost exhausted. Tanks and heavy weapons will then be immobilized, ammunition situation acute, food supplies available for a further six days.

Paulus

Paulus, his superior (the commander-in-chief of Army Group B), and General Zeitzler, Chief of Staff of the German Supreme Command, all saw the necessity of breaking out of the trap, but Hitler refused to allow this.

Despite the exceptional gravity of the decision to be taken, with the far-reaching consequences of which I am well aware, I must report that I regard it as necessary to accept General Paulus's proposal for the withdrawal of 6 Army. My reasons are as follows:

1. The supplying of the twenty divisions that constitute this army is not feasible by air.

2. Since the probable future developments do not offer any certainty of a

rapid penetration of the encircling enemy forces from the outside, the attack to relieve 6 Army cannot, in view of the time required to assemble the relieving force, be mounted before 10 December.

.... However, I believe that a break-through by 6 Army in a south-westerly direction will result in favourable developments to the situation as a whole.

With the total dissolution of 3 Roumanian Army, 6 Army is now the only fighting formation capable of inflicting damage on the enemy. The proposed direction of attack, opening towards the south-west and then being followed by the northern wing advancing along the railway from Chir to Morosovskaia, will result in a relaxation of the existing tension in the Svetnoie-Kotelnikovo area.

.... I am well aware that this proposed operation will entail heavy losses, particularly in arms and equipment. But these will be far less than those that must ensue if the situation is left to develop, as it must do, in existing conditions, with the inevitable starving-out of the encircled army as the certain result.

Colonel-General Freiherr von Weichs, C.-in-C. Army Group B

It is a crime to leave 6 Army where it is. The entire army must inevitably be slaughtered and starved. We cannot fetch them out. The whole backbone of the Eastern Front will be broken if 6 Army is left to perish at Stalingrad.

General Zeitzler

6 Army is temporarily encircled by Russian forces. It is my intention to concentrate 6 Army in the area [here followed a more precise definition of the area between Stalingrad-North-Point 137–Marinovka-Zybenko and Stalingrad-South]. 6 Army must be left in no doubt that I shall do everything to ensure that it receives its supplies and that it will be relieved in due course.

I know the brave 6 Army and its C.-in-C., and I also know that it will do its duty.

Adolf Hitler, 24 November

Supplies

6 Army can only hold fast if it is supplied with the necessities of life, fuel, ammunition and food and other clearly specified *matériel*, and if it can be assured of relief from outside the encirclement within a short period of time. What we need in the way of supplies has been stated in unambiguous terms. It is now up to the Supreme Command to calculate by means of a staff study whether these large quantities can be delivered, how, and then to issue the necessary orders. So far as 6 Army is concerned, all we can do is to report what exactly it is that the encircled troops need: it is not up to us to say how those needs can and will be met. . . . In view of the general situation, a withdrawal by 6 Army would appear the more useful course to follow, but I cannot make such a decision from 6 Army Headquarters, since it presumes an inability on the part of the Supreme Command to meet 6 Army's requirements concerning the delivery of supplies and the breaking of the encirclement from without. . . .

General Paulus, 24 November

Night after night we sat in our holes listening to the droning of the aircraft engines and trying to guess how many German machines were coming over and what supplies they would bring us. The supply position was very poor from the beginning, but none of us thought that hunger would become a permanent thing.

We were short of all sorts of supplies. We were short of bread and, worse, of artillery ammunition, and worst of all, of petrol. Petrol meant everything to us. As long as we had petrol our supply—little as it was—was assured. As long as we had petrol we were able to keep *warm*. As there was no wood to be found anywhere in the steppe, firewood had to be fetched from the city of Stalingrad by lorry. As we had so little petrol, trips to the city to fetch firewood had to be limited to the bare minimum. For this reason we felt very cold in our holes.

Until Christmas 1942 the daily bread ration issued to every man was a hundred grammes. After Christmas the ration was reduced to fifty grammes per head. Later on only those in the forward line received fifty grammes per day. No bread was issued to men in regimental headquarters and upwards. The others were given watery soup which we tried to improve by making use of bones obtained from horses we dug up. As a Christmas treat the Army allowed the slaughtering of four thousand of the available horses. My division, being a motorized formation, had no horses and was therefore particularly hard hit, as the horseflesh we received was strictly rationed. The infantry units were better off as they were able to do some 'illegal' slaughtering.

Colonel Dingler

It was my task to attempt to supply the 6 German Army by air . . . but our resources were far too inadequate. We lost over five hundred transport planes trying to bring in ammunition and food for the quarter of a million men encircled in the city. Food soon became so short that the troops had to eat horses that had been frozen in the snow for weeks. It was useless to attempt to break out once we had been surrounded because there was nothing behind us but hundreds of kilometres of open, frozen steppes. In any case we had been ordered by the Führer to hold Stalingrad. We always underestimated the Russian strength in the winter of 1942.

Lieutenant-General Pickert

On 24 November von Manstein assumed command of Army Group B, having been promoted to Field-Marshal. He thus came directly under Hitler's command.

Hitler as Supreme Commander

Now that I had come immediately under Hitler in my capacity as an army group commander, however, I was to get my first real experience of him in his exercise of the supreme command.

When considering Hitler in the role of a military leader, one should certainly not dismiss him with such clichés as 'the lance-corporal of World War 1'.

He undoubtedly had a certain eye for operational openings, as had been shown by the way he opted for Army Group A's plan in the west. Indeed, this is often to be found in military amateurs—otherwise history would not have recorded so many dukes and princes as successful commanders. In addition, though, Hitler possessed an astoundingly retentive memory and an imagination that made him quick to grasp all technical matters and problems of armaments. He was amazingly familiar with the effect of the very latest enemy weapons and could reel off whole columns of figures on both our own and the enemy's war production. Indeed, this was his favourite way of sidetracking any topic that was not to his liking. There can be no question that his insight and unusual energy were responsible for many achievements in the sphere of armaments. Yet his belief in his own superiority in this respect ultimately had disastrous consequences. His interference prevented the smooth and timely development of the Luftwaffe, and it was undoubtedly he who hampered the development of rocket propulsion and atomic weapons.

Moreover, Hitler's interest in everything technical led him to over-estimate the importance of his technical resources. As a result, he would count on a mere handful of assault-gun detachments or the new Tiger tanks to restore situations where only large bodies of troops could have any prospect of success.

What he lacked, broadly speaking, was simply *military ability based on experience*—something for which his 'intuition' was no substitute.

. . . . Hitler had a masterly knack of psychologically adapting himself to the individual whom he wished to bring round to his point of view. In addition, of course, he always knew anyone's motive for coming to see him, and could thus have all his counter-arguments ready beforehand. His faculty for inspiring others with his own confidence—whether feigned or genuine—was quite remarkable. This particularly applied when officers who did not know him well came to see him from the front. In such cases a man who had set out to 'tell Hitler the truth about things out there' came back converted and bursting with confidence.

Field-Marshal von Manstein

Having closed the trap, the Russians began to grind down the Germans within it.

On 2 December the enemy made his first attack on 6 Army. Like those which followed on the 4th and 8th of the month, it was bloodily repulsed by the courageous troops in the pocket. Fortunately the supply position now appeared more favourable than we had originally dared to expect, for on 2 December the army reported that by existing on a reduced scale of rations and slaughtering a large proportion of the horses, it could—reckoning from 30 November—manage with its present stocks for twelve to sixteen days. At the same time the state of the weather encouraged us to hope for an improvement in the rate of air supplies, a record load of three hundred tons being flown into the pocket on 5 December. (Unfortunately this was to remain an all-time high.) Nonetheless it was clear that no time must be lost in making contact with 6 Army on the ground and fetching it out of the pocket.

Field-Marshal von Manstein

The Second Winter Comes

The weather conditions were bearable during the first days of December. Later on, heavy snowfalls occurred and it turned bitterly cold. Life became a misery. Digging was no longer possible as the ground was frozen hard and if we had to abandon our lines this meant that in the new lines we would have no dug-outs or trenches. The heavy snow diminished our small petrol supplies still further. The lorries stuck in the snow and the heavy going meant a larger consumption of petrol. It grew colder and colder. The temperature remained at a steady twenty or thirty degrees below freezing-point and it became increasingly difficult for aircraft to fly in.

Colonel Dingler

Then one night the great freeze-up began, and winter was with us, the second grim winter in that accursed country. Like a black cloak the frost folded over the land. A supplies truck came round and brought us greatcoats, gloves and caps with ear-flaps. Despite this issue, we froze miserably in our funk-holes. In the morning we would be numb with cold, our rifles and guns completely coated with thick hoar-frost. As it left our mouths our breath was as dense as cigarette smoke and immediately solidified over the side-flaps of our caps its glittering crystals of ice. When shells came over, each detonation rang out with a new, hard resonance and the clods of earth which were thrown high were like lumps of granite.

Though apparently completely healed, last year's frost-bites on my heels began to be very painful again. I dared not let myself think of how long this cold would be with us, dared not remember everything would still be frozen up at the end of March.

We just lay in our holes and froze, knowing that twenty-four hours later and forty-eight hours later we should be shivering precisely as we were now, and vainly longing to be relieved. But there was now no hope whatsoever of relief, and that was the worst thing of all.

.... The day came when one realized that it was some time since a single truck had dared attempt the journey from our front to the rear base. Scattered Russian units had occupied every approach. At first they attacked any vehicle which came along only if it was night, then they attacked day and night continuously. When it came to that, all supplies columns were for a time linked up— trucks, sleighs, officers' cars—and moved off together in convoy, flanked by armoured stuff and motor-cycle units. In that way essential communications were kept going for a time. But now even this last link had been completely cut.

Frenzied counter-attacks, accompanied by huge losses, failed completely. Slowly but surely the Soviet wedges in the sides of our wedge grew broader, and the German divisions were thrown back, on the one side far beyond the Don, on the other eastwards, back on to that great mass of ruins, the city of Stalingrad.

.... The truth was slowly borne in on us, as, dragging all they had with them, the remnants of defeated division after division fell back from all sides before the on-pressing enemy, crowding and cramming into the heart of the cauldron. Gradually the columns of converging transport blocked all roads. On the road guns were blown up, and weapons of all kinds, tanks included, which had come to a standstill from want of fuel. Fully laden lorries, bogged in the snow, went up in flames. Munition dumps were sprung. Vast supplies of provisions and clothing had to become huge fireworks, not to fall into enemy hands. Installations erected at enormous effort were wiped out wholesale. The country for miles around was strewn with smaller equipment—tin hats, gas-masks in cases, ground-sheets, cooking utensils, ammo pouches, trenching tools, even rifles, machine-pistols and grenades. All of this stuff had been thrown away because it had become a mere hindrance, or because the men who carried it had become the wounded in their endless columns, with blood-soaked bandages and tattered uniforms, summoning the last vestiges of their strength merely to drag themselves on through the snow. Or else the equipment had belonged to the countless men now rigid and dead, of whom nobody took any more notice than we did of all that abandoned material.

Completely cut off, the men in field grey just slouched on, invariably filthy and invariably louse-ridden, their weary shoulders sagging, from one defence position to another. The icy winds of those great white wastes which stretched for ever beyond us to the east lashed a million crystals of razor-like snow into their unshaven faces, skin now loose-stretched over bone, so utter was the exhaustion, so utter the starvation. It burned the skin to crumpled leather, it lashed tears from the sunken eyes which from over-fatigue could scarce be kept open, it penetrated through all uniforms and rags to the very marrow of our bones. And whenever any individual could do no more, when even the onward-driving lash of fear of death ceased to have meaning, then like an engine which had used its last drop of fuel, the debilitated body ran down and came to a standstill. Soon a kindly shroud of snow covered the object and only the toe of a jackboot or an arm frozen to stone could remind you that what was now an elongated white hummock had quite recently been a human being.

Away two thousand kilometres to the west was another world, a home country, a wonderful motherland. There one imagined the glad laughter of little ones and men who were happy too. There, people slept in soft warm beds; there, at midday they sat down to eat as much as they liked from clean white table-linen. And there, on Sunday, when the church bells brought people out of doors, they all dressed in their best and the whole family took its stroll, with pet dog trundling after. Neighbours raised their hats to each other, folk asked after each other's health, forecast the weather and exchanged the latest talk of the town. And if you were a bit out of sorts, the children tiptoed and dared not speak above a whisper, and the doctor came, with most serious mien, to say you really ought not to take such things so lightly.

Bereft of initiative, we allowed ourselves to be driven, crawling ever onward, obeying senseless orders to take up ever new positions in hollow or dug-out and offer a resistance which was already totally devoid of military meaning. Mechanically we aimed our guns with frozen fingers, banging away into the ocean of snow back whence we had just come. Just as when tipsy men feel pain less, it was only dully now that we sensed the biting cold, the emptiness of our bellies, even that nagging fear of the final end. It seemed to us a matter of real indifference when the night sorties which the Luftwaffe flew to bring us in supplies became smaller and rarer, when the only warm food began to be a thin broth with rare cubes of sweetish horse-meat, or that we often had to do with no more than a couple of slices of bread all day.

We buried our heads in the snow till our breath melted the white stuff away, but still could not help hearing the bubbling sound of the enemy mortars, by old habit counting the seconds till they burst in destruction nearby. We felt the earth shudder under the H.E.s, or we watched the countless rocket volleys of the Stalin-organs as they came roaring down out of the overcast grey skies, spraying their fiery stuff over enormous areas till the very snow seemed red hot.

In spite of all this we still again and again experienced sheer astonishment when we saw that we were not the only ones whom for the time being death had spared, that there was still much tenacious life in this inferno of bellowing steel, and that that life was manifesting itself now even at that moment by sending red and violent flares into the heavens, warning of attack, warning of tanks, and urgent cries for help. And then we fired straight into the storming, yelling mass of Bolsheviks, and fired automatically as robots until at last the mammoth tanks, clattering down on us, compelled yet another withdrawal farther back still into the cauldron which with every day grew smaller.

Benno Zieser

Russian Tactics

Practically every Russian attack was preceded by large-scale infiltrations, by an 'oozing through' of small units and individual men. In this kind of warfare the Russians have not yet found their masters. However much the outlying areas were kept under observation, the Russian was suddenly there, in the very midst of our own positions, and nobody had seen him come, nor did anybody know whence he had come. In the least likely places, where the going was incredibly difficult, there he was, dug in and all, and in considerable strength. True, it was not difficult for individual men to seep through, considering that our lines were but thinly manned and strong-points few and far between. An average divisional sector was usually more than twelve miles broad. But the amazing fact was that in spite of everybody being alert and wide awake during the whole night, the next morning entire Russian units were sure to be found far behind our front line, complete with equipment and ammunition, and well dug in. These infiltrations were carried out with incredible skill, almost noise-lessly and without a shot being fired.

General von Mellenthin

Von Manstein's armies included Italians, Roumanians and other more or less willing allies of Germany.

Italians in the Snow

When it snowed we had to keep very careful look-out for sudden raids. One night while I was going round with my white shirt over my overcoat, like a ghost, I noticed a Russian patrol trying to slip round under the strong-point. I couldn't see the Russians but felt their presence a few paces from me. I stood silent and still. And they were silent and still. I felt they were looking round in the dark as I was, their weapons at the ready. I was so frightened I almost began trembling. What if they captured and took me away? I tried to control myself but the veins in my throat were throbbing hard. I really was frightened. Finally I made up my mind; I shouted, threw the grenades I had in my hand, and jumped down into the trench. Luckily one of the grenades went off. I heard the Russians running and by the flash saw them retreating into the nearest bushes. From there they opened fire with a machine-gun. Meanwhile some of Pintossi's men had arrived. We began to fire too from the top of the trench. One of us hurried off to get the machine-gun. We fired it and then moved it a few yards. The Russian patrol replied to our fire but slowly drew farther back. Then they stopped some way off and began firing continuously with a heavy machine-gun. But eventually it got too cold, they went back to their dugouts and we to ours. If they'd been able to capture one of us they might have been sent home on leave. In the morning, in sunlight, I went out to look at the tracks they'd left. They'd been farther away than I'd supposed the night before, and I smoked a cigarette and looked at their positions on the other side of the river. Every now and again one of them got up to take snow from the top of the trench. They'll be making tea, I thought. I felt I'd like a little cup, too. And I looked at them as one looks at a peasant scattering manure in the fields.

Sergeant Mario Rigoni Stern

In some respects, Russian tactics had changed little since the disastrous Finnish campaign of 1939–1940.

Russian tactics are a queer mixture; in spite of their brilliance at infiltration and their exceptional mastery of field fortification, yet the rigidity of Russian attacks was almost proverbial. (Although in some cases Russian armoured formations down to their lowest units were a conspicuous exception.) The foolish repetition of attacks on the same spot, the rigidity of Russian artillery fire, and the selection of the terrain for the attack betrayed a total lack of imagination and mental mobility. Our Wireless Intercept Service heard many a time the frantic question: 'What are we to do now?' Only a few commanders of lower formations showed independent judgment when faced with unforeseen situations. On many occasions a successful attack, a break-through, or an accomplished encirclement was not exploited simply because nobody saw it.

But there was an exception to this general clumsiness: the rapid and frequent exchange of units in the front line. Once a division was badly mauled, it disappeared overnight and re-appeared fresh and strong at some other place a few days afterwards.

That is why fighting with Russians resembles the classic contest between Hercules and the Hydra.

General von Mellenthin

On 12 *December von Manstein attacked in an attempt to relieve Paulus. On the* 18th *von Manstein, acting directly against the Führer's instructions, ordered Paulus*

*to leave Stalingrad and break out to the west, where the relieving troops were no
more than forty miles away. Paulus refused. By Christmas Eve the attempt at relief
had failed, and Manstein found the problem taken out of his hands.*

6 Army was doomed; nothing could save Paulus now. Even if by some miracle
a break-out order had been wrung from Hitler, even if the exhausted and starving troops had cut through the Russian ring, the means did not exist to get them
back across the icy steppe to Rostov. The army would have perished on the
march, as surely as Napoleon's veterans between Moscow and the Berezina.

Hitler took the Stalingrad area under his personal command; it was designated as a 'War Theatre under the Supreme Command'. He assumed direct
responsibility for everything regarding Stalingrad.

General von Mellenthin

Mass Grave

Every seven seconds a German soldier dies in Russia. Stalingrad—mass
grave.

Moscow Radio: constantly repeated propaganda broadcast

'Unless a miracle happens, the game is up.'

G.O.C., 23 Panzer Division

It was often asked, 'Is there nobody prepared to tell Paulus the truth?' To
which the answer was, 'Before 24 December there was no need, since there was
still a hope that 6 Army might break out. After 24 December there was no
point, for what is the purpose of telling a man condemned to death that he must
surely die?'

Christmas Eve

The company laughed long and loud at the reference to 'rickety old Father
Christmases'.

The man, who could only raise his right arm, then said:

'To-day is the evening men call Christmas Eve and to-morrow is the day
when, two thousand years ago, salvation was to have been brought to the world.
These two days were to bring us peace. We are faced by an enemy who does not
recognize that day or its eve. We do not know these men against whom we
fight, nor would it occur to us to shoot at them, had it not been for this war. We
are told where to go, and what to do. You are only a handful, but this evening
you should render unto God what is God's, and when this hour has passed
render once more unto Caesar what belongs to Caesar. We wish peace to our
homeland, that same peace which is the promise of Christmas Eve, we wish that
the candles on their trees may burn quietly, that the hands which are clasped
beneath the tree may be unhurried, that those at home may think not of the
winter but of the spring that is to come, that if we should return we shall find
warm hearts to welcome us, and that our homeland may hold its head high and
never need look to the front for an example.'

Five Letters from Stalingrad

My hands are done for, and have been ever since the beginning of December. The little finger of my left hand is missing and—what's even worse—the three middle fingers of my right one are frozen. I can only hold my mug with my thumb and little finger. I'm pretty helpless; only when a man has lost any fingers does he see how much he needs them for the very smallest jobs. The best thing I can do with the little finger is to shoot with it. My hands are finished. After all, even if I'm not fit for anything else, I can't go on shooting for the rest of my life. Or would I still make a gamekeeper, I wonder? That's a pretty grim kind of humour, I know. The only reason I write such things is to keep my nerves steady.

A week ago Kurt Hahnke—you may remember him from the lectures we attended in '37—played the *Appassionata* on a grand piano in a little side street by the Red Square. Not a thing one sees every day of the week—a grand piano planted in the middle of a street. The house it came from had to be demolished, but I suppose they took pity on the piano and fetched it out beforehand. Every private soldier who passed that way had thumped around on it: where else, I ask you, would you find pianos standing out in the street? Anon.

I was horrified when I saw the map. We're quite alone, without any help from outside. Hitler has left us in the lurch. Whether this letter gets away depends on whether we still hold the airfield. We are lying in the north of the city. The men in my battery already suspect the truth, but they aren't so exactly informed as I am. So this is what the end looks like. Hannes and I have no intention of going into captivity; yesterday I saw four men who'd been captured before our infantry re-occupied a strong-point. No, we're not going to be captured. When Stalingrad falls you will hear and read about it. Then you will know that I shall not return. Anon.

For a long time to come, perhaps for ever, this is to be my last letter. A comrade who has to go to the airfield is taking it along with him, as the last machine to leave the pocket is taking off to-morrow morning. The situation has become quite untenable. The Russians are only two miles from the last spot from which aircraft can operate, and when that's gone not even a mouse will get out, to say nothing of me. Admittedly several hundred thousand others won't escape either, but it's precious little consolation to share one's own destruction with other men. Anon.

To return to the present position. Of the division there are only sixty-nine men still fit for action. Bleyer is still alive, and Hartlieb as well. Little Degen has lost both arms; I expect he will soon be in Germany. Life is finished for him, too. Get him to tell you the details which you people think worth knowing. D. has given up hope. I should like to know what he thinks of the situation and its consequences. All we have left are two machine-guns and four hundred rounds. And then a mortar and ten bombs. Except for that all we have are hunger and fatigue. B. has broken out with twenty men on his own initiative. Better to know in three days than in three weeks what the end looks like. Can't say I blame him. Anon.

We have no winter clothes. There are five pairs of *ersatz valenki* per company—great big straw boots on wooden soles. They do not warm the feet and are almost impossible for walking. We have been swindled, and have been condemned to death; we shall die of the war or of frost.

Anon.

The Russian Ultimatum: 8 January 1943

To the Commander-in-Chief of the German 6 Army, Colonel-General Paulus, or his representative, and to all the officers and men of the German units now besieged in Stalingrad.

6 German Army, formations of 4 Panzer Army, and those units sent to reinforce them have been completely encircled since 23 November 1942.

The soldiers of the Red Army have sealed this German Army Group within an unbreakable ring. All hopes of the rescue of your troops by a German offensive from the south or south-west have proved vain. The German units hastening to your assistance were defeated by the Red Army, and the remnants of that force are now withdrawing to Rostov.

The German air transport fleet, which brought you a starvation ration of food, munitions and fuel, has been compelled by the Red Army's successful and rapid advance repeatedly to withdraw to airfields more distant from the encircled troops.

....The situation of your troops is desperate. They are suffering from hunger, sickness and cold. The cruel Russian winter has scarcely yet begun. Hard frosts, cold winds and blizzards still lie ahead. Your soldiers are unprovided with winter clothing and are living in appalling sanitary conditions.

You, as Commander-in-Chief, and all the officers of the encircled forces know well that there is for you no real possibility of breaking out. Your situation is hopeless, and any further resistance senseless.

In view of the desperate situation in which you are placed, and in order to save unnecessary bloodshed, we propose that you accept the following terms of surrender:

1. All the encircled German troops, headed by yourself and your staff, shall cease to resist.

2. You will hand over to such persons as shall be authorized by us, all members of your armed forces, all war materials and all army equipment in an undamaged condition.

3. We guarantee the safety of all officers and men who cease to resist, and their return at the end of the war to Germany or to any other country to which these prisoners of war may wish to go.

4. All personnel of units which surrender may retain their military uniforms, badges of rank, decorations, personal belongings and valuables and, in the case of high-ranking officers, their swords.

5. All officers, non-commissioned officers and men who surrender will immediately receive normal rations.

6. All those who are wounded, sick or frost-bitten will be given medical treatment.

Your reply is to be given in writing by ten o'clock, Moscow time, 9 January 1943. It must be delivered by your personal representative, who is to travel in a car bearing a white flag along the road that leads to the Konny siding at Kotlubanj station. Your representative will be met by a fully-authorized Russian officer in District B, five hundred metres south-east of siding 564 at 10.00 hours on 9 January 1943.

Should you refuse our offer that you lay down your arms, we hereby give you notice that the forces of the Red Army and the Red Air Force will be compelled to proceed with the destruction of the encircled German troops. The responsibility for this will lie with you.

Representing Headquarters Red Army Supreme Command,
Colonel-General of the Artillery Voronov

The Commander-in-Chief of the Forces of the Don front,
Lieutenant-General Rokossovsky

On Hitler's orders, Paulus rejected the demand for surrender.

On 16 January the Russians resumed their attacks to the west and south, and pushed forward remorselessly towards Gumrak, the last airfield remaining to the beleaguered garrison. Whenever the Russians met determined resistance they stopped and attacked somewhere else. By 19 January the ring round 6 Army had grown very tight, and Paulus held a conference with his corps commanders. It was seriously proposed that on 22 January all troops in the 'fortress' should rise as a man, and break out in small groups in an endeavour to reach the German lines on the Don. As Dingler comments, 'This was a plan which despair alone could suggest', and it was quietly forgotten.

During this period various senior commanders and staff officers received orders to fly out of the Stalingrad ring. Among these was Colonel Dingler, whose shattered 3 Motorized Division was then holding a small sector near the water tower of Voroponovo. Together with General Hube, the commander of XIV Panzer Corps, he was to leave Stalingrad and try to improve the supply position of those in the ring. It was with a heavy heart that he left his men behind, and he did not do so before discussing the order with his Divisional Commander and other officers, who saw a ray of hope in this mission. The one and only transport vehicle left to the division—a motor-cycle combination—brought him to the Gumrak landing ground; the road was covered with dead soldiers, burnt-out tanks, abandoned guns, indeed, all the debris of an army in the last stages of dissolution. The airfield presented a similar picture of destruction—a snowy desert littered with aircraft and vehicles. Everywhere lay the corpses of German soldiers; too exhausted to move on, they had just died in the snow.

General von Mellenthin

THE END

6 Army to High Command: 24 January

.... Troops without ammunition or food. Contact maintained with elements only of six divisions. Evidence of disintegration on southern, northern and western fronts. Effective command no longer possible. Little change on eastern front: eighteen thousand wounded without any supplies of dressings or drugs; 44, 76, 100, 305 and 384 Infantry Divisions destroyed. Front torn open as a result of strong break-throughs on three sides. Strong-points and shelter only available in the town itself; further defence senseless. Collapse inevitable. Army requests immediate permission to surrender in order to save lives of remaining troops.

Paulus

Adolf Hitler to 6 Army: 24 January

Surrender is forbidden. 6 Army will hold their positions to the last man and the last round and by their heroic endurance will make an unforgettable contribution towards the establishment of a defensive front and the salvation of the Western world.

Adolf Hitler

31 January

12.18 hours. The dropping of supplies on the Red Square no longer possible, on the Engineer barracks unsafe and on the tractor factory doubtful.

12.30 hours. Enemy forces directly outside the door. The end of the struggle is no longer in doubt.

15.10 hours. From 6 Army Headquarters to VIII Flying Corps and Air Signals Battalion 129 through 9 Anti-Aircraft Division:

Remainder of Stalingrad Headquarters signing off to-day. Good luck and greetings to the homeland.

Lieutenant Wachsland, 6 Army Headquarters

The Russians stand at the door of our bunker. We are destroying our equipment.

This station will no longer transmit.

6 Army Headquarters, 05.45 hours

On this day, General Paulus was promoted to the rank of Field-Marshal.

A Message to Stalin

Carrying out your order, the troops on the Don Front at 4 p.m. on 2 February 1943, completed the rout and destruction of the encircled group of enemy forces at Stalingrad. Twenty-two divisions have been destroyed or taken prisoner.

Lieutenant-General Rokossovsky, Commander of the Don Front
Lieutenant-General Malinin, Chief of Staff of the Don Front

The battle for Stalingrad has ended. Faithful to its oath to fight to the last breath, 6 Army under the exemplary leadership of Field-Marshal Paulus has been overcome by the enemy's superior force and by adverse circumstances.

German High Command official communiqué, 3 February

Captured German Officers

The most unforgettable of them was Lieutenant-General von Arnim, a cousin of the other Arnim who was to be captured in Tunisia a few months later. He was enormously tall, with a long twisted nose, and a look of fury in his long horse-like face with its popping eyes. He had a stupendous display of crosses and orders and mantelpiece ornaments. He, no more than the others, had any desire to explain why they had allowed themselves to be trapped at Stalingrad, and why they had been licked. When somebody put the question, he snarled and said, 'The question is badly put. You should ask how did we hold out so long against such overwhelming numerical superiority?' And one of the sulking ones in the background said something about hunger and cold.

But how they all hated any suggestion that the Red Army was a better army and a better-led army than theirs! When somebody suggested it, Von Arnim snorted and went almost purple with rage.

.... One thing astonished me about these generals: they had been captured only a couple of days ago—and they looked healthy, and not in the least under-nourished. Clearly, throughout the agony of Stalingrad, when their soldiers were dying of hunger, they were continuing to have more or less regular meals. There could be no other explanation for their normal, or almost normal, weight and appearance.

The only man who looked in poor shape was Paulus himself. We weren't allowed to speak to him; he was only shown us. (We could then testify that he was alive and had not committed suicide.) He stepped out of a large cottage—it was more like a villa—gave us a look, then stared at the horizon, and stood on the steps for a minute or two, amid a rather awkward silence, together with two other officers; one was General Schmidt, his Chief of Staff, a sinister, Göring-like creature, wearing a strange fur cap made of imitation leopard skin. Paulus looked pale and sick, and has a nervous twitch in his left cheek. He had more natural dignity than any of the others, and wore only one or two decorations.

Alexander Werth

Post-Mortem

Hitler: 'They have surrendered there formally and absolutely. Otherwise they would have closed ranks, formed a hedgehog, and shot themselves with their last bullet. When you consider that a woman has the pride to leave, to lock herself in, and to shoot herself right away just because she had heard a few insulting remarks,* then I can't have any respect for a soldier who is afraid of that and prefers to go into captivity. I can only say: I can understand a case like that of General Giraud; we come in, he gets out of his car, and is grabbed. But ——'

Zeitzler: 'I can't understand it, either. I'm still of the opinion that it might not be true; perhaps he is lying there badly wounded.'

Hitler: 'No, it is true. . . . They'll be brought to Moscow, to the G.P.U. right away, and they'll blurt out orders for the northern pocket to surrender

* Nothing is known of the incident Hitler refers to.

too.* That Schmidt will sign anything. A man who doesn't have the courage, in such a time, to take the road that every man has to take some time, doesn't have the strength to withstand that sort of thing. He will suffer torture in his soul. In Germany there has been too much emphasis on training the intellect and not enough on strength of character. . . .

'. . . . Here is a man who sees fifty or sixty thousand of his soldiers die defending themselves bravely to the end. How can he surrender himself to the Bolsheviks? Oh, that is ——'

Zeitzler: 'That is something one can't understand at all.'

Hitler: 'But I had my doubts before. That was the moment when I received the report that he was asking what he should do. How can he even ask about such a thing. From now on, every time a fortress is besieged and the commandant is called on to surrender, he is going to ask, "What shall I do now?". . . .'

Zeitzler: 'There is no excuse. When his nerves threaten to break down, then he must kill himself.'

Hitler: 'When the nerves break down, there is nothing left but to admit that one can't handle the situation and to shoot oneself. One can also say the man should have shot himself just as the old commanders who threw themselves on their swords when they saw that the cause was lost. That goes without saying. Even Varrus gave his slave the order: "Now kill me!" '

Zeitzler: 'I still think they may have done that, and that the Russians are only claiming to have captured them all.'

Hitler: 'No.'

After the Battle

The steep river bank covered with the black entrances to trenches and dug-outs resembled a cave town.

Over one of the dug-outs I read a sign half washed-out by rain: *General Rodimtsev's Headquarters.*

This, then, was that narrow strip of land along the river to which our troops had clung tenaciously throughout the siege, which they had held although to hold it was obviously impossible—a fortress one or two hundred yards wide. A command—spoken, not shouted—from divisional headquarters was heard by the men in the forward positions. One had to crawl from dug-out to dug-out, for to raise one's head was asking for sudden death.

A Happy New Year, Comrades! said a sign over the entrance to one of the dug-outs and I pictured them standing face to face with death, drinking to victory on that New Year's Eve. Unfortunately, I was unable to reconstruct the story of the heroes of Chuikov's and Rodimtsev's divisions, for all those who had taken part in that great battle had moved on to the west before I arrived. But I did see the monument to the Defence of Stalingrad.

It is not a monument in the accepted sense. Just a plain wall with the soot-scrawled inscription: *Here Rodimtsev's Guards Stood to the Death.*

Boris Agapov

* A small part of the German forces, under the command of Lieutenant-General Streicher of XI Corps, was still holding out north of Stalingrad at this time. This unit surrendered on the day following this conference.

Doubt

We all had friends on the Russian Front and we tried not to talk too much about them to each other. But one day an old friend of mine—Edith Wieland—wrote, begging me to visit her, as she had just lost her husband in the battle. I found, as she opened the door, a thin, old woman in black, not the proud, confident Edith I had known. She began to cry as she asked me inside.

In the lounge she showed me her husband's last letter from Stalingrad. He asked her to forgive him for anything he might ever have done to hurt her. He had never at any time wanted to hurt her. It was for her alone that he was now living and he loved her more than his life. This was no empty phrase he wrote, because they were now facing death, and it would only be a matter of days or weeks. But as long as he felt his death served a purpose he would be willing to give his life for the Fatherland. He implored her never to give up, no matter what might come, and to bring up their children—the youngest only two months old—in the spirit they had agreed upon.

I was utterly shaken. I could see him standing before me in his officer's uniform, so proud and with the Iron Cross on his chest and the stars of a *Hauptmann*. He had been a strong and virile man, honest as the day.

'Was he wounded when he wrote this letter?' I asked Edith.

'No,' she said quickly. 'I have been told he was not wounded. He met his death with open eyes. He was perfectly well and strong.'

I looked down at the carpet. What kind of death then had he met? As if Edith could guess my thoughts, she said, 'They have written that death came instantaneously. He got a bullet through the head as he came round the corner of a house.'

While I was searching desperately for the right words, Edith spoke again. 'There is one thing that haunts me. I have heard a rumour that they could have escaped, but that Hitler forbade it!'

I was frightened. I had not heard that rumour myself at the time. 'No! Impossible!' I said. 'It would be plain murder. Hitler would never do such a thing. You know that, surely?'

Very slowly Edith lifted her head. 'I am not so sure,' she said in a low voice. 'I keep re-reading that sentence in Albert's letter ("as long as I feel my death serves a purpose"), that doesn't sound a bit like Albert. It sounds as though his confidence was waning, and he was beginning to doubt.'

Else Wendel, housewife

20

THE TIDE TURNS IN THE
PACIFIC: MIDWAY

*By the spring of 1942 the Japanese had established a defensive perimeter which
ran from Burma round Sumatra and Java and along the northern coast of New
Guinea to the western Solomons, then turning north and embracing parts of the
Gilbert and Marshall groups and Wake Island. The Kurile Islands off the coast of
Siberia marked the northern extremity of the perimeter. In late March and April
Japanese naval and air forces had raided far out into the Indian Ocean, attacking
Ceylon and British naval forces with fair success and then returning to their de-
fensive ring. With freedom of action within it and inexhaustible supplies of food and
raw materials, the Japanese considered themselves in a position to fight on indefinitely.
Within a few months they had achieved their aim and had reached the zenith of their
success. General MacArthur, arrived in Australia from the Philippines, prepared to
defend the Southern Continent and plan counter-strokes.*

General MacArthur Arrives in Australia

THE President of the United States ordered me to break through the Japanese
lines and proceed from Corregidor to Australia for the purpose, as I understand
it, of organizing the American offensive against Japan, a primary object of which
is the relief of the Philippines. I came through and I shall return.

General MacArthur

*Long before the Allied victories began; while, indeed, their forces were still being
driven from Burma and the Philippines, the Japanese people in their homeland had
received grim warning of what was to come two years later. On 18 April 1942
General Doolittle flew sixteen B-25 bombers off the U.S.S. Hornet and bombed
Tokyo. This totally unexpected stroke, though isolated, administered a salutary
shock to Japanese morale, so far borne along on the flood-tide of victory. Rudimentary air-raid precautions were hurriedly instituted.*

Thirty Seconds over Tokyo

We were about two minutes out over the bay when we all of us seemed to
look to the right at the same time, and there sat the biggest, fattest-looking
aircraft carrier we had ever seen. It was a couple of miles away, anchored, and
there did not seem to be a man in sight. It was an awful temptation not to change
course and drop one on it. But we had been so drilled in what to do with our
four bombs, and Tokyo was now so close that I decided to go on.

There were no enemy planes in sight. Ahead, I could see what must have

494

been Davey Jones climbing fast and hard and running into innocent-looking black clouds that appeared round his plane.

It took about five minutes to get across our arm of the bay, and, while still over the water, I could see the barrage balloons strung between Tokyo and Yokohama, across the river from Tokyo.

There were no beaches where we came in. Every inch of shoreline was taken up with wharves. I could see some dredging operations filling in more shoreline, just as we were told we would see. We came in over some of the most beautiful yachts I've ever seen, then over the heavier ships at the wharves and low over the first of the rooftops. I gave the ship a little more throttle, for we seemed to be creeping along.

In days and nights of dreaming about Tokyo and thinking of the eight millions who live there, I got the impression that it would be crammed together, concentrated, like San Francisco. Instead it spreads all over creation, like Los Angeles. There is an aggressively modern sameness to much of it and now, as we came in very low over it, I had a bad feeling that we wouldn't find our targets. I had to stay low and thus could see only a short distance ahead and to the sides. I couldn't go up to take a good look without drawing anti-aircraft fire, which I figured would be very accurate by now because the planes that had come in ahead of me all had bombed from fifteen hundred feet. The buildings grew taller. I couldn't see people.

I was almost on the first of our objectives before I saw it. I gave the engines full throttle as Davenport adjusted the prop pitch to get a better grip on the air. We climbed as quickly as possible to fifteen hundred feet, in the manner which we had practised for a month and had discussed for three additional weeks.

There was just time to get up there, level off, attend to the routine of opening the bomb bay, make a short run and let fly with the first bomb. The red light blinked on my instrument board, and I knew the first 500-pounder had gone.

Our speed was picking up. The red light blinked again, and I knew Clever had let the second bomb go. Just as the light blinked, a black cloud appeared about a hundred yards or so in front of us and rushed past at great speed. Two more appeared ahead of us, on about the line of our wingtips, and they too swept past. They had our altitude perfectly, but they were leading us too much.

The third red light flickered, and, since we were now over a flimsy area in the southern part of the city, the fourth light blinked. That was an incendiary which I knew would separate as soon as it hit the wind and that dozens of small fire bombs would moult from it.

The moment the fourth red light showed I put the nose of the Ruptured Duck into a deep dive. I had changed the course somewhat for the short run leading up to the dropping of the incendiary. Now, as I dived, I looked back and out: I got a quick, indelible vision of one of our 500-pounders as it hit our steel-smelter target. The plant seemed to puff out its walls and then subside and dissolve in a black-and-red cloud.

Our diving speed picked up to 350 m.p.h. in less time that it takes to tell it, and up there in the front of the vibrating bomber I dimly wondered why the Japanese didn't throw up a wall of machine-gun fire. We would have to fly right through it.

I flattened out over a long row of low buildings and homes and got the hell out of there.

Captain Ted W. Lawson

Air-raid Precautions: Japan

The repeated air-raid drills took up a large part of the day when they were called. I took active part in only one of these drills and I think my neighbours were glad when I did not reappear. People looked at me instead of listening to the warden and that created too much confusion. Running uphill with pails of water, without spilling any water from the buckets, seemed to me a silly and tedious way to fight a war. We had to fill small bags with sand and stack them outside each dwelling, supposedly for use in putting out fires the air raids would start. We never knew and were never told whether that was the purpose of the sandbags or not, and I could only guess what the authorities had in mind. Additional fire protection was supplied by a large container of water outside each house and what looked like a huge fly swatter (to beat out the flames).

Sometimes a smudge pot would be placed in the lower branches of a tree, and the women would have to line up with pails of water to throw in an attempt to extinguish the smudge fire. Usually these exercises were at night when the women were exhausted from their household chores. The warden would shout 'next', and I would hear the clap-clap of the wooden clogs and then the splash of the water.

. . . . The so-called shelter each household had to prepare in its garden was often only a deep hole, exposed and damp. These holes always depressed me; they looked so like open graves, gaping expectantly at us. Kikuya had to dig ours, and our new dog Kuri did his bit, too. Like a true war dog, he worked side-by-side with Kikuya, and I longed for a movie camera to record the scene.

Besides the shelter, every household had to have on hand one rucksack filled with supplies, bandages, a few first-aid articles, rice, a cooking-pan, and the padded hoods which we were required to wear. Many people were to be badly burned because of those hoods. The padding used was made of thick cotton, and when it caught fire the wearers were unaware of the blaze until it was too late to avoid serious burns. All women were requested to wear either monpe (the Japanese 'pantaloons' I had learned to appreciate) or slacks, although slacks were frowned on as too Western. Permanents and nail polish were also considered in bad taste. But the Japanese woman, in spite of having been taught obedience from birth, rebelled at the prohibition of permanents. She continued to have her hair done, sometimes under great stress, and often incurring real danger during air raids. These governmental restrictions were short-sighted. The Japanese lady had always been a colourful, well-groomed person. She should not have been robbed of such attractiveness unnecessarily and forced to adopt drab, muddy colours in place of her gay, delightful kimono. A happy woman is a more efficient woman, even in war-time.

The men were requested to wear what was called 'the national uniform', a dull khaki affair with puttees wrapped around the trousers. This uniform included a field cap identical with the army cap except it was without insignia.

On the eighth of every month, to commemorate the beginning of the war, every man was required to wear the uniform and the women had to wear slacks or *monpe*. Anyone dressed otherwise was stopped at the exits of the stations and roundly scolded. Often some poor woman, harried and overworked, was forced to return home and dress again.

I noticed that many people cultivated flowers on top of their air-raid shelters. When the evening's work was done, they would sit in front of their shops and homes to admire the few blossoms they had been able to nurture.

Gwen Terasaki

Few nations can have enjoyed the full flush of unrelieved victory for so short a time as the Japanese. In fact, no sooner had they reached the limits of their advance within their original perimeter than the first of two battles which turned the tide of war took place.

In early May 1942 the Japanese launched the first stage of a three-fold operation to extend their perimeter. This stage was designed to begin the envelopment of northern and eastern Australia. They occupied the eastern Solomons and began to build an airfield on Guadalcanal, and then a strong naval force sailed to support a troop convoy heading for Port Moresby in eastern New Guinea. To meet them in the Coral Sea was an American force of approximately equal strength. On 4 May ensued the first naval action in history to be fought entirely in the air, in which the opposing fleets never came within sight or gunshot range of one another.

This battle of aircraft carriers ended with one sunk and one damaged on the American side and two damaged on the Japanese side, so the latter claimed the victory, but it was a hollow one, for the convoy destined for Port Moresby turned back.

THE BATTLE OF MIDWAY

Encouraged by an apparent victory in the Coral Sea, the Japanese pressed on towards the other objectives of their extending operation. One was the Aleutian islands of Attu and Kiska, cold lands in a world of fog, which they took without trouble and later abandoned. The other was the fortified atoll of Midway protecting Hawaii, towards which Admiral Yamamoto sailed with all the forces he could muster in the last week of May 1942. The decisive battle of the Far Eastern war was about to be fought.

The Battle of Midway took place on 4 June 1942. The Japanese Navy, excelling in carrier strength and flushed with victory after the Hawaiian attack, was unaware that operational secrets had leaked out. And so we fell into the trap laid by the enemy, who was forewarned of our movements. A severe defeat ensued for the Japanese. Midway was a crucial battle which reversed the whole position in the Pacific war.

Mochitsura Hashimoto

The Advance Guard sails from Japan

The fleet had formed a single column for the passage through the strait. Twenty-one ships in all, they cruised along at intervals of a thousand yards, resembling for all the world a peacetime naval review. Far out in front was Rear-Admiral Susumu Kimura's flagship, light cruiser *Nagara*, leading the twelve ships of Destroyer Squadron 10. Next came Rear-Admiral Hiroaki Abe's Cruiser Division 8—*Tone*, the flagship, and *Chikuma*—followed by the second section of Battleship Division 3, made up of fast battleships *Haruna* and *Kirishima*. (The first section of Battleship Division 3, *Hiei* and *Kongo*, had been assigned to Admiral Kondo's invasion force for this operation.) Behind *Kirishima* came large carriers *Akagi* and *Kaga*, comprising Carrier Division I, under Admiral Nagumo's direct command. Rear-Admiral Tamon Yamaguchi's Carrier Division 2—*Hiryu* and *Soryu*—brought up the rear, completing the Nagumo Force.

Presently a dozen or so fishing boats waiting for the tide hove into sight to starboard, and their crews waved and cheered as we passed. To port, the tiny island of Yurishima appeared to be floating on the surface of the sea, its thick covering of green foliage set off against the dim background of Aoshima. Beyond, the coast of Shikoku lay hidden in mist.

As the fleet steamed on, three seaplanes of the Kure Air Corps passed overhead, their pontoons looking like oversized shoes. The planes were on their way to neutralize any enemy submarines which might be lying in wait for us outside Bungo Strait.

Mitsuo Fuchida

The Interceptors

'In accordance with Commander-in-Chief Pacific Operation Plan 29-42, the *Hornet* got underway from Pearl Harbor, 28 May 1942, recovering the Air Group at sea, at 16.30, the same afternoon,' begins the *Hornet's* Action Report for the Battle of Midway. As was usual, her aircraft had been stationed ashore when the ship was in port. They flew out to roost when she was a short time out of Pearl Harbor. Minutes after the planes were aboard, the speaker system blared throughout the ship:

'This is the captain. We are going to intercept a Jap attack on Midway.'

That settled any doubts in the minds of the *Hornet* pilots.

Not all of Torpedo Eight was aboard. Six new Grumman Avengers, part of VT-8, were based on Midway. The *Hornet* pilots had been training for months, long before the ship got her final coat of paint, but not one was blooded. Their total average flying hours were somewhere around 285 each. Routine training was conducted en route, and most of the aircraft, in addition to combat air patrol, were scheduled for daily exercises. The force steamed on to a rendezvous with Rear-Admiral Frank Jack Fletcher's Task Force 17.

. . . . On 1 June, Mitscher wrote out a message for Commander Henderson to read over the bull horn: 'The enemy are approaching for an attempt to seize Midway. This attack will probably be accompanied by a feint at western Alaska.'

We are going to prevent them from taking Midway, if possible. Be ready and keep on the alert. Let's get a few more yellowtails.' Although some skippers, through oversight or intent, kept their crews in suspense, Mitscher tried to inform every man of what might be hanging beneath the next cloud.

The next day, at 14.00, the *Hornet* task force kept its rendezvous with the *Yorktown* northeast of Midway. Admiral Fletcher assumed tactical command of the entire American defensive force, but Nimitz, back in Pearl Harbor, still called the strategical signals. Halsey was ill, and Rear-Admiral Raymond Spruance had taken over Task Force 16, in which the *Hornet* rode.

Theodore Taylor

Contact

During the next hour there was a confusing succession of reported contacts on our force both by individual flying boats and by small numbers of enemy planes of unidentified type. There was also a further radio warning from *Tone's* search plane at 05.55 that fifteen enemy planes were heading towards us. The formation raised its speed to twenty-eight knots, and *Tone*, after sighting three planes overhead at 06.43, began making smoke to provide concealment against attack. Since no attack took place during this entire period, however, some of the reported contacts must have been erroneous or on our own fighters patrolling overhead. But there was no question that enemy flying boats were shadowing us, skilfully manœuvring in and out of the clouds to elude pursuit.

Each time one of the persistent PBYs was sighted, now to starboard, now to port, *Akagi's* harassed fighter director would shout orders to our combat air patrol to go after it. The enemy pilots, however, were so adept at weaving through the clouds that the fighters merely exhausted themselves to no avail. While our own movements were thus observed and reported continuously, there was still no warning from our own search planes of any enemy task force.

Mitsuo Fuchida

Midway Attacked

.... The first Japanese air strike—thirty-six torpedo aircraft, thirty-six dive-bombers, and thirty-six fighters, under Lieutenant Tomonaga, was picked up by Midway radar forty-three miles north-west of the island. The alarm was sounded, every aircraft able to leave the ground took to the air, and at 6.16 a.m., when thirty miles out, the Marine Corps fighter squadron, twenty-six aircraft in all, encountered the Japanese van, but was out-numbered and almost annihilated. 'The entire island,' wrote an American officer, 'was deadly silent after the buzz of the planes taking off. It was a beautiful sunny morning. The men all strained for a first glimpse, and I had to sharply remind the lookouts to keep the other sectors covered against surprise. Then we saw the Japs, and the tension snapped. A moment later we were in action.' Although considerable damage was done to the installations on the island, few men were killed and none of the runways was rendered unusable. At 6.50 a.m. the attack was over.

Closing for the Kill

Shortly after 07.00, while Army B-17s were unsuccessfully attempting to damage the enemy from twenty thousand feet, the *Hornet*'s fighter pilots were called to deck; then the scout bombers were manned. Finally, Waldron's torpedo planes were ready. Hitting fast ships at sea is a job for planes that go in low. Then Mitscher spoke into the bridge microphone: 'We intend to launch planes to attack the enemy while their planes are still returning from Midway. We will close to about a hundred miles from the enemy's position.'

Theodore Taylor

Surprise

Already about an hour before Tomonaga's Midway strike planes got back to the carriers, however, there had been a development which completely altered the battle situation confronting Admiral Nagumo. *Tone*'s No. 4 search plane, which had been launched a full half-hour behind schedule, finally reached its three-hundred-mile search limit on course 100° at 07.20, and it then veered north to fly a sixty-mile dog-leg before heading back. Eight minutes later its observer suddenly discerned, far off to port, a formation of some ten ships heading south-east. Without waiting until it could get a closer look, the plane immediately flashed a message to the Nagumo Force: 'Ten ships, apparently enemy, sighted. Bearing 010, distant two hundred and forty miles from Midway. Course 150°, speed more than twenty knots. Time, 07.28.'

This vital message was received by the flagship only after several minutes' delay occasioned by the relaying of the message through *Tone*. When it reached Admiral Nagumo and his staff on *Akagi*'s bridge, it struck them like a bolt from the blue. Until this morning no one had anticipated that an enemy surface force could possibly appear so soon, much less suspected that enemy ships were already in the vicinity waiting to ambush us. Now the entire picture was changed.

Lieutenant-Commander Ono, the Staff Intelligence Officer, quickly plotted the enemy's reported position on the navigation chart and measured off the distance between it and our force. The enemy was just two hundred miles away! This meant that he was already within striking range of our planes, but if he had carriers, we were also within *his* reach. The big question now was what composed the enemy force. Above all, did it contain any carriers?

Mitsuo Fuchida

Strike

There was a cloud-flecked sky as Soucek gave orders to send the *Hornet*'s stingers off. The fighters, Grumman Wildcats, were first; Rodee's scouts in the Dauntlesses followed; then Johnson's dive-bombers, also in Dauntlesses; and lastly Waldron's heavy-bellied torpedo planes.

It took almost an hour for the launching and Mitscher bent over the railing, occasionally giving an order, and following each plane off with his eyes. Once the last torpedo plane was airborne, Mitscher was practically out of touch with the fight. Radio silence was maintained. Squadron commanders were in charge, with Stanhope Ring, a senior, over them. Mitscher could not contact, advise, or 'assist. He would have to wait until they got back to find out what happened.

Last-minute teletype instructions to the *Hornet*'s air group placed the enemy at a distance of 155 miles. The fighters and bombers climbed to nineteen thousand feet, flying at 125 m.p.h. Waldron stayed below a layer of cumulus clouds, nursing his planes along at 110 m.p.h. They breezed through the morning without knowledge that Admiral Nagumo had changed the course of his carriers and was retiring. When the bombers and fighters reached their supposed position, Nagumo and his carriers were not in sight. Stanhope Ring kept the air group travelling south-west.

But Jack Waldron, down below the blanket of clouds at fifteen hundred feet, unmindful that his fighter cover was not above, rolled the torpedo squadron northward on a strong hunch. He found Nagumo and the carriers *Hiryu*, *Akagi*, *Kaga* and *Soryu*. What Waldron then did has been called foolhardy, but it was also heroic. He rode his torpedo planes in against the carriers without fighter protection; full into the ack-ack and whirling Zeros, hoping to deliver his weenies and pickles. Waldron presented fifteen solid targets to the Japanese gun gallery. Ensign Gay was shot down and hid beneath a floating seat cushion. He witnessed the Battle of Midway from that bobbing seat and was picked up later.

The *Hornet*'s bombers and fighters were running low on gas. But planes from the *Enterprise* and the *Yorktown* arrived to convert three of Nagumo's carriers into flotsam. The *Hiryu* sent her planes after the *Yorktown* in retaliation. Meanwhile, back on the *Hornet*, Mitscher stirred about the bridge uneasily. He knew little or nothing of what was going on. Communications had been spotty all morning. Action reports seeped in, but nothing to indicate any decisive combat. Some of the planes had run out of fuel and crash landed in Midway's lagoon; others had refuelled at Midway. Survivors of the *Hornet*'s snipe hunt banged down on deck to refuel. They didn't need to rearm. They hadn't fought. Mitscher pushed on, holding an easterly course at high speed to land his planes. The first wheels hit the deck at 13.20. Rodee's scouts and part of Bombing Eight fluttered in. Then they waited for the fighters and for Torpedo Eight.

Ring and Rodee went to the bridge to tell Mitscher they hadn't seen the enemy and knew nothing of Waldron. Then Quillen, the rear gunner in Ensign White's dive-bomber, reported that he thought he had heard Waldron's voice on his radio: 'What I heard was Johnny One to Johnny Two. I am quite sure it was Lieutenant-Commander Waldron's voice as I have heard him on the air a number of times. I also heard him say, Watch those fighters. Also, See that splash. Also, How'm I doing, Dobbs? Also, Attack immediately. Also, I'd give a million to know who did that. . . .'

And then there was silence. Thus they died, all except one. Fifteen planes, each with pilot and crewman.

Japanese planes were attacking the *Yorktown*. Soon a column of smoke reached into the north-west sky. Some *Hornet* fighters were over there trying to ward off the blows, and got three Zeros. The *Yorktown* was mortally wounded. One *Yorktown* pilot wobbled towards the *Hornet* and crashed down in a grind of ripping metal, his machine-guns peppering the island structure. Minutes later, the officer of the deck reported to Mitscher: five dead and twenty wounded. With Fletcher's Task Force 17 flag burning in the *Yorktown*, Rear-Admiral Raymond Spruance took local tactical command. A Japanese submarine finished the *Yorktown* later.

Spruance signalled Mitscher and the *Enterprise* to get the *Hiryu*. Her planes had destroyed the *Yorktown* and could do the same to the *Enterprise* and the *Hornet*. At 18.03, Mitscher launched sixteen bombers to join the *Enterprise* striking group. *Enterprise* pilots got there first and laid into the enemy carriers. The *Hornet* bombers circled at twenty thousand feet while nine B-17s attempted to bomb the *Hiryu*'s escorting battleships, missing by a wide margin. Then VB-8 pushed over into their dives, releasing bombs at low altitude for hits on a battleship and a heavy cruiser. The *Hornet* had finally drawn blood.

As m re action reports drifted in, Mitscher informed the *Hornet* crew, 'Four Japanese carriers are afire. Direct hits have been scored on their battleships and cruisers.'

It was growing dark, and the *Hornet*, blacked out, soon blended into the night. How could her surviving bombers find the flight deck? Two planes angled towards the task force. Then others droned up. None of the *Hornet* pilots had qualified in night carrier landings.

'Turn on the truck lights,' Mitscher ordered. The dim red beacons shone out from her masthead but the planes passed over. Mitscher knew the pilots could not possibly spot her deck. 'Let's give them more light.'

Two search beams climbed into the air over the *Hornet*; a string of lights outlined the flight deck to port.

Henderson said, 'Captain, there must be subs here.'

'The hell with the subs,' Mitscher said, straining to glimpse the aircraft as they approached and finally landed.

He had thought Stan Ring was lost. Then Ring came up to the bridge, sweaty and haggard. The surviving pilots gathered in the wardroom and pantry, happy to be alive, but the joy was tempered by concern about the still unreported torpedo-men.

Mitscher ordered Dr. Sam Osterlough to the bridge, and Sam came up with his pockets bulging and clinking. 'How are they?' Mitscher asked.

'Some are a little shaky.'

'Give them each a bottle and see to it personally that they go to bed.'

Osterlough, on the way to deliver his 'packages' to the pilots, stopped by Mitscher's cabin, pulled one of the two-ounce bottles of brandy out of his pocket, and placed it on the desk.

By now, it was obvious that Torpedo Eight was not returning. It appeared the *Hornet* had lost at least twenty-five aircraft and almost double that number of pilots and crewmen. The day's operations had not been good, but the bombers had partially recouped in the sunset attack. There were five bodies in readiness for burial from the gun accident. Luck had been very bad. Theodore Taylor

The Slaughter of the Carriers

As our fighters ran out of ammunition during the fierce battle they returned to the carriers for replenishment, but few ran low on fuel. Service crews cheered the returning pilots, patted them on the shoulder, and shouted words of encouragement. As soon as a plane was ready again the pilot nodded, pushed forward the throttle, and roared back into the sky. This scene was repeated time and again as the desperate air struggle continued.

Preparations for a counter-strike against the enemy had continued on board our four carriers throughout the enemy torpedo attacks. One after another, planes were hoisted from the hangar and quickly arranged on the flight deck. There was no time to lose. At 10.20 Admiral Nagumo gave the order to launch when ready. On *Akagi*'s flight deck all planes were in position with engines warming up. The big ship began turning into the wind. Within five minutes all her planes would be launched.

Five minutes! Who would have dreamed that the tide of battle would shift completely in that brief interval of time?

Visibility was good. Clouds were gathering at about three thousand metres, however, and though there were occasional breaks, they afforded good concealment for approaching enemy planes. At 10.24 the order to start launching came from the bridge by voice-tube. The Air Officer flapped a white flag, and the first Zero fighter gathered speed and whizzed off the deck. At that instant a lookout screamed: 'Hell-Divers!' I looked up to see three black enemy planes plummeting towards our ship. Some of our machine-guns managed to fire a few frantic bursts at them, but it was too late. The plump silhouettes of the American Dauntless dive-bombers quickly grew larger, and then a number of black objects suddenly floated eerily from their wings. Bombs! Down they came straight towards me! I fell intuitively to the deck and crawled behind a command post mantelet.

The terrifying scream of the dive-bombers reached me first, followed by the crashing explosion of a direct hit. There was a blinding flash and then a second explosion, much louder than the first. I was shaken by a weird blast of warm air. There was still another shock, but less severe, apparently a near-miss. Then followed a startling quiet as the barking of guns suddenly ceased. I got up and looked at the sky. The enemy planes were already gone from sight.

The attackers had got in unimpeded because our fighters, which had engaged the preceding wave of torpedo planes only a few moments earlier, had not yet had time to regain altitude. Consequently, it may be said that the American dive-bombers' success was made possible by the earlier martyrdom of their torpedo planes. Also, our carriers had no time to evade because clouds hid the enemy's approach until he dived down to the attack. We had been caught flat-footed in the most vulnerable condition possible—decks loaded with planes armed and fuelled for an attack.

Looking about, I was horrified at the destruction that had been wrought in a matter of seconds. There was a huge hole in the flight deck just behind the amidship elevator. The elevator itself, twisted like molten glass, was dropping into the hangar. Deck plates reeled upwards in grotesque configurations. Planes stood tail up, belching livid flame and jet-black smoke. Reluctant tears streamed down my cheeks as I watched the fires spread, and I was terrified at the prospect of induced explosions which would surely doom the ship. I heard Masuda yelling, 'Inside! Get inside! Everybody who isn't working! Get inside!'

Unable to help, I staggered down a ladder and into the ready room. It was already jammed with badly burned victims from the hangar deck. A new explosion was followed quickly by several more, each causing the bridge structure to tremble. Smoke from the burning hangar gushed through passageways and into the bridge and ready room, forcing us to seek other refuge. Climbing back to the bridge, I could see that *Kaga* and *Soryu* had also been hit and were giving off heavy columns of black smoke. The scene was horrible to behold.

Akagi had taken two direct hits, one on the after rim of the amidship elevator, the other on the rear guard on the port side of the flight deck. Normally, neither would have been fatal to the giant carrier, but induced explosions of fuel and munitions devastated whole sections of the ship, shaking the bridge and filling the air with deadly splinters. As fire spread among the planes lined up wing to wing on the after flight deck, their torpedoes began to explode, making it impossible to bring the fires under control. The entire hangar area was a blazing inferno, and the flames moved swiftly towards the bridge.

Because of the spreading fire, our general loss of combat efficiency, and especially the severance of external communication facilities, Nagumo's Chief of Staff, Rear-Admiral Kusaka, urged that the flag be transferred at once to light cruiser *Nagara*. Admiral Nagumo gave only a half-hearted nod, but Kusaka patiently continued his entreaty: 'Sir, most of our ships are still intact. You must command them.'

The situation demanded immediate action, but Admiral Nagumo was reluctant to leave his beloved flagship. Most of all he was loath to leave behind the officers and men of *Akagi*, with whom he had shared every joy and sorrow of war. With tears in his eyes, Captain Aoki spoke up: 'Admiral, I will take care of the ship. Please, we all implore you, shift your flag to *Nagara* and resume command of the Force.'

At this moment Lieutenant-Commander Nishibayashi, the Flag Secretary, came up and reported to Kusaka: 'All passages below are on fire, sir. The only means of escape is by rope from the forward window of the bridge down to the deck, then by the outboard passage to the anchor deck. *Nagara*'s boat will come alongside the anchor deck port, and you can reach it by rope ladder.'

Kusaka made a final plea to Admiral Nagumo to leave the doomed ship. At last convinced that there was no possibility of maintaining command from *Akagi*, Nagumo bade the Captain good-bye and climbed from the bridge window with the aid of Nishibayashi. The Chief of Staff and other staff and headquarters officers followed. The time was 10.46.

On the bridge there remained only Captain Aoki, his Navigator, the Air Officer, a few ratings, and myself. Aoki was trying desperately to get in touch with the engine room. The Chief Navigator was struggling to see if anything could be done to regain rudder control. The others were gathered on the anchor deck fighting the raging fire as best they could. But the unchecked flames were already licking at the bridge. Hammock mantelets around the bridge structure were beginning to burn. The Air Officer looked back at me and said, 'Fuchida, we won't be able to stay on the bridge much longer. You'd better get to the anchor deck before it is too late.'

In my condition this was no easy task. Helped by some sailors, I managed to get out of the bridge window and slid down the already smouldering rope to the gun deck. There I was still ten feet above the flight deck. The connecting monkey ladder was red hot, as was the iron plate on which I stood. There was nothing to do but jump, which I did. At the same moment another explosion occurred in the hangar, and the resultant blast sent me sprawling. Luckily the deck on which I landed was not yet afire, for the force of the fall knocked me out momentarily. Returning to consciousness, I struggled to rise to my feet, but both of my ankles were broken.

Crewmen finally came to my assistance and took me to the anchor deck, which was already jammed. There I was strapped into a bamboo stretcher and lowered to a boat which carried me, along with other wounded, to light cruiser *Nagara*. The transfer of Nagumo's staff and of the wounded was completed at 11.30. The cruiser got under way, flying Admiral Nagumo's flag at her mast.

Meanwhile, efforts to bring *Akagi*'s fires under control continued, but it became increasingly obvious that this was impossible. As the ship came to a halt, her bow was still pointed into the wind, and pilots and crew had retreated to the anchor deck to escape the flames, which were reaching down to the lower hangar deck. When the dynamos went out, the ship was deprived not only of illumination but of pumps for combating the conflagration as well. The fireproof hangar doors had been destroyed, and in this dire emergency even the chemical fire extinguishers failed to work.

The valiant crew located several hand pumps, brought them to the anchor deck and managed to force water through long hoses into the lower hangar and decks below. Firefighting parties, wearing gas masks, carried cumbersome pieces of equipment and fought the flames courageously. But every induced explosion overhead penetrated to the deck below, injuring men and interrupting their desperate efforts. Stepping over fallen comrades, another damage-control party would dash in to continue the struggle, only to be mowed down by the next explosion. Corpsmen and volunteers carried out dead and wounded from the lower first-aid station, which was jammed with injured men. Doctors and surgeons worked like machines.

The engine rooms were still undamaged, but fires in the middle deck sections had cut off all communication between the bridge and the lower levels of the ship. Despite this the explosions, shocks and crashes above, plus the telegraph indicator which had rung up 'Stop', told the engine-room crews in the bowels of the ship that something must be wrong. Still, as long as the engines were undamaged and full propulsive power was available they had no choice but to stay at General Quarters. Repeated efforts were made to communicate with the bridge, but every channel of contact, including the numerous auxiliary ones, had been knocked out.

The intensity of the spreading fires increased until the heat-laden air invaded the ship's lowest sections through the intakes, and men working there began falling from suffocation. In a desperate effort to save his men, the Chief Engineer,

Commander K. Tampo, made his way up through the flaming decks until he was able to get a message to the Captain reporting conditions below. An order was promptly given for all men in the engine spaces to come up on deck. But it was too late. The orderly who tried to carry the order down through the blazing hell never returned, and not a man escaped from the engine room.

As the number of dead and wounded increased and the fires got further out of control, Captain Aoki finally decided at 18.00 that the ship must be abandoned. The injured were lowered into boats and cutters sent alongside by the screening destroyers. Many uninjured men leapt into the sea and swam away from the stricken ship. Destroyers *Arashi* and *Nowaki* picked up all survivors. When the rescue work was completed, Captain Aoki radioed to Admiral Nagumo at 19.20 from one of the destroyers, asking permission to sink the crippled carrier. This enquiry was monitored by the Combined Fleet flagship, whence Admiral Yamamoto dispatched an order at 22.25 to delay the carrier's disposition. Upon receipt of this instruction, the Captain returned to his carrier alone. He reached the anchor deck, which was still free from fire, and there lashed himself to an anchor to await the end.

Meanwhile, uncontrollable fires continued to rage throughout *Kaga*'s length, and finally, at 16.40, Commander Amagai gave the order to abandon ship. Survivors were transferred to the two destroyers standing by. Two hours later the conflagration subsided enough to enable Commander Amagai to lead a damage-control party back on board in the hope of saving the ship. Their valiant efforts proved futile, however, and they again withdrew. The once crack carrier, now a burning hulk, was wrenched by two terrific explosions before sinking into the depths at 19.25 in position 30° 20′ N., 179° 17′ W. In this battle eight hundred men of *Kaga*'s crew, one-third of her complement, were lost.

Soryu, the third victim of the enemy dive-bombing attack, received one hit fewer than *Kaga*, but the devastation was just as great. When the attack broke, deck parties were busily preparing the carrier's planes for take-off, and their first awareness of the onslaught came when great flashes of fire were seen sprouting from *Kaga*, some distance off to port, followed by explosions and tremendous columns of black smoke. Eyes instinctively looked skyward just in time to see a spear of thirteen American planes plummeting down on *Soryu*. It was 10.25.

Three hits were scored in as many minutes. The first blasted the flight deck in front of the forward elevator, and the next two straddled the amidship elevator, completely wrecking the deck and spreading fire to petrol tanks and munition storage rooms. By 10.30 the ship was transformed into a hell of smoke and flames, and induced explosions followed shortly.

In the next ten minutes the main engines stopped, the steering system went out, and fire mains were destroyed. Crewmen, forced by the flames to leave their posts, had just arrived on deck when a mighty explosion blasted many of them into the water. Within twenty minutes of the first bomb hit the ship was such a mass of fire that Captain Ryusaku Yanagimoto ordered 'Abandon ship!' Many men jumped into the water to escape the searing flames and were picked up by destroyers *Hamakaze* and *Isokaze*. Others made more orderly transfers to the destroyers.

It was soon discovered, however, that Captain Yanagimoto had remained on the bridge of the blazing carrier. No ship commander in the Japanese Navy was more beloved by his men. His popularity was such that whenever he was going to address the assembled crew, they would gather an hour or more in advance to ensure getting a place up front. Now, they were determined to rescue him at all costs.

Chief Petty Officer Abe, a Navy wrestling champion, was chosen to return and rescue the Captain, because it had been decided to bring him to safety by force if he refused to come willingly. When Abe climbed to *Soryu*'s bridge he found Captain Yanagimoto standing there motionless, sword in hand, gazing resolutely towards the ship's bow. Stepping forward, Abe said, 'Captain, I have come on behalf of all your men to take you to safety. They are waiting for you. Please come with me to the destroyer, sir.'

When this entreaty met with silence, Abe guessed the Captain's thoughts and started towards him with the intention of carrying him bodily to the waiting boat. But the sheer strength of will and determination of his grim-faced commander stopped him short. He turned tearfully away, and as he left the bridge he heard Captain Yanagimoto calmly singing *Kimigayo*, the national anthem.

Mitsuo Fuchida

On 5 June, Mitscher launched twenty-six bombers for a strike against the still burning carriers and battleships. The planes found only oil slicks to mark the major ships but attacked a destroyer leaving the scene. Once again, they roared back over the task force in darkness, and once again, Mitscher lit up the *Hornet*. Out of gas, they sputtered in.

On 6 June, search planes fanned out to find the remnants. Running low on gas, Gee landed on the *Enterprise*, and unaware of his relative inexperience, the *Enterprise* sent him off on a long-range search mission. After a few hours he spied some ripples on the mirrored ocean and went down for a better look. Soon Gee relayed word that two groups of the Japanese fleet had been located. The pilot Mitscher had grounded in January thus vindicated himself completely.

Mitscher launched twenty-six bombers again, along with eight fighters. At 11.50, *Hornet* planes attacked two cruisers and a destroyer. The cruisers *Mogami* and *Mikuma* were sunk by dive bombing. A few weeks later, the pilots of *Hornet*'s VB-8 were nicknamed 'The Bombing Fools' because of their low-altitude drops.

A little later that day, when the planes had returned and were being re-armed for a second strike, the *Hornet*'s radio intercepted a message from a Japanese admiral saying he was being attacked (by *Enterprise* planes). The *Hornet*'s planes made the second shuttle to the fleeing enemy, and then came home for a rest. The Battle of Midway was over.

Theodore Taylor

The End

On 7 June, with no enemy in sight and his ships in need of fuel, Yamamoto called off his vain pursuit and retired towards the homeland.

Mogami, in the meantime, had continued westward in her effort to lure the enemy. Through the untiring efforts of her crew, a speed of twenty knots was achieved by 15.15 despite the heavy bomb damage she had sustained and the loss of her bow. She was fortunate that no enemy planes had appeared since *Mikuma*'s sinking, and she was able to creep out of the very jaws of death, the last Japanese warship to come clear of enemy attacks in the Midway battle. Kondo's force finally rendezvoused with cripped *Mogami* and provided escort to Truk.

Further American attempts to hit the retreating Japanese Fleet this day were made by 26 B-17s from Midway, but the foul weather thwarted these efforts and no contacts were made. Alert to the possibility of attack by planes based on Wake Island, the enemy carriers also gave up the chase, and the action was over.

Thus fell the curtain on a spectacular and historic battle. Japan's sole consolation for the defeat lay in the minuscule success of having captured two Aleutian bases. The northern operations, resumed after their earlier cancellation, had progressed smoothly and led to the occupation of the islands of Attu and Kiska on 7 June. But these unimportant acquisitions were small compensation for the devastating fleet losses suffered to the south, and in the end they were to bog us down still deeper in the quicksands of defeat.

The catastrophe of Midway definitely marked the turning of the tide in the Pacific war, and thenceforward that tide bore Japan inexorably on towards final capitulation.

Mitsuo Fuchida

For Japan, Midway was to be what El Alamein and Stalingrad were to Germany later in the same year of 1942—the turning-point of their fortunes. Japanese expansion had been stopped.

21

THE PRISONERS

While the armies contended, another battle was being fought out less sensationally but just as bitterly behind barbed wire. The prisoners of war fought boredom and frustration in many ingenious ways, trying to raise their morale and make confinement less intolerable. The more enterprising and active among them planned constantly for the day of escape.

EUROPE

The Prison

THE Tower, which at various times had housed Saxon kings, fallen women, Communists, lunatics and dissident Czechs, was in the winter of 1941–1942 the seat of six hundred prisoners of war who had been sent to it from milder places, either on account of escaping or because they had otherwise by act or word incurred German displeasure. It was called *Sonderlager* ('Special Camp') and sometimes *Straflager* ('Punishment Camp'). A beetling spot, overlooking the small town of Colditz in the very middle of Germany, it was intended to be a firm and final immurement for these prisoners whose isolation was also, in the German view, a quarantine measure.

The mingling of nationalities was the brightest feature of the Tower. The Germans too seemed to feel a shy pride in this speciality which fluttered flag-like above the sterile landscape of the captor-captive situation.

English, French, Poles, Dutch and Belgians, though they had separate quarters and spent most of their time within their own groups, were all very much aware of each other. Membership of Colditz, however earned, seemed to vouch for a prisoner and thus enjoined a fellowship that slipped past national prejudice. Over and above that, the experience by which national groups different from your own in every obvious way were sharing an identical fate exerted a restraining, if not necessarily civilizing, influence. No nation, under those circumstances, ran amok in its specialized field of lunacy. Take sport. The British, instigators of a roughish game called 'Stoolball', invited the slovenly, anaemic-looking French to play against them—and were beaten. The Poles, for whom all sport entailed a life-or-death defence of Polish honour, controlled, if they did not abandon, their most blatant grimness about defeat. The Dutch, though their rigid discipline and precision restrained them from playing much, cultivated an admiration for the English, associating themselves especially with their light sporty ways, and seemed in this to be making a deliberate effort, prompted by some new awareness, to lengthen the distance that separated them from their national neighbours, the humourless, wooden Germans.

The Belgians, who did not play at all, were the most intractably, individualistically unmilitary group. The French, worried about their own centrifugal tendencies, were genuinely scared when they contemplated the Belgians, seeing mirrored in them the extreme perils of civilization. This fear was indirectly corroborated by Commandant Flébus the cat-eater, who said often that his own soldierly character had never been properly appreciated until he came to Colditz. The Belgian Army had been very unpopular, he said, in pre-war Belgium. Girls would not dance with men in uniform, on pavements they were expected to give way to everybody, and sometimes things were thrown at them. The Belgians of Colditz, unshaven, shapeless, striking no attitude and just as placid about large matters as about small, did look like an unappreciated squad that had got captured by some mistake. Yet they were perkily, serenely alive; and their mere presence set quizzical limits to the exorbitances of their neighbours.

There were hundreds of dreary days in Colditz. The drive to escape and the campaign to harry the Germans could never be wholly successful at the point where they expressed, not their obvious purposes, but rather the resolve of the prisoners to keep themselves active and to resist succumbing to lethargy. From that point of view there was always too much against them. There were periods when the old looked old, the young did not look fit, and the ardours of defiance, never an unforced growth, failed to leap out. The Germans would find that they had quiet parades and would patter secure along the files, almost like nannies.

In such lethargic periods each nation slipped into its special groove. Dutch, Poles and Belgians seemed to hibernate, while the larger nations, the English and French, fought the malaise in larger and dissimilar ways.

In that fight the French were the better equipped. They had a knack of domesticating themselves. The British prisoner's corner was his castle only if he could get out of it. The *summum bonum* of the British cuisine was the bread pudding, impatiently kneaded and left to bake as best it might; a French prisoner could spend a happy day contriving a *baba au rhum*. In the general field of manual ingenuity there was not much to choose between them, but the French often made things for their own sake whereas the English always made them for a purpose—usually escape. The French made mouse-tanks. The tanks were toy-sized, built of small pieces of wood, and driven from inside by a mouse revolving on a ferris-wheel. The mouse visibly enjoyed this job. There was also a 'Big Wheel' for the recreation of several families of mice. Mice lay about on a beach of sand while those who were feeling more active kept the wheel spinning by getting aboard the spokes. It was the particular sport of the bigger mice to leap suddenly from sand to spoke so that their weight set the wheel flying and tipped off all the little mice. Wondrous as these mouse-machines were, the spirit of Colditz was against them, and they were readily forgotten.

The French, who had no fear of convenience, considered that *les anglais* wittingly or unwittingly believed in subjecting themselves to inconvenience. Their own way of dealing with strain was to 'exteriorize' and relax; whereas the British tended to produce more and more of it and press it down inside themselves harder and harder until they were at last exhausted and could fall virtuously asleep. British prisoners rejoiced, or said that they did, at being moved as often as possible from camp to camp, castle to castle, on the principle that moving was good for you—kept you fit and so on. It was looked at askance if anyone tried to make the corner in which he lived and slept more comfortable, personal, or home-like; such contrivances being dubbed disparagingly 'life-boats', as constituting a mode of private self-salvage. Their search for inconvenience drove the British outside to the cobbles of the Colditz yard to spitting frenzies of shadow-boxing or to a hundred press-ups before breakfast. One, who on principle and on the coldest nights would never sleep under more than a single blanket, was not imitated; yet a wiry pride was taken in his unflinching austerity.

The French, in periods when escaping slackened off, fretted little. They never were so communally single-minded about escape as the English were. They rarely counted the world—even Colditz—well lost for it. There was a case where a French prisoner of war, offered a method which involved bribery of a German and some purchases through German channels, totted up the cost and decided that it was too high. French escapes were the outcome of individuality and daring rather than of collective patience and organization; a temperamental difference not obscured, though it *was* exaggerated, by obvious differences of situation, military and political, that made the rewards of escape less alluring for the French.

The interplay of national differences contributed a resilience and *élan* that often cushioned what otherwise was only noisy and hard. Anglo-French relations, more tortuously developed than others, provided a continual diversion due chiefly to the inevitable clashing impact of French curiosity on British sluggish phlegm. The French, passionately curious about changing events and 'movements of opinion', found it incomprehensible even after months of enforced and intimate contact that their British opposites could get through the day without being bothered by events and without once changing their opinions on any subject.

There was a general pairing-off between the two groups, originally for exchanges of language-lessons, later widening into friendly acquaintances and friendships, and Anglo-French pairs would meet daily in the yard or in each others' quarters. '*Bonjour*' would lead straight to either '*Quoi de neuf?*' or '*Eh bien, qu'est-ce-que vous racontez?*' from the French side, whereupon the following dialogue (subject to variations) would develop:

'*Bonjour! Quoi de neuf?*'

'Oh, nothing particularly. Still here, I suppose.'

'Yes I think so. Have you some interesting letters lately?'

'No—o, nothing very interesting. Rather dull really.'

'But I think the situation is rather interesting at present?'

Pause. On English side, lighting and filling of pipe.

'The Germans admit to-day that they are retreating in Africa.'

'About time they did admit it.'

'Yes, I think so. It is better now than when you were at El Alamein. I think you were very anxious then, yes?'

'Oh, not really.'

'No?'

'Well, I mean we were a bit anxious, I suppose. But we never thought it would really come to anything.'

'We were very anxious. Personally I thought the Germans should take Alexandria.'

'Well, they didn't.'

'No, of course not.'

'Have a cigarette?'

'Thank you. And what about the danger from U-boats now? I think it is very serious. From the speech of your Mr. Alexander one has the impression that. . . .'

The British side would brace itself reluctantly; it certainly would not have read the speech. Yet all that was stimulating rather than irritating. The different groups in Colditz swallowed many a prejudice for the sake of this enlivening solidarity. Sometimes they did more. Once, for instance, an English prisoner suffering from jaundice coughed up some blackish ersatz German jam which he mistook for blood. He was visited by a German doctor and also by a Polish prisoner-doctor. The German was sceptical about the blood. But the Pole was enthusiastic about it; urging a muscular injection to prevent internal bleeding; he marshalled phial, needle and syringe, and said, with a contemptuous gesture at the German:

'He doesn't think this necessary. I do. You can choose.'

Seeing the sufferer inclined to refuse he became offended. The German *Arzt* smiled.

Refusal, it was plain, would precipitate Anglo-Polish discord. Poles were allies, German enemies. Polish nationalism was sensitive. The British officer endured the injection.

Giles Romilly and Michael Alexander

Tedium

It was lunch time. The biscuits had not been buttered. No one had gone for the tea water. Five morose figures sat round a naked table. Presently Pomfret spoke. 'It's a matter of principle. I've done it every day this week and now it's Friday. It's not that I mind doing it, but I've done more than my share. Clinton must do it to-day as a matter of principle.' He advanced his chin obstinately. He was dressed in the full uniform of a flight-lieutenant. His collar, ironed with a tin of hot water, was frayed round the edges.

'That's all very well,' said Bennett, 'but it's lunch time and we're hungry. You and Clinton share the duty of cook and it's up to you to see that the meal is prepared.' Bennett, apart from his odd assortment of clothes, might have been addressing a board meeting. He delivered his opinion as an ultimatum and glanced round the table for approval. His red, hairy arms were crossed upon the table. Having delivered his speech, he sucked his teeth with an air of finality.

'Well, I'm not doing it,' said Pomfret. He appeared about to cry. 'It's not fair! Just because he's digging a tunnel it doesn't mean that he can neglect all his duties in the mess. I'm fed up with doing two people's work. All they think about is their wretched tunnel. I'm sick to death of seeing them sitting in the corner whispering all evening. It was bad enough before they started the tunnel.

Clinton was always missing at meal times. But for the last two months I've done all the work. It's not right, you know.'

'That's for you and Clinton to settle between yourselves,' said Bennett judicially. 'What about our lunch? It's only a matter of buttering eight biscuits and walking over to the canteen for some hot water.'

'That's not the point!' said Pomfret. 'It's a matter of principle.'

'So the whole mess suffers for the sake of your principles,' put in Robbie, who was sitting at the head of the table disgustedly studying his finger-nails.

'It's not my principles at fault, it's Clinton's laziness.'

'I don't call it laziness to dig a tunnel for several hours a day,' said Robbie. 'Surely you and he can come to some arrangement so that you both do equal amounts of work, but his share doesn't interfere with his tunnelling.'

'You can't come to any arrangement with Clinton,' said Pomfret. 'He always forgets. He hasn't grown up yet. He's got no sense of responsibility.'

'He's not the only one who hasn't grown up,' said Robbie.

'This is all very well,' put in Bennett, 'but do we get our lunch?'

'I'm not doing it!' said Pomfret obstinately.

The five men looked at one another angrily. The food cupboard was sacred. No one but the cook was allowed to open it. It was a custom of the mess. In a life where hunger was ubiquitous, food had strict taboos. None but the high priest could approach the shrine.

'Supposing we split the mess in two,' said Barton. 'Let them mess together and we five will mess together. They can do what they like, then.' Barton spoke with a genteel accent. His whole appearance was genteel, even to the crook of his little finger as he removed the cigarette from his mouth.

'They always do,' said Pomfret fretfully.

'Well, what do you say?' asked Barton. 'I think it would serve them right.'

'Very likely buck them no end,' said Robbie.

'I think we ought to do it,' said Downes. 'Howard and Wilde can't cook, anyway.'

The party hesitated. It was a decision. Some of them had not made a decision for years. Some were reluctant to cast the three into the outer darkness of their disassociation.

'I think we should,' said Pomfret.

'Let's take a vote,' said Bennett, once more addressing the board of directors.

'I agree,' said Downes.

'So do I,' said Barton.

Bennett looked at Robbie, who thought of coping with the eccentricities of the other three. He decided not to risk it. Anyway, their tunnel would be finished soon.

'I think it's bloody childish,' he said, 'and it'll be damned inconvenient having two messes in one room.'

'Would you rather go with them, then you can do all the cooking for them?' said Pomfret spitefully.

'No, I'll go with you,' said Robbie, 'but I don't like the idea of splitting up.'

When the three came in from tunnelling they found the biscuits ready buttered and the tea water in the can. John had been working at the face, Peter half-way down, and Nigel at the tunnel entrance. John, who was yellow from head to foot with caked sweat and sand, threw himself on his bunk and closed his eyes.

'Lunch, John?' asked Peter.

'Not for the moment, thanks, old boy,' said John.

'Feeling rotten?' asked Peter.

'I'm O.K. I'll be O.K. in a minute. I'll wash before I eat.' He lay back with his eyes closed. His body was brown, but his face was colourless. His hair, matted with sand and sweat, was damp on his forehead. There were long streaks down his chest and arms where the sweat had washed away the sand. The sand was under his broken finger-nails and in his eyes. As he lay there, Peter could see that his nostrils too were filled with sand.

Pomfret cleared his throat. 'I prepared the lunch to-day,' he said.

'Thanks, old boy,' said John. 'Was it my turn?'

'It was your turn,' replied Pomfret. 'It has been your turn for the last three days. As a matter of principle I, at first, refused to do it to-day.'

'Thanks for doing it all the same,' said John. 'I'll do the dinner.'

'That will not be necessary,' said Pomfret. 'We five have decided to mess separately.'

'After due consideration,' said Bennett, addressing an audience of at least five hundred, 'we have decided that we five shall mess on our own.'

Pomfret looked at him angrily. After all, he was in the chair.

'We are tired of Clinton's impossible attitude,' Bennett continued, 'and we presumed that you three would want to be together. We have separated the food, and starting with dinner to-night, we shall cater for ourselves.'

'O.K.,' said Peter, 'that suits us.' In a way he was glad, as very soon they would begin to save their food for the escape. 'What do you say, Nig?'

'*Blond genug*, old boy,' replied Nigel.

So the mess was split into two and settled down to a new way of living.

Eric Williams

Escape

. . . . Escape is not only a technique but a philosophy. The real escaper is more than a man equipped with compass, maps, papers, disguise and a plan. He has an inner confidence, a serenity of spirit which makes him a Pilgrim.

Airey Neave

The Way Out: Germany

Valenta had put Axel Zillessen on to the Keen Type. Axel wasn't his real name, but the one he'd chosen to use if he ever escaped from the compound so that he could travel as a Swede. He got everyone to call him Axel so he'd get used to it. Actually he was a wool buyer from Bradford, a tall young man with a slightly hooked nose and kinky hair; and with a charming and infectious enthusiasm Axel could talk the leg off an iron pot almost as fluently in German as in English.

The next time Keen Type came in the duty pilot's runner went and told Axel, and Axel strolled into the dusty compound where Keen Type was patrolling. He passed him a couple of times without speaking, and on the third time gave him a casual greeting and they exchanged a few words about the weather. The same thing happened next day. The third day they spoke for about five minutes.

Keen Type came in every day, and as soon as he did the runner warned Axel. By the end of the week Axel and the ferret were walking up and down together chatting for an hour. Gradually they got on to the war, Axel staying always on neutral ground, regretting the bombing and the suffering on both sides.

'It's ridiculous,' he said. 'Here are we, two ordinary people talking as civilized people, and if I put a foot over the warning wire you have to shoot me.'

The Keen Type laughed.

'I have shot no one yet,' he said mildly.

'But you would!'

'Only in the leg,' said the Keen Type, 'and with regret.'

'That doesn't make it any more civilized.'

'The bombing is not very civilized, either'—this rather resentfully.

'We didn't start it,' said Axel, and veered off what could only be a bitter subject. 'What are you going to do after the war?'

The ferret laughed without humour. 'Why worry now? I don't think it's ever going to end, and if it does I probably won't see it.'

'Look,' said Axel, 'when it's over we're going to need the co-operation of Germans who weren't mad Nazis. You won't be an enemy then.'

The ferret considered the delicate implication but did not answer. Neither did he think to deny, as normally he automatically would, the clear inference that Germany was going to lose.

Axel took him to his room for the first time next day for a cup of coffee. 'X' gave the room a little extra ration for this and whenever they wanted hot water for a brew they could claim time on the stove, no matter how many other pots were on it.

The others in the room—Dave, Laurie, Nellie and Keith—gave Keen Type casual welcome. He sat among them with a hot brew, a biscuit and a cigarette. It was more comfortable than padding round the dust of the compound, and it was interesting to hear the British and American point of view. It is a soldier's privilege—his only one—to grumble, but you couldn't grumble in the German Army unless you were tired of life and wanted to go to the Russian Front. Keen Type had a lot that he hadn't been able to get off his chest, and now he had a sympathetic and safe audience and he spoke with more and more freedom.

'What can we Germans do?' he said, after a week, sitting with his coffee and nibbling a piece of chocolate from a food parcel. 'Against Hitler and the Gestapo —nothing.'

'I'll tell you what you can do.' Axel got up and sat down on the bunk beside him. 'You can realize that the war is lost and nothing you do can help that. The sooner it's over the better. We're not going to be enemies for ever. Start regarding us as friends now.' He added quietly, 'We won't be forgetting our friends.'

The duty pilot checked the Keen Type into the compound just after *appell* next morning and the runner slid off to warn Axel. He saw the Keen Type seemed to be following him, so he shied off. The ferret went straight into 105, knocked on Axel's door and put his head round the corner. 'Keen Type here,' he said with a friendly grin. 'Can I come in?'

He stayed a couple of hours, and then he excused himself, saying he'd better put in an appearance in the compound or Glemnitz would be wondering what he was doing. He was much more leisurely this time in his patrolling. He reported to Axel's room every day after that for a brew, and when he reluctantly went out into the compound again he had a new benevolence. After a while, Roger took him off the danger list.

Valenta had detailed a German-speaking contact to every ferret and administrative German who came into the compound. The contact made friends with his man, fed him biscuits, brews and cigarettes and listened sympathetically to his grumbles and worries.

Funny people, the Germans. When you got them in a bunch they were all Nazis (they had to be), but when you got the little people by themselves and worked on them for a while they didn't have any morale underneath. Inside they seemed naked and defenceless. You could bribe ninety per cent of them—including the officers—with a little coffee or chocolate.

In a way, I don't think you could blame them. Valenta's contacts were like white ants, nibbling away a little at a time at the German faith in victory. Hitler had said that if you tell a big enough lie people will believe it, but he rather overlooked the fact that once the lie is exposed everything else you've said is also disbelieved. It wasn't hard to get a German thinking that Hitler wasn't the angel of virtue, and then the rest of his edifice of wishful faith came tumbling down.

The contacts sympathized with their Germans that they had to fight Hitler's war, lamented with them about Gestapo persecution and poured out a stream of irresistible logic to show that Germany could never win.

'Why, then,' they said, 'regard us as enemies? Soon you will want us as friends.'

The talking wasn't only one-way. Delicate steering had the ferrets talking about the security measures they planned, about conditions in Germany, details of the area round the camp. Dozens of little snippets were picked up, and Valenta, who had done an intelligence course at Prague Staff College, put them all together with Roger.

Soon they knew all the paths around the camp, how far the woods stretched and the layout of Sagan town. They had timetables of all trains out of Sagan station and the prices of all tickets. They knew what foods were ration-free, where the Swedish ships lay in Stettin and Danzig, what guards were around them, what guards covered the Swiss frontier and the Danish frontier, and a thousand other handy hints on how to get out of the Third Reich.

'Why do you make such a bloody mess when you search the huts?' Axel asked the Keen Type.

'We have to be thorough,' said the ferret. 'Germans are always thorough. We have to take everything apart or we are in trouble with Glemnitz. And if we waste time putting everything together again we are in more trouble with Glemnitz.'

'You never find anything.'

'Orders,' said Keen Type virtuously, 'are orders.'

'Orders don't say you have to make a bloody mess wherever you go,' said Axel, who'd reached the stage where he could be a little stern with the Keen Type. 'Last time you people went through my room you pinched half the wood-shavings out of my palliasse and it was spread all over the floor. It took me half an hour to clear up.'

'It wasn't me,' the Keen Type said apologetically. 'I will do your room myself next time.' He added reproachfully: 'You must not forget that you are our prisoners. Do not expect too much.'

'Don't forget you'll be our prisoners one day,' Axel said, with flippant menace, though the Keen Type did not need much reminding. Axel had been wedging the thought into his mind for a couple of weeks.

'It'd help us all,' Axel went on, 'if we knew when we were going to be searched. We could have things a little more orderly and you wouldn't have to waste so much time going through all the mess. Be a help to you, too.'

'You ask too much,' said Keen Type, shaking his head in fright at the thought.

Axel carefully brought up the subject again next day, but it was a fortnight before he got Keen Type to tell him what huts were to be searched in the next few days, and after that it was easy. Roger nearly always got at least a day's notice of searches, and it was just a question of smuggling *verboten* stuff out of the hut next on the list, usually to the hut that was last searched. That was the safest spot of all. Once the ferrets had searched a hut it was usually immune till all the other huts had been searched and its turn came up again. It suited us.

'There's madness in their method,' said Roger with satisfaction.

.... Roger went in search of Travis and found him in his room filing a broken knife into a screwdriver.

'Can you make me a rifle?' he asked, and Travis stared at him.

'It's for show, not for shooting,' Bushell explained.

'What sort of rifle exactly?'

'German one. Imitation. We've got a new show on. D'you remember the time just before we moved they took a mob out from east camp to be deloused?'

'Yes,' said Travis. 'Someone on a new purge came in with wogs all over him.'

'That's it,' said Roger. 'I think we can put on a couple of unofficial ones. We've got to have some goons to go as escort. Guest is making the uniforms. You're going to make their guns.'

'They'd have to be terribly good to pass the gate posterns, Roger,' Travis said slowly. 'I don't know that we can do it.'

Roger swivelled his twisted eye on him. 'I want them in a week,' he said and walked out.

Travis, McIntosh and Muller tried to put on paper an accurate plan of a German military carbine and found they didn't have a clue about the detail and dimensions. Muller went and got Henri Picard out of the forgery factory. Picard, a young Belgian, was one of the best artists in the camp. Muller's idea appealed to him and he went away and cut a rough pair of calipers out of a piece of tin.

Coming off *appell* that afternoon, Muller started chatting to one of the guards and Picard stood just behind very carefully measuring with his calipers the width and depth of various parts of the carbine slung over the guard's shoulder. Then he stood beside him and calculated the length of the rifle, noting where the barrel came to about the height of his head and where the butt finished by his thighs. For the next day he cautiously trailed several guards, drawing rough detail parts of the gun.

Travis had noticed that about one in every three hundred bedboards was made of beech instead of pine and Williams toured every hut and whipped every beech board he could find. They weren't thick enough to make a rifle, so they sawed and carved out each rifle in two halves, glued them together and clamped them to set in vices made of reinforced ping-pong net-posts. They carved out in wood the parts that were supposed to be metal, barrel, breech and bolt, and rubbed and polished them with a lump of graphite brought in by a tame German till they looked like blue gunmetal. The wooden parts that were really wood they stained with tan boot polish and rubbed till it looked perfect.

The clips round the barrels Muller made from strips cut off a metal jug; he used bent nails for the sling clips and belts for the slings. Muller didn't think the polished wooden barrel looked quite perfect enough, so he melted down silver paper from cigarette packets into lead and cast a proper barrel end in a soap mould. He polished it with graphite until it *was* perfect.

By happy chance, the grey of Luftwaffe uniforms was almost identical with R.A.F. grey-blue, and Tommy Guest used old R.A.F. uniforms to cut out several *unteroffiziers'* uniforms. Six of his amateur tailors hand-sewed them.

Muller made the little eagles that went on the lapels and the belt buckles by casting melted silver paper in soap moulds, carving the eagles in the mould himself. The belt buckle was perfect. One of the contacts got his goon to take off his tunic on a hot day while he drank his daily brew, and Muller stealthily pressed the buckle into the soap to make his mould. Guest cut a bit off the tail of a terrible old shirt of Kirby-Green's to make the colour patches on the uniforms.

Tim Walenn produced several beautifully forged gate passes (the originals had been brought in by a tame guard). The *unteroffiziers* would have to show the passes to get out of the camp with their party and Walenn's staff had hand-lettered them, working non-stop on the job for about a week. He took the passes to Roger.

'Which is the real one?' he asked.

Roger peered at them for a while.

'They're bloody good, Tim,' he said. 'I don't think I could pick them apart.'

'As a matter of fact,' Tim said, 'they're all forgeries.'

And the day it was all done and thirty-two men were getting their last briefing for the break, the German *unteroffiziers* came in without rifles. They all had pistols instead, in holsters on a belt. It was a new order. *Unteroffiziers* weren't going to carry rifles any more, and there had to be an *unteroffizier* on the fake delousing party. An ordinary *obergefreiter* (lance-corporal or private) wouldn't be allowed to escort a party out of the gate.

Roger really lost his temper this time and for two days he was quite unbearable. Travis and Muller weren't much better.

One of Tommy Guest's men had been a hand-bag maker in private life and Roger put him to work making imitation pistol holsters out of cardboard. He marked the cardboard to give it a leathery grain and rubbed it with boot polish and you couldn't tell the result from a real holster. McIntosh made a couple of dummy pistol butts out of wood and fixed them so they peeped coyly out of the holster flaps.

Roger planned the break in two phases. First, twenty-four men escorted by two *unteroffiziers* were to march out of the gate (they hoped) ostensibly bound for the delousing showers. Ten minutes after they were clear, Bob Van Der Stok, a Dutchman in the R.A.F. who spoke perfect German, was to march out a party of five senior officers for a 'special conference' with the Kommandant.

Roger, Wings Day and the committee hand-picked the people to go, selecting men who'd been working hard for 'X' and who'd been behind the wire for a couple of years or more. Roger himself toyed with the idea of going, but Wings and the others energetically talked him out of it. As Wings pointed out, there was a very fair chance of the alarm being given quite quickly, in which case many of them probably wouldn't get very far, and if Roger was caught again so soon after the last time he knew what to expect.

'Wait till you can get through "Tom",' Day said. 'You'll be out of the area by train then before they wake up to it.'

Roger reluctantly agreed, partly because he was banking so much on 'Tom'. Floody wanted to go on the delousing party, too, but Roger vetoed the idea and they had a short, sharp argument. Arguments with Roger were often sharp and always short.

'We need you here for the tunnels,' he told Floody flatly.

'God, I'm sick of tunnels!' Floody groaned. 'I seem to spend my life down a stinking hole in the ground. I want a change.'

'Look, Wally,' Roger said, 'we're just getting somewhere now and everything's going like a bomb. Don't spoil it. We'll get "Tom" out in a couple of months and then you can go for your life, but *not* now. You're needed here.'

'But I'd be back,' said Floody, spreading his hands appealingly. 'They'd catch me. Nothing surer. I'll go on the delouser now and in two days I'll be back in the cooler. Then I can have a nice rest for a fortnight and come back fit. How 'bout that?'

'No,' said Roger.

It was just after two o'clock on a warm afternoon that twenty-four men fell in outside 104, carrying bundles wrapped in towels, presumably to be dumped in the steam delousers. It would be too bad if the gate guards inspected them because they contained uniform jackets and pants converted to look like civilian clothes and little packets of concentrated food cakes made from oatmeal and breadcrumbs, milk powder, chocolate and sugar. In the pockets were maps and a little German money. Two *unteroffiziers*, holsters at their waists, formed them into three ranks and they straggled off towards the gate laughing and joking with the fake heartiness people show as they climb into the dentist's chair. The atmosphere was a little electric. Roger and the envious Floody felt it one hundred yards away where they sat by a corner of a hut, unobtrusively watching.

The party stopped at the first gate and one of the *unteroffiziers* showed his pass. The guard hardly even looked at it and then the big barbed wire gates were swinging open. They marched to the next gate, the guard looked casually at the pass and in a few moments they were walking out into the road that curved into the pine wood. It was practically an anticlimax.

Three hundred yards down the road without a German in sight they turned sharply and vanished into the trees, then broke into a run for half a mile. Deep in the woods they changed into their travelling clothes and split up into ones, twos and threes.

At a quarter-past two Van Der Stok walked out of 110 with the second party and headed for the gate. Goodrich, the senior, was an American colonel of about forty, with a red, tough face and barrel chest. Beside him walked Bob Tuck, slim and elegant, a Battle of Britain ace with a D.S.O. and three D.F.C.s; then Bill Jennens, R.A.F. squadron-leader and compound adjutant with a voice like a drill sergeant and a face like a lump of uncarved granite. The other two were the lanky 'Nellie' Ellan, who looked after the camp radio, and a Polish wing-commander.

Van Der Stok showed his pass at the first gate and they walked through. At the next, the guard was a little more conscientious and turned the pass over and looked at the back. (We found out later it was only a week before that the Germans had put a new mark on the back of the gate passes in case they were ever copied.) Van Der Stok's pass didn't have the mark and the guard looked suspiciously up at him. It was only then that his brain slowly grasped the fact that he had seen this man walking round the compound as a prisoner. He raised a shout and a dozen German soldiers came clumping out of the guardhouse.

Van Der Stok bowed disarmingly and raised his hands.

Broili came over from the *Kommandantur* in response to an urgent message. He was chief security officer, a plump little major with shiny black hair, given to monumental anger when prisoners escaped and patronizing politeness when they failed to. He greeted the little group jovially.

'Mr. Van Der Stok,' he said roguishly, 'you are improperly dressed. Ah, it is too bad, gentlemen'—with a happy grin—'the fortunes of war. Perhaps you will have better luck next time.'

He congratulated the guard on recognizing Van Der Stok and the guard put his foot right in it.

'I thought it unusual, *Herr Major*, that two parties should leave the camp so close together,' he said smugly, and Broili looked suddenly older.

'Two parties?' he asked in a voice of doom, and the guard told him.

'*Mein Gott, sechs und zwanzig*,' shrieked Broili, and with a terrible look at Van Der Stok and Goodrich he ran for the guardhouse phone.

Paul Brickhill

The Tunnel

At this unhappy stage, when we were casting around to decide what to do with our tunnel, Peter Allan and Howard Gee (a newcomer), both excellent German speakers, reported the existence of a helpful Goon sentry. He was a sympathetic type, and he started smuggling for us on a small scale: a fresh egg here and there in return for English chocolate, or a pound of real coffee in exchange for a tin of cocoa, and so on. He ran a terrific risk, but seemed to do it with equanimity—perhaps too much equanimity—and we decided also to take a risk and plunge. At several clandestine meetings, in doorways and behind angles in the courtyard walls, Peter and Howard Gee primed the sentry and eventually suggested that he might earn some 'big' money if he once 'looked the other way' for ten minutes while on sentry duty.

The sentry fell for the idea. He was told that we would have to arrange matters so that he did a tour of sentry duty for a given two-hour period, on a given day, on a certain beat, and that in the ten-minute interval, between two predetermined signals, he was to stand (which was permitted) at one particular end of his beat. He was to receive an advance of one hundred *Reichsmarks* of his reward, which was settled at five hundred *Reichsmarks* (about £34), and the remainder would be dropped out of a convenient window one hour after the ten-minute interval. The sentry was told also that no traces would be left which could lead to suspicion or involve him in accusations of neglect of duty. To all this he listened and finally agreed. The escape was on!

The first escape party consisted of twelve officers, including four Poles. The French and Dutch were as yet newcomers, whereas the Poles were by now old and trusted comrades, which accounted for their inclusion. Further, the participation of officers of another nationality was decided upon for reasons of language facilities offered, and for camp morale. The Poles had been most helpful since our arrival; the majority of them spoke German fluently, some of them knew Germany well, and those of us who thought of aiming for the North Sea or Poland took Poles as travelling companions. A few decided to travel alone.

My mind was occupied with another problem—how to arrange for the entry of thirteen officers, twelve escaping and one sealing up the entry, into the canteen? During opening hours I examined the cruciform lock closely and came to the conclusion that, from the inside, I could dismount the lock almost completely, allowing the door to open.

The escape would have to be done after the evening roll-call and in darkness.

The fateful day was decided upon—29 May. I arranged to knock down the false wall the day before and extricate all our provisions and escape material. This was comparatively simple. During the two-hour lunch interval the canteen was locked. Before it was locked, however, I hid in a triangular recess which was used as a store cupboard and to which I had the key. When the canteen was locked up I had two clear hours to prepare everything. I removed the false wall, took out all our escape paraphernalia, hiding it in the cupboard, and prepared the tunnel exit so as to give the minimum amount of work for the final opening. After two o'clock, with a suitable screen of officers, I came out of the cupboard and all the stores were carried to our quarters.

The arrangements for the escape were as follows: Howard Gee, who was not in the first party, was to deal with the sentry. He would pass him the first signal on receipt of a sign from us in the tunnel. This was to be given by myself in the first instance at the opening end of the tunnel, passed to our thirteenth man on watch at the canteen window in the courtyard, who would then transmit it to our quarters by means of a shaded light. Gee could then signal to the sentry from an outside window. The 'all clear' was to be given in the same way, except that our thirteenth man had to come to the tunnel exit and receive the word from me when I had properly sealed up the exit after all were out. A piece of string pulled out through the earth served the purpose. I would be over the wall at the far end of the lawn before the signal would be transferred to the sentry.

29 May loomed overcast and it soon began to rain. It rained all day in torrents, the heaviest rainfall we had ever had, but this would mean a dark night and it did not upset our plans. The sentry was told during the course of the afternoon what post he was to occupy. He was given his advance in cash and instructed to avoid the end of his beat nearest to the canteen on receipt of an agreed signal from a certain window, and to remain away from that end until another signal was given.

As the evening approached, the excitement grew. The lucky twelve dressed themselves in kit prepared during many months of patient work. From out of astonishing hiding-places came trousers and slouch caps made of grey German blankets, multi-coloured knitted pullovers, transformed and dyed army overcoats, windjackets and mackintoshes, dyed khaki shirts and home-knitted ties. These were donned and covered with army apparel. Maps and home-made compasses appeared, and subdued last-minute discussions took place concerning routes and escape instructions. As the time passed, impatience for the 'off' increased. I became alternately hot and cold, and my hands were clammy and my mouth was dry. We all felt the same, as I could tell by the forced laughs and the nervous jokes and banter which passed around.

I remained hidden in the canteen when it was locked up for the night, and dismounted the lock. When the evening *appell* sounded, I slipped out of the door behind a well-placed crowd of officers. If a goon pushed the door for any reason whatever we were finished. A wedge of paper alone held it. Sentries were posted for the *appell* at all vantage-points, and one stood very close to the canteen. Immediately after the *appell* we had to work fast, for all the prisoners then had to disperse to their rooms, the courtyard doors were locked, and every door tried by the German duty officer. All thirteen of us had to slip into the canteen behind the screen of assisting officers while German officers and N.C.O.s were in the courtyard, and the lock had then to be remounted on the canteen door in double-quick time. The twelve escapers had to appear on parade dressed ready in their escape attire suitably covered with army overcoats and trousers. Assembled rucksacks had been placed in order in the tunnel during the lunch-time closing hours in the same way as before.

The *appell* went off without a hitch. Colonel German, who had to stand alone in front, was looking remarkably fat, for he was escaping with us. He aroused no comment. Immediately after the 'dismiss' was given, and almost in front of the eyes of the sentry nearby, the thirteen chosen ones slipped silently through the door until all were in.

'Where do we go from here?' asked one of the Polish officers who had not worked on the tunnel.

'Over the palisades!' I replied, pointing to the high wooden partition, over which sheets had already been thrown.

He grabbed them and started to climb, making a noise like a bass drum on the partition door. A loud 'Sh! Sh!' as if a lavatory cistern was emptying greeted his effort.

'For God's sake!' I said, 'you're not in Paderewski's orchestra now.'

'No,' replied the Pole dramatically from the top of the partition, 'but his spirit is living within me this night!'

Luckily the din in the courtyard covered any noise we made at this juncture.

While the lock was remounted on the door, I removed my army uniform and handled it to our thirteenth man. He was to collect all discarded clothes, conceal them in the cupboard, and remove them with assistance next day. I went straight away to the end of the tunnel, closely followed by Rupert Barry, for we were going together, and started work on the last few inches of earth beneath the surface of the opening. It was dark by now outside, and the rain was still pelting down. It began pouring through the earth covering of the exit, and within five minutes I was drenched to the skin with muddy water. The lock-testing patrol tried the canteen door and passed. Soon all was quiet in the camp. Within an hour the sentry was reported by light flashes to be at his post. I gave the signal for him to keep away from the canteen window.

I worked frenziedly at the surface of grass, cutting out my square, and then slowly heaved the tray of the exit upwards. It came away, and as it did so a shaft of brilliant light shot down the tunnel. For a second I was bewildered and blinded. It was, of course, the light of the projector situated ten yards away from the opening, which lit up the whole of the wall-face on that particular side of the Castle. I lifted the tray clear. Streams of muddy water trickled into the tunnel around me. I pushed myself upwards, and, with Rupert's assistance from behind, scrambled out.

Once out, I looked around. I was like an actor upon a stage. The floodlight made a huge grotesque image of my figure against the white wall. Row upon row of unfriendly windows, those of the German *Kommandantur*, frowned down upon me. The windows had no blackout curtains and a wandering inquisitive eye from within might easily turn my way. It was an unavoidable risk. Rupert began to climb out as I put the finishing touch to the tray for closing the hole. He was having some difficulty. He had handed up my rucksack and was levering himself upwards when I happened to look from my work at the wall in front of me, there to see a second giant shadow outlined beside my own crouching figure. The second shadow held a revolver in his hand.

'Get back! Get back!' I yelled to Rupert, as a guttural voice behind me shouted:

'*Hände hoch! Hände hoch!*'

I turned, to face a German officer levelling his pistol at my body, while another leaped for the hole. He was about to shoot down the opening.

'*Schiessen sie nicht!*' I screamed several times.

A bullet or two down that stone-and-brick-walled tunnel might have wrought considerable damage, filled as it was with human bodies. The officer at the hole did not shoot.

Germans suddenly appeared from everywhere, and all the officers were giving orders at once. I was led off to the *Kommandantur* and conducted to a bathroom where I was stripped completely and allowed to wash, and then to an office where I was confronted by *Hauptmann* Priem.

He was evidently pleased with his night's work and in high spirits.

'*Ah hah! Es ist Herr Hauptmann Reid. Das ist schön!*' he said as I walked in, and continued:

'Nobody could recognize who the nigger was until he was washed! And now that we have the nigger out of the woodpile, what has he got to say for himself?'

'I think the nigger in the woodpile was a certain German sentry, was he not?' I questioned in reply.

'Yes, indeed, *Herr Hauptmann*. German sentries know their duty. The whole matter has been reported to me from the start.'

'From before the start, maybe?'

'*Herr Hauptmann* Reid, that is not the point. Where does your tunnel come from?'

'That is obvious,' I replied.

'From the canteen, then?'

'Yes.'

'But you have been locked into your quarters. You have a tunnel from your rooms to the canteen?'

'No!'

'But yes! You have just been counted on *appell*. The canteen has been locked many hours ago. You have a tunnel?'

'No!'

'We shall see. How many of you are there?'

'So many I have never been able to count them properly!'

'Come now, *Herr Hauptmann*, the whole camp or just a few?'

'Just a few!'

'Good, then I hope our solitary confinement accommodation will not be too overcrowded!' said Priem, grinning broadly.

P. R. Reid

The Way Out: England

During the whole of the war only one German prisoner who had been confined in Britain eventually succeeded in getting back to his own country. This man was Franz von Werra, a Luftwaffe pilot who displayed unsurpassed powers of tenacity and resource. His attempts to escape from this country failed: shipped to Canada early in 1941, *he eventually crossed the border into the still-neutral United States, returning by a devious route to Germany. During one of his escapades in Britain, he posed as a Dutch pilot and made his way to an airfield with the idea of stealing an aircraft and flying it across the Channel. Realizing that the R.A.F. officer who was questioning him, known to him as 'Mr. Boniface', was about to unmask him, von Werra acted.*

Von Werra had got away from the office and 'Mr. Boniface'. But for how long? Time was now the supremely vital factor. Fractions of seconds mattered.

He sprinted back along the road he had travelled in the R.A.F. vehicle. There was not a soul in sight. When he reached the perimeter track he turned left, towards the group of camouflaged hangars and the gaggle of Hurricanes.

He slowed down to a walk near the first hangar, at the front of which construction work was being carried out. Builders looked down at him curiously from scaffolding. He dodged between a cement mixer and a heap of ballast, almost bumping into a labourer cutting open a cement bag.

He was out of sight of Headquarters. He did not start running again but walked briskly, purposefully. Past a wrecked aircraft and a row of twin-engined bombers. They were no good to him, but the wide sweep of the airfield made his nostrils twitch and his blood tingle. The orange red orb of the sun had risen above the rim of the airfield and frost sparkled on the grass.

The doors of the second hangar were wide open. It was full of aircraft in various stages of assembly.

Ahead was the group of Hurricanes. A mechanic wearing a black smock was dodging about near one of them. A trolley-acc. (accumulator trolley) was beside him. The Hurricane was about to be started up! There was only this one mechanic in sight and von Werra needed someone to explain the controls of the British fighter to him.

The mechanic looked up wonderingly as the little man in the unusual flying-suit approached.

'Good morning!' said von Werra. 'I am Captain van Lott, a Dutch pilot. I have just been posted here. But Hurricanes I have not yet flown. Mr. Boniface, the Adjutant, sent me down here so you should show me the controls and make a practice flight. Which one is ready for take-off? This one here?'

He looked the mechanic straight in the eyes and spoke with firmness and authority.

The mechanic looked puzzled. Then von Werra noticed that he was not in R.A.F. uniform, but wore civilian trousers and shirt and a striped tie.

'Haven't you come to the wrong place?' the man asked. 'This is a private firm. We have nothing to do with the R.A.F. over there.'

'I know. But Mr. Boniface said it was to you I should come. I don't have much time. . . .'

The mechanic pondered. Then the probable explanation dawned on him. The airman had said he was a 'Captain', so he must be a ferry pilot from White Waltham, headquarters of Air Transport Command. Apparently he had come to take delivery of a Hurricane. It was a common occurrence for civilian ferry pilots, known by the courtesy rank of Captain, many of them foreigners speaking hardly a word of English, to collect aircraft which had been sent to the Rolls-Royce works for modification. Moreover, when they had to fly a type of aircraft new to them they often asked for a practical demonstration of controls and peculiarities, in addition to the printed pilot's notes which were issued to them. Of course, von Werra knew none of this.

'Ah!' said the mechanic, 'then you must be a ferry pilot?'

Von Werra did not know the meaning of the word 'ferry'. But he thought it best to agree.

'Yes, of course,' he replied.

'That's different,' the mechanic said. 'You'll have to see the A.I.D.* blokes.'

* Aeronautical Inspection Directorate.

Aieyedeeblokes? Von Werra couldn't cope with it.

'Look,' he said, 'I have no time... you shall show me the controls now, yes?'

'I can't do anything until you've signed the Visitors' Book, and then you'll have to get your paper-work attended to. Hang on a minute, Captain, I'll go and fetch the manager.'

The mechanic walked across the tarmac into the hangar. Von Werra stood leaning against the fuselage of the Hurricane. A brand-new beautiful Hurricane with not a scratch on it. A colossal beast, it seemed, twice as large as the Hurricanes he had encountered in air combat. He was tempted to climb into the cockpit and try to start the engine on his own. But it was no good. There were certain controls he must be sure about before he attempted to take off. If he got into the cockpit now it might wreck his chances altogether.

Familiar, nostalgic sounds issued from the hangar, as though from a cave: the beating of metal, the whirr of electric drills, somebody singing, somebody else whistling, the musical tinkle of a ring-spanner dropped on to concrete. At any minute 'Mr. Boniface' would know the truth. The alarm would be sounded and every man on the aerodrome mobilized to hunt for him.

The mechanic came out of the hangar with a man wearing a khaki smock. They approached the Hurricane in a leisurely fashion, talking and looking at one another from time to time, apparently discussing something quite unconnected with the Dutch Captain. Von Werra remained leaning negligently against the fuselage, one arm stretched out along it, one flying boot crossed in front of the other, his body half covering the roundel painted on the side.

The man in the khaki smock, presumably the manager, smiled pleasantly and said:

'Good morning, Captain!' His manner was positive, as though his mind was already made up and he was dealing with an everyday occurrence.

'I hear you've come to collect a Hurricane,' he continued. 'If you'll come with me we'll get your paper-work fixed up.'

'It shall take long? I have little time,' von Werra replied. 'I just want to learn controls of the Hurricane.'

'I'm afraid nothing can be done until you've signed the Visitors' Book. We'll soon fix you up, though.'

Von Werra reluctantly followed the two men into the hangar. There was nothing else he could do. They walked with infuriating slowness. Fitters working on aircraft in the hangar stared down at him from staging, peered at him between undercarriages, craned their necks out of cockpits. He felt like a pickpocket at a police convention.

The mechanic remained in the works. Von Werra continued behind the manager. They reached the rear wall of the hangar and passed through a door into an asphalt yard. On the other side of it was a gate and a glass-sided lodge. A man in a blue uniform was sitting inside the lodge. Evidently a works policeman. The manager entered and spoke to him.

Through the window von Werra saw a large, solemn, white-faced clock on a wall. A couple of minutes to nine. His mouth opened and his brow furrowed as he watched the thin, central second hand sweeping round the dial. Then he bit his lip and looked away.

What was 'Mr. Boniface' doing between the time the second hand moved from three to six? Perhaps that was the decisive quarter of a minute.

Though he looked away, the pointer continued to revolve in his mind's eye. He had to glance back. He expected to find the pointer at eight, but it was nearly at ten.

If only these idiots would hurry up!

The damned clock was making him lose his nerve. He fumbled for his cigarettes and matches with moist, quivering hands. Then he looked again at the pointer: twelve. The two men came out of the lodge.

As they emerged von Werra put away his packet of Player's and the box of Swan matches, making sure that they saw them. Then he idly flicked away the match with which he had lighted a cigarette.

' 'Morning, sir!' said the policeman brightly.

' 'Morning!' von Werra replied in the same tone.

'If you'll just sign along the next line, sir. . . .'

The entry had to be made across two pages, which were divided into columns. They were already half-filled with many different styles of handwriting. As he was afraid his German style might betray him, he decided to make his entry in printed characters. The first four columns were headed, Date, Name, Nationality and Address respectively, and presented little difficulty. He wrote:

> 21.12.40.   van Lott   Dutch   Aberdeen

His anxiety not to betray himself by his entry did not prevent him from once again making the tell-tale stroke over the 'u' in 'Dutch'.

The fifth column was headed 'Order'. He had no idea what he should write under it, and the other entries in the column were indecipherable. He casually asked the policeman whether he wanted this item written out in full.

'No, it doesn't matter, sir. Just put "see A.I.D.".'

Von Werra was none the wiser for his successful ruse. He asked the policeman to spell the words, but when he did so he was all the more confused. He had to write something. The manager was watching over his shoulder. The second-hand was sweeping round the dial. Guards were probably searching every corner for him. Possibly Polish guards.

He made an entry of sorts, but the nearest he could get to 'See A.I.D.' was 'Siocioed'. The proper entry was later filled in by the policeman.

The next column was headed 'Time of Arrival'. The clock showed exactly nine o'clock, so von Werra wrote '09.00' (hours). (It must have been the policeman who subsequently filled in the time of departure—perhaps just to keep his books straight.)

'That's it, sir. Now everything's in order!' The policeman smiled happily, and von Werra's spirits soared. If 'Mr. Boniface' would only give him another five minutes! He now felt so confident that when the manager asked him for his written orders covering the collection of the Hurricane, he replied firmly and without hesitation:

'My papers, parachute—all my kit—will come on a plane which shall land here soon—any minute. I will have instruction on controls to save time, yes?'

'Right ho,' said the manager. 'We can do that all right now you've signed the book. Come with me, Captain.'

Meanwhile, the mechanic in the black smock had come out into the yard and was hanging about expectantly. The manager went over to him and told him to take the Captain back to the Hurricane and explain its instruments and controls in detail.

The manager went off in a different direction with a smile and a cheery wave of the hand.

'He'll fix you up all right,' he said as he left.

Von Werra followed the mechanic back across the yard. There was a large notice on the outer wall of the hangar: 'No smoking beyond this door.' Von Werra dropped his cigarette and trod on it.

Back through the hangar. Every second counted. Would he see a group of airmen looking for him when he emerged on to the tarmac? The mechanic did not dawdle, but von Werra felt an urge to push him along still faster. Instead, he had to keep pace nonchalantly.

Out through the open front. A glance right and left. No R.A.F. uniforms in sight!

And there was the beautiful, brand-new Hurricane, with a coating of rime on its wings and——

Hell's teeth!—the accumulator trolley was no longer beside it. Nowhere in sight. Some other mechanic must have taken it away while he was signing that blasted book. Oh, well, he would just have to hope that he could start the engine using the battery in the aircraft.

The mechanic climbed up on one side of the cockpit and slid back the perspex hood.

A couple of seconds later von Werra was sitting at the controls, the strange-feeling stick in his hands, aghast at the completely unfamiliar lay-out and instrument panel. Leaning over him into the cockpit, the mechanic carefully explained the controls and instruments.

Von Werra hung on to his every word. But there was much he was unable to follow, too many words he did not understand. He could not absorb and retain all that information in so short a time. He almost panicked. Never mind all those details—what were the essentials?

The compass. Heavens! What kind of compass was that? Nothing like a Messerschmitt's. How did you set the damned thing? (He had determined before escaping from Swanwick that 120 degrees was the most direct course to fly from the Midlands to the Continent.)

'Set the compass to 120 degrees, for instance,' he told the mechanic. The mechanic obliged. Von Werra looked from the reset compass to the sun shining through the perspex. Rubbish. It didn't make sense. He could not make head or tail of the compass. To hell with it. Take off and keep the sun to port.

The stick. A monstrous contraption. As long as he didn't stand the aircraft on its nose when trying to take off. . . .

The hydraulic brake system. Incomprehensible. He had never seen anything like it. Ah, never mind. Hope for the best. As long as he didn't stand the aircraft on its nose. . . .

The starter. Most important. Try it. The mechanic had already pointed out the starter button and the injection pump. What had he said was the proper drill? Von Werra could not remember.

It was a cold morning. Would the aircraft battery be strong enough to turn the engine through the stiff oil? If so, then in a minute he would be on the edge of the field. He would have to taxi along the perimeter road until the engine warmed up. In five minutes he would be airborne, setting course by the sun. In half an hour or so he would be approaching the familiar French coastline. Then —throw the kite flat on the deck on the cliff tops—never mind about the under-cart—before the flak started flying about. He would have made it!

He glared at the starter button. He willed the battery to be strong enough. God grant. . . . It was almost a prayer.

Before the mechanic could anticipate his move, he jabbed the button.

Whirr—whirr. The propeller revolved twice, then stuck. Not a cylinder fired.

'Don't do that!' the mechanic cried in alarm. 'Can't start without the trolley-acc.!'

'Fetch it, then!' von Werra ordered.

He must have it. He must make the mechanic get it. He must *hurry* him to get it.

'It's not available just now. Somebody else is using it.' Just who did this little man think he was?

Von Werra bit his lip. He could not possibly have more than a few minutes left. He must have the trolley-acc. He must have it. He must have it at once. But if he tried to boss and hurry the mechanic, it would probably have the opposite effect; he would sulk and deliberately take his time. Or not fetch it at all.

He turned on the von Werra smile.

'*Please* get it, yes? I really am in a hurry.'

The mechanic looked hard at the smiling Dutchman, then grinned himself. 'All right,' he said. 'I'll see if I can find it.'

The aircraft swayed slightly as he stepped down off the wing. He moved off in the direction of the hangar.

Von Werra glanced back up the perimeter of the airfield. Surely any second men would come running round by the scaffolding on the end hangar. He must not think about it, but use these last few minutes to concentrate on the controls and the instrument panel. The air-speed indicator was graduated in miles per hour. He would have to convert that into kilometres. The altimeter showed height in feet. He would have to convert that into metres.

He heard a strange whining sound and looked out of the cockpit. The mechanic was coming across the tarmac standing on an electric truck, which was pulling the accumulator trolley.

Von Werra's heart thumped madly. His hands were clammy, his throat dry. Two more minutes! God grant nobody turned up.

The mechanic manipulated the truck with conscious expertness, swinging it round the starboard wing in a graceful sweep, halting it dead, with a clatter of couplings, so that the trolley-acc. was in exactly the right position. He jumped off the truck platform, went behind to the trolley-acc. and raised the armoured cable over his shoulder, preparatory to plugging it in.

The aircraft swayed. For a second von Werra did not grasp the significance ~of the movement. He operated the injection pump a couple of times, hoping it would be enough. A voice above him on the port side said quietly:

'*Get out!*'

He jerked his head back. At eye-level on the left-hand side of the cockpit, the sun was reflected on a highly-polished button of an Air Force officer's great-coat. It gleamed too on the muzzle of an automatic pistol.

Von Werra's eye ran up the coat buttons, over a chin, a mouth twisted in a queer sort of grin and halted on a pair of cold, blue eyes.

It was 'Mr. Boniface'.

Prisoner's Return: Italy, December 1943

Descending the hill on the far side, I met three Italians on donkeys.

'Are there any Germans round here?' I asked them in Italian.

Suspiciously, they asked if I was German. Hearing I was English, their manner changed immediately. They embraced me and told me to keep going for half a mile when I would reach their village, Montenero, and find English soldiers everywhere.

'*Niente tedeschi, niente tedeschi!*' they laughed.

The sun broke through the morning mist as I came in sight of the village. Approaching it, I deliberately dawdled and finished the last mouthful of Italian bully.

'Well, here you are,' I said aloud. 'I suppose you'll remember the next minutes all your life.'

And I was quite right.

From a hundred yards away the much-battered buildings appeared deserted. Then I noticed a Bren-carrier behind a wall, a few trucks under camouflage netting in a yard. As I limped slowly into the main street, a solitary shell whistled overhead, exploding somewhere at the farther end. A group of British soldiers, the first I had seen, in long leather waistcoats and khaki cap-comforters, chatted unconcernedly in a doorway across the cobbles from me. I glanced shyly at them, but they took no notice. Just another bedraggled peasant haunting the ruins of his home. . . .

The conventional inhibited Englishman is ill-equipped by temperament for such occasions. I would have liked to dance, to shout, to make some kind of demonstration. A Frenchman, an Australian, would have done it naturally, but somehow I could not. So I walked slowly on, holding off the pleasure of the long-awaited moment, the exclamation of surprise, the greeting from a compatriot.

English voices and laughter came from a house. I crossed the threshold and found, in what had been the peasants' kitchen but was now the usual military desolation of a billet, two half-dressed privates cooking breakfast. One of them saw me, standing there grinning at them.

'Christ, Nobby, look what the cat's brought in,' he said.

I tried to be hearty but failed. 'I've just come through. I'm soaked. Can I warm up by your fire?' I heard my bored voice say politely.

Neither of the soldiers was much surprised by this sudden entry of what was, to all appearances, a dank and bearded Italian, who spoke fluent English with a B.B.C. accent. Sensibly enough, they were more interested in breakfast.

'What are you? Escaped P.O.W. or something?'

'Yes.'

It didn't cause much of a sensation and they asked no more questions. They treated me, as they might have a stray dog, with a sort of cheery kindness and without fuss. In a few minutes I was sitting naked before their fire, drinking a cup of char and feeling the warmth return to my numbed body.

A corporal and others of the section came in for their breakfast. My back view may have mildly surprised them.

'Bloke's an escaped P.O.W.,' Nobby explained.

'Lucky sod. They'll send you home,' the corporal said, offering me a Player's.

Savouring every puff of the tobacco, every sip of the tea, I wondered whether Amos was doing the same somewhere nearby. We had so often pictured just this situation in the past three months. Superstitiously, I put off asking them if they had heard of him. If they had, they would surely say so. And I didn't want to hear them say they hadn't.

Long anticipated pleasures seldom come up to expectation. Neither the tea, the tobacco nor even the warmth were now quite as delicious as I had imagined they would be. The scene was unreal, unbelievable. Though the soldiers' gossip around me was vivid enough.

'Ginger, go and swipe some clothes for him off the C.Q.M.S.'s truck,' the corporal said to one of the men.

'Do you think the C.Q.M.S. can spare me something?'

'The C.Q.M.S. won't know,' Ginger winked as he left the room.

Certainly I was back with the British Army all right.

Later, in the miscellaneous garments swiped by Ginger (the C.Q.M.S. would, I am sure, have supplied them voluntarily—but that, of course, would have been more trouble) I visited R.H.Q. in another part of the village. Nothing had been heard there of Amos and the C.O. refused at first to credit my story that I had walked through his outposts unobserved, until I traced my route for him on the map. Evidently I had indeed walked slap through C Company's position.

'Can't think why they didn't shoot you,' the colonel said irritably. 'Remind me to have a word with the company commander about that,' he added to his adjutant.

John Verney

THE FAR EAST

In Japanese eyes, a prisoner of war was not only defeated, he was also an object of contempt for having allowed himself to be captured. He had lost face; he was no longer entitled to be treated or considered as a human being. He was not.

Owing to the normal Oriental standards of treatment for the defeated, even civilians—men, women and children—who fell into Japanese hands fared little better. Starvation and brutality were their lot.

Out of three hundred thousand prisoners captured by the Japanese in the first months of the war in the Pacific one hundred thousand were already dead when the day of liberation dawned. The two hundred thousand survivors staggered emaciated and exhausted from unknown villages and prison camps scattered over the islands or in the interior of the Asiatic mainland from the rocky shores of the Banda Sea to the Burma jungle.

An almost unsurmountable barrier surrounded them. It was not only the physical prison which held them, or the enormous distances which separated them from their homes and their families and from those who were fighting to liberate them, but their complete isolation amongst a race whose language and customs were completely foreign to them. And, in addition, there was the wall of silence which their Japanese guards deliberately erected around them.

A letter took a year to reach the place of their imprisonment—and then the Japanese would often leave the post sacks lying unopened for some time.

Marcel Junod, International Red Cross

Capture

From the south the leading groups of Japanese came swiftly through the grey light towards the town. The advance scouts marched as quickly as the troops behind, scarcely bothering to watch the sides of the roads for ambushes, knowing that a properly laid ambush would be impossible to detect however hard they strained their eyes. It was easy for them to go forward so quickly and impassively, for them the issue was simple. They could either go forward and perhaps die gloriously, with the absolute certainty of eternal bliss, or not go forward and be even more certain of a swift death and utter disgrace. There were a few to whom the gift of faith in heaven had not been granted and there were some who feared the pain of dying, but they would be ground on the millstone of their own comrades if they allowed those sentiments to show, and with a certainty that made the life of a leading scout seem full of promise.

. . . . When it was light enough to see a few yards the Japanese officer got to his feet. He felt numbed with cold and his body ached with tiredness; it was so usual a condition that he no longer thought about it. Soon the vile fishy taste in his mouth would go and he would feel hungry, perhaps they would come across some water once they moved.

He told his senior N.C.O. to bring the men up to the track immediately; in the meantime he walked towards the dark patch on the dusty track that he knew was the English soldier; perhaps there were some more lying dead in the jungle. He drew his revolver from force of habit; he was convinced that there was no one hiding in the jungle, he had listened contemptuously to the cries for help and the noise they had made as they crashed down the slope; if his own men behaved like that he thought he would commit suicide.

With his foot he rolled Clifton's stiff body over and searched it, transferring everything of possible interest to his haversack. Then he went on. He found more bloodstains and left the track and pushed his way into the jungle.

When he came back the men had fallen in on the track and bowed as he reached them. He gave his instructions in a low voice and they listened stolidly.

When he finished he walked to the head of the line of men and began to pick his way through the jungle towards the ridge.

The group that he led were not picked men nor did they receive any special pay, although their tasks were much more dangerous than those that usually fell to the ordinary Japanese infantry. But even so these groups were envied by the others, it was not only more honourable, but also part of their role was to spread fear by committing atrocities and letting their handiwork be found by the other side. It was exciting and amusing to watch your enemies die bizarrely, and at the same time shocking and horrifying to listen to them begging for mercy on their knees, begging for the incomparable disaster of being taken prisoners.

As far as the Japanese were concerned such men deserved to die.

. . . . In the course of half an hour the back of the work was broken. The cooks had made tea for themselves and taken some to the two diggers; now they stood watching them as they shovelled out the hard lumps of earth, sweat running down their faces. The driver had managed to unscrew the padlock on the front door and wandered about the gloomy rooms lit by chinks of mote-flecked sun that slipped through the shutters. The place was bare except for a few rickety pieces of furniture, but he found a tattered copy of *Blackwood's* dated July 1926; he dragged an armchair to the veranda and sat drinking his tea and reading odd paragraphs that caught his eyes, his lips forming the words.

He heard a slight noise and casually looked across to his lorry, thinking that one of the wounded men might have dropped something, but the lorry was broadside on and he could see nothing. He went on reading and then something moved into his line of vision. He looked up quickly . . . a few yards away were three men in uniform coming towards him, a young man in front carrying a thin revolver. He knew at once that they were Japanese, and he got up slowly, glad that he had left his rifle in the front of the lorry because he thought that as he was unarmed they would not shoot him. He was dazed by the shock, and all he could feel was bitterness, not against the Japanese but against his own people for allowing this to happen, allowing a lorry-load of dead and wounded to go unescorted and be captured.

The officer stood on the bottom step of the veranda and said something to him. The driver shook his head: 'No speak Jap,' he said very quietly as though they were in a conspiracy together. They stood for a few seconds looking at each other, and then the officer beckoned him to walk forward. He came down the steps and they prodded him gently in the back and made signs that he should go in front of them. They walked round the bungalow and past the cookhouse towards the group of men at the grave, the two soldiers on either side and the officer a few paces behind. Dobson stared at them uncomprehendingly, wondering for a moment if he was doing wrong by digging in the rest-house garden, thinking that maybe they were civil police.

'What's up?' he called out.

'I . . . I don't know,' the driver answered, 'they're Japs.' There was a moment of frozen silence and then some dry earth pattered into the grave and one of the cooks turned quickly and started to run towards the trees that hid the river. He ran clumsily in a straight line and everyone watched him. It seemed to take a very long time to reach the edge of the trees and then there was a shot and he pitched forward and rolled against the slender trunk of one of the palms. The officer spoke harshly and waved his revolver in the direction of the lorry. They were too dazed to resist, their rifles which lay close at hand were as useless to them as twigs, movement towards them meant death and to die was unthinkable. Burns had died because he had run, they would not run and would live.

They started towards the lorry. While it was still hidden behind the bungalow they heard screams, and when they turned the corner they could see a little group of men prodding at a body on the ground. They came nearer and saw that Rasby's bandages had been torn off and his smashed jaw was being whipped at and prodded with little sticks; one man had pushed a long piece of bamboo into his mouth and was gouging at the back of his throat with the broken end while Rasby moved his head from side to side carefully, screaming when he could. The officer shouted to them and they stopped at once, shuffling back a few paces and watching the body move on the ground. The officer spoke again and one of the soldiers caught hold of the driver's shirt, ripping it down the front and dragging it off him. He rolled the shirt lengthways, and while someone held Rasby's arms he twisted it twice round the gaping mouth and jerked the knot as tightly as he could.

Some of the Japanese climbed into the lorry and threw everything out, others started tearing blankets into strips and gagged and bound the uninjured prisoners. Myler's and Rasby's clothes were torn off, and they were tied to the flamboyant tree under which the lorry stood. No one resisted, they were outnumbered and unarmed and they did not believe they would be killed. When all the baggage was thrown out of the lorry Dobson was sure that his party of Japanese knew nothing of the company marching towards them and intended driving them back to the town as prisoners. He thought it was much more likely that they would be shot by their own side than killed by the Japanese, who would have no time to waste on prisoners once they met the company. He couldn't understand why the two men should be stripped and tied to the tree so securely; it was dreadful but it wasn't happening to him.

Everything had now been thrown out and quickly examined, the tins of bully beef seemed to attract them more than anything else and their haversacks were bulging with them. He was seized roughly by two men and made to hop over to the lorry and then pushed in with the others. They lay on the floor waiting for the tail-board to be put up, but instead all the baggage started to be thrown in again, blankets first and then the heavier articles. They tried to escape from the soft suffocation of the blankets but they were only partially successful; the four of them managed to roll together to one side of the lorry, but they were smothered in blankets and heavy cases lay across them in confusion. They could hear the Japanese laughing and whispering outside and unscrewing the spare two-gallon tins of petrol. The driver was the first to interpret the sounds, but he did not understand that they were going to be burnt alive until one of the Japanese climbed into the lorry and poured petrol on the pile of luggage until it soaked into the blankets. The sudden knowledge seemed to separate his mind from his body, and he started jerking and heaving to escape from the stifling horror of the blankets, and the sounds that came from his throat and filtered through the gag infected the others and they too began to writhe in terror, strange sounds pouring from their blanket-stuffed mouths. There was a muffled explosion and they heaved their bodies this way and that, the flames reached down quickly, but to them the interval was timeless. The blankets blazed on their bodies and as the fire scorched them they made a last effort to burst loose and the driver stood upright in an oven of fire, blinded by the flames, his arms and body blazing like a torch. He managed to turn towards the open back and tried to step forward, he toppled across the burning cases and fell to the ground. His head lay in a puddle of fire. It was the last thing Myler saw before the petrol tank exploded and enveloped the whole flamboyant tree in flame.

Walter Baxter

Borneo: Civilians

Some days later in the prison compound, behind a thirty-foot wooden boarding, we listened to the first of many addresses by Japanese commanding officers, expressing the following sentiment: 'You are a fourth-class nation now. Therefore your treatment will be fourth-class, and you will live and eat as coolies. In the past you have had proudery and arrogance! You will get over it now!'

Throughout three and a half years they did their best to cure us of proudery and arrogance.

.... For a while we kept small bowls of oil with wicks floating, which we burned at night to give us light. The oil was coconut oil given as a ration. But soon the Japanese stopped giving us oil, and we got so hungry we ate what we had, and by that time we had burned up all the cloth for wicks. So then we lived in the dark.

The barrack had no glass in the windows, just solid wooden shutters. Although it wasn't the rainy season when we arrived, it rained much of the time on Berhala, the rain and wind driving furiously upon us from the sea side of the island. At such times we had to have the shutters closed tight, leaving no ventilation or light, either by day or by night.

The building itself was made of loose shakes, with cracks between, and the rain drove through. I lived on the side exposed to the ocean wind. It rained almost every night, and for six months I rolled up George's and my sleeping things nightly and moved them to a dry spot, and sat on them until the rain abated. I never could unroll them in a dry spot, because there wasn't room enough. The dry places were full of somebody else. Those nights George slept with Edith and Eddie and Mrs. Cho, the Chinese Consul's family, the four of them lying on her feather mattress which her *amah* had rescued for her.

There were two cement latrine holes in camp. These had no containers or outlets, and no manner of being emptied, so after a few experiments we stopped using them. Then the Japanese gave us two corrugated tin buckets to use, and these we stood outdoors behind a shelter.

We took turns disposing of their contents. At first we dug holes in the compound and buried the refuse, but we had no good digging tools, and there was a rock layer just under the topsoil; when it rained we couldn't get the refuse to stay below water level, and excrement floated about the compound. The compound became crowded with refuse holes, and the whole place stank. It was like nothing else I ever smelled. We didn't pass through that smell holding our noses. We simply ate, slept and lived in it.

In time the Japanese decided to permit us to empty the latrine buckets in the sea, five minutes' walk away, twice a day. The men's camp asked permission to do this work for us, but the Japanese refused, as they believed in equal rights for the sexes when it came to excrement. When it was my turn to empty the bucket, I used to carry George on one side and the bucket on the other. We carried the buckets out to the end of the wharf, experimented with the wind, dumped in the refuse. From thence it was carried back to the shore by the current, to the beach where we bathed.

It was a rule in camp that the buckets should be used for faeces only, as otherwise they filled up too fast, so one corner of the compound was used as a urinal. It did not offer the seclusion of those in Paris.

A hooded cobra was said to sleep in the latrine shelter at night, by one of the buckets. Some said they saw it, and all of us heard it. I never saw it there, but I know that there were cobras in the grass outside the compound. Whether the cobra was in the latrine or not, the idea of his being there was sufficient.

The change of diet for all of us, and a dysentery epidemic among the children, made it necessary to keep one latrine bucket in our sleeping quarters on rainy nights. The sounds of that bucket in use, the odour of it, the thought of it, make war more deadly and unendurable to me now than does the memory of all the bombs dropped over us in 1945.

.... On the island there were no officers in charge, and the eight guards were changed once a week. During the week they had complete power over us. To them island duty was a vacation; the lads relaxed in loin-cloths most of the time, bathing, doing acrobatics, throwing things at prisoners, picking their noses, beating up people, distributing largesse, or lolling in the women's barrack playing footsy-footsy.

Our barrack was one big room with a loft above it, and no partitions. Each person occupied about five square feet. If the guard wanted to occupy it with you, there wasn't much you could do except roll over. Not that the guards spent all their time lying down near us; a lot of the time they were drunk in the guardhouse.

Some of it was good clean fun, and boys will be boys. But sometimes boys are dirty boys, and one doesn't like being frisked, frolicked, bullied, chased, back-slapped or face-slapped by a young man with a gun. The gun removes the element of light-hearted gaiety from the game.

Because there were buns, rice, and privileges to be had from tolerating and encouraging the guards, and no means with which to discourage them, the fact that they treated us like tarts was sometimes justified. One good argument against collaborating was the fact that the guards had bedbugs.

They were not sadistic, or masochistic; they were not Oriental, or Occidental; they were just a gang of lowdown young hoodlums who had complete power over a hundred people who could not strike back.

Once a week a worn-out officer arrived in a worn-out motorboat, and both made a loud noise coming. He searched the guards, and us, with equal suspicion. Warned by the motor, the guards could just get their trousers on in time to reach the wharf's end and stand at attention. We could just get our forbidden diaries, books, and food hidden in the grass and the latrines. When the officer departed, everybody relaxed.

Life on Berhala was according to the whims of the guards—and they were whimsical. They could be very kind. One guard gave his own buns to the children daily, another distributed loaves of bread to them. They frequently fed us their own surplus, commenting that our food was terrible. Sometimes they let us meet our husbands openly, and sometimes they beat us for smiling at them secretly.

The first guard we had in Berhala made a speech to us after one week, on the eve of their departure. Before making it, they dictated their sentiments to me in broken English and told me to write them out in 'literary' style. The result of our effort was this:

GENTLEMEN, LADIES AND WOMEN: Nipponese soldiers are very kindly. We will pray for your health until we meet again. To-morrow we go back to Sandakan. We are very sorry for you. However, if you get conceited we will knock you down, beat you, kick you, and kill you.

I suggested that the last sentence was a trifle harsh, but they were particularly attached to it.

.... In Kuching we learned to bow seriously. We had printed instructions, demonstrations and practice. The Nipponese orders for bowing were: Incline the body from the waist to a fifteen-degree angle, with head uncovered, hands at the side, and feet together: remain thus to the count of five (silent); then recover. (If not knocked down.)

The first time we were instructed in bowing in the Kuching camp, we were being trained to present a good appearance for the visiting lieutenant-general for whom we had planted potatoes.

The day came, we were all assembled in ranks, the Sisters in front, the women and children behind, where it was hoped we could do the least harm by our frivolous ways. The order was given to bow. The Sisters had wonderful behinds, the bow made the behinds spring into sudden prominence; by standing too close and bowing too swiftly we managed to meet the behinds with our heads. Confusion and concussion reigned, and order was not restored. The lieutenant-general was hastened away to review the pigs, who had more respect for lieutenant-generals than we did, or else did not understand the meaning of the phrase 'dumb insolence', as we did. We were never again assembled together in one group to bow to a visiting general.

.... Every change was for the worse. Rules increased, food decreased, work increased, and strength decreased. Disappointments multiplied, and optimism was never verified. Hope itself seemed only a refuge for those who would not face facts.

Our food ration, then, as supplied by the Japanese per person per day, was as follows: one cupful of thin rice gruel, five tablespoons of cooked rice, sometimes a few greens, a little sugar, sometimes a little salt and tea. This was what the Japanese expected us to live on. Or did they expect us to live on it?

Additions to this diet were sweet-potato tops, which we grew ourselves. We used the tops because we were too hungry to wait for the potatoes to mature. Every square foot of the camp was in use for gardens, but the soil was exhausted, and we were exhausted. The last eight months of imprisonment it was almost impossible for us to do heavy work, but we did it. We arose before sunrise to finish the work inside camp, and then went outside the camp to work for the Japanese. By nine o'clock in the morning we were worn out.

By now soldiers were trading for and buying skinned cats and rats, people were eating snails and worms, all of us were eating weeds and grass, and plenty of us would have liked to eat each other.

I had meals of banana skins stolen from Japanese refuse barrels and boiled into soup.

. . . . Throughout their imprisonment a home-made radio was concealed— and functioned—in the British soldiers' camp.

The radio was never referred to in camp by name, but spoken of as Granny, Mrs. Harrison, the Ice Cream, the Old Lady, and several less polite terms. Knowing that the lives of its inventors and protectors were forfeit to its discovery, as well as the welfare of the whole camp, a security service of men was formed to guard the Old Lady. These kept guard on the Japanese guards with more efficiency that the guards kept guard on them. Night and day a signal system of songs, whistles, and bird noises kept the Old Lady vigilant to the approach of danger in the shape of guards, officers and *Kempi-Tai*.

At first the soldiers' camp had electric light, and while this lasted the radio was run by electricity. Later when the electricity was discontinued, the radio ceased to function for a four-months' period, during which time the men were busy at work making a hand-power generator. It took them only one month to make the generator itself, but it had taken them three to make the tools with which to make the generator.

This hand-power generator was run by a flywheel, which was disguised as a barrel top. The wheel was turned by one man, and had to revolve at the rate of three thousand revolutions per minute in order to generate sufficient power for the radio. The man who turned the flywheel was given extra food and care in camp, and developed huge muscles in one arm and side from turning it. After sixty seconds of turning, the sweat poured from him like water, and he could turn for only a few minutes at a time.

. . . . So humble were her beginnings, and so simple and inanimate the articles which finally in her being gained life and functions, that the Old Lady seems to have been truly created rather than built. The origins of her component parts were as follows:

The receiver was made from the stolen steering damper knob of a Norton motor-cycle.

The coil was made from a Gibbs' bakelite shaving-soap container.

The variable condenser was made from biscuit tins, stripped and remodelled.

The resistors and valves were made over from old hearing-aid amplifiers belonging to a deaf civilian. Without these, there could have been no Old Lady.

The resistor condenser panel was made from bakelite linen from an old map container.

The high-frequency choke was made from a Colgate's shaving-soap container.

The humdinger or small rheostat was made from stolen old brass, bakelite and wire.

Insulation was supplied by pieces of aeroplane glass stolen by soldiers working at the airfield.

The ignition coils were stolen from an old gun battery.

The rectifier was stolen by a soldier when on a working party in Kuching.

A fixed condenser was stolen from a motor-cycle in Kuching by a soldier on a working party.

And the generator was made of scrap iron, soft Swedish iron, and copper, these materials being stolen from the Nipponese stores, or salvaged from old machines, by men on working parties.

The Old Lady in the altogether was hidden in a soldier's mess tin, an unrewarding place for the only lady in the soldiers' camp to sleep.

. . . . Colonel Suga's picture of himself was as the cultured and beneficent administrator of the ideal internment camp of Kuching. He was always kind to the children, often brought them biscuits and sweets, supplied means for their teaching, gave them what liberty he could. They all liked him.

He had good and kindly impulses, and a real desire for inter-racial understanding. He was kind to me personally. I believe that he saved my husband from death.

Against this, I place the fact that all the prisoners in Borneo were inexorably moving towards starvation. Prisoners of war and civilians were beaten, abused and tortured. Daily living conditions of prison camps were almost unbearable.

At Sandakan and Ranau and Brunei, North Borneo, batches of prisoners in fifties and sixties were marched out to dig their own graves, then shot or bayoneted and pushed into the graves, many before they were dead. All over Borneo hundreds and thousands of sick, weak, weary prisoners were marched on roads and paths until they fell from exhaustion, when their heads were beaten in with rifle butts and shovels, and split open with swords, and they were left to rot unburied. On one march, 2,970 P.O.W.s started and three survived.

The Kuching prison camps were scheduled to march on 15 September 1945 had peace not intervened. It was this abandoned order which Colonel Suga had read to me on the day peace pamphlets were dropped.

I have since heard reports of other Japanese prison camps outside of Borneo: in most of them conditions were better than ours, in few were they worse.

For these black chapters in captivity Colonel Suga, commander in Borneo, must be held responsible.

What his orders were I do not know. No doubt he must obey them, or risk himself. Whether he attempted to save us I do not know, but I do know that it takes more even than physical courage to stand up for human values against patriotic zeal in wartime. Until the gun is held at your own head, until the whisper comes of 'Traitor', you cannot know what you will do.

Agnes Newton Keith

25 March 1945

First Allied planes seen to-day. Three years ago I would have been delirious with joy. To-day I have neither energy nor heart for excitement. Too little food.

Diary entry

. . . . The British soldiers' camp stretched along the side of our road. I was walking up that road on the way to Colonel Suga's office one day when something caught my attention. All over the soldiers' camp I saw small camp-fires glowing, with little pots of various sorts smoking over them. And I thought I smelled . . . chicken! I stopped and stared and sniffed. The Jap sentry near by me said nothing. All this was unusual—fires, food and silent sentries.

A miserably thin-looking soldier in a loin-cloth, so close to the barbed wire that I could see him wink at me, sang out recklessly, 'Happy days are here again!' A boy near him shouted, 'It won't be long now, lady!' Two others bellowed out the familiar camp phrase, 'They'll be coming up the river when they come!' Somebody else chanted the soldiers' favourite:

Let the Chinese and Dyaks and the Dutchmen fight about it,
They can have their Borneo. We can do without it. . . .

and all over the camp I could hear snatches of *Yankee Doodle Dandy*. I saw then that every British soldier within sight was smiling at me, and waggling thumbs up, and the Jap sentry nearby, instead of shouting and shaking his gun, just glared with gummy eyes and did nothing.

I remembered what Harry had told me. I walked on, thinking. None of the scraggy Indonesian chickens that usually fluttered about on the road between camps were visible to-day. Slowly I began to see the connection between the road without chickens, and the soldiers' camp-fires with. It had been chicken that I smelled all right!

The soldiers would not have been killing the chickens from which they occasionally got stray eggs if they did not have good reason to believe that peace had come, nor would the Nipponese sentries have been allowing them to build camp-fires. That smell of chicken cooking will always in my mind be the first harbinger of peace.

The next day the Nipponese sent us a double ration of rice and sago flour. We had already received our August rations, complained at their scarcity, and been answered, 'There is no more rice in Kuching.' When the double ration arrived we knew something had happened.

Meanwhile the Japanese officers denied the rapidly spreading rumours of peace, and the Japanese guards believed their officers, so convinced had they always been of their own invincibility.

. . . . A Douglas C-47 flew very low over camp. A door opened in the centre, and two blond airmen leaned far out, waving and shouting and laughing at us. We had crowded to the entrance of the camp when we heard the plane flying low, and now we waved back, jumping and cheering, not knowing what was happening, but sure that it was good.

The C-47 circled camp and returned, swooping even lower as she neared us. The centre door opened again, the men were leaning out waving, and suddenly, to our delight, out of the door came a long torpedo-shaped object. It shot downward; then, just before reaching the ground, a parachute unfurled above it, and the torpedo settled softly to the ground, between the entrance gates of our camp. The thirty-four kids fell upon it. On the six-foot torpedo was printed the word BREAD.

People have asked me since if we raced for this first bundle of food, and tore it open and fought over it. Such an action would have horrified us. We might have felt like it, but we could not have done it. Mean tricks we had learned in captivity, but an equal division of rations had become sacred.

In any case, half-starved though we were, that first parachute meant so much more to us than food that we were not even tempted. Even more than our bodies, our hearts had starved—for contact with our own people, for a touch of the friendly hand. The word on that parachute spelled BREAD, but it meant, YOU ARE NOT FORGOTTEN. The greatest satisfaction we could get from its contents was ours already.

Twenty-five parachutes descended that day. At first the Japanese held us back; but by the time the planes had left we had raced forward and started salvaging the parachutes themselves, which we saw would be priceless for shirts and pants. Some of those first parachutes—made speedily into pants—were walking around on children and mothers within twenty-four hours.

In addition to bread we received that day boxes containing tinned tongue, ham, rabbit, milk, butter, chocolate, biscuits, sugar, custard powder, soap, toilet paper, Red Cross medical supplies and a little clothing.

During all this people continued to go mad. George leaped into the air like a puppy, women jumped and waved and screamed, tears flowed, noses were blown, hearts pounded, laughter and cheers poured out. All but myself; I went very silent, in a cold sweat, with an asinine smile, and no words for my feelings. I could only nod my head, yes, yes, in agreement with everyone that this was the greatest moment of *our* war.

.... While awaiting liberation I was requested by Colonel King, the English medical officer who had been in charge of the British soldiers' camp during captivity, to visit their camp. If I was going to write, he said, I must know the truth. So Harry, two other civilians, and I accompanied Colonel King into camp the next day.

When I entered the soldiers' compound I was instantly struck by its utter barrenness compared to our own. It was an eroded brown wasteland crossed by washed-out gullies with row after row of withered palm-leaf huts with ragged, limping men coming from them.

.... Before Colonel King took me through the sick huts he asked me if I had a strong stomach for shocking sights. I said that I hoped I had. When I saw the conditions I was not concerned about my stomach, which had stood up to everything for years, but I was disturbed at the distress which I feared I might cause the patients. They were almost naked, covered with ulcers, and in such a state that I felt they would resent my intrusion, if they had strength for resentment. If they had any active wish now, it must be to crawl away from all eyes and die.

But I found I was wrong. Great as their physical misery was, their boredom was even greater, and this I could relieve. For they, like the stronger men in

camp, were avid for sight, sound or smell of a woman. Soon we all talked together, and examined ailments together; soon we could scarcely move through
the huts for patients describing their symptoms and showing their wounds.
Finding that they liked seeing me helped me to move naturally amongst sights
which Colonel King had properly described as shocking.

The bodies of all the men were shrunken from starvation, with the bones
showing like skeletons, the skin dried and shrivelled, while the skulls with their
deep-set eyes seemed unnaturally large.

All patients had ulcers caused by malnutrition and lack of circulation, many
covering an entire leg, chest, arm or thigh. Many had a gangrenous condition
of feet, hands, testicles. Some had a condition of the fingers and toes which can
only be described as dissolving away; the tips of the digits were open and bloody
and they seemed to be bleeding off.

I was told that of two thousand British soldiers who had been brought to
Kuching from Singapore as prisoners, seven hundred and fifty now survived.
Of this number six hundred and fifty were ill, and not thirty men in the whole
camp remained strong enough to form a working party.

Four years before, these soldiers had been fittest of the fit. This was what
a war fought in captivity had done for them. I was glad I had seen them. I would
never forget them. I wished that anyone who spoke philosophically of 'the next
war' could see them.

Agnes Newton Keith

Manchuria

The first thing we saw was a big yard around which were sheds made of
concrete.

The yard was empty and there was nothing in the sheds. Where were the
prisoners?

'They're at work,' Matsuda replied with a great display of nonchalance.

'Well, will you please take us to where they are working?'

'Oh, that's quite impossible. It's too far.'

'Perhaps we can at least see their representatives?'

'Na. Na. An unforeseen hindrance.'

Not for the first time in my career as a delegate of the International Committee of the Red Cross I felt anger rising hot in my breast. But I had to keep
calm. An unpleasant incident on this very first 'visit' might create difficulties
better avoided. And incidentally the colonel was taking us towards a building
which appeared occupied.

'And here is our magnificent hospital,' he announced with one foot on its
first step.

At the top of the steps stood four men in shirts and shorts at attention. They
were the first prisoners of war I had seen in Manchuria.

As our procession mounted the steps after him the four men bowed low, their
arms kept tightly to their sides, until their heads were almost on a level with their
knees.

In a low voice, and making an effort not to show the indignation which was
boiling up in me, I said:

'That's not the manner in which soldiers of an Occidental army salute.'

'No, it's the Japanese manner,' replied Colonel Matsuda with his eternal and impenetrable smile.

We were taken along a corridor with sick-rooms on either side. Standing by the wall near each door were three or four sick prisoners, all of whom bowed low as we approached. Those prisoners who were unable to rise were seated tailor-fashion on their beds, their arms crossed on their chests, and they too bowed as low as their bandages, wounds or mutilations would permit. When the last Japanese officer had passed they resumed the upright position, their eyes raised fixedly to the ceiling. Never once did their eyes meet ours.

The palms of my hands were wet and Margherita was as white as a sheet. This was indescribably horrible. Matsuda tried to lead us on but I stopped before a group of four prisoners, three British and an American.

'Is there a doctor amongst you?' I asked, trying to keep my voice firm and not betray the emotion I felt.

No one answered, and the Japanese behind me kept silent.

I stood directly in front of a big fellow who towered above me. I could see only his chin and his stretched neck as he looked up at the ceiling. Not a muscle stirred and I repeated my question. There was still no reply and I turned grimly to Matsuda.

'Why doesn't he reply?' I asked. 'Isn't he allowed to?'

The Japanese were stupefied at my audacity, but Matsuda was evidently unwilling to risk an unpleasant incident and he indicated one of the men standing against the wall with the others.

'This Australian is a doctor,' he said.

I went towards my Australian colleague with outstretched hand. I had to overcome a lump in my throat to get out the banal words:

'How do you do?'

The man lowered his eyes, but not to me. It was at Matsuda he looked. It was the colonel's permission he sought. After several seconds which seemed incredibly long his hand slowly rose to mine. I took it and shook it warmly, trying to convey to him all the emotion and sympathy I felt and hoping he would afterwards communicate them to his comrades.

I told him as briefly as possible who I was and why I had come and I tried to get into conversation with him. He replied slowly and in monosyllables and each time before he spoke I could see that he silently sought the approval of Matsuda over my head.

'Will you accompany me on a tour of the wards?' I asked finally.

This time Matsuda intervened.

'No,' he said. 'A Japanese doctor will accompany you.'

I felt it was impossible to insist further, and I let go the man's trembling hand which stiffened back to the attention against his side whilst his eyes rose again to the ceiling.

.... We walked towards the grey house, which was less like a prison than a miner's block in the Borinage. A long corridor went from end to end of it with doors on either side, seven on the left and eight on the right.

In surroundings which were so like the familiar surroundings we knew at

home I had difficulty in realizing that I was about to come face to face with the
hero of Corregidor, the defender of Singapore, the Governor of the Dutch East
Indies and twelve other soldiers of high rank whose armies were still fighting
everywhere in the Pacific.

And suddenly a disturbing sight presented itself.

There they stood upright and motionless in the middle of the room. I should
not have been able to distinguish their faces even if I had not involuntarily
turned my head away because they bowed low, their arms close to their bodies,
as soon as the sabre of Matsuda rapped on the floor.

It seemed to me that the last man in the row refused to submit to the
humiliation and remained upright.

'General Wainright.'

My emotion was so great that I could hardly utter the words I had to speak.
He maintained an icy reserve towards the Japanese around me. Nothing, it
seemed, had broken his spirit. His voice was still vibrant as he replied to the
pitiful and absurdly abrupt questions which were all I was allowed to ask
him.

'How are you?'

'Not bad. My right hip is giving me rather less trouble now.'

'I am happy to tell you that your family is well and that they received your
last message safely.'

'Thank you.'

His face lit up at my last question.

'Have you any request to make?'

'Certainly. Can I make it now?'

'No,' put in Matsuda at once. 'It will have to be made in writing to Tokyo.'

The ghost of a sceptical smile passed over General Wainwright's lips.

The door was closed behind us. The interview was at an end. It had not
lasted two minutes.

I left the house almost hustled out by the Japanese, who seemed to fear that
I would shout the 'goodbye' that struggled for expression. I had been able to
see them and let them see me; that was all. But at least they now knew that we
were aware of their place of detention.

Only prisoners who had been cut off from their world for three years and
had seen nothing around them but yellow faces could appreciate the full significance of that pitiful result: two months' journey from Europe to China, via
Egypt, Persia, Moscow and Siberia, for two minutes restricted conversation with
one prisoner of war in Manchuria.

Marcel Junod

EXTERMINATION

*There was another kind of prisoner whose one object was simply to survive.
These were the men, women and children of every nationality whose crimes were
political or racial: they had spoken or written or acted against the Nazis, or they
happened to belong to one of the races marked down for organized extermination.*

They went to concentration camps, where they were kept just alive while their bodies or their labour served some useful purpose, and then, if they were not dead already, they were killed.

The Jews

As far as the Jews are concerned, I want to tell you quite frankly that they must be done away with in one way or another. The Führer said once, 'Should united Jewry again succeed in provoking a world war, not only will the blood of the nations which have been forced into the war by them be shed, but the Jew will have found his end in Europe.' I know that many measures carried out against the Jews in the Reich at present are being criticized. It is being done intentionally, as is obvious from the reports on the morale, to talk about cruelty, harshness, etc. Before I continue, I want to beg you to agree with me on the following formula: We will on principle have pity on the German people only and nobody else in the whole world. The others, too, had no pity on us. As an old National Socialist I must say this: This war would be only a partial success if the whole of Jewry should survive it, while we had shed our best blood in order to save Europe. My attitude towards the Jews will, therefore, be based only on the expectation that they must disappear. They must be done away with. I have entered into negotiations to have them deported to the East. A great discussion concerning that question will take place in Berlin in January, a discussion to which I am going to delegate the State Secretary, Dr. Bechler. It is to take place in the Reich Security Main Office with S.S. Lieutenant-General Heydrich. A great Jewish migration will begin, in any case.

But what should be done with the Jews? Do you think they will be settled down in the *Ostland* in villages? This is what we were told in Berlin: why all this bother? We can do nothing with them either in the *Ostland* or in the *Reichskommissariat*. So liquidate them yourselves.

Gentlemen, I must ask you to rid yourselves of all feeling of pity. We must annihilate the Jews, wherever we find them and wherever it is possible, in order to maintain the structure of the Reich as a whole.

Hans Frank, Governor-General of Poland, Cracow, 16 December 1941

Auschwitz

I am twenty-nine years of age, from Lublin, Poland, where I was arrested on 19 May 1940 because I was a Jewess. I received no form of trial, was first kept at Lublin for a year and then was sent to Auschwitz, where I arrived in the autumn of 1941. My husband, who was not a Jew, was a lieutenant in the Polish Army and was also arrested. At the camp all our personal belongings were taken away. We had to leave our clothes behind and we were taken into a shower-bath. As my hair was cut very short I asked for a cloth to put round my head as I was freezing, and a *Kapo* who was in charge of the shower-bath started to hit us very severely. The clothes we were given consisted of a long sort of coat and a silk blouse without any sleeves. We had already had a number tattooed on our arms. For a whole day we were left naked in that sort of shower-bath, and then at last we were led into Block No. 25. There were sort of cages in three parts in this block and very often we slept seven or eight in one part of this cage, getting one blanket issued amongst eight persons. There were no mattresses or palliasses. 3.30 a.m. was the normal time to get up in the morning.

What happened when you got up in the morning?—Everybody had to leave the block for a roll-call which lasted until eight or nine o'clock in the morning. We had to stand to attention in lines of five, and if we moved we were hit in the face or had to kneel down holding a heavy stone in our arms. For the first six weeks we did not work at all as we were in a sort of quarantine. Whilst I was fetching food one day I fell down and broke my leg, and was taken to the camp reception station, and was in hospital at Christmas 1941.

What happened on the day before Christmas Day?—There was a big selection in Block No. 4, the hospital block. Over three thousand Jewish women had to parade in this selection, which was under the charge of Hoessler. We had to leave our beds very quickly and stand quite naked to attention in front of him and the doctors, Enna and Koenig. All those who could not leave their beds had their numbers taken, and it was clear to us that they were condemned to death. Those whose bodies were not very nice looking or were too thin, or whom those gentlemen disliked for some reason or other, had their numbers taken, and it was clear what that meant. My number also was taken. We stayed in Block No. 4 for a night and the next day were taken to Block No. 18. About half-past five in the evening trucks arrived and we were loaded into them, quite naked like animals, and were driven to the crematorium.

When you reached the crematorium, what happened there?—The whole truck was tipped over in the way they do it sometimes with potatoes or coal loads, and we were led into a room which gave me the impression of a shower-bath. There were towels hanging round, and sprays, and even mirrors. I cannot say how many were in the room altogether, because I was so terrified, nor do I know if the doors were closed. People were in tears; people were shouting at each other; people were hitting each other. There were healthy people, strong people, weak people and sick people, and suddenly I saw fumes coming in through a very small window at the top. I had to cough very violently, tears were streaming from my eyes, and I had a sort of feeling in my throat as if I would be asphyxiated. I could not even look at the others because each of us concentrated on what happened to herself.

What was the next thing you remember?—At that moment I heard my name called. I had not the strength to answer it, but I raised my arm. Then I felt someone take me and throw me out from that room. Hoessler put a blanket round me and took me on a motor-cycle to the hospital, where I stayed six weeks. As the result of the gas I had still, quite frequently, headaches and heart trouble, and whenever I went into the fresh air my eyes were filled with tears. I was subsequently taken to the political department and apparently I had been taken out of the gas chamber because I had come from a prison in Lublin, which seemed to make a difference, and, apart from that, my husband was a Polish officer.

After you came out of hospital, how were you employed?—In the beginning I was employed in cleaning the room of the *Blockälteste* and in washing in the laundry. Later on I was employed on latrine fatigues. With my own hands I had to clean whatever was in the latrines and there were no brooms or brushes or any sort of cleaning material given to me. It was considered a good job because sometimes we would warm ourselves near the stove, or even wash a shirt. Our food consisted of coffee in the morning, half a litre of vegetable soup for lunch, sometimes only a quarter, and in the evening a ration of bread, sometimes something with it, other times without, and sometimes coffee. For a few days I worked in the kitchen, but as the work was too hard for me I was put on a working party called 'Kanda', which consisted of sorting out the belongings which came from other people who went to the crematorium. I got this through the influence of the *Blockälteste* with whom I was working previously.

Dachau

I, Franz Blaha, being duly sworn, depose and state as follows:

I was sent as a prisoner to the Dachau Concentration Camp in April 1941, and remained there until the liberation of the camp in April 1945. Until July 1941 I worked in a Punishment Company. After that I was sent to the hospital and subjected to the experiments in typhoid being conducted by Dr. Mürmelstadt. After that I was to be made the subject of an experimental operation, and only succeeded in avoiding this by admitting that I was a physician. If this had been known before I would have suffered, because intellectuals were treated very harshly in the Punishment Company. In October 1941 I was sent to work in the herb plantation, and later in the laboratory for processing herbs. In June 1942 I was taken into the hospital as a surgeon. Shortly afterwards I was directed to conduct a stomach operation on twenty healthy prisoners. Because I would not do this I was put in the autopsy room, where I stayed until April 1945. While there I performed approximately seven thousand autopsies. In all, twelve thousand autopsies were performed under my direction.

From mid-1941 to the end of 1942 some five hundred operations on healthy prisoners were performed. These were for the instruction of the S.S. medical students and doctors and included operations on the stomach, gall bladder, spleen and throat. These were performed by students and doctors of only two years' training, although they were very dangerous and difficult. Ordinarily they would not have been done except by surgeons with at least four years' surgical practice. Many prisoners died on the operating table and many others from later complications. I performed autopsies on all these bodies. The doctors who supervised these operations were Lang, Mürmelstadt, Wolter, Ramsauer and Kahr. *Standartenführer* Dr. Lolling frequently witnessed these operations.

During my time at Dachau I was familiar with many kinds of medical experiments carried on there with human victims. These persons were never volunteers but were forced to submit to such acts. Malaria experiments on about twelve hundred people were conducted by Dr. Klaus Schilling between 1941 and 1945. Schilling was personally asked by Himmler to conduct these experiments. The victims were either bitten by mosquitoes or given injections of malaria sporozoites taken from mosquitoes. Different kinds of treatment were applied, including quinine, pyrifer, neosalvarsan, antipyrin, pyramidon and a drug called 2516 Behring. I performed autopsies on bodies of people who died from these malaria experiments. Thirty to forty died from the malaria itself. Three to four hundred died later from diseases which proved fatal because of the physical condition resulting from the malaria attacks. In addition there were deaths resulting from poisoning due to overdoses of neosalvarsan and pyramidon. Dr. Schilling was present at the time of my autopsies on the bodies of his patients.

In 1942 and 1943 experiments on human beings were conducted by Dr. Sigismund Rascher to determine the effects of changing air pressure. As many as twenty-five persons were put at one time into a specially-constructed van in which pressure could be increased or decreased as required. The purpose was to find out the effects of high altitude and of rapid parachute descents on human beings. Through a window in the van I have seen the people lying on the floor of the van. Most of the prisoners who were made use of died as a result of these experiments, from internal haemorrhages of the lungs or brain. The rest coughed blood when taken out. It was my job to take the bodies out and to send the internal organs to Munich for study as soon as they were found to be dead. About four hundred to five hundred prisoners were experimented on. Those not dead were sent to invalid blocks and liquidated shortly afterwards. Only a few escaped.

Rascher also conducted experiments on the effect of cold water on human beings. This was done to find a way for reviving aviators who had fallen into the ocean. The subject was placed in ice-cold water and kept there until he was unconscious. Blood was taken from his neck and tested each time his body temperature dropped one degree. This drop was determined by a rectal thermo-meter. Urine was also periodically tested. Some men lasted as long as twenty-four to thirty-six hours. The lowest body temperature reached was nineteen degrees C., but most men died at twenty-five degrees C., or twenty-six degrees C. When the men were removed from the ice water attempts were made to revive them by artificial warmth from the sun, from hot water, from electro-therapy or by animal warmth. For this last experiment prostitutes were used and the body of the unconscious man was placed between the bodies of two women. Himmler was present at one such experiment. I could see him from one of the windows in the street between the blocks. I have personally been present at some of the cold-water experiments when Rascher was absent, and I have seen notes and diagrams on them in Rascher's laboratory. About three hundred persons were used in these experiments. The majority died. Of those who lived many became mentally deranged. Those not killed were sent to invalid blocks and were killed, just as were the victims of the air-pressure experiments. I only know two who survived—a Jugoslav and a Pole, both of whom have become mental cases.

Liver-puncture experiments were performed by Dr. Brachtl on healthy people, and on people who had diseases of the stomach and gall bladder. For this purpose a needle was jabbed into the liver of a person and a small piece of liver was extracted. No anaesthetic was used. The experiment is very painful and often had serious results, as the stomach or large blood vessels were often punctured and haemorrhage resulted. Many persons died of these tests, for which Polish, Russian, Czech and German prisoners were employed. Altogether these experiments were conducted on about 175 people.

Phlegmone experiments were conducted by Dr. Schütz, Dr. Babor, Dr. Kieselwetter and Professor Lauer. Forty healthy men were used at a time, of whom twenty were given intra-muscular, and twenty intravenous, injections of pus from diseased persons. All treatment was forbidden for three days, by which time serious inflammation and in many cases general blood poisoning had occurred. Then each group was divided again into groups of ten. Half were given chemical treatment with liquid and special pills every ten minutes for twenty-four hours. The rest were treated with sulphanamide and surgery. In some cases all of the limbs were amputated. My autopsy also showed that the chemical treatment had been harmful and had even caused perforations of the stomach wall. For these experiments Polish, Czech and Dutch priests were ordinarily used. Pain was intense in such experiments. Most of the six hundred to eight hundred persons who were used finally died. Most of the others became permanent invalids and were later killed.

In the autumn of 1944 there were sixty to eighty persons who were subjected to salt-water experiments. They were locked in a room and for five days were given nothing to swallow but salt water. During this time their urine, blood and excrement were tested. None of these prisoners died, possibly because they received smuggled food from other prisoners. Hungarians and gypsies were used for these experiments.

It was common practice to remove the skin from dead prisoners. I was commanded to do this on many occasions. Dr. Rascher and Dr. Wolter in particular asked for this human skin from human backs and chests. It was chemically treated and placed in the sun to dry. After that it was cut into various sizes for use as saddles, riding breeches, gloves, house slippers and ladies' handbags. Tattooed skin was especially valued by S.S. men. Russians, Poles and other inmates were used in this way, but it was forbidden to cut out the skin of a German. This skin had to be from healthy prisoners and free from defects. Sometimes we did not have enough bodies with good skin and Rascher would say, 'All right, you will get the bodies.' The next day we would receive twenty or thirty bodies of young people. They would have been shot in the neck or struck on the head so that the skin would be uninjured. Also we frequently got requests for the skulls or skeletons of prisoners. In those cases we boiled the skull or the body. Then the soft parts were removed and the bones were bleached and dried and reassembled. In the case of skulls it was important to have a good set of teeth. When we got an order for skulls from Oranienburg the S.S. men would say, 'We will try to get you some with good teeth.' So it was dangerous to have a good skin or good teeth.

Transports arrived frequently in Dachau from Studthof, Belsen, Auschwitz, Mauthausen and other camps. Many of these were ten to fourteen days on the way without water or food. On one transport, which arrived in November 1942, I found evidence of cannibalism. The living persons had eaten the flesh from the dead bodies. Another transport arrived from Compiègne in France. Professor Limousin of Clermont-Ferrand, who was later my assistant, told me that there had been two thousand persons on this transport when it started. There was food available but no water. Eight hundred died on the way and were thrown out. When it arrived after twelve days more than five hundred persons were dead on the train. Of the remainder, most died shortly after arrival. I investigated this transport because the International Red Cross complained, and the S.S. men wanted a report that the deaths had been caused by fighting and rioting on the way. I dissected a number of bodies and found that they had died from suffocation and lack of water; it was mid-summer and a hundred and twenty people had been packed into each car.

In 1941 and 1942 we had in the camp what we called invalid transports. These were made up of people who were sick or for some reason incapable of working. We called them *Himmelfahrt* Commandos. About a hundred or a hundred and twenty were ordered each week to go to the shower baths. There, four people gave injections of phenol evipan, or benzine, which soon caused death. After 1943 these invalids were sent to other camps for liquidation. I know that they were killed because I saw the records, and they were marked with a cross and the date that they left, which was the way that deaths were ordinarily recorded. This was shown both on the card index of the Camp Dachau and the records in the town of Dachau. One thousand to two thousand went away every three months, so there were about five thousand sent to death in 1943, and the same in 1944. In April 1945, a Jewish transport was loaded at Dachau and was left standing on the railroad siding. The station was destroyed by bombing, and they could not leave. So they were just left there to die of starvation. They were not allowed to get off. When the camp was liberated they were all dead.

Many executions by gas or shooting or injections took place in the camp itself. The gas chamber was completed in 1944, and I was called by Dr. Rascher to examine the first victims. Of the eight or nine persons in the chamber there were three still alive, and the remainder appeared to be dead. Their eyes were red and their faces were swollen. Many prisoners were later killed in this way. Afterwards they were removed to the crematorium, where I had to examine their teeth for gold. Teeth containing gold were extracted. Many prisoners who were sick were killed by injections while in hospital. Some prisoners killed in the hospital came through to the autopsy room with no name or number on the tag which was usually tied to their big toe. Instead the tag said, 'Do not dissect.'

I performed autopsies on some of these and found that they were perfectly healthy, but had died from injections. Sometimes prisoners were killed only because they had dysentery or vomited, and gave the nurses too much trouble. Mental patients were liquidated by being led to the gas chamber and injected there or shot. Shooting was a common method of execution. Prisoners would be shot just outside the crematorium and carried in. I have seen people pushed into the ovens while they were still breathing and making sounds, although if they were too much alive they were usually hit on the head first.

The principal executions about which I know from having examined the victims, or supervised such examinations, are as follows: In 1942 there were five thousand to six thousand Russians held in a separate camp inside Dachau. They were taken on foot to the Military Rifle Range near the camp in groups of five hundred or six hundred and shot. These groups left the camp about three times a week. At night we used to go out to bring the bodies back in carts and then examine them. In February 1944, about forty Russian students arrived from Moosburg. I knew a few of the boys in the hospital. I examined them after they were shot outside the crematorium. In September 1944 a group of ninety-four high-ranking Russians were shot, including two military doctors who had been working with me in the hospital. I examined their bodies. In April 1945, a number of prominent people who had been kept in the bunker were shot. They included two French generals, whose names I cannot remember, but I recognized them from their uniform. I examined them, after they were shot. In 1944 and 1945 a number of women were killed by hanging, shooting and injections. I examined them and found that in many cases they were pregnant. In 1945, just before the camp was liberated, all *Nacht und Nebel* prisoners were executed. These were prisoners who were forbidden to have any contact with the outside world. They were kept in a special enclosure and were not allowed to send or receive any mail. There were thirty or forty, many of whom were sick. These were carried to the crematorium on stretchers. I examined them and found they had all been shot in the neck.

From 1941 on, the camp became more and more overcrowded. In 1943 the hospital for prisoners was already overcrowded. In 1944 and in 1945 it was impossible to maintain any sort of sanitary condition. Rooms, which held three hundred or four hundred persons in 1942, were filled with a thousand in 1943, and in the first quarter of 1945 with two thousand or more. The rooms could not be cleaned because they were too crowded, and there was no cleaning material. Baths were available only once a month. Latrine facilities were completely inadequate. Medicine was almost non-existent. But I found, after the camp was liberated, that there was plenty of medicine in the S.S. hospital for all the camps, if it had been given to us for use.

New arrivals at the camp were lined up out of doors for hours at a time. Sometimes they stood there from morning until night. It did not matter whether this was in the winter or in the summer. This occurred all through 1943, 1944 and the first quarter of 1945. I could see these formations from the window of the autopsy room. Many of the people who had to stand in the cold in this way became ill from pneumonia and died. I had several acquaintances who were killed in this manner during 1944 and 1945. In October 1944 a transport of Hungarians brought spotted fever into the camp, and an epidemic began. I examined many of the corpses from this transport and reported the situation to Dr. Hintermayer, but was forbidden, on penalty of being shot, to mention that there was an epidemic in the camp. He said that it was sabotage, and that I was trying to have the camp quarantined so that the prisoners would not have to work in the armaments industry. No preventive measures were taken at all. New healthy arrivals were put into blocks where an epidemic was already present. Infected persons were also put into these blocks. So the thirteenth block, for instance, died out completely three times. Only at Christmas, when the epidemic spread into the S.S. camp, was a quarantine established. Nevertheless, transports continued to arrive.

We had two to three hundred new typhus cases and a hundred deaths caused by typhus each day. In all, we had twenty-eight thousand cases and fifteen thousand deaths. In addition to those that died from the disease, my autopsies showed that many deaths were caused solely by malnutrition. Such deaths occurred in all the years from 1941 to 1945. They were mostly Italians, Russians and Frenchmen. These people were just starved to death. At the time of death they weighed fifty to sixty pounds. Autopsies showed their internal organs had often shrunk to one-third of their actual size.

The facts stated above are true: This declaration is made by me voluntarily and without compulsion. After reading over the statement I have signed and executed it at Nuremberg, Germany, this 9th day of January 1946.

Dr. Franz Blaha

The Perfectionist

The overhauling of vans by groups D and C is finished. While the vans in the first series can also be put into action if the weather is not too bad, the vans of the second series (Saurer) stop completely in rainy weather. If it has rained, for instance, for only one half-hour, the van cannot be used, because it simply skids away. It can only be used in absolutely dry weather. It is now merely a question of whether the van can be used only when it stands at the place of execution. First, the van has to be brought to that place, which is possible only in good weather. The place of execution is usually ten to fifteen kilometres away from the highway and is difficult of access because of its location; in damp or wet weather it is not accessible at all. If the persons to be executed are driven or led to that place, then they realize immediately what is going on and get restless, which is to be avoided as far as possible. There is only one way left; to load them at the collecting point and to drive them to the spot.

I ordered the vans of group D to be camouflaged as house-trailers by putting one set of window shutters on each side of the small van and two on each side of the larger vans, such as one often sees on farmhouses in the country. The vans became so well-known that not only the authorities but also the civilian population called the van 'death van' as soon as one of the vehicles appeared. It is my opinion the van cannot be kept secret for any length of time, not even camouflaged.

Because of the rough terrain and the indescribable road and highway conditions, the caulkings and rivets loosen in the course of time. I was asked if in such cases the vans should not be brought to Berlin for repairs. Transportation to Berlin would be much too expensive and would demand too much fuel. In order to save these expenses I ordered them to have the smaller leaks soldered.... Besides that I ordered that during application of gas all the men were to be kept as far away from the vans as possible, so that they should not suffer damage to their health by the gas which eventually would escape. I should like to take this opportunity to bring the following to your attention: After the application of gas several commands have had the unloading done by their own men. I brought to the attention of the commander of these S.K. concerned the immense psychological injuries, and damage to their health which that work can have for those men, even if not immediately, at least later on. The men complained to me about headaches which appeared after each unloading. Nevertheless they do not want to change the orders, because they are afraid prisoners called for that work could use an opportune moment to flee. To protect the men from those risks, I request orders be issued accordingly.

The application of gas is not usually undertaken correctly. In order to come to an end as fast as possible, the driver presses the accelerator to the fullest extent. By doing that the persons to be executed suffer death from suffocation, and not death by dozing off as was planned. My directions now have proved that by correct adjustment of the levers death comes faster, and the prisoners fall asleep peacefully. Distorted faces and excretions, such as could be seen before, are no longer noticed.

To-day I shall continue my journey to group B, where I can be reached with further news.

Dr. Becker, S.S. Untersturmführer

Sachsenhausen

These hangings take place on the parade ground, and everyone has to look on. Our Norwegian comrades have seen any number of them. Nor are these executions lacking in their 'heroic episodes'. A German was hanged for attempting to escape. He talked of freedom on the scaffold, freedom for the German people which would soon come. He turned to the Commandant, who attends the executions, and calmly said, Well, it was his turn now, before long it would be the Commandant's. When the rope was put round his neck, he raised his hand and waved and smiled to his comrades for the last time. It must be a good deal worse to look on when the unhappy man or men scream, weep and struggle. Once there were seven hanged at the same time.

Odd Nansen

Solitary Confinement

Sunday, 20 February 1944

It is Bella's birthday to-day, I have never been so heavy-hearted as in this morning hour. The whole weight of my many failures towards Bella crushes me. I have been mean, indifferent and unkind towards her—she who is the pearl of my life. What is the good of regretting it now? It is deeds which count. To-day I feel a great need to pray. I can't manage all this alone. I will pray when the bells of Holy Trinity ring. I will pray to be allowed to live and fulfil the law of life and love at Bella's side. Oh Bella! I long for you. My heart is more tender towards you than my back is from the whipping at Victoria Terrasse. Believe me, Bella, I write this in an hour which is full of pain and terrors.

The sun is shining upon a beautiful Norwegian winter day. Here at 19 M* are over three hundred good Norwegians imprisoned because they did their duty towards their country. Well—Nazism will never take root in Norway. That is worth great sacrifice. Seen in this light the fate of the individual is not worth

* The Gestapo prison in Oslo where Moen, chief of the whole Norwegian underground press, was put in solitary confinement. On his deportation to Germany in September 1944 he lost his life when the ship struck a mine. His diary, written on toilet paper with a tack, was discovered after the war (Ed.)

mentioning. But this is not *London News.** It is my diary which comforts and strengthens me. . . . One summer day when Norway is once again a free country Bella and I will walk in the woods and sing: 'What is the country where you live called?' Happiness!! Oh God, I beg for this. Bella! A new bond goes between us from 19 Møllergaten to Grini. We suffer for our cause and are comrades in what is for us a new sense of the word.

Comrade Bella.

We will live and love.

Peter Moen

* The best-known of the clandestine newspapers of the Norwegian resistance movement (Ed.)

22

THE ORDEAL OF THE CITIES: BOMBS ON GERMANY – V-WEAPONS ON ENGLAND

While German bombs were falling on England in 1940, the Royal Air Force had already begun to attack Germany's war industries and domestic morale. Until the spring of 1942 these raids achieved little, but during the same year the introduction of radar position-finding devices allowed really accurate night bombing for the first time, mainly on the Ruhr.

Woe to the One who Loses

THE worst part of the raids for me, however, was being separated from my children. Were they all right; and if I were killed what would happen to them? I did not tell Heiner of these anxieties. Perhaps I should have done but I felt it was a personal matter. We often talked about the war and the bombing of England and how long they would last out.

'Do you think they can stand much more?' I asked him one night. It was just after the bombing of Coventry. 'The whole town has gone . . . a town with two hundred thousand people in it! I should die if I thought that Wolfgang and Klaus would ever have to go through the things those English children must have suffered.'

'If you start thinking that way in a war you will end up by committing suicide,' he told me. 'You've got to be hard, and think: "It's the enemy or me and the sooner they give in the better!" '

'That's a frightful creed,' I protested.

'War is a frightful thing, and it's no use thinking about it too much when you are in the midst of one. I'm glad for that reason that I shall never be called up. I might start thinking when I was in a plane and be too paralyzed to drop the bombs.'

'But surely we needn't bomb civilians as we did at Coventry.'

'It's easier said than done. Targets are close together sometimes. Bombs fall where they are not meant to.'

I was silent.

'Coventry was a reprisal raid, anyway. For the bombing of our towns,' he added.

'I wonder who started first?' I wanted to know.

'I'll tell you after the war. No one knows the truth while it is going on,' he told me.

'But will you know the truth even after the war?'

'Oh, yes,' laughed Heiner. 'We'll know then. The man who starts a war is the one who loses it!'

'Which means England will be blamed for starting the air-raids on civilians?' I asked.

'Don't forget Hitler's speech in September when he threatened: "If they attack our cities we will destroy theirs." I'm afraid these air-raids are now such a mix-up of attack and counter-attack that one can never fix the blame fairly and squarely. This is now a total war, and woe to the one who loses it. It will be total destruction.'

Else Wendel, housewife

Security

Empty your pockets, Tom, Dick and Harry,
Strip your identity; leave it behind.
Lawyer, garage-hand, grocer, don't tarry
With your own country, your own kind.

Leave all your letters. Suburb and township,
Green fen and grocery, slip-way and bay,
Hot-spring and prairie, smoke stack and coal tip,
Leave in our keeping while you're away.

Tom, Dick and Harry, plain names and numbers,
Pilot, observer, and gunner depart.
Their personal litter only encumbers
Somebody's head, somebody's heart.

John Pudney

Bombers from Britain

If you live in Sussex or Kent nowadays (or I suppose in a good many other counties besides), you know before getting out of bed and pulling aside the black-out if it's a nice day. A clear dawn has a new clarion—the deep and throbbing roar of hundreds of planes, outward bound. They may be sailing high towards the coast, flashing or shining in the light of the sun that's not yet up over the horizon. Sometimes they look white and as graceful as gulls against the blue; at others they look black and sinister as they come and go between the clouds. But the impressive thing—the thing that makes land-girls pause in their stringing of the hopfields and makes conductors of country buses lean out and look up from their platforms—the impressive thing is the numbers. Never in the Battle of Britain, in the days when the Luftwaffe was beaten over these fields and woods, did the Germans send over such vast fleets. Never were their bombers four-engined monsters, such as these of the Americans which go out in their scores and hundreds. Sometimes you will see one big formation coming, say from the north, others from the north-east, others from the west, all heading for a common rendezvous. Their courses often converge, and a stranger to the scene might hold his breath seeing the approach of disaster as the formations close in. At the moment when it looks as if they must collide, he sees with relief that they're at different heights; and they make a brief, fascinating cross-over pattern and sail on as easily as an express train flies over complicated points. As their roar fades with them, another rises until things on the kitchen mantelshelf tinkle and rattle as they catch the vibration. Up over the beechwoods on the hill, the leading formation of a second wave of heavies appears, followed by others and still others. Some days it will go on like this pretty well all day—not all heavies, of course, but twin-engined bombers of various kinds, fighter-bombers and fighters. There are always lots of Marauders, packed together, flying very fast—reminding one of those sudden clouds of migrating birds which appear from nowhere and as quickly vanish. They have an appointment abroad, and they're keeping it.

Pat Smithers

The Last Trip

The sense of apprehension, normally dissolved as soon as they were airborne, was still with him. The last trip was always the worst. When you began a tour, risks were part of it, inevitable, natural. In retrospect, the risks seemed suicidal. His determination was worn and thinned like an old chisel. At the beginning, you did not care: you were full of expectation. Now expectation had hardened into experience. So many of your friends were dead. Sometimes their faces laughed at you from the bottom of a tankard at a mess party, momentarily. They were dead and you were alive: and, on this last trip, there was so much to lose.

. . . .'PORT GO!'

His heart stopped.

At once he rolled into a steep dive to port, conscious only of a great surge of fear.

Out of the corner of his eye he saw tracer going over their starboard wing and, ahead of them, the splutter and wink of the self-exploding cannon shells.

He heard Taffy's voice exultant, hysterical. 'Got you, you bastard, got you!'

Then the voice was cut off.

Flames were coming in puffs from the cowling of the starboard outer engine. Every moment they became thicker, feeding on the slipstream.

'Feather the starboard outer,' he shouted to the second dickey.

. . . . Jesperson turned towards him. He put his hands to his ears and shook his head.

'Feather it, you bloody fool!'

He stabbed his finger towards the feathering button. Was the man deaf, crazy? The fire was licking and leaping round the outboard motor. He cut back on the throttle and switched off the master fuel cock.

The engineer leaned over Jesperson and pressed the feathering button. With immense relief he watched the propeller steadily stopping. As it slowed the flames subsided. Looking at his instruments, he saw the aircraft was commencing to spiral and the speed was building up. Quickly he corrected, taking the load off his foot with the rudder trim. When he looked up again, the flames were out.

Jesperson was pointing to his ears.

'What is it?' Peter said. He flicked the microphone switch. 'What is it?'

He could not hear himself speak. His plug must be out. No wonder Jesperson could not hear him. He felt for the plug. It was firmly home. Again he flicked the mike switch. Silence. The intercom was dead. He was isolated, walled in by the engine noise.

He signalled 'W-W-W' on the call light.

He was alone in a nightmare world of possible emergencies.

He pressed the emergency switch on his R/T set. Still the roaring, lonely silence, swirling round him like a sea. He pressed each switch in turn on the 1196. Nothing.

He began to sweat.

Finding himself thirty degrees off course, he swung the aircraft fiercely round. Jesperson leaned towards him, took off his oxygen mask and shouted. Peter shook his head. He could not hear a thing. Then, faintly above the noise of the motors, came the words: 'My helmet is u/s.'

Rage swept over him. He felt he could take Jesperson by the throat. The dim, stupid fool, sprawled over half the cockpit, unable to feather an engine, telling me his blasted helmet is u/s when nobody in the kite can hear a thing. As if his helmet mattered; or his head.

Suddenly, like a miracle, came the wireless operator's voice, crackling at first, then clear as a bell.

'Hallo, skipper; hallo, skipper; can you hear me?'

'Loud and clear.'

Thank God. Good old Nobby.

'Bloody good show, Nobby,' he said.

Then, after a moment's pause: 'Everybody all right—rear-gunner?'

'O.K., skipper. I got him. He came so close I could have hit him with a stick.'

'Good boy, Taff.'

. . . . 'I think we'll press on,' said Peter. 'What do you feel, nav?'

'Och, we might as well. We're past Denmark. We might as well get on with it.'

'How about that turret, mid-upper?'

'It'll be O.K., skip. It works all right manually.'

Thank God that was over.

Well, we shall not be in time to do any supporting. That's one consolation, anyway. And the bombing height's only fifteen thousand. We should just about maintain that height on three motors.

'Did you use the graviner, engineer?'

'No, skip. When we feathered the engine, the fire went out by itself.'

'Was it a petrol fire?'

'Don't know.'

I would not fancy being three thousand feet below everybody else. He remembered a daylight sortie when things went wrong and bombs began falling round them and an aircraft ahead had been sliced in half. Down spun the two halves; grotesque, down, down, twisting like a leaf, while everyone waited for the white flowering of the parachutes. But there was no flowering—only of flame as the aircraft hit the ground.

Searching port, searching starboard.

Having trimmed the aircraft to fly comfortably on three engines, Peter felt master of the situation once more, though the silhouette of the feathered propeller was a stark symbol of insecurity. Jesperson no longer aroused his irritation. The aircraft was obviously a good one. Already he had an affection for it. They had a fighter to their credit—first blood on his last trip—and no serious damage: and, surely, it was unlikely that on this one operation they would run into all the bad luck in the world. He looked at the silhouette of Jesperson's helmeted head and, behind him, Dicky Wagstaffe crouched by his instrument panel. What were they thinking, he wondered, two faceless enigmas.

Always he was searching for fighters.

They were well over the Baltic now—what about a trip to the Baltic for your summer holidays?—eating up time and distance. I shall be glad, he thought, when we're coming back. I could almost wish time suspended. I could wish to freeze this stream that carries us remorselessly towards the target glare.

Searching port, searching starboard.

It must have been an isolated fighter that attacked us. We have seen no flares, no sign of other aircraft being jumped on. How stupid it would have been if we had been flicked out of the sky as if by the idle movement of some divine finger. It has happened to so many. There would be no baling out over the sea if we really started burning.

. . . . On the approach to the target—long and straight from the west—Peter trimmed the aircraft as carefully as he could. This is the last time, he thought, and we will make a good job of it. We must drive the last nail home as sweetly and truly as the rest.

In the clear September night the target seemed to be much nearer than it really was. He settled down in his seat, bracing himself against the fear which began to rise in him, fear like a dark pool, deepening with every operation and threatening always to burst the barriers of his control. The firm contact of armrest and seat and throttle enabled him more easily to master it.

Ahead the attack, a fiery parasite upon the body of a city, began to writhe terribly into life, following the cycle he had seen so often. He saw the first flares, the target markers going down, the incendiaries budding, flowering, the short bright blossoming of the bombs. He watched the searchlights swinging and swaying, and the gradual growth of the flak-cloud.

Out of the corner of his eye he saw Jesperson gazing motionless, and the feathered propeller stark beyond him.

Nearer they flew, nearer.

Slowly the glare from the ground began to fill the cockpit with that strange sinister light. To and fro went the long knives. The turbulence of the air was growing. Every so often the aircraft shook itself like a small ship struck by a wave.

He felt the tension in his stomach. He braced himself in the seat, determined, at the same time, to keep his hands and feet relaxed.

'Bomb-doors open.'

Carefully he held the heading.

Carefully he narrowed the focus of his mind down to his instruments, ex-cluding everything that waited, on the edge, to shiver his concentration into fragments.

They were shocked and jolted by the air.

Now, like the beak of a giant bird, the flak rapped at their egg-shell of metal and perspex. Imperiously the raven-fear came knocking, knocking. With all his strength he must guard the little crystal core of his will. Yet he kept hands and feet gentle. Relax, yet don't relax.

'An S turn to starboard, skipper,' came Bron's voice, eager.

Then, in an agony of haste—'Enough, enough. On heading.'

'On heading,' said Peter, his voice coming calm from the turmoil of his mind. 'Steady'—lovingly—'steady.'

The sky above was sown with fighter flares. The piercing searchlights were pale upon them. He saw a Lancaster blow up into a great slow balloon of fire.

Coax her through the turbulence. Ride her lightly through the rocking air. Keep that little pointing needle central, quite central.

'Steady, steady.'

How much longer.

It can't be much longer.

This is the last time, the last time.

He felt his control slipping little by little, as a handful of dry sand diminishes the more quickly the tighter it is grasped.

'Bombs gone.'

Henry Archer and Edward Pine

Bombs Gone

Mr. Wolter was becoming nervous. 'Have you heard?' he asked one morning, 'they are dropping bombs on West Berlin now on a bigger scale. It's serious. I had a real taste of it last night,' he added. 'They dropped bombs on the block of flats in the Bayerischer Platz. It smashed all our windows and shook the whole house. We were in the cellar, of course. The women and children didn't take it too well. The noise and screaming, it was frightful.' He looked up for sympathy.

'Yes,' I agreed. 'It's bad for the women and children.'

'It was bad enough for me,' added Mr. Wolter with a wry smile. 'I had enough, I can tell you. I couldn't sit down there scared to death with people screaming all round me. I had to go out and do something. I went along to the Bayerischer Platz. It was the most frightful sight.'

He had got up now and was pacing about on his blue carpet. I had never seen him moved in this way before. Enthusiastic, optimistic, bitter and confident. I had seen all that in my boss, but not this pity and horror.

'It's easy to say, it was just a rubble heap, and leave it at that. But to me, and I passed the place every day, you know, it was the end of the most sumptuous and beautiful block of flats in Berlin. When I went there in the middle of last night it was still burning.'

'And the tenants?' I interrupted.

'Dead! Practically all of them, I should say. They can't have lived through that heat. We worked like niggers for the rest of the night trying to dig an entrance to the cellars, but when I left to come to the office this morning they still hadn't got through. They now have tractors and cranes on the job. When they do reach the cellars they will only find burned bodies, I think.'

He was still walking nervously up and down. It took him some time to get down to work that morning. This was the first time he had seen bombing in his part of the town. It changed him in a night.

At lunch-time I went along to the Bayerischer Platz to see for myself. There were hundreds of sightseers, all people, who like me, had come to make sure that the British had really got to the heart of luxury Berlin with their bombs.

'Now we can call him "Meyer",' said a man's voice beside me. He referred, of course, to Goering's boasts in 1939 that Berlin should never be bombed while he was in charge; if it was we could call him Meyer. A woman next to the man plucked at his sleeve and pulled him away. It was an unwise thing to say aloud in a crowd.

Suddenly the cranes stopped working. A murmur went through the crowd. 'They've cleared the entrance . . . they are going in now. . . .' We stood on tip-toe, staring in horror and fascination. There was something moving, I could see at the entrance of the luxury block, something being brought out. A woman screamed sharply three times. It was the same awful scream that I heard from women later on when the Russians came.

'What's happening? What has she seen?' the people round kept asking. We surged forward to look. Police appeared and pressed us back. 'Move on, now,' they said. 'This is no sight to stare at. You'll read about it soon enough in the papers.'

Actually we didn't read the truth in the papers. What had happened in the flats was too terrible to be printed. The tenants had not been burned but scalded to death. The water pipes of the central heating system had burst, and boiling water had poured into the air-raid cellar. They found women with their arms stretched out holding their children above their heads as they died. They found people crouched on the top of piles of chairs and tables as they clambered to escape the rising, boiling water. No wonder they didn't print these facts at the time. There were hundreds of other flats similarly constructed in Berlin. Few people would have sought shelter in those cellars had they known what might happen.

Else Wendel, housewife

The Shelters

This time it was in the Berlin streets. I stood in the centre of Berlin, in the Friedrichstrasse, looking in a shop window for some things I had come up from Kladow to buy. The sirens suddenly screamed out over the city. Immediately there was a dead silence all round. Shops closed, business people and gossiping women stopped talking. Then they began to run through the street. Women with children in their arms, or pushing prams; young children quite alone; old people appeared from the houses with blankets and bags. All of them ran, and no one spoke at all. All had a look of blank fear on their faces. In a few moments the trams and buses were empty, and cars were left abandoned by the side of the street. In two or three minutes the whole life of a city seemed to have disappeared. I stood completely alone except for an air-raid warden I noticed in the porch of a house opposite. Like a scene in a film, it seemed. Then, very frightened myself, I went over to the warden.

'Where is the nearest shelter?' I asked quickly.

He replied by roaring with laughter. 'Where do you come from?' I told him, from my house outside Berlin.

He nodded. 'Don't you know the shelters are packed like sardines? Why, people queue up long before an alarm for they have a sort of instinct for trouble on the way. Mind you, it's well worth it. The shelters are quite bomb-proof— which is more than these cellars are.' He jerked his head to indicate the mass of rubble on each side of him. 'Not one soul was rescued from those cellars,' he said morbidly. 'Not one,' the warden repeated. 'So now you know why the public shelters will be full.'

I began to get more and more frightened. 'But where shall I go, then? Can I go into the cellar of this house behind you?'

'No,' he said brusquely. 'We are full too. The only thing you can do is to go back to the *S-Bahn* (Metropolitan railway) and find shelter there in one of the underground tunnels.'

'Isn't that about the most dangerous place in Berlin? Surely they always aim at the main railways?'

He shrugged his shoulders. 'It's the only advice I can give you. Now, hurry and get off the streets. The Tommies will be here in no time. *Heil Hitler!*' He turned away.

I ran myself now, this time to the *S-Bahn*, and into one of the underground tunnels. I shrank back as I tried to descend the stairs, the tunnel was packed completely full. People were standing on the long, wide platforms, tightly pressed against each other, *in silence*. A man in a brown Party uniform told me that there was no room left here, I must go to tunnel C. I pushed my way on— still that awful silence as I moved.

'Try and move forward as much as you can,' the warden of tunnel C told me. 'In a minute all the passengers of the last train will be diverted here, then it will be really crowded.'

So I walked forward on to the platform as far as I could. The passengers of the last train came down the stairs, again in silence. Soon we were tightly jammed against each other. I suppose if I had looked in a mirror I would have seen the same expression of intense fear and seriousness on my face as I had noticed in the running crowds a few minutes ago. The bombing began. We heard the bombs falling. Some were very near. We could distinctly hear the crash of the explosions and a rumbling noise of falling stones, then splintering glass— something like a gigantic cocktail-shaker.

I looked along the tunnel. The crowd stood motionless, listening. Nobody spoke. This silence! Like a vast crowd watching a funeral, it flashed through my mind. Or were we watching our own funeral? Until the air-raid ended nobody knew. Even the children amongst us did not stir. I was glad no child was near me. I could not bear the look on those tiny, pale faces, so unnaturally quiet. Suddenly there was a thundering bang right over our heads, or so it seemed to us. I felt as though the ground under my feet wavered for a second, then the lights went out and big clouds of smoke blew into our tunnel.

For the first time the crowd moved. They all surged forward towards the staircase to escape the smoke. None of us wished to be toasted alive by heat and smoke. If it was burning above our heads it was high time we got out. The lights came on again and a man in brown Party uniform stood at the top of the stairs and shouted, 'Don't move. No one is permitted to leave the tunnel!'

The crowd obeyed automatically. We stood quite still in the thick smoke and waited. Children began to cry. The grown-ups near them took it in turns to pick them up and comfort them. Only one man spoke. He bent down and whispered in my ear: 'If they manage to get a bomb in there,' he indicated with his finger the wall opposite us, 'where the Spree is flowing along, then it's good-night!'

I said nothing. I was too frightened to speak. To be drowned in that tunnel like a mouse in a bucket of water!

I went on standing motionless in silence like the hundreds round me, waiting . . . waiting . . . till at long last the all-clear sounded. Immediately Berlin became alive again. As if a spell had been lifted we all began to talk and laugh and joke again.

'That was a pretty near thing,' said the man next to me . . . in quite a different tone of voice now.

Else Wendel

Attack and Counter-attack

Our night fighters tried to adjust themselves to the new British methods, and profited by them to a certain extent because the British markers not only showed the way to their bombers but also to our pursuing night fighters. In a certain way the disadvantages of the radio and radar interference were annulled by the effect of the markers. Another means of finding the bomber stream was the burning enemy bombers which had been hit and which could be seen from a great distance. As a result of this, our night fighters found the whereabouts, course and altitude of the bombers, visible in the glow of the fires that attracted our fighters from a distance of sixty miles as a candle attracts a moth. The British bombers were pursued until they were over the target and also on their return journey. The solid system of the limited defence areas were out of date. Now the fighters 'travelled'.

Colonel Adolf Galland, Luftwaffe

In 1943 the United States Air Force operating from Britain joined in on a large scale, but their daylight raids, unescorted for lack of long-range fighters, suffered terribly.

In the course of the year 1943 the emphasis shifted more and more to action against daylight raiders. Even though numerically the British raids against Germany were still stronger than the American and were undoubtedly a great trial for the civilian population, the American precision raids were of greater consequence to the war industry. They received priority attention over the British raids on our towns.

.... The first air-raid on Schweinfurt was a shock to the German High Command. If the German ball-bearing industry, their Achilles' heel, were to be destroyed or paralyzed, then the armament production of the whole Reich would suffer heavily. Speer, in a post-war report, pointed out that with a continuation of the raids the German armament industry would have been essentially weakened within two months, and in four months would have come to a complete standstill. But luckily the first raid on Schweinfurt and Messerschmitt-Regensburg proved a disaster for the enemy: 315 Flying Fortresses reached the target area, sixty were shot down, and over a hundred damaged. For the first time the losses were sixteen per cent of the airborne force and nineteen per cent of the actual raiding force. The most important air battle of the war so far ended with a success for the German air defence. About three hundred fighter aircraft took part. They assembled in the sector of Frankfurt, outside the range of the fighter escort, and were directed against the bulk of the bombers in close formation. The success cost us twenty-five and not 228 fighters, as the American communiqué claimed. . . . These first high losses, shown by films, descriptions and many reports which were published later, caused deep depression amongst the American crews and a sort of crisis in the Command. Raids of this nature were not repeated before the fighter escort brought the solution.

Colonel Adolf Galland

In the nights of the spring and summer of 1943 the Ruhr, Hamburg and Berlin were effectively damaged for the first time by an ever-increasing weight of bombs, Hamburg being almost obliterated in a succession of raids of a violence and duration never before experienced by any city.

Die Katastrophe

On the night of 24–25 July, after midnight, about eight hundred heavy British bombers assembled over England. This mass formation, passing over Lübeck, approached from the north-east of Hamburg, the city with a million population on the Elbe, the German sea-gate to the world. A narrow, restricted area, comprising the harbour and part of the inner city, was attacked mainly with incendiaries and phosphorus canisters. The raid was carried out in close formation with the greatest precision, and was almost unmolested by the German defence. What had happened?

Not one radar instrument of our defence had worked. The British employed for the first time the so-called 'Laminetta' method. It was as primitive as it was effective. The bomber units and all accompanying aircraft dropped bundles of tinfoil in large quantities, of a length and width attuned to our radar wavelength. Drifting in the wind, they dropped slowly to the ground, forming a wall which could not be penetrated by the radar rays. Instead of being reflected by the enemy's aircraft they were now reflected by this sort of fog bank, and the radar screen was simply blocked by their quantity. The air situation was veiled as in a fog. The system of fighter direction based on radar was out of action; even the radar sets of our fighters were blinded, the flak could obtain no picture of the air situation, and the radar target-finders would not work. At one blow the night was again as impregnable as it had been before the radar eye was invented. Furthermore, during this dark night—dark also for the Reich's defence—the British used for the first time a new method of approach—the 'Bomber Stream'. This is a compromise between the loose, stretched-out formation on a broad front, as was usual for the night approach, and the tightly packed formation in which daylight raids were flown. The bombers flew in several waves on small fronts, each wave behind the other, as the single aircraft used to fly, with a synchronized course, altitude, speed and time—the E.T.A. They formed no definite formation; only occasionally two or more planes flew in visual contact. Out of many small raindrops which used to unite over the target area into a cloud-bursting bombing effect, a stream had already formed during the approach that broke through our defences in a bed five miles wide. Our already insufficient peripheral defences were powerless against this new method.

Colonel Adolf Galland

For several weeks the R.A.F. had dropped leaflets over Hamburg calling on the citizens to leave the city. No one had left; everyone was too used to official exaggeration to believe anything very seriously. I still remember every detail of the hot, sultry July night when the first large-scale raid began. At first there was nothing unusual about it; people sat cowering in their damp cellars, children wept, the whistle of falling bombs, dull thudding hits, blasts of air which tore out windows and doors.

In none of this was there anything new. But what was new was the way in which it went on; while red flames still stood above the houses and the air was black with dust and dirt and the fire engines were clanging through the streets, the sirens went again. With a deep zooming sound the squadrons returned to the city. Again the sharp and clear bark of the 88 mm. guns alternated with the deep powerful hits of the heavy bombs.

At first I was not caught in the general mood of panic. 'The British don't mean me,' I thought. I had nothing to fear. Those men up there in the sky were fighting against the Nazis, too; we had the same enemy. However stupid it may sound, I felt instinctively that no British bomb could harm me. I was firmly resolved to stay in Hamburg and see what would happen. I wanted to witness the death of the city.

Claus Fuhrmann, half-Jewish, unemployed

Suddenly the sirens sounded again. Everybody jumped up. What did the enemy want now? Hadn't they done enough?

This time the harbour was attacked, the dockyards and factories in Wilhelmsburg. This raid lasted well over an hour. When it was over Mama decided to go in search of other friends on the far side of the city, friends she had not seen for some time. Anything was better than lying here homeless on the grass. She walked and walked, carrying her suitcase and the coat. It was still very hot, and the fires behind her were still burning. But this time she found her friends safe and their home intact. She was given food, allowed to wash in a minute basin of water, and then put to bed. That night there was no air-raid, nor on the Monday.

On the Tuesday night, 28 July, the bombers came back. In that one raid over thirty thousand people in Hamburg died. Mama and her friends went down into their cellar. The air warden stored sand and water and piled up tools ready for any digging that might be necessary.

It was the worst raid Mama had ever known. For hours they huddled there, with bombs crashing nearer, and the ceaseless rumblings of falling masonry. Then there was the loudest crash of all. The air warden ran out. He came back, his face grey. 'Leave the cellar at once!' he called. 'A phosphorus bomb has fallen at the entrance door. Quick, all of you. . . .'

An indescribable panic started. Mothers grabbed children and rushed madly away. People fell over each other and Mama was separated from her friends. She didn't see them again. Out in the street people just rushed blindly away from the bomb, thinking of nothing else. An old man came near Mama, who was now standing dazed and alone. 'Come with me,' he said. She picked up her suitcase and followed him. It was unbearably hot in the street.

'I can't go through this. There's a cellar there not burning, I shall go down there,' she told him.

'Don't be a fool,' he said. 'All the houses here will catch fire soon; it's only a matter of time.'

A woman with two children joined them. 'Come on,' said the old man. 'This looks the clearest way.'

There were walls of flame round them now. Suddenly into the square came a fire engine drawn by two startled horses. They swerved aside, and one of the terrified children rushed down a side street. The mother followed, leaving her boy behind. As the first child reached a burning house some blazing wood fell near her, setting her clothes alight. The mother threw herself on top of the child to try and smother the flames, but as she did so the whole top floor of the house opposite crashed down on the two of them.

The old man grabbed the boy's hand firmly. 'You come with us,' he ordered. 'I'll wait for my Mummy,' said the boy.

'No,' said the old man, trying to make his voice sound harsh. 'It's getting too hot here. We will wait for your Mummy farther away from the fire.'

Mama intervened quickly. 'We will find the best way out, and then come back and fetch your Mummy.'

'All right,' said the little boy.

They went the same way as the horses, thinking the animals' instinct might have led them to safety. The boy fell down but got up, then fell down again.

'We can't go on like this,' said the man, pulling them towards a cellar. 'There's some water left here, pour it over your coats, and we'll put them over our heads and try that way.'

Up in the square again, the man took a hasty glance round and then grabbed the boy's hand. 'Now—come this way,' he told them. Mama grabbed her suitcase. 'Put it down,' shouted the old man. 'Save yourself, you can't bring that as well.'

But Mama would not let go. She took the boy's hand in her left hand and the case in her right. Out in the square it was like a furnace. Sweat poured down her body as they began to run. The smoke seeped through the wet coats and began to choke them. Only for a few yards could she carry the suitcase, then she dropped it in the road and left it without another thought. The little boy ran between them, taking steps twice as fast as their own. He fell again, but was hauled to his feet. Were they still on the track of the horses? They didn't know, for every moment or two they had to turn to avoid burning wood and pylons which hurtled down from the houses around. Bodies were still burning in the road. Sometimes they stumbled against them. But on they went, with the little boy's feet running tap, tap, tap between them. A dog was howling madly somewhere. It sounded more pathetic and lost than they themselves. At last they came to a small green place, and ran to the centre of it and fell on their faces, the little boy between them. They fell asleep like exhausted animals, but only for a few minutes. The old man woke first.

'Wake up,' he said, shaking them both. 'The fire is catching up with us.'

Mama opened her eyes. They were lying in a small field, and the houses on one side were now alight; worse than alight; some kind of explosive material was there as well, it seemed. A great flame was shooting straight out towards them. A flame as high as the houses and nearly as wide as the whole street. As she stared in fascination, the giant flame jerked back and then shot forward towards them again.

'My God, what is it?' she said.

'It's a fire-storm,' the old man answered.

'The beginning of one. Quick, come along, there's no time to lose. In a minute there will be dozens of flames like that and they'll reach us; quick, come on, we must run. I think there's a small stream farther over this field.'

Mama got up and bent over the boy. 'Poor little thing, what a shame to wake him.' She shook him gently. 'Get up! We must run again.'

The child did not stir. The man bent down and pulled him to his feet. 'Come on, boy,' he said. The child swayed and fell again. The man sank to his knees beside the child and took his hands.

'Oh, no!' he said in a shocked voice. 'No, it can't be. My God, he's dead!' The tears began to pour down his blackened face. He bent down lower over the little figure and began to whisper to it.

'You were a good little boy, a very brave little boy,' he said, stroking the child's face with a woman's tenderness. 'As long as Hamburg has boys as brave as you she won't die.' He kissed the child's face very gently. 'Sleep well, little boy,' he whispered. 'Sleep well; you got a kinder death than your mummy and sister. They were burnt alive like rats.'

Mama became nervous; another tongue of flame shot out from the side street. The roaring of the flames became stronger. The old man seemed quite oblivious now of their danger.

'Come on,' she called out. 'The boy is dead. We can't help him any more. Come on, we must go on.'

The old man did not look up. 'No,' he said. 'You go on by yourself. I shall die with this little boy.'

Mama yelled through the roaring wind. 'You're crazy! Come on!' The old man did not answer. He kissed the child's forehead again.

In despair, Mama grabbed the man in her arms and tried to pull him away. Sparks were now beginning to reach their coats. Suddenly a hot gust of wind blew their coats off their backs, sending them blazing through the air. This brought the man to life again. He jumped up and started to run. As they raced across the field, the flames crept behind them. Once they fell and then got up and ran on. The field seemed wider and wider as they raced towards the stream, but at last they reached it. Unable to say another word, they both fell on the banks and slept, or perhaps they fainted first and slept afterwards.

When they regained consciousness it was daylight, and they stumbled down into the stream and splashed their faces and hands. The water stung their scorched skin, but they did not mind. The old man told her he had lost two grandsons and his daughter-in-law in the fires last night. 'My son is in Russia. I don't know how I shall tell him when he returns,' he said.

After a rest they decided to walk back into Hamburg. It seemed suicidal, but they both felt they must go and see what remained of the city. It was a terrible walk. They passed through one big square where corpses were piled up, corpses burned beyond recognition. Soldiers and police were sorting them out and loading them on to trucks.

'All of them were standing in the middle of the square when a fire-storm caught them. No one escaped,' a woman said.

'Didn't I tell you?' said the old man to Mama. 'A fire-storm finished everything and everybody.'

The woman standing near them shivered. 'I heard scream after scream. I shall never forget those screams. If there were a God, he would have shown some mercy to them. He would have helped us.'

'Leave God out of this,' said the old man sharply. 'Men make war, not God.'

Else Wendel

Trees three feet thick were broken off or uprooted, human beings were thrown to the ground or flung alive into the flames by winds which exceeded a hundred and fifty miles an hour. The panic-stricken citizens knew not where to turn. Flames drove them from the shelters, but high-explosive bombs sent them scurrying back again. Once inside, they were suffocated by carbon-monoxide poisoning and their bodies reduced to ashes as though they had been placed in a crematorium, which was indeed what each shelter proved to be. The fortunate were those who jumped into the canals and waterways and remained swimming or standing up to their necks in water for hours until the heat should die down.

A German secret report

After the last bombs of this series of raids had dropped on Hamburg in the night of 2–3 August, we began to take stock: the amount of bombs dropped was approximately eighty thousand H.E. bombs, eighty thousand incendiary bombs and five thousand phosphorus canisters; a quarter of a million houses were destroyed, i.e. nearly half of the city; a million people were bombed out or fled. Shipping, industry and supply suffered great damage. The death-roll, only completed in 1951, six years after the war, numbered forty thousand, of whom five thousand were children.

A wave of terror radiated from the suffering city and spread throughout

Germany. Appalling details of the great fires were recounted, and their glow could be seen for days from a distance of a hundred and twenty miles. A stream of haggard, terrified refugees flowed into the neighbouring provinces. In every large town people said, 'What happened to Hamburg yesterday can happen to us to-morrow.' Berlin was evacuated with signs of panic. In spite of the strictest reticence in the official communiqués, the Terror of Hamburg spread rapidly to the remotest villages of the Reich.

Psychologically the war at that moment had perhaps reached its most critical point. Stalingrad had been worse, but Hamburg was not hundreds of miles away on the Volga, but on the Elbe, right in the heart of Germany.

After Hamburg in the wide circle of the political and the military command could be heard the words: 'The war is lost.'

Colonel Adolf Galland

Morale

Reports from the Rhineland indicate that in some cities people are gradually getting rather weak in the knees. That is understandable. For months the working population has had to go into air-raid shelters night after night, and when they come out again they see part of their city going up in flames and smoke. The enervating thing about it is that we are not in a position to reply in kind to the English. Our war in the East has lost us air supremacy in essential sections of Europe and we are completely at the mercy of the English.

Dr. Goebbels

By 1943 both sides were developing jet-propelled aircraft.

In May 1943, Messerschmitt informed me that the test flights of his Me.262 prototypes had now progressed so far that he begged me to fly and judge one for myself. He was convinced of the future of the developed type. . . . With the Me.262 we had a hope of being able to give the fighter arm a superior aircraft at the very moment when Allied air superiority was opening up catastrophic prospects for Germany in the war in the air because of the increased range and overwhelming number of the American fighter escort.

I shall never forget 22 May 1943, the day I flew a jet aircraft for the first time in my life. In the early morning I met Messerschmitt on his testing airfield, Lechfeld, near the main works at Augsburg.

. . . . We drove out to the runway. There stood the two Me.262 jet-fighters, the reason for our meeting and for all our great hopes. An unusual sight, these planes without airscrews. Covered by a streamlined cowling, two nacelles under the wings housed the jet engines. None of the engineers could tell us how many horse-power they developed.

. . . . The flying speed of 520 m.p.h. in horizontal flight, which was fantastic at that time, meant an advance of at least 120 m.p.h. over the fastest propeller-driven aircraft. Inferior fuel similar to diesel oil could be used instead of octane, which was more and more difficult to get.

The chief pilot of the works made a trial demonstration with one of the 'birds', and after refuelling I climbed in. . . . I took off along a runway fifty yards wide at a steadily increasing speed, but without being able to see ahead— this was on account of the conventional tail wheel with which these first planes were still fitted instead of the front wheel of the mass-produced Me.262. Also I could not use the rudder for keeping my direction: that had to be done for the time being with the brakes. A runway is never long enough! I was doing 80 m.p.h. when at last the tail rose, I could see, and the feeling of running your head against a wall in the dark was over. Now, with reduced air resistance, the speed increased quickly, soon passing the 120 m.p.h. mark and long before the end of the runway the plane rose gently off the ground.

For the first time I was flying by jet propulsion! No engine vibration, no torque, and no lashing noise from the air-screw. Accompanied by a whistling sound, my jet shot through the air. Later, when asked what it felt like, I said, 'It was as though angels were pushing.'

Colonel Adolf Galland

By the spring of 1944 long-range fighters came into service which allowed the Americans to attack escorted. Thus, in spite of improved German aircraft, radar and night flying techniques, 'round-the-clock' bombing was now possible for the first time. Even when the main Allied air effort was switched farther west to prepare the way for D-Day, Germany's respite was short and incomplete, and German war production, though never entirely crippled by the bombing, thanks to its excellent organization and plentiful labour resources, was decisively reduced. The Allied air forces had succeeded where the Luftwaffe and U-boats had failed; but at a terrible cost. Many hundreds of aircrew might be lost in a single raid; if, as sometimes happened, one in ten of perhaps a thousand attacking planes failed to return. Below them they would leave a shattered city and tens of thousands dead.

German Difficulties

The weather has to be mentioned as a last factor that destroyed, again to our disadvantage, the balance between attacker and defender which had somehow been re-established by a tremendous effort during the summer of 1943. While the attacking units flew in at an altitude of twenty-one to twenty-four thousand feet above the bad weather, in radiant sunshine high above rain, snow, or the icing-up danger zone, completing their effective raids with excellent navigational aids and bomb-sights, and while they took-off, assembled and landed again in tolerable weather conditions in England or Italy, our defending units, by force of circumstance, often had to be sent up in the very worst of weather. Neither crews nor aircraft were prepared for such demands.

. . . . The defensive fire of the bombers and the escorting fighters took great toll of our force. Numerous German pilots were sitting in their completely iced-up cockpits, half-blinded, to become an easy prey for the Thunderbolts. The appalling losses of this period were plainly due to the weather. The fact that, despite all objections, such forced actions of practically no value were demanded over and over again by the High Command shattered once more the confidence of the squadrons in the leadership.

Göring began to lay increasing blame on Fighter Command and the pilots, and as I felt I had earned the right to answer him back, we were soon at logger-heads. One meeting was particularly stormy. The *Reichsmarschall* had summoned a number of squadron leaders and pilots to discuss a raid against southern Germany in which the German fighters had scored very few victories. After some general remarks, he proceeded to comment on the Fighter Command's lack of spirit. He may have been exasperated by my replies to his previous questions; at all events, he got into such a state that he hurled reproaches and accusations at us, to the effect that we had been loaded with honours and decorations, but had proved ourselves unworthy of them, that Fighter Command had been a failure as early as the Battle of Britain, and that many pilots with the highest decorations had faked their reports to get Knight's Crosses over England.

As I listened to him I got more and more furious, until finally I tore my Knight's Cross off my collar and banged it on the table. The atmosphere was tense and still. The *Reichsmarschall* had literally lost the power of speech, and I looked him firmly in the eye, ready for anything. Nothing happened, and Göring quietly finished what he had to say. For six months after that I did not wear my war decorations.

Colonel Adolf Galland

Single Combat

.... In spring, 1944, I took part in a fighter operation of the Reich's defence together with the Inspector of the Day Fighters East, *Oberst* Trautloft. A 'Fat Dog' was reported to be approaching the Dutch coast, and we were following it, as we always did, from my little control room in Hottengrund. I ordered two Focke-Wulfs to be warmed up on Staaken Airfield and invited Trautloft to accompany me. He sprinted across the fifty yards to the Fieseler-Storch which was waiting with the engine running, and ten minutes later we took off from Staaken. Course west—climb to twenty-five thousand feet.

On the Reich's Fighter Wavelength we received details of location, course, altitude and other important information concerning a major formation of about eight hundred B-17s and the other oddments which were flying in advance or safeguarding the flanks. We had just crossed the Elbe north of Magdeburg when we first caught sight of the enemy. We let the American formation pass at a respectful distance of from five to ten miles: eight hundred bombers went by, two thousand tons of death, destruction and fire inside their silver bodies, flying to their appointed targets in the heart of Germany. Something had to be done. Wave upon wave, endless formations of four-engined bombers, and right and left above them, with and without vapour trails, a vast pack of Mustang fighters. 'The range of the enemy's fighter escort does not extend beyond the Elbe'—according to the General Staff! They had stopped talking about the Ruhr long ago, but they still refused to see what was written in realistic letters in the German sky.

Where were our combat formations? Switching over to the other command wavelength, I found that part of our force was preparing to land after completing an attack and was preparing for a second take-off to catch the enemy on their way back. The bomber formation did not look at all as if it had just been through a battle. No wonder, with such masses of bombers and their protective escort.

Further German combat formations were being assembled between Berlin and Magdeburg. I had to watch them in action. One of the last formations had just passed by, and my fingers itched. Should I be passively watching this parade? I had just banked to the left and closed in on the formation when I saw a B-17 straggler trying to join another formation to the left. 'Hannes,' I called. 'Going in! We'll grab this one!'

There was nothing heroic in the decision. We should have headed right into a complete formation and shot down the leading aircraft, but we should have been shot down for certain. Now, with this straggler, we had to act very quickly before he joined the next formation.

I was a hundred yards behind on his tail. The B-17 fired and took desperate avoiding action. The only thing that existed in the whole world was this American bomber, fighting for its life, and myself. As my cannons blazed away, pieces of metal flew off, smoke poured from the engines, and they jettisoned the entire bomb-load. One tank in the wings had caught fire. The crew was baling out. Trautloft's voice cried over the radio: '*Achtung*, Adolf! Mustangs! I'm beating it! Guns jammed!'

And then—with the first bursts from four Mustangs—I sobered up. There was no mistake about the B-17; she was finished, but I was not. I simply fled.

Colonel Adolf Galland

Bomber Hit

The explosion kicked my mind back a quarter of a century. Down. Down. We're going down. I can feel the rush of air. We are going so very fast—200, 300, 400 miles an hour. I don't know, but who in earth would? Alice in Wonderland didn't, did she? She only knew she was going down. Why do my eyes hurt so much? God, I can't see! Everything is black, black as a rook. No, raven, of course. Yes, raven, not rook. I must be blind. I've always wanted to know what it's like to be blind, and now I know. The funny thing is that it doesn't really seem any different, except merely that I can't see: there must be more to it than that. I suppose it's just that I've not got used to it yet! No! Good lord, how stupid I am! I'm not blind at all! It's that terrible flash. Yes, I'm beginning to remember now. Just in front of me. A terrible bright yellow flash. It seemed to split my eyes right open, right round to the back of my head. . . .

And the noise. Yes, what a noise! It felt as though it broke every bone in my body. But I don't think it can have; I feel more or less all right. A bit peculiar, that's all. What is it? I know, I feel sick. More at heart than anything, but it's in my stomach. We've got to jump. Jump? Yes, jump. I've never jumped in my life. I've often wanted to, but I never have. Now I've got to. It's not quite the same, though. If I was going to jump I wanted to do it in my own good time, not in Jerry's time.

. . . . God knows where my parachute is now. I hurled it somewhere in the nose when I got in, but I haven't seen it since. There were one or two there some time ago, but goodness only knows if any of them were mine. Yes, I've thought about all that from time to time, but I've always said, 'Oh, well, you won't think anything to it, because if the situation arises where you've got to jump, you'll be so bloody glad to get out you won't give a damn about anything else,' but now I know how foolish I was. The thought of jumping is worse than anything. I'd rather stay here and hope for the best.

'Have you dropped the bombs?'

What on earth made me say that? I wasn't thinking of bombs or anything like them. I didn't even mean to say it: it just slipped out. Nobody seems to answer: I don't suppose anybody's left alive. Anyway, as far as the bombs go, it doesn't matter very much. If we're going to crash the bombs may as well stay with us, and if we aren't going to crash we may as well drop them some place. What's making me cough? I haven't got a cold, have I? No, I'm sure I haven't. .... My eyes are smarting, too. What a foul smell! Bitter, like that day in the shelter when they bombed the aerodrome. If it goes on much longer I won't be able to breathe. I need a towel soaked in water. 'Desmond, get me a towel.' No, of course, Desmond isn't there. I wonder what's happened to him. Oxygen mask! That's the thing: oxygen mask. Where is it? Hanging from my neck somewhere, but where? Good, I've got it. Quick, man, quick, before it's too late.

.... Have you dropped the bombs yet?'

Nobody seems to answer. Funny, that; surely there must be someone there. Desmond wouldn't have gone off without saying cheerio. No, I'm wrong; somebody's speaking. What's he saying? I can't quite make it out. Yes, I can.

'I've been hit. I've been hit.'

I wonder who it is. I can't recognize the voice and he doesn't say his name. It must be coming from the front, not the back. Something awful has happened at the back. I don't quite know what, but most of the explosion seemed to come from behind. First of all it was in front, that terrible bright flash. And then almost immediately afterwards a much bigger explosion from behind my back. There can't possibly be anyone left alive there: so it must be coming from the nose.

.... The smoke cleared, and like a ray of sunshine my eyesight came back. I blinked once or twice, perhaps; I don't know. Anyway, I could see quite well. I looked at the altimeter: five thousand feet. Plenty of height, much more than I would have thought possible. Somehow we seemed to have been diving for ages and ages, and we were still diving now. The instruments were all haywire; they did not make sense however you looked at them. They must have been shot away behind the panel. Awkward. But when we levelled out and ceased diving they began slowly to come back to normal, so probably they were intact, after all. I rubbed my forehead between my eyes, and started to take stock of the damage. First of all, the engines and the wings. Perhaps a few pieces of twisted burned metal: not more. They must have borne the brunt of the explosion. I looked out, and, like the man who saw the table slide slowly of its own accord across the floor, sat frozen to my seat. They were running; both of them. Running as they've always run before.

.... Something was stirring. I looked up and saw there was a figure standing in the well, staring at me. The lights had fused. In the half darkness of the moon it was a grotesque figure, leaning drunkenly on an enormous pair of arms, and a pair of wide, gaping eyes, and face and shoulders streaming with blood. Who or what it was, God only knows. I didn't. I tried to work things out, but somehow had to give up. The only association I could make was with the voice that said, 'I've been hit. I've been hit.' And all the time we were staring into each other's eyes. Suddenly he looked away, down the fuselage, and uttered a strangled cry:

'Fire! The tank's on fire!'

'Well, put it out then.'

At last, thank God, I regained my senses. I don't think the figure in the well heard what I said: before I had finished speaking he had disappeared on his hands and knees down the fuselage, where the petrol tank was. And then for a long while I was left in solitude.

We were flying straight and level, at least more or less so, but something, somewhere, was radically wrong. The aircraft was wallowing and flopping around like a small boat on a gentle swell, and the controls felt as though they had come unstuck. I looked out at the engines with a song in my heart, and then back at the instruments. It was incredible, but nowhere on any of the gauges was there a sign of trouble. I could hardly believe my eyes. The compass, I noticed, was steady; so were the rest of the flying instruments. They couldn't have been damaged, then, after all. I set about synchronizing the gyro with the compass, for it was hopelessly out, and only then did I realize the truth. What a fool! What an incredible, bloody fool! We were flying almost due east, back into Germany, and down an eighty-mile-an-hour wind at that! Of all the times to forget an elementary principle! Without thinking what I was doing, I pulled the stick hard over, and again I cursed myself for being a fool. The port wing dropped, the nose reared up, and only just in time I stopped her spinning. From then on I treated the controls as though they were made of putty, and it was three minutes before we were back on a westerly course.

The thought of what I had done made me sweat, and that was comforting, because if I was capable of sweat there could not be overmuch wrong. But this comfort did not last long, and the smile came off my face. I began to notice the sweat was all on my back and not my front. What's more, my back was getting hotter and hotter all the time. By this time I was prepared to believe anything, but this was definitely not normal. I screwed my head round, and what I saw forced a quiet, unwanted curse from my lips. Thick, black, oily smoke, pouring out from beneath the petrol tank, and in the background red gashes of fire.

I did not stay looking long, for on the port and ahead of us a barrage of shells came up. They were bursting in bunches of twenty or thirty, like that Saturday over the Ruhr, only this time they seemed to make more noise, because the hatch above my head was missing and all around the perspex was torn. Instinctively I started to take evasive action, but remembered just in time. If only I knew what was wrong with the controls it would make it easier. It felt as though the cables were hanging on by a thread, but I could not be certain. Anyway, it was better to take the shells than settle everything by pulling the controls off. So I flew straight and level. A searchlight picked us up, then a lot more, and almost immediately a rattle of splinters came through the fuselage somewhere behind me. I switched on the microphone and started speaking, but no one answered. The heat seemed no worse, but I did not look round any more. Somehow, I could not take my eyes off the shells. On the floor beside me was a parachute. It was not mine. In the nose there were two others, and there was no one except me this side of the petrol tank. What if they could not put the fire out? They would never get past the tank again. I found I was clutching the control column like a drowning man at a straw, and cursed myself. Tried to fix my mind on things that mattered, but it was elusive. I could not hold it down. Curious visions again. Damn them: it's as bad as being drunk. A grotesque figure in the well. Who on earth was it? I'm sure it can't have been the voice that said 'I've been hit', because the intercom in the front was u/s. Good Lord, he's come back! I'll fix him this time. In fact I'll ask him straight who he is. I looked up at his face, but I did not have to ask him his name.

'Hello, Desmond. Where have you been hiding?'

'Can you keep her in the air?'

'What do you think?'

'That's all I wanted to know.'

'What about the fire?'

'If you can keep her going another five minutes, we'll have it under control.'

They were long, those five minutes, very long, but they got the fire out. Taffy was the first to come back: bleeding and glistening, but grinning all over his face.

.... Taffy came back and disappeared into the front turret. The shells were still as fierce as ever, but now that there had been diversion it was not quite so bad. Someone flopped down beside me. I looked up. He was squatting on the step, his head down below his knees and his arms covering his face. I leant across and pulled him gently back. Pray God I may never see such a sight again. Instead of a face, a black, crusted mask streaked with blood, and instead of eyes, two vivid, scarlet pools.

'I'm going blind, sir; I'm going blind!'

I didn't say anything: I could not have if I had wanted to. He was still speaking, but too softly for me to hear what it was. I leaned right across so as better to hear. The plane gave a lurch, and I fell almost on top of him. He cried out and once more buried his face below his knees. Because I could not stand it, I sat forward over the instruments and tried to think of something else, but it was not much good. Then suddenly he struggled to his knees and said:

'I haven't let you down, have I, sir? I haven't let you down, have I? I must get back to the wireless. I've got to get back. You want a fix, don't you, sir? Will you put the light on, please, so that I can see?'

So it was Davy. Davy: his very first trip. Someone came forward and very gently picked him up. Then came Desmond. He sat down beside me and held out his hand. I took it in both of mine and looked deep into his smiling blue eyes.

'Everything's under control.'

'God bless you, Desmond.' Never have I said anything with such feeling. 'What about Davy? Is he going to die?'

'He's O.K. Revs is looking after him.'

'Thank God. Tell me the worst. What's the damage?'

'Pretty bad.'

'Will she hold?'

'I don't know. About evens, I should say. The whole of the port fuselage is torn: there's only the starboard holding.'

'How about the controls?'

'I don't know. They look all right, but it's difficult to tell. Shall I go and look more carefully?'

'No, it makes no odds. We're going to make a break for it however bad they are. If they're damaged, I think I'd rather not know. If this ack-ack doesn't stop soon I shall lose control of myself, Desmond. I can stand all the rest, but this I can't. They've got us stone cold. We can't turn, and we can't dive, and we can't alter speed, and it's only their bad shooting that will——'

A staccato crack, and Desmond covered his face.

'Desmond, Desmond! Are you all right?'

'Yes, sure.'

'You're bleeding.'

'That's nothing. A bit of perspex, probably: the splinter missed me. Taffy's signalling. Have you still got the bombs or something?'

'Yes. Which way?'

'Right. Hard right. Go on, much farther.'

'Tell him to shut up. What the hell does he think this is? A Spitfire?'

We went on like this for some time. Turning all the time, very gently, but none the less turning, and always to the right. Then at last the bombs went. I felt the kick as they left the aircraft. Desmond stood up and went back to Revs and Davy.

'Where was it?'

'Cologne.'

Group-Captain Leonard Cheshire

Dresden

Dresden was still considered safe, possibly owing to the architectural fame of the town and the great pictures which drew people from all over the world. But in the end Dresden also received its share of bombing. There were two hundred thousand refugees in Dresden when, on the night of 13 February 1945, the fire-storms fell on the town. There are no figures of the numbers who perished that night in Dresden, for the simple fact that the chaos was so complete no one knew who was in the town and who was not. Identification being impossible, and a decent burial out of the question, petrol was poured over the corpses, and all of them were set alight. Officially it was reported by the German authorities that the casualties were four hundred thousand. The British gave the numbers as two hundred and fifty thousand. No one will ever know the truth. Most of our news about Dresden came from Evelyn, who was working there in a hospital.

Gerhart Hauptmann, the famous German poet, saw Dresden's end from one of the surrounding hills. He watched it burning for five whole days. He saw it in ruins. He had a stroke. After his recovery he wrote an appeal to the world in which he said, 'He who has forgotten how to weep, learns again at Dresden's ruin. I know that in England and America there are enough good people to whom such glories as the Sistine Madonna were well known. I am at the end of my life, and I envy my dead friends who have been saved this terrible sight. I weep, and I am not ashamed of my tears. The great heroes of old were not ashamed of tears, were they? I am nearly eighty-three years old and I am standing before God beseeching him with my whole heart to show us His love more clearly, to show mankind how to purify ourselves, to show us how to reach our salvation.'

Else Wendel

'Come on,' he said aloud, and slid down from the hill of rubble. The narrow street was not blocked. The ruins on both sides were like filigree, with the sky glimmering through. Tangles of wires hung down from above and stretched across the street. He worked his way between them, careful not to be caught in them in the dark. Ahead of him was the main-street crossing. When he got that far, he must see the open space of the Pirna Platz on the left, and the wide Johann-Georgen-Allee a few yards farther on. Just in front of him he heard the sound of falling masonry and human voices shouting. That must be the fire brigade, busy clearing the main street. People! So he wasn't alone.

When he reached the corner of the street he saw that there were a lot of houses still blazing here. The main street itself was empty and, for as far as he could see, covered with stones, charred beams, and iron bars, as though there had been a barricade battle. There was no sign of fire-service parties. A dead human body lay flat on the tramway lines. That must have been a delusion, thinking he heard voices. The only things to be heard were the crackling and sighing of the fires and from time to time the rumble of walls collapsing.

He climbed over the debris. Showers of sparks and ashes prickled hot on his face. He inhaled the smell of burnt flesh and saw a house-front ahead of him swaying to and fro like a piece of blazing scenery on a stage. He tried to run past under, but his ski boots and the suitcase caught in the wires. The wall was coming down slowly straight in front of him. He threw himself to the ground, flattening himself close behind stone blocks lying about there. There came a short thundering roar, as of big waves breaking, followed by a long-drawn-out hissing. The blast and the heat swept over him. The dust cloud got into his nose, he fought for air, and during a long fit of coughing he realized that he was apparently unhurt. The burning houses to the right and left of him now all seemed to be swaying like gigantic loose back-drops. He tore himself free again, went running and jumping over the flames that shot up out of the ground, and as he reached the open square, behind him in the street he had just left walls crashed and a yellowish, white-hot lake spread out, with fetid smoke going up from it.

. . . . He walked towards the Grosse Garten. He felt rain trickling out of the sky, thin and cold, and heard the hum of aircraft engines. There were no more air-raid signals in this city. There was no hand to work them. He stumbled over the pieces of clothing in the roadway. If he went diagonally across the park, he could be in Blasewitz by three in the morning. In front of him the bare trees towered up, a broad front. He crossed a wide street where a great many things lay scattered about. The footpath leading into the park was also littered with clothes, pieces of luggage, shreds of material and books. Two bodies glimmered where they lay sideways across the path. They seemed to be children, one lying crosswise over the other. He walked round to them, but an instant later stumbled on something soft and shapeless which gave under his feet. It was better to go across the lawn and through the trees to the other side. A wan grey light showed the vague outlines of a clearing. He fell over a smashed tree-top lying on the ground. Now he could see quite clearly that there were corpses lying about among the trees, too. They lay scattered, this way and that, at brief intervals, like huge autumn leaves blown down from the branches. There must be hundreds of them, a boundless field of the dead disappearing into the dim darkness. He decided to turn back. Suddenly he noticed how violently his right arm was aching, and the smell of burning rose into his consciousness again, and the nauseating, choking taste of it lay on his tongue. He walked a few paces back towards the street, saw close in front of him a woman's red skirt edged with black rep, and felt the blood draining out of his head. Shutting his eyes, he leaned against a thick tree trunk, slid down it, and sat on the wet, cold earth, with the feeling that now he himself was a dead man among thousands of the dead.

If he had been there twenty-four hours earlier, he would have seen them die. Adjoining the park was a hospital centre, in which wounded soldiers lay in white cots. It was a hospital for the blind and those who had lost limbs. When the fire started to rain through the trees, they let themselves drop out of the windows of the burning structure. The fireworks were noisy and colourful, and in the midst of it hopped the one-legged in their blue-and-white striped hospital smocks, dragging along by their arms those that had lost both legs.

The fire-engine that was on its way to the hospital came to a halt in the city. The motor was still running, but the firemen had suffocated. Their uniforms crumbled in the baking air and they sat naked on their seats, lined up against the metal ladder, with straps round their brown bodies and helmets on their yellow skulls.

Here in the hospital the soldiers rolled in strange antics on their stumps and tried to escape the vicinity of the glowing buildings. But they did not have the key to the gate in the high iron fence which separated them from the garden, and so they built human pyramids supported by the blind. Whoever reached the top let himself fall to the other side of the high fence. The striped smocks hopped bare-footed in the hissing embers, supporting themselves with crutches, spades and bars, and they limped or rolled, screaming and in flames, among the trees, whose old trunks split apart under the impact of the bombs. The air grew thinner and thinner, and the striped ones fell unconscious in the wet, smouldering leaves. It was a gorgeous spectacle, glittering in violet, lemon-yellow, emerald-green and raspberry-red colours, and filled with whimpers and screams, roaring and howling, as never heard before. Outside the fence stood women in smouldering skirts trying to catch those who hurled themselves from the top of the towering fence.

Bruno E. Werner

Where is the Luftwaffe?

On my arrival in Berlin, I asked for the latest figures of the fighter reserve. They had increased to nearly eight hundred, but with this good news I received orders from O.K.L. to send the total fighter reserve immediately into the defence battle in the west. That was absolutely irresponsible! They were bound to get into the stream of the retreat and be overrun, and they could no longer do any-thing to change the critical situation of the Army, even had there been a ground organization to receive them. One cannot throw fighter groups into gaps like infantry regiments! These squadrons, which consisted of eighty per cent in-experienced pilots, could have gained their experience with tolerable losses in the defence of the Reich. The order to protect the German war industry from total destruction would have justified their action in the defence of the Reich and would have made it worthwhile! But in the west they were doomed to be destroyed in the air or on the ground without achieving any operational effect.

My objection, which I raised with the Luftwaffe staff, only received the answer: 'The Führer's orders!' I could not speak to Göring, who had retired because he was 'not well'. The real reason was probably his collapse under the continuous reproaches which were levelled against him and the Luftwaffe. Until the last moment he had tried to keep the real situation hidden from those above, but now there was no longer anything to hide or to falsify. The naked facts of the war in the air spoke realistically and inexorably.

As I could no longer count on Göring, I turned to the Minister for Arma-ments, Speer. Even in this desperate situation he remained sober and as strictly realistic as ever. He asked for information as to what the fighter arm could undertake against strategic day bombing; the key industries and transport had been hit so severely that things could not go on like this for more than a week. I reported to him that the Führer had irrevocably ordered the last fighter reserves to be transferred to the retreat in the west, which was now beginning.

Speer said, 'If the *Reichsmarschall* does not act, then it is my duty to act. Please come with me immediately to the Ministry. We will fly and see the Führer at the "Wolf's Redoubt". This order must be cancelled.' Four hours later we landed at Rastenberg, and soon afterwards were standing in the Führer's bunker. Hitler gave me the impression of being very irritable, overworked and physically and mentally overwrought. Speer explained briefly and precisely the situation of transport and the armament industry, which had become more acute through the increase of the American mass attacks. As usual, he accom-panied his *exposé* with actual figures. Hitler listened with increasing irritation. When Speer requested a strengthening of the fighter forces in the Reich, even if necessary at the expense of the situation on the Western Front, and that the fighters which had just been ordered to France should be used for the defence of the Reich, he could not complete his sentence. He had just started, 'Galland has just arrived from the west, and can give you, my Führer . . .' when Hitler interrupted him like a maniac, and Speer was given a slating which was particu-larly embarrassing because it was quite unjustified. The Führer forbade any interference with his operational measures and said, 'Please look after the war industry!' Then, as an aside to me: 'See that my orders are immediately exe-cuted!' And to both of us: 'I have no time for you any more!'

We were thrown out.

Colonel Adolf Galland

A Letter to Russia

How can I write to you when there are a thousand British bombers overhead? We feel so wretched and depressed. Hans, it is high time you finished in the East, so that at least the Luftwaffe can be sent back. For if the Tommies are allowed to go on bombing us like this, soon there will be nothing left of Western Germany.

Anon.

Nothing Left

During March* the American and British raids increased, delivering an almost continuous shower of bombs. Night after night, day after day, death and destruction descended upon the ever-diminishing area of the Reich. Hardly a town remained untouched. On 12 March the largest weight of bombs ever dropped during a night raid on a German town was registered: 4,899 tons on Dortmund. The last week in March is entered as a record in the statistics of the R.A.F., the total weight of bombs dropped being 67,365 tons . On 6 April Harris stated that there were no worthwhile targets left for his strategic bomber fleet in Germany, and a day later large-scale R.A.F. air raids stopped. The bombing commission which functioned in London under the code name Jockey telegraphed to Allied Headquarters: 'Jockey has unsaddled.' Three days later, on 10 April, American four-engined bombers raided Berlin for the last time. A fortnight later 8 A.A.F. was transferred to Okinawa in order to bomb Japan in conjunction with 20 A.A.F., which was already stationed in the Far East, until she was ripe for capitulation.

V1—V2

The German people had been clamouring for revenge against England, and in the summer of 1944 their leaders and scientists gave them what they asked for—the V1 jet-propelled flying bomb and the V2 rocket. A week after D Day the first V1 crossed the English coast, and in the following three months about eight thousand were launched against London. Then the longer-range V2s began to fall out of the sky, to the total number of about a thousand. In all, about two thousand four hundred V1s got through the defences, killing and injuring ten times as many people, mostly in London. The rest were brought down. Five hundred V2s hit London, causing nearly ten thousand casualties, but Hitler's weapons of revenge had come too late to affect the course of the war.

. . . . There was a lot of talk about the wonder weapons. We learned that our scientists had developed entirely new types of planes with four to five times the present speed, and these were now ready waiting for the Führer to give the order to go into action. And the real 'wonder' weapons had shown during their trials that their power of destruction was so immense that anything we had developed before was a joke in comparison. That was why we were almost crazy

* 1945 (Ed.)

with joy when we heard that the first secret weapon, the V1, was at last being used against Britain. There was panic in London, the town was in flames, and we saw again how the Führer had kept his word. It was now only a matter of his wonderful intuition when the final onslaught was going to take place to force the proud British on to their knees and make a vast desert out of their country.

Fritz Muehlebach, Storm Trooper

Dive-bombing V-Weapon Sites

.... On our return from the Orkneys it was decided to equip some Spitfires with 500 lb. bombs and make them dive-bomb the flying-bomb sites. 602 and 132 Squadrons were to be the guinea-pigs in this experiment.

On 13 March we left with our Spitfire IXs, which we had recovered, for Llanbedr, on the North Wales coast, for the first trials.

Dive-bombing with Spitfires is a technique on its own, as the bomb is fixed under the belly of the machine, in the place of the auxiliary tank. If you bomb vertically the propeller is torn off by the bomb. If you bomb at forty-five degrees, aiming is very difficult. After various attempts Maxie evolved the following method:

The twelve aircraft of the squadron made for the objective at twelve thousand feet in close reversed échelon formation. As soon as the leader saw the target appear under the trailing edge of his wings he dived, followed by the remainder, at seventy-five degrees. Each pilot took the objective individually in his sights and everyone came down to three thousand feet at full throttle. At that point you began to straighten out, counted three and let go your bomb. It was rather rudimentary, but after a fortnight the squadron was landing its bombs inside a hundred-and-fifty-yard circle.

During the three weeks we spent at Llanbedr we were the object of visits from every V.I.P. from Inter-Allied G.H.Q.; each time we staged a demonstration. They had their money's worth. At the first visit Dumbrell's bomb landed plumb on Fox at 450 m.p.h. and the poor blighter had to bale out *in extremis*. At the second visit one bomb, McConachie's, hung up. He decided to land with it and made a run over the airfield to warn them. As he passed the bomb came free at last and exploded bang in the middle of the airfield, covering the dismayed visitors with earth and mud.

Really, apart from Max and Remlinger, who were always eager beavers and dreamt of nothing but blood and thunder, nobody was very keen on this brand of sport. We preferred to await the first results against an objective well defended by flak before making up our minds.

.... After the first bombardments, in the course of which 16,432 tons of high explosive had been dropped on the launching sites in four months, the Germans had evolved a new type of much simplified installation. They were erecting more than fifty a month, very well camouflaged and hard to detect. The total German layout consisted of nine sectors, four directed against London and the other five against Southampton, Portsmouth, Plymouth, Brighton and the harbours of Dover and Newhaven respectively.

According to the latest information the flying bomb, or V1, was a jet-propelled device capable of carrying about a ton of explosive a distance of two hundred and fifty miles at roughly 425 m.p.h., and highly accurate, i.e. to within a thousand yards.

We returned to Detling on 8 April and we waited without exaggerated impatience for our first dive-bombing trip.

13 April 1944

The day before, for the first time, Spitfires had dive-bombed the Continent. 602 and 132 had attacked the flying-bomb installation at Bouillancourt, twelve miles south of Le Tréport.

Although our objective was in an area crammed with flak, the Germans had been so surprised at the sight of twenty-four Spitfires, each carrying a 500 lb. bomb, that they had opened fire only after we were out of range.

16 April 1944

We were going to repeat the prank on a big scale. We were to bomb Ligercourt, by the forest of Crécy. It was much less funny this time, as in a radius of two thousand yards round the target there were nine 88 mm. guns and twenty-four 20 and 37 mm.—not to mention the fact that we should be within range of Abbeville's formidable defences.

We took off at 12.25 hours. We were to attack first, followed by an Australian squadron (453), while 132 covered us against possible enemy fighter reaction. We passed the French coast at ten thousand feet and Sutherland put us into our attacking positions: 'Max aircraft, echelon port, go!'

I was the tenth of the twelve and didn't feel at all happy.

'Max aircraft, target two o'clock below.'

I could see Ligercourt woods just under my wing and I recognized the target—another flying-bomb site cleverly camouflaged among the trees—from the photos we had been shown at briefing.

We were now immediately above it. With a turn of the hand I depressed the switch that fused the bomb and removed the safety catch of the release mechanism.

'Max, going down.'

Like a fan spreading out, all the Spitfires turned on their backs one after the other and dived straight down. This time the flak opened fire straightaway. Clusters of tracer began to come up towards us. Shells burst to left and right, and just above our heads a ring of fine white puffs from the 20 mm. guns began to form, scarcely visible against the streaky cirrus clouds. Our acceleration, with that heavy bomb, was terrific: in a few seconds we were doing well over 400 m.p.h. I had only just begun to get the target in my sights when the first bombs were already exploding on the ground—a quick flash followed by a cloud of dust and fragments.

Max and Skittles Flights were already climbing again, vertically, jinking hard, stubbornly followed by the flak.

My altimeter showed three thousand feet and I concentrated on my aim. I pulled the stick gently back to let the target slip under my Spitfire's nose, following our technique—a tough job at that height. I counted aloud—one, two, three—and pressed the release button.

For the next few seconds, as a result of the effect of the violent centrifugal force, I was only dimly aware of what was going on. I recovered to find myself hanging on the propeller, at full throttle, at eight thousand feet. The flak seemed to have given us up. A turn left soon showed me why. 453 were beginning their dive. The aircraft went over like a waterfall and were soon only tiny indistinct patches against the ground.

The flak redoubled. Suddenly there was a flash and a Spitfire turned over, leaving a trail of burning glycol, and crashed into the middle of the target. A horrifying sight, which I couldn't get out of my mind.

A bitter blow, one of the dead pilot's friends told me back at the airfield. It was Bob Yarra, brother of the famous 'Slim' of Malta, also brought down by flak the year before. Bob had got a direct hit from a 37 mm. between the radiators as he was diving at well over 400 m.p.h. The two wings of his Spitfire had immediately folded up and come off, tearing off the tailplane on the way and spattering with debris the aircraft behind, which had to take violent avoiding action. Three seconds later the plane crashed into the ground and exploded. Not the ghost of a chance of baling out.

Pierre Clostermann

The Guards' Chapel

Sunday, 18 June 1944. I have good reason to remember that date: it was the last day on which I walked.

I came out of the Tube station in the Strand to find Pauline waiting for me. She was always first at our meeting places but smilingly recognized the fact that service life tended to make one unpunctual.

'Where shall we go? What shall we do?' The usual questions had to be settled. On this particular day it didn't take us long to make up our minds. I don't know who suggested it, but we were in full agreement that, as it was early and as it was Sunday, a good way of starting a long day would be at divine service at the Guards' Chapel, Wellington Barracks—not far to walk, and a place loved by us both, and visited by us in other, pre-war days.

'It would be peaceful there for you,' Pauline said, 'after your sleepless night as orderly officer.'

. . . . We sauntered through St. James's Park. What did we talk about? I don't know; we nearly always talked at the same time when we met—there was so much to say. We came from the same home town, so I imagine we talked a lot of home. I wish now, for her mother's sake, that I could remember something of what Pauline said to me. But it's no use, I can't.

I do remember that we argued a bit about where we should lunch after the service, and that the siren sounded while we were arguing. After five years, its blood-curdling wail no longer had much effect on us. We sat down on a bench opposite the Barracks for a few minutes, and watched the Guards drilling on the square. When we got up to cross to the chapel, I wondered a little nervously if I should be able to return the sentry's salute as smartly as he was sure to give it.

. . . . We sat near the back of the chapel and watched the people come in. This part of the day is clearer than the earlier part, and I do remember some of the people I saw, in particular a young Canadian lieutenant who eagerly surveyed his surroundings as if to memorize the details that he might write them down in his next letter home. . . . Then there was an elderly colonel with his wife and daughters, and a section of A.T.S. girls, possibly those stationed at the Barracks. In the gallery . . . a band of Guardsmen began to play; the band, instead of an organ, was one of the special charms of this charming chapel. Military atmosphere here was very strong, and yet in some curious way it never seemed to war with the peace of God.

We sang the opening hymn. I probably enjoyed that, for my Welsh blood ensures a fondness for hymn singing. My mind must have wandered during the reading of the first lesson—it usually does. I daresay I was thinking about my forthcoming leave or of what chance I had of getting my third pip.

'Here endeth the first lesson,' the Guards' colonel who had been reading it must have said.

The congregation rose to its feet.

. . . . This is the clearest part of all. I can see what happened as clearly as I can see the last of the roses outside my window at this moment; I can hear what happened as loudly as I can hear a late thrush singing in the hawthorn tree in the lane.

In the distance hummed faintly the engine of a flying bomb.

'We praise thee, O God: we acknowledge Thee to be the Lord,' we, the congregation, sang.

The dull burr became a roar, through which our voices could now only faintly be heard.

'All the earth doth worship Thee: the Father everlasting.'

The roar stopped abruptly as the engine cut out. We were none of us then as familiar as later all London and the south was to become with Hitler's new weapon, to recognize this ominous sign. The *Te Deum* soared again into the silence.

'To Thee all Angels cry aloud: the Heavens, and all the Powers therein.'

Then there was a noise so loud it was as if all the waters and the winds in the world had come together in mighty conflict, and the Guards' Chapel collapsed upon us in a bellow of bricks and mortar.

There was no time for panic, no time to stretch out a hand to Pauline for comfort. One moment I was singing the *Te Deum*, and the next I lay in dust and blackness, aware of one thing only—that I had to go on breathing.

I have often been asked since of what I thought during those hours when I lay buried. Did I think I was going to die? And if so did my past life parade its characters and scenes before me as is said to happen to a drowning person? All I can say is that I didn't think of anything, and yet I know that I was conscious. I felt no pain, I was scarcely aware of the chunks of massed grey concrete that had piled on top of me, nor did I realize that this was why breathing was so difficult. My whole being was concentrated in the one tremendous effort of taking in long struggling breaths and then letting them struggle out again.

It may have been an hour later, perhaps two or three or more, that greater consciousness came to me. I was suddenly aware that somewhere far above me, above the black emptiness, there were people, living helpful people whose voices reached me, dim and disembodied as in a dream.

'Please, please, I'm here,' I said, and I went on saying it until my voice was hoarse and my throat ached with the dust that poured down it. To this day I can sometimes smell that acrid dust in my nostrils—I don't know what it is that reminds me of it—and when I do smell it I sometimes find my fingers curling as they did then in a vain endeavour to scrape my way out of my living tomb.

The blessed relief of light and air! Someone frantically scraped away the rubble from around my head; I learnt later that it had been difficult for rescuers to find their way into the chapel; walls and roof shut in the dead and wounded, and there seemed at first to be no entrance at all until at last one was found behind the altar.

I had until now felt no terror, but as soon as my eyes were able to take in the ghastly scene around me my ears began to do their part. Somewhere not far away from me someone was screaming, screaming, screaming, like an animal caught in a trap—and with the pain of that dreadful sound ringing in my ears came realization of the awfulness of what had happened. I could not fully take in the scene of desolation around me, but my eyes rested with horror on a bloodstained body that, had my hands been free, I could have reached out and touched. It was the body of a young soldier whose eyes stared unseeingly at the sky. The Canada flash on the shoulder nearest me glittered.

. . . . Although I was still pinned down by debris, rescue work was progressing fast and it was with wonder that I gazed idly at a leg that had been uncovered and lay in front of me. It was dressed in a khaki silk stocking and shod with a brown brogue shoe. It looked lifeless. For a moment I thought of Pauline, but no, what would she be doing with *khaki* stockings? I looked again. . . . That was *my* stocking, *my* shoe, *my* leg. And yet it was no part of me. I could not move it, I could not feel it. I tried to wriggle my toes. Nothing happened. Engulfed now with fear, I tried to convince myself that, yes, this was truly a nightmare, one from which I was bound soon to wake up. I think I must have been given a morphia injection for I still felt no pain, but I did begin to have an inkling that I was badly injured. I turned my freed head towards a Guardsman who was helping with the rescue work, and hysterically I cried out:

'How do I look? Tell me how I look!'

'Madam,' he said, 'you look wonderful to me!'

Elisabeth Sheppard-Jones

23

THE WAR AT SEA,
1941-1945

Throughout the war, in spite of the growing menace of air power and submarines, the capital ships of both sides played a vital part. In the Mediterranean and in the Atlantic their presence protected or threatened destruction for the convoys of both sides. While full-scale naval warfare between the British and Italian fleets was a feature of the fighting in the Mediterranean, the threat of German battleships sitting in their protected harbours was sufficient to tie up most of Britain's remaining large warships on the Atlantic seaboard. British command of home waters suffered a severe reverse in 1942 when the Scharnhorst *and* Gneisenau *successfully broke out of Brest and escaped to northern ports. Sometimes a German battleship would sally out into the Atlantic and wreak havoc among the convoys before it slipped back to its home port or, in the case of* Bismarck *and later* Scharnhorst, *was destroyed.*

However, even in their ports battleships were not invulnerable, as the 'human torpedoes' and midget submarines employed successfully by the Italians and British proved.

Matapan

On 27 March 1941 a British battle fleet under Admiral Cunningham sailed from Alexandria to protect British convoys bound for Greece against the Italian fleet. It consisted of three battleships, Warspite, Barham *and* Valiant, *the aircraft carrier* Formidable *and nine destroyers. In support were Vice-Admiral Pridham-Wippell's squadron of four cruisers and four destroyers. On the morning of the 28th the latter located the Italian battleship* Vittorio Veneto *and a considerable number of other enemy warships. The whole British fleet gave chase, damaging the Italian battleship and endeavouring to overhaul her. The cruiser* Pola *was also hit and stopped. Night fell.*

ADMIRAL ANGELO IACHINO was in command of the Italian fleet with his flag in the *Vittorio Veneto*. I have read his account of the operation and the night battle, and there is no doubt that he was badly served by his air reconnaissance. This is surprising to us who know how efficient the Italian reconnaissance had been on many other occasions. However, as Admiral Iachino says, the Italian naval co-operation with the air in the tactical field was very imperfect.

It appears that they were relying upon German aircraft reports before the battle, and as the weather was by no means unfavourable it is not easy to understand why their reconnaissance failed. At 9 a.m. on 28 March German aircraft from the Aegean had actually reported one aircraft carrier, two battleships, nine cruisers and fourteen destroyers in such and such a position at 7.45. This actually was our fleet, which up to that time Admiral Iachino had thought was still safely at Alexandria. However, on plotting the position given, the Admiral convinced himself that his Aegean reconnaissance had mistaken the British fleet for his own, and signalled to Rhodes to this effect. He does not seem to have become aware that the British battle-fleet was at sea until later.

On the evening of the 28th, when the *Pola* was damaged by our air attack, Admiral Iachino's information led him to believe that the nearest British battleship was ninety miles astern of him, something over four hours' steaming. With this in mind his decision to detach the *Zara* and the *Fiume* to help the crippled *Pola* cannot be questioned. He was originally urged to send destroyers; but finally decided that only a Flag Officer, Rear-Admiral Carlo Cateneo in the *Zara*, who did not survive, could take the responsibility of deciding whether the *Pola* should be taken in tow, or abandoned and sunk.

Instead of being ninety miles astern, the British battle-fleet was roughly half that distance.

. . . . At 9.11 we received Pridham-Wippell's report that an unknown ship lying stopped five miles to port of him had been located by radar. We went on after the enemy's fleet and altered course slightly to port to close the stopped ship. The *Warspite* was not fitted with radar; but at 10.10 the *Valiant* reported that her instruments had picked up what was apparently the same ship six miles on her port bow. She was a large ship. The *Valiant* gave her length as more than six hundred feet.

Our hopes ran high. This might be the *Vittorio Veneto*. The course of the battle-fleet was altered forty degrees to port together to close. We were already at action stations with our main armament ready. Our guns were trained on the correct bearing.

Rear-Admiral Willis was not out with us. Commodore Edelsten, the new Chief of Staff, had come to gain experience. And a quarter of an hour later, at 10.25, when he was searching the horizon on the starboard bow with his glasses, he calmly reported that he saw two large cruisers with a smaller one ahead of them crossing the bows of the battle-fleet from starboard to port. I looked through my glasses, and there they were. Commander Power, an ex-submarine officer and an abnormal expert at recognizing the silhouettes of enemy warships at a glance, pronounced them to be two *Zara* class 8-inch gun cruisers with a smaller cruiser ahead.

Using short-range wireless the battle-fleet was turned back into line ahead. With Edelsten and the staff I had gone to the upper bridge, the captain's, where I had a clear all-round view. I shall never forget the next few minutes. In the dead silence, a silence that could almost be felt, one heard only the voices of the gun control personnel putting the guns on to the new target. One heard the orders repeated in the director tower behind and above the bridge. Looking forward, one saw the turrets swing and steady when the 15-inch guns pointed at the enemy cruisers. Never in the whole of my life have I experienced a more thrilling moment than when I heard a calm voice from the director tower— 'Director layer sees the target'; sure sign that the guns were ready and that his finger was itching on the trigger. The enemy was at a range of no more than three thousand eight hundred yards—point-blank.

It must have been the Fleet Gunnery Officer, Commander Geoffrey Barnard, who gave the final order to open fire. One heard the 'ting-ting-ting' of the firing gongs. Then came the great orange flash and the violent shudder as the six big guns bearing were fired simultaneously. At the very same instant the destroyer *Greyhound*, on the screen, switched her searchlight on to one of the enemy cruisers, showing her momentarily up as a silvery-blue shape in the darkness. Our searchlights shone out with the first salvo, and provided full illumination for what was a ghastly sight. Full in the beam I saw our six great projectiles flying through the air. Five out of the six hit a few feet below the level of the cruiser's upper deck and burst with splashes of brilliant flame. The Italians were quite unprepared. Their guns were trained fore and aft. They were helplessly shattered before they could put up any resistance. In the midst of all this there was one milder diversion. Captain Douglas Fisher, the Captain of the *Warspite*, was a gunnery officer of note. When he saw the first salvo hit he was heard to say in a voice of wondering surprise: 'Good Lord! We've hit her!'

The *Valiant*, astern of us, had opened fire at the same time. She also had found her target, and when the *Warspite* shifted to the other cruiser I watched the *Valiant* pounding her ship to bits. Her rapidity of fire astonished me. Never would I have believed it possible with these heavy guns. The *Formidable* had hauled out of the line to starboard; but astern of the *Valiant* the *Barham* was also heavily engaged.

The plight of the Italian cruisers was indescribable. One saw whole turrets and masses of other heavy debris whirling through the air and splashing into the sea, and in a short time the ships themselves were nothing but glowing torches and on fire from stem to stern. The whole action lasted no more than a few minutes.

Our searchlights were still on, and just after 10.30 three Italian destroyers, which had apparently been following their cruisers, were seen coming in on our port bow. They turned, and one was seen to fire torpedoes, so the battle-fleet was turned ninety degrees together to starboard to avoid them. Our destroyers were engaging, and the whole party was inextricably mixed up. The *Warspite* fired both 15-inch and 6-inch at the enemy. To my horror I saw one of our destroyers, the *Havock*, straddled by our fire, and in my mind wrote her off as a loss. The *Formidable* also had an escape. When action was joined she hauled out to starboard at full speed, a night battle being no place for a carrier. When she was about five miles away she was caught in the beam of the *Warspite*'s searchlight sweeping on the disengaged side in case further enemy ships were present. We heard the 6-inch control officer of the starboard battery get his guns on to her, and were only just in time to stop him from opening fire.

The four destroyers, *Stuart*, Captain H. M. L. Waller, Royal Australian Navy; *Greyhound*, Commander W. R. Marshal-A'Deane; *Havock*, Lieutenant G. R. G. Watkins; and *Griffin*, Lieutenant-Commander J. Lee-Barber, in company with the battle-fleet, were then ordered to finish off the enemy cruisers, while the battle-fleet collected the *Formidable* and withdrew to the northward to keep out of their way. According to their own reports the destroyers' movements were difficult to follow; but they had a wild night and sank at least one other enemy destroyer.

At 10.45 we saw very heavy gunfire, with star-shell and tracer, to the south-westward. Since none of our ships was on that bearing it seemed to us that either the Italians were engaging each other, or that the destroyers of our striking force might be going in to attack. Just after 11 p.m. I made a signal ordering all forces not engaged in sinking the enemy to withdraw to the north-eastward. The objects of what I now consider to have been an ill-considered signal were to give our destroyers who were mopping up a free hand to attack any sizeable ship they saw, and to facilitate the assembly of the fleet next morning. The message was qualified by an order to Captain Mack, and his eight destroyers of the striking force, now some twenty miles ahead, not to withdraw until he had attacked. However, it had the unfortunate effect of causing Vice-Admiral Pridham-Wippell to cease his efforts to gain touch with the *Vittorio Veneto*.

Just after midnight the *Havock*, after torpedoing a destroyer and finishing her off by gunfire, reported herself in contact with a battleship near the position where we had been in action. The battleship was Captain Mack's main objective, and the *Havock*'s report brought Mack's destroyer striking force back hot-foot from their position nearly sixty miles to the westward. An hour later, however, the *Havock* amended her report to say that it was not a battleship she had sighted, but an 8-inch cruiser. Soon after 3 a.m. she sent a further message reporting herself close to the *Pola*, and, as all her torpedoes had been fired, Watkins asked whether 'to board or blow off her stern with depth-charges'.

The *Havock* had already been joined by the *Greyhound* and *Griffin*, and when Captain Mack arrived he took the *Jervis* alongside the *Pola*. That ship was in a state of indescribable confusion. Panic-stricken men were leaping over the side. On the crowded quarterdeck, littered with clothing, personal belongings and bottles, many of the sailors were drunk. There was no order or discipline of any sort and the officers were powerless to enforce it. Having taken off the crew, Mack sank the ship with torpedoes. The *Pola*, of course, was the vessel reported by Pridham-Wippell and the *Valiant* between nine and ten the night before as lying stopped on the port side of our fleet's line of advance. She had not been under gunfire or fired a gun; but had been torpedoed and completely crippled by one of the aircraft from the *Formidable* during the dusk attack.

Her sinking at 4.10 a.m. was the final act of the night's proceedings.

Reconnaissance at dawn by the *Formidable*'s aircraft, with others from Greece and Crete, failed to discover any trace of the enemy to the westward. As we discovered afterwards, the *Vittorio Veneto* had been able to increase speed and get clear away during the night.

As daylight came on 29 March our cruisers and destroyers were in sight making for the rendezvous with the battle-fleet. Feeling fairly certain in our minds that the *Warspite* had sunk a destroyer in the mêlée the night before, we eagerly counted them. To our inexpressible relief all twelve destroyers were present. My heart was glad again.

It was a fine morning. We steamed back to the scene of the battle to find the calm sea covered with a film of oil, and strewn with boats, rafts and wreckage, with many floating corpses. All the destroyers we could spare were detached to save what life was possible. In all, counting the men from the *Pola*, British ships rescued nine hundred, though some died later. In the midst of this work of mercy, however, the attentions of some German JU88s pointed the fact that it was unwise to dally in an area where we were exposed to heavy air attack. So we were compelled to proceed to the eastward, leaving some hundreds of Italians unrescued. We did the best we could for them by signalling their exact position to the Italian Admiralty. They sent out the hospital ship *Gradisca*, which eventually saved another hundred and sixty.

. . . . Although the *Vittorio Veneto* had escaped, we had sunk the three ten-thousand-ton, 8-inch cruisers *Zara*, *Pola* and *Fiume*, together with the fifteen-hundred-ton destroyers *Alfieri* and *Carducci*. The Italian loss in personnel was about two thousand four hundred officers and men, most of them being caused by our devastating bombardment at close range. The *Fiume* received two 15-inch broadsides from the *Warspite* and one from the *Valiant*; the *Zara* four from the *Warspite*, five from the *Valiant*, and five from the *Barham*. The effect of those six- or eight-gun salvoes of shell, each weighing nearly a ton, cannot be described.

Admiral Cunningham

The End of the *Bismarck*

On 24 May 1941, the Bismarck *and* Prince Eugen, *raiding in the North Atlantic, were intercepted off Greenland and brought to action. The British battleship* Hood *was sunk by the* Bismarck. *The latter was damaged and was pursued by a powerful British force, which scored several hits with torpedoes. On the 26th the* Bismarck *was stopped four hundred miles west of her base at Brest.*

Winston Churchill at the Admiralty

On this Monday night I went to the Admiralty and watched the scene on the charts in the War Room, where the news streamed in every few minutes. 'What are you doing here?' I said to the Controller, Admiral Fraser. 'I am waiting to see what I have got to repair,' he said. Four hours passed quickly away, and when I left I could see that Admiral Pound and his select company of experts were sure the *Bismarck* was doomed.

The German commander, Admiral Lutjens, had no illusions. Shortly before midnight he reported, 'Ship unmanœuvrable. We shall fight to the last shell. Long live the Führer!' The *Bismarck* was still four hundred miles from Brest, and no longer even able to steer thither. Strong German bomber forces were now sent to the rescue, and U-boats hastened to the scene, one of which, *having already expended her torpedoes,* reported that the *Ark Royal* had passed her within easy striking distance. Meanwhile the *King George V* and the *Rodney* were drawing near. Fuel was a grave anxiety, and Admiral Tovey had decided that unless the *Bismarck*'s speed could be greatly reduced he would have to abandon the chase at midnight. I suggested to the First Sea Lord, and he signalled accordingly, that he should be towed home if necessary, but by then it was known that the *Bismarck* was actually steaming in the wrong direction. Her main armament was uninjured, and Admiral Tovey had decided to bring her to battle in the morning.

A north-westerly gale was blowing when daylight came on the 27th. The *Rodney* opened fire at 8.47 a.m., followed a minute later by the *King George V*.

The British ships quickly began to hit, and after a pause the *Bismarck* too opened fire. For a short time her shooting was good, although the crew, after four gruelling days, were utterly exhausted and falling asleep at their posts. With her third salvo she straddled the *Rodney*, but thereafter the weight of the British attack was overwhelming, and within half an hour most of her guns were silent. A fire was blazing amidships, and she had a heavy list to port. The *Rodney* now turned across her bow, pouring in a heavy fire from a range of no more than four thousand yards. By 10.15 all the *Bismarck*'s guns were silent and her mast was shot away. The ship lay wallowing in the heavy seas, a flaming and smoking ruin; yet even then she did not sink.

At eleven o'clock I had to report to the House of Commons, meeting in the Church House, both about the battle in Crete and the drama of the *Bismarck*. 'This morning,' I said, 'shortly after daylight the *Bismarck*, virtually at a standstill, far from help, was attacked by the British pursuing battleships. I do not know what were the results of the bombardment. It appears, however, that the *Bismarck* was not sunk by gunfire, and she will now be dispatched by torpedo. It is thought that this is now proceeding, and it is also thought that there cannot be any lengthy delay in disposing of this vessel. Great as is our loss in the *Hood*, the *Bismarck* must be regarded as the most powerful, as she is the newest battleship in the world.' I had just sat down when a slip of paper was passed to me which led me to rise again. I asked the indulgence of the House and said, 'I have just received news that the *Bismarck* is sunk.' They seemed content.

It was the cruiser *Dorsetshire* that delivered the final blow with torpedoes, and at 10.40 the great ship turned over and foundered. With her perished nearly two thousand Germans and their Fleet Commander, Admiral Lutjens. One hundred and ten survivors, exhausted but sullen, were rescued by us. The work of mercy was interrupted by the appearance of a U-boat and the British ships were compelled to withdraw. Five other Germans were picked up by a U-boat and a ship engaged in weather reporting, but the Spanish cruiser *Canarias*, which arrived on the scene later, found only floating bodies.

This episode brings into relief many important points relating to sea warfare, and illustrates both the enormous structural strength of the German ship and the immense difficulties and dangers with which her sortie had confronted our very numerous forces. Had she escaped the moral effects of her continuing existence as much as the material damage she might have inflicted on our shipping would have been calamitous. Many misgivings would have arisen regarding our capacity to control the oceans, and these would have been trumpeted round the world to our great detriment and discomfort. All branches rightly claimed their share in the successful outcome. The pursuit began with the cruisers, which led to the first disastrous action. Then when the enemy was lost it was aircraft that found him and guided the cruisers back to the chase. Therefore it was a cruiser which directed the sea-borne aircraft who struck the decisive blows, and finally it was the destroyers who harassed and held him through a long night and led the battleships to the last scene of destruction. While credit is due to all, we must not forget that the long-drawn battle turned on the first injury inflicted on the *Bismarck* by the guns of the *Prince of Wales*. Thus the battleship and the gun were dominant both at the beginning and at the end.

The traffic in the Atlantic continued unmolested.

To the President I telegraphed on the 28th:

I will send you later the inside story of the fighting with the *Bismarck*. She was a terrific ship, and a masterpiece of naval construction. Her removal eases our battleship situation, as we should have had to keep *King George V*, *Prince of Wales*, and the two *Nelsons* practically tied to Scapa Flow to guard against a sortie of *Bismarck* and *Tirpitz*, as they could choose their moment and we should have to allow for one of our ships refitting. Now it is a different story. The effect upon the Japanese will be highly beneficial. I expect they are doing all their sums again.

Winston Churchill

The Channel Dash: 11–12 February 1942

With American and British interest shifting to the Pacific and East Indies, Raeder began to consider using the German surface fleet in the Atlantic again. The German ships *Scharnhorst*, *Gneisenau* and *Prinz Eugen* had been stationed at Brest ever since the *Bismarck* had been sunk. They had been heavily attacked by the R.A.F., and Raeder suggested to Hitler, who had himself pointed out that the protection of these ships from air attack was proving too difficult, that the Brest Group should be sent into the Atlantic against Allied convoys.

But, besides being deterred by the precedent of the *Bismarck*, Hitler had suddenly decided that the Allies were about to land in Norway.

For these reasons Hitler had refused to allow Raeder to send the surface fleet into the Atlantic, and had ordered him instead to send the Brest Group north to protect the Norwegian coast and to operate against the Russian convoys.

Raeder protested strongly; he pointed out the difficulties—the Brest Group had only two alternative routes, either by a long voyage round the British Isles, when they would almost certainly be attacked by the Home Fleet from Scapa Flow, or by the shorter but equally hazardous route through the English Channel, where they would be attacked by the R.A.F. as well as by the Home Fleet. The crews of the German ships were untrained and enervated by their long stay at Brest, and there was no question of their being able to fight a sustained action such as the *Bismarck* had encountered.

Hitler insisted that the threat to Norway was extremely serious and that the ships must be moved. He left it to Raeder to decide how, but he showed himself strongly in favour of the Channel route.

The Naval Staff set to and produced rough plans for operation 'Cerberus', the code word for the movement of the Brest ships. In view of the state of training of the crews, unfitting them for a long voyage, they decided that the ships should go through the Straits of Dover.

In the second week of January, when the plans were completed, Hitler summoned a general conference to discuss the operation.

Ciliax* . . . explained that he had decided that the ships should leave Brest under cover of darkness, making the actual passage of the Straits of Dover in

---

* Vice-Admiral Ciliax, in command of the operation (Ed.)

daylight, since they would thereby be able to have the maximum air cover. Lieutenant-General Jeschonnek, Göring's Chief of Staff, doubted whether the necessary aircraft would be available, but Hitler ordered him to see to it that they were. Hitler finally summed up:

'In view of past experience I do not believe the British are capable of making and carrying out lightning decisions. I do not believe that they will be as swift as the Naval Staff and Vice-Admiral Ciliax assumed in transferring their bomber and fighter aircraft to the south-eastern part of England for an attack on our ships in the Dover Straits. Picture what would happen if the situation were reversed, i.e. if a surprise report came in that British battleships had appeared in the Thames estuary and were heading for the Straits of Dover. Even we would hardly be able to bring up fighters and bombers swiftly and methodically. The situation of the Brest Group is like that of a patient with cancer who is doomed unless he submits to an operation. An operation, on the other hand, even though it may have to be drastic, will at least offer some hope that the patient's life may yet be saved. The passage of our ships through the Channel is such an operation. It must therefore be attempted. . . .

'There is nothing to be gained by leaving the ships at Brest; their "flypaper" effect, that is their ability to tie up enemy air forces, may not continue for long. Only as long as the ships remain in battleworthy condition will the enemy feel obliged to attack. But the moment they are seriously damaged—and this may happen any day—the enemy will discontinue his attacks. Such a development will nullify the one and only advantage derived from leaving the ships at Brest. The operation is to be prepared as proposed by the C.-in-C., Navy.'

On the evening of 11 February, the *Scharnhorst*, *Gneisenau* and *Prinz Eugen*, accompanied by destroyers and E-boats, left Brest, and, at full speed, began their dash up the English Channel.

Running the Gauntlet

It was planned that the squadron should keep an average speed of twenty-six knots, and in the beginning, with favourable tides, they were actually making about thirty knots. After rounding Ushant to the west of Brittany, the formation set course for the Channel at 1.13 a.m. As total radio silence was observed, reports of position came only from our radar stations along the French coast, which picked up the warships at intervals. Each time this was a pleasant surprise. After the loss of two valuable hours, I was fairly certain that at dawn I should have to transfer the fighter forces standing by from the Pas de Calais down to the Le Havre–Caen–Cherbourg sector. Allowance had been made for such a case in the plan, but it would have meant an additional strain on everyone concerned. Each new report showed that the warships were catching up on their initial delay until, early in the morning, it was clear that they would make up their time and, with the first light of day, would be in the prearranged position exactly to the minute.

. . . . At 6.30 a.m. decks were cleared for action on board the battleships, which were travelling at high speed through the darkness towards the Channel. Off Cherbourg a flotilla of torpedo boats joined them to strengthen the outer safety belt which so far had only been formed by destroyers. The whole unit consisted now of the two battleships, the cruiser, seven destroyers and eight to fifteen E-boats, the latter relieved from sector to sector.

The weather was cloudy, with a fifteen hundred-foot ceiling and relatively good visibility. At 8.14 a.m. the first night-fighters took off in complete darkness and were over the fleet at 8.50 a.m. From now onwards, during the whole day, fighter forces kept in continuous and direct contact with the ships. The air umbrella—a small one, of course—was opened. Our destroyer fighters were flying only a few feet above the water in order not to be detected by the English radar stations. All radio communications were, of course, silenced. At 8.54 a.m. the dawn broke. The units were off the Cotentin peninsula.

The first dramatic note crept into the operation when naval security forces discovered a previously unnoticed minefield off Dieppe only a few hours before the ships were due, and although a channel was swiftly swept by an all-out effort of four minesweepers, the decision to pass through this barely cleared path was a very risky one. But there was no alternative bar returning and calling the whole operation off. The unit passed through without incident.

The night-fighters, which flew mainly on the port side of the warships, the side towards the enemy, had been joined in the meantime by day-fighters. The operation ran according to plan. Discovery by the enemy, which, luckily, had not yet occurred, had to be avoided for as long as possible. In briefing the pilots, each commander had therefore stressed to the utmost the orders: fly at the lowest possible level and with radio silence. Those who knew the general lack of radio discipline in the Luftwaffe, and particularly among fighter pilots, can imagine how worried I now was in this respect.

. . . . At eleven o'clock Middle European Time (ten o'clock British time) an alerting radio message from a British fighter was intercepted by our listening service. It said nothing except that a large German naval formation consisting of three capital ships and about twenty warships was steaming at high speed towards the Straits of Dover, present position about fifty miles off the mouth of the Somme. The secret was out.

. . . . The German high-frequency experts took a large share in creating the obvious confusion of the British command. Usually we gave little heed to these contraptions, which always remain a mystery to the uninitiated, and indeed to quite a few laymen in the high command of the German Luftwaffe, including its C.-in-C., who once said to me that his understanding of such things was already overtaxed when operating a radio set. One should value all the more the activities of these experts, who often have to struggle against stupidity, unintelligence and even ill-will! They had created strong interference with the British radar stations by a series of installations and by different methods. They had also directed interference transmissions against the British fighter intercoms, and by special instruments in bombers had simulated radar signals giving false reports of approaching large formations, against which the British actually sent strong fighter forces. The confusion created in this way continued even when the German warships were clearly located and when practical deception was no longer possible.

At this moment [15.30 hours] the flagship *Scharnhorst* was heavily shaken:

the lights failed, and the wireless went dead. She had struck a mine, and, leaving a trail of oil behind her, now came to a standstill. The leading destroyer, Z29, was ordered alongside to take aboard the Commander and the fighter liaison. At the same time the weather was deteriorating rapidly with a cloud ceiling of five to six hundred feet, visibility half to one mile, and rain. The naval formation proceeded with *Prinz Eugen* and *Gneisenau* as well as the bulk of the destroyers and torpedo boats, the enemy concentrating on the *Scharnhorst* and the destroyer Z29. It was 3.50 p.m. Near *Prinz Eugen* an M.T.B. approached. Change of course, detonation of the torpedo a thousand yards aft. With the stopping of the *Scharnhorst* the naval formation split up. *Prinz Eugen* and *Gneisenau* proceeded with the main destroyer and torpedo-boat force, while *Scharnhorst* stayed behind.

. . . . Meanwhile, ill luck still dogged the C.-in-C. of the battleships. Since his flagship had been damaged by the mine he had been aboard the destroyer Z29, which now developed engine trouble in the port engine. Again the C.-in-C. and the fighter liaison, with a limited staff, had to be transferred. The destroyer *Hermann Schömann* was ordered to stand by, and the transfer was effected by means of a cutter, under continuous attacks by British aircraft and in a rough sea. At 6.45 p.m., while the Admiral was still bobbing up and down in the cutter, the *Scharnhorst*, which had been brought under way again, went off at full speed, trying to catch up with the flotilla. This must have been a great personal disappointment, mitigated, however, by the satisfaction of knowing that the *Scharnhorst* was now able to continue towards her destination.

Towards 7 p.m. it was getting dark. Day- and night-fighters were battling with the last Wellington bombers, which attacked incessantly and with tenacity. *Gneisenau*, *Prinz Eugen* and *Hermann Schömann* reported kills by fighters and A.A. fire. At 7.35 hours it was quite dark, and fighter action was ended for the day. Successes and losses could not yet be assessed, but one thing was clear: we had completed our task to form and maintain an air umbrella over the German warships while they were breaking through.

. . . . During the night the R.A.F. was very active. Besides intensive air reconnaissance, they were mainly busy with mine-laying operations, in order to mine the whole route right up to the German Bight and the Elbe Estuary. Our night-fighters kept in contact with the enemy, but there were no major actions.

The British mines still did some damage that night. Shortly after 9 p.m. the *Gneisenau* shook under an explosion and all her engines stopped. She had hit a mine! Yet the damage was only superficial, and after a short time she was under way again, making twenty-five knots. An hour and a half later the *Scharnhorst* hit another mine. She too could soon continue, although at first only at ten, later at fifteen knots.

It was still dark when the *Gneisenau* and *Prinz Eugen* reached the mouth of the Elbe and cast anchor. At that time the German Bight was still outside the range of British fighters. After their heavy defeat in their attack on Wilhelmshaven on 4 September and 18 December 1939, the British bombers no longer ventured during daytime into this area, which was well covered by radar stations.

. . . . The remarkable thing about Churchill's description is it shows that Hitler in his planning judged the suspected reaction of the British command absolutely correctly. Faced with the German surprise, they showed amazingly little ability to improvise. Hitler had been right in his statement that the British would not make any lightning decisions, and this was the only possible explanation which all those who took part in the venture could find for the unbelievable fact that the formation was not attacked before noon, when it had already nearly reached the narrowest point of the Channel. This was the key to our success.

. . . . The British Prime Minister describes in detail the failure of the radar organization during the operation. Until after the war, opinion in Britain was that it had been an unaccountable episode, a national misfortune. Only after the war was it discovered that the reason for this inexplicable failure was no less than a clever trick of the chief of German radio communication, Martini. Unfortunately, the German command did not draw the necessary conclusions from this victory in the radar war and did not start a rapid development of this weapon. The British learned from their defeat and developed radar interference to a perfection which later on during the bombing war became fatal for the Reich.

Colonel Adolf Galland, commanding Luftwaffe fighter cover

'Vice-Admiral Ciliax,' wrote *The Times*, 'has succeeded where the Duke of Medina Sidonia failed. . . . Nothing more mortifying to the pride of sea power has happened in Home Waters since the seventeenth century.'

The Small Killers

The Italian Navy, having been worsted in surface action in the Mediterranean, still had a trump card to play. On the night of 17 December 1941 the Italian submarine Scire *lay outside Alexandria harbour. She carried several 'pigs'—torpedo-shaped craft on which two men, sitting astride, could penetrate protected harbours undetected and plant limpet mines on shipping inside them.*

Alexandria: 18 December 1941

The plan of operations provided for the arrival of the *Scire* on a certain evening, a few thousand metres from the entrance to Alexandria harbour; as it was assumed that everything would be in darkness (owing to the black-out), it had been arranged that, in order to facilitate the submarine's landfall, the coast being low-lying and without conspicuous features, and allow her to identify the harbour (for the success of the operators' raid would depend largely on the precision with which the point of their release was determined) on the evening before, and also on the one of the action, our aircraft would bomb the harbour. The submarine would then release the operators. The latter, proceeding on courses laid down beforehand, as soon as they arrived in front of the harbour, would have to overcome the obstructions and attack the targets previously assigned to them by the commander of the *Scire*, who would base his orders on the latest data transmitted to him by radio. After attaching the charges to the hulls of the targets, the operators were to lay a certain number of floating incendiary bombs with which they had been supplied. These bombs would go off about an hour after the warheads had exploded and were intended to set alight the oil which would by then have spread from the ships which had been attacked; it was expected that this would cause fire to break out in the harbour, affecting all the vessels therein, together with the floating docks, the harbour installations and the warehouses . . . thus putting the chief enemy naval base in the Eastern Mediterranean utterly out of action.

The sea was very calm, the night dark. Lights in the harbour permitted the pilots to determine their position, which they found to be precisely as planned. They went ahead so coolly that at one point, as de la Penne relates in his report, 'as we were ahead of schedule, we opened our ration tins and had a meal. We were then five hundred metres from the Ras el Tin Lighthouse.'

At last they reached the net defences at the harbour's entrance.

'We saw some people at the end of the pier and heard them talking; one of them was walking about with a lighted oil-lamp.

'We also saw a large motor-boat cruising in silence off the pier and dropping depth-charges. These charges were rather a nuisance to us.'

While the six heads, only just above the water, were looking, with all the concentrated attention of which they were capable, for a gap in the net, three British destroyers suddenly appeared at the entrance to the harbour, waiting to go in: guide lights were switched on to show them the way and the net gates were thrown wide open. Without a second's hesitation our three assault craft slipped into the harbour with the British destroyers: they were in! They had lost sight of one another during this manœuvre, but they were now close to their targets. The latter had been distributed as follows: de la Penne was to take the battleship *Valiant*, Marceglia the battleship *Queen Elizabeth*, and Martellotta was to look for the aircraft carrier; if she were not in harbour, he was to attack a loaded tanker in the hope that the oil or petrol which would issue from it would spread over the water and thus furnish excellent fuel for the floating incendiary bombs the operators were to scatter before abandoning their 'pigs'.

Inside the harbour, after passing the interned French warships, the presence of which was well known, de la Penne sighted, at the presumed anchorage, the huge dark mass of the target assigned to him, the thirty-two-thousand-ton battleship *Valiant*. As he approached her, he encountered the anti-torpedo net barrier: he got through it *surfaced*, 'in order to lose as little time as possible, for I found that my physical condition, owing to the cold, would be unlikely to let me hold out much longer.' (His diver's suit had been leaking ever since he had left the submarine.) He had no difficulty with negotiation of the net: he was now thirty metres from the *Valiant*; it was nineteen minutes past two. He touched the hull, giving it a slight bump; in performing the evolution necessary to get beneath the hull, his 'pig' seemed to take on extra weight and went to the bottom in seventeen metres of water; de la Penne dived after it and discovered to his amazement that there was no sign of his second pilot. He rose to the surface to look for him, but could not see him; everything was quiet aboard the battleship; no alarm had been given. De la Penne left Bianchi to his fate, returned to the bottom and tried to start the engine of his craft to get it underneath the hull, as it had meanwhile moved some distance away. But the engine would not start; a rapid check-over soon showed what the trouble was: a steel wire had got entangled in the propeller.

What was to be done? All alone, with his craft immobilized on the sea-bed a few metres from the target, de la Penne resolved to try the only possible expedient: this was to drag the 'pig' by main force, finding his direction from the compass, beneath the battleship. Speed was essential, for he feared that at any moment the British might pick up his second pilot, who had probably fainted and would be floating about close by. . . . The alarm would be given, depth-charges would be dropped, his operation and those of his companions would be doomed to certain failure, for they would be at work only a few hundred metres away. With all his strength, panting and sweating, he dragged at the craft; his goggles became obscured and the mud he was stirring up prevented his reading the compass, his breath began to come in great gasps and it became difficult to breathe at all through the mask, but he stuck to it and made progress; he could hear, close above him, the noises made aboard the ship, especially the sound of an alternating pump, which he used to find his direction. After forty minutes of superhuman effort, making a few inches at every pull, he at last bumped his head against the hull. He made a cursory survey of the position: he seemed to be at about the middle of the ship, an excellent spot for causing maximum damage. He was now almost exhausted; but he used the last vestiges of his strength to set the time fuses; in accordance with the orders he had received he regulated them so as to cause the explosion at five o'clock precisely (Italian time, corresponding with six o'clock local time). He did not release his incendiary bombs, for when they rose to the surface they would reveal the presence and the position of the threat now established under the hull with the fuses in action. He left his craft on the sea-bed under the vessel and swam to the surface. The moment he got his head above water he removed his mask and sank it; the fresh, pure air revived him; he began to swim slowly away from the ship. But someone called out to him, a searchlight picked him out, a burst of machine-gun fire brought him to a halt. He swam back towards the vessel and climbed out of the water on to the mooring-buoy at the bows of the *Valiant*. He found there his second pilot Bianchi, who, after fainting, had risen to the surface like a balloon and on regaining consciousness had hidden himself on the buoy so as not risk causing an alarm which would have disturbed the work of his leader. 'Aboard they were making facetious remarks, believing that our operation had failed; they were talking contemptuously about Italians. I called Bianchi's attention to the probability that in a few hours they would have changed their minds about the Italians.' It was then about 3.30. At last a motor-boat turned up and the two 'shipwrecked' men were picked up by it and taken aboard the battleship. A British officer asked who they were, where they had come from and expressed ironical sympathy with their lack of success. The two operators, who were now prisoners of war, made clear who they were, by handing over their military identity cards. They refused to answer any other questions. They were taken in the motor-boat, separated from each other, to a hut ashore, near the Ras el Tin Lighthouse. Bianchi was the first to be cross-examined; on leaving the hut he made a sign to de la Penne indicating that he had said nothing. It was then the latter's turn: naturally, he held his tongue; the Britisher, who had a revolver in his hand, seemed to be an excitable sort of fellow, 'I'll soon find a way to make you talk,' he said in excellent Italian. The men were taken back aboard the *Valiant*: it was then four o'clock.

They were received by the commanding officer, Captain Morgan, who asked them where the charge was located. On their refusing to answer the two men, accompanied by the officer of the watch and escorted by an armed picket, were placed in one of the holds forward, between the two gun-turrets, not very far from the point at which the charge would explode.

We will now let de la Penne take up the tale.

'Our escort were rather white about the gills and behaved very nicely to us; they gave me rum to drink and offered cigarettes; they also tried to make us talk. Bianchi sat down and went to sleep. I perceived from the ribbons on the sailors' caps that we were aboard the battleship *Valiant*. When there were about ten minutes left before the explosion, I asked if I could speak to the commanding officer. I was taken aft, into his presence. I told him that in a few minutes his ship would blow up, that there was nothing he could do about it and that, if he wished, he could still get his crew into a place of safety. He again asked me where I had placed the charge, and as I did not reply had me escorted back to the hold. As we went along I heard the loudspeakers giving orders to abandon ship, as the vessel had been attacked by Italians, and saw people running aft. When I was again in the hold I said to Bianchi, as I came down the ladder, that things had turned out badly and that it was all up with us, but that we could be content, since we had succeeded, in spite of everything, in bringing the operation to a successful conclusion. Bianchi, however, did not answer me. I looked for him and could not find him. I supposed that the British, believing that I had confessed, had removed him. A few minutes passed (they were infernal ones for me: would the explosion take place?) and then it came. The vessel reared, with extreme violence. All the lights went out and the hold became filled with smoke. I was surrounded by shackles which had been hanging from the ceiling and had now fallen. I was unhurt, except for pain in a knee, which had been grazed by one of the shackles in its fall. The vessel was listing to port. I opened one of the port-holes very near sea level, hoping to be able to get through it and escape. This proved to be impossible as the port-hole was too small, and I gave up the idea: but I left the port open, hoping that through it more water would enter. I waited for a few moments. The hold was now illuminated by the light which entered through the port. I concluded that it would be rash to stay there any longer, noticing that the vessel was now lying on the bottom and continuing slowly to list to port. I climbed up the ladder and, finding the hatchway open, began to walk aft; there was no one about. But there were still many of the crew at the stern. They got up as I passed them; I went on till I reached the Captain. At that moment he was engaged in giving orders for salvaging his ship. I asked him what he had done with my diver. He did not reply and the officer of the watch told me to be silent. The ship had now listed through four or five degrees and come to a standstill. I saw from a clock that it was a quarter-past six. I went farther aft, where a number of officers were standing, and began to watch the battleship *Queen Elizabeth* which lay about five hundred metres astern of us.

'The crew of that battleship were standing in her bows. A few seconds passed and then the *Queen Elizabeth*, too, blew up. She rose a few inches out of the water and fragments of iron and other objects flew out of her funnel, mixed with oil which even reached the deck of the *Valiant*, splashing everyone of us standing on her stern. An officer came up and asked me to tell him on my word of honour if there were any other charges under the ship. I made no reply and was then again taken back to the hold. After about a quarter of an hour I was escorted up to the officers' mess, where at last I could sit down, and where I found Bianchi. Shortly afterwards I was put aboard a motor-boat, which took me back to Ras el Tin.

'I noticed that the anchor, which had been hanging at the bows, was now underwater. During transit an officer asked me whether we had got in through the gaps in the mole. At Ras el Tin we were locked in two cells and kept there until towards evening. I asked whether I could be given a little sunlight, as I was very cold. A soldier came, felt my pulse and told me that I was perfectly all right.

'Towards evening we were put into a small lorry and transported therein to a prisoner-of-war camp in Alexandria. I found some Italians in the camp who had heard the explosions that morning. We lay down on the ground without having had any food, and, though we were soaked through, we slept till the following morning. I was taken to the infirmary for treatment of my knee injury and some Italian orderlies gave me an excellent dish of macaroni. The next morning I was removed to Cairo.'

In 1944, after de la Penne and Bianchi had come back to Italy from prison, they were awarded the gold medal for gallantry in war. And he who pinned the medal on the chest of de la Penne was none other than Admiral Morgan, formerly commanding officer of the *Valiant* and at that time chief of the Allied Naval Mission in Italy.

J. Valerio Borghese

Two could play at this game.

Please report what is being done to emulate the exploits of the Italians in Alexandria Harbour and similar methods of this kind.

At the beginning of the war Colonel Jefferis had a number of bright ideas on this subject, which received very little encouragement. Is there any reason why we should be incapable of the same kind of scientific aggressive action that the Italians have shown? One would have thought we should have been in the lead.

Please state the exact position.

Winston Churchill to General Ismay, 18 January 1942

Mr. Churchill had realized that the enemy's employment of a manned torpedo was a mode of warfare particularly suited to the capabilities and needs of Britain in the dark days of 1942. Heavy capital units of the German and Italian navies were constituting a serious menace to our lines of communication and compelling large-scale strategic positioning of our own capital ships, merely by remaining safely for months on end in strongly defended anchorages.

The Navy had not been blind to this situation and was already in the process of producing a midget submarine—the X craft—to be manned by three or four men.

The British planned an attack with midget submarines on Kaafjord on the coast of Norway, where the Tirpitz, Scharnhorst *and* Lützow *lay.*

22 September 1943

Next morning the entrance of Kaafjord began; X.7 left the lee of the Brattholm islands shortly after midnight, and X.6 followed an hour later. Within three hours Place had taken his craft successfully through the first obstacle, the anti-submarine net at the entrance to the fjord. With Cameron, however, things were a little more difficult. The periscope flooded soon after they left the billet and continued to flood and reflood time and time again. It was a mystery how he conned them throughout the rest of the attack, for he could hardly see anything. But luck was with them. They surfaced in the wake of a small coaster and followed her through the nets in broad daylight. Cameron had acted in the coolest manner. They must have been invisible.

Meanwhile life in Kaafjord in general and in *Tirpitz* in particular pursued its normal course, as the following extract from the battleship's deck-log shows:

05.00–22 Called the hands.
Set normal anti-aircraft and anti-sabotage watch ashore and afloat. Boat-gate in anti-torpedo nets opened for boat and tug traffic. Hydrophone listening office closed down.

Once his craft had entered Kaafjord, Cameron went to sixty feet and proceeded by dead reckoning, taking the opportunity to strip the periscope, but without managing to effect a permanent repair. To add to the difficulties the periscope hoisting-motor brake burnt out, resulting in manual control of the brake being necessary when raising or lowering the very dimly-lensed 'stick'. It is no wonder that twice they only just avoided collisions by a coat of paint. 'Once,' wrote Lorimer, 'we passed under the bows of a destroyer, between her stem and her mooring buoy.' A few minutes later they were so close to the tanker *Nordmark*, lying half a mile from *Tirpitz*, that a periscope sight came just in time for another mooring buoy to be avoided by a very sharp alteration of course. E.R.A. Goddard was kept busy on the wheel.

By 07.05 X.6 had closed the anti-torpedo shore-net defence of *Tirpitz* and was through the boat-entrance and within striking distance of her target.

After entering the fjord at four o'clock X.7 had her first piece of bad luck when she was forced deep by a patrolling motor-launch. While she was thus temporarily 'blind' she got caught in the unoccupied square of A/T nets, once used to house the *Lützow*, but by then empty. They spent a busy, if cautious, hour or more in getting free. Place had no wish to put a diver out unless it was really necessary, especially as this was a case of getting free from a net as opposed to getting through one. After much pumping and blowing the craft shook herself free and shot up to the surface. Luckily she was not spotted during her brief moments before she dived again. All this violent action seemed to have put the gyro-compass 'off the board', as Place wrote, and the trim-pump was also out of action. Then the craft was 'hooked' again, this time by a lone wire across the periscope standard. But by six o'clock she was free once more, and although, without a trim-pump, her trim at periscope-depth was somewhat precarious, she was soon headed down the fjord for her target.

At 07.10, Place having decided in favour of passing under *Tirpitz*'s A/T net defences, X.7 endeavoured to do this at seventy-five feet (which should have been well below the maximum depth of such nets) and was surprisingly caught. Up to this point no suspicions had been aroused in *Tirpitz*, and normal harbour routine was in progress. That the two craft should have reached the innermost defences of the battleship after so long a journey and through so many hazards to arrive within five minutes of each other was a supreme credit to careful and intelligent planning and to able and determined execution.

X.6 made her way through the boat-gate, following close behind a picket-boat. Once the latter was through the gate was closed, which fact Cameron was able to discern on his periscope and report to his crew.

'So we've had it now as far as changing our mind,' joked Goddard.

The water was very calm, and it was unfortunate that the craft should run aground on the north shore of the netted enclosure. As she was at remarkably shallow depth when this occurred it was impossible for her to be freed without just breaking surface for a few moments. This surfacing was observed in *Tirpitz* but, although reported as a 'long black submarine-like object', there was a five-minute delay in passing the information on to higher authority as it was thought that the object sighted might be a porpoise. So X.6 was enabled, by some German's fear of ridicule, to close inside the range of *Tirpitz*'s main and subsidiary armament. Five minutes later their luck, hitherto so good, deserted them again. They hit a submerged rock and were pushed to the surface.

Lorimer took her down immediately, and from her position some eighty yards abeam of the battleship her head was again turned to close. But this time she had been clearly sighted and correctly identified. The gyro had been put out of action by the grounding and by the subsequent acute angles that the craft had taken, and the periscope was almost completely flooded, with the result that progress in the target's direction was blind. Indeed, Cameron was hoping to fix their position by the shadow of the battleship.

After another five minutes X.6 got caught in an obstruction which she took to be the A/T net on the far (starboard) side of *Tirpitz*, but which was probably something hanging down either from the battleship or from one of the small vessels alongside. She surfaced where she was, close on *Tirpitz*'s port bow, to be greeted with a brisk fire from small arms and hand-grenades from the deck that loomed above her. Don Cameron realized that escape was hopeless, so, directing the crew to destroy the most secret equipment, he had the craft go astern until the hydroplane guard was scraping *Tirpitz*'s hull abreast 'B' turret. There he released the charges, both of which had been set earlier to detonate one hour after release, and scuttled the craft. It was 7.15 a.m.

'Bail out!' came the order.

'This we did,' wrote Lorimer subsequently, 'and we were very sad to see X.6 go. She went down on top of the charges, under "B" turret. It was the end of an old friend.'

They were picked out of the water by *Tirpitz*'s picket-boat, which also made unsuccessful attempts to secure a tow to the X-craft before it sank.

On board *Tirpitz* and in Kaafjord the alarm had now been properly raised and it is clear from entries in the battleship's log-book that complete surprise had been achieved. 'Action stations' was sounded in the battleship, steam was ordered, and the ship prepared for sea, in order to get her outside the nets. This order was apparently not given until all the watertight doors were closed, twenty minutes after the crew of X.6 had been embarked. It is not clear why there was this delay, nor why the Germans initially took the four of them for Russians, unless because of their unshavenness, or because of their presence in such northerly waters, or both. The four of them—Cameron, Lorimer, Goddard and Sub-Lieutenant 'Dick' Kendall—were huddled together in a group while orders were shouted and divers put down over the side. Their interrogation was being left until later, but an attempt was made to warm them up after their 'dip' with generous amounts of hot coffee and schnapps. They all recall that as the time neared 8.15 there was a certain amount of anxious and surreptitious looking at watches, mingled with speculation as to what effect the charges would have, and connected, in Lorimer's mind at least, with the knowledge that the divers were still under the ship. These unfortunate men had been given the unpleasant task of examining the hull for limpet mines, although it appears that some form of charge dropped under the ship was also expected, as the extract from the log recording the preparations for sea reads: 'In order to leave the net enclosure if possible before the time-fused mines detonate.'

The interrogation was just starting when the charges went off—at 08.12.

'I was thrown off my feet with the force of the explosion,' Lorimer recalls, 'and we all ended up on the deck. I could not help thinking that the two divers must have come up much more quickly than they went down—with the aid of what I knew would be at least four tons of amatol and which I now know to have been eight.'

'There was panic on board the *Tirpitz* as our charges went off,' wrote Kendall after his return from Germany. 'The German gun-crew shot up a number of their own tankers and small boats and also wiped out a gun position inboard with uncontrolled firing. Everybody seemed to be waving pistols and threatening us to find out the number of midgets on the job. The Germans lost about a hundred men all told, mostly due to their own lack of discipline.'

Place had been disappointed to see *Tirpitz* still on the surface following the explosion. The fact that she survived at all was largely due to the limited evasive action she was able to take after the sinking of X.6. This was achieved by heaving in on the starboard cable and veering port to take the ship as far away as possible from the position in which the craft had gone down. The battleship's log records at 08.12 'two heavy consecutive detonations to port at one-tenth of a second interval'. The first explosion was abreast 'X' turret about six to eight yards from the ship, the other fifty to sixty yards off the bow in X.6's last position. The latter explosion was almost certainly composed of three charges going up together, for a subsequent examination of the sea-bed failed to discover any of the charges, or even fragments.

With the explosions the giant ship was heaved five or six feet upward, and a large column of water was flung into the air on the port side. Members of the ship's company on deck were hurled off their feet and several casualties resulted.

The ship took on an immediate list to port of about five degrees. All the lights failed. Oil-fuel started to leak out from amidships. From the damage reports compiled in *Tirpitz* during the morning after the attack the following items of the battleship's structure and equipment were put out of action: all three main engines; one generator room; all lighting equipment; all electrical equipment; wireless telegraphy rooms; hydrophone station; 'A' and 'C' turrets; anti-aircraft control positions; range-finding gear; port rudder.

One person was killed and about forty wounded by the explosion, in addition to those killed and injured by the Germans' own gunfire, and five hundred tons of water were taken aboard. In all, the final effect of the attack was completely satisfactory. Even though the *Tirpitz* was still afloat, and even though many of the minor disablements she suffered were only temporary, she was certainly immobilized as far as undertaking any sea-action was concerned. On 22 November, two months after the attack, the German *Marinegruppenkommando Nord* reported to the German Naval War Staff that 'as a result of the successful midget-submarine attack the battle cruiser *Tirpitz* had been put out of action for months'. It was, indeed, considered by the War Staff that the forty-thousand-ton ship might never regain complete operational efficiency. The truth of the estimates was borne out by the fact that it was not until April of the following year that *Tirpitz* was able to limp from her anchorage, only to be further damaged and finally destroyed by air attack.

Grudge Fight

The men who fought the war at sea were not always fighting the enemy. . . .

I was interviewing request-men one morning and had reached the last man.

'Next request is by Able Seaman Morris, sir,' said the Coxswain; then he shouted—'Able Seaman Morris . . . '*hun*. Able-Seaman Morris . . . three paces forward . . . *march*.' He looked down to consult the request book. 'Able Seaman Morris requests to see the First Lieutenant through Divisional Officer for permission to have a grudge fight with Ordinary Seaman Sweeney.'

The Coxswain completed the formal introduction—'Able Seaman Morris, sir.' Having satisfied himself that I was fully aware of the identity of the request-man before me he stood back to see how I would deal with this somewhat extraordinary request.

Able Seaman Morris saluted and got his eyes focused on a point on the bulkhead behind my left shoulder.

'Well, Morris,' I started, 'what's all this about?'

Morris spoke with suppressed emotion—' 'e pinched the end orf me banger, sir.'

'He did what?' I cried, thoroughly startled.

'Pinched the end orf me banger, sir,' repeated Morris stolidly, not shifting his sphinx-like gaze. 'Ordinary Seaman Sweeney did, sir.'

I was nonplussed. Banger, of course, was a sausage, but how one pinched the end off one, or what excuse that was for a grudge fight was beyond me. I turned to the Coxswain for enlightenment.

'Do you know anything about this, Coxswain?' I asked.

Of course he did. Coxswains know everything.

'It appears, sir,' he said, 'that number five mess—that's Able Seaman Morris's mess—don't go much for Pusser's sausages, sir, so they got some from Naafi. Naafi bangers—sausages, sir—have skins and sometimes when they're cooked the skins burst at the ends and the innards come out. Well, sir, it seems that Able Seaman Morris arranges with the cook to have a couple of bangers—beg pardon, sir, sausages—with the ends sticking out where the skin's burst. It appears Able Seaman Morris likes these end bits. . . .'

'Very partial I am, sir, to the ends of Naafi bangers, sir,' interjected Able Seaman Morris. The Coxswain silenced him with a frown and continued. 'But when he gets his ban—er—sausages down to the mess, sir, and turns his back for a minute, he finds the ends gone and Ordinary Seaman Sweeney eating them. So he wants to fight Sweeney, sir.'

I turned back to Morris. 'Anything further to add?' I queried.

'I jest goes ter get me knife, sir, and when I turns around I finds the ends gorn—nipped orf, sir, as yer might say. The best part, too. I'm very partial to the ends, sir.'

'Quite,' I said. 'So you want to fight Ordinary Seaman Sweeney?'

'Yessir. I wants me revenge, sir,' answered Morris grimly.

'What about Sweeney?' I asked. 'Does he want to fight too?'

'Yes, sir,' said the Coxswain.

'Right, request granted. Fourteen hundred to-morrow on the upper deck,' I said.

'Thank yer, sir' said Morris.

'Request granted. Fourteenhundredtomorrowuppperdeckaboutturndouble-march,' echoed the Coxswain.

As Morris doubled away I reflected that he must indeed like the 'ends orf bangers' to be prepared to suffer physical pain for their sake.

That he would suffer physical pain I had no doubt, for Ordinary Seaman Sweeney was young, active and aggressive, while Morris was one of the pillars of the Royal Navy—a three-badge Able Seaman. Aged about forty-eight, he had, either through lack of ambition, or reluctance to shoulder responsibility, never bothered to pass professionally for Leading Seaman.

There are many such 'stripeys' in the Navy. They are reliable, tolerant, staid and conservative and know all the tricks of the trade from sailmakers to 16-inch guns; from the Persian Gulf to Pompey Hard. In wartime they are invaluable in a crew to balance the younger, inexperienced ratings. Morris was a typical 'stripey'.

At fourteen hundred the next afternoon I went on the upper deck with the boxing-gloves. Quite a crowd had gathered and in the centre, but standing ostentatiously apart, were Morris and Sweeney, clad in singlets and shorts.

'Now you both know the rules,' I said as the gloves were laced on; 'carry on fighting until one of you has had enough. And after it's over shake hands, and no more quarrelling or you'll be run in.'

They nodded and took up their varied ideas of a fighting stance.

'Go to it,' I shouted.

It was obvious from the start that Morris was going to get a good hiding.

Sweeney made rings round him and was altogether too fast for the stripey's main advantage—weight—to be put to any use. However, he stuck it for nearly ten minutes before he raised his hand in surrender. He was not in the least disgruntled; he had had his grudge fight, which was all that counted. He hadn't even expected to win.

So I put the gloves away and regarded the matter as closed. Alas, I didn't know my sailor.

Four days later I was again holding request-men and Morris was the first in the line. He didn't wait for a proper introduction, but, at the first syllable of the Coxswain's order 'Able Seaman Morris . . . 'hun,' he bounded forward to the request table, saluted and blurted out—' 'e done it agen . . . 'e pinched the end orf me banger agen. So 'elp me, sir, I jest turns me back and that there young . . . hrrrrrmph . . . was stuffin' it in 'is marf. Sneaked up behind me 'e did, and nicked it right orf me plate . . . standin' there larfin' at me. . . . I wants ter fight 'im agen, sir. I wants another grudge fight. . . .' Morris was absolutely chattering with rage, the veins stood out on his forehead and he was rolling his eyes like a man possessed.

The Coxswain took advantage of his breathlessness to get in his little speech. 'Able Seaman Morris, sir, requests to have second grudge fight with Ordinary Seaman Sweeney.'

'Now, Morris,' I said, in what I hoped was a pacifying manner, for I could see he was smouldering and would shortly erupt into impassioned outburst, 'now, Morris, before you started the last fight you understood the rules. I should charge both you and Sweeney with needless, frivolous quarrelling and....

'Needless . . .? Frivolous . . .?' stuttered Morris, 'but 'e 'alf-'inched me end agen, sir, right under me nose. Cor stone the. . . .' The Coxswain silenced him with an upraised hand.

I thought for a moment. Strictly speaking, I should run both of them in as defaulters, but I was thinking ahead to the problems of making out the charge sheets and giving the reasons for the quarrel. I couldn't see the representatives of Their Lordships looking with any favour at all on a charge reading, 'Did commit an act to the prejudice of Good Order and Naval Discipline in that he did sneak the end off a N.A.A.F.I. sausage, the property of J. Morris, Able Seaman, C/JX 113037.'

'Granted. Fourteen hundred, upper deck, to-morrow,' I said.

'Granted . . . brrp . . . brrp . . . brrp . . . aboutturndoublemarch,' said the Coxswain.

At fourteen ten the following afternoon Morris wearily picked himself up off the deck and signified his surrender. There was a triumphant grin on his bloodied face. Honour was satisfied; he had had his grudge fight.

And there the matter rests for the moment. But I am uneasy. I feel as if I am living on the top of an active volcano. I'm sure that at any moment Ordinary Seaman Sweeney will succumb to the temptation and pinch another of Morris's ends. I know he'll do it again. Shall I implore N.A.A.F.I. to make their sausages without skins, or should I draft both Sweeney and Morris away for a gunnery course?

I don't know . . . I can't think. Who'd be a First Lieutenant?

Alan Vale

<h1 style="text-align:center">24</h1>

THE END IN AFRICA

After the battle of El Alamein, Rommel was driven in precipitate retreat west-wards for the last time, his army in ruins. Thanks to halts in the pursuit occasioned by breaks in the weather, the Eighth Army out-running its transport and supplies, and its commander's skill in delaying tactics, the Afrika Korps escaped encircle-ment and annihilation. By the end of November 1942 the British stood once more at El Agheila.

Rommel Retreats

WITH the Afrika Korps broken through between 15 and 21 Panzer Divisions and no more reserves left, I gave orders—with a heavy heart, because of the German and Italian formations still on the march—for the withdrawal to Mersa Matruh.

When the orders were out, we too, moved off. It was a wild helter-skelter drive through another pitch-black night. Occasional Arab villages loomed up and dropped behind us in the darkness, and several vehicles lost contact with the head of the column. Finally, we halted in a small valley to wait for daylight. At that time it was still a matter of doubt as to whether we would be able to get even the remnants of the army away to the west. Our fighting power was very low. The bulk of the Italian infantry had been lost. Of XXI Corps, part had been destroyed after a stiff resistance against the overwhelmingly superior British, and part had been overtaken in its retreat and taken prisoner; the vehicles which we had repeatedly demanded for them from the Italian Supply H.Q. had not arrived. X Italian Corps was on the march south-east of Fuka, short of water and ammunition, and, to be quite frank, with no hope of escaping to the west. Of the formations only the transport échelons were on the coast road, choking it with their traffic as they slowly trickled west. There was little we could do to get order into the columns; it would have taken time and all we had to do was to get the move over as quickly as possible.

. . . . Conditions on the road were indescribable. Columns in complete disorder—partly of German, partly of Italian vehicles—choked the road between the minefields. Rarely was there any movement forward and then everything soon jammed up again. Many vehicles were on tow and there was an acute shortage of petrol, for the retreat had considerably increased consumption.

Meanwhile, our columns were steadily streaming westwards and were now approaching Sollum. In the afternoon the Italian General Gandin appeared on behalf of Marshal Cavallero to enquire about our situation and plans. This suited me very well. I gave him a detailed account of the battle, laying particular stress on the effects of the supply crisis and the Führer's and Duce's order. I told him point-blank that with the present balance of forces there was not a chance of our

607

making a stand anywhere, and that the British could keep on going right through to Tripolitania, if they chose to. We could never accept battle, but would have to confine ourselves to trying to delay the British long enough to allow our columns, in which the utmost confusion reigned, to get across the Libyan frontier. There could be no attempt to restore any semblance of order until they arrived in Libya, because so long as they were this side of the frontier they were in constant danger of being cut off. Speed, therefore, was the one thing that mattered. We could attempt no operation with our remaining armour and motorized forces because of the petrol shortage; every drop that reached us had to be used for getting our troops out. Gandin left my H.Q. visibly shaken.

During that day*, we succeeded in forming a fairly firm front and beat off all enemy attacks. Although the enemy must have been aware of our weakness, he still continued to operate with great caution. All German troops everywhere, and some of the Italian units, made a very disciplined and good impression and appeared to be firmly in the hands of their officers. It was a personal blow to every man to have to give up all this territory we had conquered with such high hopes during the summer.

Rommel

Pursuit

Reveille would be at 5.30 a.m.; at six would come the order 'Prepare to Move'; five minutes later, 'Move'. A dim red light glowed on the Navigator's vehicle, and the rest would follow it. Soon there would be a little light; at 7.15 a.m. the chilly sun would pop into the sky; then there would be a halt, and the order 'Brew up!' A hundred little petrol fires would spring into being, and there would be a delicious breakfast of sausages, bacon, biscuits, marmalade and tea. While it was preparing, everyone would wash and shave in a mugful of water each. Off again, faster now with the advantages of daylight, the morning still crisp like a woodcock day at home, the Battalion's vehicles fanning out wide, now that they could see each other; halt and brew-up at noon, halt and brew-up again just before dark; and then five miles on a slightly different course, in case the enemy might make an intelligent guess at the location of the laager. Then the Navigator would flash 'Halt!' on his red light, the convoy would pull up, everyone would climb stiffly from his place, his face rigid with its mask of dust; and each would dig his slit trench. By half-past eight, all would be asleep except for the sentries.

Bernard Fergusson

General Montgomery to General Sir Alan Brooke: 10 November

What saved him from complete annihilation was the rain; I had nearly reached Matruh and was getting in behind all his transport when torrential rain turned the desert into a bog, and I had two armoured divisions . . . bogged and unable to move.

* 6 November (Ed.)

Mines

Nightly and gingerly our line was advanced, until the original No Man's Land of five thousand yards had shrunk by more than half.

It was here that the British made their first acquaintance with a new and nauseating type of anti-personnel mine—the 'S' mine. The Germans had little expected defeat at Alamein, but when it had come upon them they realized that the door at Agheila must be not only shut but bolted against the inevitable pursuit. That pursuit had developed quickly; and elaborate mining was the quickest means of putting the Agheila position into a state of defence. They used mines as standing patrols; to deny the use of observation posts; and to make all movement difficult and costly. The whole area was a minefield, with 'S' mines everywhere. This pestilent device leaped six feet in the air when it was set off, flinging a shower of metal in all directions, and causing casualties many feet away.

They had been laid with cunning and imagination. One night a truck-load of Middlesex hit an anti-tank mine at a point in the road where there was a deep crater. The survivors, jumping clear, found themselves in an 'S' minefield, and were killed. During the night some Camerons sent out a patrol to bring in the bodies; they were fired on, they took cover in the crater, they found it full of mines and six of them were killed. Once more the Camerons tried, but this time the Germans had attached 'S' mines to the bodies, and three more lives were lost. That particular spot is said to have cost thirty-six lives before it was finally cleared.

Bernard Fergusson

TORCH

While in early November the Eighth Army was beginning its drive to victory, a vast Anglo-American armada had set sail from Gibraltar, bound for the North African coast. 'Operation Torch', under the command of General Eisenhower, was designed to win the whole of North-west Africa from French Morocco to Tunisia, as yet occupied only by the Vichy French. Thus the Allies would obtain control of the southern Mediterranean shore, which could be a jumping-off point for future operations against Southern Europe, and also take Rommel on two sides.

It was hoped that the French in North Africa would be led peacefully into the Allied camp by General Giraud.

Because of the earnest belief held in both London and Washington that General Giraud could lead the French of North Africa into the Allied camp, we had started negotiations in October, through Mr. Murphy, to rescue the General from virtual imprisonment in southern France. An elaborate plan was devised by some of our French friends and Mr. Murphy, who had returned to Africa after his visit to London. General Giraud was kept informed of developments through trusted intermediaries and at the appointed time reached the coastline in spite of the watchfulness of the Germans and the Vichyites. There he embarked in a small boat, in the dark of night, to keep a rendezvous with one of our submarines, lying just offshore. A British submarine, commanded for this one trip by Captain Jerauld Wright of the United States Navy, made a most difficult contact with General Giraud and put out to sea. At another appointed place the submarine met one of our flying boats, and the General, with but three personal aides and staff officers, flew to my headquarters during the afternoon of 7 November. The incident, related thus briefly, was an exciting story of extraordinary daring and resolution.

General Giraud, though dressed in civilian clothes, looked very much a soldier. He was well over six feet, erect, almost stiff in carriage, and abrupt in speech and mannerisms. He was a gallant, if bedraggled figure, and his experiences of the war, including a long term of imprisonment and a dramatic escape, had not daunted his fighting spirit.

It was quickly apparent that he had come out of France labouring under the grave misapprehension that he was immediately to assume command of the whole Allied expedition. Upon entering my dungeon, he offered himself to me in that capacity. I could not accept his services in such a role. I wanted him to proceed to Africa, as soon as we could guarantee his safety, and there take over command of such French forces as would voluntarily rally to him. Above all things, we were anxious to have him on our side because of the constant fear at the back of our minds of becoming engaged in a prolonged and serious battle against Frenchmen, not only to our own sorrow and loss, but to the detriment of our campaign against the Germans.

General Giraud was adamant; he believed that the honour of himself and his country was involved and that he could not possibly accept any position in the venture lower than that of complete command. This, on the face of it, was impossible. The naming of an Allied Commander-in-Chief is an involved process, requiring the co-ordinated agreement of military and political leaders of the responsible Governments. No subordinate commander in the expedition could legally have accepted an order from General Giraud. Moreover, at that moment there was not a single Frenchman in the Allied Command; on the contrary, the enemy, if any, was French.

All this was laboriously explained to the general. He was shaken, disappointed, and after many hours of conference felt it necessary to decline to have any part in the scheme. He said, 'General Giraud cannot accept a subordinate position in this command; his countrymen would not understand and his honour as a soldier would be tarnished.' It was pitiful, because he had left his whole family in France as potential hostages to German fury and had himself undergone great personal risks in order to join up with us.

. . . . The conversation with General Giraud lasted, intermittently, until after midnight. Though I could understand General Giraud's French fairly well, I insisted on using an interpreter, to avoid any chance of misunderstanding. When we had worn out more expert ones, General Clark volunteered to act in this capacity, and though he is far from fluent in the language, we made out fairly well. One reason for this was that after the first hour of talk each of us merely repeated, over and over again, the arguments he had first presented. When, finally, General Giraud went off to bed there was no sign of his modifying, in any degree, his original demands. His good-night statement was: 'Giraud will be a spectator in this affair.' He agreed, however, to meet me at the Governor's house the next morning. The political faces in our headquarters that night were long.

Fortunately a night's sleep did something to change General Giraud's mind, and at the next morning's meeting he decided to participate on the basis we desired. I promised that if he were successful in winning French support I would deal with him as the administrator of that region, pending eventual opportunity for civil authorities to determine the will of the population.

General Eisenhower

On 8 November the Allied landings began; at Casablanca in French Morocco, and at Oran and Algiers. There were British units among the forces going ashore at Algiers, but the Americans played a predominant part in 'Torch', and it was they who were mainly involved in the heavy fighting which took place with the French at Oran and Casablanca. Unlike their comrades in the Pacific, these men had never seen battle before, but they were to be blooded and were to vindicate themselves on the battlefields of Africa and Europe. General George S. Patton was in command of the forces landing around Casablanca.

First Battlefield

In Africa, for the first time I saw the loneliest and most ominous of all landscapes, a battlefield. And I knew for the first time that strange exhilaration that grips a man when he knows that somewhere out there in the distance hostile eyes are watching him and that at any moment a bullet he may never hear, fired by an enemy he cannot see, may strike him.

General Matthew B. Ridgway

Our first battle contact report was disappointing. The U.S.S. *Thomas Stone*, proceeding in convoy towards Algiers and carrying a reinforced battalion of American troops, was torpedoed on 7 November, only a hundred and fifty miles from its destination. Details were lacking and there existed the possibility of a very considerable loss of life. Though our good fortune to this point had been amazing, this did not lessen our anxiety for the men aboard. We could get no further information of her fate that evening, but later we learned that the incident had a happy outcome so far as the honour of American arms was concerned. Casualties were few and the ship itself was not badly damaged. There was no danger of sinking. Yet officers and men, unwilling to wait quietly until the ship could be towed to a convenient port, cheered the decision of the commander to take to the boats in an attempt to reach, on time, the assault beach to which they were assigned. Heavy weather, making up during the afternoon, foiled their gallant purpose and they had to be taken aboard destroyers and other escort vessels, but they were finally placed ashore some twelve hours behind schedule. Fortunately the absence of these troops had no appreciable effect upon our plans.

General Eisenhower

CASABLANCA: 7 NOVEMBER

Fedala

Midnight. The stars are out, but it's dark as hell on deck. The *Ancon*'s engines are down to a slow throb. According to the timetable we should be easing into the transport area preparatory to going over the side. Elements of 3 Division are lining up at their deck stations adjacent to the disembarkation nets. All very orderly. They seem to know where to go and what to do. They are going over the side now. The technique seems to be to step up on a stanchion and back-climb over the rail. Weighted down with sixty-five pounds of equipment exclusive of steel helmet and tommy-gun, it is something of a trick. A landing net is a mean piece of equipment. With the outward roll of the ship it swings clear. That is fine. You can get your hands and feet into the rungs. The inboard roll is something else again. The net flattens hard against the ship's side, reducing finger and toe holds to next to nothing.

.... A steel helmet well heated by the subtropical sun, a slippery tommy-gun, a saturated uniform, trench coat, and full infantry pack are not conducive to speed, but it didn't take us long to scramble up the dune to the crest tufted with coarse grass. Beyond and behind its comforting protection stretched a wide field. It presented a curious appearance. Standing and sitting in small groups, the French officers and coal-black enlisted men of the Fedala garrison. Their rifles were stacked in neat array and most of them were smoking *jaunes*.

'What outfit is this?' we asked a French captain.

'102nd Company of the Sixth R.T.C.' (*Régiment de Tirailleurs Sénégalais*.) 'We came over to your side right after H-hour,' he said pleasantly.

'Is the whole garrison here?'

'No, some of them have gone back to the barracks.' He pointed to a row of low wooden buildings at the edge of the town.

'Fedala is yours,' said the French captain.

'In that case, what is all the shooting for?'

'Doubtless the Marine battery of seventy-fives out on the end of Cap Fedala. It's a pity, but you know how it is——' he shrugged—'our Navy has always had less comprehension than the Army.'

Two small Arab boys loped up. Smiling eyes, extended palms, they had not yet acquired the cigarette, chewing-gum refrain. It was still early.

The French captain shooed them away. He was most co-operative, but he didn't really know anything. The landing, he said, had been a complete surprise. Besides the Senegalese garrison, the only French troops in the town itself were three or four Renault tanks in charge of a Lieutenant Lefèvre, whose heart, it seemed, was in the right place. He had, the captain said, greeted our first assault wave as it landed and had delayed the giving of the alarm by at least an hour. Yes, General Noguès—the Resident-General in French Morocco—had given the order to resist, and undoubtedly reserves would be arriving from Rabat and Meknes. Meantime the French Navy, in charge of all coastal defences, are going all out.

'It is fantastic, but there it is,' the French captain said.

'And the German Armistice Commission?' Colonel Ratay asked.

'The Fedala contingent, fifteen of them, have been quartered at the hotel for some months. *Assez correctes, mais de sales types au fond.*'

Colonel Charles Codman

Confusion

Swell had been increasing during the day, and we landed about 15.00 in a pounding surf. My jeep was embedded in heavy sand within a few yards of the water's edge, and there it was to remain all night. There was much confusion on the beach, for craft destined for Green Beach were also landing on Blue. The soft, powdery sand, much worse than we had anticipated, was causing trouble. The wire netting and burlap roadways on the sand across the dunes were already ruined by traffic, but the engineers were building others and reconnoitring for better routes. Some landing craft had broached to in the surf and had been abandoned by their crews. Some weapons and equipment had been dumped into the surf, but everywhere men were working.

At the beach command post, marked only by a staff displaying the Blue Beach flag and lantern and the antenna of the beachmaster's radio, little was known of the situation inland and nothing of the situation on other beaches. There were rumours of heavy fighting inland, and a non-commissioned officer from McCarley's battalion was somewhere on the beach looking for tanks. We could barely see the transports at sea. They were beyond the range of the beachmaster's signal lamps and even his radio. However, I wrote a message to be sent off to Carleton and the Commodore when it might be possible, and went inland to learn how things were going.

In the staff half-track, we followed the trace of the 1st Battalion. Passing two light tanks and a tank destroyer on the way, we took them along. One of the tank gunners almost ended my career right then and there. When I told them to load and to follow me, one of the gunners fired an accidental burst from a machine-gun that missed my head by a hair's breadth. On the ridge just east of the southern end of the lagoon, we found McCarley's rear command post with his executive officer, Major Otto Koch, in charge. There, also, was part of Company A and part of the Regimental anti-tank company, which had established the road blocks along the Rabat Road to protect the flank. There had been fighting along the Rabat Road during the afternoon—French infantry and tanks had overrun our road blocks. Some few men had straggled in, but the company commander was missing. However, most of the company were there and in position with anti-tank guns, and Major Koch had sent to the beach for tanks. I left the two light tanks and the tank destroyer with him, and set off to find McCarley.

Leaving Bond and Netterbald with the command half-track struggling to establish radio communication with the ship and with the other battalions, Conway, Southworth and I set off on foot along McCarley's telephone line. After an hour's rugged going through the dense woods along the ridge east of the lagoon, with naval gunfire cracking overhead and the distant crash of bursting shells and clatter of machine-guns to keep us company, we found McCarley.

He had not reached the south end of the lagoon until 11.00, and his progress northward had been slow. He had been held up by machine-gun fire from along the road to the east, and had only located the source a short while before. A skirmish was in progress in that direction, and artillery shells were crashing in the woods beyond.

McCarley had not yet made contact with the 2nd Battalion, but we could hear sounds of firing along the ridge to the north not more than a mile distant. It was now almost six o'clock and the day was nearly done. I told McCarley to make contact with the 2nd Battalion during the night and to advance at daylight the next morning on the airfield. Company A would have to remain where it was to protect the south flank until I could get Semmes and his armour there, but I would send the Provisional Assault Company up to him during the night so that he would have some reserve at least. McCarley and others whom I had encountered were all in good spirits even though our plans were behind schedule.

It was nearly dark when we had retraced our steps and reached the staff car. Our radio had not been able to contact anyone. French infantry and tanks were still in the woods along the Rabat Road, and I was fearful of an attack from that direction. Stopping only to send the Provisional Assault Company to join McCarley, and to warn Major Koch of the danger, we went on to the beach. Our half-track could not negotiate the steep slope of the sand dunes in the darkness. Leaving it with Bond in charge, Conway, Netterbald and I set off on foot once more.

At the beach command post, all was dark and silent. There was only a sleepy operator listening for radio signals which he could not hear. No officers were about, but all around men were sleeping the profound sleep of exhaustion. Figures were stumbling about the beach and sand dunes in the darkness. There, shouts and oaths and calls of 'George' and 'Patton'. And there was roaring surf. But I had to find Semmes and his tanks. Sending Conway to the north and Netterbald to the south to find him, I sat down on the sand dune to wait.

When their figures disappeared into the gloom it came to me that even with hundreds all around me I was utterly alone. And I had to stay just where I was, or they would never find me when they returned with Semmes. Out to sea, much closer than when we had come ashore, signal lamps were flashing among the ships. As far as I could see along the beach, there was chaos. Landing craft were beaching in the pounding surf, broaching to the waves, and spilling men and equipment into the water. Men wandered about aimlessly, hopelessly lost, calling to each other and for their units, swearing at each other and at nothing. There was no beach party or shore party anywhere in sight. And I was chilled. Not a light could I see on shore except the dim blue lantern under which I sat. I was lonely. More than anything else right then I wanted a cigarette. There had been no enemy aircraft since early morning. A cigarette on shore could be no more dangerous than those flashing lights at sea. I lit one. In a matter of moments I was glad when other glows appeared as other lonely and uncertain men sought the comfort of tobacco. They would have been surprised to know that the Commanding General had been the first to violate the blackout order.

I was sitting there with my cigarette half smoked wondering what I was going to do next and how, when out of the gloom from the shore appeared a strange-looking figure, approaching with uncertain steps, and peering nervously from side to side. He stopped in front of me and in alien accents addressed me: 'Heyyuh, gimme a cigarette.' I handed him one from the package I held. He spoke again: 'Goddam. All wet. Gimme a light too.' I extended the lighted end of my cigarette. As he put it to his face, Conway appeared on one side, Semmes the other, both thrust tommy-guns into his midriff, and Conway challenged 'George'. And the response was instantaneous: 'George? George, hell. Me no George. My name Lee, Cook, Company C, 540th Engineers.'

General L. K. Truscott

First Sight of Patton

Near the embankment an infantryman, his tommy-gun beside him, lay face downward on the sand. With a speed surprising in so large a man, the tall figure raced to the recumbent soldier, snatched up his tommy-gun, and leaning over him, shouted, 'Yea-a-h.'

The soldier half turned over, shielding his face with his arms. 'Go 'way and lemme sleep,' he said.

'Yea-a-h.'

The barrel of his own tommy-gun was boring insistently into the pit of his stomach as the soldier decided to open his eyes. His glance climbed slowly up the cavalry boots, the wet trouser leg, the pearl-handled revolver, the deep-chested torso. Behind the butt of the tommy-gun, grey eyes blazing from an inexorable face surmounted by the dripping helmet with its two stars.

'Jesus,' he said simply.

Stepping back, General Patton examined the lock of the tommy-gun. O.K. 'Get up, boy,' he said gently.

The soldier scrambled to his feet, swaying uncertainly.

'Are you hurt?' the General said.

'No, sir.'

'I know you're tired,' the General said. 'We're all tired. That makes no difference.'

He put his hand on the man's shoulder. 'The next beach you land on will be defended by Germans. I don't want one of them coming up behind you and hitting you over the head with a sockful of silt.' Only that was not quite the word he used.

The man grinned.

'Here's your gun.' The sharpness returned to the General's voice. 'Now, get going.'

General Giraud's attempts to rally the French to the Allied cause had been a complete failure, but by chance, Admiral Darlan, Commander-in-Chief of all the Vichy French fighting forces, was present in Algiers at the moment of the invasion. Every Frenchman in North Africa obeyed him, as the representative of Marshal Pétain. He was won over, and the problem of French co-operation was solved. Darlan ordered a cease-fire, and on 13 November an armistice was concluded. The sequel both for him and for his Government was unfortunate, for he was assassinated eleven days later, and the infuriated Germans occupied Vichy France. But in North Africa, the armed forces of France joined the Allies.

Capitulation at Casablanca

General Keyes looks at his watch. His face is impassive, but around his eyes there are lines of strain.

The hum of engines. Louder. Streaking across the sky directly overhead a squadron of fighter planes. Colonel Lauris Norstad's P-40s from Port Lyautey. Out at sea a glint of wings—the Navy bombers taking off from the *Ranger*. Twelve miles distant the sleeping city of Casablanca, under whose white roofs half a million souls lie mercifully unconscious of the terrible engines of destruction closing in on them from the land, the sea, and the air.

Colonel Hammond's walkie-talkie comes to life. '3 Division C.P.?' 'Yes. Just a minute.' He hands the receiver to General Keyes.

'That you, Geoff?' The sharp, incisive voice of General Patton.

'Yes, sir.'

'Call it off. The French Navy has capitulated. Ratay has just been here. You are still in touch with Hewitt?'

'Yes, sir.'

'Good, but you'll have to work fast.'

At General Patton's first words a vigorous nod from General Keyes to Hammond, and a second radio set is already crackling its message across the water. Aboard the *Augusta* Admiral Hewitt and his staff get busy. Very busy indeed.

Outside the Casa breakwater the covering group, big guns elevated, is now plainly visible. Over the city the Navy bombers circle and circle and circle. The seconds and minutes tick off. No one speaks. Without warning the leading bomber banks and peels off. The next, the next, as the circle dissolves into a long serpentine line headed for the open sea, where the *Ranger* is poking up into the wind to receive them. Once again the roar of engines over our heads as our P-40s hit the trail for home, dipping their wings to show they have understood.

General Keyes lowers his field-glasses and with his handkerchief carefully wipes the lenses. Before starting down the stairs from the roof, he takes a last look in the direction of Casablanca.

'Thank God,' he says.

.... Shortly before three o'clock General Patton ordered a guard of honour drawn up before the hotel entrance. At the prescribed hour a black limousine with motor-cycle outrider swept up the drive. Out of it got General Noguès, trim, erect, ascetic, rather Spanish in appearance. He walked smartly up the steps, followed by General Lascroux, the compact, stoutish Commander of the Ground Forces, and General Lahoulle, Chief of the French Air Forces, whose genial, forthright aspect made an immediately favourable impression.

At the top of the steps they were met by General Keyes, who escorted them to the smoking-room, where General Patton received them.

A preliminary conference attended by Admirals Hewitt and Hall had taken place with the French Admirals, Michelier and Ronarch. Matters concerning the ports had been discussed. Michelier had been *pincé* and difficult, but thawed out more or less when Admiral Hewitt offered to shake hands.

General Patton now opened the full *séance* by expressing his admiration for the courage and skill shown by the French armed forces during the three days of battle.

'We are now met to come to terms,' he said. 'Here they are.'

As the conditions of Treaty C were read aloud and the full import of their stringency began to sink in, the faces of the French grew more and more sombre. At the end there was a strained silence, then General Noguès arose. 'Permit me to point out,' he said, 'that if these terms are enforced it means the end of the French Protectorate in Morocco.'

In the discussion which followed it became apparent that while Treaty C as drawn might reasonably be applied to a civilian set-up such as exists in Algeria, its literal enforcement here would virtually cancel the responsibility of the French Military Protectorate to maintain law and order in Morocco. If, as provided by the treaty, the French forces are disarmed and disbanded, to us will fall the entire task not only of preserving order among seven million Arabs and Berbers, but of securing the Spanish Zone frontier, the port of Casablanca, and the long and vulnerable lines of communication to far off Tunisia—now our immediate goal. Communications with General Eisenhower in Gibraltar and with General Clark in Algiers are nil. General Patton is on his own.

It did not take him long to decide. Rising to his full height, he picked up the familiar typescript of Treaty C and tore it into small strips.

'Gentlemen,' he said, 'I had the pleasure of serving with your armed forces throughout two years of World War One. Needless to say, I have implicit faith in the word of honour of a French officer. If each of you in this room gives me his word of honour that there will be no further firing on American troops and ships, you may retain your arms and carry on as before—but under my orders. You will do thus and so. We will do this and that. Agreed?'

It was.

'There is, however, an additional condition upon which I must insist.'

The faces of the French delegation, which had brightened considerably, lengthened.

'It is this,' General Patton said, signalling one of his aides, 'that you join me in a glass of champagne.'

Colonel Charles Codman

THE RACE FOR TUNIS

Meanwhile the Germans, fully alive to the dangers to them inherent in 'Torch', were unwilling to cut their losses. They began desperately to feed troops and equipment into Tunisia, as yet unoccupied by Allied forces, beginning only one day after the latters' landings farther west. The race for control of Tunisia was on, but the British 1 Army, under General Anderson, struggling eastwards towards the ports of Tunis and Bizerta, possession of which would strangle Rommel, was hampered by small numbers, appalling communications and constant, heavy German air attacks.

First contact with German troops was made on 17 November, and on the 28th the British were in sight of Tunis, but they were too late and too weak. By the end of November the Germans had fifteen thousand men in Tunisia; a force which was trebled a month later. On 1 December they were able to repulse the British advance, and further Allied attacks bogged down in the mud of winter. The force of their blow was spent, and Tunisia was held for the Axis.

Rommel Meets Hitler: November

There was a noticeable chill in the atmosphere from the outset. I described all the difficulties which the army had had to face during both the battle and the retreat. It was all noted and the execution of the operation was described as faultless and unique.

Unfortunately, I then came too abruptly to the point and said that, since experience indicated that no improvement in the shipping situation could now be expected, the abandonment of the African theatre of war should be accepted as a long-term policy. There should be no illusions about the situation and all planning should be directed towards what was attainable. If the army remained in North Africa, it would be destroyed.

I had expected a rational discussion of my arguments and intended to develop them in a great deal more detail. But I did not get as far, for the mere mention of the strategic question worked like a spark in a powder barrel. The Führer flew into a fury and directed a stream of completely unfounded attacks upon us. Most of the F.H.Q. staff officers present, the majority of whom had never heard a shot fired in anger, appeared to agree with every word the Führer said. In illustration of our difficulties I mentioned the fact that only five thousand of the fifteen thousand fighting troops of the Afrika Korps and 90 Light Division had weapons, the remainder being completely unarmed. This provoked a violent outburst in which we were accused, among other things, of having thrown our arms away. I protested strongly against charges of this kind, and said in straight terms that it was impossible to judge the weight of the battle from here in Europe. Our weapons had simply been battered to pieces by the British bombers, tanks and artillery and it was nothing short of a miracle that we had been able to escape with all the German motorized forces, especially in view of the desperate petrol shortage, which had allowed us to retreat at a rate of only tens of kilometres a day. I stated that all other armies would suffer the same fate if the Americans ever succeeded in setting foot on the Continent.

But there was no attempt at discussion. The Führer said that his decision to hold the eastern front in the winter of 1941–42 had saved Russia and that there, too, he had upheld his orders ruthlessly. I began to realize that Adolf Hitler simply did not want to see the situation as it was, and that he reacted emotionally against what his intelligence must have told him was right. He said that it was a political necessity to continue to hold a major bridgehead in Africa and there would, therefore, be no withdrawal from the Mersa el Brega* line. He would do everything possible to get supplies to me.

Rommel

* Before El Agheila (Ed.)

Allied Supply Difficulties

Supply was the absorbing problem in every headquarters in North Africa. There was still a dearth of service troops and transportation. Few units in North Africa yet had their full scale of motor transportation. The single rail line eastward from Oran and Algiers had suffered from neglect, and there was a shortage of locomotives and rolling stock. The two principal roads east from Algiers, one along the coast and the principal highway farther inland, although paved, were not in good repair; and both traversed rugged, mountainous terrain with steep grades and turns and many bridges. British supplies and equipment destined for Tunisia came for the most part from Algiers and the small ports of Bone and Philippeville. Oran was the principal American port and base. French supplies and equipment came in part from local sources, the remainder from British and American stocks. So critical was the problem of supply that the loss of a single truck was almost a tragedy, the destruction of a bridge or locomotive a catastrophe of concern even to the high command. And the Germans were employing agents already in the country and others dropped by parachute to sabotage this tenuous line of communications.

Reinforcements in men and material were arriving as rapidly as shipping permitted, but the only troops immediately available to reinforce the front were the American 1 Armoured and 1 and 34 Infantry Divisions. Both of the latter were for the most part scattered in small detachments protecting airfields and critical points on the line of communications.

General Truscott

The Race Lost

Clark and I found Anderson beyond Souk-Ahras, and forward of that place we entered a zone where all around us was evidence of incessant and hard fighting. Every conversation along the roadside brought out astounding exaggerations. 'Beja has been bombed to rubble.' 'No one can live on this next stretch of road.' 'Our troops will surely have to retreat: humans cannot exist in these conditions.' Yet on the whole morale was good. The exaggerations were nothing more than the desire of the individual to convey the thought that he had been through the ultimate in terror and destruction—he had no thought of clearing out himself.

Troops and commanders were not experienced, but the boldness, courage, and stamina of General Anderson's forces could not have been exceeded by the most battle-wise veterans. Physical conditions were almost unendurable. The mud deepened daily, confining all operations to the roads, long stretches of which practically disintegrated. Winter cold was already descending upon the Tunisian highlands. The bringing up of supplies and ammunition was a Herculean task. In spite of all this, and in spite of Anderson's lack of strength—his whole force numbered only about three brigades of infantry and a brigade of obsolescent tanks—he pushed on through Souk-el-Khemis, Beja, and finally reached a point from which he could look down into the outskirts of Tunis.

. . . . Courage, resourcefulness and endurance, though daily displayed in overwhelming measure, could not completely overcome the combination of enemy, weather and terrain. In early December the enemy was strong enough in mechanized units to begin local but sharp counter-attacks and we were forced back from our most forward positions in front of Tunis.

As soon as we ceased attacking, the situation in northern Tunisia turned bleak for us, even from a defensive standpoint. Through a blunder during a local withdrawal we had lost the bulk of the equipment of Combat Command B, of 1 Armoured Division. The 18th Infantry of the U.S. 1 Infantry Division took severe losses, and practically an entire battalion of a fine British regiment was wiped out. General Anderson soon thought he would have to give up Medjez-el-Bab, a road centre and a junction point with the French forces on his right. Since this spot was the key to our resumption of the offensive when we should get the necessary strength, I forbade this move—assuming personal responsibility for the fate of its garrison and the effect of its possible capture upon the safety of the command.

We were still attempting to mount an attack of our own. Work continued twenty-four hours a day to build up the strength that we believed would, with some temporary improvement in the weather, give us a good fighting chance to capture north-eastern Tunisia before all operations were hopelessly bogged down. 24 December was chosen as the date for our final and most ambitious attack. Our great hope for success lay in our temporary advantage in artillery, which was relatively great. But reports from the Tunisian front were discouraging; the weather, instead of improving, continued to deteriorate. Prospects for mounting another attack grew darker.

I was determined not to give up unless personally convinced that the attack was an impossibility. Weather prohibited flying and I started forward by automobile on 22 December, encountering miserable road conditions from the moment we left Algiers. Travelling almost incessantly, I met General Anderson at his headquarters in the early morning of 24 December, and with him proceeded at once to Souk-el-Khemsi. At that point was located the headquarters of the British V Corps, which was to make the attack and which was commanded by Major-General C. W. Allfrey of the British Army. The preliminary moves of the attack had already been made by small detachments, attempting to secure critical points before the beginning of the major manœuvre, scheduled for the following night.

The rain fell constantly. We went out personally to inspect the countryside over which the troops would have to advance, and while doing so I observed an incident which, as much as anything else, I think, convinced me of the hopelessness of an attack. About thirty feet off the road, in a field that appeared to be covered with winter wheat, a motor-cycle had become stuck in the mud. Four soldiers were struggling to extricate it, but in spite of their most strenuous efforts succeeded only in getting themselves mired into the sticky clay. They finally had to give up the attempt and left the motor-cycle more deeply bogged down than when they started.

We went back to headquarters and I directed that the attack be indefinitely postponed.

General Eisenhower

After a pause on the Eighth Army front, Rommel was dislodged from El Agheila on 13 December and was again in full retreat to the west. Tripoli fell on 23 January 1943.

After the capture of the El Agheila position, a staff officer from Eighth Army Headquarters was visiting Benghazi. Here he met a high personage from Cairo. They started talking about the future. The staff officer said, 'The Army Commander hopes to be in Tripoli in five weeks' time.' The reply he got was: 'Oh! that's impossible, we have just approved a Joint Planners' paper which says that a two or three months' pause is required to ensure a safe maintenance situation.'

Major-General Sir Francis de Guingand

The Poor Relations

We had still received no strategic decision from the supreme German and Italian authorities on the future of the African theatre of war. They did not look at things realistically—indeed, they refused to do so. What we found really astonishing was to see the amount of material that they were suddenly able to ship to Tunisia, quantities out of all proportion to anything we had received in the past. The urgency of the danger had at last percolated through to Rome. But the British and Americans had meanwhile multiplied their supply shipments many times over and were steadily increasing their strategic command over sea and air. One Axis ship after the other was going down beneath the waters of the Mediterranean, and it was becoming obvious that even the greatest effort could no longer hope to effect any decisive improvement in the supply situation; we were up to our necks in the mud and no longer had the strength to pull ourselves out.

The mismanagement, the operational blunders, the prejudices, the everlasting search for scapegoats, these were now to reach the acute stage. And the man who paid the price was the ordinary German and Italian soldier.

Rommel

Small Success

During January, a number of our A.A. gunners succeeded in surprising a British column of the Long-Range Desert Group in Tunisia and captured the commander of 1st S.A.S. Regiment, Lieutenant-Colonel David Stirling. Insufficiently guarded, he managed to escape and made his way to some Arabs, to whom he offered a reward if they would get him back to the British lines. But his bid must have been too small, for the Arabs, with their usual eye to business, offered him to us for eleven pounds of tea—a bargain which we soon clinched. Thus the British lost the very able and adaptable commander of the desert group which had caused us more damage than any other British unit of equal strength.

Rommel

28 December 1942

Dearest Lu,

Our fate is gradually working itself out. Supplies have been very short and it would need a miracle for us to hold on much longer. What is to happen now lies in God's hands. We'll go on fighting as long as it's at all possible. I saw this coming when we were last together and discussed the most important things with you.

Rommel

Free French

There was one other formation that was in touch with the enemy—General Leclerc's force. This fine Frenchman had moved his troops from Lake Chad across the desert and gained contact with Eighth Army about the time we arrived at Tripoli. It was a real mixture—a bit of everything. He had Frenchmen and native soldiers, some artillery of various types, an armoured car or two, machine-guns, some oddly assorted transport which by some miracle had made the journey, and even some aircraft. They were short of most things, food, clothes and material; but a wonderful spirit went a long way towards surmounting the deficiencies. I remember my first meeting with Leclerc. I was sitting in my caravan outside Tripoli when he arrived to report. At first I thought one of the characters of Wren's *Beau Geste* had come along to pay a call. His appearance personified the hardened French colonial soldier. He was thin and drawn, but intensely alert. His clothes had long since seen their day. Thin drill uniform with threadbare breeches, and old but shapely riding boots. A French *képi* completed the picture. He told me who he was and from whence he came. He said this just as you might say you had dropped over from the next village to tea. I took him along to the Army Commander, who shook hands and looked him up and down. Leclerc said, 'I place myself and my troops under your command.' Montgomery then said he accepted the offer, and told me to discuss with the French General details of his co-operation and matters affecting material and supplies. Later Montgomery told me,.'I can make use of that chap.'

Major-General Sir Francis de Guingand

THE CASABLANCA CONFERENCE

In the middle of January 1943 Winston Churchill and President Roosevelt met at Casablanca to discuss further strategy. It was agreed that after Tunisia had been won, the next Allied blow should fall on Europe itself: Sicily was to be invaded. The date of the cross-Channel invasion of Western Europe was fixed for 1944. At the same conference, unconditional surrender of the Axis powers was proclaimed as the war aim of the Allies; a declaration which was used by the Germans as propaganda to stiffen the resistance of their armies.

Unconditional Surrender

We propose to draw up a statement of the work of the conference for communication to the Press at the proper time. I should be glad to know what the War Cabinet would think of our including in this statement a declaration of the

firm intention of the United States and the British Empire to continue the war
relentlessly until we have brought about the 'unconditional surrender' of Germany and Japan. The omission of Italy would be to encourage a break-up there.
The President liked this idea, and it would stimulate our friends in every
country.

Winston Churchill, 20 January

We, the United Nations, demand from the Nazi, Fascist and Japanese
tyrannies unconditional surrender. By this we mean that their willpower to
resist must be completely broken, and that they must yield themselves absolutely to our justice and mercy. It also means that we must take all those far-
sighted measures which are necessary to prevent the world from being again
convulsed, wrecked and blackened by their calculated plots and ferocious
aggressions It does not mean, and it never can mean, that we are to stain our
victorious arms by inhumanity or by mere lust of vengeance, or that we do not
plan a world in which all branches of the human family may look forward to
what the American Declaration of Independence finely calls 'life, liberty, and
the pursuit of happiness'.

Winston Churchill, 30 June 1943

The Allied demand for unconditional surrender and the persistent claim by
the Allies that Germany must be destroyed (shades of the earlier cry, *'Delenda
est Cartago!'* during the war between Rome and Carthage) reinforced the will
of the German people to fight to the bitter end. The Allies offered no alternative.

General Hasso von Manteuffel

Another Meeting: 4 February 1943

Local note: Fast car driven by nicely turned-out Moroccan in European
clothes is stopped by American M.P. on the main road.
'Pull over to the kerb. Where's the fire?'
The Moroccan takes it calmly.
M.P.: 'Your name?'
Moroccan: 'Sidi Mohammed ben Youssef.'
M.P.: 'Your profession?'
Moroccan: *'Fonctionnaire.'*
M.P.: 'What function?'
Moroccan: 'Sultan of Morocco.'
Tableau.

THE BATTLE FOR TUNISIA

*In Tunisia both sides reinforced for the coming final battle for Africa, strong
American forces and some French units moving in to support 1 Army. In spite of
losing a large proportion of his men and supplies to Allied air and naval forces in the
Mediterranean, Rommel, now in command of all Axis forces in Tunisia, struck first
and struck hard. On 14 February he launched a powerful assault on the Americans*

in the south, his veterans driving back their gallant but unseasoned opponents through the Kasserine Pass, taking Kasserine, Feriana and Sbeitla, and threatening Tebessa.

Kasserine: 14 February

About half-past ten that night, I telephoned the Corps G-3 to ask if there was any further information about the tank battle which had been reported as imminent shortly before dark. I was told that it had apparently been only a reconnaissance as the German tanks had withdrawn to the east.

All seemed relative quiet, so I turned in about half-past eleven. But I was not to sleep for long. At one o'clock in the morning, General Fredendall telephoned, and my records show:

Fredendall reported that German tanks were fighting on edge of Sbeitla; estimates gave them eighty-nine tanks—eighty Mark IVs and nine Mark VIs. Apparently had pierced covering position five kilometres east of Sbeitla, which had been established along the line: Djebel Koumin (?)—south slope Djebel Mrhila, and had attacked in the moonlight. Considered situation extremely grave, and uncertain of ability to hold. If kicked off Sbeitla, the Thelepte-Feriana position exposed as well as valley towards Maktar. Said he had talked to McNabb earlier and had asked to be allowed to withdraw to high ground but had been refused. Said he had not reported present situation to McNabb yet.

Directed him to report situation to McNabb and let me know result.

Said Ward had just reported situation in person. Ward considered situation grave—but was doing best he could.

I had barely finished talking with General Fredendall when a message from Carleton reported that tanks were fighting in the moonlight in Sbeitla, and were all around Ward's command post. Ward was determined to fight it out there. He was uncertain of the outcome, but could not withdraw then if he wanted to do so.

At half-past one General Fredendall telephoned again:

Fredendall reported that McNabb had authorized him to withdraw. Orders had been sent as follows:

To Colonel Moore at Kasserine with one battalion 26th Infantry, four companies 19th Engineers, four 37 mm. guns, two 75 mm. guns of Cannon Company, reinforced by one company of medium tanks and 805th Tank Destroyer Battalion (less company) from Stark's command, to hold at all costs along the Oued east of Kasserine for a minimum of at least twelve hours. When forced to withdraw, to withdraw to the north and hold Kasserine Pass.

Armoured Division to move north through Kasserine Pass in direction of Thala.

Stark to pull in covering force to hold main ridge line at Feriana, leave covering force of one company infantry, one battery artillery, one company light tanks. Take remainder of command including French to ridge north of Thelepte airdrome.

Williams (Air Support Commander) informed of situation, making arrangements to remove aircraft from Thelepte at daylight.

Ward reported tank battle east edge of Sbeitla himself. Uncertain of ability to hold. Was not breaking off battle at Sbeitla because he could not if he would. He fears we have lost 1 Armoured Division.

Fredendall feels that 1 Army has not given credit to his reports as to gravity of situation.

Towards morning, there was another message from Carleton. The German attack had apparently been beaten off at Sbeitla, but there was still firing. He would report when he could find what the situation actually was.

And a message from Conway at Feriana. His radio operator had roused him from sleep to inform him that everyone had pulled out of Feriana. The headquarters was gone. He would follow and report when he could find it.

Just at daylight another message from Conway reported that our people on the airfield at Thelepte were destroying airplanes and burning fuel and other supplies. Roads were crowded with vehicles but the troops were establishing themselves on the ridge north of the airfield.

Those early hours of 17 February had been anxious hours at the Advanced C.P.—and elsewhere.

By now it was obvious even to General Anderson that this was the German offensive which intelligence officers had been so certain was to come through the passes around Fondouk farther to the north. We knew that some of Rommel's Panzer divisions were involved, and there had still been no action anywhere else on the front.

At half-past nine the morning of 17 February, Brigadier McNabb telephoned to say that one brigade of the British 6 Armoured Division with artillery and anti-tank guns had been ordered from the northern sector to Thala, and that 34 Infantry Division on the right of what had been the French sector was to hold the high ground east of Sbiba.

At 10.45, General Fredendall called to report that our troops had withdrawn from Feriana to the ridge north of the airfield at Thelepte, and that our forces were already withdrawing through Kasserine Pass. Ward was to start west at 11.00 to come through Kasserine Pass and take position south of Tebessa. McQuillin was to start at 11.00 but was to delay en route and reach Sbiba at nightfall in order to ensure protection of Ryder's (34 Infantry Division) south flank. Fredendall said, 'There is some confusion, but we are getting along pretty well. We are acting offensively in the air and have air cover over them.'

Fredendall had had another big argument with General Anderson. He said, 'He wanted me to hold all day at Sbeitla, but if I had, it (the armoured division) would have been tangled up in another dogfight. Finally I got him to agree to let me go ahead. They not only want to tell you what to do, but how to do it. Anyway, I think we are going to get our tail out of the door all right.'

Fredendall wanted a battalion of the 18th Field Artillery to replace the one that had lost its guns at Sidi bou Zid and all but some three hundred of its personnel. In answer to my question as to what else he would need, he replied that he was going to survey the situation and take inventory and would let me know. He had already asked for a battalion of tanks. Then he added, 'We are going to have to write Drake and his battalion off. I am going to get a plane over him and tell him to give in. There is no out. He is completely surrounded.'

He had two days' ammunition and two days' rations. He had been out for twenty-four hours. There is no use prolonging the agony. We have got to write him off.'

That was bitter news.

I sent messages to Carleton to report General Ward's plan in full, and to A.F.H.Q. reporting the situation and the sad news about Drake's battalion. More of General Alexander's 18 Army Group were to inform themselves of the situation. And about noon, a staff officer called from Tebessa to say:

'Hello, General Truscott. This is Colonel Arnold. Got a little point. The French railroad people in Tebessa are packing up and evacuating—apparently on orders from their higher headquarters. I wonder if something could be done to cancel this and make them stay here. They are sort of panicking the population here.'

I was hard put to answer that one. I telephoned Whitely at A.F.H.Q. He said he would find someone in authority there to deal with it, and suggested that I get after the line of communications people, both British and French, in Constantine, which I did. Then I reported the matter to Brigadier McNabb at 1 Army, and he replied:

'Yes, we have heard the rumour. I think it is fairly a rumour. I am sorry to say that I think it was started by the British Town Major in the place. I am not quite sure about the French civil. The whole thing has been started by some blasted rumour. I am after the bloke who did it. I think we have got it in hand, but I will make sure again.'

General Eisenhower had A.F.H.Q. actually scraping the bottom of the barrel, but there was little there which would help our hard-pressed troops in the battles then in progress.

General Fredendall telephoned again at half-past one that afternoon (17 February) to appeal for another regimental combat team. As he expressed it:

'I am holding a lot of mountain passes against armour with three and one-half battalions of infantry. If they get together any place a couple of infantry battalions, they might smoke me out. . . . I haven't got a damn bit of reserve. I need a combat team of infantry worse than hell. All I have got are three and one-half battalions of infantry. They are not enough. And we just got a little dope from 1 Army that indications are the enemy is going to continue the attack from Feriana with the objective of taking Tebessa.'

I explained to General Fredendall that the artillery and cannon companies of 9 Infantry Division were on their way, but that even they could not be expected for several days. The rest of the Division was moving, although it would be some time before any of its infantry regiments could reach the forward area. I suggested that he appeal to General Anderson again for infantry to help meet the emergency.

About mid-afternoon, Carleton reported heavy fighting at Sbeitla where our troops had just been attacked by twelve Me.109s. Our people were blowing up ammunition dumps and destroying supplies in preparation for withdrawing. And we had thought the withdrawal was already well under way!

....As it turned out later, Ward had held Sbeitla until three o'clock in the afternoon to cover the withdrawal, and had then withdrawn through Kasserine Pass.

We did succeed in 'getting our tail out of the door' during 17 February, and we were hopeful that the doors—Kasserine Pass and the Feriana Gap—were shut and barred so that we could lick our wounds and repair some of the damage.

On the morning of 18 February, General Fredendall telephoned to say that he wanted one hundred and twenty M-4 tanks, including the fifty-four diesels which were to come from the British, and which McNabb had already informed me the British had made arrangements to turn over to II Corps. Fredendall concluded:

'We are a little thin but if they will just reconnoitre for awhile, we'll be all set. The longer they let us alone, the better we'll be set. The air is working fine. 1 Armoured will not have its tail in until noon, so I am giving them air cover.'

So far we could only guess at the extent of our losses and what would be needed to make them good. And I was becoming doubtful of obtaining any prompt or exact report from the Corps staff. Accordingly, I charged Carleton to check with every element of 1 Armoured Division to obtain an accurate account of the requirements. Carleton's report telephoned in the evening of 18 February, and confirmed in writing the following morning, summarized what defeat in battle can mean to an armoured division. He wrote:

'Since the start of the Sbeitla battle the morning of 15 February until its close at dark 17 February, 1 Armoured Division suffered the following losses:

Medium tanks	112
Light tanks (81 Recon. Sq.)	5
Half-tracks	80
Self-propelled 105s	11
Assault 75 mm. howitzer self propelled	5
Half-tracks 81 mm. mortar mounts	5
Scout cars	15
Wreckers	7
Tank destroyer 75 mm. self-propelled gun	10

'These losses are the best information available. Scattered portions of units were still putting in their appearance and vehicles of various types that had been abandoned on the field of battle and considered lost were appearing.

'Though the loss in personnel in the division had been considerable, it has in no way been commensurate with the losses in vehicles, and trained replacements are available and are being made promptly.

'The reverses suffered by this unit in the past few days and the magnification of losses in conversation between soldiers would normally indicate a decided lowering of morale and consequent effect upon efficiency. However in the case of this division, I do not believe this to be true. A very fine spirit still exists . . . and I am convinced that they can always carry more than their own weight against the Boche under any circumstances.

'There is a definite feeling in 1 Armoured Division which it is very difficult to argue against and which I have made every effort to explain logically—that our Allies are being given A-1 modern American equipment while they must be content to fight with obsolete Mark III tanks. I do not believe this has a detrimental effect upon the morale, as might appear in stating it; however, the feeling is there. The Mark III tank has a thirty-four-degree traverse of its only effective gun—the 75 mm. In a withdrawal, it is helpless. The tank crews and the officers who man the Mark III tanks have a definite inferiority complex when opposed to the German Mark IVs. . . .'

It is to be noted that Colonel Carleton's summary of losses applied only to 1 Armoured Division. It did not include the guns and half the personnel of the 2nd Battalion, 17th Field Artillery; all of one infantry battalion and most of another one lost on the Djebels at Sidi bou Zid; the numerous half-tracks mounting the light 75 mm. guns with which the tank destroyer battalions and companies had challenged the superior German armour and armament; nor any losses in 1 or 34 Infantry Divisions or among the Corps troops. There were plenty of holes in the dikes and all too few boys' fingers with which to plug them.

On 19 February, we were 'getting set' as General Fredendall expressed it. Holding Kasserine Pass was Colonel Moore's force, the 19th Engineers, a battalion of the 39th Infantry, a chemical mortar company, a company of medium tanks, and the 805th Tank Destroyer Battalion (less one company). West of Kasserine, in the valley leading towards Tebessa, was Robinette with Combat Command B—one battalion and one company of medium tanks, 13th Armoured Regiment, the 27th Field Artillery Battalion, the 601st Tank Destroyer Battalion, and the 2nd Battalion, 6th Armoured Infantry Regiment. To the north around Thala was the remnant of Combat Command A, and in this area the 'Nick Force'—so called from its British commander, Brigadier Nicholson, 6 Armoured Division—was gathering. Nick Force included an armoured brigade of 6 Armoured Division equipped with obsolete Crusader and Valentine tanks, a reconnaissance squadron, three batteries of artillery with twenty-four 25-pounder guns, several anti-tank detachments with forty-eight 6-pounder and eight 17-pounder anti-tank guns, a battalion of infantry, and the Cannon Company of the 39th U.S. Infantry. To the east, defending the Sbiba Gap, was 34 Infantry Division (less one regimental combat team and one infantry battalion) with the 18th Regimental Combat Team of 1 Infantry Division attached.

During the day, the Germans reconnoitred along the front from Feriana to Sbiba, and on 20 February, the German Panzer divisions struck through our poorly organized defences at Kasserine Pass. Infiltrating around the small infantry forces placed too far out in front, and on to the heights behind them, and avoiding the minefield and obstacles which had been carefully marked off with tape and flags to avoid casualties among our own troops during the withdrawal, Rommel's Panzer divisions struck through the pass and then fanned out in two columns: one of Germans and Italians heading west towards Tebessa, the other stronger column northward towards Thala and Maktar. During these hours we had little information at the Advanced C.P., and most of that discouraging. To us, it seemed almost touch and go. If we had not been able to hold the strong position at Kasserine Pass, how could we hope to hold the weaker ones of the wide front between Thala and Tebessa?

From all along the front and from the rear, every gun and tank which could be brought to bear upon the enemy was being rushed to the critical area. And the whole weight of Allied air power in North Africa, including the mighty

B-17s, was brought in to support our hard-pressed troops. At nightfall, no one knew what would happen next.

That night the enemy was reported withdrawing, but he was only regrouping himself for battle. At dawn on the 21st, he renewed the attacks. In the south, the Germans and Italians drove Combat Command B back to a point only eight miles from Tebessa, but a counter-attack by the 2nd Battalion, 6th Armoured Infantry, supported by a company of tanks, in the late afternoon regained all lost ground. In the north, the Germans were stopped just short of Thala by the fires of massed artillery and the pounding of the Allied air forces..

This was not the end of the Kasserine battle, but it was to be the high-water mark in the tide of the German storm.

. . . . 23 February brought an end to the Kasserine battle.

. . . . Rommel, pounded by our vastly superior air forces and confronted by superior strength in front, had actually begun his withdrawal the night of 22 February. Attacking troops on 23 February received only light artillery fire. On the 24th there was no opposition at all—the bird had flown. We reoccupied Feriana and Sbeitla and within a few days the Germans were back on the ground from which they had begun operations the morning of 14 February. Rommel had accomplished little in the way of gaining elbow room in Tunisia and he had sustained losses which could not be replaced. He had thrown a scare into every headquarters in North Africa, and he had taught us much. More than enough to pay the cost in men and material which had fallen so heavily upon the American troops of II Corps.

General Truscott

By 28 February Rommel was back in his original positions.

General Alexander Worries

Have just returned from three days on the American and French front lines. . . . Broadly speaking, Americans require experience and French require arms. . . . I am frankly shocked at whole situation as I found it. . . . Hate to disappoint you, but find victory in North Africa is not just around the corner.

General Alexander to Winston Churchill, 27 February 1943

Dr. Goebbels Worries

We have about seventy-five thousand men in North Africa and the Italians about two hundred thousand. That is quite a concentration of troops, but it lacks weapons, fuel, and in some places even food. Only sixty per cent of the supplies reach Tunis; forty per cent must be written off as lost. What is being sent to the bottom of the ocean in the way of equipment almost baffles description; consequently we are short of these supplies at decisive points on the Eastern Front. Nevertheless the Führer has decided that Tunis must be held as long as possible and has opposed every compromise proposal.

Rommel described in detail to the Führer his difficulties with the Italians. Hearing his description, one can understand why he fell ill. In North Africa actually almost half a dozen different command points are functioning one against the other—Rommel, Kesselring, Arnim, the *Commando Supremo* in Rome, the local Italian commander, etc. It is simply hopeless to try and wage war with authority and jurisdiction in such a muddle.

. . . . If the Italians were also to lose Tunis, a very serious crisis might conceivably ensue at this critical moment.

Dr. Goebbels, 17 March

Mareth

On 21 March, having repulsed a last attack by the Afrika Korps near Medenine, the Eighth Army to the south launched its own assault on the Mareth Line, the last really formidable desert position their old enemies could hold. The Mareth Line was a bristling system of fortifications built before the war by the French against possible attack from Italian Tripolitania.

Medenine

February—we closed up to the Mareth Line, the last enemy barrier between us and the Allied armies to the north. On a cold, misty morning we moved north round Medenine and isolated the twin features of the Tadjera hills, the outposts to Mareth. Here on 6 March, Rommel, whose gambles had so frequently before been successful, tried one last throw against us.

. . . . It was a most unusual battle for us. All day Kinnaird and I sat in the A.C.V. as the reports came in from all parts of the front. I listened and marked the enemy moves on the map, and Kinnaird sat for most of the time silent, with his chin cupped in his hands. I did not know what thoughts were passing through his mind. For myself, when I had a moment to spare I could not help comparing this day with many in the past. After two and a half years of deadly struggle against an enemy who always seemed to have the power to come back, it was a new feeling to be utterly confident of the outcome of so vicious a battle. In character it was almost exactly the same as our successful defensive battle at Alam Halfa, against Rommel's final attack at Alamein. We waited, making no move, for the enemy to attack our fixed defences. But whereas the previous year, after so long a series of faults and disasters in the weary withdrawal to Alamein, we had not dared to hope that the tide had really turned and that we could in fact defeat the German tanks, now we were completely confident.

As the day passed we began to be sure, with an absolute certainty, that never again would we feel the sting of disaster, never again would the enemy be able to turn defeat to triumph. On that day we really began to know that the Germans had begun to crack. Throughout their long, skilfully conducted withdrawal it had not been very obvious, but now it showed in a number of things—some small, some big. It showed in the sterility of the German tactics—the same methods which, though they had succeeded often enough when we were outgunned, out-armoured and unco-ordinated, had proved ineffective at Alam Halfa. It showed in the hesitation of the advance of their tanks, now cautious and indecisive, a pale shadow of what they had been in the past. It showed in the failure of the German artillery and infantry to take any part in the battle. And finally it showed most clearly and convincingly in their failure to withdraw or destroy some of their tanks which were only slightly damaged, but which they allowed to fall into our hands.

Kinnaird broke his silence towards evening when the battle was clearly won. 'That's that, Tony. However long the war goes on for now, I don't believe we'll ever again have the trouble we first had with their Panzers. Come on, let's go and drink to the swiftest, shortest, surest victory I've ever seen.'

Cyril Joly

Maoris at Mareth

On the Maori front there was trouble. The tanks were unable to climb Hill 209 and sheered off to go round it. An 88 mm., cleverly placed behind the hill, knocked out five in succession and the others drew back. The right of the battalion was pinned down by heavy fire from 209 but C Company on the left, under Peta Awatere, swung right and attacked in the most spirited fashion. A lower feature of 209, later called Hikurangi, was strongly held and a bitter fight ensued on its steep slopes. The barrage had gone over, the tanks in the vicinity had lost interest or were out of touch, and the Maoris had to fight it out themselves.

I went up in a Bren carrier just before dusk and found that C Company had at last forced the Germans off the top of Hikurangi on to the reverse slope, but they were unable to stay on the top themselves under the intense fire from 209. Awatere had been wounded and the remnants of the company under one of the platoon commanders, Ngarimu, were clinging to a position just under the lip of the hill. The Germans had closed up to within twenty yards and a furious grenade and stone-throwing fight was in progress.

Brigadier Kippenberger

Gurkhas

The Gurkhas from 4 Indian Division were given a sort of roving commission in the hills towards Hallouf. Their main task was to beat up any posts, destroy any large guns which were firing from that area, and generally cause alarm and despondency. They appeared to have had excellent sport. They got busy with their knives very quietly in the dark. I don't think the Germans quite liked it. I remember one particular Gurkha situation report which finished as follows: '. . . Enemy losses ten killed, ours nil. Ammunition expenditure nil.'

Major-General Sir Francis de Guingand

DÉBÂCLE

By 26 March the Mareth Line was broken and the Germans were once more in full flight; now northwards into Tunisia. On 7 April the Americans linked up with Montgomery's men: the two arms of the nutcracker had met, after five months. In the last days of April the Allied forces, closing in on all sides, delivered the first of

*a series of great assaults. Some of the Eighth Army's strength, tied up before
Enfidaville, was switched to 1 Army to lend weight to the knock-out blow. After
much hard fighting the final break-through came on 6 May; on the 7th both Tunis
and Bizerta fell. The German front collapsed completely, and by the 13th all
resistance was at an end. The large forces which the Germans had poured so recklessly into Tunisia were trapped and destroyed almost to a man.*

Two British Armies Meet

May—and we were half-way over the mountains which separated us from
1 Army, facing the gates of Tunis. The call had been dramatic in its scope and
suddenness. At midday the previous day we were facing still the enemy positions
at Enfidaville—resigned to seeing the campaign concluded by others, impotent
in face of the natural strength of the physical barrier that held our further advance. By nightfall the tanks were already loaded on to transporters, and as
darkness closed in we moved off on a march of a hundred and seventy miles
with the beckoning prospect of being in at the kill. Over wild, unmarked tracks,
in places almost disappearing among a mass of tangled rocks and undergrowth,
in wireless silence so that our move would not be detected, we drove until we
reached the first signs of the new army which we were to join.

In two days we were together again, in an area a hundred and twenty miles
west of Tunis. Here we were issued with new tanks and new vehicles to fill the
gaps in the ranks of the sand-covered, battered columns of our units. We were
given, too, a generous share of the delicacies of their canteens—food and drink
which we had not tasted for three long years, whisky, English chocolate and beer,
English cigarettes. Only when we saw them did we realize how atrocious had
been the supplies on which we had existed so long—Egyptian beer, 'V' cigarettes,
chocolate tasting of straw.

We began to note and silently judge the Army among whom we had so
abruptly arrived. They were smarter than we were, their equipment and uniforms new and glistening with paint and polish. Their methods were different,
too. They relied to a great extent on written orders, whereas we had become
accustomed to settling all but the smallest details by conference and discussion,
swiftly convened and quickly over, the decisions just as complete and binding.

Perhaps it was most like the meeting between a mature, seasoned veteran
and a young, brilliant, eager amateur. We had learnt too much from bitter
experience to put much faith in the books and manuals; our new companions
had thought and trained for so long that they were steeped in the exact theory of
the conduct of operations. They had fought a hard, bitter war for each yard of
their advance and were not so ready as we had learned to be for moves of more
scope and speed.

Gradually we began to know each other, and some of the rough edges of our
mutual suspicion wore away under the surge of the imminence of our next
enormous task. We became less conscious of, and boasted less of, the length of
our advance; we were less aware of the difference of our garb and the colouring
of our equipment, still splashed with the dappled yellow and grey which had
served to hide us among the ridges of the desert. We began to feel less guilty of

our peculiar manners, our peculiar and barbaric phrases—all the hundred and one differences of manner, language, outlook which had grown from so long an isolation from home and been nurtured by the multiple character of the nations and races which formed our army.

'They look like novices, but they've done a good job,' was a typical, somewhat patronizing remark. It was difficult for each side not to be patronizing—their 'Of course you won't find it the same in the mountains' was no less offensive than our 'After three years we ought to be able to do something'.

Cyril Joly

The Last Days

During the final days of the Tunisian campaign two local battles in the north, one in the British sector and one in the American, gripped the interest of the entire theatre. Both positions were exceedingly strong naturally and fiercely defended, and both were essential to us in our final drive for victory. The position in the British sector was Longstop—the battle for its possession from the beginning to the end of the African campaign probably cost more lives than did the fighting for any other spot in Tunisia. In the American sector the place was Hill 609, eventually captured by 34 Division, to the intense satisfaction, particularly, of the American high command. This division had been denied opportunity for training to a greater degree than any other, and its capture of the formidable 609 was final proof that the American ground forces had come fully of age.

Following immediately upon the break-through, Alexander sent armoured units of the British 1 Army rapidly forward across the base of the Bon Peninsula, where we believed the Germans might attempt to retreat to make a last stand in the manner of Bataan. Alexander's swift action, regardless of the many thousands of enemy still fighting in confused pockets along the front of 1 Army, destroyed this last desperate hope of the enemy. From then on the operations were of a mopping-up variety. Some fighting continued until the twelfth but by the following day, except for a few stragglers in the mountains, the only living Germans left in Tunisia were safely within prison cages. The number of prisoners during the last week of the campaign alone reached two hundred and forty thousand, of whom approximately 125,000 were German. Included in these captures was all that was left of the Afrika Korps and a number of other crack German and Italian units.

Rommel himself escaped before the final débâcle, apparently foreseeing the inevitable and earnestly desiring to save his own skin. The myth of his and Nazi invincibility had been completely destroyed. Von Arnim surrendered the German troops, and Field-Marshal Messe, in nominal command of the whole force, surrendered the Italian contingent. When von Arnim was brought through Algiers on his way to captivity, some members of my staff felt that I should observe the custom of bygone days and allow him to call on me.

The custom had its origin in the fact that mercenary soldiers of old had no real enmity towards their opponents. Both sides fought for the love of a fight, out of a sense of duty or, more probably, for money. A captured commander of the eighteenth century was likely to be, for weeks or months, the honoured guest of his captor. The tradition that all professional soldiers are really comrades in arms had, in tattered form, persisted to this day.

For me the second World War was far too personal a thing to entertain such feelings. Daily as it progressed there grew within me the conviction that as never before in a war between many nations the forces that stood for human good and men's rights were this time confronted by a completely evil conspiracy with which no compromise could be tolerated. Because only by the utter destruction of the Axis was a decent world possible, the war became for me a crusade in the traditional sense of that often misused word.

In this specific instance, I told my Intelligence officer, Brigadier Kenneth Strong, to get any information he possibly could out of the captured generals but that, so far as I was concerned, I was interested only in those who were not yet captured. None would be allowed to call on me. I pursued the same practice to the end of the war. Not until Field-Marshal Jodl signed the surrender terms at Rheims in 1945 did I ever speak to a German general, and even then my only words were that he would be held personally and completely responsible for the carrying out of the surrender terms.

The outcome of the Tunisian campaign was of course eminently satisfactory, but the high command was so busily engaged in preparation of the Sicilian attack that little opportunity was available for celebration. However, a Victory Parade was held in Tunis on the 20th to mark the end of the Axis Empire in Africa.

The very magnitude of our victory, at least of our captures, served to intensify our difficulties in preparing for the Sicilian affair. We had more than two hundred and fifty thousand prisoners corralled in Tunisia, where poor communications made feeding and guarding difficult and rapid evacuation impossible. But the end of the campaign did have the effect of freeing commanders and staffs from immediate operations and allowed them to turn their full attention to the matter in hand. Preparatory planning had been going on ever since February in a special group under General Alexander. This group was now absorbed completely in General Alexander's staff and the whole process of preparation was vastly speeded up.

The Tunisian victory was hailed with delight throughout the Allied nations. It clearly signified to friend and foe alike that the Allies were at last upon the march.

General Eisenhower

I am grateful to the British soldiers—to those small humble citizens who are capable of being the greatest soldiers. But they do not talk about their deeds; they do not boast; and as soon as the war ends they will modestly disappear into their homes and cease to be heroes. Therein lies their greatest glory.

President Masaryk of Czechoslovakia,
on the occasion of the Allied victory in Tunisia

Masaryk was speaking from Britain, which he knew so well. His gratitude extended to all who were striving in the cause which would liberate his country.

25

SICILY - ITALY SURRENDERS

On 10 July 1943, two months after the last Axis troops ceased resistance in Tunisia, the British and American armies descended on Sicily by sea and air. 'Operation Husky', the first step in the liberation of Europe, had been taken.

SICILY

No war was ever fought, I think, in more ideal weather than was the Sicilian campaign. The soft spring lay upon the land like a benediction; the days were warm, the nights cool, and there was no rain. After the frying pan of Africa, the balmy weather was like heaven to the troopers who had suffered through Morocco and Tunisia. There were no insects, except mosquitoes, and these were no problem.

General Matthew B. Ridgway

The Axis Defenders

Of the two German divisions then known to be in Sicily both were pointed toward the invasion corner. 'Strictly hot mustard,' was the way Dickson described them. Fortunately, however, both were short on tanks; we estimated only eighty-five between them.

A total of six Italian static divisions defended the five hundred miles of Sicilian coastline. Known to be under strength and shabbily equipped, they had grown lazy and indolent on the beaches.

Somewhat better were the four Italian field divisions drawn back into reserve in the hills. Of these, only one was posted in the south-east corner. Two held the western end of the island and another was located in the middle. Altogether this Italian garrison was estimated by Patton's G-2 to consist of two hundred thousand men.

'When the going gets tough,' Dickson predicted, 'the Boche will pull the plug on the Eyeties and wash them down the drain.' He meant the German would ditch his Italian ally to save his own troops. And that is precisely what happened.

Of all the terrors we faced, however, none seemed more menacing than the threat of German air. For our army, huddled on a narrow beachhead, could be severely mauled should the Luftwaffe break through in strength. And a naval force concentrated offshore would offer Göring a tempting target for all-out air attack.

I was not to learn how groundless those fears were until after the invasion. During May and June the Allied air force had decimated the enemy's Mediterranean air strength.

.... In Sicily the nineteen scattered airdromes that had worried Eisenhower's planners so much the previous spring had increased to thirty-two by early May. But as Spaatz aimed the weight of his bombers against those Sicilian objectives, the Axis withdrew its aircraft to safer rearward fields. These extended as far north as Foggia, halfway up the Italian boot. To prevent enemy reinforcement through Messina, Spaatz hammered that port until its peacetime capacity of four thousand tons each day fell to a small fraction of that. By D-day eight Sicilian airports had been put out of operation. Only two fields in the western tip of the island remained operational. By smashing the enemy's air on the ground and by forcing his airfields back, Spaatz had spared us the D-day enemy air offensive we feared the most.

General Omar Bradley, G.O.C. U.S. II Corps

The Reason Why

To confuse both the enemy and garrulous officers on our own staffs, we devised a cover plan for the invasion of Sardinia. It was not an illogical diversion, for at Casablanca a plan for the invasion of Sardinia and Corsica had been quite seriously considered before we finally decided on the 'Husky' plan. In the event of a later decision to invade Italy, it was foreseen at Casablanca that Sardinia and Corsica would provide us nearby bases for fighter support. Both islands were only lightly defended with Italian troops and presumably could have been taken with a modest-sized Allied force. However, until Sicily was neutralized, Axis air would continue to terrorize our narrow ship passage through the Mediterranean to the Middle East. Not only would the seizure of Sicily ease Allied shipping shortages but an attack there, it was anticipated, might also push Italy nearer to surrender. These were the reasons that induced the planners to favour Sicily.

General Omar Bradley

'Husky'—the Beaches

During the first week in July, the Army Commander held a conference in Malta at which he made it clear that, although he was soberly confident of the success of the operation, he was under no illusions about the serious fighting that lay ahead.

On 9 July the convoys of the 7 U.S. and Eighth Armies were closing towards their rendezvous areas east and west of Malta. The sea was rough and many of the men in landing craft were suffering from seasickness. The swell threatened to make the beaching of assault craft a hazardous operation. However, during the night the wind began to slacken, and as the risk of postponing the assault was greater than the hazard of continuing it was decided to go forward with the plan.

The seaborne assault was an outstanding success, for as a result of the gale the enemy garrison, already wearied by false alerts, had relaxed vigilance. Complete tactical surprise was achieved, and though some of the beaches came under fire from enemy guns, these were soon silenced. Naval supporting fire was admirable, and artillery F.O.O.s and liaison teams in bombarding ships worked smoothly. One enemy battery at Marzamemi were captured complete, in their beds.

Major-General M. E. Dennis

Losses and Gains

The airborne assault had been the only part of the operation that had not been a great success. Yet in spite of this the troops, showing great bravery, held on to the important bridge south of Syracuse until relieved by XIII Corps. Many of the pilots of the transport aircraft had never flown an operational flight before, and coming up against flak for the first time is most unpleasant. Then the strong wind did not help matters. As a result of all this many of the airborne troops landed in the water and lost their lives by drowning. General Browning, the Commander of Airborne Forces, was always afraid that this lack of training of the pilots might face them with too difficult a test on the day itself. Between Sicily and Normandy great strides were made, and those later landings were a conspicuous success.

XXX Corps had the easiest task, and by the first evening were in possession of the peninsula and the Pachino airfield. XIII Corps had more difficulties, but secured their beaches, had pressed inland and had captured Syracuse by nightfall. The port, luckily, was found to be undamaged. We had not met any German troops so far, and the Italians—particularly the troops of the coastal divisions—were quite ready to give themselves up. The American Army was not so fortunate, and soon after landing they were counter-attacked by German troops. Some very stiff fighting took place about Gela. The situation was, however, restored by the dogged fighting of the Americans, by the U.S. Navy steaming close inshore and giving very close range support, and by the courageous leadership of George Patton, who had come ashore at the danger point personally to supervise the operations.

Major-General Sir Francis de Guingand

Commando Landing

The loudspeaker suddenly broke into harsh speech and summoned one troop to its boat-stations. The darkness on the other side of the mess-deck resolved itself into men picking themselves up and moving in single file up the gangway. They had remained unseen until then. Their departure was like a load lifted from the stomach; something was happening at last. I could hear my watch—or was it my heart?—ticking out its seconds, and my flesh bristled with anxiety. The loudspeaker commanded us up on deck and, without a word, I stepped forward; the men followed, swinging their weights of ammunition on to their shoulders.

We expected to be swept up by the spray as we stepped out into the night but we were greeted instead by a fatigued breeze and a heaven full of stars. The storm had worn itself out and the ship lay unmoved on the water, but we saw, as we stood alongside the assault craft, that the sea was still riding high in a succession of swift sinuous waves, lathered down their smooth flanks and groins with dapples of foam. The command came to load the boats, and, wishing the second-in-command 'good luck', a salute that he took, it seemed, unhappily, and glancing to make sure that the mortar barrels in their water-tight cylindrical containers were securely lashed to the stern, I stepped across the swaying gangplank, noticing the spasmodic caress of the waters against the ship's hull below, into the craft after the men. They crouched down in the narrow breadth under the gunwales and I stood upright in the bow. While we swung gently in this cradle, the dimness ahead collected into the dark outline of another ship bearing slowly down on us, and our ship sounded its siren thrice to avert an accident. This must surely wake the enemy, this harsh scream uttered in what they believed to be empty wasteland, and with a curse for such folly I held myself ready to duck as the first shell from the shore batteries struck into our midst. We rocked gently to and fro. 'Lower away!' the incisive command was given and we went down smoothly and horizontally to meet the water that, rising in an unexpected wave, struck the bottom a resounding blow and jarred each fibre of the craft. We were at once in a weltering sea that pressed on to overwhelm us or to crush us against the smooth hulk of the ship towering above like a cliff. The sailors on the deck forgot their duty to raise the davits and, as we pitched aimlessly, the cumbrous grapples lunged at our heads and once struck the stern a dull welt. The accelerating engines at last gripped the water and, drawing away out of danger into the open sea, we formed up. Signals flashed from the leading craft were picked up and repeated by the rest, and we were quickly under way in a long line. The parent ship sank down in the water and when I looked back again there was only darkness to be seen.

. . . . It was difficult at first to distinguish more than the alternating whine of the engines and the lapse or sidling hiss of the repulsed seas, but . . . I slowly became aware of the vast round our cockle shell, and heard the methodical throb of aircraft flying high overhead below the confusion of unfamiliar stars. They were either bombers, or more probably, air transports which were to drop paratroops in the enemy's rear immediately before our assault. Something will happen at any moment now, I thought, and I strained to see land through the dimness, but there was only the rhythmical repetition of the retreating waves against the skyline. I was soon cold and stiff with standing in the bows and crept into the little space that had been saved for me under the gunwales; but the stench of vomit and the retching made it impossible to stay there for long and I preferred to shiver in the spray than to be sick. I climbed up again into the fresh air and succeeded in dulling my thoughts by watching, until I was almost hypnotized, the fluctuating wakes of the craft ahead. The time insensibly passed until a singular star trembled and fell like a liquid drop from the sky on my right. I was following its quavering descent when another, bright crimson like a prick of blood, suddenly hung above it, poised momentarily, and began to fall after the first. This was the signal for spurts of light, like fiery morse-code, to lace the darkness and intersect each other's staccato lines in a geometrical pattern. The paratroops had been dropped. I saw now that we were sailing parallel to a long hump of land and warned the men to stand by.

Before I was fully aware of our position, the craft deployed and the cliff's dark bulk rose immediately before us. The landing ramp fell forward and shouting; 'Follow me!' I clambered down into the water that was disturbed into white spume by the men of the first wave struggling ashore. I lurched and stumbled forward, up to the waist in water that bellied against me, and furiously strove for the sheltering lee of the cliff to escape from the diabolic racket of machine-gun fire that whipped overhead. The smallest man in my troop fell in a pot-hole beside me and, surfacing with difficulty, unleashed an incantation of curses but still retained a firm grasp on his mortar's bipod. I made a last violent effort and found myself freed from the water and at the base of the low cliff. The cliff was not a vertical but a retreating face, up which it was easy to crawl if little weight was put on its crumbling clay jags. I climbed until it flattened out into a slope, and took cover in a sand dune as the machine-gun lashed a foot above my head along the rank of men on the skyline immediately to my front. My sergeant-major and batman joined me, and together we hurriedly ran over the rough ground along the cliff to the right, unravelling as we went the telephone cable that would be connected to the mortars on the strip of beach. Before any troop could need our fire we had to find a square house that had appeared on the aerial photographs as a solid cube, but in the darkness we could see only a foot ahead, and, when they were against the skyline, running groups of men. The wire defences were blown with a bangalore torpedo, the explosion shattering the night into a thousand fiery splinters, and we were through the reeking gap on the heels of the first troop. A track of loose stones, sheltered by a low wall and a line of rounded bushes, ran straight ahead from there along the cliff, and, slipping and cursing as the singeing cable cut our hands, we kept on until we reached the house, our objective. We fixed the telephone and, calling up the mortars, found that they were ready to fire. Lying on our bellies under cover of the house we stared ahead for the two green Verey lights to summon our fire. My heart thumped like the open palm of a hand against the ground, and my indrawn breath almost stifled me with its uncontrollable recurrence. A few shots rang out, a grenade exploded with dull percussion, and a stream of tracer fountained up into the sky, but there were otherwise few sounds of battle.

I began to get back my wind, and my senses, which had been dulled by the strenuous action, became aware again of danger. We had not examined the house in our flurry to set up the telephone, but we suddenly imagined we heard the quiet movements of someone inside. It was not the solid building which it had appeared on the aerial photograph, but a crazy hut of wattle and rushes with one door and no windows. My batman manned the telephone while the sergeant-major and I crept round to the front and flung the door open so violently that it fell off its upper hinge, at the same time covering with our revolvers the square room that our torches lit up. It was entirely empty and only the black ashes of a charcoal fire in the centre of the earth floor showed that it must have been occupied. While we were examining it, we heard the batman order the mortars into action; two green Verey lights had been sent up by the attacking troop and their signal called for supporting fire against a pre-arranged target. A dozen rounds were fired before they signalled us by a red Verey light to cease fire. The casually falling red ball thinned out and was extinguished, and immediately after its descent there were some bursts of Bren fire, the faint echo of men shouting, and then abrupt silence. We anxiously waited for any other noise by which we might guess the success of the attack, but the night had closed over the interruption as swiftly as water over a stone.

My eyes were now accustomed to the darkness, which seemed to shine with a deceptive incandescence as though it had been blown with powdered lime, and I saw a few yards away towards the cliff the enemy's deserted trenches and unbroken barricade of wire. A man or a shadow slipped quickly along the far side of the wire, and had the movement not been so stealthy I should have thought that it was one of our men lost and unable to cross the entanglement. I drew my revolver and walked slowly towards the trenches. They were all empty except for one into which a rag doll had been carelessly thrown. I had bent down to look at it more closely, imagining it might be some company mascot, before I realized too late that it was an undersized boy. He lay dead on his back. An arm and a leg were sprawled out and the other pair were oddly tucked underneath his body. His unbuttoned tunic was ripped and torn. I returned and crouched down beside the telephone again.

A light wind blew up and a heavy drift of perfume, sweet and pervasive, filled the air and mixed with the dry scent of the baked dust. A clump of pampas-grasses sent up a continuous whispering and made it difficult to distinguish other sounds. The sergeant-major laid a hand on my arm and pointed out into the darkness towards the cliff edge. I could see nothing until a head was dimly silhouetted against the skyline and behind it what appeared to be a crouching file of men. We stepped forward calling out the pass-word, but the shapes sank into the ground again without noise. The silence around us was inexplicable and our attention was so strained to catch the slightest clue that every moment was like a drop of liquid added to bowls already brim-full. A scream suddenly rang out with a violence that showed it had been long suppressed, and a voice, exasperated by pain and fear, cried 'Mamma! Mamma!' It called again and again from the seaward side of the cliff in this high pitch and slowly dwindled to a monotonous tearful moan of 'Mamma! Mamma!', like a child lulling itself to sleep in an upper room, until it fell silent. It was horrible to lie in the darkness and listen to the eerie repetitive cry.

I glanced at my watch and found I could clearly read the dial. The darkness lessened and the light gained strength like a reviving pulse. The house, walls, pampas-grasses and barbed wire stood out in hard relief and the sea crawled from beneath the sky. We heard the brittle crunch of boots on the track to our front and four men, their haggard faces begrimed with dirt and streaked with sweat, appeared carrying a troop commander on a stretcher. He lay on his face and his flattened right buttock was a bloody patch. All the attacks had succeeded, they said, and the casualties had been light. A few minutes later the Brigadier walked jauntily down the track and I reported to him that I had heard a man screaming below the cliff. He detailed off some men to search the area and they returned at once driving before them perhaps twenty Italian soldiers, who had been cowering out of sight within a few yards of the hut where we three had spent the night. One of them, the man who had called on his mother, had evidently fallen from the cliff and his face was just a raw contusion. The Italians were glad to be taken alive and, their hands above their heads, they span round in a retreating dance each time their captors threatened them with their fixed bayonets. My signaller came up from the beach with a message ordering me to report with my troop at a farmhouse farther inland, and we prepared to move on after condoling again with the wounded troop commander.

The sun's brilliant edge appeared above a low bank of violet cloud, and the light struck down with such force that the ground seemed to ring like metal under its impact. The volleying light pealed against the farthest limits of the wide air and the barrage gained in strength as the sun quickly rose into dominance. The cicadas, that had sung the night through so persistently that they had been unnoticed, fell silent, and whatever gentleness the night had put out recoiled affronted. The wide bay of lambent water was seen to be full of shipping, and landing craft plied to and from the shore carrying men and ammunition. It was a scene of intense but apparently peaceful activity, like the building of a new city on the Asian coast by ancient settlers. My men came up from the beaches singing and hailed us cheerfully; they were glad to find that we, too, were alive and that death had as yet driven no wedge into our unity. We formed up and set off along the track, that swung suddenly seawards and continued along the cliff's edge, until we came to a group of huts enclosed within a wooden palisade. A skirmish had been fought about the hutment and pieces of our own and the enemy's equipment littered the trodden ground. The gate into the palisade had been blown down and a Sicilian family was huddled together in the centre of the enclosure. The grandmother, whose toothless face was withered like a mummy's shrunken skull by sun and labour, and the mother knelt with the children kneeling before them, their hands raised in supplication to the Virgin Mary; and the father, his lips also mumbling a prayer but his eyes fixed on our every movement, stood in the middle with an arm round the neck of a shabby, moth-eaten donkey, clearly the one possession for which they were prepared to die. A small boy, the only other male, with tears streaming from his wide, fearful eyes, guarded the animal's other flank, and as we stepped through the gate to search the buildings, his fingers convulsively clutched its lousy hide. They were bundles of rags; poor scarecrows, riddled by disease and undercut by starvation; and angular bones and stringy flesh showed through the gaps in their clothing. We felt ashamed that we had been the cause of their terror. A few filthy blankets and a tin or two were strewn about the earthen floor of their living quarters, but there was not a stick of furniture or a single decency. The whole place stank of excreta and it was as much as we could bear even to glance into the huts. We left the family still praying about their donkey, but a corporal, turning round in the gateway with a curse, tossed a packet of cigarettes into their midst. Others followed suit with more cigarettes and bars of chocolate.

We found at the next hutment along the track a second donkey, undefended this time, which we attempted to harness into a cart, but the girths broke immediately, and rather than manhandle our considerable weights of weapons and ammunition any longer, we piled them into the cart and took it alone. The track, narrowing and winding tortuously between a cactus hedge and the cliff verge, was just wide enough to take the width of the cart. As we rounded a corner, we suddenly came on the corpse of an Italian soldier sprawling out and blocking the way. His open mouth was twisted into a coarse grimace and his body was stiff-

ened into a taut arch. The hedge was too high to lift the body over, but it had
to be moved if we were to pass. While I wondered how this might best be done,
the corporal who had thrown the first packet of cigarettes levered it forward with
his foot until it tumbled like a heavy branch over the cliff and fell without alter-
ing its attitude on to the rocks below. The track widened out again and, where it
turned abruptly inland to run uphill through a vineyard, the body of one of our
own men lay stretched out. His pallid face, which seemed to have been coated
with grease, was empty of all expression, and the flies, singing sharply in the
rising heat, crawled as thickly as currants over his skin. A gas-cape had been
thrown across his body and we raised it to hide his face, but as we moved it we
saw that his bowels had been torn out. We covered his face with a rag and hung
his helmet on an upright bayonet to mark his resting place.

The sun beat down intolerably and as we toiled up the track, quickly petering
out into the vineyard's soft dust, its rays could almost be heard to vibrate
shrilly like telegraph wires on an empty English road in mid-summer. Half-
way up the sloping vineyard, towards the white cubic farm buildings on the
crest, we were passed by a middle-aged woman walking quickly down towards
the sea. Her blue and white striped dress flapped about her erect figure with the
vigour of her movement as though it had been caught in a wind, and the loose
end of her kerchief fastened over her coils of black hair trailed out like a streamer
behind. She stiffly averted her face from us to conceal not the tears that ran
from her unblinking eyes but the look of implacable hate and contempt into
which her features were set. Two coastguards had been bayoneted in their post
by the man whose face we had covered up, and the hurrying woman, who may
have been wife or mother, was going too late with a handful of bandages to tend
their wounds.

When we reached the farm we were ordered to remain there until summoned
forward. The buildings, whose whitewashed walls threw back the light in a solid
glare, were apparently deserted, but we felt that every movement was watched by
furtive eyes from cracks and crannies we could not find. Each sense had now
been primed by danger and was sensitive to every stealthy movement, but the
knowledge that we were under scrutiny made us walk about with a brave
swagger. There was neither sign nor sound of battle, and each hour the enemy
delayed their expected counter-attack found the bridgehead in a stronger position. I could see, from where I stood at the corner of the farmyard, the shuttle
of the landing craft to and from the beaches, where the boxes of rations and
ammunition were steadily piling up, and the road leading inland past the foot of
the crest below me, along which marched the staggered files of the Canadian
brigade. Only a respite of twelve hours was necessary to make our grip secure.

Douglas Grant

The Pillbox

One night during the Sicilian campaign a party of commandos, accompanied
by a pioneer detachment, went ashore on a lonely stretch of coast to prepare the
way for a larger-scale landing.

It was almost dawn, and the men climbed through a pine wood until they had reached the low ridge which dominated the beaches. They moved along the ridge to clear it of any defenders, but they found only a few forlorn groups of Italian soldiers whom they rounded up silently and without any difficulty.

The men, who had been spilled ashore full of the tension and hot vigour that long training and the lack of action had bottled up in them, grew cold and bored as they trudged in silent files along the bare slopes. The two officers at their head commiserated with each other upon the lack of excitement.

The sky grew lighter. By now the main body of landing craft would be starting out from the troopships. There was no bombardment, for no considerable opposition was expected. The landing of the advance party had only been a precaution to ensure that no small groups of Italians who might happen to be hereabouts could establish themselves on the ridge to fire down on the beaches.

They came to a dip in the ridge and halted. Below them, in the saddle of ground, they saw a concrete pillbox sunk into the seaward crest of the ridge so that it commanded the beach. A man was just vanishing into the pillbox, and they saw the steel door close.

The commando officer said to his colleague, 'All right, old man. I think we can manage this one without your chaps.'

'I beg your pardon,' the pioneer replied. 'It looks to me like a job for us.' The two young men continued to wrangle over the problem.

'I'll tell you what we'll do,' the commando said, and produced a coin. They tossed, and the pioneer won. 'Ours, I think,' he announced happily, and called his men forward while the commandos retired.

The pioneer officer had just begun to dispose his men when a white flag appeared outside the pillbox and a group of Italian soldiers emerged behind it.

'Oh, damn!' The officer stood with his hands on his hips, a picture of disappointment. 'The windy rotten bastards! All that lovely training, and all this lovely gelignite, and look what they've gone and done to us!'

The commando officer, who was sitting on the slope above him with his assault rations on his knees as if he were preparing for a picnic, said, 'Tickle 'em up with the Bren, old boy, and see what happens. We don't have to worry any more about making a noise.'

The pioneer officer took a light machine-gun from one of his men and fired a couple of bursts from the hip. The Italians hesitated in bewilderment. The firing continued, and they scrambled back into the shelter of the pillbox. They continued to wave their white flag desperately. A couple more bursts sprayed the entrance, and they were forced to slam the steel door to protect themselves.

'There!' the commando said. 'Always listen to uncle. You can go ahead now, they're resisting.'

The Bren continued to fire at the slits in the pillbox. The white flag, which was protruding and wagging frantically, was withdrawn. A few moments later the inmates, blindly trying to at least keep these implacable attackers at bay, fired a few harmless shots.

'Now, my old sport,' the pioneer officer said, 'we'll give you a little demonstration in the use of high explosives, demolition. If you'll kindly pay attention.'

He and his men worked their way around the pillbox. While the commandos sat on the hillside brewing up tea, the pioneers laid their charges. They demolished the pillbox and its crew most efficiently, and made their way up the hill to join the commandos at breakfast.

A friend of mine, a mild and peaceable young man, took part in this episode and told it to me as a joke. Sometimes, when I hear myself making free with expressions like 'the humanist outlook' and 'the sanctity of life', I remember that for a couple of years after the event, I, too, continued to tell it to other people as a funny story.

Alexander Baron

The Germans Hit Back: Gela, 11 July

In defending his Sicilian shore line the enemy could not hope to hold in equal strength everywhere. For no matter how intensive beach fortifications may be, an invader coming by sea can concentrate his strength at a point of his own choosing, and force his way ashore. Knowing this, the enemy had screened his beaches lightly with third-rate Italian coastal divisions. We anticipated no trouble in cracking this crust and indeed none developed on D-day. The real threat came from behind the beaches where the enemy had concentrated his mobile field divisions as reserves. To the rear of II Corps beachhead, the Hermann Göring Division waited to repel us in a concentrated counter-attack.

Eager to have a hand in operations ashore before the enemy counter-attacked, I left Kirk's flagship on the morning of D plus 1 and headed toward the beach. . . . While running in to the beach from the *Ancon*, a signal lieutenant had spotted a stray radio jeep awash in the surf where it had been abandoned on the assault. With the aid of a bulldozer we dragged that jeep to the beach, hitched it to a truck, and towed it to Scoglitti where the lieutenant set to work repairing the set.

Off to the west in the sector of 1 Division I could hear the rumble of guns, too angry and incessant to be dismissed as a routine attack.

'How long will it be before you can get through to 1 Division?' I asked the signal lieutenant.

'An hour or so, sir, maybe more. I'm going to have to scrounge around Scoglitti for a soldering iron.'

'Bill,' I said to Kean, 'I'm going to run down to see Terry Allen. There's too much noise and dust down there. Maybe he's gotten into trouble.'

'But you probably can't get through all the way on the beach. Maybe you'd better take a boat.'

'Thanks,' I told Kean, 'but I'll grab a DUKW somewhere down on the beach.'

An invasion beach the morning after a landing is a dismal sight. This one was no exception. More than two hundred assault craft wallowed in the surf after having burned out their engines in crossing the runnels while coming ashore. Bulldozers churned through the soft sand, dragging pallets of supply from the water's edge to be piled in dumps behind the grassy dunes. A fleet of more than seven hundred DUKWs moved from ship to shore, ferrying in the bulk tonnage that would be needed for support. Everywhere along the fifteen-mile length of beach to Gela belly-wrapper lifebelts littered the sands where they had been discarded by assault troops. Behind the beaches A.A. crews were digging deeper into the dunes in anticipation of another noisy night of bombing.

Near Gela I found 1 Division fighting for its life against a Panzer counter-attack that had almost broken through to the beaches.

Three months before, on 23 April, Patton had prevailed on Eisenhower to substitute the veteran 1 Division for the 36th on this invasion. In doing so he may have saved II Corps from a major disaster. As we had anticipated, the burly Hermann Göring Panzer Division lunged down the Gela road with its tanks in a bold effort to throw Allen's division back into the sea. I question whether any other U.S. division could have repelled that charge in time to save the beach from tank penetration. Only the perverse Big Red One with its no less perverse commander was both hard and experienced enough to take that assault in its stride. A greener division might easily have panicked and seriously embarrassed the landing.

A dog-tired Terry Allen waited for me in a makeshift C.P. near the beach. His eyes were red from loss of sleep and his hair was dishevelled. His division was still under serious attack.

'Do you have it in hand, Terry?' I asked.

'Yes, I think so,' he answered, 'but they've given us a helluva rough time.' He briefed me on the start of the counter-attack.

At 6.40 on the morning of 11 July Roosevelt telephoned from the 26th Regiment to report that Panzers had broken through on that front and were headed towards the beach.

'We're going to have a helluva time stopping them,' he said, 'until we get some anti-tank stuff ashore.'

Allen's artillery and anti-tank guns were still being dragged ashore from the landing craft. But even the regimental anti-tank companies had not yet gone into the line. Meanwhile the lightly-armed infantry of 1 Division had already been overrun by tanks. Twenty Mark IVs were reported headed down the road towards Gela where the beachfront bulged with supply. Another forty tanks had cut across Allen's front towards Gela. If those columns were to converge there and break through to the water's edge, Allen's infantry would not only be cut off, but the whole beachhead would be endangered.

Now in desperate need of artillery pieces with which to fight those Panzers, Allen ordered every gun in the division rolled into position to meet the tanks at point-blank range. Trucks raced to the beach to drag up additional artillery as it rolled off the landing craft. At the same time fire-support parties called for help from the naval guns. Though overrun, Allen's infantry did not fall back. Instead they burrowed into their foxholes to let the Panzer wave wash through while they waited to repel the grenadiers advancing behind it. Fortunately that added artillery enabled the line to hold, and those tanks were stopped on the plains outside Gela. Of the sixty Panzers committed to that counter-attack more than half were destroyed.

Later that afternoon the enemy resumed his attack, though this time with fewer tanks. However, as salvo after salvo of naval gunfire split their armoured hulls, the German Panzer commanders wisely concluded that the twenty-six-ton

Mark IV is no match for a cruiser. The enemy turned and ran for the hills where the navy could not pursue him. Allen had barely squeaked through, for those tanks had advanced to within two thousand yards of the beach before they turned.

Elsewhere the Allied landings met with only spotty resistance from the demoralized Italian coastal units and casualties were unexpected light. . . . Having landed, we had now only to consolidate our beachheads and get on with the campaign.

General Omar Bradley

The Allied airborne operation in Sicily was decisive. . . . It is my opinion if it had not been for Allied airborne forces blocking the Hermann Göring Armoured Division from reaching the beachhead, that division would have driven the initial seaborne forces back into the sea. I attribute the entire success of the Allied Sicilian operation to the delaying of German reserves until sufficient forces had been landed by sea to resist the counter-attacks by our defending forces.

General Kurt Student, Wehrmacht

The British Meet the Germans: Vizzini, 13 July

Vizzini, like so many Sicilian towns, stands on top of a hill and dominates the several roads which clamber up to it. At first it was hoped that it might be possible to by-pass it without a fight, but a look at the ground showed that the main road through the town was the only possible axis for the advance. An attempt was made that night to dislodge the enemy by an independent brigade which had hitherto been part of the garrison of Malta and whose first action this was. This formation tried but failed to carry the town by an attack from the flank; and 153 Brigade was ordered to put in a new attack next morning, with some armour in support.

The more Vizzini was examined, the tougher it looked. The roads wound up to it as though to a fairy castle in a Disney film; and if the enemy were stouthearted or in strength, he would take a lot of evicting. The orders were for the Brigade to move up to the outskirts of the town (but not to enter it) on a two-battalion front, the 5th Battalion on the left and a battalion of Gordons on the right. The advance began at noon. The day was the hottest of the whole campaign, and everybody was abominably thirsty. There was artillery support, but unfortunately no smoke was available, which meant that the maximum use must be made of the meagre cover. The troops moved forward with skill, and by six in the evening, having suffered only a few casualties from shelling, they were close in under the town.

Colonel Chick Thomson spoke to the Brigadier on the radio and asked permission, despite the original orders, to send a patrol into the town before night fell. The Battalion was out of touch with the Gordons, and nobody knew how far they had got; but unless the success so far gained were followed into the town the enemy might regroup during the night and make the next day's work more difficult. The Brigadier agreed, and a company went in, with one platoon a little ahead of the rest. Spirited fighting broke out at once, and another company was sent in to reinforce. By the time it was dark both companies were firmly established, but not without loss, including two officers killed and a third wounded. The church was turned into a hospital, and the townsfolk helped willingly to tend the casualties; and by next morning the Germans were gone.

There had been one tragic contretemps during the night. The 1st and 7th Battalions had been waiting to help with Vizzini if they were required, and were close up on the 5th Battalion's flank. It seems that the success signal put up by the Gordons was misinterpreted by some Allied artillery as an S.O.S. There are varying accounts as to what actually happened; but the result was ten minutes' bombardment by our own artillery. Most of it fell on the 1st Battalion, which in that short space of time lost eight killed and twenty-eight wounded. The 5th Battalion had one officer wounded; the 7th did not suffer.

Vizzini was a sticky little battle, but it might have been very much worse. It was the enemy's first and last show of resistance before the Catanian Plain.

Bernard Fergusson

Prisoners

Within a week after the landing Patton's 7 Army had moved more than twenty-two thousand prisoners through its cages—one-fourth of them native Sicilians conscripted into the Italian Army. The task of caging and boarding this hungry multitude had become an increasingly heavy chore. Plans had been made for their evacuation by sea to camps in North Africa. From there they would be sent to the United States as prisoners of war, a prospect they did not deplore.

Meanwhile summer grain was ripening on the Sicilian hillsides without manpower to harvest it. Villages had long ago been stripped of all but aged men, their worn-looking women, and children. By caging Sicilian P.O.W.s we would deprive those people of the manpower they needed to bring in their crops. Without those crops they would probably become wards of the United States. This could only mean an even greater drain on Allied shipping. It all made little sense.

On our third night ashore Dickson reported that an Italian soldier had been captured near the corps C.P. wearing civilian clothing.

'Not an agent, I hope?'

'No sir. Not this bird, General. He's just a little *paesano* and he's scared to death. Told us he was home on furlough when the Americans came and it seemed like a good time to stay home on furlough.'

'Can't blame him for that,' I said.

'No—there are probably thousands of others that would like to change places with him. They don't care about the war. They'd much sooner go home and get to work.'

'Then why do we bother to lock them up?'

'Beats me, General.'

'Monk, why don't we see what happens if we pass the word around that any Sicilians wishing to desert may go on back to their homes. We won't pick them up as prisoners of war.'

'I'll get started on it right away, sir. We can handle it through the local gossips to start with. Let's see how well we do over the grapevine.'

I passed the suggestion on to 7 Army, but when higher headquarters learned of this bargain offer it disapproved the plan. But by then it was too late to halt the desertions that were already mounting in response to the rumour. On 18 July we broke into Caltanisetta, and Monk Dickson called on the local bishop to enlist his aid. Soon the clergy spread the word into the hills and thousands of shabby Sicilians came out of hiding. With this manifestation of good will the Sicilians welcomed us into their homes.

Eventually our recommendation for clemency found its way through channels, and on 28 July legal authority was granted us to parole Sicilian prisoners of war. Of the 122,000 P.O.W.s captured on that island by the American Army, thirty-three thousand were Sicilians paroled to their homes and farms. In town after town that we entered Fascist slogans had been scrubbed from the walls and the posters of Mussolini defaced. Angry mobs fell on local party headquarters to run their functionaries out of town and make bonfires of their files.

General Omar Bradley

Recovering from their initial surprise, the Germans withdrew into the eastern part of the island, to fight their main defensive battle around Mount Etna and the Catanian Plain. Here the fighting was to become heavy and bitter for both British and Americans.

German Difficulties

My flight to Sicily yielded nothing but a headache. I had seen for myself the total breakdown of the Italian divisions and the tactical chaos resulting from their disregard for the agreed defence plan. The west of Sicily had no further tactical value and had to be abandoned. But even so the east of the island or an extended bridgehead round Etna could only be held for a short time. The two German divisions which were bearing the brunt of the battle alone were no longer sufficient—a third was urgently needed if the 'Etna line' were to be consolidated speedily.

Field-Marshal Kesselring, 12 July

After a lull during which both sides reinforced, the Allied offensive was reopened early in August.

Troina: 4–6 August

For three days Allen's attack on Troina was thrown back by savage resistance. From a wooded mountain to the northeast of the city the enemy repelled our assaults with observed artillery fire. Each advance was answered with a jarring counter-attack until Allen was forced to withstand twenty-four of them in six days. To strengthen his attack we committed a second regiment from 9 Infantry Division, increasing to five the total number of U.S. regiments on that front. This last regiment had been ordered to dislodge the enemy from that vantage point where he held a corner on artillery observation. Troina itself was to be bombed until it surrendered or was smashed into dust.

On the late afternoon of 4 August I waited at a bend in the road, high up in Cerami, to witness this air attack, the heaviest to date in our Sicilian campaign. Across the bowl-like depression, now half obscured in dust, the fire from eighteen battalions of artillery hammered the enemy's A.A. positions.

Thirty-six fighters circled high overhead, each loaded with 500-pound bombs. The artillery slackened and the bombers peeled off in a near-vertical dive. Soon the crown of Troina was wreathed in dust. By the time a second flight of thirty-six planes had bombed that stricken city, Troina lay half obscured under a column of grey dust that partially hid the cone of Mount Etna. Once more the infantry started forward, but once more the enemy held and slashed back in counter-attack.

The following day we renewed the offensive. This time Major-General Edwin J. House, Patton's tactical air commander, accompanied me to Cerami to view the air bombing. H hour passed with no sign of air. As we were about to leave in dismay, a drone sounded far off to the south. There, high in the sky, three A-36s were high-tailing for home.

'Holy smokes,' I turned to House, 'now just where in hell do you suppose they've dropped their bombs?'

'I'll be damned if I know,' he said. 'Maybe we'd better get back to your head-quarters and see what went wrong.'

On our arrival the phone was ringing. It was Oliver Leese from British XXX Corps. 'What have we done that your chaps would want to bomb us?' he asked.

'Where did they hit?' I groaned.

'Squarely on top of my headquarters,' he said, 'they've really plastered the town.'

But by now the enemy had taken punishment enough on the *stellung* at Troina. He withdrew and our tanks rolled forward. On the sunny morning of 6 August, Allen's 16th Infantry Regiment scaled the steep sides of Troina in the face of desultory rear-guard resistance. Dazed by their week's ordeal, the Sicilians crawled out of their cellars. Already the hot sun had baked the mountains of rubble that clotted the city's streets and a nauseous odour of death settled over the town. But while the bombing had momentarily stunned Troina, few Germans had been killed.

The morning Allen drove into Troina his 1 Division was accompanied by the 39th Regiment of Manton Eddy's 9 Division. At the head of that unit trooped its bold and eccentric commander, the indomitable Colonel Harry A. Flint of St. Johnsbury, Vermont. Stripped to the waist that he might be more easily identified by his men, Paddy Flint wore a helmet, a black silk scarf, and carried a rifle in his hand. The battle at Troina marked the start of his brilliant but brief combat career.

An old-time cavalry crony of Patton, Flint first appeared at the Corps C.P. in Beja to beg a line command that he might get into the shooting war. At the time he was assigned to A.F.H.Q. in Algiers. 'Hell's bells, Brad,' he complained, 'I'm wastin' my talents with all those featherbed colonels in the rear——'

Soon after the Tunisian campaign ended Manton Eddy asked for a regimental commander to spark up his 39th Regiment, which then showed signs of sluggishness in contrast to its spirited companions.

'What we need in the 39th is a character,' Eddy said.

I sent him Paddy Flint.

After landing in Sicily, Manton reported to corps at Nicosia with Paddy Flint in tow. The 39th was to be attached to Terry Allen for the Troina attack. The remainder of Eddy's 9 Division had not yet come ashore.

'Brad,' Eddy whispered when Paddy ambled off to the G-3 tent for a briefing, 'have you seen this?'

He held Flint's helmet in his hand. On its side there was boldly stencilled 'AAA-O'.

'And just what in hell does that mean?'

'Anything, anytime, anywhere, bar nothing—that's what it means. Paddy has had this thing stencilled on every damned helmet and every damned truck in the whole damned regiment.'

I grinned.

'But haven't you issued some kind of a corps order about special unit markings?'

'Manton,' I answered, 'I can't see a thing to-day—nope, not even that helmet of Paddy Flint's.'

To help his regiment gain confidence under enemy fire, Paddy would stroll about the front, unconcernedly rolling a cigarette with one hand. With his rifle in the other he would gesture scornfully towards the enemy lines.

'Lookit them lousy Krauts. Couldn't shoot in the last war. Can't shoot in this one. Can't even hit an old buck like me.'

These antics of Flint's worried me.

'Some day, Paddy,' I once chided him, 'you're going to walk around like that and get killed. Then you're going to prove just the opposite of what you're trying to teach your men.'

He looked at me strangely for a moment. 'Hell's bells, Brad,' he said, 'you know them Krauts can't shoot——'

Paddy was killed in Normandy when a German sniper shot him in the head. I'm certain he would have called it a lucky shot, but even this satisfaction was to be denied him. For though he lived several hours, the wound had impaired his power of speech. Paddy died, a silent Irishman with a grin on his face.

General Omar Bradley

Patton—the Incident

During the attack on Troina, I drove to the headquarters of General Bradley, who was conducting the attack, accompanied by General Lucas. Just before we got there I saw a field hospital in a valley and stopped to inspect it. There were some three hundred and fifty badly wounded men in the hospital, all of whom were very heroic under their sufferings, and all of whom were interested in the success of the operation.

Just as I was leaving the hospital, I saw a soldier sitting on a box near the dressing station. I stopped and said to him, 'What is the matter with you, boy?'

He said, 'Nothing; I just can't take it.' I asked what he meant. He said, 'I just can't take being shot at.' I said, 'You mean that you are malingering here?' He burst into tears and I immediately saw that he was an hysterical case. I therefore slapped him across the face with my glove and told him to get up, join his unit, and make a man of himself, which he did. Actually, at the time he was absent without leave.

I am convinced that my action in this case was entirely correct, and that, had other officers had the courage to do likewise, the shameful use of 'battle fatigue' as an excuse for cowardice would have been infinitely reduced.

General Patton, G.O.C. 7 Army

After lunch General Blesse, Chief Surgeon A.F.H.Q., brought me a very nasty letter from Ike with reference to the two soldiers I cussed out for what I considered cowardice. Evidently I acted precipitately and on insufficient knowledge. My motive was correct because one cannot permit skulking to exist. It is just like any communicable disease. I admit freely that my method was wrong and I shall make what amends I can. I regret the incident as I hate to make Ike mad when it is my earnest desire to please him. General Lucas arrived at 18.00 to further explain Ike's attitude. I feel very low.

.... Went to church in Royal Chapel at 10.00. At 11.00 I had in all the doctors and nurses and enlisted men who witnessed the affairs with the skulkers. I told them about my friend in the last war who shirked, was let get by with it, and eventually killed himself. I told them that I had taken the action I had to correct such a future tragedy.

General Patton

A Soldier's Prayer

God of our Father, who by land and sea has ever led us on to victory, please continue Your inspiring guidance in this the greatest of our conflicts.

Strengthen my soul so that the weakening instinct of self-preservation, which besets all of us in battle, shall not blind me to my duty to my own manhood, to the glory of my calling, and to my responsibility to my fellow soldiers.

Grant to our armed forces that disciplined valour and mutual confidence which ensures success in war.

Let me not mourn for the men who have died fighting, but rather let me be glad that such heroes have lived.

If it be my lot to die, let me do so with courage and honour in a manner which will bring the greatest harm to the enemy, and please, oh, Lord, protect and guide those I shall leave behind.

Give us the victory, Lord.

General Patton

On 13 August the Germans broke off contact with the attacking Allies and withdrew swiftly across the Straits of Messina to the mainland of Italy.

Messina

It now became a race as to which Army would reach Messina first. Patton was coming along the northern coast road at a great pace. He had his whip out, and brought off a very successful little seaborne landing behind the enemy, which accelerated things.

On 15 August we occupied Taormina, but the going was very bad. The coast road clinging as it did to the steep hills made demolitions an easy matter. Bridges had to be built every few hundred yards, and in spite of the use of landing craft to circumvent the obstacles, progress was very slow. In order to speed up our advance, the Army Commander ordered a seaborne landing to be carried out at Ali on the night of 15–16 August. It was, however, too late, for the enemy had withdrawn.

The Americans won the race and entered Messina on 16 August, and some of our troops who had landed at Ali joined up with them the next day.

Major-General Sir Francis de Guingand

During the 16th, the 7th Infantry overcame the last resistance and by night-fall was on the heights overlooking Messina. About dark we emplaced a Long Tom well forward and had the pleasure of unloading the first one hundred rounds of American artillery on the mainland of Europe. Patrols entered the city during the night as the last Germans made their escape across the Straits of Messina.

.... Just after we arrived in the city, a British armoured patrol entered it from the west. General Montgomery had no doubt been anxious to beat General Patton into Messina for he had landed a patrol a few miles down the coast for the purpose of being there before us.

General L. K. Truscott

ITALY SURRENDERS

The Allied landings in Sicily precipitated a crisis in Italy. On 25 July 1943 Mussolini was overthrown by a coup d'état *and arrested. The King entrusted his government to General Badoglio. On 8 September, five days after British forces landed in Calabria, Italy surrendered. Within two days the Germans had seized control of the country and Badoglio's government was forced to flee to the Allies.*

A Message to Italy

At this moment the combined armed forces of the United States and Great Britain under the command of General Eisenhower and his deputy, General Alexander, are carrying the war deep into the territory of your country. This is the direct consequence of the shameful leadership to which you have been subjected by Mussolini and his Fascist regime.

Mussolini carried you into this war as the satellite of a brutal destroyer of peoples and liberties.

Mussolini plunged you into a war which he thought Hitler had already won. In spite of Italy's great vulnerability to attack by air and sea, your Fascist leaders sent your sons, your ships, your air forces, to distant battlefields to aid Germany in her attempt to conquer England, Russia and the world.

This association with the designs of Nazi-controlled Germany was unworthy of Italy's ancient traditions of freedom and culture—traditions to which the peoples of America and Great Britain owe so much.

Your soldiers have fought not in the interests of Italy but for Nazi Germany. They have fought courageously, but they have been betrayed and abandoned by the Germans on the Russian front and on every battlefield in Africa from El Alamein to Cape Bon.

To-day Germany's hopes for world conquest have been blasted on all fronts. The skies over Italy are dominated by the vast air armadas of the United States and Great Britain. Italy's sea-coasts are threatened by the greatest accumulation of British and Allied sea power ever concentrated in the Mediterranean.

The forces now opposed to you are pledged to destroy the power of Nazi Germany—power which has ruthlessly been used to inflict slavery, destruction and death on all those who refuse to recognize the Germans as the master race.

The sole hope for Italy's survival lies in honourable capitulation to the overwhelming power of the military forces of the United Nations.

If you continue to tolerate the Fascist regime which serves the evil power of the Nazis, you must suffer the consequences of your own choice. We take no satisfaction in invading Italian soil and bringing the tragic devastation of war home to the Italian people. But we are determined to destroy the false leaders and their doctrines which have brought Italy to her present position.

Every moment that you resist the combined forces of the United Nations— every drop of blood that you sacrifice—can serve only one purpose: to give the Fascist and Nazi leaders a little more time to escape from the inevitable consequences of their own crimes.

All your interests and all your traditions have been betrayed by Nazi Germany and your own false and corrupt leaders; it is only by disavowing both that a reconstituted Italy can hope to occupy a respected place in the family of European nations.

The time has now come for you, the Italian people, to consult your own self-respect and your own interests and your own desire for a restoration of national dignity, security and peace. The time has come for you to decide whether Italians shall die for Mussolini and Hitler—or live for Italy and for civilization.

President Roosevelt, 16 July

The *Coup d'Etat*

On the morning of 24 July a rumour spread through Rome that the members of the Fascist Grand Council had insisted that Mussolini should summon a meeting of the Council for that evening. The news was, however, received with considerable incredulity. There was talk of a plot by leading Fascists against the Duce, and it was even thought possible that it might lead to violence. As a matter of fact, the Council met and the discussion continued to a very late hour.

The next morning, Sunday 25 July, there was the sensational news that the Fascist Grand Council had demanded Mussolini's resignation. It was said that his most bitter assailants had been Ciano, Grandi, De Bono and Bottai. The proceedings were summed up in a resolution. The excitement in the city was intense; violent arguments led to brawls in the streets, Fascists being roughly handled.

In the afternoon some intimate friends came to see me. At about five o'clock the Minister of the Royal Household arrived to say that the King wished to see me urgently.

While I was changing into uniform the Minister hurriedly told me that Mussolini had gone to see His Majesty to inform him of the result of the meeting of the Grand Council. The King had forced him to resign, and as he left the palace he had been arrested and taken to a Carabinieri barracks. The King wished me to become Head of the Government. Very much disturbed by such serious news, I went to the Villa Savoia.

The King was quite calm and told me at once what had happened. What he said made so deep an impression on me that I can repeat it almost word for word.

'This morning Mussolini asked me for an interview, which I fixed for this afternoon at 4 p.m. at this villa. When he arrived Mussolini told me that a meeting of the Fascist Grand Council had been held and had passed a vote of censure on him, but he believed that this resolution was not in order. I replied at once that I did not agree with him; the Grand Council was an organ of State which he himself had created by means of a law which had been passed by the Chamber and the Senate; therefore every decision of the Grand Council was valid. "Then, according to Your Majesty I ought to resign," he said with considerable violence. "Yes," I answered, and told him that I forthwith accepted his resignation.'

His Majesty added:

'When he heard this Mussolini collapsed as if he had had a blow over the heart. "Then my ruin is complete," he muttered hoarsely.'

Having taken leave of His Majesty, Mussolini went out, and not seeing his car, he asked an officer where it had gone. 'It is standing in the shade at the side of the Villa,' the officer answered. Mussolini went in the direction indicated when suddenly he found himself surrounded by secret police who asked him to get into a motor ambulance which was standing a little distance away. 'Can't I use my car?' he asked, 'and where are you taking me?' 'To a place where you will be quite safe,' answered the officer. Without saying anything more, Mussolini got into the motor ambulance and was taken to a Carabinieri barracks.

The King then asked me to become Head of the Government; I knew that the country trusted me, that His Majesty would be embarrassed if I refused, and that my refusal would still further complicate a situation which called for immediate action. I put all personal considerations on one side and faced the terrible responsibility I was undertaking. I answered, 'I am very conscious of my lack of political experience; I have never taken any part in politics, but I under-stand the pressing needs of the moment and I accept. As for my colleagues in the Ministry, I have here a list of the politicians who have promised to collaborate and of the parties they represent.' I read to His Majesty the names of Bonomi as Minister of Internal Affairs, Casati as Minister of Education, of Soleri, of Bergamini, of Einaudi, and others.

The King was entirely opposed to this plan. He said that I would have to act with great rapidity and energy both internally and in our relations with the Germans, and that I must not be surrounded by politicians.

'You must have a Ministry of experts,' he added, 'who will carry out your orders efficiently.' 'But as a result,' I said, 'I shall be entirely cut off from public opinion and shall have no contact with the feeling of the country.' 'No', said the King, 'the whole country is with you and will follow you. I am sure that your political friends will support you even if they are not in the Ministry. Here is a list of the new Ministers; they are all experienced and capable officials, with whom you can work.'

So, as the King was determined to have his own way, I ended by agreeing.

General Badoglio

The Führer Betrayed

When I reached my home I was immediately called by telephone from the Führer's G.H.Q. The news from there sounds almost unbelievable. It is to the effect that the Duce has resigned, and Badoglio has taken over in Italy in his place. The whole situation, I was informed, was still very obscure; such news as we received had come over the radio and had been given out by Reuter. At G.H.Q. nobody can determine just what has really happened. The Führer wants me to proceed immediately to his headquarters. . . . It is simply shocking to think that a revolutionary movement that has been in power for twenty-one years could be liquidated in such a way.

. . . . In the final analysis this crisis was, of course, directed against Germany. The idea was to get Italy out of the war so as to create an exceptionally dangerous situation for the Reich. Undoubtedly the English and the Americans sponsored the crisis. The Führer was firmly convinced that Badoglio had already negotiated with the enemy before he took these decisive steps. The assertion in his proclamation that the war would continue meant exactly nothing. There was nothing else he could say, for any statement to the contrary would immediately have called the Wehrmacht into action, and Italy would then have become a theatre of war—the one thing she is now trying to avoid.

. . . . This whole episode is the greatest example of perfidy in modern history. The Führer is firmly determined to see to it that Italy does not betray the German Reich a second time.

Dr. Goebbels

Armistice

On the evening of 8 September, after I had read my proclamation of the armistice over the wireless, I went straight to the Ministry of War. I was convinced that in order to forestall a probable attack by the S.S. it would be advisable to take up my quarters there together with the royal family and the Chief of the General Staff. The Minister of War had given orders for a strong detachment of troops to be on duty inside and outside the building to protect it from a possible German attack. From it I could also communicate by telephone or wireless with everyone. After eating some food I went to lie down in a room which had been prepared for me, for I was completely worn out by the emotions of the day. At 4 a.m. I was awakened because there was serious news, and in another room I found the Minister of War, the Chief of the General Staff, and the Chief of the Army Staff, General Roatta. Roatta described to me in the gloomiest terms the situation of our troops who were being violently attacked by armoured detachments and German parachute contingents; they were already engaged in an indecisive action at the Porta S. Paolo. He was of opinion that, given the strength of the attack, the defence could not last very much longer, and therefore to avoid the capture of the King, the royal family, and the Government it was necessary that we should leave immediately by the one route which was still open, the Via Tiburtina.

It was a momentous decision which I had to take and I had to take it in the utmost haste. I had to consider all the factors. For me one question was of capital importance and overmastered all the others—that was the necessity to maintain at all costs a close and continuous contact with the Allies, so that the armistice, signed by my orders by General Castellano, might continue in operation. As long as it did so Italy would be treated, not as an enemy nation but as a nation which had solemnly declared her intention to make common cause with the British and Americans. If the Government remained in Rome its capture would be inevitable and the Germans would rapidly substitute a Fascist Government who would repudiate the armistice. This disaster must be avoided at all costs, for it would mean the complete ruin of Italy.

There was another vital question—the fate of Rome. Everything possible for the defence of the capital had been done, but the situation described by General Roatta did not admit of any delay. It was essential to take an immediate decision so as to avoid the struggle spreading to the centre of the city with the inevitable result of fire and ruin.

All these considerations brought me to one conclusion—it was to leave at all costs and try to reach the south so as to remain in touch with the Allies.

I said that I approved of the orders given by General Roatta and that I had decided to leave Rome by the Via Tiburtina.

In General Ambrosio's presence I told General Sorice immediately to inform all the ministers what I had decided and named Pescara as the place of meeting. Having given these orders, I went down to the apartment where the royal family had spent the night and communicated to the King my determination to leave Rome and try to reach Pescara by the Via Tiburtina. I did not conceal from him that it was impossible to foresee what would happen and that it was quite possible, even probable, that we should all be captured during the journey.

The King did not make any objection, but it must be clearly understood that I alone was responsible for the decision to go to Pescara.

We got into five motor-cars and went straight to Tivoli. At least three times we were stopped at control posts, but we were allowed to proceed. Tanks were on the road driving towards Rome, but though we believed that they belonged to the Militia Division, we were not sure because we heard loud shouts in German.

We finally arrived at Crecchio and were the guests of the Duke and Duchess di Bovino, and here the Minister of the Navy joined us. He said that he had wirelessed to Pola and Taranto to send the cruiser *Scipione l'Africano* and two corvettes to Pescara, but he did not know whether these orders had been received, and if they had been, whether it would be possible for them to be carried out.

In the afternoon we arrived at the airport of Pescara to be followed by General Ambrosio. I asked him for news of the Minister of War and he said that he had left Sorice in his office very much excited, but he thought that the Minister would join us. At the same time some aeroplanes under the command of Colonel Ranieri arrived, but of the cruiser and the two corvettes there was no sign.

We could not leave in the aeroplanes because the Queen had heart trouble and could not fly. But it was absurd to remain at Pescara, for the Germans could reach it without the slightest trouble. Finally, an aeroplane which I had sent on a reconnaissance flight to the north reported that there was a corvette about fifty miles distant, steaming south. We embarked in her at midnight—the royal family, I, the Ministers of the Navy and the Air Force, the Chief of the General Staff, and my most faithful private secretary, Lieutenant-Colonel Valenzano, who had been at my side ever since 1935, sharing with me good and evil fortune. Neither the Minister of War nor any other Cabinet Minister had joined us. In this cockleshell, which was the corvette *Baionetta*, we steamed south without the slightest idea where we could drop anchor.

Arrived at Bari we saw a German reconnaissance plane which circled over us for about twenty minutes at a prudent distance, sending out wireless signals all the time. Perhaps surprised at seeing so many people on the upper deck, she was calling for other planes to come and attack us. Finally we arrived at Brindisi, and having sent for Admiral Rubartelli, the Admiral of the Port, we learned that there were at Brindisi a certain number of men of an Italian Coastal Division, and at the moment there was no sign of German or British and American troops.

We disembarked and the sailors gave us a great reception, cheering the King and me.

At last we were ashore, in the city which was the first capital of the new Italy.

General Badoglio

An Anti-Fascist Leaflet

Brothers,

After thirtynine months of war, pains and grieves; after twenty years of tiranny and inhumanity, after have the innocent victims of the most perverce gang at the Government; today, September 8. 1943, we can cry at full voice our joys our enthusiasm for your coming.

We can't express with words our pleasure, but only we kneel ourself to the ground to thank Good, who have permit us to see this day.

With you we have divided the sorrow of the war, with you we wish to divide the day of the big victory.

We wish to march with you, until the last days against the enemy N.1.

We will be worth of your expectation, we will be your allied of twentyfive years ago

>Hurra the allied
>
>Hurra the free Italy

The committee of antifascist
ex fighters of the big war

The Duce will enter history as the last Roman, but behind his massive figure a gypsy people has gone to rot.

Dr. Goebbels, 10 September

The Führer Betrayed Again

The Führer anticipated Italian treason as something absolutely certain. He was really the only one who firmly counted on it. And yet, when it actually happened, it upset him pretty badly. He hadn't thought it possible that this treachery would be committed in such a dishonourable manner.

The Führer had hardly got up when he summoned me for a first conference. Contrary to my expectations, he looked exceptionally well. It is always to be noted that in times of crisis the Führer rises above himself physically and spiritually. He had had hardly two hours' sleep and now looked as though he had just come from a holiday. He regards the whole Italian problem as a gigantic example of swinishness and realizes clearly that we must exert every effort to master it. But he also considers that one never knows what the consequences will be in the long run. Something that to-day looks like a great misfortune may possibly prove a great boon to-morrow. During the early struggles of our movement and of our state, crises and setbacks, seen historically, always proved to have been for the best.

On the previous day the Führer had been in Zaporozhe to restore a semblance of order in the southern sector of our Eastern Front. He was quite favourably impressed, although our situation there is critical and our troops have to fight very hard. But during the day the Führer was overcome by a queer feeling of unrest which drove him back immediately to his G.H.Q. Hardly had he arrived here and retired than the first distressing news came from Italy. He then went to work at once.

We now began to examine the situation in detail. In the foreground naturally stood the Italian problem. Our Counsellor of Embassy, Rahn, only a few hours before the Italian treachery, had had a talk with the King, to whom he was being presented. He put a number of critical questions to the King, which the monarch answered either evasively or with absolute assurance. The tenor of their talk was that Italy would remain true to the Axis and in no circumstances desired to desert our ranks. Two days earlier, Badoglio had confirmed this expressly to

Rahn in conversation. Badoglio even gave Rahn his word of honour as an officer and a general. Now we know what to think of that!

The news of the Italian treachery reached us first via a London broadcast, an occurrence that undoubtedly is unique and without precedent in history. Exactly as we imagined and suspected, surrender negotiations had been going on for a long time and had been signed as early as 3 September. The English had insisted upon postponing publication until the moment which promised the best publicity and the greatest political effect. That explains why the Italian troops in Calabria offered almost no resistance.

The real traitor in the whole hostile clique in Italy is Badoglio. He had prepared both the fall of the Duce and the whole capitulation negotiations at long range with the evident intention of hoodwinking and cheating us. The King was his ready tool, a man without character and will and therefore most useful for Badoglio's ambitious plans.

Dr. Goebbels

26

ITALY

On 9 September 1943 Allied landings were made at Salerno, near Naples. The Germans under Kesselring counter-attacked to such effect that the American and British troops were almost thrown back into the sea, and not before a week of slaughter had passed was their foothold secure.

Embarkation Leave

Two days had to be snatched for shopping and affairs generally. We grudged them and forgot them. The other twelve I shall never forget. The weather was extraordinarily kind all the time. However tired we were it was often difficult to go to bed on those lovely warm nights, because hanging out of the window, listening to the silence that was only broken by the occasional gentle plop of a feeding fish, was so fascinating. Sometimes the war gave us a distant reminder of its existence. From our own quiet darkness we could see the flash of guns and the searchlight streaks and knew that the town twenty-five miles away was having an air raid. So far away from it, it seemed unreal, although we had both experienced the reality often enough.

I remember most vividly, perhaps, some particularly still and quiet evenings when we lay in wait for the wood-pigeon, but never fired at them because the peace of those hours was too good to be shattered. We saw them coming—looked at each other—and let them come.

A fortnight can be a very small part of a person's life, but this particular fortnight was much more than merely fourteen days. It was much more than just a rest and a change from Service life. It was to be a memory that could make the difficult times easier for both of us. In the Persian Gulf, in Iraq, Tunis and Italy, Angus could forget the heat and dust in remembering the water lapping against the old boat as we drifted home down the lake with the prevailing wind from the west. Even the flies conjured up the sweep of the moors on that 1 August; and a start at dawn was a reminder of other, cooler early mornings, when a fussy little moorhen bobbed across the lake regularly at 7 a.m. on her mysterious but obviously urgent business.

Mrs. Esther McCracken, widow of Lieutenant-Colonel Angus McCracken,
D.S.O., M.C., died of wounds 12 December 1943

SALERNO

The L.S.T. (landing-ship for tanks) No. 402, Lieutenant-Commander Sprigge, R.N.R., lay off the African coast at Bizerta, carrying a naval crew of fifty and 243 Army personnel, with heavy anti-aircraft guns and vehicles packed tightly into its capacious hold, and myself as brigade commander on the bridge beside the commander. In front of us a long stream of smaller landing-craft, laden with infantry, passed out of the harbour line-ahead and made for the open sea under naval escort with the precision of a drill manœuvre. Our engines had given trouble, and night found us still at anchor in a blackness that was impenetrable and a silence that was almost eerie. Then suddenly the bombers were all about us. The sky was aflame, starred by bursting shells and tracer and criss-crossed by searchlights, in two of which the tiny moth-like form of an attacker swayed and darted and tumbled about the sky. Fires began to glow from the environs of the town, and in slowly mounting streaks across the kaleidoscope a smoke barrage added undertones to the scene. It was a noisy and spectacular farewell to Africa.

The next day, 7 September 1943, the western coast of Sicily lay low down in the mist to starboard, and two massive 130-ton pontoons (to bridge the landing) wallowed in our wake. There was a cool sun on this Sunday morning, and, in the absence of a chaplain, the commander and I mustered all hands to the fore peak for a short ship's service, with the usual adjunct of a Union Jack spread precariously across a packing-case altar. For the lesson I chose Joshua i. 6-9; and I can still hear my voice seemingly disembodied and echoing strangely from the stark and alien steelwork and the skyward guns of the little ship as the solemn sentences followed one another into the gusty air.

'Be strong and of good courage: for unto this people shalt thou divide for an inheritance the land, which I sware unto their fathers to give them.

'Only be thou strong and very courageous, that thou mayest observe to do according to all the law. . . . Turn not from it to the right hand or to the left, that thou mayest prosper whithersoever thou goest. . . .'

The Union Jack rose in a sudden draught and subsided askew upon its box. The bare heads and blue and khaki forms in front of me stood rigid save for the slight swaying of the ship.

'. . . . Have not I commanded thee? Be strong and of a good courage; be not afraid, neither be thou dismayed: for the Lord thy God is with thee whither-soever thou goest.'

The fine resonance of the Old Testament had ever the stuff of battle in it, with just that hint of the theatre which helps a man through the first impact.

Northwards we fared across the Tyrrhenian Sea, line upon line of L.S.T.s, with larger ships and cruisers between us and the invisible coast of Italy, and a busy screen of destroyers, anti-submarine trawlers and motor launches all about us. During the night there had been gunfire over Sardinia away to the west. From the bridge beside the commander the scene was picturesque but quiet, ordered and intelligent. A signal was climbing the mast of the leading ship, and I put out my hand for the code-book. Spelling out the signal with unaccustomed eyes, I wrote on the pad ITALY HAS SURRENDERED, and turned to the commander. 'Do you see what I see?' I said to him. He took the book from me, glanced at it, and replied 'Yes, I expect so. Now what are we going to do?' I picked up the megaphone and ordered all hands aft. Army and Navy packed in below the bridge, and I told the news. There was a moment's pause, then a wild burst of cheering that was echoed from ship to ship as the word spread. The cheering died and I again put up the megaphone. 'Well, that's that. Now I am going to ask you to do a little thinking. What does Italy's surrender mean to you and me? It means just this. It means that, instead of a reception committee of a few half-hearted Italians on the beach at Salerno, we shall find a first-class German armoured corps with its back well up. We shall beat it, but to-morrow's battle will be a trifle tougher than it might have been. Each one of us. . . .' They dissolved slowly into serious little discussion-groups.

In the gathering darkness we altered course and, leaving the commander on the bridge, I went down to his tiny cabin underneath, took off my boots and immediately fell asleep. . . . A penetrating jolt, as though the ship had struck a rock, nearly threw me from the bed and a second jolt brought me to my feet. We had been closely straddled by two bombs, and as I climbed to the bridge hell was let loose. Rocket-ships were hurling blazing salvoes at the unseen coast; monitors, cruisers and destroyers were blasting the blackness and intensifying it by their lightning flashes. The first landing-craft, including one of my light batteries, were groping shorewards. The flickering night was alive with hidden activity.

Dawn, after a sudden faint start, grew slowly amidst the mist and smoke. Detached fragments of mountain began to appear in the intermittent rifts; I remember the greedy delight with which my eyes, mountain-starved by two years on African desert, feasted momentarily upon a jagged crest of the Apennines. Now we were zigzagging towards the beaches, evading the black, sinister mines which, loosened from the sea-bed around us by our devoted minesweepers, clustered like fishes' eggs amongst the waves. And now we were under shell-fire. In front of us a landing-craft with tanks aboard slowly rolled over and sank. A destroyer coming inshore to the rescue was likewise hit. Then the Navy closed in and gave the offending battery everything. (When I visited the spot later in the day, I found the German guns knocked to all points of the compass and their plucky crews splashed about them.) Meanwhile, another German battery, four 88-millimetres, had got the range of our craft over open sights as we moved slowly in, awaiting our turn at the beach. The captain of the next landing-ship beside us was killed by a direct hit on the bridge. Another ship beyond was struck forward and received a number of casualties. Our turn was next. The rounds came over in sharp salvoes and bracketed us with perfect precision, sending showers of spray over us as we changed course cumbrously to vary range. The troops lay flat on deck or were mildly screened in the hold. The naval commander and the brigade commander on the bridge took it in turns, salvo by salvo, to stand and watch the beach ahead, making the usual fatuous and self-conscious jokes which are appropriate to such an occasion, and taking turns ceremoniously also with the single tin-hat which we shared. At length the awaited sign flashed to us from the beach; the commander signalled 'full speed ahead' and we struck the beach fairly and squarely. Sprigge, R.N.R., had brought us in to a nicety.

Sir Mortimer Wheeler

Our landings were on a strip of coast about thirty-six miles long, extending from Maiori, just west of the town of Salerno, southward to Paestum and Agropoli. As the men clambered into landing-craft and the small boats manœuvred noisily into position all around us I could see flashes of gunfire on the north sector of the assault zone where British warships were laying down a barrage in front of the British X Corps' first wave. On the southern sector the American VI Corps was attempting to land quietly without previous bombardment, but there were ominous hints that the enemy was on the alert. Flares and the flames of demolition fires could be seen in that area as the 142nd Regimental Combat Team, led by Colonel John D. Forsythe, and the 141st Regimental Combat Team under Colonel Richard J. Werner—both of 36 Division—felt their landing-crafts touch bottom on the shore at 3.30 a.m.

Then, to end any doubt about surprise, a loudspeaker voice on the shore roared out in English, 'Come on in and give up. You're covered.' Flares shot high into the air to illuminate the beaches, and German guns previously sited on the beaches opened up with a roar. The assault forces came on in, but not to give up. There was resistance on every beach, and within a short time the defenders were strengthened by artillery and planes, so that our opposition increased steadily as dawn approached. Some boats in the first assault wave were unable to reach their designated beaches and had to shift to other sectors, especially Red Beach, where opposition was lighter; while many of the second-wave boats were badly damaged or had to turn back on their first attempt to get ashore. Men were separated from weapons in the confusion when their boats sank. Radio communication was difficult in most instances because of loss of equipment and the intense enemy fire.

But owing to sound basic training and countless instances of personal bravery the assault forces not only held on, but slowly advanced inland. Men squirmed through barbed wire, round mines, and behind enemy machine-guns and the tanks that soon made their appearance, working their way inland and knocking out German strongpoints wherever possible as they headed for their assembly-point on a railway that ran roughly parallel to the beach about two miles away. Singly and in small groups, they reached their first objective by devious means. Private J. C. Jones collected fifty stragglers, guided them off the beach through heavy fire, and destroyed several enemy machine-gun posts. Sergeant Manuel S. Gonzales wriggled on his belly through heavy rifle-fire and grenade-bursts, and with his own grenades killed an 88 mm. gun crew. Private James M. Logan killed three Germans who rushed at him, firing rifles, from a wall, shot near-by machine-gunners, and turned the weapon on the rest of the gun crew as they fled. Lieutenant Clair F. Carpenter and Corporal Degar L. Blackburn, manning a 75 mm. self-propelled howitzer in a defile swept by enemy fire from both flanks, knocked out a machine-gun nest and a tank before they were cut down by a heavy burst of fire. There were countless other acts of heroism.

Under great difficulties heavy weapons were being landed by dawn. Ducks brought in 105 mm. howitzers of the 133rd Field Artillery Battalion, and the 151st Field Artillery Battalion landed at 6 a.m., just in time to beat off a dangerous German tank assault on the beachhead. The veteran 531st Shore Engineers began organizing the communication and supply lines, and bulldozer men, ignoring a steady fire which inflicted many casualties among them, built exit routes for vehicles to move from the beaches through the sand dunes.

In this manner our toe-hold on Fortress Europa was gained.

General Mark Clark, G.O.C. 5 Army

Crisis: 12–14 September

The dust was uncomfortable, but nothing compared with the discomfort that the enemy was causing. The two fingers which 45 Division had stuck out towards the Ponte Sele were being badly bruised, and it appeared that they might be cut off. The 157th R.C.T., under Colonel Charles Ankcorn, which had been shifted to the British flank after being landed in the wrong sector, was instructed to advance along the Sele river to a tobacco factory on high ground near Persano, where it would be able to protect the flank of the northerly finger which 45 Division had exposed.

Ankcorn soon discovered that the Germans had infiltrated across the river and occupied Persano, and had tanks and machine-guns concealed in and around the tobacco factory, where our tanks fell into a trap and were caught in a devastating fire that knocked out five of the seven involved. Thus the high ground near Persano, which the 179th R.C.T. was unable to occupy as it struck towards the Ponte Sele, was now held by the enemy, and served as a kind of spear-thrust into the centre of our entire beachhead. If the Germans could push that spear forward to the sea they would divide the American VI Corps from the British X Corps and gain ground from which to try to turn both flanks.

Kesselring, having gathered reinforcements, immediately set out to exploit this possibility. He sent elements of 26 Panzer Division, 29 Panzer Grenadier Division and 16 Panzer Division southward against the north flank of VI Corps, while the Hermann Göring Division and units of 15 Panzer Grenadier Division and 3 Panzer Grenadier Division attempted to drive the British X Corps from the Montecorvino area. Fighting on 12 September was approaching a new peak all along the front. A strong enemy attack drove the 1st Battalion of the 142nd Infantry out of Altavilla, a vital high point in the American sector. A similar thrust on the British front forced us to abandon Battipaglia. In the centre of the beachhead heavy fighting swung back and forth round the tobacco factory, and elements of 45 Division which had been pushed back from the Ponte Sele were in danger of being isolated. It was becoming obvious that General Dawley had not been fully aware of the strength of the enemy on his left flank, and had not taken steps, or been able to take steps, to protect himself from counter-attack in that sector after the failure of our thrusts towards Ponte Sele and Battipaglia. Furthermore, as the counter-attacks developed, it was disclosed that all the troops had been committed in a cordon defence, leaving none in reserve to meet an enemy break-through. We were getting into a very tight place.

. . . . Later General Dawley telephoned me and reported that the Germans had broken through the Persano sector and were fanning out in our rear areas. It was the first word I had had that such a critical situation had developed at that point.

'What are you doing about it?' I asked. 'What can you do?'

'Nothing,' he replied. 'I've no reserves. All I've got is a prayer.'

That was the beginning of a couple of days of real nightmare for me and a lot of other people. What had happened was that Kesselring had sent a strong attack, led by tanks, against both flanks of the 1st Battalion, 157th Infantry, at Persano, where our line ran along the Sele river. In mid-afternoon German tanks hit the battalion on the left flank, and others, followed by elements of the 79th Panzer Grenadier Regiment and supported by towed artillery, hit the right flank. The fighting was intense for a couple of hours, after which German tanks slipped down a defile, caught our men by surprise, temporarily trapped the battalion headquarters, and eventually forced our lines back enough to let the main German force across the Sele river.

The enemy column divided at Persano, one part of it striking north-east against the 2nd Battalion, 143rd Infantry, which simultaneously was hit by a German attack from the opposite flank and soon became completely isolated. The main enemy thrust from Persano, however, was due south about two miles towards the Burned Bridge. In effect, Kesselring was now pushing forward the spear which had been thrust into the centre of our beachhead perimeter, and he might well drive it clear to the sea, splitting the American and British sectors. He had, furthermore, picked the sector where we were least able to meet such an attack.

Late in the afternoon the Germans pressed steadily along the dusty road towards the Burned Bridge, while their artillery moved into Persano to support the advance, and their infantry made heavy attacks on both sides of the gap to preclude any hope of closing it in time to cut them off. At 6.30 fifteen Nazi tanks reached the heavy underbrush on the north side of the Calore river, where its juncture with the Sele formed the bottom of the Sele-Calore corridor adjacent to the Burned Bridge.

At this point we were almost certainly at the mercy of Kesselring, provided he massed his strength and threw it at us relentlessly. It is possible that he never realized his opportunity, or that he feared a trap, but, considering merely the logic of the situation, it would have been agreed by any military expert that we didn't have much with which to stop him. Well, that's not quite true. There were some military men in the path of the German tank spearhead who would not have agreed. They were the men of the 189th Field Artillery Battalion, under Lieutenant-Colonel Hal L. Muldrow, junior, and the 158th Field Artillery Battalion, under Lieutenant-Colonel Russell D. Funk, both from 45 Division.

The two battalions were on the south bank of the Calore, where a gentle slope runs down to the Burned Bridge. They stripped their gun-crews to a minimum and sent men down that slope with rifles and machine-guns to dig in. They posted six 37 mm. guns to support the men. They went out on the near-by roads and began stopping trucks, jeeps, and everything else that came along. Every soldier who got out of the vehicles was given a gun and put in the line. They collected an emergency reserve of mechanics and truck-drivers to go into action at any point where a break was threatened.

There was a hill on their flank that might have offered the enemy a vantage-point; but by the time I had discovered the immediate situation there were no troops left to take it over, so I ordered a regimental band to be armed and sent there immediately. The hill hadn't any name, and there was some confusion about designating it until I pointed it out and told them to call it Piccolo Peak, because there was nobody there but the musicians.

By this time the German tanks were firing on the positions of the 189th Field Artillery Battalion in preparation for crossing the Calore near the Burned

Bridge; and by this time, too, the sweating, dust-coated men of the two battalions were ready. They opened up with everything they had.

The ford beside the bridge and the road leading to it simply went up in dust. The fields and the woods in which the enemy tanks took cover were pulverized. When the Germans tried to fight their way across the ford the fire laid down by everybody from the artillerymen to the piccolo-player knocked them back on their heels. At one time the two battalions were firing eight rounds per minute per gun, and they acted as if they could keep it up all night, if necessary, and someone passed the ammunition.

After several unsuccessful thrusts the enemy column wavered and began to fall back. By sunset the two battalions had fired 3,650 rounds, and seven guns of Battery B, 27th Armoured Field Artillery, had arrived in time to fire another three hundred rounds. A few minutes later the Germans were in full retreat from the Burned Bridge, and the artillery was feeling fine. I was feeling somewhat better myself, although I knew that we were far from being out of the wood.

When I got back to my headquarters it was obvious that we had narrowly escaped disaster that day, and that we were still in a difficult position all round the front. On the north, or British sector, the enemy had infiltrated in the direction of Maiori, and the situation was critical round Vietri Pass, with reinforcements needed at once.

.... The next day was 14 September, and all day the German attacks continued in strength against our new defence-lines, which had been drastically shortened and reorganized during the night. 36 Division was subjected to new enemy onslaughts, and 45 Division, holding a line west of the Sele river, was under heavy attack along the sector where, by our realignment, we had closed the gap between the American and British forces. On the British sector 46 Division dug in on the hills round the town of Salerno; 56 Division was in an open plain south-east of Battipaglia, where the enemy had excellent observation of its movements and was able to send repeated tank-thrusts against the Coldstream Guards of 201 Guards Brigade and the 9th Royal Fusiliers of 167 Infantry Brigade.

Early in the day, following a conference with General Dawley at 7 a.m., Sergeant Holden drove me by jeep, with my aide, Captain Warren Thrasher, to the front sectors. We drove along the highway to a small road that ran parallel to the south bank of the Sele, and thence followed the front line eastward at the critical point where the German break-through of the day before had been finally halted. We stopped at points where small units had been posted on the shortened front line; it was evident that officers and men had taken a severe drubbing and were tired. Everywhere we stopped I talked to as many of the men as possible, telling them that the situation had improved, reinforcements were arriving, and that this was where we stopped giving ground.

'There mustn't be any doubt in your minds,' I said. 'We don't give another inch. This is it. Don't yield anything. We're here to stay.'

There was plenty of spirit left in the men when they understood the situation, and I felt that they would be equal to the order of the day, to hang on, which I had issued earlier.

At one point we went forward to a hill near the spot where our most forward elements were dug in. Climbing to the top of the hill, I studied the rough terrain ahead of us in the hope of finding some of our forces still hanging on in that sector. There were no such hopeful signs, but I did see eighteen tanks beginning to infiltrate our lines. For a moment I hoped that they were ours, but, studying them through binoculars, I soon discovered that they were German. It was also obvious that they had found a weak spot in our lines, and that if they were merely the spearhead of a big tank attack we were again in the utmost danger of being split apart and crushed. Anxiously I searched the rear area for indications of other tank columns. I couldn't see any—but that didn't mean that they were not there. I could not imagine that Kesselring would fail to exploit this opportunity to rush up powerful armour and break through to the sea.

We hurried back to our own lines and called up an anti-tank unit that I had previously seen there and an engineer unit that was not far away. They were able to get into favourable positions quickly, and laid down a heavy fire that turned back the eighteen tanks. I still can't understand why such an able general as Kesselring failed to carry through on that occasion with a stronger attack force, or why he used his plentiful armour—he originally had probably six hundred tanks at Salerno—in piecemeal fashion at critical stages of the battle. I can't understand it, but I can be thankful for it. Looking back, I often feel that this lapse on the part of Kesselring was all that saved us from disaster.

General Mark Clark

Behind the Lines, near Naples: The 'Free English'

One evening the wardmaster asked me if I would see an officer who had just arrived in an ambulance, as the orderly medical officer could not be found. I went to the ambulance and brushed aside a little group around the doors. Inside was a young, fresh-faced subaltern who said that, while running a road check, he had stopped a car driven by an Italian. An American officer had alighted from the rear of the car and had shot him through the thigh. While he was telling me about his injuries I became aware that someone was trying to attract my attention, so I looked over my shoulder and saw an R.A.F. officer, who said that he could give me all the details. I arranged for the admission of the patient and the warning of the theatre, then took the R.A.F. officer into the mess.

He told me that he had been taking an airfield constructional unit in convoy and had been stopped by two Italian police in mufti with a note requesting the provision of an armed guard and an ambulance, the note being signed by an American officer of the Allied Military Government. Taking some airmen with him he had followed the Italians up the hills, where he had come across an American officer covering two British officers with an automatic, one of the officers being wounded. With commendable presence of mind the Air Force officer had placed the whole lot under arrest and disarmed them. He had then asked the British officers for their pay books, remembering as soon as he had said it that Army officers, unlike those of the R.A.F., did not have pay books, but carried identity cards instead. To his surprise they had both produced pay books. A closer inspection had revealed that the badges of rank on their uniforms were made of cardboard.

The American had then identified himself as an A.M.G. officer. He said that he had been sent up to the hills to investigate a rumour that two British officers were terrorizing a village.

He had gone in a car driven by two Italian police in civilian dress, while he had lain concealed in the back, in the hopes that the men he sought would not be scared off. His plan had succeeded very well. The two had staged a road block when they had seen the car approaching. They had told the Italians that their car was to be requisitioned: when he had emerged from the car, they had remained quite cool and had offered to take him to wherever he wanted to go. He had replied:

'You are the guys I have come to see.'

One of them had drawn his pistol. The American, however, was quicker on the draw, and had shot the Briton through the outer part of the thigh, whereupon the other had rapidly surrendered.

It later transpired that the two were private soldiers who had deserted, and, equipping themselves with home-made badges of rank and police armbands, had made tracks for this village, away up in the Apennines. Arriving at the village as the first British to visit it, they had sent for the mayor and had demanded the surrender of all arms. When this had been done they had settled down as the virtual tyrants of the place, helping themselves to anything they wanted and ruling by terror. It was only after some weeks that the absence of any contact with the Allied forces had made the Italians complain by letter sent at night by a young boy.

The American had obviously been skilled in the use of firearms, as the outer side of the thigh is devoid of vital structures such as large arteries or nerves and, after removal of the bullet and the excision of the dead tissues in its track, the man made a rapid recovery. He had been placed under arrest, but we were too busy at the hospital to be able to provide a guard, so I had asked the chief clerk to get one provided by headquarters. Fortunately he had sent a signal that remained on record, for, in spite of a telephonic promise that a guard would be provided, no one turned up. Five days after his operation, the man stole an R.A.F. sergeant's battle-dress blouse, and, in pyjama trousers, with his stitches still in his leg, deserted again. Up to the time of our leaving Salerno he had not been recaptured, and had presumably managed to join the 'Free English', as the bands of deserters in the hills were called.

Lieutenant-Colonel J. C. Watts, R.A.M.C.

Beefsteak and Potatoes

On our way to Naples we gave a lift to an American private, who, when he noticed the accent of my driver, said:

'Say, you're an American. How come you're with a Limey outfit?'

Ben Ford explained that he had volunteered for the American Army, but had been turned down on medical grounds. Our passenger asked when this had been and Ben told him 1940.

'Oh, before the war,' said the G.I. 'Gee, they take anybody now. Why, there's a guy goes up for his medical and he has no arms, but they enlist him and post him to a unit. When he gets there the adjutant says, "You got no arms. Never mind, son. There's a place for you in this Army. Just go and help those two guys over there, pumping water into buckets." "But I can't help them. I've no arms." "Never mind. Just tell them when to stop," said the adjutant. "They're both blind."'

The American continued in similar vein for the rest of his journey, claiming that he had been a fool to join up, as he was in a reserved occupation, making clutch pedals for Dodges. He firmly announced his war aims, saying:

'When I get me home I am going to rent a cabin in the woods and I am going to furnish it with beefsteak. Yes sir, beefsteak and potatoes.'

Lieutenant-Colonel Watts

Naples: Time Bombs

The German time bombs brought still another horror to the city. There is an implacable impersonal wickedness about laying time bombs among a helpless civilian population which seemed peculiarly German, or at least it represented the state of mind the Germans were reaching through these declining years of their war. They mined all places like the telephone exchange and the post office, where considerable numbers of people were likely to be hurt or killed. The explosions went off without the slightest warning, as a rule, and there very few safeguards which could be taken, as most of the mines were laid secretly at night by the last enemy soldiers to leave the city. In effect the explosions were rather like the V-2s which fell on London and northern Europe much later in the war.

I remember the gardener in our villa above the town reported to us that he had been hearing a constant ticking noise at the foot of the cliff beneath the bridge that carried the main road round the coast. One of our officers jumped into a car and called on the bomb disposal squad. 'You will have to wait,' they told him. 'We will put you on the list of suspicious noises. We have a hundred and fifty jobs on hand already.' Eventually they came and took two big charges away from under the bridge.

It was the impersonality, the cold pre-calculation of the mining that so astonished one at first. Many of us had only known the German Army in Africa, where the war had been reduced to a straight military contest between the forces in the field. In general, the Germans had behaved very well. There had been no Gestapo. But now something quite different was happening behind the German lines. One could easily understand their mining the roads and ports on their way of retreat, since that was a military device. But now for the first time in our experience they were killing civilians for no military advantage but out of a simple desire for killing, and possibly for revenge.

A hundred atrocity stories were reported, most of them greatly exaggerated, some quite true. At the announcement of the Italian armistice the German soldiers had, quite understandably, reacted strongly against their former allies. Houses and shops were entered and looted. Watches and jewellery were seized from women in the streets. Italians were impressed into labour gangs. None of all this is very remarkable in an operational zone. You cannot submit men to the brutality of war and then expect them to come out of the line and behave like little gentlemen. But the German command deliberately fostered the hatred of the Italians. The soldiers found they could go to further and further extremes without any official reprimand. Rape was winked at. Death sentences were pronounced on civilians who were merely suspected of assisting the Allies. Then the soldiers and their junior officers were licensed to carry out summary executions on the spot. That meant that you could kill on sight, kill on a whim and get away with it. If an Italian peasant refused to give you a chicken you simply shot him and took the chicken. If someone sniped at you from a village you simply lined up the inhabitants and shot them. And then, if you felt like it, you burned the village. I do not say that at this stage the German Army in the west was entirely committed to this savagery, but here and there quite definitely the assassin complex began to break out. And there was a special viciousness in it since the Italians had once purported to be their friends. The senseless burning of books in Naples was part of the same thing.

All through the war up to this point the reactions of the Allied soldier towards the enemy, and the reactions of his people at home, had been developing on broadly different lines. The divergence was particularly marked among the British. Every time any of us went home to England we were struck by the intensity of the hatred of the enemy. A number of things seemed to have contributed to this feeling—the bombing, the endless difficulties of life occasioned by the war like the blackout, the anxiety for the safety of the men abroad. Then, too, the people were under a daily barrage of propaganda. Since they had no direct physical contact with the Germans, the German soldier was little by little invested with a monstrosity and savagery that was almost inhuman.

The experiences of the soldier in the field up to this point were, in the main, quite different. As soon as he met a German prisoner he observed that to all outward appearances he was a normal human being. A bit pompous, perhaps, and wooden, but still just another man. It was rather gratifying to have fought him and caught him. Owing to a very thorough lack of newspapers and radio sets the average soldier viewed the enemy freshly and at first hand, and also in a very limited way. The war for the soldier was not a thing of imagined fears but a very simple mechanical process. The enemy was a defined and exact animal who had to be beaten by certain physical means.

Then, too, it was a very different thing being bombed in the field to being bombed at home. In the field you did not care much, and you certainly hated the German no more, if a bomb fell over the hill and destroyed a foreign village. The main thing was that it had not hit you personally or the others in your platoon. At home every bomb counted. It was a bomb on England. It expanded the hatred.

I am not speaking now of the soldier's feelings at the height of a battle (the mixture of desperation, fear, anger and hatred is quite definite on the firing-line), but of the average overall reaction to the Germans up to this time. In a word, it had none of the acidity and passion which one found at home. It was usually a waste of time for an officer to bluster to his men about the 'Boches', and call them murderers. He got far better results by simply referring to the enemy as though he were an abstract evil which had to be destroyed. And after the fight was over the reaction of the average soldier on seeing the prisoners was to think: 'Well, the poor dumb beggars, they certainly bought it. They've had it.' And he would hand out his cigarettes.

As we went into Europe we found more and more that it was the civilians who hated the Germans most, not the soldiers. But about this time the men in Alexander's armies began to notice a difference in some sections of the German Army. Whenever they overran areas where the young S.S., the Hitler Youth or the Gestapo had been they found the unmistakable evidence of atrocities— rooms where civilians had been tortured, the courtyards where firing squads operated, the houses looted and bodies lying about. The number of atrocities was in direct proportion to the condition of the German Army; where its situation was desperate the atrocities increased. This developed into a general rule during the whole retreat of the enemy through Europe.

The effect of it upon the soldier was to bring his attitude round towards that of his people at home. It was a slow process, but it began here in Italy and accelerated. The soldier began to hate the Gestapo in the same vicarious and violent way as the people in England did. The sight of the civilian bodies in a Naples street after a time-bomb explosion made him angry. The old feeling, 'We have got to fight for liberty and honour and all the rest of it' was replaced for short intervals by the more animal reaction that demanded revenge.

Alan Moorehead

A.M.G.

As the Germans withdrew in Italy, Fascist civil officials usually fled with them and left communities without normal governmental functions or means of maintaining law and order. Public utilities were disrupted by war. Transport was almost non-existent for civilian use. Food was extremely scarce, and distribution of the low food stocks was almost impossible. Communities were torn with dissension—pro-Ally against pro-Fascist—royalists against republicans— town against country—landowners against peasants—capital against labour. Throughout northern Italy, particularly, there was a strong Communist Party ready to fan the flames of dissension and to exploit every opportunity for subversion. In the Partisan movement there had been an uneasy truce among the conflicting elements, while all concentrated against the common enemy. The withdrawal of the Germans, however, was followed by a bitter struggle for power among the dissident factions which verged at times on civil war.

Allied Military Government, or A.M.G. as it was familiarly known, controlled occupied territory by establishing and supervising civil administrations. It was composed of specially selected or trained officers and men of all branches of the service of both the United States and Great Britain. The Allied Control Commission supervised execution of the armistice terms by the Provisional Italian Government and directed the military government except in areas where the Allied Armies were operating, in which case the establishment and supervision of military government was a responsibility of the Army commanders. In 5 Army, this task fell to the G-5 or Civil Affairs Officer of the Army staff assisted by A.M.G. personnel attached to 5 Army.

Brigadier-General Erskine E. Hume, G-5, 5 Army, was the staff officer responsible for the establishment and supervision of Allied Military Government in areas occupied by 5 Army. Hume and his assistants followed closely behind the troops. In each community they organized the civil administration promptly. They appointed mayors, judges and police officials. They restored public utilities—power, telephone, telegraph. They opened banks and supervised the currency; they established schools, opened factories, supervised labour, and provided for collection of food available in the localities. One of their most important functions was the distribution of food, and a very large part of the food to sustain the civilian population was obtained from Allied sources. The value of their work can hardly be overestimated.

General Truscott

Italy Turns Against Germany

Badoglio has issued an appeal to the Italian public. This appeal is about the most shameless thing that has ever come from the pen of a marshal. He calls upon the Italian people to engage in guerilla warfare; he places himself on the side of our enemies; he declares that we betrayed Italy and left the Italian divisions in the lurch on all battlefields, and that we are now plundering Italy. His aim is a strong and faithful Italy—in short, he commits to paper whatever the human tongue can fabricate in the way of lies and hypocrisy.

. . . . The Führer is determined to strip the Italian cities completely of their anti-aircraft defence. The Italians deserve nothing better than abandonment to their military fate.

Dr. Goebbels, 22–23 September

On 13 October Italy declared war on her erstwhile ally. Dr. Goebbel's comments on this have not survived.

DEADLOCK

The long and bloody grind up the Italian peninsula was about to begin. The mountainous country on the Allied line of advance to Rome was appallingly difficult, and ideally suited to defence. The weather broke, and the Germans took full advantage of what Nature offered to delay the advance and finally to halt it. The Allies were slowed down by heavy resistance at the Volturno river and came to a halt, their momentum spent, before the immensely strong German winter line running from the Sangro on the Adriatic to the mouth of the Garigliano on the west coast. Little impression had been made on the German defences before winter set in.

Incessant rains did more to delay our advance than either German demolitions, which were bad enough, or German delaying action. Along the main highways there were piles of fine big trees which the Germans felled to interlock across a road, in places where there was no way round. Booby-trapped and mined, these were formidable obstacles which required much time and labour to remove. In many places in the mountains the road passed through the narrow streets of ancient towns. Here the Germans demolished the fronts of whole blocks of old stone buildings, completely blocking the narrow streets. By-passes were rarely possible, and removal of the rubble was impossible. Our one way forward was to bulldoze new tracks across the rubble heaps often at the level of the second storeys of the gaping buildings. There was an encouraging sign, however, that the enemy might be running short of demolitions. In many places artillery shells and anti-tank mines were used for demolition purposes, and many structures prepared for demolitions lacked demolition charges. One rather unusual delaying measure which the Germans employed during this period was that of destroying mules in the countryside to prevent their falling into our hands. Obviously, the Germans had not liked our pack trains and mounted men.

General Truscott

Across the Volturno

Under ordinary conditions the Volturno was fordable at many places, but the incessant rains had transformed it into a major obstacle. We had been preparing to cross the river even before we reached it on 6 October. Few assault boats were available—not nearly enough to lift the assault battalions—so we had to improvise. We obtained life rafts from the Navy in Naples, extra water and fuel cans from our own and captured stocks, a large quantity of Italian life jackets found in storage in Naples, and other material from which we improvised rafts and ferries for crossing men, mortars and machine-guns, and even a few light vehicles. As reconnaissance indicated some places where men could wade the stream, we found miles of rope for use as guide ropes to aid in fording. There was a limited amount of waterproofing material left over from the Salerno landing. This we obtained and used to waterproof tanks, and tank destroyers, and communications vehicles for early infantry support.

Division engineers had sufficient pontoon equipment for one ten-ton bridge, capable of division loads, but not for tanks, heavy artillery or heavy engineer equipment. Provision of heavier bridges is a Corps and Army responsibility which Corps solved in this instance by attaching to the Division Company B, 16th Armoured Engineer Battalion, with pontoon equipment for a bridge capable of carrying thirty tons. Besides these two bridges we improvised another bridge from a few extra pontoons, floats, railroad iron, and matting used for landing fields, which was capable of carrying light vehicles. Because of time required for construction the light 'jeep' bridge was to be ready first, and over it would pass the light vehicles with heavy weapons, communications and supplies for the infantry battalions. Several hours later, the Division bridge would be ready for trucks and Division artillery. Still later, the thirty-ton bridge would be ready for crossing tanks, heavy artillery and heavy engineer equipment.

While these preparations were under way, the regiments were conducting intensive reconnaissance night and day to find the best crossing places and to locate every enemy machine-gun, gun emplacement and defensive position along the river line. Night after night men waded and swam the cold river, often under fire, to obtain the vital information. Meanwhile commanders and staffs worked night and day to complete and perfect all plans and preparations.

. . . . On the enemy side of the river, opposite Monte Tifata and immediately above the village of Triflisco, was the spur which marked the southern end of the long ridge leading northwest towards Teano along which the Division was to attack. This spur rose steeply to a height of more than eight hundred feet and the ridge extended northwest to Monte Grande and a series of higher hills. From the sides open to us the spur could be scaled by infantry; it was not practicable for vehicles, although vehicles could come down the crest from the north.

. . . . We knew that we were opposed by the Mauke Battle Group, at least half of the Hermann Göring Division, one of Germany's best. The Germans had fortified the two small hills opposite Monte Castellone, the line of the road and railroad, and the heights beyond. Knowing that the Triflisco area was the only suitable site for a heavy bridge, the Germans held the ridge above Triflisco in strength. Mobile reserves including tanks were in readiness in the northern end of the valley to oppose our crossing.

Our plan was simple, as all good tactical plans must be. Our aim was to clear enemy fire from the river line to permit building bridges so that the entire Division could cross over in the shortest possible period of time. We would first cross the infantry battalions with tanks and tank destroyers supported by the fire of the Division artillery emplaced south of the river. Opposite Triflisco, where the Germans expected an attack in force, we would make a full-scale feint, which, timed and co-ordinated with the British crossing at Capua and their demonstration in the area, would lead the Germans to believe that it was our main attack. While the Germans were preparing to meet this attack we would cross the 7th and 15th Infantry Regiments in the flat valley to the east to advance rapidly to the north and gain the heights in the rear of German defences.

. . . . Promptly at midnight the fireworks began, marked by the flash and rumble of guns as the feint attack and the mass of British artillery on the left opened fire. Accompanied by Major-General Geoffrey Keyes, now commanding the II Corps soon to arrive in Italy, who had come up to see the show, I went to the observation post in the old monastery to see the attack get under way. Promptly at 01.00, our Division and attached artillery began their preparation fire. On the enemy side of the river the whole area seemed filled with the flash of bursting shells, and the guns in the valley below us rumbled and roared against the surrounding mountains, drowning out all other sounds. The night was clear, but we could see little more than the flash of bursting shells as we watched and shivered in the chill night air. Five minutes before the zero hour of 02.00, white phosphorus, intermingled with the high explosive, shrouded the whole valley with a heavy pall that blotted out the landscape. Then came word that the battalions were crossing.

The crossing had just begun when Carleton telephoned that the British crossing at Capua had failed. 56 Division had crossed one company but it had encountered heavy resistance and had to be withdrawn. All further attempts to cross there were cancelled. I was not surprised, for had the British intended to make a serious effort to cross at Capua, the attempt would have been made in greater strength. Nevertheless, that left only British artillery to interfere with enemy movements on our western flank.

.... At the observation post in the old monastery soon after daylight I talked the situation over with Bill Campbell, the Division artillery commander. He was prepared to lay down the mass of the Division artillery on any threat which developed. Near the crossing site of the 7th Infantry, perhaps an hour later, a few tanks and tank destroyers were standing about in an open field and occasional enemy shells were falling in the neighbourhood but doing no damage. Across the river there were sounds of battle in the valley beyond, but all was concealed from view by the smoke. Unarmoured bulldozers had been prevented from breaking down the banks so that tanks could enter, although several operators had become casualties in trying to do so.

On my way from Sherman's Command Post, I found an engineer platoon on its way to the site of the Division bridge. In a few brief words I painted for them the urgent need for courageous engineers who could level off the river bank even under fire so that tanks could cross and prevent our infantry battalions being overrun by the enemy. Their response was immediate and inspiring. I left them double-timing towards the river half a mile away to level off the bank with picks and shovels—which they did, while tanks and tank destroyers neutralized enemy fire from the opposite bank.

.... It was then mid-morning. The 2nd and 3rd Battalions of the 15th had captured the hills on the north bank of the river, and were reorganizing under heavy fire to continue their advance. On our right, 34 Infantry Division was making slow progress. On the left, the 2nd Battalion, 30th Infantry, had still not been able to cross the river but the demonstration fire and smoke screen were being maintained. But there was word that tanks were fording the river in rear of the 7th Infantry.

Major-General Matt Ridgway arrived to see how the battle was going. Leaving him at the observation post with General Campbell, I continued on to see how the bridges were coming. The jeep bridge was almost finished. At the bridge site southwest of Caiazzo, work on the Division bridge was well under way but had stopped because of artillery fire which had damaged several pontoons, trucks and jeeps, and caused some casualties. When I explained to the engineers that the bridge had to be finished in spite of enemy fire, that gallant company returned to work as nonchalantly as though on some engineer demonstration. In spite of artillery fire which caused a number of casualties and continued until the 15th Infantry advance captured the guns which were causing the trouble, the bridge was completed during the afternoon.

Not far from this point I found General Eagles, temporarily commanding the 15th Infantry. Colonel Ritter had been injured in an accident on 6 October. There on a mountain spur, we watched German tanks approaching the flank of the 7th Infantry in the valley across the river. Eight or ten German tanks drove down the valley from the north and turned eastward well north of the road and railroad. Three or four of our own tanks were making their way northward from the river towards the road. Then concentrations of artillery landed among the German tanks. When the dust and smoke cleared so that we could see, the remaining German tanks were making off to the north still pursued by bursting shells. It was a grand sight, and I felt better. Later I was to learn that a forward observer, Lieutenant Jenkin R. Jones, 10th Field Artillery, had spotted the approaching tanks. Setting up his radio in an exposed location, he called for artillery fire and continued to direct it, under fire from the approaching tanks. When the attack was stopped, the leading German tank was within fifty yards of his position.

General Truscott

Although the breaking of the German line on the Volturno was achieved by mid-October, we were confronted during the following month with some of the most difficult terrain and the worst weather of the campaign. The rain came down in torrents, vehicles were bogged above the axles, the lowlands became seas of mud, and the German rearguard was cleverly entrenched on the hills to delay our progress. We knew from questioning prisoners that the main enemy force had retired to a *Winter-stellung*, or 'Winter Line', a strong outpost to the Gustav Line, which guarded the Liri and Rapido valleys from the south.

General Mark Clark

Visitors: French

At the end of October General Giraud came to Naples in connection with the preparations for putting French troops into the field as part of 5 Army. We were steadily adding units of different nationalities to our polyglot army, which in the end represented a score of countries. The French General was a welcome guest, and I arranged for him to occupy a van next to mine in the Caserta woods. With Lieutenant-Colonel Arthur Sutherland as his guide and interpreter, Giraud visited VI Corps Headquarters and pushed his way up to an observation post where he could witness an attack by 3 and 34 Divisions. He was the kind of officer who always wanted to know what was going on at the front, and usually felt he had to see it with his own eyes.

This was evident when he returned to my quarters and agreed to talk to the correspondents who had assembled there. We went out under the trees and stood before a map showing the front lines while photographers crowded round. Giraud asked me to point out on the map the front positions that he had visited. When I had done so he said, 'May I make an observation?'

'Certainly,' I replied.

'Your headquarters is too far behind the front lines. I'll give you some historical examples of what I mean. In the first World War, when I commanded a regiment, my headquarters was only half a kilometre behind the front line. In the beginning of this war, in 1940, I commanded an army in France, and my headquarters was only two kilometres behind the front.'

'Yes, General,' I said, 'and, as I recall, you were taken prisoner by the Germans on both of those occasions.'

General Mark Clark

Russians

It was while this fighting was in progress that I received the five Soviet Army officers who were visiting the 5 Army front. The party, including General

Vasilieff and General Solodovnek, came to my van in a jovial mood, and expressed great interest in getting a close-up of the fighting.

'We want to see what the Americans are like in action against the Huns,' Vasilieff exclaimed, after discussing the valiant stand of the Red Army on the Eastern Front and the manner in which they were slaughtering the enemy. 'We would like to get right up to the front.'

I poured him another drink of vodka, which the Russians had brought, and said, 'I'll make certain that you see some fighting.'

The Russians were accompanied by three American officers, but I assigned a British officer attached to my staff, Major Renwick, who spoke Russian fluently, to see that the party got a good look at what was going on. In fact, I emphasized to Renwick that it would be unfortunate if our visitors were given any grounds for feeling that we didn't want them to see everything, because from their questions I was sure that they had been sent to our front to find out whether the Italian campaign had drawn off from the Russian front any appreciable German strength. We knew from questioning prisoners that it had, but the Russians had trouble in believing it and were inclined to regard the Italian fighting as a picnic.

Renwick proved more than able to conduct the tour. He took them up towards the rugged three-thousand-foot-high peaks of the Camino hill-mass, where enemy artillery made travel more or less hazardous on any road. He put them astride some mules, and led them up the twisting mountain-paths where American troops were struggling to overcome mines, wired booby-traps, machine-gun nests, and mortar positions concealed deep in the rocky slopes. With the help of the elements, he saw that they were rained on most of the day, and had to slither through sticky mud when they dismounted from the mules. Finally, to complete the picture, he got himself wounded by a shell-fragment.

That night, when I saw the Soviet mission at dinner-time, they were considerably less jovial than when they started out. I might even say that they were impressed by what they had seen. Later in the evening, when I questioned them about the day's trip, Vasilieff suggested that I had misunderstood his explanation of just what the mission wished to see.

'What we're most interested in,' he said, 'is logistics. We want to see how your rear elements are organized and how your supply problems are handled.'

He took another gulp from his vodka-glass. 'After all,' he added, 'we can die for Mother Russia any day in Russia. Why should we die in Italy?'

General Mark Clark

Survey on Monte Camino

At first light on that dreaded day an officer and two sergeants set out to recce the two left-flank posts—Charlie and Don. Through Sessa, Ponte and on to Roccamonfina, where we called in at Divisional H.Q. to find out if anyone knew anything. No, we must go to Brigade H.Q. to get a clear view of the situation. On we went, and eventually arrived at Campo—a quaint little village tucked away in a fold of this great Camino *massif*, as safe as houses (we thought). Yes, we got the information we wanted: 'Jerry was occupying such and such villages' —'Last night our patrols went so far'—'We've got a platoon of infantry here'— 'In this sector the situation is rather obscure.' They say it never rains but it pours; but why on top of all my other qualms did they have to say that in the particular area I was going to occupy the situation was obscure? Personally, though, I'm a fatalist; and I know the gods don't like me, young though I am.

Following the rough, stony mule track, the three of us sweated and strained up the steep back slope of the ridge. We were bound for a point near the Monastery. Glossing over a few of the hours of my life that don't want remembering, I'll only say now that we got to the top. False crests were the bane of our lives that day, but when the job has got to be done, one doesn't bother with such trifles. Just over the top of the first ridge there was a burying party, and we pushed on, picking our way carefully over the bald boulder-strewn *massif*. Here and there a few inches of soil bore some meagre vegetation, with a tree or two on the more verdant areas of this hardened limestone mountain. The last ridge was our objective, and after crawling cautiously on hands and knees round a stony crag, we found a spot for Charlie Post. The Monastery was out of the question—it was said that the bodies were piled up inside, with no chance of getting them buried. As fast as they were interred under a few inches of rubble, Jerry sent a shell or two to dig them all up again. Shells are no respecters of persons, and both friend and enemy suffered the same.

Light was fading and we had to get back, with but a vague idea of where Don Post was going. The next day I was going out with some of the men to get the post settled and the survey initiated, if not finished. Thanks to the enemy's thoroughness in blowing up every bridge, large and small, we had to walk back six miles to Campo, where we had arranged to rendezvous with our trucks. The village was absolutely packed with infantry and carriers, some reliefs and some resting for a day or two. But there was a large stable waiting for us and something to counteract that gnawing pain I'd begun to get in my stomach; fortunately for me, too, someone had made my bed.

That night we were introduced to our mules, one per post. What staunch friends these gallant hybrids have turned out to be, never flinching come what may, and never hesitating in any weather. 'Heads, he bites you; tails, he kicks you!' was a libel invented by field artillery drivers. In the same class of faithfulness we must put the muleteers, too. They all came from North Italy and were of the best type. If they were afraid of anything on this earth, they never mentioned it to anybody.

Early next morning the mule, his master, three surveyors and myself journeyed forth into a far country (so it seemed), but unlike the Children of Israel, not into a land flowing with milk and honey. We covered the first five miles together, and then one surveyor and I went on farther to see what was what. Along the track we had already passed the bodies of seven mules which hadn't been able to 'make it' and had either died or been shot by the more humane drivers. Ours, fortunately, was still going strong. A further half-mile brought us 'over the top', the ridge at this point being only about four hundred and fifty metres high and some half-mile from Cocuruzzo. Despite the unfortunate conditions under which we viewed the scenery, we had to admit that from a purely aesthetic viewpoint it was wonderful. To the left, the great Majo *massif* rose three thousand five hundred feet above the Garigliano meandering round its foot to the sea. To the right, Monte Cassino, backed by the gigantic Monte

Cairo, hid the central mountains. Straight in front lay the main valley—Ambrogio, Pontecorvo and on to Frosinone. We could see some forty miles before a ridge, dimmed by the distant mist, blocked the view to Rome. Across this valley stretched small hillocks with farms and scattered houses breaking the level of the intervening plain. I sat for many minutes admiring it all, the war far from my mind, until suddenly that all-too-familiar whistle presaged the arrival of a shell, twenty yards above me on the hill. Egotistically I thought that shell had been meant particularly for me, but I learned later there were three gun O.P.s on the top of the ridge.

This hill, the only decent place for a flash-spotting O.P., was an obvious target for Jerry's artillery, as we came to know only too well. There was one other minor difficulty about this post. Ever since we had left Calabritto, some miles back, we had been 'hit in the face' by innumerable red notices, one every hundred yards or so: 'Keep to the Track', 'Verges not Cleared', 'Danger S Mines', etc. Even had I chanced it personally, I realized that the twelve men on my post would not necessarily step into my footsteps every time, so I wandered up and down the main path until I found what I was looking for—signs that someone else had cut across country, which was all I wanted.

I could describe the next two days' events in detail, but there's no need to dwell on how we laid about nine miles of double wire from post to rest centre, with half a crook stick; how we pitched and hid a bivouac tent on a rocky crag, three feet by two feet, to shelter the people at the post; how, at dusk, we managed to get our instruments up and hidden from the enemy who overlooked us—or could have done, had he known where to look; or finally, how we 'brewed up' at three o'clock in the morning. What of the weather? It was fairly temperate to begin with, until the wind veered to the north and made life a real hell. The sun went and the rains came. Despite wearing all the clothes available, two, perhaps three, pairs of socks, long pants, short pants, shirt (or shirts), overcoat over battle-dress, a blanket around our feet, it was still impossible on some of the colder nights to sit at the instrument for more than half an hour without walking round to revive a few odd fingers and toes and the general blood circulation. But what a contrast to get back into the tent after a spell of duty and have a tot of rum!

Sergeant V. G. Brailey, killed in action

It was not until 10 December that a bridgehead had been established over the Moro river by the Canadians. The advance from here towards Ortona was fiercely contested and the German paratroops in the town were fanatical in their resistance. By Christmas Day our line ran from just short of Ortona on the right (1 Canadian Division), Villa Grande (8 Indian Division), Arielli (5 Division), and on the left the New Zealand Division had all but captured Orsogna.

The fighting during this period had been fairly costly, and one rather wondered what we achieved. Enemy formations were certainly pulled over from opposite 5 U.S. Army, and heavy casualties had been inflicted on the Germans. With snow in the mountains and mud everywhere else, we began to think about Passchendaele. Had we gone on too long? Were the troops being driven too hard? I feel very definitely that a mistake was made in pressing the Sangro offensive as far as it was. When once the weather had broken it was extremely unlikely that we could have advanced across the mountains, even if we had reached the Pescara–Rome road. Perhaps we were still not prepared to give the weather best, resenting her behaviour after the dryness of the desert. Who should have stopped the operations—the Army or the Army Group? The Army Group, I suppose, for its job was to assess whether our contribution was proving worth while within the bigger picture.

Major-General Sir Francis de Guingand

CASSINO

Throughout the winter and the early spring the Gustav Line and especially its key point, Monte Cassino and the surrounding mountain massifs protecting the approaches to Rome, was subjected to a continual battering by British, Americans, French and Poles. This war of attrition made little or no progress in face of skilful and determined resistance.

The Battlefield, from Monte Trocchio

If the morning was clear we could see the Garigliano shining in the moonlight as it bent in and out, appearing as a series of tiny dots. Often the valley was hidden completely by drifting smoke from the generators at the station, so that I looked out over billowing clouds to the Monastery, which stood gleaming in the early sunshine. Behind soared Monte Cairo, six thousand feet high, its gullies streaked with snow, which ran down from its white pyramid. Gradually the mist thinned out as the wind veered, and in a few minutes the whole valley was clear.

At this time of day visibility was at its best. I looked down on the near part of the valley so vertically that it seemed to be spread out like a map: the river curved, each bend easily identifiable, the railway, roads and paths stretched like tapes, the farm buildings dotted among the trees and tracks in chessboard fashion. Thus map-reading was made very easy, but with the deepening perspective ridge faded into ridge until it was extremely difficult to decide, often within a thousand yards, where a particular farmhouse actually was. At first glance the Liri plain appeared to be as flat as a billiard table (its nickname was the 'Cricket Pitch'), but in reality it was honeycombed with little valleys and gullies, giving differences in height of a hundred and fifty feet in many places. A set of air photos, gridded to match our 25 maps, solved many a difficulty, and without them some identifications would have been impossible.

The relief signaller came up at mid-day with the lunch and crawled down a specially constructed shady gully, at whose entrance was a colourfully worded notice surmounted by a skull and crossbones. In the hot weather the early afternoon was the worst part of the day: one's head drooped, it seemed impossible to keep one's eyes open; the only movement was when an emerald lizard streaked over the hot stones. Then, later, a slight breeze rustled the silver leaves of the olive trees overhead, the rank, brittle grass quivered, and it was possible to concentrate once again. But there were always noises to break up the day: the infantry below singing and clattering their mess-tins; the unexpected bray of a donkey or the peck of a bird breaking a snail-shell; the sounds of guns and mortars—constant 'shellreps' to be sent back; the characteristic woof, blare and following moan of the 'sobbing sisters', which gave themselves away by their quick, fiery streaks shooting into the air; the shriek of our own close-range shelling, which seemed to skim over our heads with only a few inches to spare— once or twice those inches were missing and there was a loud crash behind us, up there on the top of the ridge.

Later in the day the sun struck across the valley slantwise, seeming to pick up all the motes in the atmosphere, so that, first, distant belts of trees and then nearby houses would be completely shrouded by haze. It was at its worst at sunset, when the valley was flooded with brilliant golden light, silhouetting the distant hills but hiding everything else completely—except the forward slopes of Trocchio, where one felt conspicuous and naked. We even went to the length of making cardboard hoods for the lenses of binoculars in case they caught the sun. Benefiting by one of Rommel's maxims, the enemy would send trucks down Route 6 at full speed, hoping to get away with it in the bad light. However, it was possible to pick out the tell-tale flare of dust in the distance and lay on a recorded target in time. After a week's persistent shelling of every truck we saw, they realized that we meant business and movement dried up entirely. The one exception to this was the gigantic ambulance armoured car; its body glittered in the sunshine with brilliant white paint, a dozen enormous flags fluttered on every side. Its progress was marked by eerie silence: it seemed as if a thousand hidden eyes were watching its slow and stately run. After a halt of a few minutes at 'Red Cross House', it would return.

Apart from this and a stray truck dashing along a lane on some important mission, I saw no movement during the month that we manned the Trocchio O.P. But great experience was gained by everyone in map-reading, learning to analyse the many new battle noises, and acquiring that light deft touch which is required in observed shooting at ranges over thirteen thousand yards (one corrected target gave the range as fourteen thousand six hundred with charge super). This lack of visible movement, when a whole day's arduous staring rewarded one with nothing at all, was made tantalizing by the night sounds—the clank of armoured cars, the whizz of trucks and motor-cycles and even the cement mixer whose grinding noises floated up to us from St. Angelo. These always seemed ridiculously near; in fact, they were so misleading that one night an O.P. signaller, on being asked by the Command Post why he was whispering into his phone, answered that his post was surrounded by the enemy.

When it was dark I would take an hour off to go down to the 'O.P. House' for dinner. A roaring fire would be burning in the great open hearth, several figures crouched over a long row of tins which hung from a rod spanning the width of the hearth; the fire caught their faces, tingeing them an even more brilliant colour than the sun and wind had been able to achieve. Soon after nine I would be on my way up again, the moon perhaps non-existent and the fireflies even more brilliant as they flitted across the faces of the rocks—tiny sparks of intermittent light. With a full moon I could read even the smallest details of a map.

Captain R. L. Banks

The Troglodytes

Cassino was almost entirely flat, and part of it in enemy hands. Existence was troglodytic, and there could be next to no movement during the day. All supplies, including water, had to be carried up at night by porters; and to minimize congestion and reduce porterage, every man that first night carried two days' rations with him. All stores such as lamps, telephones, wireless sets and Piats were taken over on the spot from the Coldstream for the same reason, and a large store of rations as well. The town was held by three battalions, two of whom, including the 6th Battalion, had a joint H.Q. and regimental aid post in the crypt of the ruined cathedral; on top of the crypt there was such an accumulation of rubbish that it could—and did—withstand direct hits from heavy guns. The signal exchange shared with an ammunition dump and part of another battalion a large nunnery which abutted on to the cathedral; but the crypt was the command post and nerve-centre of the town. All movement in and out of Cassino, all carrying-parties and evacuations were controlled from here; and the regimental police lived and ran their collecting posts in another vault of the crypt a few yards from the command post.

Bernard Fergusson

The Killing-ground

It is not easy to convey. This kind of fighting has little coherence, no design that is easy to follow. For the New Zealanders it was a mosaic of grim little fights over small distances: a lethal game of hide-and-seek in ditches, cellars, craters, mounds of rubble, sewers, and fragments of buildings that resembled stumps of teeth, but each of which concealed one or more abscesses in which a man, or a gun, or even a tank could be hidden. Enough of the prepared fortifications—reinforced cellars, gun emplacements, ground-floor bunkers—survived the bombing well enough to preserve a hard core of defence at the western end of the town, barring the way to the Liri Valley.

The New Zealanders had for days studied a town layout on maps and air photographs. The shambles into which they filed on the first day of the battle bore no relation to what they had so carefully memorized. The Germans on the other hand knew their way about. They were in strong positions prepared long before. They had no distances to cover. They could readily dart from one to another along covered ways that had been carefully constructed. They knew the ravines and walls and other covered approaches that led from the slopes of the mountains into the town. Night after night they could filter little parties of additional men into the ruins: and an area that was clear of Germans by nightfall had sprouted a machine-gun post or a few snipers by the following day.

It was the disposal of this kind of post, the capture, one at a time, of cellars concealed in heaps of debris, that kept the New Zealanders occupied for more than a week trying to advance and clear what was a ludicrously small ground area. Their difficulties can most readily be appreciated if one fills in a little of the detail that made up the complex whole.

From the first the sniper came into his own. Even in modern war there is, strangely, nothing more effective than the sniper in conditions that suit him. The rubble of Cassino was a sniper's paradise. Shelling, mortaring, and machine-gun fire provide a generalized hazard, a generalized death. It is easier to face them than the particular, personal, selective menace of the sniper. Men can be inspired to rise from cover and charge through the generalized kind of fire. It is much more paralyzing for the soldier to know that as soon as he shows himself he may be deliberately aimed at by a single, concealed marksman. Throughout this battle snipers grew overnight like weeds in different parts of the rubble, and on the lower slopes of the mountain commanding the rubble.

.... On another occasion a New Zealand battalion headquarters were mystified by the sound of a tank engine turning over quietly. It appeared to be coming from the next building, yet no tank was visible. An investigation revealed that the German tank was sealed inside the house. An officer thereupon crawled through the rubble, guiding two New Zealand tanks to a point from which they could fire at it. He was spotted and heavily mortared, but his shouted instructions got the tanks into position and they began firing at the house. A platoon then stormed it, and as soon as they entered it collapsed. Inside they found the tank intact, but the crew had been killed. The engine was still running. The tank had been used as an observation post in their very midst for five days. It explained the uncanny accuracy of the fire they had had to endure. An underground passage had been constructed from the room in which the tank stood to the cellar, and thence under a courtyard and the road to an embankment on the other side. Thus the crew could be relieved regularly and safely. It would not have been detected had the commander not been compelled to run his engine for a short while to charge his radio batteries. This was the kind of thing the New Zealanders were up against. The Germans had had a long time to prepare the Cassino defences. They had prepared them well.

.... Like the Indian Division, the men in the town suffered from the necessary torment of the smoke screen which was maintained throughout each day. 'There is no day,' one of them recorded, 'only two kinds of night—a yellow, smoky, choking night, and a black meteor-ridden night.' For the many the smoke was an insufferable addition to their other troubles, but for the few it was essential, and so it had to be kept up.

.... It was one of the more tragic features of the winter battles that so many of those who survived them with their lives were blinded or disfigured. The proportion was exceptional enough for two hospitals to have to make special arrangements to deal with these injuries. The 92nd General Hospital became partly an eye hospital, the 65th was reserved for head, facial, and neurosurgical cases.

There was, however, a more humane side to the picture. The exceptional closeness of the combatants, together with the restriction it imposed on daylight movement, led gradually and spontaneously to the practice of openly evacuating wounded men in daylight under the Red Cross flag. Nothing was arranged officially. It was done sparingly. But it was done, and both sides respected the Red Cross. It was one of those situations in which front-line soldiers, separated by a hundred yards or less, seem to develop a strange kinship in extremity. In the mountains the stretcher-bearers of both sides made these occasional day-time excursions into the boulders and thickets of no-man's-land, and sometimes they exchanged words with one another.

During the period in which the Gurkhas were isolated on Hangman's Hill their medical officer made three daylight trips up the face of Monte Cassino with a party of orderlies to bring down wounded men to his aid post in the valley. Each time he was stopped by a German post, taken to the nearest headquarters and then given permission to continue. The second time he was told not to do it any more. But he risked a third journey and was merely told that this must be positively the last.

Fred Majdalany

Americans Attack

The attack, initiated in foggy weather, was led by the 1st Battalion of the 14th Infantry, which previously had moved boats and supplies to dumps near the river. Enemy artillery on high peaks from Monte Cassino southward to be-yond the Liri river was able to fire on the Rapido front round Sant' Angelo, and the 1st Battalion found that some of its boats and other equipment had been destroyed. The men had to cross a low, muddy area, heavily mined, to reach the steep river-bank. Heavy enemy fire not only caused casualties, but destroyed the white tape that had been used to mark lanes previously cleared through the minefields. Visibility was poor, considerable confusion developed, and it was nine o'clock in the evening by the time elements of A and B Companies of the 1st Battalion had forced a way across the Rapido under heavy small-arms fire from the enemy positions north of Sant' Angelo. Under the most intense and steady resistance by hostile artillery, mortars, and *Nebelwerfer*, as well as machine-gun and rifle fire, the 1st Battalion put up a tremendous fight to secure its position. Engineers struggled with footbridges, most of which were destroyed by mines or artillery as they were being erected. From remnants of four damaged and destroyed bridges one was finally installed to permit the rest of Companies A and B to get across the river. The Company C attack put only a few men across, despite the efforts of the other two companies to silence the enemy fire along the west bank. Men were swept down the icy river. Mines on the banks and in the water took a heavy toll. Rubber boats were sunk by small-arms fire. Assault boats were knocked out by mortar fire. On the hostile bank the men who had crossed successfully encountered barbed wire, mines, machine-gun fire, and a steady artillery barrage. Both A and B Companies suffered a severe loss of officers and non-commissioned officers.

General Mark Clark

The Sentry

Occasionally there was light relief. The German artillery sent over a num-ber of pamphlet shells; the British artillery replied in kind, but the bulk of their shells fell short among the Royal Fusiliers on the Battalion's flank, who com-plained irritably that they couldn't read German. Passwords were another new feature of this theatre, and a source of annoyance to the Jocks.

'Halt! wha's that?' asked a sentry one night.

'Come, come,' said the officer, 'that's no way to challenge. Ask me the pass-word.'

'This is nae time for your bloody kiddin',' said the Jock. 'Whit's your bloody name?'

Bernard Fergusson

ANZIO

On 21 January 1944, in order to break the impasse, British and American troops landed at Anzio between Rome and the Gustav Line, planning to threaten Rome and the German rear, but they were confined to their bridgehead by powerful counter-attacks. Deadlock had been reached again.

I went ashore with my staff soon after six o'clock. Roads were congested with armour and vehicles, but everything was moving. There had been almost no opposition. The only elements encountered were two depleted battalions of 29 Panzer Grenadier Division which had just been relieved from hard fighting on the Cassino front and assigned to this quiet sector for rest. More than two hundred men were captured, many of them still in bed. By 09.00, we were firmly established on the initial beachhead line. The most serious enemy reaction up to this time had been an air raid as we were leaving the beach, but fortunately no damage was done.

In a landing operation one never knows too much of what is taking place even in his own sector, and all too little about what is happening in adjacent sectors. Information concerning other parts of the beachhead, the Rangers, and the British, was slow in reaching us. It was past mid-morning. I had sent the 1st Battalion, 7th Infantry, to occupy the ground just north of Nettuno, when the 509th Parachute Battalion arrived in the town and made contact with us. It was much later before we knew that 1 Division, which had been delayed in landing by mines and beach conditions, was finally established on its initial objective.

About 10.00 I returned to my Command Post, which had been established in a wood a few hundred yards inland from the beach, after visiting the regiments and inspecting conditions on the beach. My orderly, Private Hong, knowing that I had had no breakfast before leaving the *Biscayne*, had breakfast waiting for me —bacon and fresh eggs and toast made over an open fire as only Hong could make it. Fresh eggs were hard to come by in Italy but by means known only to an astute Chinese, he had acquired about three dozen with which he expected to see Carleton and me through until the supply channel with Naples was fully established. Needless to say, I enjoyed this first Anzio breakfast, with the hood of my jeep for a table.

I had barely finished when General Clark, accompanied by General Brann and several others, arrived to congratulate us on the success of the landing. Yes, they would love to have some breakfast, so Hong produced more bacon, eggs, and toast. Before they had finished General Lucas and his Chief of Staff arrived, and they, too, expressed a desire for breakfast. More of Hong's bacon and eggs. One after another, visitors arrived, and of course, all wanted some breakfast. More of Hong's bacon, eggs, and toast. As the last visitors left, about half-past

twelve, and I was preparing to leave the Command Post, I overheard Hong remark to Sergeant Barna, in a tone of exasperation most unusual with him:
'Goddam, Sergeant, General's fresh eggs all gone to hell.'

General Truscott

No Rear

Anzio was unique.

It was the only place in Europe which held an entire corps of infantry, a
British division, all kinds of artillery and special units, and maintained an immense supply and administration setup without a rear echelon. As a matter of
fact, there wasn't any rear; there was no place in the entire beachhead where
enemy shells couldn't seek you out.

Sometimes it was worse at the front; sometimes worse at the harbour.
Quartermasters buried their dead, and amphibious duck drivers went down with
their craft. Infantrymen, dug into the Mussolini Canal, had the canal pushed in
on top of them by armour-piercing shells, and Jerry bombers circled as they
directed glider bombs into L.S.T.s and Liberty ships. Wounded men got oak
leaf clusters on their Purple Hearts when shell fragments riddled them as they
lay on hospital beds. Nurses died. Planes crash-landed on the single air strip.

Planes went out to seek the 'Anzio Express', that huge gun which made
guys in rest areas play softball near slit trenches. The planes would report the
Express destroyed and an hour later she would come in on schedule.

The krauts launched a suicidal attack which almost drove through to the sea.
Evacuation was already beginning in the harbour when a single American battalion broke the point of the attack, then was engulfed and died. Bodies of
fanatical young Germans piled up in front of the machine-guns, and when the
guns ran out of ammunition the Wehrmacht came through and was stopped only
by point-blank artillery. One American artillery battalion of 155s fired eighty
thousand rounds of ammunition at Anzio, and there were dozens of these
battalions.

You couldn't stand up in the swamps without being cut down, and you
couldn't sleep if you sat down. Guys stayed in those swamps for days and weeks.
Every hole had to be covered, because the 'popcorn man' came over every night
and shovelled hundreds of little butterfly bombs down on your head by the light
of flares and exploding ack-ack. You'd wake up in the morning and find your
sandbags torn open and spilled on the ground.

The krauts used little remote-control tanks filled with high explosives. You
wondered how Jerry could see you and throw a shell at you every time you stuck
your head up, until you climbed into the mountains after it was all over and were
able to count every tree and every house in the area we had held. Tiger tanks
grouped together and fired at you. Your artillery thought it was a battery and
threw a concentration of shells at the tanks, and by the time your shells struck
the Tigers had moved away and were firing at you from another place.

Four American tank destroyers crossed the canal and bounced armour-
piercing shells off the turret of a Tiger until it turned its massive gun and disintegrated them with five shells.

German infantry rode their tanks into battle and the dogfaces shot them off like squirrels but they didn't get all of them—some came in and bayoneted our guys in their holes.

This wasn't a beachhead that was secured and enlarged until it eventually became a port for supplies coming in to supplement those being expended as the troops pushed inland. Everything was expended right here. It was a constant hellish nightmare, because when you weren't getting something you were expecting something, and it lasted for five months.

Bill Mauldin, American war artist

The Art of Survival

Life at Anzio was never dull, easy or quiet. German artillery and aircraft continued to strike almost daily. While mass raids of fifty or more aircraft practically ceased during April, hit and run raids by one or more planes persisted. Nor was there any part free from the daily scream of artillery projectiles in flight, the crash of bursting shells, or the thud of bursting bombs.

Life was tense as it always is when men live close to death. But we learned how to survive. The men found some means of making life more comfortable, and even discovered precarious forms of entertainment to relieve the tedium of congested living and battle tensions.

Living accommodations were, for the most part, extremely primitive: caves hollowed from canal banks, shelter halves stretched over a bit of defilade, the interior of tanks, trucks, or other vehicles. In the forward areas, a few *poderis*—plastered stone farmhouses of the Mussolini Reclamation project—remained standing. Here were housed regimental and battalion command posts, and aid stations where men from the front line companies could occasionally obtain a hot meal and dry out their clothing. There were a few tents, but not many, under cover in areas adjacent to the beaches. Division commanders for the most part had caravans or trailers to house their offices, but none of them were protected by more than a makeshift camouflage. Few of the buildings in Anzio or Nettuno had escaped damage, although the lower floors of those along the waterfront were protected to some extent by the cliff that rose behind them, and it was here the port engineers, various service installations, and the Press camp (never very large), were accommodated. The only concentration of tentage was in the hospital area which I have described. Even under these conditions, men displayed rare ingenuity in making themselves more comfortable and their humour lightened their loads. All over the beachhead signs indicated that you were approaching '42nd and Broadway', the 'Good Eats Café', '4719$\frac{1}{4}$ miles to the Golden Gate', 'Beach Head Hotel, Special Rates to New Arrivals', and such forms of soldier wit.

Division, regimental and other unit commanders had their own messes. Luncheon parties became a favourite form of social intercourse, usually interspersed with business. Each one sought to outdo the others in both fare and appointments. However the fare, except for occasional steaks or roasts from a butchered cow or pig, was usually limited to what ingenious cooks could do with rations. A lively trade went on between Americans and British—our '10 in

1' for British 'bully beef' and hard bread. Appointments normally were limited to white table cloths, usually sheets pilfered from the Navy or a hospital, an assortment of china and crockery accumulated from bombed-out buildings, and the silverware issued with the Army mess kits. Flowers, in profusion as spring came on, were used for magnificent centre-pieces; none on other luncheon tables ever approached those produced by my Corporal Hong, arranged as divisional crests or other insignia of a guest of honour.

General Truscott

The Anzio Stakes

In these static conditions, with nowhere safe for troops to go, there was little to do when off duty until beetle racing suddenly arrived. This caught on like wildfire, particularly amongst the Gunners and at Divisional H.Q. Elaborate totes were constructed and really large money changed hands in bets. A champion beetle might fetch as much as three thousand *lire* or more, and as a thousand *lire* in those days was £2 10s., it was no mean price to pay for an insect. Runners were plentiful, for beetles seemed to be one of the chief products of the beach-head. Dig a slit trench, leave it for an hour, and the bottom would be black with beetles all trying to get out. The system of racing was simple. Various colours were painted on the beetles' backs and the runners were paraded round the ring in jam jars. Just before the 'off', or I suppose one should say when they came under starter's orders, the beetles were placed under one glass jar in the centre of the 'course'. This was a circle about six feet in diameter. At the 'off' the jar was raised and the first beetle out of the circle was the winner. A difficulty arose when, for one reason or another, it became necessary to change a beetle's colours in quick time; but at one Gunner meeting the problem was solved by attaching small flags to the beetles' back with chewing gum.

Static conditions tended to make troops slack, so a great drive on smartness and saluting was instituted by the Divisional Commander. Somehow our Light A.A. Regiment incurred particular displeasure. Although their A.A. record was among the best in the beachhead, their saluting was nowhere near the same standard as their shooting. The inevitable excuse of the look-outs when confronted by an irate General was that they were too busy looking for aircraft to notice him approaching. One of the jobs of the A.A. Regiment was to construct dummy positions. One of these was put up immediately outside the main entrance of Divisional H.Q., and at the rear of the gunpit, with his eyes steadfastly on the entrance and his hand frozen in an impeccable salute, stood the dummy No. 1. This particular position was beyond reproach—and, fortunately, the Commander had a sense of humour.

Major F. C. M. Reeves

BREAKING THE DEADLOCK

On 11–12 May the U.S. 5 and the British Eighth Armies, together with other Allied forces, opened the final great offensive on the Gustav Line, and ten days later the troops on the Anzio bridgehead also burst out.

The evening of 11 May was misty after a little rain, but by the time darkness settled over the 5 Army front the sky was clear and the stars were out. Our right flank began at the junction of the Liri river and the Garigliano, with the French facing the necessity of crossing the Garigliano in that sector, although farther south their line was already across that barrier and joined with the American II Corps line near Castelforte, where we had occupied the Minturno sector taken by the British in January.

As soon as it was dark a steady movement of troops began behind the 5 Army lines, as well as behind the British Eighth Army lines to the north. Everything else went on in as near the normal routine as possible. Patrols were out. There was occasional artillery fire. It was just as it had been on the previous evening and for many evenings before. On the German side everything went on as usual, too, except that they were in earnest about it. We weren't. We were waiting and preparing for the hour before midnight.

At eleven o'clock about a thousand big guns from Cassino to the sea fired at approximately the same moment, their shells aimed with great care at enemy headquarters, communication centres, command posts, and other vital targets that had been quietly located by air reconnaissance during the previous month. The ridges in front of 5 Army seemed to stand out momentarily in a great blaze of light, sink again into darkness, and then tremble under the next salvo. It was perhaps the most effective artillery bombardment of the campaign. It simply smashed into dust a great number of enemy batteries and vital centres; so that for hours after the Germans had overcome the initial shock of an attack where they least expected it they were still confused and unable to establish good centralized direction of their defence lines.

Meanwhile the French forces had crossed the Garigliano and moved forward into the mountainous terrain lying south of the Liri river. It was not easy. As always, the German veterans reacted strongly, and there was bitter fighting. The French surprised the enemy and quickly seized key terrain, including Mounts Faito and Cerasola and high ground near Castelforte. 1 Motorized Division helped 2 Moroccan Division take the key Monte Girofano, and then advanced rapidly north to S. Apollinare and S. Ambrogio. In spite of stiffening enemy resistance, 2 Moroccan Division penetrated the Gustav Line in less than two days' fighting.

The next forty-eight hours on the French front were decisive. The knife-wielding Goumiers swarmed over the hills, particularly at night, and General Juin's entire force showed an aggressiveness hour after hour that the Germans could not withstand. Cerasola, San Giorgio, Monte D'Oro, Ausonia and Esperia were seized in one of the most brilliant and daring advances of the war in Italy, and by 16 May the French Expeditionary Corps had thrust forward some ten miles on their left flank to Monte Revole, with the remainder of their front slanting back somewhat to keep contact with the British Eighth Army.

Only the most careful preparations and the utmost determination made this attack possible, but Juin was that kind of fighter. Mule pack-trains, skilled mountain fighters, and men with the strength to make long night marches through treacherous terrain were needed to succeed in the all-but-impregnable mountain ranges. The French displayed that ability during their sensational advance which Lieutenant-General Siegfried Westphal, the Chief of Staff to Kesselring, later described as a major surprise both in timing and in aggressiveness. For this performance, which was to be a key to the success of the entire drive on Rome, I shall always be a grateful admirer of General Juin and his magnificent F.E.C.

.... Cassino was as difficult as ever, and it was a week after the offensive started before the Polish Corps seized the battered, besieged, and outflanked town of ruins. The Eighth Army's delay made Juin's task more difficult, because he was moving forward so rapidly that his right flank—adjacent to the British— was constantly exposed to counter-attacks.

It should be emphasized that the Eighth Army was going up against prepared defences. The Polish Corps fought with utter bravery and disregard for casualties, and the XIII Corps (British) advanced two miles in four days at a cost of 4,056 casualties in order to outflank Cassino on the south. The Abbey fell to 3 Carpathian Division (Polish) on 18 May, and the way into the Liri Valley was opened.

General Mark Clark

Cassino: the End

The guard didn't have to wake us at five. Chilly dawn and a brisk shower of rain proved equal to the task. It was wet and cold and misty when John laid his maps and his notes on the flat bonnet of his jeep, and gave out final orders for the battle. All the familiar phrases. Only the places and the timings different. Two companies forward . . . barrage . . . about four hundred guns . . . tie up with tanks at forming-up place . . . all the details that are so dull in retrospect, so vital at the time. More things to mark on maps beginning to get crumpled and sodden. Officers scribbling details that concern them in every kind of little note-book. Questions. 'Do you want me to push something forward to the wood after I've got the farm, sir?' . . . 'Am I responsible for the track, sir, or are "A" Company?' . . . 'Are we likely to get a meal up to-night, or does the emergency ration have to last?' . . . 'How soon can I expect anti-tank guns in my area?' . . .

The timings again, just to make sure that everyone is certain of them. From here at 07.20 so as to get to the forming-up place by 08.00, which gives us nearly an hour to get together with the tank people. Then from the forming-up place at 08.52, which should just give nice time to cross the start-line at H-hour, 09.00. Remember the barrage is doing four two-hundred-yard lifts, and staying on each one for twelve minutes. Keep close behind the barrage. Close as you can. Everybody clear? A last look through notes. Then away to the companies to pass the orders a stage further.

While the officers are receiving and giving orders the men are shaving and washing. And after they've shaved and washed they go for their breakfast, which has just arrived in containers brought up by the cooks. And while the officers are still giving out their orders, batmen surreptitiously place bowls or tins of water at hand, and the officers' shaving things. And when the officers have at last finished giving out their orders, and are reflectively re-reading their notes and thinking, 'Have I forgotten anything?' the batmen produce some breakfast, and with maternal brusqueness order the officers to eat it, as it's almost stone-cold now. The officers eat the breakfast, but the tea is too hot to drink quickly, so they start to shave and while they shave they keep having sips of their tea. And while they are shaving and sipping people keep coming up and asking them questions, and with a shaving-brush in one hand and a mug in the other the officers try to make quick, clear decisions about such varied problems as a man who has lost his nerve and refuses to participate, a vehicle that has burnt out a clutch, probable ammunition requirements that night—while the batmen look on and think, 'Can't they bloody well leave him alone for five minutes?'

It is all to the good, really, all this preliminary detail. It keeps your mind off yourself.

07.10 hours. Time to get ready. The shouts of the sergeant-majors. Jokes and curses. The infantry heaving on to their backs and shoulders their complicated equipment, their weapons and the picks and shovels they have to carry, too, so that they can quickly dig in on their objective. The individuals resolving themselves into sections and platoons and companies. Jokes and curses.

'Able ready to move, sir.'

'Baker ready to move, sir.'

'Charlie ready to move, sir.'

'Dog ready to move, sir.'

The column moved off along the track we'd taken the previous night. It was Tuesday morning. It was the fifth day of the offensive. In England the headlines were announcing that the Gustav Line was smashed except for Cassino and Monastery Hill. 'Except' was the operative word. That was our job now. To break through and cut off Cassino and the Monastery.

On the stroke of nine there was an earth-shaking roar behind us as four hundred guns opened fire almost as one. With a hoarse, exultant scream four hundred shells sped low over our heads to tear into the ground less than five hundred yards in front, bursting with a mighty antiphonal crash that echoed the challenge of the guns. It was Wagnerian.

From then on the din was continuous and simultaneous: the thunder of the guns, the hugely amplified staccato of the shell-bursts close in front, and the vicious overhead scream that linked them with a frenzied counterpoint. And sometimes the scream became a whinny, and sometimes a kind of red-hot sighing, but most of the time it was just a scream—a great, angry baleful scream. The fury of it was elemental, yet precise. It was a controlled cyclone. It was splendid to hear, as the moment of actual combat approached.

The makers of films like to represent this scene with shots of soldiers crouching dramatically in readiness, and close-ups of tense, grim faces. Whereas the striking thing about such moments is the matter-of-factness and casualness of the average soldier. It is true that hearts are apt to be thumping fairly hard, and everyone is thinking, 'Oh, Christ!' But you don't in fact look grim and intense. For one thing you would look slightly foolish if you did. For another you have too many things to do.

The two leading companies were due to advance exactly eight minutes after the barrage opened. So those eight minutes were spent doing such ordinary things as tying up boot laces, helping each other with their equipment, urinating, giving weapons a final check, testing wireless sets to make certain they were still netted, eating a bar of chocolate. The officers were giving last-minute instructions, marshalling their men into battle formations, or having a final check-up with the tank commanders with whom they were going to work.

Those who were not in the leading companies were digging like fiends, for they knew that the temporary calm would be quickly shattered as soon as the tanks and the leading infantry were seen emerging from it.

Meanwhile the barrage thundered on, and to its noise was added the roar of the Shermans' engines. A great bank of dust and smoke welled slowly up from the area the shells were pounding, so that you couldn't see the bursts any more. The sputtering of the 25-pounders rippled up and down the breadth of the gun-lines faster than bullets from a machine-gun, so numerous were they.

At eight minutes past nine they moved. Geoff led his company round the right end, Mark led his round the left end of the bank which concealed us from the enemy in front. Then the Shermans clattered forward, with a crescendo of engine-roar that made even shouted conversation impossible. The battle was on.

Geoff and Mark were to reach the start-line in ten minutes, at which time the barrage was due to move forward two hundred yards. Geoff and Mark would edge us as close to it as possible—perhaps within a hundred and fifty yards, and they'd wait until it moved on again, and then, following quickly in its wake, their bayonets and Brens would swiftly mop up any stunned remnants that survived. And while they were doing this the protective Shermans would blast with shells and machine-guns any more distant enemy post that sought to interfere.

Then the barrage would move forward another two hundred yards. The process would be repeated until the first objective had been secured—farm areas in each case. Then Kevin, who would soon be setting off, would pass his company through Geoff's and assault the final objective the code word for which was 'Snowdrop'. When Kevin wirelessed 'Snowdrop' the day's work would be largely done. Highway Six would be only two thousand yards away.

To-day was crucial. To-day would decide whether it was to be a breakthrough or a stabilized slogging-match here in the flat entrance to the Liri Valley, with our great concentrations of men and material at the mercy of the Monastery O.P.

The Boche reacted quickly. Within a few minutes of our barrage opening up the shells started coming back. The scream of their shells vied with the scream of ours. Salvo after salvo began to rain down on the farms and the groves to our rear, where our supporting echelons were massed ready to follow in the wake of the assault. The sun's rays, growing warmer every minute, cleared the last of the morning mist. The Monastery seemed to shed the haze as a boxer sheds his dressing-gown before stepping into the ring for the last round. Towering in stark majesty above the plain, where the whole of our force was stretched out for it to behold. This was the supreme moment—the final reckoning with the Monastery.

Mortar-bombs began to land on the crest immediately in front. The bits sizzled down on our positions. Ahead the machine-guns were joining in. The long low bursts of the Spandaus: and the Schmeissers, the German tommy-guns that have an hysterical screech like a Hitler peroration. There were long answering rattles from the Besas of the Shermans. Then the *Nebelwerfers*, the six-barrelled rocket-mortars, as horrific as their name. . . . The barrels discharge their huge rockets one at a time with a sound that is hard to put into words. It is like someone sitting violently on the bass notes of a piano, accompanied by the grating squeak of a diamond on glass. Then the clusters of canisters sail through the air with a fluttering chromatic whine, like jet-propelled Valkyries. . . . There were several regiments of them facing us, and the existing cacophony was soon made infinitely more hideous by scores of Valkyries. They were landing well behind. For the time being the Boche were concentrating everything on the farms and the woods, that were crammed with concentrations of trucks and tanks and supplies of all kinds.

'You may as well push off now, Stuart,' John said. A minute later the fourth company moved round the right end of the bank and went the way of the others. The first of the prisoners came in. Six paratroops. Able Company's. Four large blond ones and two little dark ones. They were sent straight back.

Smoke-shells were being poured on to Monastery Hill now in a frantic effort to restore the mist. They had some effect, but they couldn't blot it out. The barrage seemed to get a second wind and the guns seemed to be firing faster than ever. The German shells were taking their toll of the rear areas. Four farms were on fire. We could see three ammunition-trucks blazing. Three more prisoners: one wounded, the other two helping him along. A grinning fusilier in charge. Some wounded in from Baker Company. All walking cases. Running commentary from tank liaison officer—'Rear Link'. He sits in a Honey tank at our H.Q. and acts as wireless link between the squadron fighting with us in front and the tanks' regimental headquarters. 'Both companies moving well. Machine-gun has opened up on Baker Company. Freddie Troop moving round to cope.' The sharp crack of the Shermans' seventy-fives, and a burst of Besa that seems to go on for ever. That must be Freddie Troop 'coping'.

'Okay now,' says Rear Link. 'On the move again.'

The *Nebelwerfers* have quietened down. They're easy to spot. Perhaps the counter-battery boys have got on to them. Our turn now. They're shelling our ridge as well as mortaring it. Some close ones. Rear Link has news. How Troop reports that five men have just come out of a building it has been blasting for five minutes and surrendered. Able Company report all's well. Baker report all's well. Charlie Company, following up, report all seems to be well in front, some wounded on the way back from Able. Three shells just above us. A signaller is hit.

The barrage ends. The effect is like the end of a movement in a symphony when you want to applaud and don't. From now on the guns will confine themselves to steady visitations on the enemy's rear. Unless the infantry want something hit. In which case the whole lot will switch in a very few minutes on to the place the infantry want hit. The infantry want something hit now. The voice on the wireless says, 'Two machine-guns bothering me from two hundred yards north of Victor Eighty-two. Can you put something down?' John tells Harry, who is eating a sandwich. Harry gets on the wireless and says, 'Mike target— Victor Eighty-two—north two hundred—five rounds gunfire.' The shells scream over. Harry says, 'We may as well make sure.' He orders a repeat. The voice on the wireless says, 'Thanks. That seems to have done the trick. They're not firing any more.' Harry finishes his sandwich.

Rear Link has been deep in conversation with the left-hand troop commander. Rear Link thinks the companies have reached the first objective. No, not quite. It is all right on the left. But the right company seems to have run into something. Trouble from a farm. Tanks moving round to help. A lot of firing, ours and theirs. Rear Link says the tanks are pouring everything they've got into the farm. Twelve more prisoners—they look more shaken than the others. They had a bad spot in the barrage. Rear Link asks the troop commander how the battle is going on the right. The troop commander says it is a bit confused. A platoon is moving round to a flank. The farm seems to be strongly held. A reserve troop has joined in. A tank has been hit and has 'brewed up'. Baker on the left report that they are on their first objective. Charlie report they are moving up to pass through Baker. The *Nebelwerfers* again. Not as many as before. Some of them, at any rate, have been discouraged by the counter-battery fire. They seem to be going for the Bailey a mile back on the main track. Our anti-tank guns are in that area waiting to be called forward. Hope they are all right. Get Charles on the wireless and ask him. Charles says two trucks hit. One man killed and ten wounded. It has been all right since the first shelling. Able Company report that they are now firmly on first objective. Some casualties getting the farm. But they've killed a lot of Germans, and got eleven prisoners. They're digging in. The tanks are protecting their right, which seems horribly open. The tanks are in great form. They won't stop firing. They are spraying everything that could possibly conceal a German.

It has become very unhealthy behind our ridge. They are still mainly hitting the top of it. So long as they stay up there it won't be too bad. But there is always a nasty uncertainty about it. If they add a few yards to the range they'll be landing right among us. One or two have already come half-way down the slope.

Rear Link getting excited again. He's been talking to one of the troop commanders. Rear Link says Charlie appear to be on their objective. Can he signal 'Snowdrop' to his R.H.Q.? John says, 'No, not yet.' Rear Link gets another message from the tanks. Rear Link says Charlie have started to dig in. Can he signal 'Snowdrop'? John says, 'No. They haven't consolidated yet.' Kevin reports that he has arrived and is digging in. He says he has sent back more prisoners. More wounded, more prisoners, more *Nebelwerfers*, more shells, and the Monastery horribly clear. Rear Link has another conversation with the tanks. 'How about "Snowdrop", sir?' Rear Link almost pleads. 'Not yet,' John says. 'Not until they have consolidated.'

They're shelling us hard now. Not on the crest any more, but just over our heads and to our right. It is a different battery. They seem like 105s. They are coming over in eights. About every thirty seconds. The hard digging earlier in the morning is paying a good dividend. The last three salvoes landed right on our mortars, but they are well dug in and they get away without a single casualty. None of the shells has landed more than thirty yards from the command post. It is very frightening. Kevin on the wireless. Charlie Company are being counter-attacked with tanks. More shells on us. Twelve this time. Two of them within twenty yards. Behind, fortunately. Harry has taken a bearing on the guns and passed it back to the counter-battery people. Kevin on the wireless again. The leading Boche tank has got into a hull-down position fifty yards from his leading platoon. He has had some casualties. Our tanks trying to deal with it but hampered by very close-wooded country and a sunken lane that is an obstacle. Boche infantry are edging forward under cover of the fire from their tanks. More shells on the command post. The same place still. If they switch thirty yards to their left we've had it. That is the frightening thing. Wondering if they'll make a switch before they fire again. The accuracy of the guns is their downfall. John tries to get Kevin on the wireless. The signaller cannot get through. His toneless signaller-voice goes on saying, 'Hello Three, hello Three, hello Three, hello Three.' But he cannot get an answer. A closer shell blasted me against the bank. It is a queer feeling when you are brought to earth by blast. There is an instant of black-out, then sudden consciousness of what has happened: then an agonized wait for a spasm of pain somewhere on your person. Finally, a dull reactionary shock as you slowly discover you are intact. The signaller's voice again, 'Cannot—hear—you—clearly—say—again—say again—that's—better—hear—you—okay.' Kevin on the wireless. There is a tank deadlock. The rival tanks are now very close, on opposite sides of the same shallow crest. If either moves the other will get it the second the turret appears above the crest. The German cannot be outflanked. He has chosen his position cunningly. The sunken lane protects him. Kevin has had more casualties. More shells on the command post. Intense machine-gun fire from the direction of Kevin's company. Not a vestige of haze round the Monastery. This is the climax. No word from Kevin. John saying, 'Are you through to Charlie Company yet?' The signaller-voice tonelessly persevering: 'Hear my signals, hear my signals, hello Three . . . hear you very faintly. . . .' Then, after an eternity, 'Through now, sir. Message for you, sir.' It is Kevin on the wireless. A fusilier has knocked out the tank with a Piat. It has killed the crew. The tank is on fire. The others are withdrawing. The infantry are withdrawing. Charlie Company are getting some of them as they withdraw. The counter-attack is finished. Consolidation may proceed. The tension is broken.

It went from mouth to mouth. 'Bloke called Jefferson knocked out the tank with a Piat. Bloody good show! Bloke called Jefferson knocked out the tank with a Piat. Bloody good show! Bloody good show—bloke called Jefferson. . . .' It passed from one to another till all the signallers knew, the stretcher-bearers, and the mortar crews, and the pioneers: and the anti-tank gunners waiting some way behind, and some sappers who were searching for mines along the track verges. Till the whole world knew. 'A chap called Jefferson. . . .'

Kevin on the wireless. 'No further attacks. Consolidation completed.'

'Get on to Brigade,' John said, 'and report "Snowdrop".'

'Snowdrop,' the Adjutant told Brigade.

'Snowdrop,' Brigade told Division.

'Snowdrop,' Division told Corps.

'Snowdrop,' Corps told Army.

In all the headquarters all the way back they rubbed out the mark on their operations maps showing our position in the morning and put it in again twelve

hundred yards farther forward, on the chalk-line called 'Snowdrop'. It was ten
past two. The battle had been going for six hours.

'Command post prepare to move,' John said.

We advanced in extended order through the long corn, as the ground was
completely flat and without cover. The smell of the barrage still lingered, and the
lacerated ground testified to its thoroughness. Wondering how many of the farms
away to the right were still occupied by Boche; wondering how many machine-
guns were concealed in the woods and the olive groves which stretched across the
front a thousand yards ahead. Wondering if anyone had spotted our wireless aerials,
which are impossible to conceal, and which always give away a headquarters.

There wasn't a vestige of cover in the half-mile stretch to where the reserve
company had dug in. There was still a lot of firing in front, mainly from the
tanks. They were taking no chances with the open right flank. They were dosing
all the farms in turn. With nine tell-tale wireless aerials swaying loftily above the
heads of the sweating signallers who carried the sets on their backs, we pushed on
quickly through the long corn, wishing it was a good deal longer. And the
Monastery watched us all the way.

As soon as the command post was established in the area of the reserve
company, John went forward to where Kevin's company were, and he took me
with him. They had turned the area into a compact little strong-point. It had to
be compact, because there were fewer than fifty of them left out of ninety who
had set off in the morning. Besides which, the country was so thick with trees
that you couldn't see more than fifty yards ahead. They had adapted some of the
excellent German trenches to face the other way. Some were reading the highly-
coloured magazines left behind by the Boche. These were filled with lurid
artists' impressions of the Cassino fighting bearing such captions as 'Our paratroop supermen defying the Anglo-American hordes in living Hell of Cassino'.
They were all on that level. There was one copy of a sumptuous fashion magazine, which seemed slightly incongruous, and suggested that the Rhine-maidens
weren't all the drab blue-stockings the Nazis made them out to be. There was
one of the famous new steel pill-boxes: an underground three-roomed flatlet,
which included a well-stocked larder. Only its small, rounded, steel turret protruded above the ground, and this was skilfully camouflaged.

A few yards away Jefferson's tank was still burning. They were all talking
about Jefferson. They were all saying he saved the company. The tank had
wiped out a section at sixty yards' range, and was systematically picking off the
rest of the company in ones and twos until fewer than fifty were left. Then
Jefferson, on an impulse, and without orders, snatched up a Piat and scrambled
round to a position only a few yards from the tank. Unable to get in a shot from
behind cover, he had stood up in full view of the enemy and fired his weapon
standing up, so that the back-blast of the exploding bomb knocked him flat on
his back. Then he had struggled to his feet and aimed a shot at the second tank—
but the tank was hurriedly pulling back, and with it the Boche infantry. It was
one of those things that aren't in the book. Jefferson was typical of the best
Lancashire soldiers—quiet and solid and rather shy, yet able in an emergency to
act quickly without seeming to hurry. Such men are nice to have around in
battles. It was one of those deeds the full implications of which don't

really strike you till some time later, then leave you stunned and humble.
.... During the night we received orders to continue the advance at 6 a.m.
and secure the next objective-line, 'Bluebell'. This was to synchronize with the
Poles, who were to make a final attempt to work round from our old position
north-east of Cassino and cut the highway from their side.

It was well after three by the time everyone had been fed, ammunition had
been replenished, and orders for the new attack had been given out. Before he
went to sleep John said, 'I'm going to put Jefferson in for the V.C.'

At a quarter to six the earth trembled, and once again the shells started
pouring overhead so thickly that at times you fancied you could see them. At the
same time another lot of guns began to pound Monastery Hill in support of the
Polish attack. In next to no time dust and smoke and yellow flame enveloped the
Monastery itself, so that when our Dog and Baker Companies passed through
Charlie Company on the stroke of six it was hidden from view. This was the
kill. We were going in for the kill. The Poles were sweeping round from the
right: we, two and a half miles away in the valley, were on our way to seal it off
from the left. It shouldn't be long now. And once we had cut the Highway the very
qualities that had made the Monastery an impregnable bastion for so long would
turn it into an equally formidable death-trap. For so long the guardian and pro-
tector of its garrison, it would round on them in its death-throes and destroy them.

Compared with the previous day, we had a fairly easy advance. There were
some snipers and one or two isolated machine-guns, but they didn't seem disposed to resist very strongly, and by ten Baker and Dog, assisted by fresh tanks,
were nicely settled on Bluebell, another thousand yards on. We were ordered to
push on as fast as possible. So Baker and Dog advanced again to the final
objective line, 'Tulip', twelve hundred yards farther on. And Able, Charlie and
Command Post pushed on to the area just cleared by Dog and Baker. By four
o'clock in the afternoon Dog and Baker both signalled that they were established
on 'Tulip'—both had O.P.s directly overlooking Highway Six. Both asked permission to carry on and cut the road and search beyond it. We were ordered to
stay where we were, however, as the exact position of the Poles was not known
and mistakes might occur if we both started milling around by the road. We
dominated it from where we were. We had done what was required of us. We
were to stay where we were until we had further orders. The job was nearly done.

During the night Dog and Baker were told to patrol as far as the road. Not
till the following morning were we allowed to send anyone beyond it. By that
time it had ceased to be a military feat. It was a formal ceremony. So John sent a
special patrol of three corporals, all holders of the M.M. They crossed the Highway and carried out a careful search of the gullies and ruined buildings on the
far side of it, but the only Germans they could find were dead ones. Their time
was not wasted, however. Each returned with a Schmeisser gun, a camera, a
watch and a pair of binoculars of impeccable German manufacture. An hour
later the Poles entered the Monastery. As so often happens when great events
are awaited with prolonged and excessive anxiety, the announcement of the fall
of Monte Cassino was rather an anticlimax. It was Thursday, 18 May. The battle
had lasted a week. The job was done.

Fred Majdalany

The Poles

In a fortnight these two under-strength Polish divisions and their Armoured Brigade had lost 281 officers and 3,503 other ranks—of whom one-third were killed, and only 102 missing. These terrible figures speak for themselves. The gallantry of the Poles was beyond praise, and there is a particular poignancy in the inscription on the Memorial in their war cemetery which now stands on the slopes of the hill known as Point 593:

> We Polish soldiers
> For our freedom and yours
> Have given our souls to God
> Our bodies to the soil of Italy
> And our hearts to Poland.

Anzio: the Break-out

On 22 May I moved permanently into the forward echelon of my headquarters at Anzio in preparation for the break-out. . . . Almost every inch of space at Anzio was crowded with men, guns and ammunition in preparation for the attack. Any time the enemy fired a shell in our direction it was almost certain to hit something, but we had taken what precautions were possible, and most of our supplies were protected by mounds of earth.

. . . . Before dawn on the morning of 23 May I went with Truscott to a forward observation post on the Anzio front, where just before six o'clock some five thousand pieces of artillery opened up on the enemy, whose positions were concealed by a morning haze. The smoke and haze hid our movements, but in the next hour or so we could hear our tanks moving forward to the attack, and there was a dull rumble of aircraft overhead as bombers began to pour their bombs on the German positions. The beleaguered Anzio garrison was about to break out, with the town of Cisterna their first objective.

The timing of the attack from Anzio again caught the enemy off-guard. As the artillery fire suddenly ended our tanks drove through the smoke, followed by swarms of infantry that caught the enemy outposts unprepared. Some of the Germans in dugouts had to be dragged out with only part of their clothes on, completely unready for battle. Our artillery had previously been aimed at specific enemy centres, which were heavily shelled, but the morning haze interfered with the German artillery observation and gave us an opportunity of making considerable progress before meeting firm resistance. The Germans were never able to recover from this initial setback, and their later counter-attacks were weak and poorly organized.

1 Armoured Division, 3 Division, and the 1st Special Service Force fought their way towards Cisterna or on either side of the town, and by the night of 24 May they had all but isolated that centre of enemy resistance. On the following day 3 Division's 7th Infantry drove into the town to wipe out remnants of 362 Grenadier Division, while the rest of our offensive strength surged on towards Cori or swung north-westward towards the Alban Hills before the gates of Rome.

On that day, 25 May, the German defences were beginning to crumble on both fronts. On the southern front elements of 85 Division, after meeting veteran German reinforcements at Terracina, rallied and crashed into that coastal town and pushed on up the coast. The French 3 Algerian Division entered San Giovanni on our right flank; thereafter the Germans fought a delaying action on that front. The climax was approaching, and we hoped that it would not be long delayed.

I talked over with Truscott the possibility of directing the attack by 45, 34 and 36 Divisions in the direction of Velletri, which was on the edge of the Alban Hills, and at the same time pushing other elements forward on the Cori-Valmontone line, on which Alexander had insisted I had felt, as I said, that it was essential to maintain flexibility of movement at this period of the battle, and, as it turned out, it was possible to pursue both objectives. We had taken 9,018 prisoners at this point, and I felt that it would not be long before Keyes' vigorous advance through Terracina would put his forces in contact with the bridgehead.

This meeting took place even sooner than I had expected Shortly before ten o'clock that morning, when I was in my jeep, our radio picked up word that elements of the 48th Engineer Regiment and the 91st Reconnaissance Squadron were close to a junction with a task force from Anzio. The task force was from the 36th Engineer Regiment, and included American tank-destroyer elements and members of a reconnaissance unit of 1 British Division. I drove hurriedly to the sector, arriving as the two groups were meeting on the Anzio–Terracina road about a mile north-west of Borga Grappa, a little village that had been beaten almost into rubble by air attacks. The juncture was a triumph as far as I was concerned, because of the difficulties of the previous five months, although it was not of any great importance in the battle that was raging to the north-west The men were tired but grinning as they joined hands, and that was about all there was to it. Thanks largely to the great aggressiveness of Keyes and II Corps, which had come sixty miles through the mountains in fourteen days, the beachhead had at last been liberated; but in the moment of liberation everybody's thoughts were turned to Rome.

General Mark Clark

Rome

On 5 June, with Gruenther and other officers, I drove along Route No. 6 into Rome. We didn't know our way round the city very well, but General Hume, who was with us, had suggested that the Town Hall on the Capitoline Hill would be a good place for me to meet my four corps commanders for a conference on our immediate plans. We wanted to push on past Rome as rapidly as possible in pursuit of the retreating enemy and towards Civitavecchia, the port of Rome, which we direly needed for unloading supplies. There were gay crowds in the streets, many of them waving flags, as our infantry marched through the capital. Flowers were stuck in the muzzles of the soldiers' rifles and of guns on the tanks. Many Romans seemed to be on the verge of hysteria in their enthusiasm for the American troops. The Americans were enthusiastic, too, and kept looking for the ancient landmarks that they had read about in their history books. It was on this day that a doughboy made the classic remark of the Italian campaign, when he took a long look at the ruins of the Colosseum, whistled softly, and said, 'Gee, I didn't know our bombers had done *that* much damage in Rome!'

Our little groups of jeeps wandered round the streets while we craned our necks looking at the sights, but not finding our way to the Capitoline Hill. In fact, we were lost, but we didn't like to admit it, and we didn't care very much, because we were interested in everything we saw. Eventually we found ourselves in St. Peter's Square, which delighted us all and which enabled Hume to get his bearings. As we stopped to look up at the great dome of St. Peter's a priest walking along the street paused by my jeep and said in English, 'Welcome to Rome. Is there any way in which I can help you?'

'Well,' I replied, 'we'd like to get to the Capitoline Hill.'

He gave us directions, and added, 'We are certainly proud of the American 5 Army. May I introduce myself?' And he told me his name. He came from Detroit.

'My name's Clark,' I replied.

We both expressed pleasure at the meeting, and the priest started to move on. Then he stopped and took another look and said, 'What did you say your name is?' A number of Italians had gathered round by this time and were listening to our conversation. When the priest told them that I was the commander of 5 Army a youth on a bicycle shouted that he would lead us to the Capitoline Hill. He did, pedalling along in front of our jeep and shouting to everybody on the street to get out of the way because General Clark was trying to get to the Capitoline Hill. This, of course, merely added to the excitement that we had felt everywhere we had gone in Rome, and by the time we reached a point opposite the balcony where Mussolini used to appear for his major speeches the road was blocked by curious and cheering people.

We finally broke a path through and twisted up the hill to the Town Hall. The door was locked, and there didn't seem to be a soul about. Pounding on the big door, I reflected that it had been a curiously varied as well as an historic day. We had been lost in the ancient capital which we entered as liberators after a long and unprecedented campaign. We had been welcomed and taken in tow by a priest and a boy on a bicycle. We had almost been mobbed by excited, cheering crowds. But now we couldn't even get into the Town Hall. I pounded on the door again, not feeling much like the conqueror of Rome. Anyhow, I thought, we got to Rome before Ike got across the Channel to Normandy. I was right about that, too, but by a narrow margin. I didn't know it, but even while I stood there Ike's army was embarking. We had won the race to Rome by only two days.

General Mark Clark

THE LONG ROAD NORTH

The Germans retreated up the peninsula to their next major defensive position, the Gothic Line, north of Florence, fighting a series of delaying actions en route. Again the pursuing Allied armies were slowed down and halted, severely weakened by the demands of the Riviera landings. On 26 August General Alexander mounted a large-scale offensive on the Gothic Line which broke through, but by October the advance had been halted by German resistance and by the weather. On the edge of the plains of Lombardy another stalemate ensued until the spring of 1945.

Last Offensive

The final Allied offensive in Italy began in the spring of 1945. On 10 April the Eighth Army attacking towards Bologna, crossed the River Senio.

D-day dawned fine and clear. Leaving command posts and gunpits like hives buzzing with gun programmes and preparing ammunition, I now moved to join 6 Brigade H.Q., where I would have to remain so long as the Brigade was in the line. The long hours of suspense dragged slowly by, eyes turning continually to watches. At last at 13.45 hours the distant roar of heavy bombers seemed the signal for the first guns to speak. These were the 3·7s firing a line of air-bursts as markers to guide the heavies on to their target. From the broad line of the Santerno defences soon rose a great pall of smoke and dust beneath which a rumbling carpet of anti-personnel bombs pulverized the enemy reserves. This was an anxious time for us all, with bitter memories of Cassino.

A strange hush fell and the silent minutes and seconds ticked slowly by till at 15.20 hours, with a mighty crash, the gun battle began along the whole front. Shells tore into the stop-banks of the Senio from all angles, some from guns carefully sited to enfilade the reaches of the river, others crashing headlong among the mines and wire and strong-points; others searching deep into the back areas among the guns, dumps, headquarters and supply routes. Suddenly the shelling lifted from the stop-banks, stepping out in a 'dragnet' barrage. Then the guns were silent, and for ten minutes Thunderbolts, Spitfires and Kittyhawks took charge of the river, zooming up and down with bombs, rockets and machine-guns adding their staccato to the hymn of hate. Back came the guns to pound the banks, play 'dragnet' with variations and again give way to the air. In all, five gun attacks and four air attacks—till at 19.20 hours a sudden silence marked H-hour, broken only by the aircraft coming back for a dummy run to keep the enemy heads down and drown the roar of Crocodiles and Wasps clambering up the near bank to sear with flame the already blasted enemy banks. In their tracks the assaulting infantry, with their kapok bridges, struggled forward to the river in the gathering dusk.

19.30 hours; with a roar the protective barrage opened four hundred yards beyond the river line and held there for thirty minutes, a curtain of steel behind which the infantry completed their grisly task. Fresh platoons leapfrogged through, and at H+40 moved forward with the barrage. There was no stopping now; four thousand yards to go and, apart from short spells to cool the guns, a steady slog for the Gunners till midnight.

Back at Brigade H.Q. common sense suggested a few hours' sleep for me, for there would be no rest after the barrage stopped at midnight. But the excitement was too intense as progress reports came in from the infantry biting deeper and deeper into the heart of the German 98 Division. In the eerie artificial moonlight provided by searchlights throwing their beams into the sky, the sappers were already busy at the bridging sites, while tanks, anti-tank guns, mortars and the whole assembly of supporting arms formed up in long queues waiting to carry their strength to the expanding bridgehead.

Although all was going well at the guns, with nothing coming back at them, the approaches to the river and the bridging parties seemed to be getting it— not as hotly as they might, perhaps, had the enemy not wasted so much ammuni- tion a few nights ago. On the right the Indians were across, but counter-attacks were hampering them and the flank of 5 Brigade. The Poles on our left, attacking across a dirtier section of the river, were having a hard time. Our left flank was well ahead of them now and meeting trouble here and there. All was well on the front, but there were Tigers about. The tally of prisoners mounted steadily.

24.00 hours and the barrage stopped. Voices rang loud in the stillness. Soon both brigades reported themselves on the final objective. All counter-attacks had been overcome and now seemed to be dying down. But to the left flank was a worry, with our troops three thousand yards ahead of the Poles in their tiny bridgehead. Defensive fire tasks were checked and extended to cover the gap. A reserve battalion was sent over to cover up till the Poles, who would pass over our bridges as soon as the last of our supporting arms were over, could attack outwards and extend their gains.

At dawn on the 10th our batteries slipped forward in turn to the prepared positions behind the banks of the Senio and, tired but jubilant, Gunners were ready to cover the infantry to the Santerno river line.

Lieutenant-Colonel S. W. Nicholson

After the Attack

The next morning I went forward with the General to the Senio. The narrow dusty road which led towards the stop-bank ran for its last quarter of a mile through country which was only now losing that chill, suspended, deadened atmosphere of ground which is being fought for. The shell-pitted fields, grass torn and trampled, or else lush and evil, covering unseen minefields, the shat- tered farm-houses still marked with the Red Crosses of the regimental aid posts, the signs marking company headquarters, troops wearing their steel helmets and carrying their arms, two wounded men walking back by the road edge, and over all the marks of the shelling—smashed and splintered trees, like plants broken off half-way up their stems, shallow craters, with their dead, dried sterile earth, their burnt black edges, and littered jagged shrapnel covering the fields like the scabs of some ugly disease, all were there.

We made our way through the transport, New Zealand and Polish, which packed the road, through the gap in the stop-bank, and across the Bailey bridge marked 'Raglan' on the plan. On the far side the road ran aslant to the top of the stop-bank. Tracks, trodden clear by many feet, wound straight up from the water's side. We walked up one of them, treading carefully, our eyes probing the ground for anything which might be mines. Behind us, dirty, brown and meagre, the Senio swirled away between its black earthen banks. It looked contemptible enough between its cratered dykes, and with all the litter of war

strewn around—German rifles, ammunition belts, old grenades, rags, paper—
the inevitable paper which covers every battlefield, with here and there the
crumpled grey shape of a dead German.

The flaming had left great burnt strips at intervals along the bank. On the
east bank a bulldozer was still at work clearing the approaches. The driver wore
a khaki felt hat bent up at the sides like an Australian, and a green jersey. They
were always given to individuality, these bulldozer drivers. He gave the General's
figure and red-banded cap no more than a glance.

Around us were the smashed remains of the stunted wire entanglements.
Under this dark earth were the mines. It seemed unbelievable that the infantry
had got across these banks with hardly a single mine casualty. The barrage had
torn the fields about in part, but the main thing had been the daylight. There
had been still light enough to allow the infantry to see the tracks already made
by the Germans, and to run up them to the unmined top. The flame-throwing
and the bombardment had kept down the heads of the enemy till our men were
on top of them. Had we had to make this attack in the full darkness this would
not have been possible. They would have had to move up the bank anywhere,
through minefields as well as along tracks. But now the mine bogy of the Senio
was laid. There were other bogies a-plenty ahead, but this one at least was
conquered.

The western face of the far bank sloped down to the countryside below. In
it the trees and houses and orchards and roads, torn by fire, lay dense and rich.
We looked ahead over a sea of green tree-tops, with here and there the white and
red island of a farmhouse. To our left, distant in the haze, were the foothills
above Route 9. Beyond them, invisible now, were the Apennines, where 5
Army, mostly Americans, with some South Africans and British troops, waited
to attack towards Bologna. I placed my map on the bank top and orientated it.
Bologna itself lay about half-left, eighteen miles distant, swallowed up utterly in
the greenness and the haze. To our right, equally unseen, was the township of
Cotignola, which 9 Brigade had captured that morning and were now handing
over to the follow-up force, and beyond it again was the town of Lugo, which the
Indians were due to take. Straight ahead our forward infantry and tanks were
now along the line of the Lugo canal, waiting for word to advance to the Santerno, and staring warily in the meantime either side of them. For we were now
well ahead of the other Allied forces. We were thrust out . . ., if not like the
proverbial sore thumb, certainly like an aggressive forefinger, reaching out for
the enemy's throat along the line of the Santerno.

Geoffrey Cox, New Zealand Intelligence Officer

A Nazi Officer: April 1945

At the new area a group of partisans with red scarves were waiting. They had
been stopped by our own troops down by the river bank as suspicious characters.
Enthusiastically (they were not yet disillusioned) they explained that they wanted
to help. They had been told that there were several Germans hiding in this area.
One, they said, was patently an officer. Gold braid had been seen on his
shoulders. Could they not carry on with the search?

It took only five minutes to get their papers checked and to set them loose. At the same time we put part of the Headquarters Defence Platoon out on the same quest. 'Any prisoners you can get will be valuable,' I told the bearded partisan leader. He grinned. '*Si, si. Prigionieri,*' he said.

Half an hour later there were shots down by the river bank. An hour later the partisans were back. They had found the Germans, three of them. One was certainly an officer. Where was he? Ah, he had tried to escape. A very foolish fellow. '*Molto stupido, molto stupido.*' But here were his documents. And they handed over a blood-stained bundle.

I opened the top pay-book. *Hauptmann.* So he was an officer all right. An anti-tank gunner. Two passport photographs fell out of the book. The face on them might well have come from a stock propaganda shot of the stern S.S. man. Here were those deep-set eyes, that hard thin mouth, that cheek crossed with duelling scars, that sleek yellow hair, that square German head of the ideal Nazi type. Every detail in the book bore out the picture. The man had been in the S.S. from the early days of Hitlerism; his list of decorations filled a whole page at the back. 'Medal for the *Einmarsch* into Austria: Medal for the *Einmarsch* into Czechoslovakia: Medal for the Polish campaign: Iron Cross Second Class in France. Served with the infantry in Russia: Transferred to the anti-tank gunners at the end of 1943: Iron Cross First Class in the Crimea for destroying two '*feindlicher Panzer Kampfwagen*'. The medal of the Iron Cross, its ribbon stained crimson brown above its red, black and white, lay amongst the papers.

The *Hauptmann*'s book was full of photographs of Storm Troops and of soldiers, of sisters in white blouses and dark skirts, of a heavy-built father with close-cropped hair, of other young officers with the same relentless faces. This was the type Hitler had loosed on Europe, brave, desperate, efficient. And now he had come to his end in an Italian field, shot down by an Italian farmer's boy with a Sten gun, shot in the back, I learned later, as he crouched in hiding.

Geoffrey Cox

27

PACIFIC ADVANCE

ATTACK ON PORT MORESBY

In spite of their crushing defeat at Midway, the Japanese doggedly persisted in their attempt to expand their perimeter towards northern Australia. Undeterred by the Coral Sea failure, they tried another approach to Port Moresby, beginning an advance overland from Buna on the north-eastern coast of New Guinea on 22 July 1942. Their prospects seemed fair. Fighting conditions in the Owen Stanley ranges of Papua were the worst of any in the Far Eastern war, and the Australian troops available to defend Port Moresby were completely untrained.

In New Guinea the great mountain ranges with their high peaks and deep gorges, the dense jungles which cover almost all of the huge island, the reeking *nipa* and mangrove swamps—'a stinking jumble of twisted, slime-covered roots and muddy "soup"'—the hazardous jungle trails, the vast patches of *kunai* grass, with its sharp-edged blades growing to a height of six or seven feet, the swollen streams, the ever-present mud, the dangerous off-shore reefs, most of them uncharted, the poor harbours—these terrain characteristics exerted a constant and adverse influence on troops and military tactics.

The problem of climate and health were no less severe. The penetrating, energy-sapping heat was accompanied by intense humidity and frequent torrential rains that defy description. Health conditions were amongst the worst in the world. The incidence of malaria could only be reduced by the most rigid and irksome discipline and even then the dreaded disease took a heavy toll. Dengue fever was common, while the deadly blackwater fever, though not so prevalent, was no less an adversary. Bacillary and amoebic dysentery were both forbidding possibilities, and tropical ulcers, easily formed from the slightest scratch, were difficult to cure. Scrub typhus, ringworm, hookworm and yaws all awaited the careless soldier. Millions of insects abounded everywhere.

MacArthur historical records

.... If the High Command had been conducting war games and had searched for the ultimate nightmare country, Papua must have been the inevitable selection. There was something cynically malignant about the weather and the geography. ... Through the deep ravines and gorges of these mountains innumerable rivers rush down to muddy coastal plains, smothered in dense tropical forests. This was the country where the Engineers were to build and repair air strips, harbours, bridges, roads and trails.

General Casey, U.S. Army engineers

Port Moresby

. . . . A native village, huts on 'stilts' in the shallow coastal waters; a few ware-houses and go-downs; tropical cottages with wide verandas and corrugated iron roofs; a few administration buildings and police barracks . . . hard-eyed native constabulary, strong men in military blouses terminating incongruously in a red blanket-like sarong.

The First Australians in New Guinea

Making every allowance for the state of affairs existing in Australia at the time of the outbreak of the Japanese war, the condition which manifested itself immediately after the arrival of (the *Aquitania*) convoy calls for severe censure of the persons responsible for the loading of the troops' camp equipment. The troops were of the average age of eighteen and a half years, and had received no proper training. They were in the charge of inexperienced officers who appear to have had little or no control over them. They were inadequately equipped in every way; in particular, they were without much of the equipment necessary to give them any reasonable prospect of maintaining health in an area such as Port Moresby. In (the) general state of unpreparedness, that may have been inevitable, but no excuse is apparent . . . for the gross carelessness and incompetence which resulted in the stowing of camp equipment at the bottom of the holds, so that when the troops were disembarked there were no facilities to enable them to be fed and encamped. These conditions (the blame for which cannot be ascribed to the Commandant or his staff) had a grave effect upon the morale of the troops, and contributed in no small measure to the disorderly and undisciplined conduct which was prevalent for some weeks after their arrival.

Barry Report

. . . . The Militia units were a measure of the general unpreparedness of Australia to defend itself. Their ranks were a mixture of the extremely brave and the extremely confused. They faced the enemy in the opening battles of the South-west Pacific, when the enemy was strong, confident and merciless. Instead of a gradual immersion into the trials of war, they were plunged into terror and exhaustion, under circumstances which would try the best and most seasoned troops. They deserved the pity and sympathy of the guilty community which had allowed them to remain unprepared, and which had passed laws purporting to keep them at home. Instead, their efforts were held to scorn, and they were unjustly blamed for our early shortcomings.

Brigadier Porter, A.I.F.

. . . . On 27 January, the day of the call-up, Major-General Morris addressed a message to the commanding officers of the units responsible for the defence of Port Moresby. He gave them specific orders: 'No position is to be given up without permission; outflanked positions must continue to resist; even the smallest units must make provision for counter-attack. . . . We have the honour of being the front-line defence of Australia. Let us show ourselves worthy of that honour.'

The Japanese advance collided with the Australians at Kokoda in the Owen Stanleys, where the latter gave a good account of themselves.

In the advance to Kokoda the Japanese vanguard wore green uniforms and steel helmets garnished with leaves. Some wore scarlet helmets. They carried abundant supplies of ammunition, mess tins of cooked rice, and equipment which included a light shovel slung across the back and a machete for cutting a pathway through the jungle.

Their tactics appeared to follow a definite pattern. A mobile spearhead advanced rapidly until opposing forces barred further progress. While the spearhead deployed and engaged the opposition, support troops would site a machine-gun, and might also bring up one or more mortars. Feint or deliberate attacks disclosed the width and strength of the defensive position by drawing the enemy's fire. For this purpose, advance scouts often risked and forfeited their lives. The stronger support elements, coming forward, cut their way round their opponents' flank, either to force a withdrawal or to annihilate the defenders in a surprise attack from the rear.

Raymond Paull

Japanese at Kokoda

As dusk approached, we advanced to within seventy metres of the Australians, who concentrated an intense fire on the platoon. Our formation was faulty, and the rain hindered us, so that we were unable to carry out the charge and decided instead to attack at night. Then the men were not properly assembled, and valuable time was wasted in the torrential rain and darkness. Even the section leaders could not be lined up.

We began the night attack at 10.20 p.m., advancing stealthily on hands and knees. We were moving in closer to the Australians but suddenly encountered their guards in the shadows of the large rubber trees. Corporal Hamada killed one of them with his bayonet and engaged the others, but the Australians' fire finally compelled us to withdraw. The platoon was scattered, and it was impossible to repeat our charge. 1st Class Private Hirose was killed, but the soldier I had grappled with was wounded on the leg by a grenade thrown by Corporal Hamada.

Hamada, because of the darkness, was unable to assemble the men remaining. I went to the rear and tried myself to assemble them, but I turned in the wrong direction in the darkness, and with two of my men, suddenly realized that we were within forty metres of the Australians' lines and grenades were thrown at us. The night attack ended in failure. 1 Platoon attacked at 3 a.m. and was unsuccessful also. Every day I am losing my men, and I could not restrain tears of bitterness. So I rested, struggling against hunger and the cold, and waited for the dawn.

Second Lieutenant Hirano

The Loss of Kokoda

Dusk fell early, a grey, misty, cheerless evening though the moon was at the full. Jap scouts had already been reported, and about 7.30, cat-calls and a stray mortar shot or so came ringing across the Mambare. Thereafter, there was increasing noise and salvoes of firing, mostly I think from the Japs, who had a big mortar with them, at shorter and shorter intervals. By midnight the firing on both sides had become almost continuous. It was warm and comfortable in the lounge, and I slept secure in the knowledge that I would be called when wanted.

About one o'clock on the 29th a hand touched my shoulder. It was Brewer, with news that Colonel Owen had been wounded. The moon was now in full strength, and shone brightly through the white mountain mist as I hurried with Brewer past the old magistrate's house, now the H.Q., where we picked up a stretcher and several bearers.

We crept down a shallow communication trench leading forward to a firing pit at the very edge of the escarpment. The C.O. was propped up in the narrow space, struggling violently yet more than semi-conscious, quite unable to realize where he was or to help us get him out. Removal was difficult, but we got him on to the stretcher at last and carried him to the R.A.P. where Wilkinson [W.O. John Wilkinson] was waiting with a lantern and the instruments laid out for operating. Lieutenant-Colonel Owen had received a single G.S.W. [gun-shot wound] at the outer edge of the right frontal bone just above the eyebrows. There appeared to be no wound of exit, and a little bleeding was controlled by gauze packing. Skull and brain had, of course, been penetrated. He was now quite unconscious, with occasional convulsive seizures which lessened as he grew weaker. At the time of our withdrawal he had become quite still and was on the point of death. He probably did not survive another fifteen minutes.

Major Watson came in to see him, and then we had four or five casualties in rapid succession who, when dressed, were told to get back to Deniki as soon as they could. Wilkinson held the lantern for me, and every time he raised it a salvo of machine-gun bullets was fired at the building. This particular enemy machine-gun was as yet a little below the edge of the escarpment, probably just behind Graham's back premises, so its range was bound to be too high, and while the roof was riddled those working below could feel reasonably safe.

. . . . Outside the mist had grown very dense, but the moonlight allowed me to see where I was going. Thick white streams of vapour stole between the rubber trees, and changed the whole scene into a weird combination of light and shadow. The mist was greatly to our advantage; our own line of retreat remained perfectly plain, but it must have slowed down the enemy's advance considerably, another chance factor that helped to save the Kokoda force. After a hasty look round the almost deserted plateau, I walked into the rubber. The firing was still heavy, coming, I suppose, from the Japs, as many of our men had left. I stayed awhile on the edge of the rubber, hoping to strike someone in authority, but as all the men were hurrying out to Deniki I slowly followed them.

. . . . Looking back on the Japanese assault on Kokoda, I can now see that by withdrawing we took the wisest course. That we were considerably out-manned by the enemy was only too certain; we had but about ninety combatants, not counting a detachment of the P.I.B., whereas the Japanese force was variably estimated at from three hundred to five hundred men. Besides this advantage in numbers they had others, particularly in that our line of retreat was practically undefended and open to them had they worked around to our rear. In that case the entire force would have been surrounded, and capture or death the fate of every individual. By withdrawing in good time we saved men who later held up the Japs till reinforcements arrived, a very good example of the military axiom that the only conclusive victory consists in the complete annihilation of enemy forces.

Dr. Vernon

MacArthur at Moresby

At the time of my arrival in July 1942, we felt we would be lucky if we didn't have to fight the Nip in Australia. When I went up to Port Moresby for the first time, the plane stopped rolling just long enough for me to get out. It took off before the enemy could catch it on the ground. Shortly after that the Nip came over and strafed the airfield. I may have had a lot of plans and ideas but this attack crystallized one of them—the determination to clear the enemy off our lawn so that we could go across the street and play in his yard.

General MacArthur

Late in August a strong Japanese force attempted to establish airfields at Milne Bay at the eastern tip of New Guinea, but had been wiped out by the second week in September. At the same time the Japanese in the Owen Stanleys had reached the end of their tether, halting not far short of their objective.

The Milne Bay area is rapidly being cleared of the enemy. Australian combat troops, ably commanded by Major-General Clowes, and brilliantly supported by American and Australian air units, have thrown the enemy back into the narrow confines of the peninsula north of the bay, where he is rapidly being reduced. His losses have been heavy. Remnants of his forces were probably saved from destruction by evacuation by naval warcraft under cover of darkness. All of his heavy supplies and equipment, including tanks, were lost. This operation represents another phase in the pattern of the enemy's plans to capture Port Moresby. This citadel is guarded by the natural defence line of the Owen Stanley Range. The first effort was to turn its left flank from Lae and Salamaua, which proved impracticable. The enemy then launched an attack in large convoy force against its rear. This was repulsed and dissipated by air and sea action in the Coral Sea. He then tried to pierce the centre by way of Buna, Gona and Kokoda, subjecting himself to extraordinary air losses because of the extreme vulnerability of his exposed position. His latest effort was to try to turn the right flank by a surprise attack at Milne Bay.

General MacArthur, communiqué

The Japanese Halt

More than a month has elapsed since the Shitai departed from Rabaul, following the gallant Yokoyama Advance Butai. We have crushed strong positions at Isurava, Iora, the Gap, Efogi, etc., advanced swiftly and, after a fierce battle, destroyed the Australians' final resistance at Iorabaiwa. We now hold securely this high hill, the most important point for the advance towards Port Moresby.

Each Tai has marched over mountains and through deep valleys, conquered great heights, and pursued the Australians for more than twenty days. We have waded through deep rivers, scaled breath-taking cliffs, uncomplainingly carried heavy burdens of guns and ammunition, overcome the shortage of provisions, and thereby triumphed over the reputedly impregnable Owen Stanley Range. . . . The reason why we have halted is to regain our fighting strength before striking a decisive blow at Port Moresby. . . . Fortify your morale, and make your preparations complete, so that the Shitai is strong for our next operation.

Japanese order of the day, 20 September

The Japanese advance over the Owen Stanleys, from a military point of view, was a triumph of discipline and rugged determination. Allied air-strafing undoubtedly made the maintenance of supply difficult, but I imagine that the inefficiencies of Japanese headquarters planning were equally guilty in the situation. Fortitude is admirable under any flag, and those Japanese foot soldiers had it. They pressed on—ill and hungry. They had no way to evacuate their sick and wounded. Sanitation was wretched, and they suffered from tropical fevers and exhaustion.

There is a limit to human faithfulness and fervour. Men must be rested and fed. The Japanese reached the Imita range, and there a halt was called.

General Robert L. Eichelberger, U.S. Army

GUADALCANAL

Meanwhile, on 7 August 1942 the Americans had struck the first counter-blow by land at the Japanese threat to Australia. A division of Marines landed on Guadalcanal (and on nearby islands in the eastern Solomons) and seized the airfield the Japanese were building there. The latter reacted violently to this unexpected attack. Both sides tried to pour reinforcements into Guadalcanal. The Japanese, operating from their massive bases at Rabaul and Truk, made repeated attempts to cut up American supply convoys. The latter's naval covering force was shattered at the battle of Savo Island on 9 August, but though the American marines were left on their own as a result, they held out, and the series of terrific naval battles in surrounding waters which ensued were evenly fought. The land battle centred on the struggle for Henderson Field, as the erstwhile Japanese airfield had been renamed. This jungle airstrip was vital to both sides, and the Americans hung on to it by the skin of their teeth. The climax of the battle came in October.

The code name of Guadalcanal Island was Cactus, and God knows it was a thorny spot. I don't remember the code name of the operation, but it should have been called Shoestring. The Navy and Army commanders charged with seeing it through made repeated requests for additional troops and ships, but Europe was Washington's darling; the South Pacific was only a stepchild. None the less, the Marines landed on Guadalcanal and Tulagi on 7 August. They might have won a reasonably quick victory if we had been able to protect them, supply them, and reinforce them, but we weren't. We didn't have the ships, either cargo or combat, and the enemy did.

Admiral William F. Halsey

Guadalcanal Landing

Mare Island Naval Hospital

Dear Mother and Dad: Excerpt from diary . . .

It is 6 August. Just released from the ship's hospital after a bit of surgery. Nothing serious. The decks are humming with industry. Marines all over are cleaning machine-guns and filling belts for 30s and 50s, making head nets and camouflage nets for their helmets, getting their combat gear shipshape. Those that have finished spend hour after hour sharpening their sheathknives on the soles of their rough calf-skin field shoes.

Every face is a picture in grimness. There is no laughter anywhere. Last minute instructions are being given by platoon leaders. Maps of our objectives are being distributed among squad leaders and runners, with enemy positions marked out from aerial photos. We are issued pamphlets telling of the Jap weapons, explosive bullets, tactics. My instructions are to land with the first platoon. We will be the second wave to hit the beach (Red Beach). We will take cover and I shall immediately contact Lieutenant —— by moving along to the right, then come back and lead the first platoon to the rest of the company which has been made a machine-gun company.

The sea is very rough. I have an errand that takes me to the forward deck. Waves are dashing over the ship. The climb down is slippery and precarious. I cling to a cable as the wind nearly sweeps me into the ocean. I literally throw myself from cable to cable. The cables hold some groups of landing boats to the deck. I try to take shelter under them, but almost get drowned by a wave that breaks like a ton of bricks. Sailors and Coast Guardsmen are getting the Lewis machine-guns attached to the gun turrets on landing boats. They're in slickers. Waves dash over them every few seconds. You can almost hear their curses above the howling gale.

Coming back from the forward well deck, the going is worse. Working back with no cover and fifteen feet between cables, water swirling over the deck knee high. Work my way up to the boat deck, then a fifty-foot dash across that slippery deck against a sixty-mile side-sweeping gale to the ladder leading up to the promenade deck. I drag myself up to the enclosed half section and proceed to the exposed part where we are quartered. Change to dry dungarees. Sit down on a coil of rope and try to be comfortable. The cold is biting and the wind so strong you can't hear yourself talk. The ship is plunging so that if I stand up I'll be pitched overboard. I stay there for a couple of hours sharpening my sheathknife and bayonet to razor edges. I make the vicious journey to the mess hall only to find that the place reeks with many seasick men.

I met Paul Taylor and Steve Hanasack. We hadn't seen each other since the old Quantico days when I was attending camouflage school. Paul is also an artist and a good one. He's from Brooklyn, too. We talk of old times in the art colonies and of the folks back home. Night is falling. We go to the boat deck talking of the work we both love—painting. Finally we try to sleep on a hatch covered with men. No cover or pillow on this ship. The deck for a bed, our helmets for pillows. After two hours we still can't sleep. The wind gets stronger all the time.

We get to the enclosed part of the promenade deck, drenched. It's full of men packed in like sardines. It's pitch dark and we hold on to each other, stumbling over heads, chests and arms. Then we lie across four other guys and sleep till 3 a.m. . . .

Later: after landing.

My boot camp (Parris Island) platoon is reported wiped out. The only ones I'm sure of, however, are: [mentions the names of ten men whom he saw killed, among them 'Woodie, who was always laughing']. They were all good friends of mine and I used to dream they were talking to me.

Love, John

The Defence of Henderson Field: 24 October

Before we could get set up darkness came and it started raining like hell. It was too black to see anything, so I crawled along the ridge-front until it seemed I had come to the nose. To make sure I felt around with my hands and the ridge seemed to drop away on all sides. There we set up.

With the guns set up and the watches arranged, it was time for chow. I passed the word along for the one can of 'Spam' and the one can of 'borrowed peaches' that we had with us. Then we found out some jerk had dropped the can of peaches and it had rolled down the ridge into the jungle. He had been too scared to tell us what he had done. I shared out the 'Spam' by feeling for a hand in the darkness and dropping into it. The next morning I sent out a couple of scouts to 'look over the terrain'. So we got our peaches back.

That night Smitty and I crawled out towards the edge of the nose and lay on our backs with the rain driving into our faces. Every so often I would lift up and call some of the boys by name to see if they were still awake and to reassure myself as well as them.

It must have been two o'clock in the morning when I heard a low mumbling. At once I got Smitty up. A few minutes later we heard the same noise again. I crawled over to the men and told them to stand by. I started figuring. The Japs might not know we were on the nose and might be preparing to charge us, or at any moment they might discover our positions. I decided to get it over with. As soon as the men heard the click of my pin coming out of the grenade, they let loose their grenades too.

Smitty was pulling out pins as I threw the grenades. The Japs screamed, so we knew we had hit them. We threw a few more grenades and then there was silence.

All that second day we dug in. We had no entrenching tools so we used bayonets. As night came I told the men we would have a hundred per cent watch and they were not to fire until they saw a Jap.

About the same time as the night before we heard the Japs talking again. They were about a hundred yards from the nose. It was so damned quiet, you could hear anything. I crawled around to the men and told them to keep quiet, look forward and glue their ears to the ground. As the Japs advanced we could hear the bushes rustle. Suddenly all hell broke loose.

All of us must have seen the Japs at the same time. Grenades exploded everywhere on the ridge-nose, followed by shrieks and yells. It would have been death to fire the guns because muzzle flashes would have given away our positions and we could have been smothered and blasted by a hail of grenades. Stansbury, who was lying in the foxhole next to mine, was pulling out grenade-pins with his teeth and rolling the grenades down the side of the nose. Leipart, the smallest guy in the platoon, and my particular boy, was in his foxhole delivering grenades like a star pitcher.

Then I gave the word to fire. Machine-guns and rifles let go and the whole line seemed to light up. Pettyjohn yelled to me that his gun was out of action. In the light from the firing I could see several Japs a few feet away from Leipart. Apparently he had been hit because he was down on one knee. I knocked off two Japs with a rifle but a third drove his bayonet into Leipart. Leipart was dead; seconds later, so was the Jap. After a few minutes, I wouldn't swear to how long it was, the blitz became a hand-to-hand battle. Gaston was having trouble with a Jap officer, I remember that much. Although his leg was nearly hacked off and his rifle all cut up, Gaston finally connected his boot with the Jap's chin. The result was one slopehead with one broken neck.

Firing died down a little, so evidently the first wave was a flop. I crawled over to Pettyjohn, and while he and Faust covered me I worked to remove a ruptured cartridge and change the belt-feed pawl. Just as I was getting ready to feed in a belt of ammo, I felt something hot on my hand and a sharp vibration. Some damned slopehead with a light machine-gun had fired a full burst into the feeding mechanism and wrecked the gun.

Things got pretty bad on the second wave. The Japs penetrated our left flank, carried away all opposition and were possibly in a position to attack our ridge-nose from the rear. On the left, however, Grant, Payne and Hinson stood by. In the centre, Lock, Swanek and McNabb got it and were carried away to the rear by corpsmen. The Navy boys did a wonderful job and patched up all the casualties, but they were still bleeding like hell and you couldn't tell what was wrong with them, so I sent them back. That meant that all my men were casualties and I was on my own. It was lonely up there with nothing but dead slopeheads for company, but I couldn't tell you what I was thinking about. I guess I was really worrying about the guns, shooting as fast as I could, and getting a bead on the next and nearest Jap.

One of the guns I couldn't find because it wasn't firing. I figured the guys had been hit and had put the gun out of action before leaving. I was always very insistent that if for any reason they had to leave a gun they would put it out of action so that the Japs wouldn't be able to use it. Being without a gun myself, I dodged over to the unit on my right to get another gun and give them the word on what was going on. Kelly and Totman helped me bring the gun back towards the nose of the ridge and we zig-zagged under an enemy fire that never seemed to stop. While I was on the right flank I borrowed some riflemen to form a skirmish line. I told them to fix bayonets and follow me. Kelly and Totman fed ammo as I sprayed every inch of terrain free of Japs. Dawn was beginning to break and in the half-light I saw my own machine-gun still near the centre of the nose. It was still in working order and some Japs were crawling towards it. We got there just in time. I left Kelly and Totman and ran over to it.

For too many moments it seemed as though the whole Japanese Army was firing at me. Nevertheless three men on the right flank thought I might be low on ammunition and volunteered to run it up to me. Stat brought one belt and he went down with a bullet in the stomach. Reilly came up with another belt. Just as he reached the gun, he was hit in the groin. His feet flew out and nearly knocked me off the gun. Then Jonjeck arrived with a belt and stopped a bullet in the shoulder. As I turned I saw a piece of flesh disappear from his neck. I told him to go back for medical aid, but he refused. He wanted to stay up there with me. There was not time to argue, so I tapped him on the chin, hard enough so that he went down. That convinced him that I wanted my order obeyed.

My ears rang when a Jap sighted in on me with his light machine-gun but luckily he went away to my left. Anyway, I decided it was too unhealthy to stay in any one place for too long, so I would fire a burst and then move. Each time I shifted, grenades fell just where I had been. Over the nose of the ridge in the tall grass, which was later burned for security, I thought I saw some movement. Right off the nose, in the grass, thirty Japs stood up. One of them was looking at me through field-glasses. I let them have it with a full burst and they peeled off like grass under a mowing machine.

After that, I guess I was so wound up that I couldn't stop. I rounded up the skirmish line, told them I was going to charge off the nose and I wanted them to be right behind me. I picked up the machine-gun, and without noticing the burning hot water jacket, cradled it in my arms. Two belts of ammo I threw around my shoulders. The total weight was about a hundred and fifty pounds, but the way I felt I could have carried three more without noticing it. I fed one of the belts off my shoulders into the gun, and then started forward. A colonel dropped about four feet in front of me with his yellow belly full of good American lead. In the meantime the skirmish line came over the nose, whooping like a bunch of wild Indians. We reached the edge of the clearing where the jungle began and there was nothing left either to holler at or shoot at. The battle was over with that strange sort of quietness that always follows.

The first thing I did was to sit down. I was soaked in perspiration and steam was rising in a cloud from my gun. My hand felt funny. I looked down and saw through my tattered shirt a blister which ran from my fingertips to my forearm. Captain Ditta came running up, slapped me on the back and gave me a drink from his canteen.

For three days after the battle, we camped around the nose. They estimated that there were a hundred and ten Japs dead in front of my sector. I don't know about that, but they started to smell so horribly that we had to bury them by blasting part of the ridge over on top of them. On the third day we marched twelve miles back to the airport. I never knew what day it was, and what's more I didn't care.

Sergeant Mitchell Paige, U.S.M.C.

Scraping the Barrel

In the Solomons, with heavy losses in fighting ships and planes, Americans were seeking to maintain a precarious foothold on the advanced beachhead at Guadalcanal. I still recall the dismal August day when Admiral Leary told me the results of the Battle of Savo Island. We had five heavy cruisers and a group of destroyers there to protect our Guadalcanal transports. The engagement lasted eight minutes. The Japanese had no losses. We lost four of our cruisers— the *Quincy*, *Vincennes*, *Astoria* and *Canberra* (Royal Australian Navy). The fifth cruiser, the *Chicago*, was damaged. It took considerable optimism in those days to believe we were on the winning side of the fight.

General Eichelberger

We now were down to our last carrier, the *Saratoga*, and it was sometimes temporarily unavailable because of damage received. We had new ones coming along rapidly, but at this moment we were skating on thin ice. Our hold on Guadalcanal was precarious. The enemy also had suffered heavily in carriers, and naval action was becoming more and more a continuing battle between surface craft. There seemed to be a conspicuous lack of air support for our ground and sea forces.

Admiral William D. Leahy

We were living off captured rice and driving our trucks on captured fuel. Our A.K.s [cargo ships] were loaded with the stuff we needed, but every time there was a Condition Red [enemy air raid], they had to up-anchor and get out. First the planes pounded us, and then the battleships. During thirty-six hours on 13 and 14 October, the *Kongo* and the *Haruna* gave us a thousand rounds of 14-inch. But it wasn't that; it was the hopelessness, the feeling that nobody gave a curse whether we lived or died. It soaked into you until you couldn't trust your own mind. You'd brief a pilot, and no sooner had he taken off than you'd get frantic, wondering if you'd forgotten to tell him some trivial thing that might become the indispensable factor in saving his life.

Lieutenant-Commander J. E. Lawrence, U.S. Air Combat Information Officer

The last of the series of major naval encounters, the five-day Battle of Guadal-canal in November, ended with victory for the Americans, and was decisive.

This battle was a decisive American victory by any standard. It was also the third great turning point of the war in the Pacific. Midway stopped the Japanese advance in the Central Pacific; Coral Sea stopped it in the South-west Pacific; Guadalcanal stopped it in the South Pacific. . . . If our ships and planes had been routed in this battle, if we had lost it, our troops on Guadalcanal would have been trapped as were our troops on Bataan. We could not have reinforced them or relieved them. Archie Vandegrift would have been our 'Skinny' Wainwright, and the infamous Death March would have been repeated. (We later captured a document which designated the spot where the Japanese commander had planned to accept Archie's surrender.) Unobstructed, the enemy would have driven south, cut our supply lines to New Zealand and Australia and enveloped them.

Admiral Halsey

In the end it was the Japanese who failed to reinforce their Guadalcanal garrison adequately, even by means of Admiral Tanaka's 'Tokyo Express'—a force of fast destroyers and other craft. By January 1943 the Japanese garrison was in desperate straits, and resorted to suicidal tactics.

Reinforcements Sunk

The Japanese were crowded together on board their transports like herrings in a cask. The two ships that went down at the first attack had left a sheet of water about three-quarters of a square mile in area covered with soldiers in khaki, who gradually disappeared. The bombs smashed the bridges and exploded on the over-crowded between-decks, leaving a pulp of mangled human beings. While the burning transports continued to advance imperturbably on Guadalcanal, according to their orders, the pilots flew back to restock their machines with fuel and projectiles, and returned to bomb and machine-gun them.

Georges Blond

Suicide Attack

On 22 January Japanese units had made suicide sorties. That of the Inagaki unit was thus described in the paper *Yomiuri*:

'On the eve of the sortie, at midnight, all the assembled men sing the *Kimigayo* ["Your Majesty's reign will last ten thousand and one generations. Until the pebble becomes a rock and is covered with moss."], the sad and solemn hymn to the Emperor, then give three *banzais* [cheers] for his eternal prosperity. The company bows in the direction of the Imperial Palace. While the American loudspeakers, which are set up above the lines, continue to repeat in Japanese the invitation to capitulate, the two hundred men, including the sick and the wounded who have still survived, rush towards death in a supreme attack. . . .'

At the end of the month Admiral Tanaka's destroyers were sent to evacuate the survivors; in three runs twelve thousand were taken off and Guadalcanal was at last in American hands.

THE FIRST VICTORY

As a deadly stalemate ensued in New Guinea and in Guadalcanal in late 1942, the Japanese High Command began to draw in its horns. Reinforcements destined for New Guinea were diverted to Guadalcanal, and the hapless Japanese in the Owen Stanleys were left to dispute a bitter and long drawn-out retreat back to Buna with the Australians, and the Americans who had reinforced them.

It left us momentarily dazed to have to retreat from our present position, after advancing so close to our goal at the cost of enormous sacrifices and casualties.

Second Lieutenant Hirano

It is a sorry thing that we must leave the bodies of our comrades and the ground that we won so dearly. Sleep peacefully, my friends. Farewell! We shall meet again in Heaven!

Lieutenant Sakamoto

Buna was the first Allied Ground Force victory in the Pacific (the Buna campaign was ended before the fall of Guadalcanal), and it was bought at a substantial price in death, wounds, disease, despair and human suffering. No one who fought there, however hard he tries, will ever forget it. I am a reasonably unimaginative man, but Buna is still to me, in retrospect, a nightmare. This long after, I can still remember every day and most of the nights as clearly as though they were days and nights last week.

Buna Village and Buna Mission are god-forsaken little places on the in-hospitable northern coast of New Guinea. A few score native huts and the coconut plantations around them represented, before the war, Buna's sole claim on an indifferent world's attention. The climate there is insufferable; the man-made gardens on the edge of swamp and jungle are only judicious scratchings on the rich earth near the ocean: the Australian planters (before they were dis-possessed by the Japanese) didn't want to get very far away from the sea breeze which alone made life tolerable. In times of peace a package of used razor blades might be—in terms of barter—a reasonable price for a native hut in Buna Village. But Buna cost dearly in war, because possession of the north coast of New Guinea was vital to future Allied operations.

General Eichelberger

The effect of jungle fighting in New Guinea against the Japanese was as demoralizing to the newly-arrived Americans as it had been to the Australians.

'Bob,' said General MacArthur in a grim voice, 'I'm putting you in command of Buna. Relieve Harding. I am sending you in, Bob, and I want you to remove all officers who won't fight. Relieve regimental and battalion commanders; if necessary, put sergeants in charge of battalions and corporals in charge of com-panies—anyone who will fight. Time is of the essence; the Japs may land reinforcements any night.'

General MacArthur strode down the breezy veranda again. He said he had reports that American soldiers were throwing away their weapons and running from the enemy. Then he stopped short and spoke with emphasis. He wanted no misunderstandings about my duties.

'Bob,' he said, 'I want you to take Buna, or not come back alive.' He paused a moment and then, without looking at Byers, pointed a finger. 'And that goes for your chief of staff, too. Do you understand?'

'Yes, sir,' I said.

General Eichelberger

Buna

The troops were deplorable. They wore long dirty beards. Their clothing was in rags. Their shoes were uncared-for, or worn out. They were receiving far less than adequate rations and there was little discipline or military courtesy.

. . . . When Martin and I visited a regimental combat team to observe what was supposed to be an attack, it was found that the regimental post was four and a half miles behind the front line. The regimental commander and his staff went forward from this location rarely, if ever.

Troops were scattered along a trail towards the front line in small groups, engaged in eating, sleeping, during the time they were supposed to be in an attack. At the front there were portions of two companies, aggregating a hundred and fifty men.

Outside of the hundred and fifty men in the foxholes in the front lines, the remainder of the two thousand men in the combat area could not have been even considered a reserve—since three or four hours would have been required to organize and move them on any tactical mission.

U.S. Intelligence Officer

The first thing I found out was that troops in the front-line positions had no trustworthy knowledge of Japanese positions. Our patrols were dazed by the hazards of swamp and jungle; they were unwilling to undertake the patrolling which alone could safeguard their own interests. To get accurate information was almost impossible—and yet men die if orders are based on incorrect information.

Actually, this long after, I'm inclined to believe that the men were more frightened by the jungle than by the Japanese. It was the terror of the new and the unknown. There is nothing pleasant about sinking into a foul-smelling bog up to your knees. There is nothing pleasant about lying in a slit trench, half submerged, while a tropical rain turns it into a river. Jungle night noises were strange to Americans—and in the moist hot darkness the rustling of small animals in the bush was easily misinterpreted as the stealthy approach of the enemy. I can recall one night hearing a noise that sounded like a man brushing against my tent. It turned out that a leaf had fallen from a tree and struck the canvas side. The stem of the leaf was as thick as my thumb. It measured two and a half feet long by one and a half feet wide.

General Eichelberger

The Americans: a Japanese View

The enemy has received almost no training. Even though we fire a shot they present a very large portion of their body and look around. Their movements are very slow. At this rate they cannot make a night attack.

They hit coconuts that are fifteen metres from us. There are some low shots but most of them are high. They do not look out and determine their targets from the jungle. They are in the jungle firing as long as their ammunition lasts. Maybe they get more money for firing so many rounds.

The nature of the enemy is superior and they excel in firing techniques. Their tactics are to neutralize our positions with fire power, approach our positions under concentrated mortar fire. Furthermore, it seems that in firing they are using treetops. During daytime mess, if our smoke is discovered, we receive mortar fire.

The Battle

I watched the advance from the forward regimental command-post, which was about 125 yards from Buna Village. The troops moved forward a few yards, heard the typewriter clatter of Jap machine-guns, ducked down, and stayed down. My little group and I left the observation post and moved through one company that was bogged down.

I spoke to the troops as we walked along. 'Lads, come along with us.'

And they did. In the same fashion we were able to lead several units against the bunkers at Buna Village. There is an ancient military maxim that a commander must be seen by his troops in combat. When I arrived at Buna there was a rule against officers wearing insignia of rank at the front because this might draw enemy fire. I was glad on that particular day that there were three stars on my collar which glittered in the sun. How else would those sick and cast-down soldiers have known their commander was in there with them? They knew, being sensible men, that a bullet is no respecter of rank. As I wrote to General Sutherland that evening: 'The number of our troops who tried to avoid combat to-day could be numbered on your fingers.'

The snipers were there all right. On one occasion all of us were pinned to the ground for fifteen minutes while tracer bullets cleared our backs with inches to spare. Fifteen minutes, with imminent death blowing coolly on your sweat-wet shirt, can seem like a long time! Later a sniper in a tree opened fire at a range of about fifteen yards. My companions returned the fire with tommy-guns, although, in that green and steaming jungle, they couldn't see the sniper. Someone scored a direct hit.

. . . . There had been one important success in that day's fighting. A platoon of G Company, 126th Infantry, had found a crevice in the Japanese defences and had driven through the sea on the narrow spit of land between Buna Village and Buna Mission. The commander of the platoon was Staff-Sergeant Herman J. Bottcher, a fine combat soldier. The break-through was, possibly, lucky: the holding of the position was accomplished by intelligence and sheer guts.

Bottcher had only eighteen men with him, and he was sure that next morning his foothold on the shore would be attacked from both sides by infuriated Japs. He kept his men at work all night in the darkness. They dug themselves in. Before morning I managed to see to it that ammunition and a few additional men were sent in to the spot. Their one machine-gun was emplaced in the sand. It seemed unlikely that this small force could hold off an attack from two sides. But Bottcher, in his calculations, accepted gambler's odds. It was a narrow beach, and he guessed that there would not be simultaneous attacks because of enemy lack of communications.

Bottcher was right. Japanese from Buna Village attacked about dawn, and the machine-gun discouraged them. Japanese from Buna Mission attacked in force a while later, wading across the shallows from the other direction. With his hand on the hot machine-gun Bottcher was able to mow them down like wheat in a field. It was sharp and clear daylight when the last attack took place. For days after, the evidence of Sergeant Bottcher's victory rolled in and out with the tide—the evidence was the sea-carried and drifting bodies of Japanese soldiers.

Because American newspaper and magazine photographers appeared some days later to snap grim, realistic pictures of the Japanese dead, that stretch of sand between Buna Village and Giropa Point is now identified as Maggot Beach, and, if I may say so, with reason.

. . . . Bottcher's platoon at Buna had absorbed some of his devil-may-care attitude. Byers, whom I had appointed to succeed the wounded Waldron as commander of the forward elements of 32 Division, went forward on the morning of the 6th to confer with the troops who had achieved that heartening success. He chatted with the friendly, bear-like Bottcher, who said they could hold out. Then Byers talked with the thin group of doughboys. He was prepared to promise deliveries of—figuratively speaking—peacock tongues and garlic pickles and hot sausages and beef steaks and turkey, if they would just maintain their hard-won position on the sea.

'What do you need?' Byers demanded.

The American soldier is unconventional and unpredictable. One member of Bottcher's platoon gave the answer. He turned a half-somersault on the sand and held his pose. Swamp water had rotted away the seat of his trousers and his naked buttocks were exposed.

'Pants,' said the G.I. 'For God's sake, General, pants!'

. . . . On 18 December tanks and troops jumped off. It was a spectacular and dramatic assault, and a brave one. From the New Strip to the sea was about half a mile. American troops wheeled to the west in support, and other Americans were assigned to mopping-up duties. But behind the tanks went the fresh and jaunty Aussie veterans, tall, moustached, erect, with their blazing tommy-guns swinging before them. Concealed Japanese positions—which were even more formidable than our patrols had indicated—burst into flame. There was the greasy smell of tracer fire from the snipers' seats in the trees and heavy machine-gun fire from barricades and entrenchments.

Steadily tanks and infantrymen advanced through the spare, high coconut trees, seemingly impervious to the heavy opposition. There were a hundred and fifty Japanese bunkers on Cape Endaiadere. Three tanks were destroyed; casualties were extraordinarily high. I have never seen Australian official figures, but I'm sure that Aussie battalion lost nearly half its fighting force in killed and wounded. Nevertheless, the job was done. The sea was reached, and mopping up began.

The next day the attack changed direction, and the Americans and the Australians pushed the surviving enemy towards Buna Mission. Now Allied troops of the right flank were on dry ground at last.

General Eichelberger

Japanese Morale Declines

Morale of troops is good because we feel reinforcements will come.

Received word of praise from Emperor to-day. We will hold out to the last.

. . . . Our troops do not come. Even though they do come, they are driven away by enemy planes. Every day my comrades die one by one and our provisions disappear.

We are now in a delaying holding action. The amount of provisions is small and there is no chance of replenishing ammunition. But we have bullets of flesh. No matter what comes we are not afraid. If they come, let them come, even though there be a thousand. We will not be surprised. We have the aid of Heaven. We are the warriors of Yamamoto.

How I wish we could change to the offensive! Human beings must die once. It is only natural instinct to want to live; but only those with military spirit can cast that away.

With the dawn, the enemy started shooting all over. All I can do is shed tears of resentment. Now we are waiting only for death. The news that reinforcements had come turned out to be a rumour. All day we stay in the bunkers. We are filled with vexation. Comrades, are you going to stand by and watch us die? Even the invincible Imperial Army is at a loss. Can't anything be done? Please God.

A Japanese soldier

Because of the food shortage, some companies have been eating the flesh of Australian soldiers. The taste is said to be good.

Lieutenant Sakamoto

22 December—I am getting a little better. This must be due to the grateful aid of the Gods. . . . Horita has died. I respectfully pray for his peace and happiness. Yamashita is wounded in the leg by shell fragments, but it is not much of a wound. I wonder if I have peritonitis? I took out a picture of Mother and Father and thought about home, and I prayed that they may be well. Enemy planes flew overhead all day. There were no provisions brought in to-day. If we have a little, and make it last a while, we will not starve, although seven *shaku* (eighty per cent barley) is a little hard on the body. Only ten days of this year left. To have spent over five months on this island of distress and sorrow, enduring starvation and hardships and carrying on a battle, is good training which comes but once in a lifetime for a man. Released from the Narita Tai on the 20th and placed under command of the Field Hospital platoon.

23 December—If I eat to-night, I may not be able to eat to-morrow. It is indeed a painful experience to be hungry. When we made our first attack, I had no consideration for life or death. When we advanced, I felt I had done my job well enough as a signal soldier and that I had lived these twenty-eight years just for this one battle. I was willing to die at any time, but nowadays, somehow I am full of the desire to go back home alive just once more. To-day, again, enemy planes flew overhead from early morning. Five *shaku* of rice was distributed this evening. Fierce enemy attack with artillery and rifle fire. Everyone alert. Seems the enemy plans to annihilate Giruwa by Christmas.

24 December—Our troops expect to make a general attack, beginning the night before Christmas and lasting till to-morrow morning. I am praying for our complete success. Seems that there will be no rice to-day. Supper consisted of coconut and octopus. No rice. Ate snakes. Okazaki on sentry duty. Intense enemy artillery fire. Wish I could eat rice by the *go*. I hope our troops will hold out.

25 December—I suppose the enemy is not having much of a Christmas either. A handful of rice for supper. Our mess area was blown to bits by enemy artillery fire during the morning, and our mess kits were damaged. Provisions arrived—one *go* three *shaku* of barley for three days.

1943—1 January—I greeted the New Year. I spent the last days of 1942 in the jungle amidst bursting shells. I greeted the New Year in the same way, soaked through and midst artillery fire. We must make this year a good year. The comrades in the front line are hoping only for this. Received one *go* of rice for New Year. I ate breakfast and did not have enough for supper. Woke up early and prayed. Not a single one of our planes flew overhead, and enemy strafing was very fierce. Providential help comes to naught when the opportunity is lost. I greet the New Year in the jungle and think about my native land. . . . New Year's Day ended with me still being alive, although with an empty stomach. Prayed for Mother's and Father's health.

11 January—Last night's rain was terrific. The floor, which was raised five inches, is under water. Everything is soaked. Enemy shelling becoming increasingly intense. While I am able to think quietly, I feel discouraged and wretched, feeling that this may finally be the last day at Giruwa. But I am a soldier of the Imperial Army! I will live proudly to the last. If I am to believe General Oda's instructions, the situation should gradually be turning in our favour now. Caught six crabs and ate them raw. One *go*, five *shaku* of rice to-day. Fortunately, three of us, Kinoshita, Okazaki and I received rice. It is said that one division and three battalions have landed at Mambare.

12 January—I wish Okazaki would come. It is said that weak characters left alone will do bad deeds, but it is difficult to control evil thoughts when alone, especially when the rice bag is left by my side when I am so starved. So I ate into Kinoshita's and Okazaki's rice rations, and ate it raw. I am troubled. I am troubled. The enemy planes have been overhead since morning, and the fire is terrific. One *go* of rice costs seven *yen*. I wish I had a thousand *yen* and could buy a lot of rice.

13 January—This must be the rainy season in New Guinea. Cannot stand living in water every day. All of my equipment and clothes are wet. I went to the beach to get supplies to-day. The road is mostly under water and often above my waist. It was evening when I returned.

17 January—Was in a terrible situation yesterday. The enemy came as far as the L. of C. Hospital and we barely escaped. I thought that No. 1 Section of No. 4 Platoon could get on the boat, but the boat for Nos. 3 and 4 Platoons had been postponed. Spent the night in the vicinity of the Tomita Butai. Sergeant Shoji was sent back with the patients, and I am left to take charge in his place. My responsibility is heavy but my stomach is a little better and I feel relieved. Warrant-Officer Akiyoshi is on the boat. Takaishi is left behind. Too bad, but we stay together. We think that to-night will be the last night for Giruwa, and talked about swimming together to Lae. Fortunately the day dawned. I wonder if we can get away to-night? Wakaichi will not leave us behind.

18 January—We looked forward to getting on the boat to-night, but the wounded were put on first and we could not go. It is regrettable. Heavy rain is falling to-night. Reinforcements have not come. There are no provisions. Things

are happening just as the enemy says. It is a difficult situation, but I don't think Wakaichi will leave us behind.

Private Wada

In those early days we consistently underestimated the enemy. Intelligence guessed there were three hundred Japanese at Buna, and there were three thousand. Intelligence guessed there were five hundred Japanese at Sanananda, and there were five thousand. However you look at it, the task was tough. Japanese casualties mounted up to about eight thousand dead. There were some high-ranking Japanese officers who did not become casualties at Buna and Sanananda. They dumped their wounded out of motor-barges and saved their own skins by departure by sea.

What did it cost us? I have before me the casualties of 32 Division from 26 September 1942 to 28 February 1943. Killed in action and died of wounds: 690. Total deaths, including disease: 707. Wounded in action: 1,680. Fever and disease cases (including shell shock and concussions): 8,286. The Australian casualties should be added to the high purchase price for inhospitable jungle. Between 25 September and 22 January, a period which covers their pursuit of the Japanese over the Kokoda Trail, 3,359 Australians were wounded and 1,602 were killed in action or died of wounds.

We had our victory, and we were started back.

General Eichelberger

While the Australians and the Americans were learning to fight side by side in New Guinea, the latter were arriving in Australia in large numbers. They were new to the Australians, and the Australians were new to them. Inevitably, the alliance took time to shake down, but good soldiers of any nationality, like water, find their own level.

Australia Hotel, Sydney

Lofty put a boot like a steam shovel on the brass rail and leaned an elbow on the bar as he'd leaned it on innumerable bars from Ypres to Milne Bay. He spat with deliberation and mumbled under his breath that he could run a bloody war with one hand tied behind him better than the whole of this flash-tailored bunch with their fancy buckled shoes, bent on doing an honest digger in for his beer.

A hard-faced barmaid with a hennaed pompadour and a permanent smile was pulling beer rapidly.

'Pass us over a couple,' Blue whispered persuasively.

Lofty commented adversely upon the collar that foamed over the top.

'Cripes,' Blue whispered at him, 'you been stuck up there in the jungle that long you don't know there's a war on. If you're not careful she won't serve you at all.'

The barmaid continued to fill glasses and slide them across the counter.

'Here you are, gentlemen,' she said, directing her smile over Blue's shoulder.

A hand reached out, passed over a ten-shilling note, and took a middy from her. 'Keep the change, sister.' She rang up the sale on her register and pocketed the change.

Blue repeated his order. She ignored him again.

Lofty glared over his shoulder: 'Whaddaya expect,' he muttered bitterly to Blue, 'from the coves what murdered Phar Lap as soon as they got him to the States?'

There was a rustle along the counter. The barmaid's smile lost some of its brilliance.

'Lay off the Yanks,' Blue warned, 'and keep your mind on the beer.'

'Listen, lady,' Lofty said, resting two arms on the counter and sticking out his bony jaw, 'we asked for two beers.'

The girl darted her eyes over his faded green uniform, flashed her smile at two G.I.s, who breasted the bar beside him, and slid the next glasses to the newcomers.

'What the flamin' . . .' Lofty began.

'Take it easy,' Blue pleaded, putting a hand on Lofty's arm as he began to unwind himself with a deliberation Blue knew only too well. 'Pass 'em over, girlie,' he begged, 'we got here before them other blokes.'

'You wait your turn!' she snapped as though hearing him for the first time, 'like the others.'

'Christallbloodymighty!' Lofty bellowed, bringing his fist down on the counter with a thump that set the glasses rattling. 'Has a bloke got to stand here and be insulted in his own country, while a bunch of refugees from Pearl Harbor mop up all the beer?'

There was an ugly murmur behind them and a clank of glasses along the counter. The barmaid retreated; the girl next to her cast a startled eye in the direction of the disturbance and whispered to the useful, who disappeared round the corner of the bar.

Blue shut his teeth and groaned. 'I suppose you know them's fightin' words?'

He picked up an empty bottle by the neck and slid it down beside him, turning his back to the counter and calculating with the expertness of long experience the distance and the opposition between them and the door. He looked sideways at Lofty, who had also turned and was leaning with his back against the bar, one heel on the rail, fists slowly clenching, while a smile spread across his face.

'Fightin' words?' he drawled. The murmur died down. 'What's wrong with sayin' they beat it from Pearl Harbor?'

The murmur swelled to a roar, the crowd pressed forward. A rangey young G.I. shaped up to him: 'If you don't take that back,' he shouted, 'I'll, I'll. . . .' Lofty stuck a knobbly fist under his nose. 'Take a Captain-Cook at that, buddy. One more squeak out of you and I'll knock yer bloody block off.'

The boy lashed out at him. Lofty's open hand caught him in the chest and sent him staggering back against his mates. A stocky airman made a swipe at Blue.

'Job him one, Blue,' Lofty called encouragingly.

'Go easy, pal.' A tall, wiry sergeant pushed his way through to Lofty, a smile creasing his atabrined face. 'Say, buddy, weren't you at Milne Bay?'

Lofty glared at him from under lowered brows. 'What's that gotta do with you?'

'Well, if you were,' he laughed, 'I reckon you're the guy that sold me a phoney Nip flag.'

Lofty stared at him hard: 'Christ Almighty,' he shouted, 'so y'are. I didn't know y' at first, yer lost that much weight.'

The young G.I. made another lunge.

'Lay off, kid,' Lofty said in a lordly fashion. He slid an arm round the American sergeant's shoulders. 'Listen, you blokes,' he shouted, 'it was all a mistake. It was some other blokes I meant. Yer serg here and me was pals at Milne Bay, and any Yank what's been at Milne Bay with me can 'ave all the beer in Sydney, for all I care.'

'It's O.K., buddies,' the sergeant called, 'he's a white guy. It's just he don't speak English too good.'

Dymphna Cusack and Florence James

APPROACH TO THE PHILIPPINES: NEW GUINEA

By early 1943, the first breaches had been made in the Japanese island perimeter in New Guinea and the Solomons.

From June of that year General MacArthur worked steadily westwards along the northern coast of New Guinea, his spearhead pointing towards the Philippines. His forces were faced with a long and horrible task. A year's heavy fighting saw the capture of Salamaua, Lae and Finschafen, and then in April 1944 Wewak was by-passed by American and Australian forces 'leap-frogging' to Aitape and Hollandia. Before the end of June the final bound had been made to Biak Island, where the Japanese put up a ferocious struggle.

Successful Evacuation

The Japanese are now speaking of a successful evacuation of Salamaua. These 'successful evacuations' are getting the upper hand with the Axis. I don't believe we shall be able to use the expression much longer; it makes us more of a laughing stock each time. The Axis powers in the course of one year have done so much more successful evacuating that a large part of their former war potential was lost in the process. We must finally start giving a clear picture to our people and the world about our situation and our methods in this war.

Dr. Goebbels

'Leap-frogging'

My strategic conception for the Pacific Theatre contemplates massive strokes against only main objectives, utilizing surprise and air-ground striking power supported and assisted by the fleet. This is the very opposite of what is termed 'island hopping', which is the gradual pushing back of the enemy by direct frontal pressure with the consequent heavy casualties which will certainly be involved. Key points must of course be taken, but a wise choice of such will obviate the need for storming the mass of islands now in enemy possession. 'Island hopping' with extravagant losses and slow progress is not my idea of how to end the war as soon and as cheaply as possible. New conditions require for solution, and new weapons require for maximum application new and imaginative methods. Wars are never won in the past.

. . . . The system is as old as war itself. It is merely a new name dictated by new conditions given to the ancient principle of envelopment. It was the first time that the area of combat embraced land and water in such relative proportions. Heretofore, either the one or the other was predominant in the campaign. But in this area the presence of transportation of ground troops by ships as well as land transport seemed to conceal the fact that the system was merely that of envelopment applied to a new type of battle area. It has always proved the ideal method for success by inferior in numbers but faster moving forces. Immediately upon my arrival in Australia and learning the resources at my command, I determined that such a plan of action was the sole chance of fulfilling my mission. For its application it demanded a secure base from which to anchor all operations. Australia was plainly the only possible base. . . . The first actual physical by-pass was probably when I had Halsey's forces, which had been placed under my operational control, by-pass the lines of Guadalcanal along the west coast of Bougainville. Probably the first time it attracted general public attention was the Admiralty landings.

General MacArthur

. . . . This was the type of strategy we hated most. The Americans attacked and seized, with minimum losses, a relatively weak area, constructed air fields and then proceeded to cut the supply lines to our troops in that area. Our strongpoints were gradually starved out. The Japanese Army preferred direct assault after the German fashion, but the Americans flowed into our weaker points and submerged us, just as water seeks the weakest entry to sink a ship.

General Matsuichi Ino, 8 Army Staff

Hollandia: the Jungle Turns Against the Japanese

22 April 1944: Resigned to death, I entered the muddy jungle. Enemy airplanes are flying overhead. I am hungry and am beginning to become alarmed about the situation. I plunged through the jungle because I believe it is dangerous to remain here. The vast expanse of the jungle cannot be expressed in words.

2 May 1944: At a small creek. There is no end to this life. We are still roaming aimlessly on the thirteenth day. Perhaps this is part of our fate. We hoped that we would meet our commander and his amiable staff. We are beginning to hate everything in this world. We live each day sympathizing with one another. At times, we see someone in our group shedding tears.

24 May 1944: . . . The jungle is everywhere, and there is absolutely no water in this area. We must reach Kotabaru or we will all die.

26 May 1944: In the wilderness. As we proceeded farther we met our troops. This force was retreating from Aitape. They were shouldering rice which they stole from Kotabaru supply depot. I heard the news from the commanding officer. It was terrifying news. They had marched ahead with the men falling dead one by one.

A Japanese soldier

Wakde Island

Wakde Air Field was bombed and put out of commission, while every airplane was destroyed. Sewar Air Field was also raided and the airplanes were destroyed. The American Air Force has definite air supremacy. Sarmi H.Q. has been greatly damaged. A three-thousand-ton freighter which was in Sarmi Harbour was hit by three bombs and sank. Rations (Division's one-year rations), which were piled up, were almost completely burnt by an incendiary bomb. Heard that many men were killed or missing. Total number of airplanes for today was three hundred. Some were shot down but it is nothing compared to the damage our forces received.

26 May 1944: The rain is cold and there is nothing to eat.

27 May 1944: The present strength of my platoon is sixteen. Am trying hard to get rations.

25 June 1944: Under the existing situation, we are helpless. 'Let us be the guardian spirits of the Empire,' said one Sergeant —— before he killed himself. There were about thirty of us wounded soldiers left in the cave. Those who could move assisted others. They all shouted 'Long live the Emperor' before leaving this world. My friend Nagasaka stabbed his throat with a knife, but he did not succeed in killing himself. I finally decided to assist him so that he could rest in peace. I stabbed my own brother in arms. Who could understand my horrible predicament? I still have two hand grenades; one to destroy myself and one for the enemy. I don't know whether or not my rations will last till we are rescued. I determined to kill myself before I lose the power to pull the grenade pin. I want to restore my health so that I can die on the battlefront and follow Nagasaka.

25 June 1944: Long live the Emperor!

Father and Mother, please forgive me for dying before you do. I hope that you will be able to live the rest of your lives in peace. I wish you good health. I have done my duty to my country. My dearest parents, I am committing suicide with a hand grenade, my ashes will not reach you.

A Japanese soldier

Biak

Americans who fought at Biak, just off the coast of upper New Guinea, remember that sun-baked island as something as unreal and frightening as Conan Doyle's *Lost World*. The geography was scarred and pitted by the accidents of Nature's past, and some of the cliffs and limestone terraces along its southern shore seemed as barren as the mountains of the moon.

Biak is an island of innumerable caves—caves with the dimensions of a narrow dark hallway, caves as deep and large as five-storey tenement buildings and with as many levels of connecting galleries, caves with weird stalactite and stalagmite formations reminiscent of the Carlsbad Caverns of New Mexico. It is also an island of subterranean streams, and scarce (and evil-tasting) surface water. Soldiers fought for the precious water-holes, and more than one American died as he crawled forward in the night to replenish his water-bottle.

. . . The inland route was difficult. The jungle at Biak was never as thick as it was at Buna or in the rain-forest at Tanahmerah Bay. But there were evergreen trees which grew as high as one hundred and eighty feet; there were long, spidery vines which encompassed the trees like thick cobwebs in a dream, and there was high *kunai* grass in the open spaces. There was no water. Troops emplaced on the hills had to be supplied with both food and water, and human pack trains did the job. Back at Bosnek the artillery laid it on supposed enemy positions and lived a reasonably comfortable life in daylight. Their troubles started just about dusk when enemy planes began making passes at our rich supply dumps and continued throughout the dark watches. The pack-train lads lived miserable lives—day and night. As they struggled up the hills, Japanese soldiers fired from ambush or leaped out to engage them in hand-to-hand fighting. Men fought with pistols, knives and fists.

The Japanese at Biak were trained and excellent troops. Captured records show there were nearly ten thousand troops on the island; not all of them in the beginning resisted our invasion. On the southern shore the combat troops belonged to 22 Infantry Division (veterans of the China campaign); there was also a detachment of Japanese Marines—always bigger and taller and braver than any other enemy troops. The commander of the island defences was a certain Colonel Kuzume. Documents reveal that in case of invasion he planned to use his service troops to reinforce the infantry, and he did. The Americans invaded with only two combat regiments. Ordinarily, considering the hazards of attack, a three to one advantage in troop strength for the invaders is set up by the military textbooks as a fair and equal fight. 41 Division had not, in my opinion, done badly.

. . . . It was plain that Biak could not belong to us before we had captured the caves. The first riddle—no one had solved it before 1 Corps arrived—was to find the *main* caves. Where were they? Where were the entrances and exits? Aerial photographs were of no help in locating them. Our maps told us nothing.

Colonel Bill Bowen, my operations officer, and his assistants risked their lives on tours of exploration and discovery. For several days, in unarmed Cub planes, they flew repeatedly over the Japanese positions at low altitudes until they sighted and charted the entrances to the enemy's unbelievable underworld. There were the East Caves directly above Mokmer Village, and there were the caves, farther down the coast, at the Ibdi Pocket. Both were as full of troops as a New Guinea Fuzzy-Wuzzy's unwashed head is full of nits.

Most important of all, however, were the West Caves. (We referred to these as The Sump.) Although we did not know it then, Colonel Kuzume had his headquarters there; it was the arterial centre, the heart, of the Japanese defences. As long as The Sump was occupied, the airstrips were neutralized. The enemy was adequately prepared for siege. The Japanese had plenty of supplies, plenty of ammunition. While our soldiers thirsted, their soldiers filled their drinking-bottles at underground brooks. In the adjoining chambers at The Sump there were electric lights provided by petrol generators; there were wooden floors as insurance against the damp, and deep in the ground there were wooden houses for the comfort of the officer echelon. Ladders and passageways connected the chambers, and troops could be sent in many directions to meet attacks.

There were several frontal entrances to the West Caves. There was also the main sump itself. This was a pothole about eighty feet deep and a hundred feet across. Once it had been a cave, but the roof of earth had worn away and the great hole was open to daylight. Down at the bottom were the caverns which led off to the underground maze.

. . . . Flame-throwers were now used against The Sump but with only limited success. They could not penetrate far enough in the long, winding cavern to be effective. Also, striking internal walls, they often flashed back with resultant American casualties. We industriously searched out crevices and cracks which led underground and poured hundreds of barrels of petrol in them. The petrol was ignited. Eventually a series of dull explosions were heard—the burning petrol had met up with the enemy's ammunition stores.

The next day infantry captured the lip of the main sump. Under protection of machine-gun fire and tank-gun fire, engineers lowered an eight-hundred-and-fifty-pound charge of T.N.T. into a cave entrance by means of a winch. The charge was exploded electrically.

Unknown to us, Colonel Kuzume had conceded defeat in the early morning hours of 22 June. He assembled his officers around him and ordered all able-bodied soldiers to leave the caves and launch a final counter-attack. He distributed hand grenades to the wounded so that they might destroy themselves. In an impressive ceremonial, he burned all documents and the regimental flag. Then, in the Samurai tradition, he knelt and disembowelled himself with his own warrior's sword.

Just at daybreak some of the survivors issued from the cave and launched a *banzai* attack. They encountered a rear unit of the 186th Infantry. None of the Americans panicked. There were only twelve soldiers on guard at the spot, but they stood firm and fought as the screaming Japanese swept frenziedly down the trail. Machine-guns, rifles and grenades were used calmly and effectively—how effectively the statistics make very clear. Morning light disclosed that one hundred and nine enemy soldiers had been killed. We lost one man; a Japanese leaped into his foxhole and exploded a grenade which killed them both.

. . . . We didn't enter the Sump Caves for several days and continued to belabour them with explosives. But we knew we had won the fight there. When we did enter the caves on 27 June the stench of the dead was intolerable. Bullets, grenades, petrol, T.N.T.—each had done its work. It was hopeless in that almost unimaginable purgatory even to attempt an accurate count of bodies. They littered almost every square foot of ground. There were a few of the living still in the far recesses.

General Eichelberger

Farther to the east, the Americans were 'leap-frogging' their way westwards through the Solomons towards Rabaul. By March 1944 this stronghold had been by-passed and cut off.

New Georgia: Japanese Attack

Attack came suddenly—the nerve-shredding *brhhh-brhhh* of an automatic rifle a few yards away. Within seconds every machine-gun on the perimeter opened up. One felt rather than heard the sound. It was like a multitude of tiny hammers upon the spine.

Five of us jumped into the foxhole together. Bullets ripped gashes of moonlight in the inky drape of the tent roof. A grenade exploded with jarring concussion.

Two men were burrowing into the rotten coral ahead of me. Two others crouched over my awkwardly twisted legs. It was agonizing, but to have made them move would have exposed the others or myself to the withering Japanese fire. The hole was too shallow and small for five. The bullets were whining only an inch or two overhead. After awhile I peered at my watch and said, 'Half-past seven.'

The man on my knees answered, 'Who the hell cares what the time is? It's my birthday.'

'Many happy returns. Happy birthday,' said the man lying across my ankles. Silence. The firing was cut off.

The moon floated above the trees. The moon of New Georgia is very bright and in its light the forest was a stark, speckled black and white. The insect chorus diminished. The cry of the hunting birds was more abrupt and harsh. Then a new sound came out of the cold, white moonlight—the sound of Japanese voices, shrill and high toned.

I was surprised and affronted. They chattered, shouted to one another arrogantly, groaned, screamed, and broke sticks. For men who so often died from making a noise, the noise they made had almost an obscene quality to it. They sounded like apes with human tongues.

The first burst of cross-fire from our guns had hit hard. They had withdrawn a hundred yards into the thickets and made no fresh move for thirty minutes. It was the longest half-hour I have lived. I wanted to get out of the hole and go quietly away into the bush, but I knew I would never get through the perimeter alive. There was nobody above ground but the Japs.

I thought they were setting up mortars as they so often did in these night attacks. And 90 mm. mortar fire at a hundred yards' range would be very deadly, even against men in far better, deeper foxholes than ours.

But the next move was not mortar fire. Even though the first bursts of our guns must have pinpointed our perimeter positions clearly, the enemy was still uncertain of our strength and disposition. They sent in close reconnaissance.

One Japanese hid himself in a gully about thirty yards out and began squalling ludicrously: 'Aid, aid, doc! Give aid to me. I am wounded!' He just screamed the words because he had been taught to scream them, parrot fashion. Their pitch was as blood-chilling as the cry of an epileptic. A few nights before the troops might have fired on him, and the muzzle flashes would have betrayed their position. Not now.

Apart from the noise made by the squalling 'tactician' in the deadfall, the stillness of the jungle now became deathly. The birds were quiet. Even the frog chorus seemed hushed. Inch by inch I lifted my head. One rustle and a grenade might have been tossed at me out of a bush, but I couldn't stand the blindness any more. I peered over the parapet.

In a little patch of moonlight about fifteen yards away a Japanese soldier was standing upright, as still as a statue. I could see the shapeless folds of his uniform, the rifle he held, the glint of the bayonet, the peaked, shoddy cap on his head. I saw him and perhaps twenty other men saw him—but no one fired. We knew he stood there deliberately inviting death, for a reason.

Somewhere behind him were two or three of his comrades with grenades ready. If anyone had fired they would have lobbed the grenades at the flash. Four or five Americans might have died in exchange for one Japanese life.

I would have liked the courage to keep watching the human bait while he waited for honourable death, but I lacked it. Inch by inch I put my head down.

There was a soft, metallic click. The man lying across my knees cocked his pistol. I twisted my mouth against his ear and breathed: 'Don't shoot! Grenades!'

He whispered back: 'Only if he jumps into the hole. They've been doing that lately.' But he didn't jump in.

The posts on the jeep track opened up furiously for thirty seconds. This time the screams were genuine. Afterwards the man who had been screeching 'Aid, aid!' withdrew to a greater distance and began imitating the cry of a stabbed man, calling after each shriek: 'Christ, he's got me in the guts! I'm stabbed! Water, water!'

He kept this up for half an hour at thirty- or forty-second intervals. Then he crept in close again and began calling: 'Buddy, are you there? Please, please answer me!'

The main body of the enemy, still a hundred yards away, broke out chattering anew. They had suffered sobering losses. They abandoned close attack and put snipers in the trees. Every few seconds there would be a sharp whack and a bullet would come singing out of the thickets. One or two Japanese, working alone, edged up and threw grenades blindly. Two bounded off the earth at the ends of our foxhole and exploded, but no one was even scratched.

Osmar White, Australian war correspondent

Japanese attempts to reinforce and supply their beleaguered or isolated garrisons were frequently intercepted and smashed by Allied aircraft and warships, including submarines.

Supply Ship Sunk

All I ever saw of the first ship we sank was a wisp of smoke and a dark shape on the horizon. That was nearly a month after our first patrol began, and two weeks after we had lost our first target.

. . . . We were running on the surface, recharging our batteries, and there were three lookouts on the bridge with me, each with a third of the horizon's circle to watch. Keeter, behind me on the cigarette deck, had the after third.

Motor Machinist's Mate D. C. Keeter was a good man to have on lookout, for he was one of the most alert lookouts I ever saw. He had a habit of freezing every now and then, like a good pointer that has come on a covey of quail, while he studied some speck on the horizon. At first it was distracting; you would forget to watch anything but Keeter, waiting to see him go on point. But it was a fine example of concentration on the job, and it paid off that night. Keeter froze, pointed, and sang out, 'Smoke on the horizon. Bearing one hundred and twenty starboard.'

We turned towards it in the bright moonlight. I watched long enough to make out a dim hull shape before I called the captain and ambled with studied unconcern down to the control room. It was the first enemy ship I had actually seen.

It was a freighter of the *Keiyo Maru* class, six thousand five hundred tons, as it turned out, and we ran towards it for half an hour on the surface and then submerged for a periscope attack. He seemed to be on a south-eastward course, making twelve knots, but every now and then he would stop and lie to. After a while we guessed why: he was waiting for his escort. At five minutes after midnight, when our tracks were very close together, we began to swing left for a stern tube shot.

. . . . Suddenly as we swung around we began to hear pings on the sound operator's loudspeaker.

Someone was echo-ranging, and freighters don't have echo-ranging equipment. Up there in the moonlight, then, an escort ship was sending out sonar signals. If they bounced off our hull loud enough for him to pick up the echo, he would have us spotted.

I don't want to use the word claustrophobia, because I've never felt that or known anyone who did in a submarine, but as those ominous pings began we did have a sensation of groping—a lonely feeling that we were blind, unsafe because we couldn't see, and that somewhere up there a destroyer, a ship built to sink subs, was looking for us.

'Stand by to fire.'

The words were low in the conning-tower, but in the silence of the control room every man could hear them, and every man breathed a sigh of relief. The captain had what he decided was a good set-up, the outer doors were opened on the torpedo tubes, the long wait was almost over.

'Stand by for final bearing. . . .' And again that sudden dryness in the mouth.

'Mark bearing . . . set . . . fire One!'

The boat shuddered as the first torpedo went out. Then, at the captain's commands, it was followed by a second, and a third.

We were firing from the freighter's starboard quarter, three-quarters of the way around from the bow. But he swung left just as we fired—probably by chance, for it is more likely that at that moment neither he nor his escort even knew we were there. The fact we could hear the escort's pinging did not necessarily mean he had contacted us; indeed, the continuing cycle of louder and softer pings indicated he was merely scanning the area and had not yet spotted us. Still, he might pick us up at any second, and we didn't even know where he was.

The torpedoes missed, all three of them.

But the turn that had saved the target from them was also to be his doom. Round and round he swung until we were off his port beam.

'Fire Four!'

Again the boat shuddered, and again we waited. That torpedo's run should have been a minute and twenty seconds. A short time, but as you listen, it is an eternity.

The periscope was down now. All action had halted. Silent, suspended in the water, we waited. . . .

Boom!

First came the loud explosion. The breaking-up noises followed, small explosions piling one on top of another, sounds that made you see bulkheads caving in, water pouring through great jagged wounds in the hull. We heard the first explosion through the hull of the submarine itself; the smaller ones came over the listening equipment in the conning-tower, but they were loud enough.

That one hit was sufficient. We picked up the freighter in the periscope again in time to see him listing heavily to port. Before we left the scene, he had sunk.

Now came the punishment. The periscope, swinging around, picked up the escort, a small destroyer, with a bone in his teeth, headed right at us.

'Down periscope! Flood negative!'

We started for deep submergence, trying to get deep and away from that spot. For the moment we weren't trying to be quiet, as we had during the tedious moments of the approach and the attack. All we wanted now was to get somewhere else, and fast.

'Rig for depth-charge attack.'

Now was the time to get quiet again. Every piece of machinery that made any noise, everything we could do without, was cut off. The air-conditioning, installed to protect electrical equipment, stopped circulating its cooling breeze. The heat of engines, motors, and relays began to creep through the boat. The planesmen and helmsmen, who had been controlling electric motors, shifted to hand control; the sweat poured down them now as they strained to turn and control the giant fins and rudder by the strength of their own backs. The flappers in the bulkheads and on the ventilation system were closed, so that if a compartment was flooded it could be isolated—an empty gesture, as we all knew, because any flooded compartment will sink you in deep water.

And then, while we were still going down and going fast, even before we were mentally prepared for it, the first depth charge went off.

It was the worst, because the escort still knew just about where we were. We could hear—through the hull this time, not on the listening gear—the propellers of the freighter's avenger going overhead. And suddenly, on the sound gear, we heard a splash. The first depth charge had hit the water.

An exploding depth charge has three noises. First there is a click. Then comes a clang or crashing sound, like someone hitting your hull with a million sledge-hammers. Finally there is a swishing noise, as though water is falling over a waterfall or pouring into a cavity the charge has created. The closer the charge is, the more closely together these noises come. When it is very close, you hear one horrible *clang!*

The first one was that way. Cork and paint chipped off the bulkheads. A light bulb shattered near my head. The boat shook. There was the jarring head-swimming, detached feeling such as you get in an automobile crash, or from a stiff right to the jaw, a feeling that this is happening to you, all right, but that you are somehow above and away from it in spirit, looking down objectively at your body, which is taking the punishment.

He dropped about a dozen charges before we began creeping away from him, running deep and silent and a little dazed. If we could get a couple of miles away, we thought, we could lose him in the darkness, surface in safety, and sneak away.

We eased farther and farther from the depth charges and surfaced about a mile from him. He sighted us in a minute, and started at us.

There was a rain squall on the horizon, and we headed for it at full speed. Rain squalls were very helpful in such a situation, especially at night. Once we were on the surface and running away from him, his sound equipment was practically useless for finding us, and we could make much better speed than we could submerged as we ran for cover. Of course, when we went fast the boat threw up a luminous wake—in some areas of the Pacific you can stand at the after part of the bridge and read a newspaper at midnight from the wake of your boat—but the rain squall would hide us and our wake long enough to lose him.

At least that was the plan, and it worked. He was closing on us as we entered the squall, but he was not close enough to do anything, and we changed course and came out the other side. In a little while he was out too, but by then we had skirted around and were ready to enter it from another place. This time, when we came out, we had lost him. Our eerie game of hide-and-seek there on the darkened ocean had ended; our prize for winning was our lives.

Looking back on it later, that first attack and depth-charging were to seem almost laughably tame. But at the time we were drunk with exhilaration and pride.

George Grider, U.S. submarine officer

Kiwi Earns Leave

The other incident involved the New Zealand corvette *Kiwi*. (A corvette is roughly equivalent to a gunboat.) Three of the *Kiwi*'s officers—the captain, the medical officer and the chief engineer—were famous from the Solomons to Auckland. Everyone knew them, at least by sight. Not only were they the most mastodonic men I ever laid eyes on—their combined weights were close to eight hundred pounds—but whenever the *Kiwi* put into Noumea, these monsters would stage a three-man parade through the town, one of them puffing into a dented trombone, another tooting a jazz whistle, and the third playing a concertina.

On 29 January,* the *Kiwi* was patrolling off Guadalcanal when a big Japanese sub suddenly surfaced close aboard. The skipper immediately put his helm over and rang up full speed on his telegraph, which so astonished the chief that he yelled up the speaking tube, 'What's the matter, you bastard? Have you gone crazy?'

'Shut up!' the skipper yelled back. 'There's a week-end's leave in Auckland

* 1943 (Ed.)

dead ahead of us! Give me everything you've got, or I'll come below and kick hell out of you!'

The big sub turned out to be the I-1, half again as long as the *Kiwi* and with twice the fire-power. None the less, the *Kiwi* charged in, with her little guns popping, and rammed the I-1 amidships.

'Hit her again!' the skipper yelled. 'It'll be a *week's* leave!'

They hit her again.

'Once more, for a fortnight!'

The third time the *Kiwi* rammed her, the I-1 sank.

It was a bold attack, bold enough to deserve recognition, so I notified the skipper and the chief that I was recommending them for Navy Crosses, our Navy's highest award. When they reported to my office to be decorated, it was in a spirit that might be described as 'picnic'. In fact, I had to support them with one hand while I pinned on the Crosses with the other. They thanked me, saluted, and rumbled away. The last I saw of them, they had picked up the medical officer and their musical instruments, and were forming another parade.

Admiral Halsey

Allied strategy depended on knowledge of the direction and strength of Japanese forces moving over vast areas of sea and between innumerable islands. Much valuable information was provided by the 'Coastwatchers'.

Coastwatchers

One of the most interesting and unconventional military outfits I ran into during the Pacific War is almost unknown to the American public. Members of the outfit—many of them middle-aged civilians and nearly all volunteers—were called the 'Coastwatchers'. This small group of venturesome men, at top strength numbering only a few hundred, risked their lives—and frequently lost them—in order to supply the Allies with accurate and first-hand information from the widely scattered tropical islands the Emperor's troops had occupied.

The code name of the organization was 'Ferdinand', and the title was peculiarly apt. Ferdinand, as you may recall from the American nursery book, was a completely unaggressive bull; he liked to sit under a tree and smell flowers. The Coastwatchers avoided combat except in dire extremity. It was their duty, figuratively, to sit inconspicuously under a tree, gather information and send it out.

Equipped with bulky tele-radios, difficult both to conceal and to transport, the Coastwatchers sat in some extremely uncomfortable spots. Throughout the period of the war they lived among the Japanese, hiding in the jungles of Papua, New Guinea, the Solomons, moving from place to place with their cumbersome and risky equipment. White men can't pass themselves off as natives, nor can they exist in the jungle without help. The Coastwatchers on their hazardous assignments were obliged to trust the natives who served them. Too often the trust was misplaced and they were betrayed to torture and death.

General Eichelberger

Execution of an Intelligence Officer

In a little over twenty minutes, we arrive at our destination and all get off.

Major Komai stands up and says to the prisoner, 'We are going to kill you.' When he tells the prisoner that in accordance with Japanese *Bushido* he would be killed with a Japanese sword and that he would have two or three minutes' grace, he listens with bowed head. He says a few words in a low voice. He is an officer, probably a flight-lieutenant. Apparently, he wants to be killed with one stroke of the sword. I hear him say the word 'one'; the Major's face becomes tense as he replies, 'Yes.'

Now the time has come and the prisoner is made to kneel on the bank of a bomb crater, filled with water. He is apparently resigned. The precaution is taken of surrounding him with guards with fixed bayonets, but he remains calm. He even stretches his neck out. He is a very brave man indeed. When I put myself in the prisoner's place and think that in one more minute it will be good-bye to this world, although the daily bombings have filled me with hate, ordinary human feelings make me pity him.

The Major has drawn his favourite sword. It is the famous *masamune* sword which he had shown us at the observation station. It glitters in the light and sends a cold shiver down my spine. He taps the prisoner's neck lightly with the back of the blade, then raises it above his head with both arms and brings it down with a powerful sweep. I had been standing with muscles tensed, but in that moment I closed my eyes.

A hissing sound—it must be the sound of spurting blood, spurting from the arteries; the body falls forward. It is amazing—he has killed him with one stroke.

The onlookers crowd forward. The head, detached from the trunk, rolls forward in front of it. The dark blood gushes out. It is all over. The head is dead white, like a doll. The savageness which I felt only a little while ago is gone, and now I feel nothing but the true compassion of Japanese *Bushido*.

A corporal laughs: 'Well—he will be entering Nirvana now.' A seaman of the medical unit takes the surgeon's sword and, intent on paying off old scores, turns the headless body over on its back and cuts the abdomen open with one clean stroke. They are thick-skinned, these *keto* [hairy foreigner—a term of opprobrium for a white man]; even the skin of their bellies is thick. Not a drop of blood comes out of the body. It is pushed into the crater at once and buried.

Japanese diary

APPROACH TO THE PHILIPPINES: THE PACIFIC

In November 1943, while the Japanese were slowly being winkled out of their positions in New Guinea and the Solomons, Admiral Nimitz began the assault on another part of the ring of Japan's island conquests, far to the east in the open waters of the Pacific. First on the list was Tarawa in the Gilberts, an outpost of Truk, the Japanese naval base in the Carolines. On 20 November Marines landed on Tarawa, going on to win the first of many dearly-bought island victories. Their casualties were appalling.

The specific plan to counter an American invasion of the Gilberts was as follows: . . . Aircraft from the Bismarcks would attack the invasion forces and then land at fields in the Marshalls-Gilberts area. . . . Warships at Truk would . . . move to the Gilberts. . . . Two factors radically changed these plans. The first was the serious damage received by several Second Fleet cruisers at Rabaul by carrier air attack on 5 November 1943. . . . The second was the intensified air war in the Solomons . . . which absorbed our air forces already in the western Solomons and also required employment of the short-range planes which were being held at Truk for defence of the Marshalls-Gilberts.

Consequently, the original plans for the defence of those islands could not be carried out when American forces invaded in November, because there was insufficient surface and air strength available to make effective resistance.

Captain Toshikazu Ohmae, Japanese Naval General Staff

Tarawa: First Day

By 03.30 the Marines had begun loading the outboard boats for the first wave. The sergeants were calling the roll: 'Vernon, Simms, Gresholm. . . .' They needed no light to call the well-remembered roll, and they didn't have to send a runner to find any absentees. The Marines were all there. One of the sergeants was giving his men last-minute instructions: 'Be sure to correct your elevation and windage. Adjust your sights.'

At 04.00 I went below. I stood outside the wardroom as the first and second waves walked through and out to their boats. Most of the men were soaked; their green-and-brown-spotted jungle dungarees had turned a darker green when the sweat from their bodies soaked through. They jested with one another. Only a few even whistled to keep up their courage.

. . . . They were a grimy, unshaven lot. The order had gone out: they must put on clean clothing just before going ashore, in order to diminish the chances of infection from wounds, but now they looked dirty. Under the weight, light though it was, of their combat packs, lifebelts, guns, ammunition, helmets, canvas leggings, bayonets, they were sweating in great profusion. Nobody had shaved for two or three days.

. . . . The first battleship had fired the first shot. We all rushed out on deck. The show had begun. The show for which thousands of men had spent months of training, scores of ships had sailed thousands of miles, for which Chaplains Kelly and MacQueen had offered their prayers. The curtain was up in the theatre of death.

We were watching when the battleship's second shell left the muzzle of its great gun, headed for Betio. There was a brilliant flash in the darkness of the half-moonlit night. Then a flaming torch arched high into the air and sailed far away, slowly, very slowly, like an easily lobbed tennis ball. The red cinder was nearly halfway to its mark before we heard the thud, a dull roar as if some mythological giant had struck a drum as big as Mount Olympus. There was no sign of an explosion on the unseen island—the second shot had apparently fallen into the water, like the first.

Within three minutes the sky was filled again with the orange-red flash of the big gun, and Olympus boomed again. The red ball of fire that was the high-explosive shell was again dropping towards the horizon. But this time there was a tremendous burst on the land that was Betio. A wall of flame shot five hundred feet into the air, and there was another terrifying explosion as the shell found its mark. Hundreds of the awestruck Marines on the deck of the *Blue Fox* cheered in uncontrollable joy. Our guns had found the enemy. Probably the enemy's big 8-inch guns and their powder magazine on the south-west corner of the island.

Now that we had the range the battleship sought no longer. The next flash was four times as great, and the sky turned a brighter, redder orange, greater than any flash of lightning the Marines had ever seen. Now four shells, weighing more than a ton each, peppered the island. Now Betio began to glow brightly from the fires the bombardment pattern had started.

That was only the beginning. Another battleship took up the firing—four mighty shells poured from its big guns on to another part of the island. Then another battleship breathed its brilliant breath of death. Now a heavy cruiser let go with its 8-inch guns, and several light cruisers opened with their fast-firing 6-inch guns. They were followed by the destroyers, many destroyers with many 5-inch guns on each, firing almost as fast as machine-guns. The sky at times was brighter than noontime on the Equator.

. . . . No sooner had we hit the water than the Jap machine-guns really opened up on us. There must have been five or six of these machine-guns concentrating their fire on us—there was no nearer target in the water at the time—which meant several hundred bullets per man. I don't believe there was one of the fifteen who wouldn't have sold his chances for an additional twenty-five dollars added to his life-insurance policy. It was painfully slow, wading in such deep water. And we had seven hundred yards to walk slowly into that machine-gun fire, looming into larger targets as we rose on to higher ground. I was scared, as I had never been scared before.

. . . . Another young Marine walked briskly along the beach. He grinned at a pal who was sitting next to me. Again there was a shot. The Marine spun all the way around and fell to the ground, dead. From where he lay, a few feet away, he looked up at us. Because he had been shot squarely through the temple his eyes bulged out wide, as in horrible surprise at what had happened to him, though it was impossible that he could ever have known what hit him.

'Somebody go get the son-of-a-bitch,' yelled Major Crowe. 'He's right back of us here, just waiting for somebody to pass by.' That Jap sniper, we knew from the crack of his rifle, was very close.

A Marine jumped over the seawall and began throwing blocks of fused T.N.T. into a coconut-log pillbox about fifteen feet back of the seawall against which we sat. Two more Marines scaled the seawall, one of them carrying a twin-cylindered tank strapped to his shoulders, the other holding the nozzle of the flamethrower. As another charge of T.N.T. boomed inside the pillbox, causing smoke and dust to billow out, a khaki-clad figure ran out the side entrance. The flamethrower, waiting for him, caught him in its withering stream of intense fire. As soon as it touched him, the Jap flared up like a piece of celluloid. He was dead instantly but the bullets in his cartridge belt exploded for a full sixty seconds after he had been charred almost to nothingness.

. . . . Our casualties had been heavy on the first day, but well over half the dead, and practically all of the wounded, had been shot, not in the water, but after they had reached land and climbed the seawall. Those wounded more than lightly in the water had little chance of reaching shore. The amphibious operation up to that point, therefore, could have been called better than successful. The hell lay in the unexpectedly strong fortifications we had found after we landed.

It was not possible—and never will be possible—to know just how many casualties the three assault battalions had suffered on D-Day. Most officers agreed afterwards that thirty-five to forty per cent was as good a guess as any. Effectively they were groggy if they had not been knocked out, because their organization was ripped to pieces. Their percentage casualties among officers had been heavier than among the men, and key men such as platoon sergeants, virtually irreplaceable, had been killed or wounded.

Second Day

. . . . The second day was even more critical than the first, and it was the day the tide finally turned in our favour.

05.30: The coral flats in front of us present a sad sight at low tide. A half-dozen Marines lie exposed, now the water has receded. They are hunched over, rifles in hand, just as they fell. They are already one-quarter covered by sand that the high tide left. Farther out on the flats and to the left I can see at least fifty other bodies. I had thought yesterday, however, that low tide would reveal many more than that. The smell of death, that sweetly sick odour of decaying human flesh, is already oppressive.

. . . . The machine-guns continue to tear into the oncoming Marines. Within five minutes I see six men killed. But the others keep coming. One rifleman walks slowly ashore, his left arm a bloody mess from the shoulder down. The casualties become heavier. Within a few minutes more I can count at least a hundred Marines lying on the flats.

07.30: The Marines continue unloading from the Higgins boats, but fewer of them are making the shore now. Many lie down behind the pyramidal concrete barriers the Japs had erected to stop tanks. Others make it as far as the disabled tanks and amphtracks, then lie behind them to size up the chances of making the last hundred yards to shore. There are at least two hundred bodies which do not move at all on the dry flats, or in the shallow water partially covering them. This is worse, far worse that it was yesterday.

. . . . We can see the light now. We are winning, but we've still got to dig out every last Jap from every last pillbox, and that will cost us a lot of Marines. I reflect: isn't that true of our whole war against the Japs? They haven't got a chance and they know it, unless we get fainthearted and agree to some peace with them. But, in an effort to make us grow sick of our losses, they will hang on under their fortifications, like so many bedbugs. They don't care how many men *they* lose—human life being a minor consideration to them. The Japs' only chance is our getting soft, as they predicated their whole war on our being too luxury-loving to fight.

.... A grimy Marine seated alongside us muses: 'I wonder what our transport
did with those sixteen hundred half-pints of ice cream that was to be sent ashore
yesterday after the battle was over.'

.... A surgeon grunts and rises from where he has been working feverishly
over a dozen wounded Marines who lie on the beach. His blood-plasma containers hang from a line strung between a pole and a bayoneted rifle stuck upright into the ground. Four deathly pale Marines are receiving the plasma through
tubes in their arms. 'These four will be all right,' the doctor thinks, 'but there
are a lot more up the beach that we probably can't save.' He continues, 'This
battle has been hell on the medical profession. I've got only three doctors out
of the whole regiment. The rest are casualties, or they have been lost or isolated.
By now nearly all the corpsmen have been shot, it seems to me.'

Third Day

This was the day the Japs fell apart. There were many factors in this rout.
Another company of light tanks and a few thirty-two-ton tanks had a field day
with the Japs, who cowered in their pillboxes and waited for death. Armoured
half-tracks, mounting 75-mm. guns, paraded up and down Betio all day, pouring high explosives into pillboxes, carrying Marine riflemen who killed Japs
whenever they dared stick their heads up. The men with the flamethrowers
killed many hundreds in their fortifications, or outside their fortifications. Our
line across the island had held during the night, preventing any fresh Japs from
filtering towards the scenes of the toughest fighting.

.... During the day I saw the first five of many Japs I saw who committed
suicide rather than fight to the end. In one hole, under a pile of rubble, supported
by a tin roof, four of them had removed the split-toed, rubber-soled jungle
shoes from their right feet, had placed the barrels of their ·303 rifles against their
foreheads, then had pulled the triggers with their big toes. The other had chosen
the same method some five hundred Japs chose on Attu: holding a hand grenade
against his chest, thus blowing out the chest and blowing off the right hand.
From the time he was a baby the Jap had been told that he was superior to the
white man, and all he had to do to win was to fight aggressively. When he found
that this was not true, and the white man could fight aggressively, too, he became
frustrated. He had never been taught to improvise and his reflexes were hopelessly slow; if his plan of battle failed, as the Jap plan on Tarawa failed when the
first Marines made the shore, he was likely, under pressure, to commit suicide.
He didn't know what else to do.

.... Said Colonel Edson, the hero of Guadalcanal: 'This is the first beachhead they have really defended. They had no choice but to defend here—they
had no interior position to retreat to; it was all exterior. Anyway,' he smiles, 'it
won't last as long as Guadalcanal.'

Captain 'Frenchy' Moore, the Navy doctor who is division surgeon, shakes
his head. 'I was on Guadalcanal. And it was duck soup.'

Carlson: 'This was not only worse than Guadalcanal. It was the damnedest
fight I've seen in thirty years of this business.'

.... The bulldozer scoops a long trench, three feet deep. Its Seabee driver pays scant attention to the sniper who fires at him occasionally. The bodies, not even covered by a blanket or poncho, are brought over and placed in the trench, side by side, while Chaplains MacQueen and Kelly supervise their identification and last rites. This is no dignified burial—a man's last ceremony should be dignified, but this isn't. The bulldozer pushes some more dirt into the Marines' faces and that is all there is to it. Then the bulldozer starts digging a second trench.

Tarawa was not perfectly planned or perfectly executed. Few military operations are, particularly when the enemy is alert. Said Julian Smith, 'We made mistakes, but you can't know it all the first time. We learned a lot which will benefit us in the future. And we made fewer mistakes than the Japs did.' Tarawa was the first frontal assault on a heavily defended atoll. By all the rules concerning amphibious assaults, the Marines should have suffered far heavier casualties than the defenders. Yet, for every Marine who was killed more than four Japs died—four of the best troops the Emperor had.

Robert Sherrod, American war correspondent

After Tarawa the next landing was some five hundred miles to the north, in the Marshall Islands, of which the best-remembered are Kwajalein and Eniwetok. Once established in the Marshalls, the Americans were in a position to assail the inner ring of Japanese island defences, running through the Marianas and Carolines. Truk was hammered from the air but was not invaded, for it was to be by-passed and cut out of the battle.

Truk Destroyed

In January 1944 I was in command of submarine RO.44, and was ordered to proceed to the eastern Solomons area with the aim of cutting the enemy's rear supply lines. At this period, since many of our submarines had failed to return from such operations, special precautions were very necessary, especially in selecting the routes to be followed. Journeys were limited to areas which were expected to be free of enemy submarines and patrol aircraft. If it became necessary to pass through areas within the radius of action of enemy search aircraft, submarines had to proceed submerged both by day and by night. After crossing the Equator, the heat made conditions in the boats very trying, though air-conditioning plant was fitted to keep the temperature down to reasonable limits.

When we got near to Truk we could see the reflection of sheets of flame in the night sky. There were sounds of frequent explosions, and we soon realized that the situation was hopeless. We arrived off the reef before dawn. There was no sighting the enemy. We waited four days, patrolling off Truk, surfaced by night and submerged during daylight. By then there was little left of our month's supply of provisions. Eventually we received orders to enter Truk harbour. Finding a suitable route was tricky, for it was difficult to see a safe passage through the remains of our sunken ships. However, we got in without mishap. The sight of capsized and sunken ships, their masts sticking forlornly out of the water, was most desolate. We anchored off the submarine base. The depot ship had sunk at her moorings and all her valuable submarine supplies had gone down with her.

I went ashore to make my report at H.Q. I found the staff wondering whether we had been sunk, as no signals had been received. RO.39 had signalled from a point off Wotje, but the message was undecipherable and she was never heard of again.

The tempo of the U.S. western advance after occupying the Marshals had been fast.

The staggering enemy attack on Truk was a natural corollary to their occupation of the Marshalls. A large enemy force of aircraft carriers had attacked on 17 February 1944. Truk had held an important position as the central base for our operations in the Solomons and Marshalls and was also the Combined Fleet base, until enemy occupation of the Marshalls forced the Combined Fleet to withdraw to Palau.

At the time of the enemy attack, although our air patrols could hardly be termed completely adequate, they were making air searches in areas in which the enemy might be expected. On this particular day only half the normal number of planes had been up due to a heavy storm, and these had already returned to base. The enemy, however, made his approach during the height of the storm. Without warning, a vast number of enemy carrier-borne aircraft suddenly appeared over Truk. The first attack was concentrated on the Takeshima air base. Fighters were sent up in an endeavour to intercept—some among them without any machine-gun ammunition. These aircraft were nearly all shot down and six warships and twenty-six of our transports were sunk. Aircraft losses amounted to one hundred and eighty planes. Enemy battleships appeared outside the reef, and soon our precious oil fuel supplies were alight. They burned for several days, making a splendid illumination of the target for night attacks carried out by U.S. B-17 bombers.

Under these conditions Rabaul ceased to have any value as an air base, and the air units there were withdrawn; the Solomons were abandoned to the enemy. Thus the outer battle area had to be abandoned and defensive action taken to keep the inner zone secure.

Mochitsura Hashimoto

THE LAST RESORT

Behind the inner ring of the Carolines and Marianas lay the heart of Japan's rich empire—the Philippines, Formosa and China. In June 1944 the Americans broke the 'impregnable' ring, landing on Saipan, Tinian and Guam. By early August Japan had lost the Marianas. By mid-September the Americans had landed in the Palau Islands in the western Carolines, another two hundred miles nearer Japan's lifelines and on Morotai Island, halfway between New Guinea and the Philippines. The two thrusts which had been converging on the Philippines—one from the Pacific and one from New Guinea—were ready to be driven home. In this critical situation the Emperor agreed to the introduction of suicide weapons: Kamikaze aircraft and human torpedoes. First introduced in the battle for the Philippines, they were employed until the last days of the war.

First Order to the *Kamikazes*

The Empire stands at the cross-roads between victory and defeat. The first suicide-unit determined to triumph through the power of the spirit will inspire, by its success, one unit after another to follow its example. It is absolutely out of the question for you to return alive. Your mission involves certain death. Your bodies will be dead, but not your spirits. The death of a single one of you will be the birth of a million others. Neglect nothing that may affect your training or your health. You must not leave behind you any cause for regret, which would follow you into eternity. And, lastly: do not be in too much of a hurry to die. If you cannot find your target, turn back; next time you may find a more favourable opportunity. Choose a death which brings about the maximum result.

Pilot's Letter

Contrary to my usual habit, I woke early, at five o'clock. I did my exercises stripped to the waist. I felt extremely well.

Now one has only to place a sheet of paper into the little box which usually contains the ashes of the dead. I wonder if that is true? I wanted to send you parings of my nails and a few locks of my hair, but I had my hair cut yesterday and my nails are already too short. I am sorry, but unfortunately it is too late. Neither my nails nor my hair will grow again in one night.

I do not want a grave. I would feel oppressed if they were to put me into a narrow vault. A vagabond, such as I, has no need of it. Will you tell my parents that?

Do not weep because I am about to die. If I were to live and one of my dear ones to die, I would do all in my power to cheer those who remain behind. I would try to be brave.

11.30 a.m.—the last morning. I shall now have breakfast and then go to the aerodrome. I am busy with my final briefing and have no time to write any more. So I bid you farewell.

Excuse this illegible letter and the jerky sentences.

Keep in good health.

I believe in the victory of Greater Asia.

I pray for the happiness of you all, and I beg your forgiveness for my lack of piety.

I leave for the attack with a smile on my face. The moon will be full to-night. As I fly over the open sea off Okinawa I will choose the enemy ship that is to be my target.

I will show you that I know how to die bravely.

With all my respectful affection,

Akio Otsuka

The *Kamikazes* Strike: Leyte, 29 October 1944

I didn't know the term at the time, but I had seen a *kamikaze* before—the plane that had tried to crash the *Enterprise* during the Marshalls raid in February 1942. That plane was already doomed; its pilot would have been killed anyhow.

But the plane that struck the *Intrepid* had not been damaged; the dive was obviously a deliberate sacrifice. Intelligence had warned us that 'the Divine Wind Special Attack Corps' had been organized, but even after we had seen this sample performance, I think that most of us took it as a sort of token terror, a tissue-paper dragon. The psychology behind it was too alien to ours; Americans, who fight to live, find it hard to realize that another people will fight to die. We could not believe that even the Japanese, for all their *hara-kiri* traditions, could muster enough recruits to make such a corps really effective.

We were violently disillusioned the very next day. They missed the *Enterprise*, in Davison's group, but they hit two of his other carriers, the *Franklin* and *Belleau Wood*, killing a total of 158 men, destroying forty-five planes, and requiring the withdrawal of both ships for repairs. Our CVs were obvious targets: their huge tanks of aviation gasoline were as vulnerable as they were inflammable, their fire power was light, their armour was thin, and damage to their flight decks meant the neutralization of around a hundred planes.

Admiral Halsey

Off Okinawa: April–May 1945

At the end of each day canvas shrouds slipped into the waters off Okinawa. Death was in the air and on the face of the sea. The Divine Wind blew hot and steadily. In April, including both the task force and the invasion forces, a hundred and twenty ships received minor damages, a hundred were damaged severely, and twenty-four were sunk.

. . . . Mitscher had come to Okinawa with four task groups. Now there were only enough ships left for three. At 05.00 on 17 April, he disbanded Task Group 58.2, and augmented the other task groups. The Japanese were not winning, but neither were they losing except in equipment and personnel. An average of twenty to thirty *kamikazes* were splashed each day. He sent strikes to Kyushu and raked the fields in desperation, but the Divine Wind kept coming.

Theodore Taylor

Bunker Hill: 11 May 1945

11 May was the *Bunker Hill*'s fifty-ninth consecutive day at sea. Task Groups 58.3 and 58.4 were about a hundred miles east of Okinawa, furnishing direct air support for the Southern Attack Force ashore and providing a fighter plane cover over Okinawa. The *Bunker Hill* was still in Sherman's 58.3.

At 02.00 enemy planes were reported, and a few minutes later everyone went to general quarters. Mitscher rose tiredly from his bunk, and pulled on a light robe and the cap. G.Q. lasted until 02.55, when 'Condition One Easy' was set, which left the anti-aircraft gunners on partial alert. At dawn, 04.41, there was the usual routine G.Q. of ten minutes. After 08.00 there were reports of more bogeys, and at 09.00, G.Q. was set again, and not relaxed for forty minutes. It was often impossible to shave without interruption.

. . . . At 10.04, the radio speaker in Flag Plot tuned to fighter frequency frantically relayed: 'Alert! Alert! Two planes diving on the *Bunker Hill*!'

. . . . Almost instantly, one Zeke released his 500-lb. bomb, which went through the flight deck and out through the side of the ship, and exploded above water. Almost at the same moment the plane plunged into the flight deck in the middle of a group of fighters manned for take-off. Its fuel tank exploded and left a searing trail as the plane skidded along the flight deck and over the side.

There was more warning of the approach of the second plane. It roared past the ship at full throttle, made a steep climbing turn to port, and then dived directly for the *Bunker Hill*. The pilot released his bomb, which hit amidships and then exploded on the gallery deck, where there were many staff personnel. Flatley, on his way up from C.I.C., two decks below, had just passed the flight deck when the second *kamikaze* hit, and flame scorched his back.

The plane finally crashed on to the island, less than a hundred feet from where Mitscher stood, and more flame leaped skyward. The Admiral then stepped out on the starboard side of the flag bridge. He had not said a word during the few minutes of attack. He looked about him, then peered down towards the flight deck.

Smoke came into Flag Plot through the door and the ventilators, and Burke soon ordered everyone out. The smoke was so thick Captain Read had to follow the edge of the chart table to reach the door. Burke, the last to leave, emerged choking and coughing, unable to do anything more than gesture and wheeze for a few minutes. As he came out, a third *kamikaze* was shot down by anti-aircraft fire, and fell, burning, into the water close to another ship.

Mitscher and Burke went up to the ship's bridge to confer with Captain George A. Seitz. Then Read joined them, climbing up a pipe to reach the bridge after he had been blocked from a more usual access by flame. As his hands came over the edge of the bridge deck, someone wearing a steel helmet grasped his wrists to help him. As the man leaned out, his helmet came off, bounced off Read's face, and struck the staff communications officer on the head. So far, these were the only known injuries to the Admiral's staff.

Read saluted the Admiral and asked, 'Are you okay, sir?'

Mitscher returned the salute and said, 'Yes,' quite imperturbably.

Burke sent Read down to the flight deck to collect members of the staff and muster them. Since the ladders were red-hot and fuel from aircraft tanks was still burning on them, Read and another officer climbed over the gun-directing system to reach the flight deck.

Meanwhile, Mitscher stayed on the ship's bridge to watch the fire-fighting operations. He knew, by now, that he could not continue his command from *Bunker Hill*. By visual signal, he relinquished command of Task Force 58 to Sherman, whose flagship, *Essex*, had not been attacked.

Bunker Hill had slowed to ten knots, and was developing a slight list. The 20-mm. batteries at the edge of the flight deck were all but deserted. There was one exception, well forward on the port side, where the Marine sergeant in charge appeared to have telephone connections with the gunnery department and kept calling out bearings to his gun crew as sporadic attacks on the group of ships continued.

Aft, there were gasoline explosions among the burning planes, and as machine-gun ammunition exploded, tracer bullets set Fourth-of-July patterns. Safety valves popped off and spouted white steam into the billowing clouds of smoke. The air was thick with the unique smell of a burning ship, acrid and nauseous. Mingled with the hiss of planes and the noise of explosions were screams, and sometimes the sound of a man whimpering. Many crew members were dying of burns.

.... Meanwhile, the cruiser *Wilkes-Barre* and three destroyers had trained their hoses on the *Bunker Hill*, and were picking up some three hundred men who had been blown off the ship or forced to jump overboard to avoid the flames. About 11.30, when the fire was being brought under control, the forward elevator was put into service to bring up casualties and planes, which were spotted forward. As the sun was hot, and there was no other shade, wounded men were placed under the wings of aircraft that had not burned.

Three hundred and forty-six of the *Bunker Hill*'s crew were killed or died of wounds, forty-three were missing and 264 were wounded. Most of the ship's fighter squadron, waiting action in their ready room, were dead from asphyxiation. Thirteen of Mitscher's staff had been killed.

Theodore Taylor

Enterprise: 14 May 1945

At 6.50 a.m., the radar plotter reported an isolated 'blip', bearing 200° at eight thousand feet, range twenty miles. The rear guns were pointed in that direction, ready to fire as soon as the 'phantom' should appear. At 6.54 it came into sight, flying straight for the carrier. It disappeared for a moment in the clouds; then, after approximately three and a half miles, it emerged again, losing altitude. It was a Zero. The 5-inch guns opened fire. The Japanese aircraft retreated into the clouds. The batteries continued to fire. The crew had been at action stations since four in the morning. All the aircraft that were not in the air had been defuelled and parked below decks.

The Japanese machine approached from the rear. It was still not to be seen, as it was hidden by the clouds. Guided by radar, the 5-inch guns continued to fire at it, and soon the 40-mm. machine-guns began to fire as well. It was very strange to see all these guns firing relentlessly at an invisible enemy.

The Japanese aircraft emerged from the clouds and began to dive. His angle of incidence was not more than thirty degrees, his speed approximately two hundred and fifty knots. There could be no doubt—it was a suicide plane. It was approaching quite slowly and deliberately, and manœuvring just enough not to be hit too soon.

This pilot knew his job thoroughly and all those who watched him make his approach felt their mouths go dry. In less than a minute he would have attained his goal; there could be little doubt that this was to crash his machine on the deck of the *Enterprise*.

All the batteries were firing: the 5-inch guns, the 40 mm. and the 20 mm., even the rifles. The Japanese aircraft dived through a rain of steel. It had been hit in several places and seemed to be trailing a banner of flame and smoke, but it came on, clearly visible, hardly moving, the line of its wings as straight as a sword.

The deck was deserted; every man, with the exception of the gunners, was lying flat on his face. Flaming and roaring, the fireball passed in front of the 'island' (the funnels, the bridges, the look-outs, which are assembled in a single super-structure) and crashed with a terrible impact just behind the for'ard lift.

The entire vessel was shaken, some forty yards of the flight deck folded up like a banana skin: an enormous piece of the lift, at least a third of the platform, was thrown over three hundred feet into the air. The explosion killed fourteen men; those boys would never laugh and joke again. The last earthly impression they took with them was the picture of the *kamikaze* trailing his banner of flame and increasing in size with lightning rapidity.

The mortal remains of the pilot had not disappeared. They had been laid out in a corner of the deck, next to the blackened debris of the machine. The entire crew marched past the corpse of the volunteer of death. The men were less interested in his finely modelled features, his wide-open eyes which were now glazed over, than in the buttons of his tunic, which were to become wonderful souvenirs of the war for a few privileged officers of high rank. These buttons, now black, were stamped in relief with the insignia of the *kamikaze* corps: a cherry blossom with three petals.

Georges Blond

The kamikazes *were a grisly success, but the human torpedoes were not. Their crews, however, were imbued with the same spirit.*

The day of decisive action together with three other men on board has arrived. We are all well and in good spirits. Apra is going to be amazed. The moon is pale and the stars sparse and distant. In early January, O Miya Island (Guam), appearing to be silent in sleep, floats before me. Who knows the confusion there will be in a few hours' time. For the sake of our great country we have come to the place appointed.

Only twenty-two years of life and it is now just like a dream. The meaning of life will be shown to-day. As the point of the decisive fight between Japan and America, just to check in one blow our decline and thus to protect for ever the illustrious three-thousand-year-old history of Great Japan.

Great Japan is the land of the Gods. The land of the Gods is eternal and cannot be destroyed. Hereafter no matter, there will be thousands and tens of thousands of boys, and we now offer our lives as a sacrifice for our country. Let us get away from the petty affairs of this earthly and mundane life to the land where righteousness reigns supreme and eternal.

Lieutenant Ishikawa, on board submarine I.58, off Guam

THE STRUGGLE FOR THE PHILIPPINES

After the successful invasion of the Marianas in June 1944, there had at first been some doubt as to where the American forces would strike next. The Navy wished to by-pass the Philippines and seek air bases on the Chinese mainland which would facilitate a final drive on Tokyo. The Army wanted the Philippines. General MacArthur presented the Army's case to President Roosevelt with such eloquence that the President, who had favoured the Navy plan, changed his mind. Subsequently, strikes by American carrier task forces on and around the Philippines revealed such weak opposition that the American Navy thought again.

The Attackers

The Joint Chiefs of Staff received a copy of a communication from Admiral Halsey to Admiral Nimitz on 13 September. He recommended that three projected intermediate operations . . . be cancelled, and that our forces attack Leyte in the central Philippines as soon as possible.

The same day Admiral Nimitz offered to place Vice-Admiral Theodore S. Wilkinson and the 3rd Amphibious Force which included the XXIV Army Corps, then loading in Hawaii . . . at General MacArthur's disposal for an attack on Leyte.

General MacArthur's views were requested, and two days later he advised us that he was already prepared to land on Leyte on 20 October, instead of on 20 December as previously intended. It was a remarkable administrative achievement.

Within ninety minutes after the signal had been received . . . General MacArthur and Admiral Nimitz had received their instructions to execute the Leyte operation on the target date 20 October, abandoning the three previously approved intermediary landings.

General Marshall, Chief of Staff

The Defenders

The Philippines were in the zone of the Japanese Southern Army, which we could have called an army group. Field-Marshal Terauchi, the commander, transferred his headquarters to Manila in May 1944. At that time the 14 Army, that part of the Southern Army immediately responsible for Philippine defence, comprised only four independent mixed brigades and 16 Infantry Division, which had been fighting Chinese and Americans since 1937. Terauchi estimated that fifteen more divisions would be required for effective defence of the archipelago; but he had slight hope of getting them. The 14 Army commander, from 5 October 1944, was General Tomoyuki Yamashita, the conqueror of Singapore. He boasted to President Laurel that he would soon demand MacArthur's surrender in the same words he once used to General Percival at Singapore: 'All I want to know from you is, *Yes* or *No*.'

Samuel Eliot Morison

On 19 October an enormous armada was approaching Leyte, covered by no less than six battleships with a screen of cruisers and destroyers. The landing was made successfully on the 20th, watched by General MacArthur, who had sailed up from New Guinea in the cruiser Nashville. *He went ashore in the afternoon.*

The Battle of Leyte Gulf

Leyte was to be a long and stubborn campaign, but after a few days the progress of the ground forces became less important, from a world view-point, than events upon the sea. A final naval engagement began. It was the Battle of Leyte Gulf, one of the decisive battles of the war. A single Japanese search plane had sighted the great American amphibious force and reported its presence to

Admiral Kurita's Singapore fleet. Approximately sixty per cent of Japan's naval units were under Kurita's command. For a period of many months our Navy had endeavoured to entice Kurita into combat. He would not be enticed. With great good sense he had harboured his carriers and battle-wagons.

But now the warlords in Japan made their decision to commit the fleet in a final gamble to prevent America's return to the Philippines.

General Eichelberger

The battle situation has become more serious . . . . However, we are confident that the enemy's operations are growing more difficult because his lines of communication are becoming extended. . . . Because the operational strength of base air forces is insufficient, Mobile Force is expected to exert its utmost strength. . . . It must make a desperate effort to defeat the enemy.

Chief of Staff to Admiral Toyoda, C.-in-C. Combined Japanese Fleet

Shortly before dawn on 23 October, I received a dispatch from a Seventh Fleet picket submarine, the *Darter*: MANY SHIPS INCLUDING 3 PROBABLE BBS [battleships] 08–28 N 116–30 E COURSE 040 SPEED 18 X CHASING. This position is near the south-western tip of the Philippine group, and the course is towards Coron Bay and Manila. The main strength of the Japanese Fleet was based, we knew, at Singapore and at Brunei, in Borneo. If it stayed holed up there we planned to go down and dig it out. On the 22nd, however, our submarines and patrol planes had reported that enemy units were restless, and the *Darter*'s dispatch was proof that a major movement was afoot.

Admiral Halsey

Three engagements made up the Battle of Leyte Gulf, one of the decisive battles of the war: Surigao Strait on the night of 24–25 October, and Cape Engaño and Samar, which both began on the 25th.

The Japanese aim was to draw off the American fleet protecting the Leyte landings and then to smash the latter while the covering forces were absent. On the 23rd and 24th two Japanese battle fleets began to converge on Leyte. One approached the San Bernardino Strait north of the island of Samar, intending to pass through the strait and sail down the east coast of Samar to its objective. The other pincer made for Surigao Strait to the south of Leyte itself. At the same time a third force, far away to the north-east of Luzon, was to lure away the defenders. At first all seemed to go well for the Americans. The fleet aiming at San Bernardino Strait turned back after being heavily punished, and in Surigao Strait the Japanese were met and shattered by Admiral Kinkaid.

Ambush in Surigao Strait

. . . . Vice-Admiral Nishimura's Force 'C' of No. 1 Striking Force included the two battleships. Its mission was to arrive off Tacloban in Leyte Gulf just before dawn (which as the Japanese reckoned dawn was at 04.30, the first glimmer of light), at the same time as Kurita's Centre Force. This timing was essential to the success of Admiral Toyoda's SHO-1 battle plan, which called for a pincer movement on the American amphibious forces in Leyte Gulf. Whether Nishimura imagined he could get through Surigao Strait without a fight, we do not know; but any hope he may have had of joining Kurita in a merry massacre of amphibious craft and transports, which he believed to be present in great abundance, must have vanished around 18.30 24 October when he received Admiral Kurita's signal of 16.00 to the effect that Centre Force had been delayed by the air battle of the Sibuyan Sea. Nishimura, nevertheless, maintained course and speed, and felt confirmed in this decision around 19.00 by Toyoda's order: 'All forces will dash to the attack.'

A frantic signal told of the reception the Japanese had encountered.

Urgent Battle Report No. 2. Enemy torpedo boats and destroyers present on both sides of northern entrance of Surigao Strait. Two of our destroyers torpedoed and drifting. *Yamashiro* sustained one torpedo hit but no impediment to battle cruising.

Admiral Nishimura

When the Southern Force pushed into Surigao soon after midnight of the 24th, it pushed into one of the prettiest ambushes in naval history. Rear-Admiral Jesse B. Oldendorf, Kinkaid's tactical commander, waited until the enemy line was well committed to the narrow waters, then struck from both flanks with his P.T.s and destroyers, and from dead ahead with his battleships and cruisers. He not only 'crossed the T', which is every naval officer's dearest ambition; he dotted several thousand slant eyes. Almost before the Japs could open fire, they lost both their battleships and three destroyers. The rest fled, but Kinkaid's planes caught and sank a heavy cruiser later in the morning, and Army B-24s sank the light cruiser the following noon. One of Oldendorf's P.T.s was sunk, and one destroyer was damaged.

Admiral Halsey

The devastating accuracy of this gunfire was the most beautiful sight I have ever witnessed. The arched line of tracers in the darkness looked like a continual stream of lighted railroad cars going over a hill. No target could be observed at first; then shortly there would be fires and explosions, and another ship would be accounted for.

U.S. naval observer

Meanwhile Admiral Halsey with the main covering force, confident that both the Straits were safe, contacted and engaged the Japanese decoy fleet in the distant north. This may well have constituted a third attacking group.

Cape Engaño: the Decoys Caught

If the enemy slipped past my left flank, between me and Luzon, he would have a free crack at the transports. If he slipped past my right flank, he would be able to shuttle-bomb me—fly from his carriers, attack me, continue on to his fields on Luzon for more bombs and fuel, and attack me again on the way back. I had to meet him head-on, and I was trusting the *Independence*'s snoopers to set my course.

They began to report at 02.08: CONTACT POSIT 17–10 N 125–31 E x 5 SHIPS 2 LARGE 2 SMALL 1 SIZE UNREPORTED.

At 02.14: CORRECTION x 6 SHIPS 3 LARGE 3 SMALL COURSE 110 SPEED 15.

At 02.20: ANOTHER GROUP 40 MILES ASTERN OF FIRST.

At 02.35: SECOND GROUP 6 LARGE SHIPS.

We had them!

Later sightings, in daylight, established the composition of the Northern Force as one large carrier, three light carriers, two hermaphrodite battleships with flight decks aft (a typical gimcrack Jap makeshift), three light cruisers, and at least eight destroyers.

I ordered TF 34 to form and take station ten miles in advance, and my task-group commanders to arm their first deckload strike at once, launch it at earliest dawn, and launch a second strike as soon afterwards as possible. Our next few hours were the most anxious of all. The pilots and aircrewmen knew that a terrific carrier duel was facing them, and the ships' companies were sure that a big-gun action would follow.

The first strike took off at 06.30. An hour and a half passed without a word of news. . . . Two hours . . . Two hours and a quarter. . . . God, what a wait it was! (Mick admitted later, 'I chewed my fingernails down to my elbows.') Then, at 08.50, a flash report reached me: ONE CARRIER SUNK AFTER TREMENDOUS EXPLOSION x 2 CARRIERS 1 CL [light cruiser] HIT BADLY OTHER CARRIER UN-TOUCHED x FORCE COURSE 150 SPEED 17.

Samar: the Lost Chance

But while Halsey pursued the Japanese diversionary force, and though Kinkaid had hammered one arm of the pincer, the second arm came within an ace of accomplishing its mission. Last seen sailing away from San Bernardino Strait, it now turned in its tracks and, passing quickly through the Strait, bore down the coast of Samar towards Leyte and the defenceless beachhead. In its path were only the small carriers and escorting light vessels of Admiral Sprague, hopelessly outclassed and far from aid. The Japanese set upon them and tore them to pieces.

I was puzzled by the Central Force's hit-and-run tactics and still more puzzled when I learned the complete story. Four battleships, six heavy cruisers, two light cruisers, and eleven destroyers had survived our air attacks on 24 October and had transited San Bernardino that night. When they were sighted next, at 06.31 on the 25th, they were only twenty miles north-west of Sprague's task unit. His seventeen-knot escort carriers were no match for the enemy in either speed or gun power, and at 06.58 he was taken under fire at a range of thirty thousand yards.

Sprague immediately turned east, into the wind, launched his available planes, and ordered all ships to make smoke. The enemy formation now divided, the heavy ships advancing to his port and the light to starboard, thereby forcing him around to the south-west, in the direction of Leyte Gulf. When the cruisers had closed to fourteen thousand yards, Sprague ordered his screen to fall back and deliver a torpedo attack. Two destroyers, the *Hoel* and *Johnston*, and the destroyer escort *Samuel S. Roberts* reversed course, ran within ten thousand yards of the battleships, and fired a half-salvo, then fired the other half within seven thousand yards of the cruisers. Smoke concealed the effect of their torpedoes, but it lifted to show that all three of these heroic little ships had been sunk.

The enemy continued to close, and presently his fire began to take toll. If he had had the elementary intelligence not to use armour-piercing projectiles, many of which ripped through our ships' thin skins as if through a wet shoebox, without detonating, he might have annihilated Sprague's unit, since every ship in it suffered hits. As it was, except for the three ships from the screen, Sprague's only loss to the guns was the carrier *Gambier Bay*. At 08.20 she dropped astern under continuous fire, and after being riddled with 8-inch shells from the murderous range of two thousand yards, she blew up at 09.00.

For these first two hours, Sprague's gallant men fought entirely alone, at such close quarters that his CVEs' single 5-inchers were registering hits on the cruisers, and with such valour that his Avengers, their bombs and torpedoes expended, were making dummy runs to distract the battleships.

Admiral Halsey

We circled the heavy cruisers for three turns to gain a cirrus cloud cover and attacked from out of the sun and through this cloud at about 09.05. We caught the second heavy cruiser (*Mogami* class) in column completely by surprise as we received absolutely no anti-aircraft fire. At this time we had only four torpedo-bombers as the twelve fighters and other torpedo-bombers had fallen out of formation in the thick weather. We completed all dives in about thirty-five seconds, scoring five hits amidships on the stack, one hit and two near-misses on the stern and three hits on the bow. The third plane hitting the stern sent the heavy cruiser into a sharp right turn. After pulling out of the dive, I observed the heavy cruiser to go about five hundred yards, blow up and sink within five minutes.

Commander R. L. Fowler, *Kitkun Bay*

The *Johnston*

The Japanese destroyer squadron, as soon as it had fired torpedoes, concentrated on *Johnston*. She was observed from *Heermann*, her mast shot away and hanging over the superstructure deck, and on fire amidships. She was almost done for. Lieutenant Hagen thus records her end:

'We checked fire as the Japanese destroyers retired, turned left and closed range on the Japanese cruisers. For the next half-hour this ship engaged first the cruisers on our port hand and then the destroyers on our starboard hand, alternating between the two groups in a somewhat desperate attempt to keep all of them from closing the carrier formation. The ship was getting hit with disconcerting frequency throughout this period.

'At 09.10 we had taken a hit which knocked out one forward gun and damaged the other. Fires had broken out. One of our 40 mm. ready-lockers was hit and the exploding shells were causing as much damage as the Japs. The bridge was rendered untenable by the fires and explosions, and Commander Evans had been forced at 09.20 to shift his command to the fantail, where he yelled his steering orders through an open hatch at the men who were turning the rudder by hand.

'. . . . We were now in a position where all the gallantry and guts in the world couldn't save us. There were two cruisers on our port, another dead ahead of us, and several destroyers on our starboard side; the battleships, well astern of us, fortunately had turned coy.* We desperately traded shots first with one group and then the other.'

Shortly after this an avalanche of shells knocked out her one remaining engine room and fireroom. Director and plot lost power. All communications were lost throughout the ship. All guns were out of operation with the exception of the No. 4 5-inch, which was still shooting by local control. All depth charges were scuttled. At 09.45, five minutes after the ship went dead in the water, the captain gave the order 'Abandon ship'.

The Japanese destroyer squadron, whose torpedo attack *Johnston* had thwarted, now made a running circle around her, shooting at her 'like Indians attacking a prairie schooner'. At 10.10 she rolled over and began to sink. One destroyer closed to give her the *coup de grâce*. One of her swimming survivors saw the Japanese skipper on the destroyer's bridge salute as *Johnston* went down.

But now, with Sprague crippled and victory in sight, Admiral Kurita once more turned about and retreated. He knew of the disaster in Surigao Strait, was badly knocked about himself, and did not know that the diversion had been successful. Unsupported, he thought that Halsey and Kinkaid were converging on him. He lost his chance, and in retreat was battered to pieces by American air and sea reinforcements, which had now had time to arrive.

At 09.25 my mind was occupied with dodging torpedoes when near the bridge I heard one of the signalmen yell, 'Goddamit, boys, they're getting away!' I could not believe my eyes, but it looked as if the whole Japanese Fleet was indeed retiring. However, it took a whole series of reports from circling planes to convince me. And still I could not get the fact to soak into my battle-numbed brain. At best, I had expected to be swimming by this time.

Admiral Sprague

Now came an intermission during which the offensive passed to us, but at 10.50 the enemy's shore-based air struck again, this time on Sprague's wounded, exhausted carriers. One plane plunged into the *Kalinin Bay*'s flight deck, causing a small blaze; another crashed through the *Kitkun Bay*'s catwalk; a third dropped a bomb on the *Saint Lo* and itself crashed close aboard. The *Saint Lo*'s

---

* The enemy Main Body had reversed course and was retiring.

fires could not be controlled; she was abandoned with heavy losses. The enemy still did not exploit his overwhelming advantage, and soon it was gone forever. At 13.10 McCain's planes arrived. In the emergency, he had launched them from far outside their range of return; after their attacks, they had to land and rearm at Tacloban and Dulag Fields on Leyte, which had fallen to MacArthur only a few days before. Together with planes from TG 77.4, they sank a light cruiser and a destroyer and damaged most of the other ships. Sprague had lost five of his thirteen ships. TG 77.4 had lost 105 planes.

The Central Force was in full retreat by late afternoon, and by 22.00 it was re-entering San Bernardino, with my force still two hours away.

.... McCain's and Bogan's planes were harrying the Central Force's scattered remnants, still fleeing westward, while our ships searched east of Samar for other stragglers and for our airmen who had ditched the day before. We found no Jap ships, but Jap swimmers were as thick as water bugs. I was having breakfast when Bill Kitchell burst in and cried, 'My God Almighty, Admiral, the little bastards are all over the place! Are we going to stop and pick 'em up?'

I told him, 'Not until we've picked up our own boys.'

We chartered their position, along with wind and tide data, and when we had recovered all the Americans, I ordered our destroyers, 'Bring in co-operative Nip flotsam for an intelligence sample. Non-co-operators would probably like to join their ancestors and should be accommodated.' (I didn't want to risk their getting ashore, where they could reinforce the garrison.) The destroyers brought in six.

.... Thus ended the three-day, threefold Battle for Leyte Gulf. Six of our ships had been sunk and eleven damaged. Twenty-six enemy ships had been sunk, and twenty-five damaged. In my official report, I was able to write with conviction that the results of the battle were: '(1) the utter failure of the Japanese plan to prevent the re-occupation of the Philippines; (2) the crushing defeat of the Japanese fleet; and (3) the elimination of serious naval threat to our operations for many months, if not forever.'

Admiral Halsey

To all intents and purposes, the Battle of Leyte Gulf had meant the end of the Japanese Navy. The results were startling.

After long miles and weary months of The Hard Way Back, all of us had the heartening news that Japan's stolen marine empire had been broken asunder. During the next weeks the Great Fleet roamed at will from Hong Kong to Indo-China, pounding away at shore facilities and shipping. It destroyed almost everything in the way of war vessels which Admiral Kurita had been able to salvage from the disaster of Leyte Gulf.

General Eichelberger

War on Leyte

In spite of their crushing defeat at sea, the Japanese hung grimly on to Leyte for nearly two months, reinforcing their troops there and fighting savagely for every inch of ground. They counter-attacked by air and land, but though their resistance delayed the American descent on Luzon, the intermediate stepping-stone, the island of Mindoro, was captured during December.

The naval defeat added greatly to Terauchi's difficulties in transporting troops from one island to another. It did not reduce his stubbornness and determination. He intended to fight, and he decided he would do a lot of his fighting in the rice paddies and mountains of Leyte. He relieved Lieutenant-General Shigenori Kuroda, and put General Tomoyuki Yamashita in charge. This was the same Yamashita who had conquered Singapore and who had taken over the Philippines early in the war when General Homma could not capture Bataan. For his victories Yamashita had been given the First Area Army in Manchuria, one of the most important Japanese field commands.

When Yamashita took over from Kuroda he sent this message to General Makina, head of the Japanese 16 Division on Leyte: 'The Army has received the following order from His Majesty, the Emperor: Enemy ground forces will be destroyed.'

. . . . Despite the efforts of General Kenney's land-based fighters and Admiral Halsey's carrier-planes, the Japanese continued to land formidable reinforcements. One of the outfits which came in was the Japanese 1 Division, a crack aggregation from the Kwantung Army. This made it obvious that Yamashita was committing his finest troops. The 1 Division had been in China when 6 Army's expedition against Leyte was discovered; it had been speeded by transport from Shanghai to Manila and then on to Leyte.

. . . . Yamashita, the rainy season, and evil terrain made Leyte hard going for the military calendar-keepers. When G.H.Q. set 7 December as the date when command would be taken over by 8 Army, General Krueger came to see me. He expressed, with considerable eloquence, his concern at handing me what the younger members of my staff might have called a 'hot potato'. Certainly, the results at that time were indecisive. And the opposition was rugged: the experience of 24 Division offers convincing evidence. A combat force of the 24th, then and later excellent fighters, landed on 7 November at Carigara Bay on the north coast of Leyte. The force struck south from Pinamapoan and ran into 1 Japanese Division at a circle of hills ideal for defence. This position became known as Breakneck Ridge. After several weeks of fighting the ably commanded 24th had got only two or three miles inland. Later 32 Division took over the same positions and found forward movement equally slow.

In the end, G.H.Q. set a later target date for the Lingayen Gulf assault and asked General Krueger to finish his Leyte campaign by 25 December.

. . . . In late November I attended an important conference which was concerned with planning for the landing on Mindoro Island. Mindoro lies immediately south of Luzon, and possession of it was vital to the success of any Luzon operation. It was at this meeting that General Kenney admitted to General MacArthur (despite previous bold promises) that his Leyte-based planes would not be able to protect an amphibious landing if the day were overcast. This came as somewhat of a surprise to those who earlier had heard General Kenney argue that Admiral Halsey's carrier-based planes were no longer necessary to the Leyte operation.

Surprises are a commonplace of war—and reconsidered opinions too. As a result of Kenney's testimony, General MacArthur urged Admiral Kinkaid of the Seventh Fleet (under MacArthur's command) to wheel his old battleships and small aircraft carriers through the narrows to cover the invasion. Kinkaid objected violently. He pointed out that to get to Mindoro his fleet must pass through Surigao Strait and the Sulu Sea, where the vessels would be clay pigeons for Jap land-based planes. In the end, of course, Kinkaid accepted the assignment, and Seventh Fleet did its usual fine job.

There were repeated Jap air-raids during this heated conference. The finer points of the discussion were frequently blurred—to me, at least—by the persistent roar of American ack-ack. I was interested and somewhat entertained by the fact that General MacArthur chose to ignore the air-raids. Since the Supreme Commander was deaf to the violence around him, the rest of us maintained the elaborate pretence that we couldn't hear any bombs falling either.

Rain and raids were now everyday occurrences. There was little in the way of recreation even for troops not immediately in the line. Tacloban, capital of Leyte, had a population of about thirteen thousand and was the only town of any size or modernity on the island. Few combat troops got there, and it wasn't very exciting for them when they did. So, in camps and headquarters along the coasts, privates and generals alike often sat gladly in a pouring rain to watch an outdoor movie. There was a recognized technique for a rainy night: you adjusted your poncho around yourself and your chair and put a helmet liner on your head so the water wouldn't drain down in your eyes. Thus, with vision clear, you were a proper and appreciative audience for the artistry of Gloria Gumm in *Passion's Darling*.

The Americans had developed a device which protected the movie screen and the movie projector so they could not be seen from aloft. This, of course, was a precaution against raids. One night when General Byers and I and innumerable soldiers sat contentedly in the moist darkness, a covey of our planes came in all lighted up from some strike. It was an old story to us. Our planes always came in lighted because the pattern of light made their identity clear.

That evening an ingenious enemy pilot made capital of the custom. All of us saw one straggler plane come in belatedly, circle over us a number of times, and ease out of the spiral at two hundred feet. Then—boom, boom—we heard a series of explosions, and the lone plane was quickly away. Tenuan Airstrip, a few miles up the coast, had been bombed without a round of American ack-ack being fired. It was a bad bombing, too. The enterprising Japanese had got on the tail of our homeward-bound planes, and, all lights burning, had unscathedly followed them in.

. . . . Major-General Joe Swing set up his 11 Airborne headquarters not too far away from mine, and I saw him frequently. My diary of 6 December simply says: 'Raids again.' But Joe Swing had a different story, and I heard it next day. Swing had eaten his supper and, looking for a breath of cool air, was sitting outside his tent in his underwear. It was dusk. Indifferently he watched a flight of Japanese bombers flying high over three nearby airstrips. Then two flights of

Japanese transport planes came in slowly at seven hundred and fifty feet. Japanese parachutes began to swell and float in the Leyte evening. It was an all-out attack on our strips and Swing's headquarters. Several miles away were the 44th General Hospital and the Signal Centre which controlled Fifth Air Force communications throughout the Philippines.

11 Airborne never had a more confusing night. The attack was, of course, a complete surprise, but the confusion of our troops was hardly a patch on the confusion of the Japanese; in the growing darkness it was hard to tell friend from foe. Anticipating this, the enemy had devised a system of identification for assembly on the ground which included bells, horns, whistles, and even distinctive songs for each small unit. This was ingenious but not too effective. Many of the Japanese were killed before they could take up fighting positions.

We know now that the parachute drop was part of a co-ordinated plan of attack which involved the Japanese 26 Division and the remnants of the Japanese 16 Division. Some four hundred and fifty paratroops were airlifted from southern Luzon. They were supposedly crack troops and they were provided with bottles of liquor to sharpen their morale. Labels on the bottles gave the firm instruction that the contents were *not* to be drunk until the planes were in the air.

Many men were killed on both sides during that bedlam night. Flames leaped high in the sky as the Japanese burned American planes and supply dumps. The attack was upon the headquarters, and two artillery battalions and an engineer battalion functioned as infantry that night. In other sections of the dark battlefield cooks and clerks were the fighting men. Eventually dawn came. Some three hundred Japanese were killed the next day, and the remainder were hunted out in surrounding areas and killed over a period of three days.

. . . . This long after, I think of the Japanese parachute attack as a near thing. It had no military importance, but, with better luck, it might have had.

. . . . 8 Army took over Leyte on Christmas Day. There were eight divisions fighting there when I assumed command. When 32 Division and 1 Cavalry broke through on a narrow front, G.H.Q. described the Leyte campaign as officially closed and future operations as 'mopping up'.

Actually the Japanese Army was still intact. I was told that there were only six thousand Japanese left on the island. This estimate was in serious error, as subsequent events proved. Soon Japanese began streaming across the Ormoc Valley from eastern into western Leyte, well equipped and apparently well fed. It took several months of the roughest kind of combat to defeat this army. Between Christmas Day and the end of the campaign we killed more than twenty-seven thousand Japanese.

Many others, evacuated safely by *bancas* (small boats), reappeared to fight 8 Army on other islands in later campaigns. I called these singularly alive veteran troops the Ghosts of Leyte.

General Eichelberger

While some Japanese escaped from Leyte, others were not so lucky. As organized resistance broke down, the Japanese units slowly disintegrated into a scattered mass of starving refugees.

Flotsam

'What, are you here again?' I heard a voice behind me.

I turned round and saw the expressionless face of a middle-aged soldier called Yasuda whom I had met that morning on my way from the hospital. He was suffering from tropical ulcers and one of his legs had swollen to the size of a huge club. On the shin was an ulcer as large as a biscuit, in the centre of which the bone was exposed like a grain of boiled rice. Yasuda had adopted the local remedy of wrapping the leaf of an aromatic plant round his leg, applying a small piece of tin over the leaf and securing it all with a piece of cotton.

'That's right. They wouldn't take me back in my company. They sent me back here again.'

'It won't do you much good coming here, you know,' said Yasuda.

. . . . 'I had nowhere else to go,' I said vaguely.

I looked round and counted my companions-in-despair, who were sitting here by the edge of the forest. We were eight soldiers in all; of the six who had been here when I had passed in the morning, one had left, and there had been two new arrivals apart from myself.

Only one of us was completely immobile. He was a young soldier who had been thrown out of the hospital a few days before in the last stages of malaria for having annoyed one of the orderlies. The others were suffering from diarrhoea, beri-beri, tropical ulcers, bullet wounds or a combination of these complaints; they could have left at any time, had they known of a worthwhile destination.

Like me, they were the rejects, the debris of a defeated army. At this stage of the campaign, they could be of no possible military use. Once these men had been discarded from their own units, why should the hospitals bother to take them? Yet somehow the field hospital remained in their imaginations, from the days when they had still been on active duty, as the soldier's final haven, his last resort; and so they hovered near the compound, knowing full well that they could die in agony before they would ever be admitted.

. . . . Shortly after I arrived, for instance, one of the men, who had been dozing a few yards away, stood up and came over to me.

'How much food have you got?' he asked.

He was fearfully emaciated, and I could tell that he was suffering from diarrhoea; for, even as he awaited my answer his whole body shook uncontrollably.

'Six potatoes,' I said.

The man nodded with an air of satisfaction and tottered back to his place. Evidently he felt it necessary to know exactly how much food each person had.

'Ha ha! Six spuds! You're a real millionaire, aren't you?' said a young soldier who was lying near me. He was one of the new arrivals. On his ankle was a bullet wound infested with maggots.

'I wish I'd been in your unit.' he continued. 'In my company they only give us two spuds when we're thrown out. And now I've just got one left.'

. . . . When I awoke again, it was to the sound of heavy firing. It was almost daylight. By the river in the west, the air was full of noise and smoke. The mighty concatenation of explosions approached our forest and seemed to fuse the whole surrounding sky into a narrow strip. The roar of guns grew terrifyingly close, and with it came a bellowing rumble as of distant thunder. Beyond the hills, which I had crossed the day before, I could see a single reconnaissance plane flying round in small circles, like a bird of prey watching for its victim. The bombardment seemed to be concentrated directly below the plane.

We all jumped to our feet. The doctors and orderlies hurried out of the hospital and peered beyond the hills.

Suddenly there was a whistling sound of a shell, and a moment later a huge cloud of smoke arose in the plain where yesterday I had seen the prairie fire. Someone gave an order and the doctors and orderlies dashed into the hospital, to re-emerge at once with their rifles and field equipment. They came running towards us at full speed.

The range of shell-fire was reaching steadily over the hills in our direction. The medical personnel rushed past us towards the valley, as if they could possibly outstrip the rapidly-expanding range of the shells. A few of our group followed them. The one-potato soldier with the great welt on his face took advantage of the confusion to run back to the hospital; even the roar of the shell-bursts could not deflect him from his determination to steal food. The patients began to pour out of the wards, and scattered about helplessly, each going his own way.

The malarial soldier was lying face-down on the grass without moving. I tapped him on the shoulder, then realized that he was dead.

I walked alone into the forest towards the spring where I had gone to fetch water the night before. When I reached the mountain-range, I decided to climb the foothills and make my way along them, parallel to the broad front from where the shell-fire was coming.

After scrambling about sixty yards up the zigzag path, I reached a turning from where I had an unbroken view of the whole valley. I stopped and looked down. The patients who had fled from the hospital had by now exhausted their strength and were lying motionless, scattered like little beans between the ridges of the maize-fields.

The roar of guns continued, but so far the shells had not quite reached the hospital compound. I wondered where the main firing could be coming from. This was clearly not one of the usual trench-mortar bombardments. No; it was probably a softening-up from one of the American warships offshore, preceding a concerted landing operation on the west coast. After all, we were separated from the sea by less than three miles of flat, open plains.

Smoke began to rise from one of the hospital buildings. It whirled round in little eddies, curling up from under the eaves, and finally formed a single thick, convoluted column. Through the windows I could make out a red glare. Had the orderlies fired the buildings, according to normal Army practice before abandoning a position? Or had the predatory one-potato soldier dropped a match or upset an oil-lamp by mistake?

.... Now scattered groups of soldiers began to appear from the forests on the hills and joined the road. Soon we were part of a long, serpentine formation with enough men to make a whole company.

When the road emerged into open country, we broke formation and hurried between the bordering trees until it once more entered the shelter of the woods. As our column passed through the virgin forests, they became as bustling and congested as the shopping quarter of some city.

The condition of the troops had deteriorated unbelievably since I had last seen them. Their uniforms were in shreds, their shoes broken, their hair and beards absurdly long. In the soldiers' pale, dirty faces only their eyes shone clearly, as they peered inquiringly at each other.

Palompon, Palompon. With that one magic word in his mind, each soldier dragged his sick, starved, exhausted body along the road, desperately trying not to lag behind the others. On the slopes on both sides were rows of soldiers who had lain down to rest, or who had collapsed and been pushed off the road.

I wondered whether the Americans knew our orders about going to Palompon. As if to answer me, the roar of a plane passed low over the forest through which we were filing. I heard the harsh staccato of machine-gun fire. We all scurried for safety. When the plane had passed, the road was littered with more bodies of the dead and wounded.

. . . . The young man was selling tobacco to the passers-by.

'Anyone want some tobacco? The normal price is three potatoes for a leaf,' he announced, 'but two potatoes will do.'

The Army's purchasing power, however, had drastically declined since the days outside the hospital, and there seemed to be no offers.

. . . . The rain beat down mechanically like a shower-bath. Sometimes it would stop abruptly, only to start again in a few minutes, as if a tap had been turned on. So it continued day in day out.

Before long we were all wet to the skin. Our sodden haversacks seemed several times their normal weight, and the sash-cords cut painfully into our shoulders. The narrow straps of the steel helmets, which we carried on our backs, began to chafe: soon the roadside was dotted with abandoned helmets.

I quickened my pace in a desperate effort to overtake the corporal and his two men, but although they could not have been very far ahead of me, I no longer had sufficient strength to make up for the time I had lost by the roadside. After two days of useless exertion, I resigned myself to abandoning the goodwill of my companions into which I had so hopefully invested my salt.

The water had begun to flow in rapid rivulets over the grass by the roadside. Some of the soldiers in the last stages of exhaustion tried to revive themselves by dipping their bodies in the water. A few lay completely inert with their faces immersed, and looked as if they had stopped breathing. As we passed one such lifeless figure, the soldier next to me said, 'Poor bastard! That's how we'll all end up.' To my amazement, the 'corpse' lifted its face, all dripping with water, and murmured, 'What's that you say?' We hurried on.

Many of the bodies had begun to swell like the ones that I had seen in the seaside village: these, I knew, were really dead. Maggots drifted on the surface of the water, and gathering in clumps of grass a few feet from the corpses, floated there in wriggling masses.

The corpses were devoid of everything but the sodden uniforms that were stretched tightly over their bloated bodies. Their shoes had been removed and their bare feet, bleached by the water, were swollen like the feet of the angels in the primitive Buddhist paintings of the Hakuchō Period.

Mixed with the sour, vegetable smell of the rain-soaked grass, that pungent odour which I knew so well began to hover over the greenery.

On the rare occasions that it stopped raining, a dazzling sun would thrust its way through the branches of the trees. Then we would strip and spread our clothes out to dry. Our bodies were filthy and emaciated; but to my eyes there was something strangely impressive about these scenes, in which the brown colour of the soldiers' naked limbs mixed on the steaming green undergrowth with the greenish-yellow of their uniforms and the white of their underclothes.

Thanks to the rain, American planes had grown scarce; but in their place our procession was constantly harassed from the flank by well-armed Filipino guerrillas. The path which we had so far taken followed the foothills to the west of the central mountain range. The guerrilla attacks, however, forced us to strike inland and to make our way northward, parallel to the coast, along the narrow mountain trails. Often when we crossed the mountain streams, which had swollen now into huge, muddy rapids, the starved and battered soldiers would be swept off their feet by the swirling waters and carried helplessly downstream.

. . . . One evening when the rain had stopped and the crimson of the sky traced the hill-tops, I climbed one of the hills—perhaps so that I might more clearly view that crimson colouring. At the summit, leaning against a solitary tree, I found a single, motionless body.

Its eyes were closed. The sun-rays, as they moved down over the western hills, shone on the green face and formed shadows in the recesses of the cheeks and chin. Then I perceived that the body was alive. The man opened his eyes. He seemed to be looking directly into the sun. His lips moved and words came forth.

'It's burning,' he said. 'It's burning! Quickly it's sinking, really quickly! The earth is turning round. That's why the sun is sinking, you know.'

He looked at me. There was the same gleam in his eyes as I had seen when the soldier brushed past me with his cry of 'Oh!'

'Where have you come from, fellow?' he said.

I sat down next to him, but did not answer. The sun hid itself in the hill opposite, and from between the trees that lined its summit, the rays splashed forth in stripes. Only the clouds still shone golden as they hung in the sky. For some time they illuminated the two of us.

'The Western Paradise! Buddha is Amida. One is one. Two is two. I join my hands in prayer.'

He put his hands together and on them leaned his bearded chin. With a rustling sound, the rain began to fall.

'Uh, uh!' he said, lifting his face and laughing. He put back his head and let his mouth fall open to receive the rain-drops. His throat rumbled. Only when he was actually swallowing did the sound of his voice cease entirely.

'Hey,' I said. 'Let's leave here!'

'Leave? There's no reason to leave. A plane's coming to fetch me from

Formosa. Don't you understand? They'll be landing right here by heli-copter.'

I looked at him. He was in his forties. His uniform, though discoloured by sun and rain, showed him to be an officer; but he carried neither sword nor revolver.

'Uh, uh!' he kept saying. The movement of his chin whetted my appetite.

When the darkness covered our hilltop, he finally grew silent. Then his stertorous breathing told me that he was alive.

I did not sleep.

What first startled me in the morning light were the swarms of flies that covered the officer's face and hands. With a whistling sound of 'Hee-e-e', he awoke. The flies buzzed off, as though frightened by the sound, and circled in mid-air and the whirring of their wings became louder; then they settled on him once more.

He opened his eyes, swept the flies away and bowed deeply.

'Your Imperial Majesty,' he intoned. 'Great Emperor of Japan, I humbly implore you to let me return home! Aeroplane, come and fetch me! Land here in a helicopter. . . . Goodness, but it's dark,' he broke off, lowering his voice. 'So awfully dark! It's not yet morning.'

'Certainly it's morning,' I said. 'Can't you hear the birds singing?'

It was a rainless morning. The busy voices of various types of birds came from the surrounding trees and from within the forest at the bottom of the valley. On the opposite hills, I could see them darting back and forth like arrows in the spaces between the trees.

'Those aren't birds,' said the officer. 'They're ants! That's the buzzing of ants. You're a fool, you know!'

He grasped a handful of earth from between his knees and stuck it into his mouth. There was the smell of urine and excrement.

'Aha, aha!'

He closed his eyes. As though this were their signal, the flies closed in from far and near with a great whirring of wings. His face, his hands, his feet—every exposed part of his body was covered by swarms of murmuring insects.

They began to attack my body too. I shook my hands, but they evidently made no distinction between me and the dying man—was I, in fact, dying too? —and my movements did not bother them in the slightest.

'It hurts! It hurts!' he said. Then from the sound of his regular breathing I gathered that he had fallen asleep again.

It began to pour. The rain streamed over the officer's body. The flies lost their foothold and slipped off one after another. In their place, large mountain leeches fell on him from the trees, accompanying the rain-drops. Some, which had landed a short distance away, moved along the ground, folding their bodies up completely like canker-worms as they advanced on their prey.

'Your Imperial Majesty, Great Emperor of Japan,' said the officer, bowing and shaking his head, from which the leeches dangled like tatters, 'I want to go home. Let me go home! Stop the war! Save us, O merciful Buddha! Buddha of mercy! I join my hands in prayer.'

Yet once before he died he fixed me with the clear eyes of a policeman, and in an access of lucidity, such as visits patients at the moment of their death, said, 'What, are you still here? You poor fellow! When I'm dead, you may eat this.'

Slowly he raised his emaciated left arm and slapped it with his other hand.

Shohei Ooka

Manila

On 9 January 1945 American forces went ashore at Lingayen Gulf on Luzon, north of Manila—the same spot chosen by the Japanese for their main landing three years earlier. Resistance was feeble at first, but stiffened as the Americans drew nearer to Manila. Two more landings were made, and the city was surrounded. The Japanese put up a desperate defence, which was not finally crushed until March.

As the year 1945 was ushered in—with, I might add, a minimum of joy and jollity on the combat fronts—a new American assault force was assembled at sea east of Leyte. It moved through the Surigao Strait and into the Mindanao and Sulu Seas and then swung north to pass through the very heart of the Philippine Archipelago. Two years before, the Japanese Navy and Air Force had maintained unquestionable control of those land-surrounded waters; 6 Army with air cover and fleet protection was on its way to Lingayen Gulf, which had always been considered Luzon's point of greatest vulnerability.

On 9 January, I Corps and XIV Corps hit the beaches. General Marshall has written: 'Japanese forces on the island, harassed by guerrillas and by air, drove north, south, east, and west in confusion, became tangled in traffic jams on the roads, and generally dissipated what chance they might have had to repel the landing-force. . . . By nightfall sixty-eight thousand troops were ashore and in control of a fifteen-mile beachhead six thousand yards deep. . . .

'The landing had caught every major hostile combat unit in motion with the exception of 23 Infantry Division to the south-east of the beachhead in the central Luzon plain and its supporting 58 Independent Mixed Brigade twenty-five miles to the north of Lingayen Gulf. Yamashita's inability to cope with General MacArthur's swift moves, his desired reaction to the deception measures, the guerrillas, and General Kenney's aircraft combined to place the Japanese in an impossible situation.

'The enemy was forced into a piecemeal commitment of his troops. The Japanese 10 and 105 Divisions in the Manila area which were to secure Highway No. 5 on the eastern edge of the Luzon plain failed to arrive in time. The brunt of defending this withdrawal road to the north fell to 2 Japanese Armoured Division, which seemingly should have been defending the road to Clark Field.

'General MacArthur had deployed a strong portion of his assault force in his left or eastern flank to provide protection for the beachhead against the strong Japanese forces to the north and east.

'In appreciation of the enemy's predicament 6 Army immediately launched its advance towards Manila across the bend of the Agno, which presumably should have been a strongly held Japanese defence line.

'The troops met with little resistance until they approached Clark Field. The I Corps, commanded by Major-General Innis P. Swift, had heavy fighting on the east flank, where the Japanese were strongly entrenched in hill positions. For the time being they were to be held there to keep the supply-line for the advance on Manila secure.'

General Eichelberger

Japanese attempts to move by sea had been as ill-fated as their scurryings on land.

We left Manila on 8 November. As the enemy outnumbered us considerably, we put off our departure for two hours and did not leave port until nearly noon. On the 9th, towards three in the afternoon, we learnt that a twin-engined American aircraft was approaching us, but nothing happened. Suddenly, towards 5 p.m., we were attacked by Lockheed fighters, which appeared from behind the mountains. We had just entered the Gulf of Ormoc. The planes dived at us vertically, peppering us with machine-gun bullets and shells; then they dropped their bombs. One of these fell beside my ship, the *Kashi Maru*, and upset the whole of the electric system. At the second attack—I was the officer on duty—they came straight for the bridge. On my right, a soldier and the cadet Akiguchi were wounded: one seriously, the other slightly. Corporal Kimura was killed near the funnel while he was firing the anti-aircraft gun, as well as two soldiers who were manning the machine-guns. Many soldiers were seriously wounded and the funnel of the ship was pierced by forty-six shells.

Four Lockheeds and B-25s took part in the fourth attack, but no damage was done. The sun had gone down and night was beginning to fall. I was on the look-out. There was no light on the bridge. The waters of the sea around us were tinted with blood, and a few wounded men were floating on them. I arranged for Kimura's possessions to be packed up and told the doctor to cut off the little finger of his left hand and pull out two of his teeth, in order to send them to his family. The finger was cremated, and the next day we dropped his body overboard in the open sea off Ormoc.

We were told that the port of Ormoc was a veritable hell. Orders were given to land on the shore, a kilometre to the south, and disembark the men there, but the boats which had been prepared for this operation had all been cast on to the sands by the hurricane of the previous day.

We knew that we would be attacked at dawn and we found ourselves in an unpleasant situation. At last, towards three in the morning, we put the men ashore in the coastguard vessels. This operation was completed at 7 a.m. All that was left to be done was to land the ammunition, but for that purpose we would have to use the launches. This was impossible, and we decided, therefore, to return to Manila. The ship sailed about 10.40 a.m. When we arrived at the spot where the enemy had attacked us the day before, our planes and the Lockheeds started a dog-fight in the clouds just above us. We realized the danger and steamed off as rapidly as possible. In vain—through my field-glasses I could clearly pick out thirty B-25s on their way back from a raid . . .; they were flying towards us.

They advanced rapidly parallel to our convoy, flew over our bows and attacked us from starboard in pairs. The first couple were shot down, and crashed in flames into the sea. But the ship was shaken by the bombs which were falling all round us. The second time, two B-25s attacked the bridge with 13 mm. machine-guns. Bullets whistled round our ears. With the third wave two machines almost grazed our funnel as they dropped their bombs. Then there was a fourth attack: four bombers, splitting up into two groups, made for our bows and our stern. The first bomb fell on the first section, the second on the first hatchway; the fourteen men under the command of Kishimoto were reduced to pulp. The bomb which fell into the hatchway set fire to one hundred and eighty cans of petrol. In the stern of the boat, near the sixth hatchway, there was a hole big enough to have let a horse pass through. Another bomb shook up the cases of mortar ammunition, which exploded. Sergeant Fujimoto and Corporal Minato were killed on the spot, and the fire spread to other cases of ammunition on the bridge. The vessel was beginning to break in two, and the captain gave the order to abandon ship.

As I could not swim, I gave up the idea of saving my life. Nevertheless, so as to obey orders I went on to the bridge, wearing my life-saving jacket and carrying my flask, the bag containing my toilet things, with my sword at my side. The ship was now a mass of flame and the enemy planes continued to pepper this furnace with their machine-guns. There was nothing left now to protect me from the bullets. I lit a cigarette.

I ordered the soldiers, who were running distractedly in all directions, to throw everything that could float into the sea. They heaved boards and casks overboard, while the ship began to sink.

The captain came and asked me to abandon ship. I went back to the bows, where I saw the dead bodies of Fujimoto and Minato, and I watched the soldiers jumping into the sea. It was to that part of the bridge I used to come and dream of my native village while I watched the stars. Finally, remembering the captain's orders, I jumped overboard last of all, for I did not want to make myself ridiculous, even though my rank was not very high. When a ship goes down it is the rule that the men who cannot swim jump in first, so as to get as far away as possible from the whirlpool which sucks down everything. But I had men under my command, so I did not want to be the first to jump. I knew that Kumiko would be proud to know that I had died nobly.

The soldiers had all left the bridge and the ship was keeling over. I slid down, holding on to a rope, having covered my hands with the cotton gloves I had prepared. I had quite forgotten that I could not swim. I had done my duty. From the water I looked at the ship and I saw, just above my head, her name: *Kashi Maru*. As I tried to paddle, I heard a voice calling to me: 'Hi, sir. Hi, sir!' I called back, 'Yes', and started to move my arms and legs again, but I made no headway. I thought this was very peculiar and turned round. Then I saw Sasugawa, who was holding on to my sword with both hands. I called to him: 'I can't swim!' 'It doesn't matter,' he replied. Floating on my back, I attempted to get away from the ship, so as not to be sucked down by the whirlpool. A little farther on I came upon Lieutenant Shimokura, who was holding on to a big board. He called to us, telling us to join him. He could not swim either. All three of us held on to the board and began to paddle. But the petrol flowing from the ship encircled us. We had been floating for less than ten minutes when I had the impression that the surface of the water was lit up and slowly the oil began to burn. The sea was transformed into a sheet of flame. So as not to be burnt alive we tried to go forward against the wind, but the fire spread so quickly that it singed our faces. I thought: 'This is the end. . . . I don't mind dying here.' I had all the photographs of my loved ones on me; I did not care.

When the fire reached the sixth hatchway there was a tremendous explosion. Boards and scraps of iron were thrown up to the sky. The resultant blast extinguished the fire. It was then that we had to struggle away with all our strength. Then the oil began to burn again, but by this time we were already far and I felt relieved.

Towards 2 p.m. we reached a cargo boat transporting troops and we were thrown ropes and taken aboard. When night fell we were given a bowl of rice, and then we stretched ourselves out in a lifeboat. I was so tired that I was unable to sleep or even to think. At last I dozed off in my soaking clothes.

A Japanese officer

New Landing: the Drive to Manila

At dawn on 31 January I was aboard the command ship *Spencer* with General Swing and Admiral Fechteler. Visibility was excellent, and from the deck we could see both the white beaches of Nasugbu and the green mountains of Luzon. Destroyers and rocket-firing L.C.I.s pounded the shore for an hour, and on the landing-craft, to quote the graphic phrase of a service report, 'stomach butter-flies nervously flapped their wings'.

Then the landing-craft went in, and the troops waded ashore in shallow water. There was sporadic machine-gun fire and some artillery fire. But it was quickly evident the Japanese intended to follow their usual pattern—little defence at the beachhead and tough defence at prepared positions in the hills. By 9.45 that morning the town of Nasugbu and the important airstrip were ours.

The 11 Airborne troops must have dragged their feet as they passed through the town on their way to the hills. Nasugbu was almost untouched by war, and it was the only town of any consequence they had seen in the Pacific. There was a tremendous welcome; Filipinos lined the streets and gave away such precious and hoarded food stocks as eggs, chickens, bananas, papayas. There was a village square and a bandstand, and a lot of cheering and chatter. But 11 Airborne moved on and reached a huge, sprawling sugar *central* about six miles to the east. The Japanese had intended to destroy this combined industrial plant and warehouse, and a seven-man demolition squad was assigned to the job. A stray de-stroyer shell discouraged them, and they retired without setting off their explosives.

At the *central* the Americans found a Lilliputian railroad. It had narrow tracks and cars about the size of a living-room sofa, and it had been used, in peace-time, to transport sugar to the coast. The tiny locomotives burned alcohol, and we captured six thousand gallons to fuel them. The miniature rail-way was immediately put to work hauling supplies and soldiers inland.

Three hours after the initial landing I decided, because of the limited resistance, that we would hit and not run, and ordered the floating reserve to be put ashore. Indeed, so speedy was the advance inland that the Navy had to chase the Army to turn over command. General Swing remembers that in that afternoon he espied a very dusty jeep approaching his command-post near the Palico River bridge. A very dusty Admiral Fechteler was the passenger.

'Thank God I've caught you, Joe,' said the Admiral. 'Thought I might have to chase you all the way to Manila. I'm tired of playing hare-and-hounds in a jeep. Please take over and let me get back to my ships.'

. . . . I went ashore early on the second day and motored to the front. I found the troops fighting at the picturesque Cariliao-Aiming-Batulao defile. Here the highway passes between three mountain peaks—Mount Cariliao, Mount Batulao, and Mount Aiming—and the Japanese had prepared this ideal defensive terrain for their first determined stand. The battle had begun in the moonlight, and was being waged hotly at midday. The highway was bracketed by enemy artillery fire. There were dugouts and caves in and between the three wooded mountains, and they were interconnected by trenches. There were deep tank traps across the road; our adversaries did not realize how quickly bulldozers could fill the excavations.

11 Airborne was living up to its reputation. The troops stood up unflinchingly under artillery fire and performed flawlessly. In twenty-eight hours ashore they had advanced nineteen miles on foot. All combat equipment had been unloaded, a port and an airstrip had been established. I was satisfied that the dash on Manila should be undertaken and, after a conference with General Swing, personally gave the order for the parachute drop on Tagaytay Ridge. I set it for 3 February, two days away.

The Battle of the Peaks was to continue through 2 and 3 February. This engagement was of vital importance to the monumental bluff we were running against the Japanese. Our vehicles went roaring up and down the road, raising never-ending clouds of dust. By the generous use of what artillery we had, by our heavy and confident assaults, by repeated strikes from the air, we gave the enemy the impression that a force of army proportions—complete with an armoured division—was invading southern Luzon. This impression was not lessened by the fact that American radio announced the news that '8 Army' had landed there.

We numbered, even when four more battalions later joined us by air, only about seventy-eight hundred men. Actually the task-force was a small light division, understrength and even undermanned. There had been no replacements for our Leyte losses. But if we were to capitalize on our bluff we had to crack the line in front of us. Otherwise the confused Nipponese would come back out of the hills, cut our supply route, and isolate us.

Air support at this time—it was to dry up when we were engaged in even heavier fighting at the outskirts of Manila—was expert and heartening. A-20s of the 3rd Attack Group were coming over low and dropping parachute bombs just ahead of our soldiers. P-38s were blasting enemy positions near the village of Aga. I remember an unidentified and mysterious civilian, wearing a handsome monogrammed silk shirt, who warned me he had recently visited Aga and that there were thirty thousand troops there. I asked him, somewhat acidly, if he recommended I retreat. My answer was a blank look. It should be remembered that at this time I had four small battalions—and one of them was at the rear guarding the base at Nasugbu.

. . . . We were ready for the dash on Manila. Thousands of Japanese remained in the hills around us, but they were so demoralized they did not attempt aggressive action for many days. I pressed forward with the infantry, and my headquarters was set up in what had once been the annexe of the Manila Hotel. It was a bare and looted building, but the view was just the way I remembered it. And just as beautiful.

I could see the city of Manila gleaming whitely in the sunshine. I could see Corregidor, and the hook of the Cavite peninsula, which curves into Manila Bay. In another direction I could see Balayan and Batangas Bays on the sea, and, inland, Lake Taal in the crater of an extinct volcano and the shimmer of Laguna de Bay. It was strangely like a homecoming. But soon tall plumes of smoke began to rise in Manila, and at evening the tropical sky was crimsoned by many fires. The Japanese were deliberately destroying the magical town which had been traditionally called the 'Pearl of the Orient'.

. . . . At ten o'clock that night, after an exciting jeep ride, I set up my head-quarters in Parañaque, the entrance to Manila. Our gamble had been successful. Four days after landing at Nasugbu we had a beachhead—as someone has described it—'sixty-nine miles long and five hundred yards wide', and we had penetrated the right flank of the Genko Line.

At five the next morning we crossed the partially destroyed bridge at Parañaque, and I made the official announcement to G.H.Q. that we were in Manila. There had been fighting all night near the bridge, and Colonel I. R. Schimmelpfennig, the 11 Airborne's beloved chief of staff, had been killed by machine-gun fire. Earlier that day he had promised amiably to bring my toilet kit forward from the Manila Hotel annexe. He kept his promise. When they found him, my safety razor was still in his pocket.

For an outfit without heavy guns and heavy equipment necessary to breach a line there was hard fighting ahead. My headquarters was a building on Manila Bay which had been used as a Japanese hospital and is now the Malibu Beach Club. During my five days there, when not actually up forward, I could watch the fighting at Nichols Field from the building's cupola. All the Japanese guns along Dewey Boulevard down to the Manila Hotel kept us under constant fire, and there was never a quiet moment.

On 7 February General MacArthur announced that Manila was secured—although some weeks of fighting were to follow before the last Japanese defenders could be liquidated. On 9 February I returned to 8 Army headquarters in Leyte to push the campaign in the central and southern Philippines. Next day command of 11 Airborne passed to 6 Army.

I like to recall one story about the spirit of Joe Swing's irrepressible para-troopers. In the thick of the struggle for Manila they found that the outer rim of the enemy's position was protected by 5-inch naval guns, removed by the Japanese from warships and mounted at strategic spots. Hard pressed and under heavy bombardment, a company commander passed on the information to headquarters in this message:

'Tell Bill Halsey to stop looking for the Jap fleet. It's dug in on Nichols Field.'

General Eichelberger

*The 8 Army's extraordinary activity in the conquest of the Philippines epito-
mizes the great achievements of all American forces in the Pacific war.*

8 Army set up an all-time record for swift amphibious movements during
its Victor Operations. There has never been another army just like it. 8 Army
took over the island of Leyte on Christmas Day. It had fifty-two D-days between
that date and the Japanese surrender. In one forty-four-day period alone these
troops conducted fourteen major landings and twenty-four minor ones, thus
rolling up an average of a landing every day and a half. There was never a time,
during this action-packed interlude, when some task-force of my command was
not fighting a battle. And most of the time, hundreds of miles apart, separate
task-forces were fighting separate battles simultaneously.

8 Army fought on Leyte, on Luzon, on Palawan and the Zamboanga
Peninsula, on Panay and Bohol and Negros, on Mindanao, Mindoro, and
Marinduque, on Cebu and Capul and Samar. And on a score of smaller islands
which even now are remembered by most G.I.s only as 'faraway places with
strange-sounding names'. These separate battles—though sometimes bewilder-
ing to the troops themselves—were all logical pieces in the jigsaw puzzle of the
Philippines operation.

General Eichelberger

Murder on Panay

Enemy garrison troops, as the result of a panicky, last-minute decision, had
fled to the hills. In one instance, they found time to be thorough. At a Japanese
military hospital in an Iloilo suburb there were fifty bedridden patients. All fifty
of them were given a narcotic injection; then the Japanese set fire to the hospital.
A few of the patients escaped cremation by crawling out of the burning building
before the narcotic took effect—and that is how I know the story. The Japanese
had not been so thorough in other ways. Two-thirds of Iloilo was in ruins, but I
was able to inform General MacArthur by radio that the docks were intact and
the harbour clear.

General Eichelberger

Surrender

*Island by island the Philippines were recovered, but although the battlefront had
moved on inexorably towards the mainland of Japan, General Yamashita was still
in the field at the end of the war. He finally gave in on 25 August 1945.*

On 7 August—the day of the fall of the first atomic bomb—an American
pilot was forced to abandon his disabled plane and parachute behind the Japanese
lines in northern Luzon. He was picked up by an enemy patrol the next morning
and taken after five days of forced marches to General Yamashita's headquarters,
then south-west of Kiangan.

There he was subjected to vigorous and prolonged interrogation. He was
threatened with physical violence when he steadfastly refused to answer questions. On 16 August—the Emperor first offered to capitulate on 10 August—the

attitude of the Japanese interrogators abruptly changed. The pilot received medical treatment for his parachute-jump injuries and was extended many small courtesies. The next day the American was guided towards the American lines; when the Japanese soldiers had gone as far as they dared, they gave the flier a letter, written by Yamashita himself, which explained the circumstances of the pilot's capture and commended him for his military spirit and devotion to duty.

On 24 August the same pilot flew an L.5 liaison plane over the area in which he had been held and dropped a message of thanks to General Yamashita and two signal panels of great visibility. The message, written by General Gill of 32 Division, suggested that if Yamashita were in the mood for surrender negotiations he should display the two signal panels as evidence of his willingness to parley. The following morning another pilot found the panels staked out according to instruction; also on the ground were many cheering, hand-waving Japanese soldiers, who beckoned the plane to land. Instead, a second message was dropped. It suggested that Yamashita send an envoy to the American lines to receive detailed instructions for his surrender.

Late in the afternoon of 26 August a Japanese captain, carrying Yamashita's answer, entered the American lines under a flag of truce. The letter, which was written in English, follows:

General Headquarters
Imperial Japanese Army in the Philippines
25 August 1945

To:
General W. H. Gill,
Commanding-General Kiangan-Boyombong Area,
United States Army in the Philippines

1. I have the honour to acknowledge receipt of your communication addressed to me, dropped by your airplane on 24 August as well as your papers dropped on 25 August in response to our ground signals.

2. I am taking this opportunity to convey to you that order from Imperial Headquarters pertaining to cessation of hostilities was duly received by me on 20 August and that I have immediately issued orders to cease hostilities to all units under my command insofar as communications were possible. I also wish to add to this point the expression of my heartfelt gratitude to you, fully cognizant of the sincere efforts and deep concern you have continuously shown with reference to cessation of hostilities as evidenced by various steps and measures you have taken in this connexion. To date of writing, however, I have failed to receive order from Imperial Headquarters authorizing me to enter into direct negotiations here in the Philippines with the United States Army concerning the carrying out of the order for cessation of hostilities, but I am of the fond belief that upon receipt of this order, negotiations can be immediately entered into. Presenting my compliments and thanking you for your courteous letter. I remain, yours respectfully,

(Signed) T. Yamashita

Tomoyuki Yamashita, General, Imperial Japanese Army,
Highest Commander of the Imperial Japanese Army in the Philippines.

Our defeat at Leyte was tantamount to the loss of the Philippines. When you took the Philippines, that was the end of our resources.

Admiral Yonai, Japanese Navy Minister

THE FINAL BLOWS

Iwo Jima

Although in a hopeless position, the Japanese would not admit defeat. The island of Iwo Jima in the Bonin group lay across the path of the American long-range bombers which were pounding Japan from the Marianas, and its capture was essential if the air assault was to be fully effective. On 19 February 1945 American amphibious forces landed, to face over a month of the most savage and bloody fighting they had encountered so far.

Reflecting on the thirty-six days of unrelenting effort needed to crush the Japanese on Iwo Jima, Admiral Spruance concluded that 'in view of the character of the defences and the stubborn resistance encountered, it is fortunate that less seasoned or less resolute troops were not committed'.

The struggle raged on eight square miles of barren volcanic ash and soft rock newly formed from volcanic mud. Iwo Jima is less than a half century old, having only recently risen up from the sea. Its terrain features are wrinkled and jumbled, and this plus more than twenty thousand Japanese troops made its seizure hell for the marines. Only in one respect, despite its semi-tropical latitude, did it fall short of ideal for the defenders. The island was still growing and fissures of steam caused by subterranean heat were evident. Surely the enemy was hot, for he was dug in.

. . . . The capture of Iwo is the classical amphibious assault of recorded history. In this operation the Japanese managed to take a toll of American casualties equal to their own dead, a feat not earlier accomplished nor later repeated. Three reinforced marine divisions attached to V Amphibious Corps and led by Major-General Harry Schmidt were employed, the largest body of marines ever brought under a single tactical marine command. 4 and 5 Marine Divisions landed in beach assault, followed by 3 Marine Division in support; but the terrain was such that the fighting seldom varied, on the beach or inshore. There was little cover. Iwo was, in effect, all beach. Defences were so skilfully arranged and so expertly manned that despite the tremendous impact gained on hitting the coast, little momentum was achieved after the first two days of fighting. Iwo was taken by marines and by their demolitions and flamethrowers; the men inched forward in tanks or crawled on their stomachs, seldom seeing an enemy in the flesh and alive.

. . . . After 18 February, most of the support rendered the marines was neutralizing rather than destructive in effect. It was largely up to tanks and rifle and demolition assault squads to seize the island gun by gun, pillbox by pillbox, and blockhouse by blockhouse. While concurring that the final arbiter of battle is the man with a rifle, to a far greater degree than was necessary, taking Iwo Jima was like throwing human flesh against reinforced concrete.

Radio Tokyo announced eight days after the assault on Iwo Jima began that the American portion of the island was 'not more than the size of the forehead of.a cat'. Figuratively, this statement was too true for the comfort of the marines. By that time, upwards of seventy thousand men and many thousand tons of equipment and supplies had poured ashore. These were crowded on to the waist of the island, and it was hard for Japanese rockets, artillery, and mortars to miss.

.... No marine on Iwo had anything but respect for Nipponese marksmanship. 'Whenever a man showed himself in the lines it was almost certain death,' testified one battalion commander.

.... Mottled and naked, Suribachi resembled the head of a fabulous serpent, with fangs ejecting poison in all directions from its base. Surrounding the cone of Suribachi was harder than scaling the summit. The Japanese were in several hundred emplacements, principally pillboxes, blockhouses, covered guns, and grottoes around the base of the mountain, giving way to intricately constructed tiers of caves along the slopes.

'Harry the Horse' Liversedge and the 28th Marines of 5 Division began their attack against Suribachi itself early on the morning of 20 February. Tanks, flamethrowers, rockets, and demolitions were used, and after more than three days of hard fighting the mountain was encircled by noon, 23 February. Four hours earlier, the first American flag was raised on Suribachi. This was a small flag from a ship's boat, and raising it aloft on a short section of Japanese pipe found on the spot was the idea of some of the men who made the assault to the crest. Then at thirty-seven minutes past ten o'clock, the first flag was replaced by a larger one, erected on a more substantial staff. . . . Unfurling the larger and more visible flag was an event which increased the confidence of all hands and provided a picture which stirred the country.

Okinawa

The last and greatest of the island assaults was launched on 1 April against Okinawa in the Ryukyu archipelago. Okinawa lay only three hundred and fifty miles from Japan. From here, aircraft of any size could reach and batter the cities and factories of the homeland. Its harbours offered fine fleet anchorages. It was a perfect springboard for the invasion of Japan itself, if this became necessary, and whoever possessed it commanded all the waters round Japan most vital to her survival. Not surprisingly, both sides committed all their available resources to the battle. By the end of the battle, eighty-two days after the first landing, about four hundred and fifty thousand American ground troops had been poured into the island, of whom fifty thousand became casualties. The garrison of over a hundred thousand of Japan's finest troops was almost completely annihilated. The Japanese flung in suicide aircraft in reckless, unprecedented numbers, sacrificed the last of their air force, and also immolated the remaining vestiges of their naval power, in the shape of the battleship Yamato. *The* kamikazes *succeeded in sinking or damaging four hundred Allied vessels.*

Okinawa was defended with a fury equalled only by the defence of London. For reckless disregard of human life, Okinawa's defence by the Japanese is unparalleled in history. The charge at Balaclava was a paltry sacrificial offering in comparison with the Divine Wind of the suicide *kamikazes*.

The task-force assignment was to support the landings of the Marines and 10 Army on Okinawa and adjacent islands. To carry out this assignment, Mitscher planned strikes against fields on Kyushu, and on the Amami and Minami Daito groups. In addition, the force was to give air support to the troops ashore. Every man on the staff knew that the task force was shackled to Okinawa. 'There was nothing to do but take it—the suicide attack—and fight back like hell,' Mitscher said later at a Press conference.

The *kamikazes* were bad enough, but on 21 March, Admiral Clark reported the Japanese had a new weapon. Two dozen fighters from his group were launched to intercept a flock of bogeys and shot down thirty-two Bettys and about half that number of single-engined planes. The twin-engined Bettys were slower than usual and somehow looked odd. Intelligence photos revealed a small plane or winged bomb carried under each fuselage. This was the first appearance of what Allied forces called the *Baka* bomb, '*Baka*' being the Japanese word for 'fool'. It was a 'guided missile' employing a young suicide pilot instead of an electronic brain. Apparently the Imperial Command was now committed to *hara-kiri* on a mass basis.

Theodore Taylor

Yamato Sunk

.... On 6 April an estimated four hundred *kamikazes* visited Task Force 58, and an estimated 233 of them were splashed by fighters. Perhaps ninety more fell to ships' guns. On the same day the *Yamato* left Tokuyama, in the Inland Sea, bound for Okinawa on a suicide mission. Few of her crew, according to Japanese accounts, felt they would live past 8 April, her estimated time of arrival off Okinawa. With the battleship was a cruiser and eight destroyers. A submarine reported them in Bungo Channel, between Kyushu and Shikoku.

.... At dawn, Mitscher's search planes fanned out over the sea east of Kyushu. The weather was squally. Meanwhile, both submarines and flying boats had been tracking the oncoming enemy force. Down in the ready rooms, the pilots were impatient. Word of the friendly rivalry with the battleship guns had reached them. The pilots had heard that Admiral Mitscher 'planned to ram this one through'.

'We knew we'd get it for him if he gave us the chance and we thought he would,' said Major Long.

A few minutes after 08.00 one of Admiral Clark's *Essex* search planes found the suicide fleet, steaming southward. The report was relayed back to the *Bunker Hill* by a series of communications linking planes, another Mitscher innovation for the task force, introduced because of the relatively short range of aircraft radios. It fanned out to all the task groups and to Admiral Spruance, who ordered Deyo to push his battleship fleet to the attack. At the same time Mitscher had sent off a force of sixteen planes to cover and track the approaching enemy, but it would be more than an hour before they could make contact. Planes were manned, and as soon as the search aircraft disappeared, Mitscher gave orders to attack the Japanese fleet. It was now 10.00. As the planes, from groups 58.1 and 58.2, orbited, joined up, and sped away, the Admiral watched in silence. A few minutes after they were out of sight, he turned to Burke.

'Inform Admiral Spruance that I propose to strike the *Yamato* sortie group at 12.00 unless otherwise directed.'

'But,' said a British observer, 'you have launched before you can possibly be sure of their location.'

'We are taking a chance,' explained Burke, 'we are launching against the spot where we would be if we were the *Yamato*.'

Actually, with submarines, flying boats, and carrier-based aircraft on the *Yamato*'s trail, the chances of finding the enemy were good, even though the weather was thick. But if the planes could not find her, there wouldn't be enough red paint in the fleet to match the colour of Mitscher's face. His launch order to destroy the enemy fleet by aircraft ran contrary to Spruance's desire to let the battleships slug it out in what would probably be the last opportunity for a big-ship gunnery fight, then and forever more.

From 10.00 until noon, Mitscher's position there on the wing of the *Bunker Hill* bridge was thoroughly uncomfortable. As time stretched by, there was still no signal from Spruance countermanding Mitscher's orders. At last the planes were so close to the *Yamato* that recall would serve no purpose except to save a few dollars' worth of fuel. The Avengers carried torpedoes; the dive bombers (Curtiss Helldivers) carried mixed loads of 1,000- and 250-lb. bombs; each fighter had a 500-lb. bomb as well as a long-range droppable fuel tank. Estimated distance to the target was two hundred and forty miles.

Shortly after noon, planes from the Clark and Sherman task groups found the Japanese fleet and circled it for the kill. The weather was still bad, with clouds ranging from fifteen hundred to three thousand feet, and intermittent rain. The low ceiling and large number of planes—nearly three hundred arrived simultaneously—made co-ordination impossible. Heavy ack-ack began bursting. Even the *Yamato*'s 18-inch guns were elevated to attempt blasting the Yankees from the sky.

The weather made it impossible to see results, and Japanese jamming made it impossible to hear over the voice radio.

. . . . However confused the Americans were, the Japanese were worse. A *Yamato* gunnery officer who survived told American interrogators that the combination of dive bombers and torpedo planes made it impossible to take evasive action. The first two waves, he said, left three bomb hits forward of the great turret on her stern, and three torpedo hits in the hull. In later attacks she was hit by at least seven more torpedoes, according to his account.

At any rate, when Admiral Radford's strike group, which was launched late, arrived, the *Yamato* was listing, and his planes struck her on the high side. She finally blew up and sank, joining the cruiser *Yahagi* and four destroyers on the bottom. Photographs were handed Mitscher showing the sinking while Admiral Deyo was just getting well into his northward charge with the old battleships. A short while later, after Mitscher had signalled that the enemy had been met and dealt with, Spruance countermanded the previous order sending the ships to destroy the Japanese fleet.

When Admiral Deyo got word of Mitscher's successful attack, he good-naturedly broadcast regrets that his force wouldn't have 'Japanese scrambled eggs for breakfast'. Mitscher's losses were four bombers, three torpedo planes, and three fighters. Personnel losses were held to four pilots and eight aircrewmen by virtue of quick rescue work.

Theodore Taylor

The End on Okinawa

17 June. Admiral Minoru Ota, Commander Naval Base Force, was found with his throat cut, sitting in a ceremonial pose in a cave in the 4th Marines' zone on the Oroku Peninsula.

18 June. Lieutenant-General S. B. Buckner was killed by enemy shell-fire while observing an attack.

19 June. The collapse of Japanese defences was evident across the entire line. At 04.40/1 [Okinawa time] Major-General Roy S. Geiger, U.S.M.C., assumed command *vice* the late General Buckner.

20 June. Civilians surrendered in masses.

21 June. Major-General Geiger announced that organized resistance had ceased.

27 June. The bodies of Lieutenant-General Ushijima and Lieutenant-General Cho, Commanding General and Chief of Staff of the Japanese forces on Okinawa, were found with indisputable evidence of *hara-kiri*.

Admiral Halsey, war diary

Alas! The stars of the generals have fallen with the setting of the waning moon. . . .

Gathered around their chiefs, members of each section bow in veneration towards the eastern sky and the cheer of 'Long Live the Emperor' echoes among the boulders. . . . The faces of all are flushed with deep emotion and tears fall upon ragged uniforms, soiled with the dirt and grime of battle. . . .

Four o'clock, the final hour of *hara-kiri*; the Commanding General, dressed in full field uniform, and the Chief of Staff in a white kimono, appeared. . . . The Chief of Staff says as he leaves the cave first:

'Well, Commanding General Ushijima, as the way may be dark, I, Cho, will lead the way.'

The Commanding General replies, 'Please do so, and I'll take along my fan since it is getting warm.' Saying this he picked up his Okinawa-made fan and walked out quietly fanning himself. . . .

The moon, which had been shining until now, sinks below the waves of the western sea. Dawn has not yet arrived and, at 04.10, the generals appeared at the mouth of the cave. The American forces were only three metres away.

A sheet of white cloth is placed on a quilt. . . . The Commanding General and the Chief of Staff sit down on the quilt, bow in reverence to the eastern sky, and Adjutant J—— respectfully presents the sword. . . .

At this time several grenades were hurled near this solemn scene by the enemy troops who observed movements taking place beneath them. A simultaneous shout and a flash of a sword, then another repeated shout and a flash, and both generals had nobly accomplished their last duty to their Emperor.

A Japanese eye-witness

Though with the last arrow gone,
My blood dyes heaven and earth,
My spirit shall return, shall return
To defend the motherland.

> Poem left by Lieutenant-General Ushijima,
> G.O.C. Okinawa, before committing suicide

Japanese Survivors

We secured at 21.10, and I went down to the brig with Bill Kluss for a look at three Jap flyers who had been picked out of the drink early this morning by the destroyer *Melvin*. A Marine guard admitted us. The prisoners were in separate cells. When they spotted our collar insignia they stood up, and I saw that all three were young and quite small. One, an ensign, had a slight wound in his cheek; the others, enlisted men, seemed unharmed. Bill interrogated them in Japanese, but the ensign could read and write a bit of English, because the guard showed me a pad which he had been using for an interrogation of his own.

He had written: 'My name Richard. I am Marine. Why you fight us?'

The answer, in a laborious hand, was as despondent as it was evasive: 'I no win.'

On the next page the guard had written: 'You know B-29?'

The Jap ensign had sketched one extremely well; its characteristic tail was especially accurate. The bomb bay was open, and bombs were falling. The caption was: 'Tokyo burn.' Also on this page was a sketch of a Pete, a Jap float-plane. 'He says he flew 'em,' the guard explained.

He had written on the third page, 'We treat you good,' but the ensign had not made a comment.

> Lieutenant-Commander J. Bryan III

In the spring and summer of 1945 the American carrier fleets, supported by a British task force, were continually at sea. The fast carriers mustered twelve hundred aircraft, which incessantly assailed Japan, Formosa and any shipping they could find. The Japanese submarine fleet, like the rest of the Imperial Navy, had almost ceased to exist, but scored one last success with the sinking of the U.S. heavy cruiser Indianapolis *on 29 July.*

As soon as we were fully submerged I gave the orders—'Ship in sight'—'All tubes to be ready'—'*Kaitens** stand by.' It was 11.8 p.m. After diving we had altered course to port and the black shape was now right ahead. I was still watching through the periscope, from time to time scanning the rest of the field of view but there was nothing else in sight. Gradually the supposed enemy seemed to be getting closer. We were ready to give a salvo of six torpedoes. The dark shape continued on a course which was bringing it straight towards us. Was it a destroyer coming on for a depth-charge attack, having already detected our existence? Even if it was not, it would be difficult to score a torpedo hit if it came straight on over the top of us. I had some bad moments when thinking it might be a destroyer. In the darkness of the conning-tower it was impossible to tell the

---

* Human torpedoes (Ed.)

colour of the people's faces and if the others detected that the captain was feeling uneasy, they could only surmise this from his voice! We couldn't estimate the range as we didn't know the class of ship. We couldn't yet hear anything on the hydrophones. The round black spot gradually became triangular in shape. The time was 11.9 p.m. 'Six torpedoes will be fired.' I decided to fire from all tubes in one salvo.

.... The target began to assume the appearance of a large warship and the uppermost part of the triangular black spot had resolved itself into two portions. There was a large mast forward—'We've got her,' I thought. The fact that the enemy was now visible in two distinct portions made it less likely that she would pass right over us, and the class of ship was now apparent. I was able to assess the masthead height as ninety feet. She was either a battleship or large cruiser. The range fell to four thousand yards. The expected range at time of firing— two thousand yards—and the bearing—green forty-five degrees—were set. A hydrophone report gave the enemy speed as moderately high. I used this estimate for the moment, but visual observation didn't put it so high, and I altered the setting to twenty knots. As for the *Kaitens*, I had been so occupied with the ordinary torpedoes that I hadn't given the orders for standing by to launch, though the *Kaiten* crews kept coming to ask about it. A *Kaiten* attack at this stage of the moon would be difficult and I determined not to use them unless the ordinary torpedo attack failed.

We had the moon behind us and the enemy ship was now clearly visible. She had two turrets aft and a large tower mast. I took her to be an *Idaho* class battleship. The crew were all agog, awaiting the order to fire the torpedoes. All was dead quiet. In such circumstances the eyes of the boat were in the captain's head, and the hydrophones supplied the ears. Without him, the crew could know nothing of what was going on outside. They waited tensely for the next order. Questions kept coming from the *Kaiten* crews: 'What about the enemy?' 'Where's the enemy?' 'Why can't we be launched?' The favourable moment for firing was approaching. I altered the setting of the director to green sixty degrees, range fifteen hundred yards and began the approach for firing. At last, in a loud voice, I gave the order 'Stand by—Fire!' The torpedo-release switch pressed at intervals of two seconds and then the report came from the torpedo room, 'All tubes fired and correct.' Six torpedoes were speeding, fan-wise, towards the enemy ship. I took a quick look through the periscope, but there was nothing else in sight. Bringing the boat on to a course parallel with the enemy, we waited anxiously. Every minute seemed an age. Then on the starboard side of the enemy by the forward turret, and then by the after turret, there rose columns of water, to be followed immediately by flashes of bright red flame. Then another column of water rose from alongside Number 2 turret and seemed to envelop the whole ship—'A hit—a hit!' I shouted as each torpedo struck home and the crew danced with joy. There was still nothing else in sight and the enemy was stopped, but still afloat. I raised the day periscope and gave the conning-tower crew a sight. Soon came the sound of a heavy explosion, far greater than that of the actual hits. Three more heavy explosions followed in quick succession, then six more. The crew, not realizing the cause, were shouting 'Depth-charge attack', so I hastily reassured them that it was our target exploding and that there was no other enemy in sight. I saw several flashes aboard the enemy, but she showed no signs of sinking. I therefore stood by to give her a second salvo. From the *Kaitens* came the cry, 'As the enemy won't sink, send us.' The enemy certainly presented an easy target for them in spite of the dark, but what if she should sink before the *Kaitens* reached her? Once launched they were gone for good, and it seemed a pity to risk wasting them. I therefore decided not to use them this time. I intended to take my time, but a report came that the enemy was using her underwater detector apparatus—no doubt trying to get our range. Realizing that the enemy would get a good contact, I decided to dive deep while reloading for the second salvo, and I lowered the periscope, relying on the hydrophones and underwater detector apparatus for keeping track of the enemy. In actual fact we heard after the war that she was just on the point of sinking, but at the time this was still in doubt. We had certainly scored hits with three torpedoes, but these had so far failed to sink her. Next another report came that the sound of the detector apparatus had ceased. As we were reloading there was a list on the boat, and it would be dangerous to rise to periscope depth. As soon as reloading was completed we surfaced and raised periscope only to find there was nothing to be seen. I made for the spot where I thought she would have sunk, but still couldn't see anything. However, it was over an hour since the first action and I was certain now that she had sunk. A ship so damaged could not have got away at high speed. Even had she got away she would still have been in sight. I wanted, however, some proof that she had definitely sunk, but it was difficult to spot any flotsam in the darkness. With feelings of regret, I made off to the north-east for fear of reprisals from ships or aircraft which might have been in company with our late enemy, and after running on the surface for an hour we dived to prepare for the next encounter. The ship we had sunk turned out to be the *Indianapolis*.

Mochitsura Hashimoto

JAPAN

Only victories were broadcast. This involved such obvious contradictions that even the more simple-minded listeners became doubtful. Everyone who could think at all realized that the country was in a more and more desperate state, its back to the wall. When it became impossible to hide the truth longer, the broadcasters would announce a battle or an island lost, and each time they did so the programme was ended with music. It was always the same—the sad, sweet strains of *Umi Yukaba*, a well-loved old song. All over the nation people would bow their heads while someone quietly turned off the radio. The conviction of ultimate defeat had become widespread but everyone was careful not to speak his opinion; each carried on silently lest his doubts prevent another from doing his best.

By many little signs I knew how desperate things had become for the Japanese. I saw little boys of ten and twelve unloading the freight from the trains. Children were employed in all kinds of factory work from clothes-making to riveting aeroplane parts together; they were mobilized through their schools and taken from there to their jobs each day by the teachers.

Gwen Terasaki

28

RETURN TO BURMA

Winston Churchill's own words best sum up the position at the opposite extremity of the Japanese perimeter, when in December 1943 the Allied counter-attack was launched in this sector. The Fourteenth Army which was to drive the Japanese from Burma was commanded by General William Slim.

FOR more than eighteen months the Japanese had been masters of a vast defensive arc covering their early conquests. This stretched from the jungle-covered mountains of Northern and Western Burma, where our British and Indian troops were at close grips with them, across the sea to the Andamans and the great Dutch dependencies of Sumatra and Java, and thence in an easterly bend along the string of lesser islands to New Guinea. The Americans had established a bomber force in China which was doing good work against the enemy's sea communications between the mainland and the Philippines. They wanted to extend this effort by basing long-range aircraft to attack Japan itself. The Burma Road was cut, and they were carrying all supplies for them and the Chinese armies by air over the southern spur of the Himalayas, which they called the 'Hump'. This was a stupendous task. . . . They pressed as a matter of the highest urgency and importance the making of a motor road from the existing roadhead at Ledo through five hundred miles of jungles and mountains into Chinese territory. . . . In order to build the road to China the Americans wanted us to reconquer Northern Burma first and quickly.

. . . . I disliked intensely the prospect of a large-scale campaign in Northern Burma. One could not choose a worse place for fighting the Japanese. Making a road from Ledo to China was also an immense, laborious task, unlikely to be finished until the need for it had passed. . . . The need to strengthen the American air bases in China would also, in our view, diminish as Allied advances in the Pacific and from Australia gained us airfields closer to Japan. On both counts therefore we argued that the enormous expenditure of man-power and material would not be worth while. But we never succeeded in deflecting the Americans from their purpose.

. . . . [The campaign] opened in December 1943, when General Stilwell, with two Chinese divisions which he had organized and trained in India, crossed the watershed from Ledo into the jungles below the main mountain ranges. He was opposed by the renowned Japanese 18 Division, but forged ahead steadily, and by early January had penetrated forty miles, while the road-makers toiled behind him. In the south a British Corps began to advance down the Arakan coast of the Bay of Bengal.

Winston Churchill

The Hump

These Americans had one aim only and that was to get the war over as quickly as possible. Each one of them felt that if he could fit just one more flight into a day by reducing the time he spent on the ground, the war would be that much shorter. They were flying all day for seven days a week with little rest during their eighteen months in Burma. Every day was just twelve hours long, from six in the morning to six at night, and during this time they spent two and a half hours on the ground, unless by their own exertions they could reduce that time. Most of the flying was at ten thousand feet or higher because of the mountain ranges over which they had to fly; for these men, in the normal way, were flying over 'the hump' into China. The aircraft were not pressurized and the crew had no oxygen.

They were a tired, drawn-looking lot, unshaven and dirty. They worked and flew stripped to the waist, except for the Captain of Aircraft, who wore a scruffy bush jacket. They all lived for their work and had no interest outside it. At night they slept wherever they happened to be, while other Americans slaved during the hours of darkness to keep their aircraft in flying order. At this time two armies were being supplied by these American crews in their Commandos, supported by a few Dakotas of the R.A.F. There were never enough of them; the demands on the time and energy of both crews and machines were terrific. One would have thought that it was almost beyond their powers of endurance to meet them and yet—I was to learn later—they never failed to squeeze the last ounce of carrying capacity out of their tattered machines. Even as I stood on the edge of the field watching the aircraft swallow up the men and the mules and the baggage, amazed at the desperate energy of the crews, I realized how much the soldiers owed these men.

Arthur Campbell

ARAKAN

The Arakan, that narrow coastal strip of Burma running down from Chittagong almost to Rangoon, was a tangled mass of bamboo and jungle growing on small steep hills. The only clear-cut feature was the high Mayu range, which split in two the northern half of the strip. There was a thin belt of land between this range and the sea. Behind it lay a deep valley and beyond that the jungle, stretching for hundreds of miles to the north and to the east; to the north over the Chin Hills; to the east over unknown tracts of the Arakan Yomas falling vertically into the great Irrawaddy Plain.

A year earlier, a British attempt to recapture the port of Akyab had been repulsed by the Japanese.

We were careful in our plan to guard against the fatal errors of the 1943 campaign—attacks on narrow fronts and the neglect of an enemy outflanking counter-stroke. The intention was to advance with two divisions, not only on both sides of the Mayu range, but along its spine as well, while 81 West African

Division, moving down the Kaladan Valley well to the east, would provide a flank guard and would, I hoped, be in its turn a threat to the Japanese flank and their west to east communications.

General Slim

Parajutes

In whatever way our plans developed there would be great demands on air supply. 81 Division, Wingate's Force,* and half a dozen other commitments would moreover call for a large measure of dropping, as distinct from landing, supplies. For this we should need vast numbers of parachutes. Just as 81 Division was committed I received the unwelcome news that the despatch of parachutes from India would be much less than we had been led to expect, and would indeed fall far short of our requirements. It was useless to hope for supplies from home. We were bottom of the priority list there, for parachutes as for everything else. The position was serious. Our plans were based on large reserves of parachutes for supply dropping; if we had not got them we risked, if not disaster, at least a drastic slowing up and modification of those plans. I went for a walk in the comparative cool of the evening and did some hard thinking. Next morning I assembled Snelling and one or two of his leading air supply staff officers and explained the position. If we could not get proper parachutes of silk or other special cloth we must make them of what we could get. I believed it possible to make a serviceable supply-dropping parachute from either paper or jute. There are great paper mills in Calcutta; all the jute in the world is grown in Bengal and most of it manufactured there. I despatched officers forthwith to Calcutta to explore possibilities. The paper parachute, although I still believe it quite practicable, we could not obtain, because the manufacturers could not produce the kind of paper required in the time. With jute we were more fortunate. My assignment officer visited some of the leaders of the British jute industry in Calcutta, told them our difficulty, and asked their help. He warned them that to save time I had sent him direct and that my need was my only authority. I hoped they would be paid, but when or how I could not guarantee. The answer of these Calcutta businessmen was, 'Never mind about that! If the Fourteenth Army want parachutes they shall have them!' And have them we did. Within ten days we were experimenting with various types of 'Parajutes' as we called them. Some fell with a sickening thud; others had a high percentage of failure. By trial and error we arrived at the most efficient shape and weave for the cloth. In a month we had a parajute that was eighty-five per cent as efficient and reliable as the most elaborate parachute. It was made entirely of jute—even the ropes—and was of the simplest design. It dispensed with the vent at the top of the normal parachute as the texture of the jute cloth was such that the right quantity of air passed through it to keep the parajute expanded and stable. Instead of having one large vent it had innumerable tiny ones. It would have been risky to drop a man in a parajute, or a particularly valuable or fragile load such as a wireless set, but for ordinary supplies it worked admirably. It had in addition another advantage. The cost of a parajute was just over £1; that of a standard parachute over £20. As we used several hundreds of thousands of parachutes

* The Chindits (Ed.)

we saved the British taxpayer some millions of pounds, and, more important even than that, our operations went on. My reward was a ponderous rebuke from above for not obtaining the supply through the proper channels! I replied that I never wanted to find a more proper channel for help when in need than those Calcutta jute men.

General Slim

Dust . . .

Units erected their tiny bivouac tents among the glens east of the main road, they stretched large tarpaulins on bamboo frameworks and camouflaged their habitations as best they could. Black leeches, an inch long, sucked men's blood and had to be evicted from the flesh with a glowing cigarette end. Tracks had to be made off the road, the gunners dug their gun pits and kept on improving them, and signallers toiled up and down hills laying miles of telephone cable or carrying pack wireless sets on their backs.

The dust of the one and only road reminded veterans of certain tracks in the Desert. Each day parties of Arakanese, dressed in gaily coloured shirts and skirts called *longyis*, threw water on the road surface to subdue the billowing dust. While little boys ran up and down, having great fun with tins of water that they fetched from nearby pools or from a muddy *chaung*, the men and even their women worked on this never-ending job of repair and maintenance. Wide wicker hats shaded them from the sun that beat down on the landscape, shone upon white palm flowers waving on long stalks, and brought out the rich colours of paddy and watercourse, bamboo plant and palm tree.

. . . and Mud

Drenching rain misted the ridge of Mayu and swamped the New Year, transforming the dusty roads into such deep mud that only brigadiers and the wounded might use jeeps; all else was carried by mule, certain men rode on horseback, and the rest walked. I borrowed ponies for my linemen and dispatch riders, several of whom rode with style, having been trained as horse orderlies. Rain cascaded down the hillsides, dripped hastily from the trees and thudded upon our tents throughout these first three days of January, until the sun burned from a cloudless sky and drew steam from the sodden earth. It was during the early part of this month that, while 123 Brigade maintained their hold upon the peaks and foothills of the Mayu range, 161 Brigade under their wholly delightful commander Freddie Warren, who by his lovable personality had earned the name of 'Daddy', battered their advance among the thick-grown hillocks west from the road, and drove the enemy from Hathipauk and Point 124, a small green hillock that had offered fierce resistance.

Antony Brett-James

Each little scrub-covered hilltop had rings of trenches dug round the summit, and each was covered by the fire of at least one machine-gun from another hillock. When a particular hill was attacked by our men, the defenders would fire a red

Verey light and at once take cover. This was the signal for all other Japanese posts giving covering fire to open up with machine-guns on the post being attacked. The enemy soldiers holding the post would lob showers of grenades over the parapet, when the assaulting troops were only five or ten yards from the crest.

Antony Brett-James

Maungdaw

After two days we moved from Bakkagona into the remnants of Maungdaw, a desolation and an acrid stink for our nostrils. Among half-ruined shacks and the stronger brick buildings that had been chipped or shaken by bullet and bomb, from the cool white hospital and the prison to the *chaung* where Indian sappers worked to repair the damaged bridge, in every corner of this derelict town mingled the rotted oozings from burst tins of food, perished rubber of abandoned gas masks, dilapidated beams and rubbled bricks, with the scattered debris of our stores of a past campaign. Grass grew tall over the cracked verandas; doors and windows had vanished; even the Arakanese were absent, having removed their chattels to other villages.

Downstream, within sight of the broad Naf River and the misty hills behind Teknaf, stood the steamer station with its wooden piers bleached and mouldy; muddy water lapped at the green slime level, and the red iron hut waited empty, not hopeful of seeing again one steamer moored to this pier.

The two streets, now dusty tracks upon which eager weeds encroached, forked at the southern entrance to Maungdaw. If the form of this place seemed confused, the atmosphere was indeed deadly, as though for many months no clean wind had blown through the houses and no fresh rain fallen upon the rottenness and ruin. No trace of a bazaar could be seen, and the principal buildings alone showed how Maungdaw must have appeared before the enemy came for the first time into its midst. Only trees and weeds seemed unconcerned and living. Maungdaw was like a town of the dead, into which soldiers had brought their temporary presence and vivacity, cleaning such parts as their comfort demanded, waiting until those from further behind should take care of the place and give it a form of livelihood and spirit, when the inhabitants should return, encouraged to rebuild, retrieve and start anew, burdened at once by memory, loss and bitterness.

Antony Brett-James

The Tortoise

With Maungdaw safely in the bag, Briggs and his 5 Indian Division set about the keep of Razabil fortress—the Tortoise. This was the first time we had assaulted an elaborate, carefully prepared position that the Japanese meant to hold to the last and we expected it to be tough. It was. The attack was preceded by heavy bombing from the strategic air force and dive bombing by R.A.F. Vengeances, directed by smoke shells from the artillery. After this pounding, which left the Japanese apparently unmoved, medium and field artillery took up the task and pumped shells from their accumulated dumps into the smoking, burning, spouting hillsides. Then the guns suddenly paused and the Lee-Grant tanks roared forward, the infantry, bayonets fixed, yelling their Indian war cries, following on their tails. The Dismal Jimmies who had prophesied, one, that the tanks would never get to the line, two, that they could never climb the hills and, three, if they did the trees would so slow them up that the Japanese anti-tank guns would bump them off as sitting targets, were confounded. The tanks, lots of them—'the more you use, the fewer you lose'—crashed up the slopes and ground over the dug-in anti-tank guns. All was going well, but as the infantry passed ahead of the armour for the final assault the guns of the tanks had to cease firing for fear of hitting our own men. In that momentary pause the Japanese machine-gunners and grenadiers re-manned their slits and rat-holes. Streams of bullets swept the approaches and a cascade of bombs bounced down among our infantry. The attacks of the first three days shaved the Tortoise bare and cost us many casualties, but they did not shift the Japanese, burrowed deep into the hill, with their cunningly sited, wonderfully concealed and mutually supporting machine-guns. It was the old problem of the first World War—how to get the infantryman on to his enemy without a pause in the covering fire that kept his enemy's head down. It was solved in Arakan—and copied throughout the Fourteenth Army—by the tanks firing, first, surface-burst high explosive to clear the jungle, then delay-action high explosive to break up the faces of the bunkers thus exposed, and lastly solid armour-piercing shot as the infantry closed in. With no explosion, the last few yards were safe, if you had first-class tank gunners and infantrymen with steady nerves, who let the shot whistle past their heads and strike a few feet beyond or to one side of them. We had such tank gunners and such infantrymen—and they had the confidence in one another, even when of different races, that was needed. Gradually, bit by bit, Tortoise was nibbled away, until only in its very heart a few desperate Japanese, with a courage that, fanatical or not, was magnificent, still held out.

General Slim

> Japs on the hilltop
> Japs in the *chaung*
> Japs on the Ngakyedauk
> Japs in the *taung*
> Japs with their L. of C. far too long
> As they revel in the joys of infiltration.

But the Japanese had laid their own plans as well, and they were not defensive. In February 1944 the British advance into Arakan was halted by a bold Japanese counter-attack, aimed at capturing Chittagong—one of two prongs of a drive which aimed at no less an objective than India itself.

On the morning of the 4th, not feeling too bright myself, as I had just had my ninth daily emetine injection for dysentery, I was out at a reinforcement camp a few miles from Comilla watching a demonstration of the, to us, new lifebuoy flamethrower, when a motor-cycle despatch rider roared up with a message. It told me that the Japanese had suddenly swept down out of the blue and rushed Taung Bazaar, five or six miles in rear of 7 Division. The situation was obscure, said the signal, but it was clear that the enemy were in considerable strength.

The only thing I can think of more depressing than the effect of a series of emetine injections is the receipt of a message such as this. I had expected ample warning of the Japanese move, but this meant they had passed right round 7 Division unobserved, and were within two or three miles of the Ngakyedauk Pass and the Administrative Box, which I knew was prepared for nothing more than raids. I was angry and disappointed that all our precautions had failed to give warning of the enemy move, but, trying not to look as anxious as I felt, I quickly got back to headquarters and telephoned Christison.

.... On the 8th, I flew down to Christison's headquarters, which had been subjected to several jitter raids by parties of infiltrating Japanese. With my approval he pulled his headquarters back a couple of miles to Bawli Bazaar behind the river, where it was easier to protect. He was going to have a tough battle to fight, and it would not help if he and his staff were standing to alarm posts half the night. I knew only too well what that meant.

The situation was now fairly clear. Thanks to the Japanese habit of carrying orders and marked maps into action, we had an almost complete picture of their general plan. It was, as we would expect from them, tactically bold and based on their past experience of the effects of cutting our communications. They intended to destroy XV Corps and capture Chittagong as, it seemed, the first stage of an invasion of India.

.... The basic idea was that the British divisions, when . . . cut off, would behave as they had in the past, and, deprived of all supplies, turn to fight their way back to clear their communications. 7 Division would be destroyed as it tried to scramble to safety through the Ngakyedauk Pass. All the Japanese forces would then turn on the wretched 5 Division and annihilate it as it struggled to escape across the Naf River. Chittagong would be the next stop for the victorious Sakurai. There the local population, rallied by the Indian National Army, would rise and Bengal would lie open to the invader. The much-heralded 'March on Delhi' had begun.

The operation was planned to a strict time-table under which the total destruction of the British forces was billed to be completed in ten days. The Japanese administrative arrangements were based on capturing our supplies and our motor transport by that time, and thence onwards using them. So confident of success were they that they brought with them, in addition to a considerable artillery, units of gunners without guns to take over ours. None of our transport was to be destroyed; it was all wanted intact for the March on Delhi. The Japanese radio had evidently been issued with a copy of the programme, as for the first ten days of the battle it announced the destruction of our forces strictly in accordance with the time-table.

.... Meanwhile Kubo Force pushed north towards Goppe Bazaar, and, dropping a detachment to close the road south, turned directly west to cross the Mayu range. There was no track; the ridge was almost precipitous for a thousand feet. The Japanese, ant-like, dragged their mortars and machine-guns up the cliff and lowered them the other side, until they burst out on the main Bawli-

Maungdaw road, much to the surprise of certain administrative units peacefully pursuing their daily tasks. Bridges were blown up, camps fired on, XV Corps Headquarters harried, and for forty-eight hours 5 Division was, like the 7th, cut off from all access by road. Well might Sakurai congratulate himself on the success of his blow, while Tokyo Rose crooned seductively on the wireless that it was all over in Burma.

Actually it was just starting.

.... The Japanese knew they *had* to destroy 7 Division in the next few days and they were going to spare nothing to do it. As their reinforcements arrived they flung them to the attack on the Administrative Box or against our entrenched brigades. The fighting was everywhere hand-to-hand and desperate. The Administrative Box was our weak spot. Commanded from the surrounding hills on all sides at short range, crowded with dumps of petrol and ammunition, with mules by the hundred and parked lorries by the dozen, with administrative troops and Indian labour, life in it under the rain of shells and mortar bombs was a nightmare. Yet the flimsy defences held, held because no soldier, British, Indian, or Gurkha, would yield; they fought or they died where they stood. How some of them died will be for ever a black blot on the so often stained honour of the Japanese Army. In the moonless dark, a few hundred yelling Japanese broke into the Box and overran the main dressing station, crowded with wounded, the surgeons still operating. The helpless men on their stretchers were slaughtered in cold blood, the doctors lined up and shot, the Indian orderlies made to carry the Japanese wounded back and then murdered too. A counter-attack next morning exacted retribution, but found the hospital in a shambles, the only survivors a few wounded men who had rolled into the jungle and shammed dead.

Such an outrage only steeled the resolve of our men. Typical was the spirit of a battery of medium artillery pent up in the Box. An air pilot reported he had seen their 5-inch guns firing at a range of four hundred yards as the enemy pressed home an attack. He thought their situation desperate. A wireless signal was sent to the gunners asking how things were with them. 'Fine,' was the answer, 'but drop us a hundred bayonets!' The bayonets were dropped—and used.

.... By the middle of February the Japanese had shot their bolt; a week later Hanaya accepted defeat and, too late, attempted to pull out his disorganized units. Under cover of suicide detachments, who hung on to the last, Sakurai Force broke up into small groups and took to the jungle. But our 7 Division had already passed to the offensive, the 5th was battering through the Ngakyedauk Pass, which was fully opened on the 24th, and from the north swept down, on both sides of the ridge, 26 and 36 Divisions. The hammer and the anvil met squarely, and the Japanese between them disintegrated. Kubo Force, among the cliffs and caves of the Mayu range, was destroyed to the last man in a snarling, tearing dog-fight that lasted days, with no quarter given or expected. Of Sakurai's seven thousand men who had penetrated our lines, over five thousand bodies were found and counted; many more lay undiscovered in the jungle; hundreds died of exhaustion before they reached safety; few survived. The March on Delhi via Arakan was definitely off!

.... This Arakan battle, judged by the size of the forces engaged, was not of great magnitude, but it was, nevertheless, one of the historic successes of

British arms. It was the turning point of the Burma campaign. For the first time a British force had met, held, and decisively defeated a major Japanese attack, and followed this up by driving the enemy out of the strongest possible natural positions that they had prepared for months and were determined to hold at all costs. British and Indian soldiers had proved themselves, man for man, the masters of the best the Japanese could bring against them. The R.A.F. had met and driven from the sky superior numbers of the Japanese Air Force equipped with their latest fighters. It was a victory, a victory about which there could be no argument, and its effect, not only on the troops engaged, but on the whole Fourteenth Army, was immense. The legend of Japanese invincibility in the jungle, so long fostered by so many who should have known better, was smashed.

General Slim

THE CHINDITS

The British also planned an advance into northern Burma from Assam in conjunction with General Stilwell's drive to re-open communications with China, but the Japanese were to forestall this with the second and more dangerous prong of their 'March on Delhi'. Part of the British offensive plan was to throw several independent brigades behind the Japanese lines by forced marches and by air, cutting the Japanese communications near Indaw and so dislocating their supply system and drawing off troops facing the Fourteenth Army and Stilwell. The imminence of the Japanese offensive did not change the plan for the descent of the Chindits, as the raiders under their leader Orde Wingate were nicknamed, and it duly took place in February and March. The Chindits established themselves in a jungle stronghold which they named 'White City' from the multitude of supply parachutes which soon festooned the trees.

Training

We moved to the jungles of Central India for our training which consisted of hard living, learning our weapons and infantry jungle tactics of a specialized nature. To many of the older gunners the arrival of ponies and mules perhaps in some ways compensated for the loss of our guns; in fact, after our campaign it was found a harder task for the limber gunner to say goodbye to his mule than it was to see his gun returned to ordnance. Our future role would be to march and work behind the Japanese forward elements, and we were told that our line of approach would be from the north, where the enemy was believed to be weak. ....The equipment carried by every officer and man was substantially the same. We were 'self-contained', each man wearing web equipment with large pack containing all personal belongings, two grenades, ammunition for automatics and Brens, mess tins and five days' rations—'American Ks'. An average pack weighed between seventy-five and eighty pounds.

As our training progressed 'the jungle became our friend'. In open country we felt insecure and uncertain. And at the end of three months we were considered fit for the tasks ahead of us.

Lieutenant-Colonel R. C. Sutcliffe

Take-off

On the morning of Sunday, 5 March, I circled the landing ground at Haila-kandi. Below me, at the end of the wide brown air-strip, was parked a great flock of squat, clumsy gliders, their square wing tips almost touching; around the edges of the field stood the more graceful Dakotas that were to lift them into the sky. Men swarmed about the aircraft, loading them, laying out tow ropes, leading mules, humping packs and moving endlessly in dusty columns, for all the world like busy ants round captive moths.

I landed and met Wingate at his temporary headquarters near the air strip. Everything was going well. There had been no serious hitch in the assembly or preparation for the fly-in, which was due to begin at dusk that evening. For some days previously, our diversionary air attacks had been almost continuous on Japanese airfields and communication centres to keep his air force occupied. Meanwhile, ostentatious air reconnaissances over the Mandalay district had been carried out in the hope of convincing the enemy that any air-borne expedi-tion would be directed against that area. The attacks on air fields were effective in keeping Japanese aircraft out of the sky, but the false reconnaissances, as far as I ever discovered, had little effect.

Just a month earlier, on 4 February, Stratemeyer, the American Commander of the Eastern Air Command, and I had issued a joint directive to Wingate and Cochrane, the American commander of No. 1 Air Commando. In this, Wingate's Force was ordered to march and fly in to the Rail Indaw area (*Rail* Indaw to distinguish it from another Indaw not on the Mandalay–Myitkyina railway) and from there to operate under direct command of Fourteenth Army, with the objects of:

1. Helping the advance of Stilwell's Ledo force on Myitkyina by cutting the communications of the Japanese 18 Division, harassing its rear and pre-venting its reinforcement.
2. Creating a favourable situation for the Yunnan Chinese forces to cross the Salween and enter Burma.
3. Inflicting the greatest possible damage and confusion on the enemy in North Burma.

The tactical plan for getting the force into position behind the enemy was based on four assembly places:

'Aberdeen', twenty-seven miles north-west of Indaw;
'Piccadilly', forty miles north-east of Indaw;
'Broadway', thirty-five miles east-north-east of Indaw;
'Chowringhee', thirty-five miles east of Indaw.

These places were all away from roads and uninhabited. They were selected because there was enough flat ground to make the building of an air strip pos-sible in a short time and because there was water in the immediate vicinity. They were in fact fancy names written on the map, within striking distance of Indaw.

It was intended that in the first wave 16 Brigade should march to Aberdeen, 77 Brigade fly in two halves to Piccadilly and Broadway, and 111 Brigade land at Chowringhee. The remaining three brigades, 14, 23, and 3 West African, were to be held for the second wave which it was expected would be required to relieve the first in two to three months.

As the afternoon wore on, the atmosphere of excitement and suspense at Hailakandi grew, the old familiar feeling of waiting to go over the top, intensified by the strangeness and magnitude of this operation. Everyone, even the mules, moved about calmly, quietly and purposefully. Except perhaps for those patient beasts, it was, all the same, obvious that everyone realized that what was up to this time the biggest and most hazardous airborne operation of the war was about to begin.

During the morning the gliders had been loaded with supplies, ammunition, engineer equipment, signalling stores and men's kits. In the late afternoon the first wave, 77 Brigade headquarters, the leading British and Gurkha infantry and a small detachment of American Airfield Engineers emplaned. Each Dakota was to take two gliders. This was a heavy load, and, as far as I know, never before had these aircraft towed more than one. There was a clash of opinion among the airmen themselves on its practicability. Cochrane, in charge of the gliders, was confident it could be done; Old, whose Combat Cargo planes would provide the tugs, maintained it was unsound. Various airmen, British and American, took sides and argument was heated. Eventually, after experiments, Wingate agreed with Cochrane, and then Baldwin and I accepted the double tow. Now as I watched the last preparations I was assailed by no doubts on that score. The Dakotas taxied into position. The tow ropes were fixed. Everyone was very quiet as the roar of engines died down and we waited for zero hour. I was standing on the air strip with Wingate, Baldwin and one or two more, when we saw a jeep driving furiously towards us. A couple of American airmen jumped out and confronted us with an air photograph, still wet from the developing tent. It was a picture of Piccadilly landing ground, taken two hours previously. It showed almost the whole level space, on which the gliders were to land that night, obstructed by great tree trunks. It would be impossible to put down even one glider safely. To avoid suspicion no aircraft had reconnoitred the landing grounds for some days before the fly-in, so this photo was a complete shock to us. We looked at one another in dismay.

Wingate, though obviously feeling the mounting strain, had been quiet and controlled. Now, not unnaturally perhaps, he became very moved. His immediate reaction was to declare emphatically to me that the whole plan had been betrayed—probably by the Chinese—and that it would be dangerous to go on with it. I asked if Broadway and Chowringhee, the other proposed landing places, had been photographed at the same time. I was told they had been and that both appeared vacant and unobstructed.

Wingate was now in a very emotional state, and to avoid discussion with him before an audience, I drew him on one side. I said I did not think the Chinese had betrayed him as they certainly had no knowledge of actual landing grounds or, as far as I knew, of the operation at all; but he reiterated that someone had betrayed the plan and that the fly-in should be cancelled. I pointed out that only one of the three landing grounds had been obstructed, and that one Piccadilly, which he had used in 1943 and of which a picture with a Dakota on it had appeared in an American magazine. We knew the Japanese were nervous of air

landing and were blocking many possible landing sites in North and Central
Burma; what more likely than they should include a known one we had already
used, like Piccadilly? He replied that, even if Broadway and Chowringhee were
not physically obstructed, it was most probable that Japanese troops were concealed in the surrounding jungle ready to destroy our gliders as they landed.
With great feeling he said it would be 'murder'. I told him I doubted if these
places were ambushed. Had the Japanese known of the plan I was sure they
would have either ambushed or obstructed all three landing grounds. Wingate
was by now calmer and much more in control of himself. After thinking for a
moment, he said there would be great risk. I agreed. He paused, then looked
straight at me: 'The responsibility is yours,' he said.

I knew it was. Not for the first time I felt the weight of decision crushing in
on me with an almost physical pressure. The gliders, if they were to take off that
night, must do so within the hour. There was no time for prolonged enquiry or
discussion. On my answer would depend not only the possibility of a disaster
with wide implications on the whole Burma campaign and beyond, but the lives
of these splendid men, tense and waiting in and around their aircraft. At that
moment I would have given a great deal if Wingate or anybody else could have
relieved me of the duty of decision. But that is a burden the commander himself
must bear.

I knew that if I cancelled the fly-in or even postponed it, when the men were
keyed to the highest pitch, there would be a terrible reaction; we would never
get their morale to the same peak again. The whole plan of campaign, too, would
be thrown out. I had promised Stilwell we would cut the communications of the
enemy opposing him and he was relying on our doing it. I had to consider also
that one Chindit Brigade had already marched into the area; we could hardly
desert it. I was, in addition, very nervous that if we kept the aircraft crowded on
the air fields as they were the Japanese would discover them with disastrous
consequences. I knew at this time that a major Japanese offensive was about to
break on the Assam front and I calculated on Wingate's operation to confuse and
hamper it. Above all, somehow I did not believe that the Japanese knew of our
plan or that the obstruction of Piccadilly was evidence that they did. There was
a risk, a grave risk, but not a certainty of disaster. 'The operation will go on,'
I said.

The leading Dakota, with its two gliders trailing behind, roared down the
runway just after six o'clock, only a few minutes behind scheduled time. The
moment one was clear the next followed at about half a minute intervals. The
gliders took the air first, one or two wobbling nervously before they took station
behind, and a little above, the towing aircraft. More than once I feared a Dakota
would overrun the strip before the gliders were up, but all took off safely and
began the long climb to gain height to cross the hills. The darkening sky was
full of these queer triangles of aircraft labouring slowly higher and higher into
the distance. Eventually even the drone of engines faded and we were left
waiting.

And an unpleasant wait it was. Sixty-one gliders had set off. The full
complement for Broadway and Piccadilly had been eighty, but we had agreed
that sixty was about the most we could hope to land on one strip in the hours of

darkness, so the rest had been held back. I sat in the control tent, at the end of the air strip, to which all messages and signals came. At the rough table with its field telephones was Tulloch, Wingate's chief staff officer, who proved himself quick, reliable and cool in crisis, and Rome, another admirable staff officer. As the moon came up, in spite of hurricane lanterns and one electric lamp, it was almost lighter outside than within. There was a pause. Then came a report of red flares, fired from the air a few miles away. That meant a tow in distress— ominous if difficulties were beginning so soon. I took a turn outside and thought I saw a red Verey light fired high up in the distance. I returned to the tent to find more rumours of gliders down or tows returning before they had crossed our lines. Not so good. Then another long wait. We looked at our watches. The leading aircraft should be over Broadway now with the gliders going in. We ought to get the first wireless message any minute. Still it did not come. Wingate prowled in and out, speaking to no one, his eyes smouldering in a pallid face. Tulloch sat calmly at the phones. A garbled report over the telephone from another airfield told us that a tow pilot had seen what looked like firing on the Broadway strip. It was the time when doubts grow strongest and fears loom largest. Then, just after four o'clock in the morning, the first signal from Broadway, sent by Calvert, came in plain language, brief, mutilated, but conveying its message of disaster clearly enough—'Soya Link'. The name of the most disliked article in the rations had been chosen in grim humour as the code word for failure. So the Japanese had ambushed Broadway! Wingate was right and I had been wrong. He gave me one long bitter look and walked away. I had no answer for him. Then more signals, broken, hard to decipher, but gradually making the picture clearer. Gliders had crashed, men had been killed, there were injured and dying lying where they had been dragged to the edge of the strip—but there was no enemy. There had been no ambush. A great weight lifted from me as I realized that this was going to be like every other attack, neither so good nor so bad as the first reports of excited men would have you believe. We had to recall the last flight, as Broadway was too obstructed by smashed gliders to accept them. The situation was still far from clear to us as I left the control tent after dawn, but I was confident that if only the Japanese did not locate them for the next twelve hours, the Chindits would have the strip ready for reinforcements by nightfall.

Of the sixty-one gliders dispatched only thirty-five reached Broadway. The airmen who said that one Dakota could not tow two gliders had been right. In practice the steep climb to cross the mountains, so close to the start, put too great a drag on the nylon ropes and many parted. It also caused overheating in the aircraft engines and unexpected fuel consumption, with dire results. Many gliders and a few aircraft force landed, some in our territory, nine in Japanese. There was a brisk battle near Imphal between the Chindits of a crashed glider, convinced they were behind the enemy lines and determined to sell their lives dearly, and our own troops rushing to their rescue. Gliders by chance came down near a Japanese Divisional Headquarters and others beside a Regimental Head-quarters far from Broadway. These landings confused the enemy as to our intentions and led to a general alert for gliders and parachutists through all his units.

Long afterwards we discovered that it was not the Japanese who had obstructed Piccadilly but Burmese tree-fellers, who had, in the ordinary course of their work, dragged teak logs out of the jungle to dry in the clearing. The firing reported at Broadway was a nervous burst from a shaken glider pilot.

Even without the enemy, that night at Broadway was tragic and macabre enough. One or two of the leading gliders, circling down to a half-seen gap in the jungle, had crashed on landing. The ground control equipment and its crew were in a glider that failed to arrive so that, until a makeshift control could be improvised, it was impossible to time landings. Some gliders hurtled into the wrecks, others ran off the strip to smash into the trees or were somersaulted to ruin by uneven ground concealed under the grass. Twenty-three men were killed and many injured, but over four hundred, with some stores, and Calvert, the Brigade Commander, landed intact. Most of the engineering equipment did not arrive, but the small party of American engineers, helped by every man who could be spared from patrolling, set to work with what tools they could muster to drag the wreckage clear and prepare the ground. Never have men worked harder, and by evening a strip was fit—but only just fit—to take a Dakota.

Next night the fly-in continued.

General Slim

Chindit Strongholds Attacked

When the Japanese attacked they kicked up a colossal din by yelling and blowing bugles, probably trying to keep contact while at the same time intimidating the garrison.

Their own lack of elementary military knowledge contributed to their successive defeats, for, after forming up out of sight, each assault came over exactly the same route, which was already ranged to a yard.

Lack of good tactics and foresight was glaringly obvious during an ambush of Major Carfrae's, a former company commander of mine, and now with the 7th Battalion. His men fired at a lorry and missed, the driver turning in time to get back. Instead of benefiting from this warning, the Japs sent a whole convoy along at exactly the same time next day, to be completely wiped out.

. . . . Although their artillery and mortars were first-rate, our chaps held that the riflemen were poor. At close quarters, many of them actually looked at the ground when pressing the trigger. But everyone agreed that the infantrymen were brave to the point of fanaticism. Wounded men had dragged up and exploded 'Bangalore Torpedoes' to sever our wire, knowing that they were committing suicide. One particular incident impressed itself upon me—a British officer in the bayonet charge spared and passed a wounded man, who immediately shot him dead from behind. The man was at once killed by the officer's batman, who was in turn shot by yet another casualty lying apparently helpless. 'Never pass a wounded Jap,' was now on everybody's lips. 'And one round's no good unless it kills them outright,' I was told. 'The bastards just get up again and come at you.'

British infantry sergeant

The Task Accomplished

. . . . Eleven days after the beginning of the fly-in, Special Force's first task had been accomplished—both the main road and rail communications to the Japanese fighting Stilwell had been cut. It was impossible for the enemy to ignore this. 53 Japanese Division was at this time arriving piecemeal in Burma and, based on the Divisional Headquarters, under Lieutenant-General Kawano, and one regiment of the division, a group known as Take Force, which never much exceeded six thousand in strength, was formed to deal with the airborne invasion. The force was an improvised one and suffered, as such expedients always do, from a lack of cohesion, transport, supporting arms, signals, and administrative staff. Kawano himself was a sick man—he died soon afterwards—and was replaced by Lieutenant-General Takeda. The first serious action was an attempt by Take Force to capture White City and destroy 77 Brigade. The Japanese delivered a series of ferocious assaults, day and night, which were everywhere beaten back in hand-to-hand fighting of the bloodiest kind. British and Gurkhas (my old regiment, the 6th Gurkhas, won two V.C.s here) proved themselves man for man the superior of the enemy. Take Force, having suffered heavily, withdrew badly shaken from White City, and they never took it.

From Chowringhee one of our columns had struck east to the Chinese frontier and then turned north towards Myitkyina, cutting the important Bhamo–Myitkyina road. Lentaigne's 111 Brigade, uniting the portions that had landed at Chowringhee and Broadway, moved well to the west of Indaw. These operations did not, as I had hoped they would, seriously disorganize the Japanese communications with the Assam front. Their chief effect, as far as the battle there was concerned, was to delay for a couple of months two infantry and one artillery battalions of the Japanese 15 Division on their way to take part in the offensive against Imphal.

General Slim

On 8 March the Japanese launched their expected assault into Assam. Units of the Fourteenth Army met them round the Imphal plain. By the end of the month the Japanese hemmed it in on four sides. To the north, the village of Kohima commanded the main route to India. Here the three defending battalions were attacked early in April, and, greatly outnumbered, withstood a bitter siege in an everdwindling perimeter for sixteen days before being relieved. Throughout May and most of June the armies stood locked in combat. At Imphal and Kohima, as in Arakan, the British forces held on because they were now supplied and reinforced by air. Meanwhile General Stilwell, who had pushed as far south as Myitkyina by the middle of May, was held up by a stubborn Japanese defence.

KOHIMA

As we walked we measured the area which was left for us to defend. Across the top of the triangle it measured seven hundred yards, down the west side nine hundred and up the east side, eleven hundred; in it were crowded two thousand five hundred troops, less than one-third of them fit to fight. The measurements did not include Jail Hill. Nobody knew what was happening up there; tomorrow we would have to find out.

The ground we were on was not of our choosing; it was all the enemy had left for us, for they had taken the features all round, except the one road leading out to Dimapur. Our orders were to hold Kohima, so we did not need the road, except to move out non-combatants and wounded and this we could do only at night because of the Japanese guns. It has ever since been a constant source of wonder to us why we were allowed to come up the road immune. We could only assume that the Japs were so surprised to see anyone come into the town that by the time they had recovered from their initial shock we were in.

The whole area was covered with tall, strong trees. Among them the undergrowth grew thin, much thinner than in the jungles of the Arakan, and consisted mostly of rhododendron bushes and small shrubs; tracks and footpaths ran in all directions through the bushes. We could see only forty or fifty yards through the trees in the daytime and at night we could see nothing, not even when the stars and the moon were shining together. The sky was shut out by the thick canopy a hundred feet above our heads, so that the days were dull and the nights pitch. But it was hot in there when the sun was shining, and sticky; though the nights were bitter cold, for we were at five thousand feet.

There were only two relieving features—food and ammunition. There was plenty of both in the F.S.D., stored there for the use of our armies fighting farther up the line towards Imphal and Tiddim, but of no use to them now, for there was no way of moving it there. There was no airfield at Kohima; there was no railway passing through; the only road had been cut by the enemy.

Arthur Campbell, 4th Battalion Royal West Kent Regiment

Night Attack

Suddenly an urgent voice came through the darkness, 'Hey! Johnny, let me through, let me through, the Japs are after me; they're going to get me.' This was an old trick—the Japs had tried it in the Arakan—but even so, Bobby prayed that none of his men would shout an answer. Then came other voices, from different directions, all shouting the same theme. 'Let me through, let me through,' but there was no answer. After the voices a single shot rang out from above them, from the top of one of the giant trees. Then came another and another, again from different directions with a long pause between each shot. This, too, was an old trick and one which they had fallen for when they were fresh to the jungle. The nervous men had fired back, blazing away with their weapons at a danger they could not see, while the flashes from their muzzles showed the Japs where they were. Now they had become used to the trick and there was no answering fire, and Bobby was glad.

The sniping continued for some time, some of it coming even from behind them. This was the hardest to bear, because they felt that somehow the Jap must have found a gap in the defences and walked through it; and where one Jap had walked, others could go. They sensed that perhaps the enemy were gathering in numbers behind them and would be waiting if they had to fall back before the frontal onslaught. As time went by, the sensation grew stronger. It was a test of nerves, and only if they held steady would the enemy fail to locate their positions. Bobby's men held steady.

They held steady until they heard the scuffling in the road and knew that the attack was launched. The Japs came as silently as they could; they wore gym shoes and any part of their equipment that might clink in the darkness was muffled with cloth or removed. But even with the sounds of the shells falling behind them, the men could hear the Japs scrambling up the bank and the loosened stones falling back on to the hard surface of the road. There was no doubt that they were attacking in large numbers. Bobby took the microphone from his signaller and called up Sergeant King to tell him that the attack was coming in. A minute later the mortars opened fire and rained bombs on to Jail Hill. This was the signal for Bobby's men to fire, their weapons laid on fixed lines down the road. The fire-plan had been thought out very carefully, so that the Japs had to cross a curtain of steel before they could reach Bobby's forward positions. With one shout he brought down this curtain. The Brens and machine-guns clattered and the riflemen showered grenade after grenade on to the road.

For once the Japs were quiet, instead of yelling and screaming and blowing bugles as was their custom. It was a good custom because when there was noise you could tell where they were, but in the Stygian darkness it was the silent enemy whom you feared most. Suddenly they passed through the steel curtain and were up on the bank. One of them appeared at the end of Scudder's rifle and he shot him dead. Then came another, and another, so that Scudder was busy with his rifle, and Bobby with his tommy-gun, and Hall left his wireless set to join the fray. All along the top of the bank was a crowd of seething, cursing, sweating men in close combat, killing, maiming, wounding. Meanwhile the mortars fired. Then the defenders slowly became aware that there were fewer of the enemy up against them, until there was only one here who had been left behind, or another there, more determined than his comrades. These were dealt with quite easily, one by one. Then Bobby wiped the sweat from his face and took the microphone again and told King to stop firing because the attackers were gone. Mortar bombs were valuable; they might be needed to stave off the next attack, or the one after that, or the one after that. Soon there was silence in the darkness, except for the groans of the wounded and the rustling of the bushes as the last defeated Jap made his way back through the jungle to where he had come from.

Counter-attack

As soon as they crossed the ridge and started down the far slope the enemy opened a blaze of fire. They were well armed with automatics and, as the attacking troops drew nearer, they showered grenades on them from the buildings. Men fell wounded and dead and the attackers went to ground, taking cover in every little fold and dip they could find. Donald called on his No. 12 platoon to increase their fire and they did this and slowly mastered the enemy in the bashas. But off to a flank were two machine-guns raking the whole of the little valley with fire and it was these that were now pinning down the attack. They were hidden in a small building in the trees, away off to the left, so that No. 12 platoon could not bring fire to bear on them.

When Lance-Corporal Harman saw the threat from these two guns, he told Mathews to move his Bren a little over to the left to give him covering fire while he assaulted the position. Mathews brought his gun to bear and saw Harman climb calmly out of his slit trench and walk towards the machine-guns. The Japanese soon saw him coming and brought fire to bear and Mathews saw the bullets clipping up the ground at Harman's feet. But he went on, quite casually, and as he walked he took two grenades from his belt and pulled out the firing pins with his teeth. When he was only thirty yards away from the building he put his rifle on the ground and lobbed the two grenades inside. The machine-guns were silent for a moment and Mathews saw Harman pick up his rifle and run forward quickly until he was under the shelter of the wall. Then he disappeared round a corner and an agonized screaming came from the building, and two single shots. Then Harman walked out, carrying one of the machine-guns across his shoulders.

All the attacking troops were watching this action, and when they saw Harman come out with the machine-gun, they broke into a great cheer and surged forward again. In a moment Lieutenant Wright's Indian sappers were up against the buildings, blasting in the walls. The men streamed in after them, shooting and bayoneting as they went. Then all was confusion, with cursing, sweating, struggling men killing each other in the narrow confines, among the piles of stores and crates and in among the ovens. Donald, who had led the attack into the first building, soon cleared it of the enemy and climbed up on the crates so that he could see what was going on around him. One by one he saw the buildings empty as his men came out, smeared with blood, with clothing scorched and torn, all exhausted after the nervous tension of the attack, the horror of the bayoneting, and the exertion of hand-to-hand combat. Because the buildings were now catching fire and the ammunition in them exploding, he made them go back across the little valley, away from the confusion and the flames. Donald looked to his right and saw that in that direction the battle had been won. Then he looked to his left; on that side things had not gone so well. There was one *basha*, a little larger than the others, in which the enemy were still holding out. The sappers had not been able to blow the walls down, but even as he looked, Lance-Corporal Harman, who had come forward into the attack without orders, disappeared into the doorway.

Harman had seen at once, with extraordinary insight, that this building was not going to fall to the main attack, so he decided that it would fall to him. He went into the building and saw that it was part of the bakery, with ten ovens inside. They were large brick ovens, each large enough to hold a man, with heavy iron covers. As he walked in he was at once shot at from two of the ovens, but the bullets flashed past. He ran out of the door and back across the valley to his own section position where grenades were stored. He seized a box and, dragging it behind him, ran back into the building, taking shelter behind the nearest oven. He smashed the box open and pulled out a grenade. He put his left hand on one of the steel covers and let go the safety lever. There was a four-second delay on the fuse, so he waited for three, then lifting the lid, dropped the grenade into the oven. As he let the lid fall back the grenade exploded. He crept round all the other nine ovens and dropped a grenade into each.

The Japs did not seem to know what he was doing, or at least if they did, they knew no way of stopping him. He had trapped them in the ovens because, if they showed their faces for a moment, he would shoot them. When he had finished, Harman removed all the lids to make sure that the men inside were dead. There were dead men in five, but in two others the Japs were still alive, though badly wounded. He pulled them out and, taking one under each arm, carried them back across the valley to his section position. As the men saw him return, they went wild with cheering. The cheering became almost hysterical after the excitement of the battle and Donald was unable to stop it.

Meanwhile the *bashas* were now all afire and in some of them were Japs not yet dead; in others were Indians whom they had captured in the depot and had forced to fire on the attacking soldiers. The Indians ran out first and Donald's men let them go. It was only when the whole area was a blazing inferno that the Japs came out and were shot down one by one by No. 12 platoon, who were waiting for them, and by some of Bobby's men who had now joined the fight from the other side. Then there was a lull in the firing until one last Jap ran into the open. He had stayed too long; his clothes were on fire and, as he ran, he tore at them desperately in jerky, agonized movements. He hurled himself into a small puddle on the ground hoping that the water would put out the fire. But the puddle was too shallow and he lay screaming and scrabbling in the mud until Mathews put a bullet into his body to take away the pain.

The fire died out quickly and the men walked through the area to see what damage they had done. They counted the bodies of forty-four Japanese lying distorted and dead in the smouldering ruins. Among them were a number of their own friends.

Snipers

Their 75 mm. guns did not look up to much—just a short piece of piping on a wooden framework with two small wheels. Although these guns could be pulled along by four men harnessed to the framework, they were efficient enough to project the shell in exactly the right direction. The snipers were specially trained to the job; they climbed to the tops of the tallest trees and roped themselves to the trunk. One sniper, sitting in a tree top, would observe three or four square yards of ground, as much as he could see through the other trees which grew round about. If anyone moved into his own patch of ground, he was quick to aim and press the trigger; and the aim was generally good. Because they tied themselves to the trunk, even if we could discover where they were shooting from and fired back, we were never sure whether or not we had killed them because they did not fall out of the trees. The inexperienced soldier would fire four or five rounds instead of one, to kill a sniper, and while he was firing there were other snipers taking note of his position and passing the news down to his comrades who were due to attack that night.

The shelling and sniping meant that the men had to stay all the time, both night and day, either near or in their slit trenches and it allowed them very little sleep. As more men were wounded and killed, so there was less sleep for the ones who were left.

Rations

At four-thirty in the evening, before the evening hate started, they took the food round to the men. Colour-Sergeant Eves liked the regular habits of the Japs; the evening hate started exactly on time every day, so that he could calculate to a minute when he had to start issuing the food. The two cooks each carried two dixies, one with the stew in and the other full of the potatoes flavoured with margarine. The Colour-Sergeant followed with two more dixies full of tea. They staggered down towards the men in the front lines, dodging from bush to bush and tree to tree, taking what cover they could from the shelling and the sniping. They went first to the men nearest the enemy; men overlooked from only forty yards away by the Japs on Jail Hill. They crawled forward the last forty yards or so, pushing one dixie each in front of them, though this was not easy because the dixies were heavy and were still hot from the fire. When they reached a slit trench the two soldiers crouching inside held up their mess tins and the cook ladled the stew and potatoes into one while the Colour-Sergeant poured a little tea into the other. There was just enough water to allow each man two mouthfuls of tea. When they had fed the men in one slit trench they crawled along to the next one and then to the next, until they had fed the whole section. They then returned to collect the three dixies they had left behind and carried them off towards the next section. It took the Colour-Sergeant and his two cooks one hour, if they were lucky, to complete the company positions; for the men who fed last, those in the headquarters post, the meal was not so hot. If they were not lucky, it took more than an hour and they had to find their way back through the evening hate.

Wounded

On the way back I stopped in to see Bobby, lying in his shallow trench with the bags of *atta* and sugar piled round him. He pointed out to me the Jap mortar positions on the hills, explaining how he could watch the crews put the bombs into the mortars and could then follow the trajectory of each bomb as it turned slowly over and over on its way up to the zenith of its flight. While he watched he was convinced that each bomb was coming down on to his own stomach until, at the last moment, it swung off and crumped down somewhere else. He tried at times not to look at them, but always, when the bombing started, his eyes were drawn out to the hills, to the short gleaming barrels and to the little men busy around them. There was little else for him to do.

He could speak to the men in the slit trenches immediately to his left and right, though he could not see them. These men were as badly wounded as he was, and in as great pain, and during the thirteen days and nights they lay there side by side he came to know them very well indeed. He had these men for company and, in addition, copies of *Romeo and Juliet* and of the Bible, which

Padre Randolph had lent him to read. He found Shakespeare heavy going, but the Bible fascinated him.

There was a rusty old tin lying by his side which had once held tomatoes, and this was his lavatory, for one purpose only. There was no way of fulfilling the other need.

I asked him whether he knew how the battle was going and he said that Padre Randolph visited him each day, as indeed he did most men, both in the dressing station and on the perimeter, and kept him fully informed. The padre seemed to know exactly what was going on all the time; he knew what the men were thinking, and how they were feeling, and he had words of comfort for them all. The harder pressed they were, and the more dangerous their situation, the more often the padre visited them. Each time he came under fire he was desperately frightened, as all of us were, but not one man to whom he spoke was aware of it. He kept his fear bottled up inside himself until he mastered it. His courage was immense, and all he met drew strength from it.

A few yards to Bobby's left was one of the communal pits in which the worst wounded were crowded. Bobby could hear every word spoken by the men in this pit; he could hear the pitiful crying of those who were in great pain but could not be drugged, because drugs were in short supply. Twice, during the previous three days, shells had burst in the pit and Bobby, once the initial shock of the explosion had worn off, heard the agonized screams for help and the grunting and cursing of the stretcher-bearers and digging parties as they separated the shattered bodies not yet dead from those which had been blasted to bits, and dug out the rubble to make space for more wounded. All round him, while he lay with his own pain racking his body, with nothing to occupy his mind except the Jap mortars and his Bible and the men next door, was the stench of blood and death and rotting wounds and the sounds of anguish. But all the time we were speaking he was smiling and cheerful. Before I left him I asked him why he kept a pistol on his chest. He said, 'Oh! that's for me, in case the Japs get in.' The pistol was there for thirteen days and thirteen nights, and so was the pain and the stench and the sounds; at any time he thought he might have to put the pistol to use.

Relief

The enemy were now within one hundred yards of the command post, within one hundred yards of the dressing station, now holding no fewer than six hundred casualties.

. . . . Then the non-combatants came swarming into the dressing station, completely out of control. Bobby raised his head to see them milling round in large groups, none of them knowing where to go, all of them thinking their last moment had come. John Young and Peter Franklin were trying to produce some sort of order among them; were trying to shepherd them away from the wounded to some place where they could do no harm. One or two of the garrison officers were also with them, trying to bring them under control, shouting orders in English and Urdu. For an hour the dressing station was a shambles of wailing wounded, struggling stretcher-bearers, stampeding, fear-struck men in tattered uniforms; a hellish babble of terror and dismay. At last John Young reduced the chaos to some sort of order.

Meanwhile, into battalion headquarters came a ray of hope; a wireless message promising relief that morning, the promise supported by the sort of facts we wanted. The infantry, supported by tanks, were driving the enemy rapidly back along the road towards us.

. . . . At 13.30 hours I looked back at the road through my binoculars. The convoy was now quite close, and I could see in the leading jeep Bryn Williams and Jack Breadon, the quartermaster, bringing the precious vehicles to us.

Stopping the convoy behind Picquet Hill, they dashed up the road to reconnoitre. Peter Franklin met them at the foot of the spur and showed them how to bring six vehicles at a time into the re-entrant beneath the ridge, where they would be under cover from Jap snipers and protected from the guns on J.N.A. Hill and G.P.T. Ridge. Bryn Williams took the jeep back and brought forward the first six vehicles, while I went down to watch the evacuation. Walking up the spur I met the infantrymen of the 1/1 Punjabis, two companies strong, led by their commanding officer, 'Grim' Grimshaw. He said, 'Your chaps are in a terrible state, but what you have done is already an epic throughout the army. Cracking good show.' I sent Hefferman to guide him to the command post.

I did not witness the meeting between 'Grim' and John Laverty, but I could well imagine the immense relief as the load of responsibility slipped from John's shoulders. I learnt afterwards that the meeting was brief, because there was still much fighting to be done.

. . . . The first to leave were the walking wounded, limping down the road in tidy groups, each with a leader. The leaders were nominated from whoever happened to be there, so that some of the groups of Indian wounded were led by our privates while some of our men were led by Indian officers and N.C.O.s. As they hobbled away the enemy fired on them from the Fort and J.N.A. Hill with automatics. Some of the men fell off the road as they were wounded again, but only the few stretcher-bearers stopped to examine the bodies. Some of these were left lying, now dead, others were carried on, among them a young soldier with both legs hanging limp, whom a resourceful orderly loaded into a wheelbarrow found lying by the roadside.

. . . . On this day, the fifteenth day of the siege, we heard fighting on Terraced Hill and wondered if the Japs had once again blocked the road to Dimapur, the only road up which reinforcements could come, or down which we could pass out of Kohima. We learnt later that the Japs had blocked it by occupying a ridge from which they could fire direct on to the road. Only an astounding display of dash and courage by the Durham Light Infantry cleared it.

The following night brought fresh enemy attacks, two from the D.C.'s bungalow and one from Kuki Picquet. In the fighting Harry Smith and Tom Coath, so far uninjured, were both wounded.

Before the night was done we received cipher messages that the 1st Battalion, the Royal Berkshire Regiment would relieve us on the following day, 20 April, the sixteenth day of the siege.

All of us from the command post, except John Laverty, were early that morning at the foot of I.G.H. Spur, watching the men of the Royal Berkshires come in. They looked fresh, these men, and eager for the fray, and they took over with great efficiency, filing in orderly fashion into our posts, while our men crept out in small groups to collect behind I.G.H. Spur, ready to leave. There were sallies from the men of the Royal Berkshires aimed at our looks, our beards, our kit, but few of our men replied. They were too tired for humour, they just wanted to get out, back to a good meal and then sleep, sleep and more sleep.

Arthur Campbell

When you go home
Tell them of us and say
For their to-morrow
We gave our to-day.

Inscription on the graves of the dead at Kohima.

The Japanese had been met and held in the north as in the south. Late in June 1944 *Admiral Mountbatten telegraphed to the British Prime Minister that on the 22nd 'the 2 British and 5 Indian divisions met at a point twenty-nine miles north of Imphal and the road to the plain was open. On the same day the convoys began to roll in.' Thus ended Japan's invasion of India.*

VICTORY IN BURMA

At once the counter-attack began, and the badly battered Japanese forces were slowly but inexorably ground down and driven back the way they had come. The return to Burma had begun, and the first Japanese to suffer were the men who had been destined to invade India. Now they were all but wiped out in their desperate retreat through the jungle—and the monsoon.

Now Salomons' three battalions, West Yorkshires, Jats, Punjabis, leap-frogged down the road, the lead taken by each in turn. To describe in detail the day-to-day engagements would be tedious. Progress was reckoned by mile-stones. The enemy fought a delaying action all the way, mile by mile. His rearguard waited in concealed defence positions that commanded the winding road, opened fire on our leading infantry section, and killed or wounded several men. If the rifle company failed to oust the enemy, then mountain guns battered the position with whatever ammunition the limited airdrops had provided.

At first the Japanese were content to arrest our advance for a day or a night. But so prolonged was their resistance near the fiftieth milestone, where the road wound up the side of a hill named 'Drake', that Salomons sent for Hurri-bombers to evict them. For three days the Japanese clung tenaciously to this hill. By firing its steep slopes they denied all cover to the 3/14th Punjab, who were now leading the brigade. Twice the infantry climbed to attack. Twice they came within four hundred yards of the summit. But each time grenades and machine-guns forced them back. When one fierce assault brought Baker's platoons almost to the top, they could not stay there. The sepoys held positions on the hillside through the next night. In the tense hour before sunrise they endured a fusillade of rare intensity. An attack was expected from above. No attack came. Instead, the Japanese soldiers hurled grenades down into our trenches. Abruptly silence fell. When, at dawn on 7 August, the Punjabis crept up the bare and blackened slope they found Drake's crest deserted. The fierce outburst had been a final defiant gesture. Already the enemy was preparing to delay us a little farther down the road.

And this road—for the soldiers a long, long trail to Tiddim—bore the tracks of a retreating foe. Mud-clogged rifles and splintered packing-cases kept company with dirty webbing equipment, hand grenades and blood-stained, muddy, rain-soaked corpses. From beneath mounds of loose earth appeared legs and arms, even a solitary hand. Over all, and on almost every stretch of the road, hung the sickly smell that betrayed the presence of some dead enemy in a patch of jungle, beneath a dripping tangle of bamboo. At one road fork lay the scorched and buckled shell of a jeep that had blown up. In the bed of one stream was found a small Japanese tank, painted a pale shade of green and adorned in scarlet with the sun of Japan.

Near Drake our patrols found a site of a large Japanese hospital, and close on a hundred graves in the surrounding jungle. Among the trees within a few yards of the road lay two very long brown Japanese lorries. These contained the smashed equipment of a sterilizing unit and X-ray plant, surrounded by wicker-work hampers, chemicals and clothing, and a weighty generator. Inside, too, buzzed a host of savage hornets; one naked corpse lay there, and, pervading all, the smell of death.

Antony Brett-James

An Abandoned Divisional Headquarters

I wandered with Henchy and my orderly Mohd Shafi through acres of jungle by this former Japanese headquarters to find smashed enemy lorries painted brown, sleek staff cars of which many had been captured from our own army, and scores of shelters built of branches and tarpaulins. Scattered over the ground, or half concealed beneath bushes and scrub-oak trees, appeared petrol tins and oil drums; Japanese cookhouses were indicated by blackened grass and the ashes of a hundred fires, sodden clothing and pots and plates; we stepped among steel helmets, and tiny camouflage nets, sodden boots and damp postcards. Terry's particular quest when he visited the place was tools for our trucks, and every lorry we found was ransacked for these rusty but invaluable additions to our deficient supply. In the back of one such lorry we came upon a complete kit which appeared to have belonged to a second-class private in the Emperor's Army; white duck pyjamas, khaki suits, handkerchiefs and underpants, white socks without a shaped heel; all these items we unpacked from his packs and bags. Among a bundle of pamphlets and notebooks I drew out a parcel from Japan, as yet unopened from its brown paper wrapping; inside lay a reddy-brown woollen cardigan which I later wore in the mountains of Kashmir and Sikkim. Nearby was something that none of us had ever seen before, a lucky-charm body-belt of white silk about three feet in length, embroidered in one thousand red silk stitches with a realistic tiger, while on the front side were sewn Japanese hole-in-the-centre coins and wooden charms inscribed with red characters. We thought this an intriguing find, more original than the many photographs of enemy soldiers in training or on operations, of comely girl friends and numerous families from distant Japan; and preferable in its comparative rarity to the host of coloured postcards which littered every enemy camping-ground with extraordinary profusion. These postcards were to be found wrapped in tissue paper, in series of six, depicting many aspects of the home life of our squat and yellow foes; scenes of Japan, the blue mountains and pink fruit blossom, sheep grazing in green fields, horses and ploughing scenes, and the red-brown soil. Some cards showed two little sisters looking up at a cherry tree in full blossom, and others pictured women milking black and white cows while their children watched from the background. Whereas one favourite card portrayed a family scene, in which father smoked his pipe and read aloud a newspaper to his wife, to the cook and a row of chubby-cheeked, close-cropped boys, one of the most artistic showed two attractive young ladies reading a letter by the light of a paper lantern. In other series we found humorous cartoons or bird paintings and allegorical pictures, and in every case the colouring was pure and true to life, possessing considerable artistry. It seemed so incongruous that these fanatical, boasting and often barbaric enemies should scrawl home to their families on such peaceful and civilized postcards, a contrast of ugliness and beauty, of mass brutality and tender thoughts.

In their shelters were half-finished letters, muddy newspapers and torn military pamphlets, jumbled up with the debris of every camp and despoiled by rain and sun and filth. One such leafy arbour contained the rubber stamps, reams of paper, bottles of ink and the inevitable *bric-à-brac* of an office. From slit trenches Henchy unearthed small drums of yellow enemy cable, signalling lamps, wireless valves by the hundred, books and papers of which we could not read a word or a character. In what must have been an artillery headquarters, folded inside heavy black tin boxes, were panorama drawings, gunnery brochures, medical outfits, rolls of maps which showed every part of Eastern India, in accordance with the professed and loud-trumpeted invasion of India and the forlorn March to Delhi. As in many another abandoned camp or position, we picked up white silk flags in whose centre stood the red sun of Japan, and on which were painted, in black characters, messages of greeting. I was glad to obtain a personal seal such as many of the enemy carried with them, embossed at one end with their initials or monogram, and used to sign paybooks, savings certificates and other documents; these seals lived inside a tiny case, each possessing at one end a red ink pad.

This former Japanese divisional headquarters had been selected with immense cunning, for so completely did the woods conceal it that our bombs had caused little harm and many craters.

Antony Brett-James

Out of India

Three hundred yards beyond Milestone 75 the frontier between India and Burma was crossed, and the last enemy troops were driven from Indian territory. The ground opened out and became less hilly. Resistance weakened. The Japanese rearguards were hastening to the sheer mountainside that rose be-

tween Milestones 86 and 100, where this extraordinary road spiralled upwards
in dangerous bends. Here was a formidable natural obstacle to our advance.
Here the enemy was expected to offer stout opposition.

.... The obstacle that faced Brigadier Warren and his men would have been
formidable even in dry weather. But now, with the monsoon rains teeming
down, it was doubly so. Only four-wheel-drive trucks were allowed forward, and
even these had often to winch themselves out of ruts or up the steepest stretches.
Well might the troops call this treacherous route the 'Ladder'. The road suddenly left the valley, and in one bend after another mounted some two thousand
feet in twelve miles. Those parts of the mountain face that were bare of trees
soon became broken up by the rains, and down upon the road fell cascades of
shale and earth, of trees and rock. After each hairpin bend lorries found themselves a hundred feet or more above the spot where they had been a minute
earlier. And the intervening wall of oozing mud had to be held from collapse by
immense tarpaulins stretched out and linked together. It was hoped that these
would at least shield the bare mud from the rain. But to shield the surface of the
road itself from these torrents was quite impossible. Soon the mud was calf-
deep and so wide apart were the ruts made by trucks and lorries that jeeps had
always to advance at a sharp tilt, one pair of wheels down in the ruts, the other
pair slithering on the surface. The edge of the precipice was very close, and so
perilous did the road appear to passengers, if not to drivers, that many hung
ready to leap off if the vehicles showed signs of skidding.

At one point lorries weighed down with bridging equipment for the Sappers
were stuck for four days, patiently waiting for a day of hot sunshine to dry out
the mud sufficiently for them to proceed. One despatch rider took sixteen hours
to complete a return journey of eighteen miles between Milestones 100 and 109.
Though a spell of fine weather during the second week of September enabled
stocks of rations to be built up for British and Indian troops and for mules, very
heavy rain over the next two days so damaged the road once more that no supply
convoys could move. And the road was closed by the Provost unit to prevent its
complete ruin.

This state of affairs was to continue all through September and the first part
of October, as long as the road was in use. Men had to jump out into the squelch-
ing mud and dig the mud from round the sunken wheels. Bamboos, branches,
and sacks were laid on the mud, and pieces of rock were pressed in to support
the flailing rear wheels. In parts one-way traffic had to be enforced by the military police. Lorries that had become embedded in the mire had to be hauled to
one side before other vehicles could be steered past. Mule-drivers tugged,
sweated, shouted and swore in several languages at their muddy animals, which
struggled gamely up and down the hills with their balanced loads creaking from
the saddle. Those men who tried to keep their green trousers clean soon gave up
the effort, for boots and clothes were rapidly soaked and stained with brown.

Convoys took rations for several days when they set off up the road, for the
troops often had to spend two days and more in the open making slow and exhausting progress from one camp, traffic control post, or supply point to the
next. On bad corners the Sappers laid rows of logs that helped a little; but these
became embedded, uneven, splintered, or they vanished altogether and lorries

found temporary pits in which to sink for hours at a time. Guns had to be winched and man-handled up the slopes.

. . . . Most of the day the rain poured down, until the road's outer edge was swept away; and moving streams of shale and mud, trees and boulders, flowed across the road like lava from some volcano. Certain drivers found their way barred by a landslide that was still in motion. To clear such landslides took Sappers of the 2nd Field Company many hours. Trees were cut with explosives, and rocks broken down to a size that could be dealt with by the bulldozers.

But when the rain did cease, when the clouds were blown away from the hilltops, the view was awe-inspiring. As one Gunner officer, Major C. Morshead, M.C., wrote in a letter at the time: 'When you get on the top the ridge is open with pine trees and grass; on the lower slopes it is mostly thick scrub oak reaching to more tropical jungle below. And from the tops the view is of the kind you pay many pounds to travel to see. Rank upon rank for maybe fifty miles run long and featureless ridges of forest, steep-sided in all shades of green, shadow and sunlight. Here and there are long views down deep glens that seem to lead nowhere at all.'

Antony Brett-James

By early December the Fourteenth Army had secured two bridgeheads across the Chindwin and was preparing for its main advance into the heart of Burma. In the same month British forces in Arakan took the offensive, capturing Akyab in January of 1945.

At the end of the rainy season the British advance continued. During the period of preparation new tracks were constructed up the gorge and the old road was repaired and widened. The Tunnels area became a hive of activity. West Africans, who were destined to capture Buthidaung, mingled with troops of 25 Indian Division, whose goal was Akyab. Guns and tanks lumbered up the road through the Tunnels to harbouring areas in the Letwedet *chaung*, and at the outset of the advance there passed through a strange convoy of lorries and transporters carrying boats which were to take a brigade of 25 Indian Division from the launching site at Buthidaung down the river Mayu to Akyab. This period of activity was to prove the last time that British troops were to see the Tunnels and Point 551.

Brigadier A. G. O'Carroll Scott

We came through the bushes, and saw him there, crying.
There were fourteen holes in him, letting his life out.
    All the while he gasped, gasped a shout
    For water, gasped, and fell back sighing.
Water was short here, up here among the stones;
But one man, although it was so useless,
    Gave him a bottle, filled and cool, unless
    He should die with a curse among his groans.
He drank it all, and we watched him there, lying
With it running out of the bullet holes. He was six hours dying.

J. M. Russell

Stilwell Recalled

As we in Fourteenth Army Headquarters worked hard at our plans, and as our divisions reorganized, regrouped, and began to move into their assembly areas, above us in Supreme Headquarters, change and reorganization were in the air. In mid-October, Stilwell was recalled. The Generalissimo had insisted on it, and, in spite of pressure from Washington and from Admiral Mountbatten, had refused to yield. The only thing that was surprising was that the open breach had not come sooner. Stilwell, although Chiang's Chief of Staff, had never bothered to hide his contempt for 'The Peanut', as he usually called him in private and in public. The American had no confidence in the Chinaman's military judgment or political integrity, and announced it. He believed that the Generalissimo was more interested in using American Lease-Lend money and equipment to secure his own personal position in China than in fighting the Japanese. Stilwell, who overestimated his own indispensability to Chiang and the extent to which the American Government would go in his support, was surprised and deeply hurt. In Fourteenth Army and, I think, throughout the British forces our sympathies were with Stilwell—unlike the American 14th Air Force, who demonstratively rejoiced at his downfall. To my mind he had strange ideas of loyalty to his superiors, whether they were American, British or Chinese, and he fought too many people who were not enemies; but I liked him. There was no one whom I would rather have had commanding the Chinese army that was to advance with mine. Under Stilwell it *would* advance. We saw him go with regret and he took with him our admiration as a fighting soldier. He was replaced by three generals who divided between them his half-dozen jobs. The command of N.C.A.C. went to his loyal second-in-command, Lieutenant-General Dan Sultan, whom I already knew and liked. Wedemeyer, Admiral Mountbatten's American Deputy Chief of Staff, replaced Stilwell in China as Chiang Kai-Shek's adviser, but I gathered that the idea of building up a great American-led Chinese army to march to the sea vanished with Stilwell.

General Slim

The Invasion of Central Burma

Early in the New Year the Fourteenth Army was launched in the direction of the Irrawaddy and Mandalay, and by the end of January the Chinese and American forces farther east had re-opened the land route to China.

This advance of nearly two hundred miles in twenty days was an astonishing feat, not so much because of the opposition overcome—although that was by no means negligible—but because of the difficulty of the country. For most of the distance there was no road; the earth track built through the hills by the Japanese for their invasion of Assam had largely disappeared during the rains. 19 Division, with very little road-making equipment, had to cut the track anew. Most of the division went on foot, but guns and lorries had often to be winched and man-hauled up steep slopes, and in one place the only way to get the track round a cliff was to cantilever it out on timber supports. It was vastly exhilarating to fly over the division in a light aeroplane. Through gaps in the tree-tops that screened the hills below, I could see on every rough track files of men marching hard with a purposefulness that could be recognized from five hundred feet. Behind them gangs, stripped to the waist, were felling trees and hauling them to make rough bridges across the numberless streams and gullies that cut the route, while guns waited to move on again the moment the last log was in position. Dust rose in reddish clouds as whole companies with pick and spade dug into banks to widen the road and let the lorries pass. These men hacking out a road, dragging vehicles, pushing on with such fierce energy to get to grips with the enemy, were a heartening sight. When I came down on their hurriedly prepared airstrips and talked to them, and to Pete Rees, who was as usual in the van, my spirits soared. 19 Division had waited long enough to get at the enemy and nothing was going to stop it now.

General Slim

Preparations

The enemy knew we were about to attempt crossings, and, realizing that it was impossible to hold two hundred miles of river line continuously and effectively in strength, he did not attempt to do so. Instead, he wisely concentrated his defences at the most likely crossing places, watched the intervening spaces, and held his reserves, especially artillery and tanks, mobile and well back, until our intentions were clearer. He left certain detachments on our side of the river in the Saigang Hills and around Kabwet, some sixty miles north of Mandalay, to impede our advance, to give him observation, and if necessary to form sally ports across the river. He also organized small suicide penetration units to raid on our bank, and, by interfering with our preparations, to delay and confuse us. Generally speaking, Kimura's dispositions to meet our assault from the north were suitable, and after his tour of inspection, he probably felt that, while he might not be able to stop us crossing in some places, he should be able to destroy such forces as did manage to get over. His shortage of air support and reconnaissance was, of course, a great handicap, and must have worried him a great deal, but he made arrangements to use what he had more freely and more boldly.

If Kimura was not without anxieties, I certainly had mine. One of the greatest was shortage of equipment. I do not think any modern army has ever attempted the opposed crossing of a great river with so little. We had few power craft, and those we had were small, old, and often damaged by the long journey over execrable roads. Our handful of military boats and rafting stores had seen months, even years, of hard use and rough handling. All our equipment was very much 'part worn'. We were especially weak in outboard engines, on which we should have to rely to a great extent; most, even of those available, were underpowered for their tasks and almost all were unreliable. We tried to eke out our own equipment with a number of captured pontoons, but these were of poor type and really suitable only for bridging. Burmese country boats, of which we obtained a few, were good cargo carriers, but, to the uninitiated, extremely awkward to navigate. We strained every nerve to produce more amphibious equipment, but it was simply not there. My headquarters found all the equipment, technical units and help it possibly could, but, strive as we would, I could not provide my corps commanders with more than a fraction of what I should have liked or of what they might reasonably demand. Apart from its deplorable quality, I could not give them equipment enough to allow of more than one division at a time crossing in each corps, and, even for that one division, far too many trips would be required, the boats and rafts having to ferry back and forth many times. I was, as I said at the time, asking them to cross on 'a couple of bamboos and a bootlace'. They knew the risks quite as well as I did, but neither they nor the divisional commanders made unnecessary protests. They realized no more was available.

. . . . I drew comfort . . . at this time from quite another thought. I had, more than once, in two great wars, taken part in the forcing of a river obstacle, and I had on every occasion found it less difficult and less costly than expected. I had also read some military history, and, although I cudgelled my brains, I could not call to mind a single instance when a river had been successfully held against determined assault. As the time drew near for the first crossings, I hugged this thought to me. Historically, the odds were in my favour.

. . . . As soon as Monywa was securely in our hands, I moved my Tactical Headquarters there as it was admirably placed to control both my corps. On 8 February my Main Headquarters with the Headquarters 221 Group joined me there, and we set up a complete and very comfortable joint Headquarters, partly in the jungle and partly in some of the least battered houses on the outskirts. The Japanese had left behind a number of booby traps which were disconcerting, but my chief frights came from snakes which abounded in the piles of rubble. They seemed specially partial to the vicinity of my War Room, which lacked a roof but had a good concrete floor. It was my practice to visit the War Room every night before going to bed, to see the latest situation map. I had once when doing so nearly trodden on a *krait*, the most deadly of all small snakes. Thereafter I moved with great circumspection, using my electric torch, I am afraid, more freely than my security officers would have approved. It seemed to me that the risk of snake bite was more imminent than that of a Japanese bomb. Paying one of my nightly visits, moving slowly, and, as I was wearing rubber-soled shoes, silently, I lifted the blanket which served as a door. On the other side of the room, seated before the situation map, lit by a shaded light, were the officer on duty and a younger colleague who had recently joined the Headquarters. The older officer was speaking in the voice of assured authority. He placed his finger firmly on the map. 'Uncle Bill,' he announced, 'will fight a battle here.' 'Why?' not unreasonably asked the youngster. 'Because,' came the answer, 'he always fights a battle going in where he took a licking coming out!'

General Slim

The Crossing

At 04.00 hours on 13 February the leading flight of 100 Brigade, the Border Regiment, pushed off in silence. The night was dark but throughout the evening the wind had freshened and it now proved troublesome to heavily laden and underpowered boats. The river here was fifteen hundred yards wide, but obstructed by partially submerged sandbanks, between which ran strong currents. Several boats grounded and there was difficulty in getting them off. At first there was luckily no opposition, and it was not until some time after the first troops had landed that light and ill-aimed small arms and mortar fire was directed against them. Once the first landing had been made the rest of the brigade followed rapidly, and by eight o'clock the whole of it was over—an excellent piece of organization. A well-directed and heavy air strike on the Japanese artillery that was likely to cover the crossing places had been put down the previous day, and the enemy guns were in process of moving or taking up new positions at the critical time. A few 75-mm. shells burst on the beach with little effect. The landing could be claimed as a complete surprise and practically unopposed. By dusk on 13 February, 100 Brigade had established a small bridgehead.

32 Brigade had a longer water crossing and suffered greater difficulties from wind, currents, and sandbanks. The outboard motors were, as usual, unreliable and very difficult and noisy to start. However, here also the crossing was a surprise and by dawn the first battalion, the Northamptons, were over and digging in. All ferrying at both crossings stopped at daylight, but neither bridgehead was seriously attacked through the day. Again the Japanese were slow to recognize main crossings and to collect their troops to attack. Real opposition did not begin until the 15th when Japanese aircraft strafed the beaches, damaging a number of boats but inflicting few casualties. This was followed by a heavy night attack on 100 Brigade, during which the Japanese landed by boats behind our men and used flamethrowers. The attack was repulsed and, pushing on, our troops extended their bridgehead until it was over three miles long by half a mile deep.

Fighting now became fiercer as each enemy reinforcement arrived, to be thrown in, as usual, piecemeal. By 15 February, in spite of pressure, our bridgehead was six miles by two, so that on the 16th we were able to start ferrying by day and our build-up rapidly increased. There followed a series of suicide attacks, mainly on 100 Brigade, by waves of Japanese infantry supported by tanks, but the two bridgeheads had now joined up and they held firm. The enemy losses were heavy; five of their attacks were in daylight, and on several occasions our aircraft caught them as they assembled for the assault. Rocket-firing Hurricanes proved our most successful anti-tank weapon, and their best day was 20 February, when they knocked out thirteen medium tanks. The fiercest fighting with the heaviest casualties on both sides occurred between 21 and 26 February. When the Japanese counter-attacks were finally thrown back and they recoiled exhausted, on one sector of our defences five hundred enemy corpses were buried by bulldozers and on another over two hundred. The commander of the Japanese 33 Division, Tanaka, said later that during this period two of his battalions delivered an attack with a strength of twelve hundred men, only to lose nine hundred and fifty-three. By 27 February, fighting strongly, 20 Division had expanded its holding to eight miles by two and a half in depth. Some of the hardest fighting of the campaign had taken place in this narrow bridgehead.

General Slim

Near Pakokku, south-west of Mandalay, General Slim on 13 February de-livered a flank assault across the Irrawaddy, at a point where the Japanese were least expecting it. This was a decisive stroke.

As soon as darkness fell, equipment, boats, and all the paraphernalia for the main crossing began to move down to the water. Assembly areas were marked and the troops tramped slowly and silently from their bivouacs. The Special Boat Section made a final reconnaissance of the far bank to see if it had been occupied, and in doing so met two Japanese swimming in the river. To prevent their escape they had to be shot and it is possible that the noise put the enemy on the alert.

The night was pitch dark, a strong wind was blowing and there was a distinct lop on the water, as at a quarter to four, the leading company of South Lanca-shires got into their boats and started the long paddle across. At last their boats grounded on the opposite bank. With as little splashing as they could, they waded ashore and scrambled up the cliffs, while the boats turned and made back. By five o'clock on the morning of 14 February the company had reached the cliff top, so far without meeting any enemy. There they disposed themselves for defence and awaited the rest of their battalion.

On the west bank the remainder of the South Lancashires moved down according to programme and began to embark just as the first faint light of dawn was tinting the sky. The channels to be followed had been marked behind the first flight and things had indeed gone well, but from that moment they began to go wrong. In spite of their past experience, the Lancashire men fumbled badly at the embarkation and there was a good deal of delay and confusion. Because of noise, it was not possible to start up the outboard engines until the men were in the boats, and when the time to do so eventually came several motors failed to start. Some of the boats also were found to leak badly, having been damaged in transit. More delay resulted. Eventually the commanding officer, realizing that a start must be made, ordered the boats that were ready to move off, irrespective of whether they were in their correct flights or not. The result was that the reserve company, which should have been last, found itself when daylight came in midstream ahead of the first wave. Even then all might have been well had the boats made straight for the east bank, but the reserve company decided it would circle to take its proper place behind the others. The strong current and the wind were too much for the feeble engines and the reserve company, in confusion, began to drift downstream. The remaining boats, seeing them go and not realizing what was happening, turned to follow them. At this moment the enemy opened fire with rifles from the cliffs and with machine-guns from the water's edge. Two company commanders and the engineer officer were quickly killed, casualties grew, and several boats, including that of the commanding officer, were sunk. The guns on our bank and some of the tanks waiting to embark now opened fire, but owing to secrecy they had not registered, and at first their shooting was perforce slow. Within a short time aircraft from the cab rank were called in and under this combined cover the boats made back to our bank. The crossing, except for the isolated company, now in great danger, had failed.

Nor was this the only failure. The subsidiary crossing by 89 Brigade had met with initial disaster. The gallant patrol hidden on the east bank in Pagan had, during the night, reported that the enemy had reinforced the town and the whole of it was now occupied. The assaulting company, however, stoutheartedly decided to set out in its native craft. As they approached the far bank they came under fire and the Burmese boatmen, not unnaturally, panicked. The clumsy boats got out of control, and in spite of the Sikhs' efforts were swept downstream. At last the boatmen, urged by the sepoys, regained control and brought them back to the starting point. It would have been suicide to have tried to cross in daylight in these slow, awkward boats, and there the crossing rested.

To watch across the great river as dawn breaks over ancient Pagan is to hold one's breath at so much beauty. Pagan, once the capital of Burma, was in all its glory at the time of the Norman Conquest; now silent, ruined and deserted, it is still noble—and very beautiful. Its twelve hundred temples, madder red or ghostly white, rise, some like fantastic pyramids or turreted fairy castles, others in tapering pagoda spires, from the sage green mass of trees against the changing pastel blues, reds, and golds of sunrise. As a foreground flows the still dark yet living sweep of moving water. Yet as the officers of 89 Brigade gazed disconsolately towards Pagan in the chill of early morning, they are to be forgiven if the beauty of the scene was somewhat lost to them. They had other and less pleasant things to think about: their attempt at crossing had definitely failed. Then suddenly, to their surprise, they saw a small boat bearing a white flag put off from the opposite bank. In it were two Jiffs, who, when they came ashore, said that the Japanese had marched out of Pagan and moved hurriedly up river, leaving only troops of the Indian National Army to garrison the town. Their one wish, now the Japanese were gone, was to surrender. Quickly a platoon of the Sikhs with a British officer crossed in the only available boats. True to their word, the garrison of Pagan marched out and with smiles laid down their arms. By evening most of the Sikh battalion was established in the outskirts of Pagan. This incident was, I think, the chief contribution the Indian National Army made to either side in the Burma War.

Back at the main crossing, while all this was going on at Pagan, the Engineers were working feverishly to repair the returned boats for a new crossing. The South Lancashire company on the east bank reported it was now firmly dug in and had not so far been attacked. It was, therefore, decided to make a second effort to reinforce it. The Brigadier judged it would take too long to reorganize the South Lancashires, so he ordered a Punjabi battalion to make the crossing as soon as possible. The 4/15th Punjabis, with great calmness and in excellent order, embarked on what promised to be a most hazardous enterprise. At 9.45 a.m. their leading company set out under the heaviest covering fire that could be provided by artillery and air. As the boats chugged slowly across they were hardly fired on at all; it seemed that there were still no Japanese at the actual crossing and that even those downstream, who had taken such toll of the South Lancashires as they drifted past, had withdrawn. Some of the boats grounded on sandbanks but the men waded or swam ashore. The whole company reached the beaches intact and swarmed up the cliffs. The curtain of covering fire moved ahead of them and swept their flanks. As soon as the boats were available the rest of the battalion began to cross, and throughout the afternoon heavily laden craft continued to go to and fro practically unmolested. By nightfall three battalions were over, and ferrying had stopped as the risk of losing boats in the treacherous current in the dark became too great.

. . . . At dawn on the 15th, the crossing was resumed with increasing tempo. All day long men, mules, tanks, guns and stores poured across, and again no enemy opposed them. By evening the South Lancashires and most of 89 Brigade were in the bridgehead. The Japanese, who had now collected in some strength, were driven into caves near Nyaungu where they held out desperately in a sort of catacomb. Its entrances were blown in and sealed off, the defenders left to die inside. During the day another company of the Indian National Army surrendered. By the 16th, Nyaungu Village was in our hands and the main bridgehead, now about four miles by three, had joined up with the Sikhs at Pagan. We were over.

General Slim

Meiktila

Armoured forces from the bridgehead south of Pakokku reached the vital communications centre of Meiktila on 28 February, and a week of bitter fighting was needed to take it.

I left Cowan conducting his grim orchestra. Assured that the battle was in competent hands at the top, I thought I would go a little closer and see how it was being handled lower down. I chose 48 Brigade as, at the moment, they seemed to be cracking a particularly tough nut. We went by jeep round the north of the town and then moved forward on foot somewhat more cautiously. We had a word with various subordinate commanders on the way; all very busy with their own little battles and all in great heart. One of them told us the best place from which to see anything was a massive pagoda that crowned a nearby rise. We reached it along a path screened from the enemy by bushes, and crouching below the surrounding wall, crossed a wide terrace, where already in occupation were some Indian signallers and observation parties. Peering cautiously over the wall, we found on our right the end of the North Lake, placid and unruffled. To our left front, about a thousand yards away, the main road entered Meiktila between close-built houses, now crumbling in the dust, smoke and flame of a bombardment. We were, I knew, about to assault here, but it was the scene immediately below and in front of us which gripped the attention.

The southern shore of the lake, for nearly a mile, ran roughly parallel to the northern edge of the town. Between them was a strip, about half a mile wide, of rough, undulating country, cut up by ditches and banks, with here and there clumps of trees and bushes. Three hundred yards from us, scattered along water cuts, peering round mounds and lying behind bushes, were twenty or thirty Gurkhas, all very close to the ground and evidently, from the spurts around them, under fairly heavy fire. Well to the left of these Gurkhas and a little farther forward, there was a small spinney. From its edge more Gurkhas were firing

Bren-gun bursts. A single Sherman tank, in a scrub-topped hollow, lay between us and the spinney, concealed from the enemy but visible to us. In the intervals of firing, we could hear its engine muttering and grumbling. The dispositions of our forces, two platoons and a tank, were plain enough to us, but I could see no enemy.

Then the tank revved up its engine to a stuttering roar, edged forward a few yards, fired a couple of shots in quick succession, and discreetly withdrew into cover again. I watched the strike of the shot. Through my glasses I could see, about five hundred yards away, three low grassy hummocks. Innocent enough they looked, and little different from half a dozen others. Yet straining my eyes I spotted a dark loophole in one, around which hung the misty smoke of a hot machine-gun; I could hear the *knock-knock-knock*, slower than our own, of its firing. Searching carefully, I picked up loopholes in the other mounds. Here were three typical Japanese bunkers, impervious to any but the heaviest shells, sited for all-round defence, and bristling with automatics—tough nuts indeed. The tank intervened again. Without shifting position it lobbed two or three grenades and a white screen of smoke drifted across the front of the bunkers. One of the Gurkhas below us sprang to his feet, waved an arm, and the whole party, crouching as they went, ran forward. When the smoke blew clear a minute or two later, they were all down under cover again, but a hundred yards nearer those bunkers. A few small shells burst in the water at the lake's edge. Whether they were meant for the tank or the Gurkhas, they got neither, and the enemy gunners made no further contribution.

When I looked for it again the tank had disappeared, but a smoke-screen, this time, I think, from infantry mortars, blinded the bunkers again. The Gurkhas scrambled forward, dodging and twisting over the rough ground, until some of them must have been hardly thirty yards from the enemy. Somewhere behind the spinney, the tank was slowly and methodically firing solid shot at the loopholes. Spurts of dust and debris leapt up at every impact.

As the fight drew to its climax, we moved out of the pagoda enclosure to a spot a little forward and to the right, where, from behind a thick cactus hedge, we had a clearer view. The tank reappeared round the spinney's flank and advanced, still shooting. Gradually it worked round to the rear of the bunkers, and suddenly we were in the line of its fire with overs ricochetting and plunging straight at us. One army commander, one corps commander, an American general, and several less distinguished individuals adopted the prone position with remarkable unanimity. The only casualty was an unfortunate American airman of our crew, who had hitch-hiked with us to see the fun. As the metal whistled over his head he flung himself for cover into the cactus hedge. He was already stripped to the waist and he emerged a blood-stained pin cushion. However, he took his misfortune very well and submitted to what must have been a painful plucking with fortitude.

After this little excitement, the tank having, to our relief, moved again to a flank, we watched the final stages of the action. The fire of Brens and rifles swelled in volume; the tank's gun thudded away. Suddenly three Gurkhas sprang up simultaneously and dashed forward. One fell, but the other two covered the few yards to the bunkers and thrust tommy-guns through loopholes. Behind them surged an uneven line of their comrades; another broke from the spinney, bayonets glinting. They swarmed around the bunkers and for a moment all firing ceased. Then from behind one of the hummocks appeared a ragged group of half a dozen khaki-clad figures, running for safety. They were led, I noticed, by a man exceptionally tall for a Japanese. Twenty Gurkha rifles came up and crashed a volley. Alas for Gurkha marksmanship! Not a Japanese fell; zigzagging, they ran on. But in a few seconds, as the Gurkhas fired again, they were all down, the last to fall being the tall man. The tank lumbered up, dipped its gun and, with perhaps unnecessary emphasis, finished him off. Within ten minutes, having made sure no Japanese remained alive in the bunkers, the two platoons of Gurkhas and their Indian-manned tank moved on to their next assignment which would not be far away. A rear party appeared, attended to their own casualties, and dragged out the enemy bodies to search them for papers and identifications. It was all very business-like.

General Slim

Mandalay

At the same time the Japanese were putting up a desperate fight for Mandalay.

Japanese resistance outside Mandalay was now reduced to small parties, roaming the countryside with little knowledge of what was happening around them, but in two places the defence was still strong and well organized—on Mandalay Hill and in the city itself at Fort Dufferin.

Mandalay Hill is a great rock rising abruptly from the plain to nearly eight hundred feet and dominating the whole north-eastern quarter of the city. Its steep sides are covered with temples and pagodas, now honey-combed for machine-guns, well supplied, and heavily garrisoned. Throughout the day and night of 9 March, the fiercest hand-to-hand fighting went on, as a Gurkha battalion stormed up the slopes and bombed and tommy-gunned their way into the concrete buildings. Next day two companies of a British battalion joined them, and the bitter fighting went on. The Japanese stood to the end, until the last defenders, holding out in cellars, were destroyed by petrol rolled down in drums and ignited by tracer bullets. It was not until 11 March that the hill was completely in our hands. When shortly afterwards I visited it, the blackened marks of fire and the sights and stench of carnage were only too obvious, while distant bumps and bangs and the nearer rattle of machine-guns showed that the clearing of the city was still going on. Through all this noise and the clatter of men clearing a battlefield came a strange sound—singing. I followed it. There was General Rees, his uniform sweat-soaked and dirty, his distinguishing green scarf rumpled round his neck, his bush hat at a jaunty angle, his arm beating time, surrounded by a group of Assamese soldiers whom he was vigorously leading in the singing of Baptist hymns. The fact that he sang in Welsh and they in Khasi only added to the harmony.

. . . . The other Japanese stronghold, Fort Dufferin in Mandalay City, was a great rectangular, walled enclosure, containing one and a quarter square miles of parkland, dotted with official residences, barracks, and other buildings including the fantastic, teak-built Royal Palace of Theebaw, the last Burmese king, its upturned eaves rich with carving, vermilion, and gilding. The crenellated, twenty-foot-high outer walls of the fort were faced with thick brick-work and backed by earth embankments seventy feet wide at their base. All round lay the moat, over two hundred feet wide, water filled and studded with lotus—a picturesque but hampering weed. An immense edition of the toy fortress I used to play with as a boy, Fort Dufferin, manned by Japanese, was a very formidable object to a lightly equipped army in a hurry.

For the next few days, Rees's battalions fought their way street by street through the city, suffering heavily, especially in officers, from snipers, until on the 15th the Fort was completely surrounded. The attack on Fort Dufferin might well have been a scene from the siege of Delhi in the Indian Mutiny. Medium guns were brought up within five hundred yards to breach the walls, rafts and scaling ladders prepared, storming parties detailed, and attempts to enter made through the great pipes that ran into the moat. On the night of 16 March, in attacks on the north-west and north-east corners of the Fort, 'Forlorn Hopes' were repulsed by heavy automatic fire, and our men withdrew, after most gallantly rescuing their wounded. On the 18th and 19th, four separate attempts to cross the moat failed. Such attacks threatened to become expensive, so a more modern aspect was given to the siege by aircraft attacks on the walls. The interior of the Fort had been bombed on the 13th, and serious attempts to breach the walls with 500-lb. bombs began on the 16th. The bombs, like the 5·5-inch shells, only damaged the outer face; the great bank of earth behind was unbreached. Recourse was then had to skip bombing, when Mitchell bombers, flying low, tried to drop 2,000 lb. bombs on the waters of the moat so that they would bounce into the walls. After several days of these attacks a small breach some fifteen feet wide, up which troops might scramble, was made, but the assault would have been hazardous and certainly costly. I was, therefore, against it, as we could now by-pass the Fort, and its eventual capture was inevitable, more indeed a matter of news value than military advantage. I was prepared to wait.

However, during the night of 19/20 March there was great activity in and around the Fort, and, after the morning air strike, a group of Anglo-Burmese waving white flags and Union Jacks appeared at one of the gates. The garrison, they reported, had during the darkness crept through drains from the moat into the southern part of the town. Many were intercepted by our troops, others who hid in deserted houses were hunted down during the next few days, only a handful escaped into open country. Our men entering the Fort found large dumps of Japanese stores and ammunition, a number of European and Anglo-Burmese civilian prisoners, and a fair sprinkling of booby traps.

General Slim

The Race to Rangoon

Towards the end of March 1945, Kimura at last accepted defeat in the great battle of Central Burma, but before doing so he had used up every reserve available to him. He had run true to Japanese form; he had left it until too late.

None the less, in spite of his plans and his armies crumbling about him, he prepared resolutely and energetically to deny us the two routes to the south.

General Slim

One route lay through the town of Toungoo on the Sittang.

. . . . Kimura was driving his men as hard as Messervy and I were driving ours. He had ordered all troops in the Shan Hills to get to Toungoo with sleepless speed. Their roads were the fair-weather hill-tracks that ran roughly parallel to our route, but sixty or seventy miles to the east. Opposite Toungoo and about seventy miles from it, this track turned abruptly west and joined the Rangoon road in the town. Led by the partly reorganized 15 Division, the Japanese, ferrying fast in any kind of vehicle left to them, made for Toungoo, and it looked as if they might beat us to it. But I still had a shot in my locker for them. As it drew south their way led them through the country of the Karens, a race which had remained staunchly loyal to us even in the blackest days of Japanese occupation, and had suffered accordingly. Over a long period, in preparation for this day, we had organized a secret force, the Karen Guerrillas, based on ex-soldiers of the Burma Army, for whom British officers and arms had been parachuted into the hills. It was not at all difficult to get the Karens to rise against the hated Japanese; the problem was to restrain them from rising too soon. But now the time had come, and I gave the word, 'Up the Karens!' Japanese, driving hard through the night down jungle roads for Toungoo, ran into ambush after ambush; bridges were blown ahead of them, their foraging parties massacred, their sentries stalked, their staff cars shot up. Air strikes, directed by British officers, watching from the ground the fall of each stick of bombs, inflicted great damage. The galled Japanese fought their way slowly forward, losing men and vehicles, until about Mawchi, fifty miles east of Toungoo, they were held up for several days by road-blocks, demolition, and ambuscades. They lost the race for Toungoo.

. . . . I knew that with the loss of Toungoo, Kimura must realize that the situation in South Burma was critical. He was probably out of touch with his army commander, now a fugitive, and he could not have much left in the way of reserves. We learnt, on the 24th,* that he was moving his headquarters to Moulmein, but whether this meant that Rangoon would be abandoned or whether, as I had always feared, he would leave a garrison there, I could not tell.

General Slim

The second route lay down the Irrawaddy past Prome.

It was now the beginning of April. We were weary in body but exhilarated in spirit. The heat was growing. In six weeks the monsoon would break and Rangoon was nearly four hundred miles away. We wondered how long our transport would stand up to it. We wondered if we would be bogged down half-way by the monsoon. But I don't think anyone really doubted that we would make it when Bill Slim told us that we could and we'd got to. With 7 Indian

* April (Ed.)

Division mopping up the oilfields area around Yenangyaung, 20 Indian Division swung south-west across the plain below them to Magwe and on to Prome, and the Corps anti-aircraft artillery formed itself into an additional infantry brigade and achieved much killing in ambushes in their successful new role.

From the slow-moving jungle war, forcing our way inch by inch forward against some of the finest infantry in the world, we had now gone over to pursuit, occupying three or four positions a day, trying to catch up with a shattered enemy and kill him before he escaped from the roads and villages of the Irrawaddy valley into the misty Yomas on our left. The battle-winning factor of the jungle war, medium artillery, was no longer queen of the battlefield, leading the advance. But though I had transferred my allegiance to 25-pounders north of the Irrawaddy, my 5·5s came with us, under command, until Rangoon fell and we deployed in penny packets south of Prome to kill the Arakan Japs in their attempts to escape across the river. It was opposite Shwedaung that a Japanese officer surrendered, calling out, 'Do not shoot, I am not combatant. I am artillery officer.' Much good-humoured capital was made by the other arms out of this sorry admission before it was recognized how true, in fact, it was of the handling of the enemy artillery since the Irrawaddy crossings.

Major B. N. L. Ditmas

Rangoon

An amphibious landing was to capture Rangoon in conjunction with the Fourteenth Army's overland advance.

The overture to the landing was on D—1 Day, 1 May, when a heavy bombing attack was delivered on all located defences on both sides of the Rangoon River. Some hours later, a battalion of 50 Indian Parachute Brigade dropped at Elephant Point. A party of about thirty Japanese, either left for observation or just forgotten, offered resistance to the Gurkha paratroops. One wounded Japanese survived. Early on the same morning a pilot, flying over Rangoon, saw written in large letters on the gaol roof the words, '*Japs gone. Exdigitate*'. The R.A.F. slang was not only evidence of the genuineness of the message, but a gentle hint to speed up operations. However, it was determined, wisely I think, to continue according to plan. Early on the 2nd the weather became worse and there was some doubt whether the small landing craft could face the sea. However, it was decided to risk it and by skilful seamanship all reached and entered Rangoon River. A brigade of 26 Division, under Major-General Chambers, was landed on each bank and the advance began. Within a few hours a deluge of rain descended, making all movement arduous. Nevertheless the troops advanced several miles, and by nightfall the eastern brigade was within twelve miles of Rangoon.

While 26 Division was thus plodding forward, the pilot of a Mosquito aircraft of 221 Group, flying low over Rangoon and seeing no signs of enemy, decided to land on Mingaladon airfield at the Cantonment, about eight miles north of the city. The strip was in bad repair and he crashed his aircraft in landing, but, undismayed, he walked into Rangoon, visited our prisoners at the gaol, and assured himself that the Japanese had really gone. In the evening, commandeering a *sampan*, he sailed down the river and met the advancing 26 Division. We were rather pleased about this in Fourteenth Army. If we could not get to Rangoon first ourselves, the next best thing was for someone from 221 Group, which we regarded in all comradeship as part of the Fourteenth Army, to do it. On this confirmation of the Japanese flight, further bombing was called off and the build-up by sea, that was to follow the landing of 26 Division, was cancelled.

It was not until the evening of 3 May that the brigade on the east bank, struggling through waterlogged country, appeared on the Hlaing River, immediately south of Rangoon. It was ferried over and entered the town. The population in thousands welcomed our men with a relief and joy they made no attempt to restrain. We were back!

General Slim

SURRENDER IN SOUTH-EAST ASIA

The Japanese had now but one thought—escape; and in the following three months tried to fight their way out to the eastward. Very few succeeded. Early in September, after the Japanese Imperial Government had surrendered, Singapore capitulated to the British, and then in the same city on 12 September the final surrender of Japan in that theatre was signed in the presence of Admiral Mountbatten, his subordinate commanders and his allies. Four days later, Hong Kong followed suit. The wheel had turned full circle.

Singapore

In the doorway stood a marine sentry. For a moment dead silence filled the Admiral's dining-room. Then General Christison opened the proceedings, speaking through his interpreter.

Christison: 'What is your name, rank and appointment?'

Itagaki: 'General Itagaki, Commander-in-Chief of the Seventh Area Army.'

Christison: 'Are you entitled to speak for the Field-Marshal Count Terauchi, Supreme Japanese Commander, Southern Region, on Army matters?'

Itagaki: 'Not entirely for the whole area, but only for the landings in the Singapore area.'

Christison: 'Do you know the Terms of Agreement signed in Rangoon?'

Itagaki: 'I know of the Agreement signed in Rangoon, and furthermore I have complied with what I ought to have done in Singapore with regard to this Agreement.'

Christison: 'Do you abide by the Imperial decision to cease hostilities and are you prepared to carry out the orders of the Supreme Allied Commander, South-east Asia?'

Itagaki: 'Yes, I am quite prepared. . . .'

Christison: 'Is there any sabotage, looting or local civil disturbance taking place in the Singapore area?'

Itagaki: 'With regard to the maintenance of law and order, there are no riots of a serious nature, but there is every sign of possible looting and some sort of violence of a small nature which is under the guard of our forces now. And we have also suspicions certain societies are being formed, but we are taking every possible step to suppress them. We are also collecting information about them.'

Christison: 'I rely on General Itagaki to keep law and order until my forces take over.'

Itagaki: 'Yes, I will.'

Christison: 'My forces will act strictly in accordance with the Laws and Usages of War and International Law.'

Itagaki: 'Yes.'

The Vanquished

In Singapore on 12 September 1945 I sat on the left of the Supreme Commander, Admiral Mountbatten, in the line of his Commanders-in-Chief and principal staff officers, when the formal unconditional surrender of all Japanese forces, land, sea, and air, in South-east Asia was made to him. I looked at the dull impassive masks that were the faces of the Japanese generals and admirals seated opposite. Their plight moved me not at all. For them, I had none of the sympathy of soldier for soldier, that I had felt for Germans, Turks, Italians, or Frenchmen that by the fortune of war I had seen surrender. I knew too well what these men and those under their orders had done to *their* prisoners. They sat there apart from the rest of humanity. If I had no feeling for them, they, it seemed, had no feeling of any sort, until Itagaki, who had replaced Field-Marshal Terauchi, laid low by a stroke, leant forward to affix his seal to the surrender document. As he pressed heavily on the paper, a spasm of rage and despair twisted his face. Then it was gone and his mask was as expressionless as the rest. Outside, the same Union Jack that had been hauled down in surrender in 1942 flew again at the masthead.

The war was over.

General Slim

29

THE RUSSIAN AVALANCHE,
1943-1945

On 2 February [1943] Marshal Voronov reported that all resistance [in Stalingrad] had ceased and ninety thousand prisoners had been taken. These were the survivors of twenty-one German and one Roumanian divisions. Thus ended Hitler's prodigious effort to conquer Russia by force and destroy Communism by an equally odious form of totalitarian tyranny.

The spring of 1943 marked the turning-point of the war on the Eastern Front. Even before Stalingrad the mounting Russian tide had swept the enemy back all along the line. The German Army of the Caucasus was skilfully withdrawn, but the Russians pressed the enemy from the Don and back beyond the Donetz river, the starting line of Hitler's offensive of the previous summer. Farther north again the Germans lost ground, until they were more than two hundred and fifty miles from Moscow. The investment of Leningrad was broken. The Germans and their satellites suffered immense losses in men and material. The ground gained in the past year was taken from them.

Winston Churchill

Italians Retreat in the Steppes

We paraded again just before dawn; orders to leave everything except our arms and ammunition. My companions look at me, and showing me bundles of letters ask me, 'Can we keep these?' They look gloomy and worried; no one throws any ammunition away. 'Perhaps we're off, finally,' I say to them, 'we'll have to walk a lot and so must be as light as possible.' The officers say, 'Be quick, we're leaving.'

We walk hurriedly along. The stars soon vanish and the sky becomes as it was yesterday. A company of our battalion was missing at the parade and no one knows where it is. Later I heard that the whole of this company was taken prisoner. It was alone in the rear-guard and had delayed on its positions that morning. Columns of men in khaki had advanced across the steppes towards them and the officers had said, 'They're the Hungarians coming to take over.' But when they were on top of them they realized they were Russians. So they were caught. The only ones saved were an officer, a soldier or two, and the Captain who caught up with us later. He was drunk with brandy and shouting: 'My company are all prisoners, we're all surrounded, it's useless to fight.' But as he was drunk no one took any notice.

Now it's up to us to go and try and break out of the ring. They say that last night the divisional staff had a conference and decided we're to go on to the very last.

We all became confident, almost gay, we're convinced that we'll make it this time. I sing a song with Antonelli and Tourn. One or two passers-by look at us pityingly; they think we're mad. But we go on singing more gaily than ever. Lieutenant Cenci laughs.

.... The sun is going down, our shadows lengthen on the snow. Around us is a vast emptiness, without houses, without trees, without any sign of a living being, except for us and the column behind us which merges into the distance where the sky joins the steppe.

We walk on. Looking around I notice that ahead of us, only a little off the track, are some stray horses. I manage to catch them. We try to load the two Bredas on the strongest. But the Captain won't allow us. He says we must always have our weapons ready. And so we lead the horses along behind us and carry the guns. After a bit the Captain takes one of the horses and mounts it. He's very tired and has fever. Cenci takes a horse for his platoon. On the remaining one I load the gun-bearers' packs.

Now the sun has gone down and we're still walking. Mute, with our heads low, we sway as we go, trying to put our feet in the tracks of the man in front. Why are we walking on like this? Just so's to fall in the snow a little farther on and never rise again.

Halt. The man in front stops and we all stop. We fling ourselves down on the snow. Italian and German staff officers on a tracked vehicle near us consult maps and compasses. The hours pass, night comes and we don't move. Perhaps they're waiting for a wireless message. Being motionless we feel the cold worse than ever, and everything round is dark, both steppes and sky. Dry, hard grass sticks out of the snow. The only sound is the strange noise it makes in the wind. None of us speak. We sit on the snow near each other with our blankets on our shoulders. We're ice inside and out, and yet we're still alive. I take my reserve tin of rations out of my pack and open it, but I seem to be chewing ice, it hasn't any taste and won't go down; I manage to eat half and put the rest back in my pack. I get up and bang my feet. Lieutenant Moscioni comes towards me. Cenci is with him and we smoke a cigarette together. We only speak a few words, our vocal chords seem frozen too. But standing like this, smoking, gives a little comfort. We think of nothing, smoke and all is silent. One can't even hear Antonelli swearing.

'Get up! Get up!' comes a shout finally from somewhere. We start off again. It's difficult, very difficult to move the first steps; shoulders ache, legs ache, limbs have gone torpid with the cold and don't seem to obey. But bit by bit, slowly, slowly, the legs begin to carry the body forward.

So once again we walk on; section by section, platoon by platoon. Sleepiness, hunger, cold, exhaustion, the weight of our guns are nothing and everything. The only important thing is to walk. And it's always night, just stars and snow, snow and stars. Looking at the stars I notice that we are changing direction. But where are we going now? I realize we're getting into deep snow again. From the top of a rise we see some lights far away; a village! Antonelli begins to swear again and the Lieutenant to rebuke him and Antonelli to send him to the Verona slums. And Bodei asks me: 'Sergeant-major, will we stop there?' 'Yes, we'll stop,' I reply in a loud voice. But how can I know, I think, if we'll stop or not,

or if we'll pass by it or if the Russians are there? 'We'll stop,' I say loudly both
for them and myself. Major Bracchi pauses near us: 'Rigoni,' he says, in a voice
that everyone can hear. 'We'll find warm *isbas** there, Rigoni.'

Sergeant Mario Rigoni Stern

Hitler Explains

The débâcle of the past winter, the Führer explained, was chiefly owing to
the utter failure of our allies to do their part. Now the front was in order again.
This was a military achievement of the first magnitude, and simply cannot be
over-estimated. The Führer doesn't want to see any more allies on the Eastern
Front. He has fully made up his mind that only our own soldiers can finish off
the Bolsheviks.

Dr. Goebbels

*Early in March 1943 Von Manstein on the Donetz launched a successful
counter-attack, recapturing Kharkov, but then the spring came with its mud and
imposed another halt on major operations.*

At the end of March 1943 the thaw started on the Eastern Front; 'Marshal
Winter' gave way to the still more masterful 'Marshal Mud', and active operations came automatically to an end. All Panzer divisions and some infantry
divisions were withdrawn from the front line. . . . Advantage was taken of the
lull to institute a thorough training programme, and exercise the units on peace-
time lines.

By the spring of 1943 the military position of Germany had worsened im-
measurably. In Russia the moral comfort of Manstein's latest victory could not
obscure the fact that the whole balance of power had changed, and that we were
faced by a ruthless enemy, possessed of immense and seemingly inexhaustible
resources.

General von Mellenthin

KURSK

*With the coming of summer, the Germans got in their blow first—the last major
counter-offensive they were to launch in Russia, though it was on nothing like the
scale of their earlier grand assaults.*

In the circumstances the German Supreme Command was faced with a
grave dilemma. Should we stand purely on the defensive in the East, or should
we launch a limited attack in an endeavour to cripple Russia's offensive power?
. . . . It is true that in view of the losses suffered in preceding years there
could be no question of seeking a decision. Zeitzler's object was a limited one;
he wished to bite out the great Russian bulge which enclosed Kursk and projected for seventy-five miles into our front. A successful attack in this area would
destroy a number of Soviet divisions and weaken the offensive power of the
Red Army to a very considerable degree.

* Russian cottages (Ed.)

.... Such was my introduction to the fateful Battle of Kursk—the last great German offensive in the East.

Zeitzler outlined the plan for Operation 'Citadel', as the new attack was to be called. All our available armour was to be concentrated in two great pincers—Colonel-General Model with his 9 Army was to attack from the north, and Colonel-General Hoth with 4 Panzer Army from the south. In the initial assault Hoth was to have eight Panzer divisions and Model five; several infantry divisions were to join in the attack, and to obtain them the neighbouring fronts were to be thinned out beyond the limits of prudence. From the strategic aspect 'Citadel' was to be a veritable 'death-ride', for virtually the whole of the operational reserve was to be flung into this supreme offensive.

Because so much was at stake, hesitations and doubts were bound to arise. When the attack was originally proposed, Field-Marshal von Manstein was strongly in favour, and believed that if we struck soon a notable victory could be won.* But Hitler kept postponing D-Day, partly in order to assemble stronger forces, and partly because he had the gravest doubts about our prospects of success. Early in May he held a conference in Munich and sought the views of the senior commanders. Field-Marshal von Kluge, the commander of Army Group Centre, was strongly in favour; Manstein was now dubious, and Model produced air photographs which showed that the Russians were constructing very strong positions at the shoulders of the salient and had withdrawn their mobile forces from the area west of Kursk. This showed that they were aware of the impending attack and were making adequate preparations to deal with it.

Colonel-General Guderian spoke out and declared that an offensive at Kursk was 'pointless'; heavy tank casualties were bound to be incurred and would ruin his plans for reorganizing the armour. He warned that the Panthers, on which 'the Chief of the Army General Staff was relying so heavily, were still suffering from many teething troubles inherent in all new equipment'. But General Zeitzler was still confident of victory, and perplexed by the conflict among the experts, Hitler put off the decision until a later date.

At this conference on 'Citadel' Hitler made the significant and perfectly accurate comment, that 'it must not fail'. On 10 May Guderian saw him again and begged him to give up the idea; Hitler replied, 'You're quite right. Whenever I think of this attack my stomach turns over.' Yet under the pressure of Keitel and Zeitzler he ultimately gave way, and consented to an operation of grandiose proportions. The attack from the south was to be made by ten Panzer, one Panzer Grenadier, and seven infantry divisions; the northern thrust would be delivered by seven Panzer, two Panzer Grenadier and nine infantry divisions.†️ It was to be the greatest armoured onslaught in the history of war.

.... It is an accepted fact that plans and preparations for an operation of such magnitude cannot be kept secret for any length of time. The Russians reacted to our plans exactly as was to be expected. They fortified likely sectors, built several lines of resistance, and converted important tactical points into

---

* Manstein had pointed out, however, that there was much to be gained by adopting a strategy of manœuvre. He suggested withdrawing his right wing to the Dnieper, and then counter-attacking from the area of Kharkov. Such a conception had no appeal for Hitler.

† These totals include reserves not committed in the initial assault.

miniature fortresses. The area was studded with minefields, and very strong armoured and infantry reserves were assembled at the base of the salient. If 'Citadel' had been launched in April or May it might have yielded a valuable harvest, but by June the conditions were totally different. The Russians were aware of what was coming, and had converted the Kursk front into another Verdun.

. . . . The German Supreme Command was committing exactly the same error as in the previous year. Then we attacked the City of Stalingrad, now we were to attack the Fortress of Kursk. In both cases the German Army threw away all its advantages in mobile tactics, and met the Russians on ground of their own choosing. Yet the campaigns of 1941 and 1942 had proved that our Panzers were virtually invincible if they were allowed to manœuvre freely across the great plains of Russia. Instead of seeking to create conditions in which manœuvre would be possible—by strategic withdrawals or surprise attacks in quiet sectors —the German Supreme Command could think of nothing better than to fling our magnificent Panzer divisions against Kursk, which had now become the strongest fortress in the world.

By the middle of June Field-Marshal von Manstein, and indeed all his senior commanders, saw that it was folly to go on with 'Citadel'. Manstein urged most strongly that the offensive should be abandoned, but he was overruled. D-Day was finally fixed for 4 July—Independence Day for the United States, the beginning of the end for Germany.

. . . . The terrain, over which the advance was to take place, was a far-flung plain, broken by numerous valleys, small copses, irregularly laid out villages and some rivers and brooks; of these the Pena ran with a swift current between steep banks. The ground rose slightly to the north, thus favouring the defender. Roads consisted of tracks through the sand and became impassable for all motor transport during rain. Large cornfields covered the landscape and made visibility difficult. All in all, it was not good 'tank country', but it was by no means 'tank proof'. There had been sufficient time to make thorough preparations for the attack.

. . . . Contrary to the normal practice, we were not to attack at dawn, but in the middle of the afternoon. On 4 July the weather was hot and sultry and there was a feeling of tension along the battlefront. The morale of the attacking troops was of the highest; they were prepared to endure any losses and carry out every task given to them. Unhappily they had been set the wrong tasks.

General von Mellenthin

The Battle

The Battle of Kursk began at 15.00 hours on 4 July with an attack on the forward Russian lines, preceded by a short but sharp artillery preparation and air bombardment. On the front of XLVIII Panzer Corps, these lines ran some three miles south of the villages of Luchanino, Alexejewka and Sawidowka. Grenadiers and riflemen supported by assault guns and engineers penetrated the Russian forward line that evening. During the night the tanks were moved up and P.G.D. *'Gross Deutschland'* was ordered to advance next morning between

Ssyrzew and Luchanino. 3 and 11 Panzer Divisions were to attack on the flanks of *'Gross Deutschland'*. But as bad luck would have it, a violent cloudburst that night transformed the ground along the banks of the stream between Ssyrzew and Sawidowka into a morass. This proved of the greatest advantage to the Russian second line to the north of the stream and immensely increased its already considerable defensive strength.

On the second day of the attack we met our first setback, and in spite of every effort the troops were unable to penetrate the Russian line. *'Gross Deutschland'*, assembling in dense formation and with the swamp on its immediate front, was heavily shelled by Russian artillery. The engineers were unable to make suitable crossings, and many tanks fell victims to the Red Air Force—during this battle Russian aircraft operated with remarkable dash in spite of German air superiority. Even in the area taken by the German troops on the first day Russians appeared from nowhere, and the reconnaissance units of *'Gross Deutschland'* had to deal with them. Nor was it possible to cross the stream and swamp on the night 5/6 July. On the left flank the attacks of 3 Panzer Division against Sawidowka were as unsuccessful as those of *'Gross Deutschland'* against Alexejewka and Luchanino. The entire area had been infested with mines; and the Russian defence along the whole line was supported by tanks operating with all the advantages of high ground. Our assault troops suffered considerable casualties, and 3 Panzer Division had to beat off counter-attacks. In spite of several massive bombing attacks by the Luftwaffe against battery positions, the Russian defensive fire did not decrease to any extent.

On 7 July, the fourth day of 'Citadel', we at last achieved some success. *'Gross Deutschland'* was able to break through on both sides of Ssyrzew, and the Russians withdrew to Gremutshy and Ssyrzewo. The fleeing masses were caught by German artillery fire and suffered very heavy casualties; our tanks gained momentum and wheeled to the north-west. But at Ssyrzew that afternoon they were halted by strong defensive fire, and Russian armour counter-attacked. However, on the right wing we seemed within reach of a big victory; the grenadier regiment of *'Gross Deutschland'* was reported to have reached Werchopenje. On the right flank of *'Gross Deutschland'* a battle-group was formed to exploit this success; it consisted of the reconnaissance detachment and the assault-gun detachment and was told to advance as far as Height 260.8 to the south of Nowosselowka. When this battle-group reached Gremutshy they found elements of the grenadier regiment in the village. The grenadiers were under the illusion that they were in Nowosselowka and could not believe that they were only in Gremutshy. Thus the report of the so-called success of the grenadiers was proved wrong; things like that happen in every war and particularly in Russia.

On 8 July the battle-group, consisting of the reconnaissance detachment and assault-gun detachment of *'Gross Deutschland'*, advanced up the main road, and reached Height 260.8; it then wheeled to the west to ease the advance of the divisional Panzer regiment and the Panzer Grenadiers who by-passed Werchopenje on the east. This village was still held by considerable enemy forces and the rifle regiment attacked it from the south. Height 243.0, immediately to the north of Werchopenje, was held by Russian tanks, which had a magnificent field of fire. The attack of the Panzers and grenadiers broke down in front of this hill; the Russian tanks seemed to be everywhere and singled out the spearhead of 'Gross Deutschland', allowing it no rest.

That afternoon the battle-group on the right of 'Gross Deutschland' repulsed seven attacks by Russian armour and knocked out twenty-one T.34s. XLVIII Panzer Corps ordered the Schwerpunkt of 'Gross Deutschland' to wheel westward and bring some help to 3 Panzer Division where the threat to the left flank remained as grave as ever. Neither Height 243.0 nor the western outskirts of Werchopenje were taken on that day—it could no longer be doubted that the back of the German attack had been broken and its momentum had gone.

The slow progress of the southern pincer was disappointing, but we had in fact done much better than our comrades on the northern flank of the salient. General Guderian says of his visit to 9 Army (in Panzer Leader, p. 311):

'. . . . The ninety Porsche Tigers, which were operating with Model's army, were incapable of close-range fighting since they lacked sufficient ammunition for their guns, and this defect was aggravated by the fact that they possessed no machine-gun. Once they had broken into the enemy's infantry zone they literally had to go quail-shooting with cannons. They did not manage to neutralize, let alone destroy, the enemy rifles and machine-guns, so that the infantry was unable to follow up behind them. By the time they reached the Russian artillery they were on their own. Despite showing extreme bravery and suffering unheard-of casualties, the infantry of Weidling's division did not manage to exploit the tanks' success. Model's attack bogged down after some six miles.'

After a week of hard and almost uninterrupted fighting 'Gross Deutschland' was showing signs of exhaustion and its ranks had been thinned out considerably. On 10 July this division was ordered to wheel to the south and south-west and clean up the enemy on the left flank. The Panzer regiment, the reconnaissance detachment and the grenadier regiment were to advance towards Height 243.0 and to the north thereof; they were then to seize 247.0 to the south of Kruglik and move southwards from there to the small forest north of Beresowka where the Russians were holding up 3 Panzer Division; strong formations of the Luftwaffe were to support this attack.

The air bombardment was extraordinarily effective and the War Diary of the reconnaissance detachment describes it as follows*:

'With admiration we watch the Stukas attacking the Russian tanks uninterruptedly and with wonderful precision. Squadron after squadron of Stukas come over to drop their deadly eggs on the Russian armour. Dazzling white flames indicate that another enemy tank has "brewed up". This happens again and again.'

Supported by the splendid efforts of the Luftwaffe, 'Gross Deutschland' made

---

* The Battle of Kursk was the first occasion on which aircraft operated in force against armour and the results were highly encouraging. The famous Stuka pilot, Hans Rudel, experimented with cannon-firing Stukas, and says: 'In the first attack four tanks explode under the hammer blows of my cannon; by the evening the total rises to twelve . . . the evil spell is broken, and in this aircraft we possess a weapon which can speedily be employed everywhere and is capable of dealing successfully with the formidable numbers of Soviet tanks.' (Stuka Pilot, p. 86.)

a highly successful advance; heights 243.0 and 247.0 were taken, and Russian infantry and armour fled before the Panzers and sought refuge in the wood north of Beresowka. Trapped between 'Gross Deutschland' and 3 Panzer, it seemed as if the enemy on the left flank had at last been liquidated, and the advance to the north could now be resumed. On 11 July XLVIII Panzer Corps issued orders for the units of 'Gross Deutschland' to be relieved by 3 Panzer Division during the night; 'Gross Deutschland' was to assemble astride the road south of Height 260.8, and to stand by for an advance to the north. In view of the breakdown of Model's attack, a successful advance in this quarter offered the only hope of victory.

On the night 11/12 July the units of 'Gross Deutschland' were relieved by 3 Panzer Division according to plan, but the Panzer Grenadiers moved off with a sense of uneasiness. The last stages of the relief were carried out under heavy enemy shelling, and the men of 'Gross Deutschland' left their trenches to the accompaniment of the battle noises of a Russian counter-attack. Their fears— alas—came true, for that very night 3 Panzer Division was thrown out of its forward positions.

On the morning of 12 July 'Gross Deutschland' was assembled and concentrated astride the road south of Nowosselowka, waiting to launch the decisive advance to the north at first light on the 13th. 12 July was their first day without fighting; this breathing space was used to replenish ammunition and fuel and to carry out such repairs as could be effected in the forward area. Reconnaissance to the north reported that Nowosselowka only seemed to be occupied by insignificant forces. Heavy firing was heard to the west, and the news from 3 Panzer Division was not encouraging.

On 13 July patrolling to the north was intensified, but the expected order to advance did not come through—instead unpleasant reports were received from neighbouring formations. Strong Russian counter-attacks had been launched against the S.S. Panzer Corps and 11 Panzer Division; it was true that the number of Russian tanks knocked out on the whole front was enormous, but new tanks took the place of the casualties; faithful to their principle the Russians kept on throwing in fresh troops, and their reserves seemed inexhaustible. On the afternoon of 13 July, the Corps Commander, General von Knobelsdorff, appeared at the Battle Headquarters of 'Gross Deutschland' and gave orders which left no hope for any advance to the north: in fact the division was again to attack westwards.

By the evening of 14 July it was obvious that the timetable of the German attack had been completely upset. At the very beginning of the offensive, the piercing of the forward Russian lines, deeply and heavily mined as they were, had proved much more difficult than we anticipated. The terrific Russian counter-attacks, with masses of men and material ruthlessly thrown in, were also an unpleasant surprise. German casualties had not been light, while our tank losses were staggering. The Panthers did not come up to expectations; they were easily set ablaze, the oil and petrol feeding systems were inadequately protected, and the crews were insufficiently trained. Of the eighty Panthers available when battle was joined only a few were left on 14 July. The S.S. Panzer Corps was no better off, while on the northern flank 9 Army had never penetrated more than seven miles into the Russian lines and was now at a complete standstill. 4 Panzer Army had indeed reached a depth of twelve miles, but there were another sixty miles to cover before we could join hands with Model.

On 13 July, Field-Marshals von Manstein and Kluge were summoned to East Prussia, and Hitler informed them that 'Citadel' must be called off immediately as the Allies had landed in Sicily; troops must be transferred from the Eastern Front to deal with the invasion. Manstein had not committed all his forces and was in favour of continuing the offensive as a battle of attrition; by smashing up Russian armoured reserves in the Kursk salient we might forestall major offensives in other sectors. This situation should have been foreseen before 'Citadel' was launched; we were now in the position of a man who has seized a wolf by the ears and dare not let him go. However, Hitler declared that the attack must stop forthwith.

The Russian High Command had conducted the Battle of Kursk with great skill, yielding ground adroitly and taking the sting out of our offensive with an intricate system of minefields and anti-tank defences. Not satisfied with counterattacking in the salient, the Russians delivered heavy blows between Orel and Bryansk and made a serious penetration. With Hitler's decision to go on to the defensive, the situation on the Eastern Front became very critical. 4 Panzer Army was informed that the S.S. Panzer Corps would be withdrawn immediately for operations in Italy, while XLVIII Panzer Corps was told to release '*Gross Deutschland*' and send it to the assistance of Field-Marshal von Kluge's Army Group Centre. In the circumstances it was impossible to hold our gains in the Kursk salient, and by 23 July 4 Panzer Army had been pushed back to its start line.

'Citadel' had been a complete and most regrettable failure. It is true that Russian losses were much heavier than German; indeed, tactically the fighting had been indecisive. 4 Panzer Army took thirty-two thousand prisoners, and captured or destroyed more than two thousand tanks and nearly two thousand guns. But our Panzer divisions—in such splendid shape at the beginning of the battle—had been bled white, and with Anglo-American assistance the Russians could afford losses on this colossal scale. (Marshal Koniev afterwards described the Battle of Kursk as 'the swan-song of the German armoured force'.)

With the failure of our supreme effort, the strategic initiative passed to the Russians.

. . . . The flower of the German Army had fallen in the Battle of Kursk, where our troops attacked with a desperate determination to conquer or die. They had gone into the battle with a spirit no less determined than that of the storm troops of 1918, and it might be thought that a weakening of morale would follow our withdrawal from the ill-fated salient of Kursk. Actually nothing of the sort occurred; our ranks had been woefully thinned, but the fierce resolution of the fighting troops remained unshaken. This is not the place for a detailed discussion of this question, but it is obvious that the character of our adversary had much to do with the unyielding spirit of the troops. The Churchill-Roosevelt demand for 'Unconditional Surrender' gave us no hope from the West, while the men fighting on the Russian Front were well aware of the horrible fate which would befall Eastern Germany if the Red hordes broke into our country. So whatever the strategic consequences of the Battle of Kursk— and they were grave enough—it did not produce any weakening in German determination or morale.

General von Mellenthin

The heat of the summer had now returned, to the discomfort of the troops; and the orders and comments from the rear still showed no signs of recognizing the facts which the German soldiers could see written on the wall.

Old Soldiers

The main fighting line which the division was holding in the marshy lagoons of the river Gurka on the Kuban bridgehead was more in the water than out of it. The soldiers, living on bundles of reeds and rafts, were plagued by mosquitoes, midges, fleas and lice; and the inevitable scratching resulted in skin rashes which instead of healing got progressively worse and worse. We saw almost incredible things: men who hadn't a single healthy patch of skin left on their legs. The patients didn't come to us when the trouble started; they were hardened campaigners who never reported sick until they couldn't bear it any longer. By that time their skin was usually in such an appalling state that they had to be sent to a hospital in the rear—which is precisely what they had been trying to avoid. They knew from experience that they were better off with their own unit than anywhere else; their services were valued there and they knew that there they could depend on the next man and that he would really know his job. They had officers, too, who for many years had shared the hardships of campaign after campaign with them.

These old soldiers were the backbone of the army. They were vastly experienced in battle, imperturbable, had a matchless sense of humour. At that time a story was going around, its irony a typical reflection of their wit. It was a forecast of the victorious entry through the Brandenburger Tor: first a company of Field-Marshals marching in ponderous step; then the Supremo clad entirely in gold with a mammoth Knight's Iron Cross with laurels on a self-propelled carriage behind him; behind, an unending stream of derisive caricatures, which I have since forgotten. Finally, at the very end, an ancient corporal from the steppes, enormously bearded, very bedraggled, weighed down by gas-mask, entrenching tools, groundsheet, mess tins, hand grenades, a rifle. When asked what he's doing there, he replies: '*Nix ponemayu.*' He has been in Russia so long that he has forgotten his German.

'*Ponemayu*' means 'Do you understand?' It has been known to happen that a fisherman from the Friesian Isles and a wine-grower from Styria could understand each other best if they conversed in Russian. There was one occasion, for example, when we had such a Styrian peasant on the operating table, a strapping, black-haired fellow of immense physical strength. He had been given a whiff of ether on account of a trivial injury and our four men had hardly been able to hold him down. My orderlies couldn't, of course, abstain from bawdy comments on his manly prowess. As the Styrian came round after the anaesthetic and it gradually dawned on his stolid brain that it was Prussians who were thus maltreating him, he raised himself up on the operating table, looked darkly at each of us in turn, and then said in his broad accent: 'We Austrians loathe your bloody Prussian guts! *Ponemayu?*' We understood all right.

Peter Bamm

The S.S. Carries On

What happens to a Russian, or to a Czech, does not interest me in the slightest. What the nations can offer in the way of good blood of our type we will take, if necessary by kidnapping their children and raising them here with us. Whether nations live in prosperity or starve to death interests me only in so far as we need them as slaves for our *Kultur*: otherwise, it is of no interest to me. Whether ten thousand Russian females fall down from exhaustion while digging an anti-tank ditch interests me only in so far as the anti-tank ditch for Germany is finished.

Himmler, October 1943

To lock men, women and children into barns and set fire to them does not appear to be a suitable method for combating bands, even if it is desired to exterminate the population. This method is not worthy of the German cause and hurts our reputation severely.

Alfred Rosenberg to the Reich Minister
for the Occupied Eastern Territories, June 1943

The activity of the labour offices, that is, of recruiting commissions, is to be supported to the greatest extent possible. It will not be possible always to refrain from using force. During a conference with the Chief of the Labour Commitment Staffs, an agreement was reached stating that whatever prisoners can be released should be put at the disposal of the Commissioner of the Labour Office. When searching villages, when it has become necessary to burn down these villages, the whole population will be put at the disposal of the Commissioner by force.

As a rule no more children will be shot.

Secret S.S. order, March 1943

The Two Trains

Köln *Hauptbahnhof*. The scene was much the same as when five young *Unterärzte* had left for Normandy. Bombing raids had altered the appearance of Cologne somewhat, but the huge roof still arched across the station; steam and smoke still lingered among the steel girders. The loudspeaker blared: 'Special troop express for Maastricht, Liège, Paris is standing at Platform Four.' The harsh, precise voice paused. 'Special troop express for Hanover and Berlin, with connections to Warsaw, Brest-Litovsk, Smolensk will leave from Platform Three.'

A train stood at each side of the broad platform, and around the doors and windows of each train stood the crowds of civilians who had come to see their menfolk off. But there could have been no greater contrast between the two sets of people. On one side there were loud farewells, laughter, joking, excited instructions regarding what the soldiers must bring home from Paris when next they came on leave. People said 'Good luck!' and it was only words. On our side there was little talking, no laughter. It seemed that everything had already been said. Women wiped tear-filled eyes and the partings were sober and deliberate.

Heinrich Haape

THE RUSSIAN OFFENSIVES: 1943

While the fateful battle of Kursk was still in progress the Russians attacked strongly near Orel, and the German salient about the latter town could not be held. To the north the Germans fell back on Smolensk, which fell later in September. The second major Russian offensive opened early in August, when Kharkov was recaptured again and the Germans rolled back to—and beyond—the Dnieper. Their forces in the Crimea were cut off. Early in November, Kiev was retaken.

Scorched-Earth Retreat

Farther to the south . . . Generals Malinovsky and Tolbukhin pierced the defences along the Donetz and on the Mius river; at the end of August our XXIX Corps was encircled in Taganrog and had great difficulty in breaking out. On 3 September von Manstein flew to Hitler's Headquarters to warn him that Army Group South was facing catastrophe, and to demand a change in the conduct of operations. The interview was a stormy one, and led to no result. The situation at the front became increasingly critical, for early in September the Russians captured Stalino and smashed their way into the Donetz industrial area. Moreover, Koniev resumed his offensive on the sector of 4 Panzer Army. XLVIII Panzer Corps was the target of strong attacks, and the Russians broke through on our left flank, while they also severely handled the northern wing of 8 Army on our right.

Not until then, when Army Group South was in imminent danger of breaking up into isolated groups, did the Supreme Commander of the Wehrmacht give permission for a withdrawal behind the Dnieper. But Hitler had refused to permit the construction of any fortifications on the river bank, on the ground that if his generals knew there was a reserve line they would at once fall back there. Thus it was very doubtful whether we would be able to stop the Russians on the Dnieper, and to make matters worse there were only five crossings available. The situation could only be mastered if the Russian advance was delayed.

As is well known the Russians make very limited use of supply columns, and their troops live mainly on the country. Their method is not new; it is essentially similar to that of the Mongols of Jenghiz Khan, or the armies of Napoleon. The only means of slowing down armies of this kind is to totally destroy everything that can be used to feed and house them. In the autumn of 1943 the German Army deliberately adopted this policy, and R. T. Paget remarks very appropriately [in *Manstein*, p. 63]:

'Some five years later, lawyers were to argue for hours as to the legality of the demolition and requisitions carried out by the Germans during their retreat, but I am afraid that no law that conflicts with an army's capacity to survive is ever likely to be effective.'

General von Mellenthin

The extremely difficult conditions under which these movements had to be carried out made it imperative that we should take every possible measure likely to impede the enemy. It was essential to ensure that when he reached the Dnieper he could not immediately continue his offensive while still enjoying the advantages of pursuit.

Consequently it was now necessary for the Germans, too, to resort to the 'scorched earth' policy which the Soviets had adopted during their retreats in previous years.

In a fifteen-mile zone forward of the Dnieper everything which might enable the enemy to go straight over the river on a broad front was destroyed or evacuated. This included anything affording cover or accommodation for Soviet troops in an assembly area opposite our Dnieper defences and anything which might ease their supply problem, particularly in the way of food.

Field-Marshal von Manstein

On 27 September XLVIII Panzer Corps had abandoned the bridgehead at Kremenchug, and stood safely on the southern bank of the Dnieper. The river itself was a comforting obstacle, about four hundred yards wide at this point, and with the bank considerably higher on our side of the stream. However, thick reeds extending some distance into the water made it relatively easy for the Russians to hide boats and camouflage their preparations. Moreover, it has been most wisely said that, 'few indeed are the instances in history of a river line athwart the advance of a superior army proving an effective defence' [W. S. Churchill, *The World Crisis: The Eastern Front* (Butterworth, 1931), p. 318].

. . . . The next fortnight passed quietly on our front; the scorched earth tactics were bearing fruit and the Russians were still unable to mount an offensive on a large scale in this sector. XLVIII Panzer Corps was under command of 8 Army, which held a front of over two hundred miles from Kremenchug to south of Kiev. This army was commanded by General Wöhler with the highly capable General Speidel as his Chief of Staff. The only Russian bridgehead on the front of 8 Army was the one which XLVIII Panzer Corps was containing to the south of Pereyaslav. There was no doubt that the Russians would attack again in this quarter, and reconnaissance and intelligence reports showed that a constant stream of reinforcements was moving into the bridgehead. They had thrown several bridges across the Dnieper, and such was their skill at field engineering that they actually built bridges below water level on which troops or animals could wade across.

General von Mellenthin

Defence of the Dnieper

At 06.30 on 16 October the Russians launched their attack against the positions of XLVIII Panzer Corps; I happened to be in one of the forward observation posts of 19 Panzer Division, and had to stay there for fully two hours. The artillery bombardment was really quite impressive. No movement was possible, for two hundred and ninety guns of all calibres were pounding a thousand yards of front, and during these two hours the Russians expended their normal ammunition allowance for one-and-a-half days. The bombardment reached as far back as divisional battle headquarters, and the two divisions holding the corps front were shelled with such intensity that it was impossible to gauge the *Schwerpunkt*. Some Russian guns fired over open sights from uncovered gun emplacements. After the two hours' bombardment our trench system looked like a freshly ploughed field, and in spite of being carefully dug in, many of our heavy weapons and anti-tank guns had been knocked out.

Suddenly Russian infantry in solid serried ranks attacked behind a barrage on a narrow front, with tanks in support, and one wave following the other. Numerous low-flying planes attacked those strong-points which were still firing. A Russian infantry attack is an awe-inspiring spectacle; the long grey waves come pounding on, uttering fierce cries, and the defending troops require nerves of steel. In dealing with such attacks fire-discipline is of vital importance.

The Russian onslaught made some headway but during the afternoon the armoured assault troops, whom we were keeping in reserve, were able to wipe out those Russians who had penetrated the defence system. We only lost a mile or so of ground.

On subsequent days the Russian break-through attempts were repeated in undiminished strength. Divisions decimated by our fire were withdrawn, and fresh formations were thrown into the battle. Again wave after wave attacked, and wave after wave was thrown back after suffering appalling losses. But the Russians did not desist from their inflexible and rigid methods of attack. On our side artillery and armour bore the main burden of the fighting. Our fire plans were flexible, allowing for concentrations where they were most needed, and designed to break up the Russian columns before they could advance to the attack. Wherever a deep penetration occurred it was quickly patched up, and a few hours later counter-attacks by our tanks were delivered against the flanks of the bulge. This battle continued for more than a week and the defensive strength of XLVIII Panzer Corps began to dwindle. 8 Army moved up its last reserve— 3 Panzer Division—to the danger point.

At this time General von Knobelsdorff was away on leave and General von Choltitz was acting commander of XLVIII Panzer Corps. Day after day he spent most of his time in the foremost lines and personally conducted the battle in any sector where the situation was most dangerous. One fateful evening he talked to me about the way things were going, and expressed his anxiety at the terrific pressure on our front. Then he had a vision. He saw how the Soviet masses would close in on us like giant ocean waves. All the dams built to stem their onrush would be shattered and the Russians would go on and on and eventually submerge Germany. He wanted to go and see Hitler himself and tell him the facts about this unequal struggle and of the untenable situation at the front. He declared he would resign and by his resignation give the danger signal which would compel Hitler to make new decisions.

I did my best to convince the General by quoting sober figures, to show that even the flood of Russian manpower was bound to run dry. I pointed to the incredibly high losses the Russians had suffered at the hands of his corps, which had fought with unrivalled bravery and courage, and I told him that one day even the Russian attacks would peter out. My arguments made little impression and he remained unmoved in his decision. He did not believe that our front would hold on the following day. He wanted to spare his troops this terrible ordeal; they were growing weaker and weaker and there was no hope of getting replacements or reinforcements. The next morning he drove away from Corps Headquarters, still determined to put his views before Hitler.

Two days after General von Choltitz had left, the Russian attacks on the front of XLVIII Panzer Corps broke down. It seemed that the General had been unduly pessimistic, but during the winter of 1945, when the Soviet hordes broke over my country, I often thought of this memorable conversation.

. . . . The great Russian offensive along the line of the Dnieper was now in full swing. XLVIII Panzer Corps had brilliantly repulsed the attacks south of Pereyaslav, but on our flanks matters did not go so well. By mid-October General Koniev had gained three bridgeheads east of Kremenchug, and he then struck heavily towards the important industrial centre of Krivoyrog, as famous for its iron ore as Nikopol for its manganese. Dnepropetrovsk fell on 25 October, and it looked as though we would soon lose the Dnieper bend. Indeed, it would have been fortunate if we had done so at this stage. By insisting that the retention of Nikopol and Krivoyrog was essential to German industry, Hitler forced Army Group South to adopt dispositions which were nonsensical from the strategic point of view.

To the south of Zaporozhe General Tolbukhin captured Melitopol, and thrust past the Perekop Isthmus towards the mouth of the Dnieper. Manstein wanted to evacuate the great bend of the river, but Hitler insisted that he should counter-attack to save Nikopol and Krivoyrog. Manstein did so on 2 November and tactically the operation was a notable success; Koniev's columns were caught in flank and flung back towards the Dnieper. But three hundred miles to the north-west, Marshal Vatutin's Army Group crossed the river in great force on both sides of Kiev; on 3 November he broke out of his bridgeheads with thirty infantry divisions, twenty-four armoured brigades and ten motorized brigades. The German defence was swamped and on 6 November a Special Order of the Day from Marshal Stalin proclaimed the capture of Kiev.

General von Mellenthin

Beyond Kiev, the Germans counter-attacked and stabilized their front there in November, but they had only stopped the Russians temporarily.

We had inflicted terrific losses on the Russians; on the front of 4 Panzer Army, of which we were the spearhead, more than seven hundred tanks and 668 guns were captured during this period. Of the three Russian groups which flooded across the Dnieper in November, the first at Brussilov had been smashed as an organized force, the second in the Zhitomir-Radomyshl area had been utterly destroyed, and the third east of Korosten had been so badly mauled that it was no longer capable of offensive operations.

It is true that Russian reinforcements kept pouring through Kiev, and with their help the broken armies were reformed. But the quality of the new levies left much to be desired. Fifty per cent of the prisoners whom we captured in December were lads between fifteen and eighteen years old, and some were mere children of thirteen. Moreover the other half was largely composed of Asiatics, dragged from the deepest recesses of the Soviet Empire, or of old men more suited to the fireside than the battlefield. There were no really strong, young people.

There is no doubt that at this stage of the war the Russians collared for their ordinary infantry divisions anyone, regardless of training, age or health—and sometimes of sex—and pushed them ruthlessly into battle. The fitter men were held back for their Guard corps and assault divisions. When a force was cut off they strove at all costs to preserve the officers and N.C.O.s to serve as cadres for the future. Nevertheless, in this grim month of December 1943, the German soldiers in the Ukraine felt a flicker of hope, for it was clear that the limits of Soviet manpower were being reached; the Russians could not continue to suffer these huge losses indefinitely and 'the bottom of the barrel' was already visible.

. . . . I shall never forget that extraordinary Christmas Day. A signal came through from 19 Panzer: 'Am attacked by thirty enemy tanks. No petrol. Help, help, help'—then silence. General Balck absolutely refused to send '*Leib-standarte*' into action in dribs and drabs, even if this meant the total loss of 19 Panzer Division. Eventually, after nearly six hours of anxious waiting, a signaller handed me a most welcome message from 19 Panzer: 'We are withdrawing to the west in tolerable order.'

. . . . Intelligence reported that the Russians were advancing in great strength, and thrusting straight of Zhitomir. On 27 December we expected very strong attacks, and awaited them with much anxiety. But the Russian columns did not appear. Whether they had been made cautious by the bold thrust of 1 Panzer, whether they had too many formations moving on the same road, or whether their forces had been thrown into confusion in trying to envelop ours, I cannot say, but the fact remains that they did not attack and this greatly eased our situation.

General von Mellenthin

The three great Russian offensives of 1943 marked the ruin of the German armour on the Eastern Front, and their morale suffered sharply.

The wounded from our own division were in very low spirits; indeed, morale had sunk to zero. We had a succession of self-mutilation cases where men had shot themselves through the hand. In such cases of point-blank injury the edges of the wound are usually serrated in a characteristic manner: there are traces of blackened powder all around the wound and the fine hairs of the skin have been singed. Most experienced soldiers knew this; and from time to time, too, the Russians dropped leaflets which gave instructions on how to effect a self-mutilation that was not recognizable as such. But in practice this is virtually impossible; the expert can almost always recognize a self-inflicted wound. All such cases had to be reported and they usually ended with a court martial and a firing squad.

The first case was a young peasant lad flown out from Germany three days before after a training which had lasted only a few weeks. I examined his wound carefully: the edges were serrated and blackened. I touched it lightly with a swab; it wasn't dirt. Then I had a look at the patient; about eighteen and still quite beardless. It was clear that in desperation at having been flung so violently into hell he had suffered a mental black-out. It was clear, too, that he had no idea that what he had done might mean the end of his life. I thought for a moment. Gehrmann watched me attentively; Sergeant Fuchs, already holding mask and ether bottle in his hands, raised his enormous nose and peered over the patient's head to study the area on which I was about to operate. Both immediately recognized the sort of injury it was. I raised my eyebrows. If there should be an epidemic of self-mutilation—which under present circumstances was not impossible—we too would be lost.

I was hoist with my own petard. Since the beginning of the campaign I had deliberately set out to give all the members of the operating team some idea of the natural dignity of the science of medicine, of its ancient humanistic tradition, of the beneficial effect of this tradition on their work. I used to call the surgeon's knife the scalpel of Hippocrates and in the course of time my men had got into the way of using the phrase. And I had managed, too, to give them some idea of how great a man Hippocrates was.

Operating assistant and anaesthetist exchanged glances. Then Sergeant Fuchs, rubbing his great nose with the anaesthetic mask, said, 'Only old Hippocrates can put this right'; and then began to administer the anaesthetic. Gehrmann handed me the scalpel. I removed all traces of legal evidence by the only reliable method, cutting it away, and the wound became fairly extensive. In this manner the physician from Cos saved the life of a young German peasant in the Russian steppe; but in subsequent battles that winter it was no longer possible so to adhere to the spirit of his teachings.

Peter Bamm

Russian weapons—notably multiple rocket launches and mortars—and Russian skill in concealment and infiltration techniques further demoralized the Germans.

The air shimmered. Half hidden by the branches a white rag warned the initiated of the presence of a minefield. Behind the runner there was a rumble as of far-off thunder. The loneliness took hold of him and constricted his heart. He was constantly waiting for some piece of treachery. There were two possibilities. One was silent like the forest and gave no warning. It lay hidden behind a tree trunk or in the tall grass. It came like a whiplash out of the undergrowth. The blow was always fatal and had the sole advantage of being over quickly. This possibility took the form of a bundle of rags and a revolver. Half crazed with hunger and tortured by the same fear as himself, it lay in wait behind a tree trunk. A flash and a whiplash: perhaps a little puff of smoke. Then a brown figure would spring silently from its hiding place and bend over the dead man. Its fingers wrenched away the weapon and rummaged feverishly in his pockets. The useful and the useless disappeared in the hands of the tattered bundle which then vanished like a ghost. Only a dead man remained above whom the flies would dance until he were found. If there were marshy ground nearby he was never found.

The other possibility ended in the same way but it announced itself. It started with a roar of an infuriated beast in the distance, a dull groaning noise unlike anything else in the world. It echoed over a few *versts* like a hunting cry. Twice or three times it roared. Then came the creaking of a badly tuned organ. Paralysis descended upon the front line. The rattle of machine-guns fell silent. The snipers drew their rifles back behind the parapet. The mortar crews huddled close together and the words of command froze on the lips of the gunner officers. The runner slowed down his pace. Then hell was let loose. Countless flashes of fire slashed the wood. Nearly a hundred shells burst in the trees or on the ground. A deafening thunder. . . . Flames, gunpowder, pieces of copper as big as a fist, earth and mud. . . . A battery with four guns, ammunition boxes, cartridges, tools and horses was hurled into the mud. An hour later it burst on a field kitchen. The driver and his mate, the cook, the provisions for sixty men and twenty-five gallons of watery soup were strewn to the four winds. A few minutes later it wailed down on a company marching up to the lines to relieve—eighty men carefully smartened up with polished boots and oiled rifles from the rear lines on their way to the front. The forty men who reached the trenches were filthy dirty, blood-stained and demoralized. Two hours, two days, two weeks. . . . Somewhere a tank detachment was on the move preparatory to action. In the shelter of a hollow the commander assembled his troops to give them their final orders. A swish on the horizon. Five or six seconds of oppressive silence and then the shots burst out of the blue. Screams. . . . Shrapnel rained down on the empty tanks. The junior officer had great difficulty in finding enough drivers to bring back the twelve tanks with their dead crews inside. And everyone who had felt the earth shudder and had seen the smoke of the explosions in the sky thanked— each in his own fashion—destiny or God that someone else had caught it and that he had been spared once more. The runner, too, who had knelt down and held his hands before his face thanked his foresight. This, then ,was the nature of the second possibility.

The runner pressed on along the footpath with his reports and the sunflower seeds in his pocket. He had covered about half the journey and there was no necessity to hang about any longer than necessary. The droning above the trees increased in volume. The artillery batteries joined in. The forest thinned out with occasional paths, luxuriant undergrowth and poisonous toadstools. The footpath came to an end and gave place to a well-beaten track which the rain had turned into a welter of mud. On one side was a burnt-out *panje* cart—mouldering leather reins and the skeleton of a horse. On either side of the road were weather-beaten cardboard notices covered with mysterious signs. They indicated the whereabouts of a howitzer battery field telephone, that over there in the clearing almost underground a flak gun could raise its long barrel to the sky. Occasionally an amateurish skull and bones warned of land mines.

Suddenly something gurgled down from the sky. The runner flung himself to the ground. The blast of an explosion swept over him. A gigantic net which he had taken for a pile of dry bananas started to billow with the withered foliage. In a fountain of dust the barrel of the gun hidden beneath the net began to wobble. It stood for a moment upright before collapsing. Someone whom the shell had not hit cursed God and another called for stretcher-bearers.

The runner stood up and plodded on. He thought how seldom a call for a stretcher-bearer must be here. The track broadened out and the ruts grew deeper. A soldier came towards him. Leather satchel, dusty boots, drawn features and deep-set eyes: a runner who after two hours of safety was on his way back to hell. A nod, a tired answering smile and he disappeared. . . .

The runner hurried his pace in order to catch up with a cart that was creaking along ahead of him. It wobbled in the deep ruts. The cloud of dust which it threw up in its wake settled like a veil on the runner and he felt a furry taste on his tongue. Canvas groundsheets covered the load in the cart which was pulled by a shaggy horse. Only when the runner stretched out his hand to the backboard to hoist himself did he recognize the cargo. Under the canvas stiff hands rapped against the muddy floor and bare heads nodded to and fro. The stiff-legged travellers kicked each other in the belly. They were frozen into positions which no living man could have adopted. Two were in fraternal embrace while others grinned with distorted faces. The runner dropped the backboard like a hot brick.

He squatted in the sand until the cloud of dust had disappeared round the next bend. The clatter of an approaching shell brought him to his senses. Again he came across notices, guns and bandoliers of empty cartridges by the roadside. They were left behind. . . .

At last the field with the thistles and the damp patches which never dried up came into view and then the endless rows of beechwood crosses. The cart laden with corpses had pulled up outside the cemetery. A number of figures with shaven heads were digging. A few of them were busy unloading the cart while others dragged a dead body through the grass.

Behind the last rows of graves he could see the village. Squat huts, blockhouses of logs covered with weather-beaten wooden tiles on both sides of the road . . . a well and nearby on a mast the battalion's metal flag.

The runner stumbled into the building. The adjutant was standing by the door. He saluted and took his reports from the leather satchel.

At this very moment the runner began to fall asleep. As in a dream he turned round, staggered back along the corridor, planted his feet like a sleep walker on the steps of the entrance. He slumped down on the wooden bench near the well. Weariness descended upon him like a black pall. From company headquarters to the battalion—orders carried out.

Gert Ledig

Birnam Wood Comes to Dunsinane . . . .

The fact must be emphasized that in this Indian-type warfare the Russians were far superior to the Germans. They were truly masters of devising means of camouflage. For example, on one occasion, there was a small forest a considerable distance ahead of our position. During the day the woods seemed to be closing in on us, but we believed that our eyes were deceiving us and paid no attention to the matter. After a few days, this wood suddenly erupted with fire which engulfed our position. An entire Russian artillery battalion had been concealed behind this movable wood and had worked its way up to within close range. This example of the art of camouflage on a very large scale gives an idea of the mastery achieved by the Russians in the camouflage of men, equipment and movements.

The most unbelievable things were done. For example, an artificial grave with a little embrasure in front cost many German lives until it was finally discovered where the shots were originating.

A German battalion commander

The Russian soldier, on the other hand, was comparatively impervious to mental strain.

Experience shows that the Russian soldier has an almost incredible ability to stand up to the heaviest artillery fire and air bombardment, while the Russian Command remains unmoved by the bloodiest losses caused by shelling and bombs, and ruthlessly adheres to its pre-conceived plans. Russian lack of re-action to even the heaviest shelling was proved though not explained during Operation 'Citadel'. The question is worth considering, and the following factors may influence their attitude.

The stoicism of the majority of Russian soldiers and their mental sluggishness make them quite insensible to losses. The Russian soldier values his own life no more than those of his comrades. To step on walls of dead, composed of the bodies of his former friends and companions, makes not the slightest impression on him and does not upset his equanimity at all; without so much as twinkling an eyelid he stolidly continues the attack or stays put in the position he has been told to defend. Life is not precious to him. He is immune to the most incredible hardships, and does not even appear to notice them; he seems equally indifferent to bombs and shells.

Naturally there are Russian soldiers of a more tender physical and psychological structure, but they have been trained to execute orders to the letter and without hesitation. There is an iron discipline in the Russian Army; punishment meted out by officers and political commissars is of a draconian character and unquestioned obedience to orders has become a feature of their military system.

General von Mellenthin

The Fatal Strategy

In spite of the disasters of 1943, Hitler refused to allow the construction of strong defensive lines now that the Wehrmacht's 'elbow-room' was dwindling, and at the same time forbade strategic withdrawals.

In this conference on 27 December, one can trace the root of all the disasters which befell the German armies in the Ukraine in the next three months. Just at the time when Russian manpower was strained to the limit, Hitler persisted in holding a front which was strategically indefensible.

General von Mellenthin

In January 1944 Hitler invited me to breakfast with the words: 'Somebody's sent me a teal. You know I'm vegetarian. Would you like to have breakfast with me and eat the teal?' We were alone together at a small round table in a rather dark room, since the only light came from one window. Only his sheepdog bitch, Blondi, was there. Hitler fed her from time to time with pieces of dry bread. Linge, the servant who waited on us, came and went silently. The rare occasion had arisen on which it would be possible to tackle and perhaps to solve thorny problems. After a few opening remarks the conversation turned on the military situation. I brought up the matter of the Allied landings in the West which were to be expected for the coming spring, and remarked that our reserves at present available to meet them were insufficient. In order to free more forces it was essential that a stronger defence be established on the Eastern Front. I expressed my astonishment that apparently no thought had been given to providing our front there with a backbone in the form of field fortifications and a defensive zone in our rear. Specifically it seemed to me that the reconstruction of the old German and Russian frontier fortifications would offer us better defensive possibilities than did the system of declaring open towns as 'strong points'— which declarations, incidentally, usually came at the last moment when it was too late to take measures which would justify the phrase. With these remarks I soon saw that I had stirred up a hornet's nest.

'Believe me! I am the greatest builder of fortifications of all time. I built the West Wall; I built the Atlantic Wall. I have used so and so many tons of concrete. I know what the building of fortifications involves. On the Eastern Front we are short of labour, materials and transport. Even now the railways cannot carry enough supplies to satisfy the demands of the front. Therefore I cannot send trains to the East full of building materials.' He had the figures at his fingertips and, as usual, bluffed by reeling off exact statistics which his listener was not for the moment in a position to contradict. All the same, I disagreed strongly. I knew that the railway bottle-neck only began beyond Brest-Litovsk and I tried to make clear to him that the building I had in mind would not affect transports travelling to the front, but only those going to the line of the Bug and the Niemen: that the railways were quite capable of shouldering this burden: that there could scarcely be a shortage of local building materials and local labour: and finally that it was only possible to wage war on two fronts with success if at least temporary inactivity could be assured on one front while the other was being stabilized. Since he had made such excellent preparations for the West there was no reason why he should not do likewise for the East. Thus cornered, Hitler proceeded to bring out his much-repeated thesis, namely, that our generals in the East would think of nothing save withdrawal if he permitted the building of defensive positions or fortifications in their rear. He had made up his mind on this point, and nothing could bring him to change it.

General Guderian

*Throughout the winter and the spring of 1944, the Germans were given no
respite. By the end of February, Leningrad was finally relieved. In the western
Ukraine the Russians pushed the Germans back towards the Polish frontier, and in
the south the latter were driven across the Dniester into Roumania. On this front,
Hitler relieved von Manstein in March. Only the spring thaw brought the Germans
relief, and that was fleeting.*

In mid-January the Red Army resumed the offensive. The front of XLVIII
Panzer Corps held firm, and the Russians made little progress in the western
Ukraine. Farther to the east they gained important successes, and Nikopol fell
on 8 February. By this time our 8 Army was holding a most perilous salient,
which enclosed Korsun and extended as far as the Dnieper. Hitler insisted on its
retention, and the result was a miniature Stalingrad. Marshal Vatutin's 'First
Ukrainian Front' and Marshal Koniev's 'Second Ukrainian Front' broke through
on both sides of Korsun, and trapped over fifty thousand troops in the pocket.
With great difficulty Manstein succeeded in extricating about thirty-five thousand
men, but the losses were heavy, particularly in artillery. Most of the guns had to
be abandoned in the mud.

. . . . XLVIII Panzer Corps succeeded in concentrating west of Tarnopol,
where it assisted in establishing a firm front. Meanwhile 1 Panzer Army had
been entrapped by Zhukov in a pocket at Skala to the south-east of Tarnopol.
At the beginning of March this army was on the right flank of Army Group
South, and holding positions near Kirovograd. When Zhukov's offensive got
under way, 1 Panzer Army was moved west by forced marches to try and stem
the Russian flood, but found itself encircled at Skala. The army was cut off for
weeks and had to be supplied by air; however, its determined resistance tied
down strong Soviet forces, and as a result Zhukov's dangerous thrust into
northern Roumania lost momentum and was brought to a halt. On 9 April 1
Panzer Army succeeded in breaking out to the west and reaching the main
German front in Galicia. It was a brilliant feat of arms, for the army saved all
its heavy equipment.

The encirclement of 1 Panzer Army at Skala brought about the final crisis
between Hitler and Field-Marshal von Manstein. Hitler at first refused permission for the army to break out, and on 25 March von Manstein flew to East
Prussia in a mood of desperation. After heated arguments he offered to resign,
and finally got permission to make plans to extricate 1 Panzer Army. He flew
back to his Headquarters, but within a week was removed from his command.

General von Mellenthin

I left our headquarters in Lwow on 3 April 1944. All my faithful comrades
had come to the station to see me off. The train had already begun moving when
someone called out to me. It was my personal pilot, Lieutenant Langer—the
man who had flown me safely through every imaginable kind of weather. Now
he had volunteered for the fighter arm, in whose ranks he was soon to give his
life. For me his words were a last salute from my comrades.

'*Herr Feldmarschall*,' he cried, 'to-day we took the Crimean Shield—our
victory sign—off the aircraft!'

Field-Marshal von Manstein

The spring thaw brought operations on the Eastern Front to a close, but we had every reason for viewing the future with anxiety. The sands were running out; the war of two fronts, dreaded by German strategists since the days of von Schlieffen, was about to assume its final and fatal form.

General von Mellenthin

THE SANDS RUN OUT

Finland

The Russian summer offensive for 1944 opened early in June in the far north, in Finland. Here one of the minor tragedies of the later stages of the war was played out. Having been beaten by the overwhelming forces of Russia once, Finland found herself being brought in again, willingly or unwillingly, by Germany. Their troops fought together in the forests. There ensued a campaign which had no bearing on the outcome of the war, but which was just as real and important to those who fought in it as any greater battle.

The Amenities of War

In spite of the dreariness of the landscape up here in the North, we never felt lonely or lost as long as we were with Finnish troops; in fact, we felt more like brothers of one family. I felt this particularly strongly once when Lieutenant Schleiermacher and I visited a Finnish cornet in his forest bivouac. In the large black Finnish tent stood a little tin stove, the stove pipe leading out into the open. And I thought my eyes must be deceiving me when I saw the most beautiful girl standing by the stove, making tea. She was tall, her hair the colour of corn, her skin that of a peach, and she had large, shining eyes, almost green in colour; she was a real beauty. I gasped with surprise, and the lieutenant opened his surprised eyes wide and was speechless for a moment. So that is the way the Finnish soldiers live, I thought.

She even spoke German, this Finnish beauty queen. We were quite overwhelmed. The friendly little cornet noticed our astonishment and smiled.

The lovely girl was one of the famous 'Lottas', of whom we had heard so much. We had even seen some of them already, but never at quite such close quarters. There were many of these Lottas, very unselfish young women, who looked after the Finnish soldiers. They wore grey linen dresses, a linen cap and on their bosoms (and what bosoms!) the Lotta-badge. . . . They looked after the wounded, of course, but they did a lot more. They cooked, they washed, they sewed—and all this voluntarily. And whatever we may have thought before meeting them had been wrong: they enjoyed the highest esteem and respect, almost like vestal virgins. Although they lived in close contact with the troops, there were no occurrences of licentiousness. The girls were subject to extremely strict discipline, and during the whole of my stay in Finland I have never once experienced the slightest indication of an abuse of these relations.

A German soldier

The Forest

The Finnish cornet spoke with great frankness.

'You have no idea,' he said, and he became even more outspoken as he helped himself to the brandy which we had brought him. 'You have no idea what you have let yourselves in for up here. You people are trained for fighting from concrete bunkers and are quite useless in this murder in the woods. You'll see.'

And we did see.

The patrol stood ready to move off. We stared into the vast forest in front of us. Somewhere in this forest Captain Bern and his men were lying, either dead and finished, or at any rate in a pretty hopeless position, surrounded by the Ivans.

We were a forlorn hope—that was certain, everything else was uncertain. The lieutenant was very calm. And very calmly he explained the position to us. 'We shall advance through the wood in wedge-shaped formation,' he said slowly as if weighing each word. 'I shall walk in front with Meier, machine-gun at the hip. You will follow at about five-yard intervals, covering the left and right. Ammunition carriers in the centre. As soon as we meet Ivan, we charge. Machine-guns to fire from the hip. We will take no notice of what happens to the left or right. We go on storming through the wood until we meet our own people. If I should drop out, Zech will take command, and if he falls, Brügmann. In that case, I shall be left lying. This applies to everyone. We can't worry about the dead or wounded. I must tell you this quite frankly. And there is another thing: anyone who does not follow or keep up with us will be shot in accordance with military law. That is a promise. Now, let's go.'

Not a very rosy prospect.

In open formation we started traversing the wood. We did not have to wait long, for after covering barely three hundred yards we were fired on. Close to me, Lieutenant Schleiermacher shouted, 'Get ready to charge!' As we ran forward we noticed large figures climbing out of their holes who had so far been hidden by the dense undergrowth. Flames shot from all our muzzles. Thus, less than ten minutes after falling in, we were in close combat with the Russians; it was the first time we had got so near to them. I wish to God I could describe what it was like. I felt as if I were enveloped in a great heat from head to foot; I heard myself shout and scream; I pointed my machine-pistol towards the enemy and felt it tremble under the bursts of fire. Then a huge man appeared in front of me; he appeared as suddenly as if he had grown out of the earth. I held the machine-pistol against his belly, I shouted at the top of my voice, and as miraculously as he had risen, the man fell down again.

Of course we were lost. The wood teemed with gigantic strange figures.

And then, as if in a dream, I saw, some fifty yards ahead, some newly thrown-up heaps of earth and heard the unmistakable hammering of a German machine-gun. We had made it! We had reached Captain Bern. And now everyone was shouting, 'Our own troops . . . own troops.'

As if by magic, the enemy disappeared again. Instead, a thin lieutenant stood up in front of me, shouted something; I stumbled forward and fell round his neck.

We were completely out of breath. We sank into the gun pits and gasped. I was still burning with heat from head to foot, and I shook and trembled all over; suddenly I sobbed.

Russian Attack

. . . . At last I saw them. The first of the tall brown figures were visible between the tree trunks. Bending down, they darted forward, threw themselves on the ground, jumped up again. There weren't single men any longer, but whole packs who gave me the horrible feeling that a horde of gorillas was approaching. There was something evil and ghostlike in the approach of these leaping, shouting attackers.

Their battle-cry sounded strange and uncanny. One of them, a sort of cheer-leader, intoned the 'Ourrah' in a high tenor voice, and then the others joined in the shouting, taking it up in a monotonous voice, repeating the sound at regular intervals.

There was now frantic shooting from our side, and the figures nearest to us started collapsing. None of the Ivans got any nearer than about twenty yards. Lieutenant Schleiermacher shot from a kneeling position, the muzzle of his machine-pistol circling from right to left and back again. I lay three paces behind him, saving my bullets for the moment when I might have to defend my lieutenant from these fellows. With a peace of mind quite out of keeping with the situation I surveyed the whole scene every now and again. It occurred to me that if any more Russians came, we would be done for.

The *ourrah*-cries became less frequent. The brown figures which were still standing up, lying or kneeling amongst the trees, or which were trying to close in, no longer shouted. I could see mounds of dead Russians.

And then a single, solitary, strangely plaintive *ourrah*-cry broke through the wood. Our weapons answered here and there and then they too fell silent. I stared towards the front in amazement; the attack had been repulsed and we had survived it.

Captain Bern jumped up and called, 'Good work, boys.'

I watched the grimy, sweat-covered, bearded faces turn towards him and break into a grin. The old man had praised them.

Rearguard

Lieutenant Schleiermacher led and I brought up the rear of our little group. Suddenly I bumped into the man in front of me, who had stopped, and I heard a brisk exchange of whispers.

What had happened?

I passed the men and went up to the lieutenant in front; I was completely dumbfounded when I heard the strange N.C.O., who was with us, say in an undertone: 'No, *Herr Leutnant*! We're not going on. We're not going to commit suicide. The Russians will get us, sure as fate. Everybody is retreating; only we have to be sacrificed as the rearguard.'

Lieutenant Schleiermacher did not reply. I felt as if someone had poured ice-cold water down my back, and I broke out into a sweat that poured under my uniform; at the same time a thousand and one thoughts raced through my mind. Open mutiny! In the face of the enemy! And then I thought: the N.C.O. is right, the man is quite right. These poor bastards here, on the go for weeks past, starved and never able to get a proper sleep, always out on a limb, always on a forlorn hope, faced with a bestial enemy . . . and the lieutenant and myself were not a wit better off.

I heard the panting, hoarse voice of one of the men say: 'Herr Leutnant, what are the Finns to us . . . we can't go on . . . let's wait here a few hours. . . .'

Another one whispered breathlessly: 'Herr Leutnant, what's the point of it all? Why not wait here for reinforcements. Then we can go back. For weeks we haven't had a decent meal. . . .'

Then the man burst into tears.

'We can't go on . . .' he sobbed, 'Herr Leutnant, I can hardly stand on my legs any more! Most of the lads are dead, and now you want us to stay here and be killed!'

Another started crying.

Still Lieutenant Schleiermacher said not a word.

It was unbelievable. There we were standing in this dreadful forest in pitch darkness; scarcely two hundred yards in front of us the Russians and Finns were engaged in close combat, shots rang out, wounded men were crying out dreadfully, and here . . . it was unbelievable.

But when I screwed up my eyes, came nearer and got a better view in the darkness, I saw something even more unbelievable: unobtrusively but quite unmistakably the men had trained their weapons on the lieutenant.

Stepping back a little in the direction of the lieutenant, I lifted my machine-pistol. I had no idea what the next few minutes held in store. But now, at last, after a seeming eternity, Lieutenant Schleiermacher began to speak. He spoke calmly and quietly: 'That is impossible,' he said. 'Quite impossible. We cannot leave the Finns in the lurch. I am just as worn out as you are; my N.C.O. and I came here straight from hospital. Besides, they're expecting us up forward, comrades. . . .' He stopped.

Nothing was audible but the panting of the men. 'Comrades,' the lieutenant said, 'I don't mind your speaking your minds. I'm not offended. But don't let the Finns down. We are on our way there for a good reason, we are going to help them so that they can break away from the enemy. There is good sense behind this order, boys, so don't let me down.'

And then he added: 'You have forgotten that we shall all be court-martialled if we remain here and wait. No, boys, it's quite impossible!'

But it was no good. The men were through. They did not care what happened. They had had enough.

As if in delirium the strange N.C.O. reiterated: 'But you could report that we had run into the Russians and had had to fight our way out. We shall all say the same, Herr Leutnant. You can rely on us. We wouldn't mind it if the Russians shot us straight away, but they'll butcher us like beasts!'

'Shut up, you,' I burst out. I was shaking all over. I couldn't listen to this talk any longer. Not because of the mutiny—what did that amount to compared with all we had been through?—but my nerves were at breaking point.

The lieutenant spoke again, and his soft voice was monotonous and as if lifeless: 'You forget one detail, corporal. You forget that I am an officer and you cannot expect me to put in a false report. And that applies to you, too!'

'Yes, *Herr Leutnant*,' the N.C.O. replied stupidly.

Now there was a slightly vicious tone in the lieutenant's voice as he said, still quite calmly: 'Corporal Schmidt, I shall continue to lead and you will bring up the rear. We're going forward. Should any man fall behind, you will shoot him at once. If you do not execute my order, I myself will shoot you. Off we go! Forward!'

The lieutenant took a few steps; I followed close behind him.

It was no good.

Not one of the men made a move. The lieutenant turned back. The men stood motionless. They were just a bunch of men overcome by desperate fear and utter physical exhaustion. Their attitude was infectious. I suddenly felt the whole force of this misery and never-ending wretchedness; it gripped me like an iron fist and pressed on my head, until for next to nothing I would have dropped my machine-pistol and howled like a dog.

It was only my friendship for Lieutenant Schleiermacher . . . which kept me from giving in. I was much older than the lieutenant, and to see this fine young man in such a damnable situation hurt me deep down inside.

But all I could do was stand there and wait and jump to help him if they went for him. I was determined to do that. Everything else he had to do himself. In spite of the ugly situation in which we all found ourselves at this moment, it struck me as rather funny that this would have been considered a kind of text-book test for an officer.

A miniature mutiny a hundred yards from the enemy. A mutiny by men completely worn out, dog-tired and broken, who might not have fought death if it came quickly. There was no high-ranking officer here who could have intervened with a thundering voice of authority. All the mutineers needed to do was take a few steps into the darkness of the forest to become invisible and disappear. In a situation like this, words like 'court martial' and 'military law' had little meaning, words which normally would have made one's blood run colder. Now they were empty, meaningless words.

Lieutenant Schleiermacher now showed his mettle. Slowly he raised his machine-pistol.

'I shall count three,' he said in a flat voice, 'and then I shall shoot.'

Everyone stood as though hypnotized. Although I could not see it in the darkness, I could feel in my every sinew how the right index finger of the lieutenant pulled the trigger slowly back. 'One . . . two. . . .'

At that frightful moment the N.C.O. lifted his hands and let the machine-gun which he had been carrying fall to the ground. Between clenched teeth and in a choked voice he said, 'Fire away, *Herr Leutnant*! Go on, shoot; then it'll all be over.'

Almost at the same moment one of the men started crying again, threw himself down and sobbed: 'I can't go on . . . I can't stand any more . . . I'm going mad. . . .'

There was a moment of unbearable silence; then the lieutenant lowered his machine-pistol and said in an unnaturally calm voice: 'All right. Go to hell. Beat it then, you bastards. You're leaving our Finnish comrades and me in the lurch. Beat it, I never want to set eyes on you again. Report back that you've lost me and my corporal in the dark. We two will go forward alone.'

He shouldered his weapon, then added scornfully: 'Go on. The two of us will get through. And you needn't be scared when I return. Never fear, gentlemen, I shan't split on you. The whole affair is too petty and dirty. I hope you'll keep fit. Greetings at home!'

With a few quick steps he disappeared between the trees, and I followed him closely. My throat felt paralyzed. In my opinion, the young man had got out of a nasty spot with flying colours.

My opinion was confirmed a few minutes later. We stopped abruptly when we heard voices calling out behind us. Then they came stumbling, one after the other. The N.C.O. in front, and close at his heels the man who was still carrying the mail-bag.

'We will come with you,' the N.C.O. panted. 'All we ask is not to . . . .'

'Shut up,' Lieutenant Schleiermacher interrupted. 'The affair is closed. Not another word. I should have been very surprised if you really had let me down.'

The N.C.O. almost sobbed when he stammered: 'No . . . never . . . *Herr Leutnant* . . . never. . . .' And the other poor bastards behind him laughed with relief; but it was the laughter of men in hell.

Prisoners

Two Finns brought in an Ivan. He was trembling all over, his legs would not support him and he had to be held up under his armpits.

The prisoner was led away and a strange silence reigned for a few minutes. It was suddenly broken by deafening screams, shouts and rifle shots. Hand grenades were thrown, and machine-pistols rattled off bursts of fire. When the noise died away a little we could make out the piercing screams of a man; a man in peril of death. The Finnish lieutenant stood up, stock-still, and listened.

'A friend of ours,' he whispered.

As far as one could see, all the Finns near the battle H.Q. were standing up, listening.

Not far from us a Russian voice was heard, calling out to us. Lieutenant Nikonen translated everything in a hurried whisper. The Russians gave the name of the man who had just been taken prisoner and demanded his release. If he wasn't returned at once, they would kill a Finnish soldier whom they had just taken.

A ghastly silence ensued.

The Russian prisoner had to call out his name. But the Russians demanded the name of an officer whom, so they said, the Finns had taken an hour ago.

Lieutenant Nikonen replied that they did not know an officer of that name and that the Finns had not taken any Russian officer.

Quiet again.

Then a scream that did not seem to originate from a human being tore through the wood.

Lieutenant Nikonen's head sank on his chest. 'Is comrade of ours,' he whispered.

Another scream, and another, and another; until it seemed as if the vast dark wood would be ripped to shreds by these terrible screams of agony.

The lieutenant covered his eyes with his hand; the Finns stood like statues, their faces turned towards the other side. Now we could hear the Finn sob out words.

'Cut off ears . . . .' whispered Nikonen. After a short silence the Finn began again. His head bent low, the Finnish lieutenant said: 'Now nose. . . .'

I saw Lieutenant Schleiermacher press his knuckles into his mouth; I was bathed in a cold sweat. A man was being tortured. There were a few more cries, then sobs, whimpering, and then silence. It was ghastly.

Lieutenant Nikonen took off his steel helmet; the other Finns did the same, and so did we. They made the sign of the cross, and in an undertone the Finnish officer said a prayer, in which his men joined softly.

Although I had witnessed the terrible scenes in this Karelian wood, I shall never forget this one as long as I live. It was the worst of them all.

What happened next was like a bad dream. The Finns put on their steel helmets, and like one man they rushed forward into the darkness of the wood. We followed, the lieutenant and I, firing our machine-pistols. Shoulder to shoulder with us ran the mutineer-corporal, firing his machine-gun from his hip. After taking barely ten steps I was hit in the left shoulder and lost consciousness.

That, thank God, was the end of the war in Karelia for me.

A German soldier

In the last week of June the Russians attacked from the direction of Smolensk towards the Baltic States. Minsk fell on 6 July, and the Germans were swept beyond the Pripet Marshes to the Niemen. Here, in mid-August, a halt was called. On the central front the Russians poured into Poland, and after crossing the Vistula on 30 July, paused while the Poles of Warsaw, encouraged to rise by their supposedly imminent approach, fought the Germans and lost. But late in August Roumania was overrun, and in September the Russians reached the Hungarian border.

Death of a Regiment

A new spring and a new summer swept across Europe into Russia and the Red Army launched a mighty offensive against the dogged German Army. On 28 June 1944, 6 Division was encircled near Bobruisk. At their backs flowed the river of Napoleon's final defeat—the Beresina. And on the other bank, between 6 Division and their homeland, stood the Russians. The last order was given: 'Redundant weapons to be destroyed; only iron rations and ammunition to be carried. Code word "*Napoleon*"—every man for himself.' The men of Infantry Regiment 18, every man of the proud 6 Division fought like devils. Little Becker fell, so did *Oberfeldarzt* Schulze. Major Höke fought and died at the head of his regiment; heavily wounded, he saved his last bullet for himself. A few crossed the river and slipped through the Russian trap; most died on the banks of the

Beresina; a small remnant was captured and marched away into captivity. Perhaps a hundred men, not many more, struggled through the Pripet Marshes and reached their homeland—a hundred from the eighteen thousand men who had marched into Russia under the Bielefeld crest. 6 Division, the heroic Regiment 18, had ceased to exist.

Heinrich Haape

At the beginning of August 1944 the German Reich seemed to be in imminent danger of a total collapse. In Normandy the Americans had broken through at Avranches, and Patton's 3 Army was about to set out on its tremendous sweep into Brittany and Anjou. In Italy the Allies had reached the line of the Arno, and Florence was about to fall. In Germany the bomb explosion at Hitler's Headquarters on 20 July was to be followed by a murderous blood-bath, seriously affecting the command of our armed forces. Finally there was the catastrophe in the East, where our whole battlefront threatened to dissolve.

On 31 August Hitler said at a conference: 'I really think one can't imagine a worse crisis than the one we had in the East this year. When Field-Marshal Model came, the Army Group Centre was nothing but a hole.'* Towards the end of July Marshal Bagramyan, commanding the First Baltic Front, broke through our line south of the Dvina and reached the Gulf of Riga; the effect of this thrust was to cut off Army Group North. On 2 August the Polish Underground Army rose in revolt and seized the greater part of Warsaw. To complete the picture, Marshal Koniev's Army Group had reached the Vistula on a broad front and was threatening to drive a wedge between 1 and 4 Panzer Armies.

Later in August:

. . . . The general situation in Poland had improved considerably. The uprising in Warsaw had looked very threatening, but tension eased when the Russians failed to push through to link up with the insurgent Poles. The German 9 Army, which was fighting in this sector, formed the impression that the Russians had outrun their supplies of petrol and ammunition and were too weak to break our line. However this may be, the Red Army did nothing to help the Poles and their resistance was systematically overcome.† In the Baltic provinces the situation had also improved. Guderian, the new Chief of Staff, persuaded Hitler to order the evacuation of Estonia and Latvia, and on 16 September a German attack from Courland broke through to Riga, and enabled Army Group North to join hands again with Army Group Centre. In this fighting my old friend, Colonel Count Strachwitz, particularly distinguished himself.

Unfortunately the situation in Roumania took a disastrous turn. Marshal Antonescu was a sincere friend of Germany, and also showed a shrewd grasp of the military situation. He proposed that Moldavia and Bessarabia should be

* Model had been put in command of Army Group Centre in July, while still retaining command of Army Group Northern Ukraine. . . . On 21 July Guderian replaced Zeitzler as Chief of the General Staff.

† The Russian refusal to allow the Anglo-Americans to use their airfields for supplying the Poles certainly puts the worst possible interpretation on their actions. But as Guderian aptly says, 'This is a matter for the former Allies to sort out among themselves.'

evacuated and a strong front should be formed along the Carpathians and then across to Galati and the mouth of the Danube. Some such course was now essential, as German reserves had been moved northwards to restore the situation in Poland. There were also ugly rumours of treachery in Roumania, which made it desirable to concentrate the German troops in Wallachia. Nothing was done, and when the Red Army attacked on 20 August the Roumanian divisions went over to the Russians and turned their guns against the retreating Germans. Our former allies seized the crossings over the Danube and the Prut, so that sixteen German divisions were completely destroyed. Our position in the Balkans went to pieces; Bulgaria and Roumania were occupied by the Russians, and in September they invaded Hungary.

General von Mellenthin

This is the last picture of the German armies on the Eastern Front which presents any signs of military competence and control. Desperately short of men and arms, assailed by Russian armies of vast size and admirable efficiency, they simply fell apart. By January 1945 Hungary, Poland and East Prussia had been submerged by the victorious Russian flood, which then ran over into the Reich itself. Only the heroic defence of Breslau, though all too tragic in itself, showed the last signs of the inspiration which had so often raised German military effort far beyond any reasonable expectation. It began in February and lasted until the eve of final surrender.

Reinforcements

. . . . At that time Himmler was simultaneously Commander-in-Chief of the Training Army, commander of Army Group Upper Rhine (an organization for defending that river and for catching fugitives and deserters), Minister of the Interior, Chief of the German Police and National Leader of the S.S.; he harboured no doubts about his own importance. He believed that he possessed powers of military judgment every bit as good as Hitler's, and needless to say far better than those of the generals. 'You know, my dear Colonel-General, I don't really believe the Russians will attack at all. It's all an enormous bluff. The figures given by your department "Foreign Armies East" are grossly exaggerated. They're far too worried. I'm convinced there's nothing going on in the East.' There was no arguing against such *naïveté*.

General Guderian, Chief of the General Staff

The Beginning of the End

On 20 January the enemy set foot on German soil. This was the beginning of the last act. Early that morning I learned that the Russians had reached the German frontier at a point east of Hohensalza. My wife left Deipenhof in the Warthegau a half-hour before the first shells began to fall. She had had to stay until the last possible moment, since her earlier departure would have been the signal for the civilian population to flee. She was under constant supervision by the Party.

General Guderian

By 27 January the Russian tidal wave was rapidly assuming, for us, the proportions of a complete disaster. South-west of Budapest they had gone over to the offensive once again. In the Hungarian capital street-battles against what was left of the German garrison continued. In the Upper Silesian industrial area the situation was growing more critical. Russian forces were advancing on the Moravian Gates, on Troppau, Moravska-Ostrava and Teschen. Developments in the Warthegau and East Prussia were particularly grim. Posen was encircled and one of its forts already lost. The enemy was moving on Schönlanke, Schloppe, Filehne, Schneidemühl and Usch. Nakel and Bromberg had been captured. He was moving forward west of the Vistula towards Schwetz. At Mewe he also crossed that river. In Marienburg a battle was fought for the beautiful old Ordensburg. Himmler had moved his headquarters to the Ordensburg Croessinsee. From there, and without the approval of the O.K.H., he ordered the evacuation of Thorn, Kulm, and Marienwerder. Hitler this time made no comment. By reason of this independent decision of Himmler's the Vistula line was lost without a fight. It was only a matter of days before the troops still east of that river must inevitably be cut off.

General Guderian

The Siege of Breslau

For the defence of Breslau we had a number of badly organized battalions and batteries, and approximately fifteen thousand People's Army troops, poorly armed. The civilian population still numbered two hundred and fifty thousand. The supply situation varied. Food was ample because Silesia had served as the nation's storehouse. But arms and ammunition were totally inadequate. Transportation was in complete confusion. The freight yards were packed with abandoned trains. Truck traffic was in disorder. There was enough coal to last to the end of March. All industry had closed down. There were no fortifications except a few small infantry entrenchments dating back to 1914.

On the other hand, among our assets at the end of February was the will of the troops and the civilian population to hold Breslau.

. . . . Immediately after Breslau's encirclement, Schörner promised to bring in by air an adequate supply of ammunition. The possession of the airport in the suburb of Gandau, and its upkeep, thus became crucial for the defence of the city. The construction of an emergency landing strip had been started on the so-called Frisian Meadow, but was not yet completed.

The Russian front was so close to the Gandau airport that any landing there during the day was impossible. The weather and the growing strength of Russian anti-aircraft batteries soon made the landing of cargo planes difficult and uncertain even at night. In addition, there were not enough cargo planes, and fighter planes had to help out. But the fighter planes, because of their high landing and starting speeds, could not use the airport and had to drop their cargo by parachute. Collecting the parachuted ammunition took much time. Part of it dropped into the Oder River, or even into enemy territory. The ammunition supply was a constant hand-to-mouth affair.

The enemy attacked without delay. Bitter fighting developed in the southern part of the city. It speaks for the tenacity of the defenders that the Russians required ten days—from 20 February to 1 March—to fight their way one and a half miles deep into the centre. The street fighting was violent and dogged. The Russians first set fire to the corner building of a block, with incendiaries of all kinds. When the fire drove the defenders out, the Russians jumped forward with strong shock troops carrying fire-extinguishing equipment and took possession of the corner buildings. Thus they moved forward step by step. We had to set fire to the houses ourselves, in order to prevent their use by the enemy. In one area where our defence could try to make a stand we burned all the important houses down. This measure was particularly burdensome for the population.

Once the enemy had entered the southern part of the city, the sewer mains, over six feet high, had to be blocked.

By the end of February, shelling and aerial bombing of city sectors not directly in the battle zone increased from day to day. Lack of ammunition made it inadvisable for us to fire at the planes.

Late in February a Russian propaganda trick succeeded in spreading serious confusion among the civilians. Immediately after the morning news bulletin of the German Reich Radio, and on the same wavelength, the following special message for Breslau came over the air: 'People of Breslau! The hour of liberation has come. Two battle-tested armoured divisions have broken through the Russian encirclement in the south of the city. Hurry south, all of you, to meet your liberators!' The message was believed even by many officials. Only at the last moment was it possible to prevent the mass migration southward from walking into a Russian military barrage.

At the beginning of March the northern sector of the Russian forces, quiet until then, moved to the attack. Although these attacks were repelled, they placed a serious strain on a defence that was short of ammunition and reserves. But Schörner sent orders instead of ammunition. One of his last orders ran: 'The number of shirkers is rising at a disturbing rate. Accordingly, every unit will daily set a rearmost line behind which no soldier may go without written orders. Those found behind that line without such orders will be shot on the spot by their next superior in rank.' This order meant organized murder. In Breslau, it was not followed.

General von Ahlfen, G.O.C. Stronghold Breslau

Breslau held out for ten weeks, finally capitulating on 6 May.

Danzig, that major port in the Polish Corridor which had been used as an excuse for beginning the conflict over five years before, saw the last of the Germans in March.

Flight from Danzig

I don't think I'll ever forget that 9 March in Danzig as long as I live. . . . We had found a place to stay with a woman whose name was Schranck. Then, at seven o'clock in the evening, the sirens started to howl. The crashing started right away, the floor shook and the windows rattled. We rushed down the stairs and ran for the nearest air-raid shelter.

The shelter was so crowded we barely squeezed inside. Several hundred refugees had been living in it for days. When we finally dared to come out the sky was red, and over the houses were piles of black smoke. Then we saw that our house was burning, too. We had lost even our baggage.

The fires hissed and crackled. Some horses had torn loose and were galloping down the pavement. Children got under their hooves. Rafters fell down from burning houses. We finally fled back into the air-raid shelter. Next morning we went out again into the ruined streets, and looked for another place to stay. We found someone we knew, and they took us in. We slept on the floor. Mother was out almost all day trying to find something for us to eat.

That night, more refugees came and wanted to crawl under. Very late in the night came still another woman with a little baby on her arm. The baby was white in the face, its skin looked transparent and all wrinkled. The baby's right thigh had been torn off, and the little stump was wrapped in bloody rags.

The woman must have been young, but she wore old, torn clothes and looked fifty. She was very shy. She made me think of a scared animal. She had nothing with her, only the child. For a long time she said nothing, only sat there on her chair.

Then she said, 'God Almighty, I never thought I'd get as far as this. We were between the Russians all the time. We're from Marienburg. The first wave of Russians came. They shot Father. They took our watches, and with us they did, oh, what they do. . . .'

She went on: 'The first lot moved on. Many of them knew a little German, and they told us we should get out because those who came after were even worse. So I took my child and left. I went after them. I thought these are through now, and the next wave will take a little while. I just wanted to stay between the two waves. I walked and I walked. Tanks kept coming, and the Mongols on them, and then it started again. My Joachim lay beside me, crying all the time. When it was over we went on walking. In the evening a couple of trucks caught up with us. I wanted to hide in the snow in the ditch but then I saw they were Germans. I ran out on the road and begged them to take me along. I told them about the tanks, and they cursed and swore.

'On the truck there were other women with their children. We got near a clump of woods. Someone shot at us. The soldiers drove on into another wood, and got off. They did not want to go on, they said, they wanted to surrender to the Russians. We were terribly frightened and cried and wept and begged. But they just said, Do you think we want to get away from Ivan just to be strung up by the chain dogs*? Then a corporal pulled an automatic pistol on them and said, "You yellow bastards, if you don't get moving with those women right away I'll shoot you down." But they just grinned at him, and one of them said, "Go ahead and shoot, you couldn't get that truck moving, could you? You're stuck, too."

'But at last some of them drove on with us. All of a sudden there was a crash. The truck stopped and we were thrown all over each other. Some women were

---

* Soldiers' slang for military police and S.S. commandos rounding up 'shirkers'. (*Translator's note.*)

lying on the floor of the truck and bleeding. Then another crash. Joachim had disappeared. So I grabbed this child and ran away. Later I met a soldier and he bandaged it. I don't know its name. But I'm calling him Joachim. All night I walked, then a truck took me for a while, then I walked again.' She was silent. After a while she suddenly started to sob, and then she said, 'I'm so tired.'

An S.S. patrol came next morning and confiscated the house. By noon we were out in the street. We were not allowed to go back into the air-raid shelter. The people who had come on their carts could at least crawl into the straw. We went from door to door looking for a place. Many people slammed the door in our faces when they heard we were from old German territory. They called us Nazis, and blamed us for everything that had happened to Danzig. One man shouted at us: 'Why did you have to take us into your Germany! We were better off before! Without the likes of you we'd still be at peace! If only the Poles would come back quickly!'

So we were out on the street. There were Russian fighter planes. There were so many, the city had given up sounding the alarm. When it got dark we went into a hallway, put our blankets on the floor, and huddled together for the night. The cold from the stone floor got through the blanket and through our clothes. My teeth rattled and I had shivers. Later in the night a soldier came by and gave us his blanket. He said, 'Don't stay here, by to-morrow their artillery will have got the range. I bet they'll be here in a week. Get out into a suburb, or to the coast. There are still some ships with East Prussians sailing from Pillau, and some of them stop in here. . . .'

Next day we spent in the broken trolley cars that were lined up in one place. There were many refugees there. Most of us had not eaten properly for days. Some woman pulled out a cold boiled potato, and everybody envied her. The farmers on the wagons were better off. And the people of Danzig had food, too. But we came from a different section and the shops didn't want to sell to us on our ration tickets. Two little boys fought over a piece of bread.

In the evening we got into the railway station and somehow found a place on a train going north to Oliva. In Oliva we found a house that was deserted. But we were awakened before morning. Russian artillery was shooting away, and from the road we heard the tramping of soldiers and of the many people who were fleeing south into Danzig. When it got light and I saw such a lot of soldiers, I thought the Russians simply couldn't get through. But the soldiers with whom I spoke just sneered and asked me how I expected them to stop the Russian tanks—they had beautiful field guns, to be sure, but no ammunition, they couldn't shoot their buttons, and the tanks wouldn't stop out of respect for the orders of the stronghold commander. They said the Russians were only a mile and a half away. We were so frightened!

We stood in our cellar door, not knowing what to do. Other refugees came along, dragging their feet.

Then a soldier came by with a truck; he said he was driving to Neufahrwasser and would take us along. So we went. It was getting warmer and the streets were mud. Trucks blocked the road all the way. In one place, soldiers were digging trenches right next to the road. We saw many of the search commandos of the military police and the S.S. leading away soldiers they had arrested. And this constant flow of ragged people rushing past. I'll never forget it—sometimes one of those faces comes back to me in a dream.

We drove across the airport; there was nothing there but a few shot-up machines. Russian planes came over several times but they did not shoot. Then we got to the port. There were no ships. People said that all the Navy evacuation ships were now sailing from Gdynia. The sea looked grey. There was just a few small private cutters that had got out of the Navy confiscation order somehow or other. In front of the port commander's place people stood in long lines. He looked at us sadly and said, 'I have no more ships for you. Over there, in the barracks, there are thousands already, waiting.' Then he smiled grimly and said, 'A few cutters are still sailing. But I'm afraid you can't afford them. They charge a thousand marks a head.'

Mother still had eight hundred marks for the three of us.

'All I can tell you,' said the port commander, 'is to wait here in camp. Perhaps you'll be lucky . . . perhaps. . . .'

So we went into the camp. We opened the door of one of the wooden barracks. A cloud of stench came to meet us. Hundreds of people sat in there, crowded together on filthy straw piles. The washing hung from strings across the room. Women were changing their children. Others were rubbing their bare legs with some smelly frost ointment. My brother pulled Mother's coat and said, 'Please, Mummy, let's go away from here.' But we were grateful to find room on a pile of straw next to an old, one-armed East Prussian who had come down along the Frische Nehrung.

Near me lay a very young woman whose head was shorn almost to the skin and whose face was all covered with ugly sores. She looked terrible. Once when she got up I saw that she walked with a cane. The East Prussian told us that she had been a woman auxiliary; the Russians had caught her in Roumania in the autumn of 1944 and had taken her to a labour camp. She had escaped somehow and trekked up here. He said she was only eighteen or nineteen. I tried not to, but I couldn't help looking at her.

A few hours later we couldn't stand the barracks any more and ran away. We preferred the cold. We went to the port. Mother tried to make a deal with one of the skippers. But he would not take anyone aboard for less than eight hundred marks a head. He'd rather go back empty. Mother was ready to kill him with her bare hands.

By the time it got dark we were so cold that we went back to the barracks in spite of everything. We found just enough room to sit back to back. Next to us sat a woman whose child had just gone down with dysentery. Next morning it lay there, so little and pale.

An Italian prisoner of war who worked on the piers told us that a small ship from Koenigsberg had arrived and was docking a little farther up the coast. The woman next to us went to take the ferry and go over there. She left the child behind with us and promised to come back and fetch us. She kept her word, too. When she came back she told us that she had met an acquaintance from Koenigsberg who for five hundred marks and her ring had promised to smuggle her and her child on the ship. He could do nothing for us, but she would not forget us. And she did not forget us. We ran away from the barracks for the second time and paid an Italian to row us over to the dock where the ship was. He looked at us sadly, and said in his poor German he would like to go home, too. On the dock we waited near the ship, and finally our 'neighbour' from the barracks—she made out we were her real neighbours—persuaded her acquaintance to smuggle us aboard, too.

Most of those on the ship were from Koenigsberg. Some of them had gone ashore and were now coming back. We walked along with them as if we belonged. Then we hid in the cold, draughty hold of the ship. We huddled close together, but still we were terribly cold. But we did not dare to move, let alone go up, for fear they would recognize us as stowaways.

The night went by. The rumble of artillery over Danzig grew very loud. A man who had been up on deck said the sky was all red with the fires. We were so happy and grateful that we could lie in the draughty hold of the ship. But we were shaking with fear that we would be found out and put ashore.

Then the ship pulled out, and we breathed again.

Hans Gliewe, sixteen

Planning for National Suicide: March 1945

At this time Speer, whose attitude towards the course of events was becoming one of increasing scepticism, came to see me. He brought me the information that Hitler intended to arrange for the destruction of all factories, water and electrical installations, railways and bridges before they should fall into enemy hands. Speer rightly pointed out that such a crazy deed must result in mass misery and death to the population of Germany on a scale never before seen in history. He asked for my help in ensuring that no such order be carried out. I readily agreed to give it him and I immediately set to work drafting an order in which I laid down the defensive lines that were to be held throughout Germany and specifically ordered that only immediately in front of these few lines might demolitions be carried out. Nothing else whatever in Germany was to be destroyed. All installations that served to feed the populace and to provide it with work were to remain untouched. On the next day I took my draft to Jodl, who had to be informed of its contents since it dealt with a matter which concerned all parts of the Armed Forces. Jodl submitted my draft to Hitler, but unfortunately not when I was present. When I saw him again on the following day, and asked him what Hitler's reaction had been, he gave me an order of Hitler's to read which was the exact contrary of Speer's and my intentions. . . . Hitler's reaction to this memorandum of Speer's, with the conclusions of which I too had identified myself, culminated in these words:

'If the war should be lost, then the nation, too, will be lost. That would be the nation's unalterable fate. There is no need to consider the basic requirements that a people needs in order to continue to live a primitive life. On the contrary, it is better ourselves to destroy such things, for this nation will have proved itself the weaker and the future will belong exclusively to the stronger Eastern nations. Those who remain alive after the battles are over are in any case only inferior persons, since the best have fallen.'

. . . . While we were talking a man came in and informed Hitler that Speer wished to see him. Hitler replied that he could not receive him that night. And once again I had to listen to his now almost stereotyped outburst, 'Always when any man asks to see me alone it is because he has something unpleasant to say to me. I cannot stand any more of these Job's comforters. His memoranda begin with the words: "The war is lost!" And that's what he wants to tell me again now. I always just lock his memoranda away in the safe, unread.'

General Guderian

30

NORTH-WEST EUROPE: INVASION AND LIBERATION

The possibility of a Second Front was discussed on both sides of the hill in 1943. The Germans recognized how serious an invasion would be for them by appointing as Commander-in-Chief Western Command Field-Marshal von Rundstedt. His area of responsibility extended from the Low Countries to the Bay of Biscay, and to defend it he had sixty divisions.

The Defenders

As the tempo of the Allied air attacks increased, his staff grew worried for the Field-Marshal's personal safety, though he himself took no notice of the raids. While he was absent from his headquarters an air-raid shelter was rapidly built in the garden of his house at St. Germain and most effectively camouflaged. But when the old gentleman saw it he declared quite categorically that nothing would ever induce him 'to set foot inside the thing'. However, one evening Allied bombers dropped marker flares over St. Germain and it seemed likely that a rain of bombs would follow. I therefore ordered Rundstedt's son, who was acting as his father's aide-de-camp, to take the Field-Marshal to the shelter. Young Rundstedt succeeded eventually, and after meeting considerable opposition, in carrying out this order. As it happened the bombers hit a neighbouring suburb; I was much occupied on the telephone, and I forgot all about the Commander-in-Chief. An hour later my telephone rang. It was the Field-Marshal who simply asked, in his usual courteous fashion:

'Zimmerman, can I please come out now?'

. . . . Towards the end of 1943 Hitler assigned Rommel the task of inspecting the coastal defences in the West, from Denmark to the Spanish frontier. He had no troops, save his highly competent staff. Supreme Headquarters, however, expected valuable help from Rommel's initiative, experience and sound technical knowledge. In addition, it was hoped that his presence in the West would be useful as a propaganda weapon.

I recall his first conference with Rundstedt, in Paris, shortly before Christmas. Rundstedt outlined the situation briefly and sceptically, speaking of the poor quality of the troops, the dangerous weakness of the Air Force, the almost total absence of naval craft and stressing particularly the main defect of our defensive organization, namely the complete lack of a powerful central reserve. He ended with the words: 'It all looks very black to me.'

German staff officer

The Attackers

The Allies had decided that the shipping and supply problems inherent in mounting the invasion were so great that they would not be ready before 1944, and towards the end of 1943 their preparations began seriously.

Operation 'Overlord'

(a) This operation will be the primary United States–British ground and air effort against the Axis in Europe. (Target date, 1 May 1944.) After securing adequate Channel ports, exploitation will be directed towards securing areas that will facilitate both ground and air operations against the enemy. Following the establishment of strong Allied forces in France, operations designed to strike at the heart of Germany and to destroy her military forces will be undertaken.

(b) Balanced ground and air force to be built up for 'Overlord', and there will be continuous planning for and maintenance of those forces available in the United Kingdom in readiness to take advantage of any situation permitting an opportunistic cross-Channel move into France.

(c) As between Operation 'Overlord' and operations in the Mediterranean, where there is a shortage of resources, available resources will be distributed and employed with the main object of ensuring the success of 'Overlord'. Operations in the Mediterranean theatre will be carried out with the forces allotted at 'Trident' (the previous Conference at Washington in May), except in so far as these may be varied by decision of the Combined Chiefs of Staff.

We have approved the outline plan of General Morgan for Operation 'Overlord', and have authorized him to proceed with the detailed planning and with full preparations.

Report of the Chiefs of Staff, first Quebec Conference: 19 August 1943

The Conference: . . . .

(4) Took note that Operation 'Overlord' would be launched during May 1944, in conjunction with an operation against Southern France. The latter operation would be undertaken in as great a strength as availability of landing-craft permitted. The Conference further took note of Marshal Stalin's statement that the Soviet forces would launch an offensive at about the same time with the object of preventing the German forces from transferring from the Eastern to the Western Front.

The Teheran Conference: 1 December 1943

Very early in the morning of 24 December,* I was woken up to be given a signal from the War Office to say I was to return to England to succeed General Paget in command of 21 Army Group, the British Group of Armies preparing to open a 'second front' across the Channel. . . . It was a relief and an excitement: a relief because I was not too happy about the overall situation in Italy and considered we had only ourselves to blame for the situation which now faced us. No

* 1943 (Ed.)

grand design for the opening of a new theatre of operations; no master plan; no grip on the operations; a first-class administrative muddle—all these had cumulatively combined to impose such delay on the operations that we failed to exploit the initial advantages which we had gained before the winter closed in upon us.

. . . . For these reasons I was not sorry to leave the Italian theatre. I made a quiet resolve that when we opened the second front in North-West Europe we would not make the same mistakes again: so long as I had any influence in the responsible circles concerned.

Field-Marshal Montgomery

Both Sides Prepare

Our intention was to assault, simultaneously, beaches on the Normandy coast immediately north of the Carentan estuary and between that area and the River Orne, with the object of securing as a base for further operations a lodgement area which was to include airfield sites and the port of Cherbourg. The left or eastern flank of the lodgement area was to include the road centre of Caen.

General Eisenhower had placed me in command of all the land forces for the assault. For this we had two armies—2 British Army under Dempsey and 1 American Army under Bradley. Later, two more armies would come into being —1 Canadian under Crerar and 3 American under Patton. It is important to understand that, once we had secured a good footing in Normandy, my plan was to *threaten* to break out on the eastern flank, that is in the Caen sector. By pursuing this threat relentlessly I intended to draw the main enemy reserves, particularly his armoured divisions, into that sector and to keep them there—using the British and Canadian forces under Dempsey for this purpose. Having got the main enemy strength committed on the *eastern* flank, my plan was to make the break-out on the *western* flank—using for this task the American forces under General Bradley. This break-out attack was to be launched southwards, and then to proceed eastwards in a wide sweep up to the Seine about Paris. I hoped that this gigantic wheel would pivot on Falaise. It aimed to cut off all the enemy forces south of the Seine, the bridges over that river below Paris having been destroyed by our air forces.

All our work was linked to this basic plot, which I explained at many conferences from February onwards.

Field-Marshal Montgomery

Last February Rommel took command from Holland to the Loire. . . . It is now clear that his intention is to defeat us on the beaches. . . . He is an energetic and determined commander; he has made a world of difference since he took over. He is best at the spoiling attack; his forte is disruption; he is too impulsive for a set-piece battle. He will do his level best to 'Dunkirk' us—not to fight the armoured battle on ground of his choosing but to avoid it altogether and prevent our tanks landing by using his own tanks well forward. . . . We must blast our way on shore and get a good lodgement before he can bring up sufficient reserves to turn us out. Armoured columns must penetrate deep inland and quickly. . . .

The land battle will be a terrific party and we shall require the support of the air all the time—and laid on quickly.

Field-Marshal Montgomery

Before D-Day one Seine bridge after another was destroyed by systematic air attack. Little bridging material was available to us and the mobility of the armoured units became more and more circumscribed. I proposed the construction of under-water bridges, such as we had used on the Eastern Front. These were extremely difficult to recognize from the air. However, my proposal was turned down.

. . . . Estimates of probable enemy action varied considerably. Both Jodl and von Rundstedt's Chief of Staff doubted whether the invasion would materialize at all, regarding the Allied announcements as merely a bluff. The staff of my Panzergroup West held differently, arguing from our knowledge of the British mentality, especially as we knew that the King had inspected the invasion forces, and it was quite evident that the British monarch would not be asked to demean himself by taking part in a mere farce.

. . . . We estimated that if the invasion occurred in the Normandy area, some thirty enemy divisions might be employed; about ten or twenty in Southern France, and another twenty-eight for the Channel coast or whatever other point of attack the Allies might select. We calculated the hostile tank strength as about ten to one, armoured reconnaissance material at fifteen to one, but we had no yardstick for estimating the degree of air superiority to be expected. Already in February 1944, the battle for air command had been fought and lost. The number of trained enemy airborne divisions was also uncertain, ranging from eight to ten at the outside.

Von Rundstedt's G.3 Branch had no illusions about the combat quality of our infantry divisions. All suffered from shortage of anti-tank, artillery and supply units. The standard of the German armoured divisions was calculated at only $33\frac{1}{3}$ per cent of the 1939 standard, but nevertheless they were far superior to the Panzer formations which took part in the 'Battle of the Bulge' in December 1944.

Jodl, in Berchtesgaden, von Salmuth, the C.-in-C. of 15 Army, and Rommel were all three of them sure that a second and main landing would take place in the Pas de Calais area. It was not until a week after D-Day that this belief began to be shaken—and by the time 15 Army was ready to move towards Normandy it was too late to influence the result of the battle there. As for the situation in the air, this was quite hopeless from the start.

With regard to the date of the invasion, we had a rough guide from a notice which appeared in the London *Times* and which appeared to have escaped the censor. The paragraph concerned the rate of compensation to be paid to British farmers by the American Government for injury to farm-land during armoured night exercises. The censor apparently disregarded agricultural news as being a possible source of information for the Germans! From this article it was evident that the invasion could not take place before mid-April 1944 at the earliest. As time passed more and more evidence was accumulated regarding the probable date of the invasion.

General Baron Leo Geyr von Schweppenburg, C.-in-C. Panzergroup West

In May, all the Allied troops who were to cross the Channel were ready and moving slowly to their concentration areas.

The Infantry

When we returned from Embarkation Leave, they were sharpening bayonets.

'Guess who?' leered the Armourer Sergeant.

. . . . We stood rigidly to attention before our kit. A sergeant stepped forward.

'The Company Commander will now inspect you and your kit for the last time before you go overseas. He is a man of vast experience. He will ask each of you a question of vital importance to see if you are really ready for battle. You *must* know the answer to that question. It may save your life one day.'

The Major looked at my kit and walked all the way round me. He now stood before me. I stared, frozen-faced, at his Adam's apple. It moved.

'How many needles in that housewife of yours?'

. . . . The train pulled slowly out of Halesworth Station. Our old Platoon Sergeant, grim-faced, saluted.

'Gawd!' said someone. 'He'll be presenting arms in honour of the dead next!'

As the train gathered speed past the end of the platform, we saw a sentry—at the 'Present'.

We felt ill.

. . . . Two or three days were spent in British-occupied Aldershot, then we were paraded to draw French money. The conveyor belt was moving us on-wards. Next day our train pulled into Eastleigh, near Southampton. The usual long and apparently unnecessary wait was followed by a short march which brought us to a pleasant camp amid the trees.

The first thing which met our eyes was a large board giving details of the ever-open N.A.A.F.I. and the continuous film show. This should have put us on our guard, but our suspicions were finally confirmed when . . . we marched to our quarters. There, beneath the trees, were neat two-man tents, each with two American Army cots—and sheets.

'Lofty' stared, then roared:

'I'll bet we're not here long. The condemned man ate a hearty bloody breakfast!'

He was right.

R. M. Wingfield

The Armour

Our destination was Southampton, eighty-seven miles away by direct route, but well over a hundred by the way we were required to take to conform with the traffic arrangements which spread like a cat's cradle over the whole of southern England. According to the book this far exceeded the maximum mileage water-proofed vehicles were supposed to cover, but in fact they all stood the strain well except the three-ton lorries, which boiled constantly, and the 146th Battery's 'slave charger' which completely disintegrated.

The first event was a disappointment. So much was supposed to happen at the R.C.R.P., in our case situated just outside Winchester, that when the advance party drew up importantly it was a shock to find nothing but a caravan beside the road containing one private who had never heard of the Regiment, and whose sole immediate ambition was to complete his shaving. We were deeply distressed, and in our state of excitement and nerves we imagined some awful disaster which would preclude our ever going abroad at all. We were not comforted by the arrival of an officer who assured us that officially we did not exist, but that he would try to fit us in somewhere. We lay on the grass half asleep after our long drive while he chattered on the telephone.

Just as Tom Geddes was setting out on his motor-cycle to stop the convoy somewhere by the roadside, so that they would not pile up at the R.C.R.P., news came through that accommodation had been found for us in Camp 19. Thus by three o'clock in the afternoon we had got to the marshalling area on Southampton Common, the drivers remaining with their vehicles while the remainder were firmly imprisoned within barbed wire. Everyone who had been in the main column was suffering from eye strain, varying from a minimum slight soreness to Lieutenant Pothecary, who lost his sight completely and for some time had to be led about. This disturbing and painful ailment was brought about partly by the dust, and partly by the diesel fumes thrown up by M.10s travelling head to tail, for the roads approaching all South Coast ports carried so much traffic that normal road discipline was abandoned and the order was 'close up and get on'.

British tank officer

After an agonizing appraisal of the adverse weather reports, General Eisenhower, the Allied Commander-in-Chief, gave the order for the armada of four thousand ships to sail on the evening of 5 June for the biggest amphibious operation in history.

Waiting

For three days the ships lay at anchor in the Solent while the men of the 5th Battalion, who by now had left excitement far behind them, settled down to make themselves comfortable in yet another home.

They lounged at the rails and sprawled in groups on the decks, sleeping, eating, playing cards and talking. They slept soundly and ate heartily, as if eating were a pastime in itself. Men were haunting the ship's galley all day long, cadging extras, and sneaking back into the meal queues for second helpings. The talk was of everything but the war—much of it, indeed, consisted of grumbling at the food—except when, two or three times a day, a rumour would sweep through the troop decks that the time had come to up anchor. The card players took up most of the deck space. They squatted in little groups, their upturned berets lying on the deck between their knees to hold their money; for once neither N.C.O.s nor officers interfered with their gambling.

. . . . There was no sentimental talk, no soft singing or playing of harmonicas, no writing of farewell letters, no men sadly gazing at the distant shore. Three days with nothing to do but eat, sleep and gamble was an event in the lives of the men of the 5th Battalion. They made the most of it, and thought of nothing else.

Alexander Baron

The Sailing

By evening the convoy was on the move, the endless lines of ships passing slowly down the Solent while Spitfires from airstrips which were plainly visible on the shore swooped and snarled overhead. The men felt the ship vibrating and saw the coast moving past them, looked at each other meaningly, and bent again to their cards.

A couple of hours later they were out in the open Channel. A few of the men stood listlessly at the rails, watching the Needles slowly drop back and become indiscernible in the dusk. There was a strange, flat feeling, a sensation as of living suspended between two planets, as the ship crawled with maddening slowness across the grey, bleak sea, against the grey, bleak, evening sky. There was no shore to be seen, only the walls of purple dusk creeping in from the farthest limits of the sea; no sound to be heard but the thudding of the engines below decks and the snarling of Spitfires in the clouds that thickened overhead.

Alexander Baron

Hazards

The instructions on the cans said, 'Light the wick with a match or cigarette-end.' We did. Half the cans immediately exploded violently, scattering burning soup over the immaculate decks. Nobody told us anything about puncturing the cans before lighting the wick. Resigned sailors came to hose the decks. We assisted verbally.

Next we turned our attention to the 'Tommy Cookers'. Within a short time there was a dreadful smell as the tar in the deck seams began to run. The sailors left us to it.

It was still dark when the metallic voice of the ship's Tannoy woke us.

'Information has just been received about a new Jerry mine. It has no official designation, but the Yanks call it "the 50-50 mine". It has the general characteristics of the "S" mine, but, instead of the ball-bearings, a sharp steel rod flies up. The name is derived from your chances. If you hit with the right foot, the rod flies up past your right side. If you hit it with the left, you'll be singing tenor.'

R. M. Wingfield

After the ships had sailed, the three airborne divisions—two American and one British—which were to land in the small hours of 6 June began their loading.

British Paratroops

Three hours before dusk we paraded. Fantastically upholstered, our pockets bulging with drugs and bandages, with maps and money and escaping gadgets, we stuffed ourselves into our jumping jackets and waddled, staggering under the weight of stretcher-bundles and kitbags, to the lorries waiting to take us to the airfield. And there, formidably arrayed on the tarmac runway, was the line of camouflaged Dakotas, stretching away into a yellowish sunset streaked with bars of black cloud. We had already met the crew of our aircraft, and they had assured us that the flight would be 'a piece of cake'—a little flak over the French coast, but really nothing to worry about. Now I thought they looked less confident, their Air Force charm a little strained. The captain was a very small man, his flying suit threadbare at the seat as though he had worn it out on the office stool. As we donned our Mae Wests and parachutes, and tested the quick-release devices that would enable us to lower our burdens to the ground and land unencumbered, the captain stood a little apart, watching us with studied nonchalance. In his gaze we all became self-conscious, sheepishly matter-of-fact like people on newsreels, and physically ill at ease in our jumping harness.

. . . . It was nearly midnight by the time we took off, and I felt a sudden spinal chill when the fuselage quivered under pressure of the slipstream and the power took hold of us. With our burdens to nurse, in addition to all the clothes we were wearing, it was cramped and stuffy inside the aeroplane. As the last light faded off the landscape that fell away into a misty horizon, the glow of our cigarettes grew brighter. Other aircraft in the formation were no longer visible, dipping and swaying in the wind-flukes. Trails of sparks were the only indication that we were not alone.

James Byrom

American Paratroops

We flew in a V of Vs, like a gigantic spearhead without a shaft. England was on double daylight-saving time, and it was still full light, but eastward, over the Channel, the skies were darkening. Two hours later night had fallen, and below us we could see glints of yellow flame from the German anti-aircraft guns on the Channel Islands. We watched them curiously and without fear, as a high-flying duck may watch a hunter, knowing that we were too high and far away for their fire to reach us. In the plane the men sat quietly, deep in their own thoughts. They joked a little and broke, now and then, into ribald laughter. Nervousness and tension, and the cold that blasted through the open door, had its effect upon us all. Now and then a paratrooper would rise, lumber heavily to the little bathroom in the tail of the plane, find he could not push through the narrow doorway in his bulky gear, and come back, mumbling his profane opinion of the designers of the C.47 airplane. Soon the crew chief passed a bucket around, but this did not entirely solve our problem. A man strapped and buckled into full combat gear finds it extremely difficult to reach certain essential portions of his anatomy, and his efforts are not made easier by the fact that his comrades are watching him, jeering derisively and offering gratuitous advice.

Wing to wing, the big planes snuggled close in their tight formation, we crossed to the coast of France. I was sitting straight across the aisle from the doorless exit. Even at fifteen hundred feet I could tell the Channel was rough, for we passed over a small patrol craft—one of the check points for our navigators—and the light it displayed for us was bobbing like a cork in a millrace. No lights showed on the land, but in the pale glow of a rising moon that was a little more than a quarter full, I could clearly see each farm and field below. And I remember thinking how peaceful the land looked, each house and hedgerow, path and little stream bathed in the silver of the moonlight. And I felt that if it were not for the noise of the engines we could hear the farm dogs baying, and the sound of the barnyard roosters crowing for midnight.

A few minutes inland we suddenly went into cloud, thick and turbulent. I had been looking out the doorway, watching with a profound sense of satisfaction the close-ordered flight of that great sky caravan that stretched as far as the eye could see. All at once they were blotted out. Not a wing light showed. The plane began to yaw and plunge, and in my mind's eye I could see the other pilots, fighting to hold course, knowing how great was the danger of a collision in the air.

You could read concern on the grim, set faces of the men in my plane as they turned to peer out the windows, looking for the wink of the little lavender lights on the wing tips of the adjoining planes. Not even our own wing lights showed in that thick murk. It was all up to the pilots now.

. . . . Beside the door, a red light glowed. Four minutes left. Down the line of bucket seats, the No. 4 man in the stick stood up. It was Captain Schouvaloff, brother-in-law of Boris Chaliapin, the opera singer. He was a get-rich-quick paratrooper, as I was, a man who had had no formal jump training. I was taking him along as a language officer, for he spoke both German and Russian, and we knew that in the Cotentin Peninsula, which we were to seize, the Germans were using captured Russians as combat troops.

A brilliant linguist, he was also something of a clown. Standing up, wearing a look of mock bewilderment on his face, he held up the hook on his static line— the life line of the parachutist which jerks his canopy from its pack as he dives clear of the plane.

'Pray tell me,' said Schouvaloff, in his thick accent, 'what does one do with this strange device?'

A bell rang loudly, a green light glowed. The jump-master, crouched in the door, went out with a yell—'Let's go!' With a paratrooper, still laughing, breathing hard on my neck, I leaped out after him.

General Matthew B. Ridgway, G.O.C. 82 Airborne Division

D-DAY: THE PARATROOPS

The cathedral clock of St. Lô struck midnight. At that moment several officers of the staff of LXXXIV Corps entered the main room of the operations bunker. . . . It was the birthday of their commanding officer, General Erich Marcks. . . . He disliked all forms of celebration, so he looked surprised; his gaunt, strong-willed, deeply lined face might have been that of a scientist or scholar. He had lost a leg in Russia and the joint of his artificial limb creaked as he stood up; he raised his hand in a friendly, but nevertheless cool gesture. We each drank a glass of Chablis standing, and the little ceremony was over in a few minutes.

The General bent over the two documents which were laid before him by the Corps Intelligence officer. . . . The first was a map showing the disposition of the Allied forces in southern England: more than thirty enemy divisions were indicated; across the Channel from east to west the Canadian, British and American sectors stood out clearly. Five airborne divisions were specially marked. The

General looked thoughtfully at the coloured flags, the red and blue lines and curves, the cross-hatched ovals and the overlapping areas.

The second was a graph summarizing the aerial position during the last few months. What we had long been forced to acknowledge was here neatly depicted: the slow but systematic gaining of superiority in the air by the British and Americans in their several sectors. . . . The destruction of even quite small bridges over the Seine between Paris and Rouen, and over the Loire between Orléans and Nantes, betrayed the enemy's intention of blocking both rivers and so isolating the area occupied by 7 Army.

. . . . At 01.11 hours—an unforgettable moment—the field telephone rang. Something important was coming through: while listening to it the General stood up stiffly, his hand gripping the edge of the table. With a nod he beckoned his chief of staff to listen in. 'Enemy parachute troops dropped east of the Orne estuary. Main area Bréville–Ranville and the north edge of the Bavent forest. Counter-measures are in progress.' This message from 716 Intelligence Service struck like lightning.

Was this, at last, the invasion, the storming of 'Festung Europa'? Someone said haltingly, 'Perhaps they are only supply troops for the French Resistance?'

. . . . The day before, in the St.-Malo area, many pieces of paper had been passing from hand to hand or had been dropped into the letterboxes; they all bore a mysterious announcement: La carotte rouge est quittée. Furthermore, our wireless operators had noticed an unusually large volume of coded traffic. Up till now, however, the Resistance groups had anxiously avoided all open action; they were put off by the danger of premature discovery and consequent extermination.

Whilst the pros and cons were still being discussed, 709 Infantry Division from Valognes announced: 'Enemy parachute troops south of St.-Germain-de-Varreville and near Ste.-Marie-du-Mont. A second drop west of the main Carentan–Valognes road on both sides of the Merderet river and along the Ste.-Mère-Eglise–Pont-l'Abbé road. Fighting for the river crossings in progress.' It was now about 01.45 hours.

Three dropping zones near the front! Two were clearly at important traffic junctions. The third was designed to hold the marshy meadows at the mouth of the Dives and the bridge across the canalized Orne near Ranville. It coincided with the corps boundary, with the natural feature which formed our northern flank but would serve the same purpose for an enemy driving south. It is the task of parachute troops, as advance detachments from the air, to occupy tactically important areas and to hold them until ground troops, in this case landing forces, fight their way through to them and incorporate them into the general front. Furthermore in Normandy they could, by attacking the strongpoints immediately west of the beach, paralyze the coastal defences. If it really was the task of the reported enemy forces to keep open the crossings, it meant that a landing would soon take place and they were really in earnest!

The Divisional Intelligence Officer ordered the immediate closing down of the French postal network. Soon the attached units announced their first prisoners. Near Caen the presence of 3 Parachute Brigade was established, and this meant 6 British Airborne Division, which was a first-line formation, and there was no question of reinforcements for the F.F.I.* The parachute troops in the area of our 709 Infantry Division were Americans: to the south 101 Airborne Division (501st and 506th Parachute Regiments) and to the north 82 Parachute Division (505th Parachute Regiment). That meant that approximately seventy-five per cent of the parachute and airborne troops which were known to us as stationed in southern England had been employed.

. . . . At the beginning of June several of these conditions [considered essential for invasion] coincided. Our weather experts, however, had predicted such heavy seas for 6 June that a landing seemed practically impossible. 7 Army wished to make use of this respite; all the generals, accompanied by two of their subordinates, were summoned to Rennes for a final sand-table exercise. Furthermore, Field-Marshal Rommel, Commander-in-Chief of Army Group B which was responsible for repulsing an invasion, was on his way to the Obersalzberg to report. 'Official' opinion was that since May had passed, an invasion was unlikely before August. Therefore the most important regimental officers were away on this particular morning.

The Corps Command post resembled a disturbed beehive. At last the suspense was over, the constant round of 'stand to' and partial or full 'state of readiness'. Since the middle of April this had kept the troops in suspense, and they had in the end got so used to it that it wasn't taken seriously any more. Priority messages were sent in all directions. They were intended to hold the divisional commanders at their command posts and to recall immediately those who had already started out for Rennes. Most of them answered: Kraiss, Count von Schmettow, Richter and Hellmich. Only von Schlieben and Falley could not be found.

The commander of our 91 Airborne Division, Major-General Falley, noticed while he was on his way the heavy air attacks and the roar of aircraft, so he turned back. The driver raced across the departments first of Ille et Vilaine and then Manche; he drove his divisional commander straight to his death. When Falley jumped out of his car in the yard of his quarters at the Château Haut, north of Picauville, it was already occupied by the Americans. A few shots rang out, and the general was killed beside his driver, without having issued a single order. Soon afterwards, this enemy group of the 508th Parachute Regiment were wiped out, and the divisional command post reverted to German hands. The General was buried in the paddock at the back of the main building.

German staff officer

The Other Side of the Coin

My own little command group of eleven officers and men set up division headquarters in an apple orchard, on almost the exact spot we had planned to be before we left England. Hal Clark's boys had not failed us. They had put us down on the button.

The Germans were all around us, of course, sometimes within five hundred yards of my C.P., but in the fierce and confused fighting that was going on all

* Forces Françaises de l'Intérieur (Ed.)

about they did not launch the strong attack that could have wiped out our egg-shell perimeter defence.

This was in large part due to the dispersion of the paratroopers. Wherever they landed they began to cut every communication line they could find, and soon the German commanders had no more contact with their units than we had with ours. When the German commander of 91 Division found himself cut off from the elements of his command, he did the only thing left to do. He got in a staff car and went out to see for himself what the hell had gone on in this wild night of confused shooting. He never found out. Just at daylight a patrol of paratroopers stopped his car and killed him as he reached for his pistol. The lieutenant commanding the patrol told me the story with great glee.

'Well,' I said, 'in our present situation, killing division commanders does not strike me as being particularly hilarious. But I congratulate you. I'm glad it was a German division commander you got.'

For a while, had I thought about it, the chances were probably fair that I would suffer the same fate my German counterpart had met. We had nothing but hand weapons with which to defend ourselves, rifles, pistols, grenades, and light 2·36 bazookas. The guns we desperately needed, the 57-mm. guns that could stop a tank, were to come in with the glider serials that were to bring four thousand more men into the zone at daylight. They came just as the first streaks of day began to show in the east, but the morning mist rising from the marshy land hung low over the hedgerows, and many a glider was smashed on landing. The fragmentary news that was coming in was both good and bad. By daylight the division's first objective, the town of Ste. Mère-Eglise, was in our hands, and was never lost thereafter. The news from the gliders was less cheering. Twenty-four landed, and nearly all were badly smashed up. Some went into the trees that topped the hedgerows. Others went down in swampy places, where men sank armpit deep into the muck as they tried to bring out the heavy radios and the anti-tank guns.

. . . . In addition to our personnel losses, we were sadly handicapped in our communications. We couldn't get in touch with anybody—neither the troops that were supposed to be coming in over the beaches by now, nor with anybody back in England, nor with anybody afloat.

General Ridgway

British Welcomed

A shadow darted from a nearby tree, and I was joined in the open by the huge Sten-gunner with the black face. The whites of his eyes gleamed in the moonlight, and for all my weariness I found myself on the verge of giggles.

'You speak the lingo, tosh? All right then, you go up and knock on the door, and we'll give you coverin' fire. I'll stay 'ere and my mate'll creep round the other side of the yard so's to cover you proper.'

A dog barked at my approach. From the corner of my eye I could see a stealthy figure flit from behind a haystack into the shadow of the barn door. There was no answer to my first knock. The household was obviously fast asleep.

I knocked louder, and this time I heard a scurrying on the stairs and a sudden clamour of French voices. Footsteps approached the door, withdrew, hesitated, then approached again. The door opened.

On the way I had been searching for suitable words with which to introduce ourselves—some calming, yet elegant, phrase worthy of the French gift of expression and of their infallible flair for the dramatic moment. But at the sight of the motherly, middle-aged peasant the gulf of the years disappeared, and I might have been back in 1939, an English tourist on a walking tour dropping in to ask for a glass of cider and some camembert.

'*Excusez-nous, Madame. Nous sommes des parachutistes anglais faisant partie du Débarquement Allié.*'

There was a moment of scrutiny, then the woman folded me in her arms. The tears streamed down her face, and in between kisses she was shouting for her husband, for lamps, for wine. In a moment I was carried by the torrent of welcome into the warm, candle-lit kitchen. Bottles of cognac and Calvados appeared on the table, children came clattering down the wooden stairs, and we found ourselves—an evil-looking group of camouflaged cut-throats—surrounded and overwhelmed by the pent-up emotions of four years. The farmer and his wife wanted us to stay and drink, to laugh and cry and shake hands over and over again. They wanted to touch us, to tell us all about the Occupation, and to share with us their implacable hatred of the Boche. It seemed that the moment so long awaited could not be allowed to be spoilt by realities, till every drop of emotion was exhausted. I was nearly as much affected as they were. Warmed by the fiery trickle of Calvados, I rose to this—certainly one of the greatest occasions of my life—so completely that I forgot all about the Drop, all about the marshes and the Battery. It was the sight of my companions, bewildered by all this emotion and talk, automatically drinking glass after glass, that suddenly reminded me of what we had come for. I began politely to insist on answers to questions which had already been brushed aside more than once: Where were we? How far away were the nearest Germans? Once more the questions were ignored. '*Ah, mon Dieu, ne nous quittez pas maintenant! Ah, les pauvres malheureux! Ils sont tous mouillés!*'

James Byrom

A General, too, is Human

I woke with the first light, sore and stiff but refreshed, filled my helmet with hot water, and started to shave, with one of these little injector razors with a rotating head that a paratrooper likes because it is small, all in one piece, and takes up not much more room than a pencil. I had gotten a leather-cased field telephone in by this time, and when I was about half through shaving, it rang—a battalion down by the river reporting on the night's activities. When I put down my phone and reached for my razor again, it was gone. Some S.O.B. had stolen it.

General Ridgway

D-DAY: THE BEACHES

With one exception, the beach landings went smoothly, encountering compara-
tively little opposition, and in the next five days a rapid advance of up to ten miles
inland followed, until a continuous bridgehead was formed from north of the
Carentan estuary to the mouth of the Orne. The Allies had achieved surprise in both
place and time; the Germans had been expecting the attack across the Straits of
Dover, and did not believe that it would be launched in anything but the most
favourable weather. By chance, the landing of American troops at Omaha Beach
coincided with the arrival of a strong German force engaged on an active invasion
exercise, and the ensuing battle was bitter.

Germans

And then it struck: H-Hour. The Ia,* composed as always, read out:
'06.30 hours: landings in the area of 352 Division on the Calvados coast between
Vierville and Colleville.' These landings were followed by others towards 07.00
and 07.30 hours north-east of the Carentan peninsula at Les Grandes Dunes and
in the right-hand sector of the Corps between Port-en-Bessin and Riva Bella, at
different times, according to when the flood-tide waters reached the beach. It
was further reported that after the first wave of attackers, others followed, landing at half-hourly intervals. It was about 09.30 hours before the situation became at all clear. The location of the landing north of the Carentan estuary could
be fixed exactly. This was in the sector of the 919th Infantry Regiment. . . .
Strong point 5 was the first to be in immediate contact with the enemy, . . . the
garrison of which got buried and had to be dug out by the Americans.

. . . . The minutes dragged by. Nerves were tense. One individual report
followed another; they confirmed or contradicted each other. Army or Army
Group H.Q. were constantly telephoning. But all the Corps staff could do was to
wait, wait—wait until the confused overall picture had been clarified, until the
main centres of the dropping and landing zones had become apparent, until we
had heard from strongpoints either encircled by the enemy or by-passed by him,
or until reconnaissance thrusts had brought in important statements by prisoners.
What complicated matters was that all reports came from the Army exclusively.
Support from our own Air Force was non-existent from the very first minute.
That was why facts as they became apparent did not add up to a fixed overall
picture.

German staff officer

British

Some of the men were talking, some smoking, some vomiting quietly into
brown bags of greaseproof paper. The wind was bringing to them now the sound
of shells bursting ashore. Each man could feel each thudding detonation somewhere inside him. The talking stopped. Men took up their rifles and machine
carbines; there was the clack of bolts being drawn and rammed home. The slow,

---

* Chief staff officer (Ed.)

wallowing motion of the craft eased; they were coming into shallower water. Orders were being shouted in the stern and a marine heaved himself up over the side and began to take soundings. There was smoke sprawling across the beach ahead, and the black plumes of explosions, each with a cherry-red flicker of flame at its heart, were leaping up in front of the high bows.

The landing craft nosed inshore through a mass of floating rubbish. A dead sailor came floating out to sea, face and legs under water, rump poking upwards; then a dead soldier, his waxen face turned up to the sky, his hands floating palm upwards on the water; he was kept afloat by his inflated lifebelt. Ahead of them lay beached landing craft, some wrecked, scattered untidily along the waterline.

There was a jarring explosion beneath the bows and the whole craft lurched forward. Men toppled forward in a heap, clambered to their feet as the ramps crashed down, and ran splashing down into the water. They had no time to stop for the two men who had been caught by the mine exploding beneath the bows and whose blood stained the dirty seawater as the boat began to submerge. They were all away now, and wading with weapons held above their heads towards the wet sand ahead.

. . . . There was a tangle of wire ahead, with German mine warnings poking up everywhere and a few British dead lying with their faces in the sand. They followed the tape along a path torn through the wire and came on to a narrow track running laterally. In front of them now were gentle, dreary dunes rising from pools and runnels of water, with grass growing scantily on their upper flanks. On each side of them sappers were rooting up mines as hastily as potatoes, and a little away to the right a beach dressing station had just been established, with a row of loaded stretchers waiting on one side and a row of corpses laid out on the other, each a still mound under a grey blanket, with big boots protruding at the end. Some pioneers were trying to dig in along the far side of the road, in the wet sand.

They moved on. There was the sudden *wheep-wheep* of bullets. Paterson could not see where they were coming from; then the grating, shrieking descent of their first shell. They flopped, pressing themselves frantically into the sand, then staggered to their feet and went lumbering after Paterson.

Someone was whimpering loudly; it was like the crying of a spoilt child. Sergeant Shannon stopped and looked round. Little Alfie Bradley was lurching about in a wide circle, well away from the tape, pressing his hands to his face. The sergeant raced after him and pulled him down to the ground.

As the boy felt the pressure of the sergeant's hands on his shoulders he tried to stifle his crying; he kept on sniffling jerkily. There was a red pit where one of his eyes had been. Blood welled darkly from the other.

'I can't see,' he whispered, 'I can't see.'

The sergeant comforted him.

'All right, lad, there's nowt t'worry about. Yer eyes are full of blood. You'll be all right when they've washed them.' He whipped out the boy's field dressing, his hands already bright with fresh blood. He knew the boy would never see again. He bound the dressing tightly over the boy's face. It began to stain red at once.

'There, lad,' he said soothingly, 'that'll do just t'keep dirt out.' He steered the blind boy back to the tape, forced him down to his knees and put the tape between his fingers.

'Foller this back, lad,' he said gently. 'When yer get on t' that road again you'll be by the dressing station. They'll take you in.'

He stood for a moment watching Little Alfie crawling back towards the beach on all fours, the tape between his fingers. Then he stooped, wiped his bloody hands in the sand and doubled after the platoon.

Most of the 5th Battalion were across the beach. As the last of them clambered up a steep bank of sand, sticking close to the tape for fear of mines, they moved aside cautiously to pass Corporal Shuttleworth.

He was sitting, dazed, on his pack by the tape. Where his right boot had been there was a raw, red stump. 'Mind the mines,' he muttered dreamily to the men passing him, 'or you'll get what I got.'

No one had time to stop for him. One after another the riflemen looked curiously at him, as if they had never known him, and hurried on. The blood was draining away from him fast. There was no pain and he was becoming sleepy. Some of the men trudging past him were his friends; sometimes one of them would stoop over him and tell him apologetically that the stretcher-bearers would be along in a moment to look after him. He would shake his head drunkenly, and once he giggled. One of his old comrades from the Green Howards, bending over him, heard him snigger, 'Half a man, half a bloody man. The cow, she'll get my pension.' The blood was running away from him into the thirsty sand. He shook, as if enjoying some great secret joke. He mumbled something and toppled forward across the tape. The last rifleman of the 5th Wessex stepped over the body and plodded on.

Alexander Baron

Americans: Omaha Beach

Many men, even among the seasick, were keyed up by the occasion. One officer remembered his troops chatting about 'What a shambles the beach would be from the bombs and ships' guns', although his own impression was: 'It looked like another big tactical scheme off Slapton Sands, and I couldn't get the feeling out of my head that it was going to be another miserable two-day job with a hot shower at the end.'

. . . . The landing craft came in under the comforting thunder of the tremendous fire support from naval guns, as well as the tank and artillery pieces firing from L.C.T.s. Up to within a few hundred yards of the water's edge, there was every reason to hope that the enemy shore defences might have been neutralized. Then, many of the leading craft began to come under fire from automatic weapons and artillery, which increased in volume as they approached touchdown. It was evident at H-Hour that the enemy fortifications had not been knocked out.

. . . . The Army-Navy Special Engineer Task Force had one of the most important and difficult missions of the landing. . . . Men burdened with equipment and explosives were excellent targets for enemy fire as they unloaded in water often several feet deep. Of sixteen dozers only six got to the beach in working condition, and three of these were immediately disabled by artillery hits. Much equipment, including nearly all buoys and poles for marking lanes, was lost or destroyed before it could be used. Eight navy personnel of Team 11 were dragging the pre-loaded rubber boat off their L.C.M. when an artillery shell burst just above the load of explosives and set off the primacord. One of the eight survived. Another shell hit the L.C.M. of Team 14, detonating explosives on the deck and killing all navy personnel. Team 15 was pulling in its rubber boat through the surf when a mortar scored a direct hit and touched off the explosives, killing three men and wounding four. Support Team F came in about 07.00. A first shell hit the ramp, throwing three men into the water. As the vessel drifted off out of control, another hit squarely on the bow, killing fifteen of the team. Only five army personnel from this craft reached shore. . . . Casualties for the Special Engineer Task Force, including navy personnel, ran to 41 per cent for D Day, most of them suffered in the first half-hour.

. . . . Perhaps the worst area on the beach was Dog Green directly in front of strongpoints guarding the Vierville draw and under heavy flanking fire from emplacements to the west, near Pointe de la Percée. Company A of the 116th was due to land on this sector with Company C of the 2nd Rangers on its right flank, and both units came in on their targets. One of the six L.C.A.s carrying Company A foundered about a thousand yards off shore, and passing Rangers saw men jumping overboard and being dragged down by their loads. At H + 6 minutes the remaining craft grounded in water four to six feet deep, about thirty yards short of the outward band of obstacles. Starting off the craft in three files, centre file first and the flank files peeling right and left, the men were enveloped in accurate and intense fire from automatic weapons. Order was quickly lost as the troops attempted to dive under water or dropped over the sides into surf over their heads. Mortar fire scored four direct hits on one L.C.A., which 'disintegrated'. Casualties were suffered all the way to the sand, but when the survivors got there, some found they could not hold and came back into the water for cover, while others took refuge behind the nearest obstacles. Remnants of one boat team on the right flank organized a small firing line on the first yards of sand, in full exposure to the enemy. In short order every officer of the company, including Captain Taylor N. Fellers, was a casualty, and most of the sergeants were killed or wounded. The leaderless men gave up any attempt to move forward and confined their efforts to saving the wounded, many of whom drowned in the rising tide. Some troops were later able to make the sea wall by staying in the edge of the water and going up the beach with the tide. Fifteen minutes after landing, Company A was out of action for the day. Estimates of its casualties range as high as two-thirds.

The smaller Ranger company (sixty-four men), carried in two L.C.A.s, came in at H + 15 minutes to the right of Vierville draw. Shells from an anti-tank gun bracketed Captain Ralph E. Goranson's craft, killing a dozen men and shaking up others. An enemy machine-gun ranged in on the ramps of the second L.C.A. and hit fifteen Rangers as they debarked. Without waiting to organize survivors of the boat, sections set out immediately across two hundred and fifty yards of sand towards the base of the cliff. Too tired to run, the men took three or four minutes to get there, and more casualties resulted from machine-guns and mortars. Wounded men crawled behind them, and a few made it. When the

Rangers got to shelter at the base of the cliff they had lost thirty-five men.

.... Company F came into the beach almost on its scheduled target, touching down in front of the strongly fortified les Moulins draw (D-3). The three sections to the east, unprotected by the smoke, came under concentrated fire and took forty-five minutes to get across the exposed stretch of sand. By this time half their number were casualties; the remnants reached cover in no state for assault action. The other sections had better fortune, but had lost their officers when they reached the shingle bank and were more or less disorganized.

.... One of the spectacular disasters of the day was suffered by L.C.I. 91, approaching Dog White about 07.40 and carrying the alternate headquarters of the 116th R.C.T. Handled by a veteran crew with experience at Sicily and Salerno, the L.C.I. was struck by artillery fire as it made a first attempt to get through the obstacles. Backing out, the craft came in again for a second try. Element 'C' was barely showing above the rising tide, and the L.C.I. could not get past. The ramps were dropped in six feet of water. As some of the officers led the way off, an artillery shell (or rocket) hit the crowded forward deck and sent up a sheet of flame. Clothes burning, men jumped or fell off into the sea and tried to swim in under continued artillery fire. It is estimated that no personnel escaped from No. 1 compartment of the craft out of the twenty-five carried there.

.... Wherever an advance was made, it depended on the presence of some few individuals, officers and non-commissioned officers, who inspired, encouraged or bullied their men forward, often by making the first forward moves. On Easy Red a lieutenant and a wounded sergeant of divisional engineers stood up under fire and walked over to inspect the wire obstacles just beyond the embankment. The lieutenant came back and, hands on hips, looked down disgustedly at the men lying behind the shingle bank. 'Are you going to lay there and get killed, or get up and do something about it?' Nobody stirred, so the sergeant and the officer got the materials and blew the wire.

.... Colonel Taylor summed up the situation in terse phrase: 'Two kinds of people are staying on this beach, the dead and those who are going to die—now let's get the hell out of here.'

.... Casualties for V Corps were in the neighbourhood of three thousand killed, wounded and missing. The two assaulting regimental combat teams (16th and 116th) lost about a thousand men each. The highest proportionate losses were taken by units which landed in the first few hours, including engineers, tank troops and artillery.

Whether by swamping at sea or by action at the beach, material losses were considerable, including twenty-six artillery pieces and over fifty tanks. . . . On the Navy side, a tentative estimate gives a total of about fifty landing craft and ten larger vessels lost, with a much larger number of all types damaged.

Beach Secured

Trucks and jeeps pulling trailers loaded with ammunition bumped and skidded past the Company, and a newly arrived tank platoon clanked up the rise, looking dangerous and invincible. M.P.s were waving traffic on, Engineers were building roads, a bulldozer was scraping out a runway for an airfield, jeep ambulances, with wounded on stretchers across the top, were sliding down the rutted road between the taped-off minefields to the clearing stations in the lee of the bluff. In a wide field, pocked with shell-holes, graves registration troops were burying American dead. There was an air of orderly, energetic confusion about the entire scene that reminded Noah of the time when he was a small boy in Chicago and had watched the circus throwing up its tents and arranging its cages and living quarters.

When he got to the top of the bluff Noah turned round and looked at the beach, trying to fix it in his mind. Hope will want to know what it looked like and her father, too, when I get back, Noah thought. Somehow, planning what he was going to tell them at some distant, beautiful, unwarlike day made it seem more certain to Noah that that day would arrive and he would be alive to celebrate it, dressed in soft flannels and a blue shirt, with a glass of beer in his hand, under a maple tree, perhaps, on a bright Sunday afternoon, boring his relatives, he thought with a grin, with the long-winded veteran's stories of the Great War.

The beach, strewn with the steel overflow of the factories of home, looked like a rummage basement in some store for giants. Close off-shore, just beyond the old tramp steamers they were sinking now for a breakwater, destroyers were standing, firing over their heads at strongpoints inland.

'That's the way to fight a war,' Burnecker said beside Noah. 'Real beds; coffee is being served below, sir; you may fire when ready, Gridley. We would have joined the Navy, Ackerman, if we had as much brains as a rabbit.'

Irwin Shaw

Views of Battle

A battle exists on many different levels. There is the purely moral level, at the Supreme Headquarters perhaps eighty miles away from the sound of guns, where the filing cabinets have been dusted in the morning, where there is a sense of quiet and efficiency, where soldiers who never fire a gun and never have a shot fired at them, the high Generals, sit in their pressed uniforms and prepare statements to the effect that all has been done that is humanly possible, the rest being left to the judgment of God, Who has risen early, ostensibly, for this day's work, and is impartially and critically regarding the ships, the men drowning in the water, the flight of high explosive, the accuracy of bombardiers, the skill of naval officers, the bodies being thrown into the air by mines, the swirl of tides against steel spikes at the water's edge, the loading of cannon in gun emplacements, and the building far back from the small violent fringe between the two armies, where the files have also been dusted that morning and the enemy Generals sit in different pressed uniforms, looking at very similar maps, reading very similar reports, matching their moral strength and intellectual ingenuity with their colleagues and antagonists a hundred miles away. In these places, in the rooms where the large maps with the acetate overlays and the red and black crayon markings are hung on the walls, the battle swiftly takes on an orderly and formal appearance. A plan is always in process of being worked out on the maps. If Plan I fails, Plan II is attempted. If Plan II is only partially successful, a pre-arranged modification of Plan III is instituted. The Generals have all studied from the same books at West Point and Spandau and Sandhurst, and many of them have written books themselves and read each other's works, and they all know what Caesar did in a somewhat similar situation and the mistake that Napoleon made in Italy, and how Ludendorff failed to exploit a break in the line in 1915, and they all hope, on opposite sides of the English Channel, that the situation never gets to that decisive point where they will have to say the Yes or the No which may decide the fate of the battle, and perhaps the nation, and which takes the last trembling dram of courage out of a man, and which may leave him ruined and broken for the rest of his life, all his honours gone, his reputation empty, when he has said it. So they sit back in their offices, which are like the offices of General Motors or the offices of I.G. Farben in Frankfurt, with stenographers and typists and flirtations in the halls, and look at the maps and read the reports and pray that Plans I, II and III will operate as everyone has said they will operate back in Grosvenor Square and the Wilhelmstrasse, with only small, not very important modifications that can be handled locally, by the men on the scene.

The men on the scene see the affair on a different level. They have not been questioned on the proper manner of isolating the battlefield. They have not been consulted on the length of the preliminary bombardment. Meteorologists have not instructed them on the rise and fall of the tides in the month of June or the probable incidence of storms. They have not been at the conferences in which was discussed the number of divisions it would be profitable to lose to reach a phase line one mile inland by 16.00 hours. There are no filing cabinets on board the landing barges, no stenographers with whom to flirt, no maps in which their actions, multiplied by two million, become clear, organized, intelligent symbols, suitable for publicity releases and the tables of historians.

They see helmets, vomit, green water, shell-bursts, smoke, crashing planes, blood plasma, submerged obstacles, guns, pale, senseless faces, a confused drowning mob of men running and falling, that seem to have no relation to any of the things they have been taught since they left their jobs and wives to put on the uniform of their country. To a General sitting before the maps eighty miles away, with echoes of Caesar and Clausewitz and Napoleon fleetingly swimming through his brain, matters are proceeding as planned, or almost as planned, but to the man on the scene everything is going wrong.

'Oh, God,' sobs the man on the scene, when the shell hits the Landing Craft Infantry, H-Hour plus two, one mile out from shore, and the wounded begin to scream on the slippery decks, 'Oh, God, it is all screwed up.'

To the Generals eighty miles away, the reports on casualties are encouraging. To the man on the scene the casualties are never encouraging. When he is hit or when the man next to him is hit, when the ship fifty feet away explodes, when the Naval Ensign on the bridge is screaming in a high, girlish voice for his mother because he has nothing left below his belt, it can only appear to him that he has been involved in a terrible accident, and it is inconceivable at that moment to believe that there is a man eighty miles away who has foreseen that accident, encouraged it, made arrangements for it to happen, and who can report, after it has happened (although he must know about the shell, about the listing Landing Craft Infantry, about the wet decks and the screaming Ensign) that everything is going according to plan.

'Oh, God,' sobs the man on the scene, watching the amphibious tanks sink under the waves, with perhaps one man swimming up out of the hatch and screaming, and perhaps no one swimming up out of the hatch. 'Oh, God,' he sobs, looking down at the queer, unattached leg lying beside his face and realizing it is his. 'Oh, God,' as the ramp goes down and the twelve men in front of him pile up in the cold two feet of water, with the machine-gun bullets inside them. 'Oh, God,' looking for the holes on the beach he had been told the Air Force was going to put there for him, and not finding them, and lying there face down, with the mortar shell dropping silently on top of him. 'Oh, God,' he sobs, seeing the friend . . . blow up on a mine and hang across a barbed-wire fence with his back wide open from neck to hip.

Irwin Shaw

Reinforcements for the German forces at the bridgeheads were slow in arriving, owing to the Allied air forces which had shattered land communications leading to Normandy, and to the Germans fear of landings farther north. When their reinforcements trickled in, they were disorganized by the continual hammering from the air. Though dogged and effective in defence, especially before Caen and in the bocage *country farther west, nowhere were the Germans able to concentrate a massive counter-attack.*

Chief-of-Staff Western Command emphasizes the desire of the Supreme Command [Hitler] to have the enemy in the bridgehead annihilated by the evening of 6 June, since there exists a danger of additional sea- and airborne landings for support. In accordance with an order by General Jodl, all units will be diverted to the point of penetration in Calvados. The beach-head there must be cleaned up by not later than to-night.

Western Command to 7 Army

I first knew that the invasion had begun with a report that parachutists had been dropped near Troarn a little after midnight on 6 June. Since I had been told that I was to make no move until I had heard from Rommel's headquarters, I could do nothing immediately but warn my men to be ready. I waited impatiently all that night for some instructions. But not a single order from a higher formation was received by me: realizing that my armoured division was closest to the scene of operations, I finally decided at six-thirty in the morning that I had to take some action. I ordered my tanks to attack the English 6 Airborne Division which had entrenched itself in a bridgehead over the Orne. To me this constituted the most immediate threat to the German position.

Hardly had I made this decision, when at seven o'clock I received my first intimation that a higher command did still exist. I was told by Army Group B that I was now under command of 7 Army. But I received no further orders as to my role. At nine o'clock I was informed that I would receive any future orders from LXXXIV Infantry Corps, and finally at ten o'clock I was given my first operational instructions. I was ordered to stop the move of my tanks against the Allied airborne troops, and to turn west and aid the forces protecting Caen.

Once over the Orne river, I drove north towards the coast. By this time the enemy, consisting of three British and three Canadian infantry divisions, had made astonishing progress and had already occupied a strip of high ground about ten kilometres from the sea. From here the excellent anti-tank gun-fire of the Allies knocked out eleven of my tanks before I had barely started. However, one battle group did manage to by-pass these guns and actually reached the coast at Lion-sur-Mer, at about seven in the evening.

I now expected that some reinforcements would be forthcoming to help me hold my position, but nothing came. Another Allied parachute landing on both sides of the Orne, together with a sharp attack by English tanks, forced me to give up my hold on the coast. I retired to take up a line just north of Caen. By the end of that first day my division had lost almost twenty-five per cent of its tanks.

Lieutenant-General Feuchtinger

On 7 June our division received orders to leave the marshalling area in Thouars and to move to the invasion front in Normandy. Everyone was in a good and eager mood to see action again—happy that the pre-invasion spell of uncertainty and waiting was snapped at last.

Our motorized columns were coiling along the road towards the invasion beaches. Then something happened that left us in a daze. Spurts of fire flicked along the column and splashes of dust staccatoed the road. Everyone was piling out of the vehicles and scuttling for the neighbouring fields. Several vehicles were already in flames. This attack ceased as suddenly as it had crashed upon us fifteen minutes before. The men started drifting back to the column again, pale and shaky and wondering how they had survived this fiery rain of bullets. This had been our first experience with the '*Jabos*' (fighter-bombers). The march column was now completely disrupted and every man was on his own, to pull out of this blazing column as best he could. And it was none too soon, because an hour later the whole thing started all over again, only much worse this time. When this attack was over, the length of the road was strewn with splintered anti-tank guns (the pride of our division), flaming motors and charred implements of war.

The march was called off and all vehicles that were left were hidden in the dense bushes or in barns. No one dared show himself out in the open any more. Now the men started looking at each other. This was different from what we thought it would be like. It had been our first experience with our new foe—the American.

During the next few days we found out how seriously he was going about his business. Although now we only travelled at nights and along secondary roads rimmed with hedges and bushes, we encountered innumerable wrecks giving toothless testimony that some motorist had not benefited from the bitter experience we had had.

Staff officer, 17 S.S. Panzer Grenadier Division

Pushing Inland

The infantrymen plodded along at the roadside while the tanks, each enveloped in its own clattering roar, hurried past them. The men were dusty and sodden with sweat, marching in straggling single files, each man keeping his own uneven step.

. . . . A shell would burst in the fields a hundred yards away and the earth come pattering down on the helmets of the men sprawled in the dust, and on the backs of their necks. Then they would be up on their feet again and raggedly marching. A shell would explode across the roadway, obliterating half-a-dozen men; but the files, dispersed, would coalesce again and plod onwards past the shallow crater and through the vanishing brown smoke.

A wood echoed with the nervous clamour of machine-guns; a farmhouse burned. Desperate little fights flared up and ended suddenly, for a barn, for a hedgerow honeycombed with weapon pits, for a roadside cottage, section against section, platoon against platoon; ten, perhaps twenty men on each side, rarely more. Wary riflemen hunted snipers in the cool gloom of vaulted cellars among the great cobwebbed cider barrels. Men died on the warm dungheaps with hens fluttering in a panic about them. An old French peasant woman lugged a dead German on to her cabbage patch and began to dig his grave there, 'to enrich the earth, m'sieur'. This was the battle on D-Day Plus One.

Alexander Baron

Small Battle

Upstairs, in the bedroom of the master and mistress of the house, Rickett, Burnecker and Noah covered a lane between the barn and the shed where a plough and a farm wagon were kept. There was a small wooden crucifix on the wall and a stiff photograph of the farmer and his wife, rigid with responsibility on their wedding day. On another wall hung a framed poster from the French Line showing the liner *Normandie* cutting through a calm, bright blue sea.

There was a white embroidered spread on the lumpy four-poster bed, and little lace doilies on the bureau, and a china cat on the hearth.

What a place, Noah thought, as he put another clip in his rifle, to fight my first battle.

There was a prolonged burst of firing from outside. Rickett, who was standing next to one of the two windows, holding a Browning Automatic Rifle, flattened himself against the flowered wallpaper. The glass covering the *Normandie* shattered into a thousand pieces. The picture shivered on the wall, with a large hole at the water line of the great ship, but it did not fall.

Noah looked at the large, neatly-made bed. He had an almost uncontrollable impulse to crawl under it. He even took a step towards it, from where he crouched near the window. He was shivering. When he tried to move his hands, they made wide senseless circles, knocking over a small blue vase on a shawl-covered table in the centre of the room.

If only he could get under the bed he would be safe. He would not die then. He could hide, in the dust on the splintery wood floor. There was no sense to this. Standing up to be shot in a tiny wall-papered room, with half the German Army all around him. It wasn't his fault he was there. He had not taken the road between the hedges, he had not lost contact with L Company, he had not neglected to halt and dig in where he was supposed to; it could not be asked of him to stand at the window, next to Rickett and have his head blown in.

'Get over to that window!' Rickett was shouting, pointing wildly to the other window. 'Get the hell over! The bathtards're coming in. . . .'

Recklessly, Rickett was exposing himself at the window, firing in short, spraying bursts, from the hip, his arms and shoulders jerking with the recoil.

Now, thought Noah craftily, when he is not looking. I can crawl under the bed and nobody will know where I am.

Burnecker was at the other window, firing, shouting, 'Noah! Noah!'

Noah took one last look at the bed. It was cool and neat and like home. The crucifix on the wall behind it suddenly leapt out from the wall, Christ in splinters, and tumbled on the bedspread.

Noah ran to the window and crouched beside Burnecker. He fired two shots blindly down into the lane. Then he looked. The grey figures were running with insane speed, crouched over, in a bunch, towards the house.

Oh, Noah thought, taking aim (the target in the centre of the circle, remember, and resting on the top of the sight, and even a blind man with rheumatism can't miss), oh, Noah thought, firing at the bunched figures, they shouldn't do that, they shouldn't come together like that. He fired again and again. Rickett was firing at the other window and Burnecker beside him, very deliberately, holding his breath, squeezing off. Noah heard a high, wailing scream and wondered where that was coming from. It was quite some time before he realized that it was coming from him. Then he stopped screaming.

There was a lot of firing from downstairs, too, and the grey figures kept falling and getting up and crawling and falling again. Three of the figures actually got close enough to throw hand grenades, but they missed the window and exploded harmlessly against the walls. Rickett got them all with the same burst of a gun.

The other grey figures seemed to glide to a stop. For a moment there was silence and the figures hung there, motionless, reflective, in the clayey barnyard. Then they turned and began running away.

Noah watched them with surprise. It had never occurred to him that they would not reach the house.

. . . . 'This is an order from Lieutenant Green,' the Lieutenant said. He giggled. Then he caught himself and looked firm. 'I have assumed command,' he said formally. 'Command.'

'Is the Captain dead?' Rickett asked.

'Not exactly,' said Green. He lay back suddenly on the white spread and closed his eyes. But he continued talking. 'The Captain has retired for the season. He will be ready for next year's invasion.' He giggled, lying, with his eyes closed, on the lumpy feather bed. Then, suddenly, he sprang up. 'Did you hear anything?' he asked anxiously.

'No,' said Rickett.

'Tanks,' said Green. 'If they bring up tanks before it gets dark, French-fried with ketchup.'

. . . . It was nearly dark when Noah saw the tank. It moved ponderously down the lane, the long snout of its gun poking blindly before it.

'Here it comes,' Noah said, without moving, his eyes just over the window-sill.

The tank seemed to be momentarily stuck. Its treads spun, digging into the soft clay, and its machine-guns waved erratically back and forth. It was the first

German tank Noah had seen, and as he watched it he felt almost hypnotized. It was so large, so impregnable, so full of malice. . . . Now, he felt, there is nothing to be done. He was despairing and relieved at the same time. Now, there was nothing more that could be done. The tank took everything out of his hands, all decisions, all responsibilities. . . .

'Come on over here,' Rickett said. 'You, Ackermann.'

Noah jumped over to the window where Rickett was standing, holding the bazooka. 'I'm gahnta see,' Rickett said, 'if these gahdamn gadgets're worth a damn.'

Noah crouched at the window, and Rickett put the barrel of the bazooka on his shoulder. Noah was exposed at the window, but he had a curious sensation of not caring. With the tank there, so close, in the lane, everybody in the house was equally exposed. He breathed evenly, and waited patiently while Rickett manœuvred the bazooka around on his shoulder.

'They got some riflemen waiting behind the tank,' Noah said calmly. 'About fifteen of them.'

'They're in for a little thurprise,' Rickett said. 'Stand still.'

'I am standing still,' Noah said, irritated.

Rickett was fussing with the mechanism. The bazooka would have to throw about eighty yards to reach the tank, and Rickett was being very careful. 'Don't fire,' he told Burnecker at the other window. 'Let'th pretend we are not present up here.' He chuckled. Noah was only mildly surprised at Rickett's chuckling.

The tank started again. It moved ponderously, disdaining to fire, as though there was an intelligence there that understood its paralyzing moral effect that hardly needed the overt act of explosion to win its purpose. After a few yards it stopped again. The Germans behind it crouched for protection close to its rear treads.

The machine-gun farther off opened fire, spraying the whole side of the building loosely.

'For Christ's sake,' Rickett said, 'stand still.'

Noah braced himself rigidly against the window frame. He was sure that he was going to be shot in a moment. His entire body from the waist up was fully exposed in the window. He stared down at the waving guns of the tank, obscure in the growing shadows of dusk in the lane.

Then Rickett fired. The bazooka shell moved very deliberately through the air. Then it exploded against the tank. Noah watched from the window, forgetting to get down. Nothing seemed to happen for a moment. Then the cannon swung heavily downwards, stopped, pointing at the ground. There was an explosion inside the tank, muffled and deep. Some wisps of smoke came up through the driver's slits and the edges of the hatch. Then there were many more explosions. The tank rocked and quivered where it stood. Then the explosions stopped. The tank still looked as dangerous and full of malice as before, but it did not move. Noah saw the infantrymen behind it running. They ran down the lane, with no one firing at them, and disappeared behind the edge of the shed.

'It works, ah reckon,' Rickett said. 'Ah think we have shot ourselves a tank.' He took the bazooka off Noah's shoulder and put it against the wall.

Irwin Shaw

The Dead

I saw a great deal of death that day. Soon after the burial of Private Blank I was sent with a stretcher party to pick up what was left of a patrol of Panzer Grenadiers who had been practically annihilated by our battalion for the loss of one officer. As we drove over the shell-scarred road that was the perimeter of our Brigade positions, Canadian paratroopers were lying all long the ditch with their machine-guns pointed across the road. They had a bored, alert look, and one of them called out to Vic, who was sitting on the bonnet brandishing a Red Cross flag: 'Mind how you go, boys, Jerry don't recognize no fuggin' Red Cross!' We were not worried. One had to be a medic to trust the Red Cross, which was the psychological equivalent of the soldier's rifle. Yet it was a queer feeling to be driving along between the enemy and our own front line. The early foliage of the trees and hedges was brilliantly green, all the earth's forms lost in luxuriance and, once past the machine-gunners, we might have been going down a Kentish lane.

We stopped with a jerk—all stopping and starting in war was jerky—and climbed over a stile into a field. At first sight we seemed to have walked into an ambush of German soldiers, sitting, crouching or lying in ditches. Then I saw that they were nearly all dead, and surrounded by the litter of paper and equipment which *A Farewell to Arms* had taught me to expect. They had been killed in the act of using their weapons, creeping under cover or prying through the hedges to obtain a better field of fire. What startled me was not their rigidity but the colour of their faces. They were waxy white or mottled green: and the green of their camouflage smocks clashed horribly with the surrounding foliage. They were like waxworks dressed up for some hideous tableau at Madame Tussaud's. Somewhere in the back of my memory was the traditional picture of the battle-fields of the first World War—a picture derived from films like *The Four Horsemen of the Apocalypse* and the early paintings of Nash and Nevinson. I remembered a flat, cicatrized landscape, blasted and barren, set with tree stumps and twisted firs. The dead in those pictures were already part of the angularity and distortions of the bleak perspective, like rotting cabbage-stumps in an abandoned allotment. But here was no distortion or desolation, and the dead simply did not fit in. The last feverish gesture of devotion to duty was passionately eloquent in this mute, vegetable setting. One of them was sitting on a bank with a machine-gun tripod between his knees, staring along the barrel with a glassy eye already rimmed with flies. Another was kneeling at a gap in the hedge, his hand arrested in mid-air beside his head, killed apparently in the act of throwing a grenade. A third, crouching beside him, clawed at his belt, with his body arched lightly backwards. Whatever expression his face had worn at the moment of death, he now had a cunning, almost triumphant look, with half-closed eyes and the grim suggestion of a smile.

. . . . Shortly after dawn, stretcher-bearers brought into the barn where I was on duty a German boy of about seventeen, moaning and tossing on the stretcher to which he had been roped face down, because of the terrible wound in his back. His arrival disturbed a discussion between two doctors about the iniquity of the Germans. Instead of coming to examine him at once, which was their plain duty, they went on talking, and showed not the slightest flicker of interest. I drew attention to the patient's serious condition, for he was moaning in a half-delirium of physical and mental anguish: *'Weh, weh . . . das ist der Tod!'*

'Tell him to keep quiet,' said the doctor on duty, turning away to continue his conversation. While I was doing what I could to make the boy easier, the stretcher-bearers told me that he had been shot while trying to give himself up, a white handkerchief in his hand.

I insisted again, trying for the patient's sake to keep my anger within military limits. At last I got one of the doctors to stroll over and examine him. But by that time the struggle was over. His head had fallen forward into the straw that lined the stretcher. The doctor shrugged his shoulders. 'Nothing I can do. Take him over to Resuscitation.'

As they carried him over one of the stretcher-bearers said, 'It's a bloody shame. A kid like that!' Before putting him in the mortuary we went through his pockets. There was a love letter from a girl in Mulheim: 'Always thinking of you when I lie down at night. I pray, we all pray, you will come home safely.'

James Byrom

The Meadow

There was a placid meadow, rich with clover and tall, wet grass. The 5th Battalion had gone but its dead remained, littered about the field, staring up at the sky with the flies buzzing over them and their big boots poking up in the long grass.

They were silent and still. All the field was dreadfully still. Nothing stirred in the field but the petals of the pink hedge roses which fluttered in the helmets of the dead.

Alexander Baron

Bayeux 'Liberated'

On Sunday I divided my time between three meetings. The notables at Bayeux, General Leprince at Cherbourg, and Churchill in London. It is at Bayeux that Coubot, representing the King of Bourges, Commissaire of the bridgehead, has taken up his quarters. The town is undamaged, the shops, empty of everything else, have pyramids of Camembert cheeses in their windows. All the ancient richness of devastated Normandy—butter and cheese—remains on its hands. Coubot invited me to meet the notables at nine o'clock in the morning: judges, lawyers, priests, schoolmasters, clerks of the court, and estate owners came to hear me speak. They liked Pétain and the National Revolution very much. They gave me a glacial reception. France has already inflicted on them a war and an occupation—not a very rigorous one, however—and now the new France and Symbole have selected, together with the Allies, their beaches and their fields for the greatest operation in history. It is altogether too much for them. I took aside a cattle grazer whom Coubot had pointed out to me as the only member of the Resistance in the town. He looked rather sour, too. I questioned him.

'De Gaulle's all very fine,' he said, 'but you summoned us at nine o'clock in the morning: you must know that that's the hour for Mass.'

Emmanuel d'Astier

No Strategy

As the success of this operation became more and more probable, Rundstedt and Rommel agreed that the time had come for Hitler to decide personally what we must do next and how we were to go on fighting the battle in the West; in a word what *our* strategy was to be. It was clear to the Field-Marshals that limited measures could no longer hope to change the situation as it now stood. The only course open to us was to seal off Normandy along a favourable line, well to the rear of the present front. Along such a line it should be feasible once again to create a strong defensive position, which would enable us to withdraw our mobile reserves from the fighting and thus make them available for the sort of operations for which they were intended.

German staff officer

THE BATTLE OF THE HEDGEROWS

The bocage *country through which the American and British infantry in much of the Normandy bridgehead forced their way was about as unpleasant as any which men on their feet were ever asked to penetrate: disliked as much by defenders as attackers, and comparable in this respect with the Far Eastern jungles. The American advance towards and capture of St. Lô, known as the 'Battle of the Hedgerows', in which the best part of twelve divisions were employed on either side, was typical of this fighting.*

Look at an infantryman's eyes and you can tell how much war he has seen.

Bill Mauldin, American war artist

German Strategy

The battle area was the hedgerows of the *bocage*—an undulating, lush covered landscape, interspersed with apple orchards and pasture. For a defensive action such as LXXXIV Corps had to fight it was extremely favourable. Its peculiarities offset somewhat the enemy's superiority of armour and air. Characteristic were the many corners, the earth banks about three feet high out of which sprouted bushes or rows of trees. These banks divided the area into hundreds of little rectangles. The sunken tracks, mostly completely overgrown, were of paramount importance; they formed natural trenches and made it possible for troops to move their position in daylight without being seen.

. . . . Since obviously we were going to be on the defensive, our infantry had plenty of time to dig in along the sunken roads. Machine-guns and mortars were sited in such a way that all the tracks and gaps in the hedgerows were under observation and zeroed. Particular attention was paid to the open corners of the square pastures, for this is where the gates were usually situated. Every fighting unit, down to section level, sited its automatic weapons in depth, and cut passages through the bushes in order to be able to withdraw quickly without having to climb over any natural obstacles.

There was one fact which was of enormous help in our defence. Each section leader could see no more than a hundred to a hundred and fifty yards to the front and pretty well nothing to the flanks. The defended localities were staggered, and often they had little contact with their neighbours. Thus the defenders withdrew one by one only when the enemy pressed too hard at close quarters or penetrated the immediate flanks. Since an officer could not be everywhere at once, it depended on the N.C.O.s whether their sections lived up to the training which they had had for fighting in the *bocage*. To give our corporals and lance-corporals their due, they came through the test. Discipline and toughness proved their worth all over again. Without the drive which advance and success bring, and with the old feeling of the invincibility of the Wehrmacht fading, still nothing managed to break the character and entity of our regiments.

. . . . The nature of the terrain favoured anti-tank defence. Anti-tank rifles, the *Panzerfaust** and anti-tank bombs were all brought into use at close quarters. What is needed in close combat, however, is opportunity and men; these two factors on our side did not always coincide.

. . . . Both in armament and armour our tanks were superior to the enemy's. The long 75 mm. gun was excellent. But the local conditions back-fired on us, because the Panthers in the closely confined battle area lost the advantage which their longer range gave them. Every counter-attack we mounted therefore quickly suffered losses and bogged down.

. . . . Two other circumstances made life more difficult for our armour. The enemy's air superiority forced us to site the repair squadrons far back. Often damaged tanks which were only just non-runners could therefore not be towed away, but had to be dug in and used as armoured strongpoints. Furthermore, the armoured divisions never got any rest. They were constantly moved about as a defensive weapon, as 'hole pluggers' in the front, to intercept enemy thrusts or to regain lost territory by threatening the enemy's flanks. The enemy's constant pressure did not give us enough time to assemble strong armoured forces or to drive home any worth-while counter-attack.

. . . . The Americans developed a technique in the *bocage* which we called 'chess-board tactics'. Seen from the air the landscape resembled a chess board with thousands of squares; each measured a hundred by a hundred and fifty yards. The enemy's advanced elements overran this country field by field; they used Combat Groups, made up of armour, engineers, gunners and infantry. First artillery and fighter bombers worked over the whole area of the objective. Then engineers blew gaps in the embankments to enable the tanks to drive into the next square. The troops coming in with the tanks dealt with what German resistance remained; then the follow-up took over the ground. The next detachment to jump off assembled immediately behind the point which had been reached, and the same drill was repeated.

There was really no forward thrust, no attacking movement in these chess-board tactics; all they amounted to was the constant occupation of one small square previously softened up by gunfire. Even more than in the first World War everything depended on the mechanics of ground fighting, on sledgehammer tactics. Equipment and sweat were more important in the long run than courage and blood.

German officer

* Anti-tank missile projectors (Ed.)

Basic Principles

I don't make the infantryman look noble, because he couldn't look noble even if he tried. Still there is a certain nobility and dignity in combat soldiers and medical aid men with dirt in their ears. They are rough and their language gets coarse because they live a life stripped of convention and niceties. Their nobility and dignity come from the way they live unselfishly and risk their lives to help each other. They are normal people who have been put where they are, and whose actions and feelings have been moulded by their circumstances. There are gentlemen and boors; intelligent ones and stupid ones; talented ones and inefficient ones. But when they are all together and they are fighting, despite their bitching and griping and goldbricking and mortal fear, they are facing cold steel and screaming lead and hard enemies, and they are advancing and beating the hell out of the opposition.

They wish to hell they were someplace else, and they wish to hell they would get relief. They wish to hell the mud was dry and they wish to hell their coffee was hot. They want to go home. But they stay in their wet holes and fight, and then they climb out and crawl through minefields and fight some more.

Bill Mauldin

Problem

There were just three ways that our infantry could get through the hedge-row country. They could walk down the road, which always makes the leading men feel practically naked (and they are). They could attempt to get through gaps in the corners of the hedgerows and crawl up along the row leading forward or rush through in a group and spread out in the field beyond. This was not a popular method. In the first place, often there were no gaps just when you wanted one most, and in the second place the Germans knew about them before we did and were usually prepared with machine-gun and machine-pistol reception committees. The third method was to rush a skirmish line over a hedgerow and then across the field. This could have been a fair method if there had been no hedgerows.

Usually we could not get through the hedge without hacking a way through. This of course took time, and a German machine-gun can fire a lot of rounds in a very short time. Sometimes the hedges themselves were not thick. But it still took time for the infantryman to climb up the bank and scramble over, during which time he was a luscious target, and when he got over the Germans knew exactly where he was. All in all it was very discouraging to the men who had to go first. The farther to the rear one got the easier it all seemed.

Of course the Germans did not defend every hedgerow, but no one knew without stepping out into the spotlight which ones he did defend.

It was difficult to gain fire superiority when it was most needed. In the first place machine-guns were almost useless in the attack because about the only way they could be used was to fire from the hip. If you set them up before the advance started, they had no field of fire and could not shoot the enemy. If you carried them along until you met the enemy, still the only way to get them in position was to set them up on top of a hedgerow bank. That was not good because the German was in the next bank and got you before you set the gun down. Anyway, it had to be laid on the bank, no tripod, just a gun barrel lying unevenly on its stomach. On the other hand the Germans could dig their guns into the banks in advance, camouflage them, and be all set to cover the roads, trails and other bottlenecks our men had to use.

The artillery was the major fire support weapon. But it suffered certain handicaps. In the first place it had to be adjusted from the front line by forward observers. These sometimes had difficulty knowing just where they were, and the trees frequently delayed adjustment because of the short vision. If you found the enemy in the next hedgerow he was frequently less than a hundred yards from you, and that was too close for artillery fire, particularly since short rounds would probably burst in the trees over your men in your own hedgerow. If the enemy was two or more hedgerows ahead of you, that wasn't so good either, because the mere delay in getting to him through the last hedgerow just in front of him gave him time to rise up and smite you after the artillery lifted. The mortars were effective providing you knew just what to shoot at and where it was, but the infantryman still had the delay and exposure of getting through the last hedgerow.

The Germans, being on the defensive, profited by these minor items of the terrain. They could dig in, site their weapons to cover the approaches, and prepare tunnels and other covered exits for themselves. Then when our men appeared, laboriously working their way forward, the Germans could knock off the first one or two, cause the others to duck down behind the bank, and then call for his own mortar support. The German mortars were very, very efficient. By the time our men were ready to go after him, the German and his men and guns had obligingly retired to the next stop. If our men had rushed him instead of ducking behind the bank, his machine-gun or machine-pistol would knock a number off. For our infantrymen, it was what you might call in baseball parlance a fielder's choice. No man was very enthusiastic about it. But back in the dugout I have often heard the remark in tones of contempt and anger: 'Why don't they get up and go?'

The tanks are no better off. They have two choices. They can go down the roads, which in this case were just mud lanes, often too narrow for a tank, often sunk four to six feet below the adjacent banks, and generally deep in mud. The Class 4 roads were decent in spots, but only for one-way traffic, with few exits to the adjacent fields. An armoured outfit, whether it is a platoon or an armoured army, attacking along a single road attacks on a front of one tank. The rest of the tanks are just road-blocks trailing along behind. When the first tank runs into a mine or an 88 or 75 shell, it always stops, and it usually burns up. And it efficiently blocks the road so the majestic column of roaring tanks come to an ignominious stop. The next step is to try to find out where the enemy gun or tank is, and wheel up a tank or so to shoot at him. The only trouble is that probably only the men in the first tank saw his gun flash, and they aren't talking any more. The tanks trying to get into position to do some shooting are easily seen and get shot before they can do much about it. I have seen it happen. In the hedgerows it is almost impossible to get firing positions in the front row, and in the rear you can't see the enemy anyway, so no one bothers. Usually the tanks waited for the infantry to do something about it.

Instead of charging valiantly down the road the tanks may try to bull their way through the hedgerows. This is very slow and gives the enemy time to get his tanks or guns where they can do the most good. Then he just waits. And in the solution there is always a minor and local problem to be solved, a problem which caused a certain amount of irritation, and that is, who is going over the hedgerow first, the infantry or the tank? It is surprising how self-effacing most men can be in such situations.

. . . . German counter-attacks in the hedgerows failed largely for the same reasons our own advance was slowed. Any attack quickly loses its momentum, and then because of our artillery and fighter-bombers the Germans would suffer disastrous loss. In fact, we found that generally the best way to beat the Germans was to get them to counter-attack—provided we had prepared to meet them.

American infantry officer

Answer

Twenty minutes later what was left of the Company got up from the line of foxholes and advanced to the positions from which they had withdrawn to give the planes a margin for error. Then they broke through the hedge and started across the bomb-marked field towards where the Germans were theoretically all dead or demoralized.

The men walked slowly in a thin, thoughtful line across the cropped pasture grass, holding their rifles and tommy-guns at their hips. Is this the whole Company, Noah thought with dull surprise; is this all that's left? All the replacements who had been put in the week before, and who had never fired a shot, were they already gone?

In the next field Noah could see another thin line of men, walking with the same slow, weary thoughtfulness towards an embankment with a ditch at its bottom that made a sharp traversing line across the green landscape. Artillery was still going over their heads, but there was no small-arms fire to be heard. The planes had gone back to England, leaving the ground littered with shining silver bits of tinsel that they had dropped to confuse the enemy's radar equipment. The sun caught the strips of brightness in sparkling pin-points among the rich green of the grass, attracting Noah's eye again and again as he walked side by side, close to Johnny Burnecker.

It seemed to take the line a long time to get to the cover of the embankment, but finally they were there. Automatically, without a signal, the men threw themselves into the small ditch, against the safe grassy slope of the shielding embankment, although there still hadn't been a shot fired at them. They lay there, as though this had been a dear objective and they had fought for days to reach it.

'Off your arse!' It was Rickett's voice, the same tone, the same vocabulary, whether he was snarling at a man to clean a latrine in Florida or to charge a machine-gun post in Normandy. 'The war ain't over. Get up over that there ditch.'

Noah and Burnecker lay slyly, with heads averted, against the soft sloping grass, pretending that Rickett was not there, that Rickett was not alive.

Three or four of the replacements stood up, with a jangle of equipment, and started climbing heavily up. Rickett followed them and stood at the top shouting down at the rest of the men. 'Come on, off your arse, off your arse. . . .'

Regretfully, Noah and Burnecker stood up and clambered up the slippery six feet. The rest of the men around them were slowly doing the same thing.

. . . . Then, without warning, the machine-guns started. There were the high screams of thousands of bullets around him, the men falling before he heard the distant mechanical rattling sound of the guns themselves.

The line hesitated for a moment, the men staring bewilderedly at the enigmatic hedge from which the fire came.

'Come on! Come on!' Rickett's voice yelled crazily over the noise of the guns. 'Keep moving!'

But half the men were down by now. Noah grabbed Burnecker's arm, and they turned and raced, crouching low, the few yards back to the edge of the embankment. They flung themselves down, sobbing for breath, into the green safety of the ditch. One by one the other men came tumbling back over the edge to crash, sobbing and exhausted, into the ditch. Rickett appeared on the brink, swaying crazily, waving his arms around, shouting something thickly through an arching spurt of blood that seemed to come from his throat. He was hit again and slid face-down on top of Noah. Noah could feel the hot wetness of the Sergeant's blood on his face. He pulled back, although Rickett was clinging to him, his hands around Noah's shoulders gripping into the pack-harness on his back.

'Oh, you bathtards!' Rickett said distinctly, 'oh, you bathtards!' Then he relaxed and slithered into the ditch at Noah's feet.

'Dead,' Burnecker said. 'The son of a bitch is finally dead.'

. . . . When Green and the other man got closer, Burnecker said, 'Holy God, two stars.'

Noah sat up and stared. He had never been this close to a Major-General in all his months in the Army.

'General Emerson,' Burnecker whispered nervously. 'What the hell is he doing here? Why doesn't he go home?'

Suddenly, with sharp agility, the General leaped up the side of the embankment and stood at the top, in full view of the Germans. He walked slowly along the edge, talking down at the men in the ditch, who stared up at him numbly. He had a pistol in a holster, and he carried a short swagger-stick under one arm.

Impossible, Noah thought, it must be somebody dressed up like a General. Green is playing a trick on us.

The machine-guns were going again, but the General did not change the tempo of his movements. He walked smoothly and easily like a trained athlete, talking down into the ditch as he crossed in front of the men.

'All right, Boys,' Noah heard him say as he approached, and the voice was calm, friendly, not loud. 'Up we go now, Boys. We can't stay here all day. Up we go. We're holding up the whole line here and we've got to move now. Just up to the next row of hedges, Boys, that's all I'm asking of you. Come on, Son, you can't stay down there. . . .'

As he watched, Noah saw the General's left hand jerk, and blood begin to drop down from the wrist. There was just the slightest twist of the General's mouth, and then he continued talking in the same quiet but somehow piercing tone, grasping the swagger-stick more tightly. He stopped in front of Noah and Burnecker. 'All right, Boys,' he was saying kindly, 'just walk on up here. . . .'

Noah stared at him. The General's face was long and sad and handsome, the kind of face you might expect to see on a scientist or a doctor, thin, intellectual, quiet. Looking at his face confused Noah, made him feel as though the Army had fooled him all along. Looking at the sorrowful, courageous face, he suddenly felt that it was intolerable that he, Noah, could refuse a man like that anything.

He moved and, at the same moment, he felt Burnecker move beside him. A little, dry, appreciative smile momentarily wrinkled the General's mouth. 'That's it, Boys,' he said. He patted Noah's shoulder. Noah and Burnecker ran forward fifteen yards and dropped into a hole for cover.

. . . . Twenty minutes later they had reached the line of hedge from which the enemy machine-guns had been firing. Mortars had finally found the range and had destroyed one of the nests in a corner of the field, and the other sections had pulled out before Noah and the Company reached them.

Wearily, Noah kneeled by the side of the cleverly concealed, heavily sand-bagged position, now blown apart to reveal three Germans dead at their wrecked gun. One of the Germans was still kneeling behind it. Burnecker reached down with his boot and shoved at the kneeling dead man. The German rocked gently, then fell over on his side.

Noah turned away and drank a little water from his canteen. His throat was brassy with thirst. He hadn't fired his rifle all day, but his arms and shoulders ached as though he had caught the recoil a hundred times.

He looked out through the hedge. Three hundred yards away, across the usual field of bomb holes and dead cows, was another thick hedge, and machine-gun fire was coming from there. He sighed as he saw Lieutenant Green walking towards him, urging the men out once more. He wondered hazily what had happened to the General. Then he and Burnecker started out again.

Irwin Shaw

Night

Rain began to fall about seven o'clock in the evening. By nine o'clock it was a steady downpour and men slept in the dugouts along the sunken road. Presumably the posted guards were on duty and presumably they would awaken the men who were to relieve them, though their function seemed useless; the land was a sodden morass under the driving rain and the night was so dark that you moved by feel and sound rather than by seeing.

. . . . The commander of Company A, which was still one officer short, assigned Drew the First and Second Platoon on the left. He called in the platoon sergeants, Papracki of the First and O'Shea of the Second, to meet him. Both were big men, older than he, and they stared at him impassively, figuring he was fresh from O.C.S. and something new for the meat wagon. They stumbled together along the sunken lanes which composed the platoons' lines behind a

dozen hedge-enclosed fields. It was not a solid straight line, of course. There
were gaps, theoretically covered by fire points, and there were forward and rear
positions. They had been assigned their territory and they were covering it as
best they could. Papracki and O'Shea knew their business.

He tossed his gear into Papracki's dugout because there was room for him
and Papracki invited him. By the dim light of a lantern suspended from a beam
he saw a man, a boy actually, asleep. He lay on his back, spread-eagle, his mouth
open. You could not see his breathing; you would have thought him dead if his
hands had not fluttered occasionally.

They went out of the dugout into the rain and darkness again. O'Shea came
too, even though the First was not his platoon. There was no shelling or small-
arms or mortar fire; there was no sound except the rain and the mud sucking at
their feet. Occasionally Papracki would pause and silently indicate a darkened
dugout to Drew. He stepped down into most, he did not know exactly why,
except that Papracki seemed to wish him to. You could not see the sleeping men,
but you could hear them. Few snored, but there was much whimpering and
moaning, as in a hospital ward. Occasionally one would cry out or mumble a
few incoherent words or fart loudly in his sleep. When a man parted his lips
suddenly, seeking air, it sounded like a bubble popping. But the worst sound
was of men grinding their teeth as they slept. You could not see them, but you
could hear them and you could smell them, too. Wet clothing and sweat and the
rank smell of dirty wet feet and urine and, here and there along the sunken
road, the stench of human faeces. For they had fallen in here about five o'clock
and they'd got out their wounded and got in ammunition and cold rations. But
they weren't digging straddle trenches or doing all the folderol the book
prescribed, because they had had three days of hard fighting and they were
exhausted. They pitched down in the places the Germans had left and they
slept, for to-morrow they had to go ahead again.

Charles Mercer

The Leader Comes—and Goes

In circumstances of extreme secrecy Hitler arrived at his old command post,
at Margival, between Soissons and Laon. It was a particularly well-hidden
installation, and there he met the two Field-Marshals with their Chiefs of Staff.
Their first reports on the situation certainly impressed him and he promised to
lay down the necessary directives which they required for the next stage of the
campaign at once. But when the conversation turned on the consequences to be
drawn from the successful Allied landing, his mood changed. Rommel expressed
himself with particular force, demanding that political conclusions be drawn
from the military situation in the West. Hitler became angry, took Rommel's
arguments ill, and ordered him to concern himself with military, not political,
matters. The gist of Hitler's remarks seem to have been that in any case no one
would make peace with him.

During the course of this conference a message was received describing a
new and serious crisis which was developing in the area south of Cherbourg.
American armoured forces had broken out of their Carentan beachhead in a
north-westerly direction and in a large encircling movement were threatening

the fortress itself. Hitler announced his intention of visiting this sector personally next morning.

He did not do so. Later that day a V-1, fired at London, went astray, circled and exploded not far from Hitler's command post. All the security forces began feverishly to investigate the mishap. Hitler himself immediately flew back to Berchtesgaden with a powerful fighter escort.

German staff officer

CAEN

By late June the Germans were involved in the dilemma which had been prepared for them: should they hold the British and Canadians at Caen and prevent the direct threat to Paris, or should they hold the Americans farther west and prevent an overspill which might spread across France? They had not the resources to do both; they chose the first alternative.

On 26 June the British launched Operation 'Epsom', immediately west of Caen. It was designed as a slogging-match to draw the full strength of the enemy, and it succeeded, for within four days it was containing six Panzer divisions, almost the whole of the German armour in the West, flung against it in a furious counter-attack.

First Call

After nearly a fortnight the little field was showing signs of having been very much lived in. The grass was almost worn away and in the surrounding woods it was difficult to walk without bumping into notices which said 'FOUL GROUND'. Manuals on Sanitation in the Field were being dragged out into the light of day and worried Troop Leaders were beginning to recite in their sleep an alphabetical list of fly-borne diseases.

And then one afternoon the buzz of the flies was shattered by the high-pitched scream of a scout car being driven much too fast.

We stopped in our various tasks to watch a little four-wheeled, armour-plated vehicle roar into the middle of our field and skid to a halt in a cloud of dust. It bore the markings of Brigade Headquarters and we wondered who from that exalted level had come to visit us.

The dusty driver stood up, revealing red gorget patches on his battledress. It was the Brigadier himself, and he pushed back his goggles and beamed benevolently at us.

'You lucky people!' he bawled delightedly. 'I've bought you a battle! Where's yer commanding officer?'

John Foley

Infantry

In the misty dawn, with the rain battering upon them and the ground trembling beneath the artillery, the men of the 5th Battalion slithered up the muddy, sodden banks behind which they had been crouching and lurched forward, heads down against the rain, into the attack.

Tanks rumbled across the fields, the infantry moving behind them in scattered groups. As the daylight crept across the countryside the enemy artillery and mortars came into action. Exploding shells flung their pillars of smoke up towards the black, low-bellied rainclouds. Tanks were hit, heeling into the soft ground on their broken tracks, burning fiercely, so that the fog of smoke ahead of the infantrymen thickened into a dense wall out of which, as some burning tank exploded, would come sailing ribbons of white smoke and bright coloured lights that vanished in the driving rain. The riflemen, plodding across the broad ploughlands, seemed to ignore the din, the explosions that leaped about them, the rising crackle of small-arms fire. These things were only incidental—the real burdens that oppressed them were the rain that trickled on to their collars from the rims of their helmets, the slippery ground on which they tried to keep their balance, the muck that clung in great, clotted masses to their boots, making them as heavy to lift from the furrows as if they were soled with lead.

The leading platoons were moving towards the gentle, wooded slopes on which waited the first German outposts, little groups of men dug cunningly in among the trees and bushes, crouching unseen in narrow pits under the hedges behind the thin barrels of their machine-guns. The British infantrymen came trudging in among the trees, miserable and sodden; bewildered at first as the mines with which the ground was sown exploded beneath their comrades' feet and the bullets came whining among them; then spreading out rapidly and moving from tree-trunk to splintered tree-trunk, crouching, alert, angry; angry with the rain, with the mud, with boredom and fatigue, and closing in to vent their anger on the enemy. To many of the Germans who tried to surrender at the last possible moment they gave short shrift; others were fortunate enough to escape with a kick in the stomach or a blow in the teeth with a rifle butt before they were sent stumbling to the rear, while the rest of the 5th Battalion came streaming past.

It took an hour for them to clear the slopes and the rest of the morning before they had moved down the narrow lanes beyond the crest to take the village which nestled in the next hollow; an eternity of weary marching and of lying in the ditches, under the dripping hedgerows, in strange, sudden lulls when each man was assailed by an unutterable loneliness, a feeling of timeless unreality, a sense of muddy, sodden desolation, when the patter of rain sounded louder than the thudding guns; until the obstacle ahead had been battered into the ground by tanks or artillery and the infantrymen were able to heave themselves up out of the mire and trudge onward.

. . . . Throughout the day they trudged on, soaked and tired, sickened and stunned by the smoke and the din, until in the evening, with the German defences broken behind them, they halted. Numbed with fatigue, they pulled the spades from beneath their packs and began to dig. Later, while a relieving battalion passed forward through them to continue the attack, they sat in their shallow pits at the roadsides, huddled in their waterproof gas-capes, while on the little tommy-cookers that they sheltered between their feet they brewed boiling, life-preserving tea in their mess tins.

They had been on their feet for ten hours, marching and fighting. On the map, their advance measured precisely three miles.

Alexander Baron

Tanks

But eventually the infantry released us and the artillery began to put down smoke to cover the withdrawal of the tanks. This should have been the easiest part of the whole show. Just a case of traversing our guns over our tails and going flat out back to Hill 112. And then I noticed *Angler* wasn't with us.

Frantic calls on the B set elicited no response, and Sergeant Atkins said he thought he saw them going off to the left, but it might have been a Churchill from another troop.

There was nothing else for it; we had to swing around and cast about looking for my missing Troop Corporal. Luckily we didn't have to search for long; looming out of the smoke came *Angler* with Smith 161 breathing fire and slaughter from the driving seat. The engine had stalled and, in *Angler*'s own inexplicable way, had refused to start again for five minutes.

I heaved a sigh of relief and looked around for the way back to Hill 112. And then I realized we were lost.

Gone were the comforting cobblestones of the little road, gone were the tumbling outlines of Bon Repos; we were plunging slowly through a pall of ever-increasing smoke in a completely unknown direction.

I switched the selector knob to A.

'Hullo, Peter Five,' I called. 'I've temporarily lost my bearings. Can you send up a white Verey light to guide me back?'

Promptly a white signal flare burst in the sky behind my right shoulder, and I whistled appreciatively at Alan's promptness.

'Hullo, Peter Five,' came Alan's voice out of my earphones. 'That light you just saw was sent up by the enemy—well, you asked for it, didn't you, making a request like that over the air?'

I hoped the crew couldn't see me blushing and, for want of something better to do, I halted the troop and we sat there in the smoke while I tried to reconcile my map with the contours of the ground and the few stars I could see.

To help matters along a few stray shells started bursting amongst us, but I was hugely comforted to hear other Troop Leaders complaining on the air that they, too, were lost in the smoke.

And then a broad finger of light stabbed up into the clouds from somewhere on the horizon.

'Hullo, all stations Peter,' said Alan's voice. 'Head for that searchlight and you'll soon be home.'

Almost instantly another searchlight soared up into the night sky—a German one. I gave the enemy full marks for prompt action, but headed determinedly towards the first light. Other people did the same, and somewhere on the return journey the ether was enlivened by a rollicking chorus of *Lead Kindly Light*. Nobody would admit to this afterwards, so we put it down to German interference; but it sounded awfully like a dark brown baritone to me.

. . . . Then I saw B Squadron on the other side of the hill, and, the shelling having now stopped for a few minutes, I walked across, turning over in my mind some witty phrases with which to point out Tommy Tucker's slowness.

They told me Tommy Tucker was dead, his tank having been hit by a 88

mm. anti-tank gun. Immediately afterwards his Troop Sergeant and Corporal
had, between them, destroyed the gun; but it gave me much food for thought.

On the way back to Five Troop I heard another issue of shells coming over
and, casting dignity to the winds, I leaped into a shell hole. It was a fairly large
shell hole because there were four people in there already. In the reflected light
of the searchlight I saw that they were a sergeant and private in the Wiltshires,
and two Germans. My immediate reaction was that the two Germans were
prisoners, and then I saw that they were still wearing their steel helmets and one
of them clutched a rifle and bayonet.

It took me about ten seconds to realize I was sharing a shell-hole with four
dead men, and then I decided to take a chance on the shelling and make a bee-
line for *Avenger*.

. . . . For ten days we lived in our tanks, cooking, eating, drinking and sleeping. We did almost everything without getting out. And I mean almost everything.

Under the blazing sun the mud quickly turned to dust; and under the impact
of this dust we drank a fair amount of liquid. Since our natural functions didn't
cease just because we were living inside a round, armour-plated wall with shells
bursting around us from time to time, we found an unorthodox use for empty
shell cases. They were just the right shape for emptying out of the turret hatch.
When more solid relief was necessary there was nothing else for it but to wait
for one of the occasional shell-free spells and get out and seek an unoccupied
shell hole.

But whenever possible this operation was carried out under cover of darkness. Especially after the case of Jim Steward.

The afternoon was unusually quiet and I was leaning out of the top of the
turret getting a much-needed breath of fresh air. Some of the crews had dismounted and were stretching their legs while the slave carrier charged their tank
batteries.

I saw Jim climb out of his tank, calmly take a spade from the clips on the
engine-hatch, and set off across the hill.

I knew he wasn't going gardening. In those days people sought solitude with
a spade for one purpose only.

I breathed a sigh of relief that I wasn't feeling that way myself right then,
because the air was deceptively quiet. And since certain functions should be
carried out in private I turned my attention to other things.

The wireless crackled and spluttered at my elbow and I wondered if we were
flogging our batteries too much. And then I heard Alan's voice on the air and
for once he'd lost his air of unhurried calm.

He was sending an urgent and peremptory message for a scout car to take
away a casualty, and when I popped my head out of the turret I saw a group of
men helping Jim back to the security of his tank.

The short point was that while Jim had been communing with nature he had
been shot by a German sniper. He had his back to the enemy lines at that moment
and the bullet had penetrated the fleshy part of his buttock, missing all the vital
spots and making a not-too-serious wound.

The only lesson to emerge from that incident was that, despite propagandists' edicts to the contrary, the Germans have a sense of humour. That sniper could equally well have drilled Jim through the back of the head, but he chose the larger and (he no doubt thought) funnier target.

John Foley

Counter-attack

It was scheduled to begin at seven o'clock in the morning, but hardly had the tanks assembled when they were attacked by fighter-bombers. This disrupted the troops so much that the attack did not start again until two-thirty in the afternoon. But even then it could not get going. The murderous fire from naval guns in the Channel and the terrible British artillery destroyed the bulk of our attacking force in its assembly area. The few tanks that did manage to go forward were easily stopped by the English anti-tank guns. In my opinion the attack was prepared too quickly. I wanted to wait another two days, but Hitler insisted that it be launched on 29 June.

General Paul Hausser, G.O.C. II S.S. Panzer Corps

After 'Epsom'

. . . . The whole battlefield was little more than ten square miles, and every inch of it was torn and scarred and slashed. There were few corners where it was possible to escape the smell of death and decay, aggravated by the hot sun. Panthers and Mark IV Specials lay drunkenly half across ditches where the anti-tank guns had caught them, their plates already rusting from the sharp summer showers, and the cloud of flies buzzing round the open turrets a grim reminder that no one had had the time or the inclination to do anything about the remains of the crews inside. Epsom Downs in fact was a horrible place, but in the first week of July to the men who had come back from the Haut du Bosq it seemed fair enough.

British tank officer

The Price of Failure

. . . . Rommel drafted yet another very grave report for Hitler on the situation. Rundstedt gave his approval to this. So, too, did General Freiherr Geyr von Schweppenburg, who expressed his own views concerning the senseless attrition of his Panzer divisions in the Caen beachhead and who demanded a reappraisal of German operational tactics. The two Field-Marshals requested another interview with Hitler, which took place at Berchtesgaden towards the end of the month.

The Field-Marshals were treated with a marked lack of courtesy and were kept waiting for several hours. When at last Hitler received them, he treated them to a lengthy monologue concerning the effects to be expected from the new 'miracle weapons'. The Field-Marshals left in a very bad temper indeed. Back at his headquarters, Rundstedt telephoned Keitel and told him that they had better find a younger man to continue the battle: he himself was too old. When Keitel asked him what he thought they should do, Rundstedt replied loudly and clearly: 'End the war, you fools!'

As Rundstedt had foreseen and desired, he was relieved of his command.

German officer

I knew all along that the German position in France was hopeless and that eventually the war would be lost. But if I had been given a free hand to conduct operations, I think I could have made the Allies pay a fearful price for their victory. I had planned to fight a slow retiring action exacting a heavy toll for each bit of ground that I gave up. I had hoped that this might have brought about a political decision which would have saved Germany from complete and utter defeat. But I did not have my way. As Commander-in-Chief in the West my only authority was to change the guard in front of my gate.

Field-Marshal von Rundstedt

Rundstedt's successor, Field-Marshal von Kluge, who took over on 6 July 1944, was no happier.

I arrived here with the firm intention of carrying out your orders to hold fast at all costs. But when one realizes that the price which must be paid consists of the slow but steady annihilation of our troops . . . then one cannot help entertaining the gravest doubts as to what the immediate future holds in store for this front. I can report that up to now, despite daily losses of ground, the front has been held, thanks to the magnificent bravery of our troops and to the firmness of will of our officers, particularly the junior ones. Nevertheless, despite all our fervent efforts, the moment is approaching when this sorely tried front will be broken. Once the enemy has penetrated into open country, organized operations will no longer be possible to control owing to our troops' lack of mobility. As the responsible commander on this front, I regard it as my duty to draw your attention, my Führer, to the consequences which will ensue.

At the commanders' conference south of Caen my closing words were: 'We shall hold fast, and if no help arrives in time to improve our position fundamentally, then we shall die an honourable death on the field of battle.'

Field-Marshal von Kluge

The German Soldier Still Hopes

. . . . The incredibly heavy artillery and mortar fire of the enemy is something new, both for the seasoned veterans of the Eastern Front and the new arrivals from reinforcement units. Whereas the veterans get used to it comparatively quickly, the inexperienced reinforcements require several days to do so, after which they become acclimatized. The average rate of fire on the divisional sector is four thousand artillery rounds and five thousand mortar rounds per day. This is multiplied many times before an enemy attack, however small. For instance, on one occasion when the British made an attack on a sector of only two companies they expended three thousand five hundred rounds in two hours. The Allies are waging war regardless of expense. In addition to this, the enemy have complete mastery of the air. They bomb and strafe every movement, even single vehicles and individuals. They reconnoitre our area constantly and direct their artillery fire. Against all this the Luftwaffe is conspicuous by its complete absence. During the last four weeks the *total* number of German aircraft over the divisional area was six.

. . . . Our soldiers enter the battle in low spirits at the thought of the enemy's enormous material superiority. They are always asking: 'Where is the Luftwaffe?' The feeling of helplessness against enemy aircraft operating without any hindrance has a paralyzing effect, and during the barrage this effect on the inexperienced troops is literally 'soul-shattering', and it must be borne in mind that four-engined bombers have not yet taken part in attacking ground troops in this division's area. It is, therefore, essential for troops to be lifted out of this state of distress the moment the counter-attack begins. The best results have been obtained by the platoon and section commanders' leaping forward uttering a good old-fashioned 'hurrah', which spurs on the inexperienced troops and carries them along. The revival of the practice of sounding a bugle call for the attack has been found to answer the purpose, and this has been made a divisional order. An attack launched in this manner is an experience which new troops will never forget, and stimulates them into action again.

General von Lüttwitz, G.O.C. XLVII Panzer Corps

The Bombing of Caen: 7 July

To those of us who watched from the ground in safety there was a sinister yet inspiring majesty about the scene. The earth was already in the shadow of night, and the sky itself was that electric blue which follows a day of cloudless heat. But the long line of bombers stretching back towards England as far as we could see was still in sunlight, and their metal twinkled like fairy lights against the darkening sky. The pathfinders dropped their markers over the target and wheeled away to the right. The flares they used were a kind of golden rain, which dropped slowly in widening cascades like a shower of jewels reluctant to obey the force of gravity. Soon the sky was dotted with puffs of flak, like a giant net through the meshes of which the bombers flew on apparently undisturbed. In fact, they must have been racked by the explosions and torn by a million fragments, but from below they seemed to take no notice. Next there was a mushroom of black smoke from the target area, shot with red and yellow flames, which climbed into the sky as slowly as the flares had seemed to descend. Over it the bombers still streamed in, and I remembered only one which banked away, stricken, to seek a landing-place. Even tail-end Charlie, appearing stubbornly a quarter of an hour after his last comrade had turned for home, passed safely through the renewed storm of flak.

British tank officer

Into the City

They came over the brow of the hill. Ahead of them stretched the city of Caen. The British had been trying to take it for a month, and after looking at it for a moment, you wondered why they had been so anxious. Walls were standing,

but few houses. Block after block of closely packed stone buildings had been
battered and knocked down, and it was the same as far as the eye could reach.
Tripe à la mode de Caen, Michael remembered from the menus of French
restaurants in New York, and the University of Caen, from a course of Medieval
History. British heavy mortars were firing from the jumbled books of the
University library at the moment, and Canadian soldiers were crouched over
machine-guns in the kitchens where the tripe had at other times been so deftly
prepared.

They were in the outskirts of the town by now, winding in and out of stone
rubble. Pavone signalled Michael to stop, and Michael drew the jeep up along
a heavy stone convent wall that ran beside the roadside ditch. There were some
Canadians in the ditch and they looked at the Americans curiously.

We ought to wear British helmets, Michael thought nervously. These damn
things must look just like German helmets to the British. They'll shoot first and
examine our papers later.

'How're things?' Pavone was out of the jeep standing over the ditch, talking
to the soldiers there.

'Bloody awful,' said one of the Canadians, a small, dark, Italian-looking man.
He stood up in the ditch and grinned. 'You going into the town, Colonel?'

'Maybe.'

'There are snipers all over the place,' said the Canadian. There was the
whistle of an incoming shell and the Canadians dived into the ditch again.
. . . . 'Every three minutes,' the Canadian said bitterly, standing up in the
ditch. 'We're back here on rest and every three bleeding minutes we got to hit
the ground. That's the British Army's notion of a rest area!' He spat.

'Are there mines?' Pavone asked.

'Sure there're mines,' the Canadians said aggressively. 'Why shouldn't there
be mines? Where do you think you are, Yankee Stadium?'

He had an accent that would have sounded natural in Brooklyn. 'Where you
from, soldier?' Pavone asked.

'Toronto,' said the soldier. 'The next man that tries to get me out of Toronto
is going to get a Ford axle across his ears.'

Irwin Shaw

The Abbaye aux Hommes

The inside of the church was very dark after the brilliant sunlight outside.
Michael smelled it first. Mixed with the slight, rich odour of old candles and
incense burned in centuries of devotion, there was a smell of barnyard and the
sick smell of age and medicine and dying.

He blinked, standing at the door, and listened to the scuffle of children's
feet on the great stone floor, now strewn with straw. High overhead there was a
large, gaping shell-hole. The sunlight streamed down through it, like a powerful
amber searchlight, piercing the religious gloom.

Then, as his eyes grew accustomed to the darkness, he saw that the church
was crowded. The inhabitants of the city, or those who had not yet fled and not
yet died, had assembled here, numbly looking for protection under God, waiting
to be taken away behind the lines. The first impression was that he was in a

gigantic religious home for the aged. Stretched out on the floor on litters and on blankets and on straw heaps were what seemed like dozens of wrinkled, almost evaporated, yellow-faced, fragile octogenarians. They rubbed their translucent hands numbly over their throats; they pushed feebly at blanket ends; they mumbled with animal squeaky sounds; they stared, hot-eyed and dying, at the men who stood over them; they wet the floor because they were too old to move and too far gone to care; they scratched at grimy bandages that covered wounds they had received in the young men's war that had raged in their city for a month; they were dying of cancer, tuberculosis, hardening of the arteries, nephritis, gangrene, malnourishment, senility; and the common smell of their disease and their helplessness and their age, collected together like this in the once-shelled church, made Michael gasp a little as he regarded them, lit here and there in a mellow and holy beam of sunlight, dancing with dust motes and shimmering over the wasted, fiercely hating faces. Among them, between the straw paliasses and the stained litters, between the cancer cases and the old men with broken hips who had been bedridden for five years before the British came, between the old women whose great-grandchildren had already been killed at Sedan and Lake Chad and Oran, among them ran the children, playing, weaving in and out, swiftly and gaily shining for a moment in the golden beam from the German shell-hole, then darting like glittering water-flies into the rich pools of purple shadow, the high tinkle of their laughter skimming over the heads of the grave-bound ancients on the stone floor. . . . 'I think,' he began, 'we had better get out of here. The British got this, let them worry about it. . . .'

Two children came up to Pavone, and stood in front of him. One was a tiny, frail four-year-old girl, with large, shy eyes. She held on to the hand of her brother, two or three years older than she, but even more shy.

'Please,' the little girl said, in French, 'may we have some sardines?'

'No, no!' The little boy pulled his hand away from hers angrily and slapped her harshly on the wrist. 'Not sardines. Not from these. Biscuits from these. It was the others who gave sardines.'

Pavone grinned at Michael, then bent down and gently hugged the little girl, to whom the difference between Fascism and Democracy was merely that from one children might expect sardines and from the other hard-tack. The little one fought back tears. 'Of course,' he said in French. 'Of course.' He turned to Michael. 'Mike,' he said, 'go get a K ration.'

. . . . 'I have just come back from the front,' [the Frenchman] announced. 'Someone told me, on the bridge across the river, in the middle, between the British and the Germans, there is an old woman lying. Go and see if it is your wife. I went and looked.' He paused and stared up at the damaged church steeple. 'It was my wife.'

He stood in silence, stroking the jeep. Neither Pavone nor Michael said anything. 'Forty years,' the Frenchman said. 'We were married forty years. We had our ups and downs. We lived on the other side of the river. I suppose she forgot a parrot or a hen and decided she must go look for it and the Germans machine-gunned her. Machine-gun for a sixty-year-old woman. They are inconceivable, the Germans. She is lying there, with her dress up over her legs and her head down. The Canadians wouldn't let me go out to get her. I will have to wait until the battle is over, they told me. She has on her good dress.' He began to cry. The tears ran into his moustache, and he swallowed them wetly. 'Forty years. I saw her half an hour ago.' He took out his wallet again, crying. 'Even so,' he said fiercely, 'even so. . . .' He opened the wallet and kissed the tricolour bunting under its celluloid cover, kissed it passionately, insanely. 'Even so.'

He shook his head and put the wallet away. He patted the jeep once more. He moved off down the street, vaguely, past the torn iron of the shopfronts and the carelessly piled stones, moved off without saluting or saying goodbye.

Irwin Shaw

Rommel is Wounded

As he did every day, Marshal Rommel on 17 July made a tour of the front. After visiting 277 and 276 Infantry Divisions, on whose sectors a heavy enemy attack had been repulsed the night before, he went to the headquarters of the II S.S. Armoured Corps and had a conversation with Generals Bittrich and Sepp Dietrich. We had to be careful of enemy aircraft, which were flying over the battlefield continually and were quickly attracted by dust on the roads.

About 4 p.m. Marshal Rommel started on the return journey from General Dietrich's headquarters. He was anxious to get back to Army Group B headquarters as quickly as possible because the enemy had broken through on another part of the front.

All along the roads we could see transport in flames: from time to time the enemy bombers forced us to take to second-class roads. About 6 p.m. the Marshal's car was in the neighbourhood of Livarot. Transport which had just been attacked was piled up along the road and strong groups of enemy dive-bombers were still at work close by. That is why we turned off along a sheltered road, to join the main road again two and a half miles from Vimoutiers.

When we reached it we saw above Livarot about eight enemy dive-bombers. We learnt later that they had been interfering with traffic on the road to Livarot for the past two hours. Since we thought that they had not seen us, we continued along the main road from Livarot to Vimoutiers. Suddenly Sergeant Holke, our spotter, warned us that two aircraft were flying along the road in our direction. The driver, Daniel, was told to put on speed and turn off on to a little side road to the right, about three hundred yards ahead of us, which would give us some shelter.

Before we could reach it the enemy aircraft, flying at great speed only a few feet above the road, came up to within five hundred yards of us and the first one opened fire. Marshal Rommel was looking back at this moment. The left-hand side of the car was hit by the first burst. A cannon-shell shattered Daniel's left shoulder and left arm. Marshal Rommel was wounded in the face by broken glass and received a blow on the left temple and cheek-bone which caused a triple fracture of the skull and made him lose consciousness immediately. Major Neuhaus was struck on the holster of his revolver and the force of the blow broke his pelvis.

As the result of his serious wounds, Daniel, the driver, lost control of the car. It struck the stump of a tree, skidded over to the left of the road and then turned over in a ditch on the right. Captain Lang and Sergeant Holke jumped out of the car and took shelter on the right of the road. Marshal Rommel, who, at the start of the attack, had hold of the handle of the door, was thrown out, unconscious, when the car turned over and lay stretched out in the road about twenty yards behind it. A second aircraft flew over and tried to drop bombs on those who were lying on the ground.

Immediately afterwards, Marshal Rommel was carried into shelter by Captain Lang and Sergeant Holke. He lay on the ground unconscious and covered with blood, which flowed from the many wounds on his face, particularly from his left eye and mouth. It appeared that he had been struck on the left temple. Even when we had carried him to safety he did not recover consciousness.

In order to get medical help for the wounded, Captain Lang tried to find a car. It took him about three-quarters of an hour to do so. Marshal Rommel had his wounds dressed by a French doctor in a religious hospital. They were very severe and the doctor said that there was little hope of saving his life. Later he was taken, still unconscious, with Daniel to an Air Force hospital at Bernay, about twenty-five miles away. The doctors there diagnosed severe injuries to the skull—a fracture at the base, two fractures on the temple and the cheek-bone destroyed, a wound in the left eye, wounds from glass, and concussion. Daniel died during the night, in spite of a blood transfusion.

A few days later Marshal Rommel was taken to the hospital of Professor Esch at Vesinet, near St. Germain.

Captain Lang, Wehrmacht

BREAK-THROUGH

Once the British around Caen had successfully drawn off the greater part of the German strength, the stage was set for the Americans to mount their great offensive from St. Lô and throw their wide 'left hook' towards Paris, cutting off the Germans in Normandy. Other spearheads struck into Brittany.

Assault from St. Lô

We sure liberated the hell out of this place.

American soldier

When 2 Panzer Division was finally relieved in the Caumont sector on 20 July, after having been steadily in the line since 12 June, it did not mean that we were to be given a rest. The British having been stopped in the Caen area on 19 July, it was expected that they would soon start again. To meet this attack my division was moved to Bretteville on 24 July, while 116 Panzer Division, newly arrived from the Pas de Calais, was sent to Rouvres. There we waited in reserve, some five miles behind our front line south of Caen, for another attack to begin. The two divisions, 2 Panzer and 116 Panzer, possessed between them about two hundred tanks and were comparatively strong. But instead of the offensive coming from the British, it suddenly broke loose on 25 July on the American sector near St. Lô where I had just come from. We had been fooled as to your intentions. By placing this large armoured reserve south of Caen we completely wasted it and weakened our front west of the Orne River. Highly chagrined, the High Command quickly moved us back to the St.-Lô area on 26 July, but by that time it was too late to prevent the break-through of the Americans.

General von Lüttwitz

By about 23 July, U.S. troops had gained suitable jump-off positions for their offensive and had taken St. Lô. Panzer Lehr Division held a six thousand-yard sector west of the town and, by allocating only weak reserves, had formed a defence zone of four thousand yards in depth. The fifty or sixty tanks and self-propelled anti-tank guns still remaining to the division were deployed in static positions as armoured anti-tank guns and the Panzer Grenadiers were well dug-in on their field positions.

On 24 July, four hundred American bombers attacked our sector, but without doing much damage. My A.A. battalion even managed to shoot down ten of their aircraft. The expected ground attack did not come.

But on the next day, there followed one of the heaviest blows delivered by the Allied air forces in a tactical role during the whole of the war. I learnt later from American sources that on 25 July a force consisting of sixteen hundred Flying Fortresses and other bombers had bombed the Panzer Lehr's sector from nine in the morning until around midday. Units holding the front were almost completely wiped out, despite, in many cases, the best possible equipment of tanks, anti-tank guns and self-propelled guns. Back and forth the bomb carpets were laid, artillery positions were wiped out, tanks overturned and buried, infantry positions flattened and all roads and tracks destroyed. By midday the entire area resembled a moon landscape, with the bomb craters touching rim to rim, and there was no longer any hope of getting out any of our weapons. All signal communications had been cut and no command was possible. The shock effect on the troops was indescribable. Several of the men went mad and rushed dementedly round in the open until they were cut down by splinters. Simultaneous with the storm from the air, innumerable guns of the U.S. artillery poured drum-fire into our field positions.

During this time I myself was located at a regimental sector command post near La Chapelle-en-Juger, in the centre of the bombardment. Housed in an old Norman château, with ten-foot walls, we were rather better protected than the others. Again and again the bomb carpets rolled towards us, most of them passing only a few yards away. The ground shuddered. Quick glimpses outside showed the whole area shrouded by a pall of dust, with fountains of earth spewing high in the air. For many hours we were unable to leave the cellar, and it was afternoon before I was able to get out of the château and ride back on my motor-cycle to Division H.Q. (I had long since learned to prefer a motor-cycle to a car, having had six cars shot up during the invasion battle and several drivers killed.) We were repeatedly troubled by fighter-bombers on the way back.

When I arrived at Division H.Q. the first reports were just coming in of enemy infiltrations into the bombed area. Resistance was offered by the few surviving detachments of my division, but most of these groups were wiped out by the tactical air support rolling forward in front of the attack. Some weak reserves from other sectors tried to halt the avalanche by counter-attacks, but their attempts were smashed by the enemy artillery and air force in the forming-up stage and came to nothing. By the following morning, the American break-through was complete.

The Americans continued their advance south all the morning, using in-fantry with bomber and fighter-bomber support, and then in the afternoon brought their tank packs up into the lead. In the course of this move they over-hauled the last pitiful remnants of my division, which had fallen back, together with the divisional staff, to the south. I lay with my headquarters in a Norman farmhouse, set in typical Normandy country, criss-crossed with hedges, low hills and sunken roads, when suddenly scouts reported U.S. tanks advancing in our immediate neighbourhood. Soon the tanks were rolling past us. On sighting our vehicles, which we had parked a little way off in the bushes, the American tankmen opened fire and shot every one of them into flames. The front room of our house was immediately hit by an H.E. shell. I lay with five men in the next room. It was impossible to leave the house, for American machine-gun fire was swishing past the house door. The window at the back was barred and so we were caught like rats in a trap. Gradually the tanks moved on and the firing ceased. We were now behind the American lines. Evening brought a chance to slip away to our own troops. For hours I trekked back through sunken roads, until at about midnight I came across a stray vehicle of my division, which car-ried me on to the rearward elements of my otherwise annihilated formation.

But the Americans were now pouring through into the open country with nobody to stop them—just as Rommel had predicted. After turning west to Coutances they sealed off and annihilated our forces fighting in the Cotentin peninsula, leaving a vast hole torn in the German front, through which Patton's army poured into the heart of France.

General Bayerlein, G.O.C. Panzer Lehr Division

While the Americans broke out into open country with half France before them, the British moved on to capture the lynch-pin of Normandy—its highest hill, Mont Pinçon. This was a bloody affair.

Mont Pinçon

At the end of the first week of August 1944, the Allied armies in Normandy were at last on the move after two months of bloody fighting.

On the right the American armour had broken through and was rumbling southwards across the base of the Breton peninsula towards the Loire. In the centre British troops, massed secretly and striking suddenly, were battering down from Caumont into the switchback of the *bocage*, the thickly-wooded hill country. Towards the left of the line, the British divisions which had been fighting for weeks over the same strip of ground, from Tilly down to the Odon, and from the Odon down to the Orne, pushed forward at last, an army of tired, muddy, battle-drunk men leaving behind them Hottot and Hill 112 and a score of other shell-pitted hills and smashed villages. Every night as these men moved forward there was yet another hill or yet another village to take, yet another stream to cross under fire; every night they summoned fresh reserves of strength and will from their exhausted bodies and went forward against the mortars and the Spandaus and the eighty-eights. This time nothing was going to stop them.

Then they came to the last obstacle between their tanks and the flat lands of the French interior, the gateway to the Big Push, the last and highest ridge that forms the southern border of Normandy. For months they had pointed to this ridge on their maps, talked about it, read with foreboding the Intelligence reports of the fortifications that the enemy had installed here. Now it lay before them, twelve hundred feet above sea level; and the battalions of British infantry moved forward once more to the attack.

. . . . On the map the ridge was easy to distinguish; a little bar of chocolate-brown set in a nimbus of lighter shades. Many times in the preceding weeks it had attracted the attention of the commanders of the brigades and battalions moving south towards it.

Now that they faced it it looked less distinctive, less dangerous, a ridge of woodland and meadow looking less than its actual twelve hundred feet, a false horizon beyond the lines of gentler hills.

It lay athwart several roads vital to the British advance. With the hilltop in their hands the Germans were in a position to paralyze any movement by the British for several miles in almost any direction. Possession of this feature was the key to the communications of a wide area on this sector of the front.

The hill rose rather more steeply from the west than from the east, where the approach was across fairly open ground. On the western side the ground was close, covered with orchards and woods, and with streams cutting irregular gullies across the main approach roads.

The Germans, with every advantage of ground, could drench with fire any force that tried to establish a footing on the lower slopes. The wooded banks on either side of the road from the west offered ideal machine-gun positions from which a withering cross-fire could be poured across the bridge bottle-necks. With whatever superiority in numbers an assault might be made, this country called for the greatest staunchness and courage by the infantry, since the difficult slopes would extend to the full their staying power.

So it turned out.

The assault was launched at brigade strength, with the 5th Battalion of the Wessex Regiment in reserve during the first phase.

The first infantry attack went in from the south-west, with a group of tanks in support. Close orchards and woods, and irregular ground, made the going terribly heavy. The narrow tracks imprisoned the tanks. The area had been widely mined and there was a river in their path, meandering across the lower slopes, over which the bridge had already been blown up. Pioneers, working under enemy fire, rooted up mines like potatoes and strove to build a tank crossing across the river bed, with the rubble of the demolished bridge. In a half-hour they had nearly all been killed and the tanks, grinding desperately forward, were hit one by one and burned fiercely. Meanwhile the Germans shelled and mortared the British infantry. Hidden observation posts reported every movement to the enemy artillery. Each time the infantry surged up out of the folds in the ground in which they crouched they were met by intense shelling. Only here and there were men able to get forward, moving in twos and threes, sprinting forward in short bounds separated by long periods during which they were pinned tight to the ground. In vain the tanks tried to get across the river. Only the first few outposts of the enemy had yet been encountered, but already the assaulting battalion had suffered heavy casualties.

.... The men lying along the sunken lanes felt the morning breezes die away, and as the sun rose in the sky the daylight grew radiant and the summer's heat became intense. The chill and the fatigue fell away from them and they felt a momentary surge of confidence as their own artillery opened fire on the ridge with high explosive and smoke-shells that wrapped the enemy positions in a blinding white screen.

Then they moved forward.

They advanced across the meadows, unchallenged for the first few yards and filled suddenly, as they always were at such moments, with the wild, unreasoning hope that this time it was going to be easy; until the first shell quavered down on them and they were out there, soft, human flesh clad only in khaki serge, with the angry splinters of steel whining among them, searching the ground, seeking them out, cutting them down, widening the gaps in their scattered ranks, and each man found himself suddenly alone amid the noise and the smoke, lurching blindly forward to gamble with blind death; doubly bewildered because the enemy machine-guns were firing not only from the front but from the flanks.

A hundred yards in front of them was the stream and across the stream a narrow, stone-walled bridge, too small for tanks but treacherously inviting for infantry. There was no room in their minds for the enemy waiting on the upper slopes; now there was only one objective—to cross the bridge, to put the stream behind them. Men goad themselves on with strange illusions, with mad freaks of fancy, and their illusion was that somehow this field they were now crossing was the source of all their peril, that the bridge was a bridge to safety, that life lay on the far bank of the stream. They stumbled forward against the machine-guns and toppled forward, faces upturned in agony, hands clawing at the sunlight; more men came sprinting on, without even a downward glance at the littered dead, and fell writhing among them.

A half-dozen men reached the bridge; none of them got across. There were no more men moving across the open ground now. Only the dead and wounded sprawled in the open; the rest of the battalion was scattered, in little groups, cowering in ditches, in gullies, against the banks of sunken sun-baked lanes, in shallow folds in the ground, under the probing machine-gun fire.

.... Radio-telephone message, 5th Battalion to Brigade Headquarters, 13.40 hours:

Attack held up on start point. Leading troops under very heavy machine-gun, mortar and artillery fire. Battalion commander killed. Not possible for leading troops to advance.

Brigade Headquarters to 5th Battalion, 13.46 hours:

Advance to crossroads two hundred yards beyond river.

5th Battalion to Brigade Headquarters, 14.10 hours:

Forward troops under heavy fire and still on this side (behind) river. Fired on from woods to south-west.

Brigade Headquarters to 5th Battalion, 14.15 hours:
Advance to crossroads two hundred yards beyond river.
5th Battalion to Brigade, 15.05 hours:
Not possible for leading troops to move.
Brigade to Battalion, 15.10 hours:
Advance to crossroads.

. . . . Battle has its own strange chemistry. The courage and endurance of a group of men is greater than the sum total of the courage and endurance of the individuals in the group; for, when most of the group have reached the limits of human endeavour, there is always one among them who can surpass those limits, who will hold the others together and drive them on. It is not the romantic picture of war; but it is the truth of war.

And broken men, thus driven forward, can become—at the last pitch of exhaustion—whole and strong again; for movement generates its own strange inspiration.

The 5th Battalion swept across the stream. As the men stumbled up the slopes beyond they came within sight at last of the dark, German helmets moving in the folds in the ground, the thin black barrels of the machine-guns quivering against the grass. All the pent-up fury and bitterness they had felt towards their own commander was transferred to the enemy. In twos and threes they rushed forward, up and down, moving and firing, a dozen yards at a time, up the bare hillside. Now they were closing in; their anger swept them up and they went forward, all together, at a run.

Radio-telephone message, 5th Battalion to Brigade Headquarters, 16.45 hours:
Have crossed river and reached crossroads two hundred yards beyond. Consolidating.

. . . . All the evening the remnants of the battalion clung to the hillside, while a pitiless fire, like waves sweeping away the clusters of men clinging to the mainmast of a sinking ship, obliterated one group after another.

All through the evening little parties of men went stumbling up the hill, to be beaten down into the ground again.

And each time there came a few moments of quiet and the men rested their heads in their arms in blessed relief, Major Norman, half-mad with despair, his eyes burning, lurched in among them, goading them to open fire again and draw down upon themselves the nightmare fire from the crest.

. . . . At eight o'clock in the evening the Brigadier's attack went in from the south-west. Protected by dusk, mist and an artillery smoke-screen, the assaulting troops were able to work their way steadily up the hill.

They were already desperately tired, having been fighting for days before, and having marched several miles in full kit to take up their positions for this attack. They met heavy opposition at first, in spite of the fact that the Germans were unprepared and were already weakened by the tenacious attacks of the 5th Battalion.

It was dark already when a troop of British tanks gained the crest; and within an hour the infantry, heartened by the sight of the tanks, had overrun the summit.

The moon had risen when an officer of the victorious battalion went forward over the hill top in search of the 5th Wessex.

His own men were trying to dig in, and as he passed through them he saw that they were so exhausted that they were falling asleep over their spades.

He moved cautiously down the opposite slope. He could see no sign of life. He halted and raised his hand to his mouth.

'Hallo, Wessex!' he called. His voice echoed in the green moonlight, among the broken trees.

'Hallo-o-o!'

He picked his way forward another few yards, fearful of the mines with which the ground was still thickly sown.

'Ahoy there, Wessex!' he shouted.

'Wessex—ahoy!' There was no reply.

Two hundred yards in front of him a man rose from a fold in the ground, slowly and silently, like a corpse from the grave. Another man rose, and another. As more and more men rose to face him the officer felt as if a legion of ghosts was springing from the earth.

None of them spoke.

They began to move towards him. Silently, like sleep-walkers, they began to make their way up the desolate, moonlit slopes, towards the summit.

Alexander Baron

Patton's Gallop

In early August the British forces, with 1 Canadian Army, now operational under General Crerar, and the Polish Armoured Division were still closely pressing the German 7 Army, while the Americans had reached the sea at Avranches, passed on and already captured Mayenne and Laval, fifty miles to the south-east. Hitler ordered a counter-attack on the American communications at Mortain to hold this calamitous threat to his forces further towards the north-east, now threatened with encirclement.

The General knows exactly what he is doing, and if at times the higher staffs turn green around the gills when across their astonished situation maps flash the prongs of seemingly unprotected spearheads launched deep into enemy territory, it is only because they have yet properly to gauge the man's resourcefulness. As for his subordinates, more than one corps and division commander, in the course of a whirlwind visit from the Old Man, has felt a sinking in the pit of his stomach on finding himself and his command catapulted into outer space, but all of them have learned that he never lets them down. They know that if the unexpected happens, he will find a solution, and what is more, he will be up front to see that the solution is applied.

Three times in the last few days, in as many tents and wooded fields, the same dialogue with minor variations:

Division commander: 'But my flanks, General?'

The General: 'You have nothing to worry about. If anything develops—and it won't—our tactical Air will know before you do, and will clobber it. That will give me plenty of time to pull something out of the hat.' A pat on the shoulder. 'Get going now. Let the enemy worry about his flanks. I'll see you up there in a couple of days.'

Colonel Charles Codman

The General Keeps in Touch

. . . . Codman, Stiller, and I decided to find 6 Armoured Division. Stiller
rode in the armoured car to lead the way and Codman and I followed in the jeep,
moving via Avranches, Pontorson, Combourg, and Merdrignac. We met a very
excited liaison officer who told us that the road was under fire. Afterwards we
found out that the poor boy was slightly touched in the head. However, proceeding down a road for over fifteen kilometres in country known to be occupied
by the enemy, and not seeing one of our soldiers, was rather exciting. Finally we
caught up with the Command Post of the division.

Next day, at the briefing, I learned with considerable perturbation that I had
driven right through a German division. I did not wish to chagrin our G-2 by
telling him I had not been able to find it.

General Patton

'I have been walking for five days now,' the young Middle-Western voice
had said next to the jeep, 'and I ain't fired a shot yet. But don't get me wrong, I
ain't complaining. Hell, I'll *walk* them to death, if that's what they want. . . .'

And the sour-faced ageing Captain in Chartres, leaning against the side of a
Sherman tank across the square from the cathedral, saying, 'I don't see what
people've been raving all these years about this country for. Jesus Christ on the
mountain, there ain't nothing here we can't make better in California. . . .'

And the chocolate-coloured dwarf with a red fez dancing among the Engineers with minesweepers, at a crossroads, entertaining the waiting tankmen, who
cheered him on and got him drunk with Calvados they had taken as gifts from
the people along the road that morning.

And the two drunken old men, weaving down the shattered street, with
little bouquets of pansies and geraniums in their hands, who had given the
bouquets to Pavone and Michael, and had saluted and welcomed the American
Army to their village, although they would like to ask one question: Why it was,
on 4 July, with not a single German in the town, the American Army had seen
fit to come over and bomb the place to rubble in thirty minutes?

And the German lieutenant in the 1 Division prisoner-of-war cage who, in
exchange for a clean pair of socks, had pointed out on the map the exact location
of his battery of 88s to the Jewish refugee from Dresden who was now a sergeant
in the M.P.s.

And the grave French farmer who had worked all one morning weaving an
enormous 'WELCOME U.S.A.' in roses in his hedge along the road to cheer the
soldiers on their way; and the other farmers and their women who had covered
a dead American along the road with banks of flowers from their gardens, roses,
phlox, peonies, iris, making death on that summer morning seem for a moment
gay and charming and touching as the infantry walked past, circling gently
around the bright mound of blossoms.

And the thousands of German prisoners and the terrible feeling that you
got from looking at their faces that there was nothing there to indicate that these
were the people who had torn Europe from its roots, murdered thirty million
people, burned populations in gas ovens, hanged and crushed and tortured

through three thousand miles of agony. There was nothing in their faces but weariness and fear, and you knew, being honest with yourself, that if they were dressed in O.D.s, they would all look as though they came from Cincinnati.

And the funeral of the F.F.I. man in that little town—what was its name?—near St. Malo, with the artillery going off all around it, and the procession winding behind the black-plumed horses and the rickety hearse up the hill to the cemetery, and all the people of the town in their best clothes, shuffling along in the dust, to shake the hands of the murdered man's relatives who stood at the gate in a solemn line. And the young priest, who had helped officiate at the funeral services in the church, who answered, when Michael asked him who the dead man was, 'I don't know, my friend. I'm from another town.'

And the carpenter in Granville, who had been born in Canada and had worked on the German coastal fortifications, who had shaken his head and said, 'It makes no difference now, friend. You've come too late. 1942, 1943, I'd've have shaken your hand and greeted you gladly. Now. . . .' He had shrugged. 'Too late, friend, too late. . . .'

And the fifteen-year-old boy in Cherbourg who had been furious with the Americans. 'They are fools,' he had said hotly. 'They take up with exactly the same girls who lived with the Germans! Democrats! Pah! I give you democrats like that! I, myself,' the boy boasted, 'have shaved the hair off five girls in this neighbourhood for being German whores. And I did it when it was dangerous, long before the invasion. And I'll do it again, oh, yes, I'll do it again. . . .'

And the brothel with the girls dressed in short skirts, and the Madame at the counter, taking the money from the line of soldiers, and giving them a towel and an infinitesimal piece of soap, saying, 'Be gentle to the little girl, my dear, remember to be gentle.' And the soldiers going up to the rooms, still carrying their M-1s and their tommy-guns.   Irwin Shaw

Counter-blow: Mortain

The Führer has ordered the execution of a break-through to the coast in order to create the basis for the decisive operation against the Allied invasion front. For this purpose further forces are being brought up to the army.

On the successful execution of the operation the Führer has ordered depends the decision of the war in the West and with it perhaps the decision of the war itself. Commanders of all ranks must be absolutely clear as to the enormous significance of this fact. I expect all corps and divisional commanders to take good care that all officers are aware of the unique significance of the whole situation.

Only one thing counts, unceasing effort and determined will to victory.

For Führer, Volk and Reich.

                                        General Paul Hausser, 7 August

We made a swift advance of about ten miles and suffered only three tank losses. 116 Panzer Division, our left-hand neighbour, made only limited progress. The morning of 7 August had dawned bright and clear. It was a perfect flying day. Suddenly the Allied fighter-bombers swooped out of the sky. They came down in hundreds firing their rockets at the concentrated tanks and vehicles. We could do nothing against them, and we could make no further progress. The next day the planes came down again. We were forced to give the ground we had gained, and by 9 August the division was back where it started from north of Mortain, having lost thirty tanks and eight hundred men.

General von Lüttwitz

THE HELL OF FALAISE

Now the long pocket from Falaise to Mortain, crammed with eight German divisions and all their paraphernalia, was under assault from three sides. Despite desperate resistance the Americans from the south and west and the British and Canadians from the north and north-east closed in on the Germans, who tried to flee eastwards through the narrow Falaise gap—their only escape route. Cooped into the ever-shrinking salient, they were battered continuously from the air as they retreated.

On 3 August my division of about eight thousand men was finally told to move to Normandy, after having waited just north of the Somme for a second landing since the day the invasion began. Our destination was Falaise. I decided that, since speed was essential, my fighting troops would travel from Amiens to Rouen by train, while my supply troops would make a three-day journey on foot by road. I expected that the fighting element of the division would reach Rouen, about a hundred and twenty kilometres away, in about twenty-four hours. I went off to Rouen in advance to make preparations for my division's arrival, only to find that three days later my butchers and bakers and hygiene men arrived on schedule but my infantry was nowhere to be found. It seems that the first of the twenty-eight trains carrying my division was derailed south of Amiens, and as a result the men were sent by a long circuitous route to Rouen. They were shunted around France for days on end, and it took them no less than nine days to make this hundred and twenty-kilometre journey by rail. By the time they arrived and were ready to move off again, the battle for Falaise was lost and the retreat of 7 Army had begun.

General Schwalbe, G.O.C. 344 Infantry Division

I got out of my car and my knees were trembling, the sweat was pouring down my face and my clothes were soaked with perspiration. It was not that I was particularly anxious about myself, because my experiences of the past five years had accustomed me to the fear of death. I was afraid because I realized that if I failed now, and if I did not deploy my division correctly, the Allies would be through to Falaise, and the German armies in the West would be completely trapped. I knew how weak my division was and the task which confronted me gave me at that time some of the worst moments I have ever had in my life. Before me, making their way down the Caen–Falaise road in a disorderly rabble, were the panic-stricken troops of 89 Infantry Division. I realized that something had to be done to send these men back into the line and fight. I lit a cigar, stood in the middle of the road and in a loud voice asked them if they were going to leave me alone to cope with the enemy. Hearing a divisional commander address them in this way they stopped, hesitated, and then returned to their positions.

General Meyer, G.O.C. 12 S.S. Panzer Division

.... We had to retreat in a great hurry. All the other units pulled out without firing a shot and we were left to cover them. . . . I wonder what will become of us. The pocket is nearly closed, and the enemy is already in Rouen. I don't think I shall ever see my home again. However, we are fighting for Germany and our children, and what happens to us matters not. I close with the hope that a miracle will happen soon and that I shall see my home again.

German corporal, in a letter to his wife

Closing the Falaise Gap

The task of closing this Gap devolved mainly upon General Simonds' two armoured divisions, 4 Canadian and 1 Polish. On 16 August both were directed south-east in the general direction of Trun, an important road-junction about twelve miles east of Falaise, to cut the enemy's main escape route. On the following afternoon General Montgomery instructed the Canadian Army to push the Poles on as quickly as possible past Trun to Chambois, some four miles farther to the south-east. Early on the 18th Canadian troops got into Trun, and that day there was violent and bloody fighting by units of both divisions striving to reach Chambois, the Poles from the north, the Canadians from the north-west.

The German withdrawal through the Gap had assumed the aspect of desperation. The enemy's dire circumstances were driving him to attempt something which our superiority in the air had not allowed him to think of for months past: mass road movement in daylight. On 17 August began 'three days of the largest scale movement, presenting such targets to Allied air power as had hitherto only been dreamed of'. During these bright summer days our fighter-bombers struck at the packed roads hour after hour, turning the whole area of the Gap into a gigantic shambles; while our artillery, moving up within range, poured thousands of shells into the killing-ground. In that seething bloody cauldron which the Germans were to remember as 'der Kessel von Falaise' one of the haughty armies that had terrorized Europe was perishing miserably.

The American formations had now regrouped. General Patton's columns, meeting little resistance to the eastward, had rushed on through Chartres and Orléans and were soon on the edge of Paris. As early as 17 August his patrols reached the Seine at Mantes-Gassicourt. On 18 August the Argentan front was transferred to 1 U.S. Army. On the 17th the Americans here had resumed their northward advance. 90 U.S. Infantry Division and 2 French Armoured Division, beating down fierce opposition, drove slowly forward towards Chambois. At 7.20 p.m. on 19 August came the long-awaited contact between Allied forces north and south of the Gap, when, as a 1 Canadian Army situation report put it, the 10th Polish Mounted Rifle Regiment with the 10th Polish Motor Battalion 'captured Chambois and were joined by 90 U.S. Infantry Division forces'. It was an historic moment.

Colonel C. P. Stacey, Canadian Army

Inside the Cauldron: '*Jabos*'

When the Spitfires arrived over the small triangle of Normandy, bounded by Falaise, Trun and Chambois, the Typhoons were already hard at work. One of their favourite tactics against long streams of enemy vehicles was to seal off the front and rear of the column by accurately dropping a few bombs. This technique imprisoned the desperate enemy on a narrow stretch of dusty lane, and since the transports were sometimes jammed together four abreast it made the subsequent rocket and cannon attacks a comparatively easy business against the stationary targets. Some of the armoured cars and tanks attempted to escape their fate by making detours across the fields and wooded country, but these were soon spotted by the Typhoon pilots and were accorded the same treatment as their comrades on the highways and lanes.

Immediately the Typhoons withdrew from the killing ground the Spitfires raced into the attack. The tactics of the day were low-level strafing attacks with cannon shells and machine-guns against soft-skinned targets including all types of trucks, staff cars and lightly-armoured vehicles. Here and there amongst the shambles on the ground were a few of the deadly Tiger tanks, and although the cannon shells would have little effect against their tough armour plate, a few rounds were blasted against them for good measure. As soon as the Spitfires had fired all their ammunition they flew back at high speed to their airfields, where the ground crews worked flat out in the hot sunshine to re-arm and re-fuel the aircraft in the shortest possible time.

'Johnnie' Johnson

The Victims

Vehicles pile up. Cars, heavily laden with officers' gear, honk a way through the jam, twisting past lorries in their effort to make better time. Guns are abandoned and blown up. Heavy tractors stop for lack of fuel: a couple of grenades in the engine and that's that. The huge Mercèdes diesels of a workshop company are hit by rockets. The soldiers on the tanks cannot make out where these powerful, ultra-modern machines can suddenly have come from. The men have never seen their like before. 'Christ, we should have had them earlier.'

Electrical fitting machines, lathes, automatic welders, workshops on wheels, the very best transporters, capable of moving two tanks at once, searchlight trucks with anti-dazzle equipment for night driving. Lorry-loads of spare parts, dental trucks, a mobile film unit, dredgers. The fighters are having a field day; they hedgehop above the road, the engines screeching. Empty ammunition belts fall from them, rockets, grenades, machine-gun bullets, bombs, everything is thrown at the stream of vehicles.

'It beats me why these bastards are allowed to go joy-riding in broad daylight,' Haase remarks to Lingen. He sits beside Lingen on the hatch cover and shakes his head.

'If you'd been to Officer School, you'd know all about it,' says Lingen.

Karlludwig Opitz

A Break-out Attempt

On the evening of 19 August, large numbers of our troops were crowded together in the restricted area of Fourches—Trun—Chambois—Montabord. Some of them had already made repeated attempts to escape to the north-west with vehicles and horse-drawn columns. Quite apart from attacks from the air, the entire terrain was being swept by enemy artillery fire and our casualties increased from hour to hour. On the route leading into St. Lambert-sur-Dives from Bailleul where my division was collected, a colossal number of shot-up horses and vehicles lay mixed together with dead soldiers in large heaps which hourly grew higher and higher. That evening the order was given to force a break-through near St. Lambert. I ordered all my remaining tanks (there were fifteen left of the hundred and twenty with which I arrived in Normandy) and other armoured vehicles to form a vanguard behind which we intended to break through from Bailleul to St. Lambert, a distance of less than ten kilometres. But ground reconnaissance had established the fact that driving would be impossible in total darkness owing to the large numbers of destroyed vehicles that were lying about. Thus we were only able to start leaving the Bailleul area at four in the morning when there would be more light.

I had expected that this route would be under such a raking fire that it would be hardly possible to extricate any considerable numbers from the pocket. But for some unknown reason enemy artillery fire had practically ceased on the evening of 19 August and remained quiet until the next morning. In this lull we began to move in the early morning mist of 20 August. As a narrow lane near St. Lambert was known still to provide an escape route across the Dives river, columns of all the encircled units were streaming towards it, some of them driving in rows of eight vehicles abreast. Suddenly at seven o'clock in the morning the artillery fire which had been so silent, now broke out into a storm such as I had never before experienced. Alongside the Dives the numerous trains of vehicles ran into direct enemy fire of every description, turned back, and in some cases drove round in a circle until they were shot-up and blocked the roads. Towering pillars of smoke rose incessantly from petrol tanks as they were hit, ammunition exploded, riderless horses stampeded, some of them badly wounded. Organized direction was no longer possible, and only a few of my tanks and infantry got through to St. Lambert. At ten in the morning these elements reported to me that they had cleared an escape route and were providing cover south and north of it at Trun and Chambois.

By noon I had managed to reach St. Lambert myself, and from the church in the town I directed the evacuation of my men. The crossing of the bridge over the Dives was a particularly ghastly affair. Men, horses, vehicles and other equipment that had been shot-up while making the crossing had crashed from the bridge into the deep ravine of the Dives and lay there jumbled together in gruesome heaps. Throughout the whole afternoon enemy tanks tried to break through again into St. Lambert from Trun, while other tanks kept the road leading north-east from St. Lambert under constant fire. I formed separate small groups of my men, placed them under energetic officers and ordered them to march north-east. At nine in the evening of 20 August I broke out myself, but enemy infantry had by this time entered St. Lambert and the Falaise Gap was closed.

General von Lüttwitz

The Seine Crossings

I was in the Argentan–Falaise pocket, and I still don't know how I got out of it. We were running in wild fiery circles with artillery and aerial bombs dropping amidst us. After I got out of there I had to fight partisans and our own soldiers to get on to the ferry across the Seine. Just accidentally I met my old battery again, after having been on my own for ten days. Naturally it is very euphemistic to call whatever is left a battery. There is not even one gun left.

A German soldier's letter

The Canadians were up well before dawn, and the first pair of Spitfires retracted their wheels as the first hint of a lighter sky flushed the eastern horizon. The Germans were making strenuous efforts to salvage what equipment they could from the débâcle and get it across the Seine. Such enemy action had been anticipated: some of the Typhoon effort was diverted to attacking barges and small craft as they ferried to and fro across the river. Once more the Spitfire pilots turned their attention to the killing ground and attacked all manner of enemy transports wherever they were to be found. They were located on the highways and lanes, in the woods and copses, in small villages and hamlets, beneath the long shadows of tall hedges, in farmyards and even camouflaged with newly-mown grass to resemble haystacks. During the previous night many of the enemy had decided to abandon a great proportion of their transports: they could be seen continuing the retreat on foot and in hastily commandeered farm carts. Sometimes the despairing enemy waved white sheets at the Spitfires as they hurtled down to attack; but these signs were ignored; our own ground troops were still some distance away and there was no organization available to round up large numbers of prisoners.

'Johnnie' Johnson

The End of the Battle

. . . . Hundreds of men were coming towards me. They were German. They were from the Falaise Gap.

I never want to see men like them again.

They came on, shambling in dusty files. Every few yards there was a single British infantryman. Even that guard was unnecessary. The shuffling wrecks just followed the Bren carrier in the lead. They were past caring. The figures were bowed with fatigue, although they had nothing to carry but their ragged uniforms and their weary, hopeless, battle-drugged bodies.

R. M. Wingfield

The Falaise Pocket had been crushed, and the German 7 Army within it had almost ceased to exist.

By the morning of 22 August fighting had virtually ceased in the area where the Gap had been. The whole vicinity of St. Lambert was covered with the human and material débris of an army which had suffered the greatest disaster in modern military history. At many places the bodies of German soldiers literally carpeted the ground; one observer spoke of 'hundreds of dead, so close together that they were practically touching'. Masses of destroyed or abandoned tanks, lorries and cars blocked the roads and filled the ditches; while some eight thousand dead horses, which had drawn the vehicles of the German infantry divisions, lay offending the air. In the carnage of the Pocket and the Gap at least eight German divisions had been destroyed, and about twice as many more had suffered crippling losses. The remnants of the armoured formations—small remnants in most cases—had saved themselves at the expense of the infantry, who were left to their fate. One armoured formation, however, had actually fought to annihilation. Meyer's 12 S.S. Panzer Division had still had a few men left after the fall of Falaise, but the last survivors, sixty strong, were overrun in the Gap west of Trun.

Colonel C. P. Stacey

Before the battle ended, von Kluge, like Rundstedt before him, had lost his job.

Kluge took his dismissal quite calmly. That night he wrote a letter to Hitler imploring him to end the unequal battle in the West. Early on the 18th he said good-bye to his staff officers and set out by car for Germany. At Metz he ordered his driver to stop. He took poison there, and was carried to Metz hospital a dying man.

German staff officer

ANVIL

On 15–16 August, American and French forces detached from the Italian front landed in the South of France and thrust up the Rhône valley. On 11 September they joined forces with the Allied armies advancing down France from Normandy. The severest fighting in the early stages took place in Toulon, where French troops were engaged in a bitter and bloody struggle with the German garrison.

French Shock Troops at the Battle of Toulon: 22 August

But for the shock troops that was not yet all. Their 4th Company was busy at the Poudrière—the hardest task of the day and perhaps of the whole battle for Toulon. Let us recall the position of this fortification, a sort of reef on which, here and there, the 1st and 3rd Battalions of the 3rd R.T.A. had stranded; with its back to the western slopes of the Las valley, it was surrounded by a raised wall, bordering the road from Revest to Toulon. In its forecourt, four dark holes marked the openings of four wide galleries plunging deep into the earth. An improvised garrison of all sorts of troops—infantrymen, gunners, marines, sappers, radio operators, arsenal workers, quartermaster's men, cooks and bakehouse workers—had transformed the galleries into a fortress which they defended madly.

On the 22nd, at daybreak, Colonel de Linarès' first care was to tighten his ring about the stronghold. The 3rd Battalion of the 3rd R.T.A. blocked it to the north and west, and the 1st Battalion to the south. Only the east side remained to be dealt with, that is to say, the slopes of the Faron facing the entrance to the workings. The Torri Company was established there by 09.30 hours. One of its platoons was detached for the attack, but each time a group sought to approach the entrance, very dense fire came from the galleries, and with a loud noise of motors two tanks came out like a jack-in-the-box. Furthermore, a hundred marksmen were clinging to the superstructure, and we had to settle accounts with them first. For the chasseurs and tirailleurs it was like target-practice and the 2nd Group of the 67th Artillery Regiment hammered them tirelessly. Only the dead stopped fighting.

At 17.00 the situation was as follows. One gallery seemed empty, another had fallen in, and from the third the tanks, probably damaged by incendiary grenades thrown in by assault groups of shock troops, dared no longer come out. The fourth remained, and there the bulk of the garrison held out, defending the approaches without sign of flagging. Trucks were burning in the inner courtyard. On the superstructure thirty stubborn men continued to prevent the tirailleurs from overlooking the entrances to the galleries. It was time to finish.

From the area he held in Toulon Linarès brought two tanks of the 3rd R.S.A.R. and two tank-destroyers of the 7th R.C.A. With a platoon of the 1st Company of the 3rd R.T.A., these machines advanced as close as possible and swept the centre of the upper defences of the Poudrière with all their weapons. Blasted at point-blank range, the remaining outside defenders at last waved a white flag. We climbed up on to the fortifications.

But we were not yet inside. The tirailleurs who reached as far as the courtyard were driven back by grenades. Moreover, the defenders in the galleries had seen the surrender of their comrades on the superstructures and made haste to shorten the range of their artillery. A violent bombardment fell upon the attackers at once.

It was 20.30. Night had almost fallen. Second-Lieutenant Laflèche went under machine-gun fire to reconnoitre a passage across the mines for his leading tank-destroyer, then turned round and brought it into a good position. This was the end. Firing from a few dozen yards, the 76·2 mm. gun sent its shells full blast into the galleries. At 21.00 the southern gallery blew up. The greater number of its occupants were burned to death. The survivors attempted a mass sortie, which our machine-gunners stopped. Then, taken by the same impulse, tirailleurs and shock troops, with their grenades and machine-guns, and sappers with their flamethrowers, hurled themselves forward in a final assault. Every man who did not at once surrender was destroyed. At 21.45 it was all over: the Poudrière was conquered.

The interior of the fortification was no more than an immense débris-filled charnel-house, where a horrible stench of death prevailed and which was being devoured by the flames which threatened at every moment to involve the ammunition boxes. Two hundred and fifty corpses were scattered about the floor, although the number of prisoners totalled only a hundred and eighty, of whom more than sixty were gravely wounded. It was a Dantesque sight, and in a flash it brought back to my mind the most tragic memories of Douaumont and Thiaumont in 1916. And it was admirable that our men, for many of whom this was the first battle, were the immediate equals of the veterans of Verdun. They had faced enemies who were not inferior to those whom their fathers had vanquished: 'We defended ourselves and that's that. . . . I am an officer, a lieutenant. That's war for me as well as for you, gentlemen,' one of the defenders answered when asked the reason for such heroic and desperate resistance.

Marshal de Lattre de Tassigny

RETREAT ON PARIS

While the Falaise Pocket was being ground down, the greater part of the American forces swept east and north-east on Paris, meeting little resistance, while the British, also moving eastwards through Normandy, met stronger opposition before Rouen. The German armies had been committed in Normandy, so there were no fresh, organized troops left to hold the line of the Seine. Those units deputed to do so had no chance and were destroyed. The Americans followed the Germans across the river and Paris was encircled. The French underground in the capital rose in arms and fierce street battles raged between the resistance and the German garrison. On 25 August the French armoured division attached to the Americans liberated the city.

There was no plan available at this stage for an orderly fighting withdrawal. At first it was hoped to fall behind the Seine, but with the Americans already on the outskirts of Paris this had to be abandoned. It was then decided to use the Seine as a mid-way position to delay the enemy and give the retreating troops sufficient time to build a line on the Somme. The Seine was expected to hold for at least seven days, and then defensive positions were to have been taken up on the so-called Kitzinger Line which was to have been built by General Kitzinger across France through Abbeville–Amiens–Soissons–Epernay– Châlons–St. Dizier–Chaumont–Langres–Gray–Besançon to the Swiss border. These defensive positions had been designated as far back as 1943, but the line had only been completed on the right flank between Abbeville and Amiens. Even though this line existed in theory only, nevertheless we had been ordered to hold it. But there were no troops available to man either the Seine or the Somme, and the Allies cut through France with little opposition.

General Blumentritt, Chief of Staff, West

All I was told at the time was that the three divisions, 331, 344 and 17 Luftwaffe Field, were to take up defensive positions about ten miles south of Evreux. I never knew, until I was shown a captured order by an Allied interrogator, that our task was to cover the withdrawal of 7th Army to the Seine.

It would not have mattered in any event, whether I knew this or not, since the life of my division was so short. In trying to cross the Seine, air attacks were so bad that it was only possible to move my formation piece by piece over the river. As a result I was never able to have my complete division together. Nor were we ever properly dug in for a defensive fight. No sooner had we reached our intended positions when we discovered the Allies were already there. We attempted to withdraw but we were new, and chaos resulted instead. The vehicles jammed every road in all directions and planes attacked us constantly. In one of these attacks my own vehicle was destroyed. It was no longer healthy to drive about these roads in a motor car. I therefore was forced to travel between my units with the only safe vehicle I still had—a bicycle. My corps commander was so anxious about Allied air attacks in this area that he used to have two men sitting on the hood of his car and one on the rear bumper to act as aircraft spotters.

In a little over a week my division ceased to exist as a fighting formation. I lost three-fifths of my men, and two-thirds of the weapons of the formation had to be abandoned. The other two divisions who went over the Seine with me suffered much the same fate. So weak were we all that it was decided to merge the three divisions into one under one headquarters staff, and with this force guard the approaches to the Rouen ferries. I do not know whose plan it was to throw good divisions after bad into the cauldron west of the Seine. These thirty to thirty-five thousand men might have performed a useful function organizing the defence of the Seine river itself instead of being dissipated in a few days in a hopeless situation. I had untried troops under my command and my orders were vague and impossible. I never knew exactly where my division was, what its task was supposed to be and what was taking place all about me. Disastrous results under such circumstances were inevitable.

General Schwalbe

Letters Home

We have no vehicles or guns left, and whoever is still alive will have to fight as an infantryman. But I won't stay with them very long. I really don't know what we are still fighting for. Very soon I shall run over to the Tommies if I am not killed before I get there. . . .

Others found humour in their situation—

My total estate now fits into my little bag as I have lost everything else. The words 'hot meal' sound like a foreign language. We are gaining ground rapidly but in the wrong direction.

Paris Rises

As the front drew steadily nearer to Paris at the beginning of this week, and when we heard the news that conditions in the city itself had considerably deteriorated, we went in again on Tuesday (22 August) to get an idea of the situation. We knew that the garrisons of the strong-points remaining behind in Paris had to fight in every part of the town in ceaseless skirmishes, against the followers of de Gaulle on the one hand and against the Bolshevist-controlled Resistance on the other. We saw barricades in the side-streets, sandbags piled high, vehicles driven into one another, pieces of furniture heaped together to form barriers . . . somewhere a machine-gun chattered from time to time . . . but we came through unchallenged to the well-defended German strong-points and reached the Champs Elysées. Here the change which had come over this city was even more noticeable. It was a little after midday. But this street, usually crowded at this time of day with people and vehicles, was empty. On the way from the obelisk to the Arc de Triomphe we counted just over fifty people.

Dr. Toni Scheelkopf, German war correspondent

The Conquerors

We didn't have a damn thing to do with the taking of Paris. We just came in a couple of days later when somebody got the bright idea of having the parade and we just happened to be there and that's all there is to it. What can you do, though—that's just the way it goes. And after all, we did a helluva lot of things that we didn't get credit for.

As long as I live I don't guess I'll ever see a parade like that. Most of us slept in pup tents in the Bois de Boulogne the night before, and it rained like hell and we were pretty dirty, so they picked out the cleanest guys to stand up in front and on the outside. I had a bright new shiny patch, so they put me on the out-side. It was a good place to be, too, because every guy marching on the outside had at least one girl on his arm kissing him and hugging him.

We were marching twenty-four abreast down the Champs Elysées and we had a helluva time trying to march, because the whole street was jammed with people laughing and yelling and crying and singing. They were throwing flowers at us and bringing us big bottles of wine.

The first regiment never did get through. They just broke in and grabbed the guys and lifted some of them on their shoulders and carried them into cafés and bars and their homes and wouldn't let them go. I hear it was a helluva job trying to round them all up later.

Private First Class Verner Odegard

Return to Paris

I then went to find a locksmith to force the door of my flat. The *concierge*, a very old woman with warts on her forehead, was dead. The new one knew nothing: she was pessimistic: 'So many people have been there . . . very odd, some of them. The last was a singer from Brussels.'

Indeed, what struck me first on entering was the new sediment left by the strangers. A piano cumbered the library, a wooden negro carried a golden torch in the hall; the displaced furniture affronted my memory, though I was not able to determine immediately its previous positions.

I did not know where to begin. I went into my bedroom. The last time I had looked at myself in the looking-glass above the chimney-piece, I was five years younger. I was paler, thinner, but younger; more anxious, too. Those five years have partly delivered me from myself. I have found peace in them: something which had weighed on my life for twenty years has been dissipated.

The last time I lay on the bed—my bed—was 13 June 1940.

Emmanuel d'Astier

Dear Ike: To-day I spat in the Seine.
                    General Patton to General Eisenhower, 26 August

St. Aubin d'Aubigné: August 1944

It was only a small place and they cheered us too much,
A couple of allies, chance symbol of Freedom newfound.
They were eager to beckon, to back-slap, even to touch;
They put flowers in my helmet and corn-coloured wine in my hand.

The boy from Dakota and I, we had suffered too little
To deserve all the flowers, the kisses, the wine and the thanks.
We both felt ashamed; till the kettledrum clangour of metal
On cobble and kerbstone proclaimed the arrival of tanks.

Who saw them first, the exiles returning, the fighters,
The Croix de Lorraine and the Tricolor flown from the hull?
Who saw us moving more fitly to join the spectators,
The crazy, the crying, the silent whose hearts were full?

It was only a small place, but a bugle was blowing.
I remember the Mayor performing an intricate dance
And the boy from Dakota most gravely, most quietly, throwing
The flowers from his helmet towards the deserving of France.

                                                        Paul Dehn

Postscript

The Germans often accuse us of being low plagiarists when it comes to
music, and that we cannot deny. Our musical geniuses at home never did get
around to working up a good, honest, acceptable war song, and so they forced
us to share *Lili Marlene* with the enemy. Even if we did get it from the krauts
it's a beautiful song, and the only redeeming thing is the rumour kicking around
that 'Lili' is an ancient French song, stolen by the Germans. It may not be true,
but we like to believe it.

'Lili' got a couple of artillerymen in trouble in France. They were singing it
at a bar the day after this particular town had been taken. Some local partisans
came over and told them to shut the hell up. The guys understood, apologized,
and bought drinks all around.

                                                        Bill Mauldin

THE BOMB PLOT

*While the fighting in Normandy was reaching its climax, a number of Hitler's
generals and prominent civilians who had seen the writing on the wall attempted to
overthrow their master by assassination, an extreme measure which, they hoped,
would open the way to peace negotiations which would save something from the
wreck.*

Taken as a whole, our generals bear no resemblance to the Italians. Treason such as the Italians generals committed against Mussolini is impossible considering the mentality of the German and especially the Prussians generals.

Dr. Goebbels, 23 September 1943

A Proclamation Unproclaimed

Germans!

In recent years terrible things have taken place before our very eyes. Against the advice of experts Hitler has ruthlessly sacrificed whole armies for *his* passion for glory, *his* megalomania, *his* blasphemous delusion that he was the chosen and favoured instrument of 'Providence'.

Not called to power by the German people, but becoming the Head of the Government by intrigues of the worst kind, he has spread confusion by his devilish arts and lies and by tremendous extravagance which on the surface seemed to bring prosperity to all, but which in reality plunged the German people into terrible debt. In order to remain in power, he added to this an unbridled reign of terror, destroyed law, outlawed decency, scorned the divine commands of pure humanity and destroyed the happiness of millions of human beings.

His insane disregard for all mankind could not fail to bring our nation to misfortune with deadly certainty; his self-imagined supremacy could not but bring ruin to our brave sons, fathers, husbands and brothers, and his bloody terror against the defenceless could not but bring shame to the German name. He enthroned lawlessness, oppression of conscience, crime and corruption in our Fatherland which had always been proud of its integrity and honesty. Truthfulness and veracity, virtues which even the simplest people think it their duty to inculcate in their children, are punished and persecuted. Thus public activity and private life are threatened by a deadly poison.

This must not be, this cannot go on. The lives and deaths of our men, women and children must no longer be abused for this purpose. We would not be worthy of our fathers, we would be despised by our children if we had not the courage to do everything, I repeat everything, to ward off this danger from ourselves and to achieve self-respect again.

It is for this purpose that, after searching our conscience before God, we have taken over power. Our brave Wehrmacht is a pledge of security and order. The police will do their duty.

Each civil servant shall carry out his duties according to his technical knowledge, following only the law and his own conscience. Let each of you help by discipline and confidence. Carry out your daily work with new hope. Help one another! Your tortured souls shall again find peace and comfort.

Far from all hatred we will strive for inward reconciliation and with dignity for outward reconciliation. Our first task will be to cleanse the war from its degeneration and end the devastating destruction of human life, of cultural and economic values behind the fronts. We all know that we are not masters of peace and war. Firmly relying on our incomparable Wehrmacht and in confident belief in the tasks assigned to man by God we will sacrifice everything to defend the Fatherland and to restore a lawful solemn state of order, to live once more for honour and peace with respect for the divine commandments, in purity and truth!

Germans!

Hitler's despotism has been broken.

This proclamation was to have been broadcast after the assassination of Hitler on 20 July, 1944. It was never to be heard, for it was the Führer himself who came on the air soon after midnight.

Hitler Speaks

'If I address you to-day,' the Führer said, 'I am doing so for two reasons. First, so that you shall hear my voice and know that I personally am unhurt and well; and second, so that you shall hear the details about a crime that has no equal in German history.'

Then he described the crime:

'An extremely small clique of ambitious, unscrupulous, and at the same time foolish, criminally stupid officers hatched a plot to remove me and, together with me, virtually to exterminate the staff of the German High Command. The bomb that was placed by Colonel Count von Stauffenberg exploded two metres away from me on my right side. It wounded very seriously a number of my dear collaborators. One of them has died. I personally am entirely unhurt apart from negligible grazes, bruises, or burns.'

The plot, Hitler asserted, resembled the Badoglio coup against Mussolini. The group perpetrating it 'believed it could thrust a dagger into our back as it did in 1918'.

Hitler naturally tried to minimize the plot's importance:

'The circle that comprises these usurpers is extremely small. It has nothing to do with the German armed forces. . . . It is a very small clique of criminal elements, that will now be exterminated mercilessly.

'This time,' he continued, 'we will settle accounts in such a manner as we National Socialists are wont.' And then, shouting in typical Hitlerian style, he adjured his followers to 'counter these elements at once with ruthless determination and either arrest them at once or—should they offer resistance anywhere—wipe them out'.

In conclusion, the Führer proclaimed the outcome of the plot to be 'a clear sign of Providence that I am to carry on with my work'. And he did carry on to the bitter end.

When Colonel Count Claus Schenk von Stauffenberg left Berlin for Hitler's secret headquarters in East Prussia on the morning of 20 July he carried with him detailed plans for creating several new front-line divisions out of the Replacement Army (*Ersatzheer*) by scraping the bottom of the German man-power barrel. But the bulge in his briefcase was not due solely to these plans and papers. It concealed a bomb, of a kind made in England and smuggled into German-occupied countries for the use of saboteurs. The compactness and ingenious construction of these bombs had proved so interesting to the German police that they had turned them over for study to the Abwehr, the German intelligence and counter-intelligence service. The bombs had no tell-tale clock mechanism. They were exploded by causing a glass capsule containing acid to break in a chamber in which was fixed a taut wire that held the firing pin back from the percussion cap that would set off the explosive material. The wire's thickness determined the time required for the acid to eat through the wire and release the firing pin. Several of these bombs had been set aside some time before by Stauffenberg's confederates in the Abwehr and stored at Berchtesgaden with General Helmuth Stieff, one of the plotters. For it had been planned to make the attempt on Hitler's life in his mountain retreat. When Hitler moved to his East Prussian headquarters the bombs were taken from Berchtesgaden and delivered to Stauffenberg in Berlin.

Stauffenberg had tried twice before to assassinate Hitler. On 11 July he had flown to Berchtesgaden; but he did not place the bomb, because neither Himmler nor Göring was present, and it was the desire of the plotters to kill them as well as Hitler. Several of the highest army officers, notably Field-Marshals von Kluge and Rommel, had agreed to go along with the plot only if both Göring and Himmler were assassinated at the same time as Hitler.

The second attempt was to be made on 16 July, when another meeting was called at Hitler's headquarters. Again the plan miscarried. At the last moment Hitler did not attend the conference, nor did Himmler and Göring.

Stauffenberg's failures were severely critized by his fellow conspirators. On 16 July, counting on the success of the coup, troops in the neighbourhood of Berlin, under the command of members of the conspiracy, had been alerted to move on Berlin. It had been difficult to find an innocent excuse for this alert, but the officers did manage to pass it off as a practice manœuvre in home defence.

The nerves of the conspirators were now strained to the breaking point, for there was grave danger of a leak and they were not sure that Himmler did not know of their plot. In fact, some months earlier Himmler had told Admiral Wilhelm Canaris, chief of the Abwehr, who unknown to Himmler was privy to the conspiracy, that he, Himmler, knew a considerable number of officers were toying with the idea of an uprising. Himmler indicated he was so fully informed about them he could afford to await the most favourable moment to arrest them. He had even mentioned the names of two ringleaders—General Ludwig Beck and Carl Friedrich Goerdeler. On 17 July one of Himmler's chief criminologists, Arthur Nebe, who was in the conspiracy, reported that a warrant was to be issued for the arrest of Goerdeler and that he must go into hiding at once. He did so. Julius Leber, one of the leading Social Democrats in the conspiracy, had already been arrested. About the same time a naval officer in the Abwehr, who was aware of the plans for the plot, attended a party given by one of the social leaders of Potsdam, Frau von Bredow, granddaughter of Bismarck, whose personality was so vigorous she was called 'the only male descendant' of the Iron Chancellor. There the naval officer, to his astonishment, heard a young fellow officer say quite openly that an attempt on Hitler's life was being planned.

It was obvious there was no time to lose if the conspirators were to strike before Himmler did.

Stauffenberg had been chosen to place the bomb because he was the only member of the inner circle of conspirators who, without danger of being searched, had ready access to Hitler. As liaison between the commanders of the Replacement Army and Hitler's headquarters, his presence was required at some of the High Command's staff meetings, which Hitler generally attended.

The choice was somewhat unfortunate, for Stauffenberg had been severely wounded in Africa. His left arm and two fingers of his right hand were missing and the sight of his left eye was impaired. He was unable to shoot if necessary, or to do anything but set the detonator and place the bomb. But there was no question of his personal courage. He had offered to remain in the room when the bomb exploded if that were desirable. His associates vetoed such a sacrifice on the ground that he was too able an organizer to be expended in this way. Further, since Stauffenberg had helped prepare the plans for the use of the Replacement Army, he knew the units that could be counted upon by the conspirators and the reliability of their various officers. Above all, his personal popularity among his subordinates and his ability to assume an important command in the Army, made Stauffenberg indispensable to the success of the *putsch*. He was often described as the 'manager of the conspiracy'.

The conspirators had several confederates at Hitler's headquarters in East Prussia. Chief among them was General Erich Fellgiebel, who was in charge of the Army's Signal Corps. His task was to inform the conspirators in Berlin as soon as the bomb had exploded and then to wreck the communications centre at headquarters and thus interrupt all telephone, radio and teletype connection with the outside world. Thereby the conspirators would have time to get control of the governmental apparatus in Berlin before anyone in Hitler's entourage could set counter-measures in motion.

After the second failure, of 16 July, Stauffenberg determined that on the next opportunity no matter what happened or who was present he would place the bomb if Hitler was there. But even General Beck, the head of the conspiracy, was sceptical. 'A horse that refuses a jump twice,' he said, 'is not likely to go over a third time.' However, everyone realized these particular conspirators would never have a fourth opportunity.

Stauffenberg's chance came on 20 July. Hitler had left Berchtesgaden for the East Front, and his headquarters, near Rastenburg, were deep in a pine forest near one of the innumerable lakes which dot that part of East Prussia. It bore the code name '*Wolfschanze*', i.e., wolf's fort.

The day was hot, and the conference was shifted from one of the well protected concrete bombproof shelters, in which a bomb would have maximum effect upon human beings, to a flimsy wooden barracks. Neither Himmler nor Göring attended. As a matter of fact, Göring's advice had not been sought on military matters for some time. But the usual yes-men who surrounded Hitler were there, including Field-Marshal Wilhelm Keitel and General Alfred Jodl. General Karl Bodenschatz, who was attached to Göring's headquarters some forty miles away, had arrived at Wolfschanze a few minutes before the meeting began in order to prepare the Führer for discussions with Mussolini and Graziani, who were to arrive that afternoon. When Bodenschatz finished his report Hitler asked him, according to Bodenschatz's later testimony, to come along to the usual noon briefing. 'I didn't want to go,' said Bodenschatz, 'but I went, and fifteen minutes later the attempt at assassination occurred.'

The only circumstantial and detailed account of what took place during these few crucial minutes has been given by Heinz Buchholz, one of Hitler's confidential secretaries, who was taking notes of the meeting. Here is the essence of what Buchholz told American interrogators at Nuremberg:

The 20 July briefing of the Führer was held at the usual time, 12.30 p.m. It began punctually with a statement by Lieutenant-General Heusinger about the situation on the Eastern Front. Field-Marshal Keitel, a few minutes late, arrived about 12.35, accompanied by several officers—among them Colonel Count Claus von Stauffenberg. 'I remember Count von Stauffenberg,' said Buchholz, 'as a tall, slender man, dark-haired and dark-complexioned. He had driven over a mine during the African campaign and had been seriously injured. One of his arms was amputated, and on the day of the bomb attempt he wore a black patch over one of his eyes.'

Stauffenberg had not been a frequent participant at these briefings, and Hitler did not recognize him. Keitel introduced him to the Führer and stepped up to the table at the Führer's left. Stauffenberg placed his briefcase under the map table, around which everyone was standing, scarcely six feet to the right of Adolf Hitler, then moved somewhat into the background. An operations officer on the General Staff, Colonel Brandt, standing near the briefcase, found that it was in the way of his feet and moved it slightly to the right and farther away from Hitler. As a result, one of the table supports was directly between Hitler and the briefcase.

Stauffenberg, however, was unaware of this fact because, a moment earlier, at about 12.40, he had been called to the telephone. It was later proved by the switchboard operator that Stauffenberg's adjutant, Lieutenant Werner von Haeften, had called him to give him an excuse to get out of the room. Only a few minutes after he went out the bomb exploded. 'I remember it as thunder connected with a bright yellow flame and thick smoke,' Buchholz recounted. 'Glass and wood splinters shot through the air. The large table on which all the situation maps were spread and around which the participants were standing—only the stenographers were sitting—collapsed. After a few seconds of silence, I heard a voice, probably Field-Marshal Keitel's, saying, "Where is the Führer?"'

Supported by Keitel, Hitler was able to walk from the barracks to his quarters. After him staggered the others, injured, bleeding, hands and faces blackened and burned, hair singed and yellowed, uniforms torn and stained.

Most of those present, including the Führer himself, at first supposed the bomb had been thrown into the room from the outside, as the windows were open, or that it had been planted under the floor. But this second hypothesis was quickly eliminated because the floor boards had been pressed down and not blown up by the explosion. The investigations, concluded that same afternoon, left little doubt that the explosive had been brought into the conference room in Stauffenberg's briefcase.

When the bomb exploded Hitler was leaning over the maps, his right arm resting on the table. This arm was partly paralyzed, and his right leg was burned and injured. Both eardrums were damaged, and his hearing was affected. Though not critically wounded, he never fully recovered from the physical and mental shocks.

A score of officers were injured and later received from their Führer a special decoration inscribed: 'Hitler—July 20 1944.' Four were killed: Major-General Schmundt, Chief Wehrmacht Adjutant to the Führer, who kept his military diary; General Korten; Colonel Brandt; and Heinrich Berger, one of the stenographers. Berger has often been referred to as Hitler's 'double' because of a rather close physical resemblance, but there is no evidence that he was ever used to impersonate the Führer.

Meanwhile Stauffenberg had passed the guards unchallenged and reached the automobile assigned to him. There, in the parking lot, a few hundred yards from Hitler's barrack, he waited. General Fellgiebel, the chief representative of the conspiracy at the East Prussia headquarters, joined him. Together they counted off the minutes before the explosion. Then, confident that Hitler was dead, that his own work was done, Stauffenberg drove to the airfield, some fifteen minutes away, where a courier plane was waiting to fly him back to Berlin.

At this point one of the critical, and for the plotters fatal, mistakes occurred. General Fellgiebel did not blow up the communication centre. Whether he lost his nerve when he saw Hitler still alive or there was some technical failure down the line will never be known. He was executed shortly thereafter, and his secret died with him. In any event, Fellgiebel's failure enabled Hitler's aides to communicate with the outside world, and, even more important, to learn what was going on in Berlin.

The Führer's first idea was to conceal the attempt at assassination from the German people. It was twelve hours later, in fact well on into the night, that he made his broadcast. By that time proof had reached the Rastenburg headquarters that Stauffenberg's bomb was not an isolated incident. Orders were being issued from the conspirators' Berlin headquarters. Berlin, Paris, Vienna, Prague, Belgrade, and many other parts of Germany and of German-occupied countries were in ferment. Frantic inquiries were pouring in to Hitler's headquarters. The Führer's voice, over the undamaged communication facilities, was a vital weapon in quelling the rebellion and in bringing the timid and faltering back into line.

By a strange coincidence Hitler had granted Mussolini, who had long been importuning him, an interview for that very day. A few hours after the attack, Hitler, with his right arm bound up, met Mussolini and Graziani at their train. They had been accompanied from northern Italy by an S.S. officer, *Sturmbannführer* Eugen Dollmann, who can best be described as a kind of diplomatic envoy in Italy of the S.S. (originally a Nazi élite guard and later practically a state within a state), and S.S. liaison with Mussolini. Dollmann has given a vivid description of the macabre meeting between *Il Duce*, then almost an outcast in his own country, and the Führer, who had so narrowly escaped assassination. How different from those meetings at Salzburg, Venice, and the Brenner, when the two dictators were dividing up Europe!

Hitler's inner circle, according to Dollmann, had now reached his side. Ribbentrop, who had a headquarters nearby, had arrived; so had Himmler and Göring. They were not a gay party. Hitler, still white, told Mussolini he had just had the greatest piece of luck in his life. Together they inspected the mass of debris at the scene of the explosion. At five o'clock they started their conference. The Führer was silent and for a long time sat gazing into space, munching the vari-coloured pills supplied him by Professor Theo Morell, the quack he made his physician. But the others, more or less ignoring their Italian visitors, began to quarrel, and to blame one another because the war had not yet been won. Ribbentrop raged against the generals and insisted on being called *von* Ribbentrop. (Only adoption in 1925 by his spinster aunt, Gertrud, had given him the right to use *von*.) Göring threatened him with his marshal's baton. Keitel tried to make excuses. Mussolini was aghast, and tried to maintain his dignity among the barbarians of the north.

In some way, Dollmann was not sure how or by whom, the blood purge on 30 June 1934, when Roehm was assassinated, was mentioned. That roused Hitler from his lethargy. He leaped up, and, with foam on his lips, shouted at the top of his voice that Providence had shown him once more that he was chosen to shape world destiny. He would take his revenge even on women and children! It was an eye for an eye and a tooth for a tooth if anyone set himself up against divine Providence.

This went on for half an hour, according to the S.S. officer, until Mussolini became quite shaken. Then footmen, in white uniforms, came in to serve tea, and Hitler calmed down. Field-Marshal Graziani made an effort to change the subject and started talking to Keitel about the Italian anti-aircraft units which the Germans demanded for the slaughterhouse of the East.

At this point someone telephoned from Berlin to say that order had not yet been restored there. Hitler took the telephone himself and again began to shriek. He gave the S.S. in Berlin full power to shoot anyone they wished and completely lost his temper when he heard that Himmler, who had only just left East Prussia to take over in Berlin, had not yet arrived there.

Then Hitler calmed down, and started a monologue of self-pity. The German people, he said, were unworthy of his greatness, and no one appreciated what he had done for them. This elicited emphatic denials from his henchmen, who vied with one another to convince the Führer of their loyalty. Göring recounted what he had done for the Nazi cause and the Air Force. Doenitz extolled the heroism of the Navy. But then Göring and Ribbentrop started quarrelling again. And so it went until the S.S. officer led the bewildered Italian visitors away.

While this mad tea party went on in East Prussia, in the rest of Germany the blood purge began. Thousands were rounded up, arrested, tortured and killed in order that Hitler's Thousand-Year Reich might survive another two hundred and ninety days.

Allen Welsh Dulles

Field-Marshal Rommel was suspected of being in sympathy with the plotters, and in spite of his reputation, he was not to escape.

The Death of Rommel

Manfred Rommel, the Field-Marshal's son, begins:

On 7 October a signal arrived in Herrlingen. Field-Marshal Keitel asked my father to go to Berlin for an important conference on 10 October. A special train would fetch him from Ulm. 'I'm not that much of a fool,' my father said when he saw it. 'We know these people now. I'd never get to Berlin alive.' He spoke openly of the matter to Professor Albrecht, the brain specialist at Tübingen University, under whose care he was, whereupon the Professor immediately certified him as unfit to travel. He also tried to persuade my father to go into his clinic, where he would not be so easy to get at. My father said he would keep the offer in mind.

But events moved rapidly. My father's refusal to go to Berlin lengthened his life by only four days.

. . . . When my parents arrived back at Herrlingen again after the long car journey, they found a telephone message awaiting them to the effect that two Generals were coming next day to talk to my father about his 'future employment'.

My battery, to which I had returned several weeks before, had given me leave for 14 October. I left the gun position very early in the morning and arrived at Herrlingen at 7.00 a.m. My father was already at breakfast. A cup was quickly brought for me and we breakfasted together, afterwards taking a stroll in the garden.

'At twelve o'clock to-day two Generals are coming to see me to discuss my future employment,' my father started the conversation. 'So to-day will decide what is planned for me; whether a People's Court or a new command in the East.'

'Would you accept such a command?' I asked.

He took me by the arm, and replied: 'My dear boy, our enemy in the East is so terrible that every other consideration has to give way before it. If he succeeds in overrunning Europe, even only temporarily, it will be the end of everything which has made life appear worth living. Of course I would go.'

Shortly before twelve o'clock, my father went to his room on the first floor and changed from the brown civilian jacket, which he usually wore over riding-breeches, to his Africa tunic, which was his favourite uniform on account of its open collar.

At about twelve o'clock a dark-green car with a Berlin number stopped in front of our garden gate. The only men in the house apart from my father, were Captain Aldinger, a badly wounded war-veteran corporal and myself. Two generals—Burgdorf, a powerful, florid man, and Maisel, small and slender—alighted from the car and entered the house. They were respectful and courteous and asked my father's permission to speak to him alone. Aldinger and I left the room. 'So they are not going to arrest him,' I thought with relief, as I went up-stairs to find myself a book.

A few minutes later I heard my father come upstairs and go into my mother's room.

Frau Rommel takes up the story:

As he entered the room there was so strange and terrible an expression on his face that I exclaimed at once, 'What is the matter with you? What has happened? Are you ill?' He looked at me and replied: 'I have come to say good-bye. In a quarter of an hour I shall be dead. . . . They suspect me of having taken part in the attempt to kill Hitler. It seems my name was on Goerdeler's list to be President of the Reich. . . . I have never seen Goerdeler in my life. . . . They say that von Stülpnagel, General Speidel and Colonel von Hofacker have denounced me. . . . It is the usual trick. . . . I have told them that I do not believe it and that it cannot be true. . . . The Führer has given me the choice of taking poison or being dragged before the People's Court. They have brought the poison. They say it will take only three seconds to act. . . . I would not be afraid to be tried in public, for I can defend everything I have done. But I know that I should never reach Berlin alive.'

Manfred Rommel:

He was standing in the middle of the room, his face pale. 'Come outside with me,' he said in a tight voice. We went into my room. 'I have just had to tell your mother,' he began slowly, 'that I shall be dead in a quarter of an hour.' He was calm as he continued: 'To die by the hand of one's own people is hard. But the house is surrounded and Hitler is charging me with high treason. "In view of my services in Africa",' he quoted sarcastically, 'I am to have the chance of dying by poison. The two generals have brought it with them. It's fatal in three seconds. If I accept, none of the usual steps will be taken against my family, that is against you. They will also leave my staff alone.'

The men who had come to arrest Rommel took no chances.

We observed in the meantime that the house was surrounded by at least four or five armoured cars. The cars were apparently occupied by armed civilians, so that the eight men on duty-watch in the house, who had only two machine-guns, would be powerless. After my father had said good-bye to me and the orderly officer, he left the house, in uniform, wearing a leather cloak and with marshal's baton and cap. We accompanied him to the car where the generals saluted him with the 'Heil Hitler' greeting. We saw an S.S. man at the wheel of the car. My father climbed in first and took a seat in the back, then the two generals followed.

The car went off in the direction of Blaubeuren. Fifteen minutes later we received a call from the Reserve Hospital Wagner-Schule in Ulm to the effect that my father had been brought in by the two generals, apparently having had a brain stroke.

Manfred Rommel

In the Field
16 October 1944

Accept my sincerest sympathy for the heavy loss you have suffered with the death of your husband. The name of Field-Marshal Rommel will be for ever linked with the heroic battles in North Africa.

Adolf Hitler

Führer's Headquarters
26 October 1944

The fact that your husband, Field-Marshal Rommel, has died a hero's death as the result of his wounds, after we had all hoped that he would remain to the German people, has deeply touched me. I send you, my dear Frau Rommel, the heartfelt sympathy of myself and the German Luftwaffe.

In silent compassion, Yours,

Göring, *Reichsmarschall des Grossdeutschen Reiches*

The Funeral

Only a hypercritical observer would have asked why Marshal von Rundstedt stumbled in reading his speech, as though it had been given to him only a few minutes before. Why did he make no attempt to speak to Frau Rommel? Why, on passing Strölin and von Neurath, did he raise his eyes and give them so queer a look? 'He knew or guessed,' said Strölin, 'and hated the part they had made him play.' He must also have disliked his lines. For von Rundstedt was a soldier and a gentleman, with a long-standing contempt for Hitler and the Party. There was a soldier of another sort who also had his doubts. 'What was the matter with that funeral?' asked an S.S. officer of Strölin's acquaintance. 'Somehow I had a feeling that there was something not quite right about it.'

The Question

The next question is: what should have happened? To this I can only reply: a very great deal has been spoken and written about resistance to the Hitler régime. But of those men who are still alive, the speakers and the writers, who had access to Hitler, which of them did, in fact, even once, offer any resistance to his will?

General Guderian

31

NORTH-WEST EUROPE: STALEMATE BEFORE THE RHINE

ADVANCE ON TOO MANY FRONTS

Through the autumn and winter months of 1944, the Germans in their extremity showed their martial ability by an improvised defence which exploited the lack of a single-minded, concentrated offensive on the part of their enemies.

THE dismal and tragic story of events after the successful battle in Normandy may be boiled down to one fundamental criticism. It is this—whatever the decision, it wasn't implemented. In Normandy our strategy for the land battle, and the plan to achieve it, was simple and clear-cut. The pieces were closely 'stitched' together. It was never allowed to become unstitched; and it succeeded. After Normandy our strategy became unstitched. There was no plan; and we moved by disconnected jerks.

The rightness or wrongness of the decision taken is, of course, open to argument. But what cannot be disputed is that when a certain strategy, right or wrong, was decided upon, it wasn't directed. We did not advance to the Rhine on a *broad* front; we advanced to Rhine on *several* fronts, which were unco-ordinated. And what was the German answer? A single and concentrated punch in the Ardennes, when we had become unbalanced and unduly extended. So we were caught on the hop.

Field-Marshal Montgomery

While the British and Canadian forces—2 British Army and 1 Canadian Army —were to be directed at the Low Countries, the American 1 and 3 Armies farther south were also to advance on the Rhine, striking first in the direction of the Meuse Crossings. By 1 September Patton's 3 Army had stormed its way to Verdun on the Meuse. By the 12th, 1 Army had penetrated part of the West Wall (Siegfried Line) south of Aachen, and had been the first Allied troops to set foot on German soil.

It was our plan to attack north-eastward in the greatest strength possible. This direction had been chosen for a variety of reasons. First, the great bulk of the German Army was located there. Secondly, there was the great desirability of capturing the flying-bomb area, not only to remove this menace to England, but also to deny to the enemy the propaganda which he enjoyed on the home front and in the army from the attacks on London and talk of new weapons which would decide the war. A third reason for the north-eastward attack was our imperative need for the large port of Antwerp, absolutely essential to us logistic-ally before any deep penetration in strength could be made into Germany. Fourthly, we wanted the airfields in Belgium. Finally and most important, I felt that during the late summer and early autumn months the Lower Rhine offered the best avenue of advance into Germany, and it seemed probable that through rapidity of exploitation both the Siegfried Line and the Rhine River might be crossed and strong bridgeheads established before the enemy could recover sufficiently to make a definite stand in the Arnhem area.

General Eisenhower

Inscription on a Wall of the Fortress of Verdun

Austin White—Chicago, Ill.—1918
Austin White—Chicago, Ill.—1945

This is the last time I want to write my name here.

Also on 1 September the Canadians re-entered Dieppe, thus settling an old score. After Dieppe, they hammered on up the French coast against an enemy who would not admit final defeat, investing or taking the Channel ports one by one.

Return to Dieppe

The advance from Rouen went so swiftly that I had a frantic time getting to Dieppe on time with the Division. We had expected that it would take several more days to get into the port, and I was still cleaning up the story of the Canadians in Rouen and the advance on Dieppe when the word flashed back from the front that the 'recce' were at Totes and the road to the port was practically clear.

. . . . It may have been the wind that put tears in my eyes as I drove into Dieppe to the crowds and the flowers and the memories, to the acclaim of a town which had lived for the day the Canadians returned.

I went through the throngs on the streets to the central square and stopped near an armoured car of the 8th Recce. In ten seconds Beattie and I were sur-rounded by laughing, extravagantly happy civilians. An old lady tottered up to my scout car with a huge bouquet of flowers. A pretty girl pressed through the crowd and gave us another bouquet she had picked that morning from the gardens of the town. A hundred Dieppe people crushed around the car, wanting to shake our hands, to kiss us and tell us how welcome we were.

. . . . Our scout car was decked with flowers. Even in Rouen we had not collected a floral display like this. I shook hands for half an hour and spluttered, '*Merci, merci, mes amis*' in high-school French which had improved little in the rush across France.

It was the same with everyone who entered Dieppe that day. They were literally mobbed by the crowd, taken off to cafés and to homes to be plied with liberation wine and to be applauded like the victors they were.

. . . . I wandered around the place all day like a man in a dream. First, with a French guide, I went down to the harbour. The enemy had carried out some demolition there and sown some sea mines but had not had time to destroy the installations completely. The Army and Navy were able to get Dieppe operating, as a matter of fact, within a few weeks of its capture.

I walked past the ruined tobacco factory on the Esplanade. The factory had been set on fire during the raid and it was only a skeleton. All the buildings along the front were fortified and my guide and I went through a concrete pillbox out on to the Esplanade where the fiercest fire had raged during the Canadian attack. The Esplanade was covered with thick barbed wire and was mined from one end to the other. The pier jutting out on the west side of the harbour was mined and criss-crossed with wire. The main beach was piled with obstacles and wire and every foot of it was mined. The Casino, which the 'Rileys' had fought for and captured at the western end of the Esplanade, had been demolished to give a clear field of fire for the coast guns in the cliff face of the west headland.

. . . . Major Bult-Francis was down near the Esplanade, too. And it was there that he found the French girl who had bound his wounds in 1942 when he fell near the houses by the beach. She remembered him, and no woman of France was as surprised as she when he walked up to greet her.

All the civilians in the town seemed to have been there two years before. All they would talk about was the raid.

. . . . The mayor pointed out a plot of grass near the church where he, then an air-raid warden, had talked with some of the Canadians during the heat of battle and they had given him cigarettes. 'One of your men was hit right there,' he said. 'He lay on the grass and we could not reach him and he died there. We buried him with the other Canadians up on the hill behind the town.'

The French people of Dieppe had buried the Canadian dead. They took their bodies from the beaches and from the Esplanade and the streets of the town, and made a cemetery for them on the hill behind the town. Over each grave they placed a plain unpainted wooden cross and they gave their record of the names to the Division when it came back.

Ross Munro, Canadian war correspondent

Germans Trapped

7 September, 44. Encircled in Boulogne. For days I knew that there was no getting out of it for us. It is very hard to get used to the thought of having one's span of life nearly finished, and not to see one's wife and children again. If Fate is favourable I may become a prisoner of war. . . .

9 September, 44. Last night was comparatively quiet. Yesterday, late in the afternoon, enemy bombers attacked the forward defensive positions of Boulogne. My God, how long will it be until the town itself will be the target? Can anyone survive after a carpet of bombs has fallen? Sometimes one can despair of everything if one is at the mercy of the R.A.F. without any protection. It seems as if all fighting is useless and all sacrifices in vain. . . .

13 September, 44. Alcohol is the only thing which can comfort anyone in our position. . . . This afternoon more heavy air attacks on the outer defences of Boulogne. Most of the civilians have wandered off with bits of their belongings. What a tragic spectacle. When will tormented humanity have peace again? . . .

15 September, 44. I wonder how my family is? No mail from home now for six weeks. That is the hardest of all to take. . . .

17 September, 44. It is nine months to-day since I last went on leave. What a good time I had. And to-day what a contrast. I was just ready to go to breakfast when we had to run for shelter and we have been there ever since. The bombardment by bombers and artillery was terrific. It is four o'clock in the afternoon now. I am looking at your pictures, my loved ones. I am quiet now and resigned to my fate whatever it may be. Farewell, my dear ones, I pray to God that He may protect and guide you. . . . All afternoon a heavy artillery barrage fell on our positions. We could not move. Then we heard tanks approaching and had to surrender.

A German officer

An orderly retreat became impossible. The Allied motorized armies surrounded the slow and exhausted German foot divisions in separate groups and smashed them up. . . . There were no German ground forces of any importance that could be thrown in, and next to nothing in the air.

General Speidel, Chief of Staff, Army Group B

Antwerp fell on 4 September after a runaway advance, but then, at the end of the first week of the month, the long pursuit came to an end. It had been extended to its limit, and now, on the Belgian-Dutch frontier, met heavier and heavier opposition from reorganized German defences. Both sides brought up reinforcements to fill the gaps caused by the bitter fighting. For the Germans this meant the Landwehr, *and an increasing use of their élite paratroops as infantry.*

Landwehr

To-day I was transferred to the 42nd Machine-gun Fortress Battalion, as a messenger. Destination West Wall. This battalion is composed of Home Guard soldiers, half crippled—I found many among them quite obviously off mentally. Some had their arms amputated, others had one leg short, etc.—a sad sight. 'V-2, V-3' they jokingly call themselves. A bunch of fools.

The diary of a young German soldier

Headquarters,
11 October 1944

Certain events among units have impelled me to point out that discipline and *esprit de corps* among the troops must be raised in the shortest possible time. For this, all formation commanders, in particular company commanders, will be held personally responsible to me.

. . . . It cannot be tolerated that a formation commander should get drunk, then wander about the woods at night shouting and firing his pistol at the sentry.

It shows little discipline in a company when members of the company call each other 'cheats' during a discussion about captured loot.

A unit shows little *esprit de corps* if a soldier can declare that owing to difficulty in walking he can no longer serve with the artillery since he could not escape quickly enough if the Tommy arrived. Such a statement is a basis for defeatism and this case should be dealt with by courts-martial.

It shows lamentable carelessness if one soldier while cleaning his arms injures four comrades by sheer negligence and in such a way that they will be unable to do any duty. Before cleaning weapons, in particular new weapons, sufficient instruction must be given in stripping and assembling so that everyone who may have to use these weapons is fully conversant with their use.

. . . . During the last eight days no less than eleven desertions have been reported, seven of whom went over into enemy lines. . . . Reports about desertions are lamentable and generally arrive too late. In one particular case a soldier deserted his unit on 29 September 1944, and the official report was not made until 10 October 1944.

Major-General Gerhard Franz, G.O.C. 256 Volksgrenadier Division, Holland

10 September 1944

Certain unreliable elements seem to believe that the war will be over for them as soon as they surrender to the enemy.

Against this belief it must be pointed out that every deserter will be prosecuted and will find his just punishment. Furthermore, his ignominious behaviour will entail the most severe consequences for his family. Upon examination of the circumstances they will be summarily shot.

Himmler

German Paratroops

We felt quite a professional affection for these paratroops. They were infantry trained, like us, to use their own initiative. They had the same system of 'trench-mates'. They fought cleanly and treated prisoners, wounded and dead, with the same respect they expected from us. If our uniforms had been the same, we would have welcomed them as kindred spirits.

On one occasion the paratroops acquitted themselves as the honourable gentlemen we later knew them to be. It was the first time many of us had ever seen them. We never forgot them.

We had attacked a wood and been thrown out. The platoon was being 'stonked' in a ditch. Two of our stretcher-bearers went out to collect a casualty hit in the leg by a splinter. As soon as the Medics appeared, small-arms fire stopped as if turned off at the main. Unfortunately the German mortars could not see the target and sent over one more bomb before the 'cease-fire' reached them. That bomb hit one of the stretcher-bearers in the leg. One stretcher-bearer was left in No Man's Land with two casualties and one stretcher.

Immediately two German paras burst out of the woods, holding up their hands to show that they were not armed. They ran to the group in the field. They loaded the two casualties on to the stretcher in sitting positions, and, under the direction of the surviving Medic, they carried the men to safety in our lines. Waving farewell, they doubled back to the wood. We cheered them all the way back. A twelve-hour truce followed. No one had the heart to spoil this gesture by firing. So, temporarily, the war stopped. Next morning they were gone.

R. M. Wingfield

American Reinforcements Embark on the *Queen Elizabeth*

Everything about the scene was sufficiently moving to bring forth sentiments of patriotism or rushes of free verse if ever they were to come. On the brackish cement pier, companies of infantrymen were lined up, facing the grey steel wall of the ship. Naked electricity bulbs cast down a harsh, lonesome light, and shadows made by steel helmets turned even the most commonplace faces dramatic. In the dark harbour boats mooed sadly, a bell tolled. I listened particularly to hear what the men were saying.

'Well, this is it, fellas.' 'Yeah, I guess they got us this time.' 'Jeez, I'm sweatin'.' 'Wish the f—— they'd let you smoke.' 'I hope we don't pull any K.P., that's all I hope, I hope, I hope.' Red Cross women had appeared to give out coffee and doughnuts, and the youngest of them drew wolf calls and appreciative whistles. 'Hey, look at the ass on that one. Ooh, my f——in' back!'

Though the autumn night was mild we were dressed in a new long underwear, new woollen uniforms, sweaters, field-jackets and overcoats. Stonelike full field packs were strapped to our backs; gas masks were slung on; our belts were heavy with ammunition, bayonet, entrenching tool and filled canteen. As our names were called out over an amplifier, we answered, hoisted up the heavy duffle bag, grabbed the rifle and, in single file, began to toil up the long gritty cement staircases. On the first landing, as a boost to morale, a swing band comprised of garrison soldiers was playing *Amapola, my pretty little poppy*. Staggering up the stairs like beasts of burden, the infantrymen cursed them roundly and bitterly. 'Goddam 4-F bastards!' 'Lucky sons of bitches!' 'Hope the f—— they git you too!' The golden instruments glittered and seemed to laugh.

All at once in the dimness I came face to face with a short, steeply inclined gangplank, and as I set my foot on it I heard behind me on the stairs the loud, desperate Texan voice of little illiterate Shorty Witherspoon bawling out in farewell, 'Youah boyas will *nev-ah leave these shores!*'

Lester Atwell

By mid-September the American advance, too, had been extended to its utmost, and was encountering stiffening resistance. Metz and the upper Moselle had been reached by 16 September, but there General Eisenhower ordered a slowing-down, to the irritation of Patton especially. Meanwhile, the American 7 Army and the French 1 Army from the South of France had joined 1 and 3 Armies.

Plus ça change . . . .

On 20 September 1944 General Balck and I arrived at the Headquarters of Army Group G, then situated at Molsheim in Alsace. It was our unpleasant duty to relieve the Army Group Commander, General Blaskowitz, and his Chief of Staff, Lieutenant-General Heinz von Gyldenfeldt. As we drove up to the Headquarters, with the wooded crests of the Vosges rising above, I thought of my last visit to this region—the break-through of the Maginot Line, the fiercely contested advance on Donon, the drive to the Headquarters of the French XLIII Corps, and the formal capitulation of General Lescanne and his staff. Then I had been Ia of a division at the end of a brilliant and victorious campaign, now I was Chief of Staff of an Army Group, which had barely escaped annihilation and was facing as difficult a crisis as could be imagined.

General Blaskowitz was an officer of the old school, with all the staunch virtues associated with his native province of East Prussia. He had just extricated his Army Group from the south of France under extremely difficult conditions, but his offence was that he had quarrelled with Himmler, first in Poland and recently in Alsace.

. . . . Before taking over command Balck had reported to Hitler, and was treated to a long harangue on the military situation. According to the Führer the Anglo-American advance was bound to come to a stop on a line running from the mouth of the Scheldt along the West Wall to Metz, and from there to the Vosges. Supply difficulties would force the enemy to halt, and Hitler declared that he would take advantage of this pause to launch a counter-offensive in Belgium. He mentioned the middle of November as a likely date for this opera- tion—in fact it was delayed about four weeks—and then went on to discuss the affairs of Army Group G. In a voice ringing with indignation Hitler severely criticized the way in which Blaskowitz had commanded his forces, and re- proached him with timidity and lack of offensive spirit. In fact, he seems to have thought that Blaskowitz could have taken Patton's 3 Army in flank and flung it back on Rheims. (The absurdity of this criticism soon became clear to us.) Finally Hitler announced his formal orders: Balck was to hold Alsace-Lorraine in all circumstances—the political situation demanded that the old Reichs provinces should be retained—he was to fight for time, and on no account must he allow a situation to develop in which forces earmarked for the Ardennes offensive would have to be sidetracked to Army Group G.

. . . . Those of us who had come from the Russian front, where the German formations were still in tolerable fighting order, were shocked at the condition of our Western armies. The losses in material had been colossal; for example, 19 Army had possessed 1,480 guns, and lost 1,316 in the withdrawal from southern France. The troops under our command provided an extraordinary miscellany— we had Luftwaffe personnel, police, old men and boys, special battalions com- posed of men with stomach troubles or men with ear ailments. Even well- equipped units from Germany had received virtually no training and came straight from the parade-ground to the battlefield. Some Panzer brigades had never even done any squadron training, which explains our enormous losses in tanks.

. . . . In our training we concentrated on night fighting, for it was obvious that attacks in daylight were futile in view of the overwhelming American air superiority. Our plans were based on the principle of elastic defence, whose value had been fully proved in the great battles in Russia. Troops packed into forward positions were doomed to destruction by artillery and air bombardment, so we issued instructions that when an attack appeared imminent the forward troops were to withdraw to a line some miles in rear. Only patrols were to remain in the forward area. In this way the enemy might be induced to 'off-load' his destructive fire on empty trenches, and our troops could be conserved for the main battle.

General von Mellenthin

Patton Checked

Since our progress from now on had to be along the lines of what General Allen calls the 'rock soup' method, I will describe it. A tramp once went to a house and asked for some boiling water to make rock soup. The lady was interested and gave him the water, in which he placed two polished white stones. He then asked if he might have some potatoes and carrots to put in the soup to flavour it a little, and finally ended up with some meat. In other words, in order to attack, we had first to pretend to reconnoitre, then reinforce the reconnaissance, and finally put on an attack—all depending on what fuel and ammunition we could secure.

There was a rumour, which officially, I hoped was not true, that some of our Ordnance people passed themselves off as members of 1 Army and secured quite a bit of fuel from one of the dumps of that unit. To reverse the statement made about the Light Brigade, this is not war but is magnificent.

.... On the 20th,* at Bradley's Headquarters I saw a map study which completely confirmed the line of advance which Bradley and I had favoured since the beginning, namely, to drive through with two corps abreast and the third one echeloned to the right rear on the general axis, Nancy—Château Salins—Saarguemines—Mainz or Worms, then north-east through Frankfurt. It was evident that 3 Army should have an increase of at least two infantry divisions and retain four armoured divisions. I was convinced then, and have since discovered I was right, that there were no Germans ahead of us except those we were actually fighting. In other words, they had no depth. It was on this day that I definitely decided not to waste time capturing Metz, but to contain it with as few troops as possible and drive for the Rhine.

On the 21st, things picked up so far as fighting was concerned, but one of my staff, who had been with General Devers' Sixth Army Group, had heard Devers remark that he was going to take a lot of troops from 3 Army, so I flew to Paris to argue against it with General Eisenhower. Events proved my trip useless, but at the time I thought I had done something.

.... The 23rd was one of the bad days of my military career. Bradley called me to say that higher authority had decided that I would have to give up 6 Armoured and also assume a defensive attitude, owing to lack of supplies. General Devers had told General Eisenhower that he could supply XV Corps via Dijon by 1 October, and therefore demanded it. Both Bradley and I felt that he would eventually get it, which he did. When I told my sorrows to General Gay, he said, 'What price glory?' meaning that after the Moroccan victory, the Tunisian victory, the Sicilian victory, and finally now in France, we had always been whittled down. However, I had the optimism to remember that all through my life, every time I had been bitterly disappointed, it worked for the best. It did in this case, although at the time I didn't know it.

General Patton

* September (Ed.)

ARNHEM

However, General Eisenhower still had hopes of crossing the Rhine at the northern end of the front. Montgomery planned to seize the Rhine crossing at Arnhem with 1 British Airborne Division, while two American airborne divisions captured the crossings of the Waal and Maas at Nijmegen and Grave, and held the road between Eindhoven and Grave. All these were vital points on the road to Arnhem, along which part of the British 2 Army was to make a dash, linking up with the airborne troops and thus driving a long salient forward to the Rhine. Operation 'Market Garden', launched on 17 September 1944, was to be the biggest airborne operation in history.

The whole operation as I have said already was given the code name of 'Market Garden'. It was certainly a bold plan. Indeed, General Bradley has described it as 'one of the most imaginative of the war'. But the moment he heard about it he tried to get it cancelled, lest it should open up possibilities on the northern flank and I might then ask for American troops to be placed under my command to exploit them. He was an advocate of the double thrust—the Saar *and* the Ruhr. So was Patton. Whenever Eisenhower appeared to favour the Ruhr thrust, Patton used to say he was the best general the British had.

Field-Marshal Montgomery

Eindhoven and Nijmegen: Americans in the Air

I flew in a borrowed B-17 that hovered some two hundred feet above the transport planes below, and I remember thinking how big a target we must make up there, and how slow we were flying. Over Holland, in the clear light of that sunny Sunday, the flak began to come up heavily, and planes began to go down. My pilot was also well aware of the hazards of our situation. One of those brave, light-hearted men who, like Ulysses' mariners, 'ever with a frolic welcome take the thunder and the sunshine', I could hear him talking to his crew over the inter-com.

'Boy, did you ever see anything like that?' he was saying. 'I never saw the stuff coming up like this before. I'm going to tell my grandchildren about this.'

His uneasiness was understandable, for he was used to flying upstairs, at twenty thousand feet or so, and this slow, wobbly flight eight hundred feet above the ground was new to him. I remember hoping fervently that he did survive to tell his grandchildren about that ride.

The drop was beautiful, the best we'd ever done. Despite the fact that planes were being lost to A.A. fire, those magnificent pilots of the 52nd Troop Carrier held formation perfectly, and hit their drop zones on the nose. As we circled wide, watching the skies fill with thousands of coloured chutes, we could look down into the streets of the little villages. The people were all out in their Sunday best, looking up, as the great sky train, five hundred miles long, went past. The little houses were all intact, and I felt a great pang of regret, knowing that these fine Hollanders were all unaware of the tragedy that was soon to strike.

Up to this time the German occupation had brought little of war's devastation to that peaceful countryside, but I knew the German reaction would be quick and violent.

General Ridgway

On the Ground

17 September was a Sunday and a beautiful late summer's day. My headquarters had been established for some days in a cottage at Vught, south of S'Hertogenbosch. The front line was quiet. Just before noon, hostile air activity became considerable. From the cottage I noted numerous formations of fighter-bombers and heard the noise of dropping bombs and A.A. guns. About noon I was disturbed at my desk and went on to the balcony. Wherever I looked I could see aircraft; troop transports and large aircraft towing gliders. They flew both in formation and singly. It was an immense stream which passed quite low over the house. I was greatly impressed by the spectacle, and I must confess that during these minutes the danger of the situation never occurred to me. I merely recalled with some regret my own earlier airborne operations, and when my Chief of Staff joined me on the balcony I could only remark: 'I wish I had had such powerful means at my disposal!'

A few hours later the complete hostile operations orders were on my desk. They had been captured in a glider which was shot down near Vught. The importance of this capture was immense, for we learned at once of the enemy's strength and intentions, and the speed and comparative success of our counter-action was to no small extent due to our early knowledge of the hostile moves.

General Kurt Student, C.-in-C. German paratroop forces

Arnhem: the Landing

It is hard physical labour flying a glider in the slipstream of another aircraft, but our tug pilot was very skilful in avoiding the hundreds of other planes making for Holland. He had to fly completely out of formation and at the wrong altitude to achieve that, but we encouraged him and praised him all the way.

. . . . Soon I recognized the Lower Rhine, and a moment later could see our L.Z.—two small squares of wooded land pieced together at one corner only. Our landing was to be just where the woods joined together. It looked exactly like the photographs they had shown us at the briefing. I never imagined they could possibly look so much alike.

This was the moment to cast off:

'Hello Tug. . . . We are getting ready to cast off now. . . . Thanks for the wizard ride.'

'Best of luck, Matchbox. . . . See you soon.'

'O.K. Tug. . . . Same to you.'

Mac pulls the lever which releases the cables from our wings and we are in free flight. The tug banks off to the right as Mac pulls up our nose to gain height and reduce our flying speed. As we settle to our normal gliding speed, all the noise dies away and it seems unbelievably peaceful and calm in our cockpit. We can't think of it as other than one of our many mass landing exercises. We are now slowly losing height, and as we cross the river we can clearly see the bridge at Arnhem which is our ultimate objective.

Louis Hagen, glider pilot

Our arrival was deceptively peaceful. As Iain Murray started his landing glide, I gazed over his shoulder at the ordered, brown and green landscape below, where already many gliders now lay. Others, as they touched down, kicked up clouds of dust from the dry, sandy earth. I could see the troops hastily assembling their jeeps and guns and making for cover; here and there was a Dutch family on the way home from church.

Not a shot was being fired.

I liked the look of this landing zone—flat, spacious and sheltered by the screens of pine woods. A few gliders had somersaulted, and I noticed that one Horsa had careered into the pines fringing the patchwork of potato and turnip fields and heather moor.

. . . . As we descended, a Horsa ahead to our left landed awkwardly, stirring dust, and pitched over on its nose. A Hamilcar somersaulted; another slewed as it touched down, straightened, appeared to be going over and then righted itself. I saw one glider finish up among the trees, its wings snapped like twigs. We were about half a mile from the landing zone when the tug shook us off; I was fascinated watching the rope falling away from the nose of the glider and still attached to the tug aircraft.

Now we could see the smoke signals and yellow markers laid out by Boy Wilson's men, whose earlier appearance had provoked hardly any opposition. It was just like an exercise in Hampshire. So confident was the Independent Company about the outcome that they had taken quantities of metal and boot polish for the liberation celebrations and the victorious entry into Germany. Wilson had packed his best battledress and highly-polished brown shoes into his parachutist's leg-bag which also contained one bottle each of whisky, gin and sherry for the entertainment of Dutch Resistance leaders.

General Urquhart, G.O.C. 1 Airborne Division

Reception Committee

It was early on the Sunday afternoon of 17 September. The cinemas in the small Dutch towns were slowly filling up, and the streets and highways, along the canals and small streams, were crowded with young people on bicycles. And then out of the blue sky roared several hundred enemy fighter-bombers. Their aim was to attack the German defensive positions and locate the flak positions. Barely had they disappeared beyond the horizon when, coming from the west across the flooded coastal areas, appeared the planes and gliders carrying regiments and brigades of the enemy's airborne army. . . . The first parachute landings were made on a front of about seventy kilometres and approximately a hundred kilometres behind our lines. The troops bailed out from a very low altitude, sometimes as low as sixty metres. Immediately after that the several hundred gliders started to land. In those first few minutes it looked as if the downcoming masses would suffocate every single life on the ground.

.... Shortly after the landings of the British and American divisions, our reconnaissance troops went into action. By searching the countless forests and large parks in that area, cut by numerous small streams, they had to ascertain where the enemy intended to concentrate his forces; only then could a basis for our counter-attacks be established. The telephone lines were cut. The reconnaissance cars could move forward only slowly. Some of the enemy dug themselves in near their landing places and brought weapons into position. Others moved up to the houses and barricaded themselves, using the furniture inside the buildings. From there they tried to dominate the bridges and beat back our counter-attacks. Elements of the Dutch population assisted the enemy in their task.

Erwin Kirchof, German war correspondent

Eindhoven: the Ground Troops Follow Up

We slowed to a stop and the wireless crackled. The tank commander stuck his head out.

'Royal Tiger tanks a mile ahead. Get under cover. Tiffies have been called.'

His calm words were immediately drowned by the scream of aircraft engines as our Typhoon fighter 'cab-rank' peeled off from their constant circling above our heads. They skimmed overhead, steadied themselves by the huge bulk of the Philips works and let fly with their rockets. They banked and let fly again. The projectiles, like foreshortened lamp-posts with plumes of smoke bursting from the back, vanished behind the works. Seconds later came a dull explosion and a dirty plume of black smoke jetted up. A black object sailed lazily upwards and disappeared into the smoke. It was a tank turret, complete with gun.

Our tank commander swallowed hard. We moved on.

R. M. Wingfield

Hospitality

We parked our Churchills on either side of a wide road on the outskirts of the town.* The houses bordering the road were neat and well-kept, but not unduly pretentious.

Ian and Jim went off to find billets in the town, but before leaving they said it might be a good idea to erect the bivouacs just in case they didn't have any luck.

At first sight there wouldn't appear much that anyone can say in favour of sleeping on pavements; but if you think about it a bit it's a considerable improvement on a wet, shell-torn field. So 5 Troop were quite cheerfully putting up the bivouacs and swapping good-humoured badinage with the Dutch children. And then I felt a nervous touch on my arm. I looked around and saw a large, homely, blue-eyed housewife. She was middle-aged, comfortably plump and looked for all the world like an advertisement for somebody's starch, complete with sparkling white apron.

She pointed a stubby finger at the crew, wrestling with the main sheet.

* Eindhoven (Ed.)

'Vot is dey doink?' she said.

'For sleeping,' I smiled. '*Schlaffen!*' And I placed my hands together against my cheeks in the traditional international sign for slumber.

For a minute I thought she had interpreted it as an improper suggestion. She backed away with eyes ablaze, her complexion growing pinker every minute.

'Here?' she cried. 'On der floor?'

I nodded pleasantly. That did it! She flew away in a cloud of petticoats and high-pitched Dutch, hammering on every door and jabbering madly to the householders. Doors were flung open and a host of men and women surged out on to the road, swarming in amongst the tank crews and gesticulating fiercely towards their houses.

By the time Ian and Jim returned with the news that they had found a cinema in which we could sleep for the night, every man had a bed in one of the nearby houses—complete with clean sheets and pillowcases. I daren't think how many of the good folk of Eindhoven spent that night in armchairs or on sofas, but every man in the regiment was accommodated like a king.

I found myself in the house of the motherly soul who had organized the accommodation. The bed looked inviting and the sheets smelled of lavender. But before I was allowed to go to bed she asked me if I would like a cup of tea.

I stood in the middle of the spotlessly clean living-room wondering if I ought to be polite and say no thank you. The chances were they were short of tea, but the kettle was singing on a trivet and a tray was laid with cups of egg-shell china and little plates of cakes. It had so obviously been prepared long in advance that it would have been churlish to refuse. So I lowered my haversack to the floor smiled in what I hoped was a winning manner and looked around for the least clean chair in which I could park my grubby self.

It wasn't bad tea, at that. A bit weak, perhaps, but then I'd been used to Army tea, which is likened to a most obnoxious fluid if it doesn't stain the cup brown. And as we sat and sipped our tea more and more people crowded into the room. The rose-spattered tea-pot seemed to become the ceremonial centre of the evening; conversation stopped abruptly every time my hostess reached out for the tea-pot. But we talked about the war, and I told them about the raids on London and other places, and in this way the evening passed until I felt I had justified the production of the best china and I began to make a move towards bed.

It was not until the next morning that things were explained to me. We were stowing our gear on the tanks and talking about the excellence of our several bedrooms the previous night, when a young, dark-haired man stopped beside *Avenger* and smiled at me. I remembered seeing him at the tea-drinking cere-mony the previous night and, in fact, had addressed most of my remarks through him, for he spoke very fluent English.

'Good morning,' he said cheerfully. 'Did you enjoy your tea last night?'

'Yes, indeed,' I said. 'Very nice tea.'

He nodded and turned to walk away; then he hesitated and came back to me.

'The housewife bought that tea five years ago,' he said quietly. 'It was the last in Eindhoven. And she swore she would keep it for when the English came, because the English so love tea. Goodbye!'

He waved his hand quickly and strode away. I thought how near I had come to saying 'No, thank you', and mopped my brow in relief.

But before we rolled out of Eindhoven we broke several different kinds of regulations by thrusting upon the reluctant housewife several tins of best bully beef.

'It's pretty rough,' commented McGinty. 'But it's not so rough as all that. So what's she crying for, sir?'

John Foley

Arnhem: the End of the First Day

Not far down the road, unknown to us, the troops of Reserve Battalion 16 who had been stationed in Oosterbeek and who had done more than any other Germans to delay us, were just being joined by the battle group 'Spindler' from 9 S.S. Panzer Division. This must have been encouraging for the redoubtable commander of Battalion 16, *Sturmbannführer* Sepp Krafft: his defence of the Worfhezen–Oosterbeek area had been costly. Earlier, he had said, 'The only way to draw the teeth of an airborne landing with an inferior force is to drive right into it.' This he had virtually done. One company had moved into the attack while the rest of the battalion had formed a defence line. Krafft had collected every tank and self-propelled gun he could get.

General Urquhart

Second Day

.... The local people, who offered us great encouragement and later practical help, came into the streets bearing fruit and drinks for the rear companies of passing soldiers. Orange-coloured armbands and favours were in evidence and had obviously been carefully set aside for just such an occasion as this. Even the children were out in force, marching imitatively alongside the paratroopers, thrilled by the pats of the head and the bars of milk chocolate. In some cases, housewives came out with pots of steaming *ersatz* coffee: it was a most precious commodity at this time in Holland.

All this was very impressive and moving, but I was conscious of the precious seconds it was costing in view of the need for a rapid follow-through to the Bridge and for the securing of established positions by the time Shan Hackett's 4 Parachute Brigade were dropped later in the morning.

General Urquhart

Third Day

And now, in this fateful afternoon of Tuesday 19 September, everything began to go awry. The Airlanding Brigade, to the west and north-west, was under severe attack; there were all the distant signs that Hackett was in some difficulty to the north, and in the town casualties mounted among the units making separate bids to break through. From every side we could hear the sounds of battle. The imagination of some of the troops not yet engaged was working overtime. Rumours spread—wild, fantastic rumours with no basis in fact. There were small parties of hurrying soldiers, obviously uncontrolled, and then twenty or more, under a young officer, dashed across the lawn in front of the Hartenstein shouting, 'The Germans are coming!' With Mackenzie, I moved to intercept them. They were young soldiers whose self-control had momentarily deserted them. I shouted at them, and I had to intervene physically. It is unpleasant to have to restrain soldiers by force and threats, as now we had to do. We ordered them back into the positions they had deserted, and I had a special word with the tall young officer who in his panic had set such a disgraceful example.

. . . . One of the medical officers, Jimmy Logan, advised Father Egan, the padre with the party, that one young soldier had only a quarter of an hour to live. As Egan knelt by the youngster's side with words of comfort, he reckoned that the soldier could not be more than twenty years old.

'If you'll bring a couple of stretcher-bearers along, Padre,' the young man said quietly, 'I can handle a rifle. Just let them put me in position.'

Already in this battle, Egan had seen much gallantry. 'I'm sorry,' he said disarmingly, 'but the stretcher-bearers are too busy just now.'

Presently the soldier was placated, but remarked: 'I only hope the others don't think I'm letting them down.'

Egan stayed with him until he died.

During another bombardment, Egan found himself sharing a house with a number of soldiers, one of whom remarked unoriginally: 'Well, Padre, they've thrown everything but the kitchen stove.' A moment later the room was showered with laths and plaster as the ceiling came down—with, incredibly, a cooker. As the dust was settling, and the last bits of masonry collapsed, the soldier surveyed his colleagues, who were picking themselves up, and then the wreckage, and said, 'I knew the bastards were close, but I didn't think they could hear us talking.'

. . . . We set out on foot just as another mortar 'hate' was working up. Casualties had been mounting fast, and the hotel which was being used as a dressing-station now had several annexes among the neighbouring houses. Even so, the place was choc-a-bloc with wounded, some too badly hurt for conversation, others eager for encouraging news as I approached. I stopped by one man with a reddening head bandage and an arm in a sling. I asked him where he had run into trouble. 'In the town,' he said ruefully. 'One of those bloody S.P.s, sir. How's 2 Army getting on?'

Everyone in the ward who was conscious knew as well as I did that we were almost beyond the accepted time limit for an airborne division to survive without reinforcement. Standing so that all could hear, I said: 'We haven't much in the way of news, but I'm sure it's only a question of a very short time before we link up.' Walking among these wounded men, I sensed their irritation at having been put out of the battle so early. As I left, they were wishing *me* good luck and the orderlies were removing a corpse.

General Urquhart

One got skilled in avoiding being hit, and as time went on our casualties became fewer, though we were desperately tired and thought less about personal danger. But we had acquired a kind of sixth sense and somehow did the right things automatically. In moments of half dozing, while manning my attic position, I felt terribly pleased and grateful for this newly discovered ability. No one can know or can influence his reactions to great personal danger beforehand. And this feeling of pride and pleasure compensated a little for the hatefulness of the whole bloody business. I hate war, I can't stop thinking of the friends and relatives of anyone who has been hit. I know the Germans. I have seen them do the more vile and frightful things. I know that they have destroyed millions of Jews and political opponents. But I do not enjoy killing or wounding anyone. Once I'm forced to fight, however, the whole affair becomes a matter of skill and a job that needs all my powers of concentration. I no longer consider the effect it has on my opponent.

Louis Hagen

Supplies Go Astray

. . . . Another fleet of supply planes came over to drop urgently needed ammo and food. The cold-blooded pluck and heroism of the pilots was quite incredible. They came in in their lumbering four-engined machines at fifteen hundred feet searching for our position. The ack-ack was such as I have only heard during the worst raids on London, but concentrated on one small area. The German gunners were firing at point-blank range, and the supply planes were more or less sitting targets. The rattle of the machine-guns from the scores of planes, the heavy ack-ack batteries all round us, the sky filled with flashes and puffs of exploding shells, burning planes diving towards the ground, and hundreds and hundreds of red, white, yellow and blue supply parachutes dropping all in this very small area, looked more like an overcrowded and crazy illustration to a child's book. This was war on such a concentrated scale that it made you feel terribly small, frightened and insignificant: something like an ant menaced by a steam roller. All activity on the ground seemed to be suspended and forgotten on both sides. One could do nothing but stare awe-inspired at the inferno above.

Louis Hagen

There were even more setbacks to come this day. Our signals requesting changed dropping points for supplies were not received, so now we were forced to witness the first act of the re-supply tragedy of Arnhem as the R.A.F. crews flew through violent and intense flak in order to drop their loads accurately—on dropping points which we no longer held. On the ground, the troops tried by every means possible to attract the attention of these gallant crews: they waved, they paid out parachute material, they lit beacons.

General Urquhart

Fourth Day

In the hotel we now moved the operations room into the cellars. It was a tight squeeze. Down the aisle running through the main wine cellar, an arched dungeon from which coal was moved to make room for us, we had the ops table laid out with maps. A duty officer sat close up against it in order to make room for others to move between his chair and a roof support. My place was in the right-hand corner of the cellar between one of the blocked-up ground-level window grilles and a wine rack. Next to me was an officer of the Phantom Reconnaissance Unit, who had a direct wireless link to the War Office; then the chief clerk. On the far side of the cellar in a four-feet-deep recess leading to the other grille, which overlooked the gravel path outside, were several strangers, including two R.A.F. officers who had been shot down during the re-supply operations.

By now, the over-populated hotel and its grounds were taking on the more objectionable aspects of such confined fighting. Everyone had been living and sleeping in the same clothes since we landed, and as the Germans had long since cut off our water supplies, the lack of washing facilities meant a good deal of body odour. There were only two lavatories in the hotel, both of which were blocked. As they could not be flushed either, we were forced to use the grounds where proper latrines were out of the question. It was more than slightly disturbing to be caught in the open on such occasions by the odd shell and mortar bomb.

General Urquhart

The life we had led at Arnhem was nearer to an animal existence than anything we could have conceived, and yet the more savage the fighting got, the more civilized the men seemed to become. By civilized, I don't mean having baths and being clean and shaving and eating with a knife and fork, but the relations between man and man. They became increasingly polite and helpful. There was such gentleness and friendship among them as would have made any of them almost uncomfortable back on the station. Although they were fighting like tigers, and in that fight had to be completely ruthless, there was no tough behaviour or coarseness of speech. It was almost uncanny. The familiar Army swear words and idiom were absent from their conversation, probably for the first time since any of them joined the service. They were courteous, kind and considerate, without any self-consciousness. I remembered the awful moment when I had had to admit that it was I who had thrown those grenades into the next house. Ten days before, if I had trodden on the toe of one of those men, a stream of filthy abuse would have been hurled at me. Now, all they did was to point out gently and with no recriminations, that I wasn't very clever. I remembered Cooper being shot by the Pole, and the quiet way he and the others took it and even felt sorry for the weeping soldier who had wounded him.

Louis Hagen

Casualties

. . . . In order to fulfil Bittrich's order to re-take the Bridge, the Germans suffered many casualties: it had been an expensive business for them. There was hardly a building in the Bridge area that had not been badly hit or burnt. It was a scene of devastation. And now the Germans, who were using phosphorus shells, set the big building on fire. It was in danger of collapse. The two doctors, Logan and Wright, informed Gough that he had the option of surrendering the wounded or having them burned alive in the cellars. There was no question of choice. Two of the medical personnel presently walked out with a Red Cross flag and arranged for the removal of the wounded. This was agreed, and both sides held their fire as the Germans began to collect the wounded men. The paratroopers still in action moved back while the removal progressed. Then Gough and his companions saw that the Germans were coming right into their positions and moving towards the jeeps that were still intact. Gough ordered that they were not to come any closer. 'We cannot remove your wounded unless we use your jeeps,' came the German reply.

Gough had no counter to this ultimatum.

The work went on.

When the wounded were out of the way, the shooting started again.

. . . . Soon the wounded lay all over the ground floor of the house, some on stretchers, others on the ground, and the medical bombardier had then been led upstairs by Mrs. Ter Horst, who indicated that he should help her take the mattresses and blankets off her beds for the wounded. He refused. 'We don't want to spoil your fine things,' he said.

Whereupon she insisted and threw open the doors of the linen cupboard. The bedclothes were stacked ready for use, but later the bombardier showed Mrs. Ter Horst a bale of blankets which had come in with the re-supply aircraft. Mrs. Ter Horst was moved by the determination of these airborne soldiers not to inconvenience her more than was absolutely necessary. They even refused to accept the food she offered them. Once during a lull in the mortaring she had gone outside and noticed a soldier lying between two jeeps. Anxiously, she touched his forehead. His eyes opened. 'I'm all right,' he assured her. 'I'd just gone off to sleep.'

And as the mortaring increased and the house shook under the blast, the tall slim Dutchwoman with the blonde hair and the calm ice-blue eyes was torn between her family of youngsters in the cellar and the badly hurt soldiers above. Somehow, she found the strength and will to satisfy both loyalties: she consoled the children in the cellar, putting them to sleep with a fairy tale, and then she climbed the stairs to inspire and help the wounded.

General Urquhart

Rations

In the cellar of the Hartenstein, the sergeant-major was going round with a mess tin. He had appointed himself guardian of the rations for the duration and was making absolutely sure that there was a fair and equal distribution of whatever was going. When he reached me, he said, 'Two this time, sir.'

I collected my ration of two boiled sweets.

General Urquhart

Signal: 24 September

Must warn you unless physical contact is made with us early 25 September consider it unlikely we can hold out long enough. All ranks now exhausted. Lack of rations, water, ammunition, and weapons with high officer casualty rate. . . .

Even slight enemy offensive action may cause complete disintegration. If this happens all will be ordered to break towards bridgehead if anything rather than surrender. Any movement at present in face of enemy is not possible. Have attempted our best and will do so as long as possible.

General Urquhart to H.Q. 21 Army Group

Withdrawal: 25 September

Next to appear was Warrack. He gave me the latest casualty situation and told me of his experiences over on the German side. I had already decided that all doctors would stay behind to look after the wounded. The withdrawal would certainly involve more casualties and a senior officer would be required to organize their collection after the rest had gone.

'I have some important news, Graeme,' I said. 'To-night we're pulling out. You know what that will mean. You will be needed here with the wounded. I expect all the doctors to remain.'

No man with his mind and legs in good repair can possibly look with equanimity upon capture, but Warrack covered up whatever feelings he experienced at this moment. I had rarely seen this massive, good-natured officer without a smile on his face. He even raised one now.

'What time do you propose to go?' he asked.

I told him we would start crossing at 10 p.m.

'I'll try to see you again before then,' he said, and left to begin his own preparations.

. . . . From the Hartenstein Lieutenant Hardy, one of our signals officers, released the last of the carrier pigeons we had brought. One of these birds presently reached VIII Corps carrying Hardy's message:

'Have to release birds owing to shortage of food and water. About eight tanks lying about in sub-unit areas, very untidy but not otherwise causing us any trouble. Now using as many German weapons as we have British. M.G.s most effective when aiming towards Germany. Dutch people grand but Dutch tobacco rather stringy. Great beard-growing competition on in our unit, but no time to check up on the winner.'

The time for our going from the Hartenstein was close. The padre bade us Godspeed. We burned all our papers. In my pack I found a forgotten bottle of whisky. I handed it round; everyone in the party, I think, had a nip. The sergeant-major, still careful about equal shares, distributed benzedrine pills. I put mine in a pocket intending to take them, but forgot. Finally, I went among the wounded lying in the cellars in their bloody bandages and crude splints and said good-bye to those who were aware of what was happening. Others, morphia-injected, were mercifully out of it. I wished them well, and one worn-out soldier, propping himself against the cellar wall, murmured, 'I hope you make it, sir.'

. . . . The night was made for clandestine exits. It was very dark with an inky sky and there was a strong wind and persistent heavy rain. In their muddy ditches and foxholes and slit trenches, saturated men found themselves glad of the rain which would deaden the noise and help our chances. They ticked off the minutes until it was their time to move.

From miles away across the river, the guns of XXX Corps opened up. Someone came into the Hartenstein cellar and said, 'It seems to be going all right.' We blackened our faces with ashes and mud and muffled our boots and any equipment, such as bayonets, which might rattle. Hancock produced some curtain material and helped me to wrap it round my boots.

In the Hartenstein, the padre entered the congested cellar from which we would soon depart. Like all the other padres and doctors he was staying behind. We knelt in silent disarray where we had been standing as he said a prayer.

General Urquhart

At two minutes past ten we clambered out of our slit trenches in an absolute din of bombardment—a great deal of it our own—and formed up in a single line. Our boots were wrapped in blanket so that no noise would be made. We held the tail of the coat of the man in front. We set off like a file of nebulous ghosts from our pock-marked and tree-strewn piece of ground. Obviously, since the enemy was all round us, we had to go through him to get to the River Rhine. After about two hundred yards of silent trekking we knew we were among the enemy. It was difficult not to throw yourself flat when machine-gun tracers skimmed your head or the scream of a shell or mortar bomb sounded very close—but the orders were to 'keep going'. Anybody hit was to be picked up by the man behind him. Major Oliver had reconnoitred the route earlier on with a headquarters officer and had it memorized.

The back of my neck was prickling for that whole interminable march. I couldn't see the man ahead of me—all I knew was that I had hold of a coat-tail and for the first time in my life was grateful for the downpour of rain that made a patter on the leaves of the trees and covered up any little noises we were making. At every turn of the way there was posted a sergeant glider pilot who stepped out like a shadow and then stepped back into a deeper shadow again. Several times we halted—which meant you bumped into the man ahead of you—then, when the head of our party was satisfied the turning was clear, we went on again. Once we halted because of a boy sitting on the ground with a bullet through his leg. We wanted to pick him up but he whispered, 'Nark it; gimme another field-dressing and I'll be all right; I can walk.'

As we came out of the trees—we had been following carefully-thought-out footpaths so far—I felt as naked as if I were in Piccadilly Circus in my pyjamas, because of the glow from fires across the river. The machine-gun and general bombardment had never let up. We lay down flat in the mud and rain and stayed that way for two hours till the sentry beyond the hedge on the bank of the river told us to move up over the dyke and be taken across. Mortaring started now and I was fearful for those who were already over on the bank. I guessed it was pretty bad for them. After what seemed a nightmare of an age we got our turn and slithered up and over on to some mud-flats. There was the shadow of a little assault-craft with an outboard motor on it. Several of these had been rushed up by a field company of engineers. One or two of them were out of action already. I waded out into the Rhine up to my hips—it didn't matter; I was soaked through long ago, had been for days. A voice that was sheer music spoke from the stern of the boat, saying: 'Ye'll have to step lively boys, it ain't healthy here.' It was a

Canadian voice, and the engineers were Canadian engineers. We helped push the boat off into the swift Rhine current and with our heads down between our knees waited for the bump on the far side—or for what might come before. It didn't come. We clambered out and followed what had been a white tape up through the mud for four miles and a half—me thinking: 'Gosh! I'm alive, how did it happen?'

In a barn there was a blessed hot mug of tea with hot rum in it and a blanket over our shoulders. Then we walked again—all night. After daylight we got to a dressing-station near Nijmegen. Then we were put in trucks and that's how we reached Nijmegen. That's how the last of the few got out to go and fight in some future battle. No matter what battle that is, I know they won't let you down.

Stanley Maxted, B.B.C. war correspondent

Three-quarters of 1 Airborne Division had been lost through 2 Army's failure to reach them in time, but despite desperate German attempts to wipe it out, the narrow salient had attained if not crossed the Rhine, and there it stayed. To the south-east 2 Army now faced towards Germany on the line of the Maas. The Germans, fearing another assault towards the Rhine from this area, defended the Maas with determination through the early winter months.

Venraij; in the Peel

.... There were far more mines here than anywhere else that we were called upon to go during the campaign. Bisecting the battle area from north to south was the main road from Overloon to Venraij; crossing the area at right angles to the road was a deep dyke called the Molenbeek, and at the point where the road crossed the dyke the bridge was blown. On the right flank thick woods, the Laag Heide, which 8 Rifle Brigade had turned on the previous day, ran out like a finger in the direction of Venraij, and formed an obvious springboard for forward movement (a fact of which the enemy showed himself by no means unaware). The whole area was overlooked by the church tower of Venraij, which was still standing in spite of the battering it had received.

It was a bloody day's fighting. The infantry, making a silent crossing in the early morning, was forced to advance straight across the open fields. The armour's efforts were completely abortive. The Churchills sent down to the Molenbeek to fill the dyke with rolls of faggots either bogged down before they reached their destination, were shot up, or found their task impossible when they got there. The tanks thereupon pushed round into the woods on to the right where they were shelled and mortared for hours on end, while a recce party went forward on foot in the hope of finding some way over the obstacle. Everywhere the fair green turf was a delusion, for as soon as anything heavier than a man attempted to traverse it, it gave way. Men were caught in the fiercest concentrations, directed from Venraij church tower, as they tried to get on. The 2nd Lincolns, for example, lost seventy killed in one small field when they were observed. To make the scene more horrible, the Churchills working down to the dyke to attempt bridging operations were forced by the narrowness of the track to drive over the bodies of their fallen comrades.

British tank officer

WALCHEREN

Whatever plans were made, Antwerp was badly needed as a port, and it could not be used until the islands and coastline covering the waterways leading to it were reduced. 1 Canadian Army and British Commandos were given the difficult, bloody job of taking the island of Walcheren, the main fortress blockading Antwerp. On 31 October the attack began.

The Canadian Attack

With the south shore already virtually clear, there remained one great obstacle to our use of the port of Antwerp: the island of Walcheren. Its name was ill-omened, for it had been the scene of a famous British military reverse during the wars against Napoleon. And even isolated as it now was, it seemed likely to be a very hard nut to crack. Its defences, we have said, were extremely strong, and the only land approach was the straight and narrow causeway from South Beveland. This was singularly uninviting. Over half a mile long and less than a hundred yards wide; a brick-paved road, very badly cratered, three or four feet above the surrounding tidal flats; a single-line railway track two or three feet higher; the inevitable Dutch bicycle-path; and a row of telegraph poles—that was the causeway. To make matters worse, it was found that there was not enough water over the flats, even at high tide, to permit of an assault in storm boats; yet the flats were too saturated for movement on foot, and there were too many runnels to allow tracked amphibious 'Weasels' to operate.

. . . . Walcheren was to be attacked from three directions: across the causeway from the east; across the Scheldt from the south; and in the west by a force landed from the sea. The two latter attacks were to go in on 1 November; the causeway attack was to be delivered as soon as the causeway was reached.

During 31 October the Royal Regiment of Canada liquidated the little German pocket at the causeway's eastern end, and the Canadian Black Watch then attacked along the causeway itself. There was heavy opposition and particularly deadly mortar fire, but early in the afternoon it was reported that the Black Watch were only seventy-five yards from the west end. That night the Calgary Highlanders passed through, and after much trouble established a shallow bridgehead. But in the face of continued resolute opposition they could not enlarge it; and that evening a sudden violent counter-attack threw them out of it and back some distance along the causeway. On 2 November Le Régiment de Maisonneuve took over and re-established the bridgehead, but enemy resistance continued to be bitter, heavy shelling supplementing machine-gun and mortar fire.

Colonel C. P. Stacey

Commandos from the Sea

The landing craft tank were tossing about in three parallel lines, and far to the north we could see the *Warspite*, *Erebus* and *Roberts* steaming along in staggered formation. The dim outline of Walcheren came slowly into view. Steadily the ships drove on until the gap could clearly be seen. I wondered what the Germans were doing and hoped they had all gone to the diversionary attacks which had now been in progress for some hours. The silence was oppressive as each lived with his own thoughts.

Suddenly from the *Warspite* a cloud of dirty brown smoke erupted. Seconds later a dull rumble and columns of smoke arose from the island. The *Erebus* and *Roberts* followed suit, and broadside after broadside was poured into the north batteries. There still wasn't a sound from the island. Coming up from the right, parallel to shore and about a thousand yards off the island, we could now see the support craft with their rocket guns. The moan of the rockets could plainly be heard and the batteries on the south shore of the gap were soon wreathed in smoke and dust. Still not a sound from the island. Our spirits rose. It looked so easy.

We were getting close in now and the landing craft tank in front of us turned out of line to go farther back. It was our specially equipped hospital ship and we didn't want her in the muck yet. As it passed us, it struck a sea mine. There was a tremendous explosion and the entire ship was hurled into the air. It settled rapidly. Men jumped into the sea. Some were picked up by the following craft. Others floated face down in their lifebelts.

Pin-points of light sparkled from the south batteries. The Germans were opening up at last. The whole line of support craft broke into flame and smoke. Ships blew up and were swallowed in one gulp. Others drifted aimlessly around out of control.

An officer eye-witness

It had been a gruelling day, and the losses on the beaches, both in men, tanks, and vehicles, had been high.

. . . . The first night on Walcheren passed quietly, and at dawn No. 48 (Royal Marine) Commando moved forward towards Zouteland. H.M.S. *Erebus* shelled the town and soon after 11.00 hours its garrison of a hundred and fifty surrendered. Shortly before 13.00 hours No. 47 was able to advance and presently reached the outer defences of Flushing. Here support fire was called for and also attacks from aircraft, but these were not forthcoming owing to low clouds and rain. Q and Z Troops to the left lost about twelve killed and many wounded, including Major J. T. E. Vincent; but A and Y Troops on the right, moving along the dunes close to the sea, made good progress until they came under mortar fire which wounded three of their officers. The situation remained obscure, and that night No. 47 successfully beat off a counter-attack. Not until the following morning, the beginning of the third day on which the brigade was on shore, did the battery in the outer defences of Flushing fall. The very large number of shells which fell upon it seemed, when they did not kill, to have dazed its garrison. Many of the prisoners taken were half out of their minds, and it was noticed that the pupils of their eyes were so dilated that the whites were almost invisible.

After the capture of this battery the enemy's resistance weakened, and grew still less when a number of German officers called upon those left in the garrison to surrender.

After nine days of bitter fighting, Walcheren fell.

THE AMERICANS PUSH ON

On 8 November the American 3 and 7 Armies attacked again and crossed the Moselle, while farther north 1 Army toiled forward from Aachen towards the Roer. The weather was steady and unchangeable: rain.

Aachen

I have just returned to Brussels after four days of street fighting in Aachen. I have seen the city of German Emperors being wiped out after it had refused the offer of honourable surrender, and I found its people crushed to desperation by a double misery, by our onslaught and by the cruelties of their Nazi masters. When I first approached Aachen, the town was burning. From an American observation post just above the city I could see immense columns of smoke rising to the sky where some sixty Allied dive-bombers were freely forming up for attack and diving unmolested on their objective. As the bombs came down, red jets of flame spouted up among the houses which stood there silent without a sign of life. It was an eerie sight, no enemy guns, no movements in the streets, only the incessant rumbling of explosions. And then we went in. On both sides of the deserted streets stood empty carcasses of burnt-out houses; glass, debris and tree branches were strewn on the pavements, and almost in every street a building was burning like a huge torch.

We arrived at a huge concrete surface shelter. These shelters are ugly, gloomy constructions with many floors above and below the ground, where hundreds of civilians had been hiding for the last five weeks in darkness and stench. Army officers and the police had the entrance blocked, and no one was allowed to leave the place. In the meantime, Gestapo and soldiers were looting the town, grabbing in mad lust the property of their own people, although they had no hope to carry it away. The Army refused to open the shelter. For several hours it was besieged by American soldiers, then a German officer offered to surrender, if he was allowed to take away all his things, plus his batman.

Lieutenant Walker, a young company commander, made no effort to accept such a ridiculous offer and threatened to use flamethrowers. That helped. The doors opened and out came the drabbest, filthiest inhabitants of the underworld I have ever seen, as people came stumbling out into the light, dazed, then catching a breath of fresh air, and finally starting to jabber, push, scream and curse. Some precipitated themselves to me, brandishing their fists. Where have you been so long, they shouted. Why didn't you deliver us sooner from those devils. It was a stunning sight. These were the people of the first German town occupied by the Allies. And they were weeping with hysterical joy amidst the smouldering ruins of their homes. We have been praying every day for you to come, said a woman with a pale, thin face. You can't imagine what we have had to suffer from them. And then came the insults. Bloodhound, bandit, gangster. All this was the beloved Führer. There is no one who can hate and curse so thoroughly as the Germans, and these people were all green with hate of the Nazis. It was no trick. I certainly would not be cheated.

It was the breakdown of a nation after having played for five years on the wrong cards. Maybe it was the rage of a gangster let down by his gang-leader, but it was a hatred you find only in civil wars.

A Czech war correspondent with 1 Army

Patton: Metz, 7 November

To-morrow 3 Army once more attacks. It has been a tough week. The weather awful. The Moselle has been rising, not by inches but by feet, and acres of surrounding countryside are under water. One of the corps commanders and a division commander came to see the General early this evening to ask for a postponement. The General listened carefully.

'You feel that under present conditions you cannot undertake the attack as planned?' he asked.

'That is correct, sir,' they said.

'Would you care to make recommendations as to your successors?' he said quietly.

Changing his tone, he drew them over to the map. 'This is what we are going to do,' he said. For half an hour, into the drained reservoirs of their self-confidence he poured and pumped the elixir of his own vitality.

'And now,' he said, smiling, 'go back to your headquarters, have a big drink, and get some sleep.'

'Don't worry, General,' they said, 'the attack will go on.'

'You're goddam right it will,' the General said.

The General arose, looked at his watch. 'Ten-thirty p.m.,' he said. 'Exactly two years ago we were on the cruiser *Augusta* approaching the Moroccan coast. It was blowing hard and the question of a postponement came up. To-night it is raining even harder than it was blowing then.'

At the foot of the stairs he paused. 'I think,' he said, 'that to-day has been the longest day of my life. There is nothing I can do now but pray.' Then, seizing the banister rail, he went up to his room, briskly.

Colonel Charles Codman

Rain

Dawn came with its usual maddening slowness. You'd wonder if it actually was coming on or if your eyes were merely growing more accustomed to the dark. I ached everywhere and spasms of twitching passed over me. How soon could you safely light a cigarette? I looked down at the rifle, which in the first glimmer of light showed pale-orange streaks of rust. The rain was stopping. After a short while the men began to stir, to get up out of the foxholes, to face a tree and urinate. Cigarettes were lighted. I folded the sodden blanket and looked at the white tag in the corner. Yes, it was mine we had been using, not Dave's. It would take days to dry out.

There was not much to talk about after discussing the Billings' episode out on the road last night. The men looked ashen, dirty and unshaven. Everything was wet; there was no place to sit but on the fallen trunk of a wet rotting tree.

Half the men in the knoll were strangers and one sat next to them without bothering to talk. There was nothing to look forward to. Dave awoke leisurely and crawled out of the foxhole. Now in the clearing daylight I was depressed to see how makeshift it was. In my mind, which seemed unusually dulled, there formed the idea of working on it farther during the day, deepening it and removing the lumps. The ration of cold egg yolk and pork which I ate for breakfast began to make me nauseated; I had to throw away my cigarette.

The morning went by slowly, a grey morning, and the ground did not dry, so that there was no place to lie down. Soon the men around me began to open their luncheon rations. At the first whiff of food my stomach turned; I had to look the other way. Shortly after noon Sergeant Danowski told us we were to be relieved. The news came as a pleasant surprise. We had, he said, only an hour and a half to go.

Lester Atwell

I woke up at 03.00 on the morning of 8 November, 1944, and it was raining very hard; I tried to go to sleep, but finding it impossible, got up and started to read Rommel's book, *Infantry Attacks*. By chance I turned to a chapter describing a fight in the rain in September 1914. This was very reassuring because I felt that if the Germans could do it I could, so went to sleep and was awakened at 05.15 by the artillery preparation. The rain had stopped and the stars were out. The discharge of over seven hundred guns sounded like the slamming of so many heavy doors in an empty house, while the whole eastern sky glowed and trembled with the flashes. I even had a slight feeling of sympathy for the Germans, who must now have known that the attack they had been fearing had at last arrived. I complacently remembered that I had always 'Demanded the impossible', that I had 'Dared extreme occasion', and that I had 'Not taken counsel of my fears'.

At 07.45 Bradley called up to see if we were attacking. I had not let him know for fear I might get a stop order. He seemed delighted that we were going ahead. Then General Eisenhower came on the phone and said, 'I expect you to carry the ball all the way.'

General Patton

A Hurried Defence

. . . . In the reforming area all means were employed to get the division back on its feet. Every available officer of the divisional staff, including the divisional commander, went out cruising in the Metz area with instructions to gather troops. The officers would stand at road crossings and shanghai every passing soldier who did not have a ready answer to an inquiry as to his destination. In one instance I was directing traffic into the divisional area. The Army men, not quite satisfied about the prospect of being impressed into an S.S. unit, circled the area until they hit another road, only to run into me at the road junction again. I redirected the men into the divisional area, rather amused at the merry-go-round. When anti-tank guns were needed, an officer with a few prime-movers at hand would set up shop at a road crossing and wait for passing guns, the crews of which were not quite certain about their destination or attachment. The horses would be unhitched, the crews piled into the waiting prime-movers, and the caravan then proceeded into the reforming area.

Staff officer, 17 Panzer Grenadier Division

In our rear a special staff and labour service was working on the West Wall, and we ourselves constructed several defence systems in advance of these fortifications. Administrative services and the civil population were roped in to do the digging. Time was short, and the defences were far from ready when the Americans attacked, but even so they were a tremendous help in the bitter fighting which followed. In addition, thousands of mines were laid. (The defences of the Maginot Line were of little value to us as they faced the wrong way, but the underground shelters were useful.)

At the beginning of November our line was far stronger than a month before, and mud and slush could be relied upon to clog the movements of the American armour. Yet there was nothing really solid, and nothing dependable about our front. Under the impact of day and night bombing the supply system worked spasmodically and ammunition was woefully short. We had hardly any assault guns, and some divisions had none at all. We had a considerable quantity of field artillery, but much of it consisted of captured guns with only a few rounds of ammunition. We had a hundred and forty tanks of all types; a hundred of these were allotted to 1 Army.

Balck has been accused of being a 'notorious optimist' (Wilmot, *The Struggle for Europe*, p. 538), but he was under no illusions about the resisting power of this Cinderella among army groups. Writing to Jodl to request reinforcements, he confessed that he had never commanded 'such a mixture of badly equipped troops'.

General von Mellenthin

The Fall of Metz

On the night 8/9 November XX Corps began its attack on Metz. Units of 90 U.S. Division crossed the Moselle in assault boats to the north of Thionville and took the German defenders completely by surprise. 90 U.S. Division was commanded by General Van Fleet, who was later to win distinction in Korea. By the evening of the 9th the division had as many as eight battalions across the river, and had established a firm bridgehead. Little resistance was offered by our two divisions in this area—416 Infantry and 19 Volksgrenadier; their fighting quality was low and in any case they were stretched out on far too wide a front. (416 Division had recently come from Denmark and was nicknamed the 'Whipped Cream Division'. The average age of the men was thirty-eight, and none had ever been in battle. There were no assault guns, and their artillery consisted of obsolete fortress pieces and captured Russian 122 mms.)

At Army Group G we were extremely concerned at the rapid growth of the Thionville bridgehead; 1 Army was now without reserves and we had to ask Rundstedt for a Panzer division. But the Commander-in-Chief West could not authorize such a step on his own responsibility, and the question was referred to

Hitler; it was at this stage of the war that Rundstedt made the comment that the only troops he was allowed to move were the sentries outside the door of his headquarters. Negotiations with O.K.W. lasted more than a day, but eventually 25 P.G.D. was given to us. This formation then lay east of Trèves and had to be replenished; as there was no petrol it could not go into action until the 12th. The delay was most unfortunate, for the strong current of the Moselle and accurate German artillery fire prevented 90 U.S. Division from completing a bridge over the river until the evening of the 11th, and for three days the American infantry were without tanks or heavy anti-tank guns. Nevertheless they resisted stubbornly, beat off counter-attacks by our infantry (we did not have a single tank to bring against them), and on the afternoon of the 11th took Forts Metrich and Königsmacher by storm.

. . . . The encirclement of Metz was well under way.

This situation had been foreseen by Field-Marshal von Rundstedt, and in October he had proposed that the Metz salient should be abandoned. Balck's view was that it would be better to make the Americans fight for Metz, provided the garrison withdrew in good time. However, on 7 November Hitler settled the argument by ruling that Metz was a fortress and that the garrison was to submit to encirclement and fight to the last. But we minimized the effect of these orders by only allotting second-rate troops to the Metz garrison, and by not giving them any tanks or assault guns.

General von Mellenthin

Delaying Action

The whole front of Army Group G was under continuous pressure. The enemy was achieving important successes, but we were keeping our forces relatively intact and falling back slowly to the West Wall; I must emphasize that throughout these operations our object was to fight for time, and so enable O.K.W. to assemble reserves for the great counter-offensive in Belgium. I think that Patton would have done better if 4 and 6 Armoured Divisions had been grouped together in a single corps, reinforced possibly by the French 2 Armoured Division. These were all very experienced formations and were ably commanded; Wood of 4 Armoured Division proved himself an expert in armoured tactics, and Leclerc showed great dash in the advance on Strasbourg. I think the Americans made a grave mistake in coupling their armoured divisions too closely with the infantry; combined as a tank army under one commander, these three armoured divisions might well have achieved a decisive break-through.

While great battles were raging in central Lorraine, XX Corps advanced from Thionville towards the lower Saar, and was held up by the 'Orscholz Barrier'. This was a strong defensive position consisting of anti-tank ditches and concrete structures; the American Intelligence knew remarkably little about it and the first attempts to force a gap were easily repulsed. 21 Panzer was in mobile reserve and counter-attacked effectively. On 25 November XX Corps discontinued its attacks on the Orscholz Barrier and ordered 10 Armoured Division to thrust towards the Saar at Merzig. The Americans had made a bad mistake in dispersing this division in isolated attacks along the corps front, and the order to concentrate for an advance on Merzig was given too late to achieve an important break-through.

On 28 November we proposed to Rundstedt that Army Group G should be strongly reinforced and that 1 and 19 Armies should deliver concentric counter-attacks towards the Saverne gap in order to regain Strasbourg, and crush the enemy's salient in this area. It seemed a practicable operation if three Panzer divisions and two infantry divisions could be made available, but O.K.W. rejected it, as everything was now subordinated to the great gamble in the Ardennes.

. . . . On the afternoon of 2 December an American observation plane reported that the bridge over the Saar was still intact, and 95 Division prepared to capture it by a *coup de main*. In the early hours of the 3rd, American infantry and engineers made a surprise crossing in assault boats, avoided detection in the fog and rain, and attacked the bridge from the rear. Our garrison was overwhelmed and the bridge was captured intact. This brilliant success was rapidly exploited; the 379th U.S. Regiment crossed to Saar on the undamaged bridge and that evening had the satisfaction of capturing the first bunkers of the West Wall.

This affair caused much excitement and a great deal of moaning in high quarters. Hitler was furious and demanded a full report; he could not understand how a section of his cherished West Wall had been allowed to fall into enemy hands. O.K.W. had entirely forgotten that the West Wall had been stripped of everything that could make it formidable in favour of the ill-fated Atlantic Wall, and that in any case its fortifications were obsolete. Anti-tank obstacles lay immediately in front of the main line of defence, and the emplacements were too small for the new heavy anti-tank guns. There was no barbed wire, telephone communications did not function, and the highly complicated firing arrangements were useless because most of the troops were quite untrained. (Rundstedt himself had aroused Hitler's ire by describing the West Wall as a 'mouse-trap'.) The Führer demanded a victim, and General von Knobelsdorff, the highly capable commander of 1 Army, was sacrificed. I personally felt much affected, because I had a high regard for this very brave and distinguished officer with whom I had shared so many experiences in Russia.

General von Mellenthin

The American 1 Army emerged victoriously from one of the most horrible experiences of the war in Europe: the battle of the Hurtgen Forest, but by mid-December they, 3 Army and 7 Army had been halted. Patton had been stopped beyond the Saar by the main West Wall defences. The Rhine was still far away.

On 28 November Eisenhower came to stay a night with me at my Tac Headquarters at Zonhoven. We had long talks that night and the next morning, in the course of which we discussed the situation in which we found ourselves at that time—which, to say the least of it, was far from good.

The war of attrition in the winter months, forced on us by our faulty strategy after the great victory in Normandy, was becoming very expensive in human life. In the American armies there was a grave shortage of ammunition.

The rifle platoons in all divisions were under strength and the reinforcement situation was bad. American divisions in the line began to suffer severely from trench-foot as the winter descended on us. In my own Army Group I was concerned about the growing casualties.

Field-Marshal Montgomery

THE BATTLE OF THE ARDENNES

The last German offensive of the war was planned in early November. It opened on 16 December, driving through the Ardennes in bitter weather and achieving complete surprise.

A Secret Conference

'Gentlemen, before opening the conference I must ask you to read this document carefully and then sign it with your full names.'

The date was 3 November 1944, and I had assumed that the conference would be merely a routine meeting of the three army commanders who held the northern sector of the Western Front under Field-Marshal Model's Army Group B. . . . Each officer present had to pledge himself to preserve complete silence concerning the information which Jodl intended to divulge to us: should any officer break this pledge, he must realize that his offence would be punishable by death. I had frequently attended top secret conferences presided over by Hitler at Berchtesgaden or at the 'Wolf's Lair' both before and after 20 July 1944, but this was the first time that I had seen a document such as the one which I now signed. It was clear that something most unusual was afoot.

General Hasso von Manteuffel, G.O.C. 5 Panzer Army

The Führer's Briefing

On 11 and 12 December Hitler summoned all the commanding officers who were to take part in the forthcoming operation, down to and including the divisional commanders, to his headquarters which was called the 'Eagle's Nest', near Ziegenberg in Hesse. Half the generals came on one day, half on the other. I was summoned on the 11th, together with the commanders of my two Panzer corps, and we arrived to find Field-Marshals von Rundstedt and Model present as well. S.S. Colonel-General Sepp Dietrich was also already there.

. . . . The assembly presented a striking contrast. On one side of the room were the commanding generals, responsible and experienced soldiers, many of whom had made great names for themselves on past battlefields, experts at their trade, respected by their troops. Facing them was the Supreme Commander of the Armed Forces, a stooped figure with a pale and puffy face, hunched in his chair, his hands trembling, his left arm subject to a violent twitching which he did his best to conceal, a sick man apparently borne down by his burden of responsibility. His physical condition had deteriorated noticeably since our last meeting in Berlin only nine days before. When he walked he dragged one leg behind him.

At his side was Jodl, an old man now, overworked and overtired. . . . Keitel's manner showed that he had not been involved in working out the plans and making the manifold preparations for the 'decisive attack' to the same extent as Jodl.

When Hitler began his speech, which lasted for about an hour and a half, he talked in a low and hesitant voice. Only gradually did his style become more assured, this partially effacing the initial effect that his appearance had produced, at least for those officers who had not seen him in recent months and did not know him well. Nevertheless the impression remained that it was a sick man to whom we listened, a man whose physique and whose nerves were shattered.

General Hasso von Manteuffel

If Germany loses, it will have proved itself biologically inferior and will have forfeited its future existence. It is the West that forces us to fight to the last. However, it will transpire that the winner will not be the West, but the East.

Adolf Hitler to his generals, 11 December

The only positive contribution to the forthcoming operation which I took away from the conference was Hitler's own appreciation of the enemy. From his point of view—and he alone had access to all the intelligence sources—the prospects for a successful operation looked favourable. Hitler engraved the decisive importance of the forthcoming attack upon the hearts of the assembled officers. His fundamental thesis was that every formation should continue to advance, regardless of what might be happening on its flanks, and should push forward with all possible speed.

General Bayerlein

The German commanders knew the terrain in the Ardennes well. We had advanced across it in 1940 and retreated through it only a few months before. We knew its narrow, twisting roads and the difficulties, not to say dangers, they could cause an attacking force, particularly in winter and in the bad weather conditions which were an essential prerequisite to the opening of our operation. The main roads contained many hairpin bends, and were frequently built into steep hillsides. To get the guns of the artillery and flak units as well as the pontoons and beams of the bridging engineers around these sharp corners was a lengthy and difficult business. The guns and trailers had to be disconnected and then dragged around the corner by a capstan mechanism, naturally one at a time. Vehicles could not pass one another on these roads.

General Hasso von Manteuffel

Objective Antwerp

I strongly object to the fact that this stupid operation in the Ardennes is sometimes called the 'Rundstedt offensive'. That is a complete misnomer. I had nothing to do with it. It came to me as an order complete to the last detail.

When I was first told about the proposed offensive in the Ardennes, I protested against it as vigorously as I could. The forces at our disposal were much, much too weak for such far-reaching objectives. I suggested that my plan against the Aachen salient be used instead, but the suggestion was turned down, as were all my other objections. It was only up to me to obey. It was a nonsensical operation, and the most stupid part of it was the setting of Antwerp as the target. If we had reached the Meuse we should have got down on our knees and thanked God—let alone try to reach Antwerp.

Field-Marshal von Rundstedt

All I had to do was to cross the river, capture Brussels and then go on and take the port of Antwerp. And all this in December, January and February, the worst three months of the year; through the Ardennes where snow was waist deep and there wasn't room to deploy four tanks abreast, let alone six armoured divisions; when it didn't get light until eight in the morning and was dark again at four in the afternoon and my tanks can't fight at night; with divisions that had just been reformed and were composed chiefly of raw untrained recruits; and at Christmas time.

General Sepp Dietrich, G.O.C. 6 Panzer Army

Rundstedt Strikes

This time we are a thousand times better off than you at home. You cannot imagine what glorious hours and days we are experiencing now. It looks as if the Americans cannot withstand our important push. To-day we overtook a fleeing column and finished it. We overtook it by taking a back-road through the woods to the retreat lane of the American vehicles; then, just like on manœuvres, we pulled up along the road with sixty Panthers. And then came the endless convoy driving in two columns, side by side, hub on hub, filled to the brim with soldiers. And then a concentrated fire from sixty guns and one hundred and twenty machine-guns. It was a glorious bloodbath, vengeance for our destroyed homeland. Our soldiers still have the old zip. Always advancing and smashing everything. The snow must turn red with American blood. Victory was never as close as it is now.

Lieutenant Rockhammer, Wehrmacht; a letter, 22 December

We have been on our way through Belgium . . . without a break. No rest or sleep at all. My Christmas present, after twelve days, consisted of washing, shaving and five hours' sleep, but we are on our way again. The main thing is that the Americans are on the run. . . . We cleared an enemy supply dump. Everybody took things he wanted most. I took only chocolate. I have all my pockets full of it. I eat chocolate all the time, in order to sweeten somewhat this wretched life. . . . Don't worry about me. The worst is behind me. Now this is just a hunt.

A German soldier writes to his wife

22 December 1944

To the U.S.A. commander of the encircled town of Bastogne.

The fortune of war is changing. This time the U.S.A. forces in and near Bastogne have been encircled by strong German armoured units. More German armoured units have crossed the River Our near Ortheuville, have taken Marche and reached St. Hubert by passing through Homores-Sibret-Tillet. Librimont is in German hands.

There is only one possibility of saving the encircled U.S.A. troops from total annihilation: that is the honourable surrender of the encircled town. In order to think it over, a period of two hours will be granted, beginning with the presentation of this note.

If this proposal should be rejected; one German artillery corps and six heavy anti-aircraft battalions are ready to annihilate the U.S.A. troops in and near Bastogne. The order for firing will be given immediately after this two-hour period.

All the serious civilian losses caused by this artillery fire would not correspond with the well-known American humanity.

The German Commander
General von Lüttwitz, G.O.C. XLVII Panzer Corps

The reply to this message is generally known. It was: 'Nuts.'

Besides the great effort made by the enemy's army, the German Air Force produced their maximum contribution during the Ardennes offensive. In the first place they provided tactical support on a larger scale than had been achieved for many months, and they also carried out a somewhat desperate assault against our airfields in Holland and Belgium. This latter operation was certainly a spectacular affair. It happened on 1 January. I was back at our Headquarters in Brussels at the time, and was holding my usual morning staff conference when it took place.

I heard a certain amount of air activity around the building as I was talking, but this was nothing unusual. Then someone said, 'These aircraft are dropping things on the town.' (These turned out to be extra fuel tanks.) A few heads turned towards the window, but still no one really guessed what was happening. Then suddenly, as one aircraft flew roof-top high past the Headquarters, a shout went up, 'Christ, it's a 190!' I'm afraid there was a break in my conference as we went to see what was happening. Bombs and cannon fire were to be heard, and the air was full of German aircraft circling round and round, and then diving down to shoot up the aircraft on the Brussels airfield. Columns of black smoke were rising from that area and, sad to say, there was not a single British plane about. Eventually the attacks ceased, and later that day I went out to see the damage. It was very great—I should hate to have costed the value of the aircraft that had been written off that day. Both Montgomery's Dakota and my own lost their lives! But although a great deal of damage had been sustained, we could afford it, whilst the enemy could not stand the cost of his audacious attack. His losses amounted to over two hundred aircraft, which meant a great enemy defeat.

Major-General Sir Francis de Guingand

THE WAR

966

Stopping the Rot

Among the forces switched towards the Ardennes to hold the great threat was 3
American Army, under General Patton.

In that same fight, not long afterwards, I came upon another war-wise, war-weary G.I. He was a mortar man, down in a hole, with his weapon. He wasn't firing.

'Here,' I said. 'Get going with that mortar. Those people are right over there. Pour some fire on 'em. Let's blast 'em out of there.' He looked at me glumly.

'General,' he said, 'every time we shoot, them S.O.B.s shoot right back.'

'The hell with that,' I said. 'Get that mortar working.'

He took a sight on the opposite ridge top, dropped a shell down the tube, and the mortar belched with a bang and a smoke. Hardly had our shell exploded on the ridge opposite than there was a tremendous explosion a few yards to our left, and shell fragments screeched through the trees. Deafened by the explosion and shaken by the blast, I picked myself up off the ground. The mortar man peered warily out of his hole.

'See whadda mean?' he said.

. . . . I remember once standing beside a road leading through a pine wood, down a slope to the road junction of Manhay, where a hot fight was going on. That whole Ardennes fight was a battle for road junctions, because in that wooded country, in the deep snows, armies could not move off the roads. This particular crossroads was one of many that the Germans had to take if they were to keep up the momentum of their offensive, and we were fighting desperately to hold it. I had gone up to this point, which lay not far forward of my command post, to be of what help I could in this critical spot. As I was standing there, a lieutenant, with perhaps a dozen men, came out of the woods from the fighting, headed towards the rear. I stopped him and asked him where he was going and what his mission was. He told me that he and his men had been sent out to develop the strength of the German units that had reached Manhay, and that they had run into some machine-gun fire that was too hot for them, so they had come back.

I relieved him of his command there on the spot. I told him that he was a disgrace to his country and his uniform and that I was ashamed of him, and I knew the members of his patrol were equally ashamed. Then I asked if any other member of the patrol was willing to lead that patrol back into the fight. A sergeant stepped up and said he would lead it back and see to it that it carried out its mission.

In another hour, on that same spot, another incident occurred which I remember with regret. In the fierce fighting, the town changed hands several times. The Germans had brought up some flat trajectory guns, and they started shelling our little group. Fragments whizzed everywhere. One struck an artillery observer, who was standing by me, in the leg, and another punctured the tank of his jeep. As this shell exploded an infantry sergeant standing nearby became hysterical. He threw himself into the ditch by the side of the road, crying and raving. I walked over and tried to talk to him, trying to help him get hold of himself. But it had no effect. He was just crouched there in the ditch, cringing in utter terror. So I called my jeep driver, Sergeant Farmer, and told him to take his carbine and march this man back to the nearest M.P., and if he started to escape to shoot him without hesitation. He was an object of abject cowardice, and the sight of him would have a terrible effect on any American soldier who might see him.

. . . . That's the sort of thing you see sometimes. It is an appalling thing to witness—to see a man break completely like that—in battle. It is worse than watching a death—for you are seeing something more important than the body die. You are witnessing the death of a man's spirit, of his pride, of all that gives meaning and purpose to life.

General Ridgway

On this day* four Germans in one of our jeeps, dressed in American uniforms, were killed, and another group of seventeen, also in American uniforms, were reported by 35 Division as follows: 'One sentinel, reinforced, saw seventeen Germans in American uniforms. Fifteen were killed and two died suddenly.'

General Patton

The Big Freeze

While visiting the VIII Corps . . . I ran across two instructive incidents. In one place, elements of 17 Airborne Division were stuck on a slippery hill, and yet the officers did not have enough sense to have the men dismount and push the trucks. When this was done, the sticking completely ended. The other was that the ice and sleet had made the Germans' and also the Americans' mines inoperative, as they filled with ice right under the spider so that no pressure was sufficient to detonate the mine. It was evident that we would have many casualties when the thaw came, as troops would use the roads, which were apparently demined, and suddenly find a mine that had become operative. We used detectors to the maximum.

General Patton

The Germans were no happier.

On 2 January 1945, the Field-Marshal's car was held up during a snowstorm in the Ardennes. Several cars were stalled ahead of his, and officers in them sat snugly in their vehicles while a group of other ranks cleared the road for traffic. Suddenly Model, losing patience, became furious and bellowed 'Goddammit, what would happen now if Allied fighters were to strafe this road?' He dismounted and began to shovel the snow alongside the men. Just as the first vehicle was cleared, an indignant-looking captain appeared and, not seeing Model, demanded to know what the trouble was. Immediately the Field-Marshal snapped at him, 'And where have you been while the shovelling was going on?' The captain was forced to reply that he had been sitting in his vehicle. 'So,' replied Model, 'you would let a Field-Marshal clear the road for you while

* 30 December (Ed.)

you sit comfortably in your automobile—as from to-day, *Kamerad*, you are a private,' and with these words Model stripped the officer of his insignia of rank.

Herbert Sauer, chauffeur to Field-Marshal Model

On the 29th* I set off for 9 Panzer Division, which was in the wooded hills north-west of Houffalize; the ice-bound roads glittered in the sunshine and I witnessed the uninterrupted air attacks on our traffic routes and supply dumps. Not a single German plane was in the air, innumerable vehicles were shot up and their blackened wrecks littered the roads. When I reached my Headquarters I found that we were holding the most forward positions in the defensive line of 5 Panzer Army. Looking at the situation map I noted the violent American attacks on both flanks and the grave danger facing the Panzer divisions in the noose of the salient. But we were ordered to stay where we were and so we did, defending ourselves with mobile tactics.

Most of my men were Austrians, and in spite of heavy losses their morale was still high. The Panzer regiment was left with twenty tanks, and the two Panzer Grenadier regiments each had about four hundred men. But the artillery regiment was very strong and of high quality. We beat off the American attacks until 5 January, when orders were received to get out of this hopeless position and withdraw eastward; I was put in command of the rearguard of 5 Panzer Army. My experiences in Russia stood me in good stead; I knew all about the problems of moving through snow and ice—a subject in which the Americans still had much to learn. By day our armoured group resisted in chosen positions; all movements were carried out at night to evade the fighter-bombers, but even so concentric artillery fire on our flanks inflicted considerable casualties. By mid-January 9 Panzer Division had reached the line of the River Our, where we stood firm on the original start line of the offensive.

The results of the Ardennes fighting were more than disappointing; we had suffered excessive losses in men and material and only gained a few weeks' respite. It is true that American forces were moved from Lorraine, and the pressure on Army Group G slackened; however, this relief was only temporary (at the beginning of January Army Group G was strong enough to launch an offensive, which had some prospects of recapturing Strasbourg). The same results could have been achieved by a limited attack at Aachen, after which our operational reserves could have been switched to Poland. The Ardennes battle drives home the lesson that a large-scale offensive by massed armour has no hope of success against an enemy who enjoys supreme command of the air. Our precious reserves had been expended, and nothing was available to ward off the impending catastrophe in the East.

General von Mellenthin

At the end of a month the Wehrmacht had made its last throw, and lost. It had suffered over a hundred thousand casualties; the Americans some seventy-seven thousand. While the Battle of the Ardennes was being fought out, the last Christmas of the war had come and gone. 25 December was the day Bastogne was relieved, but on other fronts the Holy Day was quiet.

* December (Ed.)

Out of the Line

The men were taking their leggings and shoes off for the first time in weeks. The linoleum floor, which was like ice to touch, became one large bed as soon as the blankets were spread out. It was going to be a tight squeeze for all of us to lie down. We tried it, stretching out in a double row. Our feet met in a line down the centre of the room and there was just enough space to lie flat, shoulder to shoulder. Once that was settled, everyone sat up, the drink came off the stove and was passed around, poured into the canteen cups. It tasted like scorched lighter fluid, but it was burning hot, revivifying. Cigarettes were lighted, and out of the din of chatter and laughter singing began. The mournful *I'm Dreaming of a White Christmas, Silent Night, Jingle Bells, O Come, All Ye Faithful, Hark! the Herald Angels Sing, O Little Town of Bethlehem, White Christmas* again, and then, growing more secular, the Army favourites: *I've Got Sixpence, Someone's in the Kitchen with Dinah, For Me and My Gal, When You Wore a Tulip, There's a Long, Long Trail, I'm Going to Buy a Paper Doll that I Can Call My Own, Roll Me O-ver in the Clo-ver.* . . .

. . . . After a half hour of singing, *Silent Night* began again, wavered and stopped halfway. Most of the others were going to sleep. More than half the men, as everywhere in the Army, slept with their heads under the blankets. I was lying next to O'Rourke; the man on the other side I didn't know. The lantern went out, leaving a small warm ruby glow in the darkness from the open bottom door of the stove.

When everyone was asleep for quite some time, I sat up and, feeling the chill coming through the wall, put my field jacket over my shoulders and lit a cigarette. I enjoyed the sensation of privacy in being the only one awake in the snoring, crowded room. How lucky we were compared to the men who had relieved us in the Saar Valley, freezing to-night in the foxholes we had dug, standing guard or going out on patrols! They were troops even greener than ourselves and had, it was reported, marched in at attention to take over our positions, wearing ties.

. . . . 'Mass! Anyone here going to Mass? Fall out!' The tiresome routine of putting on ammunition belt, gas mask, helmet, rifle—and out on to the road. Men were coming up the street in groups, all armed, with rifles, with here and there a B.A.R., a carbine, a grease gun, coming from houses, from barns and sheds. The church bells were ringing.

It was odd to see the door of a badly smashed house open and a little boy and girl, dressed in Sunday clothes, run out, followed by a neat woman in an old-fashioned fur-collared coat, beaver hat and gloves. The children raced ahead to laugh and talk with other children, comparing, I supposed, what they had received for Christmas. There were men in overcoats, felt hats turned down all the way around, and stiff, high, polished shoes. None of the girls or women wore make-up. The civilians all kept to the sidewalk, while the soldiers roamed, talking, up the middle of the street.

The church property was surrounded by a wrought-iron fence. You went up the steps, through a graveyard and into the vestibule. Helmets came off; rifles were stacked against the back wall. All the stained-glass windows were blown out and the still air was icy and damp. There were crystal-and-brass chandeliers and a worn, patterned marble aisle. Civilians sat on one side, we on the other. An organist played unfamiliar hymns. Out of the corners of their eyes the civilians watched us and we watched them. The first few rows were filled with children, then came a row of older boys, then girls, and finally the adults.

When the bell rang for the start of Mass, the parish priest came out in handsome white vestments, the two altar boys in red cassocks, starched white lace-edged surplices and white gloves. Blasts of frigid air blew in. The children sang hymns in French, but when the priest—stocky, middle-aged and dark—ascended the pulpit, the long sermon, surprisingly, was in German. He had a fine voice, deep and clear. Occasionally he gestured towards us, and the children all turned to look, then he gestured towards the crèche.   Lester Atwell

In the Line

We stared into the night, thinking where we might have been.

'Quiet, isn't it,' said Joe, 'considering the bashing Roermond's been getting from our artillery these last few days?'

'Christmas Eve, chum,' said Tom.

We discussed the peculiar first Christmas of the first World War when the opposing sides swarmed over their trenches into No-Man's-Land and played football. Later they shelled each other's trenches to hell. We thought it stupid.

Tom gripped my arm. 'Listen!'

Faintly, from across the river, came the sound of voices singing *Stille Nachte, Heilige Nacht.*

'Their forward patrols,' said Joe.

'Shut up, Joe, and listen!'

The age-old carol gained in strength as it floated to us on the frosty air. The war was distant, almost stopped. Over all the earth the anniversary of Christ's birth was now—to-night. Jerry across the river, the British on this side, all were made in God's image, all were God's children. The river wasn't there. The world was only one huge, moonlit meadow.

The first verse ended. After a short silence the second verse began—from *our* side of the river. We listened to the voices alternating the verses back and forth across the river. At the end faint greetings could be heard intermingled: 'Happy Christmas!'—*'Fröhliche Weinacht!'*

. . . . 'Do you get any help from prayer?' asked Joe.

'Yes,' I answered.

'Could you work one out for us?'

'Why don't we all three make one up?' I suggested.

It took us half an hour.

'Oh God, look down in mercy this night on us all, friend and foe alike. Let thy fatherly hand guide those on patrol, help the wounded, strengthen the dying, and keep our families safe.'

Primitive, maybe, but comforting.

A streak of tracer flashed out on the right and the hammer of a Bren shattered the night; then silence.   R. M. Wingfield

32

THE END OF GERMANY

Over most of the front in the West, a few weeks' respite for the soldiers ensued between the end of the Battle of the Ardennes in mid-January and the beginning of the final offensive which was to spell the end of Germany.

I WENT for a walk in the woods to-day and came upon Sergeant B. lighting a wood fire underneath a dead and frozen Hun strung up to the branch of a tree. He was trying to thaw him out, in order to take off his boots. Personally, I have found the Army boots quite adequate, but most people seem to think that the type which goes almost up to the knee is warmer.

Lieutenant-Colonel Martin Lindsay, Gordon Highlanders

If you actually saw me you would lift your hands in dismay. I am ragged and filthy. I have had the same underwear on for five weeks. If one doesn't get lice it's a miracle. If only the war were over soon; it has lasted long enough already.

A German letter home

Battle Fatigue

It was then almost evening. Stars came out, and in the bitter, cold dusk a soldier approached me uncertainly. When he was close I saw that his eyes, pale in a dark-complexioned face, were fixed and dilated. He was talking in French, as if in a daze, then, half whispering, half aloud, drawing the word out, he said, 'Noi-i-se! The noi-i-se!' His eyes became even larger and he started plucking at my sleeve.

A distant shell exploded. He moistened his lips, then harkened, one finger raised. I could think only of a moving-picture actor giving a fairly good, not wholly convincing performance. Whispering in French, he started to go past me into the barn, but I said, 'You can't go in now; there's a wounded man being bandaged.' Then, thinking I might be misjudging him, I asked, 'Would you like a cigarette while you're waiting?' I had been smoking my last one before dark, cupping it.

'Yes,' he said. 'The noise. . . . The noise, you know.'

I said, 'You'll have to cup the cigarette,' and I gave him a light from the tip of mine. He bent towards it, his hands covering mine, and in the act his face was absorbed; it had lost its vacancy of expression. There was a heavy college ring on his finger. Once the cigarette was going, he said, 'The noi-i-se!'

I remained silent and he stood a short distance away, his collar turned up, hunching over to inhale. From inside the barn Preacher called, 'Anyone else out there?'

'Yes, there's one,' I said.

With that the man stepped on his cigarette, began his delirious talk in French and went inside the barn.

About five minutes later I heard the captain's voice saying near the doorway, 'Take this man over to Battalion Headquarters and tell them I said to let him rest up a few days around the kitchen. He'll be all right.'

Resting up around any kitchen meant working as a K.P. The man, who was about twenty-four, was led out past me by a medic, whispering, 'The noi-i-se. The noi-i-se!' The two figures went down the road and disappeared into the gloom.

Lester Atwell

BATTLE TO THE RHINE

Undeterred by the fate of their last offensive, the Germans decided to make their last stand with the Rhine behind them rather than in front of them. So, before General Eisenhower could throw bridgeheads across the Rhine, he first had to destroy the enemy west of it. The main attack towards the river was to be launched from Holland by the British 21 Army Group under Montgomery, supported by the 9 U.S. Army to the south. Between the Maas and the Rhine lay some of the worst fighting terrain in Europe; flooded, waterlogged fields, and then the supposedly impenetrable Reichswald Forest. The Germans recognized that Montgomery's drive was the one designed to doom them, and flung everything they had against it. February and March 1945 saw some of the hardest and most costly fighting of the war.

'An Allied attack is impending across the Maas and the Roer towards the east. Its first objective will be to reach the Rhine. If it succeeds in this, then the crossing of the Rhine will follow later, with the north wing of the English forces in the neighbourhood of Wesel. For this offensive, flank protection of 21 English Army Group with weak forces in the north between Emmerich and the Maas estuary would suffice, for the Germans have no longer means to counter-attack from Holland across the broad rivers in, for example, a strategic advance on Antwerp. Holland itself need not be attacked by the English at all. If 21 British Army Group succeeds in crossing the Rhine on both sides of Wesel it will suffice for relatively weak British forces to swing around east of the Ijssel in a northerly direction to Emden and Zwolle and automatically the whole of Holland will fall without the necessity for large-scale battles.'*

Von Rundstedt and Blaskowitz agreed with this view. But the Supreme Command of the Army, or more precisely, Hitler, rejected the proposal for a timely evacuation of Holland and, for that reason, almost all the German invasion forces in Holland later fell into the enemy's hands practically without a struggle.

General Blumentritt

---

* 25 Army intelligence summary (Ed.)

The Reichswald: Last Battle?

The Battle of the Reichswald Forest lasted three weeks, and included some of the bitterest fighting of the whole war. The Forest is shaped like a diamond, six miles from north to south and ten from east to west; its western edge is the German frontier. The Highland Division's operations were all either in its southern half, or in the country of smaller woodlands lying to the south and south-east of the Forest proper. The Siegfried Line ran through the Forest from north to south and away towards Aachen.

There was just a hope that the coming battle might be the last of the war. The enemy would not lightly yield the Siegfried Line; he might well make his last stand in it. Even if he did not intend to fight it out west of the Rhine, he might be forced to do so. The Americans in the south were to launch an offensive a day or two after the attack on the Reichswald; and a successful penetration either on the British front or on theirs might encircle the Germans before they could reach the Rhine.

Bernard Fergusson

Concentration

The move northwards took place on 4 February. All tactical signs had to be painted out and no one was allowed on the roads by day; but by night every route north for at least a week before the operation was like the Epsom Spring Meeting. It was a forty-mile journey, and a most unpleasant one, which owing to the traffic and the timings given to us could not be completed in darkness. It was daylight before we reached Nijmegen, and we all hoped we looked like half-drowned Canadians as we turned slightly southwards again into Klein Linden, an unattractive village, far too small for the King's Own and ourselves (plus some real Canadians), and completely waterlogged.

Two days remained before we were to concentrate for the battle, and they were spent in trying to get our clothes dry and peering at the Reichswald from the Canadian F.D.L.s. From the forward edge of the Groesbeek woods the ground sloped gently downhill, across open fields dotted with the crashed gliders of the American airborne troops who landed here on the extreme right flank of the Nijmegen operation of the previous September. In the valley clustered the houses of a few scruffy villages which marked the Dutch–German border, and beyond loomed the solid, forbidding bulk of the Reichswald. It was not a pleasing prospect, and as the rain poured down we could imagine what the mud was going to be like on the low-lying ground before us.

British tank officer

The Obstacle

The Reichswald looked sombre and uninviting, the black trunks of the big trees seeming as solid as if carved from granite.

'There it is,' said Ian quietly. 'That's the objective for the first day. The

Germans think the forest is an anti-tank obstacle; maybe it is, too. But you never know till you try. Personally I think we should be able to operate in there, providing we pick our trees carefully.'

'We've got to reach it first,' said Tony Cunningham. 'Is that the anti-tank ditch, that white thing zig-zagging across by the group of red houses?'

'That's it,' said Ian. 'But the funnies* are going to get us over that.'

John Foley

The attack went in on 8 February, and in spite of a terrific preliminary bombardment, was quickly in trouble.

I was nearly blasted from my blankets by a deafening barrage of noise. The ground shook with the fury of the cannonade and the walls of the sixty-pound tent whipped in and out like sparrows' wings.

It was the softening-up bombardment, and it lasted until nearly ten-thirty.

We sat up in our blankets, and by means of a mixture of shouting and sign language we agreed that we'd never heard such a noise. Sleep was quite out of the question, so we dressed and went outside the tent. Overhead a solid curtain of Bofors tracers indicated that even the 40 mm. anti-aircraft guns were being used to thicken-up the barrage, and the sky behind us was alight with the continual flicker of gunfire.

From the front of our wood it seemed that the edge of the Reichswald was a solid mass of explosions and it appeared impossible that anything could live in that inferno.

'It should be a walk-over by half-past ten!' shouted Bob Webster; but we both knew that the Germans had a peculiar aptitude for emerging unscathed from the fiercest bombardment. Still, it was an encouraging thought.

Dead on the dot of ten-thirty we emerged from our wood and headed for the Reichswald. In front of us the Black Watch moved purposefully forward; little groups of men hurrying over the ground, while others spreadeagled themselves behind what cover they could and fired their rifles and Bren guns calmly and methodically.

We had expected the start to be slow for us, because we were scheduled to wait around quite a bit while the funnies cleared lanes through the minefield. But bit by bit reports came back over the radio indicating that it wasn't the mines which were causing the delay, but the mud.

The smooth green turf quickly churned up into black, track-clinging mud. One by one the Churchills sank on their bellies, their tracks spinning uselessly around in the bog. There was one road across the battlefield, but this had quite rightly been earmarked for essential wheeled vehicles only. To have put tanks on it would soon have made it as impassable as the rest of the ground.

. . . . Then the enemy began to recover from the six-hour bombardment. Eruptions of dirt indicated mortar and artillery fire coming down on our infantry and one or two of them started coming back, stolidly plodding along while holding a bloodstained arm or shoulder. Stretcher-bearers dealt swiftly and efficiently

---

* Tanks designed for specialized operations (Ed.)

with those who couldn't walk, and still the Black Watch went forward until they reached a group of farm buildings where they were scheduled for a short halt.

We pulled into the buildings with them and I looked around for the Company Commander. He was walking along a bit of a road, quietly smoking his pipe. With his little cane and his red hackle on the side of his cap, he might well have been taking a Sunday morning stroll down Aldershot High Street, except that vicious little spurts of dust were cracking about his heels.

He raised his stick in greeting when he saw Five Troop, and completely indifferent to the bullets kicking up the dirt around him he strolled across to *Avenger* and swung up to the turret.

'Going very well so far,' he said pleasantly. 'How're your funny-boys getting on with breaching that minefield?'

'They're all bogged,' I said gloomily. 'Look here, aren't you being shot at?'

'Oh, never mind that,' he said. 'It's only got nuisance value. Well, it's a pity you can't get across that minefield. Looks like we'll have to go on without you.'

. . . . Slowly we fought our way through the interminable Reichswald Forest. And each day the great trees steadily dripped rain on to us, and succeeded in blotting out most of the grey daylight.

The fringes of the forest were shell-torn and shattered, with untidy heaps of dead Germans flung about in grotesque attitudes. Our three Churchills proved very effective de-foresters; trees of quite respectable sizes were pushed flat and we managed to show the Germans that they were just as wrong in counting the Reichswald as an anti-tank obstacle as we had been in regarding the Ardennes as one in 1940.

John Foley

First German

. . . . 'What's this striped pole across the road, sir?' said Pickford.

'The frontier!' I said, pointing to the deserted hut which had housed the frontier police and customs men.

I stared curiously at my first German civilian. He was an old man, dressed in shabby serge and an engine-driver's sort of cap. His grizzled face regarded us from above a bushy white moustache as we clattered over the broken frontier barrier. And then I heard *Angler*'s driver's hatch being thrown open, and when I looked over my shoulder I saw Smith 161 leaning out and staring questioningly at the old German.

'We on the right road for Berlin, mate?' asked Smith 161, with a perfectly straight face.

I swear the old blue eyes winked, as the man tugged at his grizzled moustache and said: '*Berlin? Ja, ja! Gerade aus!*'

'I thought the Germans had no sense of humour,' said Pickford, when we got moving again.

'I know,' I said. 'But he can remember Germany before Hitler, and probably before the Kaiser, too.'

John Foley

Robot Tank

We inspected the 'Beetle' from the cover of our ditch. A Canadian war correspondent and photographer came up and signalled for two of us to have our photographs taken inspecting the tank. We were torn between the instinct of self-preservation and the glamour of an 'action' shot. This little dear in the road might blow any minute. We decided to risk it and climbed out of our ditch to stand shrinking beside the little tank. To our annoyance, the cameraman took what seemed hours to focus. Finally the job was done. As we dived, sweating, back to our ditch we were overtaken and passed by the cameraman.

When we felt better he asked us the name of our home paper. I told him mine, but I never heard anything more. Much later I understood why. Our security was so good that he probably mistook us for Canadians, in spite of our accents. I often wonder if there was a Canadian *Wakefield Express*.

Our dumb chum, the 'Beetle' tank, was not left to rust. Canadian Engineers repaired it and sent it trundling right back at Jerry. It must have been a hell of a shock to them!

R. M. Wingfield

Meanwhile the Americans to the south were delayed, so that the British and Canadians fought on unsupported.

During the days following the launching of 'Veritable', the battle in the pine woods of the Reichswald grew in violence. Realizing now the potential danger of the new offensive, the German Command brought reinforcements forward in increasing numbers; and it was favoured by developments elsewhere. For it had become necessary to postpone 9 Army's converging operation. General Simpson's advance had been scheduled to begin on 10 February, after the capture of the Roer dams by 1 United States Army. As long as these remained in German possession, the enemy was able to flood the area opposite 9 Army at will. After heavy fighting the Americans captured the last of the seven dams on 10 February; but, meanwhile, the enemy had succeeded in opening the sluices and raising the level of the Roer some four feet. Consequently, Operation 'Grenade' could not begin on time and it was in fact to be delayed almost a fortnight. This development was an 'extreme disappointment' to Field-Marshal Montgomery. '"Veritable" had to continue alone, and against it the enemy was able to concentrate all his available reserves; it was therefore inevitable that progress was slower than had been hoped.'

The Reichswald battle now entered its crucial stage. In addition to 7 Parachute Division, the enemy threw in 6 Parachute, 15 Panzer Grenadier and 116 Panzer Divisions. He was greatly assisted by our communication difficulties. By 10 February five miles of the road from Nijmegen to Cleve, our 'main axis', was under two feet of water. Within three days the depth had doubled. In spite of the herculean efforts by the sappers, other routes broke down under the impossible strain imposed by the requirements of the advance. South of the Reichswald the only good road—that leading to Goch—was held in force by the enemy.

Colonel C. P. Stacey

Mines

We heard the pipers of the Camerons of Canada and knew that we had not far to go. Then there was a loud bang and Danny fell down with a groan.

'Everybody stand still exactly where you are,' I shouted, for it was obviously a *schu*-mine. 'Danny, how bad is it?'

I knew it was either a broken ankle or the whole foot blown off—what the doctors call traumatic amputation. Danny's language and Porter, who at great personal risk stepped two or three paces over to him and applied a first field-dressing, told me that it was not too bad. We shouted at the tops of our voices to the Canadians for pioneers with mine-prodders and stretcher-bearers. I looked around and realized now that we were in a narrow no-man's-land, only fifty yards wide, between the German and Canadian positions. Danny, Porter and I were in the middle of a minefield, but fortunately those behind us were still in the old German diggings, so I told them to go back.

A Canadian company commander came forward to a wire fence in front and said that the stretcher-bearers would not be long. He told us how pleased he was to see us as they had had seven men killed by snipers during the last week, from the position which we had just cleaned up. Danny was getting restive lying there on the ground and his language progressively worse.

'Never mind, Danny,' I shouted. 'The moonlight's lovely and I'll get you a bar to your M.C. for this day's work, you mark my words.'

But I, too, was becoming impatient for all this time I was standing on one leg—literally, and for about three-quarters of an hour—not daring to put the other to the ground. I don't think I've ever felt quite so foolish in my life. Then the Canadians came bustling up with two or three officers and four or five stretcher-bearers. I thought there was altogether too much bustle. 'For God's sake ——' I shouted, and there was another loud bang and one of them fell down, badly injured. It now took a long time to get out the two wounded men, with every footstep being prodded first. Danny had ceased to be talkative, and I learned that he had received a lot of wood splinters in the back of the head, as Porter had in the face. When the stretcher party had left, the Canadian pioneer sergeant prodded his way up to me and led me safely out of the minefield by my planting my feet precisely in his footsteps.

By this time Macpherson, who had carried on in spite of his leg wound, had been evacuated, so D had lost all its four officers in the course of the day. I formed up the company and marched them back. I was dead tired, and felt none of the elation to which I was entitled when I reported to Brigade that the road was now clear.

Lieutenant-Colonel Lindsay

Let no one misconceive the severity of the fighting during these final months. In this, the twilight of their gods, the defenders of the Reich displayed the recklessness of fanaticism and the courage of despair. In the contests west of the Rhine, in particular, they fought with special ferocity and resolution, rendering the battles in the Reichswald and Hochwald forests grimly memorable in the annals of this war.

Colonel C. P. Stacey

By 10 March the British and Americans had joined hands, and the Germans had been flung back across the Rhine. To the south, 9, 1 and 3 U.S. Armies, moving with brilliant dash, executed a lightning advance to the river in their sectors, taking both Cologne and Coblenz by 17 March. The intricate fortifications of the West Wall had not stopped them or even slowed them down appreciably. The Germans had lost their last great defensive battle.

West Wall

There were quite a number of pillboxes on the far side of the river. One, I remember, was camouflaged like a barn, and a wooden barn at that. When you opened the door through which the hay was supposed to be put, you came to a concrete wall nine feet thick with an 88 mm. gun sticking out. Another was completely built inside an old house, the outer walls of which were knocked down when it became necessary for the pillbox to go into action. The amazing thing about all these defences is that they produced no results.

During the course of these operations, 90 Division alone put out one hundred and twenty pillboxes in about forty-eight hours, with the loss of less than one hundred and twenty men. This feat was accomplished by careful reconnaissance, then smothering the embrasures with machine-gun and rifle fire, and using dynamite charges against the back door, or else by using self-propelled 155 mm. guns at short range. At three hundred yards the 155 shell will remove a pillbox for every round fired.

In the initial assault across the Sauer, we had guns on our bank firing at the enemy pillboxes across the river at ranges of from four hundred to six hundred yards. Without their assistance, the crossing would probably have been less successful. Captain Krass, a noted German counter-attack artist and head of what was called Krass's Circus, walked in and surrendered to one of our divisions. He gave his name and said he had done his best to make himself well known to the Americans. When asked why he surrendered, he said he had done all a man could do, had received all the medals for valour issued by the German Army, and was not a fool.

. . . . From one point on the road along which 76 Division had successfully advanced, fifteen pillboxes were visible in addition to dragons' teeth and anti-tank ditches. Yet this relatively green division went through them. We visited the command pillbox for the sector. It consisted of a three-storey submerged barracks with toilets, shower baths, a hospital, laundry, kitchen, storerooms, and every conceivable convenience plus an enormous telephone installation. Electricity and heat were produced by a pair of identical diesel engines with generators. Yet the whole offensive capacity of this installation consisted of two machine-guns and a 60 mm. mortar operating from steel cupolas which worked up and down by means of hydraulic lifts. The 60 mm. mortar was peculiar in that it was operated by remote control. As in all cases, this particular pillbox was taken by a dynamite charge against the back door. We found marks on the cupolas, which were ten inches thick, where our 90 mm. shells, fired at a range of two hundred yards, had simply bounced.

Pacifists would do well to study the Siegfried and Maginot Lines, remembering that these defences were forced; that Troy fell; that the walls of Hadrian succumbed; that the Great Wall of China was futile; and that, by the same token, the mighty seas which are alleged to defend us can also be circumvented by a resolute and ingenious opponent. In war, the only sure defence is offence, and the efficiency of offence depends on the warlike souls of those conducting it.

. . . . On the 6th, I decorated Private Harold A. Garman, of 5 Infantry Division, with the Medal of Honour. Garman was an attached medico in one of the battalions that forced the crossing over the Sauer river. During the action a boat with three walking and one prone wounded, paddled by two engineers, started back and was caught by German machine-gun fire in the middle of the river. The engineers, and one of the walking wounded, jumped overboard and swam for shore. The other two wounded jumped overboard, but were too weak to swim and clung to the boat while the litter case lay prone. The boat, still under a hail of bullets, drifted towards the German shore. Private Garman swam out and pushed the boat to our side. I asked him why he did it, and he looked surprised and said, 'Well, someone had to.'

General Patton

A Patton Day

Walker called up around 18.00 with a request to relieve one of his division commanders. I told him if he could name a better one he could relieve him, but he could not. I then called Eddy and gave him hell because 11 Armoured had not got anywhere. In order to make it a perfect day, I called Middleton and told him that at least he had not been cussed out, and congratulated him on his great feat in capturing Coblenz.

General Patton

Coblenz: 17 March

The fall of a city the size and importance of Coblenz was nothing as one had imagined it. The windows of all the houses were shuttered tight; a few dead German and American soldiers lay in the streets; jeeps raced by; artillery barrages screamed in, bringing houses down in a thunder of rubble; fighting continued from street to street. But there was, over all, the chaotic air of a drunken, end-of-the-world carnival. Infantrymen who had been down in the cellars ran crookedly past, firing anywhere, and shrill, over-excited young German girls, impatient of rape, ran after them through barrages, ducking into almost flat doorways as tiles fell from the roofs in crashing showers.

A Free French newspaper photographer drove up in a jeep, brandishing a revolver, and staggered out drunk to take pictures. In a shuttered house directly across the way from us we heard someone banging out *Lili Marlene* on the piano, and, going into a rage, the photographer entered and pulled open the living-room door with a shout. On the point of firing, he found himself aiming at two American soldiers: Ted Jameson at the piano and Paul Clifford standing beside him. The photographer came over to us, shaking from his narrow escape.

In another house, Jimmy McDonough and Horse-face Fogarty, an aid man temporarily taking little Jenkins' place, were looting the contents of a living room. They had learned to say, '*Achtung! Macht schnell! Kommen sie hier!*' and approximations of several other German expressions that they repeated to each other over and over. While Fogarty had his back turned, rifling through the ornaments in a corner whatnot, Jimmy McDonough, with mock German gruffness, said just behind him, '*Achtung! Macht schnell!*'

'Hey, cut it out; you make me nervous,' Fogarty said, but a moment or two passed and the harsh German voice resumed. 'Cut it *out*, I said!' Fogarty repeated. 'What the hell's the matter with you anyway, always f——in' around.' Then he felt something poke him in the back, and when he turned he saw that Jimmy McDonough was at the far side of the room, speechless and shivering, his hands trembling over his head. Four armed German soldiers had come into the room after them, and it took both Americans a few jibbering moments before they realized the Germans were poking their rifles at them in an attempt to hand over the weapons and surrender.

In a living-room up the street, a group of American soldiers were fast getting drunk. Going tipsily out into the dark hall to look for the bathroom, they found themselves, in confusion, bumping into German soldiers who had been holding wassail on the second floor and had come downstairs on the same mission. "Scuse me. Beg your pardon. Wanna get through here,' one American found himself saying to an equally drunken German in a polite, Alphonse-and-Gaston act.

Don Stoddard dashed in off the street to escape a heavy artillery barrage, and running into a dining-room, looking for the way to the cellar, he came upon one of his litter squad having sexual intercourse with the woman of the house.

At intervals between the shelling, the cobbled street just outside the hospital rang with the heavy clatter of German boots as long streams of prisoners came past. There were as many as forty or fifty at a time, hands up, being chivvied along by two small infantrymen, one of whom invariably was unsteady on his feet. Many of the prisoners themselves were drunk; their canteens were filled with cognac.

Lester Atwell

The Remagen Bridge

7 March had seen a splendid coup de main *by a few enterprising men of the U.S. 1 Army, who, seizing the chance of a moment, rushed the bridge at Remagen and unexpectedly provided the Allies with their first bridgehead across the Rhine. This stroke disorganized the Germans and drew off forces waiting to oppose the massive blow impending to the north.*

A small armoured spearhead of the 9 U.S. Armoured Division, reaching the crest of a hill overlooking Remagen, was astonished to see below it, still standing and apparently undamaged, the Ludendorff railway bridge spanning the Rhine. With the dash and courage of men who make history, an American platoon charged into the town and made its way to the bridge. Hardly had they reached it when two of the demolition charges exploded, damaging the easternmost span of the bridge but leaving the roadway intact. Despite these warnings the American infantry continued on over the bridge, while engineers quickly cut the wires controlling the remaining charges. At four o'clock that afternoon 1 U.S. Army had crossed the Rhine!

The story of the German defenders delegated to destroy the Ludendorff railway bridge combines the elements of incompetence, confusion and bewilderment which characterized most German operations in the closing months of the war. Under pain of death, a special engineer regiment had been made responsible for seeing that the bridge was blown up before the Americans threatened it. But, as in the case of General Schlemm in the Reichswald, no bridge was to be demolished too soon, since fleeing German units would otherwise be cut off from their final escape route. At Cologne a bridge prepared for demolition had been prematurely blown up by bombs falling in the neighbourhood, and as a result a large German force had been trapped and captured west of the river. It had therefore been ordered that no charge was to be placed on a bridge until the very last moment.

On 7 March the senior officer responsible for the bridge was away, and his place had been taken by a Major Schoeller. When it was finally decided that the bridge should be prepared for demolition, it was suddenly discovered that the proper charges were not in hand. Frantic efforts were made to improvise effective charges but the final product was entirely inadequate.

Even when Schoeller heard the sound of small-arms fire in Remagen, he still considered it too early to blow the bridge. Although it was expected that American infantry might soon reach the western bank, it was not anticipated that tanks would also appear—since the approaches to the bridge had been well mined and blocked. When, however, Sherman tanks unexpectedly turned up, sweeping the opposite bank with fire, the situation was beyond remedy. The fire cut some of the ignition cables and pinned down the defending troops on the other side. The last-minute demolitions were not enough seriously to affect the bridge, since the charges were too weak. Surprised and dumbfounded, the Germans watched the Americans pouring across the Rhine, too helpless to do anything but gape.

Milton Shulman

1 Army Commander to Army Group Commander . . . .

The blackout blinds were already drawn in my C.P. that evening when I came in to find that Eisenhower's G-3, Major-General Bull, was waiting for me. He had just arrived from S.H.A.E.F. with a larcenous proposal that would divert four of my twenty-six divisions to Devers for the latter's break-through into the Saar.

Suddenly my phone rang. It was Hodges calling from Spa.

'Brad,' Courtney called, with more composure than the good news warranted, 'Brad, we've gotten a bridge.'

'A bridge? You mean you've got one intact on the Rhine?'

'Yep,' Hodges replied, 'Leonard nabbed the one at Remagen before they blew it up——'

'Hot dog, Courtney,' I said, 'this will bust him wide open. Are you getting your stuff across?'

'Just as fast as we can push it over,' he said. 'Tubby's got the Navy moving in now with a ferry service and I'm having the engineers throw a couple of spare pontoon bridges across to the bridgehead.'

I pulled the long lead wire from my phone over towards the map-board. 'Shove everything you can across it, Courtney,' I said, 'and button the bridge-head up tightly. It'll probably take the other fellow a couple of days to pull enough stuff together to hit you.'

General Omar Bradley

It made a long Rhine defence impossible, and upset our entire defence scheme along the river. The Rhine was badly protected between Mainz and Mannheim as a result of bringing reserves to the Remagen bridgehead. All this was very hard on Hitler.

Reichsmarschall Göring

Well, gentlemen, I am the new V-3.

Field-Marshal Kesselring to his staff,
on becoming C.-in-C. West, March 1945

CROSSING THE RHINE

To the north of the Ruhr, Montgomery prepared the stroke which had been so long coming—the forcing of the Rhine. On the night of 23 March the British 2 Army and U.S. 9 Army crossed the river north and south of Wesel, after a shattering bombardment by land and air. At the same moment commandos cleared the Germans out of Wesel itself. On the following morning two airborne divisions—6 British and 17 U.S.—descended en masse beyond the Rhine in an enormously impressive show of force, against which the desperate German opposition was unavailing.

It is impossible to describe this tremendous sight adequately. It was even difficult to appreciate the magnitude of the huge fleet roaring so low over our heads. There were 1,572 big planes towing 1,326 gliders, with nine hundred fighters providing cover and another 1,253 fighters passing on to quieten targets east of the river. The Lancasters, Halifaxes, Stirlings, Fortresses and Dakotas flew in majestically, slowly, at eight hundred feet—a steady solid phalanx, like the pattern of a carpet in the sky, for three hours. There was haze as well as smoke over the target, and the planes gradually disappeared into it before we could see the parachutes open or the mushroom puffs of the flak which met them. We watched anxiously as the planes materialized again, their task accomplished —some, happily only a few, with their engines smoking, losing height and seeking desperately for a landing ground. One Fortress I shall never forget; it came lower and lower over our heads, glistening silver in the morning sunlight, the flames which streamed from one wing a deep orange against the azure blue. As it passed us parachutes blossomed from the side and we counted them anxiously, and watched with horror as one failed to open and plunged straight to the ground in a white streak, the man kicking desperately up to the last moment, until we knew that remaining in the blazing plane alone, whether alive or dead, was no one but the pilot.

British tank officer

It was sunny above but a misty morning in the woods and valleys as I stood there on the river bank, watching those serials come over, flying low. There was no enemy air interference at all, and behind me, to our rear, not a gun was firing. We had shut off all the British 2 Army's guns for the time being to ensure that the planes would not fly into the trajectory of our own artillery shells.

Across the river the German guns were responding angrily, however, and we had some losses from ground fire, particularly in the case of the 513th Parachute Infantry, commanded by Colonel Coutts. We did not have enough of the old workhorses, the C-47s that we had been using for paradrops, and we had to put the 513th and its supporting engineers and parachute artillery into seventy-two C-46s, a twin-engine plane capable of carrying a tremendous load. Out of those seventy-two planes we lost twenty-two from ground fire, and of these twenty-two, fourteen were flamers that caught fire in the air as soon as they were hit.

General Matthew B. Ridgway

Ground Battle

While we stood talking and smoking another wave of parachutists had broken, another plane had been shot down in flames; and now the whole sky turned above us as the gliders, released by their tugs, spiralled silently down to their landing grounds. But I was only vaguely aware of these events. I was re-adapting myself to life, slowly and with intense enjoyment.

The trees were still reeking and cracking from a well-placed salvo of mortar bombs as the Brigadier came striding up, pursued by his perspiring bodyguard, to put an end to our conversation. 'Come along, gentlemen'—his tone, as usual, was quiet and courteous—'come along now, show a little enthusiasm with those picks and shovels!' Things always began to happen when the Brigadier was on the stage. My unenthusiastic efforts to dig a hole were cut short by a babel of warning shouts followed by a tremendous crash and the splitting and rending of the forest. A glider, which had landed in the hazy distance and swept across the fields as noiselessly as its own monstrous shadow, had crashed into the pines barely thirty yards from the sandy clearing where I was grovelling. I could hardly believe my eyes when dazed soldiers came tumbling out of the shattered fuselage and the pilot was helped from his cockpit, stunned and bruised, but shielding the sun from eyes that still saw.

The sunny day was no longer a setting for self-enjoyment. A group of German soldiers came racing up, white-faced and terrified, with an ugly Canadian para-trooper prodding the stragglers in the back. Wounded men began to arrive, some carried in by stretcher-bearers, others walking unaided or supported by their comrades.

Soon there were dozens of wounded assembled in the shade. There was certainly nothing we could do for them except see that they had been given first aid. Till a nearby village had been captured there was no question of beginning surgery. There was certainly nothing we could do for Geordie, the rough little Tynesider who had slept opposite me in the Bulford barrack room. 'Follow the crowd' had been his theme whenever discussion turned on the forthcoming operation. 'I've always followed the fuggin' crowd, and I've always been all reet.' And one felt he had—as an urchin playing in the street, as an adolescent hanging about outside the cinemas, and as a volunteer for parachuting. His other phrase was 'Whose side are ye on?'—and that was the real key to his character. He had always been 'one of the gang' in a world of rival gangs and football teams. Now it was his only articulate remark as he lay on his stretcher, mortally wounded, listening to our hollow reassurances. He could already feel himself sinking into the anonymity of death, and wished to be sure that we knew who he was.

James Byrom

Slaughter of the Gliders

The situation was most confused. We were being attacked from the wood known as the Deerforsterswald, to the west, and I was evacuating the casualties east, farther into Germany, to the area held by 5 Parachute Brigade. I was still clearing the landing zone when the re-supply drop of parachute containers came in—a most alarming experience. A few parachutes failed to open, and one such landed a few feet away, the container, about four feet long and eighteen inches across, burying half its length in the ground with a squelchy thud. The landing zone looked rather like a fairground in process of closing down, the discarded parachutes resembling struck tents, and all the litter of war lying around. Only the still figures of the dead gave an air of grim reality to the scene. Several gliders were burning briskly, having been caught in a burst of machine-gun fire on landing, which had ignited the petrol in the jeep inside. The British glider was a better proposition than the American Waco, which was of fabric over a steel framework. If it crashed the occupants were trapped in a cage, whereas the British Horsa, being of wood, could be quickly chopped through, although this was usually unnecessary, as it tended to fall apart.

I saw one burnt-out Waco with the charred bodies of the occupants, the whole looking for all the world as if some monster had set a bird-cage on a bonfire.

Lieutenant-Colonel J. C. Watts, R.A.M.C.

Although the air drop had been a success and losses had been far less than pessimists had foretold, casualties nevertheless were heavy, chiefly among the gliders. Brigadier Hill's brigade, which we had just left, had suffered few casualties because their landing in trees, though uncomfortable, had given them immediate cover. 5 Parachute Brigade also escaped comparatively lightly. But the gliders had a difficult time. The morning haze and smoke over the L.Z. made their landing more difficult, and many were scattered into distant parts. The S.A.S. troops in their special jeeps and the medium bombers and fighters whose task had been to neutralize the considerable amount of flak in the area seem to have been successful with most of the 20 mms. but the 88s were either beyond their capacity or had escaped them. It was these guns, resolutely manned, which did such execution. Casualties would have been far higher if an American Parachute Battalion had not come down by mistake in the area where a few minutes later the gliders were due to land, thus occupying the attention of many of the enemy during the fatal pause when a glider is a sitting target.* Lieutenant-Colonel Allday had come down over a mile away from where he should have been, and had met the C.O. of the Airborne Recce Regiment, who was with one of his Tetrarch tanks in the same vicinity. They had walked in together, the Tetrarch reducing opposition as they went. One glider containing a much-loved battery commander of the Light Regiment came down almost on top of an 88, which, in the few seconds which must elapse before the occupants can get out, put a round of high explosive through the nose, killing them all. A battery commander of the Anti-Tank Regiment who had won a splendid M.C. in the Normandy landing was identified several days later by half his identity disc. The Anti-Tank Regiment itself could muster an effective strength of two batteries, instead of three, and H.Q. R.A. consisted of the C.R.A. and his I.O. with a few signallers. On the first day the casualties of the glider-borne troops, including missing (a number of whom found their way in later or had made forced landings before reaching the L.Z.), were reckoned at fifty per cent.

British tank officer

Link-up

It took a long time to find Bols's C.P.† There was a lot of sporadic firing going on all about, and a confused tactical situation, which is normal in an air-borne drop. We didn't know where our own people were, much less the enemy, so we had to move with a moderate degree of caution. Finally, about eleven o'clock that night, I found Bols's C.P., and we had a very satisfactory talk. He seemed glad to see the Corps commander, and his brother division commander, General Miley. So the two of them got together there over maps, evaluated the situation as best they could, and laid plans for concerting their action thereafter, with me helping at Corps in any way I could.

It was around midnight when we left, a clear night, with a half moon shining, lighting up the woods so that you could see for perhaps a hundred yards all around. There was a tremendous amount of firing going on, most of it machine-gun fire, and the bulk of it heavy stuff—50-calibre. Pretty soon, looming up in the moonlight we saw the hulk of the burned-out truck. My jeep was in the lead,

---

* Diary of Lieutenant-General Brereton: '24 March . . . Colonel Coutt's Regiment was dropped some two thousand five hundred yards north-east of its assigned zone due to an error caused by haze and smoke. The drop of the 1st Battalion was carried out in the immediate vicinity of two batteries of 88 mm. all-purpose guns, and two batteries of 20 mm. . . . Luckily this drop occurred in the area on which the British Horsas were to land. Had not these batteries been silenced prior to 6 Division landing, in my opinion and in that of Major-General Bols, the losses would have been catastrophic. The entire landing brigade might have been completely destroyed.'

† Major-General Bols, O.C. 6 Airborne Division (Ed.).

and just as we reached the truck and turned out over the same little detour we had travelled before—suddenly there was a scurrying of men in the road some twenty yards ahead. We had bumped into a German patrol. I jumped from the jeep, firing my Springfield from the hip, and I heard the first man squeal and saw him fall. Then they all hit the ground, firing, and so did we, and there was a great deal of cursing and swearing in German and English there for a while. Every gun was shooting except my jeep-mounted 50-calibre, which never fired a shot, and I wondered why the hell it didn't. I found out later they were afraid to fire. We were so mixed up there on the ground that they couldn't tell friend from foe, so they didn't cut loose with the 50. Which I guess was just as well in that situation.

I fired all five shots in my Springfield, shooting from the hip because the range was so close. Then I hit the ground to reload, rolled to get another clip out of my belt, and this threw my head right beside the right front wheel of my jeep. There was quite an explosion then, very close to me, and I felt the heat and sting of a fragment in my shoulder. Some German had thrown a grenade and it had gone off under the front of the jeep, about three feet from my head. But, by the grace of God, the wheel was between me and the blast, and all I got was one small chunk that hit me in the shoulder. It wrecked the jeep, though, broke the crankcase and all the oil spilled out on the ground.

After that explosion there was complete silence. I could hear men breathing around me in the dark, but nobody was quite sure where anybody else was, so we held our fire. Then I caught sight of a little movement to my right rear, across the ditch in a little bunch of willows, and I could vaguely see the head and shoulders of a man. I couldn't tell whether it was one of us or a German, so I eased around until I got him covered, then I called out:

'Put up your hands, you son of a bitch!'

I got a very friendly answer back in good American. 'Aaah, go sit in your hat,' he said. So I eased my finger off the trigger.

There was no more firing. The Germans had melted away into the shadows —we hoped—and we went on back, pushing my crippled jeep.

General Ridgway

The Rhine is not a strategic obstacle. It can be crossed just as the Vistula, the Dnieper, the Don, the Oder, the Elbe, the Danube, the Maas, the Marne, or any other river can be. A river is welcome as a tactical obstacle, but operationally, however, it cannot be held for long. In 1945 the Rhine was not fortified at all and only weakly garrisoned with troops who had already suffered heavily. The German Air Force scarcely existed any longer, intact Panzer divisions were not available, and the infantry divisions were exhausted.

When the Allies had crossed the Rhine the last illusory obstacle was lost and with it the war. Spirits were naturally depressed, but the troops still showed determination. Nowhere was there indiscipline or mutiny, and the spirit of the troops was much better than 1918. The divisions were tired and decimated. The staffs hoped for a more rapid advance by the Anglo-Americans, for the chief worry in our case was not in the west but in the east.

General Blumentritt

THE RUHR POCKET

On 29 March the American 1 Army burst out of the Remagen bridgehead. Two days later it linked up with 9 Army, which in company with the British was expanding the Wesel bridgehead at great speed. Germany's industrial heart was cut off from the body, and within the Ruhr pocket, trapped, lay Field-Marshal Model's Army Group B.

When I got back to my battle headquarters at Reinhardsbrunn in the Thuringian Forest on the morning of 1 April my Chief reported to me that on an order from the Führer just received my attempt to break out of the Ruhr pocket was to be called off and Army Group B was to defend the Ruhr as 'a fortress' in immediate subordination to the O.K.W.

I was more than flabbergasted by this decision of the O.K.W. It upset all our plans. The O.K.W. may have thought a break-out had no longer any prospect of success, and that an encircled Army Group might pin down enough enemy troops to prejudice a strong eastward drive. They may possibly have also believed that the Army Group could be rationed by the Ruhr and that greater supplies could thus be fed to the other units at the front.

In point of fact, however, there was only enough food in the Ruhr to feed the troops of both Army Group and population for at most two or three weeks. From a strategic point of view the Ruhr had no interest for Eisenhower; his objective lay far to the east. The only hope of pinning down strong investment forces lay in a stubborn and indeed aggressive defence, which, judging by what I had seen, was not on the face of it likely. Army Group B's three hundred thousand men could not remotely be replaced to close the gap between the Teutoburger and the Thuringian Forest.

Field-Marshal Kesselring, C.-in-C. West

Model

During the last days of the struggle I had many private conversations with Field-Marshal Model. He was an interesting character—forceful and ironical—and was well used to desperate battles; indeed, his reputation had been built up by his uncanny gift for improvisation. Time and again he had succeeded in restoring apparently hopeless situations; he had pulled the Eastern Front together after the frightful collapse in June and July 1944, and he had done the same in the West after Normandy. During April he repeatedly visited our Headquarters, and I had the feeling that he was wrestling with himself to find a solution to some inner conflict. Like all senior commanders he was faced with an insoluble dilemma; as a highly qualified officer he saw the hopelessness of further resistance, but on the other hand he was bound in duty and honour to his superiors and subordinates.

. . . . Model never digressed from the strict path of military discipline, but as a true servant of Germany he blunted the edge of senseless commands, and sought to minimize unnecessary destruction. Hitler had ordered a 'scorched earth' policy, and wanted us to wreck every factory and mining plant in the

Ruhr, but Model limited himself to purely military demolitions. The Field-Marshal was determined to preserve the industrial heart of Germany; no longer did he fight stubbornly for every building, and he disregarded the orders issued by the Führer in a last frenzy of destructive mania.

Model wondered whether he should initiate negotiations with the enemy, and put this question to me frankly. We both rejected it on military grounds. After all, Field-Marshal Model knew no more about the general situation than the simplest company commander in his army group. His ignorance sprang from 'Führer Command No. 1' of 13 January 1940, which laid down that 'no officer or authority must know more than is absolutely necessary for the execution of his particular task'. Model did not know whether political negotiations were going on, and he was fully sensible of the argument that the Western Armies must keep on fighting to the last in order to protect the rear of our comrades in the East, who were involved in a desperate struggle to cover the escape of millions of German women and children, then fleeing from the Russian hordes.

On the evening of 15 April orders were issued that small groups should be formed under selected officers, and should try to find a way through to the east. Soldiers without weapons or ammunition were to allow themselves to be over-run. On 17 April Army Group B ordered the discharge of the younger and older classes from the armed forces and the cessation of further fighting.

General von Mellenthin

After the first few days it became perfectly clear that the Germans were folding fast. Less than two miles ahead of us was the headquarters of [Field-Marshal] Model, Commander of German Army Group B. His situation was hopeless, and I knew that so shrewd a soldier as Model was well aware that he didn't have a chance. It seemed to me that here was an excellent opportunity to save many thousands of precious lives. I called in one of my personal aides, Captain Brandstetter, who spoke fluent German, gave him my instructions, and sent him to Model under a flag of truce. My message was simple. I merely told Model that he was in a hopeless situation and that further resistance could only cause needless slaughter.

Brandstetter came back with one of Model's staff officers—and Model's answer. It was to the effect that he could not consider any surrender proposal. He was bound by a personal oath to Hitler to fight to the end, and it would do violence to his sense of honour even to consider my message.

I decided to make one more try. I sat down and composed a personal letter to General Model, and think that part of the text of it might be of interest here. The date was 15 April 1945:

Neither history nor the military profession records any nobler character, any more brilliant master of warfare, any more dutiful subordinate of the state, than the American General, Robert E. Lee. Eighty years ago this month, his loyal command, reduced in numbers, stripped of its means of effective fighting and completely surrounded by overwhelming forces, he chose an honourable capitulation.

This same choice is now yours. In the light of a soldier's honour, for the reputation of the German Officer Corps, for the sake of your nation's future, lay down your arms at once. The German lives you will save are sorely needed to restore your people to their proper place in society. The German cities you will preserve are irreplaceable necessities for your people's welfare.

Brandstetter delivered this letter. He came back with Model's Chief of Staff. It was no use, they said. Model would not consider any plea whatever. That was that. I could do no more. From now on the blood was upon Model's head. His Chief of Staff was a wiser man. I told him he could go back under a flag of truce and take his chances in the disaster that was sure to come. Or he could remain in our custody as a prisoner of war. He did not debate this option long. He chose to stay.

General Ridgway

On 21 April 1945 Field-Marshal Model shot himself in my presence in a wood near Duisberg. I buried him, and I am, as far as I know, the only person who knows where his grave is. He chose death, because he had been accused of being a war criminal by the Russians. In the course of conversation I had had with him over a period of days, I expressed my opinion that the Western Powers would hand him over to the Russians—and it was this which decided him.

Senior Intelligence Officer, Army Group B

THE FLOODGATES OPEN

While Army Group B met its end, the remaining German armies everywhere crumbled away in disastrous retreat. The Americans and the French to the southward swept all before them in a series of colossal drives from the Rhine into the remotest corners of the Reich. On 29 March Patton reached Frankfurt and the U.S. 7 Army took Mannheim. 9, 1 and 3 Armies drove on Magdeburg, and on Leipzig and Bayreuth towards the Czech border, 9 Army reaching the Elbe near Magdeburg on 12 April. The Americans were sixty miles from Berlin. There has been comparatively little written which tells of these days, even from the side of the triumphant victors. From the side of the defeated there is, to date, still less. Perhaps events in the West lacked the vastness and horror of the catastrophe in the East, so providing writers with little inspiration.

The battles now beginning east of the Rhine were often obscure to us. Without an air force and with only a few tanks, without supplies, we could no longer fight as ably as formerly. The means of communication failed, there was often no communication with the corps and divisions of the Army, and many units had to act independently. Also communications with the higher echelons of command grew worse and worse. For days no orders came, often the sectors of the Army were suddenly altered, divisions were taken away, new units brought up. Firm tactical leadership was no longer possible, reconnaissance failed to an increasing extent and we frequently did not know where the enemy was.

General Blumentritt

The enormously costly battles of the last half-year and constant retreat and defeat had reduced officers and men to a dangerous state of exhaustion. Many officers were nervous wrecks, others affected in health, others simply incompetent, while there was a dangerous shortage of junior officers. In the ranks strengths were unsatisfactory, replacements arriving at the front insufficiently trained, with no combat experience, in driblets, and, anyway, too late. They were accordingly no asset in action. Only where an intelligent commander had a full complement of experienced subalterns and a fair nucleus of elder men did units hold together.

. . . . The supply situation was bad; in some areas critical. Complicated by uncertainty as to the arrival of supply trains, it made wrong distributions inevitable. The railway network was badly battered, and if further stretches of line were put out of action, could no longer be reckoned with.

Furthermore, symptoms of disintegration were perceptible behind the front which gave cause for uneasiness. The number of 'missing' was a disquieting indication that a rot was setting in. The attitude of the civilian population in several districts, particularly in the Rhine Palatinate and the Saar, confirmed this tendency. Even among military staffs political talk could be heard which undermined the solidarity of resistance and nourished defeatism at lower levels.

Field-Marshal Kesselring

I visited Colonel Allen in the hospital, as he had been recaptured when we took Weimar. His right arm had been shot off just below the elbow. He gave me some very interesting information. The surgeon who operated on him used the last ether in his possession to put Allen under, but it was insufficient, and towards the end he gave him brandy and some sort of chloral drug. Allen said he saw at least eighty Germans operated on without any anaesthetic at all except chloral and cognac; there were no sanitary arrangements, no soap or water, and the doctors and nurses were literally wading in blood. Many of the men were dragged into the operating-room by the hand, as there was a shortage of stretchers. The surgeon who operated on him was an Austrian, and, during the few days Allen was in the hospital, repeatedly gave false information as to his state of health because the Germans, having discovered that he was a colonel, were very anxious to get him to Army Headquarters for interrogation. The surgeon finally told Allen that if the worst came to the worst he would help him to escape and keep him hidden in the hills until we came up. Allen was a very sporting character and the only request he had was that he be left on duty at Army Headquarters, which request was granted.

General Patton

Into Germany

The Germans, letting go the Rhine, fell back in retreat, leaving road blocks and detachments of men to engage us in delaying actions. Sometimes during the following week, the enemy dug in to make a desperate stand only to have large numbers of its men throw down their arms and stream towards us in surrender. After a disorganized rout, collapse and retreat, more road blocks were thrown up and the wounded German Army fell back still farther.

One of the delaying actions made by the Germans, though of short duration and of obvious uselessness, stands out as one of the more ghastly episodes of the war. We were advancing down a road in convoy when a German tank drove out of a grove of trees, fired point-blank, killed two of our men, and then retreated from sight again. The convoy halted and two of our rifle companies went forward and surrounded the little grove that contained, they discovered, a platoon of German soldiers in deep foxholes. The German tank kept swivelling and firing, and after a while four of our own tanks came up. Each from a different direction sprayed the tiny stretch of woods with long streams of flaming gasoline. Within a few seconds the place became an inferno, and the shrieks and screams of the Germans could be heard through the high curtains of fire. A few, in flames, tried to crawl through, but they were mowed down by our machine-guns. Within a half hour we went on, and all that was left of the little wood was a deep bed of glowing golden coals, hideous to see and to think about in the spring sunlight.

The countryside grew extremely hilly and wooded; small towns, flying surrender flags, lay hidden in hollows. In the swiftness of pursuit, one company by mistake often seized another company's town and had to double back to take its own objective. The convoy of trucks rushed into the towns; the infantrymen hopped down, cleared out the snipers, rounded up the prisoners, jumped into the trucks again and set out for the next town. Some days, in this fashion, as many as thirty miles were covered.

. . . . The entire convoy pulled up in a higgledy-piggledy village with small, low cottages and a few round, turreted medieval buildings that seemed to have no windows. The place looked like a page from a Mother Goose water-colour book. It was full noon; the dusty road and white cottages, the bed sheets and tablecloths gave back a white glare. When the trucks stopped, the men jumped down and then there were khaki uniforms swarming everywhere over the bleached whiteness of the little street, opening gates, going into back yards searching for eggs, forcing open front doors to loot and hunt for liquor.

Not knowing how long we were to stay, we sat in the kitchen of one of the little houses, having our lunch. The old woman who lived there had just been dispossessed. . . . The kitchen was crowded with men walking about, eating and talking; Silly Willie was frying a can of C-ration hash and causing a stench.

. . . . At that moment, two line-company boys smashed down the flimsy back door of the house with their rifles and came in, asking, 'This place been looted yet?' The old woman who lived in the house had returned and there was a commotion behind me in the room. Either someone had burned the bottom out of her only good pot or she had seen someone going out of the house with her only good pot. At any rate, she set up a loud keening about it and taxed Phil, who had promised her that nothing would be disturbed. 'Hey, get her the hell outta here,' someone was saying. 'What's she bitchin' about, anyway? Go on, ya old bastard, git out! Git outta here!' She took herself off on her sore feet, whimpering and crying, followed by a few oaths and careless laughter. Sipping my tea, looking out the window at the sunlit back yard, the thought suddenly came to me, I'm tired of this, tired of war, of human beings, of everything.

. . . . And yet, only a few days before, on Good Friday, during the attack a half mile ahead on the town of Eisenach, I had seen the high wire gates of a slave-labour camp being swung open by men of our battalion, and the inmates, with a rush and a tremendous roar, had come pouring out on to the street. For me, it was one of the most thrilling moments of the war. They surrounded the handful of us who were there—I had come down the street with Phil to watch—and they crowded about to shake our hands, to thank us individually, laughing and crying and in their jubilation addressing us in their native tongues. There were no interpreters; we could only smile and smile and continue shaking hands. I offered my cigarettes around until they were gone and kept asking, 'Polski? Russki?' In time I could feel my smile growing stretched, but there was nothing to do but go on smiling and smiling and shaking hands. A few of the slave labourers, their meagre possessions slung over their shoulder, giving us a wave and a cheer as they came out, pointed to a direction—to the east, probably—and struck off without a backward glance. Then two slave labourers ran up the street, each with a bottle of liquor, and at that they all scattered and began to burst into the nearby houses in search of liquor to celebrate their freedom. The American troops were a half-step ahead of them in the search, and a fast-paced looting contest started up.

Later in the afternoon, when large numbers of German soldiers were captured and marched up the street in their long muddy overcoats, hands over their heads, some of the slave labourers ran alongside, catcalling and shouting and pointing out the S.S. troops to the American guards. Other slave labourers, by then happily drunk, were roaming up and down the street, five and six abreast, arms linked, careless of shellfire, singing their national songs. Still others, looking dazed and without plans, leaned against the wire enclosure that had been their home. A few wearily went inside. Within a few hours, all of them seemed to grow as accustomed to the sight of us as we grew to them.

Lester Atwell

Armies are composed of human beings, and few in the full flush of victory can abstain from helping themselves to the property of their enemies. Americans, British, Russians—all tended to 'live off the country' as well as their own supplies.

Luxuriating in the feel of the sun on my face, I strolled away from the tanks and wandered around the farm and outbuildings. At the end of the yard a little wooden building in a wire pen looked as if it might bear further investigation. It was a chicken run, but all the poultry had long since been liberated by the Scotsmen. But the wire netting looked as if it could be converted into a form of permane..t camouflage screen, with the judicious application of some leaves and grasses.

Casually I glanced into the hen house—and then my heart almost stopped beating as I saw, nestling warmly in a bed of straw, a delectable, speckled brown egg!

Now you must know that in those days an egg was a rare thing of great beauty; a prize to be jealously guarded and cooked with care and attention.

Beaming with pride I carried my treasure back to Five Troop, and I was soon the centre of an admiring throng of whistling tank crews. Those who were quicker on the uptake shot away to look for other hen-houses, but Five Troop just stood around making envious remarks.

'How would you like it, sir?' said Pickford. 'Boiled, fried, scrambled or poached?'

'I think I'd like it boiled,' I said. 'With a little brown bread and butter.'

We settled for biscuits and margarine, but water was swiftly put on one of the pressure stoves and brought to the boil.

At least four separate watches were used to time the cooking of this lovely brown egg, while Crosby sorted out a suitable size of socket spanner to use as an egg-cup. One of my cleaner handkerchiefs did duty as a napkin, and then with great ceremony I removed the egg from the water and settled myself for a feast.

With a great flourish I tapped the egg with my spoon—and was rewarded with a resonant and crystal-clear 'Ding!'

I tried again, mounting suspicion in my heart.

'Ding!' rang the egg.

A stunned silence lay over Five Troop, and then Crosby threw back his head and yelled: 'It's a pot egg!'

That did it. Gales of laughter swept over the assembled tank crews; people who had been cursing each other the previous day slung their arms around one another and wept tears of merriment. The reaction would have touched the heart of any E.N.S.A. comedian—and I sat in the middle of it and stared unbelievingly at the fraud in my hand.

It was a typical example of German thoroughness. Not for them the heavy, glossy object which fools British birds; my pot egg was the right weight, colour, texture, and everything. The designer of that egg had really set out to deceive the poultry, and I'll bet he succeeded.

John Foley

From motives which varied, the invaders shared their own supplies with the German civilians.

A dumpy, middle-aged German woman presented herself to ask for medicine for her mother. To Phil, acting as interpreter, she explained that her mother had *'nicht gestoolmacht'* for five days. Preacher had nothing but the large brown bombers he had given me the day we left the Saar Valley, and through Phil he told the woman that her mother was to take two immediately, and if there were no results by evening she was to take two more. With one of his rare bursts of humour he looked at me over his glasses and said, 'An' then Ah think we better be a-gettin' the hell outta town.' The woman, repeating the instructions, went off. A few hours later, from the doorway of the court, I saw her with her mother—a toothless, thin woman in her late seventies—both of them being dispossessed, making their way through the débris, bent over with Saratoga trunks on their backs, being hurried out of one smashed-up house into another by one of the battalion interpreters. German artillery fire was quite strong at the moment, and there was still small-arms fire in the streets. The interpreter, with shouts and jabs of his rifle, was trying to rush them to cover, but the old one kept turning her head to snap and crab at him. Five days of constipation, brown bombers, Saratoga trunk and all, she could still give back as good as she received.

. . . . Shortly after, two young women came along with their children, and after drawing the water they stood at the open doorway, looking into the yard, half troubled, half smiling. They did not permit the children to come in, yet something held them. We said, '*Guten Morgen!*' and they answered. One of the young women was dark-haired, fairly well built and good-looking; her companion had a waxy pinched face, tiny mouth, pale-blue eyes and masses of pale blonde hair. They pointed tentatively into the yard, and their shoulders asked questions.

'Sure! Come on in!' Jimmy McDonough said. 'We're all friends here. Come on!'

They held back at first, then the dark-haired, more adventurous one, with an embarrassed pat to her cheap clothes, as if she were stepping out on to a stage, entered and crossed quickly to the rabbit cages. Assured that the rabbits were still there, she poked in two large, wilted leaves from her pocket and hurried out with a nod of thanks. Some of the men in the meanwhile had given the children C-ration crackers, a few sticks of gum, and a hard candy or two. With laughs and *Auf Wiedersehens* the little group moved off, the women carrying their pails of water.

Phil and I were standing upstairs at our window a day or so later when the same two young women came down the passageway to draw water. When they peeked into the yard and saw that it was empty, they put down their pails and ran over to the rabbit boxes. Someone had let one of the rabbits out and it had escaped. The little blonde woman mourned, with her hand up to the side of her face. From a crumpled brown paper bag the other took out vegetable tops and poked them in between the wires.

The attention of both was attracted by someone in the window directly below ours. The women, trying to understand, looked at each other, looked back, shrugged. 'I think you might be needed as an interpreter downstairs,' I said to Phil, and I went down with him. Joe Mortara was at his window with half a chocolate bar in his hand, trying to entice one or the other of the women— perhaps both—into the bedroom. '*Schlafen?*' he was saying. '*Schlafen? Choco-lada?*'

The women, finally understanding, laughed and went out. Not too discouraged, Joe covered up the little chocolate bar, knowing he would see them come down the passageway again. Even under ordinary circumstances, I felt half a chocolate bar was niggardly, especially when the whole bar was there; but when one considered that Joe Mortara was the supply sergeant and had free access to cases of ration food, the thing was staggering.

'Now that's a damned shame,' Phil said, 'to tempt women with little kids who haven't enough to eat.' That morning on the chow line, a thin, sick-looking woman had stood silently begging, with a baby in her arms. We had passed her at our five-yard intervals and with terrible eyes she had looked from man to man. Captain Christoffsen was there with one of his lieutenants, and it had just been announced that the fine of sixty-five dollars for speaking to any German civilian was to be strictly enforced once more. For the first time in weeks, an orange was given to each man on the line. Phil took his, walked up on to the road and handed it to the woman. Immediately after, she was sent away. 'They want to fine me, court-martial me, let them!' he said. 'I don't care who they are or what they've done, if it's a woman or a child, and they're hungry, they can have half of anything I've got.'

The next time the dark-haired woman and her waxen-faced friend came for water, Joe Mortara was in the yard with the chocolate bar in his hand, trying to lure them down the cellar.

Phil was outraged. He had received four or five packages from home, and he gathered together some dehydrated soup, some tea bags, lumps of sugar, K-ration cheese, crackers and a few cans of chopped pork-and-carrot which no one could eat, and brought them down in a paper bag and gave it to the women.

'Fer der kinder,' Phil said. 'Mit obgekochter wasser: Suppe.'

The blonde woman burst into tears. The other woman, crying, 'Ah, danke! Danke,' wept also, and tried to kiss his hand. Then both hurried away with the food, leaving the pails of water behind them.

'Hey, what the hell's the matter with you?' Joe Mortara asked. 'Here I am, I got the chocolate bar all ready, you come along and spoil everything.'

'I'm sorry, Joe,' said Phil, 'but I'm going to continue spoiling it for you. If they want to go to you voluntarily, well and good; that's their business. If it's through hunger, no.'

Joe Mortara accepted it as one of his assistant's eccentricities. 'Jeez, you don't have to be so friendly with them as all that,' he said, walking back towards the house, wrapping up the chocolate for use some time again.

Lester Atwell

The great advance was not all beer and skittles. . . .

I learned that Colonel John Hines, son of my old friend Major-General John L. Hines, had been struck in the face with a solid 88 and had both eyes taken out while leading his tanks in the attack on the airfield south of Frankfurt. After he was wounded, he took the radio telephone, called the Division Commander, gave an exact statement of the situation and ended by saying, 'And also, General, you had better send someone to take my place as I am wounded.'

General Patton

My combat command, C.C. 'A' of 6 Armoured Division, had crossed the Rhine and passed through 5 Infantry Division on the left of our C.C. 'B'. Our mission was to clear the angle between the Main and Rhine rivers and attack the bridges into Frankfurt and Frankfurt itself. We had pushed through some very difficult wooded and swampy terrain, and after a brisk fight had taken the village of Morfelden.

. . . . The airport we knew had a large concentration of 88 and 105 anti-aircraft artillery and we were receiving heavy fire from them. Also we were receiving some 150 mm. artillery, probably from Frankfurt.

. . . . I remember we flushed some German infantry in foxholes who came past us to surrender. I was standing in the turret of my tank talking on the radio telephone. The tank had been swung around so that its tail end was towards Frankfurt. I had been talking first to my other task force to ascertain its progress, and then I was either talking to or trying to contact Colonel Britton and looking over the rear of my tank towards Frankfurt when a shell which I did not hear coming hit the deck of my tank and the side of the turret. I had my left hand on the hatch and was facing the shell. I remember seeing the explosion and trying to pull down the hatch with my left hand, only to find that I had lost the fingers of it. I remember dropping down into the tank and finding that I was choking from bone and shrapnel fragments in my throat and scooping them out with the fingers of my right hand. I then remember trying to call to report our situation and to have someone take my place, but I am confused as to whom I called or what I said.

Colonel John Hines

Friday, 13 April

The early morning was chill, with the sun coming up pale gold through a thin silvery fog. We had lined up at five-yard intervals on a country road, shivering and yawning, waiting for the cooks to start serving breakfast. 1st Battalion was there and the medics had formed behind them.

'Men'—an officer came quickly along the line—'I have an announcement. I'd like your attention there! I have an announcement to make: President Roosevelt died last night.'

'*What?*' You heard it from all sides. 'What? President Roosevelt? Roosevelt's *dead?*' We were astounded.

The officer's voice continued. 'We don't know any of the particulars, except that he's dead. I think it was very sudden. Probably a stroke. Truman, the Vice-President, will take over.'

'Who? Who'd he say?'

'Truman, ya dumb bastard. Who the hell you think?'

Phil was behind me and I said to him at once, 'I wonder what effect it will have on the war—whether it will make it drag out, if the Germans will take heart——'

'I don't know!'

'Just when we'd really need him! With peace conferences coming up—I wonder what Truman's like?'

Lester Atwell

Know Your Enemy

13 April 1945 was a date in the history of civilization which should never be forgotten. On that day the U.S. 3 Army reached Buchenwald, near Weimar. To the north, the Germans asked for a truce in order that the British might take over Belsen and so prevent the prisoners from escaping and spreading typhus throughout the Reich. There were other camps, but there was little to choose between them.

Buchenwald

Inside the gate is a spacious yard of rough flagstones. By prearrangement, our Military Government officer and a number of the French prisoners were waiting for us—Colonel Marhes, formerly head of the Resistance movement in northern

France, and Marvel Paul, member of the Paris Municipal Council; General Audebert of the Cavalry, and General Challe, Aviation. All of them in for 'resistance activities', for it must be understood that Buchenwald, while its inmates include many former officers and soldiers, is not a compound for military prisoners of war, but for those who have committed, or are suspected of having committed, 'crimes against the Reich'.

'You might as well see the end-product first,' the Military Government officer said, 'and then work backwards.'

While not large, the crematory is, as I remember it, the only solidly constructed building in the camp. In a smaller yard, enclosed by a wooden fence, a large wagon like a farmer's cart had just been brought in. Over it the flies buzzed lazily. Its contents, the Military Government officer explained, were part of the day's toll—thirty or forty bodies, naked, crisscrossed like matches, and about as substantial. The crematory itself is not unlike the standard variety, with certain additional features. It seems that the routine was as follows: Prisoners who died from 'natural causes' were simply carted into the ground floor of the crematory proper and tossed into six coke ovens, in which are still to be seen the charred remains of the last over-hasty and incomplete job that the arrival of our troops interrupted.

The unusual feature is the basement. Here, according to eye-witnesses whom I have no reason to disbelieve, were brought prisoners condemned of capital crimes—for example, attempting to escape, insubordination, stealing a potato, smiling in ranks—usually in groups of twenty or so at a time. They were lined up against the walls, each one under a hook fixed at a height of about eight feet from the floor. (The hooks are no longer there. They were hastily removed the day we came in, but the emplacements are clearly visible.) A short slip-noose was placed about the neck of the condemned, who was then raised by the guards the distance necessary to affix the end of the noose to the hook.

If the ensuing strangulation took too long a time to suit the mood of the guards, they beat out the brains of the condemned with a long-handled club resembling a potato masher. (Specimens of the nooses and 'potato mashers' are on view in the basement.) The remains were then placed on an elevator which lifted them directly to the crematory proper, the final run being made on a miniature railway of metal litters leading from the elevator platform to the furnace doors. Efficient.

Having seen and photographed the end-products, we proceeded to the place whence they came—the infamous Barrack 61. Exteriorly, Barrack 61 is like the other barracks, roughly a hundred and fifty feet long by thirty feet wide. Inside, four tiers of wooden shelves incline slightly towards the central corridor. In the rush season this single barrack housed twenty-three hundred prisoners jammed together on those shelves, twenty-three hundred 'non-workers' that tuberculosis, dysentery, pneumonia and plain starvation had rendered incapable of the daily twelve-hour stretch at the armament factory or nearby quarries. There were fewer when I was there. I did not count them, but the shelves were still well filled. Some of them were living human beings, but the majority were almost indistinguishable from the corpses we saw in the death cart.

On one shelf barer than the rest, three shadowy figures huddled together for warmth. Cold comfort for the outside two, since the middle one had been dead for several hours. Under the old régime he would eventually have been stripped and thrown out on to the flagstones to await the next tour of the wagon. Farther on, an emaciated spectre of a man who had managed to get to the latrine and back was attempting to crawl up on to the first shelf. It was only three feet from the floor, but he could not make it. As he collapsed, his shirt—he had no other clothing on—fell open. A living—barely living—skeleton, with a long prison serial number tattooed on the inside of the thigh. Two of the inmates who accompanied us picked him up by the shoulders and ankles, his sagging, wasted behind dribbling excrement and bloody mucus as they placed him on the shelf.

So much for Barrack 61. Barrack 47 was like it, but frankly, I hadn't the stomach.

Colonel Charles Codman

Bruce tells me that quite a nice young German hospital nurse came to see him in his Company H.Q. He showed her the pictures of the Buchenwald concentration camp. She looked horrified, then suddenly her face cleared. 'But it's only the Jews,' she said.

Lieutenant-Colonel Lindsay

Belsen

Next day, with a V.A.D., I was detailed to find Square 10, Block 61, in an enormous compound. Each square was surrounded entirely by high barbed wire, to which were attached large notices, reading 'DANGER—TYPHUS'. Every building was the same, dull-looking, of grey stone with small windows. Some had iron bars across, and a centre door. One had previously been used to house the German S.S. Panzer Division, and I was not surprised to see a large Red Cross painted on each roof. The Germans had made full use of this sign to protect themselves.

Passing through the door of Block 61, I was astonished to hear sounds of hundreds of various tongues; and the dreadful smell, only to be associated with Belsen, was indescribable. A British medical student and I, with Nurse, were able at last to overcome the feeling of nausea.

No one had been able to compile a register of patients. Many, of course, had forgotten their identity. However, with Nurse, I visited the human remains lying on the straw palliasses, covered with filthy blankets. At first glance we were unable to define their sex. Several were lying on top of the blankets, their heads shorn. The agony of their suffering showing clearly in their expression, with eyes sunken and listless, cheek-bones prominent, too weak to close their mouths, with arms extended in an appealing manner. '*Essen—essen!*' was the general cry.

There was not an open window, the floor was filthy, straw littered with human excreta. Thousands of flies were re-creating the typhus circle, by settling on potato peelings picked from the garbage-bins. Broken cups and plates held pieces of black bread, turnip tops and very sour milk.

The working personnel consisted of five Hungarian soldiers. About a hundred of these men had been left when the S.S. Panzer Division moved out. There were also two Poles, four Czechs and six Hungarians, all young girls, themselves in a convalescent stage from typhus. A Hungarian surgical specialist, Dr. Sachs, was a charming woman. She also had had typhus, had twice been removed from the gas chamber, had left-sided paralysis of the face, and a deep scar extending down her neck to the left shoulder, the result of an experiment carried out by the Germans. She was an amazing woman, working amongst the patients day and night. She was delighted to have the opportunity of speaking English again, and said she had heard no kind word for six years. Her husband was a doctor and, with their two children, was 'removed' by the enemy. She had since heard that they were dead.

With the aid of a British medical officer every patient was examined. Ninety per cent were suffering from tuberculosis, in addition to other specific fevers and post-typhus conditions. The seriously ill T.B. girls were placed in a large ward, where supervision of special diets and rest was possible.

Gradually I felt the air of fear and suspicion fading away, and with regular meals one could see a gradual improvement. A smile would flicker across a pale, thin face, a hand would try to rise in salute. *'Guten Morgen, Schwester!'* was becoming quite usual.

After seven days, writing paper and pencils were distributed. Several patients hesitated, their names temporarily forgotten, while tears poured down their faces. The letters they wrote were sent to the Red Cross, and in due course replies were received. One husband met his wife after a separation of five years.

Clothes had been collected from German families, and 'Harrods' was born. Every day several patients from each block were given slippers. As supplies were received, soap, towels, tooth brushes, combs, mirrors and cosmetics were distributed, amid great excitement. The task of supplying nearly seventeen thousand was no small matter. Several girls could not recognize their own reflections, not having encountered a mirror for years.

My patients improved, step by step, until they could be allowed to be clothed and so get into the sunshine. By this time the prison-like appearance of the camp had disappeared; to my joy the barbed wire was removed. I heard snatches of laughter and the singing of national songs.

The last three weeks of our stay were used to evacuate patients to Sweden, where they hoped to recuperate in more congenial surroundings. The British Red Cross used a large loudspeaker van to announce the names on their lists. Many friends were thus united, after long periods of separation: I saw husbands and wives with children, all of whom had thought the others dead, brought together again.

British Army medical officer

I hope that when they hang you, you die slowly.

A staff officer, British 2 Army,
to Josef Kramer, late Commandant, Belsen Camp

What to Believe?

About a week later, some rear elements of our division were present at Ordruf when the burgomaster led his townsfolk out to the concentration camp for a burial ceremony. By then the place had been considerably cleaned up. The starved and half-consumed bodies had been gathered together and placed in coffins, and there were even a few floral offerings. When the people saw what the camp was like and were led through the torture chambers and past the ovens, men and women screamed out and fainted; others were led away crying hysterically. All swore that during the past years they had had no idea of what had been going on in the camp just outside their town.

And yet, one heard other stories. One heard that it would be impossible not to know what was happening, that the greasy smoke and the unmistakable odour of burning bodies could be detected for miles around such concentration camps, that villagers got up petitions to have the camps moved elsewhere.

I never knew what to believe.

Lester Atwell

The Last Card

The Luftwaffe, broken though it was, still had one resource left.

I don't think that any of us in the field knew that the Germans had any jets, and in consequence the appearance of these aircraft came as something of a surprise—though not a shock, as we were so near victory that we did not think anything of this nature could stop us.

I saw them first one afternoon somewhere between the Rhine and the Elbe. Three of them streaked across the sky trailing their unearthly shriek behind them in the way which has now become a commonplace, but which then left us bewildered and fascinated. About a mile behind them the sky was peppered with a row of black dots as the Bofors boys went into action, baffled by the speed to which they were unaccustomed and of which they had evidently not been forewarned.

I saw them again in less comfortable circumstances. The assault crossing of the Elbe was made on 29 April, and we had to go over in the afternoon with the Grenadiers' Churchills as soon as a pontoon bridge was available. The exit from the bridge was a steep muddy defile through the blazing village of Schnaeckenbeck, and in consequence there was a monumental traffic jam. I sat in my tank in the middle of the bridge for ages. The R.A.F. had a remarkably efficient umbrella over the bridge, but while I was sitting there something went wrong and one lot of Spitfires went home before the next had arrived. In a second the Luftwaffe pounced: six jets in line astern screamed down on the bridge and plastered us with anti-personnel bombs. I felt very small, sitting in the open-top turret of my M.10. With one continuous series of explosions and spouts of water they had dropped their load: it was over in a matter of seconds. They missed all of us sitting stuck on the bridge, and were gone behind the trees. With an unsteady hand I lit a captured German cigar; I suppose I should have said to myself: 'Well, there opens a new chapter in man's achievement,' but I don't think I did.

D.F.

During the following days we were often attacked by the 262s, and more airmen were killed and more Spitfires damaged. The enemy jets came in very fast from the east, and in order to protect our airfield we carried out standing patrols at twenty thousand feet, the favourite attacking height of the intruders. But the Spitfires were far too slow to catch the 262s, and although we often possessed the height advantage we could not bring the jets to combat. Suddenly we were outmoded and out-dated. Should the enemy possess reasonable numbers of these remarkable aircraft, it would not be long before we lost the air superiority for which we had struggled throughout the war.

The complete superiority of the Messerschmitt 262 was well demonstrated to us one evening when we carried out a dusk patrol over Grave. Kenway had told us that the jets were active over Holland, but although we scanned the skies we could see nothing of them. Suddenly, without warning, an enemy jet appeared about one hundred yards ahead of our Spitfires. The pilot must have seen our formation, since he shot up from below and climbed away at a high speed. Already he was out of cannon range, and the few rounds I sent after him were more an angry gesture at our impotence than anything else. As he soared into the darkening, eastern sky, he added insult to injury by carrying out a perfect upward roll. We were at a loss to know why the enemy pilot did not attack one of our Spitfires unless he had already used all his ammunition. Later that evening Dal Russel phoned to say that some of his boys had shot down a 262. This was the first time that this type of enemy aircraft had been destroyed, and Dal and his wing were celebrating the event.

'Johnnie' Johnson

On 26 April I set out on my last mission of the war when I led six jet fighters of the J.V.44 against a formation of Marauders. Our own little directing post brought us well in contact with the enemy; the weather report was: varying cloud at different altitudes, with gaps, ground only visible in about three-tenths of the operational area.

. . . . We were flying in almost the opposite direction to the Marauder formation. Each second meant that we were three hundred yards nearer. I will not say that I fought this action ideally, but I led my formation to a fairly favourable firing position. Safety-catch off the gun and rocket-switch! At a great distance we already met with considerable defensive fire. As usual in a dog-fight, I was tense and excited, and so forgot to release the second safety-catch for the rockets, which did not go off. I was in the best firing position, had aimed accurately, and pressed my thumb on the release button with no result—maddening for any fighter pilot. Anyhow, my four 3 cm. cannons were working. They had much more firing power than we had been used to so far. At that moment, close below me, Schallmoser, the 'jet-rammer', whizzed past. In ramming he made no difference between friend or foe.

This engagement had lasted only a fraction of a second—a very important second to be sure. One Marauder of the last string was on fire and exploded. Now I attacked another bomber in the van of the formation, and saw it was heavily hit as I passed very close above it. During this break-through I got a few minor hits from the defensive fire, but I wanted to know definitely what was happening to the second bomber I had hit. I was not quite clear if it had crashed. So far I had not noticed any fighter escort.

Above the formation I had attacked last I banked steeply to the left, and at this moment it happened: a hail of fire enveloped me. A Mustang had caught me napping. A sharp rap hit my right knee, the instrument panel with its indispensable instruments was shattered, the right engine was also hit—its metal covering worked loose in the wind and was partly carried away—and now the left engine was hit, too. I could hardly hold her in the air.

In this embarrassing situation I had only one wish: to get out of this 'crate', which now apparently was only good for dying in. But then I was paralyzed by the terror of being shot while parachuting down. Experience had taught us that we jet-fighter pilots had to reckon on this. I soon discovered that after some adjustments my battered Me.262 could be steered again, and after a dive through a layer of cloud, I saw the *autobahn* below me; ahead lay Munich, and to the left Riem. In a few seconds I was over the airfield. Having regained my self-confidence, I gave the customary wing wobble and started banking to come in. It was remarkably quiet and dead below. One engine did not react at all to the throttle, and as I could not reduce it I had to cut out both engines just before the edge of the airfield. A long trail of smoke drifted behind me. It was only then I noticed that Thunderbolts in a low-level attack were giving our airfield the works. Now I had no choice. I did not hear the warnings of our ground post because my wireless had faded out when I was hit. There remained only one thing to do: straight down into the fireworks! Touching down, I realized that the tyre of my nose wheel was flat. It rattled horribly as the earth received me again at a speed of 150 m.p.h. on the small landing strip.

Brake! Brake! The kite would not stop, but at last I was out of it and into the nearest bomb-crater. There were plenty of them on our runways. Bombs and rockets exploded all around, bursts of shells from the Thunderbolts whistled and banged. A new low-level attack. Out of the fastest fighter in the world into a bomb-crater—an unutterably wretched feeling!

Colonel Adolf Galland

THE TERROR FROM THE EAST

Hopeless as the situation was in the West, it was the menace from the East which struck the coldest fear into the heart of Germany. Vienna fell to the Russians on 13 April. At the same moment they were a mere thirty-five miles from Berlin; only the defended line of the Oder lay between them and the capital of the vanishing Third Reich. On the 16th the Russians attacked, and nine days later Berlin was surrounded. On this day, too, the Americans and Russians met near Torgau on the Elbe.

THE END OF GERMANY

Hitler's Last Order of the Day: 16 April

Soldiers of the German front in the east!

The hordes of our Judeo-Bolshevist foe have rallied for the last assault. They want to destroy Germany and to extinguish our people. You, soldiers of the east, have seen with your own eyes what fate awaits German women and children: the aged, the men, the infants, are murdered, the German women and girls defiled and made into barrack whores. The rest are marched to Siberia.

We have been waiting for this assault. Since January every step has been taken to raise a strong eastern front. Colossal artillery forces are welcoming the enemy. Countless new units are replacing our losses. Troops of every kind hold our front.

Once again, Bolshevism will suffer Asia's old fate—it will founder on the capital of the German Reich.

He who at this moment does not do his duty is a traitor to the German nation. The regiments or divisions that relinquish their posts are acting so disgracefully that they must hang their heads in shame before the women and children who here in our cities are braving the terror bombing.

. . . . If during these next days and weeks every soldier in the east does his duty, Asia's final onslaught will come to nought—just as the invasion of our Western enemies will in the end fail.

Berlin stays German. Vienna will be German again. And Europe will never be Russian!

Rise up to defend your homes, your women, your children—rise up to defend your own future!

At this hour the eyes of the German nation are upon you, you, my fighters in the east, hoping that your steadfastness, your ardour, and your arms will smother the Bolshevist attack in a sea of blood!

This moment, which has removed from the face of the earth the greatest war criminal of all ages*, will decide the turn in the fortunes of war!

Adolf Hitler

The reality was very different.

There was now nothing to do but wait for the final battle in Kladow to begin. We brought the boys up from the cellar to let them play in the air and light, as they were so white and heavy-eyed from living underground. We kept the shutters across the windows, and played games, and read to them quietly. Except for the distant noises of machine-gun fire there was peace round our house on a lovely spring day. But not for long. Suddenly there was the tramp of heavy boots round the house. We peeped through the curtains, German soldiers! We opened the windows to speak to them. To my horror they wanted to come into the house to use it to fight from. Hearing my conversation the boys ran into the garden.

'Oh, you have children?' said the eldest of the group. 'All right, then we'll leave you in peace. But have you got a boat?'

'Yes, but not here. Farther down the river at the bottom of the hill,' Heiner told them.

* President Roosevelt (Ed.)

'They've all gone from down there,' said the soldier. 'We searched the whole bank.'

'Where do you want to go?' we asked.

The soldier shrugged his shoulders. 'Haven't a clue.'

'But aren't you joining up with General Wenk?' I said. 'They said so on the wireless days ago.'

To my astonishment one of the soldiers burst into tears. We all stared at him. He pushed his steel helmet well over his face, but we could see the tears pouring down over his thin cheeks. He looked not a day more than seventeen. None of the other men said a word to him. Indeed, they all looked exhausted and fed-up enough to cry.

The older soldier pushed his helmet high and wiped the sweat off his forehead. 'They've been telling us that tale about General Wenk for weeks. What do they take us for? General Wenk won't come. God alone knows where he is. The Russians are everywhere. They're just playing cat and mouse with us. And so we go on . . . fighting to the last man.' His voice rose in mockery of Hitler's speeches. 'Fighting to the last little boy, they ought to say.' He turned and looked at the weeping soldier. The awful bitterness in the soldier's voice, still urging his little group on to some kind of action, brought tears to my eyes.

And General Wenk? He had taken the law into his own hands and decided *not* to sacrifice his army by leading it into Berlin. Hitler raged and screamed in his cellar, but General Wenk stayed away and saved a few hundred thousand lives. The S.S. General Steiner did not turn up either. So Berlin was now defended only by grandfathers, boys, and invalids from the Russian front.

Else Wendel, housewife

The Bottom of the Barrel

I had four hundred men in my battalion and we were ordered to go into the line in our civilian clothes. I told the local Party Leader that I could not accept the responsibility of leading men into battle without uniforms. Just before commitment the unit was given a hundred and eighty Danish rifles, but there was no ammunition. We also had four machine-guns and a hundred *Panzerfaust*. None of the men had received any training in firing a machine-gun, and they were all afraid of handling the anti-tank weapon. Although my men were quite ready to help their country, they refused to go into battle without uniforms and without training. What can a *Volkssturm* man do with a rifle without ammunition? The men went home. That was the only thing they could do.

O.C., 42nd Volkssturm Battalion

Far up the road in the dull mustardy twilight, a procession approached: a long, double file of old men in civilian clothes, their hands up over their heads in surrender. Two infantrymen had them under guard, and as they came nearer, our old men hung back deliberately to laugh and hoot though it was time for us to turn up the street. The prisoners, members of the *Volkssturm*, many of them even older than our companions, trudged past, their eyes straight ahead. Mixed in with them were a few gawky, stunned boys in their early teens. Our old codgers choked with laughter and jeered as their townsmen went by. The prisoners had evidently volunteered to hold the town, had been run out into the woods, and there ingloriously captured. Our old men might rock with laughter, but the other old boys held themselves upright: at least they had tried.

Lester Atwell

The Coming of the Russians

When the second morning came we heard loud, hoarse shouting. It came from the Russian troops and there was the sound of rifles and machine-guns.

Heiner and I stood in the lounge and looked out. The Russians were swarming into our street, running, shooting and shouting. I nearly screamed aloud in terror, then I remembered Heiner.

'Quick,' I said to him. 'Upstairs.'

He turned round, his face ghastly pale. He flung his arms round me, and held me close for a second, then he rushed up the stairs towards his hole in the roof, and I snatched up a book from the bookcase and went down to the cellars. I was too agitated to look at the boys, but merely opened the book and began to read aloud to them. It was a fairy story book. I had grabbed it at random from the children's bookshelves in my panic.

The fairy story was about a princess who was born blind. Wolfgang and Klaus became fascinated. It wasn't often I had time to read to them nowadays. There I sat in the cellar just saying the words and trying to keep my voice steady, with one ear listening for the Russians and the other trying to hear whether all was well with Heiner.

The poor shepherd in the story had just seen the beautiful blind princess and decided to give his life so that she might see when we were interrupted by a sharp banging on the door which I had locked and bolted.

'That must be the Russians,' I said in the calmest voice I could manage. I went upstairs, telling the boys to stay absolutely silent in the cellar. Two Russian soldiers stood at the door with their rifles and guns loaded and pointing at me. I stood and stared and so did they for a second. Never shall I forget that moment.

Then, in broken German, one of them said: 'Arms up!' I held my arms up. The Russian stepped forward and searched me thoroughly for weapons. He took nothing from me, not even my wrist watch.

When they were satisfied that I was unarmed, one of them spoke again. 'Where is the man?' he asked.

'There isn't a man,' I replied.

'Yes, there is.'

'No.'

'We'll find him. Show your house!'

They indicated that I was to go through the house with them. I had to go ahead and they followed with the rifle and gun behind me. While we went through the rooms I kept wondering if someone had betrayed Heiner. Why had they said, 'Yes, there *is* a man.' Suddenly I noticed Heiner's hat hanging from a peg by the front entrance door. Had they noticed it? I was seized with cold fear.

Now they wished to see the cellar. The staircase was dark as the electricity was cut off. I could sense the Russian behind me becoming nervous. Then I felt the gun pressed against my neck. It was a clear warning that if I was leading them into a trap, I should fall first!

I opened the door into the cellar. A candle was burning there, and the two small boys were standing with their mouths wide open and staring at me and the soldiers. They looked so thin and pale and frightened they might have been carved out of stone. Immediately the Russian saw them, he took the gun off my neck and broke into loud laughter. 'Oh, children!' he shouted. The other Russian smiled and let his rifle drop to his side. Then he turned to me and indicated that the search was off, and I was to return upstairs with them. Actually I was more nervous on the way upstairs than on the way down. In reaction, my legs shook so much I nearly fell twice on the steps. They took me outside the house and stood me up against the door post, aimed and shot . . . not *at* me, but to each side of me. Then they turned and left me standing there, turned to stone now, in relief and astonishment.

Else Wendel, housewife

Not all German women were so lucky.

The first Russian columns swept in, but after they had satisfied themselves that no German soldiers were left in the village they moved on immediately. They were followed by motorized infantry and a cavalry brigade.

There were no young men left in the place; only a dozen old cripples and women and children remained. Like all of us, Ellen had disbelieved the atrocity stories about the Russians. She had gone up to a pair of Russians in the street in all friendliness. She was immediately seized, thrown on the ground and raped. When they released her she ran away into the woods and stayed there until nightfall.

The cold drove her back to the village where she hid in a barn. Her Russian 'friend' and his comrades had already been looking for her and finally discovered her hiding place. They took off their belts and beat her. Then they dragged her into a house where more than a dozen of them were billeted. All of them used her the whole night for their enjoyment.

Near daybreak they had reached such a state of drunkenness and enfeeblement that she was able to slip out and shelter with a neighbour who hid her in the stable. At noon they could hear drunken voices and knocks at the door. When there was no answer the Russians smashed it open with their rifle butts.

One of the children, a thirteen-year-old girl, was lying in bed with scarlet fever. A drunken Russian threw himself upon her and when she struggled he shot her through the throat. She bled to death. The oldest child was a girl suffering from almost complete paralysis who had been unable to move for years. Several drunken liberators threw her on the table, forced her paralysed legs apart, and raped her in turn. As she lay unconscious on the table they fired their revolvers into her from three paces' distance.

Just as they discovered Ellen four officers entered the house. They had only just arrived and were now looking round for the prettiest girls. Ellen saw that they were high-ranking officers and flung herself at their feet, hoping for their protection, which she was graciously granted.

Along with three other girls she was locked into a room in a peasant's cottage. The windows and doors were hermetically closed, the room continually lit by candlelight. They were brought food and forced to drink tumblerfuls of vodka. One of the officers had a festering wound which Ellen had to wash and dress.

These officers must have been very good friends, for they politely and calmly took their turn at sleeping with the girls. On one occasion there was a little jealousy and knives were used; but this was soon smoothed over with a few bottles of liquor.

For several days the Russians scarcely stirred out of the room. The air was thick with the fumes of liquor, sweat, the festering wound and Russian tobacco. The gramophone played continually. There was only one record—*I Can't Give You Anything But Love, Baby*. One of the girls went mad, cried for her father, laughed, babbled nonsensically and twined rags in her hair. Ellen had some kind of alcoholic poisoning and vomited continually. The Russians 'cured' her by pouring more vodka into her.

On one occasion she managed to get away, but no sooner had she got into the High Street than two Siberians clubbed her with a pistol butt and raped her while she was unconscious. They then returned her to the officers' mess.

When, after a few days, the detachment moved on and was relieved by a new one, her 'friend' with the wounded foot gave her a glowing testimonial. The result was that she was at once taken over by the next batch of officers. The whole business started all over again, the only difference being that the new gentlemen were not such good friends.

She spent one night lying motionless on the bed, on either side of her a drunken Russian, both were clutching pistols and eyeing each other with mutual mistrust. In the end the two cavaliers reached agreement and both went at her simultaneously.

The village was occupied by new relays of troops from time to time and always the same scenes ensued. After a fortnight she found she had gonorrhœa, and now she was driven twice weekly in a military car to the Russian military hospital where she received 'treatment' consisting of soap and water ablutions. The Russians were quite unconcerned.

In the end Polish troops moved in. Their discipline was far superior. There were no cases of rape. A Polish private who tried it was shot by order of the commanding officer. But to make up for this the Poles looted everything thoroughly, smashing anything that they could not take away.

But apart from the sexual angle, their treatment was much harsher than the Russians. Ellen had to wash their laundry in the courtyard. So intense was the cold that her fingers bled—if the blood dropped on the laundry she was forced to do it again.

The Poles did not stay for long. They were followed by Russians, who were slightly better behaved. The women were now put on heavy work. All day long they had to unload wagons, lay cables and carry supplies. Those who did not work got no food. The only break was the customary visit to the hospital for treatment. Of course, this was completely pointless; even if one of the girls had been cured she would have been re-infected within a matter of hours.

Heavens only knows what would have become of her if her father had not managed after a few weeks to come and take her away. He had managed to desert his unit and slip through as far as the Oder, where he was held up by Polish troops.

They took away everything that he had on him and put him into a labour camp. After a fortnight he was set free and was able to take Ellen back with him to Berlin. By now a few trains were running and they found room in one of them. On the way Russian soldiers moved in who flung several men and children out of the moving train in order to make more room for themselves.

One after another they used Ellen and another girl for their purposes while Ellen's father had to hold their luggage and rifles. Shortly before they got to Berlin they allowed the girls to dress.

                                                            Claus Fuhrmann, clerk

Cossack Custom

Almost all the women had fled, horrified by the stories of rape which had spread like wildfire over East Prussia, through which three motorized divisions of Cossacks had passed. It was not difficult to protect the few who were left. It was more difficult to prevent sudden 'visitations' in private houses. Cossacks have been waging war for generations, and the customs and habits of their profession are very well established. On one occasion I had to arrest a Cossack captain who had allowed his men to disobey orders.

'According to our custom when a town is taken by storm the men have the right to do their own individual commandeering,' the arrested *Sotnik* explained to me patiently. He was a good fellow, and he had been twice decorated. 'Long-established custom allows a Cossack to carry off as much as he can load on his horse. But you see, my men are motorized, and they interpret the custom in their own way by loading up their lorries.'

It was as much a legal point as a matter of conscience for the unfortunate captain, who found himself in line for a court martial.

                                                      Ivan Krylov, Soviet staff officer

First Feeler

On 22 April Himmler met Count Bernadotte of the International Red Cross at Lübeck. He asked the Count to convey to the Allies an offer by which the German armed forces would surrender only to the Americans and British. Five days later the offer was formally rejected.

The discussion . . . came to an end and they said good-bye. Himmler, knowing I was to accompany the Count part of the way, hoped that I would once more beg him to fly to General Eisenhower and try to arrange for him to have a conference with the General.

However, at our parting on the road near Waren in Mecklenburg, Count Bernadotte said to me, 'The Reichsführer no longer understands the realities of his own situation. I cannot help him any more. He should have taken Germany's affairs into his own hands after my first visit. I can hold out little chance for him now. And you, my dear Schellenberg, would be wiser to think of yourself.'

I did not know what to reply to this. When we said good-bye it was as though we would never see each other again. I was filled with a deep sadness.

I drove back to Hohenlychen, slept for two hours, and was then called to Himmler at about twelve-thirty. He was still in bed, the picture of misery, and said that he felt ill. All I could say was that there was nothing more I could do for him; it was up to him. He had got to take some action. At lunch we discussed the military situation in Berlin, which was steadily growing worse.

At about four o'clock, having convinced him that it would be unwise to drive to Berlin, we drove towards Wustrow. In Löwenberg we were caught in a traffic jam, troops having become involved with the unending columns of fleeing civilians which blocked all the roads between Berlin and Mecklenburg.

As we drove on, Himmler said to me for the first time, 'Schellenberg, I dread what is to come.'

Walter Schellenberg

The Battle of Berlin

24 April: Early morning. We are at the Tempelhof airport. Russian artillery is firing without let-up. . . . We need infantry reinforcements, and we get motley emergency units. Behind the lines, civilians are still trying to get away right under the Russian artillery fire, dragging along some miserable bundle holding all they have left in the world.

. . . . The Russians burn their way into the houses with flamethrowers. The screams of the women and children are terrible.

Three o'clock in the afternoon, and we have barely a dozen tanks and about thirty armoured cars. These are all the armoured vehicles left in the Government sector. The chain of command seems entangled. We constantly get orders from the Chancellery to send tanks to some other danger spot, and they never come back. Only General Mummert's toughness has kept us so far from being 'expended'. We have hardly any vehicles left to carry the wounded.

Afternoon. Our artillery retreats to new positions. They have very little ammunition. The howling and explosions of the Stalin organs, the screaming of the wounded, the roaring of motors, and the rattle of machine-guns. Clouds of smoke, and the stench of chlorine and fire.

25 April: 5.30 a.m. New, massive tank attacks. We are forced to retreat. Orders from the Chancellery: our division is to move immediately to Alexanderplatz in the north. 9 a.m. Order cancelled. 10 a.m. Russian drive on the airport becomes irresistible. New defence line in the centre. Heavy street fighting—many civilian casualties. Dying animals. Women are fleeing from cellar to cellar. We are pushed north-west. New order to go north, as before. But the command situation is obviously in complete disorder, the Führer's shelter must have false information, the positions we are supposed to take over are already in the hands of the Russians. We retreat again, under heavy Russian air attacks.

.... In the evening, proclamations of a new organization, Free Corps Mohnke: 'Bring your own weapons, equipment, rations. Every German man is needed.' Heavy fighting in the business district, inside the Stock Exchange. The first skirmishes in the subway tunnels, through which the Russians are trying to get behind our lines. The tunnels are packed with civilians.

26 April: The night sky is fiery red. Heavy shelling. Otherwise a terrible silence. We are sniped at from many houses—probably foreign labourers. News that the commander of the city has been replaced. General Weidling takes over, General Mummert takes the tank forces. About 5.30 a.m. another grinding artillery barrage. The Russians attack. We have to retreat again, fighting for street after street.

.... New command post in the subway tunnels under Anhalt railway station. The station looks like an armed camp. Women and children huddling in niches and corners and listening for the sounds of battle. Shells hit the roofs, cement is crumbling from the ceiling. ... People are fighting round the ladders that run through air shafts up to the street. Water comes rushing through the tunnels. The crowds get panicky, stumble and fall over rails and sleepers. Children and wounded are deserted, people are trampled to death. The water covers them. It rises three feet or more, then it slowly goes down. The panic lasts for hours. Many are drowned. Reason: somewhere, on somebody's command, engineers have blasted the locks of one of the canals to flood the tunnels against the Russians who are trying to get through them.

27 April: Continuous attack throughout the night. Increasing signs of dissolution. ... In the Chancellery, they say, everybody is more certain of final victory than ever before. Hardly any communications among troops, excepting a few regular battalions equipped with radio posts. Telephone cables are shot to pieces. Physical conditions are indescribable. No rest, no relief. No regular food, hardly any bread. We get water from the tunnels and filter it.

The whole large expanse of Potsdamer Platz is a waste of ruins. Masses of damaged vehicles, half-smashed trailers of the ambulances with the wounded still in them. Dead people everywhere, many of them frightfully cut up by tanks and trucks.

At night, we try to reach the Propaganda Ministry for news about Wenck and the American divisions. Rumours that 9 Army is also on the way to Berlin. In the west, general peace treaties are being signed. Violent shelling of the centre of the city.

We cannot hold our present position. At four o'clock in the morning, we retreat through the underground railway tunnels. In the tunnels next to ours, the Russians march in the opposite direction to the positions we have just lost.

1 May. We are in the Aquarium. Shell crater on shell crater every way I look. The streets are steaming. The smell of the dead is at times unbearable. Last night, one floor above us, some police officers and soldiers celebrated their farewell to life, in spite of the shelling. This morning, men and women were lying on the stairs in tight embrace and drunk. Through the shell holes in the streets one can look down into the subway tunnels. It looks as though the dead are lying down there several layers deep.

.... Afternoon. We have to retreat. We put the wounded into the last armoured car we have left. All told, the division now has five tanks and four field guns. Late in the afternoon, new rumours that Hitler is dead, that surrender is being discussed. That is all. The civilians want to know whether we will break out of Berlin. If we do, they want to join us.

.... The Russians continue to advance underground and then come up from the tunnels somewhere behind our lines. In the intervals between the firing, we can hear the screaming of the civilians in the tunnels.

Pressure is getting too heavy, we have to retreat again. . . . No more anaesthetics. Every so often, women burst out of a cellar, their fists pressed over their ears, because they cannot stand the screaming of the wounded.

German staff officer, diary

Panic had reached its peak in the city. Hordes of soldiers stationed in Berlin deserted and were shot on the spot or hanged on the nearest tree. A few clad only in underclothes were dangling on a tree quite near our house. On their chests they had placards reading: 'We betrayed the Führer.' The Werewolf pasted leaflets on the houses:

Dirty cowards and defeatists
We've got them all on our lists!

The S.S. went into underground stations, picked out among the sheltering crowds a few men whose faces they did not like, and shot them then and there.

The scourge of our district was a small one-legged *Hauptscharführer* of the S.S. who stumped through the street on crutches, a machine-pistol at the ready, followed by his men. Anyone he didn't like the look of he instantly shot. The gang went down cellars at random and dragged all the men outside, giving them rifles and ordering them straight to the front. Anyone who hesitated was shot.

The front was a few streets away. At the street corner diagonally opposite our house Walloon Waffen S.S. had taken up position; wild, desperate men who had nothing to lose and who fought to their last round of ammunition. Armed Hitler Youth were lying next to men of the Vlassov White Russian Army.

. . . . It could not take much longer now, whatever the Walloon and the French Waffen S.S. or the fanatic Hitler Youth with their 2 cm. anti aircraft guns could do. The end was coming and all we had to do was to try to survive this final stage.

But that was by no means simple. Everything had run out. The only water was in the cellar of a house several streets away. To get bread one had to join a queue of hundreds, grotesquely adorned with steel helmets, outside the baker's shop at 3 a.m. At 5 a.m. the Russians started and continued uninterruptedly until nine or ten. The crowded mass outside the baker's shop pressed closely against the walls, but no one moved from his place. Often hours of queueing had been spent in vain; bread was sold out before one reached the shop. Later one could buy bread if one brought half a bucket of water.

Russian low-flying wooden biplanes machine-gunned people as they stood apathetically in their queues and took a terrible toll of the waiting crowds. In every street dead bodies were left lying where they had fallen.

At the last moment the shopkeepers, who had been jealously hoarding their stocks, not knowing how much longer they would be allowed to, now began to sell them. Too late! For a small packet of coffee, half a pound of sausages, thousands laid down their lives. A salvo of the heavy calibre shells tore to pieces hundreds of women who were waiting in the market hall. Dead and wounded alike were flung on wheelbarrows and carted away; the surviving women continued to wait, patient, resigned, sullen until they had finished their miserable shopping.

.... We left the cellar at longer and longer intervals and often we could not tell whether it was night or day. The Russians drew nearer; they advanced through the underground railway tunnels, armed with flamethrowers; their advance snipers had taken up positions quite near us; and their shots ricocheted off the houses opposite. Exhausted German soldiers would stumble in and beg for water—they were practically children; I remember one with a pale, quivering face who said, 'We shall do it all right; we'll make our way to the north-west yet.' But his eyes belied his words and he looked at me despairingly. What he wanted to say was: 'Hide me, give me shelter. I've had enough of it.' I should have liked to help him; but neither of us dared to speak. Each might have shot the other as a 'defeatist'.

An old man who had lived in our house had been hit by a shell splinter a few days ago and had bled to death. His corpse lay near the entrance and had already began to smell. We threw him on a cart and took him to a burnt-out school building where there was a notice: 'Collection point for Weinmeisterstrasse corpses.' We left him there; one of us took the opportunity of helping himself to a dead policeman's boots.

The first women were fleeing from the northern parts of the city and some of them sought shelter in our cellar, sobbing that the Russians were looting all the houses, abducting the men and raping all the women and girls. I got angry, shouted I had had enough of Goebbels's silly propaganda, the time for that was past. If that was all they had to do, let them go elsewhere.

Whilst the city lay under savage artillery and rifle fire the citizens now took to looting the shops. The last soldiers withdrew farther and farther away. Somewhere in the ruins of the burning city S.S. men and Hitler Youth were holding out fanatically. The crowds burst into cellars and storehouses. While bullets were whistling through the air they scrambled for a tin of fish or a pouch of tobacco.

Claus Fuhrmann, clerk

The Battle Ends

During the night of 28–29 April Hitler married Eva Braun in the bunker under the Chancellery garden in Berlin. On the following day he nominated Admiral Doenitz as his successor, and then committed suicide. On 1 May the remaining German troops in Berlin surrendered.

German men and women, soldiers of the German Armed Forces. Our Führer, Adolf Hitler, is dead. The German people bow in deepest sorrow and respect. Early he had recognized the terrible danger of Bolshevism and had dedicated his life to the fight against it. His fight having ended, he died a hero's death in the capital of the German Reich, after having led an unmistakably straight and steady life.

Admiral Doenitz

From the moment when Doenitz took office he saw his foremost task in ending the war as quickly as possible, in order to avoid further senseless blood-shed on both sides.

There seemed to be two radically different possibilities. One was capitulation, the other a simple stopping of the fighting. The question whether the second solution was not perhaps the simpler and more honourable one was discussed at length. This point raised grave inner conflicts. The bitterness of un-conditional surrender, and its shocking consequences, were known.

However, after carefully weighing all factors, Doenitz decided in favour of an official surrender controlled from above. His reasons for this decision were that further loss of blood and property would be avoided, that chaos would be prevented, and that the victors would find themselves under some obligation, however vague.

The question remained how such a surrender could be accomplished.

Since Roosevelt's and Churchill's conference at Casablanca it was known that the Allies would accept nothing but unconditional surrender extended simultaneously on all fronts. Such a surrender implied that all German troop movements would stop at once.

Such a surrender was eliminated from the discussions immediately. It could not be carried out. The eastern armies would not have complied with it under any circumstances. The signature under a document embodying such terms would thereby be rendered meaningless, and the new Government would find itself unable to fulfill the obligations assumed by its very first official act.

There remained only one other possible course of action: the retreat of the eastern forces, together with as large a number of refugees as possible, to the demarcation line that was now known. This operation would require at least eight to ten days. During that time, the evacuation across the Baltic Sea from the Gulf of Danzig, from Courland, and from the pockets along the Pomeranian coast would be continued.

Meantime, efforts would be made in the west to accomplish partial surrender.

Lüdde-Neurath, adjutant to Admiral Doenitz

Berlin, 2 May 1945.

On 30 April, the Führer to whom we had sworn allegiance forsook us. But you still think that you have to follow his orders and fight for Berlin, even though the lack of weapons and of ammunition, and the situation in general, makes this fight senseless!

Every hour you go on fighting adds to the terrible suffering of the population of Berlin, and of our wounded. In agreement with the Command of the Soviet Forces I am asking you to stop fighting at once!

General Weidling, Commander of Defence District, Berlin

The artillery had been silent for some time when at noon on 2 May rifle fire too ceased in our district. We climbed out of our cellar.

From the street corner Russian infantry were slowly coming forward, wearing steel helmets, with hand grenades in their belts and boots. The S.S. had vanished. The Hitler Youth had surrendered.

Bunny rushed and threw her arms round a short slit-eyed Siberian soldier who seemed more than a little surprised. I at once went off with two buckets to fetch water, but I did not get beyond the first street corner. All men were stopped there, formed into a column and marched off towards the east.

A short distance behind Alexanderplatz everything was in a state of utter turmoil and confusion. Russian nurses armed with machine-pistols were handing out loaves to the German population. I took advantage of this turmoil to disappear and got back home safely. God knows where the others went.

After the first wave of combatant troops there followed reserves and supply troops who 'liberated' us in the Russian manner. At our street corner I saw two Russian soldiers assaulting a crying, elderly woman and then raping her in full view of a stunned crowd. I ran home as fast as I could. Bunny was all right so far. We had barricaded the one remaining room of our flat with rubble and charred beams in such a manner that no one outside could suspect that anyone lived there.

Every shop in the district was looted. As I hurried to the market I was met by groups of people who were laden with sacks and boxes. Vast food reserves belonging to the armed forces had been stored there. The Russians had forced the doors open and let the Germans in.

The cellars, which were completely blacked out, now became the scene of an incredible spectacle. The starved people flung themselves like beasts over one another, shouting, pushing and struggling to lay their hands on whatever they could. I caught hold of two buckets of sugar, a few boxes of preserves, sixty packages of tobacco and a small sack of coffee which I quickly took back home before returning for more.

The second raid was also successful. I found noodles, tins of butter and a large tin of sardines. But now things were getting out of hand. In order not to be trampled down themselves the Russians fired at random into the crowds with machine-pistols, killing several.

Claus Fuhrmann, clerk

The same evening new troops kept on dropping in to ask for women or girls. This started an ever-recurring pantomime performance which I repeated as often as necessary during the next few days. Every time I was asked for women I blew my nose, sobbed, waved my arms about and led the bewildered soldiers into the garden. Then with a tragic gesture I threw back the blanket from my two grisly corpses and burst into uncontrolled weeping and moaning. The soldiers would pull off their caps, cross themselves, pat me sympathetically on the shoulder, and often start crying themselves. They understood perfectly, the same things had happened to them. Then they would surreptitiously hand me some bread or cigarettes, show me pictures of their wives and families, beg me to bear up and have faith, and tip-toe quietly and sadly away. But their grief and sympathy usually disappeared before they were more than a few houses away and they started as keenly as ever on the grand hunt.

The atmosphere during the next few days was incredibly complicated and perplexing. We could scarcely realize our joy that the war was over because we had perpetually to be on the watch.

The Russians were celebrating everywhere: in our house, in the streets, in the gardens; their victory celebrations lasting night and day for weeks. Unluckily a huge store of wine and spirits had been found just down the road. And an unending stream of keen-eyed soldiers flowed up the street, while on the other side a rolling flood of paralytic conquerors staggered back.

They were mostly from Eastern Russia, with Mongolian faces, Chinese-looking beards and ear-rings. They were little, under-sized men from Turkestan and sturdy-looking Siberians. But one thing they all had in common—an absorbing and childish fascination in domestic gadgets and machinery.

My electric radiogram really intrigued them. But having no electric current I found it rather difficult to explain and as the machine obviously wouldn't work they showed me their displeasure in no uncertain terms—by smashing it. They were also fascinated by the water-closet, which again, in spite of my rather undignified pantomime, they completely failed to understand. They searched steadily through my library looking for pictures. They sought continually after watches although we had already paid off our share of the reparations with every watch and clock in the place. They played with two cameras and broke them immediately. With deathly calm they took a lovely antique grandfather clock to pieces, and no one has since been able to reassemble it.

The street in front of our house looked like a fairground. Dirt, rubbish, pieces of cars and tanks were strewn everywhere and amidst everything dozens of Russians were riding bicycles—obviously trying this new type of transport for the first time in their lives. They fell to left and right, but clambered back again like harmless little apes. Some, just able to stay on, began immediately to try acrobatics; others stared proudly at their rows of watches, usually extending up both forearms. Then, when they were tired of it, they let the machines lie where they fell and walked away.

We had to watch like lynxes to prevent our inquiring visitors taking too much away that interested them. And my room was full of interest. I found it a matter of some delicacy to persuade a chummy Uzbeker not to demonstrate his prowess with the pistol by shooting the Iphigenia of Tauris illustration out of my Goethe first edition.

One national trait puzzled me. This was the habit of nearly every Russian who came to visit us of relieving nature in various, and to us strange and unusual places. We discovered these faecal visiting cards in every corner, on tables, beds, carpets and one, strangest and most ambitious of all, on the top of a particularly high stove. My own theory that this was the remains of an old superstition which implied that an object could only be possessed if the owner had stooled on it, did not obtain any general currency. But I still think it a possibility in the absence of any more valid theory.

. . . . The demand for women continued unabated and the unfortunate girls had to stay hidden under the roof for a whole week. We had nothing but admiration for the physical endurance which made the Russians capable of this exercise at all hours of the day or night. Fortunately, I had a pornographic book in my library with which I managed to divert them from their more practical excursions in this sphere.

Werner Harz, journalist

The Wehrmacht Moves Out

3 May. At dawn we make an attack on a bridge leading to the west. It is under heavy Russian fire, can be crossed only at a run. The dead are lying all over it, and the wounded with no one to pick them up. Civilians of every age are trying to cross; they are shot down in rows. Our last armoured cars and trucks are forcing their way across through piles of twisted human bodies. The bridge is flooded with blood.

The rearguards fall apart. They want to go west, they don't want to be killed at the last moment. The command crumbles. General Mummert is missing. Our losses are heavy. The wounded are left where they fall. More civilians join us.

4 May. Behind us, Berlin in flames. Many other units must still be fighting. The sky is red, cut by bright flashes. Russian tanks all around us, and the incessant clatter of machine-guns. We make some headway in close combat. We meet columns of refugees drifting about lost. They weep and ask for help. We are at the end ourselves. Our ammunition is giving out. The unit breaks up. We try to go on in small groups.

German staff officer, diary

A Russian Officer Moves In

We went into Berlin by car. The smoke of fires was still in the sky over the city. Rifle fire and the explosion of hand grenades could still be heard. Our tanks were parked in the Tiergarten along the Siegesallee between the damaged statues of the Hohenzollerns, many of which had been destroyed by our shells.

A huge red flag flew over the Brandenburger Tor. The roof of the famous Hotel Adlon was wrecked. A little farther along at No. 7 Unter den Linden our Embassy had lost its lime trees. They had been cut down for anti-tank blocks, a fantastic idea on the part of Goebbels, who had been Defence Commissar for the German capital.

Our car drew up at the Embassy. It was ten years to the day that I had left that building to return to Moscow to make my report to Voroshilov in the Kremlin.

Ivan Krylov

UNCONDITIONAL SURRENDER

The British had crossed the Elbe on 29 April, and on 2 May, the same day that fighting ended in Berlin and the German forces in Italy surrendered to Field-Marshal Alexander, British and American troops met the Russians on the shores of the Baltic.

The end had come. On the following day, Admiral Doenitz sent his emissaries to Field-Marshal Montgomery's headquarters on Lüneburg Heath to negotiate surrender terms for the British sector.

The Last Days

On 30 April a German counter-attack was mounted from the area west of the Elbe–Trave Canal towards Lauenburg against VIII British Corps. The attack was carried out by one under-strength infantry division and had no success. Units of VIII British Armoured Corps, led by 11 British Armoured Division, broke out of the Elbe bridgehead at Lauenburg on 1 May and penetrated very rapidly to Lübeck, which was entered on the afternoon of 2 May. South-east of Lübeck, British forces took Wismar and the Americans reached Schwerin on the same day. The British had thus reached the Baltic coast-line and we were now completely cut off from Berlin and from the German formations in the centre and south of Germany. Russian armoured spearheads had already advanced from Rostock to the west and these made contact with the Western Allies in the Wismar region on 3 May.

During the course of the final actions *Armee* Blumentritt had entered into communication with VIII British Corps and with 2 British Army in order to regulate essential matters, and in this connection had always been met halfway by the British authorities. After 1 May there was practically no more fighting. The British troops moved forward unopposed, as *Armee* Blumentritt had given orders from the hour of Hitler's death on 2 May that no further resistance should be offered. Even earlier than this date various authorities in Hamburg had contacted British units. Among these were the Mayor of the city and the Nazi district leader, Gauleiter Kauffmann. As late as 1 May the order to defend Hamburg had been given by the Supreme Command of the Army. On the evening of 1 May my Headquarters proposed that Hamburg should be surrendered as an open city in order to avoid further sacrifices. After some shuttling backwards and forwards approval was obtained and my staff entered into communication with 2 British Army with regard to the surrender of the city. The surrender took place in a correct manner; an order from the Supreme Command of the Army that the many Flak (A.A.) positions in and around Hamburg should be blown up before the capitulation was not carried out and the batteries were surrendered undamaged. The oath which the Supreme Command of the Army ordered us to take to Grand-Admiral Doenitz was refused by *Armee* Blumentritt (as it was by nearly all formations) and was not taken.

Numerous German refugees were fleeing to the west before the Russians and we requested VIII British Corps to let them cross the Elbe–Trave Canal to the west, as we did not know how far the Russians would advance westward. The British authorities helped in this matter as far as possible.

General Blumentritt, G.O.C. *Armee* Blumentritt

That night the news came that Hitler was dead, that the German armies in Italy had surrendered, that 6 Airborne Division had linked up with the Russians at Wismar, and that an envoy had come in to the leading Coldstream troop from

Field-Marshal Busch asking to be conducted to Field-Marshal Montgomery's H.Q.

The end had come. There was to be no more fighting, but when the Grenadiers and ourselves set out from the area of Siebeneichen on the morning of the 3rd there was caution, for no one knew whether there was not some fanatic with a rifle or bazooka round the next corner or behind a nearby hedge. But by midday this caution had worn off; the front was wide open. 13 Brigade were leading with two squadrons of Grenadiers—No. 1 with K Troop and No. 3 with L Troop. No. 3 took Mölln without firing a shot, and hopes of being the first troops into Lübeck were high when 5 Division was suddenly ordered to halt. 29 Armoured Brigade were closing in from the left and the Russians were not far distant on the right, and a pause was needed to get matters straight.

Mölln had to be seen to be believed. A vast quantity of D.P.s had left their camps nearby and were roaming the streets in search of liquid refreshment; they broke about two thousand bottles and the gutters ran with wine. A number of gypsies had appeared from somewhere with their caravans. A P.O.W. camp had been opened, and R.A.F. personnel were making their way to the rear in joyful mood and any conveyance they could commandeer—those on carthorses galloping down the road seemed to be enjoying themselves most, but there were several happy parties in smart traps and gigs with slogans chalked on the sides. Through this carnival of chaos the Wehrmacht in enormous numbers, bewildered and glum, either sat by the roadside waiting for orders or walked vaguely down the road. At one point the advance was brought to a standstill by a general marching his entire division in to surrender. Soon the fields round Mölln began to fill with vast herds of field-grey, like cattle, silent, tired and beaten. Panthers, all brand new, were abandoned by their crews at crossroads; gunners manning their 88s watched the tanks go by with their hands in their pockets. The S.S. was pretending to be something else, and trying to slip away without any idea where to go.

British tank officer

Lüneburg Heath: 3 May

On 3 May Field-Marshal Keitel sent a delegation to my headquarters on Lüneburg Heath, with the consent of Admiral Doenitz, to open negotiations for surrender. This party arrived at 11.30 hours and consisted of:

General-Admiral von Friedeburg, C.-in-C. of the German Navy.
General Kinzel, Chief of Staff to Field-Marshal Busch, who was commanding the German land forces on my northern and western flanks.
Rear-Admiral Wagner.
Major Freidel, a staff officer.
This party of four was later joined by Colonel Pollek, another staff officer.

They were brought to my caravan site and were drawn up under the Union Jack, which was flying proudly in the breeze. I kept them waiting for a few minutes and then came out of my caravan and walked towards them. They all saluted, under the Union Jack. It was a great moment; I knew the Germans had come to surrender and that the war was over. Few of those in the signals and operations caravans at my Tac Headquarters will forget the thrill experienced when they heard the faint 'tapping' of the Germans trying to pick us up on the wireless command link—to receive the surrender instructions from their delegation.

I said to my interpreter, 'Who are these men?' He told me.

I then said, 'What do they want?'

Admiral Friedeburg then read me a letter from Field-Marshal Keitel offering to surrender to me the three German armies withdrawing in front of the Russians between Berlin and Rostock. I refused to consider this, saying that these armies should surrender to the Russians. I added that, of course, if any German soldiers came towards my front with their hands up they would automatically be taken prisoner. Von Friedeburg said it was unthinkable to surrender to the Russians as they were savages, and the German soldiers would be sent straight off to work in Russia.

I said the Germans should have thought of all these things before they began the war, and particularly before they attacked the Russians in June 1941.

Von Friedeburg next said that they were anxious about the civilian population in Mecklenburg, who were being overrun by the Russians, and they would like to discuss how these could be saved. I replied that Mecklenburg was not in my area and that any problems connected with it must be discussed with the Russians. I said they must understand that I refused to discuss any matter connected with the situation on my eastern flank between Wismar and Domitz; they must approach the Russians on such matters. I then asked if they wanted to discuss the surrender of their forces on my western flank. They said they did not. But they were anxious about the civilian population in those areas, and would like to arrange with me some scheme by which their troops could withdraw slowly as my forces advanced. I refused.

I then decided to spring something on them quickly. I said to von Friedeburg:

'Will you surrender to me all German forces on my western and northern flanks, including all forces in Holland, Friesland with the Frisian Islands and Heligoland, Schleswig-Holstein, and Denmark? If you will do this, I will accept it as a tactical battlefield surrender of the enemy forces immediately opposing me, and those in support of Denmark.'

He said he could not agree to do this. But he was anxious to come to some agreement about the civilian population in those areas; I refused to discuss this. I then said that if the Germans refused to surrender unconditionally the forces in the areas I had named, I would order the fighting to continue; many more German soldiers would then be killed, and possibly some civilians also from artillery fire and air attack. I next showed them on a map the actual battle situation on the whole western front; they had no idea what this situation was and were very upset. By this time I reckoned that I would not have much more difficulty in getting them to accept my demands. But I thought that an interval for lunch might be desirable so that they could reflect on what I had said. I sent them away to have lunch in a tent by themselves, with nobody else present except one of my officers. Von Friedeburg wept during lunch and the others did not say much.

After lunch I sent for them again, and this time the meeting was in my conference tent with the map of the battle situation on the table. I began this meeting by delivering an ultimatum. They must surrender unconditionally all their forces in the areas I had named; once they had done this I would discuss with them the best way of occupying the areas and looking after the civilians; if they refused, I would go on with the battle. They saw at once that I meant what I said. They were convinced of the hopelessness of their cause but they said they had no power to agree to my demands. They were, however, now prepared to recommend to Field-Marshal Keitel the unconditional surrender of all the forces on the western and northern flanks of 21 Army Group. Two of them would go back to O.K.W., see Keitel, and bring back his agreement.

I then drew up a document which summarized the decisions reached at our meeting, which I said must be signed by myself and von Friedeburg, and could then be taken to Flensburg, and given to Keitel and Doenitz.

Field-Marshal Montgomery

Rheims: 6 May

Jodl arrived in Rheims on 6 May. In his cold, impersonal manner he repeated the arguments von Friedeburg had offered. General Eisenhower's terms, he pointed out, provided explicitly that all troops were to remain in the positions they occupied at the moment of surrender. But the German High Command simply could not guarantee that the German forces facing Soviet troops would abide by this condition. This fact created a dilemma in which the German Government had in the end no choice but to abandon the thought of surrender, and to let things drift as they would—and that meant chaos. He, Jodl, had come to Rheims mainly to state this dilemma and to ask the Americans for their help in solving it.

'You have played for very high stakes,' Smith said when Jodl had finished. 'When we crossed the Rhine you had lost the war. Yet you continued to hope for discord among the Allies. That discord has not come. I am in no position to help you out of the difficulties that have grown of this policy of yours. I have to maintain the existing agreements among the Allies. As a soldier I am bound by orders.' He looked at Jodl and concluded, 'I do not understand why you do not want to surrender to our Russian allies. It would be the best thing to do for all concerned.'

'Even if you were right,' Jodl replied, 'I should not be able to convince a single German that you are.'

But the American conditions remained unchangeable. Jodl, in desperation, suggested a surrender in two stages: the Americans should set a date after which there would be no more fighting, another date after which there would be no more troop movements. The order to surrender, he pointed out, would take no less than forty-eight hours to reach the widely scattered German forces. If the surrender were signed in the afternoon of 8 May, it would not become effective until the afternoon of 10 May.

General Smith left the room to submit this proposal to General Eisenhower. He returned almost at once. Eisenhower, he reported, demanded the immediate signing of the surrender document, stated that the surrender would become effective not later than midnight of 9 May, and gave Jodl half an hour to think this over: 'If you decline, the discussions will be considered closed. You will then have to deal with the Russians alone. Our Air Force will resume operations. Our lines will be closed even to individual German soldiers and civilians.'

Jodl, pale as death, rose to his feet.

'I shall send a radio message to Marshal Keitel,' he said in a strained voice. 'It is to read: "We sign, or general chaos."'

The reply arrived at half-past one o'clock in the morning of 7 May:

'Admiral Doenitz authorizes signature of surrender under conditions stated.—Keitel.'

Juergen Thorwald

At Rheims on 7 May 1945, General Bedell Smith for General Eisenhower, General Souzloparov and General Jodl signed the document which ended Germany's second attempt to dominate the world.

The mission of this Allied Force was fulfilled at 3 a.m., local time, 7 May 1945. Eisenhower.

Telegram to the Combined Chiefs of Staff, 7 May

Americans

That evening back in Jossnitz again, Chris and I were sitting with Ken and Bill in the dimness at the green serge-covered table, eating our supper, when Norman Harris came in late. Taking the rifle off his shoulder and not quite meeting our eyes, he said tiredly, with his flat Bostonian accent, 'Well, boys, it's all over. The war's over. I just heard the announcement.'

'Really over?' I put down my spoon in the mess kit.

'Honest to God?'

He raised his eyebrows, accepting no responsibility. 'So they say. It's over.' His helmet-liner stuck a little coming off his head. 'There's to be no more fighting.'

We sat in silence. I searched for some feeling, waited for it to develop. There was hardly any sensation at all. A moment later I was aware of an inward caving in, followed by a sore-throat feeling when I thought of those who had been forced to give up their lives for this moment.

'It's funny, isn't it,' Bill Eyerly was saying, 'how you can't feel anything. "The war's over." I thought I'd be hopping all over the place.'

'And I have another cha-a-a-ming bit of news,' Norman added. 'You'll all have to work to-night. The captain wants everyone to report to the house at seven o'clock.'

Leisurely, late, we went over to the attic and worked for a few hours, getting the records in order for the following day. The radio on the second floor, tuned up high, proclaimed London, Paris, New York—the entire world—delirious with joy, and there was a New Year's Eve blare of noise, voices and horns blowing in the background. 'We switch you now to London, where the crowds in Piccadilly ——' The radio snapped off and voices downstairs talked. The clerks were planning a celebration: someone was offering to buy liquor if any could be found for sale, and someone else long ago had cached away a bottle not to be opened till this night; but we upstairs in the attic had nothing, and no means with which to celebrate.

Our voices gradually quieted as we worked, and a peculiar long silence developed. Looking down, working automatically as the service records passed before me, I saw snow falling, fine, intent and unending, out of a cold, colourless sky. Where had that been? The trenches outside Rheims? Dominic's house? The château? The schoolhouse? None of those places, and yet all.

Finishing our own work ahead of the others, Chris and I left and went down the dark stairs, out into the spring night. The streets were cool and silent and leaf-shadowed. The guards were out, walking slowly up and down, and the generator chugged away in the stillness. A plane—the first in Europe we had seen with its lights on—throbbed across the sky. The entire town was blacked out.

'Do you feel like walking down as far as the corner?'

'To celebrate?' he asked.

In Norman Harris' airless, warm bedroom we sat alone, with one short candle lighted in the *épergne*, and had a canteen cup of cider that Zubek had left for us. Norman, Ken and Jim were visiting friends in one of the rooms downstairs. The dark army blankets remained stretched across the open windows. There was nothing to do but write a letter home while the candle was still burning. Up at the front, would there be any sort of a party? we wondered.

Lester Atwell

British

On V.E. night the victorious armies got drunk according to a long-cherished plan. I think I must have been on duty, for I was as sober as a judge and I remember standing at a dormer window in the great Luftwaffe hospital at Wismar, looking at the magnificent sunset and thinking that I had now come almost full circle, back to the sea that washed the shores of Sweden.

On a ward balcony below me wounded Germans were talking quietly. Presently, as the glow of their cigarettes confirmed that it was dark, the victory celebrations began. Up from the British lines came brilliant flares, singly and in clusters, but without pattern or prodigality, as if one soldier in each platoon had been given an official coloured hat and told to fling it in the air. But farther away, in the Russian lines, the glow of bonfires steadily lit up the sky. Distance subdued the flickering, making static cones that were slightly blurred by smoke or mist; and I could fancy that they were ghost fires, the fires of other historic triumphs, so strongly did I feel them as a symbol of the unreality of victory in relation to the recurring failure to keep the peace.

James Byrom

French

When I had gone half way along the Avenue of Sighs, the Château bell began ringing loudly. It was the bell for meals, hanging thirty feet above the ground on the east wall. It had not rung for at least four years. And whoever was ringing it had that technique, which I have always envied, of disengaging the bronze clapper before each stroke. I hurried on. It was Ravelon.

'What's the matter?'

'Peace . . . it's just been announced on the radio. I promised I would ring the bell to let the people know.'

It was five o'clock by the sun. She went on till she was exhausted. But no one came from the fields, the neighbouring farms or outbuildings because it was the hour and the month in which, for the uninitiated, everything seems to be at rest, for it is a time of ripening when man does not interfere. Only Tidier ran up from the kitchen garden.

'So it's finished. . . . Well, it was time it was over.'

Standing below the bell, the three of us, Tidier, Ravelon and I, having uttered excited exclamations, fell silent as at a marriage or a funeral.

Emmanuel d'Astier

Germans

Dear Father,

Now everything is coming to an end. Those of us who will see their homes again will leave Libau to-night and sail for Kiel. I shall give this letter to Hermann Meister, a sergeant of 11 Infantry Division. I hope you will get it.

Until yesterday we still hoped that all of us would be shipped back to Germany and would keep on fighting the Russians from there. Three days ago we received a secret, oral message from our commander, General Hilpert. It said that Admiral Doenitz had made contact with the Western powers and would make peace in the west. In the east, the war would go on. Army Group Courland would be moved across the Baltic Sea and would go back into action on the Elbe front. On 6 May we were to destroy all excess equipment. An army corps was put in charge of Libau port to cover our transfer to the ships. And the block positions for a gradual withdrawal had been ready since December of last year—in case the Führer should order it.

Some officers claimed to know that the British would send ships to pick us up. It was even said that English troops would land here and attack the Russian flank together with us.

We all had expected a turn in our fortunes because of the new weapons. Then we received the news of the heroic death of our Führer—it was a terrible, bitter disappointment. But then came the secret orders about the withdrawal, and all of us took new hope. We have fought here with all we have against one enemy: Bolshevism. If we fought English and Americans, it was only because they did not want to understand the meaning of our fight in the east. So our hopes were high when we heard about a separate peace in the west—our years of war would have a purpose, even though a whole nation would have been sacrificed.

You can imagine how disappointed we are, now that we have been told that all our forces have surrendered, and that Army Group Courland has joined in the surrender. Russian commissars are expected every day now. They say the English prevented the sailing of the ships that were to come for us. But no one knows for sure who has stabbed us in the back. The Navy has sent some small ships from the Gulf of Danzig. Army Group Reserve, that is, 11 Infantry Division and 14 Tank Division, will be evacuated on these ships because they were our 'firefighters', always in the thick; they have earned it. And then, each division was allowed to send some officers or an officer and 125 men on the trip home—mostly family men. And the wounded. You should have seen how 11 Infantry Division marched through Libau, fully armed, in perfect order.

Many of the men still do not believe in the surrender. They think they will march from Kiel against the Russians. The port is cordoned by military police, to keep unauthorized personnel from entering the ships. But everything has come off in perfect order, without any panic. Just as the Army has fought. We have done our part as German soldiers, if necessary to the bitter end.

We do not know how our Führer died. We do not know what weakness and treason took place back home during the last few weeks. We only know that to this day we have fought Bolshevism, the enemy not of us alone but of all Europe. We have seen Bolshevism in action as no one else has. We have seen the Bolshevist paradise. We know what we fought for. And if it is true that the English have kept our ships from leaving port, they will remember it one day when they see and go through what we have seen and gone through.

Captain Breuninger

The King's Broadcast: 8 May 1945

To-day we give thanks to God for a great deliverance.

Speaking from our Empire's oldest capital city, war-battered but never for one moment daunted or dismayed—speaking from London, I ask you to join with me in that act of thanksgiving.

Germany, the enemy who drove all Europe into war, has been finally overcome. In the Far East we have yet to deal with the Japanese, a determined and cruel foe. To this we shall turn with the utmost resolve and with all our resources.

But at this hour, when the dreadful shadow of war has passed from our hearths and homes in these islands, we may at last make one pause for thanksgiving, and then turn our thoughts to the tasks all over the world which peace in Europe brings with it.

Let us remember those who will not come back; their constancy and courage in battle, their sacrifice and endurance in the face of a merciless enemy: let us remember the men in all the Services, and the women in all the Services, who have laid down their lives. We have come to the end of our tribulation, and they are not with us at the moment of our rejoicing.

. . . . There is great comfort in the thought that the years of darkness and danger in which the children of our country have grown up are over—and, please God, for ever. We shall have failed, and the blood of our dearest will have flowed in vain, if the victory which they died to win does not lead to a lasting peace, founded on justice and goodwill. To that, then, let us turn our thoughts on this day of just triumph and proud sorrow; and then take up our work again, resolved as a people to do nothing unworthy of those who died for us, and to make the world such a world as they would have desired for their children and for ours.

This is the task to which now honour binds us. In the hour of danger we humbly committed our cause into the Hand of God, and he has been our Strength and Shield. Let us thank Him for his Mercies, and in this hour of victory commit ourselves and our new task to the guidance of that same strong Hand.

George R.

Going Home

This time there was clean straw on the floors of the forty-and-eights, and we were not nearly so crowded as we had been on the trip into Metz. The medics had been given a box-car to themselves. All day long the wide door remained open, and to the humming *click-click-clock* of the wheels, the sunlit German countryside rolled slowly past: fields and hills fading off to smoky blue on the horizon, towns, streams and woods, waterfalls, dark-green mountains. And now, when it was all over, Preacher stayed glued to the open doorway even while eating, looking and looking, trying to drink in all he had missed. I remember him speaking only once. 'Might as well git me a look at Europe,' he said with a laugh. 'Don't rightly expect Ah'll ever be back.'

. . . . Twice a day, for fifteen minutes, the boxcars halted and the men swarmed down on to the cracked blue stone of the roadbed to relieve themselves, to get water in large, flashing ten-in-one cans or helmets, to wash and shave, to walk up and down, visiting friends in other companies. Then the little referee whistles blew and there was a scattering, a scramble to climb up. 'This our car? Look and see if that's our stuff. No, we're in the next one.' The splintery, sun-faded maroon boxcars, marked '40 *Hommes ou 8 Chevaux*', chalked with in-numerable American names, dates and towns, rolled on again, beginning to finish their second World War.

Several times on the adjacent track, boxcars filled to overflowing with former Russian slave labourers and prisoners of war passed us coming from the opposite direction on their way into the Russian zone. Men, women and children waved and smiled. Many of the women were in native costume: long full skirts, blouses, embroidered aprons and *babushkas*. How, I wondered, had they been able to hold on to them through their years of imprisonment and servitude? Boughs had been lopped from young trees and fastened to the outside of the boxcars, and flanking the open doors were huge wilting bouquets of field flowers. From within came the plink and tinkle of a balalaika, or the wheeze of an accordion and voices singing Russian folk songs. In some cars a little fire was laid on bricks and a kettle was simmering. The tops of all these cars were piled high with 'acquired' two-wheel bicycles. There might be fifteen or more of such family cars, and then came those filled with Russian soldiers who had been prisoners of war, all dressed now in new green American fatigue suits and G.I. shoes.

Once our two trains stopped, leaving only a narrow aisle between. Crowds of Russian and American soldiers swung down, milling about and beaming. 'Yay, Russky! *Tovarish!*' our men said. The Russians smiled, but seemingly could not say the equivalent in English. At first American cigarettes and parts of rations were given away, but within a few minutes bartering and selling sprang up. Halting German was the common language. The Russians wanted American wrist-watches and cigarettes. The latter were snapped up for as high as fifty cents a pack in our Invasion money; within five minutes the price had soared beyond that, and I heard one of our men asking a young Russian who had bought a carton of Camels for fourteen dollars, 'For Russky camraden?'

'Naw!' came the answer. 'Fer Deutschers!' To be resold in the black market. He was offering a German Lüger for seventy-five dollars.

Not as many Russians as Americans had hopped down. The less enterprising sat on their high bales of hay, smiling down with bright childlike interest. Some looked like overgrown infants; others were astonishingly old to be in uniform. Every racial type seemed represented. There were those who looked like stout Eskimos, others like elongated Chinese, and still others like fat, placid Turks. Many, save for the newness of their fatigues and a breadth of face, were indistinguishable from the Americans. The whistles sounded again, and the trains rolled on in opposite directions.

Lester Atwell

Tailpiece

Early the next morning on our way to breakfast a small, humorous-looking, middle-aged German saw us, grinned and came across the street towards us into forbidden territory, his hand outstretched.

'Ofer!' he said. 'War ofer. *Gut!* Friends!'

We stopped. The man he had addressed, who worked in the attic with us, looked around, saw no M.P.s and permitted his hand to be shaken.

'Now,' said the German with his codger's grin, 'togedder we fight the Russian, no?'

Lester Atwell

33

THE END

When the Philippines were lost at the beginning of 1945, Japan's situation had become hopeless. All routes to her supplies of food and raw materials were cut, and in any case her merchant navy was so depleted that she had too few ships left to bring home enough to carry on the war. Admiral Halsey had taken his carrier fleet into the South China Sea and in one week alone sank 234,000 tons of shipping. The Japanese merchant navy, which had mustered over six million tons at the beginning of the war, now possessed no more than a million tons fit to put to sea. Compared with nine hundred thousand tons of bauxite for aluminium manufacture imported in 1943, only fifteen thousand tons reached Japan in 1945. In April 1945 the supply of fuel oil coming into the homeland ceased entirely. The 2,600,000 tons of rice brought in during 1942 dwindled to eight hundred thousand tons in 1944.

The Emperor

I BELIEVE it was about February 1944 that His Majesty began to grapple with the problem of peace as the most urgent issue confronting the empire. I recall that one day after the war's end the Emperor, speaking to us, his entourage, reminisced: 'From the time when our line along the Stanley Mountain Range in New Guinea was broken through, I was anxious for peace. But we had a treaty with Germany against concluding a separate peace; and we could not violate an international commitment. This was a dilemma that tormented me.'

In February 1945 we lost Manila. The Emperor summoned Baron Wakatsuki and several other ex-premiers and also Count Makino, former Lord Keeper of the Privy Seal, on different days, one at a time, and asked for their views. All these senior statesmen said peace was desirable but difficult to attain. None offered, it is said, any concrete suggestion.

It was towards the end of May 1945 when the *Yamato*, our newest and biggest battleship, despatched to save Okinawa, was sunk and all hope gone in naval warfare. General Umezu, Chief of the General Staff, informed the Throne of the impossibility of land operations to recoup our reverses at the Yunnan and Burma fronts. His Majesty was then resolved to seek peace at all costs.

. . . . With the consent of the Prime Minister he called the Imperial Presence Conference of 22 June, at which he proposed peace.

'This is a critical moment,' said His Majesty, 'permitting no hesitation, no delay. Apart from the War Direction Basic Programme of the 8 June conference, you will consider the question of ending the war as quickly as possible.' To advocate peace, as His Majesty did, in those days of frenzied chauvinism was an act which required an extraordinary resolution, involving a grave risk even to the august person of an emperor.

A Japanese Court official

Hunger

As the two of them came down the beach on their return and neared the sea wall where there were steps leading back to the street, Terry's hand tightened on Mako's and he motioned her to stop. A man had come out of the mist in front of them and was moving towards a huge trash can, placed at the corner of the sea wall near the steps, which was filled with garbage and refuse. Before the war there had been no beggars in Japan. The little girl and her father watched. The man grabbed into the barrel like an animal, spilling litter out on to the clean beach. He found some food clinging to a paper wrapper and he pressed the paper tightly against his face to gnaw the food away. A dog slunk down the steps from the street towards the beach and the man at the trash can. The dog was hungry but afraid of the man and cowered at the man's heels, whining low. Hearing the cries of the starving dog, the man turned and patted him on the head. Then, taking courage, the dog dived into the reeking pile of refuse, scavenging side by side with the man.

Gwen Terasaki

Japanese Home Guard

In the summer of 1940 a suggestion had been made by a British peer that, in the absence of anything better, the Home Guard should be armed with pikes. This was considered a great joke. The precautions which the Japanese took five years later in the face of utter defeat did not seem so funny to them.

The *kumichō* called the meeting to order. There were two main items on the agenda. First, every person of adult age must provide himself with a bamboo spear of a certain length with which to meet the enemy when they came to invade the islands. I was so shocked by this that I sat in stunned silence.... They began to argue over the length of the spears and I was engulfed by waves of talk, most of which I could not understand. I thought of how these poor people would feel when they discovered how reckless their leaders had been. With docility and courage they were doing all in their power to stave off the inevitable, but it would come and they would know that they had never had the least chance to win.

Gwen Terasaki

Death of a Pilot: 5 March 1945

Japanese law requires that the dead be cremated immediately, but the officer in charge, knowing that Captain Kurusu had a foreign mother, ordered that the body be held for her to decide how it should be disposed of. Jaye, the dead man's sister, was in Tokyo and went out to be with her brother's body. Kurusu* was some distance away when he was informed, and he went by train to the aerodrome. As a civilian, he had to make way for shipments of military personnel and it took him five hours to go from Tokyo to Tachikawa. When he arrived, he

* The Japanese special envoy to Washington, December 1941 (Ed.).

was ushered into the room where his son's body was lying. What thoughts of the mission of 1941 he must have held!

We wept for days. Terry repeated to me the Japanese poem of the death of a little boy who caught dragon flies by weaving an ever-narrowing circle about them with his fingers until they sat dazed and helpless. The mother sang:

> How far, how far, to-day
> Has gone my little
> Hunter of the dragon fly.

Gwen Terasaki

The Art Collector

The refugees were called *sokaijin* (escaped to the country). A friend of Terry's furnished a remarkable example of someone very much *sokaijin*. He was a wealthy person who had collected Chinese art for many years and had a fine home furnished with beautiful carved furniture which he had painstakingly collected during a long sojourn on the mainland. His library contained many ancient scrolls of the T'ang dynasty in China, a period which the Japanese had regarded with awe for centuries. This gentleman had been forced to move repeatedly, and each time he was forced to pack away his delicate curios, his scrolls, and his carved furniture. They were not easily packed, and much care was required to ship them from one place to another without doing considerable damage. As it was, exercising every precaution that money and love could afford, a few mishaps occurred each time a change was made. On the first move this connoisseur had transported his possessions out of Tokyo and to a small suburb, then in a few months farther inland, then again, and yet again. In the early summer of 1945 he came to visit us at Tateshina in high spirits and announced happily to Terry:

'Terasaki-*san*, I have very good news. You know all my things that I have been moving and moving all over Japan? Well, they are all gone. A bomb hit my house and burned them all. I don't have to worry about them any more. Only this small vase is left, and I have brought it to you so I can move freely once more!'

Gwen Terasaki

THE BOMB

Beaten on land, by sea and in the air, Japan was to receive two more terrible blows. The first atom bomb was dropped on Hiroshima on 6 August 1945. The second fell upon Nagasaki forty-eight hours later. The war was over.

A fission bomb of superlatively destructive power will result from bringing quickly together a sufficient mass of element U-235. This seems as sure as any untried prediction based upon theory and experiment can be.

Report by the secret committee of the National Academy of Science,
Washington, 6 November 1941

The First Atom Bomb Test

I was one of the group of British scientific men who worked at Los Alamos in New Mexico, where most of the recent experimental work on atomic bombs was carried out, and I saw the first bomb explode. Before I tell you about this, I ought to say that I have witnessed many ordinary bomb trials. In such trials the kind of result to be expected is always known beforehand, and the trial is designed to find out just how much damage the bomb will do. The first atomic bomb test had to be approached with a totally different outlook because it was not possible to make any previous experiment on a smaller scale. None of us knew whether we were going to witness an epoch-making experiment or a complete failure. The physicists had predicted that a self-propagating reaction involving neutrons was possible and that this would lead to an explosion. The mathematicians had calculated what mechanical results were to be expected. Engineers and physicists had set up an apparatus rather like that used in testing ordinary bombs, to measure the efficiency of the explosion. But no one knew whether this apparatus would be needed, simply because nobody knew whether the bomb would go off.

Our uncertainty was reflected in the bets which were made at Los Alamos on the amount of energy to be released. These ranged from zero to the equivalent of eighty thousand tons of T.N.T. Those of us who were to witness the test assembled during a late afternoon in July at Los Alamos for the two-hundred-and-thirty-mile drive to the uninhabited and desolate region where the test was to be made. We arrived about three o'clock in the morning at a spot twenty miles from the hundred-foot tower on which the bomb was mounted. Here we were met by a car containing a radio receiver. Round this we assembled, listening for the signal from the firing point which would tell us when to expect the explosion. We were provided with a strip of very dark glass to protect our eyes. This glass is so dark that at mid-day it makes the sun look like a little undeveloped dull green potato. Through this glass I was unable to see the light which was set on the tower to show us where to look. Remember, it was still dark. I therefore fixed my eyes on this light ten seconds before the explosion was due to occur. Then I raised the dark glass to my eyes two seconds before, keeping them fixed on the spot where I had last seen the light. At exactly the expected moment, I saw through the dark glass a brilliant ball of fire which was far brighter than the sun. In a second or two it died down to a brightness which seemed to be about that of the sun, so, realizing that it must be lighting up the countryside, I looked behind me and saw the scrub-covered hills, twenty-two miles from the bomb, lighted up as though by a mid-day sun. Then I turned round and looked directly at the ball of fire. I saw it expand slowly, and begin to rise, growing fainter as it rose. Later it developed into a huge mushroom-shaped cloud, and soon reached a height of forty thousand feet.

Though the sequence of events was exactly what we had calculated beforehand in our more optimistic moments, the whole effect was so staggering that I found it difficult to believe my eyes, and judging by the strong ejaculations from my fellow-watchers other people felt the same reaction. So far we had heard no noise. Sound takes over one and a half minutes to travel twenty miles, so we next had to prepare to receive the blast wave. We had been advised to lie on the ground to receive the shock of the wave, but few people did so, perhaps owing to the fact that it was still dark, and rattle-snakes and tarantulas were fairly common in the district. When it came it was not very loud, and sounded like the crack of a shell passing overhead rather than a distant high-explosive bomb. Rumbling followed and continued for some time. On returning to Los Alamos, I found that one of my friends there had been lying awake in bed and had seen the light of the explosion reflected on the ceiling of his bedroom, though the source of it was over a hundred and sixty miles away in a straight line.

Sir Geoffrey Taylor

Hiroshima

Sixteen hours ago, an American airplane dropped one bomb on Hiroshima. That single bomb had more power than twenty thousand tons of explosive. It is an atomic bomb. It is a harnessing of the basic power of the universe. We are now prepared to obliterate more rapidly and completely every productive enterprise the Japanese have above ground in any city.

President Truman, 7 August 1945

Hiroshima means 'the broad island'. It was built on the delta of the river Ota which flows down from Mount Kamuri, and it was the seventh town in point of size in Japan. The seven arms of the Ota—seven rivers which pour their waters into the inland sea—enclose in an almost perfect triangle the harbour of the town, the factories, an arsenal, oil refineries and warehouses. Hiroshima had a population of a quarter of a million people and, in addition, there was a garrison of about a hundred and fifty thousand soldiers.

Miss Ito, Hiroshima

The town was not much damaged. It had suffered very little from bombing. There were only two minor raids, one on 19 March last by a squadron of American naval planes, and one on 30 April by a Flying Fortress.

On 6 August there wasn't a cloud in the sky above Hiroshima, and a mild, hardly perceptible wind blew from the south. Visibility was almost perfect for ten or twelve miles.

At nine minutes past seven in the morning an air-raid warning sounded and four American B-29 planes appeared. To the north of the town two of them turned and made off to the south and disappeared in the direction of the Shoho Sea. The other two, after having circled the neighbourhood of Shukai, flew off at high speed southwards in the direction of the Bingo Sea.

At 7.31 the all-clear was given. Feeling themselves in safety, people came out of their shelters and went about their affairs and the work of the day began.

Suddenly a glaring whitish pinkish light appeared in the sky accompanied by an unnatural tremor which was followed almost immediately by a wave of suffocating heat and a wind which swept away everything in its path.

Within a few seconds the thousands of people in the streets and the gardens in the centre of the town were scorched by a wave of searing heat. Many were killed instantly, others lay writhing on the ground screaming in agony from the intolerable pain of their burns. Everything standing upright in the way of the blast—walls, houses, factories and other buildings—was annihilated and the debris spun round in a whirlwind and was carried up into the air. Trams were picked up and tossed aside as though they had neither weight nor solidity. Trains were flung off the rails as though they were toys. Horses, dogs and cattle suffered the same fate as human beings. Every living thing was petrified in an attitude of indescribable suffering. Even the vegetation did not escape. Trees went up in flames, the rice plants lost their greenness, the grass burned on the ground like dry straw.

Beyond the zone of utter death in which nothing remained alive houses collapsed in a whirl of beams, bricks and girders. Up to about three miles from the centre of the explosion lightly-built houses were flattened as though they had been built of cardboard. Those who were inside were either killed or wounded. Those who managed to extricate themselves by some miracle found themselves surrounded by a ring of fire. And the few who succeeded in making their way to safety generally died twenty or thirty days later from the delayed effects of the deadly gamma-rays. Some of the reinforced concrete or stone buildings remained standing, but their interiors were completely gutted by the blast.

About half an hour after the explosion, whilst the sky all around Hiroshima was still cloudless, a fine rain began to fall on the town and went on for about five minutes. It was caused by the sudden rise of over-heated air to a great height, where it condensed and fell back as rain. Then a violent wind rose and the fires extended with terrible rapidity, because most Japanese houses are built only of timber and straw.

By the evening the fire began to die down and then it went out. There was nothing left to burn. Hiroshima had ceased to exist.

A Japanese journalist, Hiroshima

Hiroshima: the Aftermath

We were then rather less than four miles away from the Aioi Bridge, which was immediately beneath the explosion, but already the roofs of the houses around us had lost their tiles and the grass was yellow along the roadside. At three miles from the centre of the devastation the houses were already destroyed, their roofs had fallen in and the beams jutted out from the wreckage of their walls. But so far it was only the usual spectacle presented by towns damaged by ordinary high explosives.

About two and a half miles from the centre of the town all the buildings had been burnt out and destroyed. Only traces of the foundations and piles of debris and rusty charred ironwork were left. This zone was like the devastated areas of Tokyo, Osaka and Kobe after the mass fall of incendiaries.

At three-quarters of a mile from the centre of the explosion nothing at all was left. Everything had disappeared. It was a stony waste littered with debris and twisted girders. The incandescent breath of the fire had swept away every obstacle and all that remained upright were one or two fragments of stone walls and a few stoves which had remained incongruously on their base.

We got out of the car and made our way slowly through the ruins into the centre of the dead city. Absolute silence reigned in the whole necropolis. There was not even a survivor searching in the ruins, though some distance away a group of soldiers were clearing a passage through the debris. Here and there a little grass was beginning to sprout amidst the ruins, but there was not a bird or an animal to be seen anywhere.

. . . . A young Japanese doctor accompanied me to the train when I left to return to Tokyo.

On what remained of the station façade the hands of the clock had been stopped by the fire at 8.15.

It was perhaps the first time in the history of humanity that the birth of a new era was recorded on the face of a clock.

Marcel Junod, International Red Cross

A Letter from Suzuki, a Young Man whose Hands were Burned Away

Father, Mother,

You will forgive me for not having always been a very good son. I would have liked to become one, but I no longer have time; I am going to die. Despite your meagre resources you allowed me to study, first at college, then at Tokyo University, and now, at the moment when I would at last have been able to repay you for all you have given me, it is my turn to die.

My sisters have renounced marriage and preferred to become school-teachers in order to assist you. So as to pay for my studies, you worked from dawn, when the moon was still in the sky, to the hour when the stars appear. I will never be able to repay your devotion and your sacrifices. I will die. I do not know how to excuse myself.

My body will soon be dead, but my soul will remain beside you, near the Lord Buddha. Do not weep, Father, Mother, and you, my sisters, I entreat you. I will always be by your side, working, taking my meals, being happy or sad. Autumn will come, the chirping of the crickets, the forest despoiled of its foliage will remind you of my death, but do not weep. Look after your health and be brave. I wish you a long and happy life. The atomic bomb that fell on 6 August had a terrifying power. It caused burns on my face, my back and my arms. I die thanking the doctors, the nurses and all my friends for their care and their kindness.

25 August, 9 p.m.

Minoru Suzuki

A Survivor

Another who struck his fancy was a three-hundred-pound faith healer who always came at mealtime. He was a survivor of Hiroshima. When the bomb was dropped he was awaiting his *shōsen* (tramcar) at the railway station and had fallen unconscious into a drainage ditch. Some time later he awoke. The siren was stilled, the planes were gone, and there was only emptiness where the station had been, but as he related it to us it appeared his greatest concern was that his clothes had been burned off. He rose and ran to his little house four miles away. When he got there his surviving child did not recognize him for his skin was a livid black. Having no medicine, he put potato juice in a mixture made from tea leaves on his burns. His wife and one child had been killed along with almost everyone he knew. He wondered why he had been spared. He came to think that the home-made remedy he had concocted had saved him and believed that he had been endowed with special curative powers and had a mission to perform. That was how he had become a faith healer. I remember his face, covered with keloids and scars from the after-effect of the bomb. He did not understand why he could not cure his sterility, but thought that when his faith was pure and strong enough he would overcome that, too.

Gwen Terasaki

SURRENDER

On 15 August, for the first time in history, the Emperor of Japan addressed his people and his speech was broadcast. The moment the Emperor began to speak our *amah* knelt down before the loudspeaker and then stretched herself out at full length, her forehead touching the floor.

Marcel Junod

Most of the twenty or so people . . . were women and children; there were only two or three elderly men there and Terry; even the *kumichō* at whose house the meeting was held was a woman. One woman, her right leg bandaged to the hip, had fled the heavily bombed Kanda district of Tokyo with her grand-children and her daughter-in-law; another woman in her forties had brought her five children to our mountains from the city. A few farm people from the region surrounding Tateshina were there. The children were afraid, awed and quiet; they kept close, huddling around their parents.

All were grave and solemn with unspoken wonder at two things: How would the Emperor's voice, which they had never in their lives heard, sound? What was their final destiny which the voice of the *tennō* would reveal?

They sat and listened intently when the high-pitched and quavering voice began. Leaning forward with brows furrowed and heads cocked to one side, they concentrated upon the sound. There was an eeriness about it, the way the people strained as if they were deaf, for the voice was loud enough and distinct; they heard the words easily as their future life or death was announced—but they could not understand. The Emperor spoke in Court Japanese and only Terry could comprehend.

Gwen Terasaki

The Imperial Rescript

We, the Emperor, have ordered the Imperial Government to notify the four countries, the United States, Great Britain, China and the Soviet Union, that We accept their Joint Declaration. To ensure the tranquillity of the subjects of the Empire and share with all the countries of the world the joys of co-prosperity, such is the rule that was left to Us by the Founder of the Empire of

Our Illustrious Imperial Ancestors, which We have endeavoured to follow. To-day, however, the military situation can no longer take a favourable turn, and the general tendencies of the world are not to our advantage either.

What is worse, the enemy, who has recently made use of an inhuman bomb, is incessantly subjecting innocent people to grievous wounds and massacre. The devastation is taking on incalculable proportions. To continue the war under these conditions would not only lead to the annihilation of Our Nation, but the destruction of human civilization as well. How could We then protect Our in-numerable subjects, who are like new-born babes for Us? How could We ask the forgiveness of the divine spirits of Our Imperial Ancestors? When Our thoughts dwell on those of Our subjects who died in battle, those who fell as victims of their duty, those who perished by a premature death, and on the families they have left behind them, We feel profoundly upset.

. . . . It is Our desire to initiate an era of peace for future generations by tolerating the intolerable and enduring the unendurable. Capable of maintaining the national policy and placing Our trust in the perfect sincerity of Our good and faithful subjects, We will always be with you.

Let all the countries, like one single family where tradition is handed down from son to grandson, have firm faith in the indestructable character of the Land of the Gods. Remembering Our heavy responsibilities and the length of road yet to be covered, concentrating all Our strength on the construction of the future, animated by deep morality and firm honesty, We swear to hold the flower of Our National policy very high, resolved not to remain backward in the general progress of the world. We ask you, Our subjects, to be the incarnation of Our will.

Hirohito

The Emperor knows better than we do what should be done.

Tie-*san, amah*

As Terry translated and they grasped the sense of what was being said, that it meant surrender, the bandaged woman began to weep—not loudly or hysteric-ally but with deep sobs that racked her body. The children started crying and before the Emperor had finished, all his people there were weeping audibly. The voice stopped. Silently the old men, the women and their children, rose and bowed to each other, and without any sound each went along the path leading to his own house.

Gwen Terasaki

Not all Japanese were so easily resigned, but the rebellious were a small minority, and their protests came to nothing.

The following day disquieting rumours began to circulate. In Tokyo the generals were said to be contemplating a seizure of power against the decision of the Emperor. Leaflets calling for the continuation of the war to the bitter end, the total destruction of the country and the death of the last soldier, had been dropped over Yokohama. Revolts had broken out in a number of towns in the south.

Marcel Junod

Suicides

I had expected to hear of mass *hara-kiri* but it turned out that I was much mistaken. There were suicides, but nothing on the scale I had feared. The only group to commit suicide that I knew about was composed of certain officers who had unsuccessfully attempted to interfere with the Emperor's broadcast; others acted as individuals. The Chief of Staff, General Sugiyama, shot himself in his office, and upon hearing of his death, his wife donned her ceremonial kimono and took her own life in the traditional short-sword manner. The War Minister, Anami, also died by his own hand. In apology to the *Kamikaze* dead, their commandant, Vice-Admiral Onishi, killed himself. He left a message which was printed in all the newspapers and widely read by the people:

'I speak to the spirits of the *Kamikaze* boys. You have fought well. You have my abiding gratitude. You have died as Human Bullets, convinced of final victory which did not come true. I wish my death to express my regret and sorrow to you and to your loved ones left behind.

'To you young men living now in Japan:

'I shall be happy in the Beyond if my death will show you that any reckless action will only worry the Emperor. You must carry out His Majesty's wish. Bear the unbearable and do not lose pride in being Japanese. You are the treasures of Japan. Hold tight the *Kamikaze* spirit and use it for the welfare of Japan and the peace of the world.'

There was a stunned apathy on the faces of the people in the street. Everyone was starving; few had the physical stamina even to express their thoughts coherently. The people were shabby, hungry, and often physically unclean, being without fuel and soap for the bath that is the daily necessity and pleasure of every Japanese. There was sadness in every face and a kind of tired relief. They waited for what they had to face and seemed resigned to it.

Gwen Terasaki

The Victors

A day or two before we were scheduled to leave for the Empire, rumours began to hit the newspapers that the Japanese were about to surrender, and the very night before we were to leave, the news became official. Pearl Harbor was bedlam that night. Every ship in the harbour was firing guns into the air, and every admiral in Hawaii was sending out dispatches telling us all to stop it. I have always believed the *Flasher* sent out the most impressive display of all. We used our entire supply of recognition signals, firing them from a little mortar on the bridge. We fired one a second. They all had parachutes on them, and they were a beautiful sight, floating down towards the water, each of them a different colour. I invited all the old chiefs to the wardroom and broke out the ship's supply of brandy—that same variety of brandy that had tasted so awful to Roger Paine and me so long ago—and each of us took a little two-ounce bottle, poured it into a glass, and drank a toast to the peace.

The celebration continued for three or four days.

George Grider, U.S. submarine officer

Tokyo began to prepare itself to receive the conquerors. Companies of soldiers worked steadily to clear up the town, filling in craters and trenches, removing masses of scrap metal, barbed wire and fire-damaged wreckage from acres and acres of the town. Apart from modern buildings, almost all quarters of the town had been gutted, because the Flying Fortresses had dropped almost exclusively incendiaries. The flimsy Japanese houses had gone up like tinder. The only furniture which had resisted the fire was the safe installed to protect valuables and fragile goods in the event of earthquakes, and thus a strange feature of the devastated areas was the appearance of thousands of these safes standing out above the wreckage.

. . . . When I returned from camp Omori I saw the first detachments of marines pouring out of the landing boats to occupy Japan. They assembled along the banks of Tokyo Bay as though going on manœuvres. Their weapons glinted in the sun and the Japanese observed the scene with tranquil interest and showed no signs either of sadness or hostility. Indeed, they might have been watching the exercises of their own navy.

These people, who had counted it a supreme honour to have a member of their family amongst the dead, and who had been tremendously proud if a son or brother was amongst the *Kamikaze* or suicide squads, as a suicide pilot or one-man torpedo crew, did not make a gesture or say a word against the invader. Had not the Emperor declared: 'The war is over'?

When a detachment of sailors passed before us preceded by their commandant I saw an old man in a grey kimono turn his head away almost unnoticeably. His narrow eyes became slits behind his gold-rimmed glasses and a polite smile crossed his closed lips. He was too moved not to smile. A white man would have wept.

Marcel Junod

The Emperor Goes to His People

When he was permitted to go among his people freely for the first time, it was as though the Emperor had been liberated. Terry accompanied him on one trip. Immense crowds choked the line of travel as they went by car through the villages and towns and cities of Japan. The people would surge towards the car, cheering, tearful in their joy to look upon the *tennō*. An old lady held up the photo of her lost son for the Emperor to look at, saying, 'Look upon him, look upon him, I beg you. He died for you!'

Gwen Terasaki

All Over

Each man has his own particular memories; passing the regimental mule lines, and seeing all the swishing tails; the record of a nostalgic tune of Tchaikovsky played constantly in Lohardaga; the endless lines of bullock carts on the dusty roads of Burma; the varied bird life for those who had a trained eye to watch; the grazing herd of camels that chewed off long stretches of insulation from a telephone line in the Sudan; a night drive across the desert, standing with your head out of the trap-door in the roof, looking down on the road, and calling to your driver to go left, or right, or straight ahead, or to stop; bathing before breakfast in the turquoise-blue waters of the Mediterranean, and walking happily along the gleaming white sands that stretch for miles beside Burg el Arab. One will remember the fields of Cyprus in springtime, when scarlet poppies and yellow patches of daisies mingled with the green of the swaying barley. Another will be reminded of shooting duck or sand-grouse. There will be a momentary glimpse of the first Italian prisoners brought in—a bedraggled crowd of native troops wearing coloured scarves round their waists to distinguish their regiment. Or a mental picture of Sikh signalmen in Eritrea, hating the cold, muffled up in greatcoats, and bright with coloured cloths tied round their beards and over the top of their intricate *pagris*. Fishing in a stream near Gallabat; the sound of children on the Teknaf Peninsula chanting their morning prayers in the Buddhist school. Lying on one's stomach in a paddy-field on the edge of an Arakanese village, and deciphering code messages by the light of the moon. The Punjabi lance-*naik* who, when he was going away, seized his officer's hand, and said, '*Agar maine koi galati kia hai, to ap muaf kijiye*' (Please pardon any mistakes I may have made). The ecstasy with which a battalion Signals Officer could greet the discovery of two miles of telephone cable or a roll of insulating tape. The contentment of listening on a long line to clear, loud speech.

The souvenirs that a man brought back with him would vary with his taste, and above all with the force of his collecting instinct and the circumstances in which he found himself. Few were able to bring heavy items, for baggage was restricted, and very little might be carried out from the battle front. Nor had anyone the space, apart from the corner of some leather *yakdan* box, or a haversack, or a niche in a truck. Yet each man took back some little group of mementos: a Japanese sword to hang above his mantelpiece, an album with photographs and news-cuttings, lace table mats from Cyprus, brocade from Damascus, an inlaid mother-of-pearl box bought in Beirut, or an Arab headrope picked up in the bazaars of Baghdad. There might be a Persian rug stretched on the parquet floor, a copy or two of an Indian or Egyptian newspaper, a handful of foreign coins, a photograph of the man himself perched on a camel beside the Sphinx, or postcards of the Pyramids and the Gateway to India at Bombay. You might find in one of his drawers a notebook with Japanese characters scrawled on the white pages; or a musty-smelling book with his own name, a date, and Cairo or Haifa or Singapore or Nicosia written on the flyleaf—and this book would, on account of its travels, hold for its owner more intimate associations than its fellows on the shelf.

Up in the attic might be found an old canvas valise, that had been spread out night after night for him to sleep in, and rolled and fastened again with straps morning after morning through the campaigns. On the outside would be the traces of his name painted in white, and various sets of code numbers and letters that had signified one ship or unit in a convoy. In some old envelope in the drawer lies a sheaf of creased and folded maps of old campaigning areas, torn at the folds, disfigured by pencil crosses and rings that have lost their meaning, and by faintly pencilled code names for hill features and crossroads. Hanging in the cupboard is a suit of green jungle battledress that is used for gardening, and somewhere or other could be found a small cardboard box filled with dusty officer's pips, or a crown, a Divisional flash or two, bits of faded medal ribbons, and disused medal bars of various lengths.

Anthony Brett-James

Some of the events portrayed in the last few pages took place after the shooting had stopped. They are included because they are part of the ending of the struggle which, as Marshal Pétain said, had brought the whole world into conflict for the first time in history, and which had caused the deaths of thirty million people. As at Lüneburg and at Rheims the armies and people of the Third Reich had signed away their nightmare and by their submission purchased the right to future happiness, so at Manila on 2 September 1945 the representatives of the Japanese people, by the order of their Emperor, set their names calligraphically upon the document which stilled at last the thunder of the war. As their signatures were brushed upon the paper, the following words were spoken by General MacArthur:

We are gathered here, representatives of the major warring powers, to conclude a solemn agreement whereby peace may be restored. The issues, involving divergent ideals and ideologies, have been determined on the battlefields of the world and hence are not for our discussion or debate. Nor is it for us here to meet, representing as we do a majority of the people of the earth, in a spirit of distrust, malice, or hatred. But rather it is for us, both victors and vanquished, to rise to that higher dignity which alone befits the sacred purposes we are about to serve, committing all our peoples unreservedly to faithful compliance with the understandings they are here formally to assume.

It is my earnest hope . . . that from this solemn occasion a better world shall emerge . . . a world dedicated to the dignity of man. . . . The terms and conditions upon which surrender of the Japanese Imperial forces is here to be given and accepted are contained in the instrument of surrender before you.

Let us pray that peace be now restored to the world, and that God will preserve it always.

These proceedings are closed.

General MacArthur

ENVOI

For Johnny

Do not despair
For Johnny-head-in-air;
He sleeps as sound
As Johnny underground.

Fetch out no shroud
For Johnny-in-the-cloud;
And keep your tears
For him in after years.

Better by far
For Johnny-the-bright-star,
To keep your head,
And see his children fed.

John Pudney

Sure, there were lots of bodies we never identified. You know what a direct hit by a shell does to a guy. Or a mine, or a solid hit with a grenade, even. Sometimes all we have is a leg or a hunk of arm.

The ones that stink the worst are the guys who got internal wounds and are dead about three weeks with the blood staying inside and rotting, and when you move the body the blood comes out of the nose and mouth. Then some of them bloat up in the sun, they bloat up so big that they bust the buttons and then they get blue and the skin peels. They don't all get blue, some of them get black.

But they all stunk. There's only one stink and that's it. You never get used to it, either. As long as you live, you never get used to it. And after a while, the stink gets in your clothes and you can taste it in your mouth.

You know what I think? I think maybe if every civilian in the world could smell this stink, then maybe we wouldn't have any more wars.

Technical Sergeant Donald Haguall,
48th Quartermaster Graves Registration

Obscure Hillocks

One of the oddest things about a war, when all is said and done, is the immortality which it confers on remote villages, obscure hillocks, abandoned cisterns or even a map reference. Here, in the chilly print of Her Majesty's Stationery Office, were nine hundred and seventy names, of which perhaps ten per cent were known to us before the war, but each of them now of immense significance to somebody, and many of them to us. They conjure up yellow dust caking on the cheeks, or knee-deep paddy-fields, or splintered branches of the *bocage*; sullen or cheering or indifferent inhabitants; heat or cold, rain or shine, day or night, fear or exultation.

The last action on the list was fought eleven years ago, but a good deal has happened since then, with one major action—battle? engagement?—in Korea, and casualties also in Malaya and Kenya. Some time-expired soldiers were being discharged—I hate the word 'released'—in the Depot that day; and, as we drove out of it, the recruits were coming on to the square for their last parade of the afternoon.

Anon.

The Last Word

It was February 1954, and I was sitting in the War Office watching the Whitehall rain beat down into the courtyard, and talking to a young subaltern just home from Kenya.

He was explaining how, in order to combat the Mau Mau terrorists, the Royal Engineers had built log roads through the jungle.

'Oh, yes; I know the idea,' I said. 'Same as they did in the Reichswald. You weren't in that battle, were you?'

He smiled faintly.

'No, sir,' he said. 'But we heard all about it at my prep school.'

'Then that just about makes it history, doesn't it?' I said pleasantly.

John Foley

KEY TO THE SOURCES
OF EXTRACTS

FOR an explanation of how to use this Key and the following section entitled *Sources*, see page xiii.

SOURCES

The Editors wish to express their gratitude to all the publishers, authors, literary agents and others who so kindly granted permission for the reproduction of the extracts in this anthology.

Key Number

1 *Above Us the Waves (The Midget Raiders)*, by C. E. T. Warren and James Benson. Harrap, 1953; Sloane, 1954.
2 *Ack-Ack: Britain's Defence Against Air Attack During the Second World War*, by General Sir Frederick Pile. Harrap, 1949; British Book Centre, 1950.
3 *Admiral Halsey's Story*, by Fleet Admiral William F. Halsey and J. Bryan III. McGraw, © 1947 by William F. Halsey and Curtis Publishing Company.
4 *After the Battle*, by Boris Agapov. Hutchinson, 1943.
5 *Aircraft Carrier*, by J. Bryan. Ballantine, 1954.
6 *American Treasury, 1455–1955, The*, by Clifton Fadiman. Harper, 1955.
7 *And Some Fell by the Wayside*, by A. R. Tainsh. Longmans, Green, 1948.
8 *Arnhem*, by Major-General R. E. Urquhart. Cassell; Norton, 1958.
9 *Arnhem: From the Other Side*, by Colonel-General Kurt Student; *An Cosantóir: The Irish Defence Journal*, 1949.
10 *Arnhem Lift*, by Louis Hagen. Hammond, 1944; Farrar, 1945.
11 *Ball of Fire: The Fifth Indian Division in the Second World War*, by Antony Brett-James. Gale & Polden, 1951.
12 *Battle of North-West Germany, The*, by General Gunther Blumentritt; *An Cosantóir: The Irish Defence Journal*, 1949.
13 *Battle of the River Plate, The (Graf Spee)*, by Dudley Pope. Kimber, 1956; Lippincott, 1957.
14 *Before the Dawn*, by Brigadier Sir John Smyth. Cassell, 1957.
15 *Behind the Steel Wall*, by Arvid Fredborg. Harrap; Viking, 1944.
16 *Big Show, The*, by Pierre Clostermann. Chatto & Windus; Random, 1951.
17 *Black Watch and the King's Enemies, The*, by Bernard Fergusson. Collins; Crowell, 1950.
18 *Blitz, The (The Winter of the Bombs)*, by Constantine Fitz Gibbon. Wingate, 1957; Norton, 1958.
19 *Bombed But Unbeaten*, by Beatrice L. Warde. Friends of Freedom, 1941.
20 *Bomber Offensive*, by Marshal of the Royal Air Force Sir Arthur Harris. Collins; Macmillan, 1947.
21 *Bomber.Pilot*, by Group-Captain Leonard Cheshire. Hutchinson, 1943.
22 *Book of War Letters, A*, edited by Harry E. Maule. Random House, 1943.
23 *Bridge to the Sun*, by Gwen Terasaki. Joseph, 1958; University of North Carolina Press, 1957.
24 *Calculated Risk*, by General Mark Clark. Harper, 1950; Harrap, 1951.
25 *Call to Honour, 1940–1942, The*, by Charles de Gaulle. Collins; Viking, 1955.
26 *Camouflage Story, The*, by Geoffrey Barkas. Cassell, 1952.
27 *Canadian Army, 1939–1945, The*, by Colonel C. P. Stacey. Department of Public Printing and Stationery, Ottawa, 1948.
28 *Cassino: Portrait of a Battle (Battle of Cassino)*, by Fred Majdalany. Longmans, Green; Houghton, 1957.
29 *Chelsea Concerto, The*, by Francis Faviell. Cassell, 1959.
30 *Club Route in Europe*, by Ronald Gill and John Groves. Werner Degener, 1946.
31 *Colditz Story, The*, by P. R. Reid. Hodder & Stoughton; Lippincott, 1952.
32 *Collected Poems*, by Norman Cameron. Hogarth Press, 1957.

Key Number

33　*Collected Poems*, by C. Day Lewis. Hogarth Press and Cape, 1949.
34　*Come in Spinner!* by Dymphna Cusack and Florence James. Heinemann; Morrow, 1951.
35　*Command Missions*, by Lieutenant-General L. K. Truscott, Jr. Dutton, Copyright 1954 by Lieutenant-General L. K. Truscott.
36　*Commando*, by Brigadier John Durnford-Slater. Kimber, 1953.
37　*Convoy Commodore*, by Admiral Sir K. Creighton. Kimber, 1956.
38　*Courage and Fear*, by Rémy. Arthur Barker, 1950.
39　*Cretan Runner, The*, by George Psychoundakis. Murray; Transatlantic, 1955.
40　*Crisis in the Desert, May–July 1942*, by J. A. I. Agar-Hamilton and L. C. F. Turner. Oxford, 1952.
41　*Cruel Sea, The*, by Nicholas Monsarrat. Cassell; Knopf, 1951.
42　*Crusade in Europe*, by Dwight D. Eisenhower. Heinemann; Doubleday, 1948.
43　*Daedalus Returned*, by Baron von der Heydte. Hutchinson, 1958.
44　*Day After Day*, by Odd Nansen. Putnam, 1949.
45　*Day's Alarm, The*, by Paul Dehn. Hamilton, 1949.
46　*Decisive Battles of the Western World, The*, Vol. 3, by Major-General J. F. C. Fuller. Eyre & Spottiswoode; Scribner, 1956.
47　*Defeat in the West*, by Milton Shulman. Secker & Warburg, 1947; Dutton, 1948.
48　*Defeat Into Victory*, by Field-Marshal Sir William Slim. Cassell, 1957.
49　*Diary of a Young Girl, The*, by Anne Frank. Vallentine, Mitchell; Doubleday, 1952.
50　*Die Invasion*, by Friedrich Hayn. Kurt Vowinckel Verlag, 1954.
51　*Dieppe at Dawn (At Whatever Cost)*, by R. W. Thompson. Hutchinson, 1956; Coward, 1957.
52　*Dittybox, The*, No. 5. H.M.S.O., 1944.
53　*Documents on International Affairs: Norway*, by M. Curtis. Oxford, 1941.
54　*Drive: A Chronicle of Patton's Army*, by Charles Codman. Little, Brown, © 1957 by Theodora Duer Codman.
55　*Drummond Tradition, The*, by Charles Mercer. Putnam, 1957.
56　*Dunkirk*, by A. D. Divine. Faber, 1945; Dutton, 1948.
57　*Eastern Approaches (Escape to Adventure)*, by Fitzroy MacLean. Cape, 1949; Little, Brown, 1950.
58　*Eclipse*, by Alan Moorehead. Hamilton, 1945; Coward, 1946.
59　*Einen Bessern Findst du Nicht*, anon. Kindler Verlag, 1952.
60　*Escort*, by Commander D. A. Rayner. Kimber, 1955.
61　*European Victory*, by John D'Arcy Dawson. MacDonald, 1945.
62　*Fall of France, The*, by Major-General Sir Edward Spears. Heinemann; Wyn, 1954.
63　*Fatal Decisions, The*, by Werner Kreipe and others, edited by Seymour Freidin and William Richardson. Joseph; Sloane, 1956.
64　*Fire on the Beaches*, by Theodore Taylor. Norton, copyright 1958 by Theodore Taylor.
65　*Fires on the Plain*, by Shohei Ooka. Secker & Warburg; Knopf, 1957.
66　*First and the Last, The*, by Adolf Galland. Hott, 1954; Methuen, 1955.
67　*Flight in the Winter*, by Juergen Thorwald. Pantheon, 1951; Hutchinson, 1953.
68　*Flight to Arras*, by Antoine de St.-Exupéry. Heinemann; Harcourt, 1942.
69　*Follow My Leader*, by Louis Hagan. Wingate, 1951.
70　*From the City, From the Plough*, by Alexander Baron. Cape, 1948; Washburn, 1949.
71　*Fuel of the Fire, The*, by Douglas Grant. Cresset, 1950.
72　*Galleghan's Greyhounds*, by A. W. Penfold, W. C. Bayliss, and K. E. Crispin. 2/30 Battalion Australian Imperial Forces Association, 1949.
73　*Gauntlet to Overlord*, by Ross Munro. Macmillan, 1945.

Key Number

74 *German Military Intelligence,* by Paul Leverkuehn. Weidenfeld & Nicolson; Praeger, 1954.

75 *German Morale 1939–1945,* by General Hasso von Manteuffel; *An Cosantóir: The Irish Defence Journal,* 1949.

76 *Germany's Underground,* by Allen Welsh Dulles. Macmillan, 1947.

77 *Goebbels Diaries, The,* by Louis P. Lochner. Doubleday, 1948.

78 *Going to the Wars,* by John Verney. Collins; Dodd, 1955.

79 *Goon in the Block,* by Eric Williams. Cape, 1945.

80 *Great Escape, The,* by Paul Brickhill. Norton, 1950; Faber, 1952.

81 *Green Armour,* by Osmar White. Allen & Unwin; Norton, 1945.

82 *Green Beret, The,* by Hilary St. George Saunders. Joseph, 1949.

83 *Grinning Face, and Other Poems, The,* by J. M. Russell. Routledge, 1948.

84 *Happy Hunted, The,* by Brigadier George Clifton. Cassell, 1952.

85 *Happy Odyssey,* by Sir Adrian Carton de Wiart. Cape, 1950.

86 *Hausfrau at War,* by Else Wendel. Odhams, 1957.

87 *Heavens Are Not Too High, The,* by Charles MacLean. Kimber, 1957.

88 *Hide and Seek,* by Xan Fielding. Secker & Warburg, 1954.

89 *History of the Argyll and Sutherland Highlanders, 5th Battalion, 91st Anti-Tank Regiment, 1939–1945,* by Major Desmond Flower. Nelson, 1950.

90 *History of the French First Army, The,* by Marshal de Lattre de Tassigny. Allen & Unwin, 1952; Macmillan, 1953.

91 *History of the Northumberland Hussars Yeomanry, 1924–1949,* by Joan Bright. Mawson, Swan & Morgan, 1949.

92 *Hitler and His Admirals,* by Anthony Martienssen. Secker & Warburg, 1948; Dutton, 1949.

93 *Hitler Directs His War,* by Felix Gilbert. Oxford, 1950.

94 *How Is It with the Happy Dead?,* by Eric Joysmith. *English Story,* 4th Series, edited by Woodrow Wyatt. Collins, 1943.

95 *Human Kind, The,* by Alexander Baron. Cape; Washburn, 1953.

96 *Hundred Years of Army Nursing, A,* by Ian Hay. Cassell, 1953. Acknowledgements to Queen Alexandra's Royal Army Nursing Corps.

97 *Ill Met by Moonlight,* by W. Stanley Moss. Harrap; Macmillan, 1950.

98 *Infantry Brigadier,* by Major-General Sir Howard Kippenberger. Oxford, 1949.

99 *In Their Shallow Graves (Road to Stalingrad),* by Benno Zieser. Elek, 1956; Ballantine, 1955.

100 *In the Thick of the Fight,* by Paul Reynaud. Cassell, 1955; Simon & Schuster, 1956.

101 *Invasion Without Laurels,* by General Baron Leo Geyr von Schweppenburg; *An Cosantóir: The Irish Defence Journal,* 1949.

102 *Invisible Flag, The,* by Peter Bamm. Faber; John Day, 1956.

103 *I Saw the Fall of the Philippines,* by Colonel Carlos P. Romulo. Doubleday, 1942; Harrap, 1943.

104 *Italy in the Second World War,* by Pietro Badoglio. Oxford, 1948.

105 *I Walk on Wheels,* by Elizabeth Sheppard-Jones. Bles, 1958.

106 *I Was Graf Spee's Prisoner,* by Captain Patrick Dove. Withy Grove, 1940.

107 *I Was There,* by Fleet Admiral William D. Leahy. Gollancz; McGraw, 1950.

108 *Journal of the War Years,* by Anthony Weymouth. Littlebury, Worcester, 1948. Acknowledgements to the Public Trustee and the Society of Authors.

109 *Jungle Road to Tokyo (Our Jungle Road to Tokyo),* by Lieutenant-General Robert L. Eichelberger. Odhams, 1951; Viking, 1950.

110 *Last Days of Sevastopol, The,* by Boris Voyetekhov. Cassell; Knopf, 1943.

111 *Last Enemy, The (Falling Through Space),* by Richard Hillary. Macmillan. Acknowledgements to the Estate of Richard Hillary; St. Martin's, 1942.

112 *Last Flight From Singapore,* by Arthur G. Donahue. Macmillan, 1943.

113 *Last Letters From Stalingrad.* Coronet, 1955; Methuen, 1956.

Key Number
114 *Leningrad in the Days of the Blockade*, by A. Fadeyev. Hutchinson, 1946.
115 *Leyte*, by Samuel Eliot Morison. Little, Brown, © 1958 by Samuel Eliot Morison.
116 *Lofoten Letter*, by Evan John. Heinemann, 1941.
117 *Look Down in Mercy*, by Walter Baxter. Putnam, 1952; Heinemann, 1953.
118 *Lost Victories*, by Field-Marshal Erich von Manstein. Methuen; Regnery, 1958.
119 *MacArthur, 1941–1951: Victory in the Pacific*, by Major-General Charles A. Willoughby and John Chamberlain. McGraw, 1954; Heinemann, 1956.
120 *Magnificent Mitscher, The*, by Theodore Taylor. Norton, copyright 1954 by Theodore Taylor.
121 *Mailed Fist*, by John Foley. Panther, 1956.
122 *Malayan Postscript*, by Ian Morrison. Faber, 1942.
123 *Maquis (Waiting in the Night)*, by George Millar. Heinemann, 1945; Doubleday, 1946.
124 *March Out, The*, by James Shaw. Hart-Davis, 1953.
125 *Memoirs of Cordell Hull, The*, Vol. 2. Hodder & Stoughton; Macmillan, 1948.
126 *Memoirs of Field-Marshal the Viscount Montgomery of Alamein*. Collins; World, 1958.
127 *Memoirs of Field-Marshal Kesselring, The (Kesselring: a soldier's record)*. Kimber, 1953; Morrow, 1954.
128 *Memoirs of Marshal Mannerheim, The*. Cassell, 1953; Dutton, 1954.
129 *Men of Arnhem, The*, by Stanley Maxted and others; *The Listener*, 1944.
130 *Merchantman Re-armed*, by Sir David W. Bone. Chatto & Windus, 1949.
131 *Midway: The Battle that Doomed Japan*, by Mitsuo Fuchida and Masataka Okumiya. U. S. Naval Institute, 1955; Hutchinson, 1957.
132 *Modern Anabasis, A*, by General Baron Leo Geyr von Schweppenburg; *An Cosantóir: The Irish Defence Journal*, 1950.
133 *Monastery, The*, by Fred Majdalany. Bodley Head, 1945; Houghton, 1946.
134 *Moscow Tram Stop*, by Heinrich Haape, Collins, 1957.
135 *My Sister and I: The Diary of a Dutch Boy Refugee*, by 'Dirk van der Heide'. Harcourt, 1941.
136 *Naked Hill, The (The Tortured Earth)*, by Gert Ledig. Weidenfeld; Regnery, 1956.
137 *Old Breed, The*, by George McMillan. Infantry Journal Press, 1949, copyright Infantry Journal Inc.
138 *Omaha Beachhead*. American Forces in Action Series, 1945.
139 *One That Got Away, The*, by Kendal Burt and James Leasor. Collins and Joseph, 1956; Random, 1957.
140 *Only Way Out, The*, by R. M. Wingfield. Hutchinson, 1955.
141 *Operation Sea Lion*, by Ronald Wheatley. Oxford, 1958, Crown Copyright.
142 *Operation Victory*, by Major-General Sir Francis de Guingand. Hodder; Scribner, 1947.
143 *Other Side of the Hill, The (The German Generals Talk)*, by Captain B. H. Liddell Hart. Cassell; Morrow, 1948.
144 *Our Vichy Gamble*, by William H. Langer. Knopf, 1947.
145 *Panzer Battles, 1939–1945*, by F. W. von Mellenthin. Cassell, 1955; U. of Okla. Press, 1956.
146 *Panzer Leader*, by Heinz Guderian. Joseph; Dutton, 1952.
147 *Partisans of the Kuban*, by P. K. Ignatov, Hutchinson, 1945.
148 *Peter Moen's Diary*. Faber; Farrar, Straus & Cudahy, copyright 1941 by Creative Press, Inc.
149 *Portrait of Patton*, by Harry H. Semmes, Appleton-Century-Crofts, 1955.
150 *Post D (Digging for Mrs. Miller)*, by John Strachey. Gollancz; Random, 1941.
151 *Private*, by Lester Atwell. Simon & Schuster, © 1958 by Lester Atwell.
152 *Private Diaries of Paul Baudouin, The*. Eyre & Spottiswoode, 1948.

Key Number

153 *Privileged Nightmare, The,* by Giles Romilly and Michael Alexander. Weidenfeld, 1954.
154 *Public Papers and Addresses of Franklin D. Roosevelt, The.* Macmillan, 1941.
155 *Recalled to Service,* by Maxime Weygand. Heinemann; Doubleday, 1952.
156 *Report My Signals,* by Antony Brett-James, Harrap, 1948.
157 *Retreat From Kokoda,* by Raymond Paull. Heinemann, 1958.
158 *Retreat, Hell!,* by William Martin Camp. Appleton-Century, 1943; Constable, 1944.
159 *Retreat in the East (Action in the East),* by O. D. Gallagher, Harrap; Doubleday, 1942.
160 *Retreat, The,* by P. H. Newby. Cape; Knopf, 1953.
161 *Retreat With Stilwell,* by Jack Belden. Knopf, 1943.
162 *Return to the Sea,* by A. H. Rasmussen. Constable, 1956.
163 *Return Via Dunkirk,* by Gun Buster. Hodder & Stoughton, 1940.
164 *Rifle Brigade in the Second World War, 1939–1945, The,* by Major R. H. W. S. Hastings and others. Gale & Polden, 1950.
165 *Road to Trieste, The,* by Geoffrey Cox. Heinemann, 1947.
166 *Rommel,* by Desmond Young. Collins, 1950; Harper, 1951.
167 *Rommel Papers, The,* edited by B. H. Liddell Hart. Collins; Harcourt, 1953.
168 *Royal Artillery Commemoration Book, 1939–1945, The.* Bell, 1950.
169 *Russia at War (Tempering of Russia),* by Ilya Ehrenburg. Hamilton, 1943; Knopf, 1944.
170 *Russian and German Tactics,* by a former German battalion commander; *An Cosantóir: The Irish Defence Journal,* 1950.
171 *Sailor Malan,* by Oliver Walker. Cassell, 1953.
172 *Sailor's Odyssey, A,* by Admiral of the Fleet Viscount Cunningham of Hyndhope. Hutchinson; Dutton, 1951.
173 *St. Lô.* American Forces in Action Series, 1946.
174 *Schellenberg Memoirs, The (The Labyrinth),* edited by Louis Hagen. Deutsch, 1956; Harper, 1957.
175 *Sea Devils,* by J. Valerio Borghese. Melrose, 1952; Henry Regnery, 1954.
176 *Sea Wolves, The,* by Wolfgang Frank. Weidenfeld; Rinehart, 1955.
177 *Second World War, The,* by Winston Churchill, Vol. 1. Houghton, 1948.
178 *Second World War, The,* by Winston Churchill, Vol. 2. Houghton, 1949. ——
179 *Second World War, The,* by Winston Churchill, Vol. 3. Houghton, 1950.
180 *Second World War, The,* by Winston Churchill, Vol. 4. Houghton, 1950.
181 *Second World War, The,* by Winston Churchill, Vol. 5. Houghton, 1951.
182 *Second World War, The,* by Winston Churchill, Vol. 6. Houghton, 1953.
183 *Second World War, The,* by Winston Churchill, Abridged Edition. Cassell; Houghton, 1959.
184 *Sergeant in the Snow, The,* by Mario Rigoni Stern. MacGibbon & Kee, 1954.
185 *Seven Times Seven Days,* by Emmanuel d'Astier. MacGibbon & Kee, 1958.
186 *Seventy Days,* by Waclaw Zagorski. Muller, 1957.
187 *Shirt of Nessus, The (20 July),* by Constantine Fitz Gibbon. Cassell; Norton, 1956.
188 *Siege, The, A Story From Kohima,* by Arthur Campbell. Allen & Unwin; Macmillan, 1956.
189 *Silent Company, The,* by Rémy. Barker; McGraw, 1948.
190 *Singapore Is Silent,* by George Weller. Harcourt, 1943.
191 *Six Against Tyranny,* by Inger Scholl. Murray; Transatlantic, 1955; Verlag der Frankfurter Hefte, G.M.B.H. (Frankfurt am Main).
192 *Skis Against the Atom,* by Knut Haukelid. Kimber, 1954.
193 *Skorzeny's Special Missions,* by Otto Skorzeny. Hale; McGraw, 1957.
194 *Slave Ship, The,* by Bruno E. Werner. Pantheon, 1951; Heinemann, 1953.
195 *Small Back Room, The,* by Nigel Balchin. Collins, 1943; Houghton, 1945.

Key Number

196 *So Few Got Through*, by Martin Lindsay. Collins, 1946.
197 *Soldier*, by General Matthew B. Ridgway. Harper, 1956.
198 *Soldier, The*, by Karlludwig Opitz. Muller, 1954.
199 *Soldier, Sail North!*, by James Pattinson. Harrap, 1954.
200 *Soldier's Story, A*, by Omar Bradley. Holt, 1951; Eyre & Spottiswoode, 1952.
201 *Soviet Staff Officer*, by Ivan Krylov. Falcon Press; Philosophical Lib., 1951.
202 *Spirit in the Cage, The*, by Peter Churchill. Hodder & Stoughton, 1954; Putnam, 1955.
203 *Stalingrad*, by Heinz Schroter. Joseph; Dutton, 1958.
204 *Still Digging*, by Sir Mortimer Wheeler. Joseph, 1955; Dutton, 1956.
205 *Suez to Singapore*, by Cecil Brown. Random, 1942.
206 *Sun Goes Down, The*, edited by Jean Lartéguy. Kimber, 1956.
207 *Sunk*, by Mochitsura Hashimoto. Cassell; Holt, 1954.
208 *Surgeon at War*, by Lieutenant-Colonel J. C. Watts. Allen & Unwin, 1955.
209 *Take These Men*, by Cyril Joly. Constable, 1955.
210 *Tarawa: Portrait of a Battle*, by Robert Sherrod. Duell, Sloan & Pearce, copyright 1944 by Robert Sherrod.
211 *Ten Summers: Poems*, by John Pudney. Bodley Head, 1944 (also in *Collected Poems*, Putnam, 1957; *Flight above Cloud*, Harper, 1944).
212 *They Have Their Exits*, by Airey Neave. Hodder & Stoughton; Little, Brown, 1953.
213 *Thirty Seconds Over Tokyo*, by Captain T. W. Lawson. Hammond; Random, 1943.
214 *This is London*, by Edward Murrow. Cassell; Simon & Schuster, 1941.
215 *This is Pearl!*, by Walter Millis. Morrow, copyright 1947 by Walter Millis.
216 *Thousand Shall Fall, A*, by Hans Habe. Harcourt, 1941; Harrap, 1942.
217 *Three Came Home*, by Agnes Newton Keith. Little, Brown, 1947; Joseph, 1948.
218 *Through the Dark Night*, by J. L. Hodson. Gollancz, 1941.
219 *Time for Decision, The*, by Sumner Welles. Hamilton; Harper, 1944.
220 *Times, The*, 9 April 1940, statement by British and French Governments.
221 *Times, The*, 2 June 1956, *We Were There: Highland Regimental Committee on Battle Honours*.
222 *Tobruk 1941*, by Chester Wilmot. Angus & Robertson, 1945.
223 *Tokyo Record*, by Otto D. Tolischus. Hamilton, 1943; Harcourt, 1943.
224 *To Perish Never*, by Henry Archer and Edward Pine. Cassell, 1954.
225 *Trial of Joseph Kramer, The*, edited by Raymond Phillips. Hodge; British Book Centre, 1949.
226 *Trial of German Major War Criminals, The: Proceedings of the International Military Tribunal at Nuremburg, 1946.* H.M.S.O.
227 *Turn of the Tide, The*, by Sir Arthur Bryant. Collins; Doubleday, 1957.
228 *Twenty Thousand Thieves, The*, by Eric Lambert. Muller, 1952.
229 *Two Eggs on My Plate*, by Oluf Reed Olsen. Allen & Unwin; Rand McNally, 1952.
230 *U-Boat 977*, by Heinz Schaeffer. Kimber, 1952; Norton, 1953.
231 *Underground Escape*, by Masanobu Tsuji. Asian Publications, 1952.
232 *Under the Iron Heel*, by Lars Moen. Hale; Lippincott, 1941.
233 *Underwater Saboteur*, by Max Manus. Kimber, 1953.
234 *Unexploded Bomb*, by Major A. B. Hartley. Cassell, 1958; Norton, 1959.
235 *Unfinished Man, The*, by James Byrom. Chatto & Windus, 1957.
236 *United States Marines and Amphibious War, The*, by Jeter A. Isely and Philip A. Crowl. Princeton U. Press, 1951.
237 *Unofficial History*, by Field-Marshal Sir William Slim. Cassell, 1959.
238 *Unseen and Silent, The*, anon. Sheed & Ward, 1954.
239 *Up Front*, by Bill Mauldin. Holt, copyright 1945 by Henry Holt & Company, Inc.

Key Number

240 *Venlo Incident, The,* by Captain S. Payne Best. Hutchinson, 1950.

241 *Voices From Britain,* edited by Henning Krabbe. Allen & Unwin, 1947; Macmillan, 1948.

242 *War As I Knew It,* by George S. Patton, Jr. Houghton, 1947; Allen, 1948.

243 *War Begins at Home,* edited by Tom Harrisson and Charles Madge. Chatto & Windus, 1940.

244 *War Fish,* by George Grider and Lydel Sims. © Little, Brown, 1958.

245 *War Messages of Franklin D. Roosevelt, The.* The United States of America, 1945.

246 *Warrior Without Weapons,* by Marcel Junod. Cape; Macmillan, 1951.

247 *War Speeches of the Rt. Hon. Winston S. Churchill, The,* Definitive Edition, Vol. 1. Cassell, 1951; Houghton, 1953.

248 *War Speeches of the Rt. Hon. Winston S. Churchill, The,* Definitive Edition, Vol. 2. Cassell, 1952; Houghton, 1953.

249 *We Defended Normandy,* by General Hans Speidel. Herbert Jenkins, 1951.

250 *We Landed at Dawn,* by A. B. Austin. Gollancz; Harcourt, 1943.

251 *We're Gonna Hang Out the Washing on the Siegfried Line,* by Jimmy Kennedy and Michael Carr. Peter Maurice Music Co. Ltd.

252 *We Shall March Again,* by Gerhard Kramer. Cape; Putnam, 1955.

253 *White House Papers of Harry L. Hopkins, The (Roosevelt and Hopkins),* by Robert E. Sherwood. Eyre & Spottiswoode; Harper, 1948.

254 *Wing Leader,* by Johnnie Johnson. Chatto & Windus, 1956; Ballantine, 1957.

255 *With Rommel in the Desert,* by Heinz Werner Schmidt. Harrap; British Book Centre, 1951.

256 *Year of Stalingrad, The,* by Alexander Werth. Hamilton, 1946; Knopf, 1947.

257 *Young Lions, The,* by Irwin Shaw. Random, 1948; Cape, 1949.

MAPS

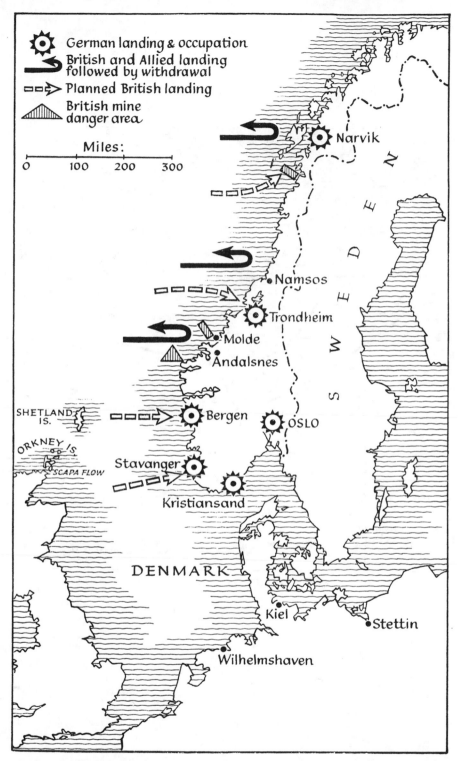

Legend:

- ⚙ German landing & occupation
- British and Allied landing followed by withdrawal
- ▭▭▷ Planned British landing
- ◭ British mine danger area

Miles:

0   100   200   300

Narvik

Namsos

Trondheim

Molde

Åndalsnes

SHETLAND IS.

ORKNEY IS

SCAPA FLOW

Bergen

Stavanger

OSLO

Kristiansand

DENMARK

Kiel

Stettin

Wilhelmshaven

SWEDEN

The Allied Campaign in Norway - 1940

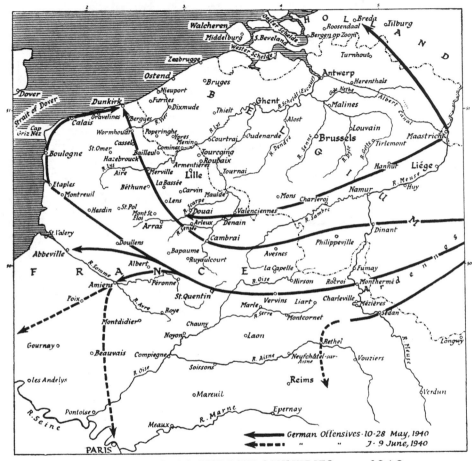

NORTHERN FRANCE & THE LOW COUNTRIES — 1940

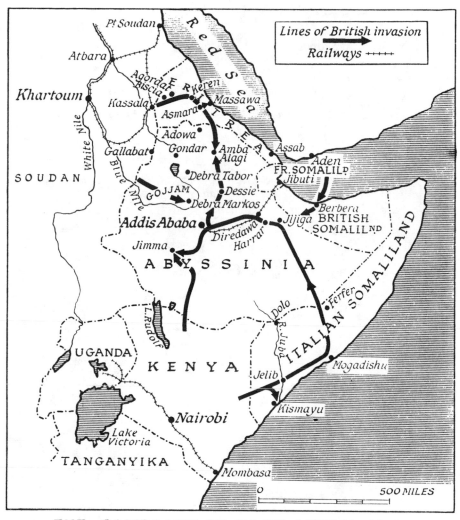

Lines of British invasion ➔
Railways +++++

Pt Soudan
Atbara
Khartoum
Kassala
Agordat
Biscia
E R I T R E A
R.Keren
Massawa
Asmara
Adowa
Gondar
Amba Alagi
Assab
Aden
FR. SOMALILD.
Jibuti
Gallabat
S O U D A N
White Nile
Blue Nile
Debra Tabor
GOJJAM
Dessie
Debra Markos
Addis Ababa
Diredawa
Harrar
Jijiga BRITISH SOMALILND.
Berbera
Jimma
A B Y S S I N I A
ITALIAN SOMALILAND
Dolo
Ferfer
L.Rudolf
UGANDA
K E N Y A
Jelib
R.Juba
Mogadishu
Nairobi
Lake Victoria
Kismayu
TANGANYIKA
Mombasa
0   500 MILES

THE CAMPAIGN IN EAST AFRICA 1941

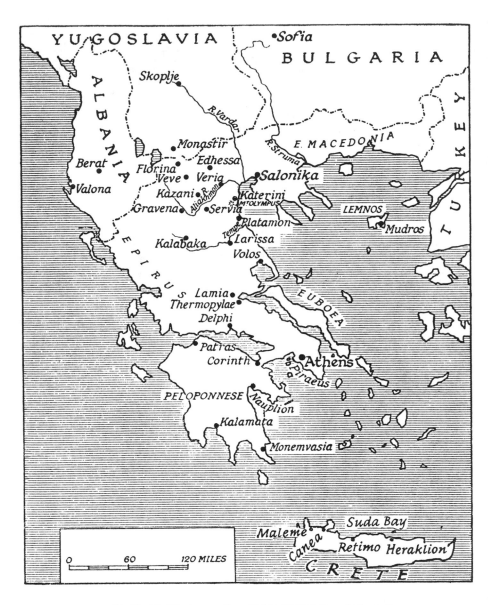

GREECE & CRETE 1941

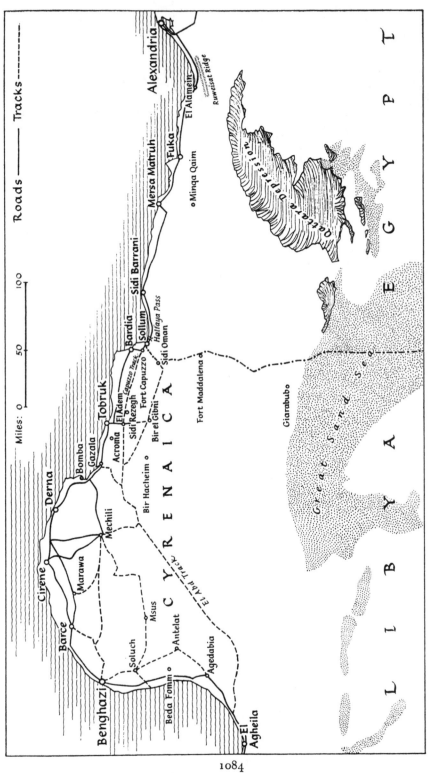

NORTH AFRICA – The Swaying Battle, 1940–42

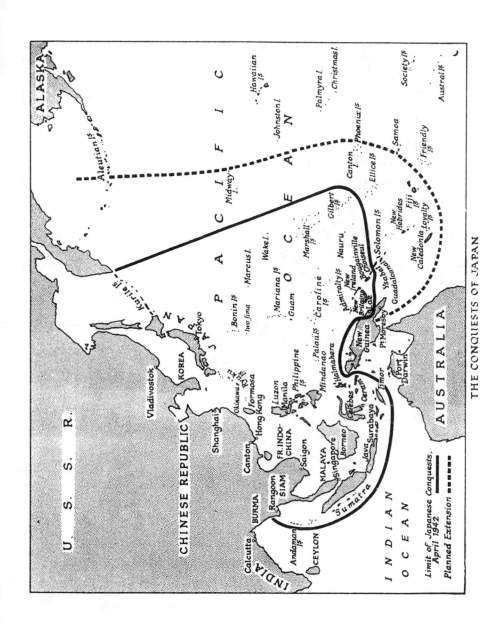

THE CONQUESTS OF JAPAN

Limit of Japanese Conquests.
April 1942 ⸻
Planned Extension ▪▪▪▪▪▪

Lake Ladoga
Leningrad
Approx. Front, April 1942
Maximum German gains
Front, March 1943
0
300 MILES
Lake Ilmen
Rzhev
MOSCOW
Velikie Luki
Vyazma
Smolensk
POLAND (1939)
Briansk
Orel
Voronezh
Kursk
R. Don
Stalingrad
Kharkov
Kiev
R. Donetz
R. Volga
R. Dnieper
Stalino
Rostov
R. Bug
CASPIAN SEA
ROUMANIA
Maikop
Nalchik
Grozny
Sebastopol
Novorossisk
Tuapse
Tiflis
Baku
BLACK SEA
Batum

THE FRONT IN RUSSIA, APRIL 1942-MARCH 1943

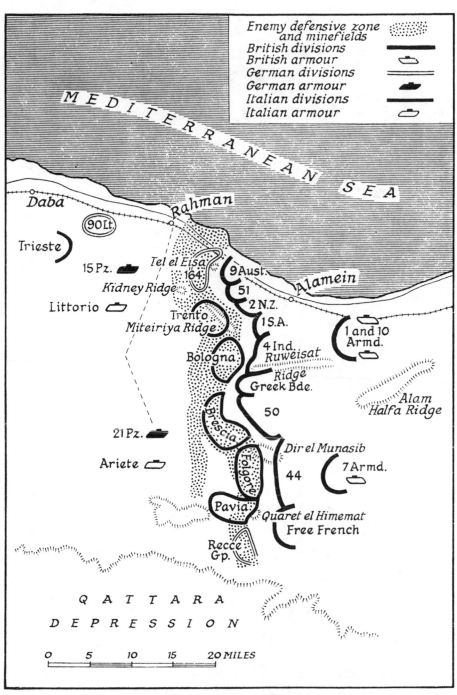

THE ALAMEIN FRONT: OCT. 23, 1942

THE END IN AFRICA. 1942-1943

British/U.S. action
Parachute landing

500 MILES

1088

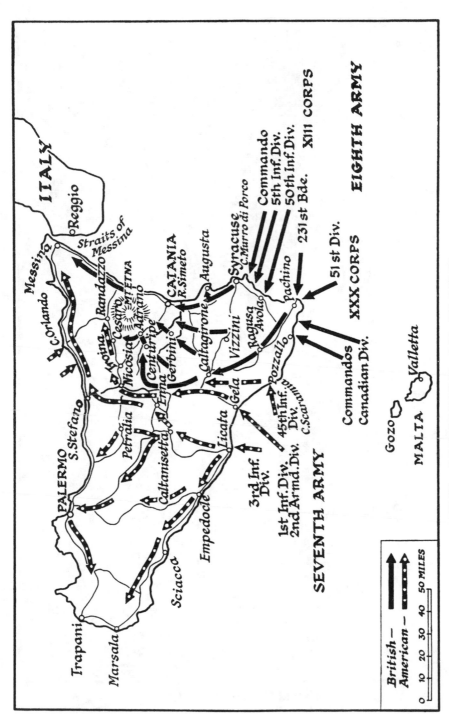

THE CONQUEST OF SICILY

ITALY

Reggio

Straits of Messina

Messina

C. Orlando

S. Stefano

PALERMO

Trapani

Marsala

Sciacca

Empedocle

Petralia

Caltanisetta

Licata

Gela

C. Scaramia

45th Inf. Div.

3rd Inf. Div.

1st Inf. Div. 2nd Armd. Div.

Randazzo

Troina

Cesaro

Nicosia

Adrano

MT. ETNA

Enna

Centuripe

Gerbini

Caltagirone

Vizzini

Ragusa

Pozzallo

Randazzo

Bronte

CATANIA

R. Simeto

Augusta

Syracuse

C. Marro di Porco

Avola

Pachino

Commandos Canadian Div.

51st Div.

XXX CORPS

Commando 5th Inf. Div. 50th Inf. Div. 231st Bde. XIII CORPS

EIGHTH ARMY

SEVENTH ARMY

Gozo

MALTA Valletta

British —
American —

0 10 20 30 40 50 MILES

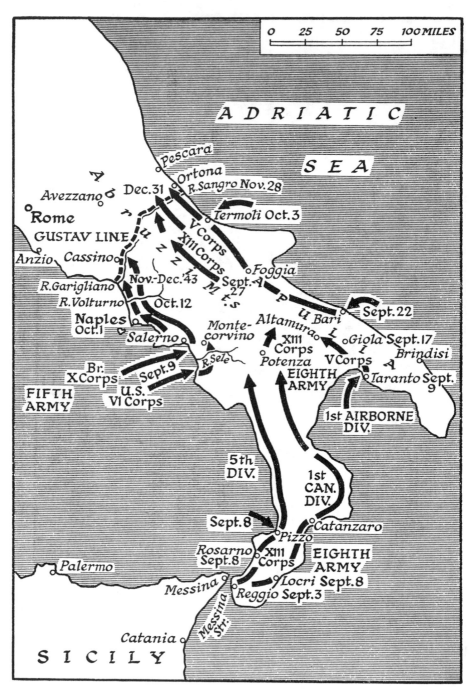

SOUTHERN ITALY

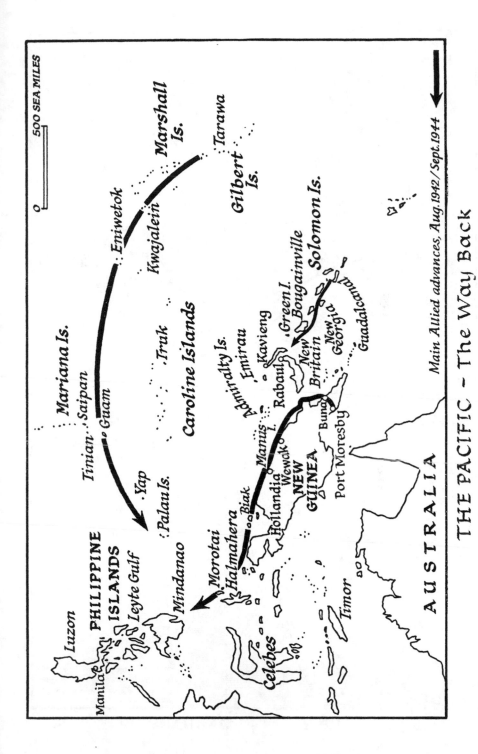

500 SEA MILES

Luzon

PHILIPPINE
ISLANDS

Manila

Leyte Gulf

Mindanao

Mariana Is.

Tinian· Saipan

Guam

Yap

Palau Is.

Truk

Caroline Islands

Eniwetok

Kwajalein

Marshall
Is.

Tarawa

Gilbert
Is.

Morotai

Halmahera

Biak

Hollandia

Wewak

NEW
GUINEA

Buna

Port Moresby

Celebes

Timor

Manus
I.

Admiralty Is.

Emirau

Kavieng

Rabaul

New
Britain

Green I.

New
Georgia

Bougainville

Solomon Is.

Guadalcanal

AUSTRALIA

THE PACIFIC ~ The Way Back

Main Allied advances, Aug.1942/Sept.1944

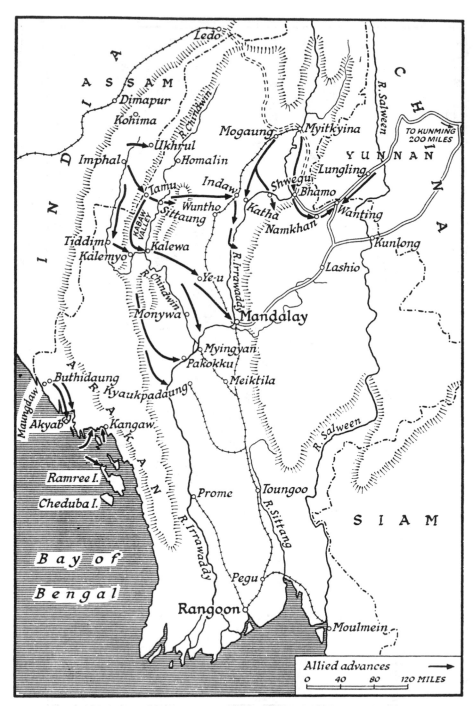

BURMA, JULY 1944 – JANUARY 1945

Legend

Front July 1, 1943	▬▬▬▬
Front Dec. 31, 1943	▬ ▬ ▬ ▬
German attacks	⇨
Russian attacks	➡
Russian pursuit	▪▪▪➤
International frontiers	·—·—·

0   100   200 MILES

OPERATIONS IN RUSSIA, JULY–DEC. 1943

To Murmansk
L. Onega
FINLAND
L. Ladoga
Viborg
G. of Finland
Leningrad
Tallinn
ESTONIA
L. Peipus
Pskov
SWEDEN
BALTIC SEA
Riga
COURLAND
LATVIA
U. S. S. R.
Vitebsk
Smolensk
LITHUANIA
Kovno
Königsberg
Tilsit
R. Niemen
Vilna
Minsk
Mogilev
Danzig
E. PRUSSIA
Grodno
Bobruisk
Stettin
Gomel
Schneidemühl
GERMANY
Berlin
R. Oder
Posen
R. Vistula
Warsaw
Pinsk
R. Pripet
POLAND
MARSHES
UPPER
Breslau
SILESIA
Oppeln
Sandomir
Kovel
Kiev
Prague
Cracow
R. San
Jaroslav
Lemberg
R. Dnieper
CZECHOSLOVAKIA
Przemysl
R. Bug
CARPATHIAN MOUNTAINS
Stanislav
R. Danube
Cernowitz
R. Dniester
Vienna
AUSTRIA
Budapest
Jassy
R. Pruth
Odessa
L. Balaton
HUNGARY
TRANSYLVANIAN
ALPS
Crimea
R O U M A N I A
Belgrade
Ploesti
BLACK
YUGOSLAVIA
Bucharest
R. Danube
SEA
BULGARIA

OPERATIONS ON THE RUSSIAN FRONT, JUNE 1944–JAN. 1945

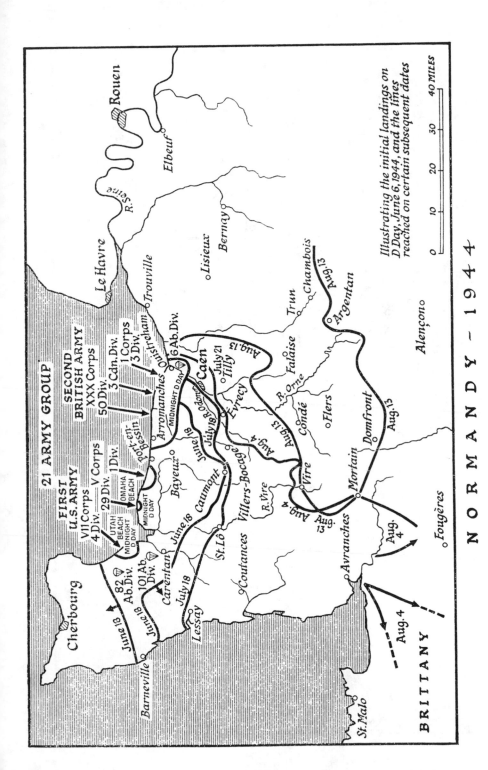

Illustrating the initial landings on
D Day, June 6, 1944, and the lines
reached on certain subsequent dates

40 MILES

NORMANDY - 1944

ADVANCE TO THE RHINE, 1944

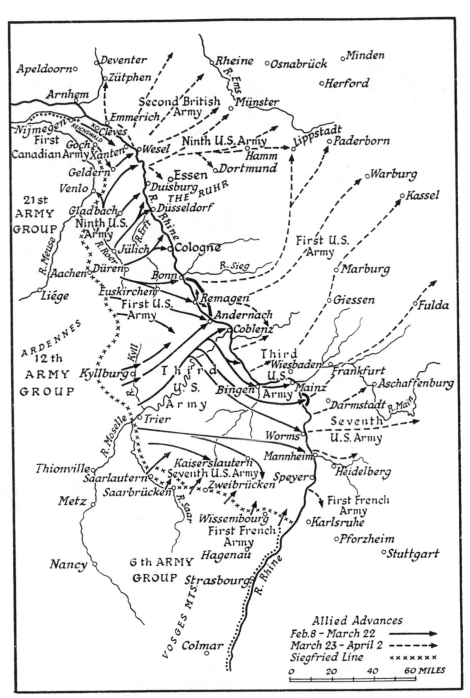

CROSSING THE RHINE

THE INVASION OF GERMANY

INDEX

INDEX

For the convenience of the reader, this index includes names of persons quoted in extracts, as well as most of the authors' names appearing at the conclusion of the extracts. Such names are distinguished by an asterisk.

Other titles of interest

SAINT-EXUPÉRY
A Biography
Stacy Schiff
559 pp., 40 illus.
80740-8 $18.95

IN SEARCH OF LIGHT
The Broadcasts of
Edward R. Murrow,
1938–1961
Edward Bliss, Jr.
402 pp.
80762-9 $14.95

MEMOIRS
Ten Years and Twenty Days
Grand Admiral Karl Doenitz
Introd. and Afterword by
Jürgen Rohwer
New foreword by John Toland
554 pp., 18 photos, 5 maps
80764-5 $16.95

THE BITTER WOODS
The Battle of the Bulge
John S. D. Eisenhower
New introduction by
Stephen E. Ambrose
550 pp., 46 photos & 27 maps
80652-5 $17.95

THE BRAVEST BATTLE
The 28 Days of the Warsaw
Ghetto Uprising
Dan Kurzman
400 pp., 51 photos
80533-2 $14.95

**THE COLLAPSE OF
THE THIRD REPUBLIC**
An Inquiry into the Fall
of France in 1940
William L. Shirer
1,082 pp., 12 maps
80562-6 $22.95

DEATH DEALER
The Memoirs of the SS
Kommandant at Auschwitz
Rudolph Höss
Edited by Steven Paskuly
Translated by Andrew Pollinger
New foreword by Primo Levi
416 pp., 42 photos & diagrams
80698-3 $15.95

THE FALL OF BERLIN
Anthony Read and David Fisher
535 pp., 17 photos, 5 maps
80619-3 $16.95

GESTAPO
Instrument of Tyranny
Edward Crankshaw
281 pp., 12 photos
80567-7 $13.95

THE GI's WAR
American Soldiers in Europe
During World War II
Edwin P. Hoyt
638 pp., 29 illus.
80448-4 $16.95

GOEBBELS
A Biography
Helmut Heiber
398 pp., 19 photos
80187-6 $9.95

**THE GUINNESS BOOK
OF ESPIONAGE**
Mark Lloyd
256 pp., 100 photos
80584-7 $16.95

JAPAN'S WAR
The Great Pacific Conflict
Edwin P. Hoyt
560 pp., 57 photos, 6 pp. of maps
80348-8 $16.95

**THE LUFTWAFFE
WAR DIARIES**
The German Air Force in
World War II
Cajus Bekker
447 pp., 119 photos, 20 maps
80604-5 $15.95

**THE MEMOIRS OF
FIELD MARSHAL MONTGOMERY**
508 pp., 61 photos
80173-6 $10.95

THE MIGHTY ENDEAVOR
The American War in Europe
Charles B. MacDonald
621 pp., 78 photos, 10 maps
80486-7 $16.95

THE 900 DAYS
The Siege of Leningrad
Harrison E. Salisbury
635 pp., 28 photos
80253-8 $16.95

NOW IT CAN BE TOLD
The Story of the Manhattan Project
Gen. Leslie R. Groves
New introd. by Edward Teller
482 pp.   80189-2 $14.95